CARL
SANDBURG

CARL
SANDBURG

A BIOGRAPHY

---- ✳ ----

Penelope Niven

A ROBERT STEWART BOOK

✳

Charles Scribner's Sons
New York

Maxwell Macmillan Canada
Toronto

Maxwell Macmillan International
New York Oxford Singapore Sydney

Charles Scribner's Sons
Macmillan Publishing Company
866 Third Avenue, New York, NY 10022

Maxwell Macmillan Canada, Inc.
1200 Eglinton Avenue East, Suite 200
Don Mills, Ontario M3C 3N1

Macmillan Publishing Company is part of the
Maxwell Communication Group of Companies.

Library of Congress Cataloging-in-Publication Data

Niven, Penelope.
Carl Sandburg: a biography/Penelope Niven.
p.   cm.
"A Robert Stewart book."
Includes bibliographical references and index.
ISBN 0-684-19251-9
1. Sandburg, Carl, 1878–1967—Biography.   2. Poets, American—20th
century—Biography.   3. Biographers—United States—Biography.
I. Title.
PS3537.A618Z785   1991
811'.52—dc20
[B]   90-20664   CIP

Macmillan books are available at special discounts for bulk purchases for sales
promotions, premiums, fund-raising, or educational use. For details, contact:

Special Sales Director
Macmillan Publishing Company
866 Third Avenue
New York, NY 10022

10 9 8 7 6 5 4 3 2 1

Printed in the United States of America

Permissions begin on page 839.

To
Olin *and* Eleanor Hearon Niven,
my parents,
and
Jennifer Niven McJunkin,
my daughter

✻

I never knew any more beautiful than you . . .
I shall never find any
greater than you.
—CARL SANDBURG, "The Great Hunt"

Out of the silent working of his inner life came forces no one outside himself could know; they were his secret, his personality and purpose, beside which all other facts of his comings and goings were insignificant.

—CARL SANDBURG on Abraham Lincoln

Contents

*

PART IV **THE CONNEMARA YEARS**

Preface

Ain't it hell the way a book walks up to you and makes
you write it?—Don't you feel almost predestinarian?
—Carl Sandburg to Amy Lowell about his biography
of Lincoln and hers of Keats, March, 17, 1925

I came to Carl Sandburg reluctantly. Immersed in nineteenth-century
American literature, I shared the prevailing critical views of Sandburg, that maverick among American writers: his work had drifted
into justifiable eclipse; his poetry was timeworn, glib, chaotic, hardly
worth notice in contemporary anthologies. I knew only fragments of
Sandburg's immense body of work—the poem "Chicago"; portions of
Abraham Lincoln: The Prairie Years and *The War Years*. I had heard about
Sandburg the celebrity, the showman, the living legend. Beyond that I
knew little of the poet and nothing of the man. Then, one summer day
nearly a decade after his death, I went to his Carolina mountain home.

In 1945 Carl and Paula Sandburg moved from their native Midwest
to Connemara—a 245-acre farm in Flat Rock, North Carolina, enfolded
in the solitude and hovering mists of the Blue Ridge Mountains. Among
mountain people, Paula Sandburg was respected as a successful breeder
of champion dairy goats, work she began as a hobby when she was fifty-
two, in part out of the loneliness and isolation of her life on the dunes
of Lake Michigan. She was sixty-two when she came to Connemara,
and quickly became known about the mountains as "the goat lady."

The Sandburgs brought three adult daughters and two grandchildren
with them to live at Connemara. There was mystery about two of the
daughters, sheltered for reasons not clear to their mountain neighbors.
The third daughter, Helga, was the youngest, twenty-seven years old,
divorced, the mother of two young children. She worked with her mother
on the farm, it was known, and later married a young man who had
worked briefly as her father's secretary.

The family had many friends in the Carolinas, but among some of
the mountain people, the old poet gained a reputation for arrogance and
indolence. Some of his neighbors understood and affirmed the work of
his dairy farmer wife, but could see no great value in the work Sandburg

did, if he did any at all. Rumor had it that he left the hard labor of the farm to his patient wife and his mysterious daughters, that he himself was lazy, unfriendly and odd.

Surly and suspect as he may have seemed to some of his mountain neighbors, Sandburg had as early as 1922 been baptized the Poet of the People. After his death, his Carolina mountain home became the "people's house." Today you can walk through its twenty-two rooms, look from its spacious porch to the distant miles of mountain peaks, hike fragrant trails to the crest of Big Glassy Mountain, contemplate the bright stillness of high summer, the white solitude of mountain winter.

At first Paula Sandburg thought of giving the government the mansion, the dependencies, the dairy, the acres of forest, meadows and mountain. Instead, her attorneys advised her to sell it to the Department of Interior to put aside money for the future of the two dependent daughters, Margaret and Janet, who were fifty-six and fifty-one when their father died on July 22, 1967, of a surfeit of years and struggle with ailing lungs, heart and mind. His family relinquished Connemara to the National Park Service in 1968, and in 1973 the Carl Sandburg Home was officially opened to the public as a National Park and National Historic Site.

✳

My first encounter with Sandburg came on the summer day in 1976 when I explored Connemara as a tourist. I saw a writer's workshop, the accrued evidence of books, papers and other tools of the literary life. His presence was palpable in almost every room. Spiders spun daily webs between the rough wood shelves arranged like library stacks in the cool stone cellar. The house was burdened with books, more than ten thousand of them, arranged in comfortable order on shelves reaching to the high ceilings. Sandburg's papers spilled from desks to sturdy wooden fruit crates to tattered cardboard cartons from the grocery store. Within easy reach on cluttered desktops were letters from Robert Frost, John Kennedy, Archibald MacLeish, H. L. Mencken. Sandburg's creased hats were there, his canes, his guitars, and buckeyes, smooth stones, dried ginkgo leaves, pine cones—talismans of a thousand strolls by day and night on the paths lacing his property.

I left Connemara haunted by Sandburg's presence in this house and compelled by the evidence of his work and character. Back home in Maryland in my own busy life, I could not forget Sandburg. Never mind that I had long ago dismissed him as a celebrity more than a serious figure in American letters. I was curious now about the shadow whose spirit seemed so alive in Flat Rock.

From the outset of his long career, I discovered, Sandburg was a literary outsider, despite (and sometimes because of) his great public popularity. For decades he carried on small wars with the literary elite, particularly certain poets and critics whom he called the Abracadabra Boys. When Sandburg's work first appeared in *Poetry: A Magazine of Verse* in 1914, he was deemed too radical. By the twenties he was considered too dated and propagandistic.

Taking aim at Sandburg, Robert Frost mused that writing free verse was like playing tennis without a net. William Carlos Williams wrote a review in *Poetry* in 1951 so profoundly negative that it haunts Sandburg's reputation to this day. He lacked development as a poet, Williams charged in the little magazine which had launched Sandburg's career almost forty years earlier. He articulated no coherent poetic theory, Williams wrote. Consequently, he believed, Sandburg had produced a "formless mass" of work.

Some of the Beat poets of the sixties admired Sandburg's work and built on it, but by the late seventies there was a generation of Americans who had not read his poetry. Yet visitors were coming in a steady procession to Connemara, exploring the books and artifacts of Sandburg's life, climbing to the musty third floor workroom where he had finished his only novel, *Remembrance Rock*, in 1948, prepared *Complete Poems* in 1950, and written his autobiography *Always The Young Strangers* in 1953. I had stood there myself, irrevocably, almost mystically drawn to the papers, the books filled with markers on which were visible the bold, cryptic notes he had written to himself.

Impulsively, I wrote to the superintendent of the Carl Sandburg Home that autumn of 1976, asking if I could work at Connemara with Sandburg's books and papers, offering as credentials a master's degree in American literature and a long teaching career. For a time I did not mail the letter, convincing myself that I should stay with teaching and leave Sandburg to the Sandburg experts, who were surely already at work there.

Yet Sandburg would not leave me alone. I mailed the letter, and received a quick, positive response. The National Park Service staff had to restore the physical property, make the old house safe for thousands of visitors who were coming in an ever-growing pilgrimage. Resources were committed to reclaiming the farm and forest land, rebuilding the goat herd with offspring of Paula Sandburg's Saanen, Nubian and Toggenburg goats, refurbishing the beauty of the estate. No one was working yet on the papers. They could not pay me, but I was welcome to come to work as a volunteer.

The summer of 1977 was unusually hot and humid in the Blue Ridge Mountains. I spent most of those sweltering weeks on my hands and knees at Connemara searching for Sandburg papers under the eaves, in the attic, in the cellar. It was a job others had begun and abandoned as too grueling and protracted to be worthwhile. I spent day after day battling mold, mildew, mice and time for custody of Carl Sandburg's papers, the remaining documents of this writer's prolific life and work.

Sandburg had sold his working library to the University of Illinois in 1956 for thirty thousand dollars. Librarians then moved four and a half tons of books and papers from Connemara to Urbana, taking particular interest in Sandburg's remarkable Lincoln library. After his death in 1967 another major transfer occurred. Helga Sandburg shipped cartons of materials to her home in Cleveland, Ohio, and Paula, Margaret and Janet Sandburg took many personal papers and books to their new home in Asheville. Certain unpublished manuscripts and letters were stored in bank vaults. Helga Sandburg kept a green velvet box full of her parents' love letters. Yet untouched boxes, cartons and files of papers remained sequestered in the old house until I began to examine them, to lift them gingerly from the old dusty boxes in which they had rested, vulnerable to heat, dampness, time and the vagaries of an aging house.

One summer was not enough to retrieve the thousands of letters, the pages of unpublished manuscripts, the private and revealing journal notes, some of them hidden, as we shall later see, under the ashes of old fires in the wood stove in Sandburg's workroom on the third floor.

I returned to Connemara in the summer of 1978 and every summer afterward until 1983, working with Sandburg's papers, that vital part of his legacy which had for so long lain unattended, even forgotten at Connemara. I joined forces with Connemara curator Warren Weber and Superintendent Benjamin Davis, careful stewards of Sandburg's house; and George Hendrick, Scott Bennett and John Hoffmann of the University of Illinois, who worked for many years to make the Carl Sandburg Collection at the university library accessible to scholars and researchers. The National Park Service, the University of Illinois Library, the National Endowment for the Humanities and the American Council of Learned Societies supported my ongoing work with the Connemara papers, until more than thirty thousand letters and manuscript pages had been retrieved, sorted and transported to my office in Lilly Library at Earlham College in Richmond, Indiana, to be catalogued. When my assistant Jody Doll and I completed that work, the papers, as Sandburg intended, went home to Illinois.

Sandburg's critics have called him a superficial, undisciplined poet and a careless biographer of Lincoln. His papers unveil a different Sandburg, however. They document his care and thought in crafting poetry and prose, his painstaking revisions, his thorough, sometimes ground-breaking scholarship, the punctual reporter's regard for deadlines and economy. They reveal Sandburg's habits of work, the identities of his colleagues and adversaries, the wide range of his public and private friendships, the nature of his family life. As I explored Sandburg's vast correspondence, names grew into personalities; identities kindled to life. There were letters from Amy Lowell, Ezra Pound, Vachel Lindsay, Edgar Lee Masters, Theodore Dreiser; presidents Franklin Roosevelt, Harry Truman, John F. Kennedy and Lyndon B. Johnson; journalists Edward R. Murrow, Harry Golden, Ralph McGill, Joseph Wershba; Sandburg's publisher Alfred Harcourt; his agent Lucy Kroll; his friend and collaborator Norman Corwin; his sisters and mother, his wife and daughters, and countless others whose lives intersected with his. There were letters from critics who assailed Sandburg's work, from women who loved and nurtured it, from those who exploited him, those who protected and revered him, those who always told him the truth about his work, even when the truth disappointed him.

Lowell, Pound, Lindsay, Masters, Dreiser and many others were gone, but with the help of Sandburg's daughters and friends, I began to search for those who would talk to me about the Carl Sandburg they had known. Consequently, I began the Carl Sandburg Oral History Project in 1980. Now there are more than 150 taped interviews with people who knew Sandburg in many different ways—his daughters; the gentle Quaker woman who was his housekeeper for a decade during his work on *The People, Yes* and *Abraham Lincoln: The War Years*; his secretary and his copy editor during the *Chicago Daily News* era; Malcolm Cowley; Sandburg's last publisher, William Jovanovich; Robert Giroux, his editor for *Remembrance Rock*, commissioned by MGM; George Stevens, Jr., and other Hollywood figures who worked with Sandburg on *The Greatest Story Ever Told*; journalists Joseph Wershba, Harry Golden and Fred Friendly; Norman Corwin, Pete Seeger, Gene Kelly, Steve Allen and other friends and associates, public and private. Only a dozen of these people had written about Sandburg, or intended to. Their illuminating recollections gave flesh to the bones, form to the spirit which had haunted me since my first summer day at Connemara.

The Sandburg daughters, each in her own way a diarist, generously shared with me the most private family letters and journals, their parents' and their own. From the outset, they and the Sandburg trustees, Maurice Greenbaum and Judge Frank Parker, extended total cooperation and complete access to all the Sandburg papers, and did not ask to see the unfolding manuscript. Because they freely granted permission to quote all previously unpublished material, this book holds many poems and letters heretofore unknown, unseen, a number of them found among the Connemara papers. The family and trustees asked nothing of me in return—only the truth, wherever it took me.

Sandburg's papers also led me to Lucy Kroll, his friend and media agent from 1958 until his death. It was she who first told me I should write this biography, and over the years became my agent, mentor and friend. I began to feel, as Sandburg said he did of the Lincoln biography, that this book walked up to me and made me write it. I began to feel "almost predestinarian."

✳

"Biography is hell," Carl Sandburg once said. "Writing biography will wear you down like no other literary work." Part of the challenge is getting to the truth, insofar as the truth of any life can be revealed to others.

The factual outline of Sandburg's life is far more easily discovered than the mysteries, the secrets, the deeply significant story of the "silent working of his inner life." To get at that exterior truth, I constructed almost daily calendars of the eighty-nine years (1074 months) of his life. I began to fathom the depth of his involvement in the turbulent events of an American century. His life is an odyssey into the American experience.

Sandburg was the maverick son of Swedish immigrants, as a boy ashamed of the name, language, clothing and poverty which at first set him apart from the American mainstream in Galesburg, Illinois, his introverted prairie hometown. He was a mischievous, restless, streetwise child. From his mother he got warm, self-effacing devotion, and the love of words and learning. From his father he received stern, sometimes harsh discipline, and a graphic daily lesson in the impact of unrelenting toil on the spirit of the American workingman. August Sandburg was one of thousands of semiliterate immigrants who came to the United States in search of the American dream, only to endure inhuman working conditions and the humiliation of a social system which was oppressive by its seeming indifference to their struggles.

From boyhood, Carl Sandburg was driven by the need to establish his identity as an American. At age eight he changed his name from the Swedish *Carl* to the more American *Charles*. He and his brother Mart and sister Mary began to spell their surname *Sandburg* rather than *Sandberg*. Young Charles Sandburg was a vagabond who quickly outgrew the boundaries of his hometown. Perhaps from his impassive father, he inherited the hunger for travel which led him first to Chicago in 1896, and then to an exploration of the American frontier as part of the vast procession of hoboes, tramps and bums who sought to find or escape work in the wake of the depression of the 1890s.

The journey left Sandburg with a permanent wanderlust. During the decade of his twenties he was a soldier, a college student, an itinerant salesman, an aspiring orator and poet, recording in dozens of pocket journals the American vernacular which would later permeate his poetry. Except for Walt Whitman, no other American poet has been so immediately responsive to the convolutions of American life. From 1900 until 1967, Sandburg's voice addressed the pivotal events of this century.

His exterior life, then, can be documented by an extravagance of published and unpublished material, enough to occupy several biographers for many years. His journals and letters let us into his soul at times, as do some of the metaphors which suffuse his poetry. He called himself a seeker, a stranger, a singer, a traveler, the Eternal Hobo. He wrote of literal and spiritual hungers, the enduring "hunger for a nameless bread." He described himself as a child of the wilderness. His visible, public sense of humor sometimes masked a profound, brooding melancholy. "Study the wilderness under your own hat," he wrote in an unpublished poem, "and say little or nothing of how you are not unaccustomed to thorns."

He was a long time coming to his authentic voice and self. He might have given up the search had it not been for the remarkable woman he married, Lilian Anna Maria Elizabeth Magdalene Steichen, whom he called Paula. His biography is also hers. As much as anyone else, she helped to shape Carl Sandburg, even urging him to reclaim his given name and affirm his Swedish roots as well as his American identity. They met in December 1907 and married six months later, after a courtship by mail and only a handful of days together. A beautiful woman of prodigious intellect, she was the sister of photographer Edward Steichen. They were fundamental forces in Sandburg's creative life.

From the first, Paula sublimated herself to Sandburg, giving him complete devotion. She was an intensely private person. Like Sophia Hawthorne, but for different reasons, she destroyed some of the papers which

would have divulged her interior life. Fortunately, her daughters intervened and persuaded her to safeguard others, including the extraordinary
Sandburg-Steichen love letters. In this unique literary family lay the seed
of much of Sandburg's lyrical poetry, his private sorrow, his motivation
for work and his joy in life.

To the end of Sandburg's life, there was the old restlessness of heart,
the constant drive to pioneer, experiment, create. Unlike many of his
contemporaries he never went abroad for a literary apprenticeship. While
other writers found their voices in Paris, London or Rome, Sandburg
turned to Milwaukee and Chicago. He grew up in a household where
Swedish was the first language and explored the American heartland in
search of his native tongue. In the process he became the passionate
champion of people who did not have the words or power to speak for
themselves. He helped the American people discover their national identity through songs, poems and that mythic national hero Abraham Lincoln. The apparent incoherence of his early experience fed a literary
explosion and launched an unorthodox poet whose immense work deserves reconsideration, if not rediscovery.

In his last book of poetry, *Honey and Salt*, published when he was eighty-
five, Sandburg spoke of his origins and his destiny:

> . . . older than the rocks and
> fresh as the dawn of this morning today are
> the everliving roots who begot me,
> who poured me out as one more seeker . . .
> I am more than a traveler out of Nowhere . . .

This traveler out of the American dream wrote the story of his first
twenty years in *Always The Young Strangers*, published in 1953 when he
was seventy-five. The book was embedded with vivid details at once so
particular to nineteenth-century life in the American heartland and to
universal rites of passage that readers in diverse cultures have found their
own life journeys reflected there. When Sandburg resurrected his prairie
roots, he turned to scrapbooks kept by his sisters, to public records and
his own private journals, and to his vast, rich memory. This excavation
of self was hard work. As he wrote in the poem "Scroll," used as an
epigraph in the book, he sometimes had to "wreck" the images in his
memory and "proceed again to reconstruct/what happened and how,/the
many little involved answers/to who? what? when? where?/and more
involved than any/ how? how?"

The autobiography begins with carefully chosen details. He was a "welcome man-child" born on a corn-husk mattress in a three-room cottage near the railroad tracks. He was born January 6, 1878, one hundred years to the day after the birth of Thomas Lincoln, father of his hero Abraham Lincoln. Sandburg dismissed that coincidence of birth date as meaningless, one of those "odd facts" that "stick in the mind even though they prove nothing." Nevertheless, he recorded it at the outset of *Always The Young Strangers*.

Certain boyhood episodes haunted him. He wrote about them in manuscript pages that are nowhere to be found in the published book, drafts more poignant than the final, edited version of the story. He was trying to decipher the "how" of his life and work. "If it can be done it is not a bad practice for a man of many years to die with a boy heart," Sandburg wrote at the end of *Always The Young Strangers*, his own boy heart intact, alive with memories, love and pain . . .

PART ONE

THE PRAIRIE YEARS

———— ✳ ————

1869–1895

1. The Young Stranger

> . . . the new people, the young
> strangers, coming, coming, always coming.
>   It is early.
>   I shall yet be footloose.
>
> —Carl Sandburg, "Broken-face Gargoyles,"
> *Smoke and Steel*, 1920

He was seventy-two and famous, reclaiming his boyhood: "When a man looks backward to things that happened to him 50 or 60 years ago," Carl Sandburg wrote in an unpublished manuscript, "he can often tell exactly what he saw and heard. Some words and actions get burned in his memory." In the solitude of the Carolina mountains, he resurrected his Illinois prairie youth: "to tell what those words and actions did to his mind and heart, what changes went on inside of him because of those words and actions, what new darkness or fresh lights became part of his personality, there the story of his life and growth goes winding into mysteries of the human mind and secrets of character, will, vision and hope that never come perfectly clear."

He was at work on *Always The Young Strangers*, published when he was seventy-five, suffused with details of his boyhood in the American heartland during the last two decades of the nineteenth century. From the time when his fingers "first found how to shape the alphabet," he

1

wanted to write. There were early signs of his lifelong fascination with the meanings and mysteries of language. He loved words, collected them, savored their shapes and sounds. He spoke Swedish before he spoke English. The first book in his memory was his father's Swedish Bible. August Sandberg read aloud from it, sometimes to the accompaniment of the winds sweeping Galesburg, Illinois, during the desolation of long prairie winters. Young Charlie Sandberg would hold the Bible in his hands, wondering how the inscrutable "black marks on white paper could be letters your eyes would pick off into words and your tongue would speak."

He was named Carl August Sandberg for his father, a Swedish immigrant who worked ten hours a day, six days a week, for thirty-five years as a blacksmith's helper for the Chicago, Burlington and Quincy Railroad (the C.B.&Q.) in Galesburg. August Sandberg's real name was a matter of mystery and dispute long after his death in 1910. When he came to the United States to escape the hardships of peasant life in Sweden, he bore a common Swedish name—Danielssen perhaps, or Johnson or Holmes or Sturm. Family memory varies and there are no official records to clarify the matter. There were other Swedes with the same name on the labor gangs building the railroads interlocking the American promised land. Their paychecks and mail were often mistakenly delivered to others with identical first and last names.

Tired of the confusion, August changed his last name to *Sandberg*, leaving behind no clues to his christened name or birthplace. The reporter who wrote his obituary in 1910 called him "Andrew" rather than "August." In death, as in his patient, industrious life, he had the name of a stranger. August was a laborer who read his Swedish Bible and his weekly Swedish newspaper, *Hemlandet*, but seldom read and never learned to write the English language which became his son's passion. He died before his son's great fame.

August was a frugal, hardworking man with a constant "Dread in his blood and brain" about the dangers of poverty and failure that drove him from Sweden to the new world to labor on the railroad. He was about twenty-three years old when he joined the exodus of thirty thousand Swedes to the United States in 1869, many of them fleeing the draft. An orphan, he had supported himself as a chore boy and then a teamster at a distillery in Sweden. Eventually he saved money for steerage passage to the United States "where there was a better chance." His first American job was in a cheese factory in Herkimer, New York. There he heard from his cousin Magnus Holmes of Galesburg, Illinois, urging him to come west. Holmes had lived in Galesburg for years and could vouch for the opportunities there. Thus August Sandberg joined the migration of Swedes to the prairie settlements of the upper Midwest.

He and Clara Anderson traveled different routes at different times in search of a better life in the United States. When they met in Bushnell, Illinois, in 1874, she was a hotel maid. He came to town to work on the C.B.&Q. Railroad line. Her baptismal name and genealogy and her parish in the homeland are a matter of record. She had been called Clara Andersdatter in Appuna, Sweden, where her father was a farmer and gooseherd. She was six years old when her mother died. Her father remarried, and she did not get along with her stepmother. Clara left home as a teenager to work as a hired girl, and was drawn to the new country by glowing letters from kinsmen who had settled in Illinois. She saved her money until there was enough in 1873 for the crossing. Steerage passage to New York was inexpensive, partly to encourage a steady supply of cheap labor. The oppressive conditions of the voyage were small price to pay for access to the streets of gold.

Clara made the arduous, confusing journey from Appuna to Illinois, where she quickly found her job as a hotel maid. There she met thirty-year-old August Sandberg, a "black" Swede with straight, dark hair and eyes that looked black or hazel, depending on the light and his mood. His dark good looks masked a sober reserve for which Clara's calm, cheerful spirit was a lifelong counterpoint. She knew immediately that August was her "chance" for home and family. When he saw her golden hair bound up neatly from the smooth neck, the soft blue of her eyes, and the rich, firm curve of her breasts, he knew good fortune had brought him to Bushnell, Illinois. They had Swedish blood in common, the bonds of language and homeland, and the desire and stamina to work hard and make something of life.

They were married on August 7, 1874, and settled in a three-room cottage in Galesburg two blocks east of the C.B.&Q. roundhouse and shop where August worked. They seldom left Galesburg again, not even to go to the World's Columbian Exposition of 1893, just 160 miles away in Chicago. Mary, their first child, was born May 30, 1875. In all, seven children were born to the Sandbergs, each sleeping at first on a corn-husk mattress in the cradle near their parents' bed, wearing diapers Clara cut and sewed from whatever was handy, often Pillsbury's Best Flour sacks.

On January 6, 1878, Clara gave birth to her second child and first son. When the Swedish midwife smiled and announced *"Det är en pojke"*

("It is a boy"), the couple rejoiced. He was Carl August, a "welcome man-child." He and Mary were followed by brothers Martin, Emil and Fred, and sisters Esther and Martha.

The Sandbergs were one of many thrifty, industrious Swedish families in Galesburg. Many of the men, like August, were laborers on the railroad. By the 1850s so many Swedes had settled in Galesburg that they comprised a sixth of the town's population and formed a "village" of their own within the town, with their own churches, lodges and newspaper. The *Hemlandet*, the first Swedish newspaper in the United States, was edited by Galesburg Lutheran minister T. N. Hesselquist. Swedish immigrants in Galesburg congregated in their neat neighborhoods near the C.B.&Q. shop and switching station on the raw edge of town, away from the gracious homes and wide, quiet streets where the establishment families lived. There were other immigrants—many Irish Catholics, a handful of Chinese and Italians, a few Japanese students at Lombard, the small Universalist university. There were many black citizens in Galesburg, which had been a sanctuary on the Underground Railroad routes north.

For all the diversity in his hometown, however, Carl grew up deeply aware of the traits which set him and his family apart. From boyhood, he had a profound need to be American, not Swedish. He wanted to belong. At an early age he began to call himself the more American "Charles" or "Charlie." Eager to be fully Americanized, he and Mary and Mart in grammar school changed the spelling of their name to "Sandburg" and the rest of the family gradually followed suit. Most of all, Charlie was sensitive to the words and lingo which set his family and their Swedish neighbors apart. He thought of himself as a stranger, an outsider. His clothes and speech often embarrassed him. Then he was ashamed of himself for being embarrassed to be the child of immigrants, living on the outskirts of the small town which was then his universe.

Galesburg was a vital, unique American town, founded in 1834 by the Reverend George Washington Gale, who had established the Oneida Manual Labor Institute in New York in 1827. He and the other town fathers were pilgrims as well as pioneers, missionaries, they felt, who were led by God into the wilderness of Illinois to spread the gospel of austere Christian morality and hard labor. The town was conceived as the site of a religious manual labor college, one of many such endeavors to civilize the "hell-roaring West." Pleased that God had led them to the cheap, fertile Illinois prairie, Gale and his colleagues purchased twenty sections of land in Knox County, Illinois. Knox Manual Labor

College was officially chartered by the state of Illinois in 1837, the nucleus of a town whose settlers were zealously committed to abolition, education and temperance. By the 1880s, Galesburg was the largest city within a forty-mile radius. The city fathers had wrested from nearby Knoxville the railroad rights which made the town grow and prosper.

With its robust dependence on the burgeoning railroads, its avid attention to politics, its reverence for the powers of education and religion, and its population of pioneers and immigrants, Galesburg was a microcosm of nineteenth-century American life. "The small town of Galesburg, as I look back at it, was a piece of the American Republic," Sandburg wrote of the place that "burned" in his memory. "Did I know America, the United States, because of what I knew about Galesburg?" His imagination and identity took root there, until the character of this town was intertwined with his own. "I was born on the prairie and the milk of its wheat,/the red of its clover/the eyes of its women, gave me a song and a slogan," he wrote many years later in the poem "Prairie."

✳

When he was twelve years old, Charlie Sandburg solemnly pledged himself to a life of total abstinence from alcohol, profanity and tobacco. His parents never bought wine and only occasionally bought liquor, but it was frugality rather than moral impulse which kept the "perils of alcohol" from their house in Galesburg's Swedish enclave. August relished a couple of teaspoons of grain alcohol in his coffee after dinner, but he could make a pint of whiskey last an entire winter.

Not surprisingly, Galesburg citizens, at least publicly and officially, vociferously opposed drinking, dancing, card-playing and all other "devilish" amusements. The local temperance society stood prestigiously in the forefront of Galesburg institutions. Its leader in 1890 was Mary Allen West, school superintendent and soon-to-be president of the Illinois Women's Christian Temperance Union. Her father was Nehemiah West, abolitionist and one of Galesburg's founders. He and the other town fathers had stipulated, in every deed to local real estate, that land upon which "intoxicating drink" was made or sold would revert to Knox College, the visionary center of their settlement. Thus the city was literally rooted in the principle of abstinence.

In sheer numbers, churches dominated bars and taverns in Galesburg, but the city stayed locked in righteous combat, the "war between home and saloon." The stern real estate prohibition clause was never enforced, however. In that town of eighteen thousand people, there were thirty saloons, most hidden away on side streets, mysterious with sin and forbidden glamour. They were supposedly rife with debauchery, gambling and loose women—especially on market days when thirsty farmers came to town, or on days when the railroad pay cars came to dispense wages to the quarter of the town's population employed in one way or another by the railroads. Now and then, Charlie took a hard-earned penny to a Main Street candy shop and invested in a piece of candy that melted on his tongue to a sweet, burning center of rum. But when a local preacher attacked the candy as an "insidious menace" to innocent children, the candymaker immediately stopped selling it. Galesburg was that vigilant, and Charlie was swept up in the ongoing fervor of the temperance crusade.

Every Sunday afternoon that fall and winter of 1890, he and his older sister Mary and younger brother Mart walked two blocks from their house on Berrien Street to the Seminary Street Mission, home of the Junior Christian Endeavor Society. A hundred boys and girls, most of them children of immigrants, spent their Sunday afternoons at the Mission. Unlike the Swedish Lutheran Sunday school classes the Sandburg children attended in the morning, Mission classes were conducted in English, by students from Knox College. Nellie Stowell, a local beauty, taught Charlie's class of twelve- to fifteen-year-old boys.

She directed plays and musicals at the Mission. Charlie sang in a quartet, played the part of a tramp in a one-act drama, and had his first public speaking experience in the Demorest Silver Medal Declamation Contest. Like thousands of American children, he was given the Demorest Medal Book replete with speeches declaiming the "evil of alcohol." The contest was named for a millionaire easterner, a "total-abstinence man." Charlie pored over his book, and chose the shortest speech in it to memorize for the contest. He would do his part to vanquish "Demon Rum," and hoped to win the Demorest Silver Medal for his efforts. If he won, he might get to go to Chicago to compete for the gold medal, maybe even a diamond medal. He practiced his speech for days, winding it up dramatically with the ringing words, "The world moves!"

Two hundred people crowded into the Mission on the night of the contest. Charlie and Mary Sandburg and six other contestants sat in a self-conscious row facing the audience. August Sandburg was there, stern and quiet, his wife, Clara, at his side, smiling at her children waiting nervously to give their speeches. When Charlie's turn came, he rose before his "parents, playfellows, friends and countrymen." As he spoke, he began to look at the rows of faces watching him. He began to think of how he must sound to them, how he looked.

Suddenly he forgot his speech. He struggled to remember the words. He could only stand there, paralyzed and mute. The prompter gave him a cue, and he stumbled through to the end. With a subdued "The world moves!" he returned to his chair, knowing he had given the worst performance of the evening. The medal went to his sister Mary.

Later, alone, he brooded about his public disgrace. Long afterward, he could recite the speech perfectly. In his Connemara study in the early 1950s, Sandburg pulled that "burning" memory onto the pages of a draft of *Always The Young Strangers*. He wrote out the painful details of his boyhood failure on the Mission stage, and then put the pages away. That hidden draft did not make its way into his published memoirs. It revealed, far more clearly than the published episode, how he was stung by the audience's laughter: "Of course I know they didn't laugh at my ideas and my language. And yet—they laughed at me."

The laughter haunted him: "They laughed because I hesitated," he wrote sixty years later, "because I did not remember my piece, because I couldn't go on till a prompter told me the words I needed to go on, because I lacked an excellent literal memory, because I was a poor fish when it came to learning words out of a book and spilling them forth to an audience in a smooth even flow of shimmering syllables."

Ashamed that his memory failed him, Charlie resolved at the age of twelve that it would not happen again. When he filled milk pails and delivered newspapers in the chill prairie dawn, he practiced reciting facts and poems until he had a memory he could trust. If he could not have that coveted Demorest medal, he was glad it had gone to Mary. But there were other medals to be won, and he intended to win them. He vowed that the next time he stood on a platform to speak, he would keep his mind on his words. He would make syllables shimmer. Any laughter which came his way in the future would come because he invited it.

✻

Throughout his boyhood, Charlie slept to the pulsing rhythms of the trains coming and going through the prairie night. He sometimes amused himself at the depot watching trains bound to and from far places. He idled with hoboes and tramps who traveled furtively on the rods or the treacherous tops of freight and passenger cars.

He and his family did not have to go out of Galesburg then in search of America. America came to Galesburg. The railroad saw to that. The farsighted Galesburg businessmen who stubbornly connived to steer the railroad their way secured the cultural as well as the economic future of their city, for the trains brought vaudeville entertainers, politicians, opera stars, magicians, circuses, evangelists—and such luminaries as William Jennings Bryan, Elbert Hubbard, John L. Sullivan and James O'Neill, father of playwright Eugene O'Neill. The railroad brought the faces and voices of American life to the very doorstep of the town.

August had signed up to work for the C.B.&Q. in the days of rapid expansion between the Civil War and the Panic of 1873. He toiled "day on day swinging sledges and hammers on hot iron on an anvil." Years of hard, rote work left "layers of muscle making a hump on his right shoulder," and those thousands of anvil strokes wore indelible calluses on his hands. The C.B.&Q. blacksmith shop was a vast, busy place, for Galesburg was a railroad hub.

Eastbound trains thundered into town bearing hogs and corn, more than twice as much cargo as before the war. The trains discharged that cargo and filled their bellies with lumber and sundries for the westward runs. Of the twelve railroads carrying goods into Chicago, the C.B.&Q. carried the most corn, oats, wool, hides, cattle, sheep and hogs. The rails August helped to maintain groaned with the weight of livestock en route to the city which, years later, his son celebrated as the "City of the Big Shoulders," "the Hog Butcher of the World."

To Charlie, the railroad meant adventure, mystery and possibility. As soon as he grew old enough to understand its purpose, he begged his father to get him the free railroad pass to which the family was entitled. Then he could go to other, more exotic places—Peoria, Keokuk, even Chicago. But August, worn down by the grueling daily toil of expediting the travels of other men, had no patience with his son's hunger to travel. Charlie was sixteen before August finally relented and let him use the C.B.&Q. pass for a ride to Peoria fifty miles away. Charlie felt "important and independent," saw the State Fair and the Illinois River and real steamboats, and drank sulphur water. He was a traveler seeing the world. He wanted to go as far as the railroad lines would take him.

His father frowned on such hopes. Travel, like books, was a luxury. There was work to be done, money to be saved. Consequently, there was the inevitable, stormy conflict between a stern father and a son growing toward independence. Charlie's gentle mother was their intermediary. One night Charlie made his way home during a "wild downpour" with a pail of milk and an umbrella. A "fast twister of wind" turned the umbrella inside out. "I picked it up and ran to the house," he remembered. "What I got from my father was a hard slam on the side of the head and some furious words about an umbrella costing money that didn't come easy. Mama spoke gently and stepped between us. That was one of the few times he laid a mean hand on me. The hurt of the blow was easier to take than his bitter words of blame."

Charlie often watched his father at work in the after-hours at home, noting the pleasure August took in his small Swedish hammer. "Ah! dat iss Svedish steel," he would say, convinced that the Swedes made the best steel in the world. Sometimes, when August was "pushing a plane or driving a hard hammer blow, his lips drew away so that all his upper and lower front teeth were flashing to make a terrific fighting face." Charlie thought he looked as though "he could kill or smash anyone or anything against him." He was afraid of his father then. "At first I was terrorized that he might turn on me and I was ready to run. When I got used to it I laughed at him, but I didn't let him see me laughing."

Between the work-worn, sometimes volatile father and the bright, restless son, there was a complicated relationship. They came to stand on opposite sides of many matters, from books and education to politics, work and travel. The train was a symbol of the distance between them. To August it was taskmaster and livelihood, the controlling weight in a burdened life. To Charlie it was romance, adventure, freedom, the escape from Galesburg to all the wide world beyond.

＊

Charlie had his mother's face, clarified with his father's sharp cheekbones. His hair was thick and brown. His eyes were a blend of her blue and his father's dark ones, hazel, with flecks of brown and dark green. In certain lights they were sea-green. They were changeable, capricious and congenitally weak. He worried in later years that he would go blind.

He was wiry and strong, with the easy grace of the natural athlete. Until he cut his foot severely playing baseball, he wanted to be a professional ballplayer. When there was mischief in Galesburg, Charlie was usually at its center. His wide, engaging grin often masked a painful shyness. Despite the warmth and love he shared with his mother and sisters, he was awkward with girls far into his manhood, although women knew that he liked and understood them. He kept in memory an album of the faces of girls he had loved from afar. "I enjoyed their loveliness in my boy's mind in ways they could never have guessed," he wrote in *Always The Young Strangers*. His first love was a girl with a haunting face, "classic as Mona Lisa and a better-rounded rosy mouth." He was twelve or thirteen; she was the daughter of customers on his milk route. He was too shy to speak more than a few words to her, even on the summer night that he mustered the courage to walk her home from revival services at the Knox Street Congregational Church. "I was more bashful than she," he remembered. "It was a lost love from the start. I was smitten and she wasn't. And her face went on haunting me. . . . I asked for nothing and she promised the same. I could say I had known my first love. It was a lost love but I had had it."

∗

August and Clara sold their cottage on Third Street in 1879 and rented "another three-room one-story house" six blocks away on South Street. By 1881, they had managed by hard work and habitual thrift to buy a ten-room house on Berrien Street. There the family had more room, and August "set himself up, with due humility and constant anxiety, as a landlord." He divided the house into two apartments in addition to his family's living quarters, and also rented out two upstairs rooms, so that for years the house was full of tenants. "Two Swede families live downstairs and an Irish policeman upstairs, and/an old soldier, Uncle Joe," Sandburg wrote many years later in the poem "House."

> Two Swede boys go upstairs to see Joe. His wife is dead, his only son
>   is dead, and his two daughters in Missouri and Texas don't want him
>   around . . .
> Joe tells the Swede boys all about Chickamauga and Chattanooga, how
>   the Union soldiers crept in rain somewhere a dark night and ran for-
>   ward and killed many Rebels . . .
> The two Swede boys go downstairs with a big blur of guns, men, and hills
>   in their heads. They eat herring and potatoes and tell the family war
>   is a wonder and soldiers are a wonder.
> One breaks out with a cry at supper: I wish we had a war now and I could
>   be a soldier.

In 1883 August paid one hundred dollars down for a quit-claim deed to the house and lot on South Street where he and the family used to live. The purchase would cost him dearly years later, but for the present, his renters there and at home helped him pay for his property. With his own strength and skill, and the help of his sons, he was "a carpenter, a bricklayer, a house painter, a paperhanger, a cabinet maker, a truck gardener, a handyman restless and dissatisfied unless there was something to fix or improve on the property he owned or was paying for." Charlie was his father's chore boy, cleaning cisterns, helping to repair the roof or the pump or the furniture, running errands. August worried constantly about money. He practiced daily self-denial, allowing himself only meager pleasures—one five-cent cigar a month, smoking just an inch or two of it each Sunday to make it last from one payday until the next; wearing his one good suit Sunday after Sunday for years until it was threadbare from meticulous brushing.

He was paltry with praise and affection, too, living with a "fear of want, a dread in his blood and brain that 'the rainy day' might come and in fair weather he hadn't prepared for it."

He was a careful steward, always mending, fixing, using his manual cleverness to prolong the life of tools and furniture. August seldom smiled or sang, was never idle, even at the end of his ten-hour workday when he came home "fagged and worn" and soaked with sweat. He kept a plug of tobacco to help ease the tension when things were hard at work. He could be generous with his anger, raging in his "deep, passionate baritone" at a child's prank or innocent mistake. Whereas gentle Clara would slap or pinch a naughty child, August gave his sons his "powerful side fist." Most often it was waste, "breakage or spoilage" which provoked his anger—a helpless fury at spilled molasses, broken toys, garnered warmth escaping through an open door—the thoughtless indifference to the "proputty" for which he worked so hard. Yet he never uttered profanity in front of his children, never visited the town's saloons, was faithful to his wife.

August had a love for music which seemed aberrant in his dour nature. He bought a cheap accordion on which he learned to play a few tunes in private. For several years a blind accordion player passed through Galesburg, playing a few days on a street near a pool room. August would stand for half an hour listening to the "gravel baritone" of the black balladeer. He particularly enjoyed a song about Jesse James, and would pull a hard-earned nickel from his pocket, look at it "with real respect," and then drop it into the singer's tin cup, asking for "de Yesse Yames song." Later, when Charlie learned that song and tried to sing it for his father to please him, August was "only mildly interested."

Clara was as generous with affection and patience as her husband was penurious. Only twice, to Charlie's knowledge, did she ever defy his father; both times, she did so to buy books for her children. She had "visions and hopes" and an "eagerness about books" which her two oldest children avidly shared. Mary was an excellent student, and as soon as Charlie learned to read in Miss Flora A. Ward's first-grade class at the Seventh Ward School, he wanted to have books to read whenever he chose.

Despite August's angry charge that she had wasted precious money, Clara bought the *Cyclopaedia of Important Facts of the World* from a traveling book salesman, who persuaded her that the book would give her children education and the power of knowledge. The book cost seventy-five cents, more than half a day's pay of $1.40. The next one Clara bought was three times as big, twice as expensive and full of pictures. It was *A History of the World and Its Great Events*, giving special attention to the famous battles of all time.

When August learned of the book which cost more than he earned in a day's toil at the C.B.&Q. shop, he "stormed and hurled reproaches, and cried aloud" that his family was heading for the Knoxville Poorhouse.

Charlie realized that "printed words, written sentences, had no charm or mystery" for his father. "They were outside his needs, prayers, or wishes." With his mother it was different. She shared his love for books and words, understood when he exulted about the beauty of nature, the mystery of stars, explained only in part of the erudite pages of the *Cyclopaedia of Important Facts of the World*. When he tried to tell his father about what the dearly bought books said about the distance of stars, August replied, "We won't bodder about dat now, Sholly," leaving his son feeling that if, as the book said, the stars were millions of miles away, similar great distances could separate people. Even walking down the street, holding his father's hand, Charlie felt that there were "millions of empty miles" between them.

✳

By the time Charlie finished the second grade in 1885, he had convinced everyone he knew, even his teachers, to call him *Charles* or *Charlie* instead of *Carl*, because "Carl would mean one more Swede Boy while the name Charles filled the mouth full and had 'em guessing." Charlie's teacher that year was Miss Maggie Mullen, who fostered his love for reading, especially the life stories of famous men. After supper, when his chores were done, Charlie read biographies such as J. T. Headley's *Napoleon and His Marshals*. He encountered another famous general in 1885 when U. S. Grant died and Galesburg, like many other American towns, honored the deceased President with a funeral parade. When Charlie could not see in the throng of thousands who lined Main Street, August lifted him to his shoulders for a better view of the Galesburg Marine Band, the uniformed veterans of the Grand Army of the Republic, the Negro Silver Cornet Band and two real cannon, pulled by horses.

The somber parade was different from the exuberant circus parades which were more customary in Galesburg, and from Republican and Democratic torchlight rallies which heralded election days. Like most Swedes in Galesburg, August was a staunch Republican, and in his early

youth Charlie followed his father's example. He often accompanied August to Republican rallies, where men wore red-white-and-blue oilskin
capes and carried lighted torches and flambeaux. Charlie was a "young
Republican, a six-year-old Republican." He was not swayed for long by
his father's views, however. In his teens he was arguing his way toward
Populism, and then toward socialism, angering his father yet again in
the process.

August took pride in the work which encumbered his life ten hours
a day, six days a week, with no yearly vacation, a schedule he followed
from 1870 until 1904. Charlie figured that if his father could have worked
eight hours a day instead of ten, he would

> have had in those years many days amounting to two or three years of
> time for work of his own choice, for rest, for play and talk with his children
> and friends, for his accordion and his Bible. In those added two hours a
> day across those years his personality would have reached out and down
> and up, would have struck deeper roots in the good earth and sent higher
> branches toward the blue sky.

August maintained that "Hard work never hurt anybody." He had
little interest in the millions of working people in America who labored
under similar conditions, heard of but paid no attention to the Eight
Hour Movement which advocated eight hours for work, eight for sleep
and eight for recreation and education. When in 1888 railroad engineers
struck the C.B.&Q. line in Galesburg, a division point for the railroad,
Charlie instinctively sided with the strikers. When a Pinkerton guard
hired by the railroad shot a striking engineer, Charlie and his friends
saw the very spot on the sidewalk where the victim fell mortally wounded
and "his blood turned dry and rusty on the wooden boards."

"How or why I was completely against the railroad, I don't know,"
he reflected in later years.

> The boys I ran with, the striking engineers whom I knew to speak to, the
> wild and furious talk against "scabs," hit deep in me. I was a partisan. I
> could see only one side to the dispute though my little head did no thinking
> and had no accurate information about what lay behind the crying and
> shooting. . . . And why was I all for the strikers and against the railroad?
> It could be that I knew some good men among the strikers and they were
> human and I liked them, whereas the Q. railroad was a big unhuman
> Something that refused to recognize and deal with the engineers who in
> all weathers took their locomotives out along the rails hoping to pull
> through without a collision or a slide down an embankment. I was a little

ten-year-old partisan. I took a kind of joy in the complete justice of the cause of the strikers.

When he told his mother how he felt about the strike, she listened patiently, but warned him: "Be careful you don't talk about it to Papa. It worries him." Father and son never discussed the strike, nor did Charlie hear August discuss it with anyone else. He knew that his father "didn't like quarrels and this one had brought fist and club fighting to Galesburg."

Charlie's early, instinctive identification with the worker illuminates much of the work he later produced in a multifaceted career as political activist, journalist and poet. His poems reverberate with images of people who, like August and Clara, bent their lives to the weight of the work they had to do, "patient and toiling, more patient than crags, tides, and stars; innumer-/able, patient as the darkness of night. . . ."

In later years Sandburg made poem portraits of individuals trapped in lives of hard labor:

> He worked thirty years on the railroad, ten hours a day, and his hands
> were tougher than sole leather. . . .

The boy who sided with the strikers became the champion and the celebrant of the laborer, men like August, "the great brave men, the silent little brave men" who took pride in their work and their hands,

> . . . clutching the knuckles of their fingers into fists ready for
> death and the dark, ready for life and the fight, the pay and the
> memories—O the men proud of their hands.

✳

Growing up in Galesburg, Illinois, in the 1880s could be fun for a boy with a sense of adventure and fifty cents in his pocket. Charlie and Mart and their friends made a summer ritual of walking the four and a half miles from Galesburg to the Knox County Fair, striding barefooted over the country roads, shoes in hand. They put their shoes on at the fair for protection against being stepped on in the crowds that filed past such wonders as the Edison Talking Phonograph, the largest Knox County rutabaga of the year, and the prize "stallions and mares, bulls and cows, boars and sows, cocks and hens" who provided their chief lessons in sex education.

Charlie went to the C.B.&Q. yards at dawn on the days when the circus came to Galesburg. If he could, he got a job carrying water for the elephants or boards for the audience to sit on in the big tent pitched in a pasture near the city limits. A few hours of work earned a free ticket to the big show in the afternoon, a ringside view of clowns, acrobats, trapeze artists and hippodrome chariot races. Charlie gaped at the side-show freaks—the man with elastic skin, the tattooed man, the Oriental dancing girl, the Wild Man of Borneo, Jo-Jo the Dog-faced Boy, the dwarf and the giant, the armless man who wrote with his feet.

He liked the dark of the theater even better than the gaudy side show of the circus. He saw the Kickapoo Indians dance, watched mesmerists appear to split great rocks and dismember and reassemble live human beings. He heard about vegetarianism and saw a diorama of the Battle of Gettysburg. He saw *Hamlet* performed and heard speeches by congressmen and other politicians. In particular he liked the quiet, thoughtful oratory of gubernatorial candidate John Peter Altgeld.

When the old opera house burned, a new auditorium was built. Almost every Broadway hit heading west by train to Omaha and Denver stopped to play there. Charlie worked backstage to earn his ticket to special features. John L. Sullivan played in *Honest Hearts and Willing Hands*. Charlie met the train which brought African explorer Henry M. Stanley to lecture. He saw world-champion boxer Gentleman Jim Corbett; James O'Neill in *The Count of Monte Cristo*; the dramatic version of *Uncle Tom's Cabin*; burlesque and minstrel shows. The C.B.&Q. carried more than hogs, lumber and corn through Galesburg. The trains brought culture, music and art, a feast for a shy boy who loved to look and listen, and then try to imitate the wonders he had seen, by himself or with his brother Mart in their attic room.

Clara's fifth child, Esther, was born in 1888, the year that local scandal surpassed the features at the auditorium as the foremost "entertainment" in Galesburg. The death of the popular pastor of the First Swedish Lutheran Church brought a new minister to Galesburg. He was young, tall and handsome, his wavy blond hair swept into an unministerial pompadour. Just before his official election to the Galesburg ministry, he was charged in a bastardy suit in a nearby town. The trial in the Knox County Courthouse in Galesburg, replete with the colorful testimony of the curvaceous victim, magnetized the townspeople. The new minister vigorously maintained his innocence.

Charlie and his friends were in avid attendance at the trial, which resulted in acquittal. But the leaders of the First Swedish Lutheran Church did not wait for the verdict to inform the newcomer that he could not minister in their sanctuary. He decided to organize his own church in Galesburg. After painstaking deliberation, August Sandburg chose to break with the old church and join the new Elim Lutheran Church, named for the biblical desert refuge. The new minister eventually moved on to Chicago, leaving behind rancor, debts and several trusting Swedes who had signed promissory notes so he could build his Elim Church. The young Swedish-American Charlie Sandburg was so disillusioned by a minister who was a hypocrite and fraud that he never again affiliated with any organized church. August, a reverent and devout churchman, was deeply shaken by the schism. The Elim Church was defunct, but he and Clara no longer felt at home in the old First Swedish Lutheran Church and from that time on attended church services randomly, often at the Swedish Methodist Church, reading their Bible at home and privately keeping "to a faith that served them to the end."

✳

By the time he was in fourth grade at Seventh Ward School, Charlie had become a consistently good student. As a fifth-grader he walked a mile to the grammar school where all Galesburg children went after fourth grade. There he flourished under the care of Miss Lottie Goldquist, one of his favorite teachers. He averaged 95 in geography and arithmetic that year, 97 in language and 88 in reading. He was eleven then, in a year that marked in ways beyond his control the end of his boyhood. Ever after, Charlie and his family thought of 1889 as the Year of the Sleeping Mortgage.

Back in November 1883, in his careful quest for "proputty," August had purchased Hoover lot eight in Congers Subdivision on South Street, west of Pearl. He made a hundred dollar down payment for the house and lot then, and had the quit-claim deed to prove it. By 1889, to his pride, he owned the lot outright. This had not been an easy purchase with his wages of fourteen cents an hour, thirty-five dollars a month. Even when that was augmented by income from boarders and wages the children earned, it was difficult to support a family of seven, let alone own property.

In February 1889, five years and three months after he acquired the lot, August learned to his consternation that the lot had always been encumbered with a lien. On August 10, 1869, when August had just come to the new promised land, and long before he laid eyes on lot eight, the man who then owned it used the lot as security for a loan, giving a mortgage to William C. Grant, a man August never knew. Never in nineteen and a half years did Grant ask for payments due for interest on the mortgage, or communicate with August or the man who had sold him the lot in 1883. It was a double misfortune that Grant died just six months before the Illinois statute of limitations would have outlawed the old mortgage, rendering it worthless and no threat to frugal, industrious August Sandburg.

As it was, Grant died and passed the terrible document on to his heirs, who turned it over with all the other papers of the estate to their lawyers, who then brought a routine and impersonal suit against August Sandburg. Intimidated and embarrassed by the legal documents he could not interpret, August put on his one Sunday suit and took several costly days away from work to consult lawyers, one of them Forrest Cooke, future mayor of Galesburg, and the other future circuit court judge George Thompson. Despite their expert defense the court "granted judgment so that under the compulsion of law on June 8, 1889, August Sandburg laid on the line a borrowed $807.24 to redeem the mortgage of $556.40 and to pay every last nickel and copper of the interest, $250.84." This new debt added impossibly heavy weight to all he carried. Inexorably the money would be "wrung from the horny hands of August Sandburg." It was "the hardest worry" he ever had. Clara told her children he was "going through a terrible trouble."

He could not fully understand the intricate legal processes which indentured him and stripped him of his pride in owning property. He accepted his fate with a terrible quiet resignation which saddened his family. Sandburg resurrected the pain of that time in *Always The Young Strangers*:

> He had nothing of the actor in him, couldn't put on a bold front, had never practiced at the role of the accused or wronged, and the moment came, I am sure, when his dark and worn heart told him, "I stand mute —and I will pay—what you ask I will pay." There can be moments of assumptions against a man when the only recourse is an armor of si- lence. . . . He sat for hours at a west window of the kitchen in a wooden chair with no armrests, looking straight ahead to the east wall, dropping his eyes to the floor, then again looking straight ahead at the east wall. . . . Now besides his old debts he had a new one. He could study about how soon with a family of seven and a paycheck of thirty-five dollars a month he could wipe out this fresh debt load of eight hundred dollars. . . . A degree of trust that he had had in mankind was shadowed into something else.

In 1889, Charlie was only a boy. There was little he could do except measure the cost of the Sleeping Mortgage in his father's increasing silence and distance from him. August was even slower to laugh, to trust, to express love or kindliness. He worked harder, drove himself longer, denied himself more.

The Sleeping Mortgage made tough times even harder for the family. Charlie resolved to help his brooding father in the one way he could see that would count for something. He found his first regular job, sweeping the office and emptying the spittoons at the Callender and Rodine Real Estate firm, for twenty-five cents a week. From Callender and Rodine he went to school, and after school, six days a week, he delivered the *Galesburg Republican-Register*. His newspaper route took an hour and a half after school, depending on the weather, and paid a dollar a week. Most of what he earned he gave to his father to help with the debt.

As the need to work grew more urgent, Charlie's school performance suffered. His older sister Mary was an excellent student, despite the economic difficulties which usurped time and energy at home. August and Clara already looked forward to her graduation so she could begin working full-time, perhaps as a teacher.

August maintained his unswerving focus on the daily obligations which kept him hard at work fourteen to sixteen hours daily, six days a week. While he heard talk of the larger economic crisis threatening the country and the world, he knew simply the weight of his own incessant struggle to pay off the unexpected mortgage. The bitter acceleration of tension between capitalists and labor was a remote abstraction for him. Of the vast consequences of unfettered speculation, expansion and overcapitalization which plunged seventy-four railroads into bankruptcy in the desperate summer of 1893, he knew only the personal consequence of a work week curtailed, wages pared in half, even tighter austerity at home.

He was just one figure out of millions caught in the Panic of 1893 and the ensuing years of depression. Bad times had worsened into "hard times." Despite his arduous labors to shelter and protect his family, the long feared "rainy day" had come.

It became clear at last that the family could not afford to send two children to high school. Mary, with her head start and outstanding grades, deserved to stay until she graduated. Charlie's destiny would be sealed by the need to work. Like most of the children in Galesburg's Swedish population, he was conscientious about his work, not as studious and obedient as Mary, but still an above-average student. The Swedish-American children held their own in the academic circles of the town, and more Galesburg commencements than not listed a Swedish name for salutatorian or valedictorian. But going on to high school was a luxury to be denied Charlie. He would have to content himself with books.

He had devoured them during his school days and in the Galesburg Public Library. In the winter, he read in an overcoat in the north window of the unheated third-floor room he shared with Mart. He had an early taste for biography and history—John S. C. Abbot's two-volume *The History of Napoleon Bonaparte*; J. T. Headley's *Washington and His Generals*; Charles Carleton Coffin's American history series, especially *The Boys of '76*, which he read several times. Methodically he read all the public library books by Oliver Optic and Horatio Alger, and went to the YMCA library for *The Life of Mason Long, Gambler*. For fun he read *Toby Tyler: Or, Ten Weeks with a Circus*, detective stories, Mark Twain's *Huckleberry Finn* and *Tom Sawyer*, and the novels of Charles Dickens. His teacher Lottie Goldquist introduced him to the work of Eugene Field, who had studied at Knox College in Galesburg. According to Miss Goldquist, England had Shakespeare and Milton, New England had Longfellow and Holmes, but "Illinois and the Corn Belt had Eugene Field." She gave Charlie a love of the rhythms and deeper meanings of poetry.

One day on his way to school Charlie found a small biography of Civil War general Pierre Gustave Toutant de Beauregard. This miniature book was the first biography he ever owned. It was one of a series of fifty books packaged in Duke's cigarettes. You had to buy the cigarettes to get the books, unless you were as enterprising as Charlie, who found two local men who smoked the cigarettes and promised to save the biographies for him. He came to own cigarette biographies of Sarah Bernhardt, Cornelius Vanderbilt, George Peabody and Robert Ingersoll. He especially liked stories about "poor boys who have become rich."

✳

At the end of his eighth-grade year, Charlie left public school for good. He had spent more time that year reading and working at his several paying jobs than studying arithmetic, which he failed with an average of 55. His grammar grade dropped to 74. Like many students his age, he finished eighth grade but did not go on to high school. He had hoped to "get his first good suit when he completed the eighth grade," but there was no money for clothes. *Always The Young Strangers* omits the story that with "nothing but his old, tattered clothing to wear," he could not "bring himself to attend the graduation program and receive his diploma." It was June 1892. He was fourteen and had "more hopes than he knew what to do with." But hard times forced him to go to work.

Fortunately, he had the stamina to carry several jobs at once, and he knew how to work hard. He swept out and cleaned showcases at Harvey Craig's Drug Store, lingering secretly over two private pleasures. When he could snatch a free moment, he pored over the huge *Pharmacopoeia* in the pharmacy's prescription room, liking the complicated words. And he broke his solemn pledge of abstinence, sworn in the presence of beautiful Nellie Stowell at the Seminary Street Mission. In charge of refilling medicine bottles from the barrels of wine and casks of whiskey and rum stored in the drugstore cellar, Charlie had his "first taste of port wine and claret and found they tasted better" than he expected. He tasted whiskey and disliked it, but discovered a twenty-year-old rum which was "so grand and insinuating and soft and ticklish" that he saw its danger right away and "never took more than a half-mouthful of it in one day."

Charlie kept his *Galesburg Republican-Register* route, earning a dollar a week from the afternoon rounds. The newspapers gave him a tangible connection with the world beyond Galesburg, especially when he began to deliver the *Chicago Tribune, The Inter-Ocean,* and Victor Lawson's *Record* and *Chicago Daily News.* He held in his hands the particulars of momentous events—the tariff, free trade, pauper labor in Europe. He tried to imagine the perils of pauper labor in faraway Europe, but gave up because it was "hard enough to understand the ten-hour workday" in the C.B.&Q. shops at home. With his wagonload of Chicago papers, Charlie was a witness and a messenger, bringing news of the world to the familiar front porches of his hometown.

He found other work as he could. When he heard that the state of Illinois, in an effort to overcome a pestilence of English sparrows, was paying a penny for each dead bird, he made a leather sling and went after the bounty. He killed more than thirty sparrows before he decided he did not care for the job.

*

In the fall of 1892 Charlie began a regular job working for George Burton, who ran a dairy two miles out of town. Clara called him at five-thirty each morning, and he joined his father for a breakfast of "buckwheat cakes, fried side pork, maybe applesauce or prunes, and coffee." For a nickel he could have ridden a trolley car halfway to the Burton farm, but he walked two miles each way to save money. He worked seven days a week as a milk-wagon helper, with no vacations, no holidays, and a salary of twelve dollars monthly. From seven in the morning until one in the afternoon, he went from one Galesburg house to another with his milk cans, filling the waiting pails.

Burton was a stern, impassive man with a retreating chin and no sense of humor. He was gruff and insensitive to the boys and men who worked for him. Therefore Charlie did not complain when in late October he was ill with a sore throat. Only when he was weak with a high fever did he stay at home in bed. The illness spread through the Sandburg household, putting Mart in bed for several days. Seven-year-old Emil and two-year-old Freddie were soon so ill with sore throats that they could not swallow. Clara put her two youngest children together in a narrow bed moved from upstairs to the kitchen, the one room in the house with a stove. There the little boys tossed feverishly and rapidly grew worse. When their swollen throats turned pink and red and then "a grayish white," the Sandburgs called the doctor, even though a house call cost a dollar and a half.

The city health commissioner nailed a large red quarantine sign to the Sandburgs' front door late in October: DIPHTHERIA. Three days later, as his family kept watch in the waning afternoon light, Freddie died. Tears raining down her face, Clara touched her son. "He is cold," she wept. "Our Freddie is gone."

Emil was older, more rugged. They watched his struggle for breath, hoping he would pull through, but within an hour after Freddie stopped breathing, Emil died.

"It was all over," Sandburg wrote years later of the funeral day.

> The clock had struck for two lives and would never strike again for them. Freddie hadn't lived long enough to get any tangles in my heart. But Emil I missed then, and for years I missed him and had my wonderings about what a chum and younger brother he would have made. I can see now the lights in his blue eyes and over his wide freckled face and his quick beaming smile from a large mouth. There have been times I imagined him saying to me, "Life is good and why not death?"

Charlie carried milk from house to house despite his exposure to the highly contagious illness which finally killed his brothers, and despite the alarm of Galesburg matrons who knew about the quarantine at the Sandburg house. George Burton had no patience with errant workers or mysterious diseases, and Charlie worked every day except the days his brothers died and were buried.

Their two small white caskets stayed in the center of Clara's front room until after a simple Lutheran funeral service. For Charlie and Mart, now his only brother, there were no public tears. They were impassive, taking that posture as a sign of strength. Later, together in the bed they shared, they cried for their lost brothers.

When Charlie walked the two miles back to Burton's dairy there were no words of compassion from his boss. He worked despite his sorrow, but there grew within him an angry resentment toward Burton and the hard times which had reduced his father's work day to four hours, his monthly paycheck to less than sixteen dollars. Sadly, there were two less mouths to feed now, two small bodies less to clothe. But August still had to make the mortgage payments. It cost money to keep Mary in high school. To the old debts were added new ones to the doctor, the undertaker, the cemetery for the lot which held the two caskets. The twelve-dollar salary George Burton paid Charlie each month was essential to the family's survival. That was known and appreciated in the house on Berrien Street.

"I shall cry over the dead child of a stockyards hunky," Sandburg wrote years later, evoking the spectre of his brothers' deaths and the aftermath of intensified economic struggle for the family:

His job is sweeping blood off the floor.
He gets a dollar seventy cents a day when he works
And it's many tubs of blood he shoves out with a broom day by day.

Now his three year old daughter
Is in a white coffin that cost him a week's wages.
Every Saturday night he will pay the undertaker fifty cents till the debt
    is wiped out . . .

I have a right to feel my throat choke about this.
You take your grief and I mine—see? . . .

That winter was savagely cold, bitter with ice and snow. There was even less chance of money for carfare. Charlie walked his daily milk route, plus the four miles to and from the dairy, his feet wet, often numb, painful with chilblains. Once when he was ten minutes late, Burton chastised him. "My feet were near frozen," Charlie explained, "and I had to stop to warm them." In those frigid days there was not a dollar to spare for overshoes, much less two dollars for warm felt boots like those which protected George Burton from the fierce prairie winter of 1893.

✳

When her two youngest sons died of diphtheria, Clara was in the first weeks of her seventh pregnancy. The baby girl Martha Clara was born on April 21, 1893. There were other comforts during those months. Charlie found solace in his sister Mary's company, and the bond between them grew with the years. She was preparing for high school graduation that spring, and Charlie proudly contributed money to buy her a pretty white dress, so that she "looked as good as any of them on Graduation Day when she stepped out and bowed and took her diploma." She was going to be a teacher. Her thirty-dollar-a-month salary meant that she would be a help and no longer an expense to the family. She practiced teaching Charlie, who was eager to get all he could from her high school texts. Together they read and discussed Irving's *Sketch Book*, Scott's *Ivanhoe* and Hawthorne's *The Scarlet Letter*. Charlie ignored Mary's algebra and Latin books, but devoured her history text, John Fiske's *Civil Government in the United States*, which gave him his first sense of the dynamics of American government.

Charlie and Mart's rare leisure hours were spent with a gang of friends called the Dirty Dozen, seven of them sons of Swedish Americans, one the son of a Frenchman and four the offspring of oldtime Galesburg families. They often got into mischief. Seven of the Dirty Dozen, including Charlie and Mart, got a special ride in the Galesburg police wagon one hot summer Sunday afternoon for swimming in the nude in the old brickyard pond just inside the city limits. Sandburg described the incident in *Always The Young Strangers*:

> There was my nice brother Mart opposite me, the first time any Sandburg in Galesburg had been arrested! There was Bohunk Calkins and "Jiddy" Ericson and Charlie Bloomgreen from their nice homes and decent people on Berrien Street and now in a wagon watched by two policemen, on their way in broad daylight on a Sunday to be hauled to the Cherry Street calaboose and thrown into stinking cells with the Saturday-night drunks and disorderlies.

The boys were released after four hours confinement with seven "sweating and puking drunks." In court the next morning they were dismissed with a reprimand.

Charlie and his friend John Sjodin once ventured into the mail-order business. John convinced Charlie that if *The Comofort* mail-order catalogue in Augusta, Maine, could reach a million subscribers, there were other mail-order fortunes to be made. John bought a little printing press for less than ten dollars, Charlie invested nearly three dollars in savings, and from the Sjodin hayloft the two boys issued Charles A. Sandburg's first printed work, a mail-order journal called *Not a Cent*, after their policy of charging nothing for subscriptions. *Not a Cent* died after two issues, which offered the sixty Galesburgians who received copies "slightly used" knives and books, and a "slightly used" Waterbury watch.

With John, Charlie found companionship "having color and mystery." From him, Charlie learned clog dancing and Chicago lore, for the Sjodins had lived and worked in Chicago before moving to Galesburg. John also taught Charlie to think about politics, business, crime and the problems of the American working class. John and his father were the first "hard-and-fast political action" radicals Charlie met. John's father was a journeyman tailor, "an anarchist, a Populist, and a Socialist." He and his son predicted that out of a great "tide of feeling among the masses" of the American people would come the power to break the oppressive domination of corporations, wealth and special privilege which in their view strangled the lives of the American labor class.

Charlie relished John Sjodin's good humor, his reverence for life, his passionate idealism. He was a catalyst for Charlie's own early idealism. Years after Charlie left Galesburg and found his own platform for socialism and reform, John Sjodin lived in their hometown working as a painter, a leader in his union and in the Galesburg Trades and Labor Assembly, and an organizer of the Galesburg local branch of the Socialist Party. He ran a grocery store far more successfully than he had run the hayloft mail-order business, and was for years the Socialist candidate for mayor of Galesburg. In the 1890s, the stimulating talk around the Sjodins' kitchen table made Charlie think hard about the issues of his times and the ferment of the "widespread American scene."

✳

The big C.B.&Q. railroad whistle apportioned the hours of daily life in Galesburg, blowing at seven in the morning when the work day began; at noon and one, the common dinner hour; and at six in the late afternoon to proclaim the day's work finished. Not even the railroad whistle escaped the "doom and fate" of hard times. With the C.B.&Q. facing severe financial problems in 1893, the whistle blew twice daily, at eight and at noon, marking the curtailed work day.

When they could no longer afford butter, the Sandburgs put lard and salt on their bread, and molasses or sorghum when the lard was gone. They depended on the yield from the garden in back of the house, and took part in a neighborhood food cooperative to buy and butcher an occasional hog. August gave his sons haircuts to conserve money, and mended the family's shoes with scraps of leather. Clara patched and repatched clothing and socks, made brown bread, added a little freshly ground Arbuckle's coffee to leftover coffee for several days in succession. Like most of their neighbors, the Sandburgs learned even more about how to make do.

As the stronger older son, Charlie was responsible for bringing fresh water several times daily from the temperamental pump fifteen steps outside the back door of the house, making the trip thousands of times. He also tended the small coal-burning kitchen stove, filling it with cheap coal which, unlike regular soft bituminous coal, had to be regularly screened for lumps. He carried the heavy coal hods and emptied countless pails of ashes. "The past is a bucket of ashes," he wrote many years later in several poems. Ashes may seem to be weightless ephemera of vanished fires, but a bucket filled with ashes is a heavy burden, not easily carried, much less forgotten or flung to the wind. The abiding weight of the past deceptively encumbers the present.

"I was no boy hero of the late 1880s and early 1890s," he wrote in *Always The Young Strangers*, "but it helped sometimes for me to imagine I was a heroic struggler amid continuous and monotonous obstacles of circumstance."

✳

Early in 1893, Charlie quit his job with George Burton, resisting the urge to say, "You know where you can stick this stinkin' job I've had with you." With his formal education behind him, he knew he had to learn a trade. There was little hope of finding work with the railroad, with so many workers laid off. Charlie tried to apprentice himself to plumbers, carpenters and house painters, but business was too slack. Finally he took a job as a barbershop porter at the Union Hotel for three dollars a week plus shoeshine money and tips. He decided to become a barber. Barbering was a trade which allowed you to travel and work from coast to coast, with the outside chance that you might one day shave a man who would give you a better job.

Charlie mopped floors, cleaned windows, mirrors and cuspidors, waited on customers, shined shoes and began to imbibe the political lore of western Illinois. Once he shined the shoes of Eddie Foy, the great showman, but his usual customers were businessmen, politicians, Civil War veterans or old pioneers. The Union Hotel barbershop was one forum where he got "education in scraps and pieces of many kinds," but he soon decided he was no barber, and got another dairy job, this time with Sam Barlow, a good barn-dance fiddler and a genial man. For the next sixteen months, Charlie worked for Barlow, earning twelve dollars a month plus dinner every day, cleaning horse stalls and driving the milk wagon for two daily deliveries in Galesburg.

He began to tinker with homemade musical instruments in his spare time, partly because Barlow loved the fiddle. Charlie made a willow whistle, a comb with paper which sounded like a harmonica, and a cigar-box banjo. He bought a kazoo and a concertina and a two-dollar pawn-shop banjo. He paid a quarter for three banjo lessons, and one of the Dirty Dozen taught him to sing minstrel tunes and popular songs and ballads. He had discovered in his love of music a lifelong avocation. Years later, as the troubadour poet of the people, he would sing and play his way across the country many times.

Then, at age seventeen, he worked ten-hour days to help support the family. His friends were laborers like himself who had been out of school for several years, doing whatever work the lean economy offered. They often hovered about the Knox and Lombard campuses, where more fortunate young people enjoyed college life. En route to his daily job at Barlow's dairy, Charlie walked through the Knox College campus, where Abraham Lincoln and Stephen Douglas had debated in October 1858. There, on a bronze plaque on the east front of Old Main Building, Charlie first read Lincoln's written words, and they were soon etched in his memory. He regularly stopped to read "what Lincoln said to twenty thousand people on a cold windy October day: 'He is blowing out the moral lights around us, when he contends that whoever wants slaves has a right to hold them.' " Charlie Sandburg studied Abraham Lincoln's words "in winter sunrise, in broad summer daylight, in falling snow or rain, in all the weathers of a year."

1896–1898

2. The Dust of the Traveled Road

> I SHALL foot it
> Down the roadway in the dusk,
> Where the shapes of hunger wander
> And the fugitives of pain go by . . .
>
> The dust of the traveled road
> Shall touch my hands and face.
>
> —Carl Sandburg, "The Road and
> the End," *Chicago Poems*, 1916

C harles August Sandburg was eighteen years old in 1896 when he first saw Chicago, the city of his destiny. Until then, he had never traveled farther than fifty miles from Galesburg, despite his father's access to the C.B.&Q. pass which entitled him and his family to free journeys by train to all other cities on the line. Charlie had been to Monmouth, Illinois, for the Junior Epworth League convention when he was eight. When he was fourteen he and some of the Dirty Dozen bought two cheap horses for a fifty-mile trek to the Illinois River. When he was sixteen, August let him ride fifty miles to Peoria on the train to see the State Fair. He felt like a "traveler seeing the world." Once he tasted the "dust of the traveled road," he was hungry for exploration and discovery. As a restless adventurous boy, he embarked on a lifelong quest for the open road. He would never be content to travel vicariously.

The Sandburgs had attended stereopticon lectures which took them on imaginary trips to China, the Holy Land and Rome, the Eternal City. As hard times began to ease somewhat, August even bought the family a stereoscope and a dozen photographs so they could make foreign jour-

27

neys in their own front room. In *Always The Young Strangers*, Sandburg recalled the impact of his favorite stereoscopic photographs, views of a barge on a river in Hamburg, Germany: " 'So this is a ship,' I said, 'and this is a river and this is what you would see if you went to Hamburg.' To a kid who had never been out of Knox County, Illinois, Hamburg was many weeks' traveling over the wide and crazy Atlantic Ocean. 'And Asia,' we said, 'Asia, that's too far off to think about.' "

Charlie was restless in Galesburg, sometimes hating and sometimes loving his hometown, but always chafing at the narrow boundaries which confined him there. He loved the arc of the prairie, the clean open contours of fields falling away to the horizon, but he wanted to explore other places. His father finally gave in to his begging for the railroad pass, and Charlie set out for Chicago, "traveling light," carrying only what would fit in his pockets—a knife, a piece of string, a pipe and tobacco, two handkerchiefs and a dollar and fifty cents he had carefully saved for the trip. John Sjodin knew how to live cheaply in Chicago, and helped Charlie plan the itinerary for his three-day excursion to make his money last as long as possible.

Charlie had formed his own opinions of the city, drawing images from the newspapers he read avidly, and from the stories he heard from the Sjodins and other friends who had actually seen the place for themselves. In his short lifetime, the population of Chicago had nearly quadrupled, to more than a million inhabitants in the 1890s, 77.9 percent of them of foreign parentage. Demographically Chicago was a cross-section of the world. Economically, the city was the commercial lifeline of the United States, as its web of railroads intertwined the financial power of the East and the agricultural riches of the West. Culturally, Chicago was on the verge of an era of thoroughly American experimentation in architecture, the visual arts and literature. There Carl Sandburg was to find both subject and setting for his major work as a journalist and poet. But on his first journey to Chicago he had just three days and a dollar and a half to spend. He was enthralled.

✳

All his life he would prefer the train to every other mode of travel. Geography and circumstance determine the route and the vessel when you are seduced by dreams of escape, romance and freedom. For the prairie vagabond, the trains were not only more accessible than ships at sea; they were just as exciting, in their novelty as well as in their power to transport.

From the window of the passenger car, Charlie watched the train's swift dissection of what seemed to be one vast, contiguous cornfield reaching for miles toward Chicago. The occasional stark farmhouse leaning into the horizon was usually dwarfed by a barn or silo. The train moved through the sparse beauty of the prairie to the homogeneous façades of tranquil prairie towns—Galva, Kewanee, Mendota, Aurora, and then to the clamor of Chicago, its jagged profile thrust against the eastern sky.

The city was a shock and an exhilaration to the senses. Charlie walked for miles. He reveled in the city's vigor and Lake Michigan's beauty, walking along Michigan Avenue and looking for hours at his first view of "shimmering water. . . . Those born to it don't know," he said, "what it is for a boy to hear about it for years and then comes a day when for the first time he sees water stretching away before his eyes and running to meet the sky."

Charlie walked through the Loop to the Board of Trade, under the vibrating Elevated lines, out to the Des Plaines Street Police Station, from which he traced the route to the site where eight policemen had been killed by an anarchist's bomb during the Haymarket Riots in 1886. He wanted to see the State Street department stores and the buildings where they published the Chicago newspapers he carried in Galesburg. At the Eden Musée on South State Street, he spent ten cents for a ticket to see "in wax Jesse James, several murderers, a line of faces showing what syphilis does to your face at first and then later if you don't get cured." John Sjodin had told him where to stay and where to have fun, so he rented a room in a cheap hotel on State Street, went two nights to a vaudeville show, and ate at Pittsburgh Joe's on Van Buren Street near Clark or in a free-lunch saloon.

Charlie had "heard so much about Chicago saloons, their free lunches and funny doings" that he did not want to leave Chicago without "seeing the inside of a saloon." He had heard about Chicago prostitutes, too, and had seen but not fully comprehended the cartoons which depicted Chicago "as a tall robust woman with a big bosom and over her forehead a crown with the words, 'I will.' " He described his first tentative encounter with a young, hard-faced Chicago prostitute:

> She smiled a hard smile and said, "What are yuh doin'? Lookin' fer a good time?" I said, "I'm polishing nail heads for Street and Walker." It was a saying then. If you were out of work and looking for a job you walked the streets where the wooden sidewalks had nail heads sticking up and your shoes polished those nail heads. Her face lighted up and she blazed it at me: "I'm goin' to polish your nail head fer yuh!" She was terribly alive and the words came hard through her teeth and her pretty mouth.

Awkwardly, Charlie replied, "You're up the wrong alley, sister. I ain't got but two nickels and they wouldn't do you any good." The prostitute moved on with a cheerful "All right," and Charlie returned to Galesburg, brimming with the power and excitement of Chicago, eager to travel again. From that time on he was never content in one place for too long.

Back home in Galesburg, he bristled more than ever at the dead-end jobs with no future in the monotony of his hometown. Still awkward with girls, his shyness made him lonely, despite his place in a large family and his links with the Dirty Dozen. "I had my bitter and lonely hours moving out of boy years into a grown young man," he reflected. "I can remember a winter when the thought came often it might be best to step out of it all." His brief contemplation of suicide gave way to his irrepressibly buoyant good spirits. His melancholy lifted as he considered how he might kill himself. He had read in detective stories about carbolic acid and prussic acid, but doubted he could get a prescription for the only two poisons he knew about. His sense of humor returned as he imagined how awkward it would be to shoot or hang himself. He had to laugh at the macabre prospect that if he strangled himself by hanging, his tongue might slide over his underlip, making him "too ugly a sight" to think about. "You have to work at several chores to hang yourself," he concluded. "It is more bother than any other way of killing yourself."

He considered drowning himself in a local lake, but figured he would instinctively swim for shore and live on. Finally he decided that the best way would be to throw himself in front of the C.B.&Q. fast mail train. He even visualized the headline: *Sandburg Boy Killed By Train.*" He speculated that this method would spare his family embarrassment and disgrace. Charlie emerged from these deliberations on his own death "actually feeling a little cheerful." His voracious reading helped him to see that life was not easy even for "all the best men and women" he had known in his life and in the books he read, that all sensitive people had "bitter and lonely hours," and that any growth of "new strengths of body and mind" came through struggle. He concluded that while there was such a thing as luck, "if the luck didn't come your way it was up to you to step into the struggle and like it."

Thus Charlie tried to throw his considerable energy into work and the daily life of the town which seemed to be growing smaller as he grew older. He heard Abraham Lincoln's son Robert Todd give a thoroughly forgettable speech at the thirty-eighth anniversary of the Lincoln-Douglas Debate at Knox College on October 7, 1896. Sam Barlow encouraged Charlie to read and talk politics that election year. Back at work after his Chicago trip, he found that his milk wagon turned out to be a congenial place for reading, whether on the loping journeys from house to house or in the lulls when he stayed with the horses and wagon while the others delivered the milk from porch to porch on foot. In those intervals he read Victor Lawson's *Chicago Record*, not imagining that one day he would write for a big Chicago newspaper, with Lawson himself as his boss. In 1896 Charlie Sandburg was just a restless, hungry young man trying to learn about the world from his vantage point on the seat of a Galesburg, Illinois, milk wagon.

He fed on books. He read Thomas E. Watson's *The People's Party Campaign Book* and decided he preferred the Populists to the Democrats or the Republicans. He concluded that the rich had become too rich, the poor too poor. He became a pessimist as he read of thousands of farmers losing their farms, millions of workers losing their jobs in the economic cataclysm of the 1890s. He feared there was "hell to pay all down the line" and wondered how the depression was going to end.

William Jennings Bryan became Charlie's hero. He heard Bryan give a speech on a platform near the C.B. & Q. tracks, and later rode the cowcatcher of a C.B.&Q. engine to Monmouth, Illinois, to hear Bryan speak again, sharing the journey and a pint of blackberry brandy en route with Frenchy Juneau. Young Bryan was tall and extraordinarily hand-some, with thick black hair. His clear-eyed sincerity coupled with his resonant, deep voice made him a compelling orator, charismatic, evan-gelical. Charlie read and reread Bryan's Cross of Gold speech and decided that he was unequivocally in support of Bryan and the free and unlimited coinage of silver. He found the courage to argue politics with his father that summer of 1896. August remained, of course, a staunch Republican who would not for a moment consider voting against William McKinley. Although later in his life Charlie concluded that Bryan was "a voice, an orator, an actor, a singer, and not much of a thinker," father and son "had it hot and heavy over the supper table" during the 1896 election. It was the first time in his life that Charlie "enjoyed argument just to be arguing."

When Mary told him he was so effective at putting "the other side in a hole" that he ought to become a lawyer, Charlie sent away for the prospectus of the Sprague Correspondence Schools of Law and Journal-ism. He studied the brochures and "half decided" he would make a better journalist than lawyer.

At eighteen approaching nineteen, he was searching for himself, for a direction for the future. Charlie knew far more about what he did *not* want than about what he did. He wanted a profession, not a dead-end job, but he had no idea what that profession should be. He wanted to travel, not to stay forever in Galesburg, but he did not have a destination in mind, much less the wherewithal to support a journey. He was doing his best to educate himself. He had worked as a tinner, a potter's turner, a water boy, a floater and ice handler for the Glenwood Ice Company. He had delivered newspapers and milk. He had a steady job at Sam Barlow's dairy, but he needed a raise.

"My bones tell me I'm not getting anywhere," he told Barlow after a year and a half at the dairy. "I hate to leave you. You're the best man I ever worked for but I can't see I'm getting anywhere." To their mutual regret, Charlie left Barlow's employ, although they kept their friendship until Barlow died.

In June 1897 Charlie Sandburg was nineteen. He weighed 142 pounds. His shock of dark hair fell over his high forehead, shadowing the hazel eyes which could change, chameleon-like, from gray to blue-green, from teasing to brooding. As he grew taller, his high cheekbones emerged dramatically to give him a handsome profile. His face was still boyish when he laughed, as he did often. He was usually suntanned from work in the open air, and although his body was lean, he had his father's wiry, virile strength.

He thought about becoming a mercenary in Cuba to help "the scrabbling little armies" of the people win their independence from the cruelties of the Spanish general Weyler. He abandoned that plan as impractical, and looked for other ventures to take him away from Galesburg and into the real world.

Once again the train was his conduit. In June 1897 he joined a procession of thousands headed West to find work in the distant wheat fields of Kansas. The ensuing journey affected him profoundly, and its consequences reverberated through the rest of his life. The journey forced him toward "the isolation, the brooding and the reverence and the solemn moments that are often a requisite to personal development." It left him infatuated with hoboes, bums and tramps, with their lingo and songs, the ragtag romance of the open road. It marked the first time that he chronicled his life in that writer's reflex, the private journal. And it deepened his empathy for the common man, his fellow strugglers in that great faceless democracy of the displaced.

Charlie had talked to the hoboes and tramps who inhabited the "jungles" near the railroad tracks in Galesburg enough to know that there was a hierarchy of vagabonds. There were tramps, hoboes and bums. The "three species of the genus vagrant" included the tramp, who would dream and wander, usually following the main lines of the railroads.

There were subspecies of tramps—the professionals and the amateurs, called "gay-cats," who would break down and work sometimes in hopes of finding regular jobs. Some tramps were runaway boys, infected with wanderlust. Then there were hoboes, who worked and wandered, usually riding the rails illegally to work on farms at harvest time, or in the cities, the mines or the railroad section houses. Finally there were the bums, who drank and wandered, frequenting barrel houses and saloons. As a matter of principle bums never worked, and were inveterate beggars and sometime con men.

Charlie intended to be a hobo and a gay-cat, hunting for work on the way West. He had seen enough of the tramps, hoboes and bums who passed through Galesburg to know that a throng of men and boys, and occasionally women, restlessly, sometimes hopelessly followed the narrow course of the railroad through the prairie to the vast plains and the high mountains, and sometimes on to the far West. There were thousands of men searching for work, displaced by hard times. There were thousands of other wanderers content with handouts and occasional odd jobs. There were able-bodied men who had no desire to work, but who loved the anonymous freedom of life in the hobo jungles skirting the railroads which offered escape, and sometimes perilous adventure. There were bums, derelicts and outcasts who could not or would not work, but who moved in a ceaseless migration from coast to coast, first in the wake of the Civil War, and then in the economic wasteland following the depressions of 1873 and 1893.

When Charlie Sandburg set out from Galesburg on a bright June afternoon in 1897, he joined an army of strangers who numbered from sixty thousand to six hundred thousand, depending on whose estimate you believed. The first significant wave of American vagrants came during Reconstruction—errant soldiers who had "become so enamoured of camp life" that they would not return to mundane life at home. These bands of "marauding veterans," as some states called them in postwar vagrancy legislation, were joined after the Panic of 1873 by legions of unemployed. By the mid-seventies, vagabonds had begun walking the better-kept railroad beds instead of the rugged turnpikes, and the next logical step was to hop aboard boxcars and ride instead of having to "drill" (walk) over the ties. By 1880 vagrants riding trains illegally were accepted by the railroad companies as "an unavoidable nuisance on railroad property."

By the 1890s the American vagabond, whether hobo, tramp or bum, was part of the last migration to the American West. American newspapers worried over "the growth of a horde of paupers, beggars and tramps." Journalists and reformers in the late 1890s believed that the "tramp problem" endangered the nation's cities and towns, its railroads and its penal system. By the turn of the century, the railroads estimated that their combined losses from property damage, "robbery, obstruction of tracks, interference with signals, stopping of trains," injuries to employees and damage suits attributable to tramps surpassed twenty-five million dollars.

Social critics blamed the nation's army of tramps for soaring crime, and the resulting overload on police work, the criminal courts and the benevolent societies of the country. Some European countries had established labor colonies to house the homeless and unemployed, and there were advocates for a similar system in the United States, where many tramps (including Charlie Sandburg and Jack London) were temporarily relegated to jails or penitentiaries.

Jack London, a skilled tramp himself in the early 1890s, believed that tramps were an essential part of the "surplus labor army" which was an "economic necessity" in American society. "Into the surplus labor army are herded the mediocre, the inefficient, the unfit, and those incapable of satisfying the industrial needs of the system," London wrote. He and Sandburg shared innocent motives in taking to the road. They were high-spirited, restless young men, tired of dead-end jobs, thirsty for adventure and excitement. London "beat" East in 1892, while Sandburg struck out for the West in 1897.

The hobo journey was for Sandburg an exploration of his own frontier. He was a pioneer helping to tame a new part of the nation. The journey was a pilgrimage, replete with fellow travelers whose vivid company stimulated Sandburg, as well as London, to become a storyteller. The successful hobo had to be an artist, according to London:

> For know that upon his ability to tell a good story depends the success of the beggar. . . . He must create spontaneously and instantaneously—and not upon a theme he reads selected from the plenitude of his own imagination, but upon the theme he reads in the face of the person who opens the door. . . . I have often thought that to this training of my tramp days is due much of my success as a story-writer.

Sandburg reflected in a similar vein in *Always The Young Strangers*:

> I was meeting fellow travelers and fellow Americans. What they were doing to my heart and mind, my personality, I couldn't say then nor later and be certain. I was getting a deeper self-respect than I had had in Galesburg, so much I knew. I was getting to be a better storyteller. You can be loose and easy when from day to day you meet strangers you will

know only for an hour or a day or two . . . I was working out of my bashfulness.

Charlie called himself "a young stranger meeting many odd strangers" on his hobo journey. Drawing on the journal he kept then, he recalled them many years later in his autobiography. He absorbed and digested the stories his fellow pilgrims shared, and wove them into his poetry and prose. There was the "Noo Yawkah" who generously shared his "lump" or handout of food, as well as his life history. He was a product of a Brooklyn orphan asylum who had "taken to The Road" and never worked a day in his life. "The real tramp can't even think about work," he told Charlie, "and it gives him a pain in the ass to talk about it." He introduced Charlie to tramp lore and lingo, advising him to stay away from "horstyle" or hostile towns. Charlie stayed away from the Noo Yawkah after he made a homosexual advance, and quickly became astute in judging his compatriots in hobo jungles from Iowa to Colorado.

He began to learn the songs of the road—"Shovelin' Iron Ore" and his perennial favorite "Hallelujah, I'm a Bum," which he first heard "at the water tanks of railroads in Kansas in 1897." His ears were full of the vernacular of the road, its vivid slang as well as its plaintive music. He was becoming a keen listener and observer, filing away the rhythms of a diverse language and the faces of the men who told him their stories, false or true.

Charlie passed up a chance to join the Gold Rush to the Klondike. He found honest, decent men like himself in the hobo jungles, victims of hard times who chose working over begging. He found panhandlers, petty thieves and pimps. He met men much older than he who were hoboes for the love of the open road, who liked to sleep under the stars and explore new terrain.

Hard times were beginning to ease in 1897. McKinley and the Republicans had won the election of 1896, restoring confidence in the stability of the currency. An extraordinarily abundant American wheat crop in 1897 coincided with a price increase from fifty-three cents to a dollar a bushel, yielding $500 million for the wheat harvest Charlie Sandburg and thousands of hands helped to thresh on rejuvenated Western farms. As farmers paid their mortgages and had money left over to spend, the renewed demand for manufactured goods stimulated factories to reopen, hire back laid-off workers, even expand. Back home in Galesburg, August Sandburg could afford to buy Clara a parlour organ, a fancy family Bible and a horsehair sofa for the front room.

In the fellowship of a variegated company of hoboes, Charlie was seeing firsthand other men who, like his father, intensified his awareness of the problems of his times and, although he had not yet found the name for it, further prepared him to become a socialist.

Charlie was discovering the dangers as well as delights of the open road, for tramping could be a perilous occupation. In 1895, 6,136 people died in railroad accidents in the United States—1,811 employees, 170 passengers and 4,155 "other persons"—trespassers; mostly tramps, hoboes and bums. Nearly six thousand "other persons" were injured on the railroads that year alone. The hoboes who successfully rode the rods, blinds or roofs of trains exerted skill, ingenuity and constant vigilance to do so. Railroad "shacks" or brakemen sometimes extorted money, shoes, watches or other goods from hoboes caught in the act of "holding down a train," but exasperated "shacks" could turn to cruel and dangerous tactics to "ditch" a hobo, or throw him off a train.

Charlie had his own narrow escape on a Colorado Midland train eastbound from Canyon City to Denver. The experience was vivid in his memory half a century later:

> It was night. There wasn't an empty boxcar on the train, and for the first time I was riding the bumpers late at night. I didn't know what a stupid reckless fool I was. My feet were on those bumpers and there was no danger in that. My hands were on the brake rod so in case my feet should slip I could hold on and not go under the wheels. Suddenly I was saying to myself, "You damn fool, you've been asleep." My numb brain was saying that when you go to sleep on the bumpers you're in luck if your hands don't loosen and topple you down under the moving train.

When he nearly fell asleep again, Charlie kicked himself and beat the side of his head with his fists in an effort to stay awake. "An hour of that," he wrote, "and the train stopped and I got off and thanked God and the everlasting stars over the Rockies."

There were dangers on land as well as on the tracks, and certain towns were widely known to be brutally hostile to hoboes. Unlucky tramps were sometimes forced to run a gauntlet of clubs from one end of town to the other. In other places, they were pelted with stones or manhandled by police, who often beat them brutally or threw them into jail. Charlie had his own encounters with "horstyle shacks." A plainclothes cop at the railroad division point in McCook forced Charlie to leave with a "We don't want the likes of you in this town." He was beaten by a shack on another train when he refused to pay the shack "two bits" to stay in an open coal car where he thought he had concealed himself.

Not surprisingly, the vagrants who risked their necks riding the rails in such unorthodox positions formed a close company. There was camaraderie in the hobo jungles strung across the country as tawdry appendages to railroad breaking points and watering stations. This was the world Charlie Sandburg entered when he left the clean, comfortable house on Berrien Street in Galesburg and rode a freight train boxcar to Fort Madison, Iowa, having his first look at a state other than Illinois, as well as the Mississippi River, which he had long had a "sharp hunger" to see.

For three and a half months, Charlie worked his way West, blacking stoves; cooking at a small lunch counter; working on a railroad section gang for two weeks in Bean Lake, Missouri; washing dishes for two weeks in a restaurant in Kansas City; harvesting hay and broom corn in Lindsborg, Kansas; threshing wheat in Larned and Lakin, Kansas; washing dishes in Denver, where he got paid for it, and in Omaha, where he did not because the hotel went under before he left.

By late September 1897 he was road-weary and "a little homesick for the faces and streets of Galesburg." Rather than move on to the West Coast, he turned east. In Nebraska City, he chopped wood at a large brick house owned by a lawyer, who took a look at his ragged clothes and gave him an iron-gray all-wool suit, secondhand but better than Charlie had ever had in his life. Charlie "thanked him and offered to chop more wood" but the lawyer laughed and sent him on his way. That night, even with the warm new suit, Charlie was too cold to sleep in the empty boxcar he occupied with four other hoboes. The five of them "marched to the city calaboose" and requested permission to sleep in jail that night, where a marshal allowed them to spread newspapers on the stone floor and sleep until morning.

In Omaha en route to Galesburg, Charlie almost enlisted in the regular army, but the required three years of service discouraged him. When he reached Galesburg on October 15, he had more than fifteen dollars in the stiff pockets of the lawyer's good wool suit. He was glad to be home in the "only house in the United States where I could open a door without knocking and walk in for a kiss from the woman of the house."

The trip had changed him, given him self-confidence and a new ease with friends and strangers. "Away deep in my heart now I had hope as never before," he reflected. "Struggles lay ahead, I was sure, but whatever they were I would not be afraid of them." The hobo journey opened his eyes and ears to the problems of his times. He began to listen for authentic voices, and to record the experience. He was discovering his country, his countrymen, himself. No one place could contain him now.

"I leave you behind—" he wrote in a later poem:

You for the little hills and the years all alike,
You with your patient cows and old houses
Protected from the rain,
I am going away and I never come back to you;
Crags and high rough places call me,
Great places of death
Where men go empty handed
And pass over smiling
To the star-drift on the horizon rim . . .
There is no pity of it and no blame.
None of us is in the wrong.
After all it is only this:
  You for the little hills and I go away.

*

Home again in Galesburg, Charlie found a full time job at Daniel and
Louisa Schwartz's dairy farm three miles east of town. Louisa Schwartz
fed the men a big breakfast, and Charlie drove the milk wagon into town
to make the deliveries. On the plodding journey to and from town, he
studied the Home University lecture series prepared by University of
Chicago professors and serialized in the *Chicago Record*. Louisa Schwartz
encouraged his reading and told him he was going to make something
of himself. Only she and his mother and sister Mary had ever expressed
that confidence in him.

Charlie was twenty years old in January 1898. He was tall and thin;
the hobo journey had worn him down to 136 pounds, but with regular
sleep and the good food he ate at the Schwartz table and at home on
Berrien Street, he gained sixteen pounds. As much as he liked the
Schwartz family, he was restless again by February, and keenly aware
that he needed a trade more than a job. He apprenticed himself to "a
blank-faced Swede" to learn to be a house painter, and spent tedious
ten-hour days scraping paint and sandpapering wood to prepare it for the
painter's brush.

During that oppressive winter, working as "one more apprentice" six
monotonous days a week for his forgettable boss, Charlie was excited by
the news of the explosion of the battleship *Maine* in Havana harbor on
February 15, 1898. He devoured Chicago newspapers which kept Galesburg citizens aware of the growing national clamor for war, the liberation
of Cuba, the achievement of Manifest Destiny. Like most Americans,
Charlie believed that the Spanish deliberately perpetrated the explosion
of the *Maine*, despite the fact that the cause of the disaster was never
proven and the Spanish had been cooperating with the American am-

bassador in Madrid, General Stewart Lyndon Woodford, to rectify Spain's oppressive Cuban policies. The Spanish expressed regret at the disaster and cooperated fully in the efforts to rescue the *Maine* survivors, but most American newspapers, particularly William Randolph Hearst's *Journal*, blamed the Spanish for an outright act of war. A *Journal* extra of February 18, 1898, carried a headline proclaiming WHOLE COUNTRY THRILLS WITH WAR FEVER YET THE PRESIDENT SAYS "IT WAS AN ACCIDENT."

The midwestern and far western states were particularly strong proponents of war with Spain, but President McKinley opposed the war, even after the *Maine* disaster. By April 11, however, intense national pressure, combined with the influence of his own political advisers (including Theodore Roosevelt, militant, exuberant Assistant Secretary of the Navy) led McKinley to send Congress a request to use "the military and naval forces of the United States" as might be necessary to protect "endangered American interests."

The same press which at times acted irresponsibly to heighten war fever had conveyed to the country the plight of thousands of Cubans held by the Spanish government in concentration camps where many of them were victims of disease, brutality and starvation. Charlie was "going along with millions of other Americans who were about ready for a war to throw the Spanish government out of Cuba and let the people of Cuba have their republic." Furthermore, he resolved during those boring days on the painter's crew, if war did come and "men were called to fight it," he would be among the first to enlist.

President McKinley declared war on Spain April 24. Two days later Charles August Sandburg was sworn into Company C, Sixth Infantry Regiment, Illinois volunteers, Galesburg's contribution to the State Militia. The Sandburgs had worried about Charlie when he hoboed his way West. Now they dreaded to see him go off to war. He went off cheerfully anyway, clad in the completely impractical army issue of heavy blue wool shirt, dark blue wool coat, light blue wool pants, the honorable and serviceable uniform which had warmed privates under Grant and Sherman in Civil War winters, but which was cruelly unsuitable for the tropical summer ahead of the Illinois men bound for Puerto Rican and Cuban battlefields. Charlie's enlistment papers described him as "twenty-one years of age, five feet ten inches high, ruddy complexion, gray eyes, brown hair, and by occupation a painter." He would not be twenty-one for ten months, but had claimed to be, and therefore to be a full-fledged citizen and soldier.

More than ten thousand Knox County citizens swarmed around the men of Company C as they assembled at the Galesburg Armory and then at the C.B.&Q. station for the journey to Springfield, then Washington and war. As Charlie's eyes roamed the crowd and found his mother weeping, he "waved to her with a laugh and she laughed back through her tears." He set out with intentions to write regular letters home to his family and his friends John and Vic Sjodin, but after one letter, gave up his idea of writing reports for the *Galesburg Evening Mail* when he found out that another Galesburg soldier was going to write for the newspaper.

Company C of the Sixth Illinois was one of hundreds of army units quickly embroiled in the contradictory and confused management of the "splendid little war" which gave up more American sons to tropical disease than to death in battle. Of 5,462 casualties in 1898, 379 died fighting enemy troops; 5,083 succumbed to malaria, yellow fever and other tropical maladies in Cuba and Puerto Rico.

The daily problems besetting Charlie and the other men of Company C were symptomatic of the management of the whole war: poor communications, ambivalent orders, scarcity of food and supplies, poor training of troops. Charlie began to chronicle his war experience in a small pocket notebook. In his free hours during basic training, he explored the state capital and walked past Lincoln's home. His company was transported by train to Falls Church, Virginia, where they marched two miles to Camp Alger. There they trained and drilled throughout May and June. Charlie wrote of the irony of living seven miles from Washington and the Department of the Army headquarters and seeing the company cook "patiently cut away from a flitch of pork about a quarter of it that was alive with maggots." As the summer heat intensified, disease began to spread from the stench and "swarming flies" of open latrines.

Charlie made friendships within Company C which lasted all his life; in later years he valued his membership in the Veterans of Foreign Wars and attended several Company C reunions. Before the war was over for the men in Company C, most of them had come to dislike and some of them to openly defy and criticize their captain, "a second-rank Galesburg lawyer, a tall heavy man with a distinct paunch, heavy jaws, and a large mustache slightly graying." While his troops were getting along on bean soup and infested meat, the captain and his St. Bernard dog ate sirloin steaks, often within sight of the men.

When Company C marched five miles from their bivouac at Camp Alger to the shores of the Potomac River for an encampment, Charlie had his first swim in the river which wound through the capital city down to the Chesapeake Bay and on to the Atlantic Ocean. He paid his respects to Lincoln sites in Washington, seeing Ford's Theater "outside and inside," standing outside the Peterson House across the street, and reciting for a fellow soldier the poem he had memorized because of Lincoln, "Oh, Why Should the Spirit of Mortal Be Proud?"

In early July the men of Company C exchanged state militia caps for wide-brimmed felt hats and Springfield rifles for Krag-Jörgensens, and traveled by train to Charleston, South Carolina. There Charlie swam in the Atlantic, swallowing seawater just to taste the salt.

On July 11, Company C and five other companies of the Sixth Illinois boarded the *Rita*, "a lumber-hauling freighter" and the first Spanish ship captured by the American navy in the war. When they could not sleep in the hot, humid bunkroom below deck, Charlie and several hundred others slept on the upper decks.

The *Rita* reached Guantanamo Bay, Cuba, on the evening of July 17, the day that former Confederate general "Fighting Joe" Wheeler aided Colonel Teddy Roosevelt and his Rough Riders and the unsung black heroes of the Ninth and Tenth Cavalry units in the capture of Santiago. That victory, and the threat of four hundred troop cases of yellow fever, resulted in a change of orders for Colonel Jack Foster and the men of the *Rita*, who anchored for several days in Guantanamo Bay with the *Oregon*, the *Indiana* and the *Iowa*. The ships set sail under the command of General Nelson A. Miles, who had served under Grant in the Civil War.

The Miles expedition reached Puerto Rico early on the morning on July 25. In full battle gear, Charlie and the soldiers of six companies of Illinois volunteers left the *Rita* in rowboats to wade ashore at Guánica. The shooting was so near that white puffs of smoke were visible from the volleys. With battle imminent, Private Charlie Sandburg was assigned company detail. He saw exploding shells and watched regulars advancing through the sugarcane fields rimming Guánica, saw soldiers firing and cutting down fences with machetes, while he played his mundane role in the day's battle. He carried pork and beans and other provisions for the company cook, and then made a special trip back to the *Rita* in a rowboat to bring his captain's well-fed dog safely to shore.

The darkness of the first night brought confusion to the American troops in the sugarcane fields of Guánica. They were marched to a site where an expected battle failed to materialize; they marched back to their camp, where edgy soldiers aimed their Krag-Jörgensens "at an unseen enemy," some of their bullets hitting the transport where General

Miles slept. For the rest of their sojourn, the men of the Sixth Illinois had for enemies not Spanish soldiers but prostrating tropical heat, torrential rains, mosquitoes so large that they seemed to come "in brigades, accompanied by bugle corps." Charlie and many other men were bitten until their eyes were swollen closed. Through the oppressive August heat, soldiers of the Sixth Illinois marched, laden with rifles, bayonets, up to fifty pounds of ammunition per man, blanket rolls, half a canvas pup tent each, coats and rations. They still wore the "heavy blue-wool pants of the Army of the Potomac in '65 and thick canvas leggings laced from ankles to knees." Cases of sunstroke, heat prostration and fever mounted day by day.

By the time they completed the grueling march to Yauco and Ponce, those towns had surrendered. As the men straggled up the steep, rough grades into the Adjuntas Mountains, Charlie and his buddies diverted themselves by singing and picking up some practical Spanish phrases. They enjoyed "elegant" native cigarettes and sampled native fruits— rich coconuts, succulent mangoes—and ate raw sorghum and sugar.

Heat, sickness and mosquitoes did not quell Charlie's exuberant spirits or his tireless curiosity. He packed the small pocket journal with observations to take home, notes about the Puerto Ricans, the landscape, the "arrogance" of militiamen, the excellence of the chaplain's sermons, the "hazing of a camp thief." He described a killing march up an eight-mile grade in blazing heat. He had been a keen observer during his hobo journey. Now he instinctively chronicled the events of the war as he saw them, in fragments as if to reconstruct the story later.

The military excursion was shorter than Charlie had anticipated. They learned at Utuado that the August 12 armistice had been signed, and started back down the steep mountain roads for the return to Ponce. By the time the Sixth Illinois returned to the *Rita*, most of them were ill and thin. Charlie, a robust 152 pounds when he enlisted in April, boarded the *Rita* in August twenty-two pounds lighter. The homeward voyage allowed for some recovery time, despite the steady diet of "cold canned beans, occasional salmon, and the reliable hardtack" and the regular necessity of inspecting for lice, the nearly invisible "gray-backs" which had to be painstakingly picked from clothing and crushed. "Underwear and pants were more of a problem," Charlie noted. "In camps we boiled them occasionally when there was time and a big kettle of water. But only a bath all over with sizzling hot water would get those armpits and other hideouts where they were dug in. This I had learned the year before in hobo jungles."

By the time the men of Company C reached the port of Weehawken, New Jersey, in late August, they were "lean, somewhat faded and ragged, tanned by sun and sea, with perhaps a touch of malaria, hard-bitten by circumstance and insects." They were treated like heroes in New York, and back in Springfield where they mustered out in mid-September, and then back home in Galesburg, where the Army and Navy League and the Presbyterian Ladies' Society vied to entertain them at banquets.

Years later, reporter Carl Sandburg covered Theodore Roosevelt's speech at the Chicago Stockyards Pavilion and heard him say of the Spanish-American conflict, "It wasn't much of a war but it was all the war there was." Sandburg wrote in those later years that the Spanish-American campaign in Cuba was "a nightmare of blood, fever and blunders."

But on September 21, 1898, Private Charles August Sandburg, American soldier and citizen, was welcomed home from his first war a hero. August Sandburg did not take time off from work to join the throng at the C.B.&Q. station who greeted the men of Company C, "emaciated and worn, bearing the marks of great hardships and suffering," as the newspaper reported the scene. Clara and Mart told Charlie later about the deep, quiet pride his father took in his military service. With a son fighting for his country, August felt once and for all time truly Americanized.

As Charlie gave his father fifty dollars of his muster-out (or discharge) pay of $103.73, he noted that August was walking more slowly, that his shoulders were "more bony so that the hump of muscle on the right shoulder stood out more." His father was aging, he could see after the months of distance from him. Their reunion was as warm a time together as they would ever share. August was grateful for the money and impressed at the handsome salary his country paid its soldiers for their work. He would never understand or approve of his son's vagabond life, but he took great pride in Charlie's military service. He read with awe the discharge papers which testified, however perfunctorily, that Charles August Sandburg had been "a good soldier, service honest and faithful." Later, August framed the certificate and hung it in a place of honor in the front room of the Berrien Street house.

For all the bravado in his Spanish-American War journal and his published account of the experience in *Always The Young Strangers*, Sandburg took his fears to Puerto Rico. In the loneliness of night guard duty he spoke to "audiences of shadows and stars" the lines of Gray's "Elegy," Longfellow's "Psalm of Life" and Robert Ingersoll's oration at the grave of his brother. "I had one eye closed by mosquito bites one night camped in a ravine near Yauco," he wrote,

> and as I walked back and forth on guard duty I spoke to
> an audience of mosquitoes—
> > "The boast of heraldry, the pomp of power,
> > And all that beauty, all that wealth e'er gave,
> > Await alike the inevitable hour;
> > The paths of glory lead but to the grave."

Along with the poetry and songs embedded in his memory Charlie apparently took passages of Shakespeare with him to Puerto Rico, as a frayed pocket dictionary among his papers suggests. More than half a century later he gave it to his grandchildren, with a note of explanation: he had carried the pocket dictionary to Puerto Rico and back in 1898, he told them. Pasted on the flyleaf were two passages from Shakespeare, one from *Love's Labor's Lost*, and another from the third act of *Measure for Measure*:

> *Claudio*: The miserable have
> No other medicine, but only hope:
> I have hope to live, and am prepar'd to die . . .
> > *Duke*: Be absolute for death: either death or life
> Shall thereby be the sweeter . . .
> > > Yet in this life
> Lie hid more thousand deaths: yet death we fear,
> That makes these odds all even.

He had gone off to war hoping to live, prepared to die. He had survived to tell about it. His life in Galesburg just before the war had taught him something about the "thousand deaths" hidden in ordinary life. "Joy always,/Joy everywhere," he wrote in a later poem. "Let joy kill you!/ Keep away from the little deaths."

✳

The night of his return from the war, Charlie went home with his sister Mary to the farmhouse near Dahinda, Illinois, where she had a job as a teacher. After months of laying his bedroll on steep hillsides, rough campgrounds and the splintering decks of troop transports, he found it impossible to sleep in the soft depths of a four-poster feather bed. He tossed and turned for a while in the unaccustomed clean comfort of the bed, and then stretched out on the rag carpet on the floor. There he slept immediately, a weary former hobo, ex-soldier and young stranger, come home again.

＊

1898–1902

3. **An Independent Drifter**

> . . . I had wonderings and hopes but they were vague
> and foggy. I couldn't see myself filling some definite
> niche in what is called a career. I might become a
> newspaper reporter, a foreign correspondent, an author of
> books, an advertising copywriter—or an actor, a Lyceum
> lecturer, an agitator, an orator—maybe a Congressman,
> or an independent drifter defiant of all respectable
> conformists. This was all misty.
>
> —Carl Sandburg, *Ever the Winds of Chance* (1983)

Charlie Sandburg never expected to go to college, even though he had grown up roaming the lawns and buildings of the two colleges in Galesburg. As a boy he often explored nearby Lombard College after he learned that "you could go in free." He and his friends would run barefooted up the narrow stairs to the gallery of the college chapel on the third floor of Main Building, where they could eavesdrop on commencement exercises and chapel speakers. On the second floor they discovered a glass case which contained "a tall human skeleton" and spent hours in furtive, whispered contemplation of the skeleton's clean bones and grinning teeth, conjecturing about the fate which led him to permanent public display at Lombard.

The need to work had closed the door of public education for Charlie when he was thirteen. Ironically, it was the monotony of dead-end work which impelled him to enlist in the army, and it was his status as a veteran which entitled him to free tuition at Lombard College. He wrote about the college years in a sequel to *Always The Young Strangers* which was still incomplete and unpublished at his death in 1967, although it was finally published in 1983. He entitled this autobiographical fragment *Ever the Winds of Chance*, after a line by humorist George Ade: "We are all wisps, and the winds of chance blow in many directions." Charlie believed that "in nearly every life come sudden little events not expected that change its course." His neighbor and Company C comrade George Longbrake was the instrument for changing the course of Charlie's life. It was Longbrake, a Lombard student, who proposed that Charlie seek free college tuition as a veteran, even though he did not have a high school diploma. Thus Charlie gained admission to the preparatory school of the small Universalist college. He was granted permission to take some college courses as well, and as the ripe prairie autumn enfolded Galesburg, Charlie signed up for Latin and English. He went to Lombard, he said, "a seasoned soldier and a raw scholar."

"I do not remember that at that time there was anything particularly distinguished in his appearance," his favorite college professor, Philip Green Wright, reflected a few years after he met Charlie Sandburg,

> anything, that is, to suggest incipient genius. He looked like one of the "prolitariate" rather than one of the "intellectuals" . . . just a rough featured, healthy boy, possessed of indomitable energy and buoyancy of spirit. But it is just these rough featured boys whose faces take on with the years the impress of that indefinable quality we call character. I suppose the "god within" can achieve more lasting results with granite and bronze than with clay and putty.

Charlie's friends quickly began to call him "the Terrible Swede," not such a bad characterization, Wright wrote, "for it is a quality of this old viking blood that it enables its possessor to land on his feet in any and every environment." Charlie would need that ability, as well as his remarkable stamina, to sustain the schedule he mapped for himself at Lombard. As always, he needed to earn money to support himself and help his family. His friend Wiz Brown got him a job as call man at the Prairie Street fire station in Galesburg. With some of his army muster-out money, Charlie bought a bicycle and a blue fireman's shirt with "two rows of pearl buttons of silver-dollar size," and moved into the Prairie Street station, where his boss, Chief Jim O'Brien, believed a former soldier would make a good fireman.

Charlie had to make a quick exit from his Lombard classes when the fire whistle blew, but his professors were tolerant. Thus, after years of getting his education in "scraps and pieces," at odd jobs and on the road, Charlie settled down to get a formal education. His family had moved across Berrien Street into a larger house than the one they had occupied for seventeen years. The house had conveniences they found luxurious —"a second floor bathroom with a long tub," "a wooden pump and well close to the house, an indoor pump for the soft rain water," and a furnace with registers. "We were very near to being Middle Class," Charlie mused, "though the Old Man was still a blacksmith's helper, ten hours a day at 14 cents an hour." His enterprise had begun to pay off; after his work day, August labored at gardening, and buying and fixing up property to rent at a profit. After classes and between fires, Charlie helped his father with the extra jobs. He and Mart worked through many nights from seven until midnight, tiring before their father did. "The Old Man was thinking of the profit that did come to him from selling the house and lot," Charlie realized, "but he couldn't have worked the way he did unless he truly enjoyed work for the sake of work itself." That was a principle Sandburg would incorporate into his own true work when he found it.

Mary's teaching income helped to lift the family "very near" to middle class, as did the contributions Mart and Charlie made to the family treasury. August's skepticism about Charlie's college studies was muted, therefore, so long as he was earning money. Clara, on the other hand, was "always smiling and cheerful."

"You do the best you can, Charlie," she would tell her hard-working son, "and maybe you make a name for yourself. It don't do any hurt to try."

✳

Unfinished as it was at the time of Sandburg's death, *Ever the Winds of Chance* promised to be more revealing of the interior person than of the general experience of coming into manhood at the turn of the century, as was the thrust of *Always The Young Strangers*. Sandburg seemed inclined in *Ever the Winds of Chance* to admit his readers past the embroidered surface of exterior details to some perception of his evolving interior life. "Often did I look back at past years and see that I had been many kinds of a fool—and that I had been happy in being this or that kind of fool," he wrote. He had "seen a good deal of the world," Professor Wright noted, "some of it, I believe, from the under side of box-cars." But Sandburg entered college, as he confesses in *Ever the Winds of Chance*, keenly aware that he "had a mind that was slow and hard driven here and there where other students took it fast and easy." At twenty, he was older than the other students in the preparatory school, and older than many of the students in the college classes. He saw the unexpected boon of a college education as his bridge to a far better life than he could expect as a Galesburg tradesman. As he moved from the fire station to his classes to the constant chores at home, he was working as hard as he had in the odd jobs before the war. The difference was that he had a passion for books and was discovering the limitless horizons of the life of the mind.

"I was a human struggler in a new loneliness good to know and good to grapple with for whatever might come of it," he wrote. He had no ideas yet about a definite profession, but from the first weeks at Lombard found himself increasingly drawn to "fooling around with pens, pencils and papers."

Although he slept at the Prairie Street firehouse nearly every night for the next three and a half years, Charlie set up a study for himself at the end of an upstairs hallway in the new Berrien Street house. There he began to spend methodical hours reading, writing and thinking. Only five feet wide and eight feet long, the room had a single window which overlooked "a tall, noble tulip tree" and all of Berrien Street. Charlie used the room to study and write, smoking "endless pipes of Scraps, the crushed and cheap but pure tobacco leaves." In February of his first year at Lombard, he sat bundled up in a turtleneck sweater, a jacket and an overcoat in his unheated study to read Robert Louis Stevenson's *Dr. Jekyll and Mr. Hyde* and write an assigned paper about it, searching himself for "Jekyll and Hyde streaks" and finding "several Hyde streaks that it wouldn't do to write about." He was groping, experimenting, struggling to understand himself. He entered fully into college life at Lombard and found it exhilarating, but there was in the background "an endless un-rest." He read Thomas Carlyle's account of a man who slit his throat one morning while shaving when "it came over him that life would be damned monotonous shaving every morning as long as he lived." "I would study about monotony," Sandburg wrote, "and whatever I died of, it was not going to be monotony."

✻

Knox College was the older, more prestigious institution in Galesburg, with twenty-six faculty members and 672 students in the late 1890s. Lombard was newer and smaller, with 175 students and a faculty of nineteen. Yet there was an air of intellectual and religious freedom about the thirteen-acre Lombard campus which suited Charlie. Lombard was an unorthodox college, and he was not a conventional student. Most of the students came as he did "from plain folks mainly, from the working class and middle class," and most of them worked as hard for their keep as he did.

Knox College was thirteen years old when the Spoon River Association of the Universalist Church voted to found a college which would be a liberal alternative to the narrow sectarianism then typical of Knox and many other church-supported colleges. Christened the Illinois Liberal Institute, the college had its first home in a building in the southeast part of Galesburg. When that building burned and a Universalist named Benjamin Lombard gave money for a new structure, the college was renamed Lombard. It became a university when the divinity school was added. From 1899 until 1902, Lombard was the site of Charles August Sandburg's formal education.

When he enrolled in Dr. Frank Hamilton Fowler's English course in October 1898, Charlie was not only older than most of his classmates, but still somewhat shy and awkward. His hands were rough from eight years of full-time labor at menial jobs. He was insecure about his intellectual ability, although his travels as hobo and soldier had given him more self-assurance. The fact that he was a war veteran gave him a certain immediate stature on campus, and he quickly became a visible and popular member of the Lombard student body. A natural athlete, he led the Lombard basketball team "to a series of remarkable victories," and later on was elected editor-in-chief of the college paper, the "most coveted honor" at the college. Despite the fact that he lived off-campus in the fire station and took most of his meals at home rather than in the college dining hall, he was soon one of the best known and liked men at Lombard.

In the fields which interested him, Charlie was an eager, hungry student. One of the most important experiences of his first year was his English class with Dr. Fowler, already bald at age thirty-two, whose flowing mustache did not fully conceal a retreating chin. Dr. Fowler had been educated at Johns Hopkins University and the University of Chicago; his students had their "suspicions that his learning weighed him down, there was so much of it."

Despite Fowler's ponderous teaching methods, Charlie was profoundly stimulated by the reading he had to do. He was introduced to British and European literature, and the encounter was explosive. There he met the work of Robert Browning, the first poet to influence him deeply. He committed long sections of Browning's work to memory. He liked the "stormy" writing of Thomas Carlyle and discovered Francis Bacon, John Bunyan, Joseph Addison and Daniel Defoe. He disliked the "pretentious, stupid, overly fancy" work of Dryden, the "overdone" prose style of Addison. He was haunted then and throughout his life by the "dark bittersweet" music he found in the essays and letters of Charles Lamb, and sought the source of the power of Lamb's descriptions. He marveled that "in the Illinois Corn Belt, in a classroom looking out on pastures and farm wagons hauling hogs, hay, tomatoes, turnips," he could get from Lamb "the feel and the smell and noises of London a hundred years before." He was learning that "books and writers can cross oceans carrying the heart's blood of men who write."

The English anthology which was required reading in Dr. Fowler's class included only five American authors—Irving, Hawthorne, Emerson, Lowell and Holmes. At the turn of the century, most American writers were still too unknown and unappreciated to be included in standard literary anthologies. In a book of essays by critic Brander Matthews, Charlie discovered the American poet Walt Whitman. He bought "a ragged, second hand edition of *Leaves of Grass*, read it when it was not 'required reading,' " and decided to "read it again and read it slow." It was the beginning of a lifelong association, personal, idealistic and poetic, with Whitman. At about the same time, he began independently to read the work of William James, where he came upon ideas which had a far-reaching impact on his later work as poet and politician. From James, Charlie got the image of the unbroken cords linking vanished prehistoric creatures with their evolutionary progeny, including contemporary man. He recorded in his notebooks passages from James, including this one: "Bone of our bone, and flesh of our flesh, are these half-brutish pre-historic brothers. Girdled about with the immense darkness of this mysterious universe even as we are, they were born and died, suffered and struggled."

He explored that concept in poetry, early and late, probing in his poems the profound repercussions of that radical idea, evolution. "I am the deer and the weasel, the tiger, the eagle—/I am thy brother and one of thy kin," he wrote in one of his first poems, "The Plow Ox: The Spanish Bull," published in 1904. In "Wilderness," published in 1918, he wrote of the zoo, the menagerie "inside my ribs, under my bony head, under my red-valve heart . . ."

> There is a fish in me . . . I know I came from the salt-blue water-gates . . .
> I scurried with shoals of herring . . . I blew waterspouts with por-
> poises . . . before land was . . . before the water went down . . .
> before Noah . . . before the first chapter of Genesis . . .

In the last volume of poetry published in his lifetime, Sandburg was still exploring the "everliving roots" of life in the universe. His last published poem "Timesweep," which closed *Honey and Salt* (1963), is in many ways a synthesis of ideas born in him when he discovered William James during his college days:

> Who are these people I come from who follow the ways
> of long-gone time and long-gone fathers? . . .

Am I, are you, kin to these everliving roots? . . .
I have been woven among meshes of long ropes
and fine filaments: older than the rocks and
fresh as the dawn of this morning today are
the everliving roots who begot me,
who poured me as one more seeker. . . .

From James, he also drew the image of the heroic struggle of "over-whelming numbers of human beings" striving up the evolutionary spiral.

For Charlie it was a stunning conception that he was bound bone to bone and flesh to flesh to the long, evolutionary processional which wound back to the beginning of time and being. The political extension of this metaphysical idea undergirded his instinctive socialism, as he tried to articulate the "human heroism lying roundabout" him, beginning in the continuous daily toil of his father's life.

In an early essay entitled "The Average Man," he echoed James:

The average man does the work of the world. . . . So when you're drawn by any spell of fascination toward him, it's a very deep and quiet heroism that attracts you, a heroism as profound and undemonstrative as the ocean during a gray rain. . . . We may put up structures that touch the sky, build touring cars that outstrip the wind, and if as a nation we have not caught the broader meanings of that word "comrade," . . . we have come short of a really great civilization.

Charlie probed in depth the ideas of writers such as James, Whitman and Lamb. The rest of his reading was random, eclectic, superficial. An examination of his Lombard transcript reveals that he did not take the standard, required courses for a degree. He chose courses instead which interested him, concentrating on literature, elocution and history. He liked a course in Anglo-Saxon because of his love of language. He was fortunate that neither the rigor of his Lombard curriculum nor the obligations of his jobs deprived him of time to think and write. He liked the dictum of English painter P. G. Hamerton that "the first requisite of a liberal education is one year of downright idleness." Later, he gave himself a half year of that requisite, but as he moved from day to day during his first year at Lombard, he began to wonder if getting an education was a waste of time, if instead "it would pay you to sit quiet and alone in a room and ask yourself questions about who and what you are inside of yourself and what are the outside forces doing to you?"

He continued to read and study in the small workroom on Berrien Street, at the Prairie Street fire station, and at the pine table in the Lombard College bell tower. He began to read not only for fellowship with the minds of the authors whose books he read, but, in a significant step toward his future, to "try to get at what it is that makes good writers good."

"Maybe what I mostly believed then," he wrote, "was that I wouldn't be scared to try my hand at writing in any field. There was always the consolation that if I didn't like what I wrote I could throw it away or burn it—as so definitely happened, and often."

✳

As the hobo-turned-soldier-turned-student instinctively moved toward becoming a writer, he was greeted one bright May morning in 1899 by four of his local army comrades. They brought him exciting news. Congressman George W. Prince of the Tenth District of Illinois was offering an appointment to the United States Military Academy at West Point to one man to be chosen by the officers of Company C, Sixth Illinois Volunteers. On the basis of his Spanish-American War service, Charlie was selected for the honor. By June 6, 1899, he was at West Point to stand examinations to make his conditional appointment permanent. "I never had any dreams about being a general, colonel, or major," he wrote of the incident in *Ever the Winds of Chance*,

> but there was a pull about it. If I didn't pass I could come back to Lombard. There was something about the way the Company C officers picked me out of ninety and more others—I had to go along with them. Con Byloff said, "We're proud of you. You're the bird for this." It was like they were pinning an award of merit on me, a private, never even a corporal.

With barely three weeks to review for the examinations, Charlie tried to refresh himself on "what I had forgotten, if I ever knew, of history, geography, arithmetic, grammar." At the same time in Milwaukee a potential classmate was completing an arduous campaign for appointment to the Academy. The son of an army general, he was an accomplished athlete and a brilliant scholar. He had flunked an earlier physical examination for admission because of curvature of the spine. His ambitious mother had moved from Texas to Milwaukee to take advantage of a family friendship with the district congressman and to have her son's spinal problem corrected by a Milwaukee specialist. She had him tutored intensively for the exam to be given in early June of 1898. He scored 700 out of a possible 750 points for an average of 99⅓, and won his appointment to the Academy in 1899 when, his spinal curvature greatly improved, he passed the West Point physical. His name was Douglas MacArthur.

Charlie Sandburg managed to prepare on his own as best he could. He traveled to West Point by train that June, riding smoking car wicker seats to Chicago, and then on to the Academy, where he was "measured, pounded, squeezed, stethoscoped, given the works, and pronounced physically fit to be an officer of the United States Army." The academic examinations were another matter. Unlike most of the men who took the examinations, Charlie had not completed high school. He had finished only a year at the Lombard College preparatory school. MacArthur and Ulysses S. Grant III were among the successful candidates for admission to the Academy in 1899. Charlie Sandburg failed.

The word came to him in his room, on a half-sheet of paper. An official letter went out to August Sandburg June 13: "It is with much regret that the Superintendent of the Military Academy directs me to inform you that your son Charles A. Sandburg, conditionally appointed as a Cadet in the service of the United States, has been pronounced by the Academic Board as not qualified in Arithmetic, and Grammar for admission into the Military Academy."

Charlie's note from the officer in charge of candidates ordered him to settle any accounts with the treasurer, and then to take his departure. He was keenly disappointed, and embarrassed. He telegraphed Mart, in care of Schultze's Cigar Store back home in Galesburg: "FAILED EXPLAIN SHORT PREPARATION TO [Congressman] PRINCE FOR REAPPOINTMENT IF POSSIBLE." As he rode the train homeward, Charlie reflected on his "deficiency" in mathematics and grammar. For a would-be writer it was the latter failure which rankled. "You had the insatiable desire to succeed all right," he said to himself ruefully over the stump of his pipe. "But where was your indomitable will? . . . Where in the hell was your indomitable will?"

✳

In September 1899 Charlie resumed his unorthodox life at Lombard, choosing courses impulsively, following his enthusiasms rather than the Lombard curricular requirements. He worked hard on the *Lombard Review*, kept his part-time jobs, and began to distinguish himself as an athlete. He gave up football when he "found that after being slammed to the ground a few times" he had no interest in his studies. He abandoned baseball after he dropped a flyball which landed right in his hands; his mistake convinced him that he had lost his earlier knack for the game. Basketball intrigued him from his first season at Lombard in 1899, when the game was just eight years old.

His teammates remembered "the Terrible Swede" because he played with contagious energy and zest, using wicked tactics to exhaust and confuse opponents. "He wore the fixed grin of a fighter who fought from sheer exuberance and the fun of it," one of his teammates recalled, "and we all caught the spirit."

∗

In February 1900 Charlie competed in another arena. He had joined Lombard's Erosophian Society, a literary and debate forum. He admired the performance of student orators there and in the elocution classes at the university. He was growing out of his shyness and feeling more at ease. He decided to study elocution. Perhaps he could, once and for all, train his unreliable memory and harness his voice to his desire for self-expression. He began to study with Maud Minor of the Lombard faculty. A statuesque beauty from Chicago, she taught in the Lombard Department of Elocution and Dramatic Expression, preparing ministers in the Lombard Divinity School to deliver effective sermons and offering instruction for "any person who desires to give better manifestation of inward truth or power, whether it be on public stage, on the street, in railroad car, or in private drawing room." Under her direction Charlie and his classmates studied Vocal Culture, Philosophy of Expression, Analysis, Physical Training, English Literature, and Shakespeare and other authors.

She also prepared the men of the Erosophian Society for the college's coveted Swan Oratorical Contest, with its prize of fifteen dollars for the best oration. Charlie wrote a speech entitled "Historical Parallels" to compare the Scandinavian polar explorers Nansen and Andrée to the Vikings. He prepared the oration carefully, and then rehearsed it over and over, en route to class from the fire station, in the privacy of the bell tower, in his Berrien Street study.

On contest night, he began the oration skillfully, and got nearly halfway through it before, once again, his memory betrayed him. The humiliating lapse was a disappointing repetition of that night a decade earlier when his boy's mind had let him down. "I did well enough in the first half of my oration," he wrote of the ordeal, "when of a sudden I couldn't think of the next sentence. I stood dumb for a few seconds, then looked toward Miss Miner in the wings. She gave me the sentence and I plowed on, knowing I had no chance at the $15 first prize."

Charlie's friend Frederick Dickinson of Chicago took the honors that year with his speech on Robert Burns. When Maud Minor moved on to Chicago in 1900 she was succeeded by Amanda Kidder, who "had wide experience in the field of dramatic expression, having appeared before more than five hundred audiences in recital work." Under her guidance Charlie prepared for the 1901 Swan Oratorical Contest, and learned a fundamental lesson which he heeded from that time forward: he was at his best on the lecture platform when he was passionate about his subject.

He chose to speak about John Ruskin, entitling his oration "A Man with Ideals." He was "lit up and somewhat intoxicated" about Ruskin, the English art critic and social theorist whose critique of industrial society was in part expressed in *Fors Clavigera*, his letters to working men. His discovery of Ruskin's ideas crystallized Charlie's own views of the problems of American society. His excitement about Ruskin's theories energized his writing and his speaking. He embraced Ruskin's words as if they were his own. Ruskin made men see the truth Charlie had witnessed in his father's life, "that the laborer is not a machine, but that he has a soul and that his soul has a right to see and enjoy the clear sky, works of art, health, sanity and beauty."

Charlie experimented with the merger of the written and spoken word, and began crafting his prose so that it would be aurally effective, measuring its cadence and emphasis for their impact on an audience who would *hear*, not *see* the words. He rehearsed this oration so many times that he could "roll out any part of it without thinking what it was about."

The Lombard gymnasium was packed with students, faculty and townspeople on February 22, 1901, for the Swan Contest, "one of the features of the college year." There were speeches on John Quincy Adams, Abraham Lincoln, Alexander Hamilton, the "Liberty of Man." Then Charles A. Sandburg rose to give his audience "A Man with Ideals," the first speech of his life to marry his "insatiable desire" to excel on the lecture platform and his passionate idealism. He began with a sketch of the scientific and industrial progress of the nineteenth century, a material progress, he asserted, which "in the main, satisfied only the wants of the body." Looking back on a century just barely closed, Charlie charged that "factories crush the human body and darken the human soul. Men by thousands are killing each other, driven by greed and covetousness."

The oration closed with a dramatic recitation from Ruskin's preface to *The Crown of Wild Olive*: a call for "Free-heartedness, and graciousness, and undisturbed trust, and unrequited love, and the sight of the peace of others, and the ministry to their pain." Eloquent with enthusiasm for his subject, he held his memory and his audience. They stayed with him throughout "A Man with Ideals." At last, he won a first prize in oratory. The Swan victory was a turning point, giving him new confidence in himself and his memory. It enhanced his stature in the small Lombard community, and stimulated his appetite for oratory, for composing words on paper to be brought to life in front of an audience. Most important, it showed him what he could do when he truly meant what he said, when he spoke from the conviction of his mind and spirit.

He was growing toward a more coherent vision of himself. The Swan Prize affirmed his instincts toward oratory. He studied each lecturer he heard, the "power and quaver" of Booker T. Washington's voice; Robert Ingersoll's "faultless and finished diction." He admired the "passionate words" and "portentous voice" of Eugene Debs, just out of Woodstock Jail. He was impressed with the "deep bass voice" of American Federation of Labor president Samuel Gompers, "cigar-maker, Jew, scholar, a master politician."

Oratory was then a widely admired art and a powerful source of education, edification and entertainment in American society. The nineteenth-century orator was the counterpart of the twentieth-century radio, television and film performer. While the Puritan reform preacher, the itinerant revivalist, the camp meeting evangelist and the temperance crusader contributed to the evolution of the nineteenth-century orator, the primary stimulus for national interest in oratory came from the lyceum movement, founded in 1826 by Josiah Holbrook, a popular lecturer on science. He designed a plan for local, state, national and international lyceum bureaus to sponsor lectures. Curtailed by the Civil War, the lyceum movement was resurrected near the end of Reconstruction in the form of talent bureaus and professional lecture bureaus. One of the foremost of these was Redpath, founded by Scottish immigrant James Redpath, who represented such successful lyceum lecturers as Mark Twain, Artemus Ward and Josh Billings—and, in the twentieth century, Carl Sandburg.

Another prolific breeding ground for oratory was the chautauqua movement. Organized in 1874 at Lake Chautauqua, New York, as a Christian retreat center, it quickly expanded into a national institution, attracting thousands of visitors each summer for vacations given over to secular lectures as well as to religious reflection. Theodore Roosevelt called the retreat at Lake Chautauqua "the most American place in America." Chautauqua speakers were famous throughout the nation— William Jennings Bryan, Susan B. Anthony, Booker T. Washington, Robert La Follette, Ida Tarbell, Clarence Darrow, Henry Ward Beecher, Grover Cleveland, Oliver Wendell Holmes, James Russell Lowell, and a host of others.

Touring groups of lecturers and entertainers modeled after the original chautauqua began to travel the country, some of them as circuit or tent chautauquas, touring one town after another with a cycle of programs.

The network of professional lecturers expanded with the progress of the railroads, and a seemingly endless procession of experts on science, health, religion, philosophy, literature, politics and art carried culture directly to the listening public. Galesburg citizens listened avidly to lecturers at Knox, Lombard and the city auditorium, or in the chautauqua tent erected at the Knox County Fairgrounds. When Charlie heard Robert Ingersoll, he went home impressed that a man could do nothing but lecture for years and make money at it.

He was particularly impressed by the work of Elbert Hubbard, the successful soap salesman who turned to writing, printing and directing the Roycroft Movement. After Hubbard's Galesburg lecture, Charlie went up to shake his hand and to have a closer look at "the long hair framing a smiling, kindly face." Charlie heard Danish immigrant and reformer Jacob Riis lecture on "How the Other Half Lives" and saw vivid stereopticon slides of squalid New York tenements as proof of the conditions Riis described. Charlie was profoundly impressed by the social issues Riis laid before serious Galesburg citizens. Riis "had fought politicians and landlords and had come through with results for humanity." He was the first lecturer to demonstrate to Charlie that an orator could have a tangible influence on society.

And so Charlie proudly joined the roster of championship Swan Orators at Lombard. He was part of a great tradition, one of many American college students excelling at the "oratory game." He completed six courses in Lombard's Department of Elocution and Physical Culture. He enjoyed the exuberant debates of the Erosophian Society. He acted in Lombard plays. He began to think of his voice as an instrument, and worked to use it with calculated effect. He began to write with the ear as well as the eye, composing words which he intended people to *hear.* That strong aural sensibility stayed with him, and grew. Years later it figured in his poetry, which was meant to be *heard* as well as read. His future was still "all misty," but he was taking concrete steps to delineate it. Would he become "a newspaper reporter, a foreign correspondent, an author of books, an advertising copywriter—or an actor, a Lyceum lecturer, an agitator, an orator"? Time would tell.

✳

There was another profound, catalytic and even more constant influence on him: Charlie dubbed him the "Illinois Prairie Leonardo." In a providential convergence of teacher and student, Charlie found his model and mentor in Professor Philip Green Wright.

"He was lean and spare of body, erect and graceful in movements,"

Charlie said of his favorite professor, "almost acrobatic in the way he could move back and forth in a demonstration in mathematics." Once after he had covered a long blackboard with equations, Wright smiled and told his class, "And the beauty of it is that it is of no use whatsoever." He infected Charlie with the joy of learning for its own sake.

From 1892 until 1912, Wright was professor of mathematics at Lombard, also offering classes in astronomy, economics and English. The versatile professor oversaw the Lombard athletic program and served as secretary of the college. He was the grandson of radical abolitionist Elizur Wright, who later instigated national reforms in the life insurance industry and served as commissioner of insurance in Massachusetts.

Wright "knew more than anyone on the campus about creative writing and how to get it out of the students if they had it in them." Charlie took Wright's "Daily Themes" course, producing the required one- or two-page essay which Wright and other students could critique. Wright taught Charlie how to analyze writing, his own and the work of others, whether fellow students or established writers—Baudelaire, Mallarmé, Turgenev. Wright was a poet as well as mathematician and economist, and an idealist whose philosophy "ran toward the radical and extreme," Sandburg wrote later. Actually, Wright was a socialist closer in tenet to English craftsman and poet William Morris than to Marx or Engels.

Wright was happily married to his cousin Elizabeth (his grandfather had sired eighteen children) and lived in a comfortable house near the Lombard campus. There, the Wrights hosted a regular Sunday-night gathering of a dozen English students for a "lively free-for-all" literary discussion, followed by hot chocolate and Nabisco wafers. In Charlie's senior year, Wright organized the Poor Writers' Club which included Charlie and Athol Brown, who were writing poetry, and Howard Lauer, who was writing skits for the *Lombard Review*. "We are poor, and we are writers," Wright said, "so why not?"

From the first, Wright took a keen interest in Charlie Sandburg. He recognized in this raw, eager student special characteristics of mind, noted the potential for something original in his writing, some "Viking force" in his character which set him apart from other Lombard students. The diminutive man with the Vandyke beard, gentle blue eyes and "richly stored mind" was mentor and friend to the lanky, dark-haired Swede, who played basketball, gave speeches and wrote poems with equal drive and intensity.

Charlie saw Professor Wright almost daily for four years, and came to count him as one of the three chief influences in his life. Wright was a "great friend and an invaluable beneficient influence."

"And there never was a time," Sandburg later said of Wright, "when he didn't deepen whatever of reverence I had for the human mind and the workings of a vast mysterious Universe."

✳

In 1901 Charlie and Fred Dickinson received free tuition for editing the yearbook commemorating Lombard's half-centenary celebration. Dickinson had a good business sense, and during the summer of 1899 had worked in Nebraska, where he made over two hundred dollars selling Underwood and Underwood stereoscopic photographs and viewers as a door-to-door salesman, and had a good time doing it. One spring day in 1900 he invited Charlie to go with him to meet an Underwood and Underwood representative at Brown's Hotel in Galesburg. Before he knew it, Charlie had signed up for a summer's work "selling views."

He was assigned exclusive rights to sell Underwood and Underwood stereographs and stereoscopes in Bureau County, Illinois, during the summer of 1900. In the second week of June, Charlie left Galesburg on his bicycle carrying a suitcase and his black leatherette agent's canvassing case. It was lined with blue plush and contained one stereoscope and two dozen choice stereographs. Charlie traveled through Wataga, Oneida, Galva and Kewanee to the village of Neponset, where he registered in "the best hotel, a two-story wooden building" where a room let for three dollars weekly and meals cost twenty-five cents each. He soon found that his oratorical experience helped him win over reluctant farmers in the hot summer fields, and busy housewives interrupted by his methodical calls from house to Bureau County house.

He was a good salesman. At summer's end, he rode his bicycle back to Galesburg with a profit of a hundred dollars and some leftover views. He kept fifty dollars for himself, and gave the rest to his father, who gave Charlie a rare smile in return, along with his hopes: "Maybe sometime you be a good businessman, Sholly."

Charlie liked the stereographic business so well that he tried it again often during the next four years. He got much more out of it than money. He liked the freedom of the open road, liked living here and there, seeing new towns and people. He liked the lazy ambles from town to town under the bright summer sky, the leisure to think and dream. He liked bringing the world to the people on the prairie farms. And he liked the stereographs themselves, the technical ingenuity which created them and brought the world to the eyes and fingertips of people who inhabited remote farms and quiet, half-forgotten villages like those he frequented in his "exclusive territory." The photographs stimulated him, and with the views in the leatherette bag began his lifelong interest in the visual image, whether in stereographs or in other photography, or later, in the art of the motion picture. In more ways than one, they were illuminating, these views he sold for Underwood and Underwood. And they gave him a new independence that he appreciated, and held on to as long as he could.

✳

Fred Dickinson and Charlie Sandburg were officially named editors of the *Cannibal*, the yearbook celebrating Lombard's half-centenary, and received the year's tuition in return for their labors. President Nash made the appointment, which, for Charlie, had the long-range benefit of teaching him some of "what goes into the making of a book." Fred and Charlie named themselves the managing editor and editing manager, respectively, and set to work in January 1901 to produce a book that would be "tall and lean, using glossy paper for the many half-tones." The book contained biographical sketches of famous graduates, as well as faculty and patrons of the college. There was a history of Lombard; text and photographs depicted college life at the turn of the century. The yearbook took its name from an operetta written and staged by Professors Wright and Fowler. The experience was worth "any two courses in the college," Charlie concluded when the *Cannibal* was complete. He and Dickinson had "edited and written thousands of words, had practiced at biography and history, had learned about type, zinc and half-tone cuts, proofreading, and the ways of printers."

They had a ten-dollar surplus in their budget after the *Cannibal* was completed, and they decided to celebrate by taking two Lombard coeds out to a restaurant for dinner. Charlie fell in and out of love several times at Lombard, but when a relationship threatened to become too deep and serious, as in the case of one girl with a "homely, freckled, sweet face" and a "lean and beautiful body," he drew back. After all, he could make no commitments when his "future was so misty." But he enjoyed the company of Nelly Clanton Turner, who had played Cleopatra to his Marc Antony in a Lombard dramatic evening, and invited her to the *Cannibal* celebration.

Charlie sent a copy of the book to Elbert Hubbard, who thanked him in a letter. "I must congratulate you on the Year Book," he wrote. "It is certainly very good stuff, and shows the best of taste throughout."

Charlie put his yearbook experience to immediate use on the *Lombard Review* when he was elected editor in 1901. The *Review* went out several times a year and exacted "more keen interest and hard work on the job" than any previous work he had done. He intended for the journal to be "loud, slangy, even undignified," "a Live College Journal." He wrote editorials and reprinted significant speeches by college speakers. His own winning Swan oration appeared in March 1901. As editor, he was free to "write in any and all styles . . . and get it printed." He wrote rhymed verse, fragments of fiction and humor. In a column he called "sidelights" and signed Karl August, he commented on socialism, the anti-saloon movement and other current issues.

Early in that exhilarating, productive spring of 1901, his vision began to trouble him. By June, he found it so difficult to see that he turned to "the best known eye man in town." The doctor's diagnosis was grim: he found a film covering both eyes, a growth called pterygium. Continued growth would cause blindness.

Charlie submitted that June to then-dangerous surgery to remove the film from his eyes. For days afterward, except when a nurse removed the bandages to put medicine in his eyes, he lay in total darkness.

When he was released from the hospital nearly two weeks after his operation, he had to wear thick smoked glasses to protect his bloodshot eyes. His vision sharpened as the surfaces of his eyes slowly began to clear. He was jubilant as his vision improved. Still wearing smoked glasses, he set out to join Fred Dickinson in Michigan to sell stereoscopic photographs, or "views." With new zest and gratitude, Charlie sold pictures of the wonders of the world to the people of Plymouth, Romulus and Ann Arbor, Michigan.

Although his eyes gradually healed, he kept the latent fear that someday he might lose his vision, and he had chronic problems with his eyes. He resolved to sharpen his powers of observation, to probe beneath surfaces, memorize the contours of faces and landscapes, so that he could see, really see. More than two decades later, when he was writing fairy tales for children, he created a character called the Potato Face Blind Man who had a sign reading "I Am Blind *Too*" because, he explained, "Some of the people who pass by here going into the post-office and coming out, they have eyes—but they see nothing with their eyes. . . . They are my blind brothers. It is for them I have the sign that reads, 'I Am Blind *Too*.' "

✳

Charlie Sandburg and his friend Fred Dickinson had high hopes of going to the Pan-American Exposition to sell views during the summer of 1901, but other Underwood and Underwood agents had saturated that territory.

They settled for Detroit instead. Still it was an exuberant summer, spent loafing, swimming, reading and arguing politics as well as peddling their wares. They enjoyed weekend jaunts to Detroit and an endless, spirited debate about politics and philosophy. Dickinson took the conservative point of view, Sandburg the radical. They educated each other that summer "without convincing each other of anything except that each was stubborn and partisan and maybe prejudiced."

From Galesburg, Charlie's elder sister Mary wrote to him of her deep need to get away from home. He answered sympathetically. He understood far too well, but the richness of his experience at Lombard had tempered his own impatience with his hometown. "You say G. [Galesburg] is for you a synonym of despair and disappointment," he wrote his sister. "It might be another word for uncongeniality and lack of appreciation but despair is quite strong. If you are expecting a full, complete and just estimate of your work and influence anywhere on earth, your hopes are askew."

Charlie urged Mary to read Elbert Hubbard, one of his current idols, believing that Hubbard's perspective of the inherent value of work would help his sister. "I believe you are strong enough to read Hubbard," Charlie wrote, "that you are able to throw yourself into work with such spirit that earthly phantoms can not mock you. There is talk of love and art and beauty, but there is no joy compared to that of doing a work however small and doing it well."

Charlie had admired Hubbard since he heard him lecture at Lombard, prized Hubbard's letter about *The Cannibal*, called him "one of the greatest men the world ever saw" and a great writer.

During his fourth year at Lombard, Charlie was a "big man on campus," a star athlete and orator, a member of the Glee Club, the editor of *The Cannibal* and the *Lombard Review*, popular with faculty and classmates alike. Reading, writing and oratory were his principal enthusiasms. His fortuitous relationship with Philip Green Wright crystallized his desire to write. But as a student he was a dilettante, enrolling in four history courses, six elocution courses and twelve English courses. He took Latin, a smattering of mathematics and science, and several courses in the "newborn science" of sociology. Provisionally accepted in the college preparatory department in 1898, he had been permitted to take college courses, too. In his fourth year at Lombard, however, he quite simply did not have the required credits to stand for college graduation.

Sometime in the spring of his fourth year, he decided he would not continue for the additional year or two a degree would require of him. He was twenty-four, older than most of his classmates. He had enjoyed

Lombard to the hilt, but he was ready to move on. From the outset of the college experience, which had come to him after all by serendipity, the diploma had not been his goal. He knew he had grown and changed. He had "not only respect but reverence" for the minds of his fellow students, and had been particularly fortunate in the quality of the small but distinguished faculty at the unorthodox little university where he had discovered the worlds of literature and rhetoric, the history of civilization, intellectual and moral philosophy, elocution, and the value of "books, diligence, decency."

Only a minority, an estimated two percent of the population of the United States attended college at the turn of the century, and attrition was high. The majority of students enrolled in American universities and colleges dropped out before graduating. Charlie was fortunate to have attended Lombard. He had gotten what he wanted from the experience. He "puzzled and wondered" about what he would do after college until he "actually enjoyed the puzzlement and wondering." In his last weeks at Lombard he went to the museum he had visited so often as a boy, and stood before the "tall elegant human skeleton." He seemed to hear a "low and thin whisper as its jaw dropped ever so slightly, 'Whither goest thou?' " Charlie whispered back, "I can't tell you but I know if you could tell me you would."

"What was I headed for in the big world beyond college days?" he wondered. He was still struggling with the "ten men" inside himself, but his Lombard experience had brought him to one profound discovery: "I was only sure that in the years ahead I would read many books and I would be a writer and try my hand at many kinds of writing."

1902–1904

4. Reckless Ecstasy

I try to express myself sensibly, but if that fails, I will use
the reckless ecstasy. As Kipling has one of his untamed
children of the forest say, "I will be the Word of the
People. Mine will be the bleeding mouth from which the
gag is snatched. I will say everything."

—Charles A. Sandburg,
In Reckless Ecstasy, 1904

I n 1905, when he was twenty-seven and failing to connect "with
anything in particular, neither business nor writing," Charles Sandburg was haunted by a recurring dream of collapsing horses. "I was
on a horse and the horse was galloping in good time;" he wrote in *Ever
the Winds of Chance*:

I was riding him bareback, the going fast. I was doing well to stick on his
back as he flew along the road. One night he was a bay, other nights
sorrel, black, roan. He was doing his best to get to wherever it was I was
going. Then all of a sudden where were we? We had been going along
the road to the Krans Farm [the Galesburg home of Clara Sandburg's
cousins]. And at the split second when the horse reached the gate to the
Krans farm he collapsed, went to pieces under me. He changed from
something to nothing. And in another split second I was on another horse
of another color. I didn't get off one horse and on another; one horse that
I had been riding somehow went to pieces, and for a split second I stood
on my feet feeling bad about losing a good horse but in no time at all I
was on another horse, riding hell bent for leather to wherever it was I
was going. So it went on. I had one horse after another sink and go to
pieces under me as though of a sudden he was a stuffed animal. Along
about the fourth or fifth horse I would come awake and I wouldn't ride
my collapsible horse again till the next week or the next month. Sometimes
I wondered whether I would ever dream of trading one of my collapsible
horses for a regular, non-collapsible nag.

The years from 1902 to 1907 were fraught with collapsible horses, three in the main: the steeds of salesmanship, writing and oratory. Charlie called himself a "hustler," trying to sell views, peddle poems and make speeches to earn his living. He was a "migratory roadster" who wandered through Illinois, Indiana, Michigan, Wisconsin, New York, New Jersey, Pennsylvania and Delaware in search of himself and a "regular, non-collapsible" horse to ride. "There are ten men in me," Charlie declared, "and I do not know or understand one of them." For the most part he was alone, and keenly aware that he was disappointing his family back home in Illinois, who had their own conventional hopes for his future. His older sister Mary and younger brother Mart had settled down to steady jobs. Charlie's family had no faith in a future given to selling stereoscopic views. It was to Mary rather than his gentle mother or his stern father that Charlie spoke his self-doubts: "Some way I feel as tho I am not doing as much as you had expected me to—that I have fallen short of the standard of achievement you had your eye on for me."

With others he could be full of bravado. "I am like Keats at least in this, that the roaring of the wind is my wife, and the stars thru the windowpane are my children. As for posterity, I say with the Hibernian, 'What has it ever done for us?' " He could be flippant, jaunty, "gay and chipper," but confessed to Professor Wright that his good humor was often a pose, "only a back-action, the kick of my melancholy, when I really don't 'care a dam for men or fate.' " At times he was overwhelmed with the surge of "the joy of life," sure that he was the captain of his soul. At other times, he was deeply uncertain about the moves he should make "in this game I am playing with the world." If he was consistent in one thing, it was his dogged resolve to maintain his independence; he "disdained harness."

Charlie wrote to Mary that he was "evolving a small-sized *aura*. I find that people think about as highly of me as I do of myself, so I am begetting a self-respect that borders on conceit." He wrote to Professor Wright of "that vagrant, restless imagination back of my egotistic viewpoint." He resolved to write a worthy biography of his namesake, King Charles XII of Sweden, the early-eighteenth-century monarch who was defeated after invading Russia, was imprisoned in Turkey, and died in battle in Norway in 1718. Sandburg admired and tried to emulate the "noble self-denial" and "sublime self-confidence" he perceived in Charles XII, who ate common soldiers' fare with his men and slept with them on the "frozen, wind-swept prairie." Self-confidence was a particular problem for Charlie. He vacillated between a growing conviction of his own powers and promise, and profound discouragement.

Alone in Wisconsin in the autumn of 1902, Charlie began what he termed "a sort of apprenticeship in salesmanship and dealing with people." All the time, he persisted in reading, writing, and thinking, telling his skeptical family, and himself when doubts caused him to despair, that "it takes time for big results." His reading convinced him that "no great, lasting triumph has ever been accomplished without that ardor which had to go slowly and measurably, imperturbably, and without applause." Much of the time his buoyant spirits and equanimity were veneer for self-searching doubt and struggle. "Take up your cross and go the thorn way," he wrote in his notebook. "If a sponge of vinegar is passed you on the end of a spear, take that too. Souls are woven of endurance."

Charlie Sandburg appeared to be a late bloomer, finding his difficult way through a prolonged adolescence, coming late to college and vocation. In reality, his progress toward maturity was confounded by the multiplicity of possible selves within him. He was aware of "the ten men" he carried inside himself, and struggled mightily to harness and express them. He was drawn to an eclectic company of mentors and writers— Zola, Hugo, Whitman, Hubbard, Stevenson, his professor Philip Green Wright. Once he left college he lived and worked in virtual isolation, except for the company of his own reading and study.

After Fred Dickinson left the stereographic circuit for law school in September 1902, Charlie traveled through Wisconsin for a few weeks, headed south for Indiana, and then took the train eastward to New York. In a letter home to Mary he exulted over "that vast organism known as New York," and the "mightiest material works of America—these subways, bridges, railroads, buildings." He found a room in a cheap Greenwich Village hotel, and made an appointment with the New York sales manager for Underwood and Underwood, hoping to find a job in Manhattan. The manager took him out for a hearty lunch of lamb chops and apple pie à la mode, but told him there were no Manhattan openings. He offered him a job in the Underwood and Underwood territory in Vineland, New Jersey, instead.

Charlie was determined to stay in Manhattan. "I have canvassed the situation a little today," he wrote Mary in December, "—enough to make me feel, dear sister, so hopeful for the future." He visited former Lombard student Lee Fairchild, now living in New York and editing *The Thistle*, a pocket-sized magazine modeled after Elbert Hubbard's *The Philistine*. Charlie had published some of Fairchild's poems in the *Lombard Review*, and now Fairchild reciprocated. Late in 1902 *The Thistle* carried "The Falling Leaves," Charles A. Sandburg's first published poem. It was undistinguished, with conventional rhyme, bland, predictable imagery, an occasional trite choice of word:

> The trees now stand in stranger tints
>   Than all the summer knew,
> Why took they on these golden glints
>   That autumn mists bedew?
>
> The ground is strewn with russet leaves,
>   Aweary seemed their fall;
> Why fall these days the autumn leaves,
>   Whence comes this yearly thrall?
>
> A leaf I loved one summer day
>   Lies shrivelled on the ground;
> What mandate spoke its doom, I pray,
>   And where does praise redound?
>
> Thus earth-bound soul protests and grieves,
>   Yet down beneath its pride,
> Yet deeper than the hint of leaves,
>   Speak slow, "Have faith! Abide!"

Except for the affirmation of faith in life in the last two lines of the poem, there was little of his future poetic vision in "The Falling Leaves." Maverick that he was in most ways, Charlie was a conformist then as a poet, modeling his first poems on the standard patterns of poetry he encountered in his college anthologies, in his eclectic reading and study after Lombard, and in Philip Green Wright's work.

In *Ever the Winds of Chance*, Sandburg devoted a chapter each to two of the vital forces in this seminal period of his life—Philip Green Wright and Elbert Hubbard. To his great delight, he was able to visit Hubbard at his Roycroft complex in East Aurora, New York, on Christmas Eve 1902.

As much as anyone he knew of then, Hubbard embodied the life Charlie wanted. He was a phenomenon, a successful businessman turned best-selling author, a publisher, an advertising genius, a charismatic lecturer and vaudeville performer. Like Charlie, Hubbard had been born in Illinois. When Charlie paid his Christmas call, Hubbard was forty-six and riding the crest of the amazing success of *A Message to García*, the fifteen-hundred-word pamphlet he had composed quickly the evening of February 22, 1899, after he and his seventeen-year-old son, Bert, finished a debate about the real hero of the Spanish-American War. In Bert Hubbard's view, that hero was the messenger Rowan who performed his job with no questions asked when given the dangerous mission of taking a message from President McKinley to the Cuban insurgent leader García, who consequently acted to aid American troops. The New York Central Railroad management wanted its employees to read about such selfless devotion to duty and paid for the printing of several million copies of Hubbard's *Message*, which would be reprinted in forty million copies in Hubbard's lifetime. He used his Roycroft colony to produce books, furnishings and crafts in the tradition of English artist, poet, designer and socialist William Morris, whom he had visited twice in England and celebrated in his popular essay series *Little Journeys to the Homes of the Great.*

Charlie arrived at Roycroft eager to see Hubbard again, and in awe of the world he had created there. Hubbard took him on a personal tour of the Roycroft shops. Later Charlie helped Hubbard deliver Christmas turkeys as gifts, and then enjoyed Christmas Eve supper and a vaudeville evening with the Hubbards and other Roycrofters. With Hubbard, his son Bert and a few others, Charlie took a night walk "over the plank road out of town two miles and back." Hubbard autographed a small book for Charlie, who went away convinced that "when the future generations weigh in the balance the life of Elbert Hubbard, they will pronounce him one of the greatest men the world ever saw."

Back in New York, Charlie continued his fruitless job search. In his hotel room on West Twenty-second Street he wrote for hours in a small pocket notebook he entitled "Links and Kinks," filling it with quotations from his wide reading, aphorisms inspired by Hubbard, one-liners he overheard in cheap diners and on the city streets. During those years of his apprenticeship, he poured observations into his notebooks. He was an instinctive and inveterate journalist, in the root meaning of the word. He jotted down ideas for poems and lectures, lists of books to be read. He covered notebook pages with lists of words he was inducting into his own vocabulary: auto-da-fé, ecce homo, radicle, imprimatur, gudgeon, coriaceous, treacle, parietal, wattled. Scrupulously he recorded pronunciations and meanings. He made notes on his reading of Robert Louis Stevenson, and thought he might write a biographical study of Stevenson as well as of Charles XII. He recorded facts and statistics, and wrote down jokes and quips which turned up more than thirty years later in his epic poem *The People, Yes.*

Charlie savored the color, excitement and vernacular of the city, but had no luck finding suitable work. By January 19, 1903, he was writing to Mary from Vineland, New Jersey, that he "could have had several things in N.Y. far better than anything I could get in Galesburg, but I believe I'll stay with the U. & U. another year—perhaps less—and see what happens."

Charlie found Vineland a pleasant town with a "wide Main Street and good people." He spent two or three days a week canvassing in and around Vineland, selling stereoscopes and stereographs, devoting the rest of his time to "walking, loafing on the grass under the trees at the edge of town, reading Shakespeare, Emerson, Whitman, Ibsen, and Zola's *Nana* and *Drink*." Carefully he reread the Book of Job, Proverbs, Ecclesiastes, the four Gospels, and Saint Paul. He was becoming a more serious, methodical student, reading with greater focus and discipline. He was writing poetry and sending it to his sister Mary and Professor Wright in Galesburg, sometimes without keeping copies for himself. When he needed more money, he canvassed his territory aggressively.

Charlie could be a loner, at ease in his own company, but he was becoming more gregarious, less shy. He enjoyed a good time and discovered he made friends easily on the road. He often found himself "rioting in social functions" in the towns where he stayed temporarily as he worked his Underwood and Underwood territory. He moved to Millville, New Jersey, in February because "Vineland was nigh a Capua for Hannibal Cannibal Sandburg."

The appalling labor conditions he saw in Millville infuriated him. Local factories worked such hardship on employees, especially children, that Charlie called the town "the avatar of Gomorrah." Angrily, he wrote to Professor Wright, "I wonder (but do not cast censure) at the God who wove the underlings who weave the cotton there." Millville haunted Charlie with images he expressed in both poetry and prose. His essay "Millville" was significant for its looming socialism and its emerging prose style. Empowered by his passion for the subject, he was writing strong, clear, almost poetic prose before he found his subject or voice in poetry. "Down in southern New Jersey, they make glass," the piece began:

By day and by night the fires burn on in Millville and bid the sand let in the light.

Millville by night would have delighted Whistler, who loved gloom and mist and wild shadows. Great rafts of wood and big, brick hulks, dotted with a myriad of lights, glowing and twinkling every shade of red. Big, black flumes shooting out smoke and sparks; bottles, bottles, bottles, of every tint and hue, from a brilliant crimson to the dull green that marks the death of sand and the birth of glass.

From each fire, the white-heat radiates on the "blowers," the "gaffers,"
and the "carryin'-in-boys." The latter are nine to eighteen years of age,
averaging about fourteen, and they outnumber the adult workers. . . .

The glass-blowers union is one of the most perfect organizations in the
country. The daily wage runs from five dollars to twenty dollars, and from
four to eight hours is a day's work. But the "carryin'-in-boys" work nine
and ten hours and get two dollars and a half and three dollars a week.
Passing back and forth in the pale, weird light, these creatures are imps
in both the modern and the old-time sense of the word. They are grimy,
wiry, scrawny, stunted specimens, and in cuss-words and salacious talk,
they know all that grown men know. . . .

The piece on Millville, foreshadowing Sandburg's work as an investigative reporter, was published in his first book, *In Reckless Ecstasy*, in
1904. The children indentured to that factory and all others were the
subject of a later poem, "Mill-Doors," published in 1916 in *Chicago
Poems*. By then Sandburg had found his free-verse style and his
subjects—working-class people struggling with the harsh realities of daily
life.

> You never come back.
> I say good-by when I see you going in the doors,
> The hopeless open doors that call and wait
> And take you then for—how many cents a day?
> How many cents for the sleepy eyes and fingers?
>
> I say good-by because I know they tap your wrists,
> In the dark, in the silence, day by day,
> And all the blood of you drop by drop
> And you are old before you are young.
> You never come back.

✳

Now estranged from his family, Charlie retreated in late February 1903
into a prolonged and uncharacteristic silence. He gave himself up to
books and writing, neglecting his sales work and letting his correspondence lapse. From late February until late May he lived in Millville,
immersed in studies and silence. When at last his sister Mary protested
in a stern letter in May, he defended himself vigorously. She was right
that he had neglected his family, but he justified his silence:

You perhaps know of other periods in my life when I was undergoing
experiences that I considered developmental to a high degree—and which
time proved to be such—but which at the time, I did not think would
interest you and of which, I therefore did not write . . . And I hope this

is an explanation that explains that sometimes, "I am doing a work and cannot come down," in which I hope I am not a second Jonah . . . I am a fool, but I know which way I am going.

During the last three months, I have let a great deal of letter-writing lapse. I will not let correspondence, or anything else that is not eternally vital, rob me of the sleep or recreation that I must have if I am to have health, do my work, and carry on my studies . . . My problems and difficulties are enough without intensifying them by writing them to any-body. So you can depend on it that of all the good-cheer, happiness, sympathy, love, or whatever in me is worth your having, you are getting all I can give without hurting myself in a way you would not care to have me.

He did not write to her of the careful, probing studies he was making, the experiments in reading and writing, the steady practice of developing his vocabulary so that he could achieve the "beauty of a clear simplicity" and "the just and exact use of language."

He was becoming a poet during this self-imposed exile. His great appetite for books led him to forage widely, but he kept coming back to one American poet for sustenance, drawn more to his idealism than to the free-verse form which, later, Sandburg would mold to his own voice. "I have been conferring with Walt Whitman lately on what constitutes life and death and Eternal Verity," he told Philip Green Wright in 1903. Charlie's explosive encounter with Whitman galvanized his experiments in poetry in those crucial developmental years. He copied pages from Whitman's poetry and essays in his journals, tinkered with the free-verse form, was "haunted" by Whitman's style and subjects. Charlie turned to Philip Green Wright for guidance. His poems lacked something, he said, asking Wright for a "designation of which way crudity lies."

There is no complete record of Charlie Sandburg's correspondence during this seminal period, but he wrote to two people who valued his letters enough to save them—Professor Wright and his sister Mary. After Mary's reprimand, he wrote to her faithfully, confiding his worries and sending drafts of poems and essays for her to keep for him as he traveled from town to town selling views. He entrusted his writing to her, he told her, "because you have been true to me, all thru college-years and this year, never complaining unjustly, and because you trust me, even tho you don't understand me." He was not trying to raise her estimate of him, he wrote, but to make her feel that he had "not wasted days," had "not advanced rearward."

When he wrote to Professor Wright, he usually put the best face on his daily life, and sent along his poems and essays for the candid criticism he had learned to expect from Wright at Lombard. "I know you under-stand me and I feel better," Charlie wrote. "Thank you for your criticism of my 'stuff.' The great, long-suffering—yet also wheedling, babyish—public shall have a chance at it one of these years."

By late spring he was emerging from his silence and solitude. He moved back to Vineland in late May or early June 1903, confiding to Wright on June 22 that he planned to leave in July to escape "two Delilahs and four Cleopatras" in Vineland, as well as "several Salomes" who would have his head if he did not move soon. Charlie had begun to take more interest in his clothes, wearing an ascot because he "had seen pictures of painters, sculptors, poets, wearing this type of tie." He was "hard as hickory" from his year-around passion for long walks outdoors—some-times twenty miles or more a day. The summer sun tanned him deeply, burnishing the dark sweep of hair. His eyes could be fierce and luminous. There was an intensity about him which women found attractive. He met them more confidently than he had at Lombard, enjoyed their company, and often had to thwart their serious interest in him, resorting sometimes to subterfuge.

There is no confirming evidence of a prolonged, serious love affair during this time, and no record of Sandburg's early sexual experience. "I met a tall school teacher who had class features; I had seen her before in magazine illustrations of love stories," he recalled in *Ever the Winds of Chance*. "I met the daughter of a banker, a lovely Scottish lassie who had a noble head and face, brown eyes, more than a Cupid's bow mouth, a strong nose—a sensible young woman who would make the right man a wonderful wife. I met a Philadelphia church singer, a soloist on Sundays, rather proud of her voice and face. . . ."

That litany of faces was all Sandburg shared of his early love life, but he was visualizing the Ideal Woman, writing about her in his journals and in letters to Wright: "If I could only meet The Ideal Woman, I believe I could pull myself together and set the world by the ears. . . . I have silenced quite effectively the superbouyancy of a young coquette at the house where I am rooming by telling her she reminds me very much of my first wife!"

Dickinson came to the rescue July 3, 1903, arriving for another summer selling views. After the solitary months, Charlie reveled in Dickinson's company. They plunged into a summer of moonlight picnics, sightseeing in Philadelphia and the familiar heated arguments. They experimented with fad diets, took long walks, swam. "Being young and not very full of days," Charlie wrote to Professor Wright, "we have been rejoicing in the days of our youth."

They concentrated on some serious canvassing, taking their Underwood and Underwood leatherette bags from house to house in Vineland, New Jersey, and Dover, Delaware. Despite the diversion of Dickinson's company, Charlie kept working on his poetry. In late summer he sent Wright seven quatrains suggested by his reading of Zola's "L'Assomoir." His poetic style was lagging far behind his prose. The aspiring poet chose trite words and stilted, pedestrian structures to express himself:

> I do not gild my words with attic salt,
> You think; and yet that's surely not my fault;
> I would be fresh as winds that sweep the sea
> And pack my words to last like God's basalt.

He had written other quatrains, he told Professor Wright, but sent him the best ones (and, he suggested ruefully, if these were the best, "what must the others be?"). One stanza commented on the greed of certain capitalists:

> I stood me near the mart and watched them flow
> To worship gold and all the things that glow
> And force; and no man came away and smiled
> And softly said, "I have enough, I'll go."

Bound as he was to traditional poetry, Charlie was beginning to experiment with social themes in the quatrains. Whitman would soon help him break free from rhymed verse once and for all.

After Dickinson departed for law school at the University of Michigan in September, Charlie canvassed hard through the Delaware countryside, saving money. He soon relapsed into his solitary schedule, however, working just enough to earn a subsistence wage, and giving the rest of his time to his studies and writing. He spent Thanksgiving in Dover, and planned to go to Galesburg for Christmas.

He had not been home for nearly a year and a half. Letters from his mother, his sisters Mary and Esther and his brother Mart followed him from one general delivery post office address to another in his East Coast "wanderjahre." He wrote affectionate, encouraging letters to Mart and to Esther, now a pretty high school senior. To Mary he confided his worries and plans, confessed his self-doubts, entrusted his manuscripts and private papers, gave advice to bolster her own ambitions. Between Charlie and his father, there was silence.

Charlie had demonstrated his own affinity for brooding silence in the mute solitude of the spring of 1903, but the weighty distance between him and his father was bitter and seemingly insurmountable. August

Sandburg was about fifty-seven in 1903; he had worked for the C.B.&Q. Railroad for more than thirty years, sublimating himself to the goal of modest material security. His children Mary and Mart worked near home at jobs he understood and approved, Mary as a teacher and nurse, and Mart as agent for the Adams Express Company in Galesburg. August had been proud of Charlie's military service and, despite his skepticism about the value of a college education, he was disappointed when Charlie quit college to become a fast-talking salesman with no trade, no steady prospects, no visible business sense. Mary and Mart supported themselves and contributed money to the family. Charlie never even came home to account for himself, much less to help with family expenses.

Despite his promise to spend Christmas in Galesburg, Charlie changed his mind by late December. He felt "something of a brute," he wrote Mary, but he was not coming home. He gave Professor Wright a jaunty explanation, writing from Dover on December 23:

> I am not unlike the captain of police who died thru having lost his life. I am here thru not having gone. You see, I consulted the auguries, opening 13 English walnuts, but got no results. Then I consulted an oracle who said I would go West at the time of the Yule-tide. Being more desirous of seeing Virginia and Washington, D.C. at present than going home, I told the oracle she was mistaken.

In a letter written two days earlier, he gave Mary the truth about why he would not come home for Christmas:

> I don't lack the carfare, but I wouldn't have a kopek for the old gentleman —it seems almost unnatural sometimes to say "Father." I haven't any resentment toward him, but neither can I make any affection blossom. And there is that in me, be it right or wrong that will not permit me to face him again till I can have some of that Stuff to hand him.

Charlie was twenty-five, poor, and sensitive about his family's image of him. He had no affection for his father, he claimed, and enough stubborn pride to stay away until he could give August what he believed he valued most—money. By memory or design, Sandburg softened his view of his father when he wrote about him fifty years later in *Always The Young Strangers.* "There was always a bond of understanding with the mother," he wrote in the final chapter. "With the father it was different." When Sandburg in his seventies reconsidered his father's life, he had tolerance and compassion for the obstacles and struggles which hardened his father's manner, and could write in reconciliation "Peace be to your ashes, Old Man."

For now there was helpless anger at his own powerlessness to affect the economic barriers thwarting his father's hopes and his own. Once more Charlie entrusted his self-doubts to Mary. "It is enough to say that literary aspirations were what knocked my financial hopes," he confessed. He regretted that he had not been able to do anything in a year for her "material favor." He hoped, he said, to see her before summer and to meet her friends, but worried:

> It's a pity tho to have to tell them I am a canvasser, just a solicitor, one who changes persons' minds. . . . Frankly, if I had been a canvasser all the time, I would have a thousand banked now. But I have been a canvasser only about ¼ the time, a scholar, a poet-taster, an athlete and a social lion (or cub) the rest of the time.

" 'I have become a name for always roaming with a hungry heart,' " he told Mary in January 1903. Some days he was defensive in his despair, eager to persuade Mary, others, himself that he was not wasting time. Some days he was exuberant with confidence in his destiny. Always he was full of an "infinite variety of zigzagging hopes and plans." Yet when Charlie tried to see 1903 as a whole, he was convinced that it had been "the most ragged, glorious, tempestuous year" he had ever known.

✳

Sometime in 1903 Philip Green Wright purchased a small Truddle-Gordon handpress, installed it in the cellar of his Galesburg house, and, in the tradition of William Morris of the Kelmscott Press and Elbert Hubbard of the Roycroft Press, created his own printing trademark, the Asgard Press. His wife, Elizabeth, and young son, Quincy, helped him set type, run the press, cut and bind pages and take orders for the modest circulation of the books they published.

In February Wright printed copies of two Sandburg poems, "Complacency" and "Austerity." Charlie was flattered. "I am delighted that you should choose to put a literary effort of mine into such a charming and delectable environment of paper and type," he told Wright. "Needless to say I shall treasure it." The poems revealed some development toward his own poetic style. Laden as they are with ponderous words ("What men would cozen progress, lave it with the blood of love . . ."), they are remarkable for two departures from his earlier poems: The assertion of a social or philosophical viewpoint growing from his conscience, and the use of free verse. "Complacency" warns against the status quo:

> . . . What men would cut into the noon day sun, the deeps of night,
> And fling their manhood into frays for righteous things

Like war-mad soldiers surging to the fore,
Were't not that thy ne'er absent aspect,
Soft and luring, riseth up to murmur, lip to lip,
"Not even now, not yet the while, for all the world's so still, so calm,
    so bright,
So dear, so fair, so good to you—stay thus!"

Despite its awkward romanticism, "Austerity" is the forerunner of Sandburg's free-verse hymns to nature with their metaphorical, sometimes Emersonian revelations for the conduct of human life. Sandburg evoked such timeworn images as "lean, wan pilgrim spirits . . . straggling to thy mountain fanes," but juxtaposed them to other, more original images, harbingers of the work to come: "The chastity of stars, the lift and rise of peaks and crags . . . the way-worn eagle's cry. . . ."

He asked Professor Wright to send his mother a copy of his poems, and, in jest, sent Wright an advertising blurb because, he said, "you know I've studied advertising." The mischievous mock copy read:

ASGARD PRESS ANNOUNCEMENT
COMPLACENCY: AUSTERITY
By Keats Yeats Sandbrough
Two bits of blank verse for two bits!!

✳

Charlie was becoming a writer, and he had the writer's instinctive tactile and aesthetic response to the textures of the printed page. He took a keen interest in the entire publishing process, always cared about how his work looked on the page, and, in the printer-artisan tradition to which Morris, Hubbard and Wright belonged, thought carefully about the design and materials for the book cover. "Now if I were to offer a suggestion—unasked—as to improvement in any further work the Asgard Press may essay," he told Wright, "I would say that maroon cord might be better—might harmonize more—with cream paper than blue ribbon. Blue, I think, is well with white. This may be only a personal liking."

"Complacency" and "Austerity" were turned out on cream paper trimmed with blue ribbon, and would appear later in Charlie's first small book, *In Reckless Ecstasy* (1904), a product of Wright's growing enthusiasm for his Asgard Press. The press was just one component of his visionary plan for an "arts-craft" movement in Galesburg, with a People's Industrial College as the focal point. Charlie added to Wright's scheme his own vision "clear in its fundamentals, but misty and varying in the details," for a journal he wanted to edit, "a publication which would be bold, reckless, joyous, gleeful, yet sometimes sad and austere and mock-ing, in dealing with socialism, 'New Thought,' sexuology, and themes" on which he had "decided convictions."

Meantime, he had an overriding plan: he wanted to go abroad. He intended to go to England to begin a "developmental tour" of Europe. Therefore he would have to defer his involvement in Wright's arts-craft movement until he returned. He was "set on a European tour" of work and study which would "require at least two years." If that tour did not materialize, he would work with Wright part of the year and spend the rest of the time lecturing on the Lyceum circuit. Like Hubbard, he would combine oratory, writing, printing, and arts-craft, "an almost holy word," said Charlie, to those who understood its significance. Wright and Sand-burg were not yet sure just what they would make or how they would market it, but they were serious dreamers—and, said, Charlie, "Only the select few know that the true dreamer is the great doer."

When Wright decided to publish a volume of his own poetry, Charlie asked to write the foreword to "enhance the readers' appreciation." "This is merely a piece of work for my own good," he told his professor, "and should you not think it suitable, as in Eng. 7, I would abide by your hints." One afternoon in late April, Charlie "dulled the nib of a pen in great shape" and on four sheets of stationery bearing the name "The Prudential Insurance Company of America, Newark, N.J.," he wrote a tribute to Wright which appeared as the preface to Wright's *The Dial of the Heart* (1904), a collection of thirty-six poems.

"It isn't often I like my own prose," Charlie told Wright, "but I am pleased just now with this 'foreword' I have executed." In part he had written,

> Of the making of verses, doggerel, yawps, and blats, there is no end. Rare is the one who has approached his task saying, "I want to make something fine, something that will show the best and truest of myself, something which will be a gratification to the highest and strongest in me." Yet that's the spirit in which I believe Philip Green Wright has written out these pieces of poetry. . . . [Cut these words and they will bleed. There is a man back of them.]

He was projecting onto Wright's work his own growing conviction that writing was an intensely personal manifestation of the soul, that the greatest artists managed to approximate in their work "all the varied sides of what is bright and choice" in their souls, as he had put it.

In addition to his prose pieces, Charlie continued to send Wright his poetry, his "blankety-blank verse" as he called it. When he was not writing or selling views, he was "playing with oratory" and "investigating lyceum possibilities." In May 1904 Sandburg wrote to Wright that he was "breaking away more and more from the habit of writing." His tendency, he said, was "now more toward oratory." His appetite for variety and his romantic attraction to what he perceived as the exotic careers of oratory and writing contributed to the fragmentation of his life then. He was torn between "horses"—the need to write and the urge to perform. His multifaceted nature exacerbated his dilemma. Part of him loved the solitary work of the writer. Part of him relished the audience in the lecture hall. Neither enterprise paid a living wage, but Charlie found he could still earn enough money selling views to live modestly and keep reading and writing. For fifty cents a day he could buy enough fresh fruit, cheese and stale bread to "eat well and keep well." He paid a dollar and a half to two dollars weekly for room rent. He could, therefore, earn his keep with just two or three days a week "canvassing and delivering" Underwood and Underwood products. In late May he was so inclined toward oratory that he cleaned out his writing files and sent everything to Wright, including "some of the 'stuff' I would not read to anyone except in self-burlesque." Those were his only copies of his work, he told Wright, giving him leave to do what he wanted with them.

In June 1904 Charlie thought his dream of living and studying in England was about to come true. Eagerly he and Dickinson awaited a July sailing. They were going to canvass England, supporting themselves as stereograph salesmen abroad. As had become his pattern, Charlie would canvass enough to earn living expenses and give the rest of the time to his studies and "developmental" experiments in writing. He had worked hard all that spring to save money for the trip, telling Wright he would "eschew all literary effort to lay up treasures for my Kingdom in England." To his great disappointment, plans for the trip fell through at the last moment. There is no record of the reason.

Denied the chance to see the homeland of Robert Louis Stevenson, Robert Browning, George Bernard Shaw, Charles Lamb, Thomas Carlyle, William Morris and others who served as models for his poetry and idealism, Charlie had to stay in New Jersey and explore sites close at hand. He spent some time with Philadelphia socialists, "acknowledged revolutionists," but found them "admirable, tiresome and laughable. So cocksure, so dead certain, so damnably positive, about an experiment untried in all history, that I don't wonder 'socialist' is a kind of by-word and hissing to people." He read Jack London's "Sea-Wolf" in *The Cen-*

tury, admiring London's work as a writer and his posture as an "avowed revolutionist." "I rank Hubbard, highest among contemporary writers," Charlie told Wright, "but among artists, I place London even above Tolstoi. London, the coal-heaver, the gold-hunter, the tramp, the war-correspondent, keep your eyes on him, Professor. He bids fair to outclass anything in all America's literary output."

Charlie was effusive in his praise of Frank Norris's novel *The Octopus*, which convinced him of how the "railroad octopus and its relentless fangs may do its worst." He admired Eugene Debs, whom he found "more sane than most of the rainbow-chasers following him. He makes one feel that the Socialist is the rarest piece of clownery that ever made a fool of himself in the ring of Time, and that he will yet take the whips from the ringmasters."

He was beginning to call himself C. A. Sandburg, or, simply, Sandburg, and to take a close, personal look at political as well as literary matters. Sandburg was not a formal socialist then. He had no experience yet with political or theoretical socialism. Like many Americans at the turn of the century, his progressive and populist instincts informed his political and social views, and in 1904 any affinity for socialism sprang from his awareness of literary, aesthetic and humanistic approaches rather than classic theoretical or political philosophies.

The fledgling Socialist Party of America had been organized just three years earlier, in 1901 in Indianapolis, born, as historian David Shannon pointed out, from a "long and strong tradition of American economic heterodoxy." The American industrial revolution had produced "Grangers, Greenbackers, Populists, Single Taxers, trade unionists, anarchists, socialists" with "burning criticisms of the status quo." American socialism was a polyglot of theories, but with little direct connection to Marxism. In fact, as Shannon observed, only a few of the delegates to the first Socialist Party convention "had more than the haziest intellectual acquaintance with theoretical Marxism," despite the fact that Karl Marx had moved the headquarters of his International Workingmen's Association from London to New York in 1872. A movement of great diversity, its character and intent varying from region to region in the country, socialism was a dynamic political alternative in the early 1900s, committed in general to establishing "the cooperative commonwealth" through "political and parliamentary action," with the ballot its primary tool.

Like thousands of Americans, Sandburg was reading London, Norris, Upton Sinclair and other writers whose work exposed the human struggle against the dehumanizing forces of industrial society. Sandburg himself had written about the diffraction of contemporary socialism in a *Lombard Review* essay published in 1904, long after he had left the college:

> If you think this subject of socialism is easy, and that everybody knows what socialism is, just turn to the S's in the Brittanica [sic]. Look in the book and see. You will find that there have been as many varieties of socialists as there are wild birds that fly in the woods and sometimes go up and on thru the clouds to drink in the azure. These varied socialists do not agree perfectly as to how the money shall be divided, what they shall do when not at work, and what tunes the band shall play as they fling to the breeze the flag of Equality. But on the proposition that there is something pitifully, execrably wrong in the main works of our boasted civilization, and the average man is too complacent about it all, the socialists are a unit.

The American socialists intrigued Sandburg, but at a distance. He and Professor Wright, a trained economist, were pulled toward the artistic, aesthetic socialism of William Morris, and toward the ideal of social justice. Sandburg had only to look to his father's ordeal during the hard times of the 1890s to conclude that every man had a right to work and to be paid "full value" for his work.

When the "magnates" of industry curtailed work in factories or on the railroads, Sandburg observed, "Then the workmen are free—free to find work elsewhere or free to economize, free to go in rags, and live on bread and potatoes, and heat but one room in the house, and spend the last of the money that was being saved to buy a home."

That system would not last, Sandburg predicted.

> It can't last. We're either going back to some kind of an oligarchy, a government of, by and for moneyed men primarily, or we're going forward to a greater democracy, a system under which no man can be thrown out of work and have his plans ruined because of a national "financial depression," or because some magnate wishes to manipulate the stock market.

Like most Americans, Sandburg was caught up in the discussion of possible solutions to the problems of a volatile time. Socialism was "in the air," one of many options looming on the horizon of the new century. Sandburg examined it as he examined all new ideas, demonstrating then and always a propensity for independent, individual judgment on issues, grounded in his own thought and keen observation, his wide reading and his passionate experience as one of the people who did the daily work of the nation.

✳

Denied his developmental journey through the landscapes of the British writers, Sandburg made a pilgrimage to Camden, New Jersey, in search of the Mickle Street home of one of his favorite poets, Walt Whitman. He rode a trolley as far as he could, and then stopped a man in the street to ask for directions to Whitman's house.

"What is he, a machinist?" the man queried, not recognizing the name of the Good Gray Poet, dead only twelve years in 1904. Someone else directed Sandburg to the house, where he paid a woman a quarter to show him through. There he "saw the room where the immortal one ran his hands thru 'Sands at Seventy.' " Sandburg talked with a woman next door who said she had known Whitman. "You couldn't help but like him," she said. "He used to say, 'People don't understand what I write, but they will ten years after I'm dead!' He wouldn't let his house-keeper brush down the cobwebs in his room. He seemed to wish to let the spiders have their own sweet way."

Then she asked Sandburg, "This Whitman, they say he was an infidel. Was he?"

Sandburg quickly replied, "He was nearer to God than any man that said that."

From Mickle Street he went to Harleigh Cemetery to view the tomb "that Whitman for years had saved and scraped for to enshrine his bones and ashes." On Memorial Day 1904 Sandburg laid a rose on Whitman's tomb. He began to see Whitman not only as a model and mentor for poetry and idealism, but as a vivid subject for oratory. He set to work on a lecture about Whitman, calling it at various times "The Poet of Democracy" and "An American Vagabond." Mingled in his 1904 journal notebook are quotations from Voltaire, Milton, Cicero and Stevenson; snippets of overheard dialogue, aphorisms, quoted and original; the pains-taking details of his Underwood and Underwood orders; and long passages from Whitman's poetry.

Sandburg copied in longhand Whitman's words in the poem "Starting from Paumanok" which spoke to him about his own poetic destiny:

> I will make the true poem of riches . . .
> I will effuse egotism, and show it underlying all—and I will be
>   the bard of personality . . .
> And I will show that whatever happens to anybody, it may be
>   turned to beautiful results . . .
>
> [Whitman]

Sandburg saw his own struggle in Whitman's, although he did not presume he could approximate Whitman's force as a poet. "His work throughout is the expression of a great soul crushed by the weight of an antagonistic environment into utterance that has caused him to be regarded as the most revolutionary of modern writers," he wrote.

Sandburg projected himself into Whitman's "Song of the Open Road," compressing Whitman's sprawling lines onto the narrow pages of his journal:

> All seems beautiful to me;
> I can repeat over to men and women, You have done such good
>   to me, I would do the same to You.
> I will recruit for myself and you as I go;
> I will scatter myself among men and women as I go;
> I will toss the new gladness and roughness among them;
> Whoever denies me, it shall not trouble me;
> Whoever accepts me, he or she shall be blessed and shall bless
>   me.
>
>   [Whitman]

From Whitman, Sandburg drew heart and inspiration, an affirmation of character, will and purpose which helped to validate his own aspirations at that uncertain and crucial time. While he began to write free verse then, Sandburg's poetry was still so inhibited by convention, so stilted in theme and language, that it appears Whitman's poetry had no immediate palpable impact. Their connection at first was one of vision and spirit rather than style.

Sandburg knew that summer of 1904 that he was treading a "mazy path" with "mix-ups and windings around in all sorts and conditions of men and women." He cared deeply that he was disappointing his family, confided his worries once again to Mary, and apologized. He reminded her that she was "one of the blessings and inspirations" of his life. His reliable, steady younger brother Mart worked at two jobs, for the Adams Express Company and a local cigar company. On June 9, 1904, Mart married his Galesburg sweetheart Kate Stater. Mary Sandburg was a witness, but Charlie, distant from home for nearly two years now, stayed in New Jersey. The young couple settled into a two-room apartment at 809 Berrien Street. Sandburg's family endorsed the life they saw Mart living with his pretty wife on the familiar street in their hometown.

But Charlie was still a mystery to them. He was still a mystery to himself. In this period of the dream of collapsing horses, his quest for his voice in poetry and oratory grew out of the need to come to terms with himself. He tried one identity after another, like so many photographic poses. Not long after his homage to Whitman's house and grave, he sent Professor Wright a curious essay entitled "The One Man in All the World." It sprang in part from Whitman's celebration of the self and Elbert Hubbard's popular credo of individualism, but in largest part from Sandburg's own reading, "developmental" studies and stubborn introspection. "I am the one man in all the world most important to myself," he began:

> I am as good as any man that walks on God's green earth. I am also as bad as any creature that ever transgressed a law of life. The spirit of all benedictions is in me, and the germs of all crime. If it were not so, I could not see, believe, love, and aspire. . . . I am proud—yes I am proud, for I know no highly useful man who does not think highly of himself. . . .
>
> Above all other privileges vouchsafed us earthly pilgrims, I place the privilege of work. The brightest, most lasting happiness I know is that which comes for my earning, striving, struggling, fashioning, this way and that, till a thing is done. Ay, down in my heart somewhere is an odd little litany which says I am near the source of all Good and all Power, because I, in my way, can do, shape, and create.

The essay was a "good expression of the longings for a high selfhood," revealing both Sandburg's growing strength in the use of language and his emerging sense of self. After "hundreds of experiments" writing "all kinds of formal verse where you have to watch your rhymes and where you are allowed only an exact given number of syllables to perch on each line you write," he decided to go his "own way in style and see what would happen."

Similarly, he was seeking to "shape" and "create" an extraordinary interior life. His letters to Philip Green Wright reveal his conscious exertion toward a carefully designed personality. In words reminiscent of Emerson and Whitman, he reflected that "the more I read the more do I think that the nearer a man can come to portraying all the varied sides of what is bright and choice in his own individual soul, the greater an artist is he." Sandburg was becoming an artist whose primary creation was himself.

He was fundamentally concerned with forging the ideal character. He worked consciously from the inner core of his being outward, trying to decipher his interior life, to take stock of his strengths and weaknesses, and to emulate the virtues he discerned in people he admired. He was convinced that great art grew only from great souls. He wanted to inhabit a great soul, to honor the "god within." Consequently, he worked deliberately to become the self he imagined.

He was fiercely determined to assert himself as a singular individual soul, an artist. Sandburg believed passionately that if he tried hard enough he would "pass thru the world one of the masterpieces of God, a man." Like Charles XII, he would find strength and courage to face his destiny. Thus Sandburg consciously built his character. To become a great artist, he had to become a great soul. Then he could craft the veneer of personality. His view of himself as artist was considerably enhanced and affirmed in the summer of 1904 when Professor Wright proposed to publish a collection of his poems and essays. Sandburg was elated.

Yet for all his lofty vision, he was still torn between his desire to be "a man of thought" and a man "of action and business." He had splendid ideas, he believed, which would surely be "literary hits" if only he had time to work them out. Yet he was faced with the daily need to earn his way. In reality, he was nearly broke, and about to be embarrassed. Dickinson invited Sandburg to join him in Freeport, Illinois, where he was selling views. Sandburg had long been absent from Galesburg. Frustrated in his desire to go abroad, and seeing no real future with Underwood and Underwood in the Northeast, he shipped his few possessions to Dickinson in Illinois. Down to his last ten dollars, Sandburg outfitted himself, as in the hobo days, with a pocket knife, a handkerchief and comb, some soap, and the ever-present pipe and tobacco. He went to Philadelphia, where, instead of buying a train ticket, he waited for nightfall and a westbound train and "swung up on the bumpers of a fast freight" bound for Pittsburgh. There he took a trolley into the city for a hearty breakfast, and then rode the trolley to the McKees Rocks freight yards where he joined five other illegal travelers in a "gondola" coal car.

Two constables aborted Sandburg's trip westward toward home: they arrested all six vagrant travelers, who elected not to pay a ten-dollar fine and were sentenced to serve ten days in the Allegheny County jail. Sandburg made light of the experience in a letter to Professor Wright:

> Unshackling myself from all the conventions and elegancies, and swinging clean to the extreme of Bohemianism. I wandered across Pennsylvania along the beautiful Susquehanna, past the coal mines and along mountainsides whence I could look down on smelter-works in lurid lights much like the pits of hell. . . . At Pittsburg, I was captured by railroad police and sent to the Allegheny Co. Jail where I put in ten days. The warden gets $ .50 per day for each prisoner he is (supposed to be) feeding; and as said feeding does not entail an expense of $ .05 per day, if only enough prisoners that can't make a howl may be obtained, why he can shake the

plum tree and fill his own pockets. The charge against me was "riding a freight train without paying fare." For breakfast, we had a half loaf of bread, and a cup of hot brown water masquerading as coffee; for luncheon a half loaf of stale bread again, soup on Wednesday & Saturday; for dinner—but there was no dinner. . . . I was thrown in a cell with a young Slav who didn't know forty words of English, and a gray-headed Civil War veteran. It was a lark on the whole, and I think gave me new light on the evolution of a criminal.

The jail experience made its way into an early poem published in Sandburg's *Chicago Poems* in 1916. In the poem "'Boes" he recalled "the ten days I spent in the Allegheny County jail in Pittsburgh":

I waited today for a freight train to pass.
Cattle cars with steers butting their horns against the bars, went by.
And a half a dozen hoboes stood on bumpers between cars.
Well, the cattle are respectable, I thought. . . .
It reminded me of ten days I spent in the Allegheny County jail in
    Pittsburgh.
I got ten days even though I was a veteran of the Spanish-American war.
Cooped in the same cell with me was an old man, a bricklayer and a
    booze-fighter. . . .

By the time "'Boes" was published in 1916, Sandburg was habitually composing free verse, some of it reminiscent of Whitman's style but most of it distinctly his own creation. Sandburg always enjoyed calling himself a jailbird and enlivening the story with humor. Nevertheless, he despised the cynical system "by which police, constables, and petty officials aimed at keeping the jail packed beyond its intended capacity." The experience further crystallized his social and political sympathies for the poor and powerless victims of any corrupt system.

Sandburg served his ten days in jail, was released "feeling weak and a little dizzy," and in quiet defiance traveled the rest of the way to Freeport, Illinois, riding the rods. He arrived in Freeport dirty, tired and hungry. The clothes he had shipped ahead had arrived at Dickinson's boardinghouse, where, Sandburg recalled, "I took a bath, got into clean underwear and my best suit, and we walked out to a corner drugstore and had two large-sized chocolate ice cream sodas. I was again a respectable American citizen and aware of my rights as such."

He had lost twelve pounds on the prison diet, but quickly regained it as he and Dickinson conducted another of their experiments with nutrition: "Such menus as Dickinson and I arrange! Stale whole wheat bread spread with honey, cheese, and peaches—one meal. Force, bananas and milk are the main items generally." After the introspective and often discouraging months alone, Sandburg welcomed Dickinson's presence. "We had a gay summer, working nearly half the time, swimming in the Pecatonica River, reading good books—and arguing whether President Roosevelt in attacking Big Business was going too far, as Dick said, or not far enough, as I said."

After Dickinson returned to law school, this time at the University of Chicago, Sandburg remained in Freeport to sell views, but his enthusiasm and energy were centered on the book to be published by the Asgard Press. Wright had written the foreword, a tribute which pleased Sandburg immensely and, he said, "measures me true and 'hits me where I live.' "

Wright found in Sandburg's prose and poetry "something of the quality of a Norse saga," he wrote, "inchoate force and virility, unconscious kinship of the world with all that is beautiful and terrible in nature, and above all the delightful bloom and freshness and spontaneous expression of one who is witnessing the sunrise for the first time."

Grateful as he was to have his mentor's endorsement, Sandburg asked for some changes if the type had not been finally set. He was crafting his image, after all, and cared about how his readers would perceive him:

> Anent the foreword you wrote, if it has not yet been set up in entirety, it might be improved I have thought if you would convey the impression that after bagging enough orders to keep me alive a few days . . . I not only read, but I go in search of things that will throw light on life, and the human in particular, such things as the homes of people or generals, houses where slaves were bred, stations on the old "Underground Railway," oil-wells, lime-kilns, glass-factories, government-mints, Independence Halls—I think these take more time than books—I would have Nature stand up and say to all the world, "This is not book-worm, whatever it is!"

Accordingly, Wright's published foreword sketched a Sandburg who read widely but formed his own impressions of life:

> And when he has "bagged some orders," enough to keep him alive for a few days, he is free! Free to read, to observe men and things, and to think! He reads everything, Boccacio, Walt Whitman, Emerson, Tolstoi, and enters with appreciation and sympathetic enthusiasm into all that he reads. But literature, even the best, is but a pallid reflection of life: he prefers impressions at first hand.

Professor Wright correctly perceived that Sandburg was growing inwardly; that was his aim, the development of an interior life which would manifest itself in personal happiness and true artistic expression. Identity had become inextricably interwoven with work.

Sandburg was willing to take the gamble, with Wright's help. He was content to leave the selections to the professor: "I sent a lot of scraps of writing home last year . . . boyish mystical probings, and graceless material—yet there may be in the lot one or two pieces you will like." The pervasive ambivalence of his life led him to question whether he would write prose or poetry from then on. He told Wright, "I am not going to cast much of my thought during life, into rhythmic or verse form and rather than a volume devoted entirely to verse to begin with, I would see something of an admixture." If this seemed illogical, Sandburg said, he could only quote Whitman in retort: "Am I inconsistent? Well then, I am inconsistent."

He entitled his book *In Reckless Ecstasy* after a line by the English romantic novelist Marie Corelli (pen name for Mary Mackay). According to Corelli, Sandburg wrote in his preface, "ideas which can not be stated in direct words may be brought home by 'reckless ecstasies of language.' " As he matured as a writer, Sandburg worked to avoid effusion and to write in a spare, direct style. But as a young writer seeking his voice, Sandburg continued to indulge himself in more than an occasional reckless ecstasy, experimenting with "sonnets and triolets, long and short rhymed verse, ballads and ballades, rondeaus, pantoums, all kinds of formal verse."

Loneliness was an immutable fact of Sandburg's daily life. "Lost in flight," he grappled with the uncertainties of his life "alone and single-handed." While Sandburg persisted on his solitary way, "disdaining harness," he was hungry for fellowship like that he had enjoyed at Lombard. He wavered between his instinct for solitary, introspective work, the life of the mind manifested in writing, and for gregarious social intercourse such as that he found lecturing or joining in political rallies that election year of 1904.

"Spoke to a vast audience that marshalled twenty shining faces Sunday," he wrote to Professor Wright. "I had made preparation and had no trouble to consume an hour, and could have bombarded the ramparts of capitalism a full hour more. I have been working on an article I am going to submit to some conservative magazines, and if not acceptable to them, I think it will be to some socialist periodical."

Perhaps he should express himself on social issues, even though he did not "particularly enjoy dealing with the sinister, the pathetic, and the execrable, as one must do in socialist propaganda." He heard Wisconsin governor Robert La Follette "speak for three hours on the need for railway rate regulation" and registered "sensitively" to "the long-spun facts and figures of La Follette and his cries for equity." Sandburg's social conscience stirred him to action. He was beginning to believe that so long as "easy-going complacent people will stand idly by and be expropriated, there is nothing for it but to taunt them with portrayals of conditions—sting them with facts, as it were."

By December 13, 1904, Sandburg actually held in his hands his own first book, a slim volume with brown cover, "heavy pink wove paper," red ribbon, and, in black lettering on the cover, "*In Reckless Ecstasy/Charles A. Sandburg.*" The alternately brooding and euphoric poems and prose, much of it begun in worn pocket notebooks as Sandburg roamed the country, foreshadowed his later themes, but there was little in the form of the poetry to predict the strong free verse style which would evolve from his experiments in writing. There were shadows of Browning, Kipling, Gray, Villon and Whitman in the early poems, and some surprising lines influenced by Emily Dickinson. In particular, "A Homely Winter Idyl" echoes a Dickinson cadence:

> Great, long, lean clouds in sullen host
> Along the sky-line passed today;
> While overhead I've only seen
> A leaden sky the whole long day.
>
> My heart would gloomily have mused
> Had I not seen those queer, old crows
> Stop short in their mad frolicking
> And pose for me in long, black rows.

The closest approximation of his later free-verse style came in the poem "Experience," a disarming revelation of his personal ambivalence during those years:

> This morning I looked at the map of the day
> And said to myself, "This is the way! This is the way I will go;
> Thus shall I range on the roads of achievement,
> The way is so clear—it shall all be a joy on the lines marked out."
> And then as I went came a place that was strange—
> 'Twas a place not down on the map!
> And I stumbled and fell and lay in the weeds,
> And looked on the day with rue.
>
> I am learning a little—never to be sure—
> To be positive only with what is past,
> And to peer sometimes at the things to come

As a wanderer treading the night
When the mazy stars neither point or beckon,
And of all the road, no road is sure . . .

He might look at other men and their maps, Sandburg wrote, but he would only heed the advice of one who looked "robust, lonely, and querulous,/As if he had gone to a country far/And made for himself a map." From such a man, Sandburg would seek guidance; "I would see your map!/I would heed the map you have!"

The poems and prose were deliberately varied in subject, but if there was a predominant statement, it had to do with the quality of life for the ordinary man and woman, the simple pleasures of nature, art and intimacy, and the cruel burdens of labor and oppression. "I heard the sounding cracks of the whips of Need—the need of Power, of Wealth, of Bread, of Love," he wrote in the prose piece entitled, after Chekhov, "Pastels." "The rampant, infectious spirit of unrest, the flash and clash and cry—I thought it must ring round the world."

Throughout *In Reckless Ecstasy* there was an undercurrent of the affirmative individualism in the philosophy of Hubbard and many lyceum and chautauqua lecturers. Sandburg dedicated the book to "one who has kept a serene soul in a life of stress, wrested beauty from the commonplace, and scattered her gladness without stint or measure": his mother.

The *Galesburg Evening Mail* gave the book a good notice December 29, 1904: "This little work is purely a Galesburg product and is so meritorious as to commend itself to the earnest consideration of Galesburg people." Otherwise, the book received little attention, but Sandburg remembered that the edition of one hundred copies sold out.

He was a published author now. The book in his hands was evidence that his journey, interior and exterior, had not been a waste of time. Yet he discovered that it was chastening to see your work fixed in print. "A man's merits and faults come to him with more clearness" then, he observed. "Of course, I see all sorts of flaws in my work now, and I am grateful that they have been brought home to me."

———————— ✳ ————————

1904–1906

5. A Vagabond Philosopher-Poet

If I could only meet The Ideal Woman, I believe I could
pull myself together and set the world by the ears. As it
is, I shall continue to prepare my cocoa myself, sew on
the trouser-buttons, and be an itinerant salesman, a
vagabond philosopher-poet, and most unworthy
descendant of Leif Ericson.

—Charles Sandburg to Philip Green Wright,
December 5, 1904

harlie Sandburg was "zigzagging toward the ideal," he wrote to
his sister Mary in 1904. He was twenty-six years old, unable yet
to discern one clear course for his life, still searching for his true
"map." He was now a published author, albeit through the auspices of
his professor's obscure press. He could see himself not only as a writer,
but as orator, politician, businessman. He had an "infinite variety of zigzagging hopes and plans," and there was constant tension between his
"literary aspirations" and his "financial hopes."

He did not expect *In Reckless Ecstasy* to yield much income, and
worried about his inability to earn enough money to help himself or his
family. He missed his youngest sister Martha's "daring, piquant, half-
elfish face," took pride in Mary's and Mart's achievements, admired
Esther's beauty and wit, and her ambition to get a college education. "I
hope I will be able to do something toward your having some courses of
study at Lombard," he wrote her in October 1904. His Swedish parents,
especially his father, had instilled in him their values of frugality and
financial responsibility.

At war with that reflex, however, was Charlie's thirst for "living a
life packed with variety." He had an innate dread of monotony. When

90

Mart, settled into a conventional life in Galesburg, confessed that he was dissatisfied with his job and wanted his own business, Charlie wrote, "I couldn't think much of anyone that would slip into one place and stay there for life." He himself moved restlessly from place to place, preferring, as he wrote Professor Wright, the "canny, restless turbulent spirits of the Pittsburg jail" to one town he briefly inhabited where "there was neither aspiration nor discontent."

His strongest urge was to write, "to say everything," but he did not mean to concentrate on poetry alone. His "literary aspirations" encompassed poetry, fiction and nonfiction, especially biography. He began to feel that to develop as a man of letters, he would have to be free of all other work. He was either blessed or cursed with unbridled energy, a restless need for variety, and a compunction to try everything. He was a man of multiple selves and talents. On the surface, his recurring dream of collapsible horses intimated failure. In reality, he had the potential to achieve at least modest success in many endeavors.

Consequently, he sometimes meandered, was often locked in ambivalence, "zigzagging" as he himself said, from one enterprise and self-image to another. He had undertaken an intense, deliberate quest for the ideal—self, woman, work, life. That lofty goal considerably diminished the chance that in his mid-twenties, he would commit himself to any one persona or vocation or relationship. His appetite was strong for new work, new maps. More than ever, he wanted to write about "what is significant and inspiring" in the lives of Robert Louis Stevenson and Charles XII. They continued to haunt him as subjects for "studies"— "not biographies"—of the content and meaning of noble lives. He resolved to work on his Swedish so he could read primary sources. He wanted to surpass Voltaire in his treatment of Charles XII, to get at his heart, to write biography with a "living touch." His passion to give a "more correct and vivid portraiture of these men and their times" led him to feel that he had two choices: to drop all other work and concentrate on the project, or to give it up, "to postpone it, not touch a hair of its head—not lust after it so much as to press my lips to the rosy cheeks of its bonnie head—and get down to business and aquire [sic] a fund as will last me through."

He was driven by the "ache to utter and to see in word/The silhouette of a brooding soul." Clearly the awkward structures and melodramatic language of *In Reckless Ecstasy* clothed a rudimentary hunger for self-expression, his quest for the right map, for true North. The introductory poem responded to the doubts he faced, his own and others':

And a man's a fool if things there are
That seethe and clash in his ardent brain?
And the ache to utter and to see in word
The silhouette of a brooding soul
Is the childish play of a childish man?
To poetize?—this is the butt and the target's eye
For the by-word, fling and gibe.

He was torn between doubt and belief that his work was more than "the childish play of a childish man." Yet in the drab winter of 1904–1905, Sandburg reluctantly began to consider giving up writing for other, more dependable work, which would yield a predictable income. "I see myself approaching a parting of the ways," he reflected in a letter to Professor Wright. "There was a time I could equalize my attentions to business and literature, but of late the latter has been drawing me away from business." He was deeply reluctant to relinquish or defer the literary dream, but he did not know of "anything great and vital in literature that was done between-whiles."

He knew that Harriet Beecher Stowe wrote *Uncle Tom's Cabin* "when the housework was done," but he called Eva and Tom "egregious distortions of humankind." Theodore Roosevelt, in his opinion, was "the all 'round man, the litterateur incidentally," and Sandburg believed that if Roosevelt "could rage out his entire contribution," the world "would not be poorer a great thought." As he had learned in oratory, the key was total concentration. "Once in a while, and by a natural genius, a great, good work is penned off-hand," he said, but he could not work that way.

✳

Sandburg had been away from Galesburg for more than two years. He began to think of joining his family for Christmas 1904. He looked forward to spending time with Professor Wright, too, but tried to clarify his future plans: "I have said it before, but I've got to say 'Out! you books and pad and pencil,' in earnest now, or Destiny will hammer me into one of those short, lean, pale wretches who make a profession of literature, unceasingly perambulating with manuscripts, most miserable of wage-slaves."

He resolved to give all his attention to one "horse." When he wrote to Wright, he put the best mark on his hard decision:

So I am thinking about formulating a vow, and on New Years Eve to stand on a stack of bibles, lift my right hand toward the vault of heaven and let the gods know by wireless that they may strike me with epilepsy, then paralyse me and disembowel me if I during the coming year entertain for a moment a dream of writing anything but letters, and orders for goods.

There is no record of that Christmas reunion in Galesburg, but early in the New Year, living in a bleak room in Aurora, Illinois, Sandburg was increasingly "fuzzy-minded and troubled" because he was not "connecting with anything in particular, neither business nor writing." He was weary of living alone in cheap furnished rooms. His dollar-a-week room in Aurora that bitter Illinois winter had "no stove or furnace heat." Many mornings he had to break ice in the pitcher before he could bathe. He cooked eggs and made cocoa over a Sterno lamp. When he was not selling stereographs in the cold winter streets, he retreated to the warmth of the public library to read "poetry, fiction, folklore, philosophy." What other work could be find? He tried out a comedy routine in a small vaudeville theater. Dressed in a borrowed red stocking cap and a checked lumberjack coat, he delivered Swedish dialect stories and humorous poems. The audience loved him, and the theater manager urged him to go on another night.

But Sandburg's heart was not in vaudeville. "From the west window of my room one evening I watched a clear short winter sunset and found my eyes full of tears," he wrote in *Ever the Winds of Chance.* "I couldn't get at what the trouble was except that I was sad over how I was doing." The dream of the collapsing horses intensified. "I am living my own God-given life with no excuses to offer anywhere but in the tribunal of my own conscience," he had written in *In Reckless Ecstasy.*

Yet in late January 1905 he told Professor Wright, "By littles and littles, I am surely breaking away from artistry, love and contemplation. I feel powerfully it is all to the good." Mary had been facing her own hard choices; she sought his advice about whether to continue teaching or begin working as a bookkeeper. "Teaching is more distinctly a woman's work than accounting," he told her, but advised her to trust her deepest instincts, for "it really doesn't matter much which way you decide. Happiness has its source in the soul, in individuality." He was trying to reassure himself as well.

Sandburg had failed to support himself by writing. Now he would just learn to become a businessman, single-mindedly working for the essential economic foundation of daily life. Then he might give poetry another look. For now, that seemed just one more collapsible horse. Sandburg set out in the first month of 1905 determined to have economic independence. He knew he could make money if he worked hard selling

Underwood and Underwood views. "Any week I didn't make money was a week I didn't work at selling," he said.

Yet despite his best intentions to concentrate on canvassing, he "was no banner salesman that winter." He quickly relapsed into the old pattern of canvassing "door to door, farm to farm, office to office" two days a week. The rest of the time he was writing. Despite his resolve, he could not stay away from it. He had truly tried to exchange "one of my collapsible horses for a regular, non-collapsible nag." Instead, he confessed to Mary that spring, "I have been writing when I felt the mood and business has gone to the dogs."

For a time his life was less episodic, more centered. In March 1905 he wrote to Professor Wright, "I am sending you my two latest [poems]. I have written some thirty or more since New Years and can't see but this thing must have its course." The new poems sprang from several seeds—his talks with Professor Wright; the positive local response to *In Reckless Ecstasy*; and an interesting new forum for his work, a small Chicago magazine with a liberal slant. It was called *To-Morrow*.

From his boardinghouse in Aurora, Illinois, Sandburg made frequent trips to Chicago in 1905, making the rounds of magazines. He got to know the people at *The Lyceumite*, a journal about lyceum lectures, managers and movements. He had met A. M. Simons, editor of the *International Socialist Review*, and Charles Kerr, owner and publisher of an active Chicago-based socialist press. Sandburg was intrigued by the radical conversation and writing in progress at Kerr's and the *International Socialist Review*. He hoped that *In Reckless Ecstasy* was "revolutionary enough to gain admittance to their catalogs."

But it would not be the lyceum or socialist organs which first gave Sandburg a serious podium for his writing. Rather, it was *To-Morrow*, a magazine "For People Who Think," according to its letter-head. *To-Morrow* staffers printed poetry, fiction and commentary in "a faded and rundown" Chicago mansion owned by the magazine's founder, editor and publisher, Parker Sercombe. As a businessman-banker, Sercombe had made a small fortune, fifty thousand dollars of which he poured into *To-Morrow*. He called his headquarters the Spencer-Whitman Cultural Center after English social scientist and philosopher Herbert Spencer and poet Walt Whitman. There he published his monthly journal, housed some of his staff, "kept open house, fed the hungry, clothed the naked." One of his associates reported that "No bum ever left his kitchen door without a succulent handout." Sercombe's Center was the site of a free public forum where poetry was read, politics debated, and "the intelligentsia and the intellectual elite of the town" gathered for tea, toast and vigorous discussion.

Sandburg found at Spencer-Whitman the "same somber gladness" which entranced him "at the Roycrofters and at the Asgard." He particularly enjoyed the literary and political crossfire of the forums, visiting the *To-Morrow* office January 12, and then again on January 22, 1905, for a memorable weekend. In Sercombe and his assistant editor, University of Chicago English professor Oscar Lovell Triggs, Sandburg found an enthusiastic audience for his own idealism and poetry. After the lonely weeks in Aurora, he was deeply heartened by his reception at *To-Morrow*.

That January was momentous in more somber ways. In St. Petersburg, Russia on Sunday, January 22, thousands of workers swarmed to the Winter Palace to confront the Czar, bringing a petition for relief from economic distress and protesting the unsuccessful war with Japan. Czarist troops fired on the unarmed throng, killing hundreds and leaving hundreds more wounded. As the news of "Bloody Sunday" spread throughout Russia, thousands of workers, students and bourgeoisie protested in bloody confrontations with soldiers and police, intensifying the cries for revolution. As sketchy reports of the staggering casualties made their way to United States newspapers by cable, Sandburg reacted reflexively, for the first time merging political commentary with poetry. American newspapers had carried stories of the turbulence for several days, and Sandburg undoubtedly heard much talk and speculation about Bloody Sunday during that late January weekend in Chicago. On Sunday night, January 22, to the jostling rhythm of a late night trolley, he wrote a "quite strident" poem called "Petersburg." The next day he copied it for Professor Wright, and sent it off in white heat to *To-Morrow*:

> In Petersburg, flows on the vodka and the blood,
>   In Petersburg, and farther, far than Petersburg,
>   The desperate and thirsty battle on,
>
>   To quench the thirst for quiet thought—Vodka!
> To quell the impulse of the vodka—Blood!
> And on and ever on they surge,
> The revels and the rulers and the ruled,
>   And everywhere is Petersburg,
>   And liquor, gore, and living men.

Despite the jagged rhythms and effusive images, the poem marked Sandburg's turn toward a more economical free-verse form. His furious reaction to a contemporary event forged in the poem a coherence of voice, subject and style. He tried, in the style of Whitman, to construct a certain symmetry with the use of parallel phrases. He was pleased with the effect, especially when Triggs published the poem in the February issue of *To-Morrow*.

Sandburg gave Triggs a copy of *In Reckless Ecstasy*, which the professor praised and later reviewed in *To-Morrow*. Triggs published several Sandburg poems in March and April 1905. Encouraged to keep working at the poetry, Sandburg revised sixty poems by mid-April and planned to "fire them at the tribe of Barabbas—make them go through them anyway, and put them through the exertion required for a turn-down."

✳

Charlie Sandburg and his brother Mart, close companions in boyhood, had taken quite different approaches to life. During the last two years of Charlie's travel away from Galesburg, Mart had married and settled down, holding two jobs and getting involved in Galesburg politics. He made the night run from Galesburg to Chicago and back as an agent for the Adams Express Company. During the regular brief midnight stop in Aurora, he often let Charlie come aboard for a free ride to Galesburg. Their older sister Mary had Charlie's complete trust, although she did not fully understand what drove him to travel and to write. As the brothers spent more time together, Mart began to sympathize with Charlie's need to write, even though it was a drive alien to his own quiet, steady nature. Practically, he analyzed his brother's problems and offered a fortuitous solution: he would get Charlie a job at the Brooks Street fire station, three blocks from the Sandburgs' Berrien Street house in Galesburg. Mart thought he had enough political clout to arrange the job, which would pay seventy-five dollars a month. Except for two hours of assigned duties a day—and any time taken up firefighting—Charlie would be free to do his own work.

"What you want is plenty of time to read and write," Mart told his brother, "and you can do that in the fire station and you won't have to fuss around and worry about that damn view business."

Consequently, Sandburg went to work as a fireman once more, caring for two big bay horses, and renewing his friendship with Jim O'Brien, former chief of the Prairie Street station where Sandburg had worked during his college days. Sandburg was given a "quiet corner in the big second floor room with a table for books" where he could read, study and write between fires. He began to read *The Worker*, the "leading journal of the socialist party of New York city and state," and the Milwaukee *Social-Democratic Herald*, published weekly by and for Wisconsin socialists. He read "classics of socialism by Marx, Engels, Liebknecht," and Herbert Spencer. He read further in Darwin and Robert Louis Stevenson, followed the daily newspapers, and shared his emerging poetry with Professor Wright.

His Lombard friend Athol Brown, now editor of the *Galesburg Evening Mail*, encouraged Sandburg to write an occasional column for the paper. Sandburg named the column "Inklings and Idlings," and hoped it would be discovered by big-city editors. He wrote unsigned editorials for the *Galesburg Labor News* and an occasional vigorous letter to the local newspaper, such as his angry "Open Letter" on the abuses by a night police officer employed by the C.B.&Q. Railroad, a spirited defense of hoboes and tramps. "A bum has no redress," Sandburg argued, pointing out that the United States census of 1900 counted six million men out of work in the country. "It is from this body that the tramp is recruited," Sandburg the former hobo observed.

> Now, while a part of the tramp class is made up of petty thieves, yeggmen and degenerates there are many good fellows among them—men with possibilities, who have done hard work and expect to do more. . . . It takes very little nerve or strength or skill to handle hoboes. As a general rule, the desperate and dangerous criminal does not travel in a box car, and, however bold or strong a tramp may be, he is at a disadvantage when hunted by one who is intimately acquainted with railroad yards and the town, and has about him club, revolver and dark lantern. . . .

Sandburg had an affinity for nicknames as well as pseudonyms. After he renamed himself Charles as a boy, he was known variously to friends as Charlie, Cully or Sandy. For some of his *Lombard Review* columns, he used the names Karl August, Charles August and the Bookish Kurmujon. In June 1905, despite the fact that many people in Galesburg and Knox County who read the *Evening Mail* knew that "Inklings and Idlings" was written by Charles A. Sandburg, he wrote a column about a current volatile teamsters' strike, dramatically signing the piece "Crimson." No doubt he had noted the journalistic habit of pinning pseudonyms to controversial opinion pieces. As an aspiring columnist, Sandburg followed suit.

As his journalistic style coalesced, so did his idealism. In the pages of a small-town newspaper he had begun to write his way toward socialism. He devoted one column to the horrors of war, and its disproportionate use of the average citizen, the "farm boys, shoe clerks, railroaders, milkmen and desperadoes" who made up the ranks and took most of the casualties. His fellow townsmen seemed to take his outspokenness in stride, or ignore it, and no big-city editors clamored to syndicate "Inklings and Idlings," but he was developing a journalistic voice and style, and he found that he enjoyed the work.

Most of the time between the rare fires in Galesburg, however, Sandburg was writing poetry, persistently sending poems out to small magazines, and garnering rejection after rejection. *In Reckless Ecstasy* still got an occasional notice: in June 1905, the Mobile, Alabama, *Daily Register* commended its "virile spirit," "fresh original tone" and the "vital, original touch in every word." *To-Morrow* published a handful of poems and Sandburg's prose pieces on Elbert Hubbard and author-journalist Alfred Henry Lewis, but every other outlet he sought turned him down, although two editors encouraged him to revise poems because they saw "signs of hope" in his work.

Undaunted, Sandburg kept working over the poems and producing new ones. Once during that year of his search for proof that he was a poet, he tried an experiment:

> I showed a sheaf of the rejected poems to three well-read persons for whose opinions I had respect. In this sheaf I inserted two free verse poems from Stephen Crane's *Black Riders* and one from Emily Dickinson. And two of the well-read persons agreed with the editors in rejecting ALL of the poems. They threw Crane and Emily Dickinson into the discard along with the Sandburg. The third judge, a teacher of English, said the two poems of Crane deserved to be printed. I didn't tell them I had slipped three jokers into the deck but I learned you can't trust the judgment of good friends.

When he heard that some magazine editors would not read handwritten submissions, Sandburg bought a fifteen-dollar second-hand Blickensderfer typewriter and taught himself to type. The repercussions of the typewriter's cylinder sounded "like a ferocious rat trying to gnaw its way out of a washboiler." To that cacophony Sandburg created the early work he himself described as "earnest, mawkish, rhymed poems." At the noisy Blickensderfer in his fire station corner between alarms, Sandburg struggled to develop a free-verse style, not so much in the manner of Whitman, he said, as of William Ernest Henley. Encouraged by his reception at *To-Morrow*, he "sent on poems and articles, smartaleck philosophizings," portraits or studies of writers and political figures who caught his imagination. Sandburg would not "remain long in obscurity when once his quality is appreciated," Oscar Lovell Triggs predicted, and went on to praise the vibrant "poetic energy" of Sandburg's poems.

Thanks to his brother, Sandburg now had a steady financial base to underpin his experiments. Inexorably he was writing his way through a maze of florid images, trite themes and affected language toward the leaner, thriftier style of *Chicago Poems*. He settled on free verse as his mode of expression. He was still searching widely for subject and voice. He had written about contemporary human and political tragedy in "Petersburg." He wrote about nature with extravagant rhetoric; some of the words—plash, suspire, glistering—echo his reading of the romantic poets and Omar Khayyam. *To-Morrow* readers could try to decipher his oblique ode to the unknown, "A Fling at the Riddle":

> I think to filch a story from the Sphinx,
> Outface the old Egyptian questioner,
> And cry, "Behold! I know! I know!
> I know I do not know! . . ."

These awkward, self-conscious verses, effusive and hyperbolic as they were, advanced Sandburg's deliberate metamorphosis into a poet. The upper recess of the Brooks Street fire station was an unlikely laboratory for a poet, but Sandburg kept doggedly at it month after month, writing when he was not grooming horses, cleaning stalls or polishing equipment.

At twenty-seven, Sandburg the poet, temporarily and expediently a fireman, reflected on Charles Darwin's description of the young eagle: "The desire to ascend is there before the wings." He was working hard to develop the wings for his poetry. For eight months he had the leisure of unencumbered time, and the regular and stimulating company of Philip Green Wright, whose poetry he admired and emulated.

Galesburg was called "the Athens of the Corn Belt" then, but Sandburg grew tired of the congenial, comfortable backdrop for his experiments in poetry and prose. After eight months "as a fireman and writer" he was bitten by the old restlessness. Every other day, he recalled years later in *Ever the Winds of Chance*, "I drove my two bay horses back and forth along Brooks Street for exercise, hauling the combination chemical hose car with ladders. On the seat one afternoon I decided that after these eight months as a fireman and writer I would go to Chicago and try my luck." After he told his family of his decision, his father took him aside, his face somber. "Iss dere any money in diss poetry business, Sholly?" he asked his son.

Sandburg waited a few seconds to answer. All he could think to say was, "I guess, papa, I haven't got anything but hope."

＊

He and his father, so unlike in temperament, politics and values, knew each other then as well as they ever would. His father's chief message to him, so far as Sandburg could decipher it, was anxiety about his material future, a practical Swedish concern about money. Between Sandburg and his mother there was a deep, enduring bond of affection. Clara supported her son's hopes as well as she could, despite August's disapproval. Sandburg was grateful to Mart for the job and other encouragement. He was devoted to his sisters: Mary, his confidante; Esther, now a Lombard College student, musically gifted and pretty enough, he told her, to be a Gibson Girl; his baby sister Martha, plain, sickly and shy. Despite their love, he had outgrown Galesburg, with its "little hills and the years all alike." It was time to leave.

That departure from Galesburg in April 1906 was Sandburg's final leave-taking from home. With the metaphor of the Indian warrior who makes his passage into manhood alone in the vast wilderness of the prairie and plains, Sandburg told them good-bye in "The Red Son":

> I LOVE your faces I saw the many years
> I drank your milk and filled my mouth
> With your home talk, slept in your house
> And was one of you.
>   But a fire burns in my heart. . . .

By the time the poem appeared in 1916, Sandburg had cut through the thicket of conventional verse forms to release his own fluid free-verse style. He could convey sharp images simply, without the crutch of effusive description. Whitman stood in the background of "The Red Son" only generically, for Sandburg had become a truly original poet by the time he addressed his passage to manhood in the beautiful economy of the poem, his commemoration of the "endless mysterious command" to discover the self. "I shall go to the city and fight against it," he wrote prophetically,

> And make it give me passwords
> Of luck and love, women worth dying for,
> And money . . .
>
> There is no pity of it and no blame.
> None of us is in the wrong.
> After all it is only this:
>   You for the little hills and I go away.

For his mother, Sandburg wrote a special farewell in "An Old Woman," unpublished until long after his death:

I kissed my hand to the dim shape
Standing in the shadows under the porch
Looking good-by to her boy
And I keep a picture
Of one shaft of moonlight
Trembling near her face
Telling of wishes farther than love or death,
The infinite love of an old woman
Keeping a hope for her boy.

✳

During his fire station retreat and his subsequent exodus to Chicago, Sandburg was writing some poetry "unduly" influenced by Whitman, by his own admission some "dull" imitations of Whitman's extravagance of line and rhetoric. Those derivative poems coexisted with Sandburg's new radical forms, and he kept experimenting. In certain poems, such as "The Rebel's Funeral" and "A Fling at the Riddle," it was hard to discern whether Whitman or oratory had helped to shape Sandburg's rhetoric. It was most likely a fusion of those influences which prompted Sandburg's use of catalogue and repetition. Out of his own vision as much as his reading of Whitman came the rhapsodic themes and images in "A Fling at the Riddle":

. . . And men and women and valor and war and want,
And nowhere a soul despoiled and bankrupt
Of some dear fondling of a hope,
Some stray blithe romance, coming, coming, coming,—
Some shining gleam of a woman's hair,
Some trusty tone of a hero's voice,
Some palace, cottage, ship, or child,
Coming, coming, coming,
Coming from out of the great and beautiful Unknown.

Ironically, as Whitman propelled him toward free verse, Sandburg began to move instinctively toward a greater simplicity and economy than Whitman possessed. *To-Morrow* published three Sandburg poems in 1906 which are like Whitman's only in their free verse. Otherwise, they are all Sandburg, with shorter lines and simple word portraits of familiar scenes, the "broad blue vista" of a lake; poppies offering "thin red dollars/To the big white sun!" "In Illinois" was a quiet, lovely depiction of the landscapes Sandburg roamed in autumn:

In Illinois
The grass is at the richest of the year.

The rivers curve along the bottoms
Flashing silver faces to the sky . . .
Yellow, scarlet, russet leaves
Spangle all the woodland—
Premonitions hover in the boughs . . .
Tomatoes redden in the sun,
As proud as any flower
Of their kinship with the soil. . . .

Like most artists finding their way, Sandburg often created by some kind of osmosis, unaware himself, no doubt, of the other voices lurking in his work. One poem in particular is a smorgasbord of influences, from his reading of William James to his frequent recitations of Langdon Smith's jaunty rhymed verse "Evolution." Its chief influence, however, is Whitman's "Passage to India." Sandburg would become the Poet of the People Whitman had hoped to be, in large part because he encountered Whitman's work at a crucial time in his own journey toward creative identity and expression. Whitman gave him a model for social idealism, poetry, the life of the soul. Sandburg's unpublished poem "Fragments," dating back at least to 1906, appears to be an almost antiphonal response to Whitman's rousing challenge in "Passage to India." "O my brave soul!" Whitman wrote in the poem's finale:

O farther, farther sail!
O daring joy, but safe! Are they not all the seas of God?
O farther, farther, farther sail!

Whitman had celebrated Columbus as "History's type of courage, action, faith," and had depicted his imprisonment, "dejection, poverty, death." He reflected on the long deferral of reward for heroic struggle, urging his audience to joyous, fearless exploration "on trackless seas," which marked the triumphant voyage of the soul. In that time of his own profound struggle for self and work, Sandburg embraced Whitman's challenge. "I am Columbus," Sandburg wrote in "Fragments":

And out over seas uncharted,
I sail my fragile and battered craft;
I may wear chains and languish,
I may fall sick, to brood and curse,
But though I reach no palm-fringed, coral shore,
    I will have sailed!
I will have sped o'er the trackless blue,
I will have known the love of the sky,
Rouse of the sea and talk of the stars—

> I will have sailed!
> I have comrades, out on the seas,
> Brothers valiant, dexterous, true;
> Their crafts are moving over the tides—
> What of the Indies we shall find?

Sandburg discovered in Whitman an extraordinary alliance of spirit, and validation of his own stubborn courage and unorthodox experiments in poetry and politics. Even more important, he glimpsed in Whitman's revelations of the interior life an affirmation of his own soul's journey. The important thing was the journey, not the outcome, Sandburg concluded. He would sail the uncharted seas.

"O my brave soul!" Whitman sang, "O farther, farther sail!"

"I will have sailed!" Sandburg answered. "I will have sailed. . . . What of the Indies we shall find?"

✳

Sandburg described his first "Chicago Plunge" in *Ever the Winds of Chance*:

> I rode with Mart in the express car to Chicago. I looked up Parker Sercombe, publisher and editor of *To-Morrow* in a faded and rundown Prairie Avenue mansion. He offered me board and room, without salary, to help at editing, proofreading, and handling manuscripts. He was moonfaced, smiling, light haired, medium height, quick in motions, with powerful arms and torso. I stayed.

After his solitary tenure in countless cheap boardinghouses and his Galesburg sojourn, Sandburg enjoyed the companionship of the half dozen or so other aspiring writers who lived upstairs at Sercombe's headquarters. At *To-Morrow* they called him Saundy, a variant of his nickname *Sandy*, short for Sandburg. Life at the Spencer-Whitman Center, he decided, was "both a joy and a mild scandal," verging on the bohemian. An ardent young woman on the staff, a poet of some charm, quickly fell in love with him, but he was not seriously interested in her. He had come to Chicago for work, not for love. According to a bachelor friend of the period, he was by no means "yet ready to be caught in any woman's net."

While his job as *To-Morrow*'s associate editor paid no salary, he could submit his own poetry and prose to Sercombe and Triggs. Perhaps they would publish his work in the audacious little journal. Sandburg threw himself into life at the Center, working on all facets of the magazine's publication, and articulating his poetry and idealism in the twice-weekly forums that were held there. Someone who heard him speak observed that Sandburg got "his first chance to spiel and read his stuff at those meets."

Twice weekly Parker Sercombe opened Fraternity Hall, his large, bare parlor, for a free public forum where members of the Spencer-Whitman Fellowship and their visitors could speak on timely topics or read from their own work. Sandburg admired Sercombe's multifaceted interests:

> He could mention investments he had in Mexican mines as a businessman and was at any time ready to show his various wrestling holds though never throwing a guest to the floor. He welcomed radicals and revolutionaries but he preferred the gentle philosophical anarchists of the Kropotkin variety to the direct actionists who believed in bombs and "the propaganda of the deed."

Clarence Darrow had lectured at the center, as had H. G. Wells; Edwin Markham; Chicago educator Margaret Haley, about whom Sandburg would later write an article and poem; and the controversial young writer Jack London. During the solitary years of his apprenticeship, Sandburg's intellectual and artistic development had been arbitrarily shaped by college studies; by his mentor, Professor Wright; and by the few congenial companions he encountered, chiefly Wright, Elbert Hubbard and Frederick Dickinson. Yet he was largely self-educated, and perennially self-conscious about his intellectual powers. In Sercombe's shabby mansion on the edge of the stockyard district, Sandburg found regular affirmation, stimulation and excitement.

He filled the pages of To-Morrow with prose and poetry he wrote or edited. He listened avidly to the animated debates on Monday and Thursday night. He loved the raw exuberance of Chicago. After his months selling views in small towns and on the farms scattered sparsely over the vast prairie, he revelled in the endless variety of the city. He had easily outgrown Galesburg, his Athens until now. Chicago stretched and challenged him. He found at Sercombe's Center an unaccustomed ratification of his own emerging philosophy of democracy of thought and education, social and economic equality, intellectual freedom, simplicity, toleration. To-Morrow was the first Chicago magazine to publish his poetry. At this crucial juncture in his life, he could freely express his poetry and his politics.

*

Sandburg began to study and emulate the work of the muckrakers, who got their name from President Theodore Roosevelt's attack on current journalistic probes of corruption in government, politics and business. In a speech in the spring of 1906, Roosevelt compared the work of the advocacy press to the Man with the Muckrake in John Bunyan's *Pilgrim's Progress*, "the man who could look no way but downward with the muckrake in his hand, who was offered a celestial crown for his muckrake, but who would neither look up nor regard the crown he was offered, but continued to rake to himself the filth of the floor."

Sandburg read Upton Sinclair's exposés in *Cosmopolitan* in 1906, which came in the wake of the great success of *The Jungle*. He knew Lincoln Steffens's *The Shame of the Cities*; Charles Edward Russell's *The Greatest Trust in the World*, an attack on the beef trust; and Louis Brandeis's exposure, "The Greatest Life Insurance Wrong," in *The Independent*. Avidly, Sandburg followed the muckrakers who "were filling magazines with floodlights on state and city political corruption and the viciously unfair practices of large corporations and trusts." He admired books by Steffens, Ray Stannard Baker, Ida Tarbell and others as "sources of history, bristling with merciless and tragic facts of an era." He wrote "The Muck-Rake Man," a poem published in *To-Morrow*, replete with his still-awkward rhetoric, testifying that "Today 'tis ink has higher homage than the blood of soldiers."

Sandburg's work was conspicuous in the April issue of *To-Morrow*, and he basked in the praise. One of his colleagues told him he was "an admirable stylist whose work is certain to make itself felt with no little force." Sercombe commended Sandburg in print for his "strong, wholesome, incisive" prose. The issue introduced Sandburg's column "Views and Reviews: A Facet of Fact and Opinion." He always enjoyed conjunctive titles in the vein of "Inklings and Idlings" and "Links and Kinks," and "Views and Reviews" became a regular feature at *To-Morrow*, giving him a ready podium for commentary on everything from yellow journalism and local evangelists to the San Francisco earthquake. He also wrote vignettes of Hubbard, Triggs and others who caught his imagination. His chief contribution to the April issue, however, was a vigorous expression of his growing obsession with the fate of the common man —a long essay entitled "Jack London: A Common Man."

Sandburg had just missed the chance to meet London and his wife, who had visited the Spencer-Whitman Center shortly before his arrival in Chicago. His article probed London's personality and experience, tracing the evolution of his socialism and analyzing its expression in his fiction, particularly *The Sea-Wolf*, whose allegory Sandburg believed critics had overlooked. This early disdain for "almost every manjack of the hired scribes," as he called London's critics, foreshadowed Sandburg's own later contempt for literary critics. He frankly admired London's socialism and realism, never missed his pieces in *Cosmopolitan*, read and reread his fiction. Like London, Sandburg had served time in jail for vagrancy, had seen firsthand the impartial cruelty of poverty.

Sandburg knew London instinctively, as a kindred spirit. He admired the "many-sidedness of the fellow." He saw in London's complex experience mirrors of his own search. Like himself, London had worked at a kaleidoscope of jobs in his youth, emerging from the fragmented experience "one of high, clean, intelligent manhood," instead of a "strong, ruthless, crafty, insensate creature." Like himself, London became a vagabond, "a hobo stealing rides on freight and passenger trains, mingling with all the hopeless, degenerate life of discouraged workmen, beggars, and petty criminals." Yet, like himself, London was not "shackled by his environment." Rather, he was "a spectator but not a partaker in the degradations that surrounded him." But London had achieved what Sandburg could only aspire to—he had written books "that sent his name around the world." For London, as was increasingly true for Sandburg, the overriding subject for thought, writing and action was the common man. "He does the work of the world," Sandburg wrote, "and he is beginning to know it." He noted that London's stature as a writer had been compromised by his "notoriety as an agitator."

London "neglected no occasion to boom his theories," Sandburg wrote. Sandburg himself would later contend that a writer had an obligation to speak openly to the issues of his time. He admired London's open demonstration of alliance with the workers: dressing as a workingman in the London slums, seeking after a job, applying for relief, sleeping where he could, as he gathered material for *The People of the Abyss*. "If he were not a Common Man," Sandburg concluded, "I would call him a Great Man."

London was a dominant force in Sandburg's intellectual life during those hectic months at *To-Morrow*. He also read Markham, Thorstein Veblen, Upton Sinclair, Frank Norris and David Graham Phillips. On the work of these writers and idealists, Sandburg modeled his increasingly prolific prose in 1906. He was becoming a political agitator in his own right, using his regular podium in the lean pages of *To-Morrow* to address issues that engaged his mind or provoked his anger. He attacked the death penalty, and hypocrisy in religion and politics. Incensed when public libraries in Chicago and St. Louis suppressed Sinclair's *The Jungle*, Sandburg lashed out at book banning as "another case of mistaken propriety on the part of the people who ought to know better." It was a "standing disgrace to American democracy," he wrote, for Philadelphia libraries to bar Victor Hugo's *Les Misérables* from circulation. "The foulest blot on America's literary record is the attempted suppression of Walt Whitman's *Leaves of Grass*."

Sandburg took on the Armours and the Swifts over conditions in Chicago's stockyards. He defended the Russian writer Maxim Gorky, whose work he had studied and admired. Gorky, like London, was a realist who drew on the painful actualities of experience for the fire in his work. Sandburg believed that Gorky, unlike Tolstoy, knew real misery and poverty, and that his work was animated by that knowledge. In 1906 when Gorky arrived in the United States with his mistress and his out-spoken idealism, he was quickly vilified in the American press. Gorky spoke out in support of labor leaders "Big Bill" Haywood and Charles Moyer, and tried to raise money for the revolutionary party in Russia. In return, he faced closed doors in the United States, canceled appoint-ments, eviction from hotels and public excoriation in the press. Sandburg defended him in "Views and Reviews," raising his voice in protest in the obscure little journal which Sercombe and his staff printed in the backroom of the rundown mansion on Prairie Avenue. Insignificant as the journal may have been, it gave Sandburg a testing ground for his idealism and his prose. At a crucial time, Chicago was for him a vortex and *To-Morrow* was, briefly, its center.

Sandburg's passion for subjects and issues fed him the words he needed, burning away the verbiage to the clean ash of clarity. At *To-Morrow* he was learning to craft his prose, to sublimate style to subject, and therein to find his true voice. The experience confirmed what he had learned about oratory: if you cared passionately about your subject, your audience was far more likely to listen to what you had to say.

✳

Sandburg could be obstreperous. He began to enjoy flexing his muscles in print. In one *To-Morrow* column he chastised prominent Chicago minister Dr. Frank Gunsaulus, whose resonant voice filled the galleries of the Chicago Auditorium on Sundays. Speaking on one occasion of the furor over Upton Sinclair's *The Jungle*, Dr. Gunsaulus charged that "the leveling down process proposed by socialists is as untrue to nature as a mechanical combination in chemistry." He brought his homily to a dramatic close, exclaiming in a ringing voice, "The great God is not a socialist! The great God is not a communist!"

Audaciously, Sandburg wondered in his column

why the preacher, having such close acquaintance with God and having authority to speak for the Supreme Being, did not announce what God's politics are, whether Jehovah is a Republican, a Democrat, or a be-whiskered and disreputable Populist. If Dr. Gunsaulus is sure that Him who planned the stars and shut up the sea with doors is not a Socialist, will he kindly inform a waiting world what God's politics really are?

Sandburg's boyhood disillusionment with the organized church shaped his views on structured religion, which he recorded privately over the years in his notebooks and then asserted with exuberant conviction in *To-Morrow*: "There is a great difference between Christianity and chur-chianity. You can follow Christ without pledging yourself to listen to the mummeries of an ordained preacher." Sandburg wound up that column with a mischievous jab at evangelist Billy Sunday, whom he would later attack in poetry.

Sandburg had no patience with "churchianity," but he had a deep, inbred reverence for nature, humanity, the mystical heart of life. He filled his private notebooks with prayers by Robert Louis Stevenson, rhythmical passages from the King James Bible, his own meditations, prayers and homilies. In the impertinent pages of *To-Morrow*, after he scolded the ministers of organized religion, he printed in bold-face type his own "Little Sermon": "As the waters of rising mist and descending shower play back and forth between earth and sky incessantly and the rain makes pure and beautifies its own origin so does the shock of the glad hand and the good word return to its source, and bless him who first gave it."

London, Veblen, Gorky, Sinclair and others inhabited Sandburg's thoughts in those days, and their idealism infused his own, but he knew them only through what they wrote. Sercombe, Triggs, Hubbard, Kerr and Wright he knew in person. Because of the active *To-Morrow* lecture bureau, Sandburg met, at least briefly, Clarence Darrow, Billy Sunday, Jane Addams and Albert Beveridge, who later saw him as a rival when both were at work on Lincoln biographies. It was heady stuff, living in Chicago and having his say in that irreverent, uninhibited "monthly magazine for progressive people."

*

Sandburg discovered his voice and style in prose before he found them in poetry, in part because of his prolific output at *To-Morrow*. With all subjects he worked carefully to strip away façades, to "play hell with fakes" and to "twist the tail of conventionality." He despised the "pach-

Charles Sandburg, barbershop porter, 1893 *Carl Sandburg Collection, University of Illinois*

August Sandburg,
Carl Sandburg's father
Graham & Forrell,
Galesburg, Illinois; Carl
Sandburg Collection,
University of Illinois

Sandburg's mother, Clara
Graham & Forrell; Carl
Sandburg Collection,
University of Illinois

Martin Sandburg,
"Brother Mart"
W. B. Loomis, Galesburg;
Carl Sandburg Collection,
University of Illinois

Mary Sandburg (*left*),
"Sister Mary"
Carl Sandburg Collection,
University of Illinois

Esther Sandburg,
"Sister Esther"
Carl Sandburg Collection,
University of Illinois

Charlie Sandburg *(first row, left)* and his confirmation class, Elim Lutheran Church, Galesburg, 1891   *Carl Sandburg Collection, University of Illinois*

The three-room frame house on Third Street, the second house east of the Chicago, Burlington and Quincy Railroad tracks in Galesburg, Carl Sandburg's birthplace   *Carl Sandburg Collection, University of Illinois*

Charlie Sandburg about 1898–1899, the "many-sided self"   *Carl Sandburg Collection, University of Illinois*

Charles A. Sandburg in the
Lombard *Cannibal*, 1900–1901
*Carl Sandburg Collection,
University of Illinois*

LOMBARD UNIVERSITY.

FOOT BALL SQUAD, SEASON OF 1899.

BARTLETT, BISHOP, (L.E.). SUTLEE (L.T.). ANDREWS (L.G.). HARTGROVE (C.). MILLER (R.G.). LOTHIAN (R.T.). GINRICH (R.E.) HOLROYD (Q.B.). ROBINSON (L.H.B.). BAIRD (R.H.B.). WEEKS (F.B.).

Compliments of THE CHICAGO TIMES-HERALD.

Charles Sandburg *(last row, second from left)* and the Lombard football squad, 1899   *Chicago Times Herald; Carl Sandburg Collection, University of Illinois*

Charles Sandburg—"Lecturer, Orator" —1906   *W. B. Loomis, Galesburg; University of Virginia Library*

Professor Philip Green Wright
Carl Sandburg Collection, University of Illinois

✛ In∵Reckless∵Ecstasy ✛
Charles A. Sandburg

"I had better bring this poor, pallid epistle to a close. My vocabulary is
rampant to-night—the tide of expression foams, the combers glitter with
speech-stuff, but the spindrift is no account. Here comes another! and it
lashes this letter to its close."—*From a letter.*

"These things are as they will be, whatever I mean by that. I am like
Keats at least in this, that the roaring of the wind is my wife, and the stars
thru the window panes are my children. As for posterity, I say with the
Hibernian, 'What has it ever done for us?'"—*From a letter.*

Charles A. Sandburg's first book,
published by Professor Wright and
the Asgard Press, 1904   *Carl Sandburg Collection, University of Illinois*

Asgard Press:
Galesburg, Illinois,
1904

Incidentals, 1907, also published by Professor
Wright and the Asgard Press   *Carl Sandburg Collection, University of Illinois*

Sandburg in 1905
University of Virginia Library

Frederick Dickinson, 1905
University of Virginia Library

Dickinson and Sandburg, selling "views" *Carl Sandburg Collection, University of Illinois*

ydermis of snobbery" and moved steadily toward a confrontation with life as it was.

This impulse toward realism began to permeate his poetry as well. The small pocket notebooks which had been his sole audience for years provided material for new poems as well as his columns. After *To-Morrow* published a number of his poems, he sent eleven poems to A. S. Hoffmann of *Watson's Magazine* in New York, who rejected them for being too minutely like Whitman in style. Hoffmann asked to see more, however, writing Sandburg that his work contained "a good deal of real poetry," although it lacked rhythm, a condition Sandburg sought to improve.

Before he arrived in Chicago, Sandburg wrote poetry deeply influenced by the traditional romantic and classic poetry he read, as well as by Philip Green Wright's poems, and the free-verse styles of Whitman and Henley. Coming to Chicago transformed Sandburg's poetry, however, as if the geographical and intellectual liberation from Galesburg transfigured form and subject. Most of the surviving poems of this period have Chicago subjects, and a freer, more economical form. There is an emerging simplicity and clarity of image. The best of these appeared in *To-Morrow* in 1906 with the title "Departures," and, renamed "Docks," in *Chicago Poems* in 1916. In quietly rhythmical free verse, Sandburg portrayed departing ships with the sustained simile of the mastodon:

> Strolling along
> By the teeming docks,
> I watch the ships put out,
> Black ships that heave and lunge
> And move like mastodons
> Arising from lethargic sleep.

He described the ships as they appeared

> Shaggy in the half-lit distance,
> They pass the pointed headland,
> View the wide, far-lifting wilderness
> And leap with cumulative speed
> To test the challenge of the sea.
>
> Plunging,
> Doggedly onward plunging,
> Into salt and mist and foam and sun.

✳

Sandburg was beginning to be restless at *To-Morrow*, and made his own departure in midsummer, for several practical reasons. As always, he needed to earn more money for himself and for his family in Galesburg. His father was right to fear that there was very little money in the poetry business. Sandburg found it hard to stay in harness during the summer months, and he may have wanted more freedom and solitude after the crowded months at the Center. As time wore on, he was openly disenchanted with Sercombe and his magazine, which Sandburg called "vindictive and scatterbrained." As much as he liked the image of himself as editor/columnist/poet, he was ready to move on. He vacationed briefly in late July in Grand Haven, Michigan, at the home of Amanda Kidder, his college elocution teacher, and came away determined to sell stereographs once more to support his two overriding ambitions: to be a poet and to become an orator.

Back in a rented room in Aurora, Illinois, Sandburg set up his Blickensderfer and kept writing about Chicago. In lines suggestive of Whitman, Sandburg described the people "On State Street, Chicago":

> These faces! this parade
> Containing all the flux and flow
> Of human passion, dream achievement—
> I ask myself what unnumbered loves
> Of men and women
> Issued this steady, unremitting pour
> Of men and women . . .

He would find endless poetry in the faces and lives of Chicago's people over the next sixty years. Simultaneously, he was beginning to write more personal poems, such as "Loafer":

> . . . I lie on my back in the grass,
> And the cool unconcern
> Of the measureless night
> Has entered my heart—
> I too am burly, at ease, unafraid.

"The Road and the End," rejected by *Watson's* in 1906 and finally published by Elbert Hubbard in *The Fra* in August 1909, revealed in its cadence and clarity the gradual but certain metamorphosis of Sandburg's earlier "reckless ecstasies" into a coherent poetic style. The poem also contains one of the enduring metaphors of his life and work—the traveled road.

> I shall foot it
> Down the roadway in the dusk,

Where shapes of hunger wander
And the fugitives of pain go by.
I shall foot it
In the silence of the morning,
See the night slur into dawn,
Hear the slow great winds arise
Where tall trees flank the way
And shoulder toward the sky.

The broken boulders by the road
Shall not commemorate my ruin.
Regret shall be the gravel underfoot.
I shall watch for
Slim birds swift of wing
That go where wind and ranks of thunder
Drive the wild processionals of rain.

The dust of the traveled road
Shall touch my hands and face.

Whitman's voice echoes in these lines, along with other voices crowding Sandburg's mind during those days of his apprenticeship, but the poem is his own invention, a signal of his gathering strength and security as a poet. The poem's simplicity of style, image and rhythm mark the debut of his true poetic voice.

In those early years Philip Green Wright was the primary influence on Sandburg, but he as much as anyone urged Sandburg to find his own unique voice. He wrote about Wright's force in his life in *Ever the Winds of Chance*, as well as in "To a Poet," a poem unpublished until more than a decade after Sandburg's death. "You said I would go alone," Sandburg told his teacher in the poem:

I would find my way.
But you were the strongest person I had known.
You were the morning wind, and you were stone.
You said: I know that you will go your way.
Whatever horse you want to ride is yours,
And night is yours, and the evening gleams, and day.
I can tell you nothing you have not known.
I said, I go with you; I am your own.
But I went alone.

After Sandburg left Wright and Galesburg for Sercombe and Chicago, and then moved on from *To-Morrow*, he entrusted some of his poems to an astute literary critic, a genial, eccentric Missouri Mencken, William

Marion Reedy. He needed criticism as much as validation, and Reedy gave him both.

In St. Louis in 1891 Reedy had founded *Reedy's Mirror*, a weekly magazine for political and social commentary and literary news and criticism. By 1898 the journal was so popular that it had a national circulation of 32,250 copies, surpassing the *Dial's* 5,000, the *Atlantic's* 7,000 and the 12,000 copies of the *Nation*. When Sandburg approached him in 1906, Reedy had edited his weekly *Mirror* for fifteen years. His everwidening circle of readers persuaded some observers that St. Louis rather than New York or Chicago deserved to be called the literary center of the United States.

Despite his grounding in classical and traditional literary forms, Reedy was a literary iconoclast and a persuasive advocate for a truly native American literature. A solid journalist, a provocative political satirist, and a witty social critic, Reedy was to his even more lasting credit a discerning patron and critic of contemporary literature. By the time the *Mirror* ceased publication in 1920, Reedy's astute literary appraisals were respected at home and abroad. He had helped to launch or validate the careers of a coterie of the most distinguished literary voices of the twentieth century: Theodore Dreiser, Vachel Lindsay, Edgar Lee Masters, Ezra Pound, Edwin Arlington Robinson, Sara Teasdale, Amy Lowell, Edna St. Vincent Millay. He was the champion of naturalism as it was expressed in the works of Thomas Hardy and James Joyce. He helped to articulate the twentieth-century appreciation of such nineteenth-century enigmas as Nathaniel Hawthorne, Emily Dickinson, Oscar Wilde, J. M. Synge and Walt Whitman.

Tall and portly, Reedy was a conspicuous figure in St. Louis in more than height and girth. His three marriages paralleled the colorful intellectual pursuits of his flamboyant life. His youthful fascination with the decadence movement as epitomized by Oscar Wilde was the concomitant to his first marriage in 1893, during a night of drunken debauchery. Reedy awoke the morning after to find himself married to a notorious and affluent madam. In the three short months that they lived together, the first Mrs. Reedy made two significant contributions to her thirty-year-old husband's life. She paid for him to take the Keely Cure for alcoholism at Dr. Leslie Keely's famous institute, and she was the catalyst for an adamant series of articles by Reedy on "the social evil."

After nearly three years of separation, Addie Reedy divorced her husband on grounds of desertion. His second wife was Eulalie Bauduy, the beautiful, charming and thoroughly respectable daughter of an upstanding Creole physician, the leading neurologist in St. Louis. This marriage coincided with the growing success and security of the *Mirror*. Eulalie Reedy died suddenly in 1901, leaving Reedy distraught. By 1905 he had recovered enough to take for a mistress another St. Louis madam, Margie Rhodes, who generously, without Reedy's knowledge, loaned his company five thousand dollars in the wake of the financial crisis precipitated by the Panic of 1907. Reedy married the charming, enterprising Margie Rhodes in 1909; their congenial union lasted until Reedy's death in July 1920. Without Reedy at the helm, the *Mirror* survived only five weeks.

Perhaps because his printed work was never collected, and the many famous beneficiaries of it never gave consolidated testimony to his influence, his role as an astute literary broker and critic was not evaluated until the early 1960s. But at the turn of the century, Charles Sandburg, like thousands of other subscribers, paid avid attention to what Reedy had to say. To his great pleasure, Sandburg received Reedy's favorable notice in a review of Philip Green Wright's book of poems, *The Dreamer*. Reedy called Sandburg's Foreword an excellent specimen of "nervous, well-knit, savory prose." In 1906, earnestly seeking proof that he could be a poet, Sandburg sent some of his poems to Reedy. In a long letter offering sympathetic but straightforward criticism, Reedy declined the poems, affirming their "certain rough vigor" and the "sweep and depth" of their thought, but objecting to their "vagueness" of idea and imagery and their resemblance to Whitman. "I know that you say that you are modeled more upon Henley than Whitman," Reedy wrote,

> and yes, to be quite frank with you, I do not think that you conform to Henley's idea of rhythm. Henley has, to my thinking, a form even in his formlessness. He is a favorite poet of mine and has been for many years. His free verse, however, is not quite so free as he imagined it was. He adhered rather more closely to the old standard and methods then [sic] he thought. In your verse the Whitman idea seems to be dominant and, as I say, in the last batch of poems which you sent me there is but one thing which seems to me to be anything like poetry as I conceive it.

Reedy praised Sandburg's careful observations of character and nature, and liked the "human atmosphere" of his radicalism. "Once in a while you strike out something that is real poetry," he wrote.

Sandburg was grateful for Reedy's criticism, and took it to heart. Sometimes it seemed a slow, endless journey, becoming a poet, but he persisted. Years later, in *Smoke and Steel* (1920), Sandburg evoked those hard years with two of the dominant, unifying metaphors of his poetry —the traveled road and the "hunger for a nameless bread":

The road I am on is a long road and I can go hungry again like I have gone
 hungry before.
What else have I done nearly all my life than go hungry and go on singing?

Reedy astutely assessed the conflicting forces which split Sandburg's
attention in those early years, and proposed a prophetic solution. "I
suppose . . . that your profession is that you are more of a radical than
a poet," he told Sandburg. "It surely is not impossible that one should
be both." Once more Sandburg was trying to choose among several
"horses." Privately he labored over the poems, destroying futile ones,
crafting and rewriting others, beginning new ones. As much as he needed
the poetry, the vigorous debates at the Spencer-Whitman Center had
sharpened his appetite for the more visible medium of oratory. As his
radical idealism intensified, the lectures and debates triggered political
and literary ideas which exploded into some of his most heated essays.
The essays set off new lecture ideas. For Sandburg, Whitman embodied
the ideal in poetry and democratic action. He polished his Whitman
lecture and tried it on several audiences. A friend who heard it called
Sandburg's Whitman lecture a "jumping-off place for a rhetorical assault
upon the capitalist system."

Sandburg's forays into oratory helped transform a respectful, émigré
idealism into a more aggressive social radicalism. In Chicago he had daily
close-ups of the struggles of working men and women, most of them
immigrants like his parents, whose problems he had witnessed throughout
the helpless years of childhood. He could see that there were boundaries
to be broken in politics as well as poetry. No single medium could express
all Sandburg had to say. Was Reedy right that he could be both poet
and radical?

While he had worked with relentless diligence to find his voice in
poetry, poetry never paid his rent. Thus Sandburg turned his hopes,
idealism and energy toward oratory. In the late summer of 1906 he was
busy at the Plainfield Chautauqua "filling the days with study of how to
orate." He listened intently to a parade of orators and lecturers, analyzed
their technique and subject matter, measured audience responses. Back
in his rented room in Aurora, he worked on three lecture-recitals, "An
American Vagabond," an exploration of Whitman's life and work, culminating in a recitation of his poetry; "Black Marks," a history of written
language; and "Stars and Comrades," although no remnant remains to
confirm it, probably a discussion of socialism. A friend helped him book
three lectures in Wisconsin for twenty-five dollars for the group. Sand-

burg arranged lecture bookings in Chicago, Blue Island and Detroit, too, but the fees would barely cover his expenses.

He stood at a crossroads that autumn, "hammering away at this and that," not sure which horse to ride or which way to go. He could not sell his poems, barely broke even on his lectures. Somehow he was convinced that in oratory "a future looms up big with mighty fates and hopes." To that end he crafted his lectures. His letters to Professor Wright sang with high hopes: he would earn a thousand dollars or more a year lecturing, spending the rest of his time in Galesburg where he and Wright would publish the "pounding, smashing, happy and readable little magazine" they dreamed of.

Influenced by Elbert Hubbard's lecture circular, "a masterpiece of advertising," Sandburg designed his own lecture advertisement, poring over each detail—the dimensions, the color and texture of the paper, the print size, the text. The outcome of this painstaking attention is a significant revelation of Sandburg's self-image in 1906. A Galesburg photographer produced a stark picture of an intense young man, dark hair parted slightly off center, brooding eyes looking enigmatically away from the camera. Sandburg carefully arranged the physical image he wished his audience to see. The dramatic, somber face in the studied pose reveals the first deliberate public image the photogenic Sandburg created. He painted a calculated word portrait of himself as well: "Amid the noise & turmoil of human affairs there is nothing grander than a quiet, strong, unselfish personality. Fame is good & wealth is good, but they fade into nothing before a man or woman who is kind & radiant, with the touch of love & the look of power that come from the god within."

Embracing the ideal of "the god within," Sandburg condensed to an "apothegm or epigram" the philosophy on which he tried conscientiously to build his character. Upon that ideal he superimposed a carefully crafted physical image—the dramatic, handsome face, the pensive, inscrutable eyes contemplating the mysteries of life which he, as Charles A. Sandburg, Lecturer and Orator, would interpret for a waiting public.

---
*

1906–1907

6. Uncharted Seas

> Look at it in any line of work you please, in art, religion,
> business, or any other place of human effort, it is by
> getting away from known shores and sailing toward
> undiscovered countries and across uncharted seas, that
> men find new things that mean power or honor or love.
> —Charles A. Sandburg, *Incidentals*, 1907

D espite Sandburg's hard work that fall, his lecture bookings were erratic, the fees unpredictable. Winter was coming on. After the Christmas rush it was difficult to sell views, even if he could muster the will to brave the bitter prairie winter. One late December day, Sandburg applied for a job on the editorial staff of *The Lyceumite*, a *Variety*-style journal about the platform and entertainment circuits. After a ten-minute interview with editor Edwin L. Barker, he was hired as assistant editor and advertising manager. If there was no conflict of interest with the Lyceumite Bureau advertisers, Sandburg was free to fill lecture dates. He needed the steady wages, but even more, *The Lyceumite* job put him in the center of the lecture network. He would "cut out vagabonding for a year or so." He set to work immediately on a series of short biographical sketches called "Unimportant Portraits of Important People," most of them platform speakers and performers.

Unlike many platform performers who exploited a gullible public, Sandburg had a great respect for the American audience. He pointed out that "Lincoln and Douglas carried on their immortal debates before backwoodsmen, pioneers." In defense of thousands of Americans who went to hear lecturers, orators, ministers and self-styled experts in tents, churches and auditoriums around the country, Sandburg wrote a letter to *Talent*, a Philadelphia trade journal edited by Indiana Quaker professor and lecturer Paul Pearson, whose son Drew grew up to be a noted journalist. "Don't flatter or fool the people," Sandburg chided. "Down in their hearts they know. If you give them palaver, they know it's palaver. If you give them soul they will know it for soul, and remember what you gave them."

Sandburg drove himself hard at *The Lyceumite*, writing columns and advertising, reading proof, selling ads, laying out pages. In his few private hours, he made journal notes about orators he read and heard—Albert Beveridge, Wendell Phillips, Henry Ward Beecher, William Jennings Bryan, Elbert Hubbard. He studied technique, noting that one orator "was in constant action, but never vehement, . . . walking often to and fro, every gesture expressive, art perfectly conclusively art. It was all melody and grace and magic, all art and paradox and power." He worked diligently at his lectures. Most of all he wanted to avoid the common-place, what William James saw in the lyceum and chautauqua movements as the "dead level and quintessence of every mediocrity." Sandburg panned one of Paul Pearson's lectures on American humor as "com-monplace and so-so" rather than "brilliant or illuminative." He was even harder on himself, deciding to drop one lecture, "Black Marks," from his repertory. The lecture was a success, Sandburg told Professor Wright, but "one of those commonplace successes—'tis on the whole too neat and self-contained—I did it partly to assure myself that I could get up a modern popular lecture."

During the winter of 1907 Sandburg immersed himself in work on two lectures spawned by political convictions. In "Three Great Blunders of Modern Civilization" he attacked child labor, the penal system and war. He was determined to use "logic, fact, invective, mercy, justice," even humor to "bring these almost universally acknowledged shames and crimes of modern life right home to every soul that listens." He was convinced that his themes were "bigger than party or creed or class" and "as dramatic as blood or tears." He wanted to awaken his audiences to the horror and brutality of social problems. Embedded in the lectures were themes which would animate his prose and poetry far into the future.

"Civilization and the Mob" was Sandburg's first extended exploration of "the man across the street, the man around the corner, and the man with the dinner-pail who leaves home in the morning." He was fascinated with the figure of the man who "does not stand out large on the horizons of the world's happenings." Kernels of that lecture can be found in his pocket notebooks; polished fragments of it appear in his leaflet called *Incidentals*. He thought of publishing it as an essay, carefully writing it out in brown ink on seventeen sheets of cheap paper, which he entrusted to Professor Wright. "The common people is a big theme," Sandburg exulted as he discovered his primary subject. "He is a mob, a paradox, a multiple personality that outstretches and eludes portraiture."

Ironically, it was his orator's ear for cadence and dramatic effect which led him closer to discovery of his inner, poetic voice. He saw his father in the faceless shadows of the common people, found his own voice in their own massed, inarticulate needs. "The average man does the work of the world," he wrote, "and this is why he has but little time to study stage-setting." He spoke with economy, clarity, authority:

> He is the essence of the tragedy of lost or mistaken opportunity. . . . He is the moving shadow of what might have been. . . . In a nation where poverty has put its finger-marks of shame on the door of ten million homes we may question whether there is "democracy" or "justice" or "liberty. . . ." The Golden Rule can not be evaded. To starve another is to starve yourself. We grow by acts of fellowship.

Having found his theme and subject in the common man, Sandburg was drawn to a striking symbolic figure: Abraham Lincoln. "He came nearer the average man and the common people than any man of the century," Sandburg wrote, finding in Lincoln that "warm compelling thing found in all real leaders of men, a kind of commonness through which each man whom he met saw that Lincoln was a man like himself, only bigger and deeper." Sandburg chose Lincoln anecdotes from the anthology of Lincoln lore he had already instinctively begun to collect.

✳

That spring of 1907 was a fertile time. He began to dream about his second book, prose pieces dealing with "art, and conduct, and sociology, and politics." It would be "confessedly discursive yet careless," but "definite and clear-cut enough here and there for 'any dam fool.' " Sandburg the orator, not Sandburg the poet, was the fulcrum for the book. He was unsure whether to name it *Incidentals* or *A Vagabond Folio* or *Roads and Stars* or *Careless Essays*, but he was clear about its purpose: "It is not intended to be a single venture but to be accessory to my designs on the platform." He would pay Professor Wright to print it on the Asgard Press.

He needed time and money to complete the book, however, and poured his energy into his job at *The Lyceumite*. He spent much time reading about socialism because of his proximity to Chicago socialism, and because of his new friendship with Reuben Borough, aspiring poet and journalist now living in Michigan. They were both "militant equalitarians" who shared a "stubborn commitment to the common people and proud identification with the poor and disinherited" and were "both at war with the capitalist system." Underneath the politics was the gentler bond of poetry.

Sandburg undertook a more deliberate study of politics that spring, thinking more systematically about socialism. With Philip Green Wright he had read and discussed the work of Karl Marx. Like Wright, Sandburg could not "go along with the main analysis of the capitalist system made by Karl Marx; that system would prove more resilient and changeful than as Marx saw it." Sandburg reread Robert Hunter's *Poverty*, kept up with socialist periodicals, admired some of the socialists who wrote for *The New York Worker*. "All not out and out Marxian, they asail regardlessly, I admire the bunch of them," he told Wright. "They are doing great and needed work. It's up to us to smile at their deficiencies as they do at ours." He read John Graham Brooks's *The Social Unrest* and William James Ghent's *Mass and Class* and "Why Socialists Are Partisan." He studied William Morris, Edward Carpenter, George Bernard Shaw and other English socialists. Fragments of that reading are recorded in his notebooks, along with angry comments on the mindless extravagance of the leisure class: "Lady photographed at society wedding in N.Y. wearing $45,000 worth pearls. . . . Her pearls represent ⅓ of her jewels.—Tiffany told C.M. 19 women in N.Y. who between them own 5 millions worth of jewels. 2 hundred million worth diamonds in N.Y. city." He made notes on hot political topics of the times—the class struggle, the capitalist class, the socialist republic. He read ten-cent paperback copies of Lieb-knecht's *Socialism and What It Means*, Ferdinand Lasalle's *A Workingman's Programme* and Benjamin R. Tucker's *The Attitude of Anarchism Toward Industrial Combinations*.

As Reedy had divined, Sandburg was equally stirred by politics and poetry. Radical politics began to take precedence over radical poetry for a time, and throughout his life there was an ebb and flow between those two great passions, as well as a reciprocity. Politics and poetry merged in his work, sometimes to its detriment later on, but in 1907 the air was alive with pending change, and Sandburg was invigorated. On Sunday mornings he and Reuben Borough attended the Arthur Morrow Lewis lectures on evolution and socialism at the Garrick Theater in Chicago. On Sunday afternoons Sandburg walked to the twenty-two-story Masonic Temple skyscraper at Randolph and State streets for the turbulent meet-ings of the Chicago Anthropological Society. There he listened to "gey-sers of words about freedom." A heated one-hour lecture was followed by

a two-hour free-for-all of speeches from the floor—anarchists, single tax-ers, radical socialists, Christian socialists, criers for cooperative stores, for birth control, for the rights of labor to organize, to strike, to picket, for the rights of women to vote, for church property to be taxed, for priests and ministers to be refused 10 percent discount on railway fares, for the death penalty to be abolished, for heavy income and inheritance taxes on the rich, for war to be outlawed by international agreement.

In that great American tradition of free, peaceable dissent, Sandburg listened to Kropotkin anarchists, fanatics, zealots. He heard anarchist Anton Johannsen, organizer for the woodworkers' union; years later, when he was acquainted with Johannsen, he portrayed him in the poem "Dynamiter":

> . . . His name was in many newspapers as an enemy of the nation and few keepers of churches or schools would open their doors to him.
> Over the steak and onions not a word was said of his deep days and nights as a dynamiter.
> Only I always remember him as a lover of life, a lover of children, a lover of all free, reckless laughter everywhere—lover of red hearts and red blood the world over.

Sandburg was learning to probe events for the individual, particular drama as it played out on the broad, volatile stage of his times. That sharp, empathic vision would make him a colorful investigative reporter as well as a poet of the people. He moved continuously between worlds, immersing himself in politics, then coming up for air and diving into poetry again, until those seemingly disparate worlds began to merge into one.

Sandburg flourished in the hectic, exciting months at *The Lyceumite*. He wrote biographical vignettes of Reedy, Hubbard, Wright, talent agent Harry Holbrook, his boss Edwin L. Barker and others who intrigued him, and published them in the journal which gave him his livelihood. He lectured and kept working on the new book. When his sister Esther wrote from Galesburg about her enthusiasm for her piano studies, Sandburg sent her a letter of encouragement, telling her "what seems to me is necessary to make a success as an artist of any kind. . . . Work and love, love and work. Live as your soul tells you you ought to live. Listen to what others have to say, good and bad, about what you ought to do and then do as your own soul, your own heart, your own self tells you."

It was a theory he himself would have to test in late April when Edwin Barker sold *The Lyceumite* to a group who planned to merge it with its rival *Talent*. It may have been irrelevant that Sandburg had given *Talent*'s owner Paul Pearson a negative review in *The Lyceumite*, but he suddenly found himself out of a job. "I was tossed out of the deck like a dirty deuce," he wrote Philip Green Wright. "If I did not enjoy a scrap, I would be crestfallen, undone, down and out." He was undaunted. "Strange things blow in through my window on the wings of the night-wind," he had written, "and I don't worry about my destiny."

Hard work was always an antidote for trouble, Sandburg had discovered, and work could generate more work. He left Chicago and set out for Indiana in May 1907 to try to book lecture courses for the Midland Lecture Bureau, hoping to secure some paying dates for himself. He gave "Blunders of Modern Civilization" in Rockford, Illinois, wrote poetry and a short story, and steeped himself in the work of George Bernard Shaw, whom he pronounced the soul mate of Jeremiah, Isaiah and Mark Twain. Sandburg quickly found his Indiana territory saturated by other lecture courses and gave up on the Midland Lecture Bureau. He worked far into those May nights to finish the little book he now called *Careless Essays*, and mailed it to Wright by month's end. Somehow he had to support himself and pay for the publication.

He was a twenty-nine-year-old editor, advertising man, politico and poet, once again out of a job. But summer was coming on. With cheerful expediency, he decided to do what he had done so many summers before: roam the prairie roadways and sell views. He had some leftover stereographs in the battered canvassing bag, and quickly settled himself in Hinckley, Illinois, which drew him because "Green-crested hills surround the town and white roads lead off into gray, mysterious distances. I will be in dire peril of tossing off a poem or two."

Indeed, he found Hinckley so conducive to writing that in a week he finished a short story, several socialist editorials, and a review of Kipling's "Sons of Martha." "I have fairly weltered in ink down here," he told Rube Borough, "haven't been out with the sample case at all." He proposed that Borough type his short story for him and send it to *The Cosmopolitan*, in exchange for part of any money the story might earn. Borough was writing for the *Chicago Daily Socialist* then, and Sandburg entrusted the editorials to him, in case they could be used, which they were. He sent the Kipling review to *Wilshire's Magazine*, which published it in August.

Without his *Lyceumite* salary, however, Sandburg stood at another crossroads. He looked for a job in Chicago and found plenty of work "for the fellow who wants to line up with an establishment permanently." But if you did not want "to sign a one or three year contract, you must be a grafter." He had a chance to earn twenty-five dollars a week at a

Milwaukee advertising agency, but declined it. He was still determined to make it as an orator, to "keep up this fight a year or more yet, before even partially abandoning it."

He was discouraged, but now he looked at his unemployment as a temporary setback, not a repudiation of his hopes and talents. Now he had faith in his own powers. "There is a place for me somewhere, where I can write and speak much as I can think, and make it pay for my living and some besides," he told Professor Wright. "Just where this place is I have small idea now, but I am going to find it."

*

Before he left Chicago, Elbert Hubbard had offered Sandburg a plum of a lecture deal. In exchange for transportation and "keep," Sandburg could lecture at Roycroft in East Aurora, New York, in July. Hubbard himself would be there, with a national audience. If Sandburg did well, as he most definitely intended to do, Hubbard would write an article about him and help arrange lecture dates for the fall and winter. This was Sandburg's big opportunity to write and speak and earn a living at it.

Preparing for July, Sandburg rambled through Illinois in early summer selling stereographs and polishing his lectures. He had long admired Hubbard's style. "Oratory?" he had heard Hubbard say. "You must give your audience more than oratory. Among the impressive orator's themes must be a plea to humanity." In that vein, Sandburg revised and reworked "An American Vagabond," his Whitman lecture, so it would be "oratory flung by a voice from a platform at a living audience." Because of the haunting memory lapses during his early Galesburg orations, he wrote out his lectures. Once they were firmly memorized, he honed his platform style, speaking wherever he could for practice—to a black literary club on South State Street in Chicago; to the guardhouse prisoners at Fort Sheridan on Chicago's North Shore. As he traveled from one small prairie town to another that summer selling stereographs, he gave his lecture en route "to rows of cornstalks and acres of cabbage heads." He sold just enough views to earn the four dollars he needed for each week's room, board and clean shirt. The rest of the time he devoted to his lectures and poetry.

He pressed Wright to let him know what to revise in the manuscript for *Careless Essays* before it was set in "cool, irreparable type." He envisioned a thirty-two-page folio, or perhaps a forty-eight- to sixty-four-page booklet, which he hoped to sell by the hundreds to lecture fans in the wake of the success which surely lay ahead. The oratory and writing fed each other if a man worked them right, and Sandburg wanted to be read as well as heard.

He decided that his lecture on the blunders of modern civilization would best fit the socialist theme set for Saturday, July 13, at Hubbard's annual Convention of the Elect. For his first lecture on July 5, Sandburg offered "The American Vagabond," which not only praised and interpreted Whitman and related him to the American scene, but expressed Sandburg's rapidly emerging socialist theories. The lecture also indulged his growing flair for the dramatic. From his worn gray paperbound edition of Whitman's *Leaves of Grass*, he would give an impassioned reading from "Song of Myself" and "Song of the Open Road," Whitman's lines which described his own life:

> Afoot and light-hearted, I take to the open road,
> Healthy, free, the world before me,
> The long brown path before me, leading wherever I choose . . .

✳

In July when the summer meadows invited walking and mild starlit nights made for pleasant sleeping in tents on the Roycroft lawns, Hubbard summoned to East Aurora a diverse and stimulating company of men and women for the "Convention of the Elect." "Take the Train for East Aurory, where we work for Art and Glory," a good-natured advertisement urged.

Sandburg had seen Roycroft and East Aurora in winter, but the village lining the brick pike eighteen miles from Buffalo was at its best in summer. By 1907 the Roycroft Inn was a pleasant "architectural hodge-podge." Several connected buildings were surrounded by a peristyle which bordered the main street, enfolded in the shade of giant trees. The cool interior of the inn reflected Hubbard's emphasis on fine craftsmanship and natural materials. Bright Navajo rugs decorated the polished walls and floors crafted of mahogany, ash, oak, cherry and bird's-eye maple. Stained-glass lamps cast soft tinted light on large round tables in the dining room. Vivid murals by Alex Fournier lined the walls of the music room, where visitors could sit in the comfort of molded leather chairs in a "sanctuary of art and beauty."

The Roycroft craftsmen, in the spirit of William Morris's Kelmscott artisans, built the massive fireplaces of native stone; designed and made functional furniture, bright rag rugs, and stained glass; and created their own sculpture and paintings. The Roycroft guest book carried a litany of names famous then and later on—Clarence Darrow, Edwin Markham,

Theodore Roosevelt, Booker T. Washington, Stephen Crane, Ellen Terry, Richard Le Gallienne, Alex Fournier, Henry Ford, William Marion Reedy, C. W. Post and Major Andrew Rowan, who had carried the famous message to García which inspired Hubbard's best-selling book.

Convention week brought an overflow crowd to East Aurora. Charles Sandburg and a score of other young men slept in tents on the lawn under the summer night skies. Hubbard's journal *The Philistine* invited his vast audience to the Convention:

> There will be three formal Programs a day, but not too formal—morning, afternoon and evening—when men and women of Note will speak, sing, recite, vibrate and otherwise disturb the ether! . . . There will be gentle walks afield, tramps to the farms and the camps, and demonstrations at the Roycroft Woodpiles. As for the Ideas—everybody is welcome to all he can bring and all he can carry away. . . .

The atmosphere was a tonic for Sandburg, accustomed to working so much alone, struggling to find an audience. "To be frank and emphatic," he wrote to Professor Wright that week, "we are having a hell of a time."

He was scheduled to deliver his Whitman lecture Wednesday afternoon. "Sandburg knows his Whitman as very few men do," Hubbard had written for Sandburg's lecture circular. "He is one with Emerson, Thoreau, Tolstoi, and the modern prophets who have worked and are working for human betterment. His religion is the religion of service." That was effusive praise for an unproven young man, not yet sure of his place in the world, but Hubbard was given to hyperbole and to encouraging promising young people of ideas.

Sandburg's voice was a rich, strong baritone, used with the dramatic effects advocated by Illinois elocution teachers and successful chautauqua and lyceum lecturers. From earliest childhood he had been lulled by the rhythms of the Swedish spoken and sung by his mother, and stung by the harsh admonitions of his father. These cadences shaped the pitch and musically elongated pace of his delivery. These carefully honed platform effects now merged with a subject which set Sandburg afire— Walt Whitman, like himself an American seeker, dreamer and vagabond who loved the open road and the common man. For the Roycroft appearance, Sandburg transformed his Whitman literary lecture into a dramatic oration, a stirring plea for humanity which, by Hubbard's definition, marked true oratory.

Sandburg was ready for the Roycrofters that July day, and they were a worthy audience. "I have dreamed & welded & prayed & laughed with [the lecture]," he wrote, "and for me and for the audience it was an occasion. They drew out of me my best." Various drafts and notes for the Whitman lecture have survived, among them these lines:

> Understand me, I don't ask anybody to feel sorry for Walt Whitman. That old gray whiskered monochromic sea-dog laughs from his tomb the same laughter as Columbus or George Stephenson or Robert Fulton. . . . From their tombs these fools, these majestic destroyers of old traditions and creators of new traditions, laugh their laughter and Walt Whitman is one of these. So today there are artists who have no past nor present. All they have is the future.

There were hints of self-justification and identification with Whitman, as Sandburg began to see himself as a creator of new traditions, with no past or present, but great hope for the future. For his finale, he delivered lines of Whitman's poetry as fervently as if they were his own, the memorized words settling like seeds in the furrows of his imagination. In particular, the lines of Whitman's "To Foreign Lands" were prophetic of Sandburg's own career:

> I heard that you ask'd for something to prove this puzzle, the
> New World,
> And to define America, her athletic Democracy;
> Therefore I send you my poems, that you behold in them what
> you wanted.

As Sandburg finished his oration and sat down, someone leaned forward to congratulate him, and so turned his attention from the audience, applauding and shouting for an encore. Hubbard himself pulled Sandburg to the front to acknowledge the applause. Sandburg was elated, especially when Hubbard and the convention asked him to speak again July 6. Then on Saturday night, July 13, he spoke on socialism in Roycroft Chapel. It was a jubilant week. Confidently, Sandburg waited for new lecture bookings.

"They are sort of crazy here about the lecture on Whitman," he wrote Professor Wright. "For the tribute as far as approbation is concerned I don't care any particular dam, but that I now am sure I have trained my powers so that they can be of service to men, pleases me. It will get me a number of dates next winter." But despite Elbert and Alice Hubbard's assurances that he had a "world-beater" of a lecture, the hoped-for bookings did not materialize. By July 21, with only two lecture dates in sight, Sandburg left Roycroft and East Aurora for the Midwest, this time Michigan.

The bookings *would* come, he consoled himself. The Roycroft audience had shown him once and for all that he had real power to move a crowd.

Meanwhile, there were the reliable Underwood stereographs to fall back on, and the open roads of the prairie to travel in the waning summer sun.

∗

Throughout that frenetic year of 1907, Sandburg studied the architecture of the soul, the layers of meaning and experience which culminate in worthy character. In the omnipresent notebooks he recorded his ideas and transposed them into his lectures, which were in many ways himself articulated. While he still and always disdained harness, he knew that he had to honor and govern his own spirit: "Conquer the kingdom under your own hat," he wrote, "and all the world shall be yours."

He was developing his own religion as he went. Despite his scorn for "churchianity," he gave it another try, "listened to a goddam oleaginous preacher deliver that old stale discourse" he had heard "forty times about the conversion of Saul of Tarsus." His contempt for organized religion was matched by his affirmation of the power and mystery he perceived in man and nature. In a "Credo" reminiscent of Elbert Hubbard's Credo in the introduction to A Message to García, Sandburg wrote: "I believe in the divinity of man's intentions. I believe man is greater than anything he has made. . . . I am an idealist. I can see humanity blundering on toward some splendid goal. No day passes but I meet a man in whose eyes are the shadow and flash of heroism."

Alone in his work once more, subsisting on small profits from occasional sales of stereoscopic photographs, Sandburg revised Careless Essays and renamed the book Incidentals. In the rambling, unstructured days between sales and the infrequent lecture bookings, he took heart from Hubbard's belief in the "paradox of success through failure," a point of view he developed in his own essays. Was he a failure? He refused to think so, and kept himself going during the weeks after Roycroft with a stubborn optimism.

All his life Sandburg relied on nature for solace and reinvigoration. He had a lifelong passion for the out-of-doors, fresh air, long, rugged walks, the contemplation of nature as metaphor for the conduct of human life. "Freedom is found, if anywhere, in the great outdoor world of wild breezes and sunshine and sky," he wrote in the essays which served the triple purpose of introspection, oratory and published prose. "To get out into the daylight and fill your lungs with pure air, to stop and watch a spear of grass swaying in the wind, to give a smile daily at the wonder and mystery of shifting light and changing shadow, is to get close to the source of power." When doubts about the wisdom of his choices encroached, Sandburg held on to his indomitable will, and an exuberant sense of humor: "I have never been in such hard luck that I could not smile at myself in reproach as I thought of the man who fell down one of these elevator shafts. It was a nine story building. He was going head first and as he passed each floor, he called out, 'All right so far.' "

Sandburg resolved to keep "this boy heart of mine, with tears for the tragic, love for the beautiful, laughter at folly, and silent, reverent contemplation of the common and everyday mysteries." Of the many prayers he wrote in his notebooks, he inscribed two for *Incidentals*. One of them spoke of failure: "Failure, as the world sees it, and disgrace and defeat, O Lord we can endure. But renew in us always the child heart, alive with the hope and romance of endeavor."

✳

In late July 1907, following his sojourn in East Aurora, Sandburg rented a room in a boardinghouse in Homer, Michigan, an "idyllic, rural and bucolic" village near Marshall, where his great companion Reuben Borough lived and worked in his father's buggy manufacturing business. Philip Green Wright visited Sandburg there in August, where they talked over plans for printing *Incidentals*. Sandburg lived simply that summer on a diet of fruits, nuts, cereals and milk, still working on his lectures. He tried them out on Borough and twenty-nine other people at the Universalist Church in Marshall. The crowd was smaller than expected, but Borough assured Sandburg they were "the cream of the town," and they hired him for a return engagement two weeks later at ten dollars for the lecture. Sandburg reviewed his own performance for the August 9 edition of the *Marshall News*:

> Walt Whitman loomed large and persuasive as the spokesman of a great democracy in Charles Sandburg's lecture, "An American Vagabond" given last night at the Universalist church.
> It was a story of a big man that Sandburg told and it fascinated the men and women who heard it. There was in it a ripple of phrase, a warmth and wealth of feeling and an intensity of conviction that first lured and then convicted—it made converts.

By August 22 he was back in Chicago with another job as an editor, this time for a new lyceum journal, *The Opera House Guide*. For twenty dollars a week he wrote for the *Guide* and, in a weekly column on the Chicago theater scene, for *The Billboard*. He could set his own hours, with plenty of time left over to work on lectures and the final draft of his new book, which he turned over to Philip Green Wright in September. He called the book *Incidentals* because its ideas were essential to him but incidental to the rest of the world, "momentarials rather than eternals." He explained the title to his readers in an "Apologia": "Life is more vast and strange than anything written about it—words are only incidentals."

Sandburg spent nine days in September in Joliet, Illinois, at the International Lyceum Association convention, working on the publicity committee and trying to sell his own lectures. Billy Sunday opened the Delwood Park Chautauqua there August 30 with a sermon called "Flies and Grinders, Hot from the Bat," and on September 6 Sandburg delivered "An American Vagabond." It was "almost tiresome" meeting so many geniuses, he found, but he was enough of a hit himself to be signed by Sunday's own agent, "Hurry-up Harry" Holbrook, whose Holbrook-Barker Company would be the exclusive agents for Sandburg's chautauqua time. Holbrook promised Sandburg thirty lecture dates at fifty dollars per engagement, a prospect which seemed too good to be true, and was. Sandburg was at first elated, and hoped to convince Holbrook to give Professor Wright a start as a lecturer. By November, however, he was disenchanted with Holbrook's business practices, and broke off with him when Holbrook asked him to sign a "flimsy agreement" which was a "piece of double dealing I hadn't looked for in that particular quarter."

He tried again to book his own lecture dates, and crafted a new lecture called "Bernard Shaw: Artist and Fool" to go with "American Vagabond." He was in a hurry for *Incidentals*. It would promote his work, he was sure, embodying as it did "some of the best" of his lectures. He had high hopes for *Incidentals*, and for a new book he had in mind, a "poetization in prose of the theory of economic determinism." He called the little parable on socialism *The Plaint of a Rose*.

He was brimming with ambition and confidence. "Where I talked in ones last year I talk in tens this year and next year will talk in hundreds," he exulted. He knew he could succeed as a lecturer. It was only a matter of persistence and time.

Meanwhile, he was enjoying Chicago. He had gotten to know Joseph Joseffy, a colorful, eccentric magician and violinist who was popular on the talent circuits. Joseffy was also a vagabond and former itinerant worker, and shared Sandburg's love of ridiculous puns. In his workshop, he kept four human skeletons, his Phantom Quartette. He called them Cord, Accord, Discord and Nocord. The centerpiece of Joseffy's magic act was Balsamo the Living Skull, whom he had created of copper, with real human teeth implanted in the jaw sockets. Joseffy wired Balsamo's lower jaw so that the skull appeared to talk. His fascination with the potential applications of electricity to the world of magic tricks and illusions led Joseffy to a masterpiece of invention: he wired his Phantom Quartette so that Cord, Accord, Discord and Nocord played an unlimited repertoire on the ocarinas they clutched in their bony hands. Joseffy also made them sing, to the amazement and discomfiture of his enthralled audiences. He commissioned Sandburg to write a publicity portrait to promote his show with the animated skeletons and skull, a wondrous entertainment for Americans on the farms and in the villages of the Midwest in those days before they could turn to movies, radio or television for amusement. Sandburg set to work on *Joseffy: An Appreciation*, which Joseffy would pay Wright to print on the Asgard Press. The piece appeared in *The Opera House Guide* in 1907, long before it was finally published as a booklet in 1910.

Sandburg met many attractive young women through his work with the Chicago talent bureaus. He wrote to Rube Borough, "Since I saw you I have fallen in love and fallen out again,—the mote just dancing through the flame—with a crack violinist, a reader, an amateur palmist, an actress, a chorus girl, a newspaper woman, and at present don't know what I'll do about a live pundit and poetess.—If I had no work 'twould be dangerous." Virile, magnetic, he attracted women almost effortlessly. He genuinely liked women and trusted them, as they intuitively knew. He could be disarmingly natural and open. Briefly, at least, he shared his work and his heart with a girl he had known at Lombard College. "There are things I want to say to you but I lift the pen and sit back and think & can't get them the way I want them—they are so many & so mixed; maybe it's just as well," he wrote to her. "There are about as many things we're sorry were said as were left unsaid. And people only trust each other by their eyes & faces. Those who have known love close enough to know its follies & cruelties as well as its beauty & abandon, don't talk much on love." His solitude preyed on him, he apologized, and his loneliness and her picture induced "poetical reverie." He resolved to get back into the "hurly-burly again and crush regret between action and sleep." Then, he promised her, "you won't be bothered with any more queer literary letters."

In 1905 Sandburg had composed "Dream Girl," a poem he sent to Wright with the note that it portrayed "the kind of woman I would be if I were a woman." The poem first appeared in *The Lyceumite* in December 1906. "You will come one day in a waver of love," Sandburg wrote, and then described his dream girl. In 1905 and later, however, he doubted that he would ever find her:

> Yet,
> You may not come, O girl of a dream,
> We may but pass as the world goes by
> And take from a look of eyes into eyes,
> A film of hope and a memoried day.

Nevertheless, he enjoyed his brief Chicago romances, and, for the most part, did not take them seriously.

✳

Sandburg lost his job in September when his position at *The Opera House Guide* was cut to save money. "Once more Fate has kicked me and I am only waiting to see how far upstairs the impetus will land me," he told Professor Wright. He was undaunted. He had "several good prospects" for jobs, and, as he told Wright in a jaunty letter, he had "a good many assets left besides my honor." When the editor of *The Opera House Guide* was fired in late September, Sandburg was offered the job, but refused it. He believed he stood on the brink of supporting himself as an orator. That was where his ambition lay. A regular job would keep him from that. He decided to trust his future and take "the long look."

"I hold firm and am out of a job," he said. It was a decision he did not regret. Sandburg had learned an axiom which forever dispelled the dream of the collapsible horses. It was the need for concentration and consecration. He put it this way in *Incidentals*: "It seems to me as though the man who wins in a big way is the man who is willing to take a chance. . . . It is the trick of fixing the mind on one thing as more important than anything else in the world. Sometimes we call it consecration and sometimes abandon but it always consists in something that no man had before attempted and attained."

He threw himself into the lecture work and into reading the final proofs for *Incidentals*. Again, he paid avid attention to the smallest details of the design. Apologizing to Wright for his fussiness, he mused "I believe I have more convictions on printing matter than I have on politics." For him every aspect of the book's cover was critical, "an important proposition, as it is to lure or repel reading."

In Reckless Ecstasy had been the work of Charles A. Sandburg, poet and essayist. *Incidentals* was the prose work of Charles A. Sandburg, orator and lecturer, hot in pursuit of his multifaceted idealism. By early

November his new book was in his hands. He praised Professor Wright's handiwork, calling it a "premier piece of printing." At least a thousand copies were published for Sandburg to sell in conjunction with his lectures.

He was pleased with his work, although he could see mistakes. Already some of the "false tints" of *In Reckless Ecstasy* embarrassed him, but he had no misgivings about circulating *Incidentals* "as far as possible." After all, he said, "the only way I can learn is to make a thing and then smash it, repeating the process till I get what I want."

At last, in the lectures, he was getting what he wanted. His idealism and delivery had been tried and proven on the lyceum circuit. The awkward little boy in the Demorest Medal Contest was buried in the swaggering, brash young man who could assert with confidence late in 1907 that he was an orator. He told his professor, "I consider now that I am trying out the lyceum, not that it is trying me out. If it is not big enough for my stuff, I will not change my stuff. I will climb out of the lyceum and make it sue me for my time."

------ ✳ ------

1907–1908

7. A Gospel of Freedom
to Come

So there I was, riding the North Shore Line to
Milwaukee, where I was to join the Social-Democratic
Party not merely as a member but as an organizer, one
who "stirreth up the people." What would it be like, to
carry a soap box to a street corner, stand on the box and
call to people to come and hear a gospel of freedom to
come?

—Charles Sandburg, unpublished fragment, no date

C harles Sandburg made a triumph of a speech on October 26,
1907, to a packed auditorium in Manitowoc, Wisconsin, according to a review he wrote himself for the *Manitowoc Daily
Tribune*. The newspaper sponsored the event as part of a series for working
people. Consequently he began his hour-and-a-half-long lecture at nine
o'clock in the evening to "accommodate late workers." Chester Wright,
the witty socialist intellectual who edited the paper, arranged the lecture
and immediately befriended Sandburg, letting him write his own glowing,
front-page review. Sandburg had "reviewed" his own lectures before when
promoting himself on the lyceum circuit, and he would do so again,
partly as self-advertisement; partly as an accurate record of what he
actually said from the platform, especially on political issues; and partly
because he enjoyed the mischief of it.

Wright had lured his readers to the lecture with the promise that "An
American Vagabond" would surpass any other lecture ever heard in
Manitowoc. Sandburg was "not a commonplace man," Wright said, and
his subject, Walt Whitman, "was nearer and should be dearer to the
heart of the worker" than any other poet.

Sandburg's review, despite his seeming immodesty, probably told a good deal of truth:

> Speaking to one of the largest audiences ever gathered in this city, Charles Sandburg held a capacity audience enraptured for an hour and a half at the opera house on Saturday night. Taking his hearers through the tortuous declines and apexes of the career of Walt Whitman, drawing from each phase a lesson, finding in each event something good, with inspiration seldom equalled on the lecture platform in this city, Sandburg proved himself a man of deep thinking ability and great oratorical power.

Sandburg reproduced those words later in circulars advertising his lectures. He was good, and he knew it now. It was no easy trick to rivet the attention of a working-class audience at the end of a long working day, but he had polished the Whitman lecture until it could not fail.

He also knew how to read his audience, many of whom were constructive socialists in sympathy if not affiliation. He gave them "bold, dashing ideas of present economical and spiritual conflicts." He played his rich voice like an instrument, modulating from hypnotic intimacy to stirring power: "If America does not break down before the forces and brutalities that destroyed old civilizations and former republics, it will be because America dares to break away from the traditions that shackle her, it will be because America dares to experiment."

Using Whitman as his envoy, Sandburg gave a rousing affirmation of the future of the common man: "The man who does not believe that we are going forward to better days and greater times, that man is your blackhearted pessimist, for he has lost faith in mankind. His hope in humanity is gone and his god is only a God of despair. I am going to believe in a god who is right here and now."

Sandburg brought down the house with his "living, palpitating personality," his gift for delving into "the deepest recesses in the souls" of his listeners. He had cast a spell over his audience, they told him in Manitowoc, with his "depth of thought," his "ascending ideas," the simplicity of his language and lucidity of his message. They told him he gave them a feeling of brotherhood.

Sandburg "had a great time" in Manitowoc, and got his first close-up view of constructive socialism. The experience changed his life.

✳

The highly complex, volatile and amorphous international philosophy of socialism was becoming Americanized by 1907, particularly in Wisconsin where a diverse group of citizens and politicians was working hard to implement change through the existing political process. As historian David Shannon later pointed out, the socialist movement in the United States in the early twentieth century was an amalgam of "recent immigrants and descendants of the *Mayflower*'s passengers, of tenement dwellers and prairie farmers, of intellectuals and unlettered sharecroppers, of devout ministers and belligerent agnostics . . . of revolutionists and gradualist reformers." At the forefront of the movement were the Wisconsin socialists who believed in constructive, orderly reform. They wanted to protect the rights and welfare of women and children, give women the right to vote, improve working conditions in factories, implement a graduated income tax and generally improve the quality of American life.

The Wisconsin Social-Democrats had gained steady strength in Milwaukee and other urban centers, and were ready to organize an urban-rural coalition of socialists. Coincidentally, probably with Chester Wright's encouragement, Charles Sandburg wrote to party headquarters in Milwaukee to introduce himself. In Chicago he had met Winfield R. Gaylord, an articulate socialist orator and politician, and saw him again that autumn of 1907 in Wisconsin. Gaylord admired Sandburg's oratory and enthusiasm. He introduced Sandburg to "a socialist movement that was practical and constructive," and wanted to recommend him to organize for the Social-Democrats in the Fox River district of Wisconsin. "Organize?" Sandburg responded, surprised at the overture. "How do you organize?"

Gaylord gave him a graphic job description. He would have to hold meetings in public halls or private homes, or speak from a soapbox on street corners. He would have to seek out new members, organize a local chapter of the party where none existed, collect dues from old and new members. "Your pay will be all of the dues paid to the party by members in your district," Gaylord told him. "You will be free to keep all money you can collect at hall or street meetings and whatever profits you make from selling Social-Democratic books or pamphlets."

"So that's how you organize?" Sandburg replied, undaunted.

Gaylord gave him a prophetic smile. "Yes, if you're good at it all you do is work morning, afternoon and night."

The prospect appealed to Sandburg. "I have been in pretty close touch with the Wisconsin socialists lately," he wrote Professor Wright in November 1907. "They have a splendid constructive movement in Milwaukee, from which socialists all over the country are taking lessons. I shall probably do some organizing thru the northeastern part of the state this winter, possibly making my permanent residence in Manitowoc or Oshkosh."

Meantime, November was given over to lecturing, promoting *Incidentals* and working on the new leaflet, *The Plaint of a Rose*, to be published by the Asgard Press as soon as possible. *The Plaint of a Rose* was a prose parable of a strong, blooming rose overshadowing a "frail, ill-grown plant bearing near its top a pale, half-withered flower." The dying rose protests that "my soul is as pure and radiant and beautiful as yours. Only—it has been repressed." His overt parable of socialism could also be read as a parable of creativity, with allusions to his own struggle to write: "The spaces I have inhabited contained nothing I could reach out and nourish myself with—shadow and barrenness everywhere as far as my power would carry me—nothing to build a body in which a soul could grow . . . not water! . . . no sunlight! . . . so I faded."

The Plaint of a Rose, his third Asgard booklet, would not be published until January 1908, but Sandburg began to take advance orders for his "poetization in prose of the theory of economic determinism."

✳

It was late November of 1907 when the State Executive Board of the Social-Democratic Party of Wisconsin officially appointed Sandburg district organizer for the Lake Shore and Fox River Valley district. State secretary Elizabeth H. Thomas wrote to him about the terms: ". . . you should receive all the dues from that district and all monthly pledges that you can obtain in the district, up to $3.00 a day and expenses whenever you were away from home. If you are willing to make a trial for three months, we will see how this plan succeeds."

Sandburg set to work immediately, going first to Milwaukee to meet with Miss Thomas and Victor Berger, party chairman. Then he settled in Oshkosh, in the heart of his district and near his friend Chester Wright, ready to "batten on the epithet of 'agitator.' "

What was the nature of the socialism for which Sandburg would agitate? As usual, he shared his thoughts with Philip Green Wright:

> I shall send you the New Emancipation, an indefinite title for an impregnable argument in favor of the movement for constructive socialism. The inevitablists are losing ground & in so far as they can be made a negligible factor, the socialists will have a chance to do more and talk less. Their work in the Wis. State legislature is fine evidence of what can be done with state power.

He went to work immediately, crisscrossing his district, hustling socialism with the same fervor that sold stereographs. Now he filled his
notebooks with names of dues-paying Social-Democrats instead of Underwood and Underwood customers. From his talks with people in every
village he visited, he built a list of prospects, gleaning other names from
subscription rolls of socialist journals.

"Have never gotten quite so to the roots of the socialist movement
as of late," he told Wright at the end of 1907. "I am certain no man
can understand it till he is an active factor of the organization."

His was a personal, instinctive, eclectic socialism more than a formal,
theoretical political philosophy. Sandburg was only superficially acquainted with the socialist theories of Marx and Engels, and knew little
of the views of scientific socialists such as Enrico Ferri. He had been
stimulated by socialist debates in Chicago, and by his sporadic dialogue
with Charles Kerr, head of the most active socialist press in the Midwest,
and A. M. Simons, editor of the *International Socialist Review*, which
came to be the intellectual touchstone of the socialist movement in the
United States. Professor Wright had influenced him profoundly, but
Wright was an economist who espoused the idealistic socialism of the
arts-craft movement as William Morris manifested it in England, rather
than radical political change.

Sandburg's most regular discourse with socialists had been on the
lecture circuit. An impassioned advocate of human rights, Sandburg
embraced the Social Democracy he discovered in Wisconsin. He knew
the unrelenting demands of his immigrant father's menial job at the C.B.
& Q. Railroad shop. He had witnessed the subordination of intellect
and spirit to grueling physical labor, and the perplexing injustice of the
sleeping mortgage. He had seen gaunt children working into the night
in factories. He remembered the expectant, decent faces of working
people in his lecture audiences, people caught helplessly between the
accelerating powers of two historic events—the industrial revolution,
and the profound social and political changes inherent in modern democracy.

Sandburg's socialism encompassed both the welfare of society as a
whole and the value of the individual life. He found lyrical affirmations
of the "broadest average of humanity" in the writings of Whitman,
Emerson, William James. He understood the propaganda of the self-help
movement in oratory, and tried like his friend Elbert Hubbard to leaven
the realities of daily existence in the new industrialized society by encouraging individual initiative. In the platform of the Wisconsin Social-

Democratic Party, he found a design for the kind of society he envisioned: reformed government; the elimination of corrupted power; the prohibition of child labor; protection of rights of women in the labor force; the right of literate women to vote; tax reform, including a graduated income and property tax; urban renewal; free medical care and school textbooks; public works projects to improve the environment and provide work for the unemployed; state farm insurance; pensions; workmen's compensation; municipal ownership of utilities; higher wages and shorter hours for working people; better living and working conditions for everyone. With the Wisconsin socialists, Sandburg had found a new forum from which to "agitate and educate."

His first publication in his new job was "A Little Christmas Sermon," which appeared in Chester Wright's *Manitowoc Daily Tribune* on December 24, 1907. Sandburg had extra copies run off on brown laundry paper "to fire into the lyceum, and at soul-pardners." "Remember who you are," he encouraged his readers: "Remember you are one of the latest products of millions of years of toil and play and gurgitation of universal forces. The rain and stars and dust of a thousand worlds that have perished have contributed to the making of you." Sandburg believed that workers were entitled to join in concerted action to achieve the full dignity and possibility of life. Otherwise, they would be "damned and helpless, tied and gagged and laughed at." His idealism, radical in his time, was rooted in his witness of human events, not abstract theory.

Sandburg had a deep and prudent aversion to violence and to the work of the anarchists. As a son of immigrants, he could deplore the failures of the American dream and still ratify its possibilities, within the structure of the American political system. When he formally joined the socialist movement, he chose the right wing, the constructive Social-Democrats of Wisconsin who were pledged to the orderly incorporation of their reforms, through the ballot box. The Wisconsin socialists were highly organized, determined to achieve their programs with electoral support.

The executive committee which hired Sandburg as a party organizer acted on his visible credentials as an effective orator. His idealism was congenial with the movement, but it was largely his charisma as a public speaker which won him the job. Sandburg was one of the first party organizers to go into the fertile farm country of lake shore Wisconsin to carry out the Social-Democratic Party's mandate to organize a rural proletariat, expand party membership and elect more assemblymen to the Wisconsin legislature.

In his pocket notebooks, previously packed with notes for poems and literary lectures, politics began to dominate. In notes for a party speech, he wrote that

> no man can name the date in the future when socialism will arrive. All that we can say is that the great change will be a gradual one, that it will come a step at a time, one point gained here and another one gained there until in the end a system of industry is established in which workers, the wealth producers are the rulers. And this change will come about through the action, the education of the workers, the producing class.

At year's end, just a month into his new job, Sandburg was thin and worn from overwork. His frenetic schedule and diminishing bank account kept him from being as nattily dressed as he would have liked as Charles A. Sandburg, author and lecturer. It was just as well, for he spent most of his time with working men and women. But it was a weary and disheveled Sandburg who stopped by party headquarters in Milwaukee one late December day to talk to Victor Berger. He had to wait, for Berger was conferring with a young schoolteacher, a party member and linguist. He had asked her to translate German socialist literature into English for party distribution. Elizabeth Thomas, party secretary, kept Sandburg company while he waited, and when the young woman emerged from Berger's office, Thomas introduced her to Sandburg. Her name was Lilian Steichen.

※

"You will come one day in a waver of love," Sandburg had written in the poem "Dream Girl," published in *The Lyceumite* in 1907:

> You will come, with your slim, expressive arms,
> A poise of the head no sculptor has caught
> And nuances spoken with shoulder and neck,
> Your face in a pass-and-repass of moods. . . .

When he looked into Lilian Steichen's lustrous blue eyes that December day, Sandburg knew almost at once that he had found the dream girl he envisioned in poetry and in the privacy of his notebooks. He was thirty, used to the deprivation of heart and spirit his solitary life dictated, wondering if he would ever find "the woman with beauty and talent who has deigned her womanhood too worthy to submit to the average tawdry ideal—the kind of woman I would be if I were a woman." "You may not come, O girl of a dream," he had written in the poem:

> We may but pass as the world goes by
> And take from a look of eyes into eyes,
> A film of hope and a memoried day.

Now she stood before him. Eagerly, he asked her to join him for dinner that night. She was amused by the sudden invitation from this tall, gaunt young man. She had a previous engagement for dinner and a concert, she told him sweetly. Even a liberated woman in 1907 did not accept such an overture from a man she had just met. However, when he asked for her address, she gave it to him. He wanted, he said, to send her some of his socialist writings, to share ideas, comrade to comrade.

In early 1908, on the "eve of maturity," Charles A. Sandburg, age thirty, and Lilian Steichen, nearly twenty-five, began to write letters to each other about socialism, moral philosophy and democratic art. She was an active member of the Socialist Party and the Socialist Club of Chicago, an intellectual, theoretical socialist who read the standard socialist literature in German, French and English. He was a newly hired socialist organizer, practical as well as idealistic, basing his socialism on what he saw before his eyes. These two passionate, idealistic people had already begun to resign themselves to loneliness, doubting that the mate existed for the union of body, mind and spirit which for each of them defined true marriage. Within days of their Milwaukee meeting, Sandburg wrote to Lilian Steichen, enclosing the promised socialist tracts, his "Little Sermon," a leaflet he had named "Labor and Politics," and a few of his poems.

Immediately she saw his multiplicity, the "company of geniuses" inhabiting this one intense man. She understood from the first that he was a paradox, a "moral philosopher" and "political agitator," as well as an artist, both "poet-prophet" and "man of action," as she called him. She was fascinated.

*

Lilian Steichen taught English, Latin, elocution and drama in a high school in the northern Illinois village of Princeton, but she had grown up in Wisconsin. She liked to walk in all weather, and could be seen even on rainy days striding briskly through the elegant prairie community, apparently heedless of the splash of mud on her skirts. She often chose as her destination Bryants Woods on the edge of town. Even in ice or snow she would walk from her boardinghouse to the refuge of the woods which belonged to the brothers of poet William Cullen Bryant, and skirted their handsome homes. On sunny days, Lilian often took school-work to do, books to read or letters to write in the woods.

She was an unorthodox teacher. She looked younger than her years, and her dainty size gave a deceptive impression of softness and vulner-ability. Blue eyes shone from an uptilted face, and she usually wore her black hair in a simple Gretchen braid. She maintained school discipline with courtesy, humor and respect for the dignity of her pupils, and they reciprocated. She stimulated them to read widely, and rehearsed them in elocution contests and plays which were admired in the town. Lilian missed the lush Wisconsin farmland where her parents lived near Mil-waukee. She also loved that growing city, and the clatter and confusion of Chicago, more than a hundred miles to the east. Princeton was sur-rounded by the vast, placid sea of the prairie. Its staid brick streets were lined with houses styled after the elegant architecture of the East rather than the bland, functional structures of most prairie villages. Beyond the town, the horizon was open and completely revealing.

In the midst of the flat, uninterrupted farmland skirting Princeton, Bryants Woods was an anomaly, a beautiful remnant of an ancient riv-erbed, a ragged chasm splitting the gentle plane of the earth there. In that sanctuary Lilian wrote long letters to her parents, and to her older brother Eduard Steichen, making his name in the photographic and artistic salons of New York and Paris. In the spring of 1908, she would write to Charles Sandburg from those quiet woods.

Like him, she was the child of immigrants. She had been born on May 1, 1883, in Hancock, Michigan, where her father worked in the copper mines until his health broke, and her mother was a dressmaker and, later, a successful milliner. They were immigrants from Luxembourg. Her father's great-grandfather had been one of thirty conscripts from a single village in the Grand Duchy of Luxembourg to march with Na-poleon to Moscow where they "saw that city burned, saw men die by the thousands from cold and hunger." Only two of the thirty returned to their home village, one of them the Steichen ancestor, who lived to be 106. Longevity was in the genes. Despite many years of frail health, Jean Pierre Steichen, father of Lilian and Eduard, lived to be ninety.

The son of modest landowners, he was orphaned in 1858, at the age of four. His mother's mother reared him and his sister Elizabeth. In 1878 Jean Pierre Steichen married Marie Kemp, a strong, vivacious young woman from a peasant family. The marriage to a Steichen was a step up for her, but hard times and poor health relegated her handsome husband to keeping house for a local count. The young Steichens were living in Bivange, Luxembourg, in 1879 when their first child was born. They

named him Eduard Jean and called him Gaesjack, meaning "little Jack."
In 1880 Jean Pierre Steichen took his small inheritance, and trunks
packed with household goods and linens, and emigrated to the United
States, leaving his wife and infant son behind to join him later. The
Atlantic crossing and the discouraging search for work left him ill. He
soon discovered that one could walk for miles in the mythical streets of
gold and wait for hours in line with hundreds of applicants for menial
jobs, only to be turned away.

For several anxious months, Marie Kemp Steichen waited in Luxembourg for word from her husband, expecting him to send for her and
the baby. Time wore on and she heard nothing. She took matters in her
own hands at last and booked steerage passage for herself and their
eighteen-month-old son. She spoke no English, but with her small son
in tow, interrogated other Luxembourgers in the ghettos of New York,
asking if anyone had seen Jean Pierre Steichen. After a futile search
there, she decided to look for him in America's other large city, Chicago.
There she walked from one boardinghouse to another, frustrated but not
intimidated by the strange new city, the alien language, tracking her
husband with the fierce, persistent energy which characterized her approach to life.

When she found him at last in a shabby boardinghouse, he was ill
and nearly destitute, and had given up hope of finding work. He had
not written to his wife because he had no job, no hope of having her
join him. Piece by piece, he had traded their hand-woven linen sheets
and tablecloths for rent and food. When he looked toward the doorway
that unforgettable day, and saw her standing there, the child in her arms,
he surely thought she was an apparition. A miracle of obstinate love and
courage brought her to him in this dingy room.

From other Luxembourgers and Germans, the Steichens heard about
jobs in the Hancock, Michigan, copper mines, and settled there. Jean
Pierre, son of a cultured family in Bivange, was not cut out to be a
miner, and the work further weakened his health. He would never be
the family breadwinner. Marie set up a dressmaking business in their
small flat; Jean Pierre left the mines to work in a department store, and
when Marie began to design and make hats to augment their income,
she quickly turned her skills into a successful millinery business.

Their son, Eduard, grew up vigorously inquisitive and mischievous.
He was four when his baby sister was born. She was baptized Anna Maria
Elizabeth, and later chose Magdalene for her confirmation name. Her
family called her Lilian, Lily or Paus'l, a Belgian endearment. Just as
Jean Pierre and Marie anglicized their names to John Peter and Mary,

Eduard changed the spelling of his name and became known as Edward Steichen, one of the world's great photographers. Destined for creativity in the visual arts, his first childhood recollection was a "kind of visual memory" of seeing his father strike his mother. The incident "startled and terrified him." Mary Steichen had too much self-respect to tolerate another blow. Some family members thought later that she had intercepted a blow her husband intended for their small son.

In 1888 the Steichens sent Edward to Pio Nono College preparatory school near Milwaukee to get him away from street gangs in Hancock. Despite their initial financial struggles, the Steichens managed to live more comfortably than many immigrant families, including the Swedish Sandburgs down in Illinois. Mary Steichen placed supreme emphasis on education for her children. Her spirited son was already independent and rebellious, but tried to please his parents and his teachers. When he was given an art assignment, he doubted his own skill and traced a drawing, which his teachers took to be his own work. When they told Edward's parents that he showed artistic promise, Mary Steichen was immediately convinced that her son would become a great artist. The family moved to Milwaukee in 1889 to be nearer to his school. He decided not to confess his subterfuge, but applied himself earnestly to his artwork, drawing his own pictures from then on. That childhood deception set Edward Steichen on a true course toward his destiny. When she was old enough to start school, Lilian's parents enrolled her in a Catholic grade school in Milwaukee.

John Peter Steichen held the "old old German ideal of the father as master of the house and of the wife and of the children." Edward and Lilian believed that he was harsh and difficult, interfering in their mother's millinery business and failing to understand his wife or his children. He "simply represented so much friction to be overcome" in Mary's life. He thought his children were "rebellious, self-willed, with strange incomprehensible ambitions!" Mary always stood up for her handsome, brilliant children, giving them fierce, single-minded devotion. She defended them against their father, Lilian said, "backing them up—finally taking the reins out of his hands so as to help them realize their ambitions."

She had a "splendid peasant constitution," but years of grueling work and heavy responsibility wore her out and left her prone to illness in middle age. She was intensely emotional and Lilian believed her mother "always took things hard." There were "many agonies in her life," but her overriding ambition was to provide every opportunity for her children. She often worked until two or three o'clock in the morning trimming hats, rising at six to "do the washing or scrub the kitchen floor and get the other housework out of the way before 8 when she opened the store."

She had no help with the house, the children, or her thriving business. After the family moved to Milwaukee and Mary's millinery shop began to prosper there, John Peter gave up his job in a Milwaukee store and "took charge of the house—cooked and washed and scrubbed—did everything about the house." She soon found, however, that she had exchanged one worry for another. He was "always around and interfered in business matters he didn't understand and couldn't understand." Each time Mary moved her flourishing business, her husband's opposition had to be overcome. She earned a good income for the family. During her last years in the store, she worked six days and spent "most of Sunday in bed with headache or fever."

Lilian loved books and her piano, and was given to the quiet pursuits of reading and writing poetry. Edward was effervescent, indefatigable; his mother often tried to channel his prodigious energy into work. He peddled enough vegetables from his father's prolific garden and enough newspapers to buy himself a magical instrument he called "delicate and strange of moods"—a camera. When his mother gave him money to buy a bicycle, Edward used his ingenuity to create Milwaukee's "first rubber-tire telegram delivery service," persuading the local Western Union office to hire him at fifteen dollars a month, five dollars more than the conventional rate, to go "whizzing around" Milwaukee on his bicycle handing out telegrams. Then, intent on understanding how his bicycle worked, he took it apart and successfully reassembled it.

The first picture Edward took with his Eastman Kodak camera was of the family cat sleeping in the show window of the millinery shop. Of the fifty exposures on his first roll of film, the only clear picture was of his twelve-year-old sister playing the piano. His father "thought one picture out of fifty was a hopeless proposition," but Mary told her son the picture "was so beautiful and so wonderful that it was worth the forty-nine failures."

Edward's formal education ended in 1894 when he was fifteen. He entered a traditional four-year German apprenticeship with a Milwaukee lithographic firm, where he would work for nothing the first year, for two dollars weekly the second year, and for a dollar-a-week increase the third and fourth years. Lilian had transferred from Catholic grade school to Milwaukee Public School, Sixth District, Number 1, where she was a gifted student. Her brother praised the poetry she wrote and was convinced she was a genius. Unfortunately no copies of her poems survived, but hundreds of her letters revealed her to be a natural writer. She and her brother would give each other a lifetime of encouragement and praise. She found his early photographic experiments in the darkroom he created in their cellar to be far more exciting than her daily duties in the millinery store.

Edward's ingenuity spurred him again to revise the practice of a local business. He convinced the manager of the lithographic firm that customers would pay more for the realism of photography than the customary drawing used on advertising posters. Edward photographed real pigs and wheat fields, as well as single sheaves of wheat. His "crowning achievement" was to "make some portraits of pigs that were much admired by the pork packers," who insisted that all future advertising matter "be based on the pigs in these photographs."

Edward was fascinated by "mysterious and ever-changing light with its accompanying shadows rich and full of mystery," and tried to capture the truth of light in his photographs and paintings. In Milwaukee in the late 1890s, photography was a young science and an undiscovered art, and Edward had to depend on his own resourcefulness. His mother and sister supported his constant need to experiment.

Lilian was an eighth-grader in 1897 when Edward and some friends organized the Milwaukee Art Students' League. He became its first president and won his first art prize that year, for his design for an envelope for the National Educational Association convention in Milwaukee. He earned extra money painting watercolors of Indian heads and portraits of women. He sold his paintings in department stores, and showed up at public meetings to take snapshot portraits which his pleased subjects bought for a dollar a dozen. He helped his mother by designing lavish, outrageous hats for her store window on the theory that passers-by would be intrigued, as they were, and come in to see what else she had for sale. He photographed hats for her as well. Mother and son had the same sense of audacity and enterprise and took risks that paid off. When Mary had the chance to buy a case of artificial roses for very little, she did so, despite her husband's protests. She covered a wide-brimmed hat with roses and asked Lilian to wear it about town. She had more orders for rose-festooned hats than she could fill.

When Lilian finished eighth grade in 1898 at age fifteen, she was a beauty as well as a serious student, hungry for more education. Her father was adamant that a proper Catholic young lady had no business in public high school. Anyway, he felt she had all the education a woman needed. Heartbroken, Lilian went to work as a reluctant apprentice in her mother's store. Mary half-believed that in time Lilian would come to like the business and take it over when she retired.

Her spirited daughter had other ideas. If her father would not send her to public school, she would try getting his permission for Catholic school. When Lilian discovered that her best friend's mother had attended a Catholic convent school she learned what she could about it and then easily persuaded her family to send her there. In September 1899 Lilian began classes at Ursuline Academy in Chatham, Ontario. She was first in her class in the fifteen subjects she carried. The sisters marveled at her religious devotion as well as her scholarship. When she learned that the nuns spent whole nights in prayer, she sometimes joined them for a dusk-until-dawn vigil at the altar in the dark chill of the convent church.

*

The autumn of 1899 brought honors to both the Steichen children. The nuns sent home reports praising Lilian's academic and religious diligence. Edward achieved his first affirmation as a photographic artist when the eminent photographer Clarence White accepted two of his photographs for the distinguished Second Philadelphia Salon of October 21–November 19.

But once again the young Steichens surprised their parents with radical decisions. For years Edward had carefully saved every penny he did not invest in photographic equipment, and by 1900, when he turned twenty-one, he had enough money to work and study in Europe. There was a roar of protest from John Peter, who thought his son was crazy to give up a good job to go to Europe. Was he not earning the princely salary of fifty dollars a week, not counting his free-lance income?

Mary listened to Edward's plan and supported his decision, supplementing his savings so he could make the journey in reasonable comfort. In late spring 1900 Edward and a friend from the Art Students' League left Milwaukee for Paris, stopping en route in New York to meet the great photographer Alfred Stieglitz. To Edward's pleasure and surprise, Stieglitz bought three of his photographic prints for five dollars each. And so Edward set sail on the French Line steamer *Champlain* with the encouragement of White and Stieglitz, America's two leading photographers.

The spring of Edward's departure was a time of crisis for Lilian, who must have longed for her brother's support in a lonely decision. As her convent year wound to its close, she happened to read an *Atlantic Monthly* article on white slavery, written by Mark Twain. Stunned by the horrible details, she became convinced that God as she understood Him, had worshiped Him on the cold stones of the convent church floor, and celebrated Him at mass and meditation, would not permit something so unbearable. Feeling profoundly betrayed, Lilian announced her intention to leave the Catholic Church. She rejected all organized religion when she perceived a flaw at its heart, and began to think of herself as an atheist.

Worried over her daughter's spiritual life, Mary took her to consult a Milwaukee Jesuit priest. He listened sympathetically, perceived her intelligence and sincerity, and assured Lilian's anxious mother that "as long as her daughter believed that she was doing right, she was still religious at heart."

Lilian did not return to convent school. Just as her brother was determined to study in Europe, she was bent on a university education. She worked at home alone throughout that summer to prepare for college entrance examinations. Into three months she crammed the year's work, prescribed by standard algebra and geometry texts, as well as the year's required readings in French. She studied German grammar and read the books required for the third-year German examination. In that diligent summer she also taught herself a year's worth of Latin, botany, English, American history and ancient history. By summer's end she took the four-year high school examination for college entrance, and nervously awaited the results. She scored in the eighty-fifth percentile, and she immediately enrolled as a freshman at the University of Illinois in Urbana.

Lilian Steichen kept her pensive blue-gray eyes in her books that first year, working hard at required subjects to get them out of the way and move on to literature and philosophy. She missed her brother and his enthusiasms, as well as the affection and understanding he lavished on her. He was by then settled in a Latin Quarter studio in Paris, where the city and its riches surpassed his expectations. He discovered the work of the sculptor Auguste Rodin, who soon became his friend. Edward Steichen's photographs began to be exhibited in Europe and the United States with increasing frequency. He was a boy wonder, at age twenty-three hailed in some circles as an artistic and photographic genius, encouraged by photographers Clarence White, F. Holland Day and Alfred Stieglitz, as well as by Rodin and the Belgian writer Maurice Maeterlinck. One reviewer in 1902 called his work "the highest point to which photographic portraiture has yet been brought."

Mary kept an ever-growing scrapbook of his letters and news clippings about his work. Other women found him irresistibly handsome and exciting. He fell passionately in love with a married woman who remained hopelessly out of his reach, and there were fleeting and sometimes tragic affairs with more accessible women. In 1903 he married a beautiful American named Clara Smith and settled down to work with fierce energy, winning international awards and growing fame as a portrait photographer. His portfolio grew to include Rodin, writer Edward Everett Hale, F. Holland Day, Maeterlinck, composer Richard Strauss, Stieglitz, and playwright George Bernard Shaw. On a single day in 1903 he photographed banker J. P. Morgan and actress Eleonora Duse. In 1904 Clara gave birth to their first child, Mary, and the family moved between homes in New York, where Steichen worked with Stieglitz, and Voulagnis, France. Once there was a grandchild, the elder Steichens were called "Oma" and "Opa," in the "old-country" way of addressing grandparents.

Oma suffered when her children were away. With Edward in France and Lilian in Urbana, the separation was "hard for such an intensely maternal woman" with "no other channel for the love in her," her daughter observed. Lilian believed that if her father had been more affectionate, Oma would not have "clung so desperately" to her children.

Lilian chose the University of Illinois for its distinguished school of library science, but discovered after enrollment that an undergraduate degree was required for entrance to the program. After her freshman year, therefore, she transferred to the University of Chicago. There she studied English with Oscar Lovell Triggs before he joined Parker Sercombe in editing To-Morrow and encouraging the fledgling poet Charles A. Sandburg. She studied economics with Thorstein Veblen, the brilliant eccentric whose propensity for radical economic theory and indecorous love affairs eventually cost him his academic post. The scholarly Miss Steichen completed her college program in three and a half years, receiving the bachelor of philosophy degree on December 22, 1903, with honors in English and philosophy and election to Phi Beta Kappa. Her absent brother, who often called her Lily, sent her a great bouquet of lilies that day.

After graduation, she stayed in Chicago, renting a room and eating her meals at a nearby health food center. After she became an active member of the Socialist Party, she converted her mother and brother to socialism, although Edward Steichen took little part in politics. Lilian and her mother, however, were active party members, attending lectures and socialist picnics, doing party volunteer work, and visiting the Milwaukee headquarters of Wisconsin's Social-Democratic Party, which Mary's good friend Charles Whitnall served as treasurer.

Lilian got a job translating quotations from Latin and German into English for "a proposed new Book of Quotations to rival Bartlett's." On Saturday nights she traveled to Jane Addam's Hull House at Ewing and Halsted streets for meetings of her socialist club. They studied works such as Labriola's *Essays on the Materialistic Conception of History*, with emphasis on scientific or critical socialism. In late spring 1904 the quotation book project was scrapped and Lilian reluctantly left Chicago to join her parents, who had moved fifteen miles out of Milwaukee to a four-acre farm near Menomonee Falls, Wisconsin. Opa had always wanted to live in the country so he could be out of doors and work with the vegetables and flowers which sprang to rich life under his hands. Oma had made a comfortable living for them in her millinery business, and Edward helped support them so they could retire to the country. Despite her friendly neighbors, she was lonely after city life, and was delighted when Lilian came home to stay while she looked for a teaching position.

From New York, Steichen wrote to counsel his sister. "I am glad you are going to teach, Paus'l," he said, assuring her that

> it is better for us all just for a while to hack—hack hack.—It will help us plan and achieve a bigger goal in the end.—Paus'l—"AIM HIGH"— I felt you had missed aim when you spoke of the position in a publishing house—you could do lots of little bits of good that way—but they are drops in a bucket—big game is your hunting and you can be this best when independent.—Your life your time your where & your when must always be yours—when you marry you as a woman will be gradually forced to give these up—you will be a mother and those instincts will get the better of you—. I do not discourage you in marriage but love you in it— glorify you because it will all be love. But you will be a greater factor in humankind if you can be a mother *intellectually* and be mother to modern humankind.—

Steichen's letters to his family were sporadic, affectionate messages scrawled in a bold, nearly illegible handwriting. Yet in times of family crisis he wrote long, tender letters, full of encouragement and empathy. "I see in you things great and glorious," he told his sister, "in any way you go if you always be true to your best self.—Be it as a *Joan of Arc* or as a wife & mother. Lovingly to you all, Gaesjack."

Lilian found her first teaching job at the State Normal School in Valley City, North Dakota, where from September 1904 until June 1906 she trained high school graduates to be teachers and produced frequent plays given by students. She was an excellent teacher, "a young woman of superior ability and pleasing personality," a school official wrote, but she saw little possibility of advancement, professional or personal, in Valley City. The austere budget did not even permit a raise. After two years she resigned and was quickly hired to teach high school English and elocution in Princeton, Illinois.

At age twenty-four Lilian Steichen was a self-sufficient, independent young woman and an avid socialist. Her diminutive, graceful beauty and the quiet lilt of her voice belied the strength of her intellect and the force of her beliefs. From girlhood she had not been afraid of loneliness if that was to be a condition of independence.

At Social-Democratic Party headquarters in Milwaukee, Lilian was quickly befriended by party leader Victor Berger, twenty-three years her senior and nearly ten years married. An Austrian immigrant, Berger was a controversial, pragmatic politician with a genius for political organization which made him a national force in the socialist movement, as well as the guiding hand in Wisconsin Social Democracy. Berger took an interest in Lilian Steichen which extended beyond her skillful translations of socialist literature and propaganda.

Vigorous exercise outdoors and innate good health gave Lilian physical vitality and extraordinary stamina. Her imperfections—her nose was a little too long, her black hair too defiantly curly—were transcended by the luminous beauty of her blue-gray eyes, vividly alive, brimming with intelligence and wit. She was radiant, and people invariably said she sparkled, shone, dazzled. Loneliness and independence bred strength in her. She and her closest friend in Princeton, fellow teacher Elsie Caskey, were misfits who seldom attended church or wore hats and gloves or conformed to the traditional views of the spinster schoolteacher. They often talked about the ideal man and about marriage and family. Lilian was old enough and independent enough so that the chances were rapidly diminishing that conventional marriage to an ordinary young man would satisfy either the bride or the groom. Her devoted brother had counseled her to keep her independence and freedom.

At the beginning, at least, Charles Sandburg certainly did not stir in her any thoughts of romance, much less marriage. He was just another socialist comrade at Milwaukee headquarters. He was shabby and gaunt, she remembered, obviously overworn from his work as a party organizer. While she admired his intensity and appreciated the hardships of his work, she did not immediately think of him as a suitor. She had been wooed by older, visibly successful socialists. A young man in Chicago had recently proposed to her. In later years, when pressed for details on her love life, all she would say was that she "had been as much as engaged" to a "brilliant and elderly" writer prominent in the Milwaukee Socialist movement. There was "another vague tale of romance" that she supposedly told and, much later, retracted, about "an Important Personality in the party, also along in years" who wanted her to have his child in order to "perpetuate his acknowledged genius." She had declined all those overtures. As she settled into the winter rhythm in Princeton in 1908, she had little time or inclination to think about Charles Sandburg and their chance meeting in Milwaukee.

✳

The first letters they wrote to each other in January 1908 were formal: "My dear Mr. Sandburg," she addressed him from her room in Princeton, Illinois, after the day's classes were done. "Dear Miss Steichen," he replied from one small Wisconsin town and then another. They wrote at first of "the progress of the socialist movement," the "politics of constructive socialism," the place of art in an "age of action." "Art now-a-days . . . is by and for the privileged minority," she wrote to him in February; "it is a thing of Snobbery—a diversion of the leisure class."

She used to write poetry herself, she confided, but gave it up because she believed she had no talent for it, and even gave up reading much poetry, relinquishing "such aesthetic enjoyment" for "A Voice from the world of action." She applauded Charles Sandburg's powers of expression, especially since he was using them "in the propaganda of socialism."

He sought to impress the scholarly Miss Steichen with his socialist writings, but the memory of her sparkling blue-gray eyes, her bright uptilted face, the energy of her trim body led him to send her a copy of his poem "Dream Girl." He masked his serious intent with self-deprecating humor. He had sent her an overture of a love poem, his tentative, hopeful acknowledgment that he had found the elusive dream girl at last. Unaware of his motive, she sent him a prompt, forthright critique of the poem: "Your *Dream-Girl*—since you laugh, I may smile at her, may I not?—is indeed a dream girl—not of our world today but of the Millennial Epoch of Rest. In our Epoch of Struggle girls must be made of sterner stuff. Too bad, but it's so." She hoped that socialism would gradually create "an environment favorable to the development of such a Millennial *Dream Girl*," she said, but, meanwhile, "under capitalism your Dream Girl must be a leisure class product."

He defended his dream girl. She was millennial, he said, "formed in the mist of an impressionist's reverie. Millennial, and at this time, impossible." Then, unconsciously echoing a line from Whitman, he described his dream girl more concretely: "But, my good girl, she is not of the leisure-class, as we know the l-c. She is a disreputable gypsy, and can walk, shoot, ride, row, hoe in the garden, wash dishes, grimace, haggle, live on half-rations, and laugh at luck." Whitman had described the ideal woman in "A Woman Waits for Me" as one who knew how "to swim, row, ride, wrestle, shoot, run, strike, retreat, advance, resist."

Sandburg mailed that letter from Oshkosh, where he had taken over the district headquarters of the Social-Democratic Party. He thanked Lilian Steichen for her letters which softened "the intensity of this guerrilla warfare" he carried on as party organizer, trying to "get the hypercritical into constructive work, and to give cheer to the desperate and rousal to the stolid." He enclosed a sheaf of his newer poems, although, he told her, his poetic period was over.

Lilian's February 24, 1908, letter to Sandburg was a turning point in their personal lives and his life as a poet. She answered him immediately, exulting over his poetry:

> The poems—the poems are wonderful! They are different from the poems in the books that stand dusty on my bookshelf—how different! Yes, from the best of them too—from Shelley, from Whitman, from Carpenter! Oh, if I had a volume of your poems, dear Poet-of-Our-World-Today, it would not stand on the shelf dusty but would be read and wrestled with for the life-strength it could give.

She had seen him only once, in that fleeting introduction in Milwaukee in late December. She quickly came to admire the fervent socialist as he revealed himself in a handful of letters. But in late February she began to fall in love with Sandburg the poet. She admonished him, "Will you tell me why you've turned from poetry—you who knew all the while these poems that I read for the first time. I knew no realistic poetry till I saw yours. . . . Your poems have that elemental quality of being direct and simple."

"Have you really turned from poetry for good?" Lilian asked him. "Shaw is our dramatist—why shouldn't you be our Poet? The American movement doesn't seem to be in pressing need of a poet at the present moment—*perhaps. Perhaps!* But surely the time isn't far off when it will need its Poet."

She had advocated socialism far longer than he, was far better schooled in its history and theory, even more committed to its programs. Yet when she discovered Charles Sandburg's poetry, she did not for a moment doubt which direction he should choose. She acknowledged that "it's *great* work what you are doing now—as S.D.P. organizer! You seem to have a genius for that work too." Then she asked the crucial question: "Would it be possible to be both organizer and poet? Or is it a case of having to forego one service in order to do the other. And if you have decided to forego being a poet, why? Why?"

✳

Sandburg traversed Wisconsin that cold winter, making a two-hour speech to workingmen here, an hour-long plea there, subsisting on the dues he could collect and small fees from random lecture bookings when he talked on Whitman. Lilian's sympathetic letters warmed him, her understanding of the movement encouraged him, but even more important, her praise for the poetry filled him with new confidence and spurred him to further experimentation.

Lilian had been exposed to genius early in her life with her brother, and immediately perceived Sandburg's promise. She was honest to the core, and he knew he could trust her praise for his work. She reread the poems to assure herself that they were as good as she first thought, "that it wasn't some passing glamor that made the poems seem so wonderful." They withstood repeated readings; she found greatness in them. "Hail, poet," she saluted him.

She also apologized for her "stupid" misinterpretation of his "Dream Girl." "Of course I must retract what I said about your Dream Girl," she wrote. "I didn't interpret rightly—your explanation in your letter was a revelation, a surprise." He had "completely upset" her notions about modern poetry, she told him. The more she read of his poems, the more pleasure they gave her. "What joy for me to read and know by reading that there are more and still more such wonderful poems."

She worried that his "strenuous life as agitator" would leave him little energy for poetry. "As if it were not enough to be possessed with one sort of divine madness! You must needs add to the divine madness of poesy the diviner madness of revolutionary agitation—Bless you!"

Avidly she kept track of Sandburg's work by reading his weekly notes in the Milwaukee *Social-Democratic Herald* and by tracing on a Wisconsin map the itinerary for his "arduous labors in the faraway North!" She cheered him on his way:

> I like to get the thought of all this great great poetry in my mind—and then think of you knocking about in the "Lake Country" . . . not as a wandering minstrel, but as a plain practical S.D.P. organizer giving talks to hard-headed workingmen and organizing them for political action. Wonderful! How Shelley would have envied you! He tried so hard, poor

boy, to do what you are doing now—to be a man of action helping to carry forward the political movement of his day. But it wasn't given him to do such work—he wasn't hardheaded himself—lacked genius for practical action.—You see the gods have been very good to you!

Sandburg had initiated the correspondence with the beautiful young socialist schoolteacher. After he revealed his poetry to her, her letters grew increasingly longer and more intimate. The neat white packets awaited him in Oshkosh, Green Bay, Marinette, in party offices or general delivery windows or boardinghouses or hotels, as the long, gray winter turned toward spring. He had traveled alone since he left Lombard and Galesburg. He found in her long, faithful letters welcome companionship of intellect and spirit, and enduring praise for his poetry and his politics.

His letters to her in Princeton were fewer, sporadic, usually brief. He had few moments to himself between speeches and traveling. Now that her friend Elsie Caskey was married and living abroad, Lilian was isolated and lonely in Princeton. It pleased her to hear Sandburg say she helped him in his work. "I like to hear that," she told him. "So I shall be able to help the world on a little, through you. Directly I don't touch the world these days. Princeton is outside the bounds of the world. Oh, there is one other hope of course—that some of my boys and girls will leave Princeton when they grow up and become a part of the World. And so my work at school may count a little."

She longed to live more actively in the world; she envied Sandburg's immersion in socialist politics and encouraged him in the work. But mainly her letters stimulated him to write new poems and entrust them to her. "I see the wellspring of poetry is not dry in you," she praised him. "You have surpassed yourself!"

She admired his prose as well. It was "Strong, simple, direct, and full of joy and wisdom—it shows the noble strength and stature of your soul." When she praised his simplicity, he playfully chided her for her sometimes stilted language. "I'll try always to say 'hard work' instead of 'arduous labors' hereafter," she promised him.

> "I'll try," I say. But doubtless I'll blunder into scholasticisms now and then. That's what schooling did for me. This was the way of it. My mother tongue is Luxembourger—a German dialect. English is an acquired tongue—and as I was a bookworm from about twelve years old till I got thru college, I got my English from books, largely academic books at that.

As winter subsided into spring, she began to pour her heart and soul onto paper, defining herself for him. "I think for myself," she confided.

"I dare to have natural feelings. And I'm not afraid to speak my thoughts and feelings." She let him know she was not a conventional woman.

Despite her regular protests that she had no gift for writing, she wrote lyrical passages in her letters to Sandburg. Once after a rainstorm, she wrote, as she walked toward the sunset under an arch of elm trees, she "saw the sky aglow! And the ruts in the road caught the glow—two ribbons of burning gold." Her words painted the windswept open country, the darkening sky, the "great fields of yellow corn stubble stretching afar on both sides of the road—and the West a great lake of burning gold!"

By March the letters were flying between them. They had seen each other only once. Eagerly they began to plan to meet again. She was going home to her parents' little farm at Menomonee Falls for spring vacation. Her brother, Edward, would be there, too, to celebrate his birthday and tell them about his recent successes in New York and Paris. Could Sandburg come to the farm? The house was small and simple, she told him, and he would have to sleep upstairs in a tiny, unheated bedroom. Would he mind? Could he be comfortable there? The farm was three miles from the nearest train station. Did he like to walk? If so, she would meet him. It was a "fine walk in good weather" and she thought it would be a "fine way to begin 'the day at the farm' with this walk together." But if he did not like to walk, or if the weather was bad, she would meet him with horse and buggy.

Right away Sandburg replied, "We will *walk* to Menomonee Falls." He shared her passion for nature, long walks and vigorous exercise in the fresh air in any season.

With mounting excitement Lilian planned for their meeting at the farm, set for March 27. As usual, Edward was vague about his plans, but she thought he would arrive that day. "An artist's temperament has its drawbacks," she wrote Sandburg. "On second thought I believe that I did my brother an injustice in referring his shortcomings to his supposed artist's temperament. I'll take that back—say his shortcomings are due to plain '*cussedness.*' " She took it for granted, she teased, that Sandburg had "a peculiar brand of 'cussedness' " all his own. After all, she noted, "It's not human nor comradely to be angelic," and she speculated that Sandburg was "innocent of any such uncomradely deficiency in plain human 'cussedness.' " Her affectionate tolerance for her brother's idiosyncrasies equipped her to understand Sandburg.

They had spent only a scant few minutes face-to-face, but by March 1908, through the leisurely intimacy of letters, they were falling in love. "So glad am I that on the great wide way we have met, touched hands and spoken," he wrote. She answered that his letters filled her with wonder and hope. "To think that one day can hold so much happiness!" she exulted, "—and it's You, my Poet, so free with the warm human gifts of your dear words and rhythms, that have filled the day brimful of Joy for me!"

Expressing his love for her transformed his poetry, as if her passion for simplicity and honesty banished pretense, artificiality and affectation from the poems he wrote for her. In his poetry she believed their spirits fused. Innocently, she described a prophetic marriage of hearts:

> I have been conscious in rare poignant moments in my life of something very beautiful deep deep within me—but the voice from those depths has always been so small, so still—more a *hush* than a *voice*—that I never dreamed anyone but myself would *hear* it. But so finely attuned was that heart of yours, you caught the fine vibrant note from the depths—and—gave it strength and quality. In your poems somehow (I dare *hope—believe* it!) the sweet still hush of my heart has become blended with the clear strong proud Music of yours and so is heard! . . . But for you, the sweet small hush yearning upward toward light and utterance would have subsided back to the dark depths. . . . So glad thanks to you—for Voice! for Life!

Ten days before their meeting at the farm, she wrote to him without inhibition, her love for him apparent in every line. Before, she had addressed him as Mr. Sandburg, or Comrade, or, once, Dear Poet and Comrade. But on March 17, after she received the copy of *In Reckless Ecstasy* he mailed her, she began her letter differently: "Wunderkind! I've got to call you that even if you don't know what it means. The name has been on my lips before when I read some account of what you were doing—or when I read some splendid poems of yours."

She was subdued in her next letter, addressing him "Dear Comrade." They would see each other face-to-face in little more than a week. "This time I shall really see you," she promised. "The first glimpse I had of you was not *seeing*. That we will be good comrades I know. For the rest, we know not."

Charles Sandburg and Lilian Steichen would meet in Milwaukee at five o'clock on Friday afternoon, March 27, 1908. They would travel together to the farm. She had sent Sandburg a photograph her brother had taken of her, more to share Steichen's work than to give Sandburg a picture of herself. She wore a simple gown in the photograph. He liked seeing her in it. "Will you bring along and wear once that Graeco-Gothic white thing you have on in that picture?" he asked. She would.

He was "battering from town to town" that week, working into the night, marking off the days until he would see her again. "Dear, beautiful girl-heart," he wrote to her that week, "proud mystery-woven girl-heart . . . we see great days of big things—so shall we be like what we see."

✳

The week they spent together at the Steichen farm surpassed their hopes. After years of lonely independence, they marveled in their joyful discovery of each other. It was a festive week, with the celebration of Edward Steichen's birthday and Oma's evident pleasure in having her children at home. She greeted Sandburg warmly, although Opa Steichen was reserved if not glum in the presence of the tall intense poet his only daughter brought home to the farm. "Now she had told us that he was a poet," Edward Steichen remembered. "That's about all anybody knew about him at the time, that he had said he was a poet." Opa would look out the window of his little house, surveying his orchard and meadows. Edward "could hear him think, 'My god, another longhair. He'll never be able to be any help on this farm.' "

Sandburg and Edward Steichen liked each other immediately, and walked and talked while Lilian and her mother worked in the kitchen. After much debate, they had decided to cook a turkey for dinner because "poets when they did eat wanted something substantial and a lot of it," according to Oma. Sandburg and Steichen began a lifelong friendship during those few days on the farm. Sandburg was so impressed that he wrote to Philip Green Wright that week to tell him he was "spending a few days . . . on the Steichen farm, with the folks of Edward Steichen, the painter and art photographer." He did not mention Lilian.

Steichen entertained them with stories of his work. He was a witty storyteller, with a dramatic flair for words as well as images, and led them into his avant-garde world with accounts of the exhibit he had just arranged at Stieglitz's Photo-Secession Galleries in New York, featuring the drawings of his friend Rodin. Steichen's own one-man show of paintings and photographs had opened at the National Arts Club in New York. He would have a one-man show of photographs in April at the Photo-Secession, and his one-man show of paintings and photographs would be at the Pratt Institute April 15–22. His reputation as a portrait photographer had won him a commission from *Everybody's Magazine* to photograph Theodore Roosevelt and William Howard Taft, for the staggering fee of five hundred dollars each. The Steichens beamed at their son's success, and he, observing with affection how Lilian looked at Sandburg, made several photographs of the lanky, photogenic socialist poet.

Sandburg and Lilian spent much time apart from the others that week, walking and talking endlessly. When he first arrived, she pitied him because he looked so tired and old. After a few days' rest, he looked ten years younger, she thought. He would remember her bright blue eyes transfixed to his face, for "the light in her eyes is the miracle-light, the light of a golden hope that glimmers and glimmers always in the heart of a Poet far off." He told her about his childhood in Galesburg, the struggle of his "young days," and she understood immediately how remarkable his accomplishments were. "That boy-heart of yours undaunted, brave heroic! and good, clean, sweet! That in spite of all and thru all you developed the genius in you, is wonderful! That you developed the heart you have—the sweetness—the hope—that is more wonderful still!"

Serious talks gave way to fun. They pretended to build a house in the woods near the farm. He carried her in his arms "over the bogs of marsh on high windy days." They kept each other company on "every intellectual ascent, every play of foolery, washing dishes, watching stupidities even, and getting down to the practical and work-a-day." They walked for miles, even ran hand in hand, playing like children, to Lilian's surprise and delight. "Oh we know how to play," she told him, "—and yet I— I had not played with anyone since I was twelve—not really *played* with anyone. I had played alone—but somehow I never let myself go when anyone else was near." She found his "Gladness and Playfulness" contagious. "With you I became free and natural as the wind," she told him gratefully. "I let myself go—I laughed and played and played."

They were caught in a fierce spring thunderstorm which they called the baptismal rain as if it blessed and sanctified their love for each other. They remembered it for years afterward as the symbol of that week, "the beginning of *everything*" for them. They left each other reluctantly at night. She would watch him climb the narrow stairs to the second floor of the farmhouse, "candle in hand—saying good-night and good-night —your eyes full of love."

Sandburg's early sexual experience is still an enigma. He was infatuated easily and often, and lived an anonymous, free life on the road. His lifestyle and nature made it unlikely that he was sexually inexperienced at age thirty. But he had never before been so deeply attracted, intellectually, spiritually and physically, to one woman. Theirs was a passionate meeting of minds, and their letters and his poems after the farm meeting hint that they made love during that rapturous March week. "You gave—with your deep blue careless eyes and your/low soft careless voice you gave," he wrote to her afterward in a poem:

Your heart went thudding under your ribs like a guess
    come sure and a bird on the wing.
Your breath was a hot and cadenced pulsing, free as the
    urge of a seaward tide.
You threw down the bars to fresh wild things of unimaginable
    gardens—
Flowers impassioned and red looked out on our reckless and
    memoried moments . . .

They spoke to each other of that idyllic week in a fusion of sacramental and sexual imagery. "What a Glory that the Soul should be so transfused into the body!" Lilian exulted. "The Body no more a Hulk—no more a thing of Wood—but etherialized—a Speaking Flame! What a Consecration! A realist Pentecost! . . . Sacrifice of self for another and Consecration of self *and* of another! Annihilation and Life!" She told him he called "to the finest in me, the most spiritual . . . and calling, a Viking-son, to the most elemental in me!"

He savored her beauty: "For your face is set with glory/ And your eyes are dusky mirrors. . . ." She was his "Dream-Girl-come-true," his "Wonder-Girl."

"I love you," he told her. "Alive & roused I love you—and tired & played out & done for, you are the Pal, the Love, the Comrade, the Presence. . . ." Away from her, he was hungry for her "dear hands—good arms—soft, warm lips." She longed for "those lips, those strong arms, those good eyes!"

Afterward, when he settled temporarily into a cheap rented room in any town where his business took him, he immediately arranged her pictures on shelves and tables. "You are with me always as a redeeming, transcending Presence," he told her. "The intangible You floats about the room. I conjure scents of your hair (that copper gleam in the black!). . . . Always you are with me, giving me your smile for my failures and mistakes, accepting everything, having seen in me as I have seen in you—something last and final of sacred resolve and consecrated desire. . . . So you fill the room—always—you awaken all the purity and intensity of the dreamer in me—with you I am proud of all romance in my blood."

In spirit they were married. He celebrated the "glamor and glory of two high, superb selves intermingled." She was his "Other Self—a complement." "We are *One*," she answered. "I know what you are going to say before you speak. I see you and hear you and touch you all day long, all night long, everywhere and in all things." She told him she was not a "single separate person" any longer. "How the world has changed! The atom commingling with another atom, become a Molecule! Oh the Wonder! . . . *Me-in-Thee, Thee-in-Me.*" They were together "the Realization of the Ideal!" He found it hard to concentrate on his work after he left her, "neglected the more practical things—moved in sort of reckless and ecstatic moods." She shared his euphoria. "After a while will come a beautiful calm acceptance of the S-S [Sandburg-Steichen] —something really grander than this present exclamatory ecstasy! I've not gotten over the sheer wonderment that *we have met*! You are!"

They would see each other again as soon as they could possibly arrange it. She knew instinctively that their joined lives held a deep, prophetic meaning, for themselves and others. They could not know, she told him, "What things are shaping themselves in the dark womb of Nature." Yet she was certain that "whatever it is—it is good!"

—✳—

1908

8. Hope and Glory

The touch of your hand is hope
And the sheen of your hair is glory.
You are the sea with its mystic song,
You are the stars and dawn and morning.
You are a woman, you are a comrade. . . .

—Charles A. Sandburg, "You," 1908

They had shared nearly fifty letters and spent only a handful of days together, but Charles Sandburg and Lilian Steichen had "known each other for eons & eons" and decided by the end of that week at the farm that they would marry. They talked vaguely of saving money, but set no wedding date. For the time being, they simply contemplated the miracle of finding each other.

In the spirit of the "baptismal rain," they renamed each other. Her family called her Paus'l, she had explained to Sandburg, but Edward's little daughter, Mary, found that hard to pronounce, and called her Paula. Sandburg thought that name suited her and called her Paula ever afterward. When she learned that he had been christened Carl August Sandburg, she began to call him Carl. She understood that he had wanted to anglicize his name in childhood, but proclaimed his given name stronger, better suited to his personality. Her preference for his given name was an implicit affirmation of his Swedish roots. By 1910 he had begun to sign his work Carl Sandburg.

In the effusive private vocabulary of lovers, they used other names for each other. She called him Cully or Sandy; he called her Liz or Kitty. They often referred to each other as the S-S, not only for Steichen and Sandburg, but "for two Souls. The hyphen means they have met and are." The S-S was a symbol of their union; it meant "intensity and vibration and radiation but over and beyond these it places harmony and equilibrium."

They missed each other profoundly. Their love letters filled a book. She was "the most beautiful, graceful woman in the world," he told her, "the most splendidly equipped of heart, intellect and feeling, in all the world." He felt her spirit, "quiet, homely, brooding, steady, unfaltering —always, always mantling me day and night." After all the solitary years of wandering, searching, living in restless, stubborn independence, he was "committed to this thing, lost and abandoned with You—the Ideal—the Woman who has lived and knows—the Woman who understands—You." Back on the Social-Democratic Party circuit, his loneliness intensified.

Just after their week at the farm, she wrote him a long letter, fifty pages in all, with a detailed description of a dinner table debate on the "sex-question" and the nature of marriage. Paula and her mother had dinner with Party secretary Elizabeth Thomas and Victor Berger. Thomas, a spinster, "stood for race suicide." Mary Steichen supported the conventional church view of marriage: "Life-long mating by *contract, promise* before state or Church authorities." Berger advocated "varietism . . . the idea that a frequent change of mates is natural and desirable." Full of her love for Sandburg, Lilian spoke of their ideal of "Life-long mating . . . two people matching each other in mind & heart & body, the mates believing that they will continue till death perfect mates."

She asked Berger his opinion of Sandburg. "He said you weren't good enough for me!" she told Sandburg, "But when I put it up to him straight—he had to say, 'Honest—I don't know him.' . . . My hope is that B will like you—that you'll work together well. . . . If B—can't appreciate you—then he doesn't understand the first thing about Me—"

Sandburg answered with a furious denunciation of Berger and varietism, "stirpiculture and eugenics." "The strong, beautiful children come from strong, beautiful love," he wrote to her. "The delectable babies are yearned and thought and caressed into life. All the stirpiculturists of Europe couldn't bring a boy from Josephine from the Bonaparte house . . . so he went to Maria Theresa . . . and there was born a wraith that flickered on the borderline of imbecility and then went out. . . . Getting into a regular dissertation, Paula!—This much tho: I don't know what will be my attitude toward B. but there will be no 'patronizing' on either side—I know him in heroic and also pathetic phases, some other than you know of—but I don't expect anything else than we'll all move along fine, treating the past as 'incidentals.' . . ."

"You glorious Man!" she answered. "Good and clean and strong! . . . Surely I am blest among women—having such a mate. . . . And what you say about B and eugenics! All so virile! . . . My Carl! Such fire in your words and such wisdom in your thoughts. . . . Such indignation— splendid! And you are right—absolutely in the right."

Sandburg worked harder than ever, carrying on the heavy correspondence in the Fox River district, writing circular letters and socialist articles for local newspapers, working on three economic lectures which he planned to use on the winter lyceum circuit, reading papers and journals "to keep in touch with the world-currents," meeting with working people at noon and in the evenings, cultivating a network of business men and trade unionists, soliciting pledges to the party, overseeing the collection of dues, trying to "drag delinquents back into membership," keeping up with the records of congressmen and state legislators in preparation for the fall election campaign.

"To keep from going crazy," he told her, he would "sit by a riverside under trees and starlight and think about this wonder and glory of You —Me—the S-S."

Lilian threw herself into her work in Princeton, Illinois, but missed him desperately. She tried to arrange for him to come to Princeton to give his Whitman lecture. She spent more and more time in Bryants Woods, writing him long letters there. "Sometime we must pitch our tent in some sweet sunny spot like this—in Spring!—And be wild things together—we-two!" she wrote to him in April. She longed for them to "Sleep together under the stars!," to live simply, "keen for the beauty around us and within us—the undefiled, clean, elemental beauty of the place and of ourselves."

They worried over each other's health, each promising to take better care. Each of them had experimented with health-food diets, and with Fletcherism, the practice, advocated by nutritionist Horace Fletcher, of eating only when hungry, and then small amounts of food at a time, chewing food slowly and thoroughly. Long before they met, each had come to thrive on vigorous exercise in the fresh air, usually walks of many miles through the countryside. She wrote him a motherly letter about spending strength recklessly. "I think we-two are the sort who will do our best work between forty and sixty," she prophesied. "We-two have good constitutions and fairly good physical culture habits as a basis for a long life. . . . We have kept our childhood long—we should keep our prime long."

She told him it was important to his work that he "look fresh and strong" so he could "inspire hope and splendid discontent!" She cautioned that "a worn-out face can't radiate hope!" He was a one-time baseball player, she reminded him, who should cultivate his own "health and vigor."

En route to Oshkosh, he wrote her a prophecy:

> We stand with a choice of forty roads. We pick one, saying "This is the way and the only." It is a winding road into an untravelled country. It is a road we can learn only by touching the dust of it. . . . Down this way we go. If hell waits for us, we're ready for hell. If mountains & valleys of poetry & dreams-come-true look for our coming, we are coming! This is the way & the only way.

✳

They decided to be married during the coming summer. Sandburg began to save his earnings in an "S-S Fund." They started thinking about where and how they would live. Their home would be "One large room, a few strong, simple things," he said. She envisioned "four walls of a room— three chairs (one for you and one for me and one for Company. . . .) —also a hat rack!—and a bread box!—and an ashtray!—and some bowl or glass for wild flowers! Oh—and of course—a coffee-pot!!!"

Sandburg and Lilian Steichen were not naïve idealists playing with politics. They were mature, hard-working, deeply committed adults determined to live fully within the promise of the American dream which had drawn their parents to the New World. More grounded in European history and culture than Sandburg, Lilian was more sophisticated and worldly, despite being five years his junior. She had enjoyed the freedom of living in two of the most vital, experimental American cities of the day—Milwaukee and Chicago. Her study of philosophy, evolution, sociology and socialism led her to her own clear vision of woman's relation to man and the world. Furthermore, her mother had given her daily lessons in those prefeminist days of the power of a woman's will to succeed. Lilian had a clear, honest sense of who she was and what she valued. Already she was a world within herself, a force unto herself. She possessed a serene coherence and harmony of personality which Sandburg had yet to achieve, for he was still fragmented, pulled among a multiplicity of selves. At ease in her own identity, she would lead him to a clearer perspective of himself.

"You are a *Man!*" she wrote in April 1908. "You are all the separate intensities of Shelley—. . . . Walt Whitman—Marx—Wagner—the Vikings—Christ—Buddha—Lincoln—Heine—Browning—You are all these separate and different intensities! But *harmonized!*" She had seen "broken fragments" of him, and she could see the whole of him, so she was not "so very greatly concerned about what you will *do—what you* will *accomplish*," She told him that April. "The main thing is: *You Are. You are yourself the Achievement.*" She was convinced that together they would do great work, but she was more interested in the character of the life they would lead. "We shall do our best *to do something*—to leave some *thing* that we have produced here on earth as a bequest!" she predicted. "But we'll remember that *the life we live* is more important than the *works we leave.*"

Thus she identified herself with his work, and began, lovingly and willingly, to merge her life with his, even to the point of subordination. "Sacrifice of self for another and Consecration of self *and* of another!" she had written to him. "Annihilation and Life!" Earnestly, she wanted to participate in his work for the party, to "be identified with the movement there." She speculated that "there would be ways in which a woman could be a helper on the field—without being less of a woman for it— rather fulfilling her woman-nature." She had given successful talks to small cultural groups in Princeton and, before that, in Valley City, North Dakota, and wondered if she could give socialist speeches to women's clubs in the Fox River district of Wisconsin. Then she would "feel nearer" him and his work. "And you know," she reminded him, "we want above all things to share all our experiences good and bad as absolutely as possible! . . . I want the hardships of the pioneer work in the district to hit me as hard as you! I want to be at your side so that I'll feel the knocks as keenly as you."

She was willing to do tutoring to supplement his unpredictable income, but with her strong need to be of service, feared that "tutoring is mere money-getting like stereopticon selling—not work, service." She was willing to live "most plainly" so they could devote themselves "wholly to developing the movement" and to developing themselves for "future service in the movement."

He encouraged her immediate involvement in his work by suggesting that she write an article called "Woman and Socialism." She began it eagerly, but wrote out so many of her ideas in letters to him that her creative energy was spent in that way. She never finished the article, but Sandburg later wrote a piece which embodied many of her ideas.

As the days went by, they found the physical distance between them seeming to expand. "It's unsatisfactory business—this of being some 300 miles away from the person to whom one wants to talk all the time," she wrote him sadly. "I used to get a lot of satisfaction out of the companionship of my own soul. . . . But now it's different."

Thirty years into his life Sandburg had unrelenting independence and hard loneliness graven in his soul. For the first time ever, he could entrust himself totally, unconditionally, to another person. He poured his love for her into poems and letters. She made sometimes three trips a day to the Princeton post office in hopes of finding more of them. He promised her in a postscript, "No, I will never get The Letter written & finished. It will always need postscripts. I end one and six minutes after have to send more. All my life I must write at this Letter—this Letter of Love to the Great Woman who Came and Knew and Loved."

From the beginning her influence on him was profound. For all his occasional swagger and self-confidence, he was sensitive about his lack of a college degree, as well as the eclectic, expedient nature of his formal education. He deeply admired Paula's academic accomplishments, her facility with languages, and her intellectual powers. "You're a Teacher too—do you know?" he wrote.

> Besides Pal, in the woods—and Coach, on fletcherism, sleep, etc.—and Mate, companion, sublime woman inducing poetry . . . besides these, you're Teacher: "Forth-going," "undersong," Wunderkind, weltan-schauung, "playfellow," you put these in my head for keeps. You're a literary stylist and a pundit! While we sit idly looking on landscapes and seascapes, I shall pump you for facts . . . draw fundamentals of science & art, stray incidents, from the repository back of your forehead into mine —the yellow pages of forgotten love illumined by the gleam of your eye —you the pundit—me the pundit—boy and girl pooling all their powers.

She was not afraid to argue when they had divergent views. He regularly sent her his poems and prose in manuscript, seeking her opinion. His papers helped her to know him better, she said, "which spells—to love and love you more and more!"

Sandburg in Wisconsin and Paula in Illinois spent many solitary hours walking and thinking about their future. They shared a love for the sudden ferocity of storms. She often walked in the rain, heedless of rivulets of water on her face. He craved long, strenuous walks over the sandy "windbeaten" hills by the Wisconsin lake shore. One April night he "took a seat on a mossy, big log," lit a cigar and read aloud to Paula hundreds of miles away in Illinois. As dusk came and he rose to leave the "somber glooms" of the pine woods, he saw a single star burning in the young night sky. He named the star Paula. Back in his room in Two Rivers, he wrote to her: "Good-night, Paula, my great-heart—like the pines & stars I worshipped with to-night—Good-night, Paula—I kiss your grand face—it's a night of grandeurs—and you are its star—Paula! I kiss you as the last glory of this night of glories."

✳

Sandburg worked vigorously in his district that spring, organizing among factory workers and farmers, trying to implement Victor Berger's view that farmers were as vulnerable to the economic and social problems of the nation as factory workers, miners, railroad men and other members of the American work force, and would benefit through solidarity. Nationally, the Socialist Party had grown in membership from 29,270 in 1907 to 41,751 in 1908. Membership was on the upswing in Wisconsin, where Berger's pragmatic attention to grass-roots organization and the problems of "the here and now instead of the fine points of ideology" was winning new support and opening the door to possible victories in local elections. Sandburg and Paula watched with great interest the Milwaukee municipal elections, in which Berger and Winfield Gaylord ran ahead of the ticket in the race for alderman-at-large. Berger received 21,543 votes, and Gaylord 21,460—a fine showing for the Social Democratic Party and, with Emil Seidel's 20,907 votes, a favorable portent for years to come.

As April ended they were planning in earnest for their marriage. Paula informed her principal in Princeton that she planned to resign, and was immediately beset by doubts, not about the marriage but the timing. She was independent, self-supporting, engaged in work she loved and did skillfully. Relinquishing her job was a serious act of commitment to an uncertain future. She wondered if she had "crossed the Rubicon" too hastily and should rescind her resignation. She worried about money, for she and her brother contributed significantly to their parents' yearly income, since Mary Steichen had given up the millinery business and the little farm yielded no real profit. Had she been rash, she asked Sandburg anxiously. He scrawled a quick answer, his reassurance spilling across the page in bold black letters: "If you're going to cross the Rubican cross it! Don't stop in the middle—you'll only catch hell from both sides. Keep your head in the air. Get into the dust of the road. And if you want to sing—why, sing! sing!"

"I've done with foolishness," she answered. "The Rubicon is crossed." She was "willing to starve—to take in washing, if need be!" she teased. But she was not willing "to live the lie of separation."

✳

They began to plan a wedding "festival," "an S-S festival" with a few close friends as guests, along with their mothers and her brother, Ed— no mention of their fathers. She told him she had "always abhorred the idea of weddings—used to say I'd make the least possible noise about it—if I got married, that I'd go to a justice of the peace." She objected to society's proscription of legalities "before a marriage of hearts becomes a marriage of bodies as well."

Sandburg wanted Winfield Gaylord or Carl D. Thompson, both Congregational ministers as well as socialist colleagues, to perform a simple wedding ceremony either in Milwaukee or at the Steichen farm. He thought the farm wedding would "be a lark" and knew it would please Paula's mother. They both thought it would be fun to have the magician Joseffy there to play the violins and do tricks with Balsamo his animated skull. Sandburg had not yet told his family or Professor Wright about Paula, much less about the engagement and the wedding. He would "calmly inform" them when it was over, he said. "Merely more of the unexpected which they regularly expect." One day he would take Paula to Galesburg to meet his family. "They won't understand you any more than me—but they will love you—yes, you will be good for them," he told her.

> My mother out of her big, yearning, hungry heart will hug you before you leave and with a crystal of tears will find the soul of you. Mary & Esther and Martha will all like you deep—but they have not starved so hard nor prayed so vainly—they will get only sides of you. We should have a whole day with Wright (the Dreamer) of Asgard—he will do us a poem!

They began to save money in earnest. From the outset, Paula was the more practical one. She wanted them to have a rainy day fund and a baby fund. They knew they would live simply and frugally; they had always done that. She was not interested in trousseaus or household furnishings. "As for household goods—I say: *as little as possible!*" she declared. She preferred Oriental simplicity and design: "I have such supreme contempt for even the better class of furniture produced by our Occidental Civilization, that it will be no deprivation for me if we never *never* own a piece of it!!"

They were alike in their attitude toward possessions. "Yes," he had written, "so simple we are, so little we want, we are wise and will get what we want."

He drove himself hard that May trying to increase his income so they could enlarge the "S-S" fund. Early in the month he visited Oma and Opa Steichen at their farm. Oma greeted him warmly, fussed over him, and called him Carl, as her daughter did. Then he was off again, making socialist stump speeches and giving an occasional paying lecture. Paula tried valiantly to keep up with his schedule, posting letters to him a day or two ahead of his planned arrival in the small towns and villages of his district. He wrote gratefully from Milwaukee that he had received two letters from her in Oshkosh, ten in Schlesingerville.

They tried unsuccessfully to arrange for him to give his Whitman lecture in Princeton. They wanted another weekend together, she wanted him to meet her friends, and he wanted her to see him in action on the lecture platform. But the principal of Princeton High School at the last would not agree to engage Sandburg to lecture. Paula was furious at "these bourgeois! these conventional sticks with their sense of proprieties" who worried about the reaction Miss Steichen's pupils would have in the presence of her "betrothed." She found the principal and "his pusillanimous bourgeois heart" disgusting, she told Sandburg. Publicly, she withheld her impatience. In her letters to Sandburg she condemned the town: "Conventional on the surface—underneath, debauched, a social sink. . . . The only decency they know is Conventionality! . . . Poor poor decayed Princeton! O the pity of it!"

Disappointed that there would be no Princeton lecture, Sandburg and Paula planned to meet in Chicago in May at the National Socialist Convention, for the Wisconsin Social-Democrats had chosen Sandburg a fourth alternate delegate. Even as he plunged into preparations for the convention, he made his regular rounds of party members, trade unionists and prospective socialists, worked on election issues, and, in what would be a lifelong pattern, spent the late night hours writing. Weary but elated, he wrote to Paula at four o'clock one morning that he had been "plugging away since six o'clock last night—on the best thing I've done yet—the letter to Dear Bill—the homeliest, fairest, beautifulest piece of socialist literature, the nearest thing to Merrie England, yet done!" Modeled in part after Robert Blatchford's book on socialism, *Merrie England*, Sandburg's series of *Dear Bill* letters was published in 1909 in *La Follette's Magazine*. One was published in pamphlet form by Charles Kerr and another socialist press. The letters revealed Sandburg's political philosophy and the issues which consumed his energy as a socialist organizer. Until the nation's economy functioned so that "there will be no shirkers and all will be workers," he wrote in the voice of "a white-haired old man out in a country village," the nation would "have radicals, revolutionists, single taxers, socialists, communists, monasticists, and people with voices grown hoarse from being raised in protest." Sandburg put his own words into the mouth of his hypothetical old man:

> I have been reading history and science for forty years and from all that I have studied as to how nations are born and grow and then die, it seems

to me that just as soon as a nation gets to the point where a small part of the people are rich and a large part of the people are poor—then that nation is starting to die, the death of it is beginning. It seems to be a sort of process of slow decay and if you can't stop the process, that nation will go to its grave.

Paula was a catalyst for Sandburg's prose as well as his poetry, and he exulted in the new work she had somehow empowered. Meanwhile, she felt herself "living among shades" in Princeton, an exile, far removed from Sandburg, now the center of her life. Her place was with him, she wrote. Only with him would she be alive, at home, completely herself. Steichen sent her proofs of the photographs he had made of Sandburg in March at the farm, and it helped to see the pictures, "love them— talk to them—. . . kiss them!" She longed to hear his resonant voice, and see the lines in his face, "the tragic ones and the comic ones both." He had less time to dwell on their absence, immersed in the endless work of the Fox River district. Some of his socialist colleagues told him he earned too little to support a wife. They would "dissipate doubts and misgivings not by explanations but by actions," he reassured Paula. She was certain, too, that they could manage.

Nevertheless, they worried about money and saved all they could, hoping to have fifty dollars by their wedding day. She fretted about his health, cautioning him not to "be foolish and starve yourself to save a few dollars." He entrusted all the money to her, dubbing her the "Honorable High Turnkey of the Exchequer." He warned her to be careful how she gave him money: "I am 'a son of fantastical fortune' and a spender," he told her. "We will buy what we need. The rest goes into your hands. Now, having sent you all my money but fifty cents, I have inclination to hustle."

Paula had written to Steichen in Voulangis about her plans to marry and her concern for their parents. His career was thriving. Not only was he exhibiting and selling his work internationally, but he was masterminding exciting exhibits of modern art at 291, the innovative Little Galleries of the Photo-Secession which he and Alfred Stieglitz had founded in New York to foster and display the work of avant-garde photographers and artists. In Paris Steichen knew Gertrude and Leo Stein, as well as the Michael Stein family, who introduced Steichen to the work of Matisse. Steichen was deeply involved in arranging an exhibition of watercolors by Matisse for 291, but turned immediately from his work to reassure his younger sister about her own life. She was not to worry about money, he wrote to her:

You are evidently in a bad way as far as being in love is concerned. Prosit. Do just as your heart dictates if your good sense will permit you, and then it is sure to be all right. At any rate you have only yourself to be responsible for. Of course I will always be on hand when I possibly can to fill in the cash account on the farm. . . . The exhibition was more of a success than I had hoped and I can see my way clear for another year and of course that means that I can also take care of Ma & Pa.

Steichen liked Sandburg, and gave his full endorsement to the marriage. "Edward Steichen is an artist," Sandburg wrote to Paula in May when he saw the photographs Steichen had made of him at the farm in March. "We all know our best selves, the selves we love. And he caught a self I pray to be all the time! . . . It took more than eyes—it took heart and soul back of the eyes." They were an affectionate triangle all the rest of their lives, Paula Steichen Sandburg, her husband and her brother. Sandburg and Steichen were kindred spirits, sharing a joint artisitc vision over the long years, collaborating on projects, enjoying an exuberant friendship. Paula was the apex of that triangle, infinitely loyal, loving and tolerant, adored by both men. Sandburg called Philip Green Wright and Paula and Ed Steichen the three most important influences in his life. Steichen's photographic genius intensified Sandburg's fascination with visual art and encouraged his own experiments with "word portraits."

Like his sister, Steichen believed in Sandburg's promise. "My sister acquired a husband," Steichen wrote years later of the Steichen-Sandburg marriage. "I acquired a brother." They were not troubled in 1908 that he was a struggling political organizer and an unproven poet.

Sandburg was determined then to support his new bride himself. He refused to let her contribute her wages to their "S-S" fund. As soon as he collected his salary, he sent the money on to Paula for safekeeping. "I'm sending a five with this," he told her in a May letter. "It leaves me broke—but I can't raise money when I *have* money—and I'm going to try to have $50 or more for starting . . . if we ever save anything, ever have a good bank account or not—that's up to you, after the stuff is once in."

✳

They knew by May 24 that Carl D. Thompson would marry them, but were still undecided about where to have the wedding. Paula positively did not want wedding gifts, and thought of writing her guests that no presents would be accepted. And she most decidedly objected to wearing a wedding ring. She had given up wearing rings when she was fifteen because they seemed "relics of barbarism on a level with earrings and nose-rings!" Paula and her mother were strong, opinionated women. Between them there was an affectionate respect for the occasional need to compromise. Thus Paula listened to Mary's argument that the couple ought to wear rings. Mary had her heart set on it, she said, because the ring was "an outward and visible sign" of marriage. After all, they would be traveling together and staying in hotels. Without rings, Mary feared, their relationship would be misunderstood, particularly because they were socialists. Knowing that her mother was "more rational than the average person," Paula finally agreed that, for the good of the socialist movement, she could wear a wedding ring, no matter how barbaric she considered the custom.

She was happy to learn that men did not necessarily wear wedding rings, and sent Sandburg nineteen dollars to buy one gold band for her to wear at the wedding. She insisted on paying for the ring herself. She was the Financial Secretary, she cajoled him, knowing he would resist her plan at first. She would not allow money to be diverted from their S-S fund to buy the ring. She wanted to pay for it, but she did not want to tell Mary. "You see I *don't* want mother to know I'm buying the rings! Mother would think it very 'unwomanly' of me!"

The ring should be thin, and as cheap as possible, she told him. After all, it was not "a splurge" but "a concession to bourgeois morals—and an 'offering' to the Cause," worn to "satisfy the prejudices of the Proletariat."

In later years there was mystery about the ring. No one could remember ever seeing a wedding band that belonged to Paula Steichen. It did not appear at her wedding, and no one knew for certain whether it was ever purchased, or worn, or lost along the way. According to their family and friends, neither Paula nor Carl Sandburg ever wore a wedding ring. But just a few days before their wedding in June 1908, they were debating "the ring question," conceding Mary Steichen's point, and going a step further: "As long as we have the ring—we might as well have the one-ring ceremony if mother seems to care much about it," Paula wrote to Carl.

Paula and Sandburg shared radical ideas about love and free will. "I believe our love will outlive the stars—as you do," she wrote:

> But neither of us believes in trying to chain love with promises of eternal fidelity. We don't believe in any promises. And we know that no promises

of eternal love can make love last forever. Love *is* free: you *can't* chain it—it comes and goes freely—when it wants to go it shakes off easily all the chains that may have been put upon it and that seemed to hold it prisoner while it stayed in reality of its own free will.

These views they would keep private for now. She was not advocating free love as it was envisioned by many of their contemporaries, but "the futility of *promises* of lifelong love." To argue that question publicly, or even within the family, would distract them from their purpose, "hamper us in our chosen work." They could not confront all the world's problems simultaneously. "One thing at a time," she urged. "Socialism is *the thing* now."

They saw each other again at last in Chicago on May 15. As a member of the Wisconsin delegation to the national Socialist Party convention, Sandburg had to arrive early. Paula arrived by train after her Friday classes in Princeton, and they shared a hotel room. She was tired; "I am not at my best anyway—and shall not be this weekend," she told him demurely. He was deeply involved in the convention, but it was a joyful reunion.

The national convention convened May 10 in Brand's Hall on North Clark Street in Chicago. Glare from the big side windows and abominable acoustics led one critic to complain that a worse convention place would be hard to find. Socialist and nonsocialist journalists alike covered the convention, and delegates traveled to Chicago from all over the country to battle for the party's nomination for President. Sandburg and more than two hundred other delegates debated whether Eugene Debs, Big Bill Haywood, Carl D. Thompson, Algie M. Simons or someone else should be the party standard-bearer in the 1908 election. The fight centered on Debs, who had discouraged the nomination. His health was not good, he said, and he thought the party should support a fresher figure. He made it clear, however, that he would always do his duty, even if he had to run a third time for President. Colorful, controversial Bill Haywood, just out of prison and cleared of charges that he had murdered the former governor of Idaho, had wide early support. However, his poor performance as a public speaker, combined with a strident socialism which displeased some party leaders, effectively removed him from the race.

For Sandburg it was an enthralling week. After the lonely, frustrating work in his Wisconsin district, pitching socialism at the grass roots, he found himself part of a volatile national movement, working on committees and mingling with prominent socialists—John Spargo, Charles

Kerr, Robert Hunter, Algie and May Wood Simons, Morris Hillquit, Victor Berger and Eugene Debs himself. Paula shared Sandburg's excitement in the turmoil and purpose of the convention, chaired by Hillquit of New York. The Wisconsin Social-Democrats were highly visible. Winfield R. Gaylord headed the Constitution Committee; Carl D. Thompson chaired the controversial committee on Farmers' Programs. Elizabeth Thomas was elected to the Resolutions Committee and Charles Sandburg, fourth alternate from Wisconsin, made the important Ways and Means Committee, a credit to his success raising money in the Fox River district.

The delegates to the 1908 convention defied classification, coming to Chicago as they did from villages and cities around the nation, a coalition of diverse interests and beliefs. They disagreed adamantly on dozens of issues. Within that broad leftist movement there were extremes of right and left and many modulations of belief in between. Critic Irving Howe wondered in later years how they could all have stayed in the same party, "the stolid social democrats of Wisconsin with the fierce syndicalists of the West, the Jewish immigrant workers of New York with the inflamed tenant farmers of Oklahoma, the Christian socialists with the orthodox Marxists?"

Factions clashed daily, in every debate on every issue. Key problems —farm programs and trade unionism—prompted "a sort of battledoor and shuttlecock time of it," with "jarring" debate. "The ghost of the moribund I.W.W. seized on the convention for a last feeble stand," one observer said. All in all, however, one socialist newsman wrote, "while the rawness, impetuosity and narrow know-it-all impulse of the zealous, newly converted, crops out here and there in the debate, and quite a little misunderstanding of the broad, constructive, scientific spirit of the international movement shows itself, as a whole the convention seems to be level-headed and able to acquit itself with credit."

When the final nominating ballots were counted, Debs had the Presidential nomination for the third consecutive time. Berger and his Wisconsin delegation had voted for native son Thompson, but pledged to support Debs vigorously in the 1908 campaign. Sandburg intended to campaign with all his energy.

He and Paula were exhilarated by such high political drama. Reluctantly they told each other good-bye at the Northwestern station in Chicago that Sunday. Before she boarded her train for Princeton, she looked up into his face as if to memorize it. "Hasn't it been beautiful?" he asked her.

She corrected him emphatically. "No! *Isn't* it beautiful?"

*

Before he left Chicago, he wrote to her: "Ghosts!—Paula—ghosts around the room last night—the ghost of You—your presence—so near you are & so dear you are."

Paula was happy, sustained for the time by their "honey-sweet days" together that weekend. "The memory is so fresh and alive," she told him. "I can feel your warm breath on my cheek. I can see your clean true eyes. I can lay my head on your breast and rest—and rest." "The vivid memory of Chicago days" would tide them over during the few remaining weeks of separation while Carl was back at work in Wisconsin. "And, dear, you left some visible tokens—mementos—of wolf-tooth love! You!" She was glad, she exulted, "Glad for the unsightly blemishes! the black and blue marks!" They were "two mad feverish days together," days to "look back to and live over again." She wondered what their "real life together" would be, when there was "no feverish haste," but "time for the whole garment of love."

*

Early in their correspondence Paula had written to Sandburg about woman's dilemma, with a thoughtful perspective anticipating the modern feminist movement. She told him she saw a tragic struggle confronting the "Woman-Genius." Yet she thought "it must be glorious to be such a woman-genius these days—doing her woman's work of bearing strong children to carry forward the Movement in the next generation; and doing besides the man's work of carrying on the Movement now."

She insisted that she was no genius. In fact, people in Princeton thought her eccentric and peculiar, but accepted her as she was, she told him. She did not wear a hat, did not go to church, *did* talk socialism and radicalism. Despite her childhood ambitions to be a writer, she emphatically resolved that spring that she would never write for print. She gave him "a solemn declaration" that she would not, and held to it. She had always had "to grind every sentence out." She concluded that in literary expression, she was "about as defective" as she could possibly be. She believed she could serve the socialist cause better by washing dishes in a restaurant and giving part of her wages to the party than by trying to write socialist propaganda. "The problem of life is to find your sphere," she wrote Sandburg, "—find what you *are* qualified to do and then do it. When you're working at what you *are* qualified to do, work is a joy, though it be only sewing on buttons. But trying to do what is beyond you is sheer agony." She had great faith in her reasoning powers, but not in her powers of expression.

"Do you understand, Carl?" she asked him earnestly. "It's a serious matter. You must get readjusted to this decision of mine—this new revelation of what I am—this new self-knowledge I'm sharing with you. You *must* under*stand*. I write no leaflet. I write no review of Hunter's *Socialists at Work*. I write *nothing* for print—not *now* nor hereafter."

That said, she told him forthrightly exactly what she could do.

> Set speeches I'll be able to make—for I *have* made them. And I can lead a discussion! And I can help with correspondence. Also I'll be able to sell literature—tho *what degree* of success I'll have in this we can't tell till I actually try it this summer. But I've sold hats—so I ought to be able to sell literature about which I know so much more! and for which I feel a tremendous enthusiasm! So.—And general organization work I ought to be able to do.

This beautiful, brilliant woman tried to put herself into perspective for the man she loved. She wanted to be certain he understood; she did not want to be "a phantom girl, an illusion, a not-me." For her part, she was relieved: "To know one's limitations is a good and necessary thing for effective work in life. Now that I know what I can't do, I shall put more determination and whole-souled devotion in the work I *can* do."

✳

The feminist fervor of suffragettes and reformers, socialist and otherwise, provoked open, sometimes radical debate in those days on the topics of free love, marriage, sexuality, the respective roles of men and women, the civil rights of women and children, the problems of white slavery, abortion, abused and homeless women and children, problems as new and old as any society. Lilian Paula Steichen's vision of her womanhood sprang in part from her study of Enrico Ferri's *Socialism and Modern Science*. Her copy of the book, passed down to her daughters, contained marginal notes in her delicate handwriting. According to Ferri, it was undeniable that woman was physiologically and psychologically inferior to man. There was a Darwinian basis for that view, Ferri wrote. Woman's inferiority was a consequence of her "great biological function, maternity."

Ferri argued that "A being who creates another being—not in the fleeting moment of a voluptuous contact, but by the organic and physical sacrifices of pregnancy, childbirth and giving suck—cannot preserve for

herself as much strength, physical and mental, as man whose only function in the reproduction of the species is infinitely less of a drain."

While woman might represent "an inferior degree of biological evolution," which placed her midway between the child and the adult male
in a hierarchy of being, she deserved, according to Ferri, to exist in "a
better judicial and ethical situation." She did not deserve to be "a beast
of burden or an object of luxury." Socialism would rescue woman from
her exhaustion "in factories and rice-fields," requiring from her "only
such professional, scientific or muscular labor as is in perfect harmony
with the sacred function of maternity."

Ferri's was one of the more enlightened contemporary male perspectives of woman's place, and Lilian Paula Steichen's views were partially
derived from her reading of his work. She put her own original stamp
on her feminist philosophy, however, part romanticism, part idealism,
part pragmatism. A genuine woman, she told Sandburg, was a woman
who could love, and who was "hardy enough, intelligent enough, emotional enough to be a real mate and a real mother." She explained her
ideas in a long letter to him:

> A woman's physical organ is two-thirds destined for motherhood and
> matehood. During pregnancy and while she is suckling her child, the
> mother gives a considerable share of her vitality and nervous force to the
> child. . . . There's a week in every month when a woman's vitality is at
> its ebb—because of the functioning of motherhood-organs. One-fourth of
> the time! (think what it means in the aggregate:—if these weeks that are
> "wasted"—from the standpoint of work, that is—could accumulate so
> that one year in every four could be put down as a year of arrested mental
> development! Think what it would mean if every doctor had to stop intense
> work and rest one year in four—if every author had to take a vacation
> from *writing his best* for one year in every four!)—Of course a woman can
> think, can work during pregnancy, during menstruation . . . but the point
> is that part of her vital force is *drained away from thinking, working.* She's
> at a disadvantage compared with men. And that's the reason, I believe,
> why, on the average and in the large, women will never equal men in
> any field of *Work.* That's not saying that the sex is inferior. It's simply
> saying that man is specialized for *work*; woman for *motherhood.* To say that
> woman is inferior to man because she can't *work* as well, is as absurd as
> to say that man is inferior to woman because he can't *bear and suckle
> children.*

Paula told Sandburg that there would

> be more happiness in the world when man does more of woman's special
> function—when he approximates her *private* virtues, her power to *love*

with abandon. And there will be more happiness in the world when woman learns to do more of a man's special function—when she acquires his *public* virtues, when she learns that politics has *everything* to do with the good of her family, when she gets a social conscience, class-consciousness—and in short joins the S.D. Party!

This remarkably independent, articulate young woman was determined to have an unconventional, true marriage. "Woman must work with man—think with him—venture with him," she told Sandburg. "Then there's a comradeship and the basis for a deep and lasting love *of souls* as well as bodies."

Still it was remarkable that as soon as she discovered his uniqueness and her great love for him, she immediately decided that she would subordinate herself to his work and needs. After all, her own mother had defied the continental conventions of a wife's subservience. Nor was Sandburg exerting any pressure on Paula to conform to the typical role of the wife, for he clearly embraced her philosophy. Before they met, he had written an editorial called "Socialism and Woman Suffrage," advocating the right of women to vote because "*Woman Is the Equal of Man as a Human Being*." Though the generic woman did have equal "physical prowess," he declared, ". . . it is possible that woman, in the grand average has not the mental reach, the brain power of man." That was an opinion he would relinquish after he got to know Paula.

"We're equal, Pal!" she wrote to him. "Do you hear? Equal even tho I can't write poems!"

"What the hell do I care whether you go in for literary work or not?" he answered. "Don't we each give the other free loose for anything & everything?—We go we know not whither—All I know is you are a great woman, a splendid girl—In some way you will express yourself—*YOU decide on the way*— . . . You tell me [that] whatever way of expression I take for myself is best. What would I be to insist that I know the road of expression You should move along?" She was "great, beautiful . . . daring . . . original," he told her. Furthermore, she was "big enough to do as you damn please." And what if she could not write poetry?

Lovingly, he put her worries to rest: "I would rather be a poem like you than write poems."

✳

Sandburg did not tell his family or Professor Wright about his romance with Lilian Paula Steichen or their impending marriage. He was self-absorbed, independent and, with his family, distant, even secretive about his private life. When his sister Esther reproached him in late May 1908 for his failure to write to her, he apologized, pleading hard work. He told her he was lean from "plugging day and night for socialism and the socialist party" in Wisconsin. He gave himself to work with such intensity that he grew thin; his body seemed refined and diminished by the energy he exerted. He could concentrate wholly, to the exclusion of all extraneous people and events.

He devoted himself to Paula and socialism that spring. There was no time for anyone or anything else. He did, however, answer Esther's letter, proselytizing for socialism. Esther was a pianist; thus he thought she would understand "why almost all the great artists, painters, musicians & dramatists" were socialists or sympathetic to socialism. If she would look into socialism, he told Esther, she would find that it meant "greater art—more of music for more people."

He did not mention that he had met Paula, much less that he intended to marry her in less than a month's time. Esther asked him to meet her and Mary in Chicago for a June visit, but he said his work would keep him in Wisconsin. Instead, he urged them to come to Milwaukee for the state Social-Democratic Party convention June 13–15. He promised that they would have some pleasant hours together, although he would "have some speaking & committee work to do at the convention." He told Esther they would "meet some great people—people with fine hearts and big souls."

✳

When he snatched moments for poetry that month, he was writing poems to Paula, such as "Middle of May":

> I am young and I want you and I know you hear me calling.
> White blossom sprays on a bush, pools cool, and shadows on the
>   road,
> Raindrops on the leaves holding silver of the morning sun:
>   I am young and I want you.

In Princeton, Paula finished the work of the school year. For all her impatience with some of the elder citizens of Princeton, she loved her students. They reciprocated. On the last day of classes they filled her classroom with a "mass of flowers," covering her desk, her books, everything. Her pupils brought her bouquets of red, pink and white peonies and "a deluge" of roses.

She left Princeton for good the week of June 8, going home to the farm to prepare for the wedding planned for June 21 in Milwaukee. She and Mary planned to meet Sandburg in Milwaukee for the state convention. He had written to tell her that his sisters would be there. She looked forward to meeting them, but wished that their visit were coming a week later so they could attend the wedding.

Paula and Mary Steichen were with Sandburg in Milwaukee when his sisters arrived. They must have been astonished to learn that their brother was engaged to be married, the wedding just a week away. Independent and solitary as they knew him to be, it was in character for him to withhold personal details of his life—but they were no doubt surprised that after so many years alone, their thirty-year-old brother planned to marry at all. They immediately liked Paula and her vivacious mother.

For all the long debate about wedding plans, the event was, at the last, arranged hastily. Mary and Esther were disappointed to learn that they would miss the wedding by a week. As much as they wanted to return for the event, Mary's job would not let them. Impulsively, Sandburg and Paula decided to be married immediately so that Esther and Mary could be with them. On Monday, June 15, they hurried to the Milwaukee courthouse to obtain the wedding license, only to discover they had to apply in the bride's place of residence. Fortunately Menomonee Falls was located in Waukesha County, not far from Milwaukee. The bride and groom made a hasty trip to Waukesha, the county seat, obtained the license and a special dispensation of the usual waiting period, and returned to Milwaukee for a simple wedding at the home of Carl D. Thompson. The bride and groom asked the minister to omit the word obey from the marriage vows.

Mrs. Thompson and Mrs. Winfield Gaylord were witnesses. Mary Steichen was present, but John Peter did not make the trip into the city from the farm to attend his only daughter's wedding. Sandburg's sisters absorbed every detail so they could give the family back home in Galesburg a full account.

Charles Sandburg and Lilian Steichen, who had renamed each other Carl and Paula, were married at last in a hurried, impromptu ceremony in the Thompsons' parlor. Realizing there were no flowers for the bride, the Thompsons' small son, then four or five years old, raced upstairs in search of a bouquet for the beautiful Miss Steichen. He tore some artificial flowers from one of his mother's hats and rushed back to the parlor. A bride should carry flowers, he told her, proudly offering his gift. Paula Steichen usually hated artificial flowers, and any other artifice, but she was amused and touched by the little boy's gesture. Graciously she bent over to accept the improvised bouquet and held it throughout the quick ceremony.

They promised to love and honor each other, but not to obey. They knew they would be lovers, partners, friends, always; companions of heart, mind and soul. They had not needed a wedding ceremony to tell them that, but now it was clear to all others.

The S-S was official at last.

———— ✳ ————

1908–1909

9. Dreamers? Yes, Dreamers

Yes, we are going forward. And how long will we keep
going forward, how long will humanity continue to
advance? So long as it continues to produce dreamers.
Dreamers? Yes, dreamers. The debt of the world to its
dreamers is beyond computation.

　　　　　　　　　　—Carl Sandburg, Journal Note, 1911

T he wedding ceremony was brief because the Sandburg sisters had
　　to hurry to catch the boat bound for Chicago. The honeymoon
　　had to be abbreviated, too—a portent of years to come when
the demands of work and his innate restlessness kept Sandburg away
from home for long periods of time. It was a friend's need which took
him away from his bride after the wedding night they spent in a Milwaukee hotel. Chester Wright and the *Manitowoc Daily Tribune* had been
sued for libel. In an urgent telegram, Wright asked Sandburg to run the
paper while he stood trial. Sandburg was a loyal friend. Furthermore, he
saw in Wright's problem a "battle for freedom of the press." He trusted
Paula to understand, and left her to travel alone to the Steichen farm
while he set out for Manitowoc.

Sandburg covered the trial for the *Daily Tribune*, attacking "big business men in general and the interests which have special privileges,
notably the water and gas people." He believed they were "fighting hard
to put the Socialist editor behind bars." Businessman William Rahr had
sued Wright for libel after Wright criticized his handling of the county
fair. Even though Wright was defended by skilled attorney Daniel Hoan,
later mayor of Milwaukee for twenty-four years, the jury found the de-
fendant guilty of criminal libel. Social-Democrats pitched in afterward
to arrange a "monster lecture and dance" to raise money for Wright's
legal expenses, and he returned to the *Tribune* believing that the verdict
was part of the socialist struggle "for ultimate freedom: something to be

181

182 / Penelope Niven

endured as a part of the incentive to struggle harder and unite more firmly."

With the case settled and Wright back at the newspaper, Sandburg returned to his own work, and to Paula, joining her and her parents at the Steichen farm for what was meant to be a restful holiday. Instead, the bride and groom got a shivaree—a raucous serenade by a chorus of farmers and hired men with "cowbells, horns, tin cans and the like" who made the quiet night "hideous with discord." One of the Steichens' neighbors organized the shivaree, and everyone, including Opa, expected the groom to treat the crowd to beer and cigars. Instead, Sandburg turned the occasion into a socialist rally, and passed the hat to take up a collection for the Social-Democrats. Some of the crowd contributed, and others gave up and went home. There was "one last grand chorus of noise—a sort of infernal finale—and then a cheer for the Social Democracy."

The authoritative eyewitness account of the unorthodox Sandburg-Steichen shivaree was written by Sandburg himself. Just as socialism dominated that night, in far more serious ways it overshadowed Sandburg's poetry and his marriage for several months. His political work during the national election campaign left him very little time to write poetry. Caught up in politics, Sandburg enjoyed many benefits from his marriage and made few accommodations to it at first. Paula traveled with him some, but most of the time stayed with her parents at the farm while he kept up his peripatetic schedule. His constant travel and their limited funds made it difficult for him to take her with him. They had no real home.

At the end of July, six weeks after their wedding, Paula Sandburg wrote to her new mother-in-law in Galesburg. They still had not met, but she wanted to tell Clara Sandburg about their work and travel. "Indeed you have taken up a great work," Clara replied in lyrical, broken English. To see her letters with phrases and spelling just as she wrote them is to know her better, and to understand more about her son's achievement as an American writer. Clara Sandburg expressed herself elegantly without using punctuation, capital letters and other traditional forms: "may you be blessed with power and wisdom to hold out in your chosen position what else could be more noble and worthy," she wrote to Paula. "I am glad Charlie is not alone now he needs advise and help on one thing and another where there is love harmony and good vill and ways and means will open up for you . . . the mighty hand that helped so far is not yet too short Why should it be. the same hand that has a good work begun is able to finish."

In the hectic months before the 1908 election, the newly married Sandburgs had more work to do than they could possibly finish. While Paula's unflagging support made Sandburg's life much easier, she was quickly disillusioned about her dream of sharing fully in his work. She had not expected that there would be "any more lonely days for the S-S" after they were married, but she was clearly disappointed. "Without being together—life is simply UNTHINKABLE for the S-S," she had told him. They had talked about how they would share his work, and as they envisioned, she helped significantly with correspondence and the many practical details he overlooked in his harried travels from one small town to another. Totally caught up in his work, he had less time for the loneliness which enveloped Paula during their separations that first summer. And he had warned her: "We cannot live the sheltered life with any bars up. It is for us The Open Road."

"I can hear your voice across the hundred miles," she wrote in late summer 1908, "and I can feel your arms enfolding me—I can stroke your brow and kiss your good sweet eyes." She longed for their own home, their world together, "The world so beautiful and so good because transfused with You!" The first summer of their marriage was a blur of hard work, frequent separation and the continual love letters. "You speak to me in everything!" she told him. "When the stars shine down upon me, it is the light and love of your eyes. When leaves and flowers brush me as I pass by, it is the love-touch of your dear hands. *You* are present everywhere in everything—and everything is so good. You prove the reality and the worth of All!"

Yet much of the time he was too busy to write. While Victor Berger, Eugene Debs, Morris Hillquit and others were generals in the turbulent socialist campaign of 1908, Sandburg was a foot soldier. He very nearly wore himself out in his efforts to "agitate and educate" in his territory, as his notebooks and dozens of newspaper columns reveal. Once a week Sandburg sent off to Berger's *Social-Democratic Herald* notes for his district report. They document his labors on behalf of the party, garnering a few dollars in dues here, speaking to a handful of listeners there, recruiting new members by threes and fours.

Sandburg must have been a puzzle to the farmers and workingmen of Wisconsin as he spread the message of socialism in the factory yards at noon, in farm meeting halls or on city streets at night. He believed the movement could be all-encompassing—not only would workers under Social Democracy enjoy equitable working conditions and compensation, but they would grow in spirit. "The Socialists say frankly they want more of the good things of life for those who work," he wrote in the *Social-*

Democratic Herald. "Pictures, books, music—how many homes have these in any amount or of any quality? Men and women are 'hands' not 'souls' to the capitalist." Socialism as Sandburg saw it was both a "spiritual movement" and a "martial movement," since "the body must be decently nourished if there is to be any intellectual life."

∗

American socialism was then a multifaceted and controversial movement which brought into uneasy, often turbulent association at least "fifty-seven varieties of Socialists," as labor leader Samuel Gompers said. Shrouded in controversy, the very word generated apprehension, fear, misunderstanding and prejudice. The Communist Party of America was not organized until September 1, 1919. By then World War I had transformed socialism just as it transformed the entire pre-war world. Socialism as the Sandburgs knew it in 1908 advocated "industry of the people, by the people, for the people," drawing activists and supporters from many nations and all strata of society.

The young Sandburgs drew some perspective on the worldwide implications of the movement from their reading of British historian Thomas Kirkup's *History of Socialism* (1900). Kirkup noted that the idea was "the child of two great revolutions—the industrial revolution, and the vast social and political change embodied in the modern democracy." In 1908 there were more than three thousand socialist organizations in the United States. One of the strongest and most conservative was the Social-Democratic Party of Wisconsin, led by German immigrants with an understanding of industrial society and a working knowledge of Social Democracy. Wisconsin Social Democracy was an ecumenical movement, however, which respected all the entities it contained. There were Danish Social-Democrats and Polish socialists in Racine, and Jewish, Danish and Slavonian branches in Milwaukee, where there was a Jewish immigrant population of ten thousand, including a young woman named Golda Meyerson before it became Meir, who began her political career under the influence of the socialists. There were Finnish branches of the party in Milwaukee, Brantwood, Ironbelt, Oulu and Superior.

The German- and Austrian-Americans spearheaded the Wisconsin movement, however. Unlike Swedish immigrants who usually came from peasant stock and rural economies, the Germans in Wisconsin were often skilled tradesmen with experience in industrialized cities. German chancellor Otto von Bismarck's oppression of German socialists drove many of these skilled craftsmen out of Germany. Thousands took their politics and labor skills to Milwaukee. At the turn of the century there were

285,000 people in the city; more than 150,000 were German by birth or parentage.

The *Protokoll* of the German Social-Democrats advocated universal suffrage for men and women over twenty years of age; self-governance; free expression of opinion; free rights of assembly; equal rights for women; freedom of religion; free compulsory education, including free university education for the qualified; free medical treatment and burial; a progressive income tax. German Social Democracy organized "the frugal, hard-working and law-abiding proletariat" and sought to inspire them with the "spirit of intelligent self-sacrifice in their common cause."

Victor Berger, Austrian immigrant, teacher and journalist, was the leader of the movement to transplant those ideals to Wisconsin. The German immigrant Emil Seidel inspired others, like the Sandburgs, to believe that education was the key to the movement's success in Wisconsin. In his newspaper column Sandburg called for public libraries to stock their shelves with "a number of works on Socialism, not only for the convenience of Socialists," but for the education of those of the "upper-upper" classes who "should be made to understand that if they do not inform themselves on Social Democracy, they will never be able to fight it."

The Wisconsin Social-Democrats were patient, pedantic and pragmatic. They made shrewd use of the politics of entertainment and recreation. After all, they cared about the whole being of each man, woman and child they sought to recruit. Socialist balls and family picnics sometimes attracted thousands. Some party organizers, including Sandburg, illustrated their speeches with stereopticon slides and that new invention, the phonograph, which carried the voice of Eugene Debs into the ears of amazed working men.

In Wisconsin and beyond, the Intercollegiate Socialist Society brought vigorous political and social debate to the nation's campuses. Organized in 1905 by Upton Sinclair and others, the ISS drew members and support from a broad swath of American society—and over the years included such names as Clarence Darrow, Thomas Wentworth Higginson, Charlotte Perkins Gilman, John Dewey, Lewis Gannett, Charles Steinmetz, Jack London, Bruce Bliven, Paul H. Douglas, Zona Gale, Robert Morss Lovett and Norman Thomas.

Charles and Paula Sandburg were just two of thousands of Americans who believed in 1908 that socialism could implement the American dream. Their passionate concerns animated his oratory and news columns. He had a gift for noting the particular. "Oshkosh is such a peculiar name," Sandburg wrote after a visit there. The name rhymed so easily "with 'josh' and 'bosh,' " he wrote, "that many people think it is an imaginary place like Valhalla or the New Jerusalem." But Oshkosh was a very real place, with painfully real problems, he told his readers. There "you may see people whose teeth and jawbones have been eaten away by sulphur while they toiled in the mills of the match trust." Again, he called for education: "Millions of matches have been made in Oshkosh, but they have not given the people of Oshkosh very much light on Socialism."

✳

Sandburg grew more visible in the Wisconsin movement during the election campaign of 1908. His fiery oratory and biting news columns won him friends at party headquarters, although he felt a tension with Victor Berger that surely had to do with Berger's interest in Paula.

Sandburg was popular with farmers, workingmen and trade unionists, who were key to Social-Democratic strategy in Wisconsin. Unlike many socialist factions, the Wisconsin Social-Democrats won the trust of trade unions, to the extent that Berger's *Social-Democratic Herald* identified itself as the "Official paper of the Federated Trades Council of Milwaukee and of the Wisconsin State Federation of Labor." Sandburg's pamphlet *Labor and Politics* was widely distributed by party leaders who considered it an effective message about the party effort among unions. Sandburg wrote sympathetically of the gains made by trade unions, such as higher wages, reduced working hours and better safety measures. He deplored the vast power of capitalists over the working class.

Sandburg's many identities were dominated then by his political persona. He was a new husband, and a poet in his soul, but poet and husband were superseded by the political reformer, almost displaced by his single-minded absorption in the campaign. He moved at high speed through his district, afire with the cause. His socialist prose and oratory converged in long, dramatic, persuasive speeches. He attacked a variety of themes—the Panic of 1907, the politics of trade unions, the evils he saw in the status quo. When he was not speaking to a street corner throng, he was selling socialism man to man, doubling the membership in some local branches.

He spoke in every town, like a man possessed. Carl D. Thompson listened to him for an hour and a half and declared he had "never attended a lecture or entertainment anywhere at which such close attention was given to the lecture." Sandburg was honing his skill as a platform orator, discovering the exhilaration of captivating an audience. It was no simple feat to engage a crowd for nearly two hours, enthrall them with words

so that they stood without "a bit of noise throughout the entire address."
His zeal for socialism fused with his oratorical gifts to yield a charismatic
style. Time after time he delivered his few seasoned, stock speeches with
the fresh, seemingly spontaneous passion of the consummate actor. He
loved performing. He was hamming it up for the party, and, weary as
he was, having a wonderful time.

*

In late summer of 1908 the Marinette Chautauqua Assembly invited
speakers from the four major parties in the national election to debate
before a crowd of a thousand people. Republicans, Democrats and Pro-
hibitionists were represented, and Sandburg was the designated speaker
for socialism. "If labor will not help itself, then God help labor," he
shouted to an attentive crowd, urging them to organize, agitate, educate.
Otherwise, they would be forever "damned and helpless, tied and gagged
and laughed at." He urged them into battle, and promised it would be
"no small battle. We are bent on nothing less than capturing the government and using it for the interests of the working class." He left his
audience with a rousing plea. Only the international socialist movement
would do honor to "justice and mercy and the sacredness of humanity."

Sandburg kept up a grueling schedule before the national election.
Sometimes he used a megaphone to muster a crowd, extolling the promises of industrial democracy while balancing on top of a piano box or
the stump-speech soapbox. He would speak with equal zeal to a crowd
of twelve or several hundred, and sell them socialist pamphlets afterward.
He talked to anyone who would listen, orating until he was hoarse and
soaked with sweat.

He spoke to the Shingle Weavers' Union in Peshtigo, the Electrical
Workers' Union in Appleton, machinists in De Pere, and to hundreds
of curious onlookers who wandered in and out of his open-air meetings.
He made noonday speeches in factory lunchrooms, on the molding floor
at the Brand Stove Company, in the yard at the Schlitz Brewing Company, on corners near saloons where men ate lunch, and on street corners
wherever he could gather even a handful of listeners. Carl Thompson
reported, "The comrades say that Sandburg improves every time he opens
his face."

In the tough laboratory of the union hall, the factory yard and the
city street corner, Sandburg the orator refined the magnetic speaking
style which would support a long, successful public platform career. But
throughout the summer and fall of the election year 1908, he was only
one worker in an arduous campaign, fighting to help working people

make some sense of the economic realities governing their lives. With characteristic single-mindedness and self-absorption, he threw himself headlong into politics at the expense of his poetry, his health and his relationship to Paula.

She traveled with him when she could be a help and not a hindrance, when the schedule was not impossibly hectic and unpredictable, when there was some place where they could afford to stay, a cheap hotel or the home of other socialists. Most of the time, she had to wait at the Steichen farm, missing him terribly, swallowing her own disillusionment that they had to be apart. She busied herself with practical tasks, sewing warm flannel gowns and pajamas for the coming winter, harvesting apples from her father's orchard and mixing sweet vats of apple butter, typing Sandburg's letters and news columns, sometimes writing the column for him from notes he hastily supplied, and, always, writing him letters brimming with her passion for him, her need. Sometimes they were laced with gentle accusations, prodding him toward guilt for leaving her there while he lived in the center of events.

She had thought she was pregnant, missed two periods, and then discovered to her surprise in late summer that a baby was not on the way. She was disappointed, even though, unsettled as they were, the time was not right for children. Often she expected Sandburg to come to her at the farm, only to be left unhappy by his last-minute change of plans. Yet she understood the dynamics of the campaign and the press of the work: "I want you!—But I'm glad you promised to meet with the new local at DePere—and help start it right!—And it's great, great that you got them to form a local! Hurrah for you! For my boy!"

She had lived self-sufficiently for years before she knew him. Their courtship had roused her hopes of an ideal daily communion of work and self. It was a crushing blow to stay behind at her parents' farm, while her husband worked hard so near and yet so far away from her. The early days of their marriage made a pattern that would last. He traveled, losing himself in his work. She looked on from a distance, supporting him practically and emotionally. "I want to kiss your tired eyes and stroke your dear brow and rest your head on my breast—so—when you come home! . . . You are very near always. You can't go so far away but I can hear your foot-fall on the path just outside the door! So near you are! Carl—Heart—"

They spent a brief, unsatisfactory vacation at the Steichen farm. Her mother was ill and cross, there seemed to be tension between her parents, and Carl and Paula could not find privacy and time for themselves. They hoped that, after the election, they could settle into an apartment of their own.

Away from him, Paula found her spirits plummeting, her health suffering. He urged her to exercise at least two hours daily in the open air, and she did. "Have walked abroad my two hours today! Am returned to natural life—out-doors—etc.—You'll see how strong I'll be when you get back." Her redeeming sense of humor sometimes sustained her when his letters were scarce or he failed to come as promised. "Will you be home this Sunday? I am a-wondering. Last Sunday I looked for you— with a PERHAPS, of course—for you told me 'it depended' . . . I'm going to lay off some flesh . . . I have an unhealthy accumulation of avoirdupois! Sorry I didn't notice it sooner!"

As fall came on and the election neared, Sandburg was worn out with work. He missed Paula keenly. "The melancholy of autumn is cast over the country," he told her one day in a rare free moment. "Trees and grass and air hover with wild, somber expectancies. Something of ours, something that you and I hold high and beautiful, is interfused and kin with it." She read and reread the letter, precious because in that hectic time it was a rare, long love letter. "One tree on a wooded slope is a blaze of scarlet and brown," he wrote, "and I murmur, 'Paula.' "

> A tall slim birch lays its sheer white out across dusky, contrasting green and again I murmur "Paula." Across the dark last night . . . the lake-song swept on the wind, a restless, indefatigable song, with the plash of surf and the voices of waves—and Paula was with me, listening—and we said, "It is our song. What we hear is the vivid and reckless sea. It is the chant of our hearts, the anthem of our strivings, the oratorio that is an accompaniment of our faring-forward toward the Ideal."

✳

In September the climaxing drama of the political campaign required Carl and Paula Sandburg to subordinate the ideal of true union in marriage to the "Ideal of Social-Democracy." Eugene Debs and his Vice-Presidential running mate, Benjamin Hanford, faced formidable opponents. Democrat William Jennings Bryan had the aggressive support of Samuel Gompers. Portly Republican William Howard Taft was Teddy Roosevelt's choice of a successor.

Social-Democratic Party leader Victor Berger energized his Wisconsin troops for the finish, giving them a vision of themselves as pioneers. "We have the satisfaction of fighting in the front ranks for Socialism in the United States," Berger told his party, "not only by reason of the vote we are getting for our party and for our principles, but also because to no small degree we have to act as pathfinders and pioneers in the Socialist movement. . . . And pioneer work is very hard work." He urged them to "self-sacrifice, patience and forethought" in the face of the "dangers and hardships" they faced. It was a mark of their growing success, Berger pointed out, that their platform and methods were "beginning to get a foothold in every state of the union."

A keystone of Berger's strategy in Wisconsin was the distribution of socialist literature by "Bundle Brigades," ingeniously organized to get a "piece of socialist literature in every house every week for six weeks before every election. Such is the battle cry of the Milwaukee socialists," wrote Carl D. Thompson. Socialist tracts had to be written first, then translated into seven or more languages. Campaign literature was then meticulously distributed precinct by precinct throughout the city, the right language reaching the right household in that city which now had a population of 374,000. Each delivery was accompanied by a "good reliable comrade" to ensure that hired delivery boys did not, out of antisocialist passion, dump leaflets into the sewer.

A particularly popular piece of socialist propaganda during the fall campaign was one of Sandburg's "Dear Bill" letters, published, with Paula's help, by Charles H. Kerr's Socialist Press as You and Your Job. The letter had appeared in The Vanguard, and reprints could be ordered from the Social-Democratic Herald for ten cents each, but by fall, Paula noted that "Comrades throughout the district have said they like Dear Bill, but want a cheaper edition." Because Sandburg was frantically busy, he asked Paula to "go over that Dear Bill and get it in [manuscript] shape" for Kerr so that they could finish it together when he came to the farm for a day's rest later in the month. She made some corrections, typed the manuscript for him, and You and Your Job was soon selling for five cents a copy as part of Kerr's Pocket Library of Socialist Literature. Sandburg's pamphlet and subsequent "Dear Bill" letters were widely published. They spoke simply and frankly to working people, putting their daily problems into national perspective to show the remedies socialism offered.

Yet, beneath the propaganda of You and Your Job there was something deeply personal. Sandburg had joined past and present, drawing poignantly from childhood memories of his father's economic struggle, as well as his own daily encounters with the economic realities of 1908. His prose was spare, direct, clear, swept clean of the effusions of earlier work. He tried to make a logical, factual case for socialism, incorporating some of the rhetorical devices which served him so well in oratory—the repetitive phrase, the direct, personal question, the telling, concrete detail:

> Do you see, Bill, how your interests and mine and everybody else's are all tangled up and woven in with each other? Do you see how society, all of us together, produced Rockefeller, Thaw, and the one-legged man on the corner selling lead pencils? . . . A modern locomotive of the latest model is said to represent ideas contributed by more than eleven thousand men. . . . Our father was lucky enough to have a job most of the time, though it was a little hard back in '93 when the shops ran only four hours a day. Father worked hard and didn't get laid off, but I can remember yet that hunted, weary look he would have when he'd come home at noon, done with work for the day, and would mumble, "They say maybe we'll all be laid off to-morrow. . . ."

You and Your Job documented most of the key issues of the campaign, especially child labor, workmen's compensation and the right to work. Sandburg pointed out that "When the last United States census was taken, an army of 1,700,000 child laborers, all under fifteen years of age, was at work in this country." Socialism would be their salvation, he promised the thousands who read his pamphlet. It was orderly, constructive, not anarchistic change Sandburg promoted: "Fighting toward one end, you can send the men you choose up into the legislatures and the national Congress to write laws that will get you better working and living conditions right now."

You and Your Job reached beyond the boundaries of Wisconsin in the 1908 socialist campaign. It also formed the crux of Sandburg's campaign speeches and enhanced his visibility in the party. One reporter who covered his "ringing speech" was struck by Sandburg's "virile" delivery. He spoke that night "under the stars, in the open air," heaping indictment after indictment on the "present economic system," backing his charges with "a horde of facts" gleaned from capitalist newspapers. Only a few people knew in advance that Sandburg would speak, so he used a giant megaphone to advertise himself "with the power of his own lungs" and gathered a crowd of fifty people in less than ten minutes. An estimated 150 people drifted in and out to hear Sandburg that night, and the mayor of the town himself drove by three or four times in his buggy, "pausing to listen for a moment or two." Other buggies and two or three automobiles stopped while Sandburg attacked capitalism and preached the wonders of Social Democracy. He could go on for two hours at a time, afire as he was with the cause.

✳

Victor Berger, Carl Thompson and socialist leaders across the country predicted that Eugene Debs would win at least a million votes in the 1908 Presidential election. His campaign train, the *Red Special*, carried Debs and the socialist platform from Chicago to Spokane, Washington, and back across country to New York, a coast-to-coast whistle-stop tour of the United States. From late August until election day, Debs and his colleagues spoke to thousands of people in more than three hundred stops and in thirty-three states. For two cents a mile, supporters could ride the three-car chartered train with Debs. Local socialists joined in the speech-making at every stop.

A throng launched the train's initial departure from Chicago's Union Depot, where a fourteen-piece socialist band played "The Marseillaise" and railroad officials banned the bright red banners which decorated Debs's car, fearing that stray sparks would cause a fire. "It is impossible to describe the interest the flaming special arouses among the people," Debs told a journalist. "It is an inspiration, and the trail it leaves will blaze with Socialism that can never be extinguished." According to the national socialist press, Debs's tour was a triumph. Seven thousand people gave him a fifteen-minute ovation after he spoke in St. Paul, Minnesota. Hundreds of midwestern farmers, some carrying red banners, greeted him on horseback along the train's route. In Lead, South Dakota, miners from William Randolph Hearst's Homestake Mine got time off to join a throng of two thousand to hear Debs speak. Two thousand people marched in a parade in Duluth, Minnesota, and heard Debs say the people were "tired of the old struggle and the old strife," and "ahunger and athirst for the gospel of the coming day."

Sandburg boarded the *Red Special* in Green Bay, Wisconsin, on September 23, and traveled with the train to Manitowoc. He was elated. He wrote Paula a note en route: "All tumbled and hurried and dusty, here we are. The success of the Train has been understated, if anything. Debs is superb. Crowded houses, all kinds of enthusiasm. . . . Will sleep on the Train to-night—not very restfully, but hell, the revolution tingles and whirls around here." Paula was hungry for details, "all about the Train—and the meetings—and Debs—and the other people."

At Manitowoc, Wisconsin Social-Democrats and curious onlookers moved in a procession from the train station to Washington Park, where Sandburg and other "comrades from the train" gave street talks. The *Red Special* band gave a concert, and Debs spoke to "tumultuous applause" at a grand rally at the Turner Opera House. It was the "greatest meeting" the city had ever seen. The whole city vibrated with "the strains of Socialist music."

Sandburg was deeply affected by his brief encounter with Debs. "His face & voice are with me yet. A lover of humanity," he wrote to Paula. "Such a light as shines from him—and such a fire as burns in him—he is of a poet breed, hardened for war." He tried to express it all to Paula, and could not. "I can't talk about myself or anything tonight. . . . I am going out into the mist and winds.—A throwback from over-reaching, and being too serious, too deeply wistful—'Wanting and wanting and always wanting.' "

✳

The crush of work and travel and the loneliness of separation began to strain their young marriage that harried fall. Paula knew her husband was neglecting his health. *"Don't wear yourself out!!"* she warned. "Save your strength. Don't draw on the future. You've done that far too much already—my precious boy! Save yourself!" She hoped that after the *Red Special* they would have a few days together—but where? They still had no home of their own, not even a room. They had spent the little time they had together either at the Steichen farm or in some socialist household when they traveled together on party business. She worried about how and where they would find the peace and solitude their marriage needed.

She urged him to come to the farm anyway. Perhaps it was "impossible as a resting-place," she wrote, but she would plan things so he could rest and they could have time alone. "Early to bed—between 8 & 9," she proposed,

> and out of bed 8 in the morning—breakfast—that would satisfy Mother —Then you off to the orchard all by yourself with a few novels—and Paula. Dinner 12. Right after dinner off to orchard again—alone with novels or a hike together—Supper, very light, at 6—a short walk and to bed at 8! . . . What do you say? Shall we give the farm one more trial? . . . If we conform to meal hours, Mother will be satisfied—and there won't be that grouchiness and criticalness in the air that your nature (and mine) is so sensitive to—spoiling the rest—ruffling one all up!—

They were worried, too, about money. For all the time apart, his grueling work on the road, and her help from a distance with his newspaper notes and correspondence, he drew less than twenty-four dollars a month in salary, even at the peak of the campaign. Carl Thompson, sympathetic to the incessant financial strain facing his party organizers, offered Paula a job doing general office work for a dollar a day at party headquarters in Milwaukee, but she knew the costs of daily life in the city would exceed her earnings.

Once again, with mixed feelings, she discovered she was not pregnant. As much as they wanted children, they had no income or home for a family. She waited for him to come to her at the farm so they could make some plans for the future. They had a short reunion, and he was off again, at the center of the game while she was alone on the sidelines. He barely had time to write to her. She spent some time in Appleton with the George Foxes, looking for rooms to rent so they could be together in his assigned Social-Democratic Party district, and she could have Hopie Fox's company when Sandburg was traveling. Back at the farm, she had too many empty hours, even when she had to write up his newspaper notes because he was too busy to do it himself.

Paula had expected to share Sandburg's work and life to the full, to make a real home for them. Nearly four months into their marriage, they were still apart. "Am homesick—and homesick," she wrote. "We must have our home soon—feeling bad—No use writing." She could not summon the energy to talk to him in the habitual long letters. "This note is just to let you know that I'm not forgetting to write—simply can't write."

Then, instead of her faithful letters, there was silence. Sandburg wrote to her in alarm: "I have been sort of fumbling at times lately—groping —It is Monday evening—and I have not had a word from you since last Friday. I've thought you may be under the weather—or you sent mail to Kewaunee.—God reigns & the government at Washington lives— but I want—words, eyes, little feet—Paula!"

Two days later he wrote to her again, still trying to interpret her silence. This time he composed a real love letter, in the style of his spring floodtide of letters to her. "I don't know where you are—Paula —I don't know what you're doing. To-morrow it will be a week since I had a letter from you—I don't know what your fingers are working at nor what problems your brain is feeling its way about—But all last night your heart beat close to mine." He spoke to her of "all the great real dangers & all the great real splendors" that they had shared. "I saw you back across the years facing all the dark questions of life & always giving them answers, unafraid," he wrote tenderly, "often sad & often with high-keyed joy, but always answering, always facing them unafraid.—I remembered your low-voiced talks to me as we lay close to each other, between kisses—the rarest, highest thing I ever touched in life or work or books." She was deep and fine, he told her, "with mystic strands of

power running all thru you." "Down whatever road your soft eyes look
& your little feet go to-day," he told her, "they go with beauty and
sweetness & poise—And always and always & always I am with you and
I love you and I love you."

He closed with an apology and a promise: "Foolish and rough & often
thoughtless I have been & may be again but what there is of me—loves
and loves."

They could wait no longer to find a place of their own. They rented
three upstairs rooms at 718 Second Avenue, Appleton, Wisconsin, in
the heart of his district. Now while he traveled Paula worked contentedly.
She sewed curtains out of cheesecloth, fashioned shelves and small cup-
boards from sturdy wooden apple crates, covering some of them with
burlap, arranged the apple butter and other provisions on simple shelves.
The simplicity and frugality of their life she took cheerfully in stride. At
last they had a home of their own.

*

Eugene Debs and his *Red Special* spent the last few days before the election
in Wisconsin, the powerhouse of American socialism. The Wisconsin
Social-Democrats had organized the campaign down to the last conceivable detail. Their confidence in the outcome was "unbounded," their
prospects for victory "simply magnificent." But they were deeply disappointed. Despite the visibility of the *Red Special*, Debs received less than
half the projected million votes, just 18,000 more votes than in 1904.
Taft easily defeated Bryan and Debs. Despite the fact that official membership in the Socialist Party in America had more than doubled since
the 1904 election, the party still lost ground in certain areas.

The fact that both Democrats and Republicans ran on reform platforms
effectively defused much of the growing socialist momentum. Roosevelt
and Congress had paid attention to some of the issues raised by the
muckrakers. In 1906 the Pure Food and Drug Act had been passed, and
railway regulation was authorized under the Hepburn Act, which
strengthened and expanded the powers of the Interstate Commerce Commission. Some socialists argued that their party lost voters because labor
leader Samuel Gompers endorsed Bryan, the Republicans enacted some
socialist reforms, and unemployed workers displaced by the Panic of 1907
were unable to vote since they were away from home searching for jobs.
In Milwaukee, election results were mixed. Socialists received more votes
than in 1906, but elected fewer candidates. Their gubernatorial candidate, Harvey Dee Brown, outpolled Debs but lost the election.

For Sandburg, there was no respite from hard work after the election, or from deep anxiety about the financial outlook for the winter. His income depended on dues he collected in the Fox River district, plus any extra money he could earn writing or lecturing. In his pocket journals he kept careful accounts of dues pledged and paid—$38.10 in September, only $7.85 in October. He had burned himself out for the party, but could barely cover expenses.

Once again he was torn between purposes. His political ideals began to seem a costly luxury, since all the hard work yielded only a meager, subsistence income. He had to be practical. Perhaps he could get back to the lyceum circuit, although "monkeying with platform work" kept him from staying on top of Social Democratic Party business. There was the constant undertow of poetry, but he had little time to write, and poetry yielded no income. In his single days, he could live a vagabond life, indulging his dreams, supporting them with sporadic sales of stereographs, or other odd jobs. Now he had a wife to support. Idealism had to defer to expediency. What of Paula, working faithfully to help him in all his enterprises?

She believed in his "company of geniuses," and always she encouraged him, especially with the poetry. "The poems you send!," she wrote in those dark days. "You are the Poet, and there is none beside You!—I read and read them—and love them!—and you. You made them!" In their Appleton rooms during his absences, she lived for his work and letters, counting the days until his return from each foray out into the district—"a couple of days—and—your arms!—your eyes! your lips!" They struggled to find the emotional and financial equilibrium of their life together. Even when they were apart, she rationalized, "We both grow, when one of us grows."

As 1908 came to a close, Sandburg began to pay more attention to lectures than to politics. He ordered a hundred copies of *Incidentals* from Philip Green Wright in Galesburg, to sell after his talks were done. The shipment arrived in Appleton after he had left on a trip, and the unexpected express collect charge of seventy cents "all but broke" them financially. "Send me money, Cully—if you get hold of enough so you can spare some!" Paula stocked their pantry with fifteen quarts of homemade apple butter, whole wheat flour and unmilled wheat. She piled wood into the woodshed and made magic out of the little money they had. In a "Miracle box" she prepared nutritious food out of cheap ingredients—"dried peas are soaking in cold water overnight—to go into the Miracle box in the morning for soup for dinner," she wrote. "And you are missing all this!"

She had been briskly self-reliant before their marriage, absorbed in a busy life. Now, isolated in Appleton much of the time, she tried to explain her melancholy. She had just expected such a different life once they were married. "I have myself in hand—and am thankful for the much that we have in our love for each other which knows no barriers of time and place—instead of grieving, as I did yesterday, that our love was denied the culminating joy of actually seeing and touching each other." Consciously or not, she played on his guilt.

He wrote to her tenderly from Michigan. Somebody who heard him lecture there said that Sandburg "has either just been married or is going to be, the way he talked about love." He cherished her "tears and love and beauty," he told her. "I can't say what my heart feels—things clattering around me—but Carl knows—he knows this you fling around him—The tears of separation Monday, the bigger fresher outlook Tuesday—they were mine too, tho with such life & pictures and hustling around me, it was harder for Paula." He would be home in a week, he promised.

He was enclosing five dollars, he told her, but when the letter reached her, there was no money in it. "I hope the FIVE was not lost in the mail," she scolded gently, "for there was none enclosed in the letter. I suppose you forgot to enclose it—my forgetful Genius, You!"

Sandburg was away speaking in Michigan and Ohio, trying to reestablish himself as a lyceum lecturer. He offered three programs, "Love, Labor and Play: The Poet of Democracy," a reworking of his Whitman lecture; "Making a New Civilization," which he called a "direct, sincere, rapid-fire discussion of things that are being talked about in every city and at every crossroad in the country"; and "America and Socialism," a "fair, courteous presentation of Socialism given in the spirit of 'Come, let us reason together.' "

Who did he say he was at the end of 1908? What public image did he compose? He called himself a "thorough and eager student of humanity, a college man, a traveler, a New York police reporter, a magazine editor, a writer, and a labor agitator," as well as an organizer of the Social-Democratic Party, a delegate to the 1908 national Socialist Party convention, the author of socialist pamphlets, and a contributor to the party press. He described himself further as "a fine human character worth knowing" with "power and charm of personality."

This self-praise enlivened his lecture circular, along with tributes from others, including Elbert Hubbard. The affirmation which pleased him most came from Eugene Debs, who called him "one of the most brilliant young orators in the Socialist movement in the United States" and "a fearless exponent of the cause of truth and justice." According to Debs,

"No one who has heard Sandburg has failed to be impressed by the dignity of his presence, the force of his logic, the eloquence of his speech, and the sincerity of his purpose." From Terre Haute, Indiana, where he was recuperating at home from the campaign, Debs told Sandburg, "I remember and shall always remember the service you so freely rendered on the 'Red Special' and your fine spirit and wholesome presence."

Sandburg's prose and oratory coalesced into vigorous, confident public expression during his work as an agitator. His political and creative lives fed each other, but it was difficult to sustain either of them, beset as he was with financial worry. "We have bills!" Paula reminded him often. "We shall have to economize this winter and get things paid up and out of the way." His December income brightened the picture somewhat. He was working day and night, between his district duties and evening lecture bookings. Paula was his full-time secretary, handling correspondence and copying the "wonder poems." The politician/orator had given the poet short shrift for months, but Paula never relinquished her faith in the poems. "You know how my heart is in them," she told Sandburg, "for all-of-you is throbbing and living in them."

Her loving praise heartened him: "The Poems are great, Carl. It would be 'all wrong' to give them up. We must give the Poet every chance!" "It's only a question of time till we come into our own," she promised him. "It's all coming—dear—coming sure!" In the days of his solitary struggles, Sandburg had wrestled alone with the ten men inside himself. Now Paula helped him to affirm his complexity and multiplicity, to harness the divergent drives toward some calibration of self and work. She was sure that once he became a poet, "all the other Carls will arrive too—Orator—organizer—Terrible Kid and all the rest!"

She understood him better than he understood himself, and believed in him when he had grave doubts. "You are a Wunder-Kind in so many ways," she told him, "—so many sides there are to you! When you finally arrive (it will take you longer—there are so many of you to look after!)—but when you do arrive, what a company of geniuses you will be."

*

In February 1909, Mary Kemp Steichen wrote to her daughter's in-laws in Galesburg in her self-taught English, sharing her pride in the life Carl and Paula Sandburg had undertaken together. Like Clara Sandburg, Mary "Oma" Steichen was eloquent despite her departures from conventional spelling and punctuation. "If Lillian was [here], she would say, I was braging with my Children etc.," she wrote to Sandburg's family, "but I am just happy over them, that is all, and perhaps just a little proudt to, am onely humum, eth?" She was glad that they had a "humble but comfortable little home and are verry happy, and that is more than a grande big house." They were gypsies, however, she said, and she was "afraid the wont stay there much longer. I let them do as they please, the have to live there owne life, and learn by experience." She was right that they were gypsies. They would not stay settled in Appleton, Wisconsin, for long. They began to dream of having some land of their own, "three acres and liberty." Like her parents and like her brother, Edward, who lived in the country at Voulangis in France, Paula had farming in the blood. She thought she and Sandburg could stabilize their income if they had land where they could grow vegetables and raise chickens.

As the harsh midwestern winter enfolded them in 1909, the financial strain intensified. Sometimes when Sandburg was away lecturing, Paula spent evenings reading in the public library to save kerosene and fuel at home. She managed on one meal a day. Both of them worked as hard as they could to capitalize on his opportunities and experience. He was tiring of his district work, for after a year's struggle he could not count on a living wage. They mailed letters to midwestern chautauqua managers promoting his lectures, and a few bookings came in. As he had so many times before, Sandburg decided that he would earn extra money selling stereopticon views; then they could save money to buy land.

At home in Appleton, Paula intensified her daily economies, worked on his papers and poems, and wrote him long letters, sometimes with no idea of where to send them. She fretted about business in his district, reminding him gently of details he might have forgotten, knowing how overworked he was, not wanting to upset him. Although he did not direct it at her, she had seen his temper. She was always tactful and pacific in her discussions with him. She had watched him "rip up shirts and swear at inanimate things." Once that winter they were traveling in a buggy pulled by Fanny, her father's headstrong horse, a former racehorse. Her father delighted in giving Fanny her way, but Sandburg was more cautious. Paula praised him for being "so calm and reasonable with Fanny," half-expecting him to "swear at a horse that had got into trouble!" She confessed that she had some fears for their future chickens, who could be foolish and "try one's temper."

"But there you were, talking so gently and reassuringly to Fanny," she told him, "—doing just the *reasonable thing*—not a hint of temper— Good Sense—sheer good-sense! You're all right, Boy." " 'There's a time for swearing,' " she teased, " 'And a time to refrain from swearing' as the Preacher saith in Ecclesiastes II xii 47. It does no harm to swear at shirts. So we swear—once more—all together d—d—d—adfinitum!"

She pressed the "three acres and liberty" idea, reading every book and pamphlet she could find about "hoeing and ploughing . . . WONDER-FUL." Yet she did not want to force the idea. She simply wanted his poetry and his health to have the best support. He was an unlikely farmer, however, and the lectures were going well enough to revive his hopes of earning a living that way. Despite the hardships of traveling in winter, he found the new sights exhilarating. For him Pittsburgh was a city of "poetry and romance," with "slopes and hillsides dotted with electric lights twinkling bluish and flashing long banners of gleam along the river—and every once in a while we pass shadowy hulking sheds with yellow hell-mouths flaming—and the grim steel workers moving around like devils put to use."

He tried to support Paula's dream of a small farm, writing to her between lectures of his "love and faith—love and adoration." He offered to stop on the way home from his long February lecture tour to look at farmland in Kenosha and Racine, Wisconsin. Perhaps Paula was right about the farm. He knew they stood at a crossroads. They had given all they had to the work of the Social-Democratic Party and could barely survive on the proceeds. Political idealism had to give way to economic reality. Sandburg was heartened by Paula's unswerving commitment to "give the Poet every chance." If, as she believed, they could do that "via the Incubator-Brooder-Chick-Machine plus the Potato-Tomato-Bean-Cabbage Factory," then the least he could do was to give the "farmer" her every chance.

Ironically, they were the victims of the very economic circumstances which he attacked from the podium of the Social-Democrats. He would have to give up organizing, educating, agitating, in order to work for his own survival. It was time to "wait—and work—and pray—all in our own S-S way," she told him, and he saw that she was right.

Alone in Appleton she tried to mute her loneliness by reading about the farm she dreamed of. She managed to replace a broken "T" on their old typewriter so she could type his newest poems. She braved a snow-storm to get to the Appleton library to read *Ten Acres Is Enough*. There she saw that even in a small town such as Appleton that winter of 1909, there were homeless men and women taking refuge in the light and warmth of the public library. The "vile, stale" air of the overheated building drove her home to start a good fire "and read by the light of our good lamp," she wrote. It comforted her that Sandburg encouraged her dream, as she nurtured his. "Every day, we're a day closer to 'Three Acres and Liberty!,' " she told him, sure that their joint dreams would come true. The more she read about farming, the more she believed that she and Sandburg would love the life, "We Two—Together!"

While she delved into plans for the farm, he scouted the possibilities for lyceum and editorial work in Chicago. He sent Paula poems he wrote on the road, verses which had yet to find the vigorous directness of his emerging prose style. A few sharp, vivid lines would be quickly over-whelmed by florid language. In a poem he called "February Morning" he described the "way and will of winter," the "Finger of ice and arm of frost" with extravagant alliteration: "Silver-flung, spray shattered . . . Gleams and looms and glisters."

It was not surprising, therefore, that he had much better luck placing his prose than his poetry that year. In April 1909 his first "Dear Bill" letter was published in *La Follette's Weekly Magazine*, founded by Wisconsin congressman and governor Robert La Follette, and later called *The Progressive*. The "Dear Bill" letters were so popular that *La Follette's* provided a steady outlet for Sandburg's prose. He thought his lecture audiences would expand the market for his other prose pieces, especially *Incidentals* and *You and Your Job*, but he was disappointed, for there were not as many lecture dates as he had hoped for. Once a heavy March snowstorm "reduced the *crowd* (!) to 20 American Citizens, 3 boys, and one dog."

By April Sandburg had relinquished his job as organizer and he and Paula moved out of the Fox River district to Beaver Dam, Wisconsin, where for four dollars a month they rented the second-story rooms in a house inhabited by a carpenter and his family. The sturdy apple crates which served as furniture for the Sandburgs in Appleton functioned as moving boxes to transport their books and their few other possessions. They settled into the new quarters, full of resolve to save enough money for their farm. Paula's parents had taken a great interest in the project. Opa was full of advice; Oma wanted to experiment with some of Paula's theories on incubating chicks, but endorsed their plans nonetheless. Meantime, Sandburg concentrated on his lectures, the "Dear Bill" letters and poetry. Springtime had always been a season for selling stereoscopic views, so he canvassed the area, trying to earn extra money selling pictures from the old Underwood and Underwood kit.

No matter how hard they tried, there were not enough lecture au-diences or stereograph customers to help them produce the needed capital to buy some land. Paula was plagued that spring with a chronic and painful throat infection and had to go to Milwaukee for expensive and difficult treatment. They had to miss Esther Sandburg's graduation from Lombard College, as well as her senior piano recital in May. Sandburg was working, Paula was ill in Milwaukee, and they could not afford the trip in any case. "Dear Sister Esther," Paula wrote from Milwaukee. "I wish so much we could be with you this evening. But across the miles, we are proud of you to-night! We have great hopes for you and high expectations."

Paula said good-bye in May to Oma, who was sailing with two friends on the *Kaiser Wilhelm der Grosse* for France and a visit with Edward and Clara Steichen and their two little girls, Mary and Kate Rodina, the latter named for Steichen's friend, the sculptor Rodin. Oma had not been well, and Paula worried about how she would stand the long voyage, and how Opa would manage for weeks without her. But Oma looked forward to seeing her grandbabies and her beloved son, and having a reunion with her relatives in Luxembourg. Nevertheless she worried about Paula and Carl, her gypsies, preparing for yet another move. *Wilshire's* published Sandburg's "The Saloon Smashers" in May, and *La Follette's* would pub-lish all the "Dear Bill" letters he could supply, but that was not going to yield enough money to live on, much less buy a farm.

"The average daily wage of the American workingman is $1.44," Sandburg had written in "The Saloon Smashers." With the advent of the new eight-hour workday and a shorter work week, that came to about thirty-two dollars a month. Sandburg had been working twelve-hour days, sometimes seven days weekly, to produce an average salary of twenty dollars a month as an organizer. The erratic lecture fees helped some months, but others were bleak. "One dollar and forty-four cents a day —that is what the American workingman gets for his work," Sandburg noted in his explanation of the anti-saloon movement. Now he could speak from hard personal experience, as well as from his memories of August Sandburg's struggles and his knowledge of working people all over the country.

> Out of this sum he must buy flour, meat, potatoes, beans and prunes to nourish his body; out of this comes the rental of or the payments on his home; out of this comes clothing, boots and shoes for himself and family; out of this he must pay for tables, chairs, stoves, chinaware, and if there is anything left, carpets, pictures, books, a daily paper, and a phonograph or piano. How do we do it? Well we do it by not doing it. The average workingman does not have what he needs of even simple necessities.

Sandburg was thirty-one years old, college-educated, a published writer, lauded as a brilliant young orator by Eugene Debs. Paula was a university graduate with Phi Beta Kappa honors, rare for a woman in her time. They had dreams and expectations. But despite all their toil they did not together earn as much as the average underpaid American workingman. Dreams had to bend to reality. Thus they turned from the country toward the city, from the idealism of politics toward the pragmatism of getting ahead. In June 1909 Sandburg went to Milwaukee to try to find a job.

He found it writing advertising copy for a department store. He tried the newspapers first, but found "nothing doing at Sentinel, Free Press or Eve, Wis." A talk with the publisher of the *Milwaukee Daily News* encouraged him that in two or three weeks he might get an assignment there as a court reporter with the possibility of writing editorials. The publisher liked his "Dear Bill" letters, and "Wanted antecedents." Sandburg "confessed everything in my dark past except [that] I had been an organizer. Didn't say what my politics are. Am wondering what kind of a liar I am."

The people at Kroeger's Department Store did not like the fact that Sandburg "had no references or previous experience in store advertising," but hired him anyway. They "Took me on my bluff!" he told Paula. "It will be a better job than reporting." He would start right away as an adman earning twenty dollars a week.

Sandburg had no idea how the job would work out but urged Paula to pack their things and come to Milwaukee. He doubted that his money would hold out till she got there. "I am down to $3.00 of cash," he wrote to her, still at home in Beaver Dam. "If you can send one or two dollar bills in your next letter, well and good. It may be skimping for me by Sat. night." Nevertheless their spirits were high that June. "I miss you so, Kitty," he wrote about the time of their first wedding anniversary. "And I want you so, Kitty—But your dear great chum-heart is near me."

"Whatever comes, we are ready for it!" she answered. "It will be good whatever the future holds—as long as Paula & Carl are both alive and well!"

He settled down to work at Kroeger's, intending to be "quite a cog in the machine." He edited store news for a twice-weekly bargain circular, wrote advertising copy for six newspapers and for store window-show cards, kept advertising records. He thought the work would be pleasant enough, and he could be his own boss much of the time. He even saw certain improvements to make and thought, all in all, that it would beat newspaper work, even though it was going to be hard on his eyes. More and more often they needed treatment with eye drops and were sensitive to light.

His bosses told him they would either raise his pay or fire him within a few weeks, but Sandburg was determined to succeed. As ever, he depended on Paula's help. "I want you—you are needed—you Wonder Girl!" He wrote a short love letter during a stormy night that week alone in Milwaukee: "I want you for the sun & flowers, Paula, but I want you for the rain & the dark too."

With "lean ribs and reduced weight," Sandburg put his energy into his new job. He and Paula settled into their rented rooms in Milwaukee while he vowed to do his best for the department store advertising business. In particular, he "studied methods of direct appeal to housewives seeking bargains."

He kept the job about six weeks, but could not keep his heart in it. He was a former socialist organizer trying to promote a thriving capitalist concern. He knew he had to face reality. He could lecture and write poetry for a sideline, but he had to have steady paying work. Yet hard as he tried at Kroeger's, he was deeply uncomfortable using his gifts of persuasion to sell goods to Milwaukee housewives.

He placed the Kroeger's ads primarily in the *Milwaukee Journal*. At night he worked at home on some prose pieces and submitted six of them to the newspaper. When the *Journal* published them that summer, they were signed Armstrong, not Sandburg. He had used pseudonyms before to shield his identity. He wrestled with the problem of how to balance his political history and activism with the expediency of work at Kroeger's. He was tempted to conceal his politics, but then he could not face his comrades or himself. Ethics aside, it was surely an impossible task anyway, given his visibility in the Wisconsin Social-Democratic movement. But how could he support Paula and himself, and his poetry? Newspaper work could be an ideal solution to this economic and political dilemma, and Milwaukee had a strong, competitive array of papers.

When the *Milwaukee Journal* offered him a job, he left Kroeger's immediately to write "feature pieces" and "an occasional news-story assignment." Sandburg admired the *Journal*, the city's influential independent newspaper, and its remarkable editor L. W. Nieman. Sandburg immediately liked the newsroom atmosphere. But when he clashed with "a nervous city editor" who "had what you might call temperament, like some stage actors have," he "stepped out of the *Milwaukee Journal* one bright summer day" to take the place of vacationing editorial writer Jim Howe on the *Milwaukee Daily News*. For two weeks Sandburg filled "two full columns a day" with editorials and squibs.

From the *Daily News*, Sandburg moved to the *Milwaukee Sentinel*, and then back to the *Journal*. There he wrote commentary on tariffs, trade agreements and industrial accidents and experimented with a light news column which he called "Zig-Zags," perhaps in reference to his constant "zig-zagging toward the ideal." He filled the column, among other things, with the aphorisms he had been crafting since he discovered Elbert Hubbard. One of them captured Sandburg's mood as he wrestled with the economics of poetry: "America has many business men but no poets. The reason for this is that we are a nation of hustlers and no poet can be a hustler."

It was a curse as well as a blessing to possess so many possible selves. He was "a company of geniuses," Paula had told him. She believed more deeply than he did himself that he was first of all a poet. "All poets from Homer to Swinburne have been vagabonds, spectators of life," Sandburg wrote in "Zig-Zags." "They sat by the wayside and watched the procession go by."

He could not afford to sit by the wayside, and he had not been able to "hustle" poetry or lectures enough to survive on the income they produced. Perhaps he could be spectator and journalist, if not poet. For a time, the poetry would submerge; the poet would defer to the journalist. He stayed on as court reporter and editorial writer for the *Milwaukee Journal.*

1909–1911

10. Fugitives of Pain

I shall foot it
Down the roadway in the dusk,
Where shapes of hunger wander
And the fugitives of pain go by . . .

—Carl Sandburg, "The Road and
the End," 1908

Sandburg's boss at the *Milwaukee Journal* was a "liberal radical" who liked his style and helped him get a foothold as a journalist. Sandburg kept producing "Dear Bill" letters for *La Follette's*. Elbert Hubbard published his poem "Dream Girl" in *The Fra* in June 1909, and his essay "What Do You Think?" in August. That piece, written to inspire his lecture audiences, was reprinted in the *Denver Post* and elsewhere. Woven of notes from his pocket journals and lines from his socialist prose and speeches, "What Do You Think?" was a folksy homily to the average man and woman:

TO PITY the respectable and satisfied, and see in the heart of the jailbird
your own impulses; to be patient with the stupid and incompetent,
and chat reverently with the town fool about his religion; to give
and take no job that involves human degradation. . . .

TO SPELL Art with a capital A and enjoy paintings, poems, stories,
statues and the silent benedictions of great architecture; to love
expression; to know when to behave and when to get reckless and
forget that you're a gentleman; to hoe in the garden, split wood,
carry out ashes, get dirty and be actually useful every once in a while
if not twice; to pray and aspire and build and when you build, build
strong;

TO LIVE in a bungalow with bathrooms, music, flowers, a beautiful
woman and children healthy as little savages. . . .

His eye problems grew worse, and chronic. The newspaperman's green eyeshade, which in later years some considered an affectation, was an essential protection from bright sun and stark electric light bulbs. But newspaper work was providing a long-needed base for his instinctual work as chronicler of people and events. Even with deadlines, he had more time to study the problems he had attacked in his socialist speeches. He found he liked investigative journalism, and began to probe current issues in greater depth, underpinning with facts and statistics some of the arguments he advanced in glib, evangelical rhetoric during the election campaign. He got back in touch with Professor Wright, who was glad to hear from Sandburg "after what seemed a long silence." Sandburg sent Wright copies of his editorials and his *La Follette's* pieces.

The Social-Democrats had elected a majority on Milwaukee's Common Council in 1908, and Sandburg's party contacts paid off in his newspaper work. He was acquiring a more practical understanding of municipal politics. He undertook a leisurely and systematic exploration of social problems which might, he thought, have socialistic solutions. One of them was a major national health crisis: tuberculosis, the White Plague. Sandburg filled his notebooks with the grim facts. Tuberculosis claimed 200,000 lives a year. Socialists and others attributed the rampage of the disease to environmental and labor conditions. Sandburg discovered that sewing machine operators in sweatshops and garment factories were at great risk, along with potters, peddlers, seamstresses, wheelwrights, cigarmakers, glass blowers, boilermakers, bartenders, coopers and cabinetmakers. His research grew into an article called "Fighting the White Plague," published in *La Follette's* in October 1909.

Tuberculosis was the "one disease whose subtle, ghastly blight more than any other lowers the standards of national health," he wrote in the piece. "The bubonic plague at its worst never laid low such multitudes of victims as tuberculosis slays yearly with a wide, ruthless sickle." Contrary to what many thought, tuberculosis was no disgrace, Sandburg argued, citing a "proud and brilliant company" of consumptives—Keats, Thoreau, Chopin, Robert Louis Stevenson. He advocated education, prevention and sound common sense to combat the disease. "The important factors in a cure are a good doctor, fresh air and sunlight, good food, plenty of rest, patience and cheerfulness of mind, tenacity of will."

By late September 1909 Sandburg had left the newspaper business to join the war on tuberculosis as a full-time lecturer and coordinator of a traveling exhibit for the Wisconsin Anti-Tuberculosis Association. He was part of a "flying squadron" assigned to a whirlwind tour of Wisconsin, lecturing in forty-five cities that fall. Among other goals, they hoped to sell three million Christmas Seals in the state. Paula accompanied Sandburg to a few of the towns on his itinerary, but he usually traveled alone with an exhibit of more than two hundred posters, pictures and lantern slides. Discovering that he could not reach many people who needed the campaign because they could not speak English, he persuaded the Anti-Tuberculosis Association to provide interpreters.

Attentive audiences crowded theaters and auditoriums to hear Sandburg describe the disease and its possible cures. The free lecture and picture show was billed as "one of the biggest educational events" ever held in Wisconsin. In some towns, merchants closed stores, billiard halls and shooting galleries during the lecture. Sandburg crusaded in public schools and mass public meetings, traveled from town to town over bad roads through heavy snowstorms, and often fought illness himself as the work wore him down. As Christmas neared he gave at least one lecture daily and sometimes three, for ten days straight.

Just before New Year's, Sandburg was stranded in a crowded railroad waiting room in West Bend, Wisconsin, waiting for an overdue train. Finding a crowd of drummers, or traveling salesmen, also "chafing at the delay," he decided to entertain them. "In five minutes he was delivering an anti-tuberculosis lecture," reported a news account. The drummers and other passengers gathered to listen as Sandburg pulled out all the stops. After a rousing speech, he pasted Christmas Seals on every trunk, grip and satchel in the baggage room. Drummers told other drummers until "hundreds of traveling men" heard about Sandburg's impromptu antituberculosis lecture, and they helped boost the Christmas seal campaign with "liberal purchases." Thanks in part to Sandburg's waiting-room oratory, Milwaukee business mail was sealed with Christmas stamps from the Anti-Tuberculosis Association, which estimated that its 1909 crusade reached more than 200,000 people.

When the campaign closed, Sandburg the crusader went wearily home to "the big heart of Paula & the sweet lips and good eyes of Paula."

*

The Anti-Tuberculosis campaign renewed Sandburg's interest in the commitment the Social-Democrats gave to attacking social problems. He and Paula watched the upcoming spring municipal elections with keen interest. Soon they were deeply involved in the campaign.

In February 1910, Sandburg wrote an article for the Milwaukee *Social-Democratic Herald* to commemorate Abraham Lincoln's birthday. The short piece was revealing for three reasons: it affirmed Sandburg's commitment to the working class; it portrayed Lincoln, who became Sandburg's lifelong obsession, as a socialist, at least in spirit; and it marked the first appearance of a new byline. No pseudonym this time concealed his political history; no Americanization masked his Swedish roots. He became, once and for all, Carl Sandburg. At the same time, he tried to wrest Lincoln away from the Republicans, to make him a symbol of hope for "the common people—the working class." "Let us not forget," he wrote:

> Abraham Lincoln was a shabby, homely man who came from among those who live shabby and homely lives. . . .
>
> He came into life sad—down in the sad world of labor—labor burdened and tragic and exploited. . . .
>
> He never forgot the tragic, weary underworld from which he came—the world of labor, the daily lives of toil, deprivation and monotony. Against these things he fought. He struggled for more—more food and books and better conditions—for the workers. . . .

The Wisconsin Social-Democrats believed that the 1910 municipal election would bring them their first chance to control Milwaukee's city government. They assembled a strong slate of candidates for office, nominating Victor Berger and six others for aldermen-at-large, and for mayor the popular councilman Emil Seidel, German woodcarver and pattern-maker. The Steichens and the young Sandburgs knew and admired Seidel, and campaigned vigorously for him. In aggressive campaign speeches, Sandburg repeated the familiar motif: "Already the concentration of wealth has proceeded to the point where one-half of the citizens of the republic are homeless tenants and where . . . more than one-half of the wealth of the United States is represented at a meeting of the directors of the United States Steel Company." Only Seidel and his colleagues could save Milwaukee the graft, corruption and indifference of previous administrations, Sandburg charged. "No other way than that proposed by the Socialists will save modern civilization from the crash of disaster."

They did not get their three acres and liberty in 1910, but Sandburg and Paula took time away from the campaigning to move from furnished rooms into a little house on Hawley Road near John's Woods in Wauwatosa, a Milwaukee suburb. The house was small, plain, "almost shabby," sparsely furnished. The floors were bare, not just because carpets were expensive, but because they were more likely to breed tuberculosis, as Sandburg had pointed out during the TB campaign. Paula divided her time between politics and organizing the new house and the project she had planned for so long. She bought her chickens and became a poultry farmer. But Sandburg had little time to help her that spring, and less time for poetry. The election campaign consumed him, and he was proving himself one of the most popular and effective speakers for the Social-Democratic ticket.

✶

As the election neared, however, Sandburg's campaigning was tragically interrupted by unexpected news from Galesburg. August Sandburg died of heart failure on the twenty-second of March.

Sandburg knew his father was not well, but no one had thought the illness was life-threatening. Consequently, the death was a shock. August was nearly sixty-six years old, retired from the long, grueling years of work on the C.B. & Q. Railroad. He had busied himself as a handyman in his last years, making more money free-lancing his industry and skills than he had earned as a railroad wage laborer. The Galesburg *Daily Republican-Register* took only brief note of his death, identifying him primarily as the father of Martin G. Sandburg, the superintendent of streets in Galesburg. The funeral took place on March 24, 1910, at the house on Berrien Street. August Sandburg, a "worker on the Illinois prairie," was buried in Galesburg's Linwood Cemetery. His son Carl August did not come home for the funeral.

With just two weeks to go until the Milwaukee election, Sandburg did not break away for what would have been a long and expensive trip. His brother Martin visited Milwaukee soon after the funeral to bring Carl and Paula news of August's final illness, and of the rest of the family gathered around their mother.

At the time of his father's death, Sandburg was fighting for the rights of working people in the Milwaukee campaign, deeply committed to the nameless men and women who had come to the United States as his parents and Paula's had come, hoping to enact their dreams of a better life. Emil Seidel, far more articulate and openly loving than August Sandburg, was an avatar and champion of the working man and woman and closer to Sandburg in spirit than his own father ever had been. Sandburg and Paula had been married for nearly two years, but he had never taken her to Galesburg to meet his parents. She was far more thoughtful than he in sending letters to the family in Galesburg. There was "always a bond of understanding" between Sandburg and his mother, but there remained to the end of August's life an impassable gulf between father and son.

There is no record of Sandburg's grief or sense of loss at the time his father died, or of his reflections, if any, on their estrangement. But in

1953, forty-three years later, at age seventy-five, Sandburg wrote in *Always the Young Strangers* about his father's life. A careful reconstruction of events reveals that his facts are a little askew—his father was nearly sixty-six when he died, not sixty-four, and an accident Sandburg linked to the death occurred not months but more than a year before.

Nevertheless, his retrospective view of his father's life suggests that the son made eventual peace with whatever strife stood between them. In "Prairie Sunsets," the final chapter of *Always The Young Strangers*, Sandburg said of his father:

> It would be wrong to pity him. . . . There is a load of pathos in what I have written of him. . . . He never sought honors and had none pinned on him . . . and it seemed never to enter his mind that it would be worth while to try to be anything other than a plain honest workingman, living decently and paying his own way. . . .
>
> No glory of any kind ever came to him. . . . Yet there is an affirmative view that can be taken of his life, not merely affirmative but somewhat triumphant. . . . He was more kindly and thoughtful in the later than in the earlier years. . . . If he could see his way to board, lodging, and a roof for family and himself, that was about all he wanted. He had a hankering after thrift that was born in his peasant blood and intensified by training and pressures of need. . . . Only by comparison with the strutting fools and sinister schemers in high places, victims of nameless thirsts that will never be quenched, strumpets of fame and fortune, can I look at the days and deeds of August Sandburg and say he was a somebody rather than a nobody. . . . Peace be to your ashes, Old Man. . . .

✳

In the last days of the campaign, Sandburg campaigned for socialism day and night. Seidel had known the Steichens for years, and the more he saw of their tall, lean, charismatic son-in-law, the more he liked him. Sandburg worked tirelessly and was especially effective with Milwaukee workingmen, one-on-one or in large groups. Their support was strategic for the socialist movement as well as this landmark election. On April 5, 1910, the Republican candidate for mayor received 11,346 votes; the Democrat had 20,530. Emil Seidel with 27,608 votes was the overwhelming choice of the people of Milwaukee to be their next mayor. It was a triumph for the Social-Democratic Party.

In later years Democrats and Republicans would unite to block socialism, but they had not learned that lesson in 1910. The image of Milwaukee as a clean, progressive city had been sullied in the years of the mayor's misalliance with liquor interests, big business, utility companies. Social-Democrats smelled victory long before Republicans and Democrats smelled defeat, and when Emil Seidel became the first socialist mayor of Milwaukee, he carried into office with him a majority of the city's common council and the county's board of supervisors, as well as twelve members of the state legislature. Seidel could establish the first socialist municipal government in the nation. To the hard-working members of the Social-Democratic Party it was an "event of the first magnitude."

Socialists across the nation asserted their electoral strength in 1910, and Americans who had previously dismissed socialists as dangerous, irresponsible, anarchistic foreigners had to look again. Socialism was becoming Americanized, being tested the American way, through the existing political process. Socialists were surmounting their vast differences in background, ideology and purpose to organize election campaigns from the village to the nation, and they were beginning to see results. Eugene Debs, Victor Berger and other visionary party leaders perceived dangers inherent in their small successes, however. Debs worried that electoral progress was won by methods inconsistent with "the principles of a revolutionary party." Premature vote-getting while the party was "still in a crude state" would inevitably harm the movement, Debs believed. Berger, whose shrewd organization was at the heart of the socialist victory in Milwaukee, also recognized the dangers facing Seidel and his colleagues as they sought to translate socialist theory and campaign promises into action.

For Sandburg and others it had been a bitter campaign. Socialist Oscar Ameringer said of Milwaukee then, "Its slums were just as festering, its red-light district as foul, its justice as unevenhanded" as any of the cities the muckraker Lincoln Steffens described in *The Shame of the Cities*. "Its banks and public-service corporations were as greedy, debauched and rapacious as that of the city's neighbor, Chicago. At best the municipal government was a milk cow; at worst a criminal conspiracy to rob honest men. Gold coast and red-light district, bankster and blackmailer, pickpocket and parson, during the campaign all of them were united in the holy crusade against the 'godless Socialists.' "

Milwaukee socialists had a uniquely broad political base and Berger knew how to exploit it. Since German socialists dominated the Social-Democratic Party in Wisconsin, Seidel had been a natural choice to head the ticket. Frederick Heath, whose ancestors claimed passage on the *Mayflower*, edited the *Social-Democratic Herald* and helped to unify the more "native" American population. Polish labor leader Leo Krzycki of the Amalgamated Clothing Workers helped to solidify trade union support.

Most people, including Sandburg, thought Berger was arrogant, self-centered, pompous, stiff. Sandburg shared the public view of the man, but his private reasons for disliking Berger went far deeper, back to Berger's interest in Paula. Genial, humble Emil Seidel was another matter altogether, widely admired, even loved. Sandburg respected him deeply as a diligent worker, a fair businessman, an enlightened, humanitarian person.

While Berger and Debs were visionary, Seidel was pragmatic, so much so that left-wing socialists called his work "sewer socialism." His common sense told him that dusty, muddy streets and open sewers promoted disease; he wanted sewers to connect to the homes of workers, wanted "our workers to have pure air; we wanted them to have sunshine; we wanted planned homes; we wanted living wages; we wanted recreation for young and old; we wanted vocational education; we wanted a chance for every human being to be strong and live a life of happiness."

✳

In his first mayoral appointment, Seidel made Sandburg his private secretary. The *Journal* announced that Sandburg's salary would be $1,200 yearly. Sandburg and Paula celebrated. Sandburg invited Rube Borough to come for a visit: "I will show you City Hall. The Wonder Girl will show you 200 fluffy chicks she has chaperoned out of eggdom." Edward Steichen wrote to them, "I don't know what to congratulate you on first, the chickens or the election—I don't see how you managed to pull through the excitement of both at once and of course the chickens are all socialists—fine chickens I'm sure."

Later, aboard the *Provence* en route from New York to France, Steichen sent congratulations: "I'm sorry I wasn't in Milwaukee after the election to dig some old fossils in the ribs with an 'I told you so.'—It's great but I don't envy the fellows their job.—I only hope & wish them success! —But wonderful to think that only a few years ago—a socialist was something common & base—sort of half-criminal—The world is a great place after all."

Elated as he was at the outcome of the election, Victor Berger warned that the sight of the nation, if not the world, would be set on the Seidel administration in Milwaukee. The Milwaukee nonsocialist newspapers scrutinized Seidel's every act and word, most often criticizing him and his colleagues no matter what they did. But the Social-Democrats were determined to fulfill what Seidel called their sacred trust. He expected obstacles, disappointments, struggle, but he was, after all, a pattern-maker. While he would serve only one term as mayor, he did establish a pattern of decent, forward-looking city government that would be more fully realized in the twenty-four-year-long administration of future Mil-waukee mayor Daniel Hoan, who served Seidel as city attorney.

✳

Carl Sandburg was cast center stage in the first drama of Milwaukee socialist control. Back in Galesburg, the *Lombard Review* announced that Sandburg had "come into national prominence" through his appointment as Seidel's secretary, and predicted that he would be at "the fountain head of the administration which promises great things for Milwaukee." Sandburg plunged into the daily administration of Seidel's plans to achieve just, efficient, compassionate city government. It was an impossible agenda that the mayor outlined in his first message to the Common Council: to safeguard health, happiness and human rights; to restore honest government; to eradicate the problem of child labor and protect the rights of women laborers; to improve city transportation and utility services, streamline the budget, expand city services; to make Milwaukee a "safe place for its men and women and children, a home for its people"; to create "a great city with free, independent civic spirit"; to embody in their work the "highest ideals of humanity."

While Paula supervised her fledgling poultry business and helped with various socialist activities, Sandburg went daily to city hall, where an electric welcome sign greeted the citizens who trekked through his office in search of spoils. Inundated with requests for jobs in his new administration, an exasperated Seidel finally protested, "For the love of Karl Marx, I didn't promise every man who voted the Socialist ticket a job in the city hall."

Seidel was beset by the unrealistically high expectations of some socialists and the unfair public rebuke of some nonsocialists, as well as a generally hostile public press. His fundamental integrity made him face problems head-on, often generating conflict in the process. His enemies had a heyday over his and Berger's plan to acquire land for public parks, portraying it as a frivolous luxury rather than for what it was, an integral part of their vision of constructing a wholesome social environment to support their dreams of a healthy society.

The opposition ran the gamut from the serious to the petty. One disgruntled Milwaukee businessman sputtered, "Why, the Social Democrats eat cabbage!"

✳

Carl and Paula Sandburg settled that year into the normal domestic life she had dreamed about before their marriage. Sandburg concentrated his inordinate energy on his job at City Hall, while Paula developed her poultry business, kept house, helped her husband with party matters, and, as usual, typed and sent out his poems and prose pieces. Occasionally she visited her parents at their farm, and then it was his turn to miss her keenly: "It is just dusk. I am sitting in Juneau Park, have been writing here for an hour. It is better here than in the Lonely Room where the Little Shoes stand all in a row and empty, where the little nightie at night has nothing warm and live in it. You *must* come Thursday."

Sometime in the spring Sandburg had bought a guitar so that there would be "songs warbled and melodies whistled to the low Mexican thrumming of Paula-and-Cully's new stringed instrument." He let things go at home when she was gone: "The bungalow is all out of order. I don't eat anything at home and I am cultivating the philosophy of a lodger in a Furnished room and I am sure it will be good for you and for me when you come back. And speaking of 'coming back,' this is a very important matter and should not be neglected."

They had hoped by now to have a child. Paula confided her disappointment to her friend Elsie Caskey. "Cheer up," Elsie encouraged her. "There is plenty of time for babies bye and bye. Be thankful that you can work in the meantime."

She was working hard indeed. The *Milwaukee Journal* carried a feature story September 29: "MRS. CARL SANDBURG, WIFE OF SECRETARY TO MAYOR, FINDS PLEASURE, BUT LOTS OF WORK, WITH CHICKENS." "It is something that every woman ought to do," Paula told the *Journal* reporter. "It gets me out into the open air, and I never felt better or happier than I have this summer."

True to the plan she and George and Hopie Fox devised in Appleton, she started with an incubator and six hundred eggs, and succeeded in bringing three hundred chicks to broiler size. The work had its hazards —sleepless nights tending to eggs in the incubator, "many sorry days when little fuzzy chicks dropped dead" and the risk of other fatalities: fifteen of Paula's "carefully nurtured Plymouth Rocks and Buff Orphingtons" escaped the chicken yard to be run over by passing streetcars. The *Journal* article was accompanied by a fetching picture of the mayor's secretary's wife feeding her flock.

Paula occasionally spoke to Milwaukee women's groups. Like her husband, she offered Lincoln as an example of the true spirit of socialism.

During the campaign she told the Eighteenth District Mothers' and Teachers' Club that "If Honest Abe Lincoln, the awkward, horny-handed rail splitter, were alive today, he would be lined up with the Social Democrats in the campaign. He would feel out of place anywhere except with the labor movement struggling for better food, better clothing and better housing."

Life was exciting in the little house on Hawley Road. Family and friends came to visit. The Sandburgs had their separate work as well as their shared interest in his writing and in the work of the party. In an effort to counteract criticism from Seidel's opposition, Sandburg began to write outspoken articles for the *Social-Democratic Herald* and for Berger's propaganda pamphlet *Political Action*.

At home, after hours, he wrote about what he saw, transmuting political passion and reality into crisp prose for *La Follette's*, as well as *Political Action*, and the *Social-Democratic Herald*. Taking a particular interest in city planning, Sandburg perceived a direct link between efficiency and beauty and the welfare of the individual.

In scraps of time he worked on his poetry and found politics spilling over into the new poems, energizing them, shaping them into terse, symmetrical free-verse forms, stripped of lyricism to stark, realistic images. He was finding his subject in poetry at last, and through this burning subject, his voice. "I have seen/The old gods go/And the new gods come," he wrote in 1910 in the poem called "The Hammer":

> Day by day
> And year by year
> The idols fall
> And the idols rise.
>
> Today
> I worship the hammer.

Sandburg evoked the powerful symbolism of the workingman's tool, the hammer, with its paradoxical destructive as well as constructive force. His father's Swedish hammer had been a prized possession, an emblem of work, hope and pride. Sandburg saluted in the sparse vigor of his poem the "new god" of socialism with its commitment to working people. He was moving toward "new gods" in poetry as well, once and for all leaving the old forms and rituals behind.

Sandburg knew many politicians and few poets then. His political experience was pulling him instinctively in new directions in both prose and poetry. There was the driving need to describe what he saw before his eyes. The confluence of poetic impulse and political passion produced a strange new form on the handwritten pages which Paula then transfixed in type. Was this new work of his poetry? Paula believed so, but Sandburg could not be sure.

✳

Carl and Paula Sandburg were a visible young couple in Milwaukee in 1910. The *Milwaukee Journal* carried a profile of him with a pensive photograph:

> His viewpoint is almost six feet above the pavement and under a shag of hair that tousles around recklessly. When he talks to you he'll lean over close and use his hands much to express his points. . . . He's meandered through a good bit of the Rockies, tried his muscles in the western wheat fields and chummed with hoboes and millionaires.
>
> He has taken good money for lyceum lectures, some of which are about Walt Whitman and others of which were about this political faith. He's soap boxed and boxed others for pastime now and then.
>
> The click of the typewriter and the roll of the newspaper has lured him. . . .
>
> Sandburg is an earnest sort of chap. He can work hard and loaf just as hard when the mood hits. He loves nature, his politics and his wife.

Another writer called Sandburg "a literary genius" who was the author of "much of the good stuff that goes into the literature of the Milwaukee movement, though this is not generally known, since for some reason his name never appears in connection with his work." When Milwaukee's new City Club invited Woodrow Wilson to speak, the *Milwaukee Journal* interviewed prominent Milwaukeeans for an article called "What Leading Citizens Think of Wilson." Sandburg was one of the civic leaders interviewed. While "Governor Wilson has better stuff in him than some men who are in the national spotlight," Sandburg said, "It was very clear that Governor Wilson knows a thousand times more about businessmen and business conditions than he knows about workingmen and labor conditions."

Sandburg dressed in a handsome new tailor-made suit for his public appearances, and tried to control his thick forelock by combing his hair back and slicking it down. Nevertheless, there was "an air of informality about the new city hall crowd" and most of them were known familiarly by nicknames or first names. City Attorney Daniel Webster Hoan, destined to be Milwaukee's longtime mayor, liked to be called Dan, and "Mayor Seidel's secretary who once was Charles August is now plain 'Carl.' "

Paula, of course, was primarily responsible for Sandburg's resumption of his christened name, but it was appropriate in that pivotal year of public recognition as public servant and "literary genius" that he should feel completely free at last to establish his identity as Carl Sandburg. As a boy he had felt ostracized as the child of Swedish immigrants in Galesburg. Now he lived in a city of nearly 400,000 people, more than half of whom were immigrants. He was part of a polyglot administration with unorthodox ideas trying to reshape the American system to more fully implement the American dream. He was playing a key role in the political life of a major American city. He no longer needed to Americanize his name to demonstrate that he was an American. Never mind that he had aligned himself with a political movement that many Americans feared or scorned. He believed that his father, who had lived and died a Republican, had never achieved the dreams which brought him to America in the first place. The traditional political parties had failed August Sandburg and the rest of the working class. Sandburg was convinced that socialism, American style, would be their salvation and their future. As Carl Sandburg, he would help make the American dream come true in Milwaukee.

He summed up his political views in "A Labor Day Talk," delivered to an enthusiastic crowd and reprinted in the *Social-Democratic Herald.* Adroitly, he used the devices of parallelism, repetition, the pithy phrase and Hubbard-style aphorisms to create a spare brawny style which would characterize his journalism over the next two decades. "Prosperity for the few and hell for the many," he began.

> That's the answer. Ask us what is the matter with America, what is the matter with Wisconsin, what is the matter with Milwaukee, what is the matter with this system, where "the interests of capital and labor are identical," and that's the answer:
>
> "Prosperity for the few and hell for the many. . . ." Prosperity, luxury and magnificence for the few and death, hell, disease, misery and degradation for the many.
>
> Years ago we asked for old age pensions. . . . But the years went by, we were laughed at as agitators, and it is today as it always was—old age is a time of life to be feared.
>
> Years ago we asked for a minimum wage to apply among all workers. . . . But the years went by, we were ridiculed as impractical, and today millions of wage earners get pay so miserably low that they cannot live decently, cleanly, rightly. . . .
>
> We have learned that Labor will have to fight its own battles. From now on we trust OURSELVES. . . .

The Philadelphia Socialist Party press printed 10,000 copies of Sandburg's *You and Your Job*, calling it the "plainest pamphlet printed in America." By late November 1910 it was clear that as useful as Sandburg was at city hall, his talents as writer and speaker would be more crucial elsewhere. With six of seven daily newspapers in Milwaukee generally opposed to the Seidel administration, only Berger's *Social-Democratic Herald* could be counted on to support the far-reaching programs of the Social-Democrats. When Berger was elected to Congress that fall, Sandburg was the logical choice to take over the job as city editor of the *Herald*. Soon after the November election, Sandburg resigned as Seidel's secretary and went to work at the newspaper.

As that exhilarating, frustrating year came near its close, Sandburg was a visible journalist and propagandist, articulate and aggressive. He reported events and wrote editorials on socialist theory and municipal politics. He wrote investigative articles on graft, strikes, plant safety, the need for free public education and free textbooks. He promoted Seidel's successful programs, including the municipal dances designed "to put the low dance halls out of business" and offer decent, inexpensive recreation.

Mayor Seidel gave Milwaukee its first community Christmas tree in 1910, a festive symbol of the season and of the Social-Democratic concern for the human spirit. Seidel knew there were "many strangers within our gates who cannot be home for Christmas," and thought a tree would make them feel at home in Milwaukee. The tree was lit on a platform in the Court of Honor on the grounds of the Deutscher Club. The cold night air was filled with Christmas carols from a choir, a band and a nearby carillon.

The Sandburgs had a special reason for celebration that Christmas. At last, Paula was pregnant.

✳

Hard work and economy left Sandburg thin and haggard by the spring of 1911, and he was having serious problems with his eyes. Friends admired "the sincerity of the idealism" which animated him when he talked. Paula marched in suffragette parades that spring, despite the fact that she was six months pregnant. She was outspoken on the importance of women exercising their hard-won right to vote in the Milwaukee school board elections in March. As always, education was a cornerstone of the Social-Democratic program. "The right to vote for school directors and on school bonds is a great opportunity for Milwaukee women, and I hope they will take advantage of it," she said in a news article, where she was identified as "Mrs. Carl Sandburg, one of Milwaukee's foremost suffragettes."

Sandburg's output for the *Herald* and *La Follette's* was prolific. He kept his eyes on the individuals who forged the issues of the day, and did the best he could "writing about a page and two columns a week—hurling the shrapnel into the Daily Liars."

His family provided a gentle counterpoint to politics that spring. "We expect to have a little red, babbling heir-apparent arrive this summer, June," Sandburg wrote to Rube Borough. Long before he discovered imagism and became acquainted with the Imagist poets, Sandburg composed some vivid, innovative poems to Paula and the coming child:

Poppies

She loves blood-red poppies for a garden to walk in.
In a loose white gown she walks
          and a new child tugs at cords in her body.
Her head to the west at evening when the dew is creeping,
A shudder of gladness runs in her bones and torsal fiber:
She loves blood-red poppies for a garden to walk in.

June

Paula is digging and shaping the loam of a salvia,
      Scarlet Chinese talker of summer.
Two petals of crabapple blossom blow fallen in Paula's hair,
      And a fluff of white from a cottonwood.

One Friday evening, the Sandburgs walked to Misericordia Hospital, where the next morning, June 3, 1911, Paula gave birth to "a girl and a wonder" whom they named Margaret.

"The white moon comes in on my baby's face," he wrote that year:

. . . Her little feet will go out
On the long road from the house
One of these days.
Keep a little of your beauty
For her, White Moon,
Falling on the snow
Amid the twisted shadows.

His best tribute to his daughter came in *La Follette's* in a gentle, whimsical essay synthesizing many of the ideals for which he had struggled in politics, particularly equality for women. He called the piece "My Baby Girl":

Only seven days ago I saw her writhe and take breath, heard her first plaintive cry to her first morning in the world.

And when I walked away from the hospital in early gray daylight and a fresh rain smell in the air, treading the blown-down and scattered catalpa blossoms under my heels, I had above all else a new sense of the sacredness of life. A grand, original something the full equal of death or first love or marriage as an experience, this I knew I had touched. . . .

All that day and the next, however, I was compelled to draw on my resources of patience and humor. The remark of a startlingly large number of my friends was:

"Too bad it's a girl."

Sandburg discovered in those few days after the baby Margaret's birth that most parents wanted their first child to be a boy. "And so," he wrote,

> while a few understood my joy, some actually took it as a half-grief, a kind of sorrow, and commiserated [*sic*] me:
>
> "Too bad it's a girl."
>
> Thus at the very start of life, prejudices and dispreferences follow the footsteps of one sex as against another. . . . Tonight however, as I hold in my arms for a few moments, this new-come beginner in the game of life, I think I would as lief be this baby girl as any man alive.

Paula was elated, and, from the first, supremely, sensuously maternal. In mid-July she took the baby to the farm to visit her parents. She loved waking to nurse Margaret before dawn in the "Gray World of mists & shadows," felt that to nurse her in those quiet gray hours was to "harken back in memory to the dim beginnings of things." She found that a baby "makes you live again."

✳

By fall 1911 Sandburg's byline and his accounts of Milwaukee socialism were going out to a national audience. He took a much-needed vacation, joining Paula and the baby at the Steichen farm for "fruit season" to help make apple butter and put up the abundant yield from Opa's garden so they would have what they needed "when the wintry winds blow cold in January." With extra money from some of his articles, they splurged on a twenty-five-dollar "dandy" Victrola. Sandburg found it deeply relaxing to lie down, listen to music and rest his weakening eyes.

The autumn was mellow, a generous harvest in more than one way. He was once and for all Carl Sandburg, husband, father and writer, putting on letters and manuscripts the bold, confident signature which became his trademark. He was grappling with the important political and social issues of his time, using his voice and his typewriter to defend the platform of Wisconsin Social Democracy and to articulate his own views. Years earlier his mentor Philip Green Wright had advocated the power of being both dreamer and doer. Sandburg sought to be both.

Always, the poetry haunted him. In the quiet hours at home, while Paula cared for the baby Margaret, or both mother and child slept, he kept working at his poems, late into the night after the day's work was done, stripping away one after the other the conventions he had admired and imitated in established, traditional poets. All of his life was spilling over into the poetry. His politics permeated the poems, hard reality forged the images, his baby daughter and his wife found their lyrical way into the gentler lines. He was coming to believe that everything was matter for poetry. The primary influence by then, of course, was Walt Whitman, who was Sandburg's poetical and biographical obsession long before he committed himself to Abraham Lincoln. He had lectured on Whitman's idealism and his work since 1903, revising his lecture as he continually discovered new facets of the man. Consciously or unconsciously, he was becoming Whitman's American poet, beginning to write about "the conventional themes," the "stock ornamentation," without "legend, or myth, or romance, nor euphemism, nor rhyme," but giving "ultimate vivification to facts, to science and to common lives." Sandburg had praised Whitman as the Poet of Democracy, reminding audiences in little prairie towns and midwestern cities of Whitman's pledge: "Without yielding an inch the working-man and working woman were to be in my pages from first to last."

Even more than his sprawling, confident form and his vast, cosmic subject, Whitman's theory of democratic poetry affected Sandburg's vision and helped to shape his work. In later years Sandburg destroyed or withheld drafts of most of his early poems, but in 1916 he put some of them in *Chicago Poems*. "The Road and the End," first entitled "Lands and Souls" when Elbert Hubbard published it in *The Fra* in August 1908, conveyed the essence of Sandburg's early life and echoed Whitman's image of the traveled road:

> I SHALL foot it
> Down the roadway in the dusk,
> Where shapes of hunger wander
> And the fugitives of pain go by.
> I shall foot it
> In the silence of the morning,
> See the night slur into dawn,
> Hear the slow great winds arise
> Where tall trees flank the way

> And shoulder toward the sky.
>
> The broken boulders by the road
> Shall not commemorate my ruin.
> Regret shall be the gravel under foot.
> I shall watch for
> Slim birds swift of wing
> That go where wind and ranks of thunder
> Drive the wild processionals of rain.
>
> The dust of the traveled road
> Shall touch my hands and face.

Like Whitman, Sandburg began to explore past journeys on "the traveled road," validating his own soul, his own past as subject for poetry. "Broadway" recalled his 1902 sojourn in New York:

> I shall never forget you, Broadway
> Your golden and calling lights. . . .
>
> Hearts that know you hate you
> And lips that have given you laughter
> Have gone to their ashes of life and its roses,
> Cursing the dreams that were lost
> In the dust of your harsh and trampled stones.

Chicago Poems concludes with a section called simply "Other Days (1900–1910)," a cluster of the early poems he was willing to publish. Some of them are pensive with themes of loss:

> . . . Dreams, only dreams in the dusk,
> Only the old remembered pictures
> Of lost days when the day's loss
> Wrote in tears the heart's loss.
>
> Tears and loss and broken dreams
> May find your heart at dusk.

Others are taut portraits of working men and women. In "Old Woman" the poet looks from the window of a streetcar late at night:

> The headlight finds the way
> And life is gone from the wet and the welter—
> Only an old woman, bloated, disheveled and bleared
> Far-wandered waif of other days,
> Huddles for sleep in a doorway,
> Homeless.

But one poem is a striking summation of all Sandburg was learning from his own experience, poetic and political. There is in "I Am the

People, the Mob" a confluence of Whitman and Sandburg, to be sure, but there is above all the authentic ring of Sandburg's emerging voice and style:

> I am the people—the mob—the crowd—the mass.
> Do you know that all the great work of the world is done through me?
> I am the workingman, the inventor, the maker of the world's food and
>   clothes.
> I am the audience that witnesses history. The Napoleons come from me
>   and the Lincolns. They die. And then I send forth more Napoleons
>   and Lincolns.
> I am the seed ground. I am a prairie that will stand for much plowing.
>   Terrible storms pass over me. I forget. The best of me is sucked out
>   and wasted. I forget. Everything but Death comes to me and makes
>   me work and give up what I have. And I forget.
> Sometimes I growl, shake myself and spatter a few red drops for history
>   to remember. Then—I forget.
> When I, the People, learn to remember, when I, the People, use the
>   lessons of yesterday and no longer forget who robbed me last year,
>   who played me for a fool—then there will be no speaker in all the
>   world say the name: "The People," with any fleck of a sneer in his
>   voice or any far-off smile of derision.
> The mob—the crowd—the mass—will arrive then.

Sandburg's tone was somber, cynical. This was no celebration of the mob, the crowd, the mass, but an admonition, growing out of his political experience. Yet the passion and realism transmuted from politics into poetry revealed to him the kind of poetry he must write. His love for Paula gave him the same authenticity. Whitman's lines and themes helped Sandburg configure some of the love poems he composed for Paula then, but his passion for her transformed Whitman's influence into his own discovery:

> Paula
>
> Woman of a million names and a thousand faces,
> I looked for you over the earth and under the sky.
> I sought you in passing processions
> On old multitudinous highways
> Where mask and phantom and life go by.
> In roaming and roving, from prairie to sea,
> From city to wilderness, fighting and praying,
> I looked. . . .
>
> In the hammering shops I stood,
> In the noise of the mad turmoiling,

In the clanging steel and grime and smoke
And a dreariness numb of hand and brain.
To a heart where hope fought hard for life
You called from out of the years ahead,
Woman of a million names and a thousand faces.

When I saw you, I knew you as you knew me.
We knew we had known far back in the eons
When hills were a dust and the sea a mist. . . .

You are the names of all women who are and have been,
    Your face is the sum of all faces. . . .
And the wrongs and shames and shattered dreams
Are explained and gone like the yesterdays. . . .

Sandburg was growing toward a poetry as unorthodox and independent as his politics. He had learned from his study of Whitman that "first-class" poems "grow of circumstances and are evolutionary." Like Whitman he drew subject matter and vision from "these incalculable, modern, American, seething multitudes around us, of which we are inseparable parts!" He was discovering his own poetic style and subject in the raw material of his vibrant daily life. From those circumstances his poems were evolving. He was becoming a truly original poet, a pioneer using the tools of realism and free verse to explore the American dream.

He was fascinated with the transitory nature of language. He had lectured on the evolution of language in "Black Marks" on the lyceum circuit. Now, searching for his poetic identity, he contemplated the subject in a poem entitled "Languages":

There are no handles upon a language
Whereby men take hold of it
And mark it with signs for its remembrance.
It is a river, this language,
Once in a thousand years
Breaking a new course
Changing its way to the ocean. . . .

He was not concerned with the future, as "Languages" reveals. His was the poetry of the here and now. Thus Sandburg the poet chose to

Sing—and singing—remember
Your song dies and changes
And is not here tomorrow
Any more than the wind
Blowing ten thousand years ago.

PART II

THE CHICAGO YEARS

———————— ✳ ————————

1911–1914

11. This My City

And they tell me you are brutal and my reply is: On the faces of women
and children I have seen the marks of wanton hunger.
And having answered so I turn once more to those who sneer at this my
city, and I give them back the sneer and say to them:
Come and show me another city with lifted head singing so proud to be
alive and coarse and strong and cunning.

—Carl Sandburg, "Chicago," 1914

S andburg the dreamer watched with growing disillusionment as political realities fractured the Social-Democratic ideal in Milwaukee.
Emil Seidel and his administration were hamstrung from the first
by the Wisconsin home-rule law, which severely constricted municipal
autonomy. Republicans, Democrats and the Milwaukee capitalist press
attributed the failures of the Social-Democrats to their doctrine rather
than to the obstacles they faced, thus obscuring Seidel's earnest efforts
to implement his campaign promises.

With municipal and national elections looming in 1912, Congressman
Berger, Mayor Seidel and other Social-Democrats, including Sandburg,
believed a daily newspaper would be an essential weapon in the campaign.
Sandburg used his column in Berger's weekly *Social-Democratic Herald* to
muster support for such a paper, urging readers to contribute whatever
they could to raise a hundred thousand dollars to finance the paper,

convinced that it would be "one of the most smashing, hammering, effective guns the American Socialists could have." With nearly half the money produced by the sale of ten-dollar bonds, Victor Berger founded the *Milwaukee Leader.* The first issue appeared on December 7, 1911. Chester Wright, cartoonist Gordon Nye, Emanuel Julius and Sandburg joined the staff, and Sandburg was assigned as labor reporter and columnist.

His inordinate physical stamina enabled him to carry several jobs at once. He chaired the resolution committee at the 1912 convention of the Wisconsin State Federation of Labor. He lavished energy on the newspaper, covering labor and socialist issues and writing a column called "Bunts and Muffs." He continued to write free-lance articles, selling his prose to *New Idea, La Follette's, The Woman's Magazine,* and other periodicals. Paula typed the poems he hammered out in scraps of time, and sent them to magazines. They had far more luck selling prose than poetry. His articles brought ten dollars, even forty dollars. The poems came back with rejection notes, although some editors encouraged him to send future work. As his byline appeared more often in regional and national journals, A. M. Simons, then editor of *The Coming Nation,* remarked that Sandburg had "made good beyond his expectations."

Milwaukee Republicans and Democrats resolved to oust Emil Seidel in the 1912 mayoral election; consequently, they organized the Nonpartisan Party, a coalition which Sandburg scornfully christened the Nonpartisan Rebunkocrats. The concerted strength of the Non-partisans overwhelmed Seidel on April 2, 1912, by 43,174 votes to 30,272. In defeat, Seidel still had three thousand more votes than in his victory two years earlier, Sandburg pointed out in his newspaper column. Had there been a "three-cornered" election instead of the overpowering coalition of "Rebunkocrats," Seidel would have won, Sandburg believed. He saw in Milwaukee socialism "some kind of a new rebellion—a steady, level-headed, common-sense insurrection of the workingmen." He argued that opponents of socialism failed to grasp that "back of all politics are the conditions of human life, the price of bread and meat, the hours that men stand on their feet and break their backs at productive toil, the terrible power of an employer to take away a man's job and thrust him suddenly into the street, the ever-present threat of a miserable old age without money or work or strength for work."

In May, the Socialist Party national convention in Indianapolis nominated Debs to run a fourth time for President. Emil Seidel was nominated for Vice President. The bitter struggle for national control aligned Debs against Berger, Morris Hillquit and John Spargo, whose politics grew out of a theoretical, middle-class vantage point rather than the raw experience of the working class championed by Debs and Seidel. Sandburg supported Debs. Although he worked for Victor Berger's newspaper, Sandburg did not respect many of Berger's political positions. His long, personal dislike for Berger aside, Sandburg thought he was wrongheaded on many issues, and "an insensitive old fogie" as well. Berger thought Sandburg should concentrate on socialism and journalism rather than poetry, which he called "downright foolishness." In any fray between Berger and Debs, Sandburg's allegiance went firmly to Debs.

Long before the election, Sandburg left the *Milwaukee Leader*. He was fed up with political and economic turmoil; angry that Berger's newspaper, supported by the labor unions of Milwaukee, did not maintain a closed shop; and stung by quarrels within the Milwaukee socialist movement. The movement to which he had given himself for four years was replete with strife, and Seidel and his dreams had been defeated at the polls. Berger and Debs were at odds. The *Leader's* position on the rights of working people looked, in retrospect, hollow and hypocritical, given the labor problems in the newspaper shop. As long as the socialist dream flourished, Sandburg and Paula could withstand financial stress and political tension. But now, politically and economically, Milwaukee exacted from them more than they were willing to give.

With Paula's support, Sandburg decided it was time to leave Milwaukee. A pressmen's strike had shut down all Chicago newspapers except the socialist *Chicago Evening World*, which planned immediate expansion to fill the void. Chester Wright and other socialist journalists were headed for Chicago, and Sandburg decided to join them. The chance for a newspaper job in Chicago seemed tailor-made for him, and he took it —immediately. Paula and year-old Margaret waited behind to be sure Chicago would be "a go."

The upheaval of the last months in Milwaukee left Paula tired and nervous, but she rested at her parents' farm that summer. Margaret flourished there, Paula said, "exploring the paths in Opa's garden— plucking the silken petals of poppies (her favorites)." Paula and Carl looked forward eagerly to their reunion, and to settling down in Chicago. They rented an apartment on North Hermitage Avenue in Ravenswood, a northwest Chicago neighborhood. Sandburg moved in and waited for his family to join him. "Now it is only a couple of days till we again maintain our establishment," he wrote to Paula, "a really truly home. And unless some over particular people rake up the leaves, it will be a fine yard for a homecoming celebration." He still wrote poetic letters to her:

It's been mystically wonderful lately, that backyard, with a half moon through the poplars to the south in a haze, and rustlings . . . on the ground and in the trees, a sort of grand "Hush-hush, child." And as the moon slanted in last night and the incessant rustlings went on softly, I thought that if we are restless and fail to love life big enough, it's because we have been away too much from the moon and the elemental rustlings.

✳

The *World* was surrounded by competition once the pressmen's strike was settled that fall. In November Sandburg joined his colleagues in an effort to unionize news writers at the paper, but a week later their paychecks bounced and the *World* began to fold under the weight of its own expansion. By December 1912, with his family barely settled in Chicago, Sandburg was out of a job, walking the winter streets, looking for work.

He tried to get on the *Chicago Tribune* and newspapers there and in other cities, applying for any job he heard of. He had been broke before and often, but he had been younger then, not encumbered with responsibility. Now he had a loyal wife who never stopped believing in him, and who deserved a stable income. He had a child. His discouragement grew as the weeks wore on. There were few people in the whole city of Chicago to whom he could turn "for even a very small loan." Day after day he searched for any kind of work. He and Paula called the struggle their "Dark Period." Paula remembered it many years later as the "only really hard part" of their lives financially. They endured, Sandburg said cryptically, "tribulations various and unique at that time."

Early in the new year he found a job at last. The man who hired him was Negley D. Cochran, editor of *The Day Book*, an innovative Scripps tabloid which took "no advertising and therefore tells the truth." A tall man with dark eyes and a kind face, Cochran was a political and social reformer as well as a good journalist and editor. He moved to Chicago from Toledo, Ohio, to run *The Day Book*, which lasted from September 1911 to July 6, 1917, when the wartime economy closed it down. *The Day Book* appeared six days a week in two daily editions selling at first for a penny and then for two cents, and achieved a circulation of 24,000 paid customers. Cochran and Scripps held to the idea that "a really free press must be wholly free from dependence on advertisers." Independence was the key word in Cochran's office: *The Day Book* ranged freely over international, national and Chicago concerns, expressing fervent, often audacious views, most of them liberal if not socialist. Sandburg took to the zesty freedom of the little paper published in cramped basement quarters on the corner of Congress and Peoria streets.

For the most part, Sandburg could write what he pleased about subjects he chose, and he came to a deep, lasting respect for Cochran, who had, he said, "a humility like that of the finest Quakers, and a reverence for life like that of certain Catholics." For all the lack of orthodoxy at *The Day Book*, Cochran was a careful editor whose influence on Sandburg's writing was profound. He said Cochran "pounded it into my poor head for five years straight that there is no 'uncolored news,' " a premise which served both Sandburg the newsman and, later, Sandburg the biographer. He came to believe that "probably the best single course of instruction" he ever had as a writer was with Negley Cochran.

The job there paid twenty-five dollars a week, and he was glad to have it. He covered city politics, crime, labor issues, "the splits and cross-sections of the Socialist and labor movements." At home at night in the little flat on Hermitage Avenue he and Paula fell into a routine which sustained him through many years of hard work. After the day's salaried job was finished, he worked for hours late into the night on poetry and prose. Chicago was a powerful stimulus. He still worked alone, far from any school or salon of poets, crafting an unorthodox style which suited the realism of his subjects.

He spent some of those winter nights writing two articles on industrial accidents which he submitted to *System: The Magazine of Business*, a leading trade journal for administrators, salesmen and factory managers. *System's* editor, Daniel Vincent Casey, bought his articles and offered him a job as associate editor of the magazine for a wage of thirty-five dollars weekly. The raise was significant, and Sandburg took the job. He was defensive about it, however, and regularly used the pseudonym R. E. Coulson to sign his articles on the high cost of government. He signed his own name to pieces on accident prevention and industrial efficiency. He was sensitive to the apparent contradictions: He was a socialist writing for a capitalist trade journal. He was a poet turning out specialized prose on technical subjects. The pseudonym concealed his political as well as literary identity.

"You might say at first shot that this is the hell of a place for a poet," he wrote to Reuben Borough, urging him to come to Chicago, "but the truth is it is a good place for a poet to get his head knocked when he needs it. In fact, it is so good a place for a healthy man who wants to watch the biggest, most intense, brutal and complicated game in the world—the game by which the world gets fed and clothed—the method of control—the economics and waste—so good a place is it from this viewpoint that I think you will like it."

Sandburg's life centered on work and family. Margaret was a precocious child whose golden curls and shining eyes her mother and Uncle Edward captured in charming candid photographs. Paula, as always, served as mentor, audience and typist for Sandburg's poems. In early spring, secure in the new job at *System*, the Sandburgs decided to have another child. Paula and Margaret spent part of the summer at the Steichen farm so that Paula could rest, with her mother's help, and Oma and Opa could enjoy Margaret. The separations were difficult for all three Sandburgs. "Margaret wailed 'Come back, papa,' even in her sleep last night!" Paula wrote from the farm. "Sweetheart, I'm real lonesome for you."

As always, she reminded him of the chores which so often escaped his notice. He was to water the fern and pay the gas bill. Her practical letters were answered with loving notes:

> Dearest: The moon is shining down into the house and there's romance here to-night. I have just carried water out and sprinkled handfuls on the fern and poured a rich supply on the roots and the moon's yellow caught in the drops. Yes, there's romance around here tonight. The memories looking backward and the expectations calling from ahead shape up this romance around the place. Love—love—to the Sweethearts from the House here, The Home that's a'calling and a'calling you.

Sandburg was not completely happy at *System*, but it was a regular job on one of the largest business journals in the country. He concentrated on poetry at night, transmuting daily experiences into unruly poems he wrote out by hand on newsprint. The exuberant optimism of earlier times had been muted by his years of struggle, yet he still looked for the best, extracting poetry from the most difficult as well as the most mundane experiences. His poems were "generally written first in a pocket notebook at or near some storm center downtown in the daytime. They are then rewritten at night," he said. "This applies to those of street and action. Those of rest and nature are generally done on hikes or in loafing spells out of doors."

His job did not fulfill him, and there were growing signs that his *System* bosses were not happy with his work. Paula and the poetry sustained him, yet the poems they sent out to magazines kept coming back. That summer *American Magazine* rejected one of his newest and best, a rugged free-verse poem modeled after some American Indian poetry he had been reading. He called it "Chicago." He was dejected, but Paula's cheerful conviction that they "must sometime succeed" helped him go on.

Paula was always his anchor, and he delighted in their bright-eyed daughter, whose profile was so like his own. They looked forward to the birth of the new baby. Because Margaret's birth in the Milwaukee hospital had been easy, Paula thought a home delivery would be safe for the second birth. She engaged a homeopathic physician of good reputation. When Paula went into labor one November day, Sandburg stayed at home with her and the doctor was summoned. Their second child, a girl, did not survive the birth. "I could see the doctor killing the child right before my eyes," Paula remembered, "and there wasn't anything I could do. I couldn't speak, but I could see he wasn't doing the right thing." Sandburg neither knew how to help nor fully comprehended what was happening. Whatever the doctor failed to do for the infant, she died before her parents could hold her. The Sandburgs were torn with grief over the death of the child they were going to name Madeline.

Haunted by their loss, Sandburg expressed it in poems. "I am singing to you/Soft as a man with a dead child speaks," he wrote in the later war poem "Killers." In *Smoke and Steel* in 1920 he published this elegy, a poem called "Never Born":

> The time has gone by.
> The child is dead.
> The child was never even born.
> Why go on? Why so much as begin?
> How can we turn the clock back now
> And not laugh at each other
> As ashes laugh at ashes?

✳

Their world seemed to collapse that autumn of 1913. To the burden of personal grief was added the truth that his job was coming to an end. It had been a difficult metamorphosis from socialist activism and radical poetry to capitalist efficiency. His superiors at *System* saw that more clearly than Sandburg himself. Reluctantly they told him he did not have "the habit of thought nor the method of approach to work which would enable" him to "develop fully in this organization of ours." Sandburg's boss told him, "It seems to me that your imaginative qualities and abilities lead toward the poetic rather than the selling." F. M. Feiker, who had helped hire Sandburg, told him as he fired him, "I sincerely want to see you in a place where you can develop yourself to best advantage. It is my opinion that you cannot do this in our organization. Consequently I feel that you ought to get into another line as soon as possible."

He had spent much of his life searching for that place, that "line." Now he had lost another job. His poems had failed, time after time. He and Paula carried the grief and some guilt after their baby's death. Worn and bereft, he set out once more to look for work.

He found a stopgap job at *The American Artisan and Hardware Record*, editing the small trade journal for the "Stove Tin Hardware Heating and Ventilating Interests." Using the pseudonym Sidney Arnold, he wrote a column called "Random Notes and Sketches," commenting ironically, ostensibly about hardware interests: "To be original is a hard job. Very few of us are truly original. The man who fails when he tries to be original has many companions. There is a wide army like him. . . . To be pleasant and sincere should not be so hard. Not near as hard as to be original. And it pays."

In Milwaukee, Sandburg had been a visible, successful politician and journalist, and secondarily a poet. Now, in Chicago, he was doing hack work on a hardware journal to pay his bills, barely getting by. Ironically those circumstances both forced and enabled him to give more time to poetry. At home at night, he worked doggedly at the growing collection of poems, stopping only when his weak eyes would hold out no longer. He could pour his anger and pain into the poems, compress them to burning intensity.

In Chicago he wrote with new commitment, making poetry out of the city, its crowds of nameless faces, its buildings and statuary, its industry, crime and suffering. He made poems out of his own sense of failure and loss. Working alone late into the night, with no friends or mentors there who were poets, no audience other than his wife and his own need, he was experimenting, and before he knew the term or the theory, crafting some poems very like those the Imagists would make famous. He brought sorrow into the poems, the loss of their child, the pervasive losses which define the human condition. He wove anger into the poetry, and the frustration of failure.

Much of the poetry was somber with the inevitable progression of losses at the core of life. "Oh things one time dust, what else now is it/ you dream and remember of old days?" he wrote in "Dust." In "At a Window" he wrote what was a recapitulation of his life:

> Give me hunger,
> O you gods that sit and give
> The world its orders.
> Give me hunger, pain and want,
> Shut me out with shame and failure
> From your doors of gold and fame,
> Give me your shabbiest, weariest hunger.

But leave me a little love,
A voice to speak to me in the day end,
A hand to touch me in the dark room
Breaking the long loneliness.
In the dusk of day-shapes
Blurring the sunset,
One little wandering western star
Thrust out from the changing shores of shadow.
Let me go to the window,
Watch there the day-shapes of dusk
And wait and know the coming
Of a little love.

In that thirty-sixth winter of his long struggle, Sandburg worked painstakingly over the unorthodox shapes and subjects of the poems. His subjects were living every day before his eyes—worn shopgirls, day laborers, once-hopeful immigrants. He wrote the incessant poems in longhand, and Paula typed them neatly, regularly dispatching them to magazines and journals. Undaunted when they were returned, she sent them out over and over again. Sandburg tried the eastern magazines he admired, hoping to find an audience in New York for the poems he himself knew to be so unconventional in style and subject that they might not be considered poetry at all.

Sometime in that winter of 1914, he and Paula decided to send the poems to an ambitious, fledgling Chicago magazine, not quite two years old, with fewer than fifteen hundred subscribers. They had been reading the magazine since its first issue in 1912, but Sandburg wondered how long it could last. He noted later that there was "a little clairvoyance about the launching of it, because it marked a departure from a long period in which the writing of poetry had had a few very well standardized styles." Perhaps this strange little magazine would pay attention to his own unconventional style.

The magazine had an experimental, adventurous spirit. He and Paula would try the poems there. They chose several to show the spectrum of his work, and the small parcel of poems went to 543 Cass Street, the home of Harriet Monroe's *Poetry: A Magazine of Verse.*

✳

The *Poetry* office was emblematic of Harriet Monroe's gentility and enterprise. The spacious front room of a renovated mansion on Chicago's Near North Side accommodated two desks borrowed from her landlord and patron James Whedon; some comfortable wicker chairs and a Wilton carpet loaned by her sister; and her own antique French colored-marble clock which sat on the white marble mantel under a gilt-framed mirror. Here Harriet Monroe entertained, nurtured and guided her poets, "some living in comfort, some writhing under the burdens of life, some strictly in the rag tag and bobtail, some with querulous and vagrant minds who for all the benefits she conferred would sometimes turn and curse her."

With unrelenting tact and energy she cultivated the patrons who supported her magazine with yearly pledges ranging from ten to a hundred or more dollars. The nucleus of financial support came from a hundred prominent Chicagoans, each pledging to give her fifty dollars a year for five years. She had conceived the design for the first American magazine to be exclusively devoted to poetry as she traveled on the Trans-Siberian Railroad in 1910. She spent more than a year in polite, persistent visits to Chicago patrons of the arts to raise the money she needed. In the Chicago Public Library she searched out books and periodicals to identify famous and novice poets alike who might contribute to her magazine. She dispatched a circular letter describing her plans to more than fifty American and British poets—Floyd Dell, Arthur Davison Ficke, Vachel Lindsay, John Lomax, Amy Lowell, Edwin Markham, James Oppenheim, Ezra Pound, Edwin Arlington Robinson, Louis Untermeyer, Edith Wharton, John Hall Wheelock among the Americans; and British poets John Masefield, Harold Monro, Alfred Noyes, Ernest Rhys and William Butler Yeats, among others. She sought to foster a new vitality in the art of poetry, to "search out and assemble" exciting poets, and to "find the necessary public for them."

Monroe was the daughter of a prominent Chicago family whose fortunes had suffered after the fire of 1871. She supported herself by writing art criticism for the *Chicago Tribune*. A poet herself, her most conspicuous work was her "Ode for the Columbian Exposition," commissioned largely at her own instigation for the sum of one thousand dollars (no more "extravagant" than the fees paid to sculptors, architects and painters for the great world's fair of 1893) and read to the throng by actress Sarah Cowell Le Moyne on the day in October 1892 when the partially completed World's Columbian Exposition was dedicated. Harriet Monroe's brother-in-law John Wellborn Root had been the fair's consulting architect; she wrote his biography after his sudden death in 1891. She had worked actively for the promotion of the other arts in Chicago, and believed that poetry was the badly neglected "stepchild" of the art world. She combined her passion for poetry, her social connections and her indomitable energy to launch her magazine and sustain it until her death in 1936.

She was fifty-two in 1912 when *Poetry* was launched, a spinster who lavished affection on her poets, gave them unstinting support and honest criticism, and was probably in love with at least one of them. An unremarkable poet herself, she was a remarkable advocate of poetry and champion of poets. Mourning her death years later, Sandburg observed that her magazine "marked an embarkation into a period that would see more widespread, furious and reckless adventure and experimenting across twenty years than had been known in two hundred years before."

From Whitman she took her motto for *Poetry*, printing it on the journal's back cover: "To have great poets there must be great audiences too." She and her small, largely volunteer staff set out to bring poets and audience together. Her associate editor was poet and critic Alice Corbin Henderson, blond, blue-eyed, with a disarming wit and intellect and an astute critical sense. Harriet Monroe called her a "pitiless reader of manuscripts." It was she who screened the growing numbers of poems submitted to *Poetry*. Volunteer office girl was the poet Eunice Hammond Tietjens, who came to *Poetry* still grieving for the death of her first daughter and the breakup of her marriage to composer Paul Tietjens, who wrote the score for the musical version of *The Wizard of Oz*, which he and the book's author, L. Frank Baum, produced in Chicago. Eunice Tietjens was tall with luminous dark eyes, a poet from a creative family. Her mother was an artist, her sister a musician, her brother the inventor of the Hammond electric organ. Her own poems had first been published in *Poetry* in 1913.

Alice Corbin Henderson opened the envelope containing the poems from unknown Carl Sandburg. She and Eunice Tietjens shared an instant enthusiasm for the unconventional "sweep and vitality" of the poems, and immediately urged Harriet Monroe to publish them. The poems startled Monroe at first with their unorthodox form and their range from brutality to misty lyricism. Perceiving their "freshness and force and originality," she chose nine for inclusion in the March 1914 issue of *Poetry*, calling them "Chicago Poems" and giving them the lead.

Sandburg had been fortunate in the guidance he received from Philip Green Wright and other male mentors—Sercombe and Triggs at *To-Morrow*, Elbert Hubbard, Seidel, Cochran. But all his life he had been nurtured by women. His mother quietly trusted his unorthodox choices in life; Louisa Schwartz encouraged him during his milk route days to make something of himself; during and after his college days Amanda

Kidder of Lombard facilitated his oratory. He had unflagging support from Paula, who had resurrected the poet in him and sustained that part of his nature when he himself lost faith in it. It was entirely fitting, therefore, that Sandburg the poet should be launched by women: Alice Corbin Henderson, who discovered and affirmed the poems which made their way to Cass Street; Eunice Tietjens, who encouraged the poetry and the man; Harriet Monroe, the *Poetry* crusader herself, who became his champion.

The Sandburgs were elated. There was celebration in early March when they received a check for seventy dollars for the poems. At last Sandburg's poetry had paid—nearly three weeks' salary for nine poems.

Their lives were transformed that spring. Sandburg left *The American Artisan and Hardware Record* to return to Negley Cochran and *The Day Book*, where he could work as a journalist and use his own name. He stepped with gratitude and some awe into the fellowship of poets who frequented the *Poetry* office. He and Paula found themselves abruptly transported from the prolonged dark period into a bright circle of lively, artistic people. In late February they eagerly accepted Harriet Monroe's invitation to a landmark literary event.

✱

The great Irish poet and playwright William Butler Yeats was coming to Chicago for a week of lecture engagements. He had accepted Harriet Monroe's invitation to be her house guest and the guest of honor at a banquet March 1. Monroe told Yeats that his appearance under the auspices of *Poetry* would confer recognition on her attempt, "not unlike your efforts for the Irish Theater, to create and perpetuate beauty among us." Yeats had contributed poems to *Poetry* in its first year; his "The Grey Rock" was awarded the Guarantors' Prize of two hundred and fifty dollars as the best poem published in *Poetry* during its inaugural year. Monroe had raised a hundred dollars for a special second prize to her protégé Vachel Lindsay for "General William Booth Enters into Heaven."

Yeats acknowledged the honor, declining all but ten pounds (about fifty dollars) of the prize money. He asked that the rest go to a young American poet who could use the encouragement and the money, in particular *Poetry*'s foreign editor Ezra Pound. From Stone Cottage in the Ashdown Forest in Sussex, Yeats had written Monroe: "I suggest [Pound] to you because, although I do not really like with my whole soul the metrical experiments he has made for you, I think those experiments show a vigorous creative mind." Yeats said that he "would always sooner give the laurel to vigorous errors than to any orthodoxy not inspired."

At the time of that letter, Yeats and Pound were sharing Stone Cottage for three winter months, as they would do for three years. Pound, already vividly idiosyncratic at the age of twenty-eight, was trying to teach Yeats fencing and to engage him in Pound's new Imagist movement. Yeats was introducing Pound to spiritualism and astrology. In his supreme self-confidence, Pound set out to criticize and occasionally revise the work of Yeats, who was twenty years his senior and already firmly established as a great poet. Yeats was sometimes irritated by Pound's advice, but told his friend Lady Gregory that Pound's criticism had given him new life, helped him write with new confidence, "to get back to the definite and concrete away from modern abstractions." Yeats considered Pound an excellent critic, although sometimes a "very bad" poet, and together they introduced Harriet Monroe to the work of some of *Poetry*'s most significant "discoveries"—Rabindranath Tagore, H.D., Robert Frost, James Joyce, and William Carlos Williams.

✳

Carl and Paula Sandburg and the other guests paid $2.50 for tickets to *Poetry*'s first banquet on March 1, 1914, at the Cliff Dwellers in Orchestra Hall. It was a lustrous evening. Sandburg had been working despondently for a trade journal, practicing his craft as a poet in literary isolation. Suddenly he was an honored guest in a company of poets, dining in the presence of one of the world's great poets. Sandburg was, Tietjens wrote, "a tall, somewhat gawky Scandinavian, always badly dressed, always fomenting in spirit. But there was in him a passion or sympathy for anything downtrodden or hurt and a vitality of the spirit which made everyone love him."

When Harriet Monroe heard that Paula had no evening gown, she loaned her one. Sandburg sat down to the banquet that night with his beautiful wife, part of the fraternity of poets whose work was affirmed in *Poetry*. There were other names and faces he recognized—Mr. and Mrs. Joseph Medill Patterson of the *Chicago Tribune* family; businessmen, architects, judges, Congressman Morton D. Hull, university professors, William Morton Payne of the *Dial*, poets Maxwell Bodenheim and Arthur Ficke, Harriet Vaughn Moody, widow of the poet William Vaughn Moody, who opened her home to artists and became a particular friend of the Sandburgs.

With his reporter's eye Sandburg studied the company he had been invited to join on the strength of his poems. He listened, making notes as a seasoned reporter, as Yeats talked about poetry and praised the native American work of Vachel Lindsay. Working as he had for so long in isolation, Sandburg was deeply moved to hear the great poet speak of poetry with a vision kindred to his own, a vision shaped in part by Yeats's discourse with Ezra Pound. Yeats advocated stripping everything artificial from the rhetoric and diction of poetry, getting "a style like speech, as simple as the simplest prose, like a cry of the heart." Yeats cited as an example of the ideal one of Sandburg's favorite poets, François Villon, insisting that the poet's business was "to express himself, whatever that self may be." Yeats challenged his select audience that night to "encourage American poets to strive to become very simple, very humble. Your poet must put the fervor of his life into his work, giving you his emotions before the world, the evil with the good. . . . Poetry that is naturally simple, that might exist as the simplest prose, should have instantaneousness of effect, provided it finds the right audience." Furthermore, Yeats observed, "A great many poets use vers libre because they think it is easier to write than rhymed verse, but it is much more difficult."

Sandburg then listened enthralled as a strange young poet from Springfield, Illinois, stood up to read his new poem. As Vachel Lindsay recited "The Congo" in his haunting voice, Sandburg recognized a poet who, like himself, merged the cadences of poetry with the rhythms of evangelical oratory. Lindsay, too, was a troubadour, a vagabond poet. They would become good friends.

Harriet Monroe deemed the evening a triumph for Yeats, for Lindsay, for *Poetry* and for Chicago. For Carl and Paula Sandburg it was unforgettable, a "highspot" evening in their lives, the culmination of his years of work on the poems, and her unswerving faith in the poet.

Harriet Monroe had orchestrated a splendid evening, but she neglected to have a stenographer present to record Yeats's speech. She and Alice Corbin Henderson tried to reconstruct it from memory so they could print it in *Poetry*. Sandburg gave them his notes. "Here are the words of Yeats as I was best able to get them," he wrote Miss Monroe on March 5. "He has a way of occasionally slipping his syllables along in a most delightful Irish burr that leaves a reporter with his pencil in the air wondering what in the divil [sic] the Celtic Playboy has just been saying. The desperate thing about getting a good record of what he says is the fact that he is a wizard of accuracy in speech and shadings of thought."

✳

In high spirits, Sandburg approached journalism and poetry with new vigor that spring. He and Negley Cochran at *The Day Book* enjoyed a deepening mutual respect. In addition to the stability of his modest salary there, Sandburg had wide latitude to cover events and topics which interested him, predictably labor, socialist and reform matters. Eagerly he awaited the March issue of *Poetry* which would publish his poems, along with work by Sara Teasdale and Edwin Arlington Robinson. His poetry would appear in the magazine which had contained the work of Yeats; Pound; the great Indian poet Tagore, who had won the 1913 Nobel Prize for literature; Joyce Kilmer ("Trees"); and Robert Frost ("The Code").

Harriet Monroe discerned trends in poetry with the help of her volatile foreign editor, Ezra Pound, whom she had yet to meet face-to-face. She had first read Pound's poetry on her long 1910 journey on the Trans-Siberian Railway. From England, he sent her his own poems and poems by other Imagists, along with "gay and peremptory and violent letters, the vivid and slashing articles, the loud praises and protests. . . ."

She did not confine her vision to America poets. In addition to Yeats, she had published D. H. Lawrence and the Bengali poet Tagore, who offered her "Gitanjali" in 1913 before he won the Nobel Prize. Patriarchal in gray beard and robe, he visited the *Poetry* office during a trip to Illinois to see his son, a student at the University of Illinois in Urbana. There was room in the spacious purview of *Poetry* for established poets such as George Sterling, Ernest Rhys and Madison Cawein, and newcomers such as Pound's protégé H.D., and the then-unknown John Reed. Harriet Monroe sought out Vachel Lindsay. She published Witter Bynner and Francis Thompson. At Pound's urging she published William Carlos Williams in 1913, rejecting the first group of poems he submitted but accepting the others with forthright criticism. One poem needed revision, she told Williams, adding that it did not appeal to her as much as it did to Pound, but "his word goes a long way and I should like to see the poem again when you have given it your last touch." She and *Poetry* got off on the wrong foot with Robert Frost, recognized in England before he was known in America. She rejected the first poems Frost sent over from England, but gave him another reading, at Pound's insistence. "I don't doubt that the things Frost sent you were very bad," Pound wrote to Monroe from abroad in 1913. "But he has done good things and whoever rejected 'em will go to hell along with *Harper's* and *The Atlantic*."

*

Even Harriet Monroe found the opening lines of Sandburg's "Chicago" "a shock at first," but she "took a long breath and swallowed it." She was also "laughed at scornfully by critics and columnists" when the poem appeared as the lead in the March issue of *Poetry*:

> Hog Butcher for the World,
> Tool Maker, Stacker of Wheat,
> Player with Railroads and the Nation's Freight Handler;
> Stormy, husky, brawling,
> City of the Big Shoulders. . . .

"I was influenced by Indian poems while writing 'Chicago,' " Sandburg said later; "I wrote it in the office of *System*, a business magazine, in 1913." The bold, concrete imagery and parallel "chants" evoke oratorical devices, too: "They tell me you are wicked . . . /And they tell me you are crooked . . . /And they tell me you are brutal." "Chicago" contains a symmetry clear to the eye by its arrangement on the page, and to the ear in its sweeping cadences, meant to be spoken, to be heard. In the context of the softer, more lyrical figures of conventional poets of that period, his vivid similes and metaphors were abrasively original: the city was a "tall, bold slugger," "Fierce as a dog," "cunning as a savage." The city, in a unifying personification, was a brawny, bareheaded young man, alive, coarse, strong, cunning, shoveling, wrecking, building, laughing —a bold, sweating young man alive with the pulse and heart of the people. There was a closing unity and symmetry in the repetition of the opening lines.

Amy Lowell and others noted the alternating virility and tenderness in Sandburg's free verse. "Chicago" was juxtaposed to the impressionistic, imagistic lines of "Lost," with its gentle, lyrical simile:

> Desolate and lone
> All night long on the lake
> Where fog trails and mist creeps,
> The whistle of a boat
> Calls and cries unendingly,
> Like some lost child
> In tears and trouble
> Hunting the harbor's breast
> And the harbor's eyes.

Having painted that view of the city's harbor, Sandburg recast it in the harsher light of irony in "The Harbor," where homeless, hungry women huddle in the desolation of the dark city near the "blue burst of lake." There birds fly free in the open, their bright freedom a counterpoint to the captives of hunger in the "huddled and ugly walls" of the city.

In each of the nine poems, the free verse form was spare, the mood somber, the structure unified by the rhetorical device of repetition. Although he was not in touch with the Imagist movement, Sandburg achieved in the poem "Jan Kubelik" the economy, clarity and cadence which Pound and the Imagists advocated. The short lyric was composed "in sequence of the musical phrase, not in sequence of a metronome." The lines moved fluidly, without rigid endings, letting the "beginning of the next line catch the rise of the rhythm wave," as Pound believed should be the case.

Eunice Tietjens reported that Sandburg's poems "roused a veritable storm of protest over what was then called their brutality. Many Chicagoans were furious at seeing the city presented in this, to them, unflattering light, and Harriet received many complaints." The critical response was swift and diverse. "Chicago" was the magnet for most of the controversy, with the *Dial* leading the attack on the "hog butcher" school of poetry. "The typographical arrangement for this jargon . . . creates suspicion that it is intended to be taken as some form of poetry," the *Dial* sniffed, "and the suspicion is confirmed by the fact that it stands in the forefront of the latest issue of a futile little periodical described as a 'magazine of verse.' " The *Dial* found "no trace of beauty in the ragged lines" of Sandburg's poem, which "admits no aesthetic claim of any description, and acknowledges subordination to no kind of law."

In the May issue of *Poetry*, Harriet Monroe gave a spirited defense of Sandburg and all her poets in an editorial called "The Enemies We Have Made," noting that "Next to making friends, the most thrilling experience of life is to make enemies." Her "most outspoken enemy," she said, had been her "orthodox neighbor *The Dial*." She continued, "It is possible that we have ventured 'rashly' in 'discovering' Mr. Sandburg and the others, but—whom and what has *The Dial* discovered? We have taken chances, made room for the young and new, tried to break the chains which enslave Chicago to New York, America to Europe, and the present to the past. What chances has *The Dial* ever taken? What has it ever printed but echoes?"

In particular Harriet Monroe had taken chances with poets who wrote in the new idioms of Imagism and free verse, who broke old barriers to construct new forms and songs with a democratic freedom of style and subject. Sandburg had been working far removed from the theory and practice of Ezra Pound in London, but he was after the same elusive outcomes of expression—personal rhythms which fit the expansive sweep of his subjects rather than constricting them into conventional meters, for his subjects were unorthodox in themselves.

Sandburg sought to use the living language of modern speech and vernacular, not a pale or archaic classical language. He sought what Harriet Monroe described as the "hard clear style" of the Imagists with the elimination of "every unnecessary word, every unstructural ornament." Yeats and Emily Dickinson in their unique ways had achieved economy and intensity in poetry, paring the art to its essence. Whitman's extravagance of form had launched the free-verse movement in the United States. Sandburg was indebted to Whitman, but would carry free verse further than Whitman or Pound into the public arena of the general audience. Pound in London made profligate use of free verse, but filled it with esoteric, classical themes which spoke to quite another audience than the one Sandburg had in mind. Pound condescended toward the "mass of dolts." Sandburg celebrated the mob. His "hog butcher" school of poetry with its commitment to democratic subjects and themes would eventually reach the people, the proletariat, the very subjects of the poems themselves.

No matter that the *Dial* critics and others found his work barbaric, brutal, offensive to traditional poetic sensibilities. Sandburg the poet was launched.

∗

He reveled that spring in the company of new friends at *The Day Book* and in the *Poetry* circle. Often after work, Sandburg stopped by to sit in the poet's wicker chair and talk with Harriet Monroe, motherly and attentive; effervescent Eunice Tietjens; and Alice Corbin Henderson, whose charm left others unprepared for the thrust and parry of her wit. There were lively discussions of poetry and art, especially if the overseas mail had brought one of Pound's long, provocative, often abrasive letters, brimming with brilliance and energy, and taking the staff of *Poetry* to task for a variety of literary sins.

Poets from all over the country began to think of the *Poetry* office as "a kind of headquarters of the art," and the *Poetry* staff welcomed them all, stopping their work to talk and listen. The wicker armchair was a modest throne for a procession of poets, from Tagore to Lindsay, "who came swinging in from the wide spaces, his chin up, his curly sandy hair rampant over a beetling brow and deep-set blue eyes. There he would 'boom out' his poems in a rich, strange voice which 'shook rafters.' "
Arthur Davison Ficke came by, like Edgar Lee Masters a lawyer as well

as poet. His role as mentor and intimate friend of Edna St. Vincent Millay led to a likelier marriage of souls than that between Lindsay and delicate Sara Teasdale, whose mutually inspired love lyrics and letters overwhelmed their other work during their ill-fated courtship. John Gould Fletcher would come in from England with fresh news of Ezra Pound, and of Ford Madox Hueffer before he began calling himself Ford Madox Ford.

Carl Sandburg found himself completely at home in the poet's chair which had held such august company before him. To Harriet Monroe he appeared "a stalwart slow-stepping Swede" with "a massive frame and a face cut out of stone." He would sit solidly in her poet's chair "and talk of life and poetry with whoever might be there, weighing his words before risking utterance in his rich, low-pitched, quiet voice." Eunice Tietjens noted approvingly that Sandburg's redeeming sense of humor "always kept him from being the usual thumping radical."

Radical as he had been in politics, Sandburg immensely enjoyed his new acclaim as "the rising poet of the revolution," a rebel who had "burst into song." The *Western Comrade* reprinted two of his poems soon after their debut in *Poetry*, commenting on the "amazing boldness" of this "sledgehammer writer." The poems which affronted some Chicagoans caught the attention of daily newspapers and press associations, who depicted Sandburg as a "rugged brickyard toiler and a railroad construction worker," a "former itinerant laborer and one-time soldier in Porto Rico." Consequently the seeds were sewn for the myth, only partially true, of the son of the earth writing his raw, muscular verse for his peers, out of a spontaneous native wisdom.

The *Day Book* job provided a stable income and gave Sandburg an essential outlet for social commentary. More and more often he transmuted grim social problems into spare, compelling poem-portraits. It was the *Day Book* job which led him to a crucial literary friendship. Sandburg and Edgar Lee Masters met in Chicago not as poet and poet, but as reporter and lawyer, when Sandburg covered a labor case Masters was trying. Both men were born in Illinois, and Masters had attended Knox College in Galesburg. They shared a deep respect for William Marion Reedy of St. Louis, who had corresponded with each of them, published them both in his *Mirror*, and encouraged them—Sandburg to give up newspaper work and concentrate on poetry; Masters to stick to the excellent legal and political articles he wrote for the *Mirror* and other periodicals, but "For God's sake" to "lay off" poetry.

Yet Reedy published Masters's poetry, and when Sandburg first sought out Masters to ask for background on the labor case, he took along a copy of the *Mirror*. He and Masters talked about poetry as well as Chicago politics. Like Sandburg, Masters stood at a crossroads in his life. His success as a Chicago attorney had grown out of his partnership with Clarence Darrow, but he and Darrow had come to a stormy parting of the ways, and Masters was trying to build his own separate practice. His personal life was in disarray; he had been married for fifteen years to the daughter of a wealthy streetcar railway president. They had three children and an increasingly unhappy marriage, and Masters was in love with someone else. His wife would not give him the divorce he wanted then. When they finally divorced years later he was galled by the bitter publicity and by what he considered betrayal by his old friend and colleague Darrow, for it was Darrow who would handle Mrs. Masters's suit.

Masters gave Sandburg background for news stories; Sandburg introduced the more staid Masters to Chicago's bohemian life, and took him home to Paula for visits. Once Sandburg and Paula visited Masters at home, where he served them a simple meal, insisting "on scrambling eggs as if he were the only one who could do them." Sandburg and Masters often took long walks through the city or on the sands of the lake shore.

Enthusiastic about Sandburg's success in *Poetry*, Masters wrote his friend, novelist Theodore Dreiser, that he was going for an April "tramp to the Sand-dunes with a swede bard." Sandburg was "a new find," said Masters, and had "the right fibre." Their friendship was particularly catalytic for Masters, who experienced that spring of 1914 "a dynamic urge" to write and felt "like a snake with a new skin." He was working on some new poems, and Sandburg's direct free-verse style impressed him, stimulating him to revise his own style. In 1909 Reedy had encouraged Masters to read *Epigrams from the Greek Anthology*. Masters and Sandburg spoke of the book that spring on their walks and talks, and read and reread it. It prompted Sandburg to write "many early portrait poems," according to Paula. Masters urged Theodore Dreiser to read the *Greek Anthology*; it was, he said, a "good book for spring days." Masters sent Dreiser one of his new poems, "Theodore and the Poet," and told him that if he consulted the Greek anthology, he would see the original form which the poem imitated.

A poet's imagination is his own kingdom, overtly and subliminally shaped by exterior events. Sandburg and Dreiser were on Masters's mind that crucial spring, as was Reedy with his friendship and the book he urged Masters to read. In May, Masters's mother, Emma Jerusha Dexter Masters, visited him in Chicago. They had been estranged for years, but, harmony restored, spent their May visit reminiscing about people at home in Lewistown, Illinois, along the Spoon River. At the end of his mother's stay, Masters spent a Sunday afternoon writing several poems which he immediately sent to Reedy for possible inclusion in the *Mirror*.

Reedy had rejected most of Masters's earlier poems, cast in conventional forms, but he immediately accepted the original, free-verse poems which Masters had written in white heat and tentatively named *Spoon River Anthology*. Just as Sandburg used pseudonyms to keep his political, pragmatic and poetical identities separate, Masters the lawyer had been calling Masters the poet "Webster Ford," after two Elizabethan playwrights, or "Dexter Wallace," a combination of his mother's maiden name and his father's middle name. Surprised by Reedy's instant and enthusiastic acceptance of the poems, Masters wanted to conceal the place as well as the poet. Reedy agreed to Masters's use of the pseudonym "Webster Ford," but rejected his wish to rename the poems the *Pleasant Plains Anthology*.

Reedy, Dreiser, Sandburg and Emma Masters helped to trigger then the inspired outpouring which became Masters's greatest work, and *Reedy's Mirror* carried the first group of poems on May 29, 1914. The second group appeared in June, the third in July. These unique "serial" poems had the same galvanizing effect on the reading public that serial novels enjoyed.

Masters gave the summer to the poems, crafting them in the tranquillity of a Lake Michigan resort. *Mirror* readers wrote fan letters to Webster Ford and watched eagerly for the next installment of new poems in the series. Letters poured in from the United States and abroad clamoring to know more about the identity of Webster Ford. Ezra Pound, who had been lukewarm in his praise of Sandburg's "Chicago," hailed Masters's *Spoon River*. "At last!" he wrote, "At last America has discovered a poet." He urged Harriet Monroe to "Get Some of Webster Ford's Stuff for *Poetry*." Sandburg applauded his friend's growing success and wrote a poem to Webster Ford which he sent in November to Reedy. "I shall run your free verse to Webster Ford with great delight," Reedy answered. "I know it will also delight him. I am also going to unmask him this week, so that it will be a Webster Ford–Masters number."

Masters's poems had been running in the *Mirror* since May. Reedy cajoled him for three months before Masters would agree to reveal his identity, fearing that his new success as a poet would endanger his old and vulnerable success as a lawyer. He was right to fear that the poems would hurt his law practice, for what many readers hailed as the beginning of a new native tradition in American poetry others saw as "one long chronicle of rapes, seductions, liaisons, and perversions."

Masters conceived the *Spoon River Anthology*, he said, when his mind, "already shaken out of certain literary prejudices by the reading in *Poetry* of much free verse, especially that of Mr. Carl Sandburg, was spurred to more active radicalism through a friendship with that iconoclastic champion of free speech, free form, free art—freedom of the soul."

Sandburg saw clearly the fundamental conflict expressed in Masters's creation of the *Spoon River Anthology*—the profound internal struggle of a multifaceted nature to find its true self. It was a struggle which had defined Sandburg's own turbulent life, the agonizing effort to come to terms with multiple personalities and proclivities encased in one visible being, the "many-sided self" lurking behind the public mask. In his poem to Masters, Sandburg saluted

> the sheer brute under the clothes
> as he will be stripped at the Last Day,
> the inside man with red heartbeats
> that go on ticking off life
> against the ribs.

✳

Sandburg came into his own that year as poet and journalist. His twofold good fortune was sweet after the long years of apprenticeship and struggle. *The Day Book* was a natural vehicle for his political and journalistic interests, for newspaper tycoon E. W. Scripps wanted his experimental, adless daily to be a newspaper for the proletariat.

By the time Sandburg joined the staff permanently in 1914, the paper was well established with a circulation of nearly fourteen thousand, triple that of the previous year. Scripps had urged Cochran to see to it that the tabloid first of all entertained its readers. He wanted subscribers to enjoy at least thirty-one of its thirty-two pages: "The thirty-second page is enough to furnish all the uplift and intellectual pablum that our duty can possibly call for." Scripps warned Cochran not to cause his readers to think, not even to invite them to think. "Let them spend the time they devote to reading these pages in entire forgetfulness of rights and wrongs, ambitions and disappointments."

Into this unique climate stepped Sandburg the reporter. It was a fruitful association, just the steady base of challenging work Sandburg needed to feed his family, explore Chicago issues, nourish his poetry. Cochran was a valuable mentor. In particular he taught Sandburg the values of economy, precision, concision. He admonished his reporters to "get the most news into the fewest possible words." He advocated the art of "boiling down," compressing stories to half their original length.

Sandburg's work at the paper supported his poetry in more than financial ways. He had an ever-unfolding pageant of new subject matter. As a reporter he encountered faces, conflicts and tragedies which haunted his poems. His anger at social injustice empowered and sometimes embittered his poetry. *The Day Book* later printed at least four Sandburg poems, unpublished elsewhere, with strong messages of social protest.

As Sandburg centered down into his work as poet and journalist, he could finally unite the many divergent drives for self-expression into one strong, coherent voice. In 1914 he sat with equal ease with the poets on Cass Street and the reporters at *The Day Book*. He prowled the city in search of stories, telling them sometimes in prose, sometimes in poetry. He was always writing, on the job at the newspaper, in the long, quiet nights at home, in transit from place to place. One day he left the *Day Book* office to go down to the Loop for an interview with a juvenile court judge. He walked through Grant Park on the way and watched the fog settle over the Chicago harbor. The judge kept him waiting, and as Sandburg sat in the anteroom, he took out a pencil and scrawled some words in a haiku form on a piece of newsprint, folded twice, reporter-style, into a handy six-column notebook which just fit a vest pocket. Sandburg's pockets were habitually stuffed with odds and ends of paper he collected—news clippings, poems, shorthand notes to himself. One pocket that gray day contained "Japanese Hokus," and Sandburg wrote his own "free-going, independent American Hoku" as he waited for the judge:

> The fog comes
> on little cat feet.
>
> It sits looking
> over harbor and city
> on silent haunches
> and then moves on.

✳

Sometime during his *Poetry* days other women became an issue for Carl and Paula. There were bright, beautiful women weaving in and out of the *Poetry* circle, some poets, some socialites or intellectuals who volunteered to help the little magazine. Sandburg was lithe and handsome, like Lindsay an anomaly in the burgeoning Chicago literary world, rugged, intense, exotic in his plebeian roots and the alternating "tenderness and virility" of his powerful new poems.

He liked and trusted women, and they reciprocated. Suddenly he was the center of attention in an exciting circle. He and Paula were unprepared for the sudden change in their lives. They had been a tightly bonded couple. Sometime during 1914, they moved to a small house on South Eighth Avenue in suburban Maywood. Sandburg began spending more and more time in Chicago, while Paula tended to matters at home. "I was rather naïve," Paula would remember. "I hadn't expected all this attention. There were all these women in and out of the *Poetry* office." Sandburg could be caught up in the pleasure of unaccustomed companionship with other poets and writers, some of them vibrant women. He often went out to dinner or to parties after work, before going home to Maywood. There was conjecture about his relationship with one or two women in the *Poetry* circle. Innocent or not, his increasingly longer hours in Chicago away from his suburban home put a barrier between him and Paula.

Paula's faith in Sandburg's poetry had been justified at last, and she rejoiced in his new success. But it pulled him away from her and three-year-old Margaret. Paula was alone with the child much of the time. As his work and the new public attention preoccupied Sandburg, she may have begun to feel that he needed her less, that her role in his work had diminished. Rumors may have drifted to her ears of possible attractions to other women. There is no evidence to clarify the misunderstanding that led them to their first and only contemplation of separation. A long probe of surviving papers and memories yields no explanation for the tension between them then. They themselves spoke of it to their daughters years later without any details, only the fact that there were strains between them that had not been there even in the more difficult earlier periods of their life together.

Whatever the cause, it was Paula who confronted Sandburg. Evoking the trust and openness of their marriage commitment, she raised the prospect of freedom for them both: divorce.

Jolted, he looked at her and said no to the idea. He loved her too profoundly, relied on her too deeply. Besides, he told her, he was not about to go through all that courting again.

✳

Paula devoted most of her prodigious energy to Margaret. Always interested in education, she heard about Maria Montessori's system for educating children, recently introduced in the United States. She began to try the Montessori method with Margaret, an eager student even at age three. Margaret loved learning her letters and numbers. She would sit down, blindfold herself, and sift through sandpaper cards cut to the shape of letters. "It's a B, Mamma, it's a B!" she would call. Her uncle Ed sent her a new Easter dress, and her favorite toy was a monkey who could do "almost everything but talk."

That summer of 1914, Paula and Margaret enjoyed the beach as well as occasional visits to Oma and Opa at the farm. Her parents called Margaret their Superchild. She was already beginning to read, poring over books about Peter Rabbit and Little Black Sambo. She became such a star Montessori pupil that her picture was later used on a national Montessori promotional brochure.

Margaret played in the sand on the tranquil shore of the Lincoln Park Beach with Hopie and George Fox's four small children, far removed from the turbulence of the grown-up world her father covered for *The Day Book*. On July 28, Austria declared war on Serbia. Germany declared war on Russia on August 1. Great Britain's declaration of war on Germany came on August 4. In Voulangis, France, Edward Steichen arranged to move his wife and two daughters from their farm/studio outside Paris to the neutral safety of home in the United States. By September, Edward, Clara, Mary and Kate Rodina Steichen were safely transplanted to Sharon, Connecticut, to the immense relief of the Steichens and Sandburgs in the Midwest.

Sandburg's political and poetic reaction to the frightening world scene was swift. In new poems he began to explore his own sense of war in the abstract, and of this particular war. Through the Newspaper Enterprise Association [NEA] and United Press news reports at *The Day Book*, he tracked the rapid-fire progression of events in Europe. In November a special war issue of *Poetry* carried his "Among the Red Guns," written, Sandburg said, "After waking at dawn one morning when the wind sang low among dry leaves in an elm."

"Dreams," it ended,

> Dreams go on,
> Out of the dead on their backs,
> Broken and no use any more:
> Dreams of the way and the end go on.

*

That first year of World War I has been called, in other arenas, the year of the Poetry Revival, the Literary Revolt, the Chicago Renaissance in literature. It was the year of Dreiser's *The Titan*, and it was foremost the year of American poets. Harriet Monroe's *Poetry* had featured the work of Frost and Sandburg, and Reedy had sponsored Edgar Lee Masters. From England, Pound was urging Harriet Monroe to publish T. S. Eliot's

"The Love Song of J. Alfred Prufrock," which would finally appear in *Poetry* in 1915.

That year of literary landmarks and growing world chaos ended on a note of personal triumph for Carl and Paula. Critic and poet Louis Untermeyer sent some of Sandburg's poems to Floyd Dell at *The Masses*, but Dell could not persuade his colleagues to publish them. "But *please* send us some more!" he urged Sandburg when he returned them. "I wish we could have printed the one about Chick Lorimer. It's a perfect lyric—equal to the best things in English poetry."

In 1913 Harriet Monroe and the *Poetry* board had given prizes to Yeats and Lindsay. For 1914, Chicago attorney and *Poetry* benefactor Salmon O. Levinson had endowed an annual prize of two hundred dollars to go to the best American poem to appear in *Poetry* each year, in honor of his deceased wife, Helen Haire Levinson. From England, Pound wrote impatiently about what he called "the American citizen prize" but suggested that it should go to John Gould Fletcher or Robert Frost, or perhaps Vachel Lindsay, Orrick Johns or Skipwith Cannell. He did not suggest Sandburg, who was Alice Corbin Henderson's choice for the honor. Harriet Monroe agreed that Sandburg's poems deserved the award, but hesitated because of the controversy over Sandburg's radical free verse. Ironically it was the conservative, traditional Hobart C. Chatfield-Taylor of *Poetry*'s advisory board who swung the vote in Sandburg's favor. He gave a careful reading to all the nominated poems, and then pronounced Sandburg's Chicago poems "the best of the lot." But he was not sure that they were poetry.

Someone suggested consulting the dictionary for a definition. It was the entry in a worn copy of the *Century Dictionary* which persuaded Chatfield-Taylor and others that Carl Sandburg did indeed write poetry, which was defined as "The art which has for its object the exciting of intellectual pleasure by means of vivid, imaginative, passionate and inspiring language, usually though not necessarily arranged in the form of measured verse or numbers."

Under the provisions of that definition, Chatfield-Taylor decided that he could "vote for Sandburg with a clear conscience," and the first Levinson Prize of two hundred dollars was Sandburg's. The decision was reached in secrecy and revealed only when the November issue of the magazine was off the press with the announcement, and a press release had gone to Chicago newspapers. Eunice Tietjens was the last to leave the *Poetry* office on the November day when the magazines were to be mailed. As she locked the door, Sandburg climbed the steps to the office.

Knowing that he would have the good news the next day, Tietjens could not resist telling him herself. She tore the wrapper off a copy of the new issue of *Poetry*, opened it to the revealing page, and gave it to Sandburg.

Quietly Sandburg read the article pronouncing his "Chicago" the best American poem of the year. Even in his surprise he was restrained. He asked Eunice Tietjens to walk awhile with him, and they turned northward in the direction of the El. "I was surprised at this calm way of hearing the news," she recalled,

> for I knew it was his first big recognition, and I knew too that the two hundred dollars would mean much to him in itself. So I waited, following his lead, to see what he would do. He began at first to speak of some indifferent subject, and I followed. After what seemed to me a long time he broke off suddenly and spoke of the prize again, but only to sheer off almost at once on another tack. He repeated this several times, each time, however, speaking more directly of the prize. At last I saw that the shock of pleasure had been so great that he could not think of it at once, as one cannot put one's hand on a hot stove and leave it there. Only after the news had cooled a little in his heart could he settle down hard on it.
>
> We had by this time walked long past my station but Carl would not let me go, and we walked northward for miles. At last Carl stopped abruptly and looked me in the eyes. His own eyes, behind the thick lenses of his glasses, looked very big and blue and shining.
>
> "How do you say 'twice quadruple'?" he asked unexpectedly. "I'm not sure, but I imagine you would say 'octuple,' " I answered, wondering on what new tack his mind was running this time.
>
> "Then," said Carl, "that two hundred dollars will just octuple our bank account."

Later on when Sandburg told people about the Levinson Prize, he noted with appreciation that the *Poetry* editorial board was divided two to two on the matter of the prize, and the deciding vote in his favor was cast by Hobart Chatfield-Taylor, "a multimillionaire club man and connoisseur" who pronounced "the same judgment on the Chicago poem which has come from Bill Haywood and Clarence Darrow." He recalled that he and Paula and Harriet Monroe had been invited to dinner at Levinson's house, where Sandburg for the first time encountered "that strange vegetable you have to tear apart and dip into a sauce—yes, artichokes."

Carl and Paula Sandburg were no longer strangers in Chicago. When they had first considered the move to the city in 1912, they had worried that it might not "be a go." Already the struggle had yielded rewards beyond their imagining. As he took the wondrous news of the Levinson Prize home to his wife, Sandburg the poet was very much like the metaphorical young man who epitomized his city in his poem—"with lifted head singing so proud to be alive and coarse and strong and cunning." Carl Sandburg had made Chicago his city, and himself Chicago's poet.

———— ✳ ————

1914–1916

12. Blood, Work and War

Poetry is written out of tumults and paradoxes, terrible
reckless struggle and glorious lazy loafing, out of blood,
work and war and out of baseball, babies and potato
blossoms.

     —Carl Sandburg to Paul Benjamin, ca. 1918

W orld War I, wrote Amy Lowell, "overwhelmed us like a tidal
  wave." She predicted that as the accelerating war in Europe
  fused a stronger national identity in the United States, a
more vital native literature would emerge. As the war irrevocably reshaped global and individual life, Sandburg and other poets began to
write about it. Sandburg for one was convinced that the poet had a duty
to address the living issues of his times.

  That was a view shared at *Poetry* by Alice Corbin Henderson, who
launched a war-poetry competition with a hundred-dollar prize for the
best poem on war or peace. Harriet Monroe came home to Chicago from
a vacation in the Rocky Mountains in August 1914 to discover the contest
in progress, and quickly composed an editorial for the September issue
of *Poetry*, encouraging realistic rather than romantic war poems. "Poets
have made more war than kings," she wrote, "and war will not cease
until they remove its glamour from the imaginations of men." To their
astonishment, the ladies at *Poetry* were inundated with entries. They
received 738 war poems, "good, bad, and indifferent, but mostly very
bad." The fourteen finalists for the hundred-dollar prize included Amy
Lowell, Maxwell Bodenheim, Richard Aldington, Alice Corbin Henderson, Carl Sandburg and a newcomer, Wallace Stevens. The prize
went to Louise Driscoll for "The Metal Checks." The poets almost to a
voice expressed "genuine revolt against war."

  At the outset of the war, President Woodrow Wilson, former President

Theodore Roosevelt and most major newspapers in the nation led the way in proclaiming American neutrality. Wilson urged the American people to be "neutral in fact as well as in name" and "impartial in thought as well as in action." Inevitably in a nation whose ethnic complexity encompassed the cultures of the world, factions emerged and clashed. There were stirrings of support for the Allies and for the Germans, but in the beginning most Americans favored neutrality and isolationism. The drama of world war captured the attention of politicians, propagandists and poets alike.

Harriet Monroe argued in the September issue of *Poetry* that it was "immediately the poet's business" to join in the movement to "get rid of war." She predicted there would be a "new poetry of war," and offered as an example Sandburg's entry in the contest, "Ready to Kill." The poem, she wrote, was "significant in its huge contempt"; in it Sandburg defended the workingman who, unlike the warrior, had not been idolized for his sacrifices and service:

Ten minutes now I have been looking at this.
I have gone by here before and wondered about it.
This is a bronze memorial of a famous general
Riding horseback with a flag and a sword and a revolver on him.
I want to smash the whole thing into a pile of junk to be hauled away to
    the scrap yard.
I put it straight to you,
After the farmer, the miner, the shop man, the factory hand, the fireman
    and the teamster,
Have all been remembered with bronze memorials,
Shaping them on the job of getting all of us
Something to eat and something to wear,
When they stack a few silhouettes
        Against the sky
        Here in the park,
And show the real huskies that are doing the work of the world, and
    feeding people instead of butchering them,
Then maybe I will stand here
And look easy at this general of the army holding a flag in the air,
And riding like hell on horseback
Ready to kill anybody that gets in his way,
Ready to run the red blood and slush the bowels of men all over the
    sweet new grass of the prairie.

Sandburg's early war poems were uniquely graphic in imagery. Other American poets dealt with the theme more impressionistically. Amy

Lowell returned from England and published a poem so idealistic that it angered her friend D. H. Lawrence. Despite the fact that Lowell was his generous patron, Lawrence scolded her. "The war-atmosphere has blackened here," he wrote from England; "it is soaking in and getting more like part of our daily life, and therefore much grimmer. So I was quite cross with you for writing about bohemian glass and stalks of flame, when the thing is so ugly and bitter to the soul." Lawrence, who had not competed for the war poem prize, shared his anger with Harriet Monroe: "It put me into such a rage—how dare Amy talk about Bohemian glass and stalks of flame!—that in a real fury I had to write my war poem, because it breaks my heart, this war. I hate, and hate, and hate the glib irreverence of some of your contributors. . . . The War is dreadful." He argued that "It is the business of the artist to follow it home to the heart of the individual fighter—not to talk in armies and nations and numbers, but to track it home, home, this war."

Among the poets of his time, Sandburg kept a singular focus on the myriad individual tragedies which composed the terrible mosaic of the war. "Murmurings in a Field Hospital" commemorated a young soldier picked up "in the grass where he had lain two days in the rain with a piece of shrapnel in his lungs." The soldier's reverie is simple:

> . . . No more iron cold and real to handle,
> Shaped for a drive straight ahead.
> Bring me only beautiful useless things.
> Only old home things touched at sunset in the quiet . . .
> And at the window one day in summer
> Yellow of the new crock of butter
> Stood against the red of new climbing roses . . .
> And the world was all playthings.

As neutrality and isolation gradually gave way to debate, and then, finally, to U.S. entry into the war in 1917, poets and novelists worked privately and publicly to "track it home, home, this war," to make sense of the conflagration and their roles in it, as writers and citizens. "The welding together of the whole country which the war has brought about, the mobilizing of our whole population into a single, strenuous endeavour, has produced a more poignant sense of nationality than has recently been the case in this country of enormous spaces and heterogeneous population," said Amy Lowell. Harriet Monroe wrote about the evolution of American and British poetry from protest to patriotism, and kept her own list of the poetic casualties of the war—Rupert Brooke, Wilfred Owen, Alan Seeger, Joyce Kilmer, Robert Frost's friend Edward Thomas, and Isaac Rosenberg, who had mailed her his "somber trench poems, sent on ragged scraps of dirty paper."

Sandburg paid more attention to the war in poetry than in his journalism during 1914. His war poems were structurally lean and tight free-verse stanzas, carefully controlled with somber rhythms and the repetition of key phrases. Sandburg explored the bitter irony of man's failure to study the lessons of military history, especially in the face of the new destructive powers of modern warfare. His poem "Statistics" depicts Napoleon in his sarcophagus learning that in the present war there are " 'Twenty-one million men,/Soldiers, armies, guns,/Twenty-one million/Afoot, horseback,/In the air,/Under the sea.' "

"It is not my world answering," Napoleon says. "It is some dreamer who knows not/The world I marched in/From Calais to Moscow."

Sandburg deplores war's destruction of the past, "the great arches and naves and little whimsical corners of the Churches of Northern France." He defends the workingman-soldier, exploited by kings and generals in war and tycoons and capitalists in industry, in either case, pawns:

SMASH down the cities.
Knock the walls to pieces.
Break the factories and cathedrals, warehouses and homes
Into loose piles of stone and lumber and black burnt wood:
    You are the soldiers and we command you.

Build up the cities.
Set up the walls again.
Put together once more the factories and cathedrals, warehouses and homes
Into buildings for life and labor:
    You are workmen and citizens all: We command you.

He tried to convey the scope of the war and its impact on the individual soldier, as in "Killers":

I am singing to you
Soft as a man with a dead child speaks;
Hard as a man in handcuffs,
Held where he cannot move:

    Under the sun
Are sixteen million men,
Chosen for shining teeth,
Sharp eyes, hard legs,
And a running of young warm blood in their wrists.

And a red juice runs on the green grass;
And a red juice soaks the dark soil.
And the sixteen million are killing . . . and killing and killing . . .
    I wake in the night and smell the trenches,
And hear the low stir of sleepers in lines—
Sixteen million sleepers and pickets in the dark:
Some of them long sleepers for always,
Some of them tumbling to sleep tomorrow for always,
Fixed in the drag of the world's heartbreak,
Eating and drinking, toiling . . . on a long job of killing.
    Sixteen million men.

More and more often Sandburg's war poems appeared in journals, including *Poetry* and the *International Socialist Review*. In *Chicago Poems* Sandburg gathered them into one fierce cluster entitled "War Poems (1914–1915)." They were powerful in their juxtaposition of war to tranquillity, past to future, the perishable dreams and bodies of individual soldiers to the awesome force of quarreling kings and "millions of men following." He attacked the carnage of the war, the exploitation of many young men in battles incurred by a few old men. He reduced war to its tragic common denominator—the loss of the individual son, brother, husband, father. The May 1915 issue of the *International Socialist Review* carried Sandburg's "Ashes and Dreams," an ode to the mothers of the world whose sons and dreams were lost to war:

Silence,
Dry sobs of darkness
In the houses and fields,
O mothers of the world,
Watching.

Hour on hour
The trenches call
And the ditches want
And the shovels wait.

White faces up,
Eyes wide and blind,
Legs stiff and arms limp,
Pass them along
And pile them in
And tumble them over,
Ashes and dreams together.

(Mothers of the world,
Your waste of work.)

The distant, growing war galvanized Sandburg's poetry. The form was sparse and rugged, the images violent and often repelling, the voice apolitical in its fervent attack on war in the abstract and its vivid depiction of the minute, realistic particulars—bloody injuries, individual agony, loss, death.

In prose he stuck to the coverage of familiar domestic wars—conflicts between trade unions and management, city politicians and the people, police and the mob. William Marion Reedy published "Voices," Sandburg's article on the U.S. Commission on Industrial Relations, and asked to have more articles for the *Mirror*, yet still tried to encourage the poet in Sandburg. "I wish you would modify your socialist devotion to the extent of refusing to sacrifice yourself on *The Day Book*," Reedy admonished Sandburg, urging him to "get out into the larger writing game. You can deliver the goods, I know." From England, Sandburg was receiving even more pointed advice from Ezra Pound, writing his own unorthodox war poems as he shared Stone Cottage at Coleman's Hatch in Sussex with Yeats. *Poetry* carried Pound's word on the war in February 1915:

> He is mankind and I am the arts.
> We are outlaws.
> This war is not our war,
> Neither side is on our side. . . .

Pound admired Sandburg's work, believing he might "come out all right" even though he "needs to learn a *lot* about *How to Write*." He sought some of Sandburg's work for *The Catholic Anthology*, a book of poetry he was compiling for publication in England, to include work of many poets he admired. Pound expected fine work of H.D. and William Carlos Williams. He and Vachel Lindsay were not "really pulling the same way," he said, although they both pulled "against entrenched senility." Robert Frost, now back home in the United States, was dull, Pound thought, "but has something in him." Edgar Lee Masters needed to "comb the journalese out of his poems," according to Pound, and had some "punch but writes a little too much, and without hardness of edge." Nevertheless, Pound believed that Masters and T. S. Eliot were "for the moment the most hopeful American poets."

Self-appointed authority on modern poetry that he was, Pound worked hard to promote the careers of poets whose work he appreciated. He did not hesitate to give them detailed criticism in the process. At the same time he was persuading Harriet Monroe to publish Eliot's "The Love

Song of J. Alfred Prufrock" in *Poetry*, he was writing to Sandburg about free verse, telling him that

> free verse has no reason for existence unless by using free verse one can make more interesting cadences, and unless one gain by it, directness of speech, hardness of the image presented. One must substitute a real metric for the dead metric discarded. . . . And one must make a form, or if you like a formality out of the perfect order of natural speech, to replace the dead form of "classical" english and regular metres.

As he solicited some of Sandburg's poems for his anthology, Pound gave him a forthright picture of what their association would be if Sandburg contributed his work to the book. "I don't know to what extent you care to put yourself in the grip of my editing," Pound warned. "I must have a perfectly free hand."

As the self-ordained critic as well as champion of poets and artists, Pound worked hard to facilitate the progress of a diverse group of writers early in their careers—Eliot, Frost, Sandburg, Stevens, James Joyce. Presuming to help Sandburg as he had helped others, Pound gave fair warning of what would happen when Sandburg turned his poetry over to *The Catholic Anthology*:

> Also you might have to stand some of my own amical, severe, and even caustic criticism, for what it's worth. I don't think you've got your "form" yet in the athletic sense. I think your work will be more of a temper. Also certain phrasings leave me in doubt. I am not sure whether your "Chicago" wouldn't hit harder if it began six lines later and ended five lines sooner, for example. I am very much the grandma in these matters and numerous people dislike it.

Sandburg listened to Pound, however, and sometimes implemented the changes he suggested. He enjoyed Pound's sense of humor, as in his promise to "peck and annoy you" with "nasty details" and "justify myself with quotations from Dante."

Sandburg's output of poetry and prose was significant in 1915. In addition to his steady coverage of labor and politics for *The Day Book* (he took on the Rockefellers, Hearst, Marshall Field, Chicago mayor "Big Bill" Thompson, the city police and the Bell Telephone monopoly from April to December that year alone), he was contributing regular articles and occasional poetry to the *International Socialist Review*, published from 1900 to 1918 by the Chicago socialist publisher Charles Kerr. Under its first editor, Algie Simons, the *Review* was moderate in slant; subsequent editors Mary and Leslie March turned the *Review* into a popular magazine with strong leftist tendencies, and built the magazine's circulation to more than forty thousand by 1911. The *Review* was controversial even among socialists, and Sandburg often used pseudonyms ("Jack Phillips," "Militant") for his *Review* byline, to keep his literary, political and journalistic identities compartmentalized. For a time Jack London was a colleague at the *Review*; Sandburg compared him to O. Henry in a poem after his death:

> Both were jailbirds; no speechmakers at all;
> speaking best with one foot on a brass rail;
> a beer glass in the left hand and the right
> hand employed for gestures.
>
> And both were lights snuffed out . . . no warning
> . . . no lingering:
> Who knew the hearts of these booze fighters?

✳

"This will be a wonderful spring—when we can start growing things in our own soil!" Paula wrote to Sandburg in 1915 from Brooklyn, where she and Margaret, now four, were visiting friends after a reunion with Edward Steichen and his family in Sharon, Connecticut. Steichen had given his sister "seeds from Voulangis for vines and trailing things—scarlet morning glory and verbenas and more than I can tell!" She planned to start asparagus and strawberry beds, for the Sandburgs had just bought their small house in Maywood, Illinois, thanks to a five-hundred-dollar loan from an old friend of the Steichens. That same spring marked Robert Frost's return to the United States from England and the American publication of *A Boy's Will* by Henry Holt and Company. The Macmillan Company brought out Masters's *Spoon River Anthology*, which Sandburg reviewed in a rather ponderous article for the May issue of Margaret Anderson's *The Little Review*.

Sandburg praised Masters's poetry, and sketched the backdrop against which it had been written: "I saw Masters write this book. He wrote it in snatched moments between fighting injunctions against a waitresses' union striving for the right to picket and gain one day's rest a week, battling from court to court for compensation to a railroad engineer rendered a loathsome cripple by the defective machinery of a locomotive, having his life amid affairs as intense as those he writes of."

Reedy wrote from St. Louis to compliment Sandburg on the review, and they spoke with regret of another mutual friend and an event which exacerbated conflict over the American position on the war. On May 7, 1915, a German torpedo boat attacked and sank the British ocean liner *Lusitania*, killing nearly twelve hundred civilians, including 128 American citizens, among them Elbert Hubbard and his wife. Reedy was invited to speak at memorial services for the Hubbards at East Aurora, New York, on July 4. He told Sandburg, "I liked Hubbard always and her too. He was not the rank fakir some people thought—went off after the efficiency craze and went wrong. But he could say things with an individual tongue and he *did* lure people into larger views. He had summat of the Socialist urge in him, though he did want to direct the way it should go." Reedy and Sandburg shared an affection for the flamboyant soap salesman whose *Message to García* and other publications had touched so many lives. Hubbard had published Sandburg's poems without paying him at times, but *The Fra* offered good exposure, and Sandburg had been grateful for Hubbard's attention in the early years of his work.

The loss of the *Lusitania* had a world-shattering impact far beyond the loss of the Hubbards and the other innocent casualties of the attack. On May 10 President Wilson set the tone for the official American response: "There is such a thing as a man being too proud to fight," he said in a speech. Theodore Roosevelt and others began to call for United States entry into the War, however, and war fever intensified with the heightened debate about the nation's preparedness for war. There were layers of conflict: pacifists versus militarists; pro-Germans and pro-Allies; neutralists and interventionists. William Jennings Bryan and Robert La Follette led the attack against preparedness, which they viewed as a tool of warmongers and profiteers.

When more than eight hundred men, women and children drowned in the capsizing of the *Eastland* in the Chicago River in the summer of 1915, an irate Sandburg attacked both the Western Electric Company, which had sponsored the outing for its employees and their families on the steamship, and the U.S. Secretary of Commerce, who was responsible for certifying the safety of such ships. He wanted to know why someone did not "stop a cranky unstable ancient hoo-doo-tub like the excursion boat *Eastland* from capsizing with twenty-five hundred human lives within a few hundred yards off shore in plain view of parents and relatives of the children who were drowning?"

He concluded that "Business required it." His attack in the *International Socialist Review* appeared in his column "Lookin' 'Em Over." Later, in an unpublished poem, he mounted an even more emotional assault, extrapolating from the *Eastland* disaster the roots of all the social "disasters" which, he believed, callous government and business interests inflicted on the American working class:

The Eastland
. . . It was a hell of a job, of course
To dump 2,500 people in their clean picnic clothes
All ready for a whole lot of real fun
Down into the dirty Chicago river without any warning. . . .

Women and kids, wet hair and scared faces,
The coroner hauling truckloads of the dripping dead. . . .

I got imagination: I see a pile of three thousand dead people
Killed by the con,* tuberculosis, too much work
                    and not enough fresh air and green groceries
A lot of cheap roughnecks and the women and children of wops, and
    hardly any bankers and corporation lawyers or their kids,
    die from the con—three thousand a year in Chicago and a
    hundred and fifty thousand a year in the United States—
    all from the con and not enough fresh air and green groceries . . .

If you want to see excitement, more noise and crying than you ever
    heard in one of these big disasters the newsboys clean up on,
Go and stack in a high pile all the babies that die in Christian
    Philadelphia, New York, Boston and Chicago in one year because
    aforesaid babies haven't had enough good milk;
On top the pile put all the little early babies pulled from mothers
    willing to be torn with abortions rather than bring more child-
    ren into the world—
Jesus! that would make a front page picture for the Sunday papers. . . .
Can you imagine a procession of all the whores of a big town, march-
    ing and marching with painted faces and mocking struts
Or all the structural iron workers, railroad men and factory hands
    in mass formation with stubs of arms and stumps of legs, bod-
    ies broken and hacked while bosses yelled, "Speed—no slack—
    go to it!"?
Or two by two all the girls and women . . .
    digging into the garbage barrels to get scraps of stuff to eat?
By the living Christ, these would make disaster pictures to paste
    on the front pages of the newspapers.
Yes, the Eastland was a dirty bloody job—bah!
                  I see a dozen Eastlands
                  Every morning on my way to work
                  And a dozen more going home at night.

Sandburg took up another battle in 1915 against popular evangelist and cult figure Billy Sunday. He had first encountered Sunday, a former baseball player, during his own chautauqua and lyceumite days, had once

* Consumption.

appeared on a program with Sunday, and had come to believe that Sunday and his crowd exploited the people in the name of religious fervor. Sandburg saw Sunday as a "salesman and crowd trickster" rather than "one sent from God." Chicago alderman Mike "Hinky Dink" Kenna told Sandburg that Sunday had "bought stock in two hotels, one of them the Hotel Morrison, persistently notorious in Chicago courts for the studied and civilized vice, the commercialized night pleasure which is much harder to look at than natural depravity." Sandburg's angry, aggressive poem "Billy Sunday" appeared in September 1915 in the *International Socialist Review* and *The Masses*, and later, in a muted revision entitled "To a Contemporary Bunkshooter," in *Chicago Poems*.

> You come along . . . tearing your shirt . . . yelling about Jesus.
>   Where do you get that stuff?
>   What do you know about Jesus? . . .
> You slimy bunkshooter, you put a smut on every human blossom in reach
>   of your rotten breath belching about hell-fire and hiccupping about
>   this Man who lived a clean life in Galilee . . .
> I don't want a lot of gab from a bunkshooter in my religion.
> I won't take my religion from any man who never works except with his
>   mouth and never cherishes any memory except the face of the
>   woman on the American dollar.
> I ask you to come through and show me where you're pouring out the
>   blood of your life . . .

Sandburg attacked Sunday more for his exploitation of thousands of American working people who trusted him and gave him money than for his fundamental religious views. Years later Sandburg asked a university professor to forward a copy of the poem to Sunday himself to solicit his opinion of it. "Who is this Sandburg?" Sunday replied. "Isn't he a Red? He sounds to me like a Red."

✳

The October 1915 issue of *Poetry* carried seventeen poems by Sandburg reflecting a wide range of themes, from "blood, work and war" to "baseball, babies and potato blossoms." A gentle nocturne evoked the beauty to be discovered in unlikely places, in this instance a deserted brickyard where the moon

> Runs on the lapping sand
> Out to the longest shadows.
> Under the curving willows,
> And round the creep of the wave line,

Fluxions of yellow and dusk on the waters
Make a wide dreaming pansy of an old pond in the night.

"I do not think 'fluxions' is, as a word, good enough," Ezra Pound chided
in a letter from England, "though the desire to get a precise and 'unpoetic'
word is sound enough." Sandburg the father and Sandburg the socialist
spoke of children: "Blossoms of babies" in "Handfuls"; a harsh indictment
of child labor practices in "They Will Say":

> Of my city the worst that men will ever say is this:
> You took little children away from the sun and the dew,
> And the glimmers that played in the grass under the great sky,
> And the reckless rain; you put them between walls
> To work, broken and smothered, for bread and wages,
> To eat dust in their throats and die empty-hearted
> For a little handful of pay on a few Saturday nights.

There were other poems with socialist themes; the war poem "Killers";
and always, love poems written for Paula;

> I never knew any more beautiful than you:
> I have hunted you under my thoughts,
> I have broken down under the wind
> And into the roses looking for you.
> I shall never find any
>   greater than you.

The group included Sandburg's bold ode to joy, entitled simply "Joy":

> Let a joy keep you.
> Reach out your hands
> And take it when it runs by,
> As the Apache dancer
> Clutches his woman.
> I have seen them
> Live long and laugh loud,
> Sent on singing, singing,
> Smashed to the heart
> Under the ribs
> With a terrible love.
> Joy always,
> Joy everywhere—
> Let joy kill you!
> Keep away from the little deaths.

His poems were radically different from those of the others included
in *Poetry*, with economy of form and clarity of image. To the eye de-

ceptively shapeless, they were, to the ear, rhythmical, often musical in cadence. Sandburg's unorthodox subjects set his work apart. As his reputation widened that fall, so did the debate in poetry circles about whether his work was legitimately poetic. Pound sent him detailed criticism and some praise for the new group of poems in *Poetry*. "I think the stuff, your stuff, in the Oct. Number of 'Poetry' shows technical advance." There were reservations: a certain line should be deleted because it had a "bum cadence and clumsy order of words." Some word choices were "bully" but others were careless. Sandburg, said Pound, used too many adjectives, vain repetition, lines which were "as bad as the Miltonic ballance" in their "too even" arrangement.

Pound toyed with some revisions for certain lines, noting that there were "a dozen ways" to rewrite them. He looked at the smallest details in Sandburg's work. "Sketch" depicted the shadows of ships "In the blue lustre/Of the tardy and soft inrolling tide." Pound urged a change because "I simply want to know where you *see* the shadow." He urged Sandburg toward greater precision of imagery and more freedom of form. "Mind, I'm not grumping . . . the picture is good." Yet Pound left Sandburg a challenge: "I don't know if you care about this sort of meticulous criticism or if you want to leave off meditating about 'greve,' 'communism,' etc. to hear my jaw about technical flummery. The shadows of ships rock in the low blue lustre. It is a week's work to decide just what order of words they ought to do it in. I shan't pretend to solve it for you in five minutes." Pound had begun to suspect that wartime censors were intercepting his mail to and from the United States, but fortunately his letters reached Sandburg, who heeded some of his suggestions, discarded others, and was considerably encouraged by Pound's interest.

Amy Lowell and others noted the multiplicity of voices in Sandburg's work, which roamed a spectrum from brutality to tenderness, powerful virility to soft lyricism, graphic, almost savage realism to misty romanticism. He drew his subjects from experiences before his eyes, and his reportage continued to feed his poetry. A 1915 *Day Book* interview with the mayor of the steel town Gary, Indiana, resulted in a news article and a poem:

. . . And I saw workmen wearing leather shoes scruffed with fire and cinders,
    and pitted with little holes from running molten steel,
And some had bunches of specialized muscles around their shoulder blades
    hard as pig iron, muscles of their forearms were sheet steel . . . and they
    looked to me like men who had been somewhere.

Sandburg's work stood in the forefront of the revolutionary new poetry, "the expression of a democracy of feeling rebelling against an aristocracy of form."

It was Theodore Dreiser who first suggested to Sandburg that he collect his Chicago poems for a book. Sandburg admired Dreiser's work, especially the recently published *The Titan*, second of the controversial trilogy of novels based on the life of Chicago's street-railway tycoon Charles Yerkes. Their mutual friend Edgar Lee Masters had brought the two men together, at Dreiser's request. Dreiser wrote Sandburg in August 1915:

> Sometime ago I asked Mr. Masters to get you to gather your poems together and let me see them. Last Monday he came in bringing them and I have since had the pleasure of examining them. They are beautiful. There is a fine, hard, able paganism about them that delights me—and they are tender and wistful as only the lonely, wist-ful, dreaming pagan can be. Do I need to congratulate you? Let me envy you instead. I would I could do things as lovely. . . .
>
> My idea is that if as many as a hundred and twenty-five or a hundred and fifty poems can be gotten together a publisher can be found for them. I sincerely hope so—I mean now.
>
> Incidentally Mr. [Floyd] Dell, hearing your poem on Billy Sunday read wanted me to let him submit it for consideration at the Masses. I loaned it to him, subject to further advice from you, of course.
>
> My sincerest compliments. When I next get to Chicago I will look you up.

"Such a dandy letter as you sent along to me I can't so far think out any real good answer to," Sandburg responded. "For the fellowship and the sentiment of it, the enheartening element, I haven't got the reply now. When you are in Chicago maybe you and Masters and I can go out for a single sacramental glass of beer and square things."

When Masters got home to Chicago in late August he told Sandburg that he had submitted his poetry manuscript to an editor at the New York office of John D. Lane and Company, the British firm which published Dreiser's work. Unfortunately Dreiser was away from New York on a "motor trip" to Indiana, and by the time he returned to New York, Lane had rejected Sandburg's manuscript. Dreiser was full of regret at the mix-up. "Edgar Lee is one of my best friends," he wrote Sandburg, "and I sincerely believe that it was his enthusiasm for you that lead him to take the matter into his own hands. When I came back from Indiana, Jones and his readers had decided against them and my voice at this late date was useless. I feel so troubled about unfulfilled obligations that I write you as I do."

Sandburg was disappointed but not daunted by the rejection, for his friends Louis Untermeyer and Alice Corbin Henderson were also at work on behalf of a book of his poems. His work was attracting attention which vacillated between new fame and notoriety. Max Eastman and Floyd Dell published "Billy Sunday" in *The Masses* and when Chester Wright reprinted it in *The New York Call*, police officers in New Haven, Connecticut, seized all issues of the newspaper, forbidding its sale and distribution because the poem was deemed blasphemous.

Dreiser had had his own struggles with censorship, and knew the struggle to get a work into print. Sometimes awkward and stiff with people, Dreiser's seeming aloofness came from shyness and a deep sensitivity. Distressed by his failure to place Sandburg's book and by Sandburg's silence after his October letter, Dreiser made another overture to Sandburg at the end of November. Dreiser had been offered the job of scenario director to create projects for a new motion picture company. Sure that he could make a good deal of money and at the same time convert the new technology into an art form, Dreiser looked about for people who could contribute exciting "books, plays, poems, masques, legends, panorama, pageants . . . as well as educational, scientific and radical propagandistic features." Among others, he approached Richard Le Gallienne, H. L. Mencken and Sandburg. "As a matter of fact," he told Sandburg, "I would very much like to secure a scenario along radical or even revolutionary lines which would be poignant and provoke serious discussion. Your poems make me think that you might be the very one to work out a brilliant picture of some kind. Does the idea interest you?" He would pay even for ideas, Dreiser promised: "I for one am determined to do away with movie grafting." He sought features of "art and power."

Sandburg replied to Dreiser's letters months later, with apologies: "I perform all tasks, except certain newspaper deadline assignments, slowly. I take my time at the joy-tasks as well as the wage-jobs. . . . Masters and others will tell you I have a bum record, a criminal record, as a letter writer."

The movie project did not materialize, and Sandburg was inundated with other work in any case. Meantime Henderson and Untermeyer kept alive the prospect of a book of Sandburg's poetry. They both knew Alfred Harcourt of Henry Holt and Company, and when Harcourt visited Chicago on a bookselling trip, he tried unsuccessfully to meet Sandburg, whose work he had read and admired in *Poetry*. "Steer Carl my way," Harcourt asked Henderson. During a trip to New York she did, personally delivering to Harcourt a manuscript containing many of Sandburg's poems. Untermeyer, too, had urged Sandburg to submit his work to

Harcourt and "tempt him to gamble on a book." Sandburg was grateful for the encouragement, for he was, as always, torn between the opposing forces of politics and poetry. "Building the *Day Book*, recent live events in politics and labor, have kept me out of poetry and art interests," he told Untermeyer. "Then too, I had begun to feel what your letter calls 'the difficulty that a real radical has to get a hearing.' There is such an aloofness from life and the people on the part of most of the poets and most of the publishers that I have begun pouring all my oaths of love and hate and beauty into my newspaper writing."

Sandburg's attention was split between poetry and journalism. He was covering the Amalgamated Clothing Workers strike for the *Day Book* when Alfred Harcourt wrote expressing his enthusiasm for the poems and asking to see more. Sandburg wrote to thank Alice Corbin Henderson, then in New Mexico undergoing treatment for tuberculosis. "I am slaving now to get a book into shape to send to Harcourt of Henry Holt & Co. He wrote me on your suggestion. You were very thoughtful." But his primary energy had to go into his job. "The garment strike is hell," he said. "It's like a voyage on a submarine with ventilation machinery busted." He admired the "organization efficiency and social vision" of the Amalgamated Clothing Workers' Union, writing a story a day during their fifteen-week-long strike. For two weeks, strike leader Sidney Hillman, suffering from influenza, ran the strike from his sickbed. Sandburg visited his bedside every day to exchange news and ideas, and paid regular visits to Clarence Darrow, the lawyer who was representing the union. Sandburg managed his friendships adroitly, and so could carry on simultaneously his literary friendship with Masters and a cordial friendship with Masters's adversary and former partner Darrow.

With Paula's help, he balanced his daytime job and the nighttime work on the poetry. By early January 1916 they had prepared a manuscript of 260 poems to send to Harcourt in New York. At Alice Corbin Henderson's suggestion, Sandburg called the collection *Chicago Poems*. He had wanted her to go over the manuscript before they mailed it, but time and distance prevented that. Harcourt was pressing him for the collection, in hopes that he might get board approval to publish it that spring.

"I saw at once that it was of first importance and quality," Harcourt said of the manuscript. Yet "There was something of a skirmish to get it past the inhibitions and traditions of the Holt office, for its middle-western atmosphere, its subject matter and strength seemed to them rather raw for their imprint." That skirmish resulted in an inspired act of subterfuge. Trusting that his superiors would not actually read the book in print, Harcourt removed the Billy Sunday poem and a few other risky pages from the manuscript. Once his colleagues approved the expurgated manuscript, Harcourt restored the vagrant pages to the whole. On February 5, 1916, Sandburg signed his first book contract for "a work to contain about 40,000 words, provisionally entitled *Chicago Poems.*"

Sandburg was "away behind in sleep, and work" but he was jubilant at Harcourt's acceptance of his work. He and Paula did not tell anyone else that he was "trying to unload a book of poetry on the world."

"It is rare to have a manuscript in the shop which interests us as much as yours," Harcourt wrote Sandburg, but he told him it would have to be cut by nearly half. Harcourt recommended poems to delete or hold for future publication, but left the final selections up to Sandburg, with some editorial advice:

> For obvious reasons, we think the poems, the subjects of which are living people referred to by name, should certainly be omitted. Some of the poems are a little too "raw." These classes are small. The third class is larger. Often there are several poems with the same or very similar theme or written by the same formula . . . the effect of repetition is unfortunate. There should be some careful winnowing with this effect, and with probably a second volume in mind.

The Sandburgs celebrated the good news and shared it with Masters. "Are they going to print Billy Sunday?" he wanted to know, and then applauded Harcourt's affirmative decision: "They are going after the soul of America."

Still the Billy Sunday poem was a point of contention. Sandburg resisted some of Harcourt's suggestions about the poem, and defended it in a letter:

> . . . I saw clearly your points about certain words forming what might be taken as an irreverent contrast with the name of Jesus. And I made revisions that I believe put the Sunday poem in a class of reading enjoyable and profitable to all but the most hidebound and creed-drilled religionists. If necessary or important, which it is not, I could furnish statements from Protestant ministers and Catholic priests that this poem has more of the historic Jesus or the ideal Christ in it, than does a Billy Sunday series of exhortations. . . . There is terrific tragedy of the individual and of the crowd in and about Billy Sunday. He is the most conspicuous single embodiment in this country of the crowd leader or crowd operative who uses jungle methods, stark voodoo stage effects, to play hell with democracy. This is the main cause of the fundamental hatred which men have

for Sunday. . . . The only other American figure that might compare with Sunday is Hearst. Both dabble in treacheries of the primitive, invoke terrors of the unknown, utilize sex as a stage prop, and work on the elemental fears of the mob, with Hearst the same antithesis to Tom Jefferson that Billy Sunday is to Jesus of Nazareth.

I am writing about Sunday at this length, Mr. Harcourt, because I want you to know what sort of foundations I see the poem resting on.

Harcourt was impressed with Sandburg's shrewd, careful editing of his own work, as well as the underlying integrity which empowered him to defend his voice and style. Harcourt still held out for the deletion of expletives and the change of any names which might bring on libel suits. Otherwise he fully supported Sandburg's views and put *Chicago Poems* on his spring publication schedule. With contract signed, revisions made and publication date set, Sandburg began to share the news with other friends. "Holt & Co. are to bring out my stuff this spring under title of 'Chicago Poems,' " he wrote to Untermeyer. "Your good note in November telling me you had met Harcourt and it was your hunch that I ought to send on manuscript without delay, was a factor. It was a first-class hunch." Untermeyer promised Sandburg a good review: "I'll vilify you in every cranny and corner of print that I can find. . . . Also I have just given you a preliminary hurrah in the Review of Reviews in an article on 'The New Spirit in American Poetry.' "

Edward Steichen offered to design the cover and did so, producing a clean, straightforward piece of work which, he thought, suited Chicago, and was a departure from the fussy, art nouveau decoration of other books, such as Pound's limited edition *Catholic Anthology* ("The silly cover on Catholic Anthology suggests a reason for doing something of that kind *well*," Steichen told his brother-in-law Sandburg.)

They were committed, Sandburg in poetry and Steichen in photography, to the idea that art should become "a civilizing force" in the modern world, a great humanizing power. Steichen told Paula in 1916 that artists in all media had to work together to "organize art like armies are organized to meet the demands we make upon it.—Poetry, painting, music—the theatre can no longer stand aloof as exquisite expressions of—an individual.—We must have something bigger. There's a thumping desire to reach mankind—everywhere in the arts." With war as the backdrop, Sandburg and Steichen agreed that "We have more material at hand than ever before—more need than ever before & a greater hunger in humanity." Steichen contended that "Art has merely been a handmaiden to culture." Instead, he told the Sandburgs, art would become the "great master force in life."

Sandburg told Amy Lowell that his purpose in *Chicago Poems* was "to sing, blab, chortle, yodel, like people, and people in the sense of human beings subtracted from formal doctrines." He and Steichen were united in their conviction of art's power to touch and transform the quality of daily life, and their desire to create art which spoke from and to "the very heart of humanity."

＊

During that winter and spring of 1916, on the eve of the publication of *Chicago Poems*, Sandburg's work took him in many directions. At *The Day Book* he bore down on city and national issues, with labor matters his overriding concern. He covered the garment workers' strike; working conditions for railroad and hotel workers; Chicago's bus transportation system; Armour and Swift and various labor law violations; the Seamen's Union and the big coal combine. At the *International Socialist Review*, sometimes as Sandburg and sometimes as Jack Phillips, he contributed longer investigative pieces on the railroads, and poems: "Child of the Romans," appearing in the January issue, was an ironic measure of the distances between classes in American life:

> The dago shovelman sits by the railroad track
> Eating a noon meal of bread and bologna.
>> A train whirls by, and men and women at tables
>> Alive with red roses and yellow jonquils,
>> Eat steaks running with brown gravy,
>> Strawberries and cream, eclairs and coffee.
> The dago shovelman finishes the dry bread and bologna,
> Washes it down with a dipper from the water-boy,
> And goes back to the second half of a ten-hour day's work
> Keeping the road-bed so the roses and jonquils
> Shake hardly at all in the cut glass vases
> Standing slender on the tables in the dining cars.

At home in the evening circle of lamplight, or in moments snatched between newspaper assignments, he wrote poetry. For the February 1916 issue of *Poetry* he wrote his first extended piece of literary criticism; the subject was Ezra Pound's work. Sandburg's style as literary critic was informal, sometimes slangy. He described more readily than he analyzed, praised more readily than he condemned. He affirmed Pound's "creative art in poetry" and his influence "inciting new impulses in poetry." He defended Pound against his critics. Pound might be "named only to be cursed as wanton and mocker, poseur, trifler and vagrant," Sandburg wrote. "Or he may be classed as filling a niche today like that of Keats in a preceding epoch. The point is, he will be mentioned." If, Sandburg said, he were asked "for an offhand opinion as to who is the best man writing poetry today, I should probably answer, 'Ezra Pound.'"

Sandburg identified sympathetically with Pound's response to critics, for it was very much like his own:

> In the cool and purple meantime, Pound goes ahead producing new poems having the slogan, "Guts and Efficiency," emblazoned above his daily program of work. His genius runs to various schools and styles. He acquires traits and then throws them away. One characteristic is that he has no characteristics. He is a new roamer of the beautiful, a new fetcher of wild shapes, in each new handful of writings offered us.

The review concluded with comments on poetry which revealed as much about Sandburg's theory as about Pound's work:

> People write poetry because they want to. It functions in them as air in the nostrils of an athlete in a sprint. . . . It is a dark stuff of life that comes and goes.
>
> There are those who play safe and sane in poetry, as in mechanics and politics. To each realm its own gay madmen. . . .
>
> In a world with so high a proportion of fools, it is neither disgrace nor honor when people say of a finished work, "I can't understand it." The last word on the merits of it will be spoken in the future. . . .
>
> I like the pages of Ezra Pound. He stains darkly and touches softly. The flair of great loneliness is there. He is utter as a prairie horseman, a biplane in the azure, a Norse crag, or any symbol of the isolate, contemplative spirit of man unafraid and searching.

From London, Pound wrote his immediate approval of the review: "'Feb.' Poetry just arrived, you have done me very handsome." The piece was "very well written" and in the "one place where I disliked your idiom I find that you have Dr. Johnson on your side—so I shall sink into silence." Sandburg's review was, said Pound, "the first and only attempt anyone has made to treat my stuff as a whole."

Sandburg befriended another poet and critic in March 1916 when the portly, cigar-smoking aristocrat Amy Lowell arrived in Chicago to lecture on "The New Poetry, with Special Reference to Imagism" to a standing-room-only crowd. That week she and Sandburg laid the foundation for a lifelong friendship, despite an unlikely combination of opposite traits. She was one of the Boston Lowells, born into privilege and wealth. Sandburg was the lean, struggling son of Swedish immigrants. Her brother was president of Harvard University; his was a street department official in Galesburg, Illinois. They began to correspond and exchange poems, giving each other encouragement and advice. Sandburg told Lowell that his copy of her *Six French Poets* was "torn to pieces and thumbed by separate pages over the street cars of Chicago." She promised to send him another copy. He applauded her outspoken, opinionated work as a literary critic and standard bearer, urging her to "remember that color-bearers invite sharpshooters, and as you go further in ultimatums declaring your literary independence, there will be cross-fire."

Back in Boston recovering from jaundice, she wrote her appreciation: "Thank you for what you say about my being a colour-bearer. Sometimes the flag jerks and the nails tear, but it has not pulled away yet, in spite of all the firing, and I think it will flutter to the end, although as a mere rag of what it was."

Sandburg enjoyed Lowell's company and conversation immensely, relished the way she traveled "amid . . . furor," and told Alice Corbin Henderson that Lowell did "good work, with a brave air of a Cyrano de Bergerac facing life's inpulchritudes."

That March Sandburg met a magazine writer named Sinclair Lewis when he came to Chicago to work on some articles and his second novel, *The Job,* published in 1917. No one had taken much note of his earlier books *Hike and the Airplane* (1912), *Our Mr. Wrenn* (1914) or *The Trial of the Hawk* (1915), but his articles in *The Saturday Evening Post* and other journals were popular. Lewis told Alfred Harcourt he found Sandburg "Rough but *real.*"

Other poets and writers stimulated him, urged him on, ratified his work as he steadily produced new poems and "had a holy picnic with some gnarled massive ones I hacked out lately." Margaret Anderson published his work in *The Little Review* in April 1916; poet Alfred Kreymborg included Sandburg in *Others: An Anthology of New Verse,* published by Alfred Knopf. By the end of April 1916 he received his first copy of *Chicago Poems.*

A prefatory note thanked Harriet Monroe, Alice Corbin Henderson and William Marion Reedy "whose services have heightened what values of human address herein hold good." Sandburg dedicated the book to "My wife and Pal/Lillian [*sic*] Steichen Sandburg." From the first, the book was controversial. On a single point critics agreed: Carl Sandburg's poetry was "tradition shattering." His poetic forms were compared to those of Whitman and English poet William Ernest Henley, and even to the sculpture of Rodin.

W. A. Bradley of the *Dial* saw two Sandburgs,

one the rather gross, simple-minded, sentimental, sensual man among men, going with scarcely qualified gusto through the grimy business of modern life, which, mystical mobocrat, he at once assails and glorifies; the other the highly sensitized impressionist who finds in the subtle accords between his own ideal moods and the loveliest, most elusive aspects of the external world, material for delicate and dreamlike expression.

William Stanley Braithwaite of the *Boston Transcript* thought *Chicago Poems* a "book of ill-regulated speech that has neither verse or prose rhythms." According to Braithwaite, Sandburg had a "strong if unpleasant imagination, which is strangely woven with a tenderness that is striking" and "undoubted visual strength." According to the *New York Times* reviewer, Sandburg's work was "all alive, stirring, human. The best is very good indeed; the worst is dull and shapeless. But the worst can easily be let alone, for there is so much of the good."

Louis Untermeyer gave him the promised praise in *The Masses*. He wrote that Sandburg's book was "vivid with the health of vulgarity" and possessed "the strength of sorrow as well as the gaiety of strength." Amy Lowell reflected at length in *The Poetry Review* about the propagandistic nature of some of the *Chicago Poems*, but declared the volume "one of the most original books which this age has produced." The book received wide notice and Sandburg had his first extended encounter with the critics who could, he said, "type hap-hazard a column of words on the work of a lifetime, and assume without humility or prayer to say this is good and that is bad." He wrote appreciative notes to critics who had spoken positively of his book. "I am delighted that my small notice pleased you," H. L. Mencken responded to Sandburg's letter of thanks, and asked Sandburg to let *The Smart Set* see some of his work. "True enough, we have barred *vers libre* out of self-defense," Mencken told Sandburg, "but why not some prose? Let it come to me personally, and I'll go through it the same instant." Mencken shared with Sandburg his opinions of Chicago and New York: "The New York crowd is stale and flaccid. One never hears an idea there. I haven't been in Chicago since 1904, but I am coming again if the Devil is kind. It is the only genuinely American city. New York is now simply a provincial English town— almost a cathedral town."

Untermeyer reviewed *Chicago Poems* several times and Sandburg thanked him for the "human drive" of his reviews, liked having his work subjected to "human judgments" and "personal impressions" rather than "solemn oracular finalities." Sandburg believed Untermeyer understood his background, perceiving how he had "been in the writing game, by day jobs and by art-craft, from advertising manager of a department store to penny labor pamphleteer."

Letters of congratulations arrived from Harriet Monroe, Amy Lowell, Alfred Harcourt and a host of old friends from around the country. Among the most treasured of these were two notes from Sandburg's college professor and mentor Philip Green Wright, now professor of economics at Harvard University. Wright had enjoyed *Chicago Poems* immensely, he said. "The pictures which they bring to the mind's eye are vivid and the emotional content at once sets in vibration the reader's sympathy. The revolutionary animus is unmistakable. They ought to do good."

"The 'Chicago Poems' have come at last. Complimenti miei!" wrote Pound from England, as usual offering a mixture of praise and suggestions for improvement, revising Sandburg as he revised all other poets he knew, including Yeats and Eliot. "If you had the patience to listen to an old maid like myself and undergo these boredoms," Pound told Sandburg, "it would put more weight in your hammer."

Sandburg listened far more attentively to Amy Lowell's criticism of the propagandistic overtones of his poems. "I have, of course, a thousand points of defense of counter-offensive against the antagonism you voice," he told her, "and I'll get to those sometime with you. What you call 'prejudice' may be 'instinct,' primal immemorial heart-cry, of hate. Also I admit I may blurt this hate as one gagged or tongue-tied and therein fall short of the articulate."

On balance, Lowell approved Sandburg's work, and her opinion was influential, particularly in the East. She told Sandburg that the "lyric counterbalance" of the poems was "excellent and beautiful." The irony was "always swift as a sword, and gives me delight." She wanted to include Sandburg in her popular lecture series on contemporary American poets. "I am perfectly delighted with your book," she wrote. "I do not know when I have read anything that gives me so much pleasure."

Lowell expanded her *Poetry Review* article in *Tendencies in Modern American Poetry* (1917), recognizing Sandburg as a lyric poet but charging that "the lyricist in him has a hard time to make itself heard above the brawling of the marketplace." She praised Sandburg's virility and tenderness, his originality and strength, and asserted his importance as a democratic poet. Lowell, the New England patrician, observed that Sandburg belonged to "the new America which I have called multi-racial. He springs from the strong immigrant class which comes yearly in boatloads to our shores."

Lowell's charge that propaganda infiltrated his poetry led Sandburg to a careful examination of his motive and his work, and to an ongoing dilemma in artistic purpose. He believed then and throughout his career that a poet has an obligation to address the issues of his time, to articulate the problems in his world. But he respected Lowell's judgment. Her observations forced him to look critically at his poetry, his aesthetic theory, his philosophy as a writer, with the outcome of strengthening his purpose.

There was predictable praise from Harriet Monroe: "Carl Sandburg has the unassailable and immovable earthbound strength of a granite rock," she wrote extravagantly. She commended him for "speaking with his own voice, authoritatively like any other force of nature." She admired his "beauty and power," his "speech torn out of the heart," his gift for vividly depicting "all the unnecessary human anguish" which was "too bitter for any human being, poet or not, to endure in silence." She thought his book was a "masterpiece of portraiture" in its rendering of Chicago. She observed that his free-verse rhythms were "as personal as his slow speech or his massive gait; always a reverent beating-out of his subject." He chose rugged rhythms to match the pulse of the city; in his war poems "his rhythms pound like guns booming." She noted that Sandburg could write with a delicate touch or with "a smashing prose hammer." *Chicago Poems* had, she said, a heroic spirit "both in its joy and its sorrow."

Sandburg began to get a close-up view of literary politics as 1916 wore on. He found his work vulnerable to critics and the experience was irritating and frustrating. He had admired Pound for going ahead, in the face of critical controversy, "in the cool and purple meantime" to produce new work "having the slogan 'Guts and Efficiency.' " Sandburg took that approach himself, forging ahead with his poetry and prose despite the controversial and invigorating attention *Chicago Poems* elicited. Yet by the fall he was feeling estranged from the literary community. "Masters I haven't seen much of," he told Alice Corbin Henderson. "In fact I'm off the literary, even the poetry crowd, lately. The why of it is all huge and mixed with me but I guess more than anything else I like my politics straight and prefer the frank politics of the political world to the politics of the literary world."

Sandburg both enjoyed and resented the disparate judgments passed on his controversial book, but the attacks by some members of the literary establishment reinforced his sense of being an outsider, still a young stranger, a step removed from the establishment. Alfred Kreymborg's

Others: A Magazine of the New Verse carried these cryptic lines by Sandburg in July:

> Ivory domes . . white wings beating
> in empty space . .
> Nothing doing . . nuts . . bugs . . a regular
> absolute humpty-dumpty business . .
> pos-i-tive-ly . . falling off walls
> and no use to call doctor, lawyer,
> priest . . no use, boy, no use.
> O Pal of Mine, O Humpty Dumpty,
> shake hands with me.
> O Ivory Domes, I am one of You:
> Let me in.
> For God's sake—let me in.

If the inhabitants of the Ivory Domes of contemporary literature would not let Sandburg in, he still had the affirmation of the avant-garde and of the *Poetry* circle and the articulate easterner Amy Lowell. His unique voice and style were hard-won during years of dogged struggle, and he was not about to relinquish or modify them for a handful of literary critics.

*

Carl and Paula Sandburg had arranged the *Chicago Poems* into seven sections. The first, *Chicago Poems*, included vivid, often harsh portraits of the city and its people—the "Poor, millions of the Poor,/patient and toiling"; children working in factories; women of the night with "their hunger-deep eyes"; factory girls, cabaret dancers, policemen, a teamster en route to prison, a Jewish fish crier, Hungarian immigrants relaxing with music and beer on a Sunday afternoon; "muckers" digging ditches for the city gas mains; millionaires and cash girls; a stockyards hunky burying his child; "long lines" of working girls and men and children; anarchists and ice handlers; black workingmen, refugees from the South, "Brooding and muttering with memories of shackels." Billy Sunday's name was removed from his poem, now entitled "To a Contemporary Bunkshooter." There were portraits of women—a factory girl who died in a fire; an Indiana girl who lost herself in the impersonal city where she had come in search of "romance/and big things/and real dreams/that never go smash."

The second section, *Handfuls*, is a gentle counterpoint to the brutal reality of *War Poems (1914–1915)*. A contemplative section called *The Road and the End* gathers some of Sandburg's early poems, pensive reflections on death and loss, the meaning of the past and the possibility of the future. In *Fogs and Fires*, lyrical, sometimes imagistic poems speak to themes of love and memory and a restless searching for self and meaning.

Shadows paints haunting vignettes of the city, "Lines based on certain regrets that come with rumination upon the painted faces of women on North Clark Street, Chicago." Here there are bold indictments of the exploitation of women by men and by themselves:

> . . . Women of night life along the shadows,
> Lean at your throats and skulking the walls,
> Gaunt as a bitch worn to the bone,
> Under the paint of your smiling faces:
>   It is much to be warm and sure of tomorrow.

In "Trafficker" a prostitute smiles

> a broken smile from a face
> Painted over haggard bones and desperate eyes,
> All night she offers passers-by what they will
> Of her beauty wasted, body faded, claims gone,
> And no takers.

Was there poetry in "Harrison Street Court," in the words of the prostitute?

> ". . . If it ain't a pimp
> It's a bull what gets it.
> I been hustlin' now
> Till I ain't much good any more.
> I got nothin' to show for it.
> Some man got it all,
> Every night's hustlin' I ever did."

Sandburg explored the realities of prostitution in certain kinds of marriage in "Soiled Dove":

> Let us be honest; the lady was not a harlot until she married a corporation lawyer who picked her from a Ziegfeld chorus. . . .

This startling section of poems on lost women concluded with a poignant portrait of Chick Lorimer, "a wild girl keeping a hold/on a dream she wants." Nobody knew, Sandburg wrote, where or why she had

Gone with her little chin
Thrust ahead of her
And her soft hair blowing careless
From under a wide hat,
Dancer, singer, a laughing passionate lover . . .
Nobody knows where she's gone.

Other Days (1900–1910) is a soft-spoken denouement for a remarkably forceful and original volume of poems. In this final section Sandburg and Paula had arranged some of his earlier pieces, including "Dream Girl," juxtaposing them to sharp city portraits. There were strong evocations of "the people—the crowd—the mass," an indictment of government vice, imagistic tributes to Emily Dickinson and Stephen Crane and the enigmatic finale, "Gypsy": "Tell no man anything for no man listens,/Yet hold thy lips ready to speak."

A wide audience was beginning to listen to Carl Sandburg. He offended many, but the poems spoke in new ways to readers who still equated rhyme and romanticism with poetry. Amy Lowell characterized Sandburg and Masters as the two revolutionary American poets. At the heart of that revolution was their use of free verse and realistic subjects who spoke to the universal human experience as well as to the common themes of the American experience. Unlike Masters, Sandburg would continue to speak to and from the heart of American life, and when Louis Untermeyer pronounced him the emotional democrat of American poetry, Sandburg was well on his way to becoming the Poet of the People.

---※---

1916–1918

13. The Four Brothers

They are hunting death,
Death for the one-armed mastoid kaiser.
They are after a Hohenzollern head:
There is no man-hunt of men remembered like this.
The four big brothers are out to kill.
France, Russia, Britain, America—
The four republics are sworn brothers to kill the kaiser.

—Carl Sandburg, "The Four Brothers,"
Cornhuskers, 1918

Paula's hair had turned "iron-gray" by her thirty-third birthday in 1916. Friends described Sandburg's hair as steel-gray. They were a handsome couple whose shared struggle for recognition of his work had deepened the bond between them. They were expecting another child in June, and took particular delight then in five-year-old Margaret's development. Her intelligence and artistic talent amazed family and friends. The Montessori people used samples of her handwriting as well as her picture in their national brochure to demonstrate the success of their method. Because of her Montessori experience, Margaret could read and write, not being taught, her proud father boasted, but "exploding" into it.

At their little house in Maywood, a cherry tree in the backyard yielded fruit for pies and jelly. Paula kept a vegetable garden and produced currants for jelly and gooseberries for pies. She painted the kitchen white to make it appear larger, for the rooms in the house were small and narrow. A fireplace made the front parlor cozy. An oak cabinet and table nearly filled the dining room, but most family meals were eaten at the kitchen table covered with a practical checked oilcloth. Sandburg had a study-bedroom on the second floor, with slanting walls and a small window overlooking the cherry tree. The two small upstairs bedrooms opposite were bright with pink-and-blue-flowered wallpaper.

Each year in early spring Paula set out the crystal bowl which was a wedding gift from the magician Joseffy, and filled it with stones and paper-narcissus bulbs. She put the bowl on the dining room table in the sunniest room in the house, and soon the fragrance of unfolding flowers filled the air. There were many neighborhood playmates for Margaret, who remembered the Maywood house in later years as the happiest home of her childhood. During this time, Oma and Opa moved from their farm in Wisconsin to a yellow bungalow on Eighth Street nearby.

Janet Sandburg was born on June 27, 1916. "It's a girl," her proud father exulted to friends, "and perfection frog legs fastened to a perfection torso. Avoirdupois: 8.5 pounds. Wavy dark hair, this notably Northern French. Mother: 100%."

There was relief, after Madeline's death, that Janet was robust and healthy. She was a beautiful, happy baby, seldom fussing or crying. Margaret welcomed the baby sister and liked to help care for her and hold her. Janet had her mother's hair and face, while Margaret was the image of her father. "So," Sandburg said, "the household is at a glorious standoff." The Maywood house was further enlivened by the presence of an Irish setter, Dan, a gift from Harriet Vaughn Moody. Sandburg swore that the dog had "as immortal a soul as any of us: he's a marvelous listener."

Sandburg's love for home sang in some of his gentler lyrics, written about his wife and children, even the Irish setter pup "dozing in a half-sleep,/Browns of hazel nut, mahogany, rosewood, played off/against each other on his paws/and head." He had written of Paula and Margaret in *Chicago Poems* in a fragment called "Home":

> Here is a thing my heart wishes the world had more of:
> I heard it in the air of one night when I listened
> To a mother singing softly to a child restless and angry in the darkness.

"In your blue eyes, O reckless child," he wrote in "Margaret," "I saw today many little wild wishes,/Eager as the great morning." His poems captured moments in the child's life—her fascination with the moon, a "far silent yellow thing/Shining through the branches/Filtering on the leaves a golden sand," and her methodical work over the Montessori exercises: "The child Margaret begins to write numbers on a Saturday morning, the/first numbers formed under her wishing child fingers."

Janet, too, made her way into her father's poetry, published and unpublished, as in "Two Sisters," a quiet portrait of the familiar ordinary days which become precious in memory: "The two sisters in sleepers/ Tucked in the sheets of their trundles/Swaddled and put away in the dark,/These are sparrows under the eaves." As the children slept, Paula and Sandburg worked or read "at the evening lamp." Home was a refuge from the "sweeping, chaotic, vivid life" of the larger world.

Sandburg often wrote letters at night, sustaining in that way the literary friendships he most valued. He was particularly faithful in corresponding with Alice Corbin Henderson, knowing her loneliness and isolation in New Mexico, where she and her family now lived because of her health. He shared with her his admiration for Ezra Pound, whose newest poems had recently appeared in *Poetry*: "I am for him stronger than ever since this last sheaf in Poetry. He is so doggone deliberate and mocking and masterly in many of his pieces . . . if only his letters and personal relationships had the big ease and joy of life his art has I would hit it off great with him."

Vachel Lindsay sent Sandburg an inscribed copy of *Rhymes to Be Traded for Bread*. He read proof of Masters's *The Great Valley*. "In power, range of pictures, play of motives, it will surpass Spoon River," he wrote Henderson. "It is a terrible book and will bring a hell's storm of censure. Its art, method and craftsmanship isn't up to Spoon River. But the size, vision and assertion of it are above Spoon River."

Chicago Poems had received other negative reviews that summer and autumn, prompting Sandburg to tell Amy Lowell that "the critics are more our enemies than the poets." Masters told Sandburg that he expected his work to "be roundly swatted by critics and the author must anticipate savage jabs." Sandburg tried to insulate himself from critical attacks, but the ongoing exposure to the intricate politics of the literary world heightened his contempt, however defensive, for the power of literary criticism. He began to see it as another dynamic in the struggle of the individual against the establishment, a variation on the theme of the repression of the working man by the controlling class. He had been a maverick in politics, an outspoken idealist and champion of reform. He could play that role with equal energy in poetry. He had found his style and he would keep it, no matter what the self-appointed literary elite had to say about it. Within himself and his own experience he had found his voice and subject. "Can each see signs of the best by a look in the looking-glass? is/there nothing greater or more?" Whitman had written. "Does all sit there with you, with the mystic unseen Soul?"

Sandburg used the looking-glass image in "Chicago Poet," a wry, introspective poem about the ongoing search for the artistic self:

I SALUTED a nobody.
I saw him in a looking-glass . . .

Ah, this looking-glass man!
Liar, fool, dreamer, play-actor,
Soldier, dusty drinker of dust—
Ah! he will go with me . . .

✳

World war overpowered every other issue in the Presidential election year of 1916. Republican candidate Charles Evans Hughes, the bearded Associate Justice of the Supreme Court, ran a close race, carrying the eastern states with his charges that Wilson was a weak leader. Wilson argued that he had persuaded Congress to pass the Adamson Act as well as a Workmen's Compensation Act to benefit federal employees. He had prevented the potential paralysis of a national rail strike, and established federal farm loan banks to provide cheap mortgages to farmers. Many of these domestic programs had first been articulated in earlier years by socialists and progressives who, not surprisingly, supported Wilson's re-election campaign. He carried California to counteract his losses in the East and won the election.

Sandburg's interest in the campaign kept him from other work. "I'll bet more poetic temperaments have been violent over this election of today than any in long years," he told a friend. He supported Wilson, and by then, according to a short autobiographical sketch he provided for Henry Holt and Company, he did not belong to "any clubs or societies" and had "quit the Socialist Party as a party." After they left Milwaukee, he and Paula never renewed their membership in the Social-Democratic Party. Sandburg's political concern was as strong as ever, but he articulated it from the wider, more objective angle of the journalist and commentator rather than the immediate involvement of the activist and partisan.

Thus by 1916 Carl and Paula were no longer politically involved in socialism. Many socialists and former socialists, including John Reed, supported Wilson in 1916, and the national membership in the Socialist Party had diminished by thirty-five thousand names, a decline of nearly thirty percent since the peak membership year of 1912. The Sandburgs never again affiliated with a political party, although they supported liberal causes all their lives. But as Sandburg's identity and visibility as a journalist grew nationally, his detachment from party politics was essential to his credibility.

He had tried both politics and poetry, and decided he preferred the "frank politics of the political world," however, "to the politics of the literary world" and "politicians, saloon keepers and thieves to the general run of poets and critics for company."

*

Despite widespread critical skepticism about his poetry, Sandburg's mail and frequent requests to reprint his poems proved that many Americans liked his work. A newspaper syndicate commissioned him to write a Thanksgiving poem to be run in a national Sunday news magazine, and he complied with "Fire Dreams," "Written to be read aloud, if so be, Thanksgiving Day." At Christmas time the *Chicago Evening Post* and the *Denver Express* carried his Christmas poem, "Why Does the Story Never Wear Out?"

Unbeknown to Sandburg, Ezra Pound in London was searching for ways to provide material support for him and other poets. Pound wrote to Felix Schelling, his former English professor at the University of Pennsylvania, proposing a fellowship program for writers:

> I keep on writing in *Poetry*, a distressful magazine which does however print the few good poems written in our day along with a great bundle of rubbish. . . . I keep on writing on the subject of fellowships for creation as a substitute for, or an addition to, fellowships for research.
>
> Now that there can no longer be any suspicion of my wanting the thing for myself, I think it may be more use to write to you than to keep on addressing that many-eared monster with no sense, the reading public. . . .
>
> I have in mind a couple of youngish men whose work will stay imperfect through lack of culture. Sandburg is a lumberjack who has taught himself all that he knows. He is on the way toward simplicity. His energy may for all one knows waste itself in an imperfect and imperfectable [sic] argot.
>
> [Orrick] Johns is another case. A year in a library, with a few suggestions as to reading and no worry about their rent might bring permanent good work out of either of these men.
>
> Masters is too old and instead of rewriting *Spoon River* he has gone off into gas. Still a year's calm would do even him some good . . . It is dull repetition to say that every other art has its endowed fellowships. Poetry, which needs more than any other art the balance of study, is without them.

Unaware of Pound's interest on his behalf, Sandburg stuck to the regimen he was now accustomed to. He worked energetically at his newspaper job, and flourished in it. In the after-hours he turned out reviews and articles for the *International Socialist Review* under at least three names—Jack Phillips, Militant, and Sandburg or C.S. He wrote and rewrote the poetry, still teaching himself. He told another poet that he turned to art "between-whiles" and demanded that "it deliver rapidly." He was learning from others as well as from his own experiments in poetry, keeping inexorably on his course "toward simplicity."

Pound offered to submit Sandburg's *Chicago Poems* to a London publisher, and forgave Sandburg when he heard secondhand that Sandburg did not care for his "Three Cantos," just published in *Poetry.* "I discount Sandburg's objection," Pound said, "by the fact that he would probably dislike anything with foreign quotations in it."

For all his eccentricities, Pound had been a staunch supporter of the work of other writers. Most recently, he had persuaded his wife, Dorothy, to subsidize publication of T. S. Eliot's *Prufrock and Other Observations.* Yet Pound was profoundly discouraged in those war-ridden days about getting his own work published in the United States. He sought Sandburg's help, therefore, in securing an American firm to publish his prose.

Pound's memoir of the brilliant young sculptor Henri Gaudier-Brzeska had been well-reviewed, and he knew that Sandburg was at work on a review of the book for the *Dial.* Gaudier-Brzeska had been killed in June 1915 at Neuville-Saint-Vaast; his war letters, literally written from the trenches, opened Pound's eyes to the grim reality of the war. Heartened by Sandburg's interest and aware of Sandburg's growing reputation and his alliance with a good American publishing firm, Pound asked his assistance:

> . . . the point is that my blasts re/poetry ought to be published rather than this book on sculpture. Now the main drive of my poetic manifestos concerns America and not England. It is foolish to expect England to care about or an English publisher to be interested in an American awakening. Some American firm ought to print my prose on the decade . . . No man sits down to write an essay when he has a poem inside him. One can't be a perpetual volcano of verse. There are times when one plays tennis, fences or writes a Damn-your-eyes-and liver manifesto. . . . Just talk this up a bit, when you're not saving a slum or shooting a capitalist.

Sandburg had no success in pleading Pound's case, and the *Dial* rejected his review of Pound's book after it had already been set in galleys. "I am very sorry that your review of Gaudier-Brezeska is not suitable for *The Dial* after all the trouble you and we have taken with it," wrote a *Dial* editor. "This is not a review, but a laudatory obituary."

Disappointed for himself but most of all for Pound, Sandburg took heart from some good-humored advice from Vachel Lindsay. "I do not take to the poetry scraps a bit," said Lindsay.

They are all nonsense to me when you consider that there are one hundred million good Americans who do not know there is even an Amy Lowell. . . . As it is the more we scrap, the more ingrowing we get, and the more divorced from the normal American currents. If all the critics in the United States shouted through one megaphone, our next door neighbor would not hear, and Whitman would not be vindicated. We can all afford to unite, and charge abreast at the American people.

Sandburg took the next "poetry scrap" in stride. When Conrad Aiken attacked him in the *Poetry Journal* in an article entitled "Poetic Realism," he did not respond. Aiken granted Sandburg credit for being "individual" with the "raciness of originality." His poetry showed "Vigor, a certain harshness bordering on the sadistic, a pleasant quality of sensuousness in unexpected places, ethical irony and sentimentality." But, admonished Aiken, Sandburg was a socialist who consistently preached socialist morals. His form was deficient, displaying only a "rather rudimentary sense of balance or echo." Sandburg had concluded that it was useless to become involved in literary politics. Years later, however, when the Aiken review was included in an anthology, Sandburg wrote to the editor protesting that Aiken had been inaccurate in "forty ways, and is the only young squirt that has ever called me 'sadistic.' "

✳

The year 1917 was one of turbulence and loss, personal and global. Early in the new year came the tragic news that George and Hopie Fox's young son Randall had died of burns from a fire in a kerosene stove. The boy was trying to make a fire to be helpful and surprise his mother, but it got out of control. Knowing the depths of loss and pain inherent in a child's death, Sandburg wrote to their old Appleton friends the Foxes, now living in Michigan:

> A world that could produce a Randall can't be a crazy world . . . the Unknown and Unknowable is close to us, in touch, all the time. . . . With Janet and Margaret, I find I am ready for anything all the time. Every day I come home and find them alive I take as a day snatched from Death. I think too about how they die every week. The little fluff of a Janet we had a year ago is dead. The Margaret that was learning to talk three years ago is dead and replaced with an endless chatterer. . . . Every beautiful thing I know is ephemeral, a thing of a moment. Life is a series of things that vanish. . . . I had two brothers go with diphtheria and we had a double funeral on a bitter winter day when I was a boy. I buried a child that had not lived long enough to be named . . . We are all such little things. A day of life is a day snatched from death.

*

For Sandburg it was a year of "work and war of every kind." As United States involvement in the world war deepened, his attention turned from domestic issues to the themes of war. He had written to the Foxes, "Life is a series of things that vanish." It was a theme which permeated his work in that year of escalating war and chaos. The United States, under President Wilson's leadership, stood at the agonizing crossroads between neutrality and preparedness, and overt intervention in the world conflict. Wilson took on the thankless and probably impossible job of peacemaker, ameliorator, negotiator in the most complex and far-flung war the world had ever experienced. He championed the "silent mass of mankind every-where who have as yet had no . . . opportunity to speak their real hearts out concerning the death and ruin."

When at the end of January it became clear that there would be no immediate peace agreement with Germany, and the Germans announced unrestricted submarine warfare, Wilson broke diplomatic relations. War tension heightened. Wilson began arming merchant ships in March, despite opposition of pacifists such as Wisconsin senator Bob La Follette, who led the congressional defeat of Wilson's proposal. The March 18 sinking of three unarmed American merchantmen resulted in heavy casualties.

Strikes and food riots in Petrograd erupted into chaos, and the in-evitable revolution of Russian soldiers and workers. Czar Nicholas II abdicated on March 15. "The world must be made safe for democracy," President Wilson told the people of the United States and the world on April 2. He believed it his "constitutional duty" to "take immediate steps not only to put the country in a more thorough state of defense, but also to exert all its power and employ all its resources to bring the government of the German Empire to terms and end the war." He pronounced it a "fearful thing to lead this great peaceful people into war, into the most terrible and disastrous of all wars, civilization itself seeming to be in the balance. But the right is more precious than peace."

The day had come, Wilson told the listening nation, "when America is privileged to spend her blood and her might for the principles that gave her birth and happiness and the peace which she has treasured." On April 6, 1917, the United States declared war on Germany.

Like a slow incoming tide, the reality of war began to touch American life. Sandburg immediately began to write a column called "War Notes" for *The Day Book*. The April issue of *Poetry* contained seventeen of his new poems, more subdued and constrained than the *Chicago Poems*. "My people are gray,/pigeon gray, dawn gray, storm gray," he wrote in the introduction. "I call them beautiful,/and I wonder where they are going."

✳

Sandburg saw Robert Frost that turbulent year and liked him immediately, calling him "the strongest, loneliest, friendliest personality among the poets today." Frost gave some people the impression that he instantly disliked Sandburg. Louis Untermeyer, who knew both Frost and Sandburg well, thought otherwise. He told Sandburg he was happy to know of his admiration for Frost, "one of the finest persons still left on this crazy planet." Untermeyer told Sandburg that Frost reciprocated his admiration. "I spent a couple of days with him last week and he said so," Untermeyer wrote Sandburg, who told Alfred Harcourt he was going to write Frost "once a year; and feel the love of him every day."

Sandburg and Sherwood Anderson had become good friends by then as well. By 1913 Anderson had written four novels; one of them, *Windy McPherson's Son*, was published in 1916. When Sandburg discovered that Anderson also wrote poetry, he sent some of his poems to Alice Corbin Henderson, who pressed Harriet Monroe to publish them in *Poetry*. Henderson thought Anderson's poetry was better than his prose, "finer, more indigenous." She urged Sandburg to get more of Anderson's poems for *Poetry*, "and get them to put it on the first page. That's all. If they don't, they might as well quit."

Largely at Henderson's urging, Harriet Monroe published a group of Anderson's poems, "Midwestern Chants," in September 1917, but declined his later submissions.

Sandburg had immediate sympathy for Anderson, two years his senior, who had, like himself, come late to success as a writer and who had wrestled with the encumbrances of responsibility for a family. Anderson was a successful copywriter turned failed businessman turned copywriter again to support his wife, three children, and an unrelenting passion for writing—which led to a conspicuous nervous breakdown in 1912 and the breakup of his marriage in 1915. Anderson's second wife was the artist Tennessee Mitchell, who had been Edgar Lee Masters's mistress.

Sandburg maintained his friendship with Anderson, Henderson and Amy Lowell that spring, but otherwise still felt himself isolated from the literary world. "Glancing over some old and genuinely propaganda material of mine of ten years ago," he confessed to Lowell, "I got a sneaking suspicion that maybe you're right and maybe I have struck a propaganda rather than a human note at times." He could accept her advice because he respected her, but he still insisted that "The goddam academicians haven't got me."

At *The Day Book* the war occupied more and more of Sandburg's attention, and, over at the *International Socialist Review*, in the guise of Jack Phillips, he reflected on "The Drift of the War." He finished the war poem "Grass," whose somber, ironic lines were much quoted and reprinted:

> Pile the bodies high at Austerlitz and Waterloo.
> Shovel them under and let me work—
>   I am the grass; I cover all.
>
> And pile them high at Gettysburg
> And pile them high at Ypres and Verdun.
> Shovel them under and let me work.
> Two years, ten years, and passengers ask the conductor:
>   What place is this?
>   Where are we now?
>
> I am the grass.
> Let me work.

✳

When *The Day Book* ceased publication in July 1917, a victim of the war, Sandburg was temporarily out of a job. Scripps, consolidating the resources of his publishing company, liquidated the experimental *Day Book* and called Negley Cochran to Washington. Sandburg quickly got an assignment to cover a union strike mediation in Omaha for the National Labor Defense Council, organized to help safeguard the constitutional rights of striking union workers.

He missed Paula, from whom he had not been separated for more than a handful of days since their move to Chicago in 1912. "I write your name/And I call in the dark/For your hand," he wrote in a group of poems to her called simply "Omaha, 1917." "The lips of you are with me tonight./And the arms of you are a circle of white./The dream of it burns./And I want you and the stars./I want you and a sickle moon./The finger-tips of you/Five hundred miles away/Make a wireless crying flash."

After nearly a month away, Sandburg returned home to Chicago and was soon offered a job at the *Chicago Evening American*, owned by William Randolph Hearst, whom he had previously condemned in the same breath with Billy Sunday. Sandburg was hired to write editorials for a hundred dollars a week and the promise of freedom to write about anything and everything. At first he enjoyed the job, and produced editorials he was proud of. "I look at my scrapbook of those editorials," he wrote years later, "and can say, without bragging, that they could stand among the best of the time: I had learned my craft." But then Hearst began to request certain editorial subjects and positions. Sandburg accommodated Hearst for nearly three weeks until he "began to feel some kind of a deterioration, something happening to the deeper roots" of his personality. He realized that he was a "mismatch" at the Hearst paper. "They had their own way of doing things," he said. "My way didn't fit theirs." He resigned, and found a job, at half his Hearst pay, on the *Chicago Daily News*.

As a boy in Galesburg, Sandburg had delivered Chicago newspapers, and on his first trip to Chicago in 1896, he had walked to see "the Daily News Building, the Tribune and Inter-Ocean buildings" because he had "carried and sold so many of their papers that I wanted to see where they were made." He had "great respect for Victor Lawson and his *Record* and *Daily News*" even then, and now, in 1917, a seasoned newsman himself, he had great regard for Lawson, publisher of the *Daily News*, and knew other writers there, including colorful reporter, novelist and playwright Ben Hecht.

Sandburg immediately liked the "curious academy of mortals" who worked in the "old ramshackle Chicago Daily News building at Wells and Madison Streets." His colleagues included veteran newsmen Ben Hecht and Keith Preston, but the "human pivot of this motley and droll gang" was news editor and later managing editor Henry Justin Smith. Sandburg had a deep respect for his scholarly, bespectacled editor, who encouraged his reporters in literary pursuits beyond news writing. After an hour-long talk that summer of 1917, Smith hired Sandburg to write editorials.

It was a tumultuous time for the nation. The slogan "he kept us out of war" had helped reelect Woodrow Wilson in 1916. Consequently, there had to be a hasty and profound reconfiguration of public opinion to support the decision to enter the war in 1917. As in any volatile time, there were not simply two sides to public opinion, but many sides, all of them complex and increasingly emotional, from the militarism of Teddy Roosevelt and his National Security League to the pacifistic, socialistic People's Council of America for Democracy and Peace, organized in June to oppose conscription and the suppression of civil liberties, and to encourage a negotiated peace.

Immediately after his declaration of war, Wilson appointed a Committee on Public Information, headed by journalist George Creel and composed of the secretaries of State, War and the Navy, to mount a massive propaganda drive encouraging the American people to support the war effort. The process of mobilizing public opinion unleashed active hatred for real and perceived enemies. As there were few privately owned radios, a corps of 75,000 public speakers, dubbed "four-minute men" for their short patriotic speeches, spoke in theaters and movie houses and other public meeting places. The young medium of the motion picture displayed the first-ever, graphic, live-action pictures of war in progress, with emphasis on alleged German atrocities. American moviegoers were horrified.

In the ensuing demand for loyal "pure Americanism," immigrants and native-born Americans of foreign names or appearance were compelled to publicly affirm their Americanism, by kissing the flag, for example, or buying war bonds. War hysteria amounted to paranoia, and a virulent anti-German fever spread throughout the Midwest, where German immigrants had traditionally settled, and from coast to coast. Some states enacted laws prohibiting the teaching of German in schools and colleges, banning German books from libraries, forbidding German or Austrian musicians to perform in public, outlawing German and Austrian music altogether. German-Americans suffered attacks on property and person. Teddy Roosevelt once even advocated shooting any German-American thought to be disloyal to the United States. In Indiana a coal miner was lynched for refusing to buy a liberty bond; in Montana an IWW organizer was tortured and lynched; in St. Louis, Missouri, Germans were attacked on the streets as well as in the press. In New York, when the president of Columbia University fired two pro-German professors as a patriotic gesture, history professor Charles Beard resigned in protest.

"The world could not pass through the welter of hate and destruction of life and property of the four years of war without bringing dire results," Clarence Darrow remembered in later years. "Indeed, the war well-nigh wiped out the best products of civilization. In America it brought an era of tyranny, brutality and despotism, that, for the time at least, undermined the foundations upon which our republic was laid."

Said Sandburg, "The planet is shaken."

Within the cataclysm of the war there were millions of smaller wars fought on the interior battlegrounds of conscience, heart and soul. The Espionage Act of June 15, 1917, levied a ten-thousand-dollar fine and a twenty-year prison term on persons who interfered with the draft and encouraged disloyalty to the United States. The law was supplemented on May 16, 1918, by the Sedition Act, which prescribed the same penalties for obstructing the sale of U.S. bonds, discouraging recruiting, or uttering disloyal or abusive language about the government, the constitution, the flag or the military uniform. The country's socialists were prime targets of the new Espionage Act, and many Americans did not realize that conflict about the war was rife within the Socialist Party, as it had been in the nation at large.

Nearly two hundred socialists gathered for an emergency convention on April 7, 1917, the day after the official declaration of war. With Kate Richards O'Hare as chairman of the War and Militarism Committee, delegates met in the Planters Hotel in St. Louis to draft a socialist war platform. After vigorous debate, they adopted a majority report which stated their "unalterable opposition" to the war and challenged workers around the world to "refuse support to their governments in their wars," contending that only capitalists would gain from the war, while workers would be forced to sacrifice everything, even life itself. Victor Berger, Emil Seidel and Winfield Gaylord were among the nine or so delegates from Wisconsin. In their delegation, as in the entire convention, opinion ran the gamut from antiwar to prowar fervor.

Against his better judgment, Berger signed the majority statement. Seidel advocated the dissenting minority report. Gaylord, adamantly opposed to the majority platform, broke with the party once and for all, and Berger became the specific focus of his disenchantment. The split Wisconsin delegation could have been a microcosm for the whole, rancorous socialist dispute over the war. Absent from the April convention was Eugene Debs, too ill to make the trip, supporting the official socialist stand on the war, and watching at a distance with deep dismay as time wore on and "federal marshals corraled radicals of every nationality, faction, and ideological persuasion" under the Espionage Act. Inevitably, Debs himself would be imprisoned under the Act before the war was over.

Many socialist intellectuals left the party in 1917, if they had not already done so, to protest the St. Louis proclamation. Meyer London of New York, the only socialist in the United States Congress, had voted to support Wilson's war appropriations bill. Sandburg's friend Emanuel Haldeman-Julius took the editorship of the New Appeal, the sequel to the Appeal to Reason, and endorsed the pro-war Social Democratic League of America, a coalition of pro-war socialists which John Spargo, Algie Simons, Gaylord and Upton Sinclair helped to form. Except for Sandburg's often pseudonymous contributions to the International Socialist Review, he and Paula were removed from organized socialism long before the 1917 conflicts riddled the party's programs, alienated its leaders from each other, and further estranged the party from the mainstream of American life.

One particularly visible, effective group in swinging public support to Wilson and war was the American Alliance for Labor and Democracy, organized by Samuel Gompers of the American Federation of Labor, with financial support from the White House. This patriotic labor group hoped to transform the war opposition of many farmers and urban laborers to active support for Wilson. Gompers got important help from journalists, including Chester Wright, now editor of the socialist *New York Call*, and Carl Sandburg.

More than a thousand American citizens were indicted under the Espionage Act. Socialists received the most indictments, with IWW members next. But age, sex and affiliation were no protection against surveillance and indictment. Neighbor spied on neighbor, employee on boss, citizen on citizen. Depending on one's vantage point, Wilson's Committee on Public Information was thorough or ruthless in its pursuit of disloyal Americans. Clarence Darrow, who supported the war, was appalled at the excesses, however well-intentioned, of government officials and others who sought to implement the Espionage Act. "Men were arrested, indicted, and convicted, and sent to prison, all over the United States," Darrow said, "for daring to express their opinions by speech or press." Sandburg the reporter was struggling to make sense of it all. He wrote to Alice Corbin Henderson, apologizing for his failure to answer a letter: "I have been among strikers in the coal fields, the American Federation of Labor convention, among pacifists, Sinn Feiners and German spies, and there has been such a tumult in my head. . . ."

※

In late summer, before he left the *Chicago Evening American*, Sandburg watched a Chicago parade of the city's first draftees, marching in uniform, "whistling 'Yankee Doodle' and 'Marching through Georgia' and 'Turkey in the Straw!' " As he watched, he wondered what the war would mean to each of them. Whatever private reassessment he was giving to his own politics and war posture, Sandburg was resolute in his concern for each soldier caught up in the vast, intricate web of war. "O sunburned clear-eyed boys!" he wrote, "I stand on sidewalks and you go by with drums and guns and bugles,/You—and the flag!/And my heart tightens, a fist of something fills my throat/When you go by."

※

Like everyone else they knew, Carl and Paula confronted the reality of war and tried to cope. They had lived and worked in the German-American city of Milwaukee. Paula and her brother grew up understanding the German culture and spirit. Steichen had chosen France as his home and the setting for his development as an artist. There in Voulangis he had his studio and a profuse garden, where he grew roses and experimented with breeding delphiniums and poppies, creating an extravagance of bloom and color. As the German army had moved on Paris in the first year of the war, Steichen cabled his friend Eugene Meyer in New York for advice about whether to move his family home to the United States. "Advise strategic retreat," Meyer had immediately replied, and the Steichens managed to get out of France two days before an advance patrol of German troops arrived in the quiet village. Later in the war, a British cavalry troop camped in the ravages of his delphinium field.

Steichen, Sandburg and Paula shared the deep affection for the United States so often ingrained in first-generation citizens whose parents moved, at great cost, into another nation's culture. The sinking of the *Lusitania* had galvanized Steichen's commitment to the war, he told his sister and brother-in-law. He decided he wanted to "be a photographic reporter, as Mathew Brady had been in the Civil War," and volunteered his services. The Signal Corps, aware of his stature as one of the world's leading photographers, accepted him, and by the fall of 1917 Lieutenant Edward Steichen was in France.

He had dreamed of arriving in France in his uniform and going to call on the great sculptor Rodin. They had been as close as father and son, and Steichen had often photographed Rodin at work. He knew his arrival in military uniform would be for Rodin "a symbol of American coming over to help France." But Steichen landed at Cherbourg on November 18 only to discover that Rodin had died the day before. He attended Rodin's funeral, in uniform, representing "the American Army and General Pershing," and, he took the liberty of adding, the "Younger American Artists."

Steichen was assigned to study aerial photography, got himself transferred to the photographic section of the Air Service, and was soon working for General Pershing and General Billy Mitchell devising methods for high-altitude aerial photography, with portable battle-line photo laboratories set up in trucks to deliver as many as five thousand photographic prints overnight.

The warriors in this twentieth-century battle were developing deadly new technology: aerial bombs, nerve gas, tanks, complex munitions. In this sophisticated new war, their destructive prowess seemed complete. Having contrived new means of decimation by land, sea and air, they now experimented with ways to photograph themselves in the process of mutual destruction. In hopes of shortening the war and hastening an Allied victory, Steichen and other photographers worked to photograph the enemy in action and to develop the art of "reading lines, shadows, blurs, camouflage in the finished prints of the day's duty," and through the interpretation of those prints, to decipher the movement, strength and strategy of the enemy.

Back home, Sandburg wrote about the war and its repercussions for the *Daily News*. He reported the Minneapolis labor convention of the American Alliance for Labor and Democracy, wrote about Gompers's pro-war activities and interviewed IWW leader Big Bill Haywood "Through a steel cage door of the Cook County Jail," where Haywood and other Wobbly leaders were incarcerated, charged with "Ten thousand crimes of sabotage aimed at hindering the war effort." In the coal-mining towns of Illinois, Sandburg interviewed striking miners who had been accused of sabotaging the war effort. He wrote an editorial on freedom of speech.

For Sandburg and other journalists and writers it was a time of crucial self-discovery. Sherwood Anderson told Sandburg that he felt profoundly the difficulty facing the "radical people of America" in the current situation. For John Dos Passos, Ernest Hemingway, e. e. cummings, Dashiell Hammett, Malcolm Cowley and other young writers "the ambulance corps and the French military transport" were "college-extension courses" in 1917, said Cowley. Some writers, like Edgar Lee Masters, found it difficult to write: "I find I can live just one day at a time," he told Harriet Monroe. He said he had to "fight down a temptation to devour the days ahead. We wait and wait for an end, for a change, a release. The War has gone so thoroughly into me that I can hardly go on sometimes."

Walter Lippmann, who, like Sandburg, had been secretary to a socialist mayor, used his podium at *The New Republic* to support President Wilson's war policies. He sometimes wrote memoranda to Wilson and speeches for him, believing that Wilson was a great statesman who had "lifted the inevitable horror of war into a deed so full of meaning." Nevertheless, he cautioned the President to insure the protection of "a healthy public opinion" and free speech. Government censors should, he warned, bear in mind "the long record of folly which is the history of suppression." He came to feel that the administration's repressive measures diluted liberal support for the war as time wore on, and divided the nation's "articulate opinion into fanatical jingoism and fanatical pacifism."

He might have been thinking of Sandburg's friends at *The Masses*, which Louis Untermeyer, a contributing editor, described as "a liberal interpretation of arts and letters" and a "fusion (or confusion) of Socialism and Bohemianism." John Reed had written in *The Masses*: "I have been with the armies of all belligerents except one, and I have seen men die, and go mad, and lie in hospitals suffering hell; but there is a worse thing than that. War means an ugly mob-madness, crucifying the truth-tellers, choking the artists, sidetracking reforms, revolutions, and the working of social forces."

Some of their friends at *The Masses* provided funds so that Reed and his wife, Louise Bryant, could travel to Russia in August 1917 to report on the Russian Revolution, which Reed wholeheartedly endorsed. They covered the power struggle between Lenin and Kerensky which resulted in the November 1917 Bolshevik Revolution and the installation of the Lenin-Trotsky government, with Stalin as a minister, and the organization of a communist, all-Russian government.

In 1917 the staff of *The Masses*, including Reed, Eastman, Untermeyer and Dell, was indicted for "conspiring to effect insubordination and/or mutiny in the armed and naval forces of the United States" and "conspiring to obstruct enlistment and recruiting." Two trials ended with hung juries, and the magazine was reorganized and named *The Liberator*. Robert Frost, who had kept his distance politically and poetically from the war, wrote his friend Untermeyer that while he disliked *The Masses*, "If the Postmaster General jugs you and starts despitefully using you I am coming to N.Y. as a sort of lay lawyer to defend you as Thoreau offered to defend John Brown." Unlike Sandburg, Frost believed that a poet should not write anything but poetry, and held to that conviction during wartime. He had discovered, he said, that "do or say my damndest I can't be other than orthodox in politics love and religion." As he observed the world scene from Amherst and Franconia, he wrote to chastise Untermeyer for continuing to "mess with the Masses (or is it mass with the messes?)." While Sandburg had stated his preference for the politics of the "real" world over the politics of poetry, Frost, the son of a frustrated politician, disdained politics altogether.

Just as Frost and Sandburg wrote poetry in different forms, Sandburg had chosen a far different role in the war which transfigured life and lives, evoking orthodoxy in some, radicalism in others. Sandburg continued to examine the war with the clear, cold eye of the reporter and the burning vision of the poet, almost unique among writers of his time in his twofold coverage of World War I. The passionate antipathy to war expressed in his earlier poems gave way to a patriotic justification of this particular war in the poems he was writing in 1917. Amy Lowell observed in *Tendencies in Modern American Poetry*, published that year, that "No poet of today has touched the present war more convincingly, more poetically, than Mr. Sandburg."

While some of his poems continued to appear in the *International Socialist Review*, his prose contributions to the journal subsided. He concentrated on his work at the *Daily News*, and poured any leftover energy into a new volume of poetry that he believed "would surpass and put it all over the first one." That autumn of 1917 Sandburg was overwhelmed with "so much work and war of every kind" that it was difficult to keep up with all his projects. In October 1917 he published two items, one news story and one poem, which delineated his position on the war. In a story for the *Daily News* he openly condemned Victor Berger, implying that Berger and other German members of the Socialist Party who supported the St. Louis platform "formally opened the doors to sabotage through the elimination from its constitution of the anti-sabotage clause." Sandburg expressed his deep opposition to sabotage, a doctrine which, he pointed out, "was formally repudiated by the Socialist Party at the time the Socialists expelled W. D. Haywood, the IWW organizer."

In poetry, he demonstrated his radical change of theme in "The Four Brothers; Notes for War Songs (November 1917)," published in *Poetry* in November. The typed manuscript ran to five pages, and when Sandburg read it to Harriet Monroe, poet Muna Lee and others at the *Poetry* office one autumn day, they pronounced it a "great poem."

"Make war songs out of these;" he read in his dramatic stage baritone:

> Make chants that repeat and weave.
> Make rhythms up to the ragtime chatter of the machine guns;
> Make slow-booming psalms up to the boom of the big guns.
> Make a marching song of swinging arms and swinging legs . . .
>
> Cowpunchers, cornhuskers, shopmen, ready in khaki;
> Ballplayers, lumberjacks, ironworkers, ready in khaki;
> A million, ten million, singing, "I am ready . . ."
>
> They are hunting death,
> Death for the one-armed mastoid kaiser.
> They are after a Hohenzollern head:
> There is no man-hunt of men remembered like this.
> The four big brothers are out to kill.

France, Russia, Britain, America—
The four republics are sworn brothers to kill the kaiser . . .

Harriet Monroe sent fifty copies of the poem to newspapers across the country, and it was widely reprinted. Sandburg himself sent a copy to George Creel of President Wilson's Committee on Public Information, who wrote on October 12 to tell Sandburg he had "done a fine piece of work. . . . At your request, I am sending a copy of it to the President."

The poem was an immediate success, nationwide and abroad. Samuel Gompers had it widely reprinted for the American Alliance for Labor and Democracy. The American Library Association asked Sandburg to read the poem at their next national convention. Sherwood Anderson wrote to call the poem "a magnificent thing. . . . It sings and it has time sweep and bigness. Makes my heart jump to know we have a man like you in our town." Lloyd Lewis, then with the *Chicago Herald* and later with the *Daily News*, had criticized the last part of the poem when Sandburg showed it to him in manuscript. On seeing it in print, however, Lewis thought the whole poem stood up "majestically and beautifully." It was the best thing Sandburg had ever done, said Lewis, and "the best thing America at war has produced. . . . Whitman's 'Out of the Cradle' is the only thing of this kind I'd rank with this masterpiece of your's [sic]." He told Sandburg he could not read it aloud without weeping. Poet Edith Wyatt pronounced it a "splendid poem," and soldiers wrote to thank Sandburg for "The Four Brothers." His editor at the *Daily News* called it "the greatest poem the war has produced," praise echoed by many readers.

Sandburg received one letter which testified to the irony in his patriotic ode to "France, Russia, Britain, America—/The four republics" who were "sworn brothers to kill the kaiser." It came from Dr. Ben R. Reitman of Chicago, who was practicing medicine among the city's hobo population, treating gamblers, prostitutes, riffraff and the general poor. Reitman was a legendary hobo and tramp who doctored his way among the country's down and out until he became the lover and supporter of the anarchist Emma Goldman. He had recently left Goldman, his feelings for her and anarchy having grown "lukewarm," and had settled in Chicago with a new lover, determined to start a home and family. "Your poem 'The Four Brothers' is a great strong beautiful song of hope," Reitman wrote Sandburg. "Thank you for writing it."

A poem which can be endorsed simultaneously by a recently reformed anarchist and the President's chief of patriotic propaganda is ambiguous in its complexity, and open to several layers of interpretation. The powerful, emotional imagery of "The Four Brothers" elicits a subjective response. In the context of the other war poems of the time, "The Four Brothers" is bold and original. The cadence of the first stanza evokes Vachel Lindsay's unique chants, but the undergirding rhythm stems from the military parade, the organic, symbolic march of "The millions easy and calm with guns and steel, planes and prows," with a "hammering drumming hell to come."

The poem marks the turning point in Sandburg's attitude toward the war. Heretofore his war poetry attacked the brutality and hopeless tragedy of war—"The killing gangs are on the way." But with the United States entry into the conflict and the onset of the Russian Revolution, through which the "people of bleeding Russia" have overthrown the "last of the gibbering Romanoffs," Sandburg has changed his position. He gives his loyal support to the nation's commitment to the war, and the union of

> The people of bleeding France,
> The people of bleeding Russia,
> The people of Britain, the people of America—
> These are the four brothers, these are the four republics.

After his initial emotional response to the war, the poet says, he has carefully reconsidered his position:

> At first I said it in anger as one who clenches his fist in wrath to fling
>   his knuckles into the face of some one taunting;
> Now I say it calmly as one who has thought it over and over again at
>   night, among the mountains, by the sea-combers in storm.

This resounding evocation of God and country is structurally more rooted in oratory than in poetry. Here Sandburg the orator appeals to the emotions of his audience through graphic, compelling images:

> The death-yells of it all, the torn throats of men in ditches calling for
>   water, the shadows and the hacking lungs in dugouts, the steel
>   paws that clutch and squeeze a scarlet drain day by day—the storm
>   of it is hell . . .

The devices of oratory transcend the techniques of poetry in "The Four Brothers." Sandburg, the advocate of the working class, contends that in this particular War

> Only fighters gaunt with the red brand of labor's sorrow on their brows
>   and labor's terrible pride in their blood, men with souls asking
>   danger—only these will save and keep the four big brothers.

Only fighters, only "reckless men, ready to throw away their lives by hunger,/deprivation, desperate clinging to a single purpose imperturbable and/undaunted, men with the primitive guts of rebellion" can win for the world a "new thousand years."

"The Four Brothers" was reprinted and quoted often in that final year of the war's grip on the "blood-crossed, bloody-dusty ball of earth." But Sandburg was no longer content to stay at home and write about the war at a safe distance. At the age of forty he was not likely to be drafted, or accepted as an enlistee. "I sit in the chair and read the newspapers," he had written in his poem "Smoke":

> Millions of men go to war, acres of them are buried, guns and ships broken, cities burned, villages sent up in smoke, and children where cows are killed off amid hoarse barbecues vanish like finger-rings of smoke in a north wind.
>
> I sit in a chair and read the newspapers.

The war was a "world storm." Sandburg longed to see it for himself.

---

*

1918–1919

14. **World Storm**

Terribly big days. . . . Always I have loved watching
storms. And this world storm with all its shadows and
pain and hunger has its points . . .

> —Carl Sandburg to Paula Sandburg,
> January 30 [1919]

Through all the "blur and the chaos" of World War I, Sandburg's home was his sanctuary. "Amid the jabber of taxes, politics, and telegraph stories," he had written in the poem "May, 1915,"

And amid the war cries of the Germans smashing at Verdun . . .
Two cherry trees in an Illinois back yard put out one by one hundreds of
blossoms, jonquils broke yellow, and tulips broke red, and stood in the
sun.

He recorded the details of his home life in his diary that spring, using the imagery of war as a counterpoint to the gentle private life he lived with his family. He christened his daughters the "Homeyglomeys." "I open my eyes," he began some unpublished diary pages dated April 28, 1918:

It is daylight. . . . I hear raindrops falling on the shingles of the backroof
outside the west window two feet from my pillow. I remember this is
Sunday because last night was Saturday night and I was at Mrs. Moody's
house and went away with Robert Frost at midnight, walking thru the
black belt, promising Frost at the corner of Wabash and 18th that I would
do my best to get to his New Hampshire home next July after I read war
poems before the national convention of public librarians at Saratoga. I
have not shook all the sleep out of my head for a rainy Sunday morning. . . . I sleep more. I open my eyes. Rain still raining. A soft magnetic
rain and the grass a wild wet green. Crocus, daffodils, jonquils sing in the
garden. Drops of crystal slide along the clothesline wires. My Irish neighbor

sits at the kitchen window 200 yards away in a shirt without a collar, reading a newspaper. . . . It is a lazy half-rain that falls. Slices of light break through the west sky. It may be any kind of a day. I wiggle my right foot big toe and wonder how high is the pile of legs and arms sawed off by the hospital units on the western front last night. . . . I put on shoes and a suit of clothes I am willing to have wet through by the rain. I am going to walk in the rain, out toward Elmhurst where the frogs sing a day like this and the cabbage fields have yearnings.

I eat two apples, three pieces of bread and butter, a cup of black coffee, a hot potato with butter, a slice of jelly cake and another cup of coffee. I read the news section of the Tribune. The western front line is holding but threatened. Germany would stand to win the war if the United States hadn't gone in. On the sewing machine next to the kitchen table is a book: Cavalry of the Clouds, written by "Contact" an aviation observer. Until the hour hand of the clock points to 4, I read the good talk of an intelligent, imaginative birdman. I eat another hot potato with butter, more bread and butter and black coffee. I read on of birdmen. Between soft showers a burst of yellow sun pours into the kitchen. Then back to rain. I must go out in this wonderful soft magnetic rain. I must follow further this birdman's life. . . . I finish the book. I read till the clock says 6:30. I slip on an old raincoat and go west through Melrose Park. The sunset dies under a flotilla of light destroyers. Five blackbirds are printed against the west. How like these did Contact and his pals look flying over Bapaume and Armienterres and the Somme? I go north on a yellow macadam road with each pool and rut of water marked as a ring or stripe of light . . . I turn east and slosh through a mile of mud, then south a mile and I am back on the sidewalks of Maywood. The repeating impression in my head has been a man circling and floating high in the air with a drumming zing-zonging motor and a whirling propeller. I see men going headfirst for the earth. I wonder if there is a better memory to have in life than that of men who showed great contempt for death and the mystery of extinction.

Sandburg and Paula, hard-working as ever, had the traditional division of labor at home. Paula cared for Margaret and rambunctious Janet, with occasional help from Oma and Opa. She welcomed her parents' company, especially since she was expecting another child in December.

After his workday at the Daily News, and usually without Paula, Sandburg dropped in at Harriet Vaughn Moody's perennial open house in her mansion on Chicago's Groveland Avenue. The charming widow of poet William Vaughn Moody ran a successful catering business from her home, and, from teatime until midnight, entertained writers, artists and other interesting people living in or passing through Chicago. Because of a painful back injury, she sat on a large black rope swing in her living room, where guests might include Tagore or Yeats, Lindsay or Sandburg, or Frost.

Sandburg still took long, solitary walks for exercise and reflection. Sometimes the tall, thin poet could be seen strolling into the open country, pulling baby Janet in a wagon. He delighted in his baby daughter's spunk and spirit: "Woke in the east room, sun pouring in," he wrote in his diary Sunday, May 5, 1918:

> Heard a chortle; Janet rising in the majesty of her nightgown at the foot of her trundle. She looks like Wm. Jennings Bryan at the rear coach of a train about to orate. Only Janet is no faker. She is honestly a pig and a savage and hesitates at no use of force or cunning to achieve her purpose of dominating the house. . . . Jesus! will this two year old child gesturing and chuckling at the end of her beddie, this poem in a dimpled neck and brown hair threatening to turn bronze, will she have three or four husbands when the blackbirds and robins have chuttered to her eighty years! . . . I don't care. This shall be a wild child and take what it needs from life. I make an oath here this Sunday morning that whatever happens, whatever wrongs of life mesh her, my door shall always be open, and every sin she ever tells me as her own I shall say was a sin of mine once and I know her language. . . . I lift her to my bed. She sits pummeling my head. . . . She flops my head as a pancake . . . Enter the mother and the child is whisked away. . . . Bath and then breakfast. . . . then Janet in the four-wheeled wagon and me for the horse go to see Opa and Oma, four blocks away. We stop and talk with a goat rope-staked for street grass. How old and immutable is the goat! . . . I look at Janet who holds a dandelion between two fingers and a small thumb. She seems to have profound thoughts about the yellow splints of flower in front of her face. Her eyes half close with these thoughts, they are so profound. Her head nods. . . . I put her in the wagon and haul her home to her mother. She is given a bellyful of bread and milk and put to bed.

When they could snatch a few quiet hours together, Sandburg and Paula finished preparing the manuscript for his second book of poetry, *Cornhuskers*, a "bigger conceived and all round better worked-out book than *Chicago Poems*." He had tried to make it "very American." In May they sent it to Harcourt.

"Of course we want to publish it, and this autumn," Harcourt told Sandburg, "and on the same terms as *Chicago Poems*." Harcourt was "very short handed on account of enlistments" and could not give the manuscript the careful attention he wanted to, but asked Sandburg to cut about a quarter of it, including some of the "cosmic stuff" and some instances of "considerable repetition of a mood or a theme." Harcourt hoped they could meet in New York to discuss *Cornhuskers*, but was sure that "It is a better book than the first one, a good deal better." Sandburg offered Harriet Monroe the lead poem, "Prairie," for the July issue of *Poetry*. He had turned from the city to the prairie as setting and symbol for his poetry during that wartime winter of 1918. "I was born on the prairie and the milk of its wheat, the/red of its clover, the eyes of its women, gave me/a song and a slogan" he wrote. The struggle of life in the new, industrialized city symbolized the world-scale conflict. The abiding peace of the prairie was a welcome antithesis to the man-made clamor of war. The city constrained even that thrusting symbol of modern life, the swift passenger train, which was liberated on the prairie:

> In the city among the walls the overland passenger train is choked and
>   the pistons hiss and the wheels curse.
> On the prairie the overland flits on phantom wheels and the sky and
>   the soil between them muffle the pistons and cheer the wheels.

The city was transient, perishable; the prairie was transcendent:

> I am here when the cities are gone.
> I am here when the cities come . . .
> I last while old wars are fought, while peace broods mother-like,
> While new wars arise and the fresh killings of young men.
> I fed the boys who went to France in great dark days.
> Appomattox is a beautiful word to me and so is Valley Forge and the
>   Marne and Verdun,
> I who have seen the red births and the red deaths
> Of sons and daughters, I take peace or war, I say nothing and wait . . .

For now, the war was everywhere. In June Sandburg wrote to Alice Corbin Henderson, still exiled by her health to a long, lonely recuperation in New Mexico. ("No pals to scrap with out here," she told him. "The desert is kind, and endlessly cruel.") "Tumult," he said. "A world heavy with change. Who that can stand up wants to write anything but flash telegram letters? . . . Sometimes I feel lucky my desk hasn't been wrecked by a shell."

With *Cornhuskers* off his mind, he could turn to other ventures. He did not expect his new book to sell well during wartime, but that seemed unimportant. He told Henderson he expected "sparse sales, a meager paucity." In literature as in life, the war overshadowed everything.

Sandburg wanted to chronicle firsthand Woodrow Wilson's crusade to make the world safe for democracy. He liked his *Daily News* job, and prized his wife and daughters and the refuge of their Maywood home. But the old restless urge to travel fed his hunger to examine events with his own eyes. He covered the repercussions of war throughout that spring, his support of Wilson and the Allies offset by his consternation at certain federal programs which seemed inordinately repressive. When Judge Kenesaw Mountain Landis presided over the wholesale convictions of Big Bill Haywood and the IWW leadership for "ten thousand crimes of sabotage aimed at hindering the war effort," Sandburg wrote about the episode for the *Daily News* and as Jack Phillips, reappeared in the pages of the *International Socialist Review* with coverage and commentary of the IWW battle with the Justice Department. Sandburg told Alice Corbin Henderson that he had "many brothers in jail."

As the forty-year-old father of two little girls, Sandburg was an unlikely soldier. His brother-in-law Steichen was distinguishing himself in France, making a weapon of his art form. Steichen spent three weeks in September at the war front, "personally directing the work of the photographic section during the September drives—all photography from airplanes of German positions, locating enemy batteries, enemy movements, back lines. . . ." His services to Generals Pershing and Mitchell and to the Allies would win him the Chevalier of Legion of Honor, the Medaille d'Honneur des Affaires Etrangères, and the Distinguished Service Citation. Sandburg wanted to move closer to the center of the world storm, to capture in his reportage and his poems the war's "shadows and pains and hunger."

Sandburg's chance came in July when he received a job offer from Sam T. Hughes, editor-in-chief of the Newspaper Enterprise Association, the Scripps daily news service which served three hundred publications with a combined circulation of more than 4.5 million. Hughes proposed to send Sandburg to Stockholm as NEA correspondent to Eastern Europe. "As you know," Hughes told him,

> Stockholm is next door to both Germany and Russia. The very latest and best German news gets to Stockholm faster and better than it gets to either Berne or Amsterdam. It is much more authentic from Stockholm than it is from Holland or Switzerland.
>
> Also Stockholm is only a short run from Russia. I am convinced that the Russian news is going to be just as important, if not more important than from any other part of the world. I know that you are better fitted than most newspapermen, mentally, temperamentally and otherwise, to cover this particular place and that particular section of the world.

When the war ended, Hughes promised Sandburg, there would be a regular NEA job for him in Cleveland, NEA headquarters. Sandburg accepted immediately. "It is a go," he wrote July 15. "On hearing from you that you can finance the stunt, I will begin packing for Stockholm, and looking up Chicago ends that have connections in Eastern Europe."

"It is a go," Hughes echoed, offering Sandburg a hundred dollars a week. Sandburg wanted half his salary to go straight to Paula. He would live frugally on the remaining fifty dollars. "I was brought up on herring and potatoes," he told Hughes, "and my forefathers lived on black bread the year round, with coffee and white bread only on Easter and Christmas. So if I have to revert—o very well." Hughes assured Sandburg that he should not have to "get down to the idea of 'herring and potatoes.' We want our men to live decently, though not extravagantly." He was eager for Sandburg to get busy on the "red tape necessary to start you for the other side." He would need a passport, letters of introduction, press credentials and clearance to sail from New York as soon as possible.

Sandburg's departure from the *Daily News* was the subject of a long poem by Ben Hecht, a parody of Sandburg's free verse style, complete with repetition:

> . . . "Go, with your great black valise and
> your time tables and everything;
> "Go, where your roving spirit bids you;
> go as far as you like or as far as
> they will stake you;
> "Go swiftly, with your stockinged toes
> hanging from an upper berth and
> your slender purse under your pillow;
>
> "Go on trains, ships, taxis, baggage
> trucks, ox carts.
> "Go quickly, and return quickly, even
> though our long, glittering pay roll
> shall cease to be;
> "For our ears will yearn for your husky,
> hesitant philosophies,
> "And the languorous local room will
> seem empty, lacking the flapping
> slouch hat and the black, unsmoked
> cigar.
>
> "Hurry back, Carl." . . .
>
> Behold Carl, the plain man, sits at dinner
> in the legation, goggling at the
> silver and the liveried servants;
> Behold he drinks Swedish liquids and is
> carried out feet first.

> Behold he awakens in a narrow bedroom
>   and finds a message from his editor,
>   "Rush more stuff."
> O life! O Carl! O hell! . . .

✳

From the outset, Sandburg found himself indeed ensnarled in red tape.
As there was no official birth registry when he was born, he had to secure
an affidavit from his mother in Galesburg to document that he "was duly
and properly born in Illinois 40 years ago." He had to travel to Cleveland,
Washington and New York to apply for his passport and book passage
on one of the few ships which still embarked every week or two for
Bergen, Norway, a voyage of twelve to fourteen days, barring encounters
with enemy mines or submarines.

It was very hard to leave Paula. She saw him off at the Maywood train
station, suppressing tears, her face "luminous." He wrote to tell her that
he understood and appreciated the restraint in her good-bye:

> There were tears in it and a big gladness and a strong-hearted woman—
> my pal—in it.—What we are having is only a breath of the world storm.
> We will hope that resolves and consecrations enough have been born out
> of the millions of separations, enough for the remaking of a world.—
> What with your line about Janet waving, and Margaret's dear note, and
> the Shewolf's* kiss too, it all tugs at me tonight. I got the warm kiss of
> your calling me "Buddy" at the finish. What we know is that all the
> chances are in favor of our sitting under our own cherry tree some day
> and talking about the year Carl went away and the Third Child came
> (No Indian name. Maybe "Mary Illinois" if it isn't John Edward.) And
> when I say God keep you and God keep you I mean it in its oldest and
> deepest way.

"And again," he told her, "lovelier face never had any woman than you
in the goodby. It was a morning-glory.—Get me a picture, please!"

He urged her to take care of herself and the baby she carried, whom
they already called John: "he may see great days never known to our
eyes." As he moved deeper into the wartime confusion in Washington,
he was glad that his family was safe at home in Maywood. He missed
them, and "the guitars, the books, the manuscripts, the stove where we
fried the eggs, the autumn sun on the dear garden,—and most of all and
all the time: you and the homeyglomeys." When his friend Henry Sell
of the *Chicago Daily News* came to visit him, Sandburg felt "an awful

---

*His nickname for Paula's mother because of her protective love for her family.

pull of loneliness. I realized that I can't think honestly and vividly about Maywood and Home as a regular thing—because it hurts too much—and so maybe my letters sometimes have this neglect in them. When they do you know what it is. C'est la guerre."

He had hoped to have his passport by early August and to sail August 10 or August 24 aboard the *Stockholm*. He asked Sam Hughes in late July to provide a statement about the purpose of his trip, and "Make me important as hell." Sandburg's reporter's notebook was packed with questions he wanted to investigate when he got to Stockholm:

> How about the revolution in Finland? Are the red guards out for keeps? Are the bourgeoisie giving labor better conditions out of fear of encouraging new red guard uprisings? What are the women of Finland, who had probably the most notable feminist movement in the world, doing these days? . . . What do sailors and workmen back from Russ, Finn and German ports say? What do travelers say are the warnings issued by health authorities in Petrograd and Moscow as to the first symptoms of cholera. . . . What are the outward signs at Stockholm of the invisible web of negotiation and intrigue known to be spinning there? . . . What are the Swedish cabinet members saying about the whole drift of the world storm as it looks to them? What have been their shifts of viewpoint during the war? Has there been much of a change in the neutral countries from a sentiment of pacifism to one of militarized democracy, like our U.S.A.? . . . What control does Germany or neutral countries exercise over news and communications the Soviets try to send out from Russia? . . . And for the love of God aren't there any tramp boats bringing people from Poland who can tell what's doing there?

Sandburg was acutely sensitive to the wartime hysteria directed toward socialists, especially after Eugene Debs had been indicted for sedition for giving a speech to the Ohio state convention of the Socialist Party in Canton, Ohio, June 16, 1918. Debs was convicted and sentenced to ten years in prison.

Sandburg took steps to validate his patriotism. He did not want his political past to deter his NEA assignment. Julian Mason, managing editor of the *Chicago Evening Post*, wrote a letter endorsing Sandburg: "From the start of the war, Carl Sandburg has been strongly in sympathy with the cause of the Entente Allies and he has manifested this sympathy in his writings. We printed 'Four Brothers,' one of his poems, as a spiritual contribution looking toward the winning of the war. This newspaper recommends him to the support and help of anyone having at heart the defeat of Germany."

More red tape continued to delay Sandburg's passport, however, and he soon began to fear that other reasons were stalling the process. He had to change the name on his Spanish-American War papers from Charles August Sandburg to his legal name, Carl August Sandburg. The Illinois Draft Board had to verify that they did not intend to conscript him. "Well, I suppose I register here," he wrote to Paula, "being under 45, tho the father of two such dependent future mothers of the republic certainly automatically goes into Class IV, if Stockholm correspondence isn't an essential war industry." He soon had to amend his visa application to request passage by way of London because of a ruling that "only neutral subjects can sail on boats of the Scandinavian countries . . . because Germany served notice boats carrying subjects of belligerent countries would be torpedoed."

"No passport today," he wrote Paula August 13 from New York. He tried to write to her every day. "Out of my tumults I try to get one a day to you, one of some kind, sometimes just a Hello My Buddy." He was also seeing a bevy of New York friends, including Chester Wright, who was working three days weekly for the *New York Call* and three days a week in Washington as Samuel Gompers's assistant, editing the official organ of the American Federation of Labor.

Perplexed by the continued delay, Sandburg heard from Washington that

> they are watching Stockholm closer than any neutral point in Europe and the investigations of all applicants for passports to that town have been made more rigid, thorough and complex than to any place in Europe. The matter of my passport is now in the hands of the Department of Justice and the secret service. I get this authoritatively. The grapevine that brings it is reliable. It also says that unless a guy is a diplomatic somebody, going on official or semi-official business, he can't get by without a certain process. It seems that this process has been made more intricate and deliberate the last three months because German propaganda and intrigue is on the increase at Stockholm.

While he waited, he worked with Harcourt on the proofs of *Corn-huskers*, due out in October. He spent time with poets Alfred Kreymborg, who had a garret in Greenwich Village, and William Carlos Williams, who practiced medicine in nearby New Jersey. After an evening with John Reed, he wrote a poem/letter to Paula:

> Paula:
> I pick this for you
> on a hill near Croton.
> The evening lights of Sing Sing

flicker a brass bar . . .
. . . a living gold wire of light . . .
a flickering strip of hot gold . . .
down among rock-walled hills of the Hudson.
"There," says John Reed and his right forefinger,
"Is the point of land where Andre met Benedict Arnold"
"and" says the shifting forefinger
"straight across the river is West Point."
(And an Illinois boy's head flutters:
Grant, Lee, Gettysburg, Zachary Taylor, Chapultepec,
The Rio Grande, Pershing, Toul, Cantigny:
A boy's head flutters with names.) . . .

For the first time since his college days Sandburg walked the streets of New York's East Side. "New York tries to live more life than is livable and it plays hell with the population which is sleazier and snivellery than in any similar compass of American territory," he told Alice Corbin Henderson. He gathered impressions in his unpublished journal:

I walk on down 3d av. Near 8th st. I meet Chumley, an I.W.W. He says Jack Reed, Jim Larkin, Nuorteva etc. are going to speak in Webster hall on 11th protesting Russian intervention. He is afraid a sweeping military victory for the Allies next year will result in financial imperialists taking upper hand again in all countries. He says the military machine created under Wilson's direction will turn on the president and control him. When we part he says on my return from Stockholm a year or two years from now I shall find him in Leavenworth . . . I walk down 7th av. wondering about the East Side and Art and War.

He went to parties with artists, musicians, writers and other inhabitants of the bohemian community in Greenwich Village. After spending an evening with John Reed and Louise Bryant, just back from Russia, he told Paula, "I can see how you and I would have fitted in Greenwich Village and how we had GV in our 'organizing' days." He wrote to tell Paula that he not only loved her, he liked her "a hell of a lot."

I'm saying over again everything I ever said about your being The Best. I see Men and Wives and Men and Women—and so often the wife or the woman hasn't been The Best for the man—and the general run of 'em haven't got *Mind.* I talked with John Reed and his wife last night, Louise Bryant, and she was the first I've met in a long while with something like your range, your head and handling of things. Only, you've got Janet and Marge on top of all this woman has.

Labor Day came and went, and Sandburg was still waiting for his passport. "I can't see how the war can run beyond next year," he told

Paula. "I have come to this slowly & feel it's near a cinch.—Hughes says after peace he counts on my reaching Berlin before the western front correspondents.—Well, God be good to you and John and ours, all the time, blessed girl. I still have a picture of your face the last morning in Maywood."

He was discouraged and restless, increasingly alarmed that his socialist past was impeding his departure. He talked to a Red Cross official who had waited seven weeks for a passport, and a YMCA official who had been waiting six weeks. "I think our national war machine is tightening up on all passages, every form of non-combatant transport that has possibilities for enemy communication," Sandburg reported to Sam Hughes. He assured Hughes that he had "kept away from the Socialist and I.W.W. bunch" in New York, although he "had occasion twice to be thrown into the company of Jack Reed and both times got a lot of good pointers on how to travel, utilize aspirin and saccharin, and permits for supplies to be obtained from the Swedish embassy at Washington."

Sandburg pointed out that F. W. Kerby and J. W. Duckworth of the NEA staff were a "dues-paying Socialist party member" and a "neo-pacifist" respectively, and speculated that the association was as "complicating and implicating as any of recent record" for him. He hoped that the popularity of "The Four Brothers" and the support of people such as Clarence Darrow and Samuel Gompers would validate his credibility as an objective, loyal American journalist. But, he told Hughes, "I am never going to brag of my patriotism, like a virgin of her chastity, or a chorus girl of her shape."

When Sam Hughes wired Sandburg that the State Department was "shutting down on passports," he hurried to Washington to plead his case and try to determine if he would ever be cleared to travel to Sweden. He wrote two poems that August about the Capitol dome at sunset and "in the night and the moon." "There is . . . something . . . here . . . men die for," he reflected.

Sandburg now had the active support of Chester Wright and the American Alliance for Labor and Democracy in his quest for a passport. His editor Alfred Harcourt of Henry Holt had written to support his case, and tried to influence a friend at the Justice Department to help Sandburg. Furthermore, Sandburg was "backed to the limit by George Creel" of President Wilson's powerful Committee on Public Information. Nevertheless, he was discouraged.

"My own hunch is I don't go to Stockholm," he told Paula. "Lately I have come to feel that if I were running the war, I would refuse passports to any and all for Stockholm, permitting no one to go there except in a military intelligence connection. The whole war machine is tightening up. Such tremendous destinies hang in the balance that I can't have a distinct personal reaction about being turned down on going to Stockholm after shaping a purpose to go."

Back in New York, Sandburg continued to wait. He watched the troop ships "loading on the river. Fifty thousand men swarming in khaki on the decks waiting for night. I sent the *News* a poetic telegram on it."

Suddenly, without any explanation, Sandburg was informed that he could have a passport provided he could furnish a certificate of exemption from his local draft board. Paula attended to that immediately, sparing him a trip home to Chicago. He told her it would be hard to come back so briefly, just to have to say good-bye again. When he returned, he assured her, he wanted it to be for years, not hours.

By late September Sandburg had his passport at last. He began to pack and take his leave of friends in New York. With *Cornhuskers* due out soon and already advertised in *The New Republic* and elsewhere, Harcourt took Sandburg to dinner at the Columbia University Club to celebrate. "Have eaten at Harvard Club and Yale with other Parties," Sandburg told Paula. "Getting to be very quite-so. All the fat I've put on, which is not much, will be needed in Stockholm."

By October 2 all his arrangements were complete. He was elated. Paula, now nearly eight months into her pregnancy, gave him her full support. "Just love and all my love and Good-bye dear," she wrote from Maywood. "I am happy over it all—but anxious over having to entrust your very life to the chances of a wooden boat on a big sea with its hidden threat of mines & submarines." She also realized the deep significance of his first trip to Sweden. She had done every practical thing to expedite his journey, and had written him all the details of life in the little house in Maywood. He was ready, he assured her:

> I am taking no scrap of printed paper except my Swedish dictionaries. Am listing all things in trunk for customs men. Bought rubbers, overshoes, wool leggins, medical kit, cold cream, orange marmalade and am a man of property. . . . Whatever you do in all these events, don't hurry, don't worry. With a Woodrow Wilson in the world things will come along— Jesus, that New York speech was a hummer—sort of the finale to the Four Brothers—hurray!

He told Paula to cable him "The day John comes . . . whether it's John or another little sissenfrass. . . . The more I look it over the surer I am that we know this world we're living in and all its human trends a lot keener and deeper because of the change we made. Only those breaking pre-war roots and taking risks and being buffeted and lonely, can know."

"These are great days," he had told Alice Corbin Henderson, "the most deadly, portentous, glorious, dangerous, democratic days the world has known." Sandburg believed the Allies would win the war, although he thought it would "probably take longer and the whole course be different from the trend of dope in the papers. But Germany is already the loser. And forty ways The People stand to win all round."

∗

On October 3, 1918, Sandburg and sixteen other passengers aboard the S.S. *Bergensfjord* were detained for three days near the Statue of Liberty, and then embarked on a rough passage, with days of high seas, rain and fog. "Had an hour of sun yesterday, the first in six days," Sandburg wrote Paula on October 17; "I ate my heart for being so lonesome for you and Maywood and thoughts of the little ones."

Storing energy for his Stockholm adventure, Sandburg slept ten or twelve hours a night, ate heartily, and imbibed the news from journalists aboard and "other good talkers." He heard that it would take six weeks for news correspondence to get through from Stockholm to newspapers in the States. "We have had brief wireless bulletins daily on the ship," he wrote Paula, "all indicating the war goes well and the Kaiser will get his." He asked her to send him reviews of *Cornhuskers*, "if anything good or bad, is printed." The isolation of the ship at sea, so often shrouded in fog, evoked poetry: "Fog on fog and never a star,/what is a man, a child, a woman,/to the green and grinding sea?"

By October 18, 1918, Sandburg was in Bergen, Norway. He soon set out by train for Christiania, and then Stockholm. "There was a thrill about seeing the soil of Sweden, setting foot on it, and hearing the speech of one's forefathers spoken by everybody," he wrote Paula. He knew enough Swedish to get along, to read the newspapers and to translate articles into English. He began filling thick notebooks with observations of the country and the times. He heard on every side that the war would soon be over, but expected to have "five or six fierce months of it" before he got home again. "No telling about anything but our heartbeats," he said.

Before he left his family, Sandburg had been creating some whimsical stories, half for children, half for adults. He had begun to think of writing a book of such stories, but the war superseded them. In Stockholm, he thought of them again. "I look forward to when I can go home and have the everlasting youths tousling my hair and giving me spitty smacky kisses," he wrote Paula in November. "I want to go ahead on that Homeyglomey book. I have seen enough sophistication and ignorance to last me a good while."

✳

"Just a hasty note to assure I'm on the job," Edward Steichen wrote to his parents and sister on November 5, 1918, from Paris.

> As a matter of fact I've been so hard at it I forgot everything else.—Have been at the front for over a month helping Uncle Sam get his stranglehold on the *vital part* of the line—We have it now and its going to do the work—It will *soon be over.* Its been a hard job—and lots of fine fellows have paid the big price—. . . Will write soon now I'm back at my desk again—so heres to joy—and peace.

While Steichen was a visible, driving force in the Allied aviation photography enterprise, Sandburg was a minor figure among the horde of journalists who covered the war, yet his news agency vaunted his credentials and his presence in Sweden. "SANDBURG'S THERE," ran an NEA headline. "He Lands in Norway and Cables This Hot News Story: *Russ Reds Plot German Revolt,* and Fifty Bolshevik Agents Daily Cross Hun Borders to Aid Popular Uprising."

In Stockholm, that "center of plot and intrigue," Sandburg immediately began cultivating a network of sources for the spot news stories he would dispatch to NEA back home. He was especially interested in the revolution in Finland and in the predominant story of the Bolshevik Revolution. Inevitably he transmuted war news into poems:

> I saw roses in a street garden in Karl Johansgatan . . . & the palace of the King was on one hand & the house of the People's congress on the other . . . & the leaves of many roses lay knocked off by the rain & the requests of autumn.
>
> I crossed the street & stood in front of the Grand hotel . . . my elbows just evading the elbows of spies & diplomats in spats speaking yes-yes & ab-so-lute-ly & perhaps to each other . . .

He was a shrewd, seasoned newsman, conscious of the pervasive wartime duplicity of "spies and diplomats speaking yes-yes & ab-so-lute-ly & perhaps to each other," but events brought him face-to-face with one of the most skillful spies of the Russian Revolution. One bright November afternoon as Sandburg sat on a park bench near the Grand Hotel, he was approached by a bearded, genial man who introduced himself as Michael Borodin, formerly of Chicago, where, he said, his name had been Mike Berg. He told Sandburg about his socialist connections in Chicago, and about the successful school he had run there for the children of Russian immigrants like himself. They spoke of Borodin's former Chicago alderman Eddie Kaindl, whom Sandburg knew. Borodin offered to furnish Sandburg information and leads for his NEA stories. He could, he said, provide useful information from Russia. Sandburg accepted Borodin's offer. Later, when he had to answer telegrams from Borodin, he signed them Eddie Kaindl.

Borodin alias Berg apparently did not disclose to Sandburg all the pertinent facts of his life. As Mikhail Markovich Gruzenberg he had played a minor role in the Russian Revolution of 1905, fled in exile to the United States, found a Russian bride, studied business courses at Valparaiso University in Indiana, and then lived in Chicago from 1908 until 1918, where he ran his profitable school which also served as a cultural center for immigrants and a site of socialist activities. Like many other Russians abroad, he returned to his country in the wake of the Russian Revolution. He became an agent of Lenin's Bolshevik government, went on to become "the Bolshevik conqueror of half of China," and died in 1951 after two years of "rehabilitation" in a Russian prison camp. But in the fall of 1918 he was working for Lenin in Stockholm, assigned to transmit Bolshevik propaganda to the United States. He needed conduits, innocent or otherwise. Hearing that Sandburg was an NEA news representative in Stockholm, he used the Chicago connection as an avenue of approach, and began to feed Sandburg information for his news stories.

In addition to running a covert intelligence operation, Borodin had a special assignment from Lenin himself: the delivery of Lenin's *Letter to American Workers* to the United States. Borodin dispatched that missive in the care of another Russian who had migrated to the United States after the 1905 revolution. He was known as Sletov or P. I. Travin, but Borodin disguised him as an American sailor stranded in Denmark by the war blockade and got him passage as a ship's carpenter on a vessel bound for New York. There, Travin claimed, he was detained by immigration authorities and so jumped ship, swam to shore, and telephoned John Reed, entrusting Lenin's letter to him.

According to some sources, it was Carl Sandburg who introduced Lenin's letter to the United States. Actually, it appears to have been Travin, at Borodin's behest, who delivered three typed copies of Lenin's long letter, each with Lenin's signature. Sandburg brought back to the United States a published English translation of Lenin's *A Letter to American Workingmen from the Socialist Soviet Republic of Russia*, printed in

English by the Socialist Publication Society, stowing his copy in an interior pocket of his greatcoat for safe passage home.

According to Sandburg, Borodin "circulated among all sorts of people in Moscow" and passed on to him "all that was vague in their dreams and all that was sharp and clear in their immediate plans." Sandburg used Borodin as one of his sources for "stories regarding the immediate practical programs of the Communist government as its heads in Moscow then believed those plans would work out." Sandburg was deeply concerned about reports coming from Finland. He had heard that more than sixty-eight thousand Finnish people were held in prison camps. He told Sam Hughes about "a report of Dr. Robert Tigerstedt, head physician of the prison camp at Ekenas, with evidence that the death rate among the 8,000 there incarcerated was high as 42 per 1,000 daily." He read an "official statement of Regent Sfvinhuvud and analyses of it by Branting's paper tending to show mass executions of 10,000 persons, starvation of 12,000, parole under penalty of 60,000, and the incarceration at the present time of more than 27,000." He obtained Norwegian Red Cross photographs of the civil war in Finland, statements of prisoners escaped from Finnish "convict camps," a circular "addressed by the Finnish socialists to the workmen of England and of Germany describing 'the White terror.' "

One of his steadiest sources of information in Stockholm was Per Albin Hanson, later Swedish prime minister but then managing editor of the Swedish Socialist-Democratic Party's daily newspaper. Sandburg saw Hanson almost daily for free-ranging talks about the war. "We understood each other thoroughly," Sandburg recalled, "both being collectivists and parliamentary Socialists and the Wisconsin movement in which I had been an organizer having operated with much the same theory and viewpoint as the Swedish party affiliated with the trade-unions."

Borodin also regularly provided Sandburg "all kinds of news." He gave Sandburg details about the Bolshevik shelling of Jaroslav, Poland, and Sandburg cabled the story to NEA acknowledging as a source "Mitchell Berg, a former Chicago school teacher." In the whirlwind of events, when news was fragmentary and conflicting, Borodin was one of many contacts Sandburg cultivated. In his effort to monitor the war, Sandburg gathered every possible shred of information, stowing away pictures, films, newspapers, anecdotes, pamphlets, a thousand separate pieces of the huge insoluble puzzle. Communication was increasingly difficult. His funds began to run low. He had no idea whether NEA was running the stories he sent back to the home office, and he began to feel his news agency was treating him badly.

The last battles of the war were waged on a scale too vast to comprehend. More than a million Allied soldiers, including nearly 900,000 Americans, took Meuse-Argonne that fall. After the British broke the Hindenburg Line, Germany was torn with mutiny and revolution. In General Foch's private dining car in the Compiègne Forest on November 11, an armistice treaty was signed, providing two months to negotiate the terms of peace.

"Most of Europe—sometimes I think all Europe—is in a physical and mental condition bordering on hysteria," Sandburg wrote from Christiania, Norway, December 10.

> After talking with travelers from the eastern and western ends of the continent and scanning reports from London to Kiev and Tammerfors to Berlin, I have the feeling that unless Europe gets down to a plain old fashioned "rest cure" of some kind, then Europe will turn into a shambles and a madhouse and its ravaged lands and decimated populations will parallel the tired, worn, languid peoples of Asia and Northern Africa.

He dispatched a story about the situation in Finland:

> They have told me with sober and zealous faces, and they have published it in their papers and leaflets as a matter of fact that THOUSANDS OF FINNS MASSACRED BY THE WHITE TERROR WERE FORCED TO DIG THEIR OWN GRAVES AND WERE THEN SHOT AND THROWN INTO THE TRENCHES THEIR OWN HANDS HAD DUG.
>
> Tell this story to a well-fed American and he laughs out, "A man who knows he is going to be shot will refuse to dig his own grave." That is the way I feel about it myself. But the light in the eyes of the Finns who told me the story in Stockholm was a weird light of eyes that had seen unearthly terrors. . . .
>
> For ghastly and deliberate cruelty during the world storm the prize must go to the Finnish Mannerheim junkers who established their White Guard government and overthrew the People's Republic of Finland by the use of German battalions withdrawn from the western front during the first six months of 1918. On percentages, counting the fact Finland has only 3,000,000 people, the record of firing squad atrocities on civilians not accorded trial, and the record of men, women and children starved in prison camps, surpass all records of frightfulness contained in evidence concerning Belgium or Serbia. It may be Armenia dripped with more innocent blood and listened to more human creatures dying with a cry

of, "Bread! bread!" on their white mouths. But it is doubtful whether from any other country has come such specific and absolute evidence of the deliberate starvation of thousands of prisoners because the starvation method was the most convenient for the killing of people the Finnish Mannerheim junkers wanted dead rather than alive.

❋

Dispirited, disillusioned, cut off from communication with NEA head-quarters and home, Sandburg was increasingly lonely for Paula. He wrote brief but regular letters to her, but wartime mail was cumbrously slow at best, and undependable. By late November Paula had not received a single letter from her husband since his departure from New York. She was still calling the baby she carried John Edward; and as time for the birth approached she had difficulty arranging for a doctor and a practical nurse because of the worldwide influenza epidemic which had already closed Chicago schools for three weeks. In the epic paranoia of wartime, rumors abounded that influenza (Italian for "influence") was a vicious germ-warfare strategy perpetrated by Germany. By autumn nearly a fourth of the nation's population had been infected with the illness, which eventually killed almost half a million Americans. Nearly half as many American soldiers died of influenza in American army camps as were killed in battle overseas.

Paula and her girls stayed well, although many of her friends were ill. At six o'clock on Sunday morning, November 24, Paula gave birth to her baby, due December 5. John Edward turned out to be a "husky little new born baby girl," Paula wrote Harriet Monroe, "—as colorful and clamorous as you could wish." She called the baby Mary Ellen after Mary Ellen Bond, the girl across the street.

"My first letter from Carl came this morning," Paula told Harriet Monroe on November 29. "He landed Kristiania October 24. A stormy voyage. He writes his health has never been better. Which is the big thing I was anxious to hear about." Paula tried to let him know about his baby's birth. She had no idea when he would come home to her and have his first look at the new child. She understood the uncertainty of events, and of mail. "But it *is* long and long, sweetheart!" she had written her husband. "And it won't be everlastingly long that you stay over there!"

❋

Late in 1918 Sam Hughes asked his NEA staff to help put together "a real, informative article about the Bolsheviki, something full of facts and told in such a tone that nobody can accuse us of prejudice or of boosting." He noted that there was little reliable news about the "ruling party in Russia," and that "with the occasional scraps of information have been many scraps of misinformation."

"Do not omit the good things they do for fear of the conservatives in this country," Hughes warned. He stressed the importance of factual, objective information. In that spirit Sandburg was industriously gathering as much material as possible to take back to the United States, for by mid-December he was scheduled to sail for home.

When Olaf Scheflo, editor of the Christiania *Social-Demokraten*, offered Sandburg Bolshevik moving picture films to take back, he wrote a long letter to the military attaché of the American Legation in Norway describing the films and requesting clearance to take them to the NEA. He believed that "even if the Committee on Public Information should decide that it is against the nation's best interest to use or publish these photographs at this time, they would be of interest to officials in Washington because of information and viewpoints they contain." Sandburg also had obtained a book entitled *From Finland's War for Freedom*, photographs by Dr. Harald Natwig published "as a combined educational and propaganda presentation of the viewpoint of the present Finnish government."

"We are at war with them now," the military attaché told Sandburg of the Bolsheviks. Sandburg acknowledged that was "a literal fact so far as the military actions of a certain small detachment of troops are concerned." But he hoped that permission would be granted on the basis of President Wilson's December 2 message to Congress urging the end of cable news censorship. Sandburg insisted that the films were "distinctly different from the literature spread by agitators of the Soviets. They are what an American highbrow would call 'expository rather than argumentative' and they have more of what a newspaperman would call 'human interest' than of propaganda."

While Sandburg awaited a decision on the films, he got a tantalizing offer of Bolshevik material from another source. When Borodin learned of Sandburg's upcoming departure for the United States, he asked if he would be interested in taking back some "Russ" material. Sandburg immediately accepted a "mass of Russ pamphlets, books and newspapers." As he prepared to sail the week before Christmas, Sandburg packed two trunks full of material for NEA, so much that "It would have cost the price of five steamboat passages to cable" it all home. With slow, erratic mail service, Sandburg figured that the material would be as long as three months reaching Sam Hughes, if it got through at all. He believed he had assembled significant documentary evidence of the devastation of the war: he had filled three notebooks with "jottings on interviews with probably 200 people"; he had clippings from Swedish and Norwegian newspapers on the German and Russian situations, including Swedish accounts of "the soviets and bolshevik government" which he intended to translate; there were many documents on the Finnish situation, and the Norwegian Red Cross films of the Finnish Civil War; a 173-page book of official communiqués "of the Russian consul-general at Simla, India to the Petrograd foreign office during 1916, with light on the many drolleries and chicaneries of what President Wilson designates 'Secret Diplomacy' "; the files of the Soviet Izvestia Congress of June 1918; a copy of the three-volume Klyuchevski history of Russia; and, in his inner coat pocket, the Lenin pamphlet.

Just before Sandburg's departure Borodin asked him for one more favor. He wanted Sandburg to carry some money into the United States: four hundred kroner for his wife, Fanya, in Chicago, and "two drafts for $5,000 each, payable to Santeri Nuorteva, head of the Finnish Information Bureau in the United States, and a former member of the Finnish landtag." Sandburg agreed. He sequestered the money for Fanya in the deep, inner pockets of his coat, along with his notebooks and the Lenin document.

As he considered the bank drafts, he began to worry, and just before his departure showed them to "U.S. Minister Schmedeman in Christiania." Sandburg explained that "they were for the purpose of getting the Finns and Scandinavians of America informed of how Finland's fate in death, sickness and hunger is worse than Belgium, Serbia, Poland or any other nation that has known tragedy the past four years." Sandburg told Schmedeman that "From such a distance I was not sure what sort of service I might be rendering and that before I delivered the drafts to Nuortava I would lay the entire matter before the editor-in-chief of the N.E.A. and that I would inform New York port officials about the drafts."

The U.S. consul would inform them himself, well before Sandburg's arrival, for the government suspected what Sandburg himself did not know, that Santeri Nuorteva, posing as the representative in the United States of the People's Republic of Finland, was in reality, like Borodin, an agent for Lenin's government.

✳

Paula prepared for Christmas 1918 without her husband, trimming the tree and shopping for their three little girls. "You should be here for the burst of joy when they first see the tree and their toys!" she wrote before

Christmas, wondering whether he would spend the holiday in Berlin or Stockholm or elsewhere, not knowing that he was at that moment aboard the S.S. *Bergensfjord* bound for home.

When Sandburg arrived in New York on December 25, weary, eager for a reunion with his family and the discharge of his material to Sam Hughes in Cleveland, he was greeted by a committee of stern government officials. Dismayed, he was immediately detained by customs officers who confiscated "every piece of written or printed material on my baggage and person," even breaking open a small jar of shaving cream to see if it concealed documents. "I was grilled I was grilled," said Sandburg, "and I gave them every fact that I had." He showed them the two five-thousand-dollar bank drafts and was at first allowed to keep them as members of the War Work Committee, customs inspectors, State Department officials, officials from Military Intelligence, the War Department, the Bureau of Investigation and the U.S. Attorney of the Southern District of New York conferred about his case. On December 30 military officers took custody of the bank drafts, but Sandburg refused to tell them who had entrusted the money to him. "I told them these drafts were given to me by persons whom I cannot name."

While government officials tried to determine whether Sandburg was "unconsciously being made the instrument of conspiratorial interests inimical to the United States," a squad of workers in the censorship office analyzed the printed and manuscript material which filled his luggage.

Sandburg had not expected to make it home to Maywood and the Homeyglomeys in time for Christmas, but neither did he expect to face government officials who suspected that by "carrying funds from Norway to the Finnish Information Bureau in the United States I violated the Trading with the Enemy Act."

The mass of Bolshevik propaganda in his luggage was problem enough, but the bank drafts were seriously compromising. Sandburg had transported them in good faith, he thought, after consulting with a U.S. official in Norway. As his detention and questioning continued, Sandburg's distress grew. He was angry that his patriotism should be questioned. He was incensed at what he perceived as unfair censorship and suppression of the rights of American citizens to "communication in a human cause."

"Isn't it fine for the Government to treat such a man like a dog of a traitor?" Sam Hughes wrote to government officials in Sandburg's defense.

"The news too big and mixed forty ways for me to try to start to tell it to you," he wrote Paula that harried week. "Love to Mary Illinois. God bless you and her and the whole holy homeyglomey crew."

Sam Hughes was deeply troubled about the bank drafts. "If it had not been for that $10,000 that Sandburg brought back from the Finnish radical party, I would have raised all kinds of hell today with Washington by telegram over that censorship business," he told an NEA colleague. "I know that you haven't had a pleasant deal with the New York censor," Hughes told Sandburg, "and while that sort of thing shouldn't go with anybody, I am pretty sure that the mutts down there jumped you without realizing or knowing who you were and who you represented."

In New York Sandburg's interrogation continued, with a three-hour session one day bringing questions from "American and British Intelligence officers and an assistant district attorney." New Year's came, and Sandburg had had no word from Paula since his arrival in the States. Worried and lonely, he cabled her: "I want to know whether you have any assurances of affection, esteem—thoughts—stuff like that—the shimmer of moonbeams—a young star winking through a cobweb—send a line to your CARL."

Suddenly, just before New Year's Eve, the censors began to release some of Sandburg's material, which he immediately forwarded to Sam Hughes in Cleveland, giving NEA a "beat on all the mail stuff that will come piddling along for two months." He still had not heard from Paula. "I have a notion to wire you that you must wire back whether you love me which is what I want to know not having heard it in weeks and weeks and weeks."

Only when that message reached her did she know Sandburg was safely home again. "I have wished so hard *for this*—my wishes must have brought you home, dear!!" she exulted. On January 4, two days before Sandburg's forty-first birthday, Paula dreamed that he came home for a brief visit and then returned to Sweden. She awoke in tears, and wrote to him about her anxiety:

> Buddy if you feel you have to go again—it will be much harder for me to let you go! I'm hoping and hoping that Hughes will feel your "mission" to Eastern Europe has been fulfilled! . . .
>
> However, Buddy, I'll be game!
>
> You wonder why I have to bother my head (and heart!) about whether you are going to leave us again! Well—it's inherited from Oma! Whenever Ed comes home, her first question is when will he go again—how long will he stay! And Ed in answering, always wants to know why Oma can't enjoy the present instead of worrying about the future! . . .
>
> I want you to know, dear, that I'm game and won't hold you back if

you really feel a call to go off somewhere again! I don't want to interfere with your destiny—or your future—or any big chance for your development—or a new inspiration to write! You must be free—till the time comes when your family is sufficiently *mobile* to go with you wherever you go!—But meantime you must know *too* how we love you and need you—and so if a proposition is made to you that is *not* very attractive— if you feel 50-50 about it—throw our love & need of you into the balance, and stay home!

Paula's letters cheered Sandburg as he waited in New York, alternately anxious and impatient. Finally, in early January, the authorities released more of his material, withholding all the Swedish and Norwegian socialist and labor papers, as well as the Bolshevik pamphlets, books and news- papers. In a few days Sandburg was permitted to head west to Cleveland and meetings with Sam Hughes, who protested Sandburg's treatment in a telegram to Secretary of the Navy Josephus Daniels. Sandburg and Hughes did all they could to resolve the matter of the confiscated ma- terial, and discussed Sandburg's future. At last Sandburg was free to travel home to Chicago and Maywood.

Paula met him at the door with the new baby in her arms. "Never can I forget you opening the door and looking into my face," he told her, "and then turning your eyes to Mary Ellen Alix, the emotional arithmetician and the wop war baby."

Margaret, now seven and a half, had hoped that by Christmas her father would be home. She had missed him keenly. Toddler Janet, obliv- ious to his absence, was so active and naughty that Paula had to keep all drawers and bookcases locked and the piano and other surfaces clear of books and breakable objects. "She reaches everywhere by bringing up chairs & climbing up," Paula had written Sandburg. "I keep Mary-Ellen upstairs for safety whenever Janet is downstairs!"

Sandburg and Paula had a gentle tug of war over the new baby's name, and the metamorphosis from John Edward to Mary Ellen to Mary Illinois Alix (after the famous racehorse, her father's idea) finally gave way to his choice, no doubt an echo of Sandburg's Swedish sojourn. They began to call her Helga, and the name stuck.

There was welcome news from Edward Steichen, now a major in the army. He wrote that he had received a hero's welcome when he visited relatives in Luxembourg that winter after the Armistice. Opa's cousin Joseph Steichen, state counselor of the Grand Duchy of Luxembourg, honored him at a dinner party. Steichen visited Oma's native village, and assured his mother that all her folks were alive and "not much the worse for the German occupation but mighty glad the Prussians are *out!*"

The Kemp and Steichen relatives greeted Major Steichen as their champion. "It would have been wonderful enough if he had come as a drummer-boy!" Paula told Sandburg. "But of course this was great! Their cousin an American major! Their Liberator!"

Like everyone else, the Sandburgs found the planet of their personal lives adrift in the galaxy of world events, spun by forces out of their power to control. They could make no plans until Sandburg's legal difficulties were settled. Then they would face a decision about moving to Cleveland and NEA headquarters, or making a renewed commitment to Chicago. On January 15, Sandburg left his family to return to New York after "ten days in the middle west, with my own people, with my old neighbors and associates whose fighting and working in the war was 100 per cent." He had another "glorious homey time of it." After "two straight nights of sleeping cars," he was back in New York ready to fight for the resolution of his case, which had been turned over to the United States attorney for the Southern District of New York.

Sandburg defended himself vigorously in New York as "one who holds an honorable discharge from the United States Army of 1898 and whose loyalty is a matter of record from the day we went into the war, and whose allegiance to France and England was spoken the day the Great War started." His former boss Negley Cochran and his friend Clarence Darrow, among others, could testify that Sandburg "was not neutral but pro-ally from the start." He thought it preposterous that the government retained the Russian revolutionary literature which he had brought into the country in good faith as a journalist. More than three-fourths of it, he pointed out, had already been printed in U.S. publications or could be found in public libraries and on the nation's newsstands.

On January 28, Sandburg and the United States government reached an agreement. Sandburg signed an affidavit relinquishing custody of all the material he had brought into the United States to "the Military Intelligence, of the War Department, the Bureau of Investigation, of the Department of Justice," and "the United States Attorney for the Southern District of New York." Sandburg agreed that all government agencies could have free access to and use of the material. It was also understood that the material would be returned to Sandburg "providing an investigation by the United States Attorney or any of the other above-named departments shows that the said material if published or otherwise used, would not constitute a violation of the Espionage Law or any other law of the United States." With that, the government dropped all charges against Carl Sandburg.

Any record of the final fate of the ten thousand dollars Berg/Grusenberg/Borodin persuaded Carl Sandburg to deliver to Santeri Nuorteva has faded into the misty recesses of inaccessible government archives, but Sandburg did recall in later years giving Nuorteva a copy of the English translation of Lenin's *Letter to the American Workingman*. As for the four hundred kroner Michael Borodin asked Sandburg to deliver to his wife in Chicago, Mrs. Berg/Borodin got her money. Sandburg himself took it to her, in the company of a Chicago alderman named Rodriguez.

For Sandburg, at last, the case was closed. He could leave New York, a free man, and go to Cleveland to settle his professional fate.

By February 1919 he was in Cleveland writing stories based on the portion of his hard-won material which government censors had let him keep. "BOLSHEVIKI, GREAT AND NEAR GREAT" ran the headline over a photograph of seventeen "Bolshes" in a February 6 piece by Sandburg, "N.E.A. Staff correspondent Just Returned from Europe." "KAISER'S FIN-NISH PALS SHOOT DOWN LABOR AND RADICAL LEADERS," wrote Sandburg in a dispatch dated February 8. He was heralded as the "N.E.A. Staff Correspondent Just Arrived from Northern Europe with Pictures and Documents Never Before Published."

According to some accounts of this period, Sandburg brought back into the United States a love letter written to the Czar of Russia by the Czarina at the onset of the Russian Revolution. As Sandburg told it, he read the letter in a Stockholm newspaper which reprinted a series of "weird, incalculable letters" from the Czarina to the Czar. Sandburg sent the story and a translation of the letter back to NEA, where it caught the imagination of American readers. "The czarina letter is going big," Sandburg told Paula, "and they feel I'm a good investment." He labored over his translations of Swedish documents into English for NEA use. He commuted between Ohio and Illinois in February as he and Paula tried to decide if they should move to Cleveland.

Paula dreaded another departure, but would support whatever Carl wanted to do. "Of course if you want very much to go back to see Germany, or Russia or Finland or something I will not say 'Nay'! You shall not be tied down by the bunch of homey-glomies here!" Sandburg began to realize that he wanted to stay in Chicago. He hoped Sam Hughes would let him work there, running the Chicago NEA office and producing a regular column for the NEA syndicate. He told Paula there was "something about Chicago as a place, and Chicago people as people, that other places and people don't have. All in good time and before a durable peace is signed we will get around to where we're going to have our homey home again." Meantime he traveled wherever Hughes sent him, including Washington and New York.

Paula waited at home, her hands full with the care of the children, snatching time to write him, never quite sure where he would be. He wrote her from Washington in mock dismay: "I haven't had a line from you since I left home. Where do you think I am? Or have you quit me? Or are your hands full of trouble? Has the flu come to Our House? Or are you working for the united charities, or taking up bridge, or welcoming veterans home? . . . Here maybe two or three days, and then I hope to be through with this all-over-the-map stuff."

"Your banjo is fixed—and so is your fountain pen," Paula answered. "As for the love of the homeyglomeys for you, dear, that needed no fixing up. It's here the same as always only a few million bushels more of it!"

He was weary of travel and turmoil, ready to settle down again at home in Chicago. "Hotels lately tur-a-bul, overheated, no circulation," he wrote Paula. "Unless some assignment turns up I expect to make home by the end of next week and then stay two weeks. This depends on cyclones, wars, strikes, explosions, floods, crimes of violence, and acts of God."

Long after he left Eastern Europe, Sandburg was haunted by all he had beheld and heard of the war's savagery, the brutal costs of the colossal battle to secure the world for democracy. He had been stung by the assault on his own loyalty and patriotism, shaken by the official examination of his character. How to compute the cost, global and personal? Before he left New York for Cleveland, he tried to share his thoughts with Paula:

Every day action and action. The world turning over. A new thousand years beginning. For some weeks I felt the result in the balance, democracy defeated, checked, smothered, put off a long while. Now I can see a democratized earth on the way in about the same vague outlines that men a hundred years ago could see a republican earth on the way—and by democracy I mean *industrial*. Always so far just as I am about to have doubts of Wilson he comes through. He certainly understands the impossibilists among the reds—and the frequent testimony from all sides that he is an "enigma" is a certificate of some good stuff in him. Terribly big days. . . . Always I have loved watching storms. And this world storm with all its shadows and pain and hunger has its points—I'm for it—just as I have no criticism of all the waste and after birth gore that go with a child born.

But how to cleanse the world of the "waste and after birth gore" of the war, and how to heal? There was a paradox of hope and disillusion. Sandburg turned first to poetry, setting to work on a new poem, "The

Liars." The poem's symmetry is evident on the page. It uses a machine-gun repetition in its bitter, caustic attack on powerful political figures who deceive nations. "The Liars is a terrible piece," he told Paula, "and I guess it's just as well you don't get it for a while." After he had rewritten it three times he sent a copy to her. " 'Liars'—terrible, yes," she agreed, "but great stuff!"

He called the poem his sequel to "The Four Brothers," and headed an early draft of it with lines from a speech by Woodrow Wilson: "The forces of the world do not threaten; they operate. The great tides do not give notice that they are going to rise and run. They rise in their majesty and those who stand in their way are overwhelmed." As the represented nations of the world quarreled over the terms of peace, and President Wilson tried to preside amicably over hopelessly disparate interests, Sandburg's December prophecy seemed tragically true: the world was "a shambles and a madhouse." The sacrifice of millions of lives had not, apparently, been enough to satisfy heads of state who now bargained with words over boundary lines, territories, embargoes, trade, reparations, power to control. Those who stood in the way, in peace as well as in war, would, it seemed, be overwhelmed.

"A liar lies to nations," protested Sandburg the poet.

> A liar lies to the people.
> A liar takes the blood of the people
> And drinks this blood with a laugh and a lie,
> A laugh in his neck,
> A lie in his mouth . . .
>
> The tongue of a man is tied on this,
> On the liar who lies to nations,
> The liar who lies to the people.
> The tongue of a man is tied on this
> And ends: To hell with 'em all.
> To hell with 'em all . . .
>
> The liars met where the doors were locked.
> They said to each other: Now for war.
> The liars fixed it and told 'em: Go.
>
> Across their tables they fixed it up,
> Behind their doors away from the mob.
> And the guns did a job that nicked off millions.
> The guns blew seven million off the map . . .
>
> And now
> Out of the butcher's job
> And the boneyard junk the maggots have cleaned,

Where the jaws of skulls tell the jokes of war ghosts,
Out of this they are calling now: Let's go back where we were.
        Let us run the world again, us, us.
Where the doors are locked the liars say: Wait and we'll cash in again . . .
So I hear The People tell each other:
   Look at today and tomorrow.
   Fix this clock that nicks off millions
   when The Liars say it's time.
   Take things in your own hands.
        To hell with 'em all,
   The liars who lie to nations,
   The liars who lie to The People.

Embittered by his own experience and by the strife and suffering that characterized the supposed peace, Sandburg spoke out against any powers which abrogated the rights of The People. One thing was clear: there was no returning to "where we were." He held to the hope, shared with Paula, that somehow, out of all the world storm, there would be a birth, "A new thousand years beginning."

In a later, gentler poem, he expressed that fervent hope as a prayer:

      . . . Wandering oversea singer,
      Singing of ashes and blood,
      Child of the scars of fire,
         Make us one new dream, us who forget.
         Out of the storm let us have one star.

1919–1920

15. Smoke and Steel

In the blood of men and the ink of chimneys
The smoke nights write their oaths:
Smoke into steel and blood into steel . . .
Smoke and blood is the mix of steel. . . .

—Carl Sandburg, "Smoke and Steel,"
Smoke and Steel, 1920

"I could write five thick books on the world layout and the nearest I can get to a summary in one line is: Look for struggle and more struggle and no stability at all for ten years," Sandburg predicted in the summer of 1919. During most of the spring he had worked for the Newspaper Enterprise Association in Chicago, sending stories and ideas to Sam Hughes in Cleveland for possible national syndication. Hughes and Leon Starmont of NEA were increasingly disenchanted with Sandburg's work. "Carl, only one in a hundred knows anything at all about [John] Galsworthy," Starmont protested after reading one Sandburg interview. Sandburg defended the piece, telling his bosses they were underestimating their audience, betting that "80 per cent of the Omaha 6 o'clock trolley car riders would get his points and thank the paper that gave it to 'em." Besides, he argued, "Frisco the Jazz King tells me any man's a fool to count on getting more than 80 per cent of his audience."

Reluctantly, Sam Hughes fired Sandburg in May, telling him that he and NEA were not "hitching well together." "I hasten to say that I realize that you are a remarkable man in many ways," Hughes told Sandburg. "You are a great writer—your poems are sufficient evidence of that. You are a fine, keen thinker. But admitting all these things, you don't fit into the NEA scheme of things."

A letter from Leon Starmont hinted that Sandburg's politics and the residue of the Borodin encounter figured in the decision to fire him. "We like you, and I know I speak for all of us. We shall miss you. But we can't forget you, and I want you to remember us. Perhaps our methods can't coincide. But I don't believe you're as dangerous as some people would have us imagine, and I know we are not as stodgy as some folks would have you think."

Sandburg decided to try for another job at the *Chicago Daily News*. In a letter to news editor Henry Justin Smith on May 31, he proposed to write two or three lead stories weekly on "the organized labor field." He was deeply concerned about the lingering impact of the war on working people around the world. "How are the returned soldiers going to work and what does life mean now to the steel workers who went overseas?" he wondered. "What are superintendents and workmen saying about 'Americanization' in the steel and iron works towns?" He wanted to write about the financial fallout and the personal devastation of the war.

Smith liked Sandburg's proposal and wanted him back at the *Daily News*. In June Sandburg rejoined the staff; he would stay for thirteen years, his longest tenure ever on any salaried job. First he traveled to Atlantic City to cover the American Federation of Labor convention, and then Smith set him to work on a special investigation of racial problems in Chicago's Black Belt.

Smith was a lenient boss who encouraged staff writers in other literary pursuits, and so gave Sandburg latitude that he would not likely have enjoyed on other newspapers. Still the *Daily News* job kept Sandburg busy, diminishing the time and energy he had to spend on poetry. "But what is a poet with a family to do?" he asked a friend. "When he has daughters who are fine tigresses and he wants 'em to grow up, he can't let his daily bread job slip away even for such glad ships of passage as Foolscap."

✳

As the Sandburgs finally settled into their peacetime lives, Sandburg was able to turn more attention to poetry. His correspondence with other poets provided stimulation and literary fellowship. He exchanged letters with Amy Lowell, whom he called the "T.R. of poetry, a candidate who united the staid and sober with the lunatic fringe."

"You are one of the things that make life worth living," she told him. "I admire your work and the way you do it, and the whole spirit of the thing, and I tried the worst possible way to review 'Cornhuskers,' but somebody else was always before me with the papers to which I suggested it."

Sandburg wrote encouraging notes to Vachel Lindsay, who was work-

Carl Sandburg, journalist, 1918 or 1919   *Carl Sandburg Collection, University of Illinois*

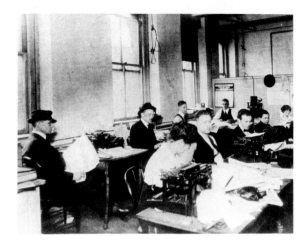

Carl Sandburg in *The Day Book*
newsroom, April 1916
Carl Sandburg Collection,
University of Illinois

Sandburg's editor, Negley D. Cochran, 1921
Carl Sandburg Collection, University of Illinois

Fog

The fog comes
on little cat feet.

It sits looking
over city and harbor
on silent haunches
and then moves on.

Carl Sandburg

"Fog," composed in 1913
Carl Sandburg Collection,
University of Illinois

Alice Corbin Henderson
Archives of *Poetry:*
A Magazine of Verse

Harriet Monroe at
Agnes Scott College,
Decatur, Georgia, in
March 1921
Poetry Archives

Eunice Tietjens
Poetry Archives

Amy Lowell
Poetry Archives

Sara Teasdale
Poetry Archives

Paula, baby Margaret and Opa, 1911 *Carl Sandburg Collection, University of Illinois*

Edward Steichen, Margaret and Paula, 1916 or 1917 *Carl Sandburg Collection, University of Illinois*

Clara Sandburg, Carl, Helga and Janet in
Elmhurst *Carl Sandburg Collection, University
of Illinois*

Janet Sandburg and her grandmother Clara
Sandburg in Elmhurst *Courtesy of Janet
Sandburg*

Carl Sandburg and his mother in the 1920s   *Carl Sandburg Collection, University of Illinois*

The Sandburgs' house on the dunes at Birchwood Beach, Chikaming Township, Harbert, Michigan   *Carl Sandburg Collection, University of Illinois*

Carl Sandburg and Eugene Debs
in Elmhurst about 1924
Carl Sandburg Collection,
University of Illinois

Carl Sandburg autographing *Abraham Lincoln: The Prairie Years* in 1926
Carl Sandburg Collection, University of Illinois

Carl Sandburg in his early forties
Will Crowell; Carl Sandburg Collection,
University of Illinois

Sandburg about 1922
Fujita; Chicago Daily News;
Carl Sandburg Collection,
University of Illinois

ing on *The Golden Whales of California* and struggling with his perennial inability to earn enough money. "The California thing is way your best—a strong vast sardonic that will bring various meanings to varied people," Sandburg told Lindsay, who thanked him for "the heartening word." "Everything seems to be lucky about that piece," said Lindsay, "including the chance to read it to you beforehand. . . . Be sure I think of you as the very pillar of Chicago, and when you are not there, the arm-chair is indeed vacant. You should be proud to have the affection and loyalty of so many. It is a wonderful thing to be a poet, and at the same time not a jackass."

Sandburg's longest, most revealing letters went to Alice Corbin Henderson in New Mexico and Louis Untermeyer in New York. With Untermeyer in particular, Sandburg discussed his views of contemporary poetry and poets. Long before Wallace Stevens's first book was published and years before his wide recognition, Sandburg admired Stevens's work, reading him repeatedly because "The music of his lines and the dusk of his implications in the phrases stays on and delivers its effect for me always in pieces like Thirteen Ways of Looking at a Blackbird." Somehow Sandburg obtained the manuscript of that poem, most likely from Stevens himself. In turn, he gave Stevens an inscribed copy of *Cornhuskers*, enclosing in the volume a typescript of his poem "Hats" with a note to Stevens: "here is one of thirteen ways of looking from a skyscraper."

"How much piffle there is in most poetry!" Stevens answered. "The blessing becomes a disease. But with you it is still a blessing and a juicy one."

Sandburg seldom saw Masters anymore, but believed that Masters's and Pound's best work was "as good as there is, by anybody." He told Untermeyer, who had criticized some of Masters's work, "If I hadn't known Masters in days when he was about the best talker in Chicago and so wonderfully democratic and companionable, before some miasmic malady of fame hit him in the midriff, I think I would go along with every line you have written." Pound, he said, "is genius of some kind," but Sandburg felt about Pound as he did when one of his children would not "do something good for it which it is told to do."

Sandburg had begun to enjoy the company of poet Lew Sarett, who taught public speaking at the University of Illinois and worked several months each year as a woodsman and guide in the American Northwest, spending so much time among the Chippewas that they named him Lone Caribou. Sarett translated American Indian poetry and wrote poetry with Indian themes. He was at work on *Many Moons*, "free renderings of tribal songs and ceremonies" which Henry Holt and Company would publish in 1920 with an introduction by Sandburg. Harriet Monroe had heard Sarett "chant a Chippewa corn dance in the original to a wild piano accompaniment of tribal music." She found his renditions "so authentically dramatic" that she urged him to translate them into free verse, and published his work in *Poetry*.

Sandburg and Sarett began to think about doing a joint lecture tour, and Sandburg approached the Pond Lecture Bureau in Chicago about representing them. "What I am day by day more sure of is that this is a field where I will have to end up because . . . I'm trained for it," he told Sarett. "I'm going to keep my eye out for dates for the two of us next fall and winter." As the Poet of the City, Sandburg would entertain with poetry and folk songs, sung to his own guitar accompaniment. As the Poet of the Wilderness, Sarett would sing and chant Indian poetry, his own and translations. By the end of 1919 they were rehearsing the joint recital.

In May Sandburg had made an important decision. Alfred Harcourt wrote to say he was leaving Henry Holt July 1 because he and Holt got on each other's nerves, especially when Harcourt published liberal or radical books. "If I am second rate I'm a fool to leave a good job," Harcourt told Sandburg, "but if I'm first rate—I'm a fool to stay. So I bet on myself." He hoped to find the capital to found his own company, and had arranged with Henry Holt that "when an author says he'd be uncomfortable here without me, that they will sell me or the publisher he turns to the rights, plates, & stocks etc. of books now in their hands." Harcourt had also edited Frost, and when Holt declined to release the copyright to books by Frost and Sandburg, Frost elected to stay with Holt. Sandburg left anyway, putting the rest of his work in Harcourt's hands at Harcourt, Brace and Howe, the company he and Donald Brace founded in 1919.

That summer of transition from job to job, publisher to publisher, also brought significant public recognition for Sandburg the poet. *Chicago Poems* and *Cornhuskers* established him as a poet of national stature. At last, he had unified his free-verse style and his realistic subject matter into a powerful, compelling poetic voice. He was no less controversial for being so visible. Largely with Sara Teasdale's support, Sandburg was awarded half of the second annual Poetry Society of America prize of five hundred dollars for the best book of poetry published in the nation in 1918. Since the Pulitzer Prizes did not yet take poetry into account, this award was given by the Poetry Society and Columbia University to fill the void.

Gentle, delicate Sara Teasdale, who had won the first award, "fought, bled and very nearly died over the Poetry Prize," seeing to it that *Corn-huskers* was nominated and persuading her fellow judges that Sandburg deserved at least a part of the prize, which he shared with Margaret Widdemer, author of *Old Road to Paradise*. Harriet Monroe congratulated Sandburg, and herself, for having the foresight to give him the Levinson Prize in 1914. "*Poetry* may be permitted to smile," she wrote in the July 1919 issue, "in remembering the clamor of journalistic guffaws which greeted its award of the initial Levinson Prize to Carl Sandburg's first *Poetry* entry, *Chicago Poems*,—his first appearance anywhere as a poet."

Like the Poetry Society of America judges, critics could not agree on the quality of *Cornhuskers*. Robert Frost told Harcourt, "Sandburg is better and better. He was a great find for you. He's man, woman and child all rolled in one heart." "Mr. Sandburg is an undeniable idealist whose very passion for his ideas prevents him from being a big poet," William Stanley Braithwaite told *Boston Transcript* readers. O. W. Firkins wrote in *The Nation* that Sandburg had "that general sense of the tremendousness of his own experience which is so stirring to its possessor and so little stirring to anybody else in the absence of confirmation of particulars."

The *New York Times* reviewer saw *Cornhuskers* as a melancholy book, a mood he attributed to the "racial soberness of the Scandinavian" and to Sandburg's view of past and future. "If to Carl Sandburg the past was as solid and vital and important as it is to Amy Lowell, he would be, we do not hesitate to say, the first American poet of his generation." A critic in *Outlook* wrote: "Art is long! One might do American literature a worse service than to pray nightly that Carl Sandburg find it out and ponder thereon. For he belongs in the front rank of contemporary American poets, well behind Robinson, but ahead of Lindsay and far ahead of Masters, neck and neck with Amy Lowell."

At the *Chicago Daily News* Sandburg's friend Ben Hecht gave him a rousing review written in slang that surpassed even Sandburg's own use of it:

. . . He's our Chicago bard, minstrel of our alleys, troubadour of the wheat patches outside our town. Homer of our sunsets and our stockyards. . . . There's more smoke to his song and kick to his heartbeat than Whitman ever coaxed out of his mellow, windbaggy soul. . . . A man in love with life is Sandburg, looking at the world through his heart. . . . The Peepul's Poet is Sandburg, poet for the great and egg-headed public who laugh at him, for the beetle browed wobblies who are sore at him because he won't throw bombs and be a regular red, for the cud-chewing pedants who perspire with rage at the right of vers libre. To all of them he makes love.

He plays their dreams on a mouth organ. He tells them their secrets on a banjo. There's a snarl and a whine to him and he sometimes writes with his fists. . . . Out of the slang of his street, out of the brotherhood hoakums and the turkey in the straw aesthetic of his day, Sandburg is making the new poetry. He doesn't belong to any of the art movements. . . . He's a movement all himself. He's the only genuine jazz motif in the letters of the day—a motif sonorous and quick, brazen and elusive.

The ache of crude passions, the snort of crude laughters, the caress of strong hands—these make love to you out of the poetry of Carl Sandburg.

✳

"Am back with the Daily News; working now on a series of articles on the Negro in Chicago," Sandburg told Alice Corbin Henderson in June 1919. There were outbreaks of racial violence throughout the country that year, tragic antecedents to the turbulence of later decades. Sandburg believed that the "Very physical hysteria of war" exacerbated racial prejudice nationwide. In many Chicago Black Belt neighborhoods, racial tensions smoldered in the mounting summer heat. Henry Justin Smith sent Sandburg to investigate.

During the war the population of Chicago's Black Belt doubled as blacks moved to Chicago from the South seeking war work. They had heard that Chicago was the "top of the world," and came in throngs in search of more freedom, more opportunity for good jobs. Between 1916 and 1919 the black population of Chicago increased from 44,103 to 190,594, yet little new housing was built. The burgeoning population of the Black Belt spilled over into adjoining, largely white neighborhoods, made frequent use of the city's parks and beaches, and did not stay within the lines of segregation drawn by some of the city's political bosses. Blacks moving into white neighborhoods risked trouble. Houses were bombed and would-be tenants harassed. Young neighborhood gangs protected boundaries with intimidation and violence. White soldiers returned from the war to find their jobs taken over by others, often black workers newly arrived from the South. Black veterans came home to Chicago, or settled there after the war, often to find their service to the country rewarded with discrimination, closed doors, joblessness, hopelessness. Clubs or gangs of white boys and young men "often armed with brass knuckles, clubs and revolvers" made frequent incursions into all-black neighborhoods, intimidating, and sometimes even murdering blacks. Policemen called the area a "pretty tough hole."

Sandburg spent days roaming the Black Belt, interviewing shopkeepers, housewives, factory workers, preachers, gamblers, pimps and many others, searching for facts to explain Chicago's version of the racial strife rampant in the country during that summer of 1919. There had been riots in Washington, New York, Omaha and other cities and towns across the nation. The return of black war veterans prompted senseless violence, as in the case of Private William Little, the subject of one of Sandburg's articles: "When Private Little returned home to Blakely, Georgia in his Army uniform, a hostile crowd of whites ordered him to remove his uniform and walk home in his underwear. Bystanders persuaded the men to release him. Little continued to wear the uniform as he had no other clothes." Sandburg reported that after anonymous notes warned Little to stop wearing his army issue, he was "found dead, his body badly beaten, on the outskirts of town. He was wearing his uniform."

This story and others by Sandburg ran in the *Chicago Daily News* in July. He kept a tight focus on the details of life in Chicago's Black Belt, investigating the roots of racial tension there, trying to place the problems in a national context. He reported the incontrovertible facts. Infant mortality was seven times higher in the Black Belt than in neighborhoods a mile to the east where housing and wages were better. Housing was critically deficient: "Under pressure of war industry the district, already notoriously overcrowded and swarming with slums, was compelled to have and hold in its human dwelling apparatus more than twice as many people as it held before the war." Hundreds if not thousands of people moved to Chicago hoping for permanent jobs and homes instead of "returning south of Mason and Dixon's line, where neither a world war for democracy, nor the Croix de guerre, nor three gold chevrons, nor any number of wound stripes, assures them of the right to vote or to have their votes counted or to participate responsibly in the elective determinations of the American republic."

Notebook in hand, Sandburg asked Chicago blacks of all ages and occupations how they saw their future in America. "We made the supreme sacrifice," black war veterans told him; "now we want to see our country live up to the constitution and the declaration of independence."

Sandburg traced the migration of Southern blacks to Chicago, gave the history of bombings which plagued black home-owners on the city's South Side, discussed the plight of black laborers in the postwar economic slump. He believed that economic equity would settle "a great deal of what is termed to-day the 'race question.'" As he spent more time in the squalor of the Black Belt, that conviction grew. The race problem, like the labor question, had economic roots, Sandburg wrote. "It is the economic equality that gets the emphasis in the speeches and writings of the colored people themselves," he reported. "They hate Jim Crow cars and lynchings and all acts of race discrimination, in part, because back of these is the big fact that, even in the north, in many skilled occupations, as well as in many unskilled, it is useless for any colored man or woman to ask for a job." He listed businesses which had "opened new doors of opportunity in Chicago" since 1917. He studied the plight of black women, writing sympathetically of their struggle for employment, and for better lives for their children. He discovered that "At the time of the greatest labor shortage in the history of this country, colored women were the last to be employed. They did the most menial and by far the most underpaid work," and often tolerated working conditions white women refused to accept. Sandburg made a strong case for education and job training. He summarized a civic housing survey which charged that housing for blacks in Chicago was "reprehensible, a menace to health and constitutes a kindling wood sufficient to keep Chicago in constant danger of disastrous conflagration."

One Sunday afternoon that July of 1919, Sandburg stood with nearly two thousand people for three hours in the hot sun at an American Federation of Labor meeting, hearing an A.F. of L. organizer tell the crowd of blacks, Lithuanians, Poles, Slovaks and Italians, "You notice there ain't no Jim Crow cars here to-day. That's what organization does." The crowd could hear the cheers from two baseball games nearby—the American Giants, a black baseball team, played in an adjoining field; the segregated White Sox played two blocks away. "The truth is," the organizer shouted over the din to his sweltering audience, "there ain't no Negro problem any more than there's an Irish problem or a Russian or a Polish or Jewish or any other problem. There is only the human problem, that's all. All we demand is the open door."

To support his belief that economics and education could solve the nation's racial problems, Sandburg interviewed Julius Rosenwald, president of Sears, Roebuck and Company, a two-hundred-million-dollar-a-year business which distributed "8,000,000 copies a year of the most widely circulated book in the United States—the Sears, Roebuck & Co. catalogue." Committed to the education of blacks, Rosenwald had founded more than three hundred Rosenwald rural schools in the South, with plans for seven hundred more.

Sandburg printed the "radical" platform of the National Association for the Advancement of Colored People, which called for a vote for every black man and woman; an equal chance to acquire an education; rights to fair trial; the right to sit on juries; defense against lynching and burning "at the hands of mobs"; equal service on trains and other public carriers; equal rights to use parks, libraries and other community services for which blacks, like whites, paid taxes; equal chance for employment; and the "abolition of color-hyphenation and the substitution of 'straight Americanism.' " He analyzed reports of race warfare in other cities in the nation, looked at crime rates involving blacks, explored the maze of gambling establishments run by blacks on South Street. He visited operations run by the likes of Louie Joe and Mexican Frank, and interviewed the unhappy neighbors who had shops, stores and apartments nearby, upset by "the proximity of the poker and craps enthusiasts." He reported on the realities of poverty—truancy, dilapidated homes, homelessness, families broken by "death, desertion, divorce, drink, promiscuous living or degeneracy."

He saw signs of hope. One day, at the corner of Thirty-fourth and South State streets, Sandburg attended a street meeting led by a black Pentecostal minister and his church choir. "New things is comin' altogether diverse from what they has been," the preacher told Sandburg, who listened as the voices of the choir "shook out irresistible and magnetic melody to a song.":

> Our boasted land and nation is plunging in disgrace
> With pictures of starvation in almost every place,
> While plenty of needed money remains in horrid piles,
> But God's going to rule this nation after a while.

Sandburg published an interview with Columbia University professor Joel Spingarn, a white man who served for six years as national chairman of the NAACP. He was an adviser to Alfred Harcourt, who arranged for him to meet Sandburg during Spingarn's trip through the Midwest that summer. "He wants to meet red shirts like yourself," Harcourt told Sandburg, "and hear for himself what these U.S.A. are thinking."

Like Sandburg, Spingarn believed the race issue to be national and federal in scope. "No city or state can solve it alone," Spingarn told Sandburg, advocating federal aid and a biracial commission to investigate racial problems across the nation. "I have fought for my country two years as a major of infantry," he told Sandburg and his readers, "and I wish to give it as my mature judgment that no barbarities committed by the Prussians in Belgium will compare with the brutalities and atrocities committed on negroes [sic] in the south. In effect, you may say that the Negroes who come north have issued from a system of life and industry far worse than anything ever seen under Prussianism in its worst manifestations."

These were some of the highlights of Sandburg's articles that hot, dangerous July. Most major newspapers in the country paid attention to racial issues during that volatile summer, but Sandburg's articles were singularly balanced and thorough, a rare firsthand account of the myriad roots of the problems. He advocated logical solutions to the social and economic ravages he saw in front of him, and called for national measures to prevent violence. His series was generally "well-received and gave a necessary balance to the more usual publication of stories involving Negroes in crimes," the Chicago Commission on Race Relations later concluded. Late in July, Sandburg was preparing to offer his readers an extensive program of "constructive recommendations." Unfortunately, there was explosive tragedy and, "as usual," Sandburg said, "everybody was more interested in the war than [in] how it got loose."

✳

During the last week of July 1919, temperatures in Chicago reached into the mid-nineties for several days running. Sweltering days gave way to still, sultry nights. In the cramped, airless rooms of tenements, it was impossible to sleep. The prolonged, intense heat short-circuited tempers and aborted daily routines. On Sunday, July 27, the thermometer climbed to ninety-six degrees, fourteen degrees hotter than normal. Blacks and whites swarmed to the city's beaches, hoping to find relief in the cooling waters of Lake Michigan where invisible barriers segregated black and white swimmers. Whites only used the beach and swam in the waters near Twenty-ninth Street, blacks only near Twenty-seventh. There were no signs or fences, but everyone understood the boundaries.

About four o'clock in the heat of that Sunday afternoon, seventeen-year-old Eugene Williams, black, entered "black" waters at the foot of Twenty-seventh Street. As he swam and drifted in the water, his attention was caught by a drama on shore: four black men walked toward the white section of beach and entered the water. A group of white men ordered them to leave, and they did, but soon returned with other blacks. There began a series of "attacks and retreats, counter attacks, and stone-throwing." Frightened women and children tried to take cover from a hail of stones.

Eugene Williams was afraid to go ashore. Not a strong swimmer, he grabbed a railroad tie floating in the water. It carried him past the invisible barrier into "white" water. As the fracas on the beach continued, stones began to come his way. Terrified, he tried to swim southward toward safety. Another swimmer approached, a young white boy, and Williams panicked. Suddenly, he went down.

Someone on the shore saw him disappear, and the contentious crowd on the beach turned its attention to the water. Several blacks accused a white man of stoning the boy in the water, and demanded that a white policeman arrest him. He refused. Meantime, several blacks and whites plunged in the water to rescue the boy. They dove for an hour without finding his body.

For a time the crowd was unified in the drama of the rescue attempt. A hundred conflicting eyewitness accounts fueled a rampage of rumors. The boy had been a dangerous interloper, some whites believed. He had been brutally stoned to death, blacks argued. When Williams's body was finally retrieved from the lake, there were no bruises to validate the story that he had been stoned to death, or that he had drowned after a stone hit him accidentally. A coroner's jury would conclude that he drowned "because fear of stone-throwing kept him from shore." But long before young Williams's body was given over to the coroner, Chicago was devastated by the worst race riot in its history. By midnight that Sunday, blacks had beaten four white men, stabbed five, shot one. Whites jumped into the battle, beating twenty-seven blacks, stabbing seven, shooting four.

Monday morning, July 28, found the city shaken and quiet, but only momentarily. Late that afternoon trouble erupted again when white men and boys who lived between the Stock Yards and the Black Belt "sought malicious amusement in directing mob violence against Negro workers returning home." Trolleys were pulled from their wires and black passengers dragged off the cars to be kicked and beaten. The police seemed powerless to stop the violence. Four blacks and one white were killed and thirty black men severely beaten in streetcar clashes. When the Black Belt retaliated, panic spread throughout the city. Police fired into a mob of more than fifteen hundred blacks, killing four and injuring dozens.

By Tuesday night, the homes of many blacks had been vandalized or burned. Rioting spread even after the mayor called in the state militia to restore order. Mercifully, at last, the weather intervened when heavy rain forced people off the streets and brought cooling relief.

Thirty-eight persons died in the Chicago race riots, fifteen whites, twenty-three blacks. Five hundred and thirty-seven persons were injured. About a thousand people, mostly blacks, were left "homeless and destitute." As the shaken city tried to return to normal, Sandburg's thoughtful coverage of the race problem seemed ironically prophetic. He was appalled at the savagery of events. "On the one hand we have blind lawless government failing to function through policemen ignorant of Lincoln, the Civil War, the Emancipation Proclamation, and a theory sanctioned and baptized in a storm of red blood," he wrote. "And on the other hand we have a gaunt involuntary poverty from which issues the hoodlum."

"It's working people killing each other, that's all there is to these race riots," a black union official told Sandburg on July 29. Sandburg used those words as the epigraph for "Hoodlums," a bitter poem he conceived during the turbulence of the riots. Later, it was revised and published in *Smoke and Steel*, but an early, unpublished draft read:

> I am a hoodlum, you are a hoodlum, we and all of us
>> are a world of hoodlums—maybe so.
> I hate and kill better men than I am, so do you, so
>> do all of us—maybe—maybe so.
> In the ends of my fingers I itch for another man's
>> neck, I want to see him hanging, one of dusk's cartoons
>> against the sunset.
> This is the hate my father gave me, this was in my mother's
>> milk, this is you and me and all of us in a world of
>> hoodlums—maybe so.
> Let's go on, brother hoodlums, let us kill and kill,
>> it has always been so, it will always be so, there is
>> nothing more to it . . .
> Lay them deep in the dirt, the stiffs we have fixed, the
>> cadavers we bumped off, lay them deep and let the night
>> winds of winter blizzards howl their burial service.
> The night winds and the winter, the great white sheets
>> of northern blizzards, who can sing better for the lost
>> hoodlums the old requiem, "Kill him! Kill him! the
>> Son of a Bitch . . ."

✳

Joel Spingarn left Chicago before the race riots, taking with him copies of Sandburg's *Daily News* articles, which he sent back to Harcourt in New York. "They ought to be printed," Harcourt told Sandburg in August, "and I think I'd like to make it the first volume of a pamphlet library we are going to start. Each bust-up in the world has been followed by an age of pamphleteering, and very often the pamphlets have the facts." At first Harcourt wanted to use "Hoodlums" as a frontispiece, but changed his mind. He proposed selling the pamphlet for twenty-five to sixty cents, and Sandburg agreed, sending Harcourt copies of eighteen articles. Harcourt asked Walter Lippmann, another of his editorial advisers at Harcourt, Brace and Howe, to write a preface. Lippmann had been one of the authors to follow Harcourt to his new firm.

Sandburg once told Amy Lowell that Lippmann deserved "a booby prize for aimless cleverness." "His nostrils are keen for the revolution everywhere except in literary style," Sandburg said. "In an electric motor age he writes like an early steam engine."

Sandburg was not entirely pleased with Lippmann's preface or with his own royalty arrangements with Harcourt, but he was eager to "get this stuff over to the country now." He told Untermeyer, "I'm surprised at the amount of solid scientific info I got into those day by day stories. I never did a harder three weeks work in my life nor enjoyed hard work more than that series." *The Chicago Race Riots* reached a wide audience, and brought Sandburg and the *Chicago Daily News* the commendation of the Chicago Commission on Race Relations for balanced coverage of the race question. Critics hailed the pamphlet as a "serious and intelligent investigation into conditions which made the race riots possible" and a "contribution to the solving of the Negro problem in any section of the country."

Chicago Race Riots: July, 1919 was Sandburg's first book published by Harcourt's new firm, as well as his first commercial book of prose. Fifty years later, it was reissued, with a preface by Ralph McGill, editor of the *Atlanta Constitution*. "How much do cities, a people, a nation learn in fifty years?" McGill wrote in 1969. "Not much." He noted, in the wake of the civil rights struggles of the sixties and the assassination of Martin Luther King, that in 1919 "Reporter Carl Sandburg's accounts were not easy to get." He believed that "Carl Sandburg's reports of half a century ago are a serious indictment of us as a people. We are again confronted with our incredible neglect of social facts and our lack of awareness of their meaning." McGill concluded that Sandburg's far-sighted reporting in 1919 was an even sadder commentary fifty years later: "It indicts us as a people addicted to folly and violent resistance to healthful social and political change."

Back in 1919, a helpless witness of war, racial hatred and mob violence, Sandburg stood bitterly disillusioned. He told Untermeyer that "it's come clear in the last two or three years

> that in a group killing of a man, in a mobbing, the event reaches a point where all rationale is gone; such a term as "anarchist" or "traitor" or "Boche" or "Englander Schwein" disappears and they babble hysterically only one or two epithets, in our language usually a tenor of "Son of a Bitch" with a bass of "Cocksucker." Since some of the finest blood of the human family goes this way poets and painters have a right to employ it or at least not kid themselves about what actually happened at Golgotha. Since I've tackled with men who were in the trenches and since I've seen race riots I am suspicious that the sponge of vinegar on the spear is a faked

legend and what probably happened, if the historicity of Jesus is ever established, is that they cut off his genital organ and stuck it in his mouth.

Inevitably Sandburg the poet transmuted the trauma of the race riots and the war into poetry. "Did I see a crucifix in your eyes/and nails and Roman soldiers/and a dusk Golgotha?" he wrote in "Crimson Changes People."

> Did I see No Man's Land in your eyes
> and men with lost faces, lost loves,
> and you among the stubs crying? . . .

In "Man, the Man Hunter," Sandburg wrote graphically about a lynching, the stark metaphor for the race riots:

> I saw Man, the man-hunter,
> Hunting with a torch in one hand
> And a kerosene can in the other,
> Hunting with guns, ropes, shackles.
>
>> I listened
>> And the high cry rang,
> The high cry of Man, the man-hunter:
> We'll get you yet,   you   sbxyzch!
>
>> I listened later.
>> The high cry rang:
> Kill him!   Kill him!   the sbxyzch!
>
> In the morning the sun saw
> Two butts of something, a smoking rump,
> And a warning in charred wood:
>> Well, we got him,
>> the   sbxyzch.

❋

In the fall of 1919, Sandburg wrote, "We suddenly picked up all our chattels and flitted away from Maywood, where we owned a place, and moved into debt at Elmhurst with wonderful pines and poplars and a chance for the daughters to sit with values of silence if they so choose."

"Why should I be the first poet of misery to be keeping out of debt," Sandburg joked in his letter to Alice Corbin Henderson. He and Paula needed "a bigger place for the kids to grow up in, and more of a chance to raise the little ones ourselves instead of having neighbor kid gangs take all their time day and night." Margaret for one sorely missed the Maywood house and the playmates of her old neighborhood.

Paula quickly put her own stamp on the house at 331 South York Street, hiring carpenters to add a porch, as well as windows for light and a view of the trees. She planted gardens to encompass the place. In his upstairs workroom, Sandburg began putting together his next volume of poetry, choosing from many new pieces as well as "many orphans and stray dogs" in his portfolio, he told Amy Lowell.

Harcourt encouraged Sandburg with the new book, but did not want to rush him. "We mustn't let our anxiety to have a book of yours on our early list induce either of us to publish before you have just the book that most nearly means you now," he told Sandburg. "You and Frost, anyway, are the longtime people, and a season more or less mustn't count."

Sara Teasdale lobbied Harriet Monroe and her committee that fall to give Sandburg *Poetry*'s hundred-dollar prize. "I know he has had the Levinson prize," she argued, "but it seems to me that this should not prevent his being eligible for another prize. And I think his Red Haw Winds the finest contribution of the year. (This, and Yeats' play)." Instead, *Poetry* honored that year the work of H. L. Davis, Marjorie Allen Seiffert and Mark Turbyfill, choosing their poems over those by Sandburg, Teasdale, Yeats, Masters, D. H. Lawrence, Lindsay and William Carlos Williams.

Sandburg was at work on a new poem then, "a smoke and steel piece, about the length of Prairie." He and Lew Sarett were preparing their joint lecture-recital for a December debut. At the *Daily News* Sandburg kept track of the trials and investigations growing out of the race riots. At work and at home, after the prolonged turbulence of the war and the riots, life resumed a more predictable ebb and flow.

That fall Nobel laureate Romain Rolland asked Bertrand Russell, Henri Barbusse, Jane Addams, Jules Romains, the poet Tagore, and other world leaders and literary figures, including Carl Sandburg, to sign an appeal calling on the "intellectual Workers of the World" to recognize "no other master other than 'the Mind.'" Waldo Frank transmitted a copy of Rolland's Declaration of Intellectual Independence to Sandburg and asked him to make copies for other "men and women of the sort who would sign this Appeal." Rolland's appeal stimulated Sandburg to try to write out his own political creed. In the midst of postwar paranoia that included the Red Scare and the Palmer Raids, Sandburg's words were bold and dangerous. The country was in the throes of an emotional reaction which blurred the distinctions between socialist and socialist, socialist and communist, dissenter and anarchist, unionist, syndicalist, agitator, radical, revolutionary. Sandburg's rhetoric could have been highly inflammatory during that time. He apparently never sent the letter, but used it as a private means of articulating his views. It is a revealing political self-portrait:

> If I have a fixed, unchangeable creed then I am saved the trouble every day of forming a new creed dictated by the events of that day. . . . I am a socialist but not a member of the party. I am an I.W.W. but I don't carry a red card. I am an anarchist but not a member of the organiza-tion. . . . I am a Francis Heney Republican and a Frank P. Walsh Dem-ocrat and a Victor Murdock Progressive but I am free to vote any ticket or back any candidate I pick in the next campaign. I belong to everything and nothing. If I must characterize the element I am most often active with I would say I am with all rebels everywhere all the time as against all people who are satisfied. . . . I am for the single tax, for all the immediate demands of the socialists, for the whole political program of the American Federation of Labor, for the political and economic measures outlined in the Progressive and Democratic party platforms, and the trend of legislation and activity voiced by Woodrow Wilson in "The New Free-dom." . . . Until the earth is a free place to free men and women wanting first of all the right to work on a free earth there will be war, poverty, filth, slums, strikes, riots, and the hands of men red with the blood of other men.

Sandburg's first political passion had been born out of his helpless witness of his father's struggle. As poet, political activist and reporter, he had documented the plight of the mass of American working people. In his brief sojourn abroad into the wartime "world storm," he learned once and for all that the struggle for human dignity was global, and his conviction deepened that the insidious root of racial, national and in-ternational conflict was economic:

> I cannot see where the people have ever won anything worth keeping and having but it cost something and I am willing to pay this cost as we go along—rather let the people suffer and be lean, sick and dirty through the blunders of democracy than to be fat, clean, and happy under the efficient arrangements of autocrats, kaisers, kings, czars, whether feudal and dynastic or financial and industrial. I cannot understand how the people are going to learn except by trying and I do not know any other way to honestly conduct the experiment of democracy than to let the people have the same opportunities of self-determination that belong of right to nations small and large. . . . In their exercise of the right of self determination I expect the people to pass through bitter experiences and I am aware it is even possible that the people shall fail in the future as they have failed in the past.

It was a year studded with violent controversy. Oliver Wendell Holmes and the Supreme Court had unanimously upheld the conviction of Eugene Debs on charges of sedition. Four hundred soldiers, sailors and marines raided the offices of the socialist *New York Call*, vandalizing the plant and beating several editors. A bomb wrecked the home of Attorney General Palmer, who began his raids in earnest in November, alleging that there was a revolutionary plot to overthrow the government. On November 11 three members of the American Legion, attempting to raid IWW headquarters in Centralia, Washington, were shot to death, and a union member was lynched in retaliation. On December 2 President Wilson urged Congress to take action to stop "the Reds." On December 21 the U.S. transport ship *Buford* sailed for Russia carrying 249 alleged Reds for deportation, among them anarchist Emma Goldman. On a single January night Palmer masterminded raids on private homes and organizations, arresting more than four thousand alleged communists in thirty-three cities.

"Many things I might have said today," Sandburg wrote in the poem "Aprons of Silence":

> And I kept my mouth shut.
> So many times I was asked
> To come and say the same things
> Everybody was saying, no end
> To the yes-yes, yes-yes,
>   me-too, me-too.
>
> The aprons of silence covered me.
> A wire and hatch held my tongue.
> I spit nails into an abyss and listened . . .
>
> I fixed up a padded cell and lugged it around.
> I locked myself in and nobody knew it.
> Only the keeper and the kept in the hoosegow
> Knew it . . .
> Here I took along my own hoosegow
> And did business with my own thoughts.
> Do you see? It must be the aprons of silence.

✳

On December 21, 1919, Sandburg and Lew Sarett gave their first joint lecture-recital. It was pronounced a "grand show!" Billed as the Poet of the City, Sandburg read his poems and, to his own guitar accompaniment, sang folk songs he had collected in his travels. He could play only two or three chords, and his mellow baritone voice, like his guitar playing, was self-taught. He crooned his songs to an enthralled audience and discovered a new way to express himself and earn money at the same time.

Lew Sarett gave the audience "Indian chants and dances, his wolf cries, his French-Canadian chanson, and remarkably refreshing poetry." Flamboyant Italian poet Emanuel Carnevali, then associate editor of *Poetry*, reviewed the show in February 1920. He liked the way the two poets "chattered and gossiped and talked" with the audience and had "as much fun as they gave to the bewildered spectators." Sandburg "most delicately and lovably" played and sang "Jesse James," "Frankie and Albert Were Sweethearts," "The Boll Weevil," and "This Morning, This Evening, So Soon." Sarett played the tom-tom and "shrieked and bellowed, snorted, squeaked and squawked, chirped and warbled—just like the many animals he had carefully listened to during his stay in the forests of the Northwest and Canada."

"Sandburg is a kingly reader," Carnevali wrote. "His reading is exactly as beautiful as his poetry and his person. He is one of the most completely, successfully alive human beings I ever saw: from his sturdy shoes to the tuft of hard gray hair over his granite eyes, to his voice and his words; from the majestic dignity of his voice to the dignity of his poems."

Another firsthand description of Sandburg in 1919 came from the pacifist British poet Siegfried Sassoon, who came to Chicago to lecture. He found Sandburg in "that dingy little newspaper room, with an old gray hat on his head, smoking a large, companionable pipe." He and Sandburg stood on the roof of a Chicago office building for a view of the city and "its canyon-like streets and facades," watching a "stormy sunset" transfigure Michigan Avenue. Sassoon told Sandburg that "it seemed funny to think of me coming to tell Chicago that war doesn't pay."

"Maybe a few of them'll believe you," Sandburg replied. "But they can't know unless they've been there themselves. Bullets, bombs, bayonets, gas, are nothing more than words to them." For Sassoon that moment was "the central point" of his time in the United States.

To literary critic Burton Rascoe, "Carl Sandburg's features aren't finely chiseled; they look as if they might have been hacked out with an adze and mattock. His countenance is not only rugged, it is rough and weatherworn." Rascoe described the inner and outer Sandburg as he perceived him during this time:

He has high cheekbones and precipitous brows, widely brambled. Two deep furrows run down his face and around the corners of his mouth, like gullies on a clay hillside. His chin juts out from square jaws, and save for his nose and forehead, he might serve as a model for a reconstructed bust of a Neanderthal man. . . . He is square-shouldered, powerfully built. . . . He is naïve and simple. Like Will Rogers, his handsome homeliness is irresistible, and he wins his way into the hearts of his audience the moment he appears on the stage.

Others who heard Sandburg were not impressed. "Is this poetry?" one listener wondered. "I thought poetry ought to be refined."

✳

There was, Sandburg observed, "a new deep solemnity coming over the labor movement of Chicago. The cynicism about existing government and morals is deeper than ever and their faith about labor doing something for itself goes deeper than I ever saw it before."

The country was jolted by strikes and lockouts disrupting the postwar economy and intensifying conflict between labor and management. Shipbuilders, railroad workers, longshoremen, cigarmakers, subway workers, mailmen, engineers, firemen, carpenters, actors, pressmen and coal miners struck for higher wages and better working conditions in 1919 and 1920. In August 1919 the new A.F. of L. steelworkers' union squared off against Judge Elbert H. Gary and the United States Steel Corporation, seeking, among other changes, the end of the twelve-hour workday. Despite President Wilson's intervention, the strike grew. After months of violence, federal troops led by General Leonard Wood interceded in Gary, Indiana. The strike wore on until January 8, 1920, when the A.F. of L. capitulated to the greater power of Gary and U.S. Steel. Sandburg covered the resolution of the strike for the *Daily News*.

Soon after the steel strike ended, Sandburg was assigned to cover the men's clothing strike of the Amalgamated Clothing Workers' Union in Chicago. Despite his own political inclinations, Sandburg could be scrupulously fair and objective in his reportage. He looked at both sides of the Chicago dispute, finding that the "Amalgamated Clothing Workers in organization efficiency and social vision are farther along than anything in the country, while Hart Schaffner & Marx is in all-around quality farther developed than any shop or factory I know." Sidney Hillman of the union and Joseph Halle Schaffner of management negotiated a forward-looking labor pact. Both men became lifelong friends of Sandburg.

Louis Untermeyer invited Sandburg to contribute poems to *A Miscellany of American Poetry*, his new anthology. He also solicited poems from Robert Frost, Sara Teasdale, Conrad Aiken and seven others, asking each poet to select and arrange his own contributions. Sandburg was reluctant at first. "I've been trying to crawl out of anthology stuff," he told Untermeyer. "Meeting too many people who think they have a fellow's number because they read some of him in an anthology. . . . However, if you and Farmer Frost can stand the gaff I can."

Sandburg was also "going along slow on another book" for the upcoming summer or fall, and he was busy with his newest literary venture—reading his poems and playing his guitar on the college and civic club lecture circuit. When his lecture agency, the Pond Bureau, closed its American offices to concentrate on British clientele, he quickly signed with a new agent, the poet and attorney Mitchell Dawson. From 1920 onward Sandburg spent many weeks each year giving lecture-recitals of poetry and folk music, thriving on the travel and the stimulation of a live audience, and gathering an ever-growing repertoire of folk music and folklore. He liked getting in touch with "a cornfed young prairie American New York has no inkling of."

By late February, however, Sandburg was overworked to the point of exhaustion, and having trouble with his eyes. He spent four days at home "sleeping nearly all the time, catching up on a heavy winter." There was little relief in his grueling schedule. He moved daily between worlds, as a journalist concentrating on the intricacies of postwar politics and labor issues, as a poet crafting his new book and publishing new poems in *Poetry*, the *Dial* and other journals. At home he managed after the day's work to "cull over and shape up" the poetry manuscripts he kept in three wire baskets in his small workroom. Most of his poems went through several drafts before he was satisfied; some he set aside for years, reworking them periodically, reshaping lines or changing words, sometimes combining two or more poems into one, and often paring, stripping, condensing. In March he sent thirty poems to Untermeyer for the anthology. "I'm sure you'll want to throw out 19, and I would rather have you throw out 20, because it's all rather a rush job," he wrote. He thought twenty pages of poems would be appropriate for the anthology because "I can deliver nearly the sum total of any poet's style and drift in 20 pages."

In March the conservative French journal *Mercure de France* printed a twenty-six-page article by Jean Catel praising the poetry of Sandburg and Frost. Catel had visited Sandburg in Chicago, where they had long walks and talks about poetry. He admired Sandburg's "broad vision, profound human sympathies," his forceful personality and his original forms. The attention of a foreign critic pleased Sandburg, particularly since Lincoln MacVeagh of Henry Holt and Company, which still held copyrights to *Chicago Poems* and *Cornhuskers*, was trying unsuccessfully to find an English publisher for Sandburg's books. At least twenty British publishers had rejected them so far. Despite Catel's enthusiasm, Sandburg's raw Americanism did not appeal to the overseas audience.

✳

Sandburg was still unhappy about his contract with Harcourt for *The Chicago Race Riots*, and told Untermeyer he was not sure "where to go with my next book this year. As I look at Harcourt slamming a 60 cent price on a 72-page cover book, and hanging me up with a royalty of 10 per cent *wholesale*, I doubt whether we'll hitch well for the long run. So why change from Holt's who already have two books of mine that are going now better than ever, thanks to you and friends."

"Say, I hear rumors that you are sore," Harcourt wrote to Sandburg. "I hear it's about the royalty on Race Riots. . . . If this matter is on your chest, why not say so, and to us first of all, and tell us what we ought to pay you for this job."

Sandburg waited nearly a month to answer Harcourt's letter:

> I wrote to you when I sent on the race riot manuscript that all arrangements would be "whatever you want." You wanted the opening story, a lurid and terrible fact narrative, a race riot curtain raiser, thrown out as "sentimental," too much like Uncle Tom's Cabin. You wanted an authentic sociological introduction. You wanted a price of 60 cents retail for a 72-page paper cover pamphlet. . . . You wanted your first contract with me in which the royalty should be 10 per cent wholesale instead of 10 per cent retail as before. You wanted all these things and you believe these things are all as they should and of right ought to be. What more is to be said?

Harcourt countered with praise for "Smoke Nights" and other new Sandburg poems he had read in journals that spring. "You're as good as they ever come," he told Sandburg. "My hat is off to you more than ever." He encouraged Sandburg to finish the new book of poetry, and traveled to Chicago in April to offer him a generous contract for his third volume of poems. "If Harcourt hadn't come along and made me a nice raise and fixed everything up," Sandburg told Untermeyer, "I suppose it would have been next winter before I got the Mss. of the third book shaped up." They decided to call it *Smoke and Steel*. Sandburg promised to deliver the manuscript by May 10.

When Lew Sarett asked Sandburg to write the introduction to *Many Moons*, his forthcoming book of poetry, Sandburg hesitated: "I am lugging several loads now and can't say when I'll get to that introduction, but it can be only when I can go to it decently. I am willing to speed up in newspaper work, for my meal ticket, but in poetry and The Arts, I shall never be anything but a loafer." He was working informally as Harriet Monroe's "Emergency Associate Editor" that winter. Paula was helping him with a Modern Library edition of the work of Walt Whitman, to be published by Boni & Liveright in 1921. He hoped his eyes would hold out for the "several loads" of work he felt obliged to do.

In his preface to the Whitman volume Sandburg was laudatory rather than critical. He wrote that Whitman was "the only established epic poet of America," and called *Leaves of Grass* a "massive masterpiece." When Sandburg appraised the work of other writers, he was characteristically supportive, accepting the style and idiom without passing judgment, except, perhaps, in private. Burton Rascoe observed later that "Sandburg has the most deficient critical sense of any writer I know. He is a man almost entirely of intuitions about which he is more or less inarticulate." But Rascoe believed that the absence of critical sense accounted for "much of the charm and impressiveness of his best poems." Sandburg's interest in editing the Whitman volume came, however, not from any critical aspirations but from his long, affectionate allegiance to Whitman's poetry and idealism.

With Paula's help Sandburg managed to shape up the manuscript for *Smoke and Steel* by early May of 1920. He believed it was his best book yet. Already he was beginning to conceive the next book, and it would be for children. He wrote Alice Corbin Henderson, "Today I feel I won't put out another book of poetry in forty years. Anyhow before another of poetry I'm going to do a Kid book. They are the anarchs of language and speech and we'll have a lot of fun whether it's a real book or not."

He shipped the manuscript of *Smoke and Steel* to Harcourt by special delivery. "It's a book of smoke, high winds, underworlds and overtones," he said. ". . . Those who holler propaganda will holler louder than ever at this."

✳

Alfred Harcourt was not alone in his confidence that he could run his own publishing firm. Sinclair Lewis had urged him on. "Don't be such a damn fool as ever again to go to work for someone else," he had told Harcourt. "Start your own business. I'm going to write important books.

You can publish them." In 1920 Harcourt, Brace and Howe published Lewis's *Main Street* and Sandburg's *Smoke and Steel.*

In Harcourt's office on West Forty-seventh Street in New York there was such excitement the day Sandburg's manuscript arrived that all other work was suspended. Harcourt's assistant Ellen Eayrs described the scene for Sandburg:

> This office has been on a complete bat today:—no one has done a lick of work. Mr. Harcourt came upstairs at ten this morning with the ms— I could not get a word out of him until 11:30 when he began to read from the ms to Mr. Spingarn; then Mr. Spingarn took part of it and read it back to him and me—They went out to lunch and when Mr. Spingarn got back at 2:30 he started on it—at 3:30 Mr. Untermeyer came in; then he and Mr. Spingarn started reading it—and now here comes Mr. Harcourt again and all four of us have begun all over again—Really—see what you have done—

Harcourt told Sandburg that he, Untermeyer and Spingarn "spent most of the day gloating over your manuscript. We have decided it is best to let it go just as it is. . . . I think we will both make a nice little dent with that book. We are very proud of it already and are going to be more so."

Untermeyer, one of Sandburg's earliest and most steadfast champions, wrote to congratulate him. "Carl, you came so damn fast you took our breath away. But, by God, you're still coming! You've not only out-stripped us all, you haven't even stopped running."

Despite the enthusiasm, Sandburg still had to focus on newspaper work. His press credentials admitted him to the headquarters of GOP Presidential candidates General Leonard Wood and Illinois governor Frank Lowden, for the turbulent Republican convention in Chicago, which would nominate the dark horse Warren G. Harding for President. In that time of Prohibition, H. L. Mencken, in town to cover the convention, drank "near beer" with Sandburg at Michael "Hinky Dink" Kenna's saloon and talked politics.

He pulled away from the convention long enough to read proof for *Smoke and Steel.* Troubled by the number of errors, he asked Harcourt to send him page proofs as well. Since the days of Philip Green Wright's Asgard Press, Sandburg had taken a keen aesthetic interest in every detail of the production of his books. He protested, for instance, the printer's change to a "narrower width of line" which resulted in the "break-overs" of certain long lines in his poems.

He dedicated *Smoke and Steel* to his brother-in-law Steichen in a significant gesture of affection. Steichen was beset with personal difficulties that summer. He and his wife, Clara, were estranged; Clara rightly suspected that her husband had been involved with other women. They were on the brink of a public and bitter divorce battle which would have international news coverage. Their daughters Mary, sixteen, and Kate Rodina, twelve, were old enough to be perceptive witnesses of the dissolution of their parents' marriage. "What can we say," Sandburg wrote Steichen, "more than that we are all tied up closer to you and with you than ever before . . . and as fate deals the cards sometimes there is reason to say, 'This is the worst of all possible worlds.' " He urged Steichen to come to Chicago to see the family, especially Janet. "She's got your own elusive way," he wrote, "and she is a hunter of beauty and will be hungry all her life. She is your kin all over.—Paula keeps more beautiful forty ways than ever before and is worth your knowing more.—If luck can come from wishing, daytime and nighttime wishing, you will have it from us out here."

✳

Smoke and Steel, Sandburg's third book of poetry, was in many ways the culmination of his work as a personal poet revealing his interior life as well as the emotional and social milieu of his times. *Chicago Poems*, *Cornhuskers* and *Smoke and Steel* were in their era highly original, forceful reflections of the soul and experience of one "common" man, metaphorically revealing in portraits of working people the problems of contemporary life and the universal themes of existence—love, joy, loss, pain, death, war, betrayal, transcendence.

After *Smoke and Steel* Sandburg became the champion and celebrant of the masses rather than the individual, of the People in conflict with the daunting forces of government, progress, injustice, time. In the poetry published after *Smoke and Steel* and before *Honey and Salt* (1963), Sandburg holds his readers at arm's length, giving them their own images in the mirrors of his poems, probing their collective experience rather than the particulars of his own soul. *Smoke and Steel* is in a sense a valedictory, a last compelling glimpse of the inner man perplexed and disillusioned by the forces of contemporary life. After this pivotal book Sandburg began to turn his readers toward their shared history and joint future.

The images of the lead poem "Smoke and Steel" (which he had earlier called "Smoke Nights") grew from his travels as a reporter to steel towns, most recently Gary, Indiana, for the coverage of the long steel strike. In the poem, workingmen, "finders in the dark," wrest steel from fire.

Some die in the process. Men and steel are simultaneously tools and symbols of the industrial society:

> The anthem learned by the steel is:
>> Do this or go hungry. . . .
> Box-cars, clocks, steam-shovels, churns, pistons, boilers, scissors—
> Oh, the sleeping slag from the mountains, the slag-heavy pig-iron will go
>> down many roads.
> Men will stab and shoot with it, and make butter and tunnel rivers, and
>> mow hay in swaths, and slit hogs and skin beeves, and steer air-
>> planes across North America, Europe, Asia, round the world. . . .

At the end, Sandburg reflects on the transience of the lives of men, and the useless, rusty permanence of the artifacts they leave behind:

> A bar of steel sleeps and looks slant-eyed
> on the pearl cobwebs, the pools of moonshine;
> sleeps slant-eyed a million years,
> sleeps with a coat of rust, a vest of moths,
> A shirt of gathering sod and loam . . .

The dramatic pronouncement of theme and the sprawling symmetry of form in "Smoke and Steel" repeat the pattern Sandburg established with "Chicago" in *Chicago Poems* and "Prairie" in *Cornhuskers*. Similarly, the lead poem is followed by a series of dark portraits of working people overwhelmed by their lives. Sandburg contemplates the resignation of work gangs who long for the oblivion of rest, sleep, even death:

> Sleep is a belonging of all; even if all songs are old songs and the singing
>> heart is snuffed out like a switchman's lantern with the oil gone,
>> even if we forget our names and houses in the finish, the secret of
>> sleep is left us, sleep belongs to all, sleep is the first and last and
>> best of all . . .

Sandburg the reporter interviewed jazz musicians while Sandburg the poet collected folk songs and studied the music of the labor movement, black church choirs, the regions of the country he explored on his lecture trips. Thus music found its way into *Smoke and Steel*, especially blues and jazz, "the red death jazz of war" in "Crimson Changes People," and the syncopation of "Jazz Fantasia": "Drum on your drums, batter on your banjoes,/sob on the long cool winding saxophones./Go to it, O jazzmen."

The group of poems entitled "Passports" drew Sandburg's journey to Sweden into *Smoke and Steel*. There were war poems; "Liars" was included, along with reflections on the aftermath of war. There were lyrical affirmations of family and home in poems for Paula and the children. He wrote of peach blossoms, birds, the landscapes he loved, and of prophecy for his daughters, as in "Helga":

> . . . The north has loved her; she will be
> A grandmother feeding geese on frosty
> Mornings . . .

For Paula there were love songs—

> . . . Your hands are sweeter than nut-brown bread when you
>   touch me . . .
> Nothing else in this song—only your face.
> Nothing else here—only your drinking, night-gray eyes.

There were beautiful cryptic meditations on love, and rare allusions to loves other than Paula, although no evidence but the poems remains to speak of other women whom he may have loved then. He wrote in "North Atlantic":

> I made a song to a woman—it ran:
>   I have wanted you.
>   I have called to you
>   On a day I counted a thousand years. . . .
>
> In the deep of a sea-blue noon
> many women run in a man's head,
> phantom women leaping from a man's forehead
>   . . . to the railings . . . into the sea . . . to the
>   sea rim . . .
>   . . . a man's mother . . . a man's wife . . . other
>   women . . .

"Put Off the Wedding Five Times and Nobody Comes to It: (Handbook for Quarreling Lovers)" is vibrant with love and mystery:

. . . Since you have already chosen to interpret silence for language and
    silence for despair and silence for contempt and silence for all things
    but love,
Since you have already chosen to read ashes where God knows there was
    something else than ashes. . . .

It will always come back to me in the blur of that hokku: The heart of
    a woman of thirty is like the red ball of the sun seen through a mist . . .

He wrote tenderly of women, as a man who knew and understood them:

> . . . Is the night woven of anything else
> than the secret wishes of women,
> the stretched empty arms of women?
> the hair of women with stars and roses? . . .

In that poem, called "Night's Nothings Again," Sandburg gave a voice and persona to Night itself:

> . . . I saw the night's mouth and lips
> strange as a face next to mine on a pillow
> and now I know . . . as I knew always . . .
> the night is a lover of mine . . .
>
> . . . I listen to Night calling:
>
> . . . I am the one whose passion kisses
> keep your head wondering
> and your lips aching
> to sing one song
> never sung before . . .

Then the poet wrote what could be read as a haunting confession of his own struggle in love and work:

> I have wanted kisses my heart stuttered at asking,
> I have pounded at useless doors and called my people fools.
> I have staggered alone in a winter dark making mumble songs
> to the sting of a blizzard that clutched and swore . . .

The most striking theme of *Smoke and Steel* is that of disillusionment. There is the despair of "a crucifix in your eyes," and the "dusk Golgotha" in "Crimson Changes People." There is cynicism in "Cahoots":

> PLAY it across the table.
> What if we steal this city blind?
> If they want anything let 'em nail it down.
>
> Harness bulls, dicks, front office men,
> And the high goats up on the bench,
> Ain't they all in cahoots? . . .

There is a pervasive loneliness ("I go hungry/Down in dreams/And loneliness") often expressed with the metaphor of hunger:

> . . .
>
> The road I am on is a long road and I can go hungry again like I have gone
> hungry before.
> What else have I done nearly all my life than go hungry and go on
> singing? . . .

There is bitterness in poems about politics, the war, the race riots. There is resignation—"And this will be all?/And the gates will never open again?" There is renunciation—"Loosen your hands, let go and say good-by./Let the stars and songs go./Let the faces and years go./Loosen your hands and say good-by." There are contemplations of death, as in "Finish":

> DEATH comes once, let it be easy.
> Ring one bell for me once, let it go at that.
> Or ring no bell at all, better yet . . .

Sandburg was forty-one as he was finishing *Smoke and Steel*, standing professionally and emotionally near the midpoint of his life. He had wearily conceded a certain defeat of dream and will. "I will read ashes for you, if you ask me," he wrote in "Fire Pages."

His most remarkable statement of disillusionment came in "Four Preludes on Playthings of the Wind." Two years before T. S. Eliot's "The Waste Land" was published, Sandburg's "Four Preludes" captured the emptiness and fragility of contemporary life, and the abatement of hope. "The woman named tomorrow" symbolizes society's failure to heed the lessons of history. Doors twisted on golden hinges suggest the spiritual and moral depletion of societies fractured by war, greed, discord. Black crows and rats herald the death of civilization.

"The past is a bucket of ashes," reads the epigraph to the poem, the line an echo from the exuberant affirmation in Sandburg's "Prairie" in *Cornhuskers* a scant two years earlier. He had written then of promise:

> I speak of new cities and new people.
> I tell you the past is a bucket of ashes.
> I tell you yesterday is a wind gone down,
> > a sun dropped in the west.
> I tell you there is nothing in the world
> > only an ocean of tomorrows,
> > a sky of tomorrows . . .

In *Smoke and Steel*, tomorrow has come, in the form of a woman taking her time, doing her hair the way she wants it. "My grandmother, Yesterday, is gone," she says. "What of it? Let the dead be dead." In the second prelude, there is the memory of golden girls who chanted "We are the greatest city,/the greatest nation:/nothing like us ever was." Repeated four times, the haunting refrain heightens the tension and unifies this tightly organized poem.

"It has happened before," the poet cautions.

> Strong men put up a city and got
>   a nation together,
> And paid singers to sing and women
>   to warble: We are the greatest city,
>   the greatest nation,
>   nothing like us ever was.
>
> And while the singers sang
> and the strong men listened
> and paid the singers well
> and felt good about it all,
>   there were rats and lizards who listened
>   . . . and the only listeners left now
>   . . . are . . . the rats . . . and the lizards.

Black crows nest over the doors which were cedar and gold and "sheets of rain whine in the wind and doorways." The final prelude of the quartet depicts the symbolic dominance of the rats over the shambles of a nation:

> The feet of the rats
> scribble on the doorsills;
> the hieroglyphs of the rat footprints
> chatter the pedigrees of the rats
> and babble of the blood
> and gabble of the breed
> of the grandfathers and the great-grandfathers
> of the rats.
>
> And the wind shifts
> and the dust on a doorsill shifts
> and even the writing of the rat footprints
> tells us nothing, nothing at all
> about the greatest city, the greatest nation
> where the strong men listened
> and the women warbled: Nothing like us ever was.

This stark disillusionment presages the spirit of modernist disenchantment for which Eliot's "Waste Land" was the touchstone. Eliot, besieged by personal difficulty (his wife's profound illness, his own financial stress and severe sensitivity, the breakdown which sent him to the refuge of a Swiss sanitorium), created "The Waste Land," with significant help from Ezra Pound, to whom he dedicated the poem. Eliot was probing the depths of personal, classical metaphysics in the context of postwar Europe. At home in the United States, Sandburg had chronicled social change and conflict for nearly two decades; he had stepped briefly into the vortex as a war correspondent. His trifocal vision as journalist, social advocate and poet animated the "Four Preludes."

Two years later Eliot's imagination turned, like Sandburg's, to appropriate symbols of transience and decay—rats, the capricious wind, doomed civilizations. Eliot, too, offers the evocative image of a woman arranging her hair. The rich layer upon layer of "The Waste Land," which was originally forty pages long in manuscript, caught the attention of the literary world when it appeared in the *Dial* and then in book form in 1922. Sandburg's "Four Preludes on Playthings of the Wind," embedded in the wider text of *Smoke and Steel* in 1920, was overshadowed by other pieces in the volume. But its message was a clear signal of change in the course of Sandburg's life.

✻

"There will be the largest unloading of cargoes of poetry this fall that America has ever seen in a season's drift," he told Alice Corbin Henderson on the eve of the publication of *Smoke and Steel*. There were books in 1920 by T. S. Eliot, Ezra Pound, William Carlos Williams, Edna St. Vincent Millay, H. D., Edgar Lee Masters, Edwin Arlington Robinson, Conrad Aiken and Stephen Vincent Benét, in addition to Sandburg. Williams's *Kora in Hell* caused a stir with its prologue delineating an American school of poetry represented by Maxwell Bodenheim, Alfred Kreymborg, Sandburg and himself, and an international school headed by Eliot and Pound, whom he called "the best enemy United States verse has." (". . . you punk out, cursing me for not being in two places at once," an angry Pound wrote to Williams; ". . . if [I] choose to write about decaying empire, will do so, and be damned to you.")

Smoke and Steel brought Sandburg congratulatory letters, and mixed critical reviews. Bodenheim, who thought Sandburg's earlier work "often flirted with platitudes and redundancy" and that he was "too fond of shouting over mud-pies" wrote to tell him, "I consider *Smoke and Steel* to be ten hundred and ninety three miles above your other books. It is like a dirty giant tearing a sunset into strips and patching the rents in his clothes."

"You know how much I have loved your work all these years," Sara Teasdale wrote, "how it seems to me more real in its tenderness and sympathy than any other poetry being written in our language today." Sandburg felt a "deep quiet thrill" when he opened a letter of praise from William Allen White of Kansas, editor of the *Emporia Gazette*. "Of all today's modern poets, it seems to me that you have put more of America in your verses than any other," White said. "The others are academic, theoretical, remote, but your verses stink and sting and blister and bruise and burn, and I love them. I am sending your book on to my boy who is in Harvard. I wish every student in America could read these verses."

From Galesburg came a letter from Sandburg's mother, full of pride in her son's work, and her own inability to comprehend all of it, in the quaint lyricism of her own language hints of the roots of Sandburg's talent: "The book of poems has come with its spicy words and deep thought it will take more than a life time to learn what it all means and is imposible for plain simple working people to understand."

Louis Untermeyer reviewed *Smoke and Steel* for the *Bookman* and *The New Republic*, describing it as "an epic of modern industrialism and a mighty paean to modern beauty." He pronounced Sandburg and Frost the nation's two living major poets. Amy Lowell wrote a generally positive review in *The New York Times*. Sandburg wrote to thank her, and to comment on several points where, he said, their "variance of viewpoint and method is perhaps a good deal like that of some cubists as against some impressionists." While she privately told a friend that Sandburg sometimes overdid his Americanisms, she wrote in the *Times* that "Reading these poems gives me more of a patriotic emotion than ever 'The star-spangled banner' has been able to do."

Not all the reviews were favorable. "Mr. Sandburg has no sense of the past, no vision of the future, and so his reality is a little huddle bunch of dried-up aspects out of which have escaped the aspects of life about which he is so passionately concerned," wrote William Stanley Braithwaite in the *Boston Transcript*. Arthur Wilson, the young critic at the *Dial*, called Sandburg a "Psychiatric Curiosity." "Either Carl Sandburg is dead or he is very sick," Wilson began. "Some of us, who announciated this great poet when his epiphanal accents crashed out in Chicago, now look up from the useless pages of Smoke and Steel with a gasp of astonished grief. Is this the latest cry of our divine bally-hoo-poet, whom we have seen and heard so often just outside the circus-tent-of-life, crudely and eloquently ranting of such God-awful splendours within?"

Wilson went on to accuse Sandburg of the same "sententious garrulity which makes nine-tenths of Whitman impossible to a man of any taste." Sandburg, he said, was "merely whoring after alien gods." "Who the hell *is* this pup, anyway?" Untermeyer wanted to know. He and his wife, the poet Jean Starr, wrote to the *Dial* to protest the running of the review.

In *The Nation*, Mark Van Doren suggested that Sandburg had "rather obviously repeated himself" and had "put himself through motions that were more profitable once than they are now." But, he asserted, "Technically, Mr. Sandburg is as interesting as any poet alive." Poet Alfred Kreymborg, a sensitive reader of the body of Sandburg's work, perceived the "many sided self-hood" expressed in *Cornhuskers* and "the tragic disillusionment of the World War" which pervaded *Smoke and Steel.* Kreymborg contrasted Whitman and Sandburg: "Whitman rose at the birth of the nation; Sandburg grew up in the midst of its vast development and vaster braggadocio, and saw that much of the vastness was hollow, many of the claims superficial. His view of the nation is fully as patriotic as Walt's. No land is in need of skepticism more than successful America." He alone of the critics seemed to hear the solemn, caustic undertones of Sandburg's latest poems.

Sandburg the poet was never deeply interested in poetics or, once he found his style, in theoretical debate about "fixed, frozen, immutable" forms. He was more interested in the poet's function, his relationship to society, his message and theme. As a poet he worked with the raw materials of human existence, seeking to synthesize his own experience and the universal experiences of life. Consequently, there was the counterplay of poetry and journalism, one feeding the other, the transmutation of common subjects into both poetry and journalism. Sandburg's poetry, deeply rooted in his passionate concern for social justice, is a singular reflection of one man's participation in his times. His poems, read in chronology and context, are a man's autobiography, a nation's biography.

Until 1920 he had thrown himself into the fray of American life, trying to communicate all he discovered and believed. He was battered now by the pain and seeming futility of it. "Beat, old heart, these are old bars/All strugglers have beat against," he wrote in a new poem:

> Beat on these bars like the old sea
> Beats on the rocks and beaches.
> Beat here like the old winter winds
> Beat on the prairies and timbers.
> Old grizzlies, eagles, buffalo,
> Their paws and beaks register this.
> Their hides and heads say it with scars.

More than any other American poet of his era, Sandburg had lived in the center of his times. Scarred, he was sick of the struggle. It was time to travel new roads.

1920–1921

16. To a Far Country of Make-Believe

. . . I travelled in a Far Country of make-believe, writing a child book.

—Carl Sandburg to A. J. Armstrong, October 13, 1921

He was forty-two years old in 1920, husband and father, respected newsman, award-winning poet of widening fame. His complicated life was, as always, kaleidoscopic, but his interior life was more centered, in harmony. "The fireborn are at home in fire," he wrote over and over again, as if that old Swedish saying explained his life. His poetry and prose had been born in the fire of passionate conviction, a vigorous exertion toward the ideal. Years of struggle with the realism of his times galvanized his poetry and prose, but, at last, wore down his ebullient spirit. He stepped into the new decade bitterly cynical and disillusioned. He had had all the reality he could stomach. He was ready for respite, refuge—for a startling change of subject and milieu.

Unlike many established writers of his time, Sandburg still migrated from genre to genre. In 1920, with three successful books of poetry to his credit and two of the most significant poetry awards of the period, he could have worked solely on further development of poetic technique, vision and theme. Yet he could not seem to confine himself to poetry. He craved variety, was incessantly reconfiguring the components of his work into different designs. His constant movement was not vacillation, or failure to commit, but the essential dynamic of his career. In 1920 he turned to his most unlikely literary venture yet.

"One satisfaction—the book of kid stories, tales of impossible villages, out next year, will be a hummer," he wrote to Alice Corbin Henderson about his new book project. "These are my refuge from the imbecility of a frightened world." After *Smoke and Steel* and *The Chicago Race Riots*, Sandburg embarked on a deliberate excursion into the realm of fancy and myth, seeking truth and meaning there, as well as consolation. He decided to create a book for children, knowing that at least for a while he had to escape graphic realism and retreat to the gentler world of his imagination. He began to write authentic American fairy tales, trying them out on his wife and small daughters in the hours at home after his *Daily News* job. As was true since the early days of his struggle, poetry paid very little. He was conscientious about his "bread and butter" job at the newspaper, for that salary supported his family. All other work had to be done when he could grab the time.

Sandburg's progression from realism toward myth coincided with a jolting family tragedy. Margaret was often sick in those days, manifesting —although they went unrecognized at first—signs of epilepsy, a mysterious affliction in the early 1920s. There was no known effective treatment then, much less cure. There Sandburg stood, on the threshold of the new decade, beleaguered by modern life, contemplating fresh responses to it. But he and Paula were parents first of all, and soon would subordinate poetry, journalism, everything to their immense love and concern for nine-year-old Margaret.

✳

During the 1920 Presidential campaign, Warren G. Harding of Ohio told the nation what it wanted to hear: "America's present need is not heroics but healing; not nostrums but normalcy; not revolution but restoration; not surgery but serenity." Harding looked like a President— handsome, dignified, smiling, photogenic. Never mind that he was, according to journalist William Allen White, "almost unbelievably ill-informed" and unable to comprehend complex issues. Harding and Calvin Coolidge, his running mate, defeated their Democratic opponents sixteen million votes to nine million. Carl Sandburg was one of 919,000 Americans to vote for Eugene Debs, who ran his campaign from Atlanta Federal Prison.

For Sandburg and Paula the vote for Debs was a gesture of support for the old idealism. Sandburg's heart was not in politics in 1920. He had turned homeward, to Paula and their three daughters. Margaret was quiet and studious. Curled up like a pretzel, she would read for hours. Sometimes, her mother said, it "required a determined effort" to make her stop reading long enough to eat her meals. Her parents often called her Marny, but her father had also nicknamed her Spink. Four-year-old Janet with her blue Steichen eyes and dark hair was a beautiful child, endlessly mischievous, but nowhere near as quick of mind as her two sisters. Her father sometimes called her Skabootch. Baby Helga, with curly blond hair and blue eyes, he later called Swipes. Sandburg wrote to Alice Corbin Henderson, "The kids are a loan, only a loan, out of nowhere, back to nowhere, babbling, wild-flying—they die every day like flowers shedding petals—and come on again."

He often read to the children from the manuscript of the stories he had been dreaming up since before the war. At the dinner table, he would ask them to choose the ones they wanted to hear, and then consider putting them in his new book. The children's stories, at first called *Liver and Onions*, were a response to years of turmoil and violence, and a sanctuary for his spirit.

He made a radical change as a journalist then as well: he relinquished the grueling reality of his newspaper beat as labor reporter and editorial writer when he agreed to substitute for W. K. Hollander, vacationing film critic at the *Chicago Daily News*. By mid-September, Sandburg had become the "cinema expert, the critic of the silent celluloid for the Daily News." Thus his fertile imagination, engrossed in the children's stories, was simultaneously energized by the potent new stimulus of the motion picture. When Hollander left the *News* for another job, Sandburg took over permanently, serving as motion picture editor for the next seven years.

He had a longtime fascination with visual images. He also enjoyed Japanese and Chinese art, literature and culture, in vogue in the United States since the teens. He was especially intrigued by the work of Japanese artists Hiroshige and Hokusai, whose inexpensive prints he brought home or gave to friends as gifts. The intensely visual nature of the work of the Chinese poet Li Po further stimulated Sandburg to try to make word photographs in his own poetry. He told Walter Yust in a *Dial* interview in 1920 that he searched for "picture words" as the Indians and Chinese did.

A keen interest in motion pictures as an entertainment form was logical for Sandburg, with his close ties to the American lyceum, chautauqua and vaudeville circuits. He enjoyed his growing popularity as a platform entertainer. He gave dramatic renditions of his poetry, read some of the new stories, and made music with his mellow baritone voice and his guitar, still a novelty to many small-town audiences. For all these reasons, Sandburg had a natural affinity for what Vachel Lindsay called *The Art of the Moving Picture*, the title of his little-known but visionary book published in 1915.

By 1910 twenty percent of all the movies in the world were produced

in Chicago, where George Spoor and Maxwell Anderson had established
their famous Essaynay (for S. and A.) studios. There Charlie Chaplin,
Tom Mix, Gloria Swanson, Wallace Beery and other stars did their early
work. Colonel Robert McCormick of the *Chicago Tribune* dubbed Chicago the "cinematic culture center of the world." Victor Lawson, Sandburg's publisher at the *Daily News*, believed that good coverage of film,
vaudeville, theater and concerts would enhance circulation and advertising revenues. Consequently, he sent his drama critic Amy Leslie to
New York and Hollywood to report firsthand on show-business luminaries, and his film critics would enjoy the same kind of excursions.

During the next few years Sandburg reviewed an average of six films
weekly, and his amiable boss Henry Justin Smith let him work out a
congenial schedule. Often Sandburg reviewed six films during the weekend, writing his week's worth of reviews all at once. That set him free
to spend the rest of the time on his own projects, and to travel to interview
movie stars. He tried to arrange his lecture and platform engagements
to coincide with his business trips. The veteran investigative reporter
turned willingly, with no regrets, from interviewing labor leaders, criminals, political bosses or inhabitants of the Black Belt, to talking to movie
star cowboys and ingénues. As journalist and poet Sandburg had painted
his times as he saw them, for better or worse. Now he chose to move
from one kind of truth to another, from the wrenching reality of "Liars"
and "Hoodlums" and *The Chicago Race Riots* to the fictional truth of fairy
tales and motion pictures. It was a sweeping change, pivotal in his career.

Postwar paranoia had reached epidemic proportions in 1920, further
reinforcing Sandburg's decision to move from the world he had chronicled, in poetry and prose, to a universe he could create and, therefore,
control. As the prolonged Red Scare continued unabated, Woodrow
Wilson, champion of democracy and the New Freedom, lay sequestered
in the White House, too ill to govern, or to restrain those who sought
to govern in his behalf. In those difficult, intolerant days, the most loyal,
patriotic citizens had to take pains to protect their credibility. Sandburg,
still sensitive about the Borodin episode, was annoyed to find himself
mistakenly identified as a member of the Communist Labor Party, and
a convicted syndicalist at that. Ironically, the error appeared in William
Marion Reedy's *Mirror*, which Sandburg had read, admired and written
for over many years. In January 1920 Reedy had published Sandburg's
article on the dangerously repressive propaganda of the times. Reedy,
blind in one eye and suffering from acute hypertension and other ailments, was too ill to oversee the work at the *Mirror*. He died in late July

1920. It was his successor Charles Finger who mistook Sandburg for a communist.

Finger, an Englishman, had covered the Chicago trial which convicted several members of the Communist Labor Party for syndicalism. One of them was a sixty-five-year-old Norwegian physician and economist, Dr. Karl F. M. Sandberg of Chicago. Finger believed the culprit to be Carl Sandburg and said so in his article. Sandburg immediately wrote to Finger about "the wayward and joyous errata of other writing men," asking him to "vamp over the following paragraphs into a Fingerian editorial":

THE TWO CHICAGO SANDB..RGS

There are two men in Chicago with names alike. One is Dr. Karl F. Sandberg, author of "The Money Trust," and member of the communist labor party. The other is Carl Sandburg, a newspaper man, author of "Chicago Poems," "Cornhuskers," "The Chicago Race Riots," "Smoke and Steel," and independent in politics and member of no party.

Karl F. Sandberg is under conviction for violation of the criminal syndicalist laws of Illinois but has not yet served time behind the bars. Carl Sandburg once served a jail sentence in Pittsburg, having been convicted of riding on a railroad train without a pass, but is not at the present moment in the status either of a martyr nor a malefactor of the law.

The two Sandb..rgs are both jailbirds, one prospective, the other retrospective.

The mail and telephone calls of the two often get mixed. Persons interested in revolutionizing banks and finance sometimes request Carl Sandburg, the poet, to lecture on currency, credits and fiat moneys, while Karl F. Sandberg, physician and communist, is sometimes asked to explain free verse and give a recital of the anapests and dythrambs thereof.

Finger was traveling when Sandburg's letter reached St. Louis. By the time he read Sandburg's letter it was too late to print a retraction, for the *Mirror* folded in September, just five weeks after Reedy's death. "To tell the truth I had always confused the two Chicago Sandb..rgs myself," Finger wrote to Sandburg by way of an apology. Sandburg sent a similar letter of disclaimer to the editors of Chicago newspapers, hoping to clear his name in a case of mistaken identity which would haunt the two Sandb..rgs for years. Dr. Sandberg's shadow even followed Sandburg on the lecture circuit in 1920. "Hand it to Beloit College and the Beloit Drama Club," Sandburg wrote Louis Untermeyer that fall. "When they arranged for me to come up there and read they were under the definite impression it was the same Sandburg who was indicted and convicted recently under the Illinois criminal syndicalist law. They said this week when I filled the date, they thought it possible for a man to be a genuine artist and a dangerous revolutionist and they would be able to forget the revolutionist in getting at the artist."

✳

The Sandburgs welcomed a special guest to their Elmhurst home in late summer 1920, when Amy Lowell swept into Chicago to read her poetry and lecture at the University of Chicago to a standing-room-only crowd. "You and Mrs. Sandburg gave me a very pleasant two evenings when I was in Chicago," she wrote in September. "I only wish we lived nearer together." She enclosed with the letter a poem entitled "To Carl Sandburg." It was a poignant sketch of her visit, with undertones of regret as if she coveted the gentle simplicity of life in "a country I knew well but had never seen."

> . . . The moon stops a moment in a hole between leaves
> And tells me a new story,
> A story of a man who lives in a house with a pear-tree before the door,
> A story of little green pears changing and ripening,
> Of long catalpa pods turning yellow through September days.
> There is a woman in the house, and children,
> And, out beyond, the corn-fields are sleeping and the trees are
>   whispering to the fire-flies.
> So I have seen the man's country, and heard his songs before
>   there are words to them.
> And the moon said to me: "This now I give you," and went on,
>   stepping through the leaves,
> And the man went on singing, picking out his accompaniment
>   softly on the black-backed guitar

Sandburg answered poem with poem: "Our letters crossed about at Erie, Pa. east and west bound," he told her. "Your poem, a good and real one, brought to a focus one that had been simmering. With the fourth revision of it I'm liking better the beats and films of it." His poem spoke of her regrets for "a lost town," for the "go-bye of streets she knew when a girl."

> . . . she regrets black branches must forget next year or the
>   year after
>   to set their white leaf drift of blossoms on the summer
>   sky
>   next year or the year after when the doomed buckeye
>   goes:

and each regret
is a high thin goose of autumn
crying south, crying south.
She fixes the millimeters of her eye-glasses herself.
She fixes the curve of her eyesight, wishing to measure
The curve of the arch of the sky of night, the curve of the
running hours on the level of night
And the curve of a moon stumble across the early
morning, testimony
     of dawn across the first light sheets.
She measures the millimeters of her eyesight with regrets
    and each regret is a grassroot
    and each regret is a high thin goose of autumn
crying south.

Amy Lowell was flamboyant and contentious and seldom allowed men to see the more vulnerable, sensitive aspects of her nature. She entrusted her memories and regrets to the Sandburgs, who served her a simple supper and treated her as one of the family. Sandburg serenaded her with some of his folk songs that late summer night, until rain broke into his rendition of "This Morning, This Evening, So Soon." Amy Lowell was, Sandburg told her, "a good neighbor as well as joyous artist."

She felt at home with the Sandburgs in their small house in Elmhurst, and later made Sandburg equally comfortable and relaxed in the grandeur of Sevenels, the Lowell family mansion in Brookline near Boston. Sandburg and Lowell respected each other. The social and poetic differences between them only enhanced their long friendship. He told her he thought it probable that both of them would "in the next ten years surpass the best we have so far done."

Sandburg seldom heard from Pound anymore, or saw Masters, Lindsay or Frost. His most regular discourse with poets came in letters exchanged with Alice Corbin Henderson and Amy Lowell. The recurring theme of his debates with Lowell had to do with the dichotomy of poetry and propaganda, and of realism and impressionism. Sandburg thought that future assessments of their work might reveal that he had put "too many realities" in his poetry, and Lowell had not offered reality enough.

For now, he was happy to leave reality behind, to explore the magical truth and illusion in motion pictures. His colleague Harry Hansen observed that Sandburg's movie criticism was "dissimilar from anything else" being written then. Like his poetry, his movie articles stayed "close to the people." "Carl saw them go into the theatres with their pennies,"

Hansen said, and "he began to speculate about the social consequences of the motion picture and its influence, proof of which was daily before his eyes." Sandburg was given "an absolutely free hand" to pass judgment on the films he saw, and "his criticism varied from sermons to vignettes, and often a strong dose of homely philosophy was thrown in after the manner of a poem in *vers libre*." Sandburg could not be influenced by theater managers or movie companies to slant a favorable review, and Victor Lawson kept a distance between the advertising and editorial sections of his newspaper which, said Hansen, was "perhaps unique in this most exploited and ungodly of all nations."

Sandburg liked Pearl White in *Tiger's Cub* that fall, and praised Harry Carey as *Sundown Slim*, although he faulted the hokum of the set and its sky "spotted with round stars like Christmas cookies," its sun "like a soft Thanksgiving pie." He enthusiastically endorsed *The Texan* with Tom Mix, who became one of his favorite actors. "The riding and shooting is heroic," Sandburg told his readers, "terrifically American, and the desert and mountain backgrounds are superb, nothing less." While he thought D. W. Griffith's *Way Down East* with Lillian Gish lacked the originality of Griffith's *Intolerance* and *The Birth of a Nation*, he found the film "thrilling entertainment," with "superb" acting by Gish, Anna Moore and Richard Barthelmess. He objected to the barn dance scene as "too terribly grandly barney and dancy."

Sandburg's own audience grew that year, as *Smoke and Steel* received wide attention. He got more frequent invitations to give his lecture-recital, and he needed the money. He was earning fifty dollars a week at the *Daily News* in a time of high prices and postwar inflation. Prices had doubled since 1914, when he earned twenty-five dollars weekly at *The Day Book*. Then he supported Paula and Margaret; now there were two more little girls, and a mortgage to pay. The lecture income was essential, and he was fortunate that his *Daily News* schedule afforded him the chance to fill occasional lecture dates. He could earn as much as a hundred dollars per lecture, plus expenses—two weeks' salary for one night's work on the lecture platform. His 1920 income-tax return reported $2608.00 in wages from the newspaper and $1159.00 in income from lectures. Royalties on his books were small, but he hoped *Smoke and Steel* would change that.

He traveled and lectured in the East in early December, and met Steichen's friends, the photographer Alfred Stieglitz and artist Georgia O'Keeffe. "That afternoon hour looking at Miss O'Keeffe's paintings and your series of photographs is still with me as a big hour," Sandburg told Stieglitz. "I went away shaken and soothed—and recalling that I had not spoken the word 'miracles' in some years." The two men exchanged inscribed books—Sandburg's poetry and *The Chicago Race Riots* and ten inscribed copies of *Camera Work*, the landmark photographic journal Stieglitz published with Steichen and others.

He had hoped for such a meeting for two years, Stieglitz told Sandburg. "You and I. Two who believe. Two workers. Perhaps two dreamers too.—It was truly a meeting. Years jammed into moments." Stieglitz gave Sandburg a copy of "The Steerage," which he had printed in an edition of one hundred copies on rare Japanese rice paper. He had been able to sell only five of them, Stieglitz said, netting $6.50. He told Sandburg he gave several others "into good hands like yours." He had kept a few prints which he would give away or try to sell for two hundred dollars each. He crumpled up sixty copies and threw them away. "The Steerage" spoke to the Sandburgs of the crossings their parents had made years earlier. They framed it and kept it in view in their house from then on.

✳

In 1920 Carl Sandburg was becoming a literary celebrity. His lectures broadened his audience and gave him the imperative and pleasure of more travel, more vagabonding. With his resonant voice and his guitar, he was a magnet for other folk musicians, balladeers and musicologists who were exploring the unmined riches of American folk music. Every lecture-recital he gave brought new songs and variations on old songs for Sandburg's ever-growing "kit bag" of music to play and sing. Wherever he went he would watch movies, make friends, discover songs. He was working steadily on the children's stories, beginning to try them out on his lecture audiences. In the background of the stories there was an imaginative fusion of fancy and reality—sober references to war, violence, political conflict; bizarre incidents gleaned from the newspapers; the fluttering images of motion pictures, the flickering lights and shadows of the great celluloid make-believe; the play and discovery of his three daughters at home.

The delightful, sometimes inscrutable nonsense of the children's book began as Sandburg's refuge and was created, in the end, to the counterpoint of family crisis. The private battles which would end the marriage of Edward and Clara Steichen became a matter of public record and notoriety in 1920 when *The New York Times* carried an account of Steichen's suit against Clara for taking art objects and antiques which belonged to him, and of Clara's alienation-of-affections suit against a prominent New York socialite. While there was no doubt of Steichen's infidelities, Clara had sued the wrong woman. Sometimes she took her daughters to court with her, compelling them to look on as their parents' failed marriage unraveled in public view. The daughters were offered their choice of which parent they wished to live with. Sixteen-year-old Mary chose her father; her younger sister, Kate, chose her mother.

The Sandburgs worried about Steichen because the war had left him depressed and searching. "The wholesale murdering was over," Steichen wrote in his autobiography.

> I had never had to come face to face with another man and [to] shoot him and [to] see him crumple up and fall, yet I could not deny to myself having played a role in the slaughter. I had never been conscious of anything but the job we had to do: photograph enemy territory and enemy actions, record enemy movements and gun emplacements, pinpoint the targets for our own artillery. . . . But the photographs we made provided information that, conveyed to our artillery, enabled them to destroy their targets and kill.
>
> A state of depression remained with me for days, but gradually there came a feeling that, perhaps, in the field of art, there might be some way of making an affirmative contribution to life. This thought restored some sanity and hope, and the desire to live took hold again.

As Sandburg retreated into the safe realm of the children's stories and motion pictures, Steichen withdrew to Voulangis for a prolonged time of "deep, earnest soul-searching." He decided to make a bonfire of his paintings and commit himself irrevocably to photography. "Painting meant putting everything I felt or knew into a picture that would be sold in a gold frame and end up as wallpaper," he said. "Photography was to be my medium. I wanted to reach into the world, to participate and communicate. . . . I was determined to reach a large audience instead of the few people I had reached as a painter."

Steichen's amazed gardener helped him pull all the paintings from his house and studio and set them afire. From then on he was Steichen the photographer. Thus Steichen, like his brother-in-law, began to reach a widening audience, and over the years the two men would work together boldly to "reach into the world, to participate and communicate." Carl, Paula and Edward were always a close-knit trio, despite the geographical distances that intervened, and family troubles only drew them closer together.

✳

Sandburg was scheduled to spend much of the winter of 1920–21 away from home lecturing in the Midwest and the South. With the help of writer DuBose Heyward, he was making final plans for a series of lectures in South Carolina. Shortly before his departure, Margaret had the first of a baffling series of attacks. She was a bright, serious little girl, nine years and eight months old that February of 1921. She loved school, where she was a painstaking student. She was a highly sensitive, responsible eldest child. During the past year she had been too thin, but had gained weight and seemed healthy. For several weeks, however, she had complained of occasional pains in her left side, so sharp that she would cry out. The pains often came just after meals, so that the family doctor diagnosed them as gas. Sharp pains in her ankles, knees and other joints had led the doctor to remove her tonsils in the summer of 1920, thinking that might eliminate the discomfort.

Margaret's pain continued, however, long after the operation. "The cramped position when reading, often immediately after eating—and the extraordinary rapidity and intense concentration with which she read," her mother conjectured, "may have had something to do with the gastrointestinal disturbance which developed later."

On Tuesday morning, February 8, Margaret got off to a slow start, hurried through breakfast, and ran to school, afraid to be late. At nine-thirty that morning, during her study period, she had a convulsion, a frightening experience which had never happened to her before. She had no memory of the seizure, which caused spasms of her head and neck and slight frothing at the mouth. An hour later there was a sharp pain in her side, and a headache which lasted all day. Alarmed, Paula kept her at home for several days. The doctor thought Margaret had suffered a gastrointestinal disturbance which he called autointoxication.

By the time Sandburg departed for his South Carolina lectures, Margaret seemed to be well. But on February 18, while her father was still away, Margaret had a second attack. Her mother made painstaking notes: "9: a.m. convulsion jerking of head & neck, no movement in legs, no frothing. Headache after." Once again diagnosing the illness as gastric, the doctor prescribed daily doses of calomel and castor oil, and a half grain of the sedative Luminal every other night. He put Margaret on a light diet, forbidding her to eat meat, fish or eggs. She recovered and seemed well over the next two weeks.

Sandburg returned from a successful Southern tour and began to prepare for an extensive trip west, where he would spend time in Hollywood lecturing and doing interviews and on-the-spot research for stories to enthrall Chicago movie fans. Shortly after his departure, Margaret experienced a third attack, a convulsion which left her with a headache and pain in her ankle and hip. Perplexed, the doctor put her on a ten-day liquid diet of milk, fermented milk to increase bacilli in her gastrointestinal tract, and broth and fruit juice. By mid-March she seemed so much better that the doctor stopped the fast and took her off Luminal. "Margaret is fine," Paula wrote Sandburg during that time, apparently seeing no reason to alarm him while he was far away. She did not describe in her letters what must have been a lonely, difficult time for her, with three young children and the daily uncertainty about Margaret's health.

There was also the lingering worry about her brother's divorce. Oma had gone to be with Steichen. She wrote "wearily about the case," Paula told Sandburg, "but she is glad she is near Ed anyway." In addition to everything else, Paula prepared their income-tax returns and supervised some renovations of the house. She enjoyed these tasks and did them well. "The porch is going up and the rooms above have skeleton walls & a floor—A great outlook from the bedrooms—Here at last we can talk to the spruce face to face!" She and Carl had achieved a happy division of labor. Her cheerful letters relieved him of any need to worry about home matters while he traveled six thousand miles over the next five weeks, working in California, Utah, Arizona, New Mexico, Texas, Arkansas and Tennessee.

Sandburg's lecture-recitals brought him the excitement and adulation of a live audience, which in turn boosted the sales of his books. His *Daily News* job as motion picture editor financed most of the trip, and gave him a refreshing change from previous newspaper jobs. The liberating whimsy of the children's stories provided a necessary respite from the intense years of writing realistically about, a world "of too much propaganda and not enough fun."

Overall, his motion picture reviews took the form of commentary more than criticism. He did not expect a film to be more or less than it was. If it was "drammer, solid melodrammer," he gave it credit if it achieved its purpose of "delivering thrills . . . good solid melodrama thrills." He had been a realist, and liked a degree of intelligent plausibility in films. He criticized scenery which was obviously artificial and actors whose costumes and makeup were implausible, found fault with an actor who maintained a "perfect unquestionable haircut" in the midst of rugged struggles in "the trackless wilds of Alaska," urged moviemakers to "let the roughnecks appear with their necks rough."

Sandburg was one of the first critics to see the educational promise of film, "the value of the celluloid reel and the white screen as a silent teacher," and the power of film to bring the world to the movie audience, just as stereoscopic pictures had introduced the wonders of the world in a far simpler way years earlier. He agreed with Griffith's remark that "In these days of Bolshevism and of tearing down we need to get back to the old-fashioned moralities."

The actor and film making the greatest impression on Sandburg during his first year of movie reviewing were Charlie Chaplin and *The Floorwalker*. He found Chaplin's art highly original and entertaining, and thought Chaplin's *The Kid* was a masterpiece. Most motion picture plays of the time were derived from books or stage plays, and Sandburg applauded the originality of Chaplin's "photoplay." He noted that Chaplin had worked on the film for a year whereas he usually made six or eight pictures in that time. Sandburg marveled at Chaplin's universal language. Chaplin stood on "an art rostrum" where he addressed the world. "He speaks to all the peoples of the earth," Sandburg said. "As an artist he is more consequential in extent of audience than any speaking, singing, writing or painting artist today."

On his first trip to Hollywood, Sandburg interviewed many people for his column, but the highlight was his visit with Chaplin. Their first meeting was at Chaplin's studio apartment overlooking the big lot where he and his company produced most of their films. As Sandburg arrived, Chaplin was just slipping out of his underclothes, preparing to take a bath. Sandburg led his *Daily News* readers right into Chaplin's bathroom: "Before starting for his bath the naked, sinewy, frank, unaffected Charlie Chaplin paused for a short interchange of thought about climate, a warm day's work, and how they had done the same thing over and over fifty times that afternoon. Whether his clothes are on or off, the impression is definite that Chaplin is clean physically and has a body that he can make obedient to many kinds of service."

Chaplin took Sandburg for a drive in the limousine he had just bought for his mother. In those days of silent films, Sandburg told his readers how Chaplin's voice sounded, low and musical, with the words coming "sometimes with terrible rapidity and then again slow and stuttering."

Before he left Hollywood, Sandburg set to work on a poem which went through several forms before its publication in *Vanity Fair* in 1922 as "Without the Cane and Derby (for C.C.)." The poem is one of the more striking instances of the movies filtering through Sandburg's imagination into poetry or prose. It is drawn directly from Sandburg's *Daily News* column about the dinner party he attended at Chaplin's mountainside house. After the Japanese cook and waiter served a sumptuous meal, Chaplin, Sandburg and other guests played Charades. Chaplin's masterful improvisations are recorded in Sandburg's poem:

. . . He sets the candle on the floor . . . leaps to the white sheet . . . rips it
back . . . has his fingers at the neck, his thumbs at the throat, and
does three slow fierce motions of strangling . . .

He stands at the door . . . peace, peace, peace everywhere only in the
man's face so dark and his eyes so lighted up with many lights, no
peace at all, no peace at all . . .

Sandburg perceived the "red gray plaster of storm" in Chaplin's eyes
and face, sensed his complexity. He noted Chaplin's ability to delight
children as well as adults. "I have heard children 4 or 5 years old bubble
and ripple with laughter in the course of a Chaplin film," Sandburg
wrote. "They answer to the child in him. *The Kid* is a masterpiece
of expression of love for the child heart—love and understanding."
Sandburg was working for that very same expression in his children's
stories.

Travel was wearying at times, but Sandburg was a vagabond at heart.
His first extended journey west was profoundly stimulating and affirming.
Everywhere, he met friendly audiences for his lectures and books. Afterward, there were parties late into the night, where Sandburg and
congenial new friends talked or made music. He entertained various
hosts, sometimes on borrowed guitars, trying out new songs he picked
up at every turn. He was a hit with "vastly different audiences," he
discovered to his amazement, for he had not believed that "such free-
for-all stuff would go over and big."

The photographer Edward Weston took pictures of Sandburg on that
trip, local newspapers along the way reviewed his performances, and
local artists sketched him. There was frequent praise for his voice—it
was "resonant," "vibrant," "thrilling." People were struck by the simplicity of his manner and his infectious sense of humor. He was hailed
as the poet of the future, the poet of America.

He always concluded his program with music, and one by-product of
his burgeoning lecture career was the enrichment of his folk music collection. His guitar and repertoire of songs provided a popular finale to
his lecture-recital. After each lecture, someone came up to offer new
songs, or variants on those he had just sung. Sandburg would transcribe
them in his own makeshift notation system, and jot down the lyrics in
his pocket notebook.

Poet DuBose Heyward, whose 1925 novel would be the basis for
George Gershwin's *Porgy and Bess* in 1935, had been Sandburg's host for
his lecture to the Poetry Society of South Carolina, and they began a

long exchange of folk music. "This whole thing is only in its beginning, America knowing its songs," Sandburg said.

> It's been amazing to me to see how audiences rise to 'em; how the lowbrows just naturally like Frankie an' Albert while the highbrows, with the explanation that the murder and adultery is less in percentage than in the average grand opera, and it is the equivalent for America of the famous gutter songs of Paris—they get it. . . . Understand, a new song learnt is worth more to me than any Jap print or rare painting. I can take it into a railroad train or a jail or anywheres.

There were critics who thought Sandburg's folk music was show business, not substance, catering to the masses. Malcolm Cowley advised him later, half in jest, to "smash that guitar." Yet for Sandburg, listening avidly for the American voice wherever it expressed itself, the American idiom was revealed in music as well as literature, film, street talk. He was discovering the American tongue in songs as well as speech, and his spontaneous fascination with the folklore and music grew into a lifelong study.

During that five-week journey, he took his lecture and songs to Santa Fe and a reunion with Alice Corbin Henderson and her family, and to Texas where English professor A. J. Armstrong handled his appearance at Baylor University. It was, he said, a "glorious" trip, profitable financially, professionally and personally. The vivid colors and sparse, rugged western landscapes haunted him, and began to displace the city and the prairie as the terrain for his poetry.

He was back home in time to attend the Society of Midland Authors dinner on April 9, 1921, at Harriet Vaughn Moody's successful Chicago restaurant, Au Petit Gourmet. Louis and Jean Starr Untermeyer were there; so were Harriet Monroe; Lorado Taft; Eunice Tietjens and her second husband, playwright Cloyd Head; and Lew Sarett. Sandburg told Untermeyer afterward that there was vitality in contemporary American literature which was "entirely lost on distant, dozing New York editors and columnists." He had seen it for himself, in his travels about the country that spring. He was part of it. For the rest of his life, as long as he was able, he would take his poetry and songs directly to the people. They were his subject and his audience. He liked seeing their faces and hearing their applause. One college student in Indiana had written of his lecture there that "by the influence of the work and personality of such men as Mr. Sandburg" the cause of modern poetry would be "advanced among the mass of people everywhere." He called Sandburg a "Poet of the People."

*

He was glad to be back in Elmhurst with the Homeyglomeys. He told them still unfolding "kid stories," and often played the guitar and sang some of the less raucous and bawdy folk songs he had collected on the journey. He plunged into work on *Daily News* columns about his Hollywood stay, and began to work and rework a long new poem which came to be called "Slabs of the Sunburnt West."

Margaret was particularly happy to have her father home again. She had been well for nearly six weeks, but on Sunday morning, April 17, she suffered a general convulsion, the worst ever. After it was over, she slipped into a deep sleep, awaking with a headache. Later that day she lost consciousness again. The doctor ordered the resumption of Luminal, and referred Margaret to a nerve specialist, who confirmed his diagnosis of "auto-intoxication." Both doctors ruled out the alarming spectre of epilepsy. Margaret had the symptoms, but they did not believe she was epileptic. The Sandburgs were deeply relieved, for there was then much stigma attached to that misunderstood illness, and no effective medication for treatment. Luminal seemed to be the best available answer. For nearly two weeks Margaret's health improved, and there were no more attacks in April.

There was good news from Harcourt in New York that month. Sandburg's lecture tour had clearly enhanced sales of his books; *Smoke and Steel* had already earned back its advance plus several hundred dollars in royalties. Harcourt pressed Sandburg for some word on the progress of the children's book, to be called *Rootabaga Stories*. The excitement about Sandburg's success was muted, however, by worry about Margaret's baffling, unpredictable attacks.

Her parents' worst fears were realized in early May when she had two attacks in one day. For the first time, she cried out at the onset of the convulsion. Afterwards there was heavy sleep and a headache. Anxiously Paula recorded each symptom in her journal and cast about for causes. Margaret had eaten six raw apples the day before. Could that have triggered the seizure? The doctor continued to treat her with Luminal every other night, and a diet free of meat, fish and eggs. After every attack Margaret was put on a liquid diet for one to three days, depending on the severity of the seizure. For the rest of May, she was fine, except for a "mild general convulsion" on May 15.

Sandburg resumed his busy schedule of work at the *Daily News* and fulfilled lecture commitments in Kansas, Illinois and Massachusetts while Paula cared for life at home and carefully monitored Margaret's health.

She was a sensitive, excitable child, and her parents worried that her emotions could trigger the dreaded attacks they tried so carefully to ward off by diet and rest. Margaret was kept home from school, in part because of her parents' concern about her health and in part because of the school's reluctance to be responsible for a child subject to seizures, never mind the doctors' opinions that she did not have epilepsy. Many nights Paula slept with or near Margaret, in case she needed her, for the attacks usually came in the early-morning hours. "After a nightly attack my throat always hurt and I had a headache," Margaret remembered, "and I would go to Mother for help and sympathy. I always tried to sleep again, hoping the throat and head would feel better afterward."

Margaret stayed well for nearly three weeks in May. Early on the morning of June 3, her tenth birthday, Paula found her lying unconscious on the bedroom floor, grinding her teeth. Margaret took a short nap after coming to, awoke with no headache, but lost consciousness again at about ten that morning. She had another attack later in the day, leaning forward in her chair and slipping slowly to the floor. Later in the afternoon she had another mild attack. Each of the two later seizures occurred just after she had opened a birthday gift.

Paula kept her on a liquid diet for three days and continued the regimen of strict diet, quiet and rest. There were no more seizures in June. The family settled into a quieter routine, with Sandburg at home. Mostly he worked on the children's stories, often reading them aloud. By the end of June, 1921, he had completed thirty-six stories. He told Alice Corbin Henderson, "When I get 100 I'll pick out a book."

✳

Paula was exhausted that summer, worn down with constant worry over Margaret's health, anxiety over her brother's problems, and the energy she gave to running a busy household and supporting her husband's complicated schedule of work. On July 4 she forgot to give Margaret her medication. She blamed herself for the attack Margaret suffered early the next morning, a general convulsion lasting about a minute. For half an hour afterward Margaret was "still grinding teeth, eyes closed." She had a headache for the rest of that day, but seemed well for the next two weeks. But Paula was so weary and ill that she spent most of July in bed.

Oma and Opa had moved to Elmhurst by this time, and lived nearby. Home from her visit with Steichen, Oma prepared meals and cared for the children while Paula recuperated. Steichen photographed his sister during those years of worry. He captured the sad, haunting beauty in her eyes. Wisps of graying hair framed her face. The lines in her brow were softened by a pensive smile.

From then on, throughout the years, Paula kept a detailed, almost dispassionate, scientific record of Margaret's diet, her treatment, her attacks. In late July Margaret suffered another seizure, and in August Janet and Helga were ill with whooping cough. Paula had gall bladder and stomach problems. Family illness superseded everything else as Sandburg, Oma and Opa cared for Paula and the girls. "The missus has had three hard weeks with gall bladder and stomach complications," Sandburg told Untermeyer. "Janet and Helga are in the second week of whooping cough with three to four weeks to go." Sandburg despaired over their problems. Margaret's attacks continued. Janet was not developing mentally. Now she and Helga were ill, Helga who had been "pink, hard, unimpeachable perfection." She was "the finest kid I ever saw or heard of," Sandburg said of his youngest child. "No sins of herself or others to expiate. Resistance 100 per cent. Then the cough came. I believed in a Hell from which comes a Personal Devil."

It was, he said, "the summer we read Job."

*

Paula was stronger by fall, but Margaret returned to school for only a week before a severe attack kept her home again. "Convulsion with cry," Paula wrote in her meticulous journal, "the second with cry." Paula and Sandburg, with their doctor's agreement, took Margaret to a psychopathologist "to see," Paula said, "if there might be any mental disturbance or irritation or unhappiness that might be a contributing factor." The family doctor ordered a Wassermann test to determine whether syphilis might be present, "although he fully expected a negative result from his examination," Paula said. "The result of the laboratory test was 100% negative," she reported. The psychopathologist "found no abnormal mental state that could be a contributing factor toward causing the convulsions or lapses of consciousness."

On September 27 Margaret had a severe general convulsion. The Sandburgs and their doctor decided it was time to "put the case in the hands of a specialist," Paula said, for the disease might indeed prove to be epilepsy. Margaret suffered a slight attack the morning of October first, and was examined by a nerve specialist that afternoon. Yes, the child had epilepsy, he told her parents, but held out hope that Margaret's condition was "favorable to cure."

"Reactions found normal to tests of nervous and muscular systems," Paula wrote in her journal. "Nervous and muscular systems declared not affected. Disease caused by disturbance in gastro-intestinal tract. Poor assimilation. Not the right balance of elements." The nerve specialist prescribed Luminal daily and a bromide twice a day. He advised denying Margaret meat and fish, but ordered one egg daily and a minimum of salt, butter and cream. He disapproved of fasting and of liquid diets.

Despite the frequent fasts and diets of the past seven months, she had gained weight "and in general Margaret was too fat," her mother said. She had serious doubts about the new doctor's treatment, but followed it conscientiously throughout October. It was a trying time. Margaret "became more and more nervous and irritable" and had attacks with increasing frequency. On October 6 she suffered "the most severe general convulsion so far." "Piercing cry at start," Paula wrote in her journal:

> Foam from mouth and nostrils. Throat working as if choking. Severe spasms of whole body. Lasted about 1-1-1/2 minutes (estimated). After convulsion began sobbing & moaning for about 5 minutes. Would not answer repeated questions as to why she was crying—seemed unconscious of questions. Cried out, "Help me!" Fell into heavy sleep. Slept till 9. Awakening said she had pain at temple and pain at throat—both continuous dull pains—not like the sudden stabbing pains in side & joints. . . . Sharp, stabbing pain under left breast, late morning. Sharp pain in left hip. Sudden pain around neck. Running pain in left fingers, afternoon.

There were five more attacks in October, the worst siege yet. On the first of November, the Sandburgs took Margaret out of the hands of the nerve specialist and turned her case over to an osteopathic physician. He confirmed the diagnosis of epilepsy, but wanted to treat Margaret with diet only, stopping all medication. In addition to a strict diet, he prescribed daily baths and massage. Within two weeks Margaret was less irritable and nervous, although there was little change in the frequency or severity of her attacks.

While Paula devoted herself to Margaret's care, Sandburg continued his work on the children's stories and some new poems, many of them about his western journey. He sometimes stayed in Chicago to work in a studio he had recently rented and shared with Dr. Emmett Angell, an author of books on children's play and an inventor of games and toys. "He and I share a work room in Chicago; travel like two friendly mules," Sandburg said. He was "strong for" the children's stories. Sandburg was having no luck placing the new poems, which several editors rejected as not up to his best work. He fell behind with correspondence and other work during that time of his and Paula's preoccupation with Margaret's illness. "It goes slow in these things because we have our living to make," he told poet Witter Bynner, "—and we are doing a book of kid stories."

Sandburg was trying to arrange a series of lecture-recitals for 1922. He told Clyde Tull at Cornell College that he had the "kid stories" in shape enough to include three or four in his lecture program. He also had a new guitar, and new ballads to offer: "Stackerlee" and "Jay Gould's Daughter," both classics, he promised, "each a child on the doorstep of neglectful parents, Mr. and Mrs. American Culture." He also proposed to lecture on the making of movies. He worked hard to line up lecture dates. More than ever, with Margaret's illness, he and Paula needed the money.

He received an honor and a windfall in early November when the Poetry Society of America awarded him half its annual prize for the best book of poetry of a year which included publications by Pound, Eliot, Williams, Millay, Robinson, Masters, Aiken and H.D. Sandburg's *Smoke and Steel* shared the honor with Stephen Vincent Benét's *Heavens and Earth*, the two poets splitting the five-hundred-dollar award. Witter Bynner, president of the Poetry Society, asked Sandburg to read at the Society's annual dinner in New York in January of 1922. On the heels of the prestigious award to *Smoke and Steel*, many lecture invitations for 1922 began to come in. While Smith at the *Daily News* still gave Sandburg and others flexibility to combine their newspaper work with literary pursuits, Sandburg tried not to exploit his freedom. "With me, it isn't merely a matter of tying up my [lecture] dates in a straight schedule," he explained to Bynner. "I have, also, to watch my newspaper job and to stay away from that beyond a certain limit of consecutive days. As between the newspaper work and the platform I always discriminate in favor of the former." His lecture fees helped to pay for "certain remorseless inevitables" and he stressed, lest there be any doubt about the nature of his lecture-recitals, that "I am a loafer and a writer and would rather loaf and write, and pick a guitar with the proper vags, than to deliver exhortations before any honorable bodies wheresoever."

He agreed to speak at the Poetry Society dinner, providing he could do his regular program and not be expected to give a formal "exhortation." But these signs of his growing fame and success were overshadowed by the ongoing reality of Margaret's illness. She grew worse in November, suffering six attacks in nine days. The osteopath recommended "an absolute fast" under the care of Dr. Hugh Conklin, an osteopathic specialist in epilepsy. On November 28 Dr. Conklin took over Margaret's case. In order to undergo his treatment, Margaret had to stay at the Battle

Creek Sanatorium in Michigan. Leaving Sandburg and Oma in charge of Janet and Helga, Paula took Margaret to Michigan immediately. "I was not ever frightened or even uneasy because mother was with me," Margaret said.

"This is only a little letter from your daddy to say he thinks about you hours and hours," Sandburg wrote to Margaret, "and he knows there was never a princess or a fairy worth so much love. We are starting on a long journey and a hard fight—you and mother and daddy—and we are going to go on slowly, quietly, hand in hand, the three of us, never giving up. And we are going to win," he promised her. "Slowly, quietly, never giving up, we are going to win."

Hopeful as he sounded, he must have felt powerless. He retreated further into the kingdom he was creating, into Rootabaga Country where "the railroad tracks change from straight to zigzag, the pigs have bibs on and it is the fathers and mothers who fix it."

The children's stories became another kind of solace, for Sandburg and for his family. He wrote Margaret a very businesslike letter about them:

> You asked me often when the stories would be ready and printed in a book for you. I am able now to vouchsafe the information and knowledge to you that this event will probably be realized in September of the year 1922, which is the year beginning on the first of next January. The title of the book will be "Rootabaga Stories." It was understood that I should let you know as soon and at the earliest possible moment I should know.

With Oma's help, Sandburg kept things going at home and wrote bright letters to Paula and Margaret, filled with details about the home life he knew they were missing. There was a new dog in residence: "Pooch learns," Sandburg wrote; "we can get him so he won't give long vocal performances; but he will never learn to stop his passionate enjoyment of scaring people by rushing them with his terrible eyes and teeth; he must have seen himself sometime in a magnifying mirror so that he imagines he is six or seven dogs in one. . . . You and your Marny, and mine, are missed all over the map."

Since August, Chicago free-lance children's book editor May Massee had been working with him on the children's stories, typing various drafts and reading them "innumerable times." In December she began trying to place some of the stories in magazines. She believed they were "great stories, among the best that have come from America and the equal of any, anywhere."

"For invention, for beauty, for nonsensical and amusing absurdities, they are second to none; for genuine humor and humanness . . . they can shake hands with Rabelais'; for sheer artistry and compactness [they] can match Maupassant at his best," she told Burton Rascoe. "They appeal to any age that has imagination and a sense of humor. . . . And they are so abso-lute-ly American. They can't be translated even into British." She believed that Sandburg had "never worked so hard on anything." With Margaret's illness there was an urgent practical motive for magazine publication of the stories in advance of the book: "Now of course Carl needs money," May Massee said. "These stories ought to bring up the children and I think they will."

As Christmas approached, Margaret was at home, but still fasting. She told her father she would not mind missing the Christmas turkey and sweets. "I don't care about them at all, for I am going to have egg on toast for Christmas and chicken broth for dinner. I don't know what for supper. Besides when there are so many surprises for Christmas, who cares for eats?"

Sandburg's friend Joseffy the magician came to entertain the family with Balsamo the animated skull. Margaret and Helga were delighted, but Janet was so frightened when the skull's mouth clicked that she hid her face in her mother's lap and cried. Joseffy put the skull back in his box then, to Margaret's great disappointment.

Sometime during the holiday season of 1921 or 1922, Paula came downstairs after being up much of the night with Margaret, only to find that pre-schoolers Janet and Helga had pulled all the ornaments off the Christmas tree. They were marching around the tree, singing, and trampling the ornaments underfoot. Not knowing whether to laugh or cry, Paula sat down on the stairs "and laughed and laughed." Then she went upstairs to tell Margaret what her sisters had done. "Virtuously indignant," Margaret did not think it was funny. "All the ornaments?" she asked in disbelief.

She was naughty in her own way that December of 1921. She ate three or four pieces of stale pastry from a Christmas box. The "terrible and forbidden indulgence" was followed by a series of attacks on Christmas Day and the day after. The Christmas Day seizures left her dazed and confused, asking her mother and the doctor if she were going to die.

By New Year's she was much better. Sandburg worked on revisions for the new book of poetry, *Slabs of the Sunburnt West,* and on the *Rootabaga Stories* "while tiding over" the crisis with Margaret's illness. "Finishing two books for publication next year," he wrote to Alice Corbin

Henderson. "Meanwhile we're thankful to be out of jails, poorhouses and asylums.—Our Margaret has been sick, has meant a lot of work, but 'she is too good to throw away.' "

"The going is all better now," he told Witter Bynner at year's end, "but it was a Christmas of grief."

—✳—

1922

17. Refuge in Rootabaga Country

> Sometime I shall do a story about a town in the
> Rootabaga Country where the money is all castanet
> clicks; they count out and pay castanet clicks in all their
> dealings; the poets are the bankers. . . .
>
> —Carl Sandburg to Lilla Perry,
> February 22, 1922

From the moment Carl and Paula Sandburg discovered that Margaret had epilepsy, they were committed to providing the best possible medical care for her, and to sheltering her, if necessary, far past their own lifetimes. They sought the most innovative therapy known in those days before Dilantin and other drugs to control seizures. While they kept their optimism that Margaret would get well, they prepared for the worst. Sandburg was driven more than ever to earn money. From that time on, his concern for his family's long-term security motivated every professional decision he made. He was often misunderstood by people who did not know that about him.

His growing success as a platform entertainer seemed incredibly providential, coming as it did just when he needed to boost his income from the *Daily News* job. In January 1922 Sandburg traveled to the Northeast for his first round of platform engagements in the new year. From then until forty years later, he traveled thousands of miles to hundreds of towns and cities, like Vachel Lindsay, "trading poems and songs for bread."

On January 24, 1922, Sandburg and Louis Untermeyer spoke at the Cosmopolitan Club in New York, with Amy Lowell and Edwin Arlington Robinson in the audience. On January 25 Sandburg was a speaker at the annual Poetry Society of America dinner, where he joined Harriet Monroe, Lowell, Witter Bynner and poets from forty states in a celebration of American poetry. There were 250 "poets and friends of poets" at the

386

dinner, with its "redundant parade of meats and sauces" and its surfeit of speeches about the state of American poetry. Now and then a speaker caught the interest of the audience who sat through the five-hour-long program. One memorable voice belonged to Dr. Chang Peng Chun, who compared American and Chinese poetry, giving classic Chinese definitions of the art—"the sound of rhythm in the voice," the "image in the mirror." Amy Lowell, Sandburg and other American poets were then experimenting with forms and images suggested by Chinese poetry and art, and when Sandburg was introduced shortly after midnight, four hours into the program, he offered his own definitions of poetry, part of an evolving series of thirty-eight which he later published in the *Atlantic* (1923) and as the preface to his book *Good Morning, America* (1928). He called poetry "a mystic sensuous mathematics of fire, smokestacks, waffles, pansies, people, and purple sunsets; a kinetic arrangement of statue syllables; the capture of a picture, a song or a flair in a deliberate prism of words."

When Witter Bynner had invited Sandburg to speak, he warned Bynner that he would read his poems and sing, but he would not make a speech. "I'd rather climb a chandelier or do a trapeze act than to make an address of *occasion*," he said. That night Sandburg skillfully did "what seemed beyond doing—brought a maimed and dying audience to life again," Dorothy Dudley wrote later in *Poetry*. Fused with his long experience as orator and lecturer was his newfound talent as a folk musician, and his charismatic stage presence. He had become a consummate entertainer. He read a new poem which he considered one of his best, "The Windy City," another dramatic evocation of Chicago. For a finale he got out his guitar and sang three folk songs, including "Jay Gould's Daughter." He was, in that august company, a hit, the highlight of a long evening.

Sandburg's winter lecture tour took him on to Boston, where he was Amy Lowell's guest at Sevenels, her sumptuous home. There her longtime companion, the actress Ada Dwyer Russell, presided as hostess to a constant parade of distinguished guests. "Buddy," Sandburg wrote to Paula on an elegant little sheet of stationery imprinted SEVENELS/BROOKLINE: "This is it—where we live the higher life—and tell all about it when we get home. Mrs. Russell gives me a good line from a letter of yours 'I married a slow man.' "

Sandburg was discovering the drawbacks as well as the pleasures of an extended lecture tour. "Raw weather and a raw throat," he wrote Paula in mid-February: "—show going well enough—but it's a fight against the bla bla and lah de dah—"

At home, Paula and Margaret were once again fighting Margaret's illness. The seizures recurred and Margaret was on an exclusive milk diet. Paula described it to her husband; "milk—milk—nothing but milk—4 oz every half hour during day—32 feedings in 24 hours, including 2 during night." Margaret had to stay in bed all the time, not allowed to read or play, consigned to absolute rest. "Believe me," Paula said, "it means little rest for the rest of us to keep her resting!!!" There was a new hired girl to help with the household work and the other children. The milk therapy was, Paula said, "an old-time Russian cure —worth a trial. Dr. Conklin approves this experiment—it may do much good—can do no harm—if it does effect a cure, it will help put Margaret in condition for another fast." Despite the deep cold of February winter, the windows in Margaret's room were kept open day and night. Paula hoped that milk, fresh air and rest would make her daughter well.

"You don't know how often I think about daddy," Margaret told her mother March 13, 1922. "Everytime I hear the front door open, I think what a beautiful surprise it would be, if it was daddy coming in." He was glad to get back to the "Homeyglomeys," and they celebrated at the news that the *Delineator* had bought ten of the children's stories for $1250.

✳

"In the making of books I've reached the peak and the breaking point for 1922," Sandburg wrote that winter when he had finished the manuscripts for *Slabs of the Sunburnt West* and *Rootabaga Stories*. "They've got my best blood and heartbeats and breath." They were also brimming with images from his kaleidoscopic world. *Slabs of the Sunburnt West*, like his other books of poetry, was intricately woven of autobiographical strands and events of the times. " 'Slabs of the Sunburnt West' has just come in, the envelope all splashed and mussy from today's big storm," Harcourt wrote to Sandburg when he received the manuscript. He suggested revising the order of the poems, beginning with "something a little more topical and easier reading for the ordinary reviewer or person who picks it up in the bookstore." He liked the book, but did not have the great enthusiasm for it which he had immediately felt for *Smoke and Steel*. Several magazine editors had already turned down some of the poems from the book as not up to Sandburg's best work.

The convergence of moving pictures, folk music, travel, home life, and the often preposterous realities of daily news events helped to shape *Slabs of the Sunburnt West*. There was an overlay of new imagery, drawn, most likely unconsciously, from the realm of the motion picture. Immersed as he was in a weekly round of films, Sandburg inevitably drew images from the new form into his work. In addition to watching at least six movies a week, he wrote background pieces to feed the avid American appetite for backstage details about the production of movies, and the private lives of producers, directors and stars. Thus the motion picture was one of the dominant forces at work in Sandburg's imagination during the decade of the twenties.

Sandburg dedicated his children's book to Margaret and Janet, using their nicknames "Spink" and "Skabootch." Many of *The Rootabaga Stories* had, of course, been created before and during World War I. "I wanted something more in the American lingo," Sandburg said of his "kid" stories. "I was tired of princes and princesses and I sought the American equivalent of elves and gnomes. I knew that American children would respond, so I wrote some nonsense tales with American fooling in them." Harry Hansen of the *Chicago Daily News* observed that Sandburg "seemed to grow perceptibly in stature on the day he first appeared before us as a teller of tales. Up to that moment he had been a strolling player, a minstrel . . . now he came to weave together beautiful prose tales that meant romance and adventure to grown men and little children."

Sandburg had introduced the Rootabaga tales to Hansen and other journalists one day at Schlogl's, a popular Chicago restaurant. Over German pancakes and wiener schnitzel, newsmen talked over current headlines and back-page gossip. The fairy-tale escapades of the Roaring Twenties were just beginning, but fairy tales in those immediate postwar years were few and far between. Into that unlikely setting, Sandburg introduced his Rootabaga stories to other newsmen.

The rutabaga is a large yellow Swedish turnip; its name is derived from words meaning "a baggy or misshapen root." Sandburg changed the spelling to "rootabaga," perhaps to Americanize it, or to emphasize its basic meaning. Home and the "Homeyglomies" provided his own root-hold. "When I look back now," Paula reflected in later years, "it seems to me that Carl and I were always surrounded by children, books and animals. The children had everything that the two of us had to give— love, attention, and, in Carl's case, the gift of imagination and humor." From that gift the stories had grown, built on everyday objects, animals and people, real or imagined, who inhabited the thoroughly plausible but highly unusual world of the Rootabaga Country.

"Carl thought that American children should have something different," Paula wrote, "more suited to their ideals and surroundings. So his stories did not concern knights on white chargers, but simple people, such as the Potato Face Blind Man who played the accordion, the White Horse Girl and the Blue Wind Boy, or commonplace objects, a rag doll and a broom handle, a knife and fork." Sandburg invented a geography, a population, even an ecology unique in American storytelling. Any map of Rootabaga Country would have to trace the Clear Green River, the Big Lake of the Booming Rollers, and the Shampoo River, the western boundary of a land whose largest city is the Village of Liver-and-Onions. The Zigzag Railroad (made that way by an invasion of zigzagging insects called zizzies) runs "forty ways farther" than off into the sky. Other major cities are the Village of Cream Puffs, formed by dissatisfied citizens of the Village of Liver-and-Onions who felt their right to eat Cream Puffs was in jeopardy; the village of Hat Pins, where the old woman Rag Bag Mammy never speaks to grown-up people, only to growing people, especially those who say "Gimme"; and a string of ball towns, populated by ball players, towns named Home Plate, Grand Stand, Three Balls and Two Strikes, Slide Kelly Slide and Paste It On The Nose.

The best modes of travel in Rootabaga Country are by train and by foot. The Golden Spike Limited train is the child of two skyscrapers. Walkers can learn the ways of birds such as gladdywhingers, bitterbasters, flummy wisters, hoo-hoos and biddywiddies; and bugs such as the zizzies who altered the railroad tracks, and the cizzywhizzies who chirp in the weeds. There are foxes, horses and pigs, and more exotic animals—the flongboo, flangwayers and hangjasts who reside on the Rootabaga prairie. There are elm trees and booblow trees, and yellow roses grow alongside necktie poppies which can be picked and attached directly to shirt collars.

People work hard in Rootabaga Country, taking pride in their work. Farmers raise corn and wheat and abundant harvests of balloons with strings for roots, picked by balloon pickers on stilts. There are dozens of ovens where clowns are baked and set out to cure and be painted. In Rootabaga Country the wind talks, as do skyscrapers and broom handles and pigeons who send telegrams. There are lovely corn fairies if you know how to recognize them, and you have to be on the lookout for magic tokens—gold buckskin whinchers which make popcorn hats, and Chinese silver slipper buckles sometimes found in squash.

Unlike many authors of children's stories, Sandburg did very little moralizing. Bimbo the Snip does get his thumb stuck to his nose when the wind changes while he is making a face at the iceman. Sandburg's mother used to admonish him with that familiar childhood threat, and in his story Bimbo the Snip regains his thumb's freedom only after it is hit six times with the end of a traffic policeman's club, a feat accomplished with the help of the comically complicated Village of Liver-and-Onions bureaucracy.

Rootabagians live by a clear, gentle and dignified ethical code and the stories are largely free of the violence typical of most fairy tales. Between the lines are glimpses of Sandburg's own life and of some of the chaos and confusion of the real world. His cities are humanized: the skyscrapers talk, feel and look beyond the city "across prairies, and silver blue lakes shining like blue porcelain breakfast plates, and out across silver snakes of winding rivers in the morning sun." The city, its skyscrapers and railroads are reduced to manageable size, compressed so that they are easy to control and cope with. Many of the characters are city people—a taxi driver, a movie actor, policemen and firemen.

One central, autobiographical character is the Potato Face Blind Man, wise and cheerful, who plays the accordion and collects silver dollars in an aluminum dishpan and a galvanized iron washtub. He wears a sign which says "I am Blind TOO" because, he explains, "some of the people who have eyes see nothing with their eyes." Sandburg's perennial worry about his own vision was transmuted into the kindly figure whom he later described to Helen Keller: "I have the impression that you are not acquainted with my Potato Face Blind Man. He is the leading character in two books . . . which I wrote for young people, meaning by young people those who are children and those grownups who keep something of the child heart." He offered to send the books to Miss Keller, "for," he said, "there are pages which travel somewhat as my heart and mind would have if I had gone blind, which twice in my life came near happening."

Government in Rootabaga Country is, on the surface, delightfully complicated. In reality, it parodies political conventions and parties, and paints a somber portrait of lynchings and war. A man is about to be hanged because he wore the wrong hat, had the wrong haircut, and sneezed at the wrong time. As fairy tales will, this story has a happy ending. Rescued by a dragonfly ship, the victim "flew whonging away before anybody could stop him." This occurred, Sandburg wrote, "long before the sad happenings that came later."

In the antiwar stories in *Rootabaga Stories* and its sequel *Rootabaga Pigeons* (1923), there are skirmishes between pen wipers and pencil sharpeners, between left-handed people and right-handed people. The Cream Puff people break away from the Liver-and-Onion people in the winter's worst blizzard, so desperate are they for the freedom to eat cream puffs if they please. The Sooners and the Boomers, once firm friends and generous allies, wage full-scale epic war over issues such as whether pink pigs should be painted pink or green, with checks or stripes; whether peach pickers must pick peaches on Tuesday mornings or Saturday afternoons; whether telegraph pole climbers must eat onions at noon with spoons. Between wars there is loud name calling (dummies, mummies, rummies, sneezicks, big bags of wind . . .). At last the Sooners and Boomers fight so long and hard in so many battles that they lose themselves and all they have in the wars.

Real, often bizarre news items made their way into Sandburg's pockets and files marked RTBGA, as did a little clipping entitled "Whose Pigeon?" with a Blue Island, Illinois, dateline, the story of a carrier pigeon, wounded on the breast and unable to fly, who had ridden into a railroad roundhouse on the brake beam of a locomotive. From that seed may have germinated the poignant story in *Rootabaga Pigeons* called "How Six Pigeons Came Back to Hatrack the Horse After Many Accidents and Six Telegrams," wherein six pigeons, six hundred miles from home, mysteriously have their wings clipped and cannot fly. The pigeons are named Chickamauga, Chattanooga, Chattahoochee, Blue Mist, Bubbles and Wednesday Evening in the Twilight and the Gloaming, called Wednesday Evening for short. Each day they walk a hundred miles homeward, sending telegrams to record a philosophical progress toward home:

1. "Feet are as good as wings if you have to. CHICKAMAUGA."
2. "If you love to go somewhere it is easy to walk. CHATTANOOGA."
3. "In the night sleeping you forget whether you have wings or feet or neither. CHATTAHOOCHEE."
4. "What are toes for if they don't point to what you want? BLUE MIST."
5. "Anybody can walk hundreds of miles putting one foot ahead of another. BUBBLES."
6. "Pity me. Far is far. Near is near. And there is no place like home when the yellow roses climb up the ladders and sing in the early summer. Pity me. WEDNESDAY EVENING IN THE TWILIGHT AND THE GLOAMING."

Embedded in the whimsical simplicity of these stories was Sandburg's attitude toward the wounds of his own life: the courage to go on doggedly by foot when "wings" fail; the knowledge that love for work or others can enable transcendence over harsh circumstances; the patient, often rewarding exactitude of "putting one foot ahead of the other"; the enduring solace of home, within and without the self.

The family heart was jolted by Margaret's illness. Rootabaga Country was a refuge from the perils of the larger world, and a temporary respite from family cares. "Some of the Rootabaga Stories were not written at all with the idea of reading to children or telling," Sandburg said. "They were attempts to catch fantasy, accents . . . sudden pantomimic moments, drawls and drolleries . . . authoritative poetic instants—knowing that if the whirr of them were caught quickly and simply enough in words the result would be a child lore interesting to child and grown-up."

Some of Sandburg's best poetry appears in these pages, as Amy Lowell and other friends were quick to see. Frank Lloyd Wright frequently read Sandburg's fairy tales at bedtime. "They fill a long felt want—poetry," he wrote to Sandburg. Wright's young associates at Taliesen devised marionette productions of the Rootabaga stories for their own amusement. "All the children that will be born into the Middle West during the next hundred years are peeping at you now, Carl—between little pink fingers," Wright told Sandburg, "smiling, knowing that in this Beauty, they have found a friend."

Alfred Stieglitz wrote from Lake George to express his delight in the book. He was "carried away by fancy & language," he said, and described Georgia O'Keeffe's pleasure in Sandburg's stories:

> In the evening late I saw O'K take up the book. I had said nothing. And I noticed her contentment while reading. It had been a very hard day for her in many ways. After a while she called out, "Alfred aren't these stories by Sandburg glorious?"—And she came into the room in which I was tinkering with some photographs & she asked whether I didn't want to hear the Story of "How the Five Rusty Rats Helped Find a New Village."—And she read.—And we both enjoyed.—Enjoyed in a way that would have given you joy had you been able to see our expressions & hear her voice. . . . At any rate we both feel you have outdone yourself & written a great book—one that will undoubtedly find its way into every home eventually—because of the sheer delight—the true poetry of life—the music in the modest volume. . . . You're a great fellow, Mr. Carl Sandburg!

Letters of praise poured in from children and their parents. Not every parent was pleased, however, especially after *Rootabaga Pigeons* appeared in 1923. From Newark, New Jersey, came a reproof:

> At breakfast this morning my daughter Grace, who is seven years old, called her little sister a "dirty sniveling snitch." Upon inquiry I found that Grace had picked up this highly elevating denunciation from a book which her mother had assured her was highly recommended and would prove amusing.

Perusal of [your] book by myself left me in a quandary. Do you consider such phrases as, "Sap-head" and "home-thief" literature for children?

The Nation reported that "One indignant child on whom Carl Sandburg's 'Rootabaga Stories' was tried, declared that 'no sensible child would so much as look at it.' " Otherwise, the reviews were positive, lauding Sandburg's sense of humor and his regard for the child's mind and imagination. He had "developed a new field in American fairy-tale conception," said the *New York Times* reviewer. His children's books would sell steadily far past his lifetime, and, translated in foreign editions, would enchant children around the world.

After years of reporting fact and circumstance, Sandburg found welcome liberation in the country he created. There he could invent language, geography, customs and people, garbed in fun and nonsense, and move them through adventures masked in whimsy but, in many instances, firmly grounded in the reality he sought to leave behind. He discovered he could tell more of the truth in his fictions for children than he could tell in the often hostile world of realities. Implicit in his "kid" book was his great respect for the child heart and imagination, and the integrity and innocence of children. He affirmed that in a poem:

> I tell them where the wind comes from,
> Where the music goes when the fiddle is in the box.
> Kids—I saw one with a proud chin, a sleepyhead,
> And the moonline creeping white on her pillow.
> > I have seen their heads in the starlight
> > And their proud chins marching in a mist of stars.
> They are the only people I never lie to . . .

✳

"The book stacks up good for looks," Sandburg told Harcourt when he saw the first copy of his fourth book of poetry. *Slabs of the Sunburnt West* begins with "The Windy City," a recapitulation of Sandburg's earlier themes in its affirmation of the American people. The poem, which had appeared in *The New Republic*, foreshadows the later volumes, *Good Morning, America* and *The People, Yes*, in the experimentation with the vernacular as a form of poetry in itself. Sandburg called "The Windy City" the "most human and simplest thing" in his new book. Evident in the ten long free-verse stanzas is Sandburg's emerging fascination with history, myth and legend. He recreated Chicago's history, beginning with the name, chosen by the Indians to describe the river intersecting it,

> the place of the skunk,
> the river of the wild onion smell,
> Shee-caw-go.

He traced the quest of the pioneers, the wagon men who "found a home-like spot, and said, 'Make a home.' " He recorded the sounds of industrial Chicago, the language and songs of the modern city, packing the poem with slang and slogans ("It ain't how old you are,/It's how old you look./It ain't what you got,/It's what you can get away with."), "the jazz timebeats" as well as the "monotonous patter" of the voices of the people.

"It is easy to come here a stranger," Sandburg wrote in stanza four, "and show the whole works, write a/book, fix it all up—it is easy to come and go away a muddle-headed/pig, a bum and a bag of wind." This was a reproof of outsiders such as editor and reformer William T. Stead of England, who had visited Chicago in 1893 and written an account of its conception in *If Christ Came to Chicago*. To know the city, you had to be one of the enduring people who "get up and carry the city,/carry the bunkers and balloons of the city,/lift it and put it down." You had to remember the late governor John Altgeld, "who gave all, praying." "Dig and/dream, dream and hammer, till your/city comes." You had to know that "the people are the city," and will perpetuate it: "Living lighted skyscrapers and a night lingo of lanterns/testify to-morrow shall/ have its own say-so." Sandburg wrote an ironic "apology" for the city:

> . . .
> The fang cry, the rip claw hiss,
> The sneak-up and the still watch,
> The slant of the slit eyes waiting—
> If these bother respectable people
>   with the right crimp in their napkins
>   reading breakfast menu cards—
>   forgive us—let it pass—let it be.
>
> If cripples sit on their stumps
> And joke with the newsies bawling,
> "Many lives lost! many lives lost!
> Ter-ri-ble ac-ci-dent! many lives lost!"—
> . . . Or the blood of a child's head
> Spatters on the hub of a motor truck—
> Or a 44-gat cracks and lets the skylights
> Into one more bank messenger . . .
> Forgive us if it happens—and happens again—
> And happens again . . .

"Mention proud things, catalogue them," he wrote in "The Windy City," and then did so:

The jack-knife bridge opening, the ore boats,
    the wheat barges passing through.
Three overland trains arriving the same hour . . .
Mention a carload of shorthorns taken off the valleys of Wyoming last
    week, arriving yesterday, knocked in the head, stripped, quartered,
    hung in ice boxes today, mention the daily melodrama of this hum-
    drum, rhythms of heads, hides, heels, hoofs hung up.

Sandburg roamed two primary landscapes then, the realism of modern times, exemplified by "The Windy City," and the timeless fantasy of Rootabaga Country. There are contrasts, almost mirror images: In Chicago, monotonous houses "go mile on mile/Along monotonous streets out to the prairies." In the *Rootabaga Stories*, Gimme the Ax and his family break away from a house "where everything is the same as it always was." The enchanting White Horse Girl and the Blue Wind Boy meet and run away together in search of "where the white horses come from and where the blue wind begins," and find the place. "It belongs to us; this is what we started for," they say. A harsh fate confronts a boy and girl in "The Windy City":

And if a boy and a girl hunt the sun
With a sieve for sifting smoke—
Let it pass—let the answer be—
"Dust and a bitter wind shall come."

The freedom and joyous civility of Rootabaga cities pose an ironic counterpoint to the disillusion and resignation of life in the Windy City where "it is easy to die alive—to register a living thumbprint and be dead from the neck up."

Yet there is a resolution in the final stanzas of "The Windy City" when the depressing realism of the city and its problems is transmuted into an affirmation of "the working men, the laughing men" who built the city and the "new working men, new laughing men" who "may come and put up a new city." There are vestiges of socialism and the war in the new poems; strands of folk music, spirituals and jazz; samples from his growing collection of folk sayings; and scenes from Sandburg's westward journey, which gave the volume its title. There are poem tributes to Robert Frost, Constantin Brancusi, Chaplin and Steichen.

"Black Horizons" reveals Sandburg's lingering pain in the long aftermath of the war:

> . . . That is all; so many lies; killing so cheap;
> babies so cheap; blood, people, so cheap; and
> land high, land dear; a speck of the earth
> costs; a suck at the tit of Mother Dirt so
> clean and strong, it costs; fences, papers,
> sheriffs; fences, laws, guns; and so many
> stars and so few hours to dream. . . .

Sandburg told *Atlantic Monthly* editor Ellery Sedgwick something of the viewpoint of *Smoke and Steel* and *Slabs of the Sunburnt West* in a letter June 30, 1922. "There is no need to rehearse for you the facts of the industrial revolution that has changed the terms of life for the human race the last 150 years," Sandburg said. "But if there is ever a history of culture and arts reporting this last century and a half, it will have to take account of the terrific acceleration of contacts of races, peoples, nations, cultures, arts, directly traceable to the shrinkage of the frontiers that no longer are frontiers because transport and communication connect human thought and feeling across such vast areas. We are in the first decade of human history in which such men as Wilson, Lloyd George, Charlie Chaplin, Einstein, speak, and reach with what they have to say, to the intelligent minorities of the people of the globe." They lived in a time of confusions and chaos, Sandburg wrote. Artists, writers, painters, sculptors, musicians who "honestly relate their own epoch to older epochs understand how art today, if it is to get results, must pierce exteriors and surfaces by ways different from artists of older times."

He was working in his own pioneering way to "pierce exteriors and surfaces" in new forms. His children's stories were among the first original, thoroughly American fairy tales. His aggressive free-verse forms and subjects defied categories, appalled and mystified some critics, but won growing recognition and applause from the American public. His movie columns engaged a large audience in an ongoing discovery that film had powers to communicate and educate as well as entertain. In fiction, poetry and journalism, Sandburg explored the American character and promise. He sang its history and diversity in the ever-growing repertoire of folk music. When *Slabs of the Sunburnt West*, dedicated to Helga, appeared in 1922, Harcourt, Brace and Company promoted Sandburg as "perhaps the most American of American poets." He was probing every "exterior and surface" for the national idiom, finding new literary frontiers for experimentation.

The final poem of his fourth book of poetry was a culmination and catharsis, and a harbinger of the work to come. There is little coherence of form or theme in the book's title poem, "Slabs of the Sunburnt West"; instead, there is a free-association display of real and surreal imagery, reactions to rich and varied stimuli—including the motion pictures. The poem is a literal and metaphorical journey by overland passenger train through the "Great American Desert," "the Santa Fe trail, the Raton pass," a scenic and metaphysical exploration of prehistory, history and the future; a delving into the innermost caverns of self. The railroad is an organic symbol for man's migration from the ancient past into modernity, the transformation and conquest of interior and exterior landscapes.

> . . . Into the blanket of night goes the overland train,
> Into the black of the night the processions march,
>> The ghost of a pony goes by,
>> A hat tied to the saddle,
>> The wagon tongue of a prairie schooner
>> And the handle of a Forty-niner's pickax
>> Do a shiver dance in the desert dust,
>> In the coyote gray of the alkali dust.
> And—six men with cigars in the buffet car mention
>> "civilization," "history," "God."

Drawing on his fascination with the evolution of mankind and of self, Sandburg speculated on the limitations of the senses, the seeming futility, imprisoned within the physical being, of searching for the meanings of life. A rider comes to the Canyon's rim, takes out a stub of a pencil and writes "a long memo in shorthand":

> ". . . Sitting at the rim of the big gap
> at the high lash of the frozen storm line,
> I ask why I go on five crutches,
> tongues, ears, nostrils—all cripples—
> eyes and nose—both cripples—
> I ask why these five cripples
> limp and squint and gag with me . . .

>> "The power and lift of the sea
>> and the flame of the old earth fires under,
> I sift their meanings of sand in my fingers.
> I send out five sleepwalkers to find out who I am,
>> my name and number, where I came from,
>> and where I am going. . . .
> They come back, my five sleepwalkers; they have an answer for me, they
>> say; they tell me: Wait—. . .

Near the close of the poem, there is a cosmic baseball game, narrated in straight prose lines:

> Eighteen old giants throw a red gold shadow ball;
> they pass it along; hands go up and stop it; they
> bat up flies and practice; they begin the game, they
> knock it for home runs and two-baggers; the pitcher
> put it across in an out- and an in-shoot drop; the
> Devil is the Umpire; God is the Umpire; the game
> is called on account of darkness . . .

Man is a rider into that cosmic darkness, through the timeless desert, under the distant stars:

> Tie your hat to the saddle
> and ride, ride, ride, O Rider.
> Lay your rails and wires
> and ride, ride, ride, O Rider.
>
> The worn tired stars say
> you shall die early and die dirty.
> The clean cold stars say
> you shall die late and die clean.
>
> The runaway stars say
> you shall never die at all,
> never at all.

On that enigmatic note, the book ends.

There is one haunting poem in the volume which caught wide attention and offered Sandburg's last biting commentary on the First World War. "And So Today" described the November 11, 1921, burial of an unknown soldier. The body lay in state under the Capitol rotunda in Washington before it was borne in a solemn procession to Arlington National Cemetery, honored by pallbearers who were generals and admirals. Woodrow Wilson and General Pershing were there. President Harding made a funeral speech honoring all the men who served and died in the first great world war. In Sandburg's poem there is a ghostly procession of "Skeleton men and boys riding skeleton horses," their ribs curving and shining with "savage, elegant curves," their bones clicking and rattling, "shining in the sun." Like a cadaverous Greek chorus the "bony battalions" of the dead hover in the background of the government ceremony. "The big fish—eat the little fish—and the little fish—eat the shrimps

—and the shrimps—eat mud," the poet has one say. While the real-life orators speak of "sac-ri-fice" (the theme of Harding's speech), a ghost of an orator lifts a "skinny signal finger" and has "nothing to say, nothing easy."

There is a cinematic fadeout of "phantom riders,/skeleton riders on skeleton horses, stems of roses in their teeth . . . grinning along on Pennsylvania Avenue . . ." with "ghostly top-sergeants calling roll calls."

Finally "they lay him away—the boy nobody knows the name of—/ they lay him away in granite and steel—/with music and roses—under a flag—/under a sky of promises."

In the poem "Caligari" Sandburg commented on the landmark film *The Cabinet of Dr. Caligari*, which he had reviewed in May 1921 as the most important and original photoplay of the year. "Caligari" was a cynical counterpoint to the more complex bitterness of "And So Today." "Mannikins, we command you," the poet/critic wrote in "Caligari":

> Stand up with your white beautiful skulls.
> Stand up with your moaning sockets.
> Dance your stiff limping dances.
> We handle you with spic and span gloves.
> We tell you when and how
> And how much.

In this instance the particular film was both metaphor and imagistic model for Sandburg's perennial theme—the terrible significance of the power to control, the timeless interplay of controller and victim, whether in economics or labor or war.

With a few exceptions—such as "The Windy City"—the poems in *Slabs of the Sunburnt West* are inferior to those in Sandburg's earlier books. He had a foretaste of the volume's critical reception in the frequent rejections of poems he attempted to place in magazines and journals in advance of the book's publication. One critic saw the emergence of a "mellower Sandburg" in the book, while the *New York Times* critic wrote that Sandburg was "already in danger of becoming the Professional Chanter of Virility." Clement Wood wrote in *The Nation* that Sandburg was uniquely himself, "Penetrating, courageous, heartening," but criticized his use of vocabulary which "limits his audience today, and does more to his lovers of tomorrow. . . . For slang is last night's toadstool growth. . . . Sandburg uses unfamiliar rhythms, and a vocabulary that tomorrow will speak only to the archaeologist." William Rose Benét praised Sandburg's "strikingly alive" language, while Arthur Guiterman deplored his lack of coherence. William Stanley Braithwaite found "All the best and all the worst of Mr. Sandburg's character as a writer of verse" in *Slabs of the Sunburnt West.*

According to Malcolm Cowley in the *Dial,* Sandburg gave a deceptive impression of "ragged ease" in his verse which "as a matter of fact is highly organized." Cowley believed Sandburg did not write free verse at all, "in the common acceptance of the word." "Rather," he said, "it is repetitive verse. He uses parallel constructions; he repeats words and phrases with skill: thereby he produces effects as complex and difficult sometimes as those of Swinburne's most intricate ballades." Cowley said that Sandburg wrote "American like a foreign language, like a language, in fact, which never existed before; the separate words existed but in the speech of no one man: Sandburg was the first to thesaurize them. More than H. L. Mencken or John V. A. Weaver or any one else he can claim the discredit of bringing a new language into a world whose tongues are too confused already."

From Galesburg Clara Sandburg wrote to her son and his family about her pleasure in the book: "Dearest Sweetest and most beloved of all! Y thank you a thousand times for the beutifull book the pretty covers as well as inside arengement. Oh how we all feel the fullness of gratitude to you and gladness that your patient work have ended in so large and so pretty book. Y wish Y could give something or do something in return." She enclosed a scrap of a crochet pattern, proposing to make some pillowcases for Paula, with a crocheted trim. She wished she could do more to show her pride in her son's work. "Y only stand bewildered and would praise God for having moulded his clay into a so beutiful piece of ornament in his kingdom," she wrote.

Sandburg had received a letter from a college student who was studying Amy Lowell's *Tendencies in Modern American Poetry.* "Amy Lowell says that two men speak in you," the girl wrote:

> —the poet and the propagandist, and that your future depends upon which finally predominates the other. . . . However, my opinion in regard to the so-called propagandist poetry is that as long as you show your extreme love and sympathy for human beings, the propaganda is more than mere propaganda—it is the interpretation of the souls of men who cannot speak for themselves. And so we are especially interested to know whether you consider your "propaganda," or your lyrics more truly the expression of your poetic genius.

"Everything is propaganda, including all things in art," Sandburg had answered. "I wrote Miss Lowell once it may be written fifty years from now that I stressed certain realities that stung my eyes too vividly while she denied some of her most vivid realities." He assumed, he said, that poems such as "Black Horizons" drew the charge of propaganda:

> "More waving of the dirty shirt," is the cry of one school of esthetes. They will do you a storm of the elements with a facile glad hand . . . but a human storm . . . mystic brooding of forces that in their coalescence or precipitation MAY blow our lights, our art, to the same limbo where the lights and art of other civilizations have gone . . . when I try my hand at this storm the esthetes cry propaganda. Let 'em.

"It is the law," he wrote in the poem "At the Gates of Tombs,"

> as a civilization dies and goes down
> to eat ashes along with all other dead civilizations
> —it is the law all dirty wild dreamers die first—
> gag 'em, lock 'em up, get' em bumped off.
>
> And since at the gates of tombs silence is a gift,
> be silent about it, yes, be silent—forget it.

He would not be silent, or forget, but this "dirty wild dreamer" would from 1922 onward articulate his vision of the world and humanity in different ways. He predicted, "In the matter of subjects and forms I know I am going to hit many new paths and roads the next ten years."

✳

On December 23, 1921, President Harding had commuted the sentences of the old socialist Eugene Debs and twenty-three other political prisoners, and on Christmas Day Debs, gaunt and frail, was released from Atlanta Penitentiary. More than 25,000 people welcomed him home to Terre Haute, Indiana. In the summer of 1922, in an effort to regain his health, Debs traveled to the Seventh-Day Adventist Lindlahr Sanitarium in Chicago. He was inundated with visitors there, and his brother Theodore had him transferred to the Lindlahr Sanitarium in suburban Elmhurst, Illinois, coincidentally just three blocks from Carl Sandburg's house. Sandburg began to visit Debs, sometimes taking his guitar and singing and playing for Debs and other patients. Paula and Sandburg invited Debs to their house, where he especially enjoyed the three little girls. There are pictures of Debs sitting in the sunlight in Paula's garden, deep in conversation with the Sandburg children.

As Debs's health improved, he signed himself out of the sanitarium to be with friends. On two different occasions, he spent spirited evenings at the Sandburgs' with Sinclair Lewis, who shared Sandburg's publisher as well as his admiration for Debs. Lewis and some friends paid a late-night visit to Debs that fall, stopping by about one o'clock in the morning to help him consume a bottle of whiskey. When Debs went to sleep about four, Lewis and company strolled over to Sandburg's house. He was out of town, but Paula greeted her husband's surprise dawn visitors. As Debs walked out of the Sandburgs' gate one day to return to the sanitarium, one of the family said, "He's a big rough flower."

∗

Sandburg kept a strenuous schedule during the fall of 1922, working late at night on revisions for the second book of children's stories, *Rootabaga Pigeons*. May Massee was helping him, and Harcourt sent his assistant Ellen Eayrs to Chicago to work with Sandburg for a few days. He wrote a long article for the *Daily News* on the publication of the report of the Chicago Commission on Race Relations, who had worked since 1919 to document the events of the Chicago race riots. "Not weeks, nor months, nor years will straighten up the race tangle," Sandburg wrote. "Tens of years, hundreds of years, maybe thousands—and patience, tolerance, intelligence—a long, long trail."

Sandburg was taking deeper, more analytical perspectives of the motion pictures he reviewed weekly, considering the intellectual and social impact of the new medium, conjecturing about what movies would do to the imagination. He deplored excessive and meaningless movie violence, advocating decent, intelligent comedy rather than "cheap, offhand horseplay." He admired the work of John Barrymore and Gloria Swanson, and was so impressed with *Nanook of the North* that he wrote several columns about it, praising it as a "brilliantly conceived travelogue" and a classic story, which he compared to *Robinson Crusoe*. Sandburg immediately saw the far-reaching value of motion picture newsreels, which brought the American people close-ups of "History in the making."

Just when his home life seemed to settle into a predictable rhythm, Margaret had another series of attacks, and had to return to Battle Creek. "Dear Daddy," she wrote on September 19, 1922. "Yesterday I began on my fast. In the morning I was awfully hungry but towards evening I wasn't so hungry. Mamma wanted to go on a fast with me but I wouldn't let her." She passed her time reading and drawing pictures and was allowed to see a motion picture from time to time. "I saw a moving picture show yesterday and today," she told her father, offering her own movie review. "Yesterday I saw 'The Bachelor Daddy,' and it is the best one I've ever seen. I'm going to tell it to you when I get home."

Paula rented a furnished room for their stay so that they could be near

Dr. Conklin's office for daily tests and treatments. Oma and Sandburg tended to matters at home, with the help of the hired girl, Lina. "I am going to shape up my work so I'll be with you at the time the fast is ending," Sandburg promised.

He wrote to Paula and Margaret about the news from home. "I am going to get tickets to *Lightnin'* for Oma and Lina at a matinee some afternoon next week when I will stay home with the shiners," he told Paula. "Margaret's letter to Lina today made us all feel she has big and deep vitality. That a girl fasting for six days could write so keenly of so many things and in such a handwriting, was testimony." He was at work on the final revisions of *Rootabaga Pigeons*. He was meeting his quota of *Daily News* reviews. He was helping Harcourt promote the children's books, and dispensing permissions for the publication of various poems, including the Billy Sunday verse which Macmillan and Company planned to include in an anthology of the great religious poetry of the world. Nevertheless, he put home matters first.

Steichen took a keen interest in his niece's illness, and when Paula wrote to tell him Margaret was improving, he offered a special way of celebrating: "Dear Paus'l," he wrote: "Hurrah & Hurrah—It looks as if you had it nailed at last.—Now it is simply a matter of patience and HEROIC COURAGE on the part of Margaret.—I'm awful proud of her and when I get rich again will buy her a marvelous hero present. In the mean time I will turn over my cross of the Legion de Honneur to her.—Love to all, Gaesjack."

It was a melancholy autumn. "Out of the window I can see the wild ruddy face of Helga with its wonderful curves," Sandburg wrote to Paula late one afternoon. "She is at the sand box. For hours those kids have been talking and laughing out there. I am only living in the present with them, which is what I am going to do with Margaret. The worst is yet to come and if it doesn't come what we get is so much velvet."

Sandburg wrote to Margaret that she was "one of the champion, long-distance, unconquerable and invincible fasters of the United States." Yet by October she was weak, depressed and very homesick. Paula concentrated all her attention on her daughter, but encouraged Sandburg to send her the manuscript for *Rootabaga Pigeons* so she could go over it thoroughly for him, "without a million interruptions," she said. Sandburg visited Margaret and Paula in Battle Creek the weekend of October 7, "renewing a mortgage on our home and helping care for a sick child," he told Ellen Eayrs in a long, handwritten letter, full of his ideas on promoting the Rootabaga books. He had hurried to Battle Creek when Margaret's fast had to be curtailed because of albumin in her urine. She had recurring pains in her side and several mild convulsions. Paula hoped that the fast had been effective anyway, and told Sandburg she would be satisfied if the fast "achieved nothing more than a break-up of the tendency to severe daytime attacks." Margaret had lost fifteen pounds in two weeks, but Paula felt she was in good condition, aside from her depression and homesickness.

Paula's detailed, scientific diaries of her daughter's problems continued throughout her lifetime. She and Sandburg were powerless to cure Margaret, could only take her to one doctor after another, subject her to the debilitating fasts which seemed at the time the most effective treatment. When Paula had to break the news to Margaret that she had epilepsy, she put it into loving perspective for her. Many famous people had it, she told her—Julius Caesar, Edward Lear. The Greeks and Romans regarded epilepsy as a sacred disease, Paula said, knowing Margaret's fascination with mythology.

The precocious Montessori cover child, who loved school and books, never attended public school again. Except for a brief enrollment as a teenager in a private boarding school, where she was acutely homesick, Margaret lived at home, educating herself on the talk of her parents and their stimulating friends, and in her parents' ever-growing library, thousands of books which spanned every academic discipline, as well as the spectrum of world literature. When she was twelve, Margaret read Shakespeare's *A Midsummer Night's Dream*, an edition illustrated by Arthur Rackham. "Don't you think she is ready for a set of Shakespeare?" Paula asked Sandburg. He agreed, and told Paula to choose one the next time she was in Chicago. The next year, for her birthday, Margaret was given a set of the works of Sir Walter Scott. Sequestered in her parents' home all her life, she would become a scholar.

In October 1922, she and her parents returned home to Elmhurst from Battle Creek for a happy family reunion. Soon after, Sandburg wrote to Harcourt with a special request:

And now a matter of a kind that I won't bother you about maybe again in a lifetime. We are buying a lot next door south of us in Elmhurst. If we don't get it somebody else will and we will have a house we may not care to look at slammed close to us. The price is $2,300, of which $1,300 must be in cash down, the rest time payments. We have paid $200 earnest and borrowed $500 and need $600. If you can find this $600 it will go into good land. It has two marvelous sugar maples in front. At the rear it has the biggest incomparable lilac bush in northern Illinois. It is the only place I have ever found glow worms. I spaded it all and raised sweet corn year before last. Our cats have their kittens there in special sunny lying-in corners. So you see we know what we're getting. And all we need is $600 spot cash greenbacks of the national government.

The *Rootabaga Stories* were selling far beyond Harcourt's expectations, and he sent Sandburg six hundred dollars immediately, an advance on royalties for "the kid book."

Edward Steichen was working on a children's book of his own that autumn. Sandburg's *Rootabaga Stories* were "real stuff," he said. He was eager for Sandburg and Paula to see his "kid's picture book," begun that summer. He thought perhaps he and Sandburg might complete it together. " 'Naturally' there never was anything like it," Steichen told his sister; "in fact I am sure kids never have had a picture book." Like Sandburg, he had deep faith in the child's imagination and found freedom and consolation in creating his own world for children.

Sandburg's public success in 1922 was a bittersweet counterpoint to the family's private anguish over Margaret's illness. His growing fame brought out crowds of people whenever he lectured. Students at Northwestern University sat on radiators, on window ledges and on the platform itself when Sandburg spoke at the Medill School of Journalism in October, to one of the largest crowds in the history of the university. They had come to hear "Carl Sandburg, the modern poet, whose verse had put Chicago on the map." William Allen White called his program "a concert, grand opera, philosophic pablum and dramatic entertainment all in one," suitable for highbrows and lowbrows. He was a famous poet now, one of the "old guard," according to Amy Lowell. His children's stories were hailed as landmark American fairy tales. Sandburg had rediscovered himself in Rootabaga Country.

The tapestry of Sandburg's *Rootabaga Stories* and *Rootabaga Pigeons* was woven from many strands—his own mystical imagination, the motion pictures he watched week by week, current events, the love and pain intertwined in his family life. After he invented and populated that fantastical realm, he took refuge there himself, feeling more at home in this imagined universe than in the harsh, real world where he had worked and struggled for years. In the unfettered landscapes of legend and myth, he found liberating truth.

The journey was rewarding in more than one way. The surprising commercial and critical success of the *Rootabaga Stories* encouraged Sandburg to think about another book for young people. There was no good juvenile biography of Abraham Lincoln, and he began to consider writing one. For years he had been collecting Lincoln material, and had enough by 1921 to set up complex files, a "classification system," as he called

it. Since boyhood, he had admired Lincoln. He had grown up listening
to the talk of people who saw Lincoln with their own eyes, and heard
him speak. Galesburg was full of Lincoln history. Sandburg and Harcourt
began to talk about a biography, four hundred pages long, written in
simple language for young people, concentrating on Lincoln's prairie
boyhood, so much like Sandburg's own. He purchased a ten-volume set
of Civil War photographs on December 21, 1922, and several biographies
of Lincoln and other Civil War figures. Deliberately, he turned toward
the past, embarking on an ambitious exploration of America history.

By year's end, Sandburg was seriously reading Lincoln.

---
*

1923–1925

18. A Certain Portrait

For thirty years and more I have planned to make a
certain portrait of Abraham Lincoln. It would sketch the
country lawyer and prairie politician who was intimate
with the settlers of the Knox County neighborhood
where I grew up as a boy, and where I heard the talk of
men and women who had eaten with Lincoln, given him
a bed overnight, heard his jokes and lingo, remembered
his silences and his mobile face.

> —Carl Sandburg, Preface to *Abraham Lincoln:*
> *The Prairie Years,* 1926

"How is the 'Lincoln' getting along?" Alfred Harcourt wrote to Sandburg in February 1923. "I hope all this traveling doesn't hinder it too much, and that it just gives the material a chance to settle into order." He asked Sandburg for a firm outline. "All this month my mind has been turning to you and that job," he told Sandburg. "It will be a great book."

"We are plowing along on the Lincoln book," Sandburg answered. "The first outline is holding firm. The road work is not interfering. The only thing liable to slow down the steady pace of the job is my eyesight. This is my last job with rigid eyesight and research requirements. Only the amazing high spots of L.'s life hold me to the job. He had more laughs and tears in him than any other human clay pot I know of."

Sandburg threw himself into the biographical study. He dug through newspaper morgues, unearthing Lincoln stories from journals of the period. He pored over bins of used books in out-of-the-way bookshops, buying relevant histories and biographies, often ripping out the sections he thought he would need, discarding the covers and remaining pages. He investigated private as well as public collections of Lincoln material. He now received more lecture invitations than he could accept, and began to plan his lecture schedule with three purposes in mind: to entertain his audiences, earn the much-needed income, and put himself close to important sources of Lincoln material.

It was already clear that the biography would not be for young people alone. It had grown far beyond that. Sandburg used three workrooms for the project. Sometimes he worked after hours in his cluttered *Daily News* office. Sometimes he worked in the rented studio in town, which he christened "The Dump" for its chaos of Lincoln material and his haphazard attention to housekeeping. Once Paula and Margaret stopped by to see him there after a visit to a Chicago doctor. Paula was "horrified" by the newspapers which littered the floor. If Sandburg tracked dirt in, he simply covered it with a newspaper, until there seemed to be a newspaper carpet. Most of the time, he worked in his study on the top floor of the Elmhurst house. In spring and summer, he often took his typewriter outside, setting it up on an orange crate behind the back fence, in the vacant lot next door. He called this arrangement his Crow Hut.

At home, after he completed the day's work at his "bread and butter" job, Sandburg worked long into the night on his evolving life of Lincoln. Sometimes he wrote until dawn, and when he was too tired to work any longer, lay down to sleep in his workroom on a narrow couch beneath a Navajo blanket. As always, Paula supported, encouraged, understood. Sometimes, lost in work, he failed to come home for dinner, or chose to stay overnight in Chicago in the rented studio. Sometimes he would stop at Harriet Vaughn Moody's to relax and talk before taking the train out to Elmhurst. Paula accepted these absences now as part of his nature and routine. When he was deep in work at home, she kept the children from disturbing him, kept visitors away. She orchestrated a smooth rhythm at home, spared him domestic worries, lent a skilled, generous hand to his research and to critical reading of manuscript drafts. Her "fine understanding," observed *Daily News* colleague Harry Hansen, "helped make Carl's married life a song."

Sandburg's lecture commitments took him to New York and Philadelphia and to other towns on the Eastern Seaboard in 1923, and back to the West Coast and the Southwest. Margaret's health was more stable, but Paula kept her on a bland diet and strict regimen of rest. Sandburg and Paula asked Harcourt for another advance that winter, this time for "interest payments on mortgages, and payments of taxes, special assessments and such." "If I can draw that amount it will save us time for work, sport and religion," Sandburg told Harcourt, who immediately forwarded a check. The thirty-eight definitions of poetry which Sandburg shared widely with lecture audiences were printed in the *Atlantic Monthly* in March, and Leon Bazalgette, the French translator of Whitman's *Leaves of Grass*, began to translate the *Rootabaga Stories* into French. Riding the crest of his success that spring, Sandburg was pleased to receive a telegram from J. M. Tilden, president of Lombard College, his alma mater, inviting him to commencement to receive an honorary degree. On May 30, 1923, Sandburg the high school and college dropout went home to Galesburg to become a doctor of letters.

✳

He had been exploring all the Lincoln sites in Illinois that spring, and was so immersed in Lincoln research that "the Big Book" was looking better than ever, he told Harcourt, although, he said, "it burns and hurts sometimes with 'growing pains.' " His schedule was strenuous. "I'm hoping you get a little rest these days between the Berkeley & Dallas dates," Paula urged. "Take best care of yourself. Everything fine at home. Margaret is in fine shape again. Good-natured & everything."

"Paula girl," he wrote in the midst of one tiring journey, ". . . in 60 more hours I'll be on the Erie Line heading home and loving home & knowing it better for this trip."

"We miss you & your voice," Paula told him, "and we don't like it at all that the guitars are silent and the hasp on your door always fastened!"

At home to stay for a while, Sandburg attended to final production details for *Rootabaga Pigeons* and he and Paula settled into a quiet summer. Margaret went away to camp in Michigan where she learned to paddle a canoe and swim the breaststroke. She was homesick, but she liked being with girls her own age, although her illness and withdrawal from school had left her out of touch with their interests. "Dear Spink," her father wrote to her, "We miss your shiny face." The camp was run by a family friend, sympathetic to Margaret's illness, who provided the oversight her health needed during her stay away from home.

Sandburg toiled at the Lincoln research. When his searches in midwestern bookstores and used-book stalls failed to turn up items he needed, he called on friends in New York and Boston, especially Ellen Eayrs at Harcourt and Amy Lowell. *Daily News* colleagues Harry Hansen and Lloyd Lewis, who shared his interest in biography and Lincoln, accompanied him on jaunts to Springfield, Illinois, Lincoln's hometown, where Sandburg talked to local people and studied materials at the Illinois State Library.

Years later, Illinois governor Adlai Stevenson vividly recalled Sandburg's visit to Bloomington, Illinois, to interview his father, Lewis Green Stevenson. Sandburg wanted to meet ex-governor Joseph W. Fifer, nick-named Private Joe for his service as a volunteer during the Civil War. Joe Fifer appreciated good whiskey, hard to come by in those Prohibition days. Armed with a pint of rare bourbon which Lewis Stevenson had sequestered in his cellar for years, he and Sandburg called on Private Joe Fifer, confident that the whiskey would warm his memory and enliven their visit. Fifer received them and their gift cordially, but to their dismay, left the tantalizing bottle uncorked on his desk while they talked. Sand-burg and Stevenson "cast frustrated glances at it throughout the inter-view."

✳

Alfred Harcourt was living through his own family tragedy in 1923. His wife, ill and despondent, committed suicide. Their young son Hastings discovered his mother's body in the kitchen of their house. Concerned by an uncharacteristic silence, Sandburg wrote to Harcourt: "You haven't written me a line in a long while. How goes it?"

"I know you haven't heard from me for some time," Harcourt apol-ogized. "I have had to be away from the office a good deal for the last year. Ellen [Eayrs] will explain to you when she sees you. I'm back now and apt, I think, to be more of a publisher than ever." Sandburg turned over the first significant segment of the Lincoln book to Harcourt in October, and he tackled it with zest.

"We've had not more than one or two books in this shop as good as this piece," he told Sandburg, "and if it keeps up it will be the brightest feather in our cap—a regular plume! You're just the boy to do this—to understand Abe and make him real in real times when Life went on so differently." Harcourt told Sandburg he wanted to keep his Lincoln book "fairly dark" so that when it was practically done he could "send a handsome announcement—all at once to everybody—of it as an event." He aimed for publication in the fall of 1924. "Do you see yourself having it done by May?" Harcourt asked. "Bless you—go on—don't get sick or anything."

Sandburg told Harcourt he believed he could finish the book by the summer of 1924. "Old Abe is now married and running for Congress," he said. "The book is about one-third done. What do you think of the title 'Abraham Lincoln and His Years'?" Sandburg promised Harcourt that the Civil War section would be "kaleidoscopic and telescopic from hell to breakfast."

* * *

Rootabaga Pigeons came out that fall to almost uniform critical approval. Anne Carroll Moore and others thought Sandburg had made a signal contribution to American literature for children. According to the *Literary Review*, Sandburg had "invented a new and rootedly American kind of fairy story." Eugene Debs wrote to Sandburg about his pleasure in the book. "No one but you could have produced this wonderful volume," he told Sandburg. "It required your peculiar genius and your marvellous imagination to conceive and execute this strikingly original and appealing production." Lonely and in waning health, Debs appreciated Sandburg's staunch friendship. "I have never for a day since leaving you and your beautiful wife and little household gods failed to think of you and return my thanks and blessings for the rest and comfort and inspiration I found there," he wrote.

Sandburg's professor Philip Green Wright, now with the Institute of Economics in Washington, D.C., wrote to congratulate him on the originality of the stories and their language. At Lake George Alfred Stieglitz and Georgia O'Keeffe, who had enjoyed *Rootabaga Stories*, read the new book with relish. Stieglitz wrote to describe O'Keeffe's delight: "O'Keeffe is sitting behind me—warming her feet on the kitchen oven. She just laughed aloud & said: Sandburg's book is too ridiculously wonderful—and now she's reading aloud to me while I'm writing—& still has no idea I'm writing to you."

Sandburg himself had little time to think about *Rootabaga Pigeons*. He had begun to arrange his lectures in a series of about ten days each, gearing his destinations to the overriding demands of his Lincoln research.

"The wife and friends are saying the job will kill me if I don't slow down," Sandburg told Harcourt at the end of his first year's work on the book. "BUT it's exactly the kind of a job that with me has to be a spurt job; if I had one of those retentive efficiency memories that took a never-let-go grip of names, dates, places, actions, I could slow down—One thing I'm sure of; the biggest part of American history has all to be rewritten; and it will be done."

✳

Soon after his forty-sixth birthday on January 6, 1924, Sandburg paid a surprise visit to his mother in Galesburg where she lived a busy life, caring for her grandchildren Richard and Charles while her widowed daughter Martha worked. Clara Sandburg wrote to Paula, "Certainly all of us were delighted to see Carl the Sunday evening his radiant face shining. I thought traveling around having a good time as it seems but as I read [in] the poem, O wondrous gifted pain teach thou The God of Love, let him learn . . . not only books, but know thyself." As his mother acknowledged in her quaint, lyrical syntax, Sandburg was not just "traveling around having a good time." His travels were purposeful, arduous, prolonged—and professionally and financially essential. He earned $2,600 from his *Daily News* job in 1924—fifty dollars a week. His Harcourt, Brace royalties totaled $3,617.89, largely thanks to the Rootabaga books. His lectures produced $1,135 in income after expenses. With three growing daughters and two mortgages, he and Paula lived as frugally as ever.

His job as *Daily News* motion picture editor took him to the West Coast again. Hollywood in 1924 faced the challenge of the home radio receiver, and retaliated against the popularity of its new rival by reducing movie admission prices and producing a spate of lavish, epic silent films. Sandburg's favorite film of 1924 was Douglas Fairbanks's *The Thief of Bagdad*, a masterpiece, Sandburg said, one of the four or five best films of all time. He wrote that Fairbanks's film was, outside of Chaplin's work, "the healthiest, boldest, most original and inspired work that has come from the film-making world since the art and industry of the cinema began doing business." Sandburg was fascinated by the production details of the film, which required an unprecedented seven months' shooting time and fourteen months to complete, using four thousand extras and several acres of specially built sets, inspired by Fairbanks's wish for an airy, ethereal backdrop for the story.

Sandburg saw his own subject on the screen when Charles Edward Bull, a Reno, Nevada, judicial officer, played Abraham Lincoln in *The Iron Horse*, the story of the "epic of the steam railroad and the locomotive crossing the great plains and connecting the Mississippi Valley with the Pacific Coast." Sandburg was critical of the historical lapses in the film: there were white-faced Hereford cattle roaming the ranges in the movie, when only longhorn were to be found during that time; and there was an incident from Lincoln's life "rather obscurely authenticated, so to speak."

Sandburg the biographer joined Sandburg the film critic in darkened movie houses watching films good and bad, plausible and artificial, and pondering the truth to be found in skillful illusion and the distortions of reality which often passed for fact or history. As the biographer lived more intimately day by day with Lincoln, the movie editor thought and wrote about art and history as entertainment for the mass audience. As a biographer he believed that the United States needed to build on its own traditions in poetry, art and human behavior. As a film critic he tried to catch the uniquely American characteristics of the young medium. The movie reviews provided the financial base for Sandburg's work on the biography, and the films he saw enlivened and sharpened his sense of dramatic and visual impact. But the biography of Lincoln was becoming the dominant reality in Sandburg's busy life. "I make my acknowledgements to you,/Jesus, Shakespeare, Lincoln," Sandburg had written in an unpublished poem. "I say you dead are more real than people I/see on streetcars, in offices and restaur-/ants, in parks and cigar store hangouts."

Sandburg traveled from coast to coast in 1924 filling lecture dates and picking up Lincoln material and new folk songs wherever he went. He asked Amy Lowell, who had just signed a contract to write a biography of John Keats, to help him get copies of the Herndon-Bartlett correspondence at the Massachusetts Historical Library. When she learned that restrictions on the letters hampered such a request she urged Sandburg to travel to Boston to examine the letters for himself, and to stay with her, "for I always love to have you stay here," she said.

He did so in early March. "Sandburg blew in for a few minutes between lectures in different cities," Lowell told Louis Untermeyer. "He was as sweet as ever, and entirely drowned in his Life of Lincoln. It will be very interesting to see what he does with a biography. I had grave doubts of his ability to do such a thing before I talked to him that night, but I must say that after we had conversed on the subject of Lincoln for some hours, both Ada and I felt that he had a great deal to say."

Lowell told Sandburg that she had spoken to a recent lecture audience about his new life of Lincoln. "Ada told me afterwards that she thought you had enjoined me to secrecy; if so I grovel on the floor," Lowell said. "I did not remember your saying any such thing, and it seemed a good opportunity to start the publicity, for the sooner the publicity for that sort of a book is started, the better."

✳

"I've been thinking about you and Lincoln," Harcourt wrote to Sandburg in the summer of 1924, about the time they had originally hoped the book would be finished. "How goes it?" He was "working like a dog at a root," but Sandburg was far from finished.

It was the private man, not the public figure, who compelled his interest. From the earliest days of his discovery of biography, he had been fascinated with the evolution of the soul, the labyrinth of the interior life. Most other Lincoln biographies of the nineteenth and early twentieth centuries concentrated on Lincoln's public life, but Sandburg announced his attention to probe the interior, private man, the "illuminated, mysterious personality," the "elusive and dark player on the stage of destiny." He experimented in biography as he did in every genre he tried. His innovative, often unwieldy, sometimes rhapsodic biography of Lincoln would offend and perplex many critics, in part because Sandburg undertook a difficult and unorthodox search for the "silent workings" of Lincoln's inner life.

He laid out his plan and purpose in the preface to the Lincoln biography. He intended to "sketch the country lawyer and the prairie politician," stressing the fifty-two years leading up to Lincoln's Presidency, because "if he was what he was during those first fifty-two years of his life it was nearly inevitable that he would be what he proved to be in the last four."

In those confusing, often cynical years after World War I, the nation still searched for a sense of its own character and purpose. "Perhaps poetry, art, human behavior in this country, which has need to build on its own traditions, would be served by a life of Lincoln stressing the fifty-two years previous to his Presidency," Sandburg mused.

Lincoln's personal history was a prism through which much of the nation's own growth could be viewed, Sandburg believed, for Lincoln was a product of his era. The "inside changes" working in Lincoln were connected to "the changes developing in the heart and mind of the country." Lincoln was irrevocably bound to his times, destined to be the spokesman for his countrymen and their rapidly changing national life. Lincoln was "lawyer, politician, a good neighbor and storyteller, a live, companionable man; these belonged to his role. He was to be a mind, a spirit, a tongue and voice."

Sandburg found a deep vein of consistency in Lincoln's pervasive simplicity of speech and life-style; his kindness and generosity; his dislike of all pretense; his humility. He was a dutiful husband and a devoted father, less ambitious than his temperamental wife, endowed with a "bigness of heart and vision." His brilliant mind transcended the limits of his backwoods education. He was an instinctive scholar, a voracious reader.

Sandburg's Lincoln portrait was studded with anecdotes, letters, memoirs, newspaper stories, hearsay, conjecture, excerpts from earlier biographies. He sketched a multifaceted man—the frontiersman, the lawyer, the politician, the orator, the storyteller, the humorist, even the poet.

He concentrated on Lincoln the politician, shrewd, smart, expedient, "cutting and scornful," but fundamentally humane and visionary. "If there had been any stubborn grandeur at all in the life of Lincoln," Sandburg wrote, "it was in his explanations of the Declaration of Independence, and his taking the words, 'All men are created equal,' not only seriously and solemnly but passionately." Lincoln understood with "Jefferson, Adams, Franklin, and the makers of the American Revolution" that "all men are not equals," that differences prevail, but that "the accent and stress was to be on opportunity, on equal chance, equal access to the resources of life, liberty, and the pursuit of happiness. To give men this equal chance in life was the aim, the hope, the flair of glory, spoken by the Declaration of Independence."

Sandburg called Lincoln the "thinker and spokesman" for the American people:

> He knew what they wanted more deeply and thoroughly, more tragically and quizzically, than they knew it themselves. He made them believe that he counted the political genius and social control of the masses of people worth more in the long run than the assumptions of those who secretly will not trust the people at all. He gained and held power, votes, friends, in many and far unknown corners and byways, because he threw some strange accent into the pronunciation of the words, "The People."

Sandburg was intrigued by Lincoln the orator and lecturer, tracing his development and giving highlights of key speeches, including the Lincoln-Douglas Debates. "Sprinkled all through the speeches of Lincoln, as published, were stubby, homely words that reached out and made plain, quiet people feel that perhaps behind them was a heart that could understand them—the People—the listeners," Sandburg wrote, giving one eyewitness account after another to establish a composite view of Lincoln on the speaker's platform—ungainly, awkward, earnest, charismatic nonetheless—"elemental and mystical," the "prophetic man of the present."

The biography is rich with accounts of Lincoln's storytelling and humor, his dark moods and melancholy, his ambivalence about organized religion, his innate spiritualism and occasional superstitions. Sandburg drew a unique portrait of Lincoln the poet, reprinting in full Lincoln's favorite poem, "Oh, Why Should the Spirit of Mortal Be Proud?," one he himself had long ago memorized because Lincoln admired it. He included the full text of some of Lincoln's own poems, along with letters he wrote about them. Lincoln's poem about his childhood home was a meditation on death and loss:

. . .

O Memory! thou midway world
   'Twixt earth and paradise,
Where things decayed and loved ones lost
   In dreamy shadows rise,

And, freed from all that's earthly vile,
   Seen hallowed, pure, and bright,
Like scenes in some enchanted isle
   All bathed in liquid light. . . .

I range the fields with pensive tread,
   And pace the hollow rooms,
And feel (companion of the dead)
   I'm living in the tombs.

Sandburg gave his readers Lincoln's autobiographical writing as well as his poems. Of his education, Lincoln had written, "Of course, when I came of age I did not know much. Still, somehow, I could read, write and cipher to the rule of three; but that was all. I have not been to school since. The little advance I now have upon this store of education I have picked up from time to time under the pressure of necessity." Describing himself as a man with "dark complexion, with coarse black hair and gray eyes," Lincoln wrote of his autobiography's brevity, "There is not much of it, for the reason, I suppose, that there is not much of me."

Growing up as he did in the wake of Lincoln's prairie sojourn, seeing places Lincoln had seen, and knowing people who had known Lincoln, Sandburg drew from his own boyhood experience to form instinctive suppositions of the forces which shaped Lincoln. The Lincoln Sandburg reconstructed was in significant ways a reflection of himself. Like the young Sandburg, exploring the mystery of words, the young Lincoln "was hungry to understand the meanings of words," "lay awake hours at night thinking about the meaning of the meaning" of language. Like the young Sandburg studying his father's Swedish Bible, Sandburg's young Lincoln pondered "the meaning of the heavy and mysterious words standing dark on the pages of the family Bible."

Sandburg, like his Lincoln, had obediently helped his father work with the tools, knew the meaning of hard physical labor from an early age, carried a burden of chores and family responsibilities in a frontier town on the verge of the wilderness, but felt most alive with "the mystery of imagination, the faculty of reconstruction and piecing together today the things his eyes had seen yesterday."

It was a prairie poet rather than a methodical historian who constructed Sandburg's "certain portrait" of Abraham Lincoln, one which critics challenged as more imagined lyricism than history. But Sandburg was recreating much of his own youth on the prairie when he rendered Lincoln's wiry physical strength, his capacity for mundane hard work, his essential loneliness. Like Sandburg, Lincoln in his passage to manhood

> was alone a good deal of the time. . . . In some years more of his time was spent in loneliness than in the company of other people. It happened, too, that this loneliness he knew was not like that of people in cities who can look from a window on streets where faces pass and repass. It was the wilderness loneliness he became acquainted with, solved, filtered through body, eye, and brain, held communion within his ears, in the temples of his forehead, in the works of his beating heart.

Sandburg's portrait of Lincoln is a mirror of his own interior life. He gave Lincoln his own passion for nature, his conviction of its capacity to heal and to reveal the metaphorical physical laws of the universe which can illuminate human conduct. "In the short and simple annals of the poor," Sandburg wrote in *The Prairie Years*, once again echoing lines from Gray's "Elegy" that he had read in youth, "it seems there are people who breathe with the earth and take into their lungs and blood some of the hard and dark strength of its mystery."

Sandburg and Lincoln were pioneers, and "pioneers are half gypsy," looking always for horizons "from which at any time another and stranger wandersong may come calling and take the heart, to love or to kill." Sandburg believed that Lincoln, too, was a dreamer who "cherished his sweet dreams, and let the bitter ones haunt him." Lincoln, like Sandburg, enjoyed reading aloud, for "words became more real if picked from the silent page of the book and pronounced on the tongue." Sandburg unconsciously used a variation of that phrase, written in the 1920s about Lincoln, to describe himself in *Always The Young Strangers* in 1953, holding his father's Bible in his hands, looking at "the black marks on white paper" which were words "your eyes would pick off into words and your tongue would speak."

Sandburg read into Lincoln's temperament the paradox of his own dual nature, "two shifting moods, the one of the rollicking, droll story and the one when he lapsed into a gravity beyond any bystander to penetrate." He discovered Lincoln in Galesburg in the places he saw and the people who had known him, but he believed he knew Lincoln intuitively because they had been nourished by the same landscapes, by kindred, simple people.

"It is toil and toil finishing up the Lincoln book . . . ," he told Clyde
Tull. "But I think that you and some others like you will say it is about
time some cornhusker had done this kind of a job."

＊

By early August 1924, Sandburg faced a crucial decision. Having completed his study of the private Lincoln "whose times and ways of life
belonged somewhat to himself," he had to confront the public Lincoln.
For nearly three weeks Sandburg wrestled with Lincoln and the Civil
War period. He realized that if he went on "with a compressed handling
of Abe in the war," he would have to write a different kind of book, in
another style, moving from the personal, sometimes lyrical intimacy of
the prairie Lincoln to the convoluted politics of Washington and war.
He and Harcourt had been planning a one-volume biography, but Sandburg began to see that "to work out the series of portraits of Abe in the
war, as I have already sketched them, would run the book beyond the
limits of even the big single volume I had expected would hold what I
planned."

He decided then that his narrative was finished. In a sense, it had
completed itself when he got Lincoln elected to the Presidency and
aboard the train bound for Washington. "It is a book, of a unity, an
entity," he wrote Harcourt.

Harcourt was away on vacation with his new wife, his assistant Ellen
Eayrs, and it was his partner Donald Brace who responded to Sandburg's
letter. "Personally, I find myself somewhat disappointed that your 'Lincoln' isn't going to be a complete 'Lincoln' in one volume," Brace told
Sandburg. He was not surprised, however: "I have had the feeling all
along that it was going to be fierce problem to do the Civil War period
on a scale which would match what you had already done." On his
return, Harcourt was initially surprised by Sandburg's view of the book,
but, on reflection, was "strongly inclined to agree." He assured Sandburg,
"I am sure that I will be convinced by the manuscript. I really believe
you've done what you set out to do in your picture of the times and the
man. This was a job you couldn't help doing, and you were the only
one who could do it. You'll do the rest of it when you can't help doing
that."

Sandburg hoped to deliver the entire manuscript to Harcourt early in
September. He searched for a title for the book, considering *Lincoln the
Western American*, *Lincoln the Prairie Man*, *The Prairie Lincoln*, and *The
Western Lincoln*. He thought, half-seriously, about *The Smooth-Faced Lin-
coln*, but somebody at the *Chicago Daily News* said, "Oh, hell, the people

don't want to see Lincoln without whiskers." "For another title," Sandburg told Harcourt, "I would submit *Abraham Lincoln and His Prairie Years.*" As Sandburg reviewed the manuscript, he doubted that he could have it "smoothed out and decently organized" by September 1, as he had promised, but thought he should take it as it was to New York in September and work it through with Harcourt, who had been an astute editor for his other books.

As a biographer Sandburg could be omniscient, holding in his hands the documents of personal and national tragedy. Burdened by that knowledge of the past, he resurrected Lincoln's life and the lives of many other people, perceiving in their drama the portents of tragedy and loss which they themselves had missed or failed to heed. By late summer Sandburg was physically and emotionally worn out by the work.

"I have been off the main job, mostly sleeping, lately," he wrote Harcourt. "The smoothing out and finishing up of the thing will take weeks yet. One thing I am sure of, and I had my doubts at first about whether it could be done. The book marches; it has good Second Wind; the last is better than the first. As soon as I get certain changes made the part tacking on to what you have will be sent on to you."

He was energized by a new and strategic friendship that fall. He met Chicago lawyer Oliver R. Barrett, who had been collecting Lincoln materials and other literary and historical documents since his boyhood in Pittsfield, Illinois. Born in 1873, Barrett, like Sandburg, had grown up hearing people talk about Lincoln and the Civil War from firsthand experience. When he was fourteen, Barrett began to write to politicians and celebrities, seeking autographs. In 1880 President Rutherford B. Hayes was amused by a "droll" request "in a boyish handwriting":

> Dear Sir, Madam, etc. I enclose you a portion of my autograph book and would be very much obliged if you would sign your name on one page and then addressing an envelope to the next person after you on the opposite page, enclosing this letter and the book. If you will, you will greatly oblige
>
> Your obedient servant,
> Oliver Barrett

Barrett included the names and addresses of Oliver Wendell Holmes, Samuel Clemens, Charles Dudley Warner, Harriet Beecher Stowe, General W. T. Sherman, President and Mrs. Hayes and others. Everyone on his illustrious list responded, and the autograph book came home to young Barrett in Illinois with handwritten responses, although Mark

Twain did grumble, writing on his envelope "Pass the damned piece of impudence to [Charles Dudley] Warner."

That boyish impudence evolved into a lifetime passion for collecting, and produced one of the foremost private Lincoln collections of the twentieth century. By the time Sandburg knew Barrett, the affable lawyer had so filled his suburban Chicago house with his treasures that he tried to fool the long-suffering Mrs. Barrett by sneaking in new acquisitions, sometimes stacking them outside a cellar window, entering the front door nonchalantly, and later hauling them in through the window to be sequestered in his cellar library.

Barrett's collection, his knowledge of Lincoln, and his robust friendship lightened some of Sandburg's solitary hours. He sacrificed sleep and pleasure to the work that fall. His correspondence went largely unattended. He churned out the requisite number of movie columns, and gave the rest of his energy to the biography. He declined to be hurried about it, knowing he had to give it time, meticulous research, patient reflection. "Forgive a hardworking sinner for not replying sooner," he apologized to a friend, "But I nearly keeled over and went under with the job I was on, which is done in the main draft and is getting smoothed out; and after I sleep with it a few months will go to a publisher. Not being a Regular Author I haven't jammed it through for the Xmas Trade."

❊

Despite his doubts that it could be done, Sandburg shipped a complete manuscript draft of the Lincoln biography to Harcourt in late September of 1924. "It's rather thrilling to have your book really here," Harcourt wrote before he had time to read it. "What was just an idea that we talked about has meant a great deal to your life for several years now. It's my guess that it will continue to mean something to both of us for a long, long time."

Sandburg filled a few lecture dates that fall, but chafed at any interruption in his writing. "I wonder how I get by to the extent I do and bet every year will be my last," he complained to Sherwood Anderson, who was trying to launch his own lecture career. "I turn the whole thing over to [lecture agent] Feakins, send him all letters of inquiry, and then get slips from him, bills of lading, such as goats and dogs in express cars have tied to them." Anderson, contemplating his own Lincoln book, heard about Sandburg's and observed that "There can't be too many of them." "That's wisdom," Sandburg told him. "I know that any Lincoln book you write will stand up proud, sad, and independent of 'em all. I am making final revisions and may have the book in Harcourt's hands by New Years."

The critic Van Wyck Brooks had joined Harcourt, Brace in 1924, and Harcourt set Brooks to work evaluating Sandburg's Lincoln. He pronounced it "Great stuff." It was Brooks who named the book *Abraham Lincoln: The Prairie Years*. Harcourt offered to pay Sandburg's travel expenses east to go over the manuscript for a day or two. Sandburg was in New York by mid-November, but the process took weeks rather than days. He stayed for a while with Steichen in Connecticut and then settled in with Alfred and Ellen Harcourt in Mt. Vernon, New York, "to stay till Thanksgiving, at least." He had brought with him cuts of photographs from Oliver Barrett's collection of Lincoln pictures. He did not want to use illustrations in the book unless he could get something "clearer and definitely better than the general run," and told Harcourt he was willing to "ditch" the photographs if they were not going to enhance the book. The illustrations were "splendid—great stuff," Harcourt thought, for a "sweet and noble book." He told Sandburg the chapters on married life were masterly.

Back at home in Illinois in December, 1924, Sandburg revised the manuscript. They had decided to publish *Abraham Lincoln: The Prairie Years* in two volumes, and in mid-December he sent Harcourt a revised draft of over a thousand pages, 300,000 words. Donald Brace's father read it immediately in order to estimate the length of the manuscript, and pronounced it the greatest book ever published by Harcourt, Brace and Company. Said Harcourt, "I am inclined to agree with him."

✳

1925–1926

19. Strange Friend

Almost there were times when children and dreamers
looked at Abraham Lincoln and lazily drew their eyelids
half shut and let their hearts roam about him—and they
half-believed him to be a tall horse-chestnut tree or a
rangy horse or a big wagon or log barn full of new-mown
hay—something else or more than a man, a lawyer, a
Republican candidate with principles, a prominent
citizen—something spreading, elusive, and mysterious—
he was the Strange Friend and he was the Friendly
Stranger.

> —Carl Sandburg, *Abraham Lincoln: The Prairie Years*,
>   1926

Carl Sandburg was a reporter and a poet, a chronicler and a minstrel. He was not an historian. He never claimed to be that.
Instead, he said, he began "tentative experiments in writing history." He was acquainted with "books elaborate with learning written
in a dull and clumsy style that oppressed the reader." He was wary of
books "where men of shallow wisdom and showman's tricks had subverted
and falsified so as to fool young people regarding events and characters
where the reality is better than the myth." Sandburg flooded his biography with realistic details of life in Lincoln's era. Only in that turbulent
context, Sandburg believed, could he paint a truthful Lincoln portrait,
for Lincoln was organically a creation of his times.

Abraham Lincoln: The Prairie Years is a vast, epic prose poem, with
Lincoln the central figure in the volatile pageant of nineteenth-century
American life. A man and a nation simultaneously came of age, for
Lincoln grew into manhood as his country faced its own great crisis of
character and identity. "The embryo of modern industrial society was
taking shape," Sandburg wrote. "The history of transportation, of world

colonization and world markets based on power-driven machinery, of international trade, and finance, and standardization, weave through the destiny of Lincoln. . . . A vast play of economic action, in whatever impressionistic manner, must move through the record of Lincoln." Sandburg brought to his study of Lincoln his own long involvement with socialism and his conviction that economics shaped human and national destinies in ways few understood.

He performed patient and humble labor as he examined Lincoln material across the country, constantly seeking new sources. Unfortunately, many Lincoln papers were inaccessible during the early 1920s, and it was not until 1953 that the Abraham Lincoln Association published *The Collected Works of Abraham Lincoln,* superseding older, incomplete and sometimes inaccurate editions of Lincoln's letters, speeches and other writing. More than a fourth of the items in the 1953 collection were newly published, many of them coming from the Robert Todd Lincoln Collection, sealed until July 26, 1947, at the Library of Congress. Many Lincoln papers were held in private collections in the 1920s, protected from public view or as yet undiscovered.

Sandburg was meticulous, painstaking and indefatigable in his quest for documents. In those days before xerography, photostatic reproduction of papers was cumbersome and expensive, if it was available. When Sandburg could afford stenographic help, he paid a typist to copy Lincoln letters. When he could not afford it, he did the work himself. Lecture dates often got him to towns where he needed to examine Lincoln papers. The money he earned from the lectures helped to support his research and to buy the books and periodicals he culled from old bookstalls, or to pay for the occasional luxury of secretarial help. His guitar and poetry produced money to help support his family and provide Margaret's ongoing medical treatment. Working under continuous constraints of time, money and multiple obligations, he drove himself relentlessly.

At home, Margaret's epilepsy presented a more predictable pattern by this time. Resigned to the fact that there was no cure or even reliable treatment, the Sandburgs constantly watched for innovative therapy for the disease, and tried to put it in perspective for their daughter. Paula helped Margaret adjust to the prospect of lifelong illness by muting discussion of it, and guiding her into a busy, if sheltered, life. The teenager spent hours reading and walking, riding her bicycle and exercising, for brisk exercise was considered important in managing epilepsy. She played with her sisters and read to them. "She was wonderful," Helga remembered, "and never discussed her illness with us." A talented musician, Margaret had studied the piano for several years, and found solace and release in music as well as books. The Sandburgs considered sending her away to a boarding school in the Ozarks to study with friends her own age. Sandburg turned to Harcourt for an advance on royalties to pay Margaret's tuition, but for some reason the plan was abandoned, and Margaret kept on with her studies at home.

The little house in Elmhurst was overflowing with the Lincoln work as Sandburg continued his writing and research. His old friend Amy Lowell understood his long toil and his frustration, as well as his sense of mission about the Lincoln book, for she had been expending her failing energy completing the two-volume biography of John Keats. Sandburg sent her thanks and praise in March 1925 when she sent him the Keats books, just two months before her death. "I am on the last long mile of the Lincoln," he told her. "Ain't it hell the way a book walks up to you and makes you write it?—Don't you feel almost predestinarian?"

Sandburg was still overwhelmed with work, trying to fill lecture commitments and to read galleys. Harcourt prodded him by long distance. "When are we going to get back the galleys of 'Lincoln'? There isn't too much time now, since the boys are to have complete samples to carry with them when they start on their travels in the middle of June." Convinced that he had a best-seller on his hands, Harcourt wanted his salesman to carry out advance word of Sandburg's book. He decided also to try to sell the serial rights to magazines. Ida Tarbell's *The Life of Abraham Lincoln*, like the work of John Nicolay and John Hay on Lincoln, had run successfully as a serial in *McClure's* magazine. Harcourt had shown Sandburg's manuscript to several journals without success. Once the book was set in galleys, he tried again, having discovered that "the best books get better when they get into cold type."

The galleys were sent at first to Harry Burton at *McCall's*, who turned them over to a young assistant book editor on his staff, Virginia Kirkus. She stayed up all night reading the manuscript, unable to put it down. The next day she urged Burton to "break precedent and serialize a serious piece of non-fiction." He would never regret it, she told her boss, predicting with the instinct that later made a success of her *Kirkus Reviews* that Sandburg's *Lincoln* was going to be a classic. Burton gave the galleys a cursory look, was not impressed, and called a messenger to return them to Harcourt.

When Virginia Kirkus heard that, she telephoned her former boss, Helen Walker of *Pictorial Review*, urging her to ask for a look at the galleys. Walker, too, stayed up all night to read Sandburg's book, and then urged editor-in-chief Arthur Vance to publish it.

Sandburg, lecturing his way from California to Texas, was out of reach and unaware of Harcourt's endeavors on his behalf, until a telegram caught up with him in Commerce, Texas, April, 4, 1925. It came from his friend Professor A. J. Armstrong at Baylor University in Waco, where Sandburg had just given a lecture-recital. "I RECEIVED ADDRESSED TO ME FOLLOWING TELEGRAM," Armstrong wired Sandburg. "IT MEANS NOTHING TO ME I AM WONDERING IF IT MEANS ANYTHING TO YOU NEW YORK CITY APRIL 3, 1925 HAVE SOLD SERIAL RIGHTS LINCOLN PICTORIAL REVIEW THEY PICK OUT FIVE INSTALLMENTS ABOUT NINE THOUSAND WORDS EACH BEGIN SEPT END JANUARY PUBLISH BOOK NEXT LINCOLN BIRTHDAY YOUR SHARE SERIAL MONEY TWENTY-ONE THOUSAND SIX HUNDRED DOLLARS GET DRUNK AND BE HAPPY LOVE ALFRED."

"HARCOURT WIRES BOOK SERIAL RIGHTS SOLD TO PICTORIAL REVIEW FOR TWENTY THOUSAND," he wired Paula. "FIX THE FLIVER AND BUY A WILD EASTER HAT."

From home in Elmhurst came Paula's answering telegram, her elation singing in the lines: "YOUR WIRE WITH BIG NEWS CAME SUNDAY OVERJOYED LETTER FROM HARCOURT TODAY CONFIRMS FIGURE OF TELEGRAM PURCHASER OF SERIAL RIGHTS WISHES FIGURES KEPT SECRET BECAUSE UNPRECEDENTED FOR NUMBER WORDS USED YOU MUST TAKE LONG VACATION FROM ALL WORK THIS SUMMER ALL JUBILATING HERE IN GAY EASTER BONNETS EVERY OPPORTUNITY ASSURED MARGARET NOW HIGH HOPES AND BUSHELS OF LOVE PAULA."

They had shared sixteen years of unremitting hard work. Paula's steady faith in him was often his only affirmation, and always his ballast. The poetry, newspaper work and lectures had carried Sandburg's voice to a wide audience, but there was never quite enough money, especially now that they faced an indefinite and often expensive struggle for treatment of Margaret's epilepsy. Sandburg's "predestinarian" Lincoln journey had brought them hope and promise. Ironically, Sandburg's sojourn in the past had secured the future, for him and his wife and children.

He told Harcourt, "This is the first time I've understood something about the emotions of holding the lucky number in a lottery."

"Vance begged that we would not tell how much they paid for the material," Harcourt wrote Sandburg. "I told him that he ought to be proud to have it known." *Pictorial Review* would pay Harcourt, Brace and Company $27,000, of which, by contract, eighty percent, $21,600, would go to Sandburg. "This, I think, is the biggest bona fide price I have heard of for an American serial," Harcourt told Sandburg, "—that is, for the number of words used. The Designer paid $50,000 for [Sinclair] Lewis' 'Arrowsmith,' but they used about 120,000 words and ran the story through an entire year."

Vance had previously serialized Edith Wharton's fiction, most recently paying $32,000 in 1924 for *The Mother's Recompense*. His offer to Sandburg was singularly high for nonfiction serial rights, however, especially for the length of the excerpts Vance published.

In mid-May Sandburg went to New York to work with Harcourt on the myriad details of producing the book. The preparation of illustrations was particularly time-consuming. Oliver Barrett and New York businessman Frederick Hill Meserve opened their prolific collections of pictures to him. When Sandburg called on Meserve the first time, he took along some of the Lincoln manuscript. As Meserve sat listening to Sandburg read aloud in his "extraordinary voice," he was moved by the "marvelous blending of poetry and history." The two men then looked through Meserve's huge collection of photographs. There were more than thirty thousand items all told. Sandburg held up one Mathew Brady negative after another, Meserve recalled, "exclaiming at their beauty, studying the prints made from them, lingering over the faces of those men and women for he knew human stories behind those faces."

*

Thanks to the money from the *Pictorial Review*, the Sandburgs were able for the first time ever to arrange a family vacation. Paula and the children went to a rented cottage in the village of Williams Bay, Wisconsin, where Sandburg planned to join them as soon as he could get away from his work. To Paula's delight, the children played quietly and contentedly, lulled by the " 'sea-change' in their natures." Helga, nearly seven, loved to paddle about in the water, and to float within the safety of her ring floater. Janet "never looked so well in her life," Paula wrote to Carl, "—actually has rosy cheeks. Margaret has a natural liking for exercise in the water—whereas out of the water, she must have others to play with or she doesn't exercise." Fourteen-year-old Margaret and nine-year-old Janet swam twice daily even on cold cloudy days. While Helga grew "rosier and chubbier," she developed a stubborn cough, which Paula attributed to her tonsils.

Sandburg's hoped-for arrival was postponed by work on the Lincoln page proofs, until he finally decided that he could not leave Chicago, even to be with his family. Disappointed, Paula worried over his health. "I hope you will somehow manage to get some rest after the book gets into page proofs," she urged him. She hoped he would take a real vacation when the page proofs were finished, and before the fall lecturing began. Paula had to curtail the vacation for the rest of the family, however, when Helga's cough persisted.

That summer of 1925 Sandburg worked on revisions and page proofs for the two volumes of *Abraham Lincoln: The Prairie Years*, nearly twelve hundred pages in all. There was no letup on his other work. He steadily met his *Daily News* commitments, reviewing Wallace Beery's *The Lost World* as a landmark film, and admiring W. C. Fields, Alfred Lunt and Carol Dempster in D. W. Griffith's *Sally of the Sawdust*, a blend of "misery and monkeyshines, and majesty." Sandburg was lukewarm, however, to Cecil B. De Mille's *The Ten Commandments*. It was, he wrote, De Mille's "masterpiece," into which he put everything he knew "about showmanship and what is called hokum." Privately, Sandburg called the film a "monument of tripe." Deeming Charlie Chaplin's *The Gold Rush* his best photoplay yet, Sandburg saw the film three times. Chaplin was, he said, "an independent artist forty ways."

The movies were welcome diversions, and by now Sandburg could turn out his reviews swiftly, almost glibly. His mind was always first and firmly fixed on the Lincoln work. Even after the book was set in galleys, he was still adding new material.

There were other Lincoln biographies on the horizon, Sandburg knew. William E. Barton's two-volume *Life of Abraham Lincoln* came out in 1925 and Sandburg thought it was "a hell of a book." Senator Albert J. Beveridge was hard at work on the two volumes of *Abraham Lincoln: 1809–1858*, which he would not live to complete. Beveridge invited Sandburg to visit him in the late summer of 1925, but Sandburg declined, pleading the press of his schedule. Beveridge apparently saw Sandburg as a rival, telling "various persons in various cities" that Sandburg's book might not be "authentic." The charges drifted to Sandburg's ears, by way of mutual friends. Angered, Sandburg wrote a long letter to Beveridge which he did not mail. Instead, he gave it to Oliver Barrett. Sandburg had discovered Lincoln's habit of ventilating his anger in letters which he never mailed, and it was a habit Sandburg came to share. "He had written angry letters filled with hard names and hot arguments," Sandburg wrote of Lincoln. "And such letters he had thrown in the stove. He gave the advice that it was healthy to write a hot letter and then burn it." Sandburg's "hot letter" to Beveridge dissipated his anger, with no affront to Beveridge, and he could resume his concentration on the last stages of the Lincoln book.

Sandburg asked Harcourt to send page proofs of the biography to Oliver Barrett and Ida Tarbell. "Yourself and Oliver R. Barrett are the only persons receiving advance sheets," Sandburg told Miss Tarbell, "as you are the two who have helped me most, which I believe is made clear in my preface."

As page proofs were being prepared, Sandburg spoke to Harcourt about a new project. "Sometime within the week a manuscript for some songs will be mailed to you. These are the ones of my collection that I want to be sure to have the right to use in a book one or two years from now. . . . There will be three versions of Franky and Johnny and some precious spirituals and other things." Sandburg asked Harcourt to help him copyright the songs "not so much that we must have exclusive use of them as that others shall not bar us from using them."

Beset as they were with the Lincoln work, Sandburg joked that "when we get around to a song book you'll have more hell yet along with me."

But all work came to a standstill for Sandburg in September of 1925. He had driven himself for years, and the past months had been intensely busy. He was still a vigorous, youthful man at forty-seven, but he had carried a heavy load of work and stress since the onset of Margaret's illness four years earlier. Overcome with fatigue, he experienced alarming chest pains. His doctor and good friend Arthur "Jim" Freese diagnosed "heart fatigue," prescribing a careful diet and much sleep and rest. He cautioned Sandburg to take better care of himself. Sandburg told Harcourt he was following doctor's orders for "a pretty strict regimen" with "little to eat and long sleeps." When he felt like working, he spent time "lazying along on songs" for the newly conceived song book.

Soon he was feeling well enough to get back to work. "I'm waiting for them doggone page proofs," he told Harcourt. "If they don't come in a day or two I'll dig up another letter of Lincoln to his wife and wire you for godsake get it in."

By the end of October Sandburg had done the last piece of work on the biography. "LINCOLN BOOK COMMITTED TO THE EVERLASTING DEEP," he wired Paula from New York. "STARTING HOME. LOVE TO YOU AND EVERYBODY."

That fall excerpts from Sandburg's Lincoln book started to appear in issues of the *Pictorial Review*. He traveled back to New York to put the final touches on the biography and to make his first phonograph record for the RCA Victor Talking Machine Company. "I breathe easier about the book now," he told Harcourt; "until this week it was always as though even if I stopped to rest I still had the crop to get in or the tunnel end to arrive at."

Harcourt aimed to have the books bound and ready for release in time for Lincoln's birthday in February 1926. There would be a handsome limited edition; Sandburg reserved sets one and two for himself, and copies for Barrett and Charlie Chaplin. Harcourt and Sandburg talked over ways to hold down the cost of the regular edition. Doing away with a gilt-edged page would save a nickel or more a set, Harcourt said. Sandburg liked the idea. The book should reflect its subject, he thought. "The gilt top of the book is easy to dispense with. Maybe it should go in the brown of butternut jeans, or an ochre of southern Indiana and Illinois clay."

As the year wound down into winter, Sandburg had to let go of the biography and "ask the Almighty to take [care] of the whole shooting match of us." For the time being, he had done all he could do. He was excited about the prospect of sending his songs into American homes by way of the records he made with RCA in December. He recorded "Elanoy" (Illinois) and other songs out of Lincoln's time in honor of his own book and Lincoln's birthday. He marveled that records could reach a million people or more who "never heard of the *New York Times.*"

The Sandburgs spent an especially happy Christmas together that momentous year. Margaret's health was the most stable it had been since 1921. The unexpected boon of the biography gave them a new sense of financial comfort and stability. They were usually joined at Christmas by Ed Steichen and beautiful Dana Desboro Glover, an actress and photographer whom he had met at the New York School of Photography. There was mystery about whether they were officially married, but they had been together since 1923. Steichen had taken a lucrative job as chief photographer for Condé Nast Publications, doing portrait and fashion photography for *Vanity Fair* and *Vogue.* Dana took some haunting photographs of Sandburg, with the focus on his burning eyes.

On Christmas Eve of 1925, Sandburg's *Chicago Daily News* column carried a summary reflection of the state of American motion pictures. His duties as film critic had exposed him to a vivid montage of films that year—the "chilling thrills" of *The Phantom of the Opera;* the "first rate" Rin-Tin-Tin movie *The Clash of the Wolves,* in which, Sandburg said, Rin-Tin-Tin rose to "heights of intelligence which even he has never before revealed"; and Chaplin's *The Gold Rush.* "Americans are at last beginning to make motion pictures their own," he wrote, achieving "what used to be impossible . . . telling stories of people's characters rather than their adventures."

That new American cinematic focus on character coincided with Sandburg's purpose in the Lincoln biography—to create a portrait of a complex character, full of "lights and shadows and changing tints." Sandburg used those very words, with their movie overtones, to state his purpose in the preface to the biography. "The wind is blowing a healthy lack of sentimentalism in pictures, a strong, lusty sense of humor that is one with American life." As a biographer, he sought the same outcome—to create a Lincoln portrait, an American portrait that was "one with American life."

✳

"A biography, sirs, should begin—with the breath of a man/when his eyes first meet the light of day—then working on/through to the death when the light of day is gone . . ," Sandburg wrote in the poem "Biography":

> . . . so the biography then is finished—unless you reverse the order
> and begin with the death and work back to the birth—
> starting the life with a coffin, moving back to a cradle . . .

Sandburg considered using that device. When the accrual of detail and insight built to the climax of Lincoln's election to the Presidency and his departure for Washington, Sandburg believed the biography had reached its logical conclusion. For a time after he had committed his book to the "everlasting deep," he had no desire or will to write further about Lincoln. Thus he conceived a preface which began with Lincoln in the coffin and moved back to Lincoln in the cradle. "I made an attempt at covering all the rest of [Lincoln's] life by the device of an introduction," Sandburg said. "This introduction would begin at the death of Lincoln and work back to the day he left Illinois. The reader could then turn to the book and begin with the birth of Lincoln."

Sandburg and Harcourt decided not to use the preface, and it was filed away in 1925. Rediscovered years later, it would be published in a limited edition for circulation among Sandburg's friends, and go on to be syndicated nationally in newspapers and journals. Part of it was woven into the address Sandburg gave to a Joint Session of Congress in 1959 on the one hundred and fiftieth anniversary of Lincoln's birth. Writing in the preface of Lincoln's death, Sandburg concluded: "The facts and myths of his life are to be an American possession, shared widely over the world, for thousands of years, as the tradition of Knute or Alfred, Lao-tse or Diogenes, Pericles or Caesar, are kept. This because he was not only a genius in the science of neighborly human relationships and an artist in the personal handling of life from day to day, but a strange friend and a friendly stranger to all forms of life that he met."

In theory, Sandburg's shift from poetry to biography indicated a move from the imaginative to the historical mode. Actually, the biography he created was poetic and highly imaginative, and therein lay its weakness and its strength. Sandburg's Lincoln biography was epic in scale, attempting to "say everything," as he had vowed to do when he was first becoming a writer. Yet his all-encompassing view of his subject sometimes overwhelmed his ability to pare and shape, to intensify by economy and restraint ("boiling down," his earlier editor Negley Cochran had called it). His occasional failure to discern and emphasize major themes and mute minor ones cost his work proportion. As he dove deeper into history, he began to relinquish the tighter focus of his earlier poetry and prose for the sprawling range of fiction and biography as he conceived them.

No history or biography could be better than its writer, Sandburg thought. The "faults and merits" of the author would "stand forth" in his work, and could not be hidden. From Cochran at the *Day Book*, he had learned that there is no such thing as "uncolored" news. Sandburg believed that the character of a biographer would inevitably be written into his work.

Biography had depleted him like no other writing he had done. It exacted of him all he knew and felt of life and the human spirit. Biographers "stood considerable wear and tear," he mused. He felt like a "battered gypsy palmist."

Harcourt mounted an expensive promotional campaign for the biography and priced the two volumes of *The Prairie Years* at ten dollars for the set. By publication day in February 1926 more than ten thousand sets had already been sold in advance. The book sales got off to a "high pressure" start, Harcourt told Sandburg, going into a fourth printing during the first month after publication. The limited edition quickly sold out, with rare-book dealers and private collectors clamoring for more, and the price already escalating. Sensing a long, successful run for the book, Harcourt began to promote it even more aggressively to capitalize on nationwide interest in Sandburg's Lincoln. In the first year alone, forty-eight thousand customers owned the set.

The "overnight" success of the biography brought a flood of invitations to lecture and write articles for journals and prefaces to books. Sandburg gave a half-hour radio address in Chicago on Lincoln's birthday; listeners called him a natural for the new medium, with his mellifluous voice and pithy Lincoln anecdotes. The Victor Talking Machine Company brought out his first recording, highlighted by Lincoln songs. For the first time in his life he had wept over a phonograph record that was the most perfect piece of reproduction he had ever heard, music critic Alfred Frankenstein told him.

With a cluster of successful projects, Sandburg stood at the apex of his career.

✳

Critical reaction to *Abraham Lincoln: The Prairie Years* was swift and divergent. Some historians and critics condemned the book because of its unorthodoxy. It did not adhere to precedent about how history should be written. There were no footnotes. There was the interjection of Sandburg's imagination and lyricism. He conjectured. He used apocryphal stories, put words into Lincoln's mouth, thoughts into his head. Some thought Sandburg had written the biography as if it were a novel or a poem.

Benjamin Thomas in *Portrait for Posterity*, his 1947 study of Lincoln and his biographers, wrote, retrospectively, "Can we accept as a Lincoln authority a poet, an author of fairy tales, a singer of folk songs, a man who thumbed his nose at the precepts of the historical professions, broke rules of literary composition with impunity and gloried in his unconventionality?" Thomas concluded that Sandburg could and should be accepted as a Lincoln authority, and believed that *Abraham Lincoln: The Prairie Years* was "entitled to high rank in Lincoln literature." Like many other critics, Thomas saw the similarities between Sandburg and Lincoln: "He grew up in the same part of the country where Lincoln spent most of his life; and he must have been attracted to him early. Like Lincoln, he is a common man with an uncommon mind. He has the same ideas about America that Lincoln had."

Sandburg's work was "one of the great American biographies and the most beautiful of all the biographies of Abraham Lincoln," wrote Fanny Butcher in the *Chicago Tribune*. Robertus Love of the *St. Louis Post-Dispatch* pronounced it "the greatest book produced thus far along in the twentieth century and in the English tongue."

Mark Van Doren told *The Nation*'s readers: "It is Sandburg the artist, the epic poet, who has attacked this largest and most complicated of all American subjects—the subject being, of course, not merely Lincoln himself, though Lincoln was complicated enough, but in addition the whirlpool of cultures out of which he was flung into fame." Van Doren found much of the "poetry" of the book annoying, and said so frankly, but believed that Sandburg's strength as a biographer rested on his immersion in the facts of Lincoln's times and his grasp of Lincoln's essential mystery. "Few men and women are truly mysterious," Van Doren noted. "Lincoln was, and in my opinion Mr. Sandburg has presented the elements of that mystery more subtly and more completely than I have ever seen them presented before." Van Doren described accurately Sandburg's strategies in composing the biography:

> He walked and talked through the many towns of Kentucky, Indiana, and Illinois where people had known Lincoln. . . . He read bundles of letters and ran his hands over shelves containing other mementos. He pushed his mind to the outermost limits of the world which was to influence Lincoln and which he was to influence—the world of European and American politics, industry, travel, science, letters, religion and art. Then he knew his imagination back to make itself at home in the civilization which actually shaped Lincoln, or helped to shape him. Here is God's plenty indeed. Here is the lining of the old Mid-Western mind. Here are the songs all people sang, the poems they recited, the proverbs they spoke, the superstitions they could not discard, the machines they used, the clothes they wore, the facts they learned in the newspapers, the gods they swore by, the dishes they ate, the jests they laughed at. As Mr. Sandburg goes on he becomes drunk with data, and in true Homeric fashion compiles long lists of things.

The *New York Times Book Review* considered the biography more important as a piece of creative writing than as a contribution to Lincoln literature, and Sandburg's achievement "an intensely individual one, suffused by the qualities which are peculiarly his own as a poet." The book would offend "superpatriots," George Currie contended, because it revealed Lincoln's imperfections.

British critic Leonard Woolf wrote in another *Nation* review that he had "rarely, if ever, read a biography which gave one such an over-powering sense of reality in the character of the biographee." Said S. L. Cool in the *Boston Transcript*, "It has done us good to read this able, rugged book. We doubt not that it has done Carl Sandburg much good to write it. Such is the blessing which Abraham Lincoln bestows on his biographers." From the London *Times*, where there had been little en-thusiasm for Sandburg's poetry, came high praise for the biography: "It says much for Mr. Sandburg's clarity of thought and expression that he makes us see American politics almost intelligibly."

Sandburg perpetuated many prevailing Lincoln stereotypes, yet his biography was lauded as a departure from the conventional Lincoln my-thology. "When so many have tried to build about the homely, lonely, awkward figure of Lincoln something of an aristocrat . . . here comes the ragged, barefooted truth, in such story-book simplicity, such brass-nailed veracity, such ax-handled sturdiness as makes it forever sure for people to know that Lincoln was a man of the people," an unidentified reviewer wrote for the *International Labor News Service*. "With glorious fidelity to the truth of the matter, Sandburg has knocked the aristocracy idea into the middle of the duck pond and it is done for." Sandburg had revealed that Lincoln was hen-pecked, that he could play "tight and rather cheap country politics," George Currie wrote in the *Brooklyn Daily Eagle*. "And Herndon, [Lincoln's] law partner, is quoted thus: 'Mr. Lincoln had a strong if not terrible passion for women. He could hardly keep his hands off a woman and yet, much to his credit, he lived a pure and virtuous life.' Moreover, the Great Emancipator once fought a legal case for a bevy of filles de joie." Reviewer after reviewer took note of what was then viewed as a uniquely balanced revelation of Lincoln's complex character.

"Sandburg's Lincoln is not the conventional Lincoln," one critic wrote, "but surely it is the actual Lincoln, the elemental Lincoln." "Out of the pages of this book emerges no heroic figure," Harry Hansen wrote, "no epic character, no titan towering above puny men. This is the book of the railsplitter, of the country storekeeper, the young lawyer, the frontier advocate, the practical backwoods politician. . . . The danger to the Lincoln legend was not from those who tried to make him less than he was; it came from those who were erecting him into a god of the new Augustan age of American commercial expansion. Lincoln was a human being of contradictions, faults and qualities."

Sandburg penetrated Lincoln's soul, critic C. M. Morrison suggested, "helped destroy the growing Lincoln myth, the demi-god legend and put a man back in its place. It is better so."

But the ink was hardly dry on the 962 pages of the two volumes of *The Prairie Years* before corrections started coming in. Sandburg attributed to Montesquieu a quotation from Tocqueville. He misspelled the name of the chief justice of the supreme court of the District of Columbia. He got De Witt Clinton's father born in the wrong place. Many readers wrote directly to Sandburg to set him straight, and other letters came to him via his publisher. A Minnesota reader sent this advice:

> The dome of the Capitol was not started until 1858. I noted some reference to the dome at the time Lincoln was running for Congress, in the version of "The Prairie Years" as printed in Pictorial Review.
>
> Please don't imagine me a captious nincompoop for whom a trifling anachronism could destroy full appreciation of your beautiful work. But I do think for the sake of enhancing faith in your "Abraham Lincoln" as history, it would be well to be right in the matter of the dome.

"Another critic of the old school tells me that the real potato bug did not cross the Mississippi coming from the West until the fifties or sixties. You have young Abe picking potato bugs off the plants. Is this an anachronism, or no?" said one letter from Harcourt, Brace and Company. "I saw a piece in some paper last week that you have Nancy Hanks singing 'Greenland's Icy Mountains' just a little time before the song was written," Harcourt told Sandburg good-humoredly. "I don't see what difference that makes—it's a good song."

Sandburg made corrections in successive editions of the biography, but stood by his sources when he was sure of them. When Lincoln biographer William Barton criticized Sandburg's description of how a rifle was loaded in Kentucky in Lincoln's time, Sandburg would not alter his account because it was "with abridgement, taken almost word for word from Audubon's autobiography; it's Audubon against Barton and we'll leave it to posterity as to which is sending an empty booming sound against the whiffletree."

✳

Sandburg sent author's copies of the biography to old friends who held his special regard. "Your Lincoln grows greater, more masterful and wonderful with each challenging and fascinating page," Eugene Debs told him, assuring him his fame "is now, if it had not been before, secure and eternal." Sandburg told Debs that he would like some time to write a biographical sketch of him that would have in it the "breath and feeling of the Lincoln." "[That] is most generous in you and flattering to me," Debs told Sandburg, "but I am sure that there is not enough of me to warrant any such venture."

From his former boss Negley Cochran came the observation that Sandburg had written himself into the Lincoln portrait. "You spent a lot of time rummaging around in old papers and things searching for fragments of Lincoln's soul so you could put them together for folks to look at—and, of course, you got his soul all mixed up with your own—then sought to have 'em trot together in double harness in a book," Cochran wrote. "In reading your book I caught your own soul peeping out from between pages, paragraphs and words. Men are like that, Carl—If they have a soul they want to pack it away some place where it will keep."

"You note that I scribbled myself through the Lincoln book," Sandburg answered. "Well, who pounded it into my poor head for five years straight that there is no 'uncolored' news?"

Alice Corbin Henderson, too, saw Sandburg in his Lincoln. "For two weeks I've been living with your Lincoln, and with you," she wrote. "I simply can't say how fine I think the book is—it's my guess that it will live as long as this civilization. . . . I was struck by things which you knew about Lincoln because you know them about yourself—as that passage about Lincoln's standing outside himself, p. 250, Vol. 2. You give such hunks of the man, and all of him—no other book has ever approached giving the whole of him as this does."

It was, said Alfred Stieglitz, "Truly a rare book—beautiful from every angle." Sandburg's longtime "friend and helper" Ida Tarbell thanked him for her copy by saying "I am hugging your book to my heart. . . . I feel as if the thing was made for me, personally."

"You have made a live boy of him," Sandburg's old champion Harriet Monroe told him after she had read the "wonderfully vivid early chapters," and continued, "I am sure he grows up into a live man. I congratulate you upon doing a grand and very human biography of a grand and very human man."

His former professor Philip Green Wright found the biography a "prose poem." "The fact is," Wright told Sandburg, "you are so much a poet by nature that poetry suffuses your ostensibly prose works, and to use this irrepressible background of poetry which gives wings to your prose is more delightful where your genius takes this form than in your confessedly poetic productions."

"I am proud of you," William Allen White wrote Sandburg. "Mondays, Wednesdays, Fridays and Sundays, I think you are a better poet than a historian; and Tuesdays, Thursdays, and Saturdays I think you are a better historian than a poet. But you are a great man, net, nothing off for cash."

"By God you pulled it off," Malcolm Cowley told Sandburg admiringly. "Your Lincoln is good; it belongs with Moby Dick and Leaves of Grass and Huckleberry Finn; it's the best piece of American prose which has been written in the last _____ years. Fill in the blank yourself, but use at least two figures."

✳

In the first quarter of the twentieth century, Americans continued to feel close to Lincoln, especially in the Midwest. There were those still living who had heard or seen the living Lincoln, and still others, like Sandburg himself, for whom Lincoln's image was indelibly stamped on mind and heart as a national symbol. Sandburg was becoming a Lincolnesque character himself; his natural, instinctive identification with Lincoln verged at times on the excessive. But his vision of Lincoln was national more than personal.

Sandburg deeply believed that the American nation needed "to build on its own traditions," to find its own sense of national identity, particularly in the aftermath of the war. Who better than Lincoln could speak in the twentieth century, as he had in the nineteenth, to a nation in the process of discovering itself?

Sandburg did not pretend that his approach was objective or scholarly. He sought to let Lincoln and his times speak for themselves. Always he held close to Lincoln, tried when possible to stand in his shoes, look out at his world through his eyes, read the books which shaped his intellect. He adhered first and foremost to the "high document" of Lincoln's letters, papers, speeches and writings, insofar as they were available in the early 1920s. In the utterances of Lincoln's hand and voice, Sandburg found his own intimacy with Lincoln's mind and heart. He gathered that evidence scrupulously, studied it deeply, and then applied to his interpretation of Lincoln the man all his own poetic and human gifts of "imagination, intuition, experience, prayer, silence, sacrifice, and the laughter next door to tears."

"Going farther month by month in stacks and bundles of fact and legend," Sandburg said in the preface, "I found invisible companionships that surprised me." He hoped those companionships would come alive for his readers as well.

Beyond the biography's astounding success was Sandburg's own growth. His exploration of Lincoln's interior life illuminated Sandburg's prolonged search for his own identity. Lincoln challenged him as a creative artist and a human being, and turned his life irrevocably toward new vistas of meaning and expression.

✳

By 1926 Carl Sandburg was articulating his expansive vision of American life in multiple forms, speaking the language of poetry, of prose, and now, of American folk music, with equal vigor and conviction. He did not pause between projects, declining to rest after the depleting Lincoln work. He loved his work, first of all, had to do it, found his release in the enthralling process of creating new forms, illuminating new subjects. Negley Cochran, long one of his mentors, recognized that fundamental fact in 1926, writing to Sandburg about it in a March 31 letter: "Man is his own God and is responsible for his own immortality. He launches his soul in a book, a poem, a song, a painting, a musical composition, an invention, a service. Michael Angelo painted his soul all over the walls of the Vatican." Sandburg had done so in his Lincoln, Cochran told him.

Sandburg jumped immediately into work on the new folk music book, believing it would "probably be of momentous importance in what is called Americanization work," he told Donald Brace at Harcourt, Brace and Company that March. He hoped it would advance "the training of those galoots Emerson had in mind when he said, 'We have persons born and reared in this country who culturally have not come over from Europe.' "

Sandburg tried then with as much energy and deliberation as any American writer to articulate the national spirit, to define the American Dream in those years after the cataclysm of world war. Pound, Eliot, Fitzgerald, Hemingway and many other American writers were living in Europe or writing about it. Sandburg the son of immigrants, once he returned from Scandinavia in 1918, stayed staunchly at home, devoting himself to journalism, poetry, children's fiction, biography and now folk music—to his "Americanization work." On the heels of his reincarnation of Lincoln, he wanted to publish the songs of the people, one more rendition of their history and spirit. For Sandburg the evocation of Lincoln and the transcription of the American idiom in folk music were one and the same mission. He had created a "certain portrait" of Lincoln and in so doing had revealed his own soul. But he was ultimately after the soul of the nation he lived in, seeking to give the people a mirror of themselves, in reality and possibility.

Endowed from boyhood with physical vigor, he was heedless of warning signs of fatigue. He spent himself totally, not pausing to reflect that the prodigious energy he had enjoyed in his teens, twenties and thirties was not guaranteed to support the rigorous schedule he laid out for himself in his forties. Sandburg wrapped up nearly four years' work on the Lincoln biography and immediately threw himself headlong into work on the songbook. He would pay the price for it in ways he did not imagine. There were warning signs he did not heed that summer, exhilarated as he was by the growing success of the biography and the promise of the new song book. He promised Arthur Vance of *Pictorial Review* that he would take a few days off in July 1926 to go sailing with him aboard his yacht *Pandora III*. By June, however, he had to renege. He was too worn out and sick even for such a pleasure trip. "I have to give up the July 27th date just as I've had to give up all meat and all wet goods for the past three weeks, including the fine mild home brew. . . . Forgive my easy assurance of some weeks back that I was getting into form for life-guard service."

He was hard at work again in August, writing for the *Chicago Daily News*. "Paper today looks like you were the whole team," Henry Justin

Smith told him on August 14, 1926. Harcourt kept him up to date on the continuing success of the biography, negotiating with a Frenchman who wanted to translate it, letting him know on August 18 that more than 15,000 sets had been sold, passing along the news that he had earned $18,000 in royalties during the first six months. When Lilla Perry visited the Sandburgs one hot August afternoon, she noted that Sandburg looked older. "People keep asking me what I am working on now," he told her, "as if a fellow didn't have to have a little while to catch his breath before tackling a new job. I usually say I'm writing a dissertation on Diogenes."

He enjoyed the company of scientist and author Paul de Kruif one August Saturday night in Chicago. They walked and looked at Chicago's "high buildings," and talked about their mutual friend H. L. Mencken, as Sandburg reported to Mencken in a letter, his normal high spirits seemingly restored. "I said that whereas Bertrand Russell was the cardinal of a sort of episcopacy of liberals who like their holy words and who are for Revolution if it will come like some of the dogs in want ads: 'Must be house broke,' . . . I said that about the time your episcopacy gets going and they enrobe you in the investitures you let a fart and the show, as such, goes bust."

※

In the decade since the publication of *Chicago Poems* Sandburg had hit his stride, personally and professionally. While his fellow poets Frost and Lindsay were, in Frost's words, "barding around" the American college and university circuit, and teaching, Sandburg was holding down his *Daily News* job, giving his lecture-recitals and working on fiction and biography as well as poetry. Frost dove deeper and deeper into poetry during that decade of Sandburg's departure into other forms, producing four volumes, winning the Pulitzer Prize for *New Hampshire* in 1924, reaping national honors for his work. Sandburg's friend Vachel Lindsay ventured far from home on recital tours, battled illness, depression and loneliness, and transmuted some of that into his drawings and his vivid, eccentric poems, publishing six books of poetry and prose from 1916 to 1926. American audiences saw a "strident" performer; British critics deemed him America's jazz poet. Lindsay hated both labels. Like Frost he was honored as Harvard's Phi Beta Kappa poet: Frost got the award in 1916, Lindsay in 1922.

In Sandburg, Lindsay and Edgar Lee Masters, Illinois gave the nation a triumvirate of poets in the first quarter of the twentieth century. Harriet Monroe's *Poetry* had honored the three midwesterners in consecutive years with its Levinson Prize in poetry: Sandburg won it in 1914, Lindsay in 1915, Masters in 1916. During the next decade, while Sandburg strode forward with his experiments in poetry, fiction and biography, Lindsay was working himself into a brilliant obscurity and Masters was seeking to reprise his masterpiece, *Spoon River Anthology*. "With *Spoon River*, Masters arrived—and left," Louis Untermeyer noted. Masters published seven volumes of poetry between 1916 and 1926, and five novels. He began to write out of a desperate and bitter expediency, for in 1923 he lost his money, property and reputation in a public divorce battle. He began to use his art as a vehicle for revenge; his former wife was his target in poetry in 1923, his former mistress in fiction in 1924.

Whether the poet's personal life is viewed as tangential to or the essence of his poetry, the private lives of these four contemporaries differ significantly. Frost's well-documented family life was torn with misunderstanding and tragedy. Lindsay, imprisoned by illness and solitude for many years, was a virginal bridegroom at forty-six when, relinquishing his long love for Sara Teasdale, he met and suddenly married a teacher much younger than he. Masters's private life was one long tragic fall after a successful career as an attorney, and a seemingly congenial marriage. The prolonged, vituperative destruction of his private life in Chicago ended his hopes for a public literary life there, and he left the Midwest for New York and a perpetual descent into anger.

There were occasional speculations about Sandburg's life beyond home, conjectures about dalliances on the road. Yet during that first decade of his literary success, the only confirmable facts of his personal life were his loyalty to Paula, his unswerving devotion to the children, his determination to do everything in his power to protect his dependent daughters. He and Paula managed, despite the growing encroachments of his fame, to sustain a warm, stable home life, a rare accomplishment among literary families of the time.

For all his success, there was an inner core of humility in Sandburg that verged on insecurity. He was still a maverick. Never mind. He had learned years ago from a jazz musician and vaudeville performer that a successful "artiste" had only to please eighty percent of his audience, and even that was quite a feat. Sandburg was writing for his countrymen now, and for himself, true to his own, independent vision, an iconoclast of forms and themes. The People seemed to be listening, no matter how vigorously certain critics had dismissed his work.

His Lincoln biography would secure his children's future and give him his own place in American letters. Born as it was from his own past, and his heart, he had dedicated it to his parents, his gentle, aging mother and his father, dead now for fifteen years. His vast, flawed, vividly alive monument to Abraham Lincoln and the American Dream began with a simple tribute:

"To August and Clara Sandburg," he wrote, "Workers on the Illinois Prairie."

PART THREE

THE LINCOLN YEARS

———— ✳ ————

1926–1929

20. American Singer

There is presented herein a collection of 280 songs,
ballads, ditties, brought together from all regions of
America. . . . It is an All-American affair, marshaling
the genius of thousands of original singing Americans. . . .
The American scene and pageant envisioned by one
American singer and touched off in one of his passages is
measurably vocal here. "Forever alive, forever forward
they go, they go, I know not where they go, but I know
that they go toward the best, toward something great."

—Carl Sandburg [with a quotation from Whitman],
Introduction to *The American Songbag*, 1927

One summer night in 1925, Sandburg and his *Chicago Daily News* cronies Lloyd Lewis and Ben Hecht and their physician friend Dr. Morris Fishbein had a rousing party for Sinclair Lewis, just home from Europe and enjoying the success of *Arrowsmith*. There was much good talk, liquor and laughter. Toward the end of the evening, Fishbein asked Sandburg to sing. Sandburg chose "The Buffalo Skinners," which Lewis described as a "great rough song, all about starvation, blood, fleas, hides, entrails, thirst, and Indian-devils, and men being cheated out of their wages and killing their employers to get even—a novel, an epic novel boiled down to simple words." Sandburg had gotten the song from Texas folklorist John Lomax. Its words, according to Sandburg, were "blunt, direct, odorous, plain and made-to-hand." The final stanza laments a fading era:

Oh, it's now we've crossed Pease River and homeward we are bound,
No more in that hell-fired country shall ever we be found.
Go home to our wives and sweethearts, tell others not to go,
For God's forsaken the buffalo range and the damned old buffalo.

Lloyd Lewis remembered that Sandburg sang the song with special pathos: "It was like a funeral song to the pioneer America that is gone, and when Carl was done Sinclair Lewis spoke up, his face streaked with tears, 'That's the America I came home to. That's it.'"

Sandburg knew only a few simple chords on the guitar, and his mellow baritone voice was untrained, but he could hold an audience transfixed when he sang a folk song. He had collected songs since his hobo days, filling his pocket notebooks with lyrics and devising his own simple notation system to jot down melodies. He hunted for nineteenth-century songbooks such as the "famous oblong songbook of the pioneer days in the middle west" which Abraham Lincoln and Ann Rutledge sang from in the Turledge tavern in New Salem, Kentucky. He gathered spirituals from Isadora Bennett Reed, DuBose Heyward, Julia Peterkin and other Southern friends. IWW leaders and labor organizers fed him prison and jail songs and labor anthems. He collected songs from five different wars, as well as the exuberant nonsense of what he called "Picnic and Hayrack Follies" and "Darn Fool Ditties."

Everywhere he lectured people flocked to him with songs. Often he sang the night away with hosts on college campuses, or in towns where he magnetized those who shared his pleasure in making music. He was curious about the vagrant past of songs which had made their way from overseas to the American highlands, prairies and frontier. He liked to study the musical migration which often mirrored the nation's history. Anonymous Americans sent him songs, as did musicologists, folklorists, and friends. Robert Frost, H. L. Mencken, Sherwood Anderson, Arthur Vance of *Pictorial Review*, Eugene and Agnes Meyer, playwright Lynn Riggs, and poets Louis and Jean Starr Untermeyer passed tunes his way. "Do you want the words and music of 'I am a Hundred Percent American'?" asked Mencken. "I have them if you do."

✳

The Lincoln biography launched, Sandburg plunged deeper into his new work as the self-appointed emissary of the American past. "I have gone hither and yon over the United States meeting audiences to whom I talked about poetry and art, read my verses, and closed a program with a half- or quarter-hour of songs, giving verbal footnotes with each song," Sandburg said of his life as a troubadour-historian. "These itineraries have included now about two-thirds of the state universities of the country, audiences ranging from 3,000 people at the University of California to 30 at the Garret Club in Buffalo, New York, and organizations as diverse as the Poetry Society of South Carolina and the Knife and Fork Club of South Bend, Indiana."

At the Eclectic Club at Wesleyan University in Connecticut, he first heard "Foggy, Foggy Dew," which became one of his favorite songs. He sang it often in public and private, for Sinclair Lewis, Sherwood Anderson and other friends. One night he sang it for Lloyd Lewis and filmmaker D. W. Griffith at Schlogl's in Chicago. Afterward, Griffith telegraphed Lewis: "SEND VERSES FOGGY DEW STOP TUNE HAUNTS ME BUT AM NOT SURE OF WORDS STOP PLEASE DO THIS AS I AM HAUNTED BY THE SONG."

In the Southwest, Sandburg picked up "I Ride an Old Paint" from poet Margaret Larkin and playwright Lynn Riggs. John Lomax had introduced Sandburg to "The Boll Weevil Song." After a 1924 recital at the University of Oregon there was an impromptu "song and story session" which lasted till five o'clock in the morning and led Sandburg to "Oh, Bury Me Not on the Lone Prairie." Cartoonist John McCutcheon and his poet wife taught Sandburg "The John B. Sails." From "midnight prowlers in Dallas and Fort Worth, Texas," he learned "Midnight Special." Relatives of Confederacy vice president Alexander Stephens sat on the front porch of their house in Pickens County, Georgia, and gave Sandburg the words to "Walky-Talky Jenny," a pre–Civil War minstrel song transmuted into a southern mountaineer "comic bucolic monologue."

Robert Frost gave Sandburg the tune and verses of "Whisky [sic] Johnny" and "Blow the Man Down," which he had learned as a boy in San Francisco "listening to sailors and dock-wallopers along the water front." Sandburg traced several versions of America's "classical gutter song," "Frankie and Albert" or "Frankie and Johnny."

From Mary Eddy, founder of the Christian Science Church, Sandburg picked up "The Drunkard's Doom," passed to her by old women who, as girls in Ohio, had heard it as a temperance song. Sandburg got a variation of the song from H. L. Mencken, whose multitude of talents included musicianship; he was pianist for Baltimore's famous Saturday Night Club, friends who gathered to play classical music, culminating with a Strauss waltz and libations at the Schellhase bierstube.

Sandburg had learned "Hallelujah, I'm a Bum," in the Kansas wheat fields during his 1897 hobo journey west. During the height of the IWW movement, it was adopted as a Wobbly theme song. Union men gave Sandburg "The Dying Hogger" and an assortment of strike songs. Indiana humorist George Ade and other members of Chicago's White Chapel Club gave Sandburg their theme song, admired by Rudyard Kipling when he was their guest, "In the Days of Old Rameses."

As Sandburg sang and lectured his way around the United States and back again, his musical "ragbag" filled to overflowing with country songs, prairie songs, war songs, jail songs, songs of love and cities and death and nonsense. Lloyd Lewis came to see in Sandburg's public performances the essence of the private man. "Sandburg may not be a great singer," he wrote,

> but his singing is great. . . . He just stands there, swaying a little like a tree, and sings . . . and you see farmhands wailing their lonely ballads, hillbillies lamenting over drowned girls, levee hands in the throes of the blues, cowboys singing down their herds. . . .
>
> Many listeners have asked him to teach them his vocal method. Always he eludes them in his slow, knowing way, understanding well enough that his method is not so much a method as a philosophy of life, a solitary art evolved in loneliness and in an eternal faith in democracy. . . .
>
> He is the last of the troubadours, is Sandburg, the last of the nomad artists who hunted out the songs people made up, and then sang them back to the people like a revelation. . . . Both his singing and his search for songs are part of his belief in the essential merit of the common man.

In the late twenties Sandburg was a conspicuous figure in American literature and culture. Thousands of Americans knew him as a charismatic platform entertainer. He had a solid reputation as a journalist. His workload was staggering and, until his late forties, his stamina to sustain it seemed limitless. His own shrewd sense of advertising and self-promotion, coupled with the meticulous advice he got from Alfred Harcourt, enhanced to the limit the outreach of many of his books. Unique in American literary history was the cross-pollination of Sandburg's work. His journalism fed his poetry, which colored his biography. The movies stimulated the fertile imagination from which he harvested more poems, children's stories and newspaper pieces. His work as biographer-historian augmented his work as folk musician, collector, performer. He and Harcourt perennially dreamed up spin-offs from his work, such as the recordings on the novel "talking machine" to complement the Lincoln biography and to coincide with the production of the book that would be called *The American Songbag*.

The Sandburg-Harcourt collaboration as writer and editor was founded on mutual respect, loyalty and a compatible sense of the marketplace. Like Sandburg, Harcourt was an enterprising promoter, and they looked together at the optimal exposure for Sandburg's work. He had learned in the earliest days of his struggle that he had to "hustle" his lectures and books, to sell them along with himself if he was to reach his audience and continue his work. Throughout his career Sandburg merged his ingenuity and enterprise with his innate capacity for sheer hard work.

Sandburg's visible public life brought rich financial rewards and public acclaim. His steady home life, supported by the devotion of a wife who worked as hard as he, if not harder, gave him serenity, harmony and freedom, as well as purpose. Some of his contemporary writers would later be admired more as writers than as human beings. In the late twenties, Sandburg was admired not only as a "poet of distinction and originality" but as a man with an unforgettable personality. He enjoyed the rare feat of being accepted and liked for himself as well as for his work.

His "tug of war for bread" was largely won. He would earn nearly thirty thousand dollars in 1926, largely thanks to *Abraham Lincoln: The Prairie Years*. His lecture fees surpassed his *Chicago Daily News* salary for the year. Invitations to lecture kept pouring in, more than he could or wanted to accept. As he crisscrossed the country in 1926, he was mining the deep natural vein of poetry in the idioms and folklore of the American people.

Sandburg tired, however, of traveling and trying to write on the road. "Just now I want to get over the feeling of battling trains, of all the time 'fixing things classified' in a traveling bag," he complained to Harcourt. He was besieged by authors who wanted him to write prefaces and introductions to their books. He had newspaper deadlines to meet in that year of the first serious attempt to combine sound with moving pictures. His job as motion picture editor of the *Daily News* was the only newspaper work he ever did that allowed him to get plenty of sleep, Sandburg teased. He had held that position for seven years, and would stay on awhile longer, but other projects were demanding more of his interest and energy. He was halfway through another children's book. He was writing a new, long poem, "Good Morning, America," possibly the title poem for a new volume of poetry. And secure in the success of *Abraham Lincoln: The Prairie Years*, he was "pegging away" at the new songbook.

From the outset, it was a difficult job, depending as it did on collaboration with dozens of musicians, folklorists and musicologists, many of them temperamental. Paula helped Sandburg as she always had, doing other literary chores for him so he could concentrate on the folk songs. She sent Harcourt a sheet of Lincoln corrections, explaining that "Carl is working hard on the Song Book, and may have it ready to send on to you in a week or two." Music critic Alfred Frankenstein worked with Sandburg from the beginning on the manuscript, and personally delivered the copy for the first, limited edition to Harcourt, Brace and Company.

"Young Frankenstein, a very pleasant fellow in spite of his ominous name, blew in today with the song book," Harrison Smith of Harcourt, Brace and Company told Sandburg. "Personally, I am very enthusiastic about it." Smith proposed calling the book *Songs of America*.

"I'm glad you think it looks something like a songbook as it now stands," Sandburg told Smith. "In the jib, the boom and the peep, it ain't such a bad songbook; there have been many worse."

Harcourt published a short, limited edition of the songbook in 1926 containing songs Sandburg had recorded for the RCA Victor Talking Machine Company so that the songs could be copyrighted. "I hear great things about the American Songbag," Untermeyer told Sandburg; "—in fact, my first glimpse at the proofs makes me feel that you are going to end your days as a Musical Authority." Harcourt and Sandburg sent a copy of the limited edition of two hundred songbooks to Clifford Cairns at RCA Victor in hopes that their records and the forthcoming, expanded *The American Songbag* could be coordinated, one of the first such "talking-book" projects in the nation. Sandburg wanted "to discuss how the records catch many shadings of tone, and many intentions of drama and character, that are too elusive to be scored or notated in a tune-book."

He had committed himself to a killing schedule through 1926 and far into 1927. A successful book could, he discovered, present its own set of problems—mail to answer, corrections to attend to, lectures and ongoing promotional events to sustain. He still had his full-time job at the *Daily News*. *The American Songbag* seemed a Pandora's box of headaches. He had to mediate endless, often petty disputes between musicians about transcriptions of songs. Harcourt proposed adding piano accompaniments to the book "else it would not be a book which could be stood up on the piano in fraternity houses and homes for ordinary folks to play the accompaniment and the rest of the crowd to sing." Then he was inclined "to let it ride," foreseeing that to add the accompaniment "would complicate the job a great deal and make it more of a musical and less of a literary book." Days later, Harcourt changed his mind again, and Sandburg set out on the grueling job of finding musicians to arrange piano accompaniments. His musical editor, Frankenstein, was in Europe, so Sandburg turned elsewhere, consulting composers Henry Joslyn and Leo Sowerby, pianist Marion Lychenheim, and composer and musicologist Ruth Crawford, who became almost a member of the Sandburg family, gave Helga and Janet piano lessons, and in later years would be the stepmother of folk musician Pete Seeger.

Sandburg had taken no vacation since completing the Lincoln biography. Now he maintained an almost frenzied schedule. In hopes of getting away from such turmoil and providing a place for the whole family to rest and play, Paula rented a summer cottage on Lake Michigan at Tower Hill, near Sawyer and Three Oaks, Michigan. Sandburg would relax there sporadically, but then, restless and compulsive about his obligations, he would push himself further. "It's a tussle, getting these harmonizations," he told Harcourt near the end of the work, understating his problems but asking for more time. He found two invaluable colleagues in Chicago composer Hazel Felman and English composer Alfred George Wathall, then living in Chicago. Wathall he discovered after the composer made orchestral settings of "The Wedding Procession of the Rag Doll and the Broom Handle and Who Was in It," one of Sandburg's *Rootabaga Stories.*

In Paris, Alfred Frankenstein learned about what he called "the sad fate of the song book," and further intensified Sandburg's anxiety. "Who in hell is the flat head that got the brilliant idea to harmonize those songs?" Frankenstein wrote angrily. "There isn't the slightest reason for publishing them so, and there are a million reasons against it." With so many hands entangled in the work, and a whole keyboard of divergent opinions on how the work should be done, Sandburg resigned himself to more delays, chafing because he carried the ultimate responsibility for the book's completion and success—or failure.

Rebecca West had recently edited the *Selected Poems of Carl Sandburg,* and the *Saturday Review* had carried her preface, "The Voice of Chicago," in the issue of September 4, 1926. She called Sandburg the voice of the Middle West, just as Robert Burns was the voice of lowland Scotland. She asserted that Sandburg, like Burns, was a national poet. "He has learned his country by heart," she wrote. "The main determinant of his art is the power of his native idiom to deal with the inner life of man." She noted that it was a "curious fact that no writer of Anglo-Saxon descent, no representative of the New England tradition, has described the break between Lincoln's America and modern industrialized America so poignantly as Carl Sandburg has." To this British novelist, critic and essayist, Carl Sandburg "evoked the essential America."

*

Sandburg was lecturing his way through the American Southwest in late December 1926. "Your Sunday morning voice had a fine undersong," he wrote Paula from the road; "—seemed both our voices were in a forget-me-not pitch." He looked forward to seeing Alice Corbin Henderson, Witter Bynner and other friends in Santa Fe. It was to Bynner's care that Martin Sandburg sent his brother a sad telegram December 30: MOTHER PASSED AWAY SUDDENLY AT SEVEN AM TODAY OF HEART FAILURE.

"Mother of Noted Author and Poet Succumbs to Pneumonia," the Galesburg, Illinois, *Republican-Register* announced. By the time Sandburg got to Galesburg for the funeral, letters of condolence were coming in from around the country.

Clara Anderson Sandburg was seventy-six when she died. She was buried on Sunday, January 2, in Linwood Cemetery in Galesburg, after a home funeral service. Aboard the train later, Sandburg wrote to Illinois: "Dearest Paula, And I think over and over of what a fine thing grew between you and Mama—and how she cherished it." On folded newsprint he jotted down lines for a poem about his mother's death. Reworked and transcribed, but never published, it read in part:

> . . .
>
> There may or may not be Pearly Gates.
> There may or may not be Gates Ajar.
> There may or may not be Doors of Heaven.
> But if she came with her record
> of so many White Pages,
> of so many Silver Entries,
> of so many Untarnished Hours,
> The Gates swung open open, she walked through those Doors
> as though she belonged,
> as though she could say,
> This is the home I never found in Sweden, in Illinois, in
> Kansas, Oklahoma.
> In corners of the mouth was a wry twist.
> She was shaking loose from the Old Works.
> She was making the grand fadeaway from an Illinois prairie
> town where the Burlington railroad rumbles with long haul
> freight trains, with commodious luxurious limited passenger
> trains for the West Coast.
> Her husband, the father of her children, took his place in con-
> struction gangs that laid the first rails, lived on bread and

> molasses while saving up the dollars to buy the gold wedding
> ring she commanded should be on the third finger of her left
> hand as she laid in the grave alongside him; her man ham-
> mered in [a] blacksmith shop twenty-four years making springs for
> locomotives weaving on main and branch lines of the Burlington.
> Now she's taking the same train he took.
>
> She wore a New Dress.
>
> The undertaker said to her son, It's better than any I've got in
> stock . . .

Not long before she died Clara wrote her own final words in lead pencil on lined paper, entitling them "Souvenir." In her skewed, musical syntax and eccentric spellings and punctuations, there are some of the roots of Sandburg's use of words. He typed his mother's "memorandum" and sent it to many friends after her death, with a note of explanation: "At one moment, weary, stifled, she called out, 'Give me liberty or give me death—I don't want to stay here,' " Sandburg reported. "She gave up the ghost as morning sun slants of a warm winter day came into the room, having spoken a little earlier the words 'It is a beautiful spring morning.' "

When he transcribed his mother's "Souvenir" to share it with family and friends, Sandburg edited her grammar and syntax, even in their flaws remarkable for an immigrant peasant woman whose English was self-taught. "My heart is so full of thoughts and feelings, so great, so much to be greatfull for, my heart at times overflow," she wrote.

> Therefore help me to be strong and patient now in present struggles for I am yet on the climbing upward path but soon I shall go down in the silence and the deep peace underground. Life is short if early days are lost. I think a bible verse each day, so deep so sweet so many of them rich in contents and wisdom for those who apply or have desire, hunger, thirst after righteousness. Sacred, mighty as ocean, the gem is called Patience. With thought and love in the home so much can be overcome. . . . Wishes is good for the soul and strength to the mind. O yes, I am yet strong and filled with the desire to live and when I think of the past, the old home and fireside when we were yet altogether, O so many pleasant memories, enough I say a thousand times enough to make me happy. All good gifts all perfect deliverance comes from above. I do look above to my deliverance, everything comes from above my complicated life to the last full measure of error. . . . Am I wrong in saying the larger wisdom that can see the use of earthly pain and sorrow and not abuse the hand behind the veil is yet strong and able to uplift the crushed. Crushed I am many times

but not yet to death. The aprons of silence is with me. Silence is a gift. Be silent. Forget it.

"Many things I might have said today./And I kept my mouth shut," her poet son had written in the poem "Aprons of Silence" in *Smoke and Steel.* " . . . The aprons of silence covered me . . . /Here I took along my own hoosegow/And did business with my own thoughts./Do you see? It must be the aprons of silence." And in "At the Gates of Tombs" in *Slabs of the Sunburnt West,* he had written, "And since at the gates of tombs silence is a gift,/be silent about it, yes, be silent—forget it."

Clara had read those poems, thought about them, found her own meanings there, perhaps merged them in her fading mind. In her written farewell to life, she chose her son's lines as her own last words.

In passages Sandburg expunged from Clara's final "Souvenir," she wrote lovingly of each of her children, enfolding in her last recorded memory the two sons who had died more than thirty years earlier of diphtheria. Of her son the poet, she wrote, "Carl with his deeper thoughts I saw allready in early childhood was not going to live for money only he wanted to do something more and better with his life his thoughts were allways with his plans in future time to come."

Clara Anderson Sandburg had understood her son, if his father never had. Among the many letters of sympathy there was a particularly welcome one from Sandburg's college friend and fellow stereograph salesman Frederick Dickinson. "As some measure of consolation may there come to you at this time a realization that your mother's latter years have been made more enjoyable and happy by virtue of the distinction and honors you have attained."

✳

"Rode back from Santa Fe a thousand miles to Illinois to bury mother," Sandburg told Alfred Harcourt in mid-January 1927. "She looked beautiful—and stately—if there are Pearly Gates they wouldn't dare stop her. She looked ready for flight." Then, confirming his mother's belief that he was interested in more than money, he relayed to Harcourt the news of another offer from William Randolph Hearst:

> I meant to write you weeks back that Hearst read the Lincoln book in California, wired Rank, the Chicago Examiner managing editor, to see me about editorial writing; they would stand a two year contract for $75,000 and said $100,000 for two years would not be "insurmountable." I told 'em to give Hearst salutations but the higher I got in figures the more sure I was that we couldn't agree on a high enough figure till I get three or four books done that must get written.

Those "three or four books" included, for the time being, the new volume of poetry, *Good Morning, America; The American Songbag*; and a third children's book. With novelist James Stevens, Sandburg talked about how a writer moves from one genre to another, speaking in particular about their shared interest in writing myth and fancy. Sandburg's latest children's book had, he said, "kicked around my workshop, my caboose for six or seven years; it is too good to print, too intelligent." He described his zany, invented characters, the spink bug and the huck, as "a little too far out of the three-dimension world for most people to get them." "The writing mood of these is so different from the mood in which a man does his more factual work," Sandburg mused,

> that the brain operates in two shifts like a day and night gang . . . fantasy, I suppose, must always be laid to one side, and "tested" and "tasted" in many ways, for a long time, before a fellow can be sure what are the good lasting high-spots. All that a fellow can do is to write his head off when the mood comes and the next day, or a week or two later, pick it up and look at it with the gravity of a lunacy commission.

By February 1927 Sandburg's fantasy tales, *Rootabaga Stories* and *Rootabaga Pigeons*, had sold twenty thousand copies, on their own merits and on the coattails of the Lincoln biography. The Pulitzer Prize for biography for 1926 went to Emory Holloway for his biography of Walt Whitman. According to the *New York Herald Tribune* art critic Royal Cortissoz, chairman of the Pulitzer committee on biography from 1925 until 1944, the committee would have been "glad if we could have given the prize to Sandburg's book." However, the Pulitzer rules on biography at that time disqualified books on George Washington and Abraham Lincoln.

Sandburg's foremost literary project in 1927 was *The American Songbag*. As he worked to finish the much-delayed book that spring, he told Vachel Lindsay, "It has mounted beyond all first plans for it. It is not so much my book as that of a thousand other people, who have made its 260 colonial, pioneer, railroad, work-gang, hobo, Irish, Negro, Mexican, gutter Gossamer songs, chants and ditties."

It was the most difficult book he had ever undertaken, kept him "tied down" long past his expectations, and wore him out physically and mentally, as well as emotionally. "Sometimes I think the reason that kind of book has not been done before," he complained, "is because so many tackle it and die on the job." He and Paula continued to monitor his "food, sleep and working conditions," but he could not recapture his customary stamina. His letters before and after that period reveal his worry about himself. "Music engraving is hell on wheels," he told a Texas friend that spring. He turned down a request to write a preface because

> there are times when a man has his work laid out before him in such a way, that he simply can't depart from his program. When I finish the song book I am on now, with all its terrible details and requisites of accuracy, I am due for a vacation of two or three months and then will have to step into the finishing up of three or four hangover jobs that are already more than half done.

Friends and family worried about his prolonged weariness. The stress from the *Songbag*, said Sandburg, "nearly put me coo coo."

Deeply concerned about Sandburg's health and temperament, as well as the well-being of her daughters, Paula decided to ensure summer solitude and rest. In December 1926, she bought the Tower Hill cottage, the vacation house they had rented, and in March 1927 purchased an adjoining lot where she had a studio built for Sandburg, a "large study and sleeping place" apart from the cottage where she and the girls would stay. She hoped he could retreat there, to rest as well as work.

Meantime, the unruly *Songbag* manuscript was in a final state of flux, and Sandburg apologized to Harcourt. "I remember vividly your remark one night about how in the old days, when authors were authors they brung and brang their manuscripts to the publisher letter perfect, from a to izzard," he wrote, "and the publisher took the book and there was no further monkeywork from the authors. . . . All I am sure of is Balzac would have a hard time getting by today."

✻

"I never was any good in synchronizing with editors or publishers, except when I was a police reporter, then I would have the murder in the paper before the corpse was cold," Sandburg once said. In March 1927, Sandburg took on new deadlines, beginning a column for the *Chicago Daily News* which he and Henry Justin Smith called *Carl Sandburg's Notebook*, a free-ranging commentary on people, events, ideas. Sandburg's years on the *Daily News* were immensely creative and productive, in part because of the flexibility of the schedule Smith arranged for him, and because of the camaraderie of fellow newsmen. The frenetic, disheveled atmosphere of the newsroom was a congenial literary retreat for Sandburg, Smith, Ben Hecht, Lloyd Lewis, Keith Preston, Robert Casey and others. Smith, managing editor of the *Daily News* from 1926 until his death in

1936, was a scholar and writer himself. He described his newsroom in *Deadlines* in 1922 and in a 1923 lecture to journalism students:

> It is a paradoxical place. At one desk a poetic genius [Sandburg] taps out reviews of moving pictures; at another a novelist rich in imagination [Ben Hecht] writes sketches of common things and people . . . at another a professor of Latin and Greek [Keith Preston] devises witty comment on books and events; at another an expert in Luxembourg folklore [Robert J. Casey] writes light verse about the folk-lore of Chicago and suburbs; and at many, many others people with imaginative gifts are expertly putting down words.

Henry Justin Smith "saw the paper as a daily novel written by a score of Balzacs," said Hecht in *Child of the Century*. Book editor Harry Hansen painted the *Daily News* in affectionate detail in *Midwest Portraits*.

Sandburg wrote his own portrait of the *Daily News* in this unpublished fragment:

> A curious academy of mortals it was with a home in that old ramshackle Chicago Daily News building at Wells and Madison Streets. Henry Blackman Sell originated the Wednesday book-page, edited it four years, then went to a bigger paying job in New York. Harry Hansen took over and ended on the New York World. . . . Lloyd Lewis, however, came as dramatic critic and stayed on for all of the New York bids, wrote "Sherman: Fighting Prophet," "Myths After Lincoln," books that will linger for quite a while. Robert J. Casey gave the front page light humor, wrote ten books across the 1920's and was to write ten more in the next ten years. . . . Tubman K. Hedrick ("T.K.H.") shaped from his column "Almost Anything" a book titled "The Orientations of Ho-Hen." . . . Ben Hecht one day after doing his uninformative but charming interview with the Theda Bara, then reigning as The Vampire of all times, strolled over to my desk where I was writing of the Chicago race riots. I asked him what he had been doing the night before. "Writing poems," Ben yawned. "What were they about?" I asked and heard the slow dreamy answer, "Same as always—the Night!"

Sandburg hailed Henry Justin Smith as the "human pivot" of the *Daily News* entourage, and trusted Smith's judgment on literary as well as journalistic matters, believing him to be as "individual and indigenous an American as Mark Twain, George Ade or Ring Lardner" and "up to them in personality and writing, only he prefers newspaper work." Sandburg willingly entrusted his column to Smith for editorial guidance. "Dear Harry," he wrote in April, "On this notebook stuff, which I have not looked over since dictating, I will leave it to you to change any verbs or adjectives you choose and to leave out such notes as the ones on Alfred Noyes and Billy Sunday, if they haven't got the right stiletto and accuracy."

Sandburg's copy editor, Donald Russell, got the column after it passed Smith's review. Sandburg wrote clean copy, Russell recalled, which needed little editing. "It was always ahead of time, there's no question about that. . . . On an afternoon paper you had to work pretty fast." Russell saw that Smith never liked to direct "the geniuses he was always hiring. He thought a genius should be let alone. And that was his attitude toward Sandburg."

✳

In the spring of 1927, months after he had hoped to finish, Sandburg was "still toiling in the depths" on *The American Songbag*, stubbornly drawing on his last reserves of energy, working with relentless discipline. His friends helped as much as they could. Mencken had sent two harmonizations of "The Drunkard's Song." "If this is horrible throw it away," he urged Sandburg. "No politeness! I am a hell of a harmonist." Sending along some extra verses, Mencken reiterated, "If the harmonization turns out to be too bad, please don't hesitate to throw it out. I spit on my hands and tried to give a show."

Sandburg was giving in to his fatigue. He apologized when he had to decline an invitation from his alma mater Lombard College. "My recital dates this season have piled up in to more than I ought to handle, considering that some books I want to write ought to take precedence over platform work." He would earn nearly seven thousand dollars in lecture fees in 1927, but the schedule was hard on him. He promised to go to Lombard the following year, and to donate his proceeds, after expenses, "to any cause, department, or purpose the College faculty should designate."

During that harried spring, he kept a number of lecture dates, arriving in one small town as expected, only to disappear "with becoming poetic temperament." "Those searching for the literary celebrity were still vainly searching at 1 o'clock," the newspaper reported, "and the Lions Club, with whom he was to have lunched at noon, were forced to solace themselves with their usual company and songs." The reporter assigned to interview Sandburg gave up, "disgusted and yet reluctantly admiring one so evidently not seeking publicity." Sandburg showed up on time for his lecture date that night in Quincy, Illinois.

Paula still hoped to give him respite and solitude on the shores of

Lake Michigan. The family looked forward to a leisurely summer on the dunes, far from the clamor and pollution of Chicago. While Sandburg went to New York in late May for "three or four weeks closing up my songbag," Paula moved the family to their new lakefront property, Wren Cottage at Tower Hill near Sawyer, Michigan. Sandburg's new studio stood nearby.

"I nearly went bankrupt in health" on the Lincoln biography, he reminded a friend. It was clear that he was starved for rest and tranquillity. Michigan summers were exhilarating. Margaret, Janet and Helga enjoyed the water or hilly shore under the blue purity of the summer sky. The lake stretched before them vast as an ocean, its tides lofting sailboats and the occasional freighter plowing along the far horizon. It was good for all of them; Margaret, Janet and Helga seemed to thrive there.

By the time Sandburg came home from New York, he was physically exhausted. Worse, he was nervous and dispirited. Paula urged him to relax, and began to take over more work on the *Songbag*. She and Howard Clark of Harcourt filled the mails between Michigan and New York with page proofs. They searched for a new printer who could do the complicated engravings of song settings with speed and accuracy. They tried to work with two printers, one in Chicago and one in Camden, New Jersey, to expedite the book. It was a ticklish job. "The plates for the 'Songbook' are going to be precious," Clark told Paula. "They are going to be hard to duplicate and as it is always the cussedness of inanimate things, it is a ten to one bet that a plate will jump the press and smash a number of others."

By late June, with Paula reading proofs in Michigan and Clark hard at it in New York, they were keeping both printers busy. They hoped to have the book ready by mid-October, at last. With Sandburg less and less able to concentrate, Paula carried most of the load, hiring a secretary so she could give the book her full attention, leaving to hired help the care of the cottage and the girls.

Sandburg was irritable when his privacy was disrupted by "invaders from Lakeside," a nearby neighborhood. "From the first," Margaret said, "we knew that we had to be quiet, or go to the beach" or to the cottage belonging to their old friends the Foxes. Sandburg's health was the family's first concern. Paula hoped that he could work and also get some rest in the new studio, surrounded by his books and papers. The studio was simply furnished, enfolded in silence, except for the music of the lake and the songbirds. For color there were Navajo serapes and the brilliant mirror of the lake, visible through the trees.

He had waited too long for rest, however, had driven himself too far, too hard. In July, too ill and tired to work anymore, Sandburg suffered a nervous breakdown.

"This is the first time I have ever felt seriously alarmed about Carl's health," Paula wrote to Harcourt that summer. "It all ties up with this Song-bag and Carl's incessant labors to make this book the best book he can possibly make. It wears him in many ways—all the details of it." He "was critically sick" at the same time with "poisoning due to kidneys not functioning at all," Paula told Harcourt, but he was "coming along better every day, responding very well to the medicine."

"You can hardly imagine how distressed I am at the news that Carl has been ill," Harcourt consoled Paula, "and I suppose I can hardly imagine how worried you've been. Of course, it is unnecessary to urge you to take care of him before you take care of the Songbag, but you may be a little more comfortable about doing that if I urge you to do so." He told Paula to ask their mutual friend Paul de Kruif, who had his own remote summer place nearby, to recommend a specialist in Chicago to help Sandburg with "the sort of thing that's troubling him."

"I have been ordered to a pretty strict regime, a long lay off," Sandburg wrote Charlie Dunning that summer. "I have a good machine, but the motor and propeller have been in the air too much and are ordered to ground work." His doctors were "dirty and domineering," he teased, but he followed their orders conscientiously. He slept alone, long hours at a stretch, in the studio. He walked the dunes contemplating the "twenty-two mile coast view," and carefully cleared his mind of work. "I have had more work, travel, fun and philosophy than the law allows and am taking a jail sentence," he mused. Paula guarded his rest and diet, managed the household, carried on his work for him.

"Two of the best diagnosticians in Chicago have given me the once-over and have decided that I am a magnificent risk, have a grand machine, a one hoss shay," Sandburg wrote Donald Brace in late August, "but they stress the word Fatigue and say if I don't work less, play more, and give the Works a chance, I'm a plain ridiculous dam fool."

There are poems from that period called "Bitter Summer Thoughts," reflections, perhaps, gathered in those long hours when he walked or rested beside the healing lake. "Beat at the bars./Cry out your cry of want," he wrote in "Bars," among that group:

> Let yourself out if you can.
> Find the sea, find the moon,
>   if you can.
> Shut the windows, open the doors.

There are no windows, are no doors?
There is no sea, is no moon?
Cry your cry, let yourself out if you can.

"Who put up that cage?" he asked in "Money, Politics, Love and Glory":

Who hung it up with bars, doors?
Why do those on the inside want to get out?
Why do those outside want to get in?
What is this crying inside and out all the time?
What is this endless, useless beating of baffled
    wings at these bars, doors, this cage?

A terse poem called "Bundles," in a cluster of poems he entitled "Timber Moon," rang with despair, almost a wish for oblivion, death:

I have thought of beaches, fields,
Tears, laughter.

I have thought of homes put up—
And blown away.

I have thought of meetings and for
Every meeting a good-by.

I have thought of stars going alone,
Orioles in pairs, sunsets in blundering
Wistful deaths.

I have wanted to let go and cross over
To a next star, a last star.

I have asked to be left a few tears
And some laughter.

In a lyrical ode, "Peace, Night, Sleep," he seemed to meditate on his passage from an exhaustion of body, spirit and will to restoration and equilibrium. A voice, perhaps Paula's, spoke:

"You shall have peace with night and sleep.
It was written in the creep of the mist,
In the open doors of night horizons.
Peace, night, sleep, all go together.
In the forgetting of the frogs and the sun,
In the losing of the grackle's off cry
And the call of the bird whose name is gone—
You shall have peace; the mist creeps, the doors open.
Let night, let sleep, have their way."

✳

By the late summer of 1927 Sandburg was stronger, more serene, and ready for the company of a few close friends. He asked Oliver Barrett, Al Hannah and Judge Henry Horner to visit him, promising that "there are swimming suits for you, a new shanty with cots where you can all be sequestrated and quarantined, and a big hardwood Liars' Log where you are invited to tell tall ones. . . . I am under orders to shun work, to play and be irresponsible as the birds, the bees, and the bums." He was trying to work again, just two or three hours a day now, "and letting things slide. But I want Good company and I'd like to see your good faces and hear you talk and talk."

Barrett, the Lincoln collector and Sandburg's lawyer, obliged immediately, promising that he would "take great pleasure in calling upon you with samples of our new fall line of fish stories and other lies. Since you will have to furnish the birds and the bees, I will provide the bums therewith, to-wit: Al Hannah and Judge Horner." After days of the healing quiet, Sandburg was ready for talk, songs and laughter with these old friends. Recuperating in Michigan, Sandburg missed a chance to see another old friend that August. "I happen to be in Chicago (for the first time in 14 years)," Theodore Dreiser wrote, enjoying the huge success of *An American Tragedy*. "If you have an hour to waste you might meet for a meal or a talk. You may or may not remember but it was to me that Masters brought & read a number of your fine poems. And it was myself who introduced him to John Lane and urged Jefferson Jones to bring them out by all means."

Slowly Sandburg began to pick up the reins again on the *Songbag*. As he, Paula and others worked over the galley proofs, Sandburg proclaimed them the "worst punished galley sheets I have ever seen. Five days we flipped & flopped them getting the inserts & line cuts located & Scotch taped. . . . On the page proofs to come we will pray."

Serene and steady, Paula watched over Sandburg's recovery, cared for Margaret, Janet and Helga with their diverse daily needs, and sustained the final work on the book. She and Sandburg decided to enroll Margaret, a shy, often lonely sixteen-year-old, in Nazareth Academy, a Catholic boarding school for girls in La Grange, Illinois. Paula had a long talk with Sister Aquinas, the directress, who welcomed Margaret, despite her epilepsy. The Sandburgs paid an additional fee to have one nun sleep in a room adjacent to Margaret's each night, in case she had one of the seizures which came most often at night or in the early dawn.

At first Margaret was happy in the companionship of other teenagers. "Dear Mamma & Daddy," she wrote. "I think I am the luckiest girl in the whole world. The girls all like me and I like them so much." With Margaret at least initially content at school, Paula could give more time to the rest of the family and to the ongoing labor over the proofs for *The American Songbag*. Sandburg was still resting, usually sleeping nine hours a night, dieting carefully. "I gained in weight," he wrote Harcourt in late September. "I cut out all meats, liquor, pastries; have handled an ax an hour a day and done puttering work of different kinds another hour and then have laid around lazy whenever I felt like it." He declined requests to lecture or write articles, explaining, "I have run on high too much and am under strict orders to double my sleep and be a lazy bum." He could not be enticed to parties "because I am under the strictest orders to double my sleep and fight shy of all shindigs."

In Sandburg's reduced workday there was little time to divert from the *Songbag*. With printers in two states working on different pages, and many different eyes proofing the results, there were constant confusions. "You mention the book being a sort of mess of knots that needs un-knotting," Sandburg wrote sympathetically to the patient Howard Clark, who was overseeing the production of the book. "My guess is that it is a batch of sausage ground to a fine point that needs only a little seasoning and wrapping in packages. You and I have climbed worse ladders than this one. We have thrown and captured wilder animals than this one."

Paula kept track of the intricate, knotted threads of the proofs that fall while Sandburg put his limited energy into reviewing the final text for the *Songbag*. On September 21 he made his first trip to Chicago in weeks, and the next day joined Hollywood publicist Charles Dunning in ringside seats provided by Jack Dempsey for his championship fight with Gene Tunney. As part of a throng of 104,943 people, they saw Tunney defeat Dempsey in a controversial decision.

The newly established Book-of-the-Month Club hoped to publish a condensed, one-volume Lincoln for the Christmas market, but Harcourt saw that Sandburg should not be rushed into such a job. "It would be nice to sell them 45,000 of it this year," he reassured Sandburg, "but it will be even nicer to do it next year and there is no sense in our breaking our necks for a single piece of business. I have just told them we can't have it ready before January. Songbag work should come first." Book-of-the-Month Club officials then countered with a proposal to publish the complete two-volume Lincoln biography in a single volume, using thin paper and fewer illustrations. Believing that the biography would be "the runaway Christmas seller this year," Harcourt persuaded Sandburg to agree to the offer. By Christmas, that edition was selling briskly.

Harcourt next planned to publish a long excerpt from the early chapters of *Abraham Lincoln: the Prairie Years*, entitle it *Abe Lincoln Grows Up*, and sell it to the juvenile audience first envisioned for Sandburg's biography. With that edition in 1928 and a condensed, one-volume version ready for Lincoln's birthday in 1929, Harcourt would shrewdly prolong sales of Sandburg's Lincoln books.

Sandburg hoped to be well enough to travel to New York in October to work with Harcourt, who invited him to stay at his new house on Long Island Sound at Greenwich, Connecticut. "There is a special lying-in corner for you where you can comfortably have the final birth pains on the Songbag or the Lincoln or anything else that comes along and for a long time."

As the interminable work on the *Songbag* proofs and plates finally diminished, Sandburg swore he had done his last collaboration. Margaret, for one, emphatically endorsed that decision. "I thought you said you would surprise me by coming out one of these days, Daddy," she wrote plaintively from Nazareth Academy. "Why don't you? I suppose the answer will be that you're too busy about the song book, but frankly, I wish that that had never been started." By mid-October Sandburg was well enough to travel east and to keep some lecture dates en route. In New York he worked on the final details of the book and traveled to Rahway, New Jersey, with Clark to see the Songbag "finally put to bed on the presses."

"Paula dearest—Songbag okeh . . . ," Sandburg wrote home. "I hope something like twilight sleep will intervene now until the child is born," Harcourt told Paula. "What a summer you've had."

"I am looking forward to the Songbag with great expectations," Mencken told Sandburg on the eve of the book's publication. "If the rest of the [piano] arrangements are as bad as mine of that drinking song, it will take its place among the masterpieces of the new music."

Sandburg took three copies of the new book to Steichen and sent author's copies to dozens of people who had helped, and sometimes hindered, his work. "Thanks over and over for the Song Bag," wrote poet Jake Zeitlin from Los Angeles. "It packs some mighty good songs. I'm sorry that you had to cut the balls out of some of them."

The Sandburgs decided late in 1927 that they wanted to live year around on Lake Michigan. The Tower Hill cottage was too small, however, and the area was too heavily populated with summer people. In November 1927 they bought a large lot a few miles away in Birchwood near Harbert in Chikaming Township, Berrien County, Michigan, with a spectacular view of the lake and dunes. They began to plan the house they would build there. Paula designed it herself, tailoring it to her family's complex routine—ample work space for Sandburg, removed from the daily household bustle; more privacy and space for the girls. It would be a simple, spacious house to enfold her family's needs, then and later. A refuge, the house would be three stories tall, jutting up from the crest of the dunes, where its many windows could open to the expanse of lake and the sandy shore. On the top floor she put Sandburg's workroom, a bedroom and a deck where he could write in the sun and air. In the basement she planned a fifteen-by-thirty-foot vault of steel and concrete, lined with shelves, where manuscripts, books and research files could be housed in fireproof, dehumidified safety.

That November after *The American Songbag* came off the press, a few of the book's contributors complained of errors. There was at least one copyright suit, promptly resolved, but otherwise the book was an immediate success. Sandburg heard on all sides that he had "done a great service, not only to the music loving people of the country, but to those who will come to know that history is not made up of the acts of statesmen or warriors." Chicago businessman and lawyer Jesse Ricks told Sandburg, "If the ink does not fade, or the paper rot, it will be useful a thousand years from now." His friend J. Frank Dobie of the Texas Folk-Lore Society pronounced the *Songbag* "a noble piece of work." In Santa Fe, Alice Corbin Henderson wrote a review for *Poetry*, and gave Sandburg her personal thanks for the book: "I wish you could see the groups that have gathered about our fire-place and sung out of the book,—with your visage hovering over us." Arthur Vance of *Pictorial Review* wondered "why in thunder you pitched [the songs] all so blamed high. It would take a double castrated pink-faced tenor voice to reach most of your musical settings and thank God my voice is not that."

The work on *The American Songbag* was "heavy and awful," Sandburg told a friend, "and it will be a long time before I ever tackle anything like it again." He wanted to keep the manuscript intact, "with its many terrible and dirty marks of toil, sacrifice and blood."

"The book nearly killed me," he reflected once it was out, "and I am just coming up from under." He told Mencken that, too, in a November letter: "The detail work on it nearly killed me and for a good many weeks I am the laziest man in the United States."

Carl Sandburg turned fifty on January 6, 1928. As he looked back over his career, he concluded that he had been "tackling books of too large a size."

*

"I have had to turn down an official invitation to be the main speaker at the Lincoln dinner February 13 [1928] of the National Republican Club of New York City," Sandburg wrote to Harcourt. "In doing so, I had to recall our common thought (It hit us both at the same time) that the Lincoln book would make us 'respectable.' However, I have accepted an invitation to deliver the Poem before the Phi Beta Kappa Chapter of Harvard University next June. They pay $100 and board you two days." For the Phi Beta Kappa poem, Sandburg decided to read "Good Morning, America," a long "piece of verse" he had been working on for three years. For five weeks during the winter of 1928 he revised the poem, and sent Harcourt the final draft in February. "It's a noble piece," Harcourt told him. "I got a thrill out of it."

They set to work then on Sandburg's next volume of poetry, and finished *Abe Lincoln Grows Up*. Sandburg's health was still fragile, and his doctors ordered him to take a winter vacation. He said he had been "advised by competent authorities to let all writing go to hellangone." With Margaret away at school and Oma and Opa on hand to care for Janet and Helga, he and Paula traveled to Florida for the first vacation they had ever spent alone together.

Margaret was doing well academically at Nazareth Academy, but was secretly more homesick than she let her parents know. There were students there who could be thoughtlessly cruel to the shy, quiet girl who had to have a nun sleep near her in case she had a seizure. Some of the sterner nuns made Margaret tense and nervous, but she turned for comfort to a gentle sister who reminded her of her mother. She longed for mail from the family. "I hope I can come home," Margaret wrote her parents that winter, "and tell Janet and Helga that I won't write ever to them because they don't write me. Also tell them I am ashamed of them for not doing it."

Janet, nearly twelve, was very slow to learn and quickly intimidated by other children. Her beautiful blue Steichen eyes gave the appearance of being crossed, Margaret remembered, "so that at times when she appeared clumsy, she simply did not see correctly." She did not wear glasses then, and eye surgery would later help her. She looked out at a world that she sometimes did not understand. At public school, nine-year-old Helga was "Janet's defender," writing in later years that Janet's "open way encouraged attacks from any bully about. Aware of this, she and I would try to get away from school early, but since a bully would also be on his toes, we seldom made it. Slinging school satchel, lunch pail or sled, I fought for our freedom." Gentle, sweet and stubborn, Janet was happiest playing with her sisters, or eating fresh-baked *Küchen* or apple pie from Oma's kitchen after school, or following the safe, familiar routines of home.

Janet was Paula's work of art, Sandburg told her. They decided to enroll Janet in a special school in Berwyn, Pennsylvania. "They will take Janet at Devereux—at the rate of $1000.00 a year—" Paula wrote Sandburg. "Dr. Adler suggests starting her in April."

At Nazareth Academy, impressionable Margaret listened to the convent sisters and "got very worried about going to Hell." She was dismayed to learn that she and her sisters had never been baptized. When her parents heard her distress about the family's spiritual welfare, Sandburg arranged for a friend, an Evangelical Lutheran minister, to baptize them. On April 6, 1928, at St. Peter's Church in Elmhurst, Illinois, the three Sandburg daughters became Margaret Mary Steichen Sandburg, Janet Mary Steichen Sandburg and Helga Mary Steichen Sandburg. Margaret's alarm was assuaged, and Oma, whose name the girls had chosen for their baptismal name, was delighted.

Margaret was no happier at Nazareth, however. In late May, when her parents and Helga were settling into the new house in Michigan, she wrote "If you want to leave me wretched and miserable in this place, you can, and I will stay here till June the seventeenth unhappy. But if, on the other hand, you want to make me happy, please come to take me away from this abominable place."

By late June she and Janet were with the family at the new house. Janet, shy and lonely, had been deeply unhappy and homesick at Devereux. On the first night in the school dining room, she shook her head when asked if she wanted milk to drink. She was never offered it again, and was too bashful to ask for it. Margaret was distressed to learn how hard it had been for Janet to spend even those few weeks away from home. "She was *very* pale, and burst into tears when she reached Mother," Margaret recalled. ". . . I had never seen her so *very pale.*"

The move to Michigan gave the whole family space and freedom. Sandburg told a friend, "I have been laying off and protecting myself from the disease called civilization—amid the sand hills of Michigan." He traveled to Harvard to read his Phi Beta Kappa poem, observing that "Harvard has more of a reputation to lose than I have." By the late 1920s many Americans recognized Sandburg's rugged face and white hair, as well as his name. He rode the crest of his literary success, his creativity and innovation evident in poetry, biography, children's fiction and

American folk music. The Harvard honor ratified his significant place in contemporary American literature. His newspaper byline further expanded his audience. Thousands of Americans heard him lecture and sing from the stage; now they could hear his distinctive voice on phonographic records and the radio.

The new house in Michigan gave him space and seclusion for his work. The Sandburgs wanted to live closely attuned to the rhythms of nature—tides, seasons, the pulse of storms. Their sturdy new house straddled a bluff steep as a fortress. They built a stairway with "resting platforms having seats" so they could have access to the beach below for daily walks or swims. The girls looked for wildflowers in the sheltering woods, where staunch pines and enduring hardwoods latched their roots to the perilous sand. The wind-battered dunes and woods protected the house in the savage winters, and spring, summer and autumn were idyllic on the lake shore.

Sandburg's years of hard work enabled him to afford this new solitude. Journalist Karl Detzer described Sandburg's solitary walks on the dunes, "a white-haired man in a disreputable old hat, knocking golf balls across the sand." Other hikers on the beach seldom glanced his way, Detzer noted, for he bore no resemblance "to either poet or biographer; he's an ordinary-looking man, and if he wants to take his lonely exercise this way, what matter is it to them?"

Behind and below the house, Paula built a double garage, where they kept their "four door sedan of Arabian sand color" which Sandburg bought straight from the Dearborn, Michigan, Ford Plant. He was not a skillful or attentive driver, being easily distracted by interesting sights along the road, but he managed to maneuver the new machine safely home to Birchwood. After futile efforts to improve his driving, Paula took over the chauffeuring chores herself. Fortunately, Sandburg could take the train to Chicago for his work at the *Daily News*.

✳

"And who made 'em? Who made the skyscrapers?" he wrote in *Good Morning, America*. "Man made 'em, the little two-legged joker, Man." The volume celebrated man's technical ingenuity, and contemplated "the short miserable pilgrimage of mankind." The book signaled a metamorphosis: After *Good Morning, America*, Sandburg did not publish another book of poetry until *The People, Yes*, in 1936. By then his immersion in American history, mythology and vernacular was complete, and his poetry was transformed accordingly. After *Good Morning, America* Sandburg's lyrical, imagistic and portrait poems were largely superseded by his need to chronicle the sweep of American history, and to draw alternately hopeful and foreboding connections between past and present. After 1928, Sandburg created vast public poems, becoming the Poet of the People en masse rather than the spokesman to and for the individual.

His friend the critic Joseph Warren Beach warned Sandburg of the dangers of self-parody: "Carl, you're imitating yourself." There are instances in *Good Morning, America* when Sandburg clearly ignored that admonition. Lines, images, whole poems seem trite, glib, overdone, hollow. The device of repetition which he had used with singular skill since the early days is reduced to tedium in "Crisscross":

> The spiders are after the beetles.
> The farmer is driving a tractor turning furrows.
> The hired man drives a manure spreader.
> The oven bird hops in dry leaves.
> The woodpecker beats his tattoo.
> Is this it? Is spring crossing over?
> Is it summer? And this always was? . . .

Mencken and other editors had turned down many of these poems in advance of the publication of Sandburg's new book, telling him that they were not up to his best work.

Good Morning, America would have been enhanced by prudent weeding and editing. It is redeemed by the originality of the title poem and the finale, "Many Hats," a sprawling, slangy celebration of the American landscape, of the "drunken, death-defying, colossal, mammoth, cyclopean, mystic . . . and imperturbable" wonders of nature, as symbolized by the Grand Canyon. In the boundaries of this one volume, Sandburg displayed his capacity for the maudlin, as well as for the poignant personal revelation. Love is a paradox, according to the poems here. "I shall take old note-books of Hokusai and Hiroshige," Sandburg wrote in "Hungry and Laughing Men":

> memoirs of the wonderful hungry laughing men, and in
> an off corner, write my code:
> Love to keep? There is no love to keep . . .

In "Explanations of Love," he writes of the "battlegrounds and workshops of love," drawing imagery from modern industrialized society: "There is a look of eyes fierce as a big Bethlehem open hearth/furnace or a little green-fire acetylene torch." "There is a place where love begins and a place/where love ends," he writes, "—and love asks nothing."

In *Good Morning, America*, Sandburg offers powerful descriptions of the artistic process, and the sacrificial birth pangs exacted of the poet, the communicator:

. . . Speech requires blood and air to make it.
Before the word comes off the end of the tongue,
While the diaphragms of flesh negotiate the word,
In the moment of doom when the word forms
It is born, alive, registering an imprint—
Afterward it is a mummy, a dry fact, done and gone.
The warning holds yet: Speak now or forever hold
    your peace.
Ecce homo had meanings: Behold the Man! Look at
    him! Dying he lives and speaks!

He writes about other poets and poetry: There is a tribute to Robert Frost in "New Hampshire Again." In "To the Ghost of John Milton," Sandburg contemplates the enduring creative drive, in lines which also reverberate with his own fear of blindness:

. . . If I then lost my eyes and the world was all dark and I
Sat with only memories and talk—

I would write "Paradise Lost," I would marry a second wife
And on her dying I would marry a third pair of eyes to
Serve my blind eyes, I would write "Paradise Regained," I
Would write wild, foggy, smoky, wordy books— . . .

The book concludes with "Many Hats," the verse about the Grand Canyon which Mencken published in *American Mercury* in 1928 before Sandburg's book came out. Part of the poem's vigor is the fusion of forces at work on Sandburg's imagination—the movies, the folk music, the "kid" stories, his travels with ears awake to the American idiom, his saturation in American history. He uses the metaphor of the processional to bring a stream of colorful figures to the Canyon's rim to speculate on its creation. Prose supersedes poetry here. Sandburg is relinquishing his own unorthodox free-verse forms for a new, controversial prose-poem style:

Comes along a hombre saying, Let it be dedicated to Time . . .

Comes along a hombre accidentally remarking, Let it be dedicated to Law and Order . . .

Comes along another hombre giving his slant at it, Now this sure was the Garden of Eden . . .

Comes along another hombre all wised up, This was the Devil's Brickyard
. . .

At the end, Sandburg himself contemplates the Canyon:

> Came a lean, hungry-looking hombre with Kansas, Nebraska, the Da-
> kotas on his wind-bitten face, and he was saying, Sure my boy, sure my
> girl, and you're free to have any sweet bluebird fancies you please, any
> wild broncho thought you choose to have . . .
> Yes, let this be dedicated to Time and Ice; a memorial of the Human
> Family which came, was, and went; let it stand as a witness of the short
> miserable pilgrimage of mankind. . . .

✳

"I feel that I must apologize for the absence of Mr. Carl Sandburg, Mr. Ezra Pound, and Mr. Edgar Lee Masters, an absence for which my own critical perversity is alone responsible," Conrad Aiken wrote in the preface to his anthology *Modern American Poetry* (1927). "The work of these three poets interests me in the mass . . . but disappoints me in the item." The late twenties marked the beginning of a new critical perspective of Sandburg's poetry. For the most part, critics were kind to *Good Morning, America*, although Edwin Seaver in *The New Republic* condemned Sandburg for "no real progression" and Percy Hutchison in *The New York Times* wished for "fresh combinations and new beauties," speculating that Sandburg had "sat too long at the feet of Walt Whitman."

The arts critic Paul Rosenfeld had cautioned in earlier years that Sandburg needed to develop a critical sense so that he could "master his own vision," "do himself justice," "penetrate his subject completely, to squeeze his poems till they are firm and solid." Rosenfeld charged that Sandburg did "not even seem to recognize where hammering and shaping is necessary," and predicted that Sandburg's "weakness of the critical faculty" would mar all his work.

"Not everybody can see the form of your poems because it is your form, and with every poem it changes," Joseph Warren Beach wrote to Sandburg. "I believe you are in for a considerable period of critical sniffing," he warned. "There is a group of young critics, who would like to be poets, who are making a great to-do over what they call classical or intellectual standards. . . . They will examine you through a spy glass and shoot their little poisoned arrows at you. It will last quite a long while. It will keep going on more or less all your life. There will be more of it than there used to be; for you have become a big mark."

✳

"Mostly I am working like hell and hiding out," Sandburg said in the fall of 1928, cloistered in the new house on the beautiful, lonely Michigan dunes. He told Sherwood Anderson he was beginning to work on *Abraham Lincoln: The War Years*, the title chosen for the second part of the biography. He was becoming the nation's foremost Lincoln spokesman. He spoke to a crowd of more than 25,000 people in Galesburg in October on the seventieth anniversary of the Lincoln-Douglas debate there. Lloyd Lewis, Henry Horner, William Allen White and many others fed him Lincoln material they came across, and he spent as much time as possible "tunneling" in Lincoln collections around the country. As he had done with *The Prairie Years*, he applied his careful habits as a reporter to his Lincoln investigations. He combined lecture-recital dates and research forays, "ransacked" libraries, and accumulated such a Lincoln library of his own that it filled tall shelves in the guest room. The family named it the Lincoln Room.

In November 1928 Sandburg became embroiled in a notable controversy over some alleged Lincoln love letters. He had a "conference with Atlantic Monthly editor [Ellery Sedgwick] on the Lincoln letters they are spilling; they're great," he wrote Paula. Sedgwick was going to press with the first installment of a three-part series called "Lincoln the Lover," based on an extraordinary group of newly "discovered" Lincoln papers which came to Sedgwick from Wilma Frances Minor, who claimed the papers had been passed down through her family. Sedgwick was convinced that the documents confirmed, once and for all, the legend that Ann Rutledge was Lincoln's great love and the inspiration for his career.

Sedgwick and Edward A. Weeks of the *Atlantic* had taken precautions, they thought, to insure the authenticity of the documents, consulting Lincoln scholars. A chemical analysis confirmed that the paper and ink seemed consistent with the purported age of the papers. At Sedgwick's invitation, Sandburg visited him in Boston just as the December issue of the *Atlantic* was coming out. Sandburg urged Sedgwick to consult Paul Angle, secretary of the Lincoln Centennial Association in Springfield, Illinois, because "Mr. Angle is so qualified, informed and situated that he is about the best person to confer with on validity and backgrounds of your material." When Sandburg saw the documents, he pronounced them "entirely authentic." Since he had used the Ann Rutledge story in *The Prairie Years*, he was pleased at this seeming verification of a controversial chapter in Lincoln's life.

Sandburg wrote an enthusiastic article about the Minor collection for the December 4 issue of the *New York World*. By that time, however, Angle, Oliver Barrett, Worthington Chauncey Ford and other Lincoln experts were publicly calling the documents forgeries, and the national press was covering the story. Sandburg's article lauded the almost "miraculous" discovery of the letters, "old fading pieces of paper that testify to this beloved lyric and tragic folk tale of the American people." On hearing from Angle and Barrett that the documents were spurious, Sandburg wrote an immediate retraction. "When I scrutinize original source material of this kind I let my emotions have full play," he apologized. "I try to do my hard-boiled analyzing later."

"Anyone can go wrong, but it takes a *man* to admit it," Angle wrote to Sandburg December 6. Already sensitive to charges that he had been indiscriminate in his use of sources for *Abraham Lincoln: The Prairie Years*, Sandburg heeded the lesson he learned from his naïveté in the Minor affair. He was particularly scrupulous in his efforts to find the best, most reliable sources for *The War Years*, to consult experts, and to "appraise the goddam witness."

Meantime, Sandburg himself was the victim of a literary hoax. To his surprise, he received a proof sheet from the editor of *Harper's Monthly*. "Somebody is spoofing us," Sandburg wrote in reply. "I have never sent you a poem entitled Gravel, of which you send me a proof. I am as sorry as you are about this conspiracy."

✳

When he turned fifty, Sandburg seemed to give himself permission, after a lifetime of arduous work, to have more fun. While he and Paula had always lived frugally, their new financial security freed them to enjoy a few well-chosen luxuries. For Sandburg, that meant the unrestricted acquisition of books, especially books about Lincoln and his century. "I have been riding on the desert, watching Charlie Chaplin work and play, and rustling through old bookshops," he told Harcourt. Wherever he went, he enjoyed the fellowship of friends. After his lecture recitals, he unwound at parties, on college campuses seeking out young intellectuals, as well as "any lads who know songs . . . that are not published, that are somewhat neglected, that even may be a little wicked." He would often reach for his guitar and sing private encores of songs from *The American Songbag*. He had found the ideal rhythm in his life—months of hibernation and work in the dune solitude, and weeks enjoying the gregarious, vagabonding life on the road.

He saw his brother Mart only on occasion in his travels, but their friendship transcended time and distance. Mart put him in touch with their boyhood friend John Sjodin in 1928. Sjodin told Sandburg his letter brought to mind "our palhood days, memory playing an old tune in my heart." Sjodin wanted to talk over "the kid days and the lapse between then and now."

Sandburg wrote frequent notes of appreciation and encouragement to other writers—Lincoln Steffens, William Carlos Williams, Countee Cullen and Vachel Lindsay, among others. Lindsay's poetic fortunes were as precarious as his health and emotional stability, and Sandburg took a sustained interest in Lindsay's work. The son of a physician, Lindsay was nearly forty-five in 1924 when he went to the Mayo Clinic for a neurological examination which revealed that he had epilepsy, and had probably suffered from it for years. From 1924 onward, he took Luminal and bromide in varying doses to minimize his seizures. He had so appreciated Sandburg's work and friendship that he had dedicated his poem "Babylon, Babylon, Babylon the Great" to Sandburg, sending him an intricate "hieroglyphic" of the poem. He and his wife, Elizabeth, urged Sandburg to visit them in his travels, and when his son, Nicholas Cave, was born in 1927, Lindsay had poured out his heart to Sandburg in a letter: "I am 48 years old in November—and now—out of the blue as one might say comes a son and *how the world changes!* . . . God bless you Carl . . . I hold you to your promise to come to see us soon. Come and teach Vachel's Baby to talk! I want my little man to meet the men."

Sandburg's best friend, of course, was Paula. Affectionately, he called Paula "Mrs. Fixit," in respect for her ingenuity and grace with all things mechanical as well as personal. It was she who designed their new house, supervised its construction, managed the money, filed the income tax, nurtured him and their daughters, ran the house, protected his freedom to work. During his frequent long absences from home, he relished the letters she and the girls sent him. "I was so glad to hear yow [sic] were coming home," Helga had written November 21, 1927. "I didn't know yow were coming at first. With very Loving love and 2,000 bushels of kisses, 20 hugs and a hello!" "Dear Swipes," he wrote to her on another journey. "My heart is glad to have your letter. . . . Love to your beautiful mother, your sweet sisters, and your angel-faced self."

"Sunday there were blue skies—and sunshine," Paula wrote to him in 1929. Their romance had taken root in letters, and twenty years later, they wrote to each other as tenderly as during their courtship. She was deeply contented in Michigan, and through the years, her letters carried the details of home life to him in all seasons, wherever he was:

> The wind was from the south-east and blew the floe ice into the lake so there was open water again to the hillocks at the second sandbar. . . . We walked to the edge of the ice and found a flock of long-tailed Squaw Duck—thirty-two of them—in a sort of cove right in front of our house—so tame we could stay within ten feet of them. . . . Beautiful swimmers & divers they are—these sea ducks that breed in the Arctic.

We all wished you were here to see them! . . . All well and here and having the best winter of our lives and I'm thanking our lucky stars and You that we can be in this lovely Winter Playground! Love and love to my Dearest.

In 1929, Sandburg was moving deeper into the work on Lincoln and the Civil War. He told Chicago composer Leo Sowerby, one of his colleagues on *The American Songbag,* that he expected to spend "six months or more" of 1929 at home in Harbert. He offered to show Sowerby the "mammoth Civil War and Lincoln library" he had collected over the years. He invited law professor and Lincoln collector Clark P. Bissett to visit him in Michigan, predicting that "It may be a five or six year job that I am now on. Lincoln ran the war."

Sandburg left home only occasionally in 1929 to lecture. He still turned out his column for the *Chicago Daily News.* But Lincoln was his passion. He spent most of 1929 at home on the Michigan dunes, with Lincoln his chief companion, turning down most public and private invitations because he was "booked for steady toil" on the biography.

---
*

1929–1933

21. A Great Bundle
of Grief

In the darkness with a great bundle of grief
  the people march.
In the night, and overhead a shovel of stars for
  keeps, the people march:
            "Where to? what next?"

—Carl Sandburg, *The People, Yes*, 1936

On Black Tuesday, October 29, 1929, Carl Sandburg was in Omaha, Nebraska, talking to the State Teachers' Association about poetry. He shared the front page of the *Omaha World Herald* with headlines about the stock market. "Heavy profit-taking halted a wild stampede of buying," the Associated Press reported. The Stock Exchange had closed for two days at the end of the preceding week to "give the over-worked brokerage organizations a rest from the crushing burdens of the last few days."

Tragically, the crushing burdens lay ahead. By 1932 there were "bread-line silhouettes" all over the country. One American out of four was out of work, a quarter of the country's working population, twelve million people. Sandburg had known firsthand the cruel reality of the "relentless meal ticket saying"

don't-lose-me, hold your job, glue your mind
on that job or when your last nickel is gone
you live on your folks or sign for relief,
And the terror of these unknowns is a circle of
black ghosts holding men and women in toil
and danger, and sometimes shame, beyond
the dreams of their blossom days . . .

474

When he concentrated on Lincoln during the 1930s, Sandburg felt a deeper kinship than ever to his perennial subject, "the plain people." The devastation of the Depression confirmed his old socialistic views about the politics of poverty. He saw economic injustice, corruption and greed at the core. He understood lives defined by

> . . . mortgages, house rent, groceries,
> Jobs, pay cuts, layoffs, relief
> And passion and poverty and crime . . .

Even as he centered down into the Lincoln research, he was always cognizant of the present reality, the

> . . . seething of saints and sinners, toilers, loafers, oxen, apes
> In a womb of superstition, faith, genius, crime, sacrifice— . . .
> The living flowing breath of the history of nations
> Of the little family of Man hugging the little ball of Earth. . . .

He had heard it said that "The people is a myth, an abstraction." "And what myth would you put in place of the people?" he replied in poetry. "And when has creative man not toiled deep in myth?"

✳

Vigorous and virile at fifty-one, Sandburg entered the most prolific, fertile decade of his life. He was working harder than ever before, characteristically writing several books simultaneously, tailoring genre to theme and intent. He would publish seven books during that Depression decade: three for children, three biographies, one long, unorthodox, epic poem. *Rootabaga Country*, a one-volume edition of his two earlier children's books, appeared in 1929, followed in 1930 by *Potato Face*, new stories for children, and *Early Moon*, a collection of his poems "for young folks." In 1929 Sandburg published a biography of his brother-in-law, *Steichen the Photographer*, and, in 1932, a biography of Lincoln's wife, *Mary Lincoln: Wife and Widow*, with Paul Angle. His book-length poem *The People, Yes*, came out in 1936, and in 1939 his long Lincoln work culminated in the four volumes of *Abraham Lincoln: The War Years*. "When at thirty-eight years of age I issued Chicago Poems," he wrote to Joseph Warren Beach in 1930, "I didn't care about fame or distinction. Each book of mine has been issued in somewhat the same spirit as I give my songs at the end of a recital; if the whole audience walks out on me I am only doing what I would be doing if I were at home alone."

Sandburg reorganized his lecture tactics, restricting himself to four bookings a week with no more than three consecutive days of lectures. He avoided traveling more than 150 miles daily, and averaged about three hundred dollars per lecture, even in the early years of the Depression. He continued to choose bookings which took him close to libraries or people he needed to see for the Lincoln research. He turned down a sailing trip with Arthur Vance, Clarence Darrow and other friends because he was "too busy with the Lincoln work."

He took a detour, however, for the portrait of his brother-in-law. The limited edition of 925 copies of *Steichen the Photographer* appeared in 1929, with forty-nine Steichen photographs handsomely reproduced by the Knudsen process. Steichen was still working, at a huge salary, as chief photographer for Condé Nast's *Vanity Fair* and *Vogue*. He and Dana established their Umpawaug Plant Breeding Farm in West Redding, Connecticut, in 1928 so that Steichen could retreat from the stress of his work and resume his avocation—breeding delphiniums. In 1926 he had suffered a breakdown of his own from working "all day and most of the night," and had retreated to the mountains of western North Carolina to recover.

Some critics, particularly leftists, read *Steichen the Photographer* as a glorification of commercial art. Paul Rosenfeld told *New Republic* readers in January 1930 that the "idealistic Sandburg, the man who heard song and expression in tough American speech, through whom Chicago was full of gestation and spiritual force, is gone." Ironically, by simply recording Steichen's views on art, Sandburg was condemned for prostituting his own art. One of the earliest charges that Sandburg was too commercial to be taken seriously as a man of letters came from some of the leftist critics who had long supported his work.

Sandburg did set his sights on a lucrative new commercial enterprise as the American economy fractured and began to crumble. In late October 1929, D. W. Griffith had called Sandburg from Los Angeles to offer him ten thousand dollars to work with him for a week on the script for a movie about Abraham Lincoln. Sandburg had frequently praised Griffith's work in his movie columns, describing him as a creative artist who was the "pioneer of motion pictures, still exploring horizons, opening up new fields, racing ahead, traveling alone in spirit, at least." Sandburg could have been describing his own artistic life. His admiration for Griffith and his love of motion pictures *and* Lincoln made Griffith's offer particularly tantalizing. Sandburg considered it overnight and telegraphed the conditions of his acceptance the next day:

DAVID WARK GRIFFITH
UNITED ARTISTS STUDIOS
LOS ANGELES CALIF.

AM KEENLY INTERESTED IN SEEING LINCOLN PICTURE DONE WHICH WILL BE
SERIES OF PERSONALITY SKETCHES SETTING FORTH HIS TREMENDOUS RANGE
OF TRAGIC AND COMIC STOP I HAVE REVIEWED OVER ONE THOUSAND PIC-
TURES AND HAVE SEEN NEARLY EVERY PICTURE YOU HAVE MADE AND KNOW
ALMOST PRECISELY WHAT IS WANTED FOR HISTORIC ACCURACY WOVEN WITH
DRAMATIC INTEREST STOP NEARLY ALL PAST PRESENTATIONS HAVE FAKED
HOKUM WHILE NEGLECTING ESTABLISHED AND ENTERTAINING DRAMATIC
VALUES OF LINCOLN STOP HAVE FOR YEARS GIVEN THOUGHT TO LINCOLN
PORTRAYAL IN STAGE PLAY OR SCREEN ONE WEEK OR TWO WEEKS OF CON-
FERENCE WITH YOU AT ANY PRICE WOULD NOT REPRESENT THE CONTRIBU-
TION WHICH I OUGHT TO MAKE IN JUSTICE TO BOTH OF US AND TO THE
PICTURE STOP I CAN ARRANGE TO DROP WORK NOW ON LINCOLN OF WAR
YEARS BOOK ALSO CANCEL TEN RECITAL ENGAGEMENTS BETWEEN NOW AND
DECEMBER FIFTEEN STOP I COULD ARRIVE IN HOLLYWOOD ABOUT NOVEMBER
TEN AND STAY TILL JANUARY TWENTY WHEN I HAVE SIX WEEKS OF RECITAL
ENGAGEMENTS AFTER WHICH I WOULD RETURN AND GIVE MY BEST TILL
PICTURE IS FINISHED STOP I WOULD BRING WITH ME A COLLECTION OF BOOKS
PICTURES NOTES DATA POSSIBLY THE MOST COMPACT AND HUMAN EVER
ASSEMBLED BEARING ON PERSONALITY OF LINCOLN STOP TERMS WOULD BE
TEN THOUSAND DOLLARS BEFORE STARTING FOR HOLLYWOOD COMMA TEN
THOUSAND JANUARY TWO NINETEEN THIRTY COMMA TEN THOUSAND ON
COMPLETION OF PICTURE A TOTAL OF THIRTY THOUSAND DOLLARS I BELIEVE
YOU AND I HAVE EVERY ESSENTIAL BASIS FOR COOPERATION STOP MANAGING
EDITOR CHICAGO DAILY NEWS COMMA MY NEW YORK PUBLISHER ALFRED
HARCOURT ALSO OUR FRIEND LLOYD LEWIS WILL TELL YOU I KNOW HOW TO
SINK MYSELF TO GET RESULTS WITH OTHERS ON A JOB STOP THIS MESSAGE
HAS HAD ALL OF MY TIME THOUGHT SINCE OUR PHONE TALK THEREFORE
DOES NOT REPRESENT SNAP JUDGMENT

CARL SANDBURG
CHICAGO DAILY NEWS

In the heyday of the movies in the late twenties that was not an exorbitant fee. Besides, Sandburg had earned more than eleven thousand dollars that year in royalties from Harcourt, Brace, about fifteen hundred dollars in other royalties and four thousand dollars in lecture fees. He was still earning seventy-five dollars weekly at the *Chicago Daily News*. He would earn nearly $22,000 in all in 1929, a handsome return on his work. A deal with Griffith would surpass that, he reasoned, but if Griffith could offer him ten thousand dollars for a week's work, why should he not pay three times that much for as much time and work as it took to do a first-rate job?

"Griffith called me on long distance from Los Angeles," Sandburg told Charlie Dunning later, "and offered $10,000 for me to spend a week with him going over the script. I thought it over and wired him the next day the arrangement would not be fair to him nor me nor the picture; that I would take on the job for thirty thousand dollars, one-third before starting, one-third at New Year's and one-third at the completion of the picture. That was the last of it."

✳

As Sandburg set out on his first round of lectures in 1930, his friend William Allen White wrote him from Emporia, Kansas: "Can't you bring Mrs. Sandburg? Much as I love your guitar, if you can't bring both, bring her. I should say with your guitar and Mrs. Sandburg, life should be one sweet song." Paula did her best to make it that way. She calibrated a complicated household and tried to sustain harmony and a comfortable rhythm for their family life. She was her husband's anchor, handling endless practical details of his work and schedule. From years of experience, Alfred Harcourt trusted Paula's reading of proofs as much as Sandburg's, and knew her to be more prompt and attentive at times than her husband was. While he lectured, gathered Lincoln material and talked to friends and colleagues around the country about "the human family and where it is headed," she tended their family and the house on the Michigan dunes.

Margaret, nineteen in 1930, was still the family invalid, her health unstable, at the mercy of the unpredictable course of her epilepsy. She enjoyed music and books, the adult conversations of her parents and their visitors, and the childhood games and enthusiasms of her younger sisters. With Helga she played "a wild game of tennis—with inexhaustible energy . . . hot sun and all," Helga remembered. Paula struggled to keep Janet ahead of Helga in school. Sandburg's secretary Betty Peterman was a great help with his *Chicago Daily News* chores, but Paula carried the brunt of his work. "I sent off the Early Moon Mss. yesterday," she wrote while he was traveling. "It looks mighty good to me."

Wherever he was, she sent news of home. "The children all feeling fine. Bosco, Jo-Jo, Frisco [the family German Shepherds] in tip-top shape. . . . Bushels of love from us all." She kept track of his mail, and helped him attend to the most pressing letters. From Rapallo, Italy, Ezra Pound sought Sandburg's contribution to an American number of *Varieties*, ". . . about the livest mag. in Europe," Pound said. "I want you in it. Can you send me your photo. some photos of farm machinery; or methods. (I've got a damn fine lot of factory photos; but I want the open air)." He also asked for a poem. They responded with several pieces, and one of Steichen's photographs of Sandburg.

Despite Margaret's illness and Janet's slowness and the problems with her vision, the Sandburgs enjoyed an idyllic existence on the dunes. Paula gave her daughters both protection and freedom. "I went in swimming today," eleven-year-old Helga wrote to her father on March 16, 1930. "I ducked twice and went up to my neck once. It was so much fun." Paula fostered in the girls a knowledgeable love for nature, teaching them to identify birds, trees, wild flowers, butterflies and moths. With the onset of spring they built birdhouses, Margaret and Helga making theirs, and Paula protecting Janet from frustration by making one for her to paint; "and then we all will have one of our own," Helga told her father approvingly.

To protect her absent husband from worry, Paula would often skim the surface of her own illnesses or minimize Margaret's in the faithful letters which followed Sandburg around the country, but she decided not to protect him from the news of his favorite dog's death. "I don't know how to tell you about Bosco," she wrote. "But he was found 4 ft. from U.S. 12 near Harbert. No bones broken—no sign of blow or injury. He was found at 4:45 P.M. At 3:45 he was playing with Jojo & Frisco in our yard. . . . I am sending this news ahead, so we won't have to break it at your dear homecoming." The daughters worried more about their father's grief at the loss of the dog than their own.

The death of his "dandy dog" was overshadowed by news of Alfred Harcourt's son's severe injuries from an automobile accident. Hastings Harcourt, on his honeymoon in South Carolina, was nearly killed by the impact. Sandburg was working with Harcourt in New York when the news came. "You have been in a realm of trial and endurance (not without its sacraments) that I have never yet had to travel in," Sandburg told him, "and in our talks I hope I was as usual something of a fool but not so far a fool as to add a feather of weight to what you are now carrying."

Hastings eventually recovered fully, and Sandburg himself was in an automobile accident on April 13. Paula cared for him and reorganized his schedule. "MR. SANDBURG WAS INJURED IN MOTOR CAR COLLISION TODAY," she wired officials at Wellesley College where he was due to speak. "FACE CUT SHOULDER BRUISED TRAVEL IMPOSSIBLE CANCELING ALL DATES NEXT THREE WEEKS SAYS TO YOU QUOTE TELL WELLESLEY I AM TERRIBLY SORRY AND WE WILL HOPE FOR BETTER LUCK NEXT YEAR." When flowers came from Wellesley, Sandburg wrote his thanks and regrets: "Fate works oddly. In ten years I have only twice had to wire I couldn't get here. The other time it was a motor car spill instead of a sideswipe."

Recuperating at home that spring, Sandburg fell behind in all his work. A month after sending the proofs for *Early Moon*, the book of poems for children, Harcourt wrote to prod him. The country's worsening financial problems were having their impact on the publishing industry; Harcourt did not want to lose his contract with the Junior Literary Guild to publish *Early Moon* as a fall selection. "Where are the proofs?" he asked Sandburg. "If you can't read them, ask Paula to."

With Carl at home and feeling desperate about "the work now in hand, which I wonder whether I will ever live to finish," Paula's days were more hectic than ever. The Sandburgs were not a conventional midwestern family, with the special needs of the daughters living at home, and his erratic schedule, unorthodox work habits and occasional outburst of temper when his work was disrupted or his materials misplaced. In July 1930, when the hired girl left, a gentle, sturdy young Quaker woman applied for the job as housekeeper for the Sandburgs and was accepted immediately. She "belonged among the kind of folks Lincoln grew up with," Sandburg told her when he met her.

She was Martha Moorman from Swayzee, Indiana, twenty-nine, pure-hearted, with a radiant face. She found the family "different but very interesting," and quickly grew to love them all. Her sensible, reliable presence in the household was invaluable to Paula, not only allowing her to sustain the "sweet song" of a daily routine, but giving her unprecedented time to concentrate on Sandburg's work and her own, and even to travel, knowing that Martha would keep home life running smoothly. She lived with the family in the big house, took the girls home with her to Indiana from time to time and took a respectful interest in Sandburg's books. She came to see if she "could stand the job" and stayed for more than ten years.

Scattering their separate ways throughout the day, the family came together for the evening meal. Afterward Sandburg would read to them—works in progress, letters, books or news clippings on his mind. When he went off to lecture or work with his publisher, the women of the house would "do the real cleaning" because, said Martha, "you always had to wait until he went away on a trip. You were never allowed to move anything. It had to be dusted and put right back where you picked it up." Mail piled up in the dining room while Sandburg was gone— letters, newspapers, boxes and boxes of books he bought in his travels and shipped home ahead of his return.

Martha Moorman fiercely defended Sandburg against the occasional rumor that he liked to work on his third-floor sundeck in the nude. "He didn't do that," she protested. "He wouldn't go that way at all. He wasn't that kind of man." There was a canvas around the deck railing to keep his papers from falling, and he loved to work there in the sun, in shorts with no shirt, deeply tanned by the end of the summer, as bronze as an Indian, Margaret remembered. On moonlit nights the family, including Martha, often walked on the beach or through the nearby ravine, called the Blow. Some evenings they sat on the terrace singing to his guitar accompaniment, learning the new songs he gleaned on every trip away from home.

Paula taught Martha to drive by showing her how to start, stop and reverse the family car, and then leaving her alone "to sink or swim." Conscientious as she was, Martha had an accident in the Sandburg car one rainy November day after she had taken Janet and Helga to school. "The car started for the ditch," she said. "It just seemed to me like these slow-motion movies you've seen. I thought, 'Is this car ever going to quit tumbling?' " She was unhurt, but worried about what the Sandburgs would say about the badly damaged car.

"Don't mind the car," Sandburg told her. "Just so you didn't get hurt."

"That's the way he was in big things," Martha said. "Little things he would fly off about, but with big things he was very calm."

✳

He would need all his composure for the work that awaited him in the thirties. "The Lincoln of the War Years comes slowly," he reported to Rupert Hughes in March 1930. "I nearly have him inaugurated and cabinet appointed; it looks like a five-years job." "Sometimes it is like a long stretch at Joliet* to go on with this job of putting down the Lincoln of the War Years," Sandburg told Fanny Butcher in June 1930. There were distractions that summer. Janet had an eye operation. He supplemented his income with an article about the little town of Santa Claus, Indiana, working on it in July for Christmas publication. He played golf and accepted another invitation to go on a sailing trip with Arthur Vance. With his young friend the Lincoln scholar Paul Angle, he and Harcourt set to work on the book about Mary Lincoln. Through it all, he plugged away at the biography.

"The work has been tumultuous this summer," he told Emanuel Hertz, who had given him total access to his private Lincoln library. "But I feel

*Joliet, Illinois, was the site of Stateville Prison, the state penitentiary.

very humble about the results. I am surer than ever that there will never be a 'definitive' biography of Lincoln and that there likely never was and never will be a 'definitive' biography of anyone."

✳

The year 1931 was studded with losses. Sandburg's youngest sister, Martha, died on January 2 after a short illness, leaving two sons, Richard, fourteen, and Charles, twelve. Her husband, Roy Goldstone, a yardmaster for the C.B. & Q. Railroad, had been killed on the job twelve years earlier. Martha Sandburg Goldstone was only thirty-nine when she died. Sandburg seldom saw his sisters, but stayed close to the family through letters and occasional visits from Mart or Mary. "We have not got so many years ahead but what we ought to be visiting oftener," he told his brother later on. But that January Sandburg was "struggling away at Lincoln of the War Years," his overriding interest. Month by month he saw more clearly that it was going to be a "long time job dark with turmoil." Already he was having serious trouble with his eyes. "A ballplayer's legs give out at thirty-five," he told a friend, "and [an] author's eyes a decade or two later." He had written about a hundred thousand words and figured he had completed about one-fifth of the book. He predicted it would go "about three volumes."

Edgar Lee Masters's controversial *Lincoln the Man* appeared that winter. His portrait was so iconoclastic as to be unbalanced, and was widely condemned. There was an effort in Congress to ban its circulation through the mails. Vachel Lindsay speculated that Masters wrote a book about Lincoln, as he had about Chicago, in part to try to upstage Sandburg. "Masters and I were close friends at the time he wrote The Spoon River Anthology," Sandburg wrote Lincoln authority William Townsend, adding cryptically, "I could do a book on phases and origins of his latest work." Sandburg decided that the "only decent thing for me to do now is say nothing of Lincoln of the War Years." He told a friend that "Masters has been a victim of increasingly deepening embitterments. His Lincoln book is one more of a series of curious reversals and treacheries. Most of his arguments are sincere for the present time though he did not hold them with such intensity and hate fifteen years ago. How and why he changed is an intricate story of which I know some essential parts."

Sandburg and Paul Angle were moving forward with their Mary Lincoln biography, Sandburg handling the text and Angle preparing source documents and notes. Angle was thorough, reliable and genial. His scholarship made him a "worthy historian and analyst," and a valuable ally in the Lincoln work. Sandburg enjoyed his company as well. "Enclosed is the marriage chapter," he wrote Angle that spring; ". . . a thick book could be done with what we have but it wouldn't solve anything special or if it did it would break all records and answer those ancient riddles, 'What is love?' and 'Is sex necessary?' "

Sandburg settled into a more leisurely routine that summer, resigned to the slow pace of the Lincoln work. He often swam at noon, played golf regularly, tried to get eight hours sleep at night. "Held down by work on Lincoln of the War Years," he was determined to garner his resources for the "long haul." He passed up a request from Robert Scripps, relayed through Harcourt, to write a biography of his father, E. W. Scripps. Lincoln would keep him tied up far into the future.

Harcourt's business was "doing pretty well," he told Sandburg then, "though of course at a slower pace than in boom times." Sinclair Lewis had just surprised him by unceremoniously breaking off his long association with Harcourt, Brace. Harcourt was forbearing, telling Sandburg privately, "I only hope Red pulls himself together and writes another good book, no matter who's to publish it." Lewis had won the Nobel Prize for literature in 1930, the first American to do so. Harcourt had been with him through *Main Street, Babbitt, Arrowsmith, Elmer Gantry* and other books. He was a significant loss to the firm.

In that year of losses, the Sandburgs watched anxiously over Oma, now 76, whose usually vigorous health began to fail. She had cancer. Paula's parents still lived in Elmhurst, where Opa passed his time working in his lush flower garden. Just as Oma planted the seeds of prodigious industry and ingenuity in her children, Opa gave them an abiding love for the land. Opa's gardening skill was transmitted to his son and daughter, who lifted it to an art form. At his Connecticut farm Steichen was putting his artist's eye and scientist's vision to the intricate task of breeding hybrid delphiniums. As illness curtailed her activities, Oma wrote loving letters to her grandchildren in Michigan, sounding out the English words she could not spell. "Dear Janet, How are you getting along in Skoll with all the escamition, be verry carful, because the end conts far the most for the passing!" she wrote; "do you like the Radio as well as ever Opa dos and I like et better than ever. . . . Udels of love from Opa and Oma."

The Sandburgs' active devotion to family and friends was not superseded by work commitments. Sandburg made a special effort in 1931 to be of help to Vachel Lindsay, knowing that he was struggling financially and personally. He had visited the Lindsays in Springfield, and encouraged Lindsay in his application for a Guggenheim Fellowship to support his work and his family. "I will go the limit for Vachel," Sandburg promised Lindsay's wife, Elizabeth, the young English and Latin teacher Lindsay had met and quickly married in 1925. She was devoted to Lindsay, but their marriage was beset from the first with financial difficulties. By 1929 Lindsay had moved his family to his boyhood home in Springfield, Illinois. The idealistic poet was a poor financial manager. A gifted platform performer, he came to despise the "Higher Vaudeville" of reciting his most popular poems on demand for lecture audiences. He doted on his wife and children but could not support them, and often made their lives unhappy with his intensity and fluctuation of moods. Few people beyond his family knew then that Lindsay had epilepsy.

On December 2, 1931, Sandburg asked William Rose Benét to send Lindsay a copy of his endorsement of his work. "Those were beautiful and forthright sentiments—a fine statement of the case of Lindsay," Sandburg said, hoping that Benét's words would lift Lindsay's spirits. Lindsay had come home from a particularly grueling lecture tour ill and exhausted, with less than seventy-six dollars for his pains. He had more than four thousand dollars in debts. He gave a final lecture to a warm hometown audience at the First Christian Church in Springfield.

During the first week in December Lindsay was taking bromide and Luminal for his epilepsy. He spent much time in bed and suffered frightening auditory hallucinations, believing he heard voices plotting to kill him and Elizabeth. While bromide allergies or an imbalance of bromide and Luminal could stimulate hallucinations and other side effects, Lindsay's bizarre behavior was attributed to instability and depression. Plausibly, the drugs he was taking may have exacerbated or even precipitated his anguish. Modern medicine would have diagnosed and effectively treated his epilepsy much earlier in his life, and minimized what appeared to be manic-depression. But in 1931, when his worried wife talked to their doctor about her fears that Lindsay would harm himself, she was told only to keep careful watch.

On December 4 Lindsay and Elizabeth had tea with friends at the Abraham Lincoln Hotel in Springfield. Lindsay was ebullient, but his spirits plummeted by nightfall. Morosely, he told his wife that his life and work were finished, that he had grown to be an old man. Later in the evening he went on a three-hour verbal rampage, threatening to leave his family, calling Elizabeth a scarlet woman. Elizabeth kept an anxious watch over him, dropping off to sleep only when, at last, he seemed relaxed and calm. Late in the night, depressed and still hallucinating, he quietly left his room, went downstairs to the dining room of the house where he had spent his boyhood, arranged pictures of his wife and two children on the table, lit two candles, and stepped into the nearby bathroom. There he poured a bottle of Lysol into a tea glass and drank it.

His wife heard him as he climbed the stairs, by then on his hands and knees. "I took Lysol," he managed to tell her. "They tried to get me! I got them first."

Lindsay's death deeply saddened the Sandburgs. His family let it be thought that a heart attack killed him, a story which stood until Elizabeth gave Edgar Lee Masters the stark details for his 1935 biography of Lindsay. When the news reached the Sandburgs, Sandburg wrote a heartfelt editorial tribute to Lindsay for the *Chicago Daily News*. In later years, the Sandburgs suggested that Lindsay's epilepsy seemed to worsen with the stress of his family life. They thought it had been unwise for him to marry and father children. Marriage could be dangerous for epileptics, they believed. As difficult and lonely as Lindsay's bachelor life was, his health had seemed better then.

Down in Springfield, Illinois, Paul Angle was a pallbearer for Lindsay's funeral and took charge of a testimonial fund, "an ambiguous term," he told Sandburg, "to cover a collection for the benefit of Elizabeth and the children. He left practically nothing. So far we have $1300, and I expect twice that amount. It's a shame the feeling behind the checks that come in wasn't made manifest during his life. . . . You should see the young son! What a boy he's going to be!"

∗

Margaret Sandburg was twenty then, dreaming of "some kind of writing career," and gradually forming her own conclusions about what her adult life as an epileptic would be like. "I had no romantic ideas or dreams of a home and family," she remembered, because she thought her epilepsy would discourage anyone from marrying her. "This was a conclusion I reached without ever thinking of Lindsay," she wrote many years later. ". . . I simply knew without thinking much on the subject that I would never marry. . . . I certainly knew that I couldn't provide for myself. If I married what could I give a husband? A lot of trouble."

Margaret was soon to suffer her own violent siege of hallucinations. In February 1932, just months after Lindsay's death, Paula took Margaret to the Mayo Clinic for treatment. Sandburg was lecturing in Florida, and Paula wrote to tell him about Margaret's latest problems: "Margaret had five light seizures—after which she dozed and then went into another series of four seizures. She has had no attacks since then—that is, for a period of six days. . . . Her freedom from seizures the past six nights must be due to the ketogenic diet—or to exhaustion following two days and three nights of bromide intoxication." Paula shared the harrowing details of Margaret's illness in a letter to Sandburg:

> During this period of intoxication she was violent part of the time throwing her legs & arms about wildly and having to be forcibly restrained; part of the time crying, worried, fearful; all this time having hallucinations: rats & snakes crawling in her bed biting her—seeing "little pink epilepsies swimming in blood on the ceiling"—crying that she had leprosy, showing her hands to prove it, screaming that a nurse is about to murder her mother. . . . Early Sunday morning in the last hour of this bromide intoxication she quieted and whispered to me as if fearful that some presences might overhear what she was confiding to me alone (altho no one else was in the room): "I have the Secret. It is the Circle. Wrap me in a ball. That's the Secret. The Circle." So I drew circles about her in the air— and she sighed with relief. She was free for a little while. A last few rats began biting her. These I picked up by the tails with pantomimic gesture and threw them out of the window. After her breakfast Sunday morning she fell asleep—and slept a deep quiet sleep, all relaxed—for five hours. This was her first sleep in 60 hours. After this sleep she awoke rational. Her mind was now perfectly clear. She remembered very little of her delirium.

Paula thought Margaret was much improved after the traumatic bromide intoxication. For months before, her sleep had seemed drugged, and she had to be forcibly aroused. Paula or Martha would wash her face in cold water to force her awake, and even then she was groggy for a time each morning. Paula hoped that the right combination of diet and medicine would control Margaret's seizures. She would stay with her at the Mayo Clinic for as long as necessary to discover that balance. Sandburg, far away, lent his support with words. "We were very happy to receive your wire Tuesday the 16th," Paula told him. "Again it was your very presence here with us. No one but you can put so much love and solace in a few words—as you can—Dearest."

Paula confronted Margaret's epilepsy with a mother's fierce, anxious love and a scientist's objective observation. Her letters are revealing documents. Her clear, dispassionate record of Margaret's response to various therapies enabled her to care for Margaret expertly at home. Helga remembered standing in the doorway looking on during Margaret's attacks of delirium. Paula had noted the "method of hot packs for the whole body followed by perspiration" used to "clear up the intoxication," along with hot water given internally "to induce perspiration and to flush the toxin out of the system." Paula and Martha would wrap Margaret in hot towels and give her hot baths, in the mode of the Mayo treatment. Sometimes, in the aftermath of such an attack and remedy, Helga would read to her older sister as she rested in bed. It was *Penrod* and I was terrified—because she was 'different,' " Helga remembered. Paula kept an enduring vigil over Margaret's diet, her daily routine, controlling her exercise, warding off events which would make her nervous or excited.

Sandburg had little choice but to leave Margaret's physical and emotional care in Paula's keeping while he worked harder than ever writing and lecturing. It was clear that Margaret and Janet would always live in the shelter of the home he and Paula could provide for them, and that would take every financial resource he could marshal. Amidst his winter lecture tours, he finished the text for *Mary Lincoln: Wife and Widow*. With Paula and Margaret settled back home, Sandburg traveled to New York to work on the project with Harcourt, who was already promoting the serial sale.

As the Depression wore on, Sandburg reduced his lecture fees, and book royalties declined with American buying power. In May of 1932, *Chicago Daily News* publisher Frank Knox ordered economy measures which included cutting all salaries in half. With his salary reduced to $37.50 weekly, Sandburg resigned, deciding it was more profitable to give his time and energy exclusively to the Lincoln work. He believed that relinquishing the job would enable him to finish the biography a year or two sooner. For the time being, he was reading proofs for the Mary Lincoln book, writing passages of the Lincoln biography and carrying forward the painstaking research for other sections. Recurring eye problems took him to his Chicago eye specialist that summer. He told a friend, "I have so worn my eyes while working on Lincoln: the War Years that it is a serious question whether they last to finish the job which is only half done, a 3 vol affair."

*

In 1932 more than a million jobless, homeless people scavenged the country in search of work. Before Black Tuesday the national unemployment rate stood at 3.2 percent. That figure had jumped to 8.7 percent in 1930, 15.9 percent in 1931 and 23.6 percent in 1932.

At least the national misery was democratic, touching almost every family in some way. Automobile sales had tumbled eighty percent since 1929. In the year that Charles Lindbergh's infant son was kidnapped and murdered, and Adolf Hitler won thirty-two percent of the popular vote for president of Germany, the Depression worsened beyond national expectation or tolerance. It was inevitable that Herbert Hoover would be defeated by the Democratic nominee, New York governor Franklin Delano Roosevelt, chosen on the fourth ballot. The year had two theme songs, "Brother, Can You Spare a Dime?" and, thanks to FDR's campaign, "Happy Days Are Here Again." In any American town men could be seen picking over garbage dumps for scraps of food or remnants of clothing. Children died of malnutrition. Millions of hopeless men, women and children stood in long bread lines or queued up at soup kitchens for one meal a day. For those who could afford one, the radio was a lifeline, especially as money for movies and vaudeville tickets disappeared. Jack Benny, Ed Sullivan, Amos and Andy, and Fred Allen diverted the American people, and when FDR promised them a New Deal, twenty-two million voters supported him, against the fifteen million who held out for Hoover.

There was another family tragedy that long, dispiriting year. Janet was struck by a car in September. At age sixteen, she was just beginning her freshman year in high school in the nearby town of Three Oaks. Her struggles in school had left Janet behind her classmates. Helga, a bright student, was two years younger than Janet but only a year behind her in school, held back because her mother did not want her to be in Janet's class or ahead of her.

Janet had just crossed the street in front of the school that September day when she realized she had forgotten her lunch pail. Without looking at traffic, she darted back across the street into the path of a car driven by the Three Oaks postmaster. The impact left her unconscious and bleeding in the street, her skull fractured.

"Our Janet was knocked down by a motorcar in Three Oaks yesterday," Sandburg told Harcourt, "had a gash in the head stitched, also stitches in one ear, has had no food in 36 hours, could only be forced to take three spoons of water in that time. The doctors say all indications are favorable to recovery, however; she won't be disfigured."

"Your letter with word of Janet's fracture sounds a tragic shame," Harcourt commiserated. "What hostages we gave to fate with our children!" Fresh from Hastings's ordeal, Harcourt shared the Sandburgs' anxiety. Hastings had recovered, and soon Sandburg telegraphed to say Janet would also. "Jesus, but I am relieved by your wire," Harcourt answered.

The injury left Janet with frequent headaches which would disrupt her education and trouble her for years. The accident became so interwoven in the family mythology that it was often given as the reason that Janet, in that brilliant family, was slow to learn. She had always been that way, but her accident intensified the problem. She could not keep up with her peers or even those a year or two younger, and Paula fretted about how to find a comfortable pace for Janet without inhibiting Helga. Janet missed most of the school year because of her accident, and failed ninth grade as Helga was promoted to tenth. Janet would not complete her high school degree until May 1938 when she was twenty-two years old.

While the family worried over Janet's accident during the fall of 1932, Sandburg was working on a "long gloom and bitterness chapter" of the Lincoln biography, an appropriately melancholy backdrop for the family drama. Sandburg was more driven than ever to earn all he could to protect Margaret, Helga and his "shy, whimsical Janet." The Sandburgs supported FDR's Presidential candidacy that fall, and rejoiced when Sandburg's close friend and horseshoe partner, Judge Henry Horner, was elected governor of Illinois. "I almost feel like getting drunk about Henry being Gov. of Ill.," he told Oliver Barrett. "And then comes the thought that for a man with his sense of justice it will be a hell of a job and shorten his life."

That winter Harcourt and Sandburg talked privately about whether Sandburg would ever be a serious candidate for the Nobel Prize, like Harcourt's former star author Sinclair Lewis. It was Sandburg's "decisive judgment" that he would never be considered because he had "failed to 'click' " in Europe, his language was "too Americanese," and in "both the poetry and the Rootabaga stories there is a batty and queer, if not crazy approach." He was sometimes mentioned as a Nobel candidate over the years, but never received the honor. In later years, when asked if he had been awarded the Nobel Prize for literature, he teased that he had, and furthermore, he had received it twice—once from John Steinbeck and once from Ernest Hemingway. Both those writers, upon winning the Nobel Prize, were quoted as saying that it should have gone to Sandburg. But Sandburg told Harcourt in 1933, "too much of my language . . . might seem almost nationalistic in its flaunting of the North American airs and syllables."

✳

During the austerity of the early Depression years, the hardest loss the Sandburgs and Steichens had to endure was Oma's death in 1933. Steichen called his mother the "guiding and inspiring influence" in his life. He wrote encouraging letters during her long illness, and Paula went to Elmhurst, Illinois, to care for her and Opa. "I hope the new radium treatment does not hurt too much," Steichen wrote to his mother; "remember radium is not like the parent who spanks the kid and says 'it hurts me more than it does you'—Radium says—'I'm sorry if it hurts but that's the way I do my job.—That's how I cure.' . . . love—& love from your only Gaesjack." Tragically, Oma received excessive doses of radium for cervical cancer.

"She had been losing ground steadily the last week," Paula wrote to her brother and Dana near the end, when her mother was unable to eat or drink, to sleep, or to recognize her family. Margaret, Janet and Helga were not allowed in Oma's room, but shortly before her death, she recognized her husband and daughter, speaking to them part in Luxembourg dialect, part in English: "Opa, Opa, Opa, Lily, Lily, Lily, stay with me."

Helga remembered Oma's death as "a terrifying time for Opa, Mother and Uncle Ed." Margaret, knowing only Oma's immense warmth and love, could not look at her body, prepared for the funeral service, which was held in a funeral parlor because the local Catholic priest had refused to participate on the grounds that Oma had not attended church in a long time. Opa was furious. The Illinois church was not like their church back in Luxembourg anyway, he said. Paula followed her mother's wishes for cremation, as Oma had feared being buried alive ever since reading the stories of Edgar Allan Poe. Afterward, Opa refused all invitations to live elsewhere. Alone in the little house in Elmhurst, he tended his beautiful garden and began to write letters to his children and grandchildren as Oma had always done. English was a crazy language, he used to say, but somehow he had learned to write it well. His brief letters gave clear details about his garden, the weather, his occasional visits to the doctor. He never spoke of his loneliness for Oma, but signed his letters, as she often signed hers, "Love and Kisses to you all."

✳

1933–1936

22. Heroes,
Did You Say?

These are heroes then—among the plain people—
Heroes, did you say? And why not? They
give all they've got and ask no questions and
take what comes and what more do you
want?

—Carl Sandburg, *The People, Yes*, 1936

Sandburg had spent his life articulating a "tangled passion about humanity." At first he watched helplessly as the Depression threatened to destroy the American Dream. Then he took a deliberate "detour" from the Lincoln biography to write a transcendent anthem to "the plain people," his ultimate affirmation of faith, *The People, Yes*. After World War I Sandburg had deliberately turned away from the heartbreaking realities of his times. He spent most of the decade of the Roaring Twenties immersed in another century, living with Lincoln and American folk music. Lincoln's strong prairie presence pervaded his life, awakening him to his own personal history. The Lincoln of the war years forced him to examine the nation's past, and once again to live squarely in the midst of his own time.

Everywhere he saw parallels in history to illuminate the harrowing drama of the Depression. He could see shadows of Lincoln's Presidency in Roosevelt's. The February 1933 issue of *Today* carried his piece on parallels between Roosevelt's New Deal and Lincoln's Emancipation policies. He frequently wrote to President Roosevelt and other public officials about the lessons of history. He told FDR he was the "best light of democracy that has occupied the White House since Lincoln."

"All the time you keep growing . . . ," Sandburg would write FDR in 1935.

Having written for ten years now on "Abraham Lincoln: the War Years," starting this year on the fourth and final volume, I have my eyes and ears in two eras and cannot help drawing parallels. . . . What many of us have come to see is that you had long preparation for what you are doing— and as with Lincoln there has been a response of the People to you: they have done something to you and made you what you could not have been without them.

He worked then in two eras, forging ahead with the Lincoln biography, but crafting all the while his poem-testament to the sheer grit of the American people, caught in one more national crisis. Almost mystically, Lincoln sustained him, fascinated him endlessly, was the source of constant discovery and revelation. He told Alice Corbin Henderson, "the man grows on me all along, has symphonic values if I can catch and gather them; he was one ecco homo prize galoot."

As he plowed further into *Abraham Lincoln: The War Years*, Sandburg found the drudgery of the research "oppressive," but loved the work "from the writing angle." As a biographer, he probed the compelling "paradox or mystery" of his subject's life and times. He was immensely disciplined, always aware that renunciation was essential if the book was to be completed. In demand as a radio performer, he declined all offers because a "ten minute broadcast is a day's work." He conserved his energy, budgeted his lecture appearances, weighed time against money. He read every book and periodical even tangentially relevant to the Civil War. He took time away from his work only for special enterprises, such as a trip down to Springfield to help dedicate the Vachel Lindsay Bridge. "At first I thought I ought not to spare the time," he said, "and then I got to thinking about Vachel and how two of his best poems are on Lincoln and Altgeld ("Sleep softly, Eagle Forgotten") and . . . I admitted it was my duty to be there."

In the course of his research, Sandburg depended on a widening network of Lincoln scholars and historians who gave him material, insights, criticism and fellowship. Oliver Barrett, Lloyd Lewis, Paul Angle and John Hervey provided continual assistance. Allan Nevins of Columbia University and James Randall of the University of Illinois agreed to furnish Lincoln material. Sandburg had encouragement from Worthington C. Ford, who had been head of the Library of Congress manuscript division, and Lincoln expert William Townsend of Kentucky. Joshua Speed, nephew of Lincoln's close friend and colleague, sent him reminiscences about his uncle and Lincoln.

The stress of the Lincoln work introduced Sandburg to "all the elations and depressed moods of the mural painters who did the interior of the

Vatican," and his lectures gave him a welcome break, some time away from home and the labor on the biography, and a chance to look for new research material. Always, he relished the fellowship and fun of the road. On March 2 he was in Los Angeles to speak to the Epsilon Phi English honorary society at the University of Southern California in a four-part series which later included Christopher Morley, Robert Frost and T. S. Eliot.

The Depression was having its effect on his lecture fees as well as on wages for all American workers. As much as he needed the income, Sandburg had to lower his fees. He wrote to his old friend Bill Leiserson at Antioch College to arrange a lecture date. "I know all about everybody around Antioch being broke just like the New York depositors in the bank of the United Snakes [*sic*]," he joked. "More than half the idea is that I stop at Antioch to see old friends and soak in more than I exude." He tried to arrange as many lectures as possible on his own without the help—and the fee—of lecture agents so that there would be no required guarantee and "no goddam contracts to sign."

Sandburg moved regularly from the Lincoln biography to lecture re-citals to work on poetry, "writing new verses and rewriting and revising old ones, shaping a book that I hope will stand alongside the others easily." Harcourt was encouraging him toward a sixth book of poems, but Sandburg told Alice Corbin Henderson, who had put his first collection into Harcourt's hands in 1916, "I'm going to wait years before committing my sixth book of verse to the frozen assets of fixed and irremediable and immitigable printers' ink."

✳

Sandburg, like Lincoln, was a creature of his times. The Depression of the 1930s resurrected the specter of the hard times of the 1890s. Sandburg knew what it was to be penniless, hopeless, emasculated by events beyond his control. The current crisis took him back to his own days as a socialist organizer, and then farther back to his childhood witness of his father's struggles. His deepening grasp of nineteenth-century American history clarified the turbulence of twentieth-century American life. "I see many striking parallels between Lincoln and Franklin Roosevelt in political method, in decision amid chaos, in reading trends, in development of policy so as to gather momentum, in resilience and acknowledgement of hazards—and much else," he wrote to New Dealer Raymond Moley.

The Poet of the People could not keep silent during the American ordeal of the 1930s. "Am sunk fathoms deep where some good poems just stepped out and wrote themselves," he told Harcourt in the summer of 1933. "One titled 'Moonlight and Maggots' has been accepted by [Archibald MacLeish at] *Fortune.* It will be the first poetry they have ever run and it seems to me the distinction of breaking in is almost equal to Maxwell Anderson's being first to arrive in The New Republic with 'sonofabitch.' "

It was poetry which brought Sandburg and Archibald MacLeish together, and although they saw each other only occasionally from 1933 until the late 1960s, nearly two hundred of their letters survive, charting one of the most significant literary friendships of Sandburg's life. Sandburg was MacLeish's senior by fourteen years. MacLeish was born in Illinois to the man who was a founder of the department store Carson Pirie Scott in Chicago and vice president of the first board of trustees of the University of Chicago. MacLeish was the aristocrat and scholar, Sandburg the swaggering self-educated son of immigrants. MacLeish had played football at Yale, while Sandburg played football and basketball at Lombard. MacLeish was a lawyer and teacher while Sandburg was a socialist organizer and newspaperman. Despite their different backgrounds, the two poets shared a deep faith in the American experience and a conviction that the poet has an obligation to address the issues of his times. Sandburg believed MacLeish to be "about the healthiest individual force in American poetry," and MacLeish returned his admiration. MacLeish's controversial *Frescoes for Mr. Rockefeller's City* appeared in 1933, the year that artist Diego Rivera, commissioned to create a mural for the new Rockefeller Center, painted Lenin into his panorama. Rivera was fired when he refused to erase Lenin's portrait, and his mural was destroyed. MacLeish dedicated *Frescoes for Mr. Rockefeller's City* to Carl Sandburg. When Mike Gold, in *The New Republic,* attacked the book as anti-Semitic, fascist and Hitlerish, Sandburg jumped to MacLeish's defense. He had his own encounter with Gold in an attack on *Steichen the Photographer.* "I kept to one issue with Mike," he told MacLeish. "I had to hold in because I have Mike's number from so many directions." *The New Republic* printed his letter supporting MacLeish, who called it a masterpiece. "And now I feel guilty," he wrote Sandburg, "because I am afraid Mr. Lincoln is still in [18]63 and may never get to '64 because of Mike and me."

*

More than fifteen million Americans were out of work in 1933, the year that Hitler became Chancellor of Germany and Roosevelt set to work waging war against the economic emergency which crippled his country. Aspiring to achieve both economic recovery and reform, Roosevelt acted swiftly, calling Congress into special session. In rapid sequence came the Emergency Banking Act, the Farm Relief and Inflation Act, the National Industrial Recovery Act, the Muscle Shoals–Tennessee Valley Development Act and the Railroad Emergency Act. FDR soon revised the nation's vocabulary, giving it the abbreviations and acronyms of his far-reaching programs—FERA, NIRA, TVA, REFC, CCC, WPA. He reminded his fellow Americans that the only thing they had to fear was fear itself. Humorist Will Rogers reminded them that FDR's administration was the only time "when the fellow with money is worrying more than the one without it." Sandburg's friend Otto Harbach had a hit Broadway show that year in *Roberta* and a hit song from the show in "Smoke Gets in Your Eyes." Jack Benny became a radio star, his dour miserliness an ironic counterpoint to the economic hardships his listeners faced.

At year's end Sandburg received a letter on White House stationery from Eleanor Roosevelt: "Miss Frances Perkins [FDR's Secretary of Labor and the first female Cabinet member] tells me that you will be good enough to come sometime for the night to play for my husband. I think a Sunday night in January will be perfect, if you and Mrs. Sandburg can come, and practically any night that you find convenient will do." While he did not expect Paula to travel with him, he responded with pleasure to Eleanor Roosevelt's invitation. He got a form letter in reply from her secretary Malvina Scheider, thanking him for his "courteous offer to give a program of songs at the White House" and telling him that "all arrangements for musicales" were in the hands of Steinway & Sons in New York, to whom "all those who kindly offer their services are referred."

In 1930 Herbert Hoover, said Sandburg, "extended me unusual courtesies in White House rambles and inspections," but it would be 1937 before FDR would give Sandburg a personal tour of the "Lincoln corners of special interest in the White House."

∗

Carl and Paula Sandburg went to Hawaii in the spring of 1934 on one of their rare journeys together. Sandburg would lecture at the University of Hawaii, but otherwise it was to be a vacation they badly needed. Paula was still grieving for Oma, and Sandburg was weary and plagued with chronic vision problems.

He had just finished typewritten page 1,958 of *Abraham Lincoln: The War Years*. It had taken him more than five years to get that far. He could not estimate how much longer the work would last. Sometimes he despaired of finishing. It seemed almost as difficult to write those years as it must have been to live through them. "Nobody will read it, it's too heavy," he brooded. "And maybe I'll never finish it. My only satisfaction is that a great and lovable character has become a reality to me. My recompense is that I've been on a long journey with one of the greatest companions of men."

Sandburg needed to get away temporarily from the intensity of the work, for it was easy to lose perspective and proportion. He had also taken to heart the punishing lesson of overwork on *The American Songbag.* Therefore, he and Paula left wintry Birchwood Beach and Harbert, Michigan, in early March 1934 for the trip to the West Coast and then the journey by ship to Hawaii. Sandburg had not taken an ocean voyage since his 1918 trip to Sweden, and Paula had never left the continent.

En route to Hawaii they saw Alice Corbin Henderson and other friends in Santa Fe. Sandburg took Paula for her first view of the Grand Canyon. The Pacific voyage was restful, and when they arrived in Hawaii, they were greeted by university officials and students who gave them bright flower leis, "more leis than could be piled around our necks," Paula wrote home.

> When we reached our room at the hotel—we piled our dresser—the tables—with leis! We hung leis over the telephone and on the beds! There was a knock at the door—and a big box (about 4 ft long) of flowers arrived for us—roses and more roses and giant gladioli and lilies and very sweet bunches of pansies! Our room is a bower! And from our windows we see the sea and the mountains—and marvelous great banyan trees—and palms!

On the homeward journey, the Sandburgs were greeted in San Francisco by composer Ernst Bacon and his wife, who entertained them for the weekend. The Sandburgs particularly wanted to visit Yosemite, which Paula had never seen. The Bacons drove them to the great redwood forest on a bright Sunday morning. As Sandburg stood in awe before one mammoth redwood, other tourists paused to watch him. He noticed the crowd gathering as if they expected some great pronouncement. Pausing for maximum stage effect, he looked the giant tree up and down.

Then he roared, in his best stage voice, "Jesus, that's a big son-of-a-bitch!"

✳

In 1933 Sandburg had been elected to the National Institute of Arts and Letters, over the protest of some of its more staid members, particularly Robert Underwood Johnson of *Century* magazine. The august membership had included Mark Twain, William Dean Howells, Augustus Saint-Gaudens, Edward MacDowell, Henry Adams, Henry James, Theodore Roosevelt, Woodrow Wilson and Julia Ward Howe, the first woman elected. As secretary of the Institute, Johnson made a personal crusade of excluding "rebel poets or cubist painters." Robert Frost had been elected in 1916, Edgar Lee Masters in 1918, Edith Wharton in 1926. Johnson had tried to exclude Stephen Vincent Benét because of the realism of *John Brown's Body*, but he was overruled. In 1933 Johnson tried to close the door on Carl Sandborg, as he spelled the name, as well as T. S. Eliot, Robinson Jeffers and H. L. Mencken. "Ye God!" Johnson wrote to a colleague. "What a quartet—Eliot, Jeffers, Sandborg and M———! Surely the radicals will soon have control. I think the only thing for me to do is resign." Nevertheless, Sandburg made it into the Institute in 1933, and into its more select inner circle, the Academy of Arts and Letters, in 1940.

In the late twenties when critic and poet Malcolm Cowley was writing portraits of authors for *Brentano's Book Chat*, he wanted to do a portrait on Sandburg. He had accompanied Sandburg when he gave a lecture recital to a Junior League, and teased him about that elite audience. After the lecture Cowley and Sandburg relaxed at an East Side beer garden and sang some folk songs "a little more scabrous than those [Sandburg] had expurgated for the members of the Junior League," Cowley said. When Cowley became "indignant about the great poet having to perform before the Junior League and other audiences," he urged him in a *Book Chat* article to smash his guitar. Years later Cowley told Sandburg it was "No use my telling the poet to smash his guitar (which you never did smash, damn you)." "No, I didn't smash the guitar like you said," Sandburg teased, "but went and bought a better one."

For all the company they gave him and all the Lincoln research he did en route, the lectures were "mainly a breadwinning exploit" for Sandburg during the harsh decade of the thirties. He told Cowley, "When you have three daughters and no sons, and one of the daughters is a semi-invalid and another not entirely recovered from a head fractured in an automobile accident, you don't travel always as you might like to, and you try not to talk about it. . . . Without the platform work, of which the guitar and songs are a part, I could not get by for a living while doing the sort of long-time books I am on. . . ."

As a poet and critic, Cowley thought that Sandburg's poetry had been dismissed by many critics and academicians during the twenties because free verse was out of vogue. He foresaw a resurgence of interest in proletarian poetry because of the Depression, telling Sandburg in 1935 that "a lot of people are talking about proletarian poetry, and always without mentioning the simple primer-book fact that almost the only good proletarian poetry in this country has been written by a guy named Carl Sandburg."

✳

With Sandburg's work occupying almost all his energy and focus, Paula and the children expanded their own interests. Paula bought an adjoining lot to have more room for gardening. Now she took the Depression-era housewife's pride in producing much of her family's food supply. She had ambitious plans to grow apples, peaches, apricots, plums and cherries. Her daughters shared her love of gardening, and Helga developed "a heavy maternal desire for a Jersey cow." The Sandburgs' "Paw-Paw Patch" was alive with animals and birds—"six giant grey Toulouse geese, a few white Pekin ducks and a flock of twenty-five White Rock pullets." There were New Zealand White rabbits and chickens for food, and Helga and her mother "became proficient at the swift kill and the skinning, plucking and eviscerating of whatever was for our table."

While Helga could be shy like her sisters, she had an ardent energy which they lacked, and she poured it all into her campaign for a cow. Martha Moorman, who knew how to milk cows and would teach her, was her ally. Helga promised to do all the work and be totally responsible for the cow. Her mother gave in at last, but Sandburg resisted.

"No," he said finally. "She can't handle a cow. And a cow's expensive. How about a goat? I knew goats in Galesburg when I was a boy. What's the girl going to do when the cow's got to be bred? Lead her down the back roads for ten miles? With a goat you can put her in the back of the flivver."

Compromising, Helga and her mother set out to search for a goat. They bought three from a dairy with a clean barn and quiet, handsome does, spending ninety dollars for the trio: Leona, a half-bred white Saanen doe; Sophie, light brown and half Toggenburg; and Felicia, the Toggenburg and the only purebred of the trio. Soon Paula bought two more goats. For years she had suffered gall bladder problems and could drink very little cow's milk. When someone told her goat's milk was good for her stomach problems, she tried it and found that it was true, and from that time on goat's milk, cheese and ice cream were staples in the family diet.

Sandburg called the summer of 1935 the season of the three Gs— "garden, geese and goats." He did not have time to help with any of them, but he was proud of the work his household did, and of the abundance of milk and food the women were producing from their enterprises. They "abolished" the milkman, getting all the milk they needed from the small herd of goats, and buying a separator to make cheese and butter. "Over 200 quarts of string beans, corn, spinach and broccoli are put up and in the cellar, and perhaps a peck of dry lima beans, more to come," Sandburg told Harcourt in awe. "For a month and more we have had cantalope unlimited and the end not in sight. Of squash and pumpkin there will be enough for many weeks after frost, besides parsnips for February and March. A pig will come next, they tell me."

Since the Milwaukee experiment with chicken farming, Paula had wanted to farm in earnest, and she went at it with zeal. "The farm here progresses beyond words," Sandburg told Oliver Barrett. Paula was building the "most colossal barn in the great state of Michigan." It was going to be a "regular Old Testament edifice" which would hold "more goats, kids and revolutionary pamphlets than any other barn in Michigan."

With the farmwork flourishing about him, Sandburg spent most of his time at home in his third floor workroom, where books were stacked everywhere and sturdy wooden apple crates continued to serve as typing table, bookshelves and filing cases. Sandburg could step out onto the adjoining deck into the sun and fresh air, or go up to the "crow's nest" to watch sudden fierce lake storms. He was hard at work in 1935 on two "long-time books," taking regular detours from *Abraham Lincoln: The War Years* to work on the long, ever-growing poem *The People, Yes*. His eyes slowed him down, and he had painful neuritis attacks, but he seldom veered from his work. He did stop to spend time with Frank Lloyd Wright, who was visiting a lake shore neighbor. It was the first time he had seen Wright in seven years, and it pleased him to hear that Wright's Taliesen apprentices were "working on an evening of marionette production of Rootabaga stories."

He lectured from the Midwest to the South to New York that fall. Back home, he concentrated on *The People, Yes*, which had begun to "effloresce," he said. He read parts of it to his family at the dinner table, and at the end of November 1935 sent Harcourt a final draft, telling him he would have a "large intelligent horselaugh" when he compared that draft to the earliest one.

He had some of his best talks about writing then with reporter Brenda Ueland of Minneapolis, a vivacious brunette divorcée whom he met through Joseph Warren Beach. In the late thirties when he was in Minneapolis, Sandburg stayed with Brenda and her family in their big, old house overlooking Lake Calhoun. A sparkling, outspoken woman of Norwegian heritage, she had lived a bohemian life in Greenwich Village before the First World War, part of the ebullient circle that included John Reed and Louise Bryant. "I was the first woman in the Western World to have my hair all cut off," she exulted. "I went to Henri in Greenwich Village . . . and I told him to cut my hair all off. He was frightened, appalled. To cut off that nice, very black, ladylike hair, with a pug! It was splendid. Wherever I went seas of white faces turned to gaze. That is just what I liked."

Despite her avant-garde life-style and her passion for romance and adventure, Brenda was a purist about love. She and Sandburg shared a deep attraction, took long walks around the lake shore near her home, and talked endlessly about politics and writing. They shared the con-strained, uniquely enriching love between a man and a woman who could consummate an emotional, spiritual bond physically, but do not. The resulting mutual respect forged a deep friendship between them, and for years they enjoyed the electricity of their meetings, in person or in letters. Brenda followed two commandments, she said: "No Cruelty. And no Lying." She believed that those two rules would take care of everything—"ignorance-inducing newspapers, advertising, war, stealing, murder, vivisection, adultery. For example, the true viciousness of adul-tery is not the romantic love—there is no objection to Tristan and Isolde—but the cruelty and the lying, for lying is so bad for the liar and it is such an injustice and cruelty to the person lied to."

She and Sandburg talked about such matters as they strode around the lake in a chill Minnesota dusk. Sandburg told Brenda he thought it was possible for a man to love many women at once, and, perhaps, impossible for him not to. But, he said vehemently, a commitment to marriage and fidelity to one woman was sacramental. In her nineties, her black eyes brilliant and fierce, Brenda looked back on her remarkable life. "I have had many glorious love affairs," she smiled, "hundreds of them. But not with Sandburg. We loved each other, it was true. But never sexually. We chose not to."

Her audacity and honesty endeared her to Sandburg, and he trusted her judgment as a writer, expressing in his letters to her some of the most thoughtful theories about the act of writing. He called her 1938 book *If You Want to Write* the "best book ever written about how to write." He revealed some of his introspection as a writer to her:

> . . . That piece "The People, Yes" grows with the faith of potatoes in June. It is now about double the length it was when you glimpsed it. I think Joe [Beach] was perfectly justified in demurrers to it. In the past I have unjustly flung unfinished things at him. . . . Once over a sheaf of

verse of mine, he said, "Carl, you're beginning to imitate yourself," and later I agreed with him perfectly. . . . Some spots in this latest piece were bad. They were miss shots. A lot of my work only gets done by many preliminary miss shots. And there are plenty of them in the finished work, the word "finished" meaning merely that I have given it every last measure of toil and devotion I could summon. . . . One impelling drive is that there is not out of all the stretches of experiment in democracy any extended handling that begins to touch the reach and majesty of the theme. Of prose treatises and oratorical discussion there is much. Whitman pioneered and was too transcendental and I will have plenty of miss shots but some poet will get it sometime. . . . And while going along on "The People, Yes" I have thought about how curiously it has been ordered that I should over and again put into a verse form (of a sort) what could also be employed in fiction or drama. The latter pay, when they get by, in dollars, a thousandfold over poetry but whenever it occurs to me to shape characters and action thru which the theme would be delivered I balk and hesitate and go back to the first scheme that came, the medium of free verse.

Despite his years of commitment to the Lincoln biography, Sandburg had a homing instinct for poetry, and for several months *The People, Yes* superseded *Abraham Lincoln: The War Years*, as the present pulled him out of the past. The poem had been a detour, he told Paul de Kruif. He described it to Supreme Court Justice Benjamin Cardozo as a poem which held "some of the chaos and turmoil of our time and of all time."

"Parts of it are superb: the creations of free imagination operating among the people," Sandburg said. "The rest of it may or may not be a songswept footnote to the stride of democracy in our era."

Whatever it was, he said, "It was the best memorandum I could file for the present stress."

After several drafts of the manuscript, Sandburg shared it with friends whose judgment he trusted. Archie MacLeish read it three times for Sandburg, once aloud. At 112 pages in manuscript, it was the longest piece of verse he had ever done. He told Malcolm Cowley it was "a ballad pamphlet harangue sonata and fugue . . . an almanac, a scroll, a palimpsest, the last will and testament of Mr. John Public, John Doe, Richard Roe, and the autobiography of whoever it was the alfalfaland governor meant in saying, 'The common people will do anything you say except stay hitched.' "

At the same time that he shared *The People, Yes* with Beach, MacLeish and Brenda Ueland, Sandburg showed the manuscript to Oliver Barrett, his mainstay for the Lincoln book. Not surprisingly, conservative Republican Barrett found disturbing political overtones in *The People, Yes*, and told Sandburg so. Barrett the conservative lawyer and Sandburg the radical Poet of the People possessed almost diametrically opposed political viewpoints, sometimes arguing so vehemently that onlookers feared they might attack each other. Their friendship not only withstood such differences, but was deepened by them.

Sandburg's disenchantment with "the masters of finance and industry in America" had deepened with "decades of passing years" since he worked the factories and farms of Wisconsin on behalf of Social Democracy. He believed in 1936 as fervently as in 1908 that they failed to realize that "the roots and sources of their holdings are in the people, the workers, the consumers, the customers, the traveling public!" He told Barrett he had never seen "greed, fear, brutality among the masses to surpass what may be seen among the rich."

Sandburg the biographer noted again the ironic parallels between past and present—for instance, the majority of strikes in Lincoln's time were against the same ten- to twelve-hour workday which wore down the twentieth-century American worker. Sandburg the historian deplored the unlearned lessons of the past: "Science, inevitable changes, inventions, moods of the people, condition the future," he told Barrett. "It is whimsical, unreadable. You and I would probably not concur on whether the present depression has essential characteristics differing from previous depressions. The Governor of the Bank of England, Norman Montagu, in taking note that it is the first known WORLD depression, emphasizes that the picture is too complicated for any one mind to grasp."

Sandburg stood in the thirties as he had all his life, "with the people as against the exploiters of the people." He had not belonged to a political party in twenty-four years, and now predicted that "Some form of controlled capitalism, pressure for good or bad results on the large financial and industrial establishments, seems to be ahead. If I could see more signs of human awareness among those now controlling these establishments, if they were showing more signs of response to some of the deeper underlying human currents of the time, I could more serenely watch the floodtide of the times."

When Barrett suggested that certain passages of *The People, Yes* were intended "to convey the thought that the laboring class are exploited by wealthy malefactors and should be made to feel hate and resentment against their employers," Sandburg argued that "if Sam Adams, Tom Jefferson and Patrick Henry had kept silence on the exploitation of other American colonists by the imbecile British crown there would have been no American revolution" and that if Garrison, Seward and Lincoln had "submitted to the rule that slavery should not be mentioned in polite society, the Southern exploiters of human chattels would have had their way." Sandburg was angry that "today the sinister and forbidden topic is something else and in the so-called best circles it is considered either bad taste or some sort of treason to mention plain and known facts and to ask where they may be leading us."

His new poem was independent and "freegoing," he admitted, a "confession of faith and in one phase autobiographic." For all his passion, Sandburg was not an aggressive or dogmatic adversary when ideas were at stake. He deeply respected Barrett, and left open the possibility that he himself might be wrong. After all, he said, "I have been wrong often in my life and have incarnated in me many kinds of fools and will die without having articulated all of them."

The Sandburgs read proofs for *The People, Yes* in June 1936 and at the same time undertook to achieve Advanced Registry for their dairy goats. The latter procedure required three responsible witnesses to attest "that Felicia, Carlotta and Meggi yielded during three milkings in a 12-hour period an amount each of more than ten pounds." Three such performances every thirty days entitled the does to Advanced Registry, Sandburg explained to Harcourt in the cover letter which accompanied the corrected galleys of *The People, Yes*. He supported Paula's progress with the small goat herd with the same enthusiasm she gave to his literary endeavors. Paula took time away from farm work to help him finish the proofs for the new book by June 8. Even after it was set in proofs, Sandburg made many additions to the book. "Those who will say it looks as tho I shovelled in every thing I had might be interested to see that about an equal mass of rejected material failed of the shovel and there was some sort of rudimentary sense of discrimination operating."

As he had worked on the gigantic sweep of the poem, he had listened to "what the Quakers call the 'dayspring of the heart' " and then hoped "to christ the music and the murmurous fall of the syllables will follow." That fall he reread the poem for the first time in three months and told a friend, "It has a curious craziness. Maybe I was a little crazy to publish it . . . On many pages the workmanship is slovenly: I would like now to go back and revise; this as the lawyers say being inadmissible." He made no apologies for the poem's political themes.

The People, Yes is indeed an anomaly of a poem, and some critics wondered if it was a poem at all. After all, Amy Lowell and other colleagues and critics in the teens had chided him for being propagandist

more than poet. But Sandburg's purpose was not to set forward an economic or political program. His friend Stephen Vincent Benét saw that
the poem was full of questions as well as convictions, warning as well as
hope. "Sometimes it goes runabout; not all of it is poetry," he wrote in
Books. "But it is the memoranda of the people. And every line of it says
'The People—Yes.' "

Sandburg, too, had called it a memorandum. The poem was outspoken
on many issues, among them "the monstrous efforts at debauching the
public mind which have gone on with increased intensity the past three
years." He praised Henry Luce for "having had no hand in it." Too many
of their fellow journalists, Sandburg charged, had "luxuriated in the
power of their rostrums, petted their passions, wreaked their whims.
They think the people lap it up," Sandburg told Luce, "and everything
is as it always was. Their conception of the public, the circulation, the
audience, does not run with mine as I have presented it in The People,
Yes. They can't monkey with the public mind as they do without consequences. To bewilder a public with lies, half lies, texts torn from
contexts, and then have that public sober and well-ordered in its processes, is not in the cards."

Sandburg was echoing a passage from *The People, Yes*, Section 102,
including Lincoln's words of July 4, 1861:

*"Accordingly, they commenced by an insidious debauching of the public mind . . .
    they have been drugging the public mind."*
. . . Can you bewilder men by the millions
with transfusions of your own passions,
mixed with lies and half-lies,
texts torn from contexts,
and then look for peace, quiet, good will
between nation and nation, race and race,
between class and class?

Sandburg's sixth book of poetry was, he said, "Affirmative of swarming
and brawling Democracy," and it attempted to "give back to the people
their own lingo." Years later, when he was writing the preface to *The
Complete Poems of Carl Sandburg* (1950), he made some notes on *The
People, Yes* which were never used: "It is dedicated to 'contributors dead
and living.' Affirmative of 'democracy' it never mentions the word. . . .
One forerunner of 'The People, Yes' was 'Piers Plowman,' seven hundred
years ago, a far better handbook and manual of democracy than either
Dante or John Donne."

✳

Sandburg believed that *The People, Yes* "would have gone to a larger audience had it been cast in a form indicating it had no relation to poetry." He was disenchanted with most poets as well with nearly all critics. "The existing prejudices and quirks regarding poetry, the aversion to it in wide circles, has a basis of a certain sort that is justifiable," he told another writer in 1936. "Part of it connects with the contradictions, quarrels, pallors, pretenses, sicklinesses, snobberies, temperaments, isolations, poverties of the poets themselves—while the critics in the main inhabit a pathetic lost world." Whether in poetry or politics, literary criticism or economic theory, Sandburg despised pretense and snobbery. Section 92 of *The People, Yes* began with one of his perennial anecdotes, the identification of the most detestable word in the English language. A group of editors charged with the task decided "the one word just a little/worse than any other you can think of/is 'Exclusive.' "

The People, Yes was epic in scope and defied a consensus interpretation. Sandburg fastened to the loose scaffolding of the poem a lifetime of experience, observation and eavesdropping on the American scene. But the transcendent opinion from attentive readers was that, in the midst of the Great Depression, the poem was a profound affirmation of the American people, a testament to their gifts for survival. Thus, to readers such as Harcourt and Archie MacLeish, *The People, Yes* was a singular public document. Someone at Harcourt, Brace told Sandburg when the book was done that the people "damned near owe you a national holiday." Harcourt considered the poem the "fruition" of Sandburg's genius, and wanted to publish it "partly as a campaign document thru the autumn."

MacLeish reviewed the book for *The New Masses*, declining to write a review for *The New York Times*. "The sad part of it is that only you and I of all the people who read it will understand what the review means," MacLeish wrote Sandburg.

> It is the full answer to Bill Benet who accuses you of getting nowhere. You get somewhere. You get where it is good to be. . . . You are the one to see that the real issue is whether or not we believe in the people. We made a revolution to believe in the people. . . . You and I have a considerable responsibility. We are poets but we are also men able to live in the political world. We cannot escape our duty as political animals. You have fulfilled that duty in your Lincoln and in this book. . . . We must now become pamphleteers, propogandists—you by your own right, I as one who can aid you somewhat.

As a citizen and a writer of conscience, Sandburg was deeply affected by the suffering the Depression exacted of his countrymen. "The people is a tragic and comic two-face," he wrote in his radical, rambling epic poem:

> hero and hoodlum: phantom and gorilla twist-
> ing to moan with a gargoyle mouth: "They
> buy me and sell me . . . it's a game . . .
> sometimes I'll break loose . . ."

Sandburg felt deeper compassion than ever for the people who had to "hold to the humdrum bidding of work and food." He worked with part of his mind on Lincoln and part preoccupied by the

> Streetwalking jobhunters, walkers alive and keen,
> sleepwalkers drifting along, the stupefied and
> hopeless down-and-outs . . .

He and Paula were reasonably secure financially, but he watched with empathy, fortified by memories of his own struggles, the anguish of people with "loans and mortgages, margins to cover,"

> Payments on the car, the bungalow, the radio, the
> electric icebox, accumulated interest on loans
> for past payments, the writhing point of
> where the money will come from . . .

He knew the terror, the hopelessness. Its memory quivered in the bones of his experience, and he recorded it in *The People, Yes*:

> And in the air a decree: life is a gamble; take a
> chance; you pick a number and see what you
> get: anything can happen in this sweepstakes:
> around the corner may be prosperity or the
> worst depression yet: who knows? nobody. . . .

The People, Yes was published as one poem, 179 pages long, with 107 free-verse sections. Sandburg introduced the book with a brief preface:

> *The People, Yes*
>
> Being several stories and psalms nobody would
> want to laugh at
>
> interspersed with memoranda variations worth a
> second look
>
> along with sayings and yarns traveling on grief and
> laughter

running sometimes as a fugitive air in the classic
manner

breaking into jig time and tap dancing nohow
classical

and further broken by plain and irregular sounds
and echoes from

the roar and whirl of street crowds, work gangs,
sidewalk clamor,

with interludes of midnight cool blue and inviolable
stars

over the phantom frames of skyscrapers.

It was the kind of jocular statement which estranged many critics and
readers, yet it was an apt description of this unorthodox, highly original
book. The poem was an amalgam of his interests and experiences, a
chronicle of the American past and present, kaleidoscopic in its moods
and themes. His subject was not confined to the American people; the
book embraced "The people of the earth, the family of man," a phrase
he had taken from Abraham Lincoln. The first section recounts the story
of the Tower of Babel, "Five hundred ways to say, 'Who are you?' " *The
People, Yes* has a great deal to say about communication, or the consequences of a lack of it, between individuals and factions of society. It is
studded with myths, songs, proverbs, folk tales and sayings. There are
anecdotes from history and from personal experience. The population of
the book ranges from the mythic to the historic to the anonymous contemporary citizen. The People is the hero, but the other characters in
the poem constitute a litany of Sandburg's reading, observation and
thought. Section 88 contains a poignant self-portrait, complete with
parodies of lines from his own poems. He describes himself as a hobo
mumbling to himself "a mumbling poem" which is a brilliant caricature
of poems in *Chicago Poems* and *Smoke and Steel*:

. . . By platoons always by platoons under a hammering,
the cries of the tongs go kling klong
to the bong bong of the hammers . . .

"Listen," he cried,
"Kling klong go the mighty hammers,
kling klong on a mighty anvil
steel on steel they clash and weld,
how long can you last? how long? . . ."

A fly-by-night house, a shanty,

a ramshackle hut of tarpaper, tin cans,
body by fisher, frames from flivvers,
a shelter from rain and wind,
the home of a homeseeker having an alibi,
why did two hungers move across his face?
    One: when do we eat?
    The other: What is worth looking at?
          what is worth listening to?
          why do we live?
          when is a homeseeker
               just one more trespasser?
          and what is worth dying for?

"The people is Everyman, everybody," Sandburg writes early in the epic. "Everybody is you and me and all others." The Depression is the setting for Everyman's pilgrimage, his hope that

    poverty and the poor shall go
    and the struggle of man for possessions
    of music and craft and personal worth
    lifted above the hog-trough level
    above the animal dictate:
        "Do this or go hungry . . ."

With empathy born of personal struggle, Sandburg writes about the universal hardships of the Depression. He saluted American workers in 1936 as he had thirty years earlier, endorsed their "hopes of a promised land, a homestead farm, and a stake in/the country,/Along with prayers for a steady job, a chicken in the pot and two cars in/the garage, the life insurance paid, and a home of your own." Parts of the poem echoed his own socialist speeches:

Those who have nothing stand in two pressures.
Either what they once had was taken away
Or they never had more than subsistence.
Long ago an easy category was provided for them:
    "They live from hand to mouth,"
Having the name of horny-handed sons of toil.
From these hands howsoever horny, from these sons,
Pours a living cargo of overwhelming plenty
From land and mill into the world markets.
    Their pay for this is what is handed to them.
Or they take no pay at all if the labor market is glutted,
Losing out on pay if the word is: "NO HANDS WANTED
              next month maybe

> next year maybe
> the works start."

"Who shall speak for the people?" Sandburg asks in section 24. He himself speaks for them, but ultimately they speak for themselves. We are told at the outset that this poem is about language, communication. Inlaid in the vast mosaic of the poem are hundreds of "shrewd and elusive proverbs,"

> The have-you heard yarns,
> The listen-to-this anecdote
> Made by the people out of the roots of the earth . . .

More than a third of the poem is devoted to myth, folklore and sayings of people around the world. For more than forty years Sandburg had been listening to the vernacular of the people, had been their scribe, storing in memory and in dozens of small notebooks the words and songs which elucidated them. In *The People, Yes* he transmuted the "plain and irregular sounds and echoes from/the roar and whirl of street crowds" into poetry. He chronicled the poetry and wisdom in words "Grown in the soil of the mass of the people." He proclaimed the universal wisdom of folk sayings, arranging them in litany after litany throughout the poem, often in discreet categories (sayings, anecdotes, yarns, tall tales, jokes, songs, superstitions, even vaudeville sketches) and sometimes in thematic clusters (greed, class struggle, war, love, marriage, hope, materialism, peace).

At first glance unstructured, incoherent, *The People, Yes* is in reality a carefully crafted modern epic poem, a pageant more than a narrative, a highly original fusion of unorthodox, seemingly disparate elements. From the outset it is a pilgrimage. The people of the earth gather to "join in a shout," "One grand hosannah, something worth listening to." God, the "whimsical fixer," suddenly shuffles "all the languages" and changes the "tongues of men." Consequently, the poem explores the difficulties of communication, the barriers words erect between brothers, lovers, worker and boss, class and class, ruler and ruled, past and present.

Sandburg roams in and out of the pages of his poem wearing his many masks. He is poet, hobo, singer, journalist, "a scholar, a clown, and a dreambook seller who had said enough for one day." Often he is "the soap boxer pleading for the proletariat," resurrecting the early themes of his socialist oratory and prose, even writing into his poem passages from the pocket notebooks he kept just after the turn of the century. He weaves into the work a long poem on Lincoln and many fragments from Lincoln's letters and speeches. His sense of humor balances his political passion. He writes with anger and bitterness about past and present social injustice, worries over the fate of "the buyers, the consumers, the customers,/the people, yes, what will we let them have?" Then, disarmingly, he asks, "What is this? Is it economics, poetry or what?"

The pilgrimage moves its characters through space and time. They come "From the four corners of the earth . . . from places where the winds begin/and fogs are born. . . ." Later, they come "From six continents, seven seas, and several archipelagoes. . . . Out of where they used to be to where they are." The people march, they revolt, they strike, they plod "in a somnambulism of fog and rain." Sometimes *The People, Yes* records the odyssey of "the wandering gypsy, the pioneer homeseeker, the singer of home sweet home." There is a migration, a search through the wilderness of history. Sometimes the people is a monolith, sometimes a mover, always a "desperate hoper." The journey, as befits a modern poem, sometimes takes place on the subway or the elevated train, where the people are "riders to work, to home, to fun, to grief." Sometimes the pilgrim is alone; sometimes he joins a mob or an army. Sometimes the poet urges his reader to join the pilgrimage, to

> pack up your bundle now and go
> be a seeker among voices and faces
> on main street in a bus station at a union depot
> this generation of eaters sleepers lovers toilers
> flowing out of the last one now buried
> flowing into the next one now unborn
> short of cash and wondering where to? what next?

Always, alone or collectively, the people are Seekers, Questers, part of "a vast field of faces,/faces across an immeasurable mural. . . ." The purpose of man's quest is to come

> To the deeper rituals of his bones,
> To the lights lighter than any bones,
> To the time for thinking things over,
> To the dance, the song, the story,
> Or the hours given over to dreaming,
> Once having so marched.

The pilgrimage does not end in *The People, Yes*, nor is its destination clear or even attainable. The people are Everyman, from all time. Despite the distinctly American idiom of the poem and its emphasis on the American Dream, it is universal in theme. A dominant metaphor is the Family of Man. The earth belongs to the family of man, we are reminded over and over, and there is a world family of nations, "the little Family of Man hugging the little ball of Earth," constant affirmation of man's "mortal kinship with all/other men." The poet envisions a "United States of the Earth," a time when men's eyes "search the earth and see no aliens anywhere,/pronouncing across the barriers the peculiar word:/'Brother.' "

The poem's title becomes a unifying refrain. The phrase "The people, yes" appears in at least fifteen of the 107 sections of the book. Some sections modulate clearly into those which follow, while others seem part of some vast free association, an impressionistic personal and national history. The first quarter of *The People, Yes* evokes the past in mythical terms. There is a long litany of present conditions, with emphasis on the hardships of the Depression. The last third of the poem examines the future where "The people, yes, the people,/Move eternally in the elements of surprise,/Changing from hammer to bayonet and back to hammer." Sandburg sees portents of revolution:

> Who can fight against the future?
> What is the decree of tomorrow?
> Haven't the people gone on and on
>   always taking more of their own?
> How can the orders of the day
>   be against the people in this time?
> What can stop them from taking
>   more and more of their own?

For all his realism, even pessimism about the struggles of the human pilgrimage, Sandburg affirms the enduring strength of the people. "The people will live on," he writes in the finale:

> The learning and blundering people will live on.
>   They will be tricked and sold and again sold
> And go back to the nourishing earth for rootholds,
>   The people so peculiar in renewal and comeback,
>   You can't laugh off their capacity to take it.

The People, Yes is an odyssey deep into the American experience, which Sandburg had begun to see as a hopeful symbol for the universal human condition. He began the poem with overtones of myth:

> From the four corners of the earth,
> from corners lashed in wind
> and bitten with rain and fire,
> from places where the winds begin
> and fogs are born with mist children,
> tall men from tall rocky slopes came

and sleepy men from sleepy valleys,
their women tall, their women sleepy,
with bundles and belongings,
with little ones babbling, "Where to now?
    what next?"

He concluded with a recapitulation of images and theme, selected proverbs and aphorisms juxtaposed to the poet's perennial question:

This old anvil laughs at many broken hammers.
    There are men who can't be bought.
    The fireborn are at home in fire.
    The stars make no noise.
    You can't hinder the wind from blowing.
    Time is a great teacher.
    Who can live without hope?
In the darkness with a great bundle of grief
    the people march.
In the night, and overhead a shovel of stars for
    keeps, the people march:
                "Where to? what next?"

In one of the autobiographical sections of the poem, Sandburg depicts
himself as

        One of the early Chicago poets
    One of the slouching underslung Chicago poets,
    Having only the savvy God gave him,
    Lacking a gat, lacking brass knucks,
    Having one lead pencil to spare . . .

and setting out a philosophy which is the nexus of *The People, Yes* and
of his life:

    "I am credulous about the destiny of man,
    And I believe more than I can ever prove
    Of the future of the human race
    and the importance of illusions,
    the value of great expectations. . . ."

The People, Yes is the culmination of Sandburg's career as a poet. After
1936 there was little significant growth or change in his poetic style,
and scant expansion of theme. With a few exceptions, the poems written
after 1936 echo those written before this immense epic poem. *The People,
Yes* is a poem and something more, something unprecedented and very
modern, an articulation of the American Dream and struggle built with

native materials. Yet here, for the first time, Sandburg's vision reaches beyond the national to the universal, embracing all the human family.

His affidavit of hope, forged out of myth and realism, heartened many of his fellow citizens during the Depression. For the critics who found the work exasperating and incoherent, Sandburg's defense was written in the poem itself, in section 101:

> The unemployed
> without a stake in the country
> without jobs or nest eggs
> marching they don't know where . . .
> they fall into a dusty disordered poetry.

✳

The present attended to, Sandburg returned to the past. "Finished revisions and additions to the People, Yes, and mailed it to Harcourt last week," he told Steichen in April 1936, "and am now reading what the hell I last wrote on the Lincoln last fall so that where I take up again the transition will be smooth as an eel swimming in oil."

---- * ----

1936–1940

23. Lincoln?

Lincoln?
He was a mystery in smoke and flags
saying yes to the smoke, yes to the flags,
yes to the paradoxes of democracy . . .

Lincoln? did he gather
the feel of the American dream
and see its kindred over the earth?

—Carl Sandburg, Section 57, *The
People, Yes*, 1936

In the late 1930s Carl Sandburg devoted his attention to Abraham
Lincoln, to his own family life on the dunes of Lake Michigan, and
to "the great human family and where it is headed." The devastation
of the American economy and spirit galvanized Sandburg's lifelong passions for justice, dignity, hope. As the Depression years wore on, and
international tensions heightened, "all the trouble of the world" haunted
Sandburg, night and day, Paula said. He found it hard to relax and sleep.
Overwork had him "down to feeling like a fumbling shadow." He had
launched *The People, Yes* with "So much honest contempt and such great
hopes," he told Ida Tarbell. He carried on a heavy lecture schedule in
the wake of its publication. As usual, there was no time to rest.

At home, the farm enterprises were burgeoning. Paula had begun right
away to breed her does, first taking two of them to "a big white horned
and pronged buck who is affirmative in his attitude toward life," Sandburg
wrote. They had built a barn to shelter the goats, who were joined now
by pigs, and a horse for Helga. Paula's gardens produced all the vegetables
the family could consume and put up for winter, and their ever-increasing
herd of goats provided an abundance of milk, butter and cheese. "Mother
was wild with power and I loved it!" Helga recalled. "We do practically
all the work ourselves," Sandburg told a friend, including himself and

Martha Moorman in the "we." He sketched this portrait of his family in the autumn of 1936:

> The eldest daughter is an invalid, the second is still below normal from being struck and run over by a careless motorist, the youngest is as good as God ever bestowed on a house; she is as nice as anything in a Russian ballet when she rides her horse out into Lake Michigan for a swim together. It is an odd corner of the world, a slow sickle of beach curving twenty-two miles to the headland where at night we see the pier lights of Benton Harbor—and in winter the splinter of the Northern Lights.

The Sandburgs enjoyed their life on the lake shore in all seasons. "The lake performs," Sandburg said. "The lake runs a gamut of all moods." They swam from early spring until the first chill of fall. One winter Helga harnessed the family dogs to a sled and taught them "to mush in true Klondike fashion," her mother said.

Sandburg's lecture schedule overwhelmed him in the fall of 1936 and the following winter. He gave thirty lectures in seventy days, traveling through a dozen states and Canada. He visited Archie MacLeish in Maine and James Thurber in Columbus, Ohio, where he and Thurber had a "fine evening; of talk and song," which Thurber later depicted in a series of cartoons. The Thurbers urged Sandburg to visit them in Litchfield, Connecticut. Thurber was heading east to New York, he said, because "Baby Tycoon Ross," his editor at *The New Yorker*, "sent me an imploring wire—I haven't done a lick in 2 weeks." Thurber took a special interest in Sandburg's *Potato Face*, and gave Sandburg a copy of his latest book, *The Middle-Aged Man on the Flying Trapeze*. "Come to Connecticut and we'll talk both books over—and sing," he urged Sandburg.

Sandburg had voted for Roosevelt that fall, believing him to be "a momentous historic character more thoroughly aware of what he is doing and where he is going than most of the commentators." He wrote to *New Republic* editor Bruce Bliven about his support for FDR in a letter he was willing for Bliven to "print or use" any way he chose.

> . . . As a political independent . . . I have been surprised at the record of substantial accomplishments in working measures, at the pettiness of the corruptions in contrast with the immense moneys spent, at the human spirit of the Administration which has permitted such sway to Ickes, Wallace, Tugwell, Perkins, Hopkins. What the underlying and dominant economic streams of the time are shaping now and are to dictate in the future, only historians decades hence can tell. In the present national chaos and international entanglements, considering the amount of combustibles lying loose every way for Sunday, I'll take Roosevelt.

Sandburg's workload kept him from being politically active, but he had "done no shadow boxing "and had "not been in any bomb-proof shelter" when it came to expressing his political opinions—in poetry or prose.

The 1936 national election coincided with Sandburg's study of Lincoln's 1864 election campaign and "the lowest gloom of th[e] war." He was probing "documents, transcripts, letters, diaries" to get the fullest picture of Lincoln and the Civil War. In his effort to suffuse the biography with authentic social context, he had to do complex "research jobs where long ago you might have believed the ground had been competently covered in special treatises." By year's end, he was exhausted. "I shall slowly pull out of it as I have done before," he assured a friend. He urged his brother Mart to watch his sleep and rest "so that in these later years of ours you can keep some of the magnificent vitality you have always had," advice he should have heeded himself.

Instead, he began the new year with a full-fledged lecture tour to the West Coast, at least twenty-four appearances in a month and a half of travel in California, Washington, Colorado, Montana, Utah, Missouri, Iowa, Illinois and Wisconsin. He came home from the West Coast with acute bronchitis. "He was very sick—ran a temperature 102.5 for several days," Paula told Steichen and Dana. "His hearing was affected. We feared that pneumonia would develop—as the prostration was severe and he was coughing up bloody mucus." He had a "hard three week siege with bronchial pneumonia" and the ear infection left him "more than half deaf in the right ear." His doctor ordered him to "keep clear of the sort of railroad jumps which shorten sleeps" and gave him no time for "outdoor oxygen." Paula felt that his long illness was "more than being worn with so many platform engagements and irregular hours, stuffy trains, etc. though all that contributed."

She knew that The People, Yes "had drained his vitality and all the trouble of the World had been in his thoughts night and day—Spain— the Floods—the strikes that were on and more that were looming." John L. Lewis of the United Mine Workers headed the new Congress of Industrial Organizations, formed in 1935 in reaction to the more conservative policies of Samuel Gompers's American Federation of Labor. Lewis spearheaded a series of strikes, many of them using the new "sit-down" strategy. Sandburg and Paula initially supported Lewis and the C.I.O., whose principles embodied their own earlier vision for American working people. Paula saw her husband's eyes fill with tears "when General Motors yielded and began negotiating with Lewis' men. Again when steel capitulated. All this had been moving him so deeply." In eighty recent platform lectures, she told her brother, Sandburg "managed to refer to our coming industrial unions—now arrived—for which he battled years ago—the Garment Workers Strike in Chicago."

Gradually, he recovered his stamina, but it was "slow going," he told Paul Angle. He eased back into the lecture schedule. He was named National Honor Poet during Poetry Week in 1937, and given a medal for *The People, Yes.* He had his most intense lecture schedule ever, partly because of his great popularity and partly because of his projected work on *Abraham Lincoln: The War Years*: "I told the [lecture] bureau to give me a heavy season this year as I would like a very light season next year when I would be in a stride of work in which I hope to go thru with the completion of a writing job that has now run ten years."

He still had his feet "in two eras." He was working on the fourth and last volume of *Abraham Lincoln: The War Years.* He was lecturing and traveling most of the time, talking "about sit-down strikes, and politics and history and the movies and the newspapers and the men who make them." When strikers were killed in a Memorial Day "massacre" at the Republic Steel Plant in South Chicago Sandburg took part in a protest meeting at the Chicago Civic Opera House. He participated in a Spanish Loyalist medical aid meeting, and the centenary of Knox College in Galesburg, "the first two for the sake of self-respect, the last for loyalties not to be thrust aside." He wrote new poems, "among them some of the best I've ever done," he told Harcourt. They "could not be put off, had to be put down." Constantly he reshaped, expanded and revised the Lincoln biography. By fall he was worn out again, "on the ragged edge," and needed "to hike away from his attic." He revealed his anxiety to Brenda Ueland: "The summer has gone heavy here what with finishing two long chapters. . . . Sometimes I find myself shrinking from people because the vital elements, the last vestiges of intestinal fortitude, have been dragged so low by the physical demands of the job. I know what I want to write and the time given to writing has been limited by the points from day to day of physical exhaustion." He thought that many would-be Lincoln biographers "contented themselves with doing patches of it because the whole scene staggered them. . . . Now I am in one more of the breakdowns, overhauling the batteries, refueling and hoping to make the usual comeback. . . ."

"Don't let the size of it overcome you," Ueland answered sympathetically, "but work long and tranquilly, like a child stringing beads in kindergarten. . . . Yes I know that nervous agony, when to talk to anybody, however dear, is being bled . . . of work energy." All he could do was write his real heart out, as he often urged other writers to do, and hope that his health would hold up for the finish of the mammoth biography.

Helga finished high school in 1937 and nestled into the farm routine at home, planning, she said, "then and there to end my formal education." Janet was in charge of the thrice-daily feedings for the kids in the growing herd, which Sandburg called one of the best in the country. Helga had a "dazzling white" new mare named Silver, who could do tricks, plow the garden and take her soaring over the dunes up and down the lake shore. Paula was putting her considerable energy into the dairy operation. Her farm was the first in Michigan to be evaluated for goat milk production. Studiously and with growing expertise, she built a herd of Advanced Registry does and sires. Park Holme Caesar A.R. #13, her Nubian buck, was the first of his breed to qualify in the United States. Paula's growing success earned her the respect of her industry. She began to attend meetings of the American Goat Society, was elected to the board of directors of the American Milk Goat Record Association, (A.M.G.R.A.), and began to publish articles in goat journals on breeding, the making of goat cheese, and high milk production. She was asked to make speeches and to consult with breeders and agriculture schools. Helga noted proudly that her mother traveled now on her own, "not following a husband . . . talking with folks who often as not had never heard of a Carl Sandburg."

Late into the night, in the circle of light at her desk, Paula pored over her goat records, skillfully planning which doe and buck to breed. Her masterful work was deeply fulfilling by its own nature. It satisfied her lifelong drive to create, investigate, serve. The tidy, meticulous calculations in her black notebooks submitted to an order and harmony not possible or even desirable in her relations with her extraordinary husband and the three beloved, homebound daughters. This was *her* creative work, something she conceived and executed on her own. Her daughters were caught up in her enthusiasm, and Margaret, Helga and Janet proved invaluable helpers with the daily chores. Isolated as their dune existence appeared to some, "It was a full life," Helga said, "replete with wonder."

The grueling lecture tours continued until the end of 1937. Sandburg's last engagements for the year were in Texas. Because the Depression economy had halved his fees, he was lucky to get $150 a lecture in 1937. The income was essential. He was putting aside funds for 1938, when he hoped to bear down on the last chapters of the Lincoln biography. He worried about whether time, money and energy would come out even, whether one or the other would curtail his work before it was done. "For the last 5 weeks I have not sat up to the typewriter and done two straight hours of decent work," he told Paul Angle at year's end. "In the next seven weeks, barring platform work, I hope to get [Lincoln] on into [18]65."

✳

Sandburg turned sixty in 1938. At an age when many people, long settled into steady patterns of work, begin to contemplate retirement, he was still moving vigorously from one genre to another. He could be one of the most popular poets in the United States and still be a pioneer, migrating from poetry to various prose forms. *Abraham Lincoln: The Prairie Years* and his children's stories were selling well in foreign translations. The February 21 issue of *Life* magazine carried his picture on the cover lauding not the poet or journalist or biographer, but Sandburg the singer. The article called Sandburg a "cowboy Paul Robeson," a "Great lover and champion of the American people" and a member of "the front rank of American writers." There were pictures of Sandburg and his bell-shaped guitar, Sandburg singing to Helga and four goats in the parlor of the Michigan house, and a picture of Sandburg and Paula gazing through a window, both of them slim, straight, handsome. In Bernard Hoffman's cover portrait, Sandburg sports the familiar hairstyle, a plaid shirt and a bandana, a wool vest, half of a cigar. The eyes are slightly averted, mischievous, shrewd, even crafty. "Sandburg Sings American," the cover caption read. He was sixty and a celebrity, torn between enjoying the attention and losing himself in the grueling work and renunciation which had made him famous. He was cautious about taking on jobs which would be "monkeywork" and would "hinder him in getting his best work done." He knew that *Abraham Lincoln: The War Years* would exact of him, before it was over, everything he had to give.

Looming in the background of that work was the unfolding reality of another world war. Roosevelt's 1937 Inaugural Address had not included a discussion of foreign affairs, so committed was the nation then to resolving its domestic crisis and staying out of foreign conflicts. At first the escalating tensions between Italy and Ethiopia, Japan and China, Fascists and Republicans in Spain, and Adolf Hitler and the rest of the European world seemed remote, almost irrelevant. "The American people surely want to stay out of the next world war," historian Charles Beard said. "It may cost the blood of countless American boys." Sandburg wrote poetry throughout the thirties contemplating the tragedy of war. In *The People Yes* he had written of

> The heroes, the cannonfodder, the living targets,
> The mutilated and sacred dead,
> The people, yes.

"The first world war came and its cost was laid on the people," he wrote in 1935. "The second world war—the third—what will be the cost?/ And will it repay the people for what they pay?" He had lived through two wars in reality and one vicariously, through his Lincoln work. The outcomes were the same, he thought: "And after the strife of war/begins the strife of peace."

Sandburg was a keen observer of the national and international dramas, some of which stirred him so deeply he could not sleep at night. *The People, Yes* had expressed his deep faith in democracy. In a powerful, prophetic poem, he assessed the world scene in 1938, drawing from Lincoln's experience and his own a somber portrait of what was about to happen to the modern world. Unpublished until 1978, "Nearer Than Any Mother's Heart Wishes" sketches earlier wars—Lincoln's, Ghengis Khan's, Napoleon's, "the chart of the fever and curse/of pre-war, war, post-war, and again later/pre-war, war, post-war." Then he described the contemporary world:

> They are changing the maps
> of Europe, Asia, and Africa—
> they are changing the maps like always.
>
> Over pieces of land they are wrangling,
> over iron and oil and fat lands,
> over breed and kin and race pride,
> over poisons, balloons, baboon reachings—
>> and the little wars are leading on
>> into the big war to come.
>
> Who could have given us the lowdown
> on why Mussolini
> poured troops and planes into Spain?
>
> Who explained why Hitler
> threw heavy guns and flying bombers
> to the help of Franco
> and the Mohammedan Moors of France
> and the cause of Liberty and God in Spain
> and the iron works
> and the mineral deposits of Spain?
>> How will his slogans die
>> and his abracadabra vanish?

He cautioned his readers to "Be steady now and keep your shirt on./Be cool as death if you can./Try to figure it out for yourself." The long poem alternates stanzas deploring the holocaust of war with stanzas meditating on the consolations of the human heart, his abiding faith in

> human wanderers with nostrils seeking
> air, oxygen, freedom, peace.
> Under the fantasies of these skulls
> runs the hope of human dignity
> somehow, sometime.

All of his experience as soldier, journalist, poet, biographer convinced him of the bitter, graphic irony of what lay ahead:

> Now babies will have baby-size gas masks.
> The time to be hard and bitter
> —is that time now?
> Or shall we insist on asking now the
> ancient question:
> "What do the people get for the wars
> they fight with each other?"
>
> . . . Men fight for dreams of freedom
> finding later they fought for
> land, for trade routes, for empire,
> for markets and controls,
> for gains in cash and dominance.
>
> Yet again men fight for dreams of freedom
> and win footholds for human rights,
> measurable gains for mankind:
> in the strife of strikes and wars
> sometimes this happens
> as a poem of action
> long remembered.

He gave lines of the poem to a consideration of what had recently happened in "Shanghai, in Bilbao, in Ethiopia/in Vienna on the blue Danube." He noted "the bloody trucks"

> and the published orders
> and the secret arrests
> and the public atrocities
> and the studied punishments
> of concentration camps.

He foresaw that "yet to come is the drama and its Act I,/Act II, Act III—and so on." He was speaking, he said, "as no prophet at all,/as a traveler taking it slow/over a mug of java with ham on rye,/as a citizen troubled over storm warnings," posing one resonant question:

> When shall men be hard and bitter,
> open and public and incessant
> in the asking of that terrible question:
> "What do the people get for the wars they fight
>   with each other?"

Sandburg's bitter, farsighted poem was chillingly accurate in its prophecy of events to come. He put it away in 1938 among poems he considered unfinished, in need of further crafting before they could "see the light of day." Published forty years later, eleven years after Sandburg's death and on the centennial anniversary of his birth, the poem ended with the fundamental, unifying, haunting reality of any war:

> Any mother might be saying now:
> "The cool music of deep hearts is on me.
> The fathoms of ancient fears are on me."
>
> Nearer than any mother's heart wishes
> now is heartbreak time.

Sandburg lived with two wars in 1938, the looming world war which he examined in poetry and journalism, and the Civil War, which he probed to the core in the Lincoln biography. It was Sandburg the reporter rather than the poet whose vision shaped *Abraham Lincoln: The War Years*. He had imbued *The Prairie Years* with poetry and lyricism, sometimes at the expense of credibility, but the poet often gave way to the seasoned journalist and historian in *The War Years*. The Civil War had its own stark reality; all he had to do was report it. He grappled with "events of wild passionate onrush side by side with cruel, grinding monotony," with a "record so stupendous, so changing and tumultuous, that anyone dealing with the vast actual evidence cannot use the whole of it, nor tell all of the story." At times it overwhelmed him. He saw "a thousand vivid parallels for the present hour in Czechoslovakia, the Sudentenland, Europe in general. . . . There are spots not easy going for the reader. But the war was often monotonous and intricate." Some periods and passages of the Civil War were "involved or cheap or monotonous," he told Lloyd Lewis, and yet they belonged in the biography, and "added years of writing and thought and craft could not make them any less involved, cheap, monotonous." War, any war, was a mystery,

Sandburg said, and much of the Civil War ran into "the imponderable and the inarticulate."

"It was a hell of a war," he told Lewis, "so often stupid, monotonous, stale, flat, stinking, hypocritical, heroic, plodding, gorgeous, hayfoot strawfoot, bang bang, the nigger the nigger, freedom, crap, gangrene, peanut politics, pus, grand slogans and lousy catchwords, every phase having its facts and stories, with motives overlapping and intertangled beyond any interpretations that wont stand further clarification and interpretation."

He was giving all he had to the Lincoln work, but he feared the past was as impossible to decipher as the future. He worried that *Abraham Lincoln: The War Years* would be "too muddy and chaotic, a bloody and murky huggermugger, to have as definite and measurable symphonic value as I would like."

Harcourt assigned Isabel Ely Lord to work as Sandburg's copy editor for *The War Years*, and Sandburg believed at last that if his health held out, he could finish the manuscript in 1938 for 1939 publication. He took time off to go with Paula to a luncheon at the Swedish Consulate in Chicago, where the Swedish minister awarded him the Order of the Northern Star, decreed by King Gustav himself. "Considering what I've written about the upper and ruling classes as such," Sandburg teased, "I can stand this if the king of Sweden can. No conditions attach. They know I am a Social Democrat, a laborite." The honor pleased him deeply, just as it would have pleased August and Clara Sandburg, had they been alive to see their son receive it.

Sandburg paid tribute himself to some friends that year. Novelist Julia Peterkin's husband died, and Robert Frost lost his wife. Sandburg wrote Mrs. Peterkin, "I cannot think of anyone more sensitive to suffering, more keen at registering to big or little tragedy as it passes, who at the same time has deep strong roots that will survive, that in the end will actually use the grief for growth." He had helped her begin her career as a writer, and kept his deep sympathy for the struggles any artist faced, but especially any artist who happened to be a woman. He told her he was haunted by her talk, "the wide range of it, the shelves of unwritten books you hold and how they have come to you because you are first of all a great hearted woman." He assured her that his hand was in hers, "in depths of faith and friendship."

Elinor Frost was still weak from breast cancer surgery when she suffered a series of heart attacks in Florida. When news came to the Sandburgs that Mrs. Frost died on March 21, 1938, Sandburg wrote to Frost right away. "Sorrow here, too," he said. "Always she was infinitely gracious to me in a way I can never forget. Your grief is deep and beyond any others knowing. Now it is past any of the sharp griefs you have sung." Sandburg did not know his words were stinging with truth, given the circumstances of Elinor Frost's death. Frost blamed himself for her heart attacks, and brooded that she died without forgiving him for the "pain and suffering he had caused her." During the last days of her final illness, he waited anxiously outside her bedroom, but she did not ask for him and, according to one account, refused to see him.

On May 24, 1938, Sandburg joined Archibald MacLeish, Ford Madox Ford, George Dillon and Sterling North at a dinner at the University of Chicago to honor Harriet Monroe and launch the Harriet Monroe Library of Modern Poetry. Monroe had died in September 1936 in the Andes. It was a death she might have chosen. Always a traveler and adventurer, she was in Buenos Aires as the first American representative to the International PEN Conference. She died in Peru and was buried in Arequipa.

At the 1938 dinner in her memory, Monroe's brother William read the section of her will which established a prize fund for American poets. George Dillon, Pulitzer Prize–winning poet who was then editor of *Poetry*, described the rare books and manuscripts which constituted the Harriet Monroe Library—inscribed first editions by Vachel Lindsay, Sandburg, D. H. Lawrence, Edna St. Vincent Millay, Robinson Jeffers, Hemingway, Ford, Hart Crane, MacLeish, Elinor Wylie, Frost, Eliot, Amy Lowell and others whose work intersected with Monroe's remarkable magazine; and manuscripts and proofs of works by Lindsay, Rupert Brooke, Millay, Tagore, James Joyce and a litany of other writers indebted to her for recognition, favors, prizes, affirmation. Ford, MacLeish and Sandburg spoke tributes. Sandburg's extemporaneous appreciation was warm and reflective. Harriet Monroe was, he said, "A slight woman physically, a little frame but a very peculiar power." He described her as "a house of many doors—all humanity could come in."

> She had an acquaintance with many very real poets, some of whom the hand of the potter shook in the making. She knew where they had created realities and she became familiar with where they verged on madness, and she loved them for all of that. . . .
>
> Poetry as a commodity does not pay its way and in this country it is a rather accepted proposition among those who own the country in the main that a commodity that does not pay its way is a sort of either outlaw or pauper or idiocy which belongs to children and to drunkards. In the Pullmans over the country you want to be careful how you mention that you are addicted to the habit of seriously writing poetry. You can talk

Carl and Paula Sandburg on their journey together in 1934
Carl Sandburg Collection, University of Illinois

Sandburg at work at Connemara
*June Glenn, Jr.; Carl Sandburg
Home*

Carl Sandburg in the living
room at Connemara
*June Glenn, Jr.; Carl Sandburg
Home*

Connemara, the Carl Sandburg Home in Flat Rock, North Carolina
National Park Service; Carl Sandburg Home

Helga's children, Karlen Paula and John Carl, with their "Buppong" in 1945
John R. Whiting; Carl Sandburg Collection, University of Illinois

Sandburg and Janet at Connemara
June Glenn, Jr.; Carl Sandburg Home

Carl and Paula and part of the Chikaming herd of champion dairy goats at Connemara   *Carl Sandburg Collection, University of Illinois*

Edward Steichen *(left)* and Carl Sandburg, 1949   *Wayne Miller, Museum of Modern Art;*
courtesy of Paula Steichen and Helga Sandburg

The Sandburgs at his seventy-fifth birthday party in 1953, also
celebrating the publication of *Always the Young Strangers*
Carl Sandburg Collection, University of Illinois

Donna Workman in 1950
Courtesy of Donna Workman

Lucy Kroll and Carl Sandburg in Hollywood to begin work on *The Greatest Story
Ever Told*   *Courtesy of Lucy Kroll*

Sandburg and John F. Kennedy
Carl Sandburg Collection,
University of Illinois

Sandburg addressing the
Joint Session of Congress,
February 12, 1959
Carl Sandburg Collection,
University of Illinois

Sandburg and Edward R. Murrow
during the 1950s
Carl Sandburg Collection,
University of Illinois

Helga and Barney and friends in the later years *Tom Merce; courtesy of Helga Sandburg*

Margaret Sandburg in the later years *Jim Callaway; Palladium-Item Photo, Richmond, Indiana*

Carl and Paula Sandburg at Connemara in the late 1950s *June Glenn, Jr.; Carl Sandburg Home*

Carl Sandburg and Abraham Lincoln   *June Glenn, Jr.;*
Citizen-Times, Asheville, North Carolina

about it as a by-play—something you do when you have had of an evening enough proper concoctions of gin. . . . I went out a few years ago to organize the North American Paw-Paw Growers Association and elected myself president of it as it is much more convenient to be that.

Now Harriet Monroe knew these two extremes of American society. . . . She effected a reconciliation of those two extremes in a finer way than anyone I have ever known.

In large measure, it had been Harriet Monroe who helped Sandburg find himself and his home in Chicago, nearly a quarter of a century earlier, when she read "Chicago Poems," and heard the music and the message in them, and shared them in the pages of her small, courageous magazine.

✳

Sandburg wrote most of *Abraham Lincoln: The War Years* at one of his reconditioned Remington typewriters perched on a sturdy wooden fruit crate in his garret workroom. On warm days, Sandburg moved some crates and a couple of chairs out onto the third-floor sundeck, where he could work in sunlight and solitude, bare-chested, the ever-present green eyeshade protecting his eyes. He took long walks on the beach, often swam around noon, fed on coffee and cigars and goat's milk, lost himself for hours and days in Lincoln's world. A Lincoln life mask and a top hat kept him company in his workroom. Margaret, Janet and Helga sorted, filed and retrieved materials for him, " 'classified,' thousands of items," he said, "and cheerfully performed many necessary petty chores." Actually, Margaret remembered, she and her sisters were not always cheerful about it, usually being in a hurry to get outside to the beach. Paula "often threw in with a rare mind and great heart."

At the heart of Sandburg's Lincoln was their joint devotion to the common people and the American dream. As early as 1906 Sandburg had been writing about Lincoln as hero, and as champion of the average man. Sandburg chose incident after incident to illustrate Lincoln's bond with the people, the national and international Family of Man. He used Whitman's words to support his theory. "For Whitman Lincoln was a great voice and a sublime doer in the field of democracy. He regarded both Lincoln and himself as foretellers of a New Time for the common man and woman." After the biography was finished, Sandburg wrote, "Look where [Lincoln] came from—don't he know all us strugglers and wasn't he a kind of a tough struggler all his life right up to the finish?" Lincoln the man haunted him even more than Lincoln the national hero. That fascination explained as much as anything why Sandburg the poet chose, in the prime of his creative life, to devote such enormous energy to biography.

The discipline and challenge demanded all of his literary skill and personal experience. "For the writing of the Lincoln I knew the Abolitionists better for having known the I. W. W.," he said. "I knew Garrison better for having known Debs." He noted in the Foreword to *The War Years* how his own experience drew him closer to Lincoln's times:

> Of the involved race question which weaves incessantly through these pages I learned as a reporter for the *Chicago Daily News*, when I covered the race riots of 1919 and did a series of articles on some of the conditions which caused the riots. It was three years later that I had a week's visit at Lang Syne Plantation near Fort Motte, South Carolina, under the guidance of the wise and vivid Julia Peterkin seeing conditions that, except for the slavery status, were somewhat like those of the 1850's.

Sandburg's foreword contains a bibliographical survey of Lincoln materials available to him at the time of his landmark work. As a vagabond poet traveling the country, he met "sons and daughters of many of the leading players in the terrific drama of the 1860's," including descendents of Sam Maverick, Alexander Stephens, Jefferson Davis, Gideon Welles and Stephen Douglas. He had worked in more than a hundred institutional libraries, and dozens of private ones. He had long-standing access to Oliver Barrett's collection, and often made himself at home at Henry Horner's Madison Park apartment, where Horner would "humorously and democratically go through a ritual of making a big grand desk collapse into a bed." If Sandburg wanted "a cheese sandwich with a little beer," Horner would provide that, too.

As Sandburg searched for that "grand human struggler" Lincoln, and for the significance of his "toils, combats, visions, and hopes," he was humbly aware of his debt to many friends and scholars, and articulated it. "You were a wholesome, steadying and kindly influence all along," he told Paul Angle, "beyond what you realized, perhaps—and that for you the job stands up counts deeply with me." Sandburg had the help of many scholars and bookmen, such as Ralph Newman of the Abraham Lincoln Bookshop in Chicago. President Roosevelt personally took him on the tour of the White House in 1937. One summer at the Olivet Writers Conference, he had long talks with Allen Tate and Caroline Gordon, who were "luminous on lights and loyalties that moved the Confederacy." Throughout, Sandburg had the unflagging help of his family, including his brother Mart, whom he thanked in the foreword for "favors, errands, loans, services. . . ."

Sandburg examined the great "wildernesses" of Lincoln papers, picking his way "carefully, sometimes drearily and with hope and patience, or again fascinated and enthralled by the basic stuff of indisputably great human action in play before my eyes." While he read every possible secondary source on Lincoln and the Civil War, he held closest to "the most essential and most formidable source"—the "record of Lincoln's utterance; his letters, notes, memoranda; the transmissions of his thoughts in his own handwriting which he signed . . . his published addresses which he wrote before delivery, as distinguished from impromptu speeches reported in the press; his arguments, declarations, meditations, remarks, or narratives noted by bystanders or participants in an interview or conference."

These documents showed Sandburg that in Lincoln's time, as his own, events were "tangled, involved" and often unfathomable. His study of Lincoln's era showed him in Roosevelt's the high personal and national costs of living in the center of "a great storm." It took all his instinct and reflex as an astute reporter, combined with the intuitions of the poet, to finish that long work tracking down "lives, deeds, consciences."

✳

Sandburg was in the home stretch on the Lincoln book in the summer of 1938. He thought he would have the first main rough draft completed by July 4. "Weaves, inserts, revisions should be done by Oct. 1," he told Harcourt. "If present health holds out your editors will have th[e] script before Jan. 1. . . . The mail is piled high and for weeks now I have answered only telegrams or the second letter asking what about the first."

His letters chronicled his progress. "Have finished now on the last day and the last night," he told Harcourt at the end of June. "Dr. Leale has smoothed the drawn face, put coins over the eyes, laid a white sheet over the body and face, stepped out of the door of the house to find cold rain falling on his bare head, remembering he left his hat in his theater seat. He looks at his detachable cuffs blood soaked and decides he will keep them as long as he lives."

By late August he was in the last chapter of the book, although he knew that "revisions and inserts of materials found since earlier chapters were written mean much heavy drudgery yet." The manuscript by then ran to over 1.2 million words. He had "faithfully plodded thru every last piece of material" he could lay his hands on, "groping" and "sifting" through a ton or two of materials, he estimated. He hoped that the book would be in print by September 1939.

There were unexpected delays. "Wilkes Booth could not be polished off as summarily as I believed," he told Harcourt in late August. "I am about half thru the final chapter, having done a more extended miniature biography of our American Judas than any other biographer has ever attempted. Remains now the obsequies and the world's greatest funeral."

He knew that portions of his biography would not be easy to read, but told Harcourt that for "the poor reader who won't go along with me on that it will be just too bad for that reader. He will just have to let the book alone and stay ignorant: there are moments when I don't give a dam whether he turns the page—which isn't saying I haven't tried to be lucid and cogent and making use of all gags and 'good theater' available." That fall he was "rewriting hundreds of sentences, scores of paragraphs," having "a big horse-laugh over things I once wrote that now must be wrecked and reorganized." He knew he could keep on and on at the work, and still not improve some sections, but he believed a biographer had to know when to stop. He told fellow biographer Lloyd Lewis that there was "a matter of timing . . . you can live with manuscripts and material still they have an unfair domination with bad results."

He pulled himself out of the Lincoln work that fall to lecture and to offer his services to Michigan Governor Frank Murphy in the fall campaign. "I belong to no party but all who know me are well aware that I am a New Dealer," Sandburg told Murphy, "that I agree with you it may be necessary to draft Roosevelt for a third term."

Paula and Helga won several blue ribbons and the Governor's Trophy for the Best Eight Head at the Illinois State Fair that summer. Sandburg was proud of their success breeding the goats. "They are sharks at genetics. Paula among the goats and kids is like her brother amid the delphiniums. It is genetics and much else."

By early 1939 Sandburg had most of the manuscript of *Abraham Lincoln: The War Years* ready to turn over to Harcourt. He had written the best book he knew how, "about a man who knew danger and throve on laughter." "Your own character gets written into your work," he had warned another biographer. Lincoln had been Sandburg's most intimate companion for years, so much so that when the book was done he said he would have to rediscover who Carl Sandburg was. Lincoln had led a disenchanted Sandburg through the past back to active participation in the present, rejuvenating his interest in contemporary politics. His long contemplation of Lincoln's times renewed his deep faith in the American experience.

Like Lincoln, Sandburg was sometimes accused of arrogance, and Sandburg explored that and other possible faults in Lincoln's behavior.

From his own experience in public life, he understood what it was to live "in terrific highlights of scrutiny and interpretation, of representations ranging from the utterly true to the unutterably false." Sandburg saw Lincoln as "a home man, a husband and father with the routine of family life in a house seldom untroubled with visitors and intruders." Lincoln was a "lonely walker and meditator" who had a "personality intricate and mysterious even to himself."

He explored Lincoln's uses of language, public and private. Lincoln's propensity for the honest, often scathing personal memo, written only for himself, was an essential, healthy ventilation of anger, frustration, despair. Lincoln loved the written word, was fond of ballads and songs, had a "remarkable and retentive" memory for lyrics, poems, facts, faces. He loved to read and recite poetry, preferred "verses from a poet of folk touch, "enjoyed puns and folk sayings, used the evolving "American language" adroitly. Lincoln preferred to speak "the plain homespun language of a man of the people, who was accustomed to talk with the 'folks.' " Lincoln "did not 'care a cornhusk for the literary critics,' " invented words for his own use, admired brevity and economy of speech, held in enduring affection and respect "that great popular assemblage" of the American working people from which he came. Lincoln chose to stay "within the direct contact and atmosphere of our whole people." He was "a President who was All-American. He embodied his country in that he had no precedents to guide his footsteps." As "frontiersman and pioneer," he broke from "a classicism of the school of the English gentleman" in his politics, becoming an American dreamer and spokesman for democracy.

Sandburg examined Lincoln's humor, his religion, his "mysticism, humility, reliance on a Power beyond himself." He wove into the biography contemporary appraisals of Lincoln, attacks heaped upon him, the extent to which "his character and personality carried the people with him." Sandburg's culminating portrait of Lincoln comes in his death, the stark immediacy of detail in "Blood on the Moon," the chapter on the assassination, and a panoramic chapter on the nation's response to the tragedy. He concluded his elegiac last look at Lincoln with a final judgment on the life and its central event, the war. It was Sandburg the quiet realist and cynic who observed:

> Black men could now move from where they were miserable to where they were equally miserable—now it was lawful for them to move—they were not under the law classified as livestock and chattels. Now too the Negro who wished to read could do so; no longer was it a crime for him

to be found reading a book; nor was it now any longer a crime to teach a Negro to read. The illiterate, propertyless Negro was to be before the law and the Federal Government an equal of the illiterate, propertyless white—and many sardonics were involved. And in spite of its many absurd and contradictory phases the Negro had a human dignity and chances and openings not known to him before—rainbows of hope instead of the auction block and the black-snake whip.

One result of the Civil War, Sandburg wrote, was that the United States took its place "among nations counted World Powers." An almost immediate consequence of Lincoln's death was that "the living and actual" man was subsumed by "the vast epic tale of the authentic Lincoln tradition mingled with legend, myth, folklore." According to Sandburg, the transmutation of man to myth and symbol was worldwide:

> Beyond any doubt, said leading men and journals, there never had been on earth a man whose death brought in all countries such quick, deep human interest, such genuine sorrow, such wide-flung discussion and commentary. Often came the statement that over the world the whole civilized Family of Man shared in regrets or grief for the loss of a common hero who belonged to humanity everywhere. . . . Some had no hesitation about one sweeping and beautiful claim: "He was humanity."

Sandburg achieved perhaps the finest, most eloquent poetry of his career in the final passages of *Abraham Lincoln: The War Years*. He had imbibed the lean, controlled, musical rhythms of Lincoln's speeches and letters, the harnessed, graceful power of Elizabethan English as the American backwoodsmen knew it unconsciously in the King James Version of the Bible. He used metaphors from his own earlier work: "Beyond all the hate or corruption or mocking fantasies of democracy that might live as an aftermath of the war were assurances of long-time conditions for healing, for rebuilding, for new growths. The decision was absolute, hammered on terrible anvils."

It had been "a storm of steel and blood" with the "melancholy and merciless crying out loud that always accompanies revolution. . . . The delicately shaded passages of the second inaugural wept over the cost of doing by violence what might have been done by reason."

Then, before the terse simplicity of the final chapter, on Lincoln's funeral, Sandburg gave one last view of the living Lincoln: "Out of the smoke and stench, out of the music and violet dreams of the war, Lincoln stood perhaps taller than any other of the many great heroes. This was in the mind of many. None threw a longer shadow than he. And to him the great hero was The People. He could not say too often that he was merely their instrument."

"Vast Pageant, Then Great Quiet," the final chapter of *Abraham Lincoln: The War Years*, is at the beginning a long prose poem. The funeral was "garish, vulgar, massive, bewildering, chaotic." It was also "simple, final, majestic, august." It was redeemed by "The People, the masses, nameless and anonymous numbers of persons not listed nor published among those present."

Sandburg juxtaposed the tragedy of Lincoln's death to the resumption of normal life:

> The ground lay white with apple blossoms this April week. The redbird whistled. Through black branches shone blue sky. Ships put out for port with white sails catching the wind. Farmers spoke to their horses and turned furrows till sundown on the cornfield. . . . In this house was a wedding, in that one a newborn baby. . . . Life went on. Everywhere life went on.
>
> In the East Room of the White House lay the body of a man, embalmed and prepared for a journey.

He traced the slow progression of the Lincoln cortege from Washington to Baltimore, Harrisburg, Philadelphia, New York and then westward to Albany, Utica, Syracuse, Cleveland, Columbus, Indianapolis, Chicago, past millions of mourners, and then home to Springfield, Illinois. More than seven million people had seen the coffin, Sandburg wrote, and "more than one million five hundred thousand people" had viewed Lincoln's immobile face: "The estimated figures were given. They were curious, incidental, not important—though such a final pilgrimage had never before moved with such somber human outpourings on so vast a national landscape."

Martha Moorman, the Sandburgs' housekeeper, had come into the workroom one day when the last page of *The War Years* was in the typewriter. Sandburg was not there, and she could not resist the temptation to read what he had written, knowing how near he was to the end. She felt as if she had lived with Lincoln, too, and she had, in a way, for nearly ten years. She had listened to Sandburg read many pages of his manuscript, but these words, which she read to herself in the quiet of his empty workroom, made her weep:

> On May 4 of this year 1865 Anno Domini a procession moved with its hearse from the State capitol to Oak Ridge Cemetery. . . .
>
> Evergreen carpeted the stone floor of the vault. On the coffin set in a

receptacle of black walnut they arranged flowers carefully and precisely, they poured flowers as symbols, they lavished heaps of fresh flowers as though there could never be enough to tell either their hearts or his.

And the night came with great quiet.
And there was rest.
The prairie years, the war years, were over.

"And the finish is symphonic," Sandburg told Lloyd Lewis; "life made it so."

✳

Sandburg had made a slightly curtailed winter lecture tour that year, setting out with the usual packet of food Martha fixed for him—homemade cheese and goat's butter on dark pumpernickel bread, and bottles of goat's milk. By June he was in New York, having delivered the final manuscript of the biography. Harcourt was delighted with the finished text, and he and Sandburg set to work on chapter titles and the table of contents. Then Sandburg went home to the dunes to write the Foreword and work on half-tone illustrations. Afterward, he would return to New York to work with Isabel Ely Lord on the copyediting.

Paula's dairy goats won their second Governor Horner Trophy at the Illinois State Fair that summer of 1939, while Sandburg focused on Lincoln. Helga, almost 21, had decided to go to college, and was enrolling at Michigan State University in Lansing. At departure time, her father was in New York finishing the last chores on the preparations to publish *Abraham Lincoln: The War Years*. Sandburg spent several days that fall with the Steichens at Umpawaug Farm, to rest and to be near New York in case Harcourt should need him. On the morning after he had corrected the last page proof, Sandburg let Steichen photograph him. "Carl sat at the breakfast table that morning with a serene and relaxed look," Steichen said, "a look that brought to mind Gardner's beautiful photographs of Lincoln made the day after the Civil War surrender. This is the only picture of Lincoln in existence which shows a real smile, a tired smile of relief, a smile of infinite warmth and tenderness." Steichen created a multiple view of Sandburg's profile which became known as "The Montage," one of Sandburg's favorite photographs of himself. Steichen's portrait of his brother-in-law appeared first in *Vanity Fair* and subsequently in many books and journals over the years.

To Sandburg's amazement, Harcourt ordered a first printing of fifteen thousand sets of *The War Years*, at twenty dollars for the four-volume set. Even at that, Harcourt had underestimated the response. Before the December 1, 1939, publication date, he had to rush a second printing for six thousand additional sets to meet the Christmas demand, and printed gift certificates for booksellers to use just in case. The Harcourt, Brace promotions staff celebrated on publication day by giving Alfred Harcourt a gold papier-mâché crown in honor of "the crowning point of his publishing career." *Abraham Lincoln: The War Years* was the apex in many ways for Harcourt and Sandburg, who had been together for nearly a quarter of a century as publisher/editor and author. Sandburg's epic biography appeared on the twentieth anniversary of his decision to leave Henry Holt and Company and entrust his career to Harcourt and his new firm.

After the four volumes of the Lincoln biography were printed, bound and boxed, Sandburg went out to the Rahway, New Jersey, plant of the Quinn & Boden Company and entertained plant personnel with his "deluxe" platform program of readings and songs "in token and appreciation of their fellowship, craftsmanship, anxiety and zeal in connection with the making of *The War Years* from a manuscript of 3,400 typewritten pages into . . . four boxed volumes" that "had from everywhere high praise as to typography presswork, illustrations, binding." He talked about the "ancient and natural partnership that exists between authors and printers, how neither can effectively get along without the other." That evening alone was unique in American literary history.

Sandburg was home at Birchwood Beach in Harbert by mid-October. Without Lincoln and Helga, the house seemed strangely quiet and incomplete. Helga was homesick for the family, and they missed her keenly. "The time when I am most homesick for you to be here is when I look at the horses," Sandburg wrote to her, "the hosses, the fellows that know your language like nobody else that talks to them. Take care of yourself . . . and maybe about a month from now we can send you the 4-vol Lincoln just to show you that it did get done."

Sandburg had not had a "real" vacation in eleven years, he told a friend on the eve of the great success of *Abraham Lincoln: The War Years*. "I am slowing down," he reflected. "There's a weariness in the bones. . . . The heave and the haul, the slime and the scum of a long voyage, is still on me."

Sandburg made the cover of the December 4, 1939, issue of *Time* magazine. "That son-of-a-gun Lincoln grows on you," he told *Time* readers. The four-volume biography of the last years of Lincoln's life immediately caught the attention of press and reviewers across the nation. "Never yet has a history or biography like Carl Sandburg's 'Abraham Lincoln: The War Years' appeared on land or sea," historian Charles

Beard wrote in the *Virginia Quarterly Review*. "Strict disciples of Gibbon, Macaulay, Ranke, Mommsen, Hegel, or Marx will scarcely know what to do with it." Beard had a clear perception of the nature and scope of Sandburg's research, observing that "few if any historians have ever labored harder in preparation for composition." Beard praised the "indefatigable thoroughness" of Sandburg's "preparations and his pages." He believed that "when specialists have finished dissecting, scraping, refining, dissenting, and adding" Sandburg's work would "remain for long years to come a noble monument to American literature."

The reviews poured in from around the country, most of them laudatory. Robert Sherwood in *The New York Times Book Review* called the work "a monumental undertaking . . . grandly realized." "Mr. Sandburg's method is unlike that of any biographer since Homer," he wrote. "Quite properly, Mr. Sandburg's great work is not the story of the one man's life. It is a folk biography. The hopes and apprehensions of millions, their loves and hates, their exultation and despair, were reflected truthfully in the deep waters of Lincoln's being, and so they are reflected truthfully in these volumes."

"The poets have always understood Lincoln," historian Henry Steele Commager wrote in the *Yale Review*, "from Whitman and Emerson to Lindsay and Benét, and it is fitting that from the pen of a poet should come the greatest of all Lincoln biographies, one of the great biographies of our literature." He praised the work's "indubitable authenticity," saw that it was "not primarily a work of scholarship," that it was "all narrative, the analysis takes care of itself, the interpretation is implicit in the material and the presentation. The technique is that of an attack in force; Sandburg masses his facts in regiments, marches them in and takes the field, and the conquest is palpable and complete."

Max Lerner observed in *The New Republic* that Sandburg was, in the Lincoln books, "reporter, poet, lover," but found the work "one-dimensional" with the detail getting the "same loving attention" as the big event, "at a considerable sacrifice of perspective . . . Sandburg is a little like a painter in the primitive style," Lerner wrote. "He is your true democratic historian. In his universe all facts, once they have been validated, are free and equal. Yet he gives his material thereby an unforced character that should cause the biographers who come after him to bless him."

Sandburg wrote to thank historian Allan Nevins for his endorsement of the biography. "You could have easily assessed a hundred serious minor errors against the book," said Sandburg, "but instead you gave a vast approval to the major and driving passion that swept through it."

Harcourt and Sandburg promoted the book aggressively. With book sales climbing, Sandburg and Paula were feted at dinners and other special occasions. Paula bought "a beautiful bright blue crepe evening dress," Margaret told Helga, and "two good daytime dresses, blue and aquamarine," not only for her husband's events, but for her own increasing involvement in A.M.G.R.A. activities. He was besieged with invitations to speak about Lincoln, and she had her own audience now, in the Midwest and as far away as Massachusetts, where she would soon travel to speak to dairy goat breeders.

After the long, solitary years of patient labor on the biography, Sandburg enjoyed the public acclaim. He was awarded the Pulitzer Prize in history in 1940, and received a garland of honorary degrees. "After the Doctor of Laws at Rollins College in February came the Diploma at Lincoln Memorial and Doctor of Letters at New York University, Lafayette, Wesleyan, Yale, Harvard," he told a friend. The Harvard citation read "Poet and reporter seeking the rhythms of America, lately Washington correspondent of the Lincoln Administration, resulting in an epic that fortifies the national faith."

He had had his quarrels with critics and the academic elite, but now he would "meet them more than half way." At the alumni dinner during Harvard Commencement in 1940, Sandburg told the audience, "When your invitation came last winter I said to myself, as I did twelve years ago when asked to read a Phi Beta Kappa poem: 'Harvard has more of a reputation to lose than I have, so I'll go.' "

The Lincoln experience had been a journey into history, a journey into self, a journey into the future of the great, worldwide "Family of Man." The long toil completed, Sandburg turned to the present. He wrote to Steichen about the current world scene: "And one little thing I am sure of about the whole goddam chaotic huggermugger—they wont straighten out the map of Europe and they wont have a basis for permanent peace, one or two generations of peace, until there has been a long war and misery and destruction lasting many years—and even at that the end may be compromises with no finality, no assurance."

He was right. It was Heartbreak Time.

———— ✳ ————

1940–1945

24. Heartbreak Time

Any mother might be hearing her boy child asking:
"Mama what is this supreme sacrifice I hear about?"
And answering, "Supreme sacrifice is when you go to
   war and die for your country."

Any mother might be saying now:
"The cool music of deep hearts is on me.
The fathoms of ancient fears are on me."

Nearer than any mother's heart wishes
now is heartbreak time . . .

      —Carl Sandburg, "Nearer Than Any Mother's Heart
      Wishes," 1938

Sometimes in those days of impending war, Sandburg looked at his "damned vast manuscript" of *Abraham Lincoln: The War Years* and saw it as "just a memorandum I made for my own use in connection with a long adventure of reading, study and thought aimed at reaching into what actually went on in one terrific crisis—with occasional interpolations of meditations, sometimes musical, having to do with any and all human times." His exploration of the past had worn him out, and he turned wearily toward the present crisis. He began his "first real vacation—and not a date ahead," he told Harcourt, "and to hell with letters and telegrams trying to use my time and keep me from doing what I want to do—which isn't definitely resolved at all yet—and may be months getting resolved."

The immediate success of *The War Years* prompted offers for radio shows, speaking engagements, other books. George Jessel wanted Sandburg to be a guest on his radio show, while Walter Schwimmer proposed a radio series based on the biography. Robert Sherwood wrote a script based on *The War Years* for the NBC Radio series "Cavalcade of America." Sandburg narrated part of the 1940 broadcast which starred

Raymond Massey as Lincoln. The mail poured into Michigan in such volume that Sandburg and Paula could not keep up with it, except for letters from friends such as Emil Seidel, his Milwaukee boss and mentor.

"Your letter arrived and I have read it slowly twice and enjoyed the breath of it and the lights of your face when you wrote it," Sandburg told Seidel in a letter. He was glad to get Seidel's address, so he could send him a set of *The War Years*. Sandburg wanted Seidel to read the chapters which dealt "with a frenzy and desperation that wore Old Abe as they wore Mayor Seidel; they deal with Office Seekers, the Uses of Patronage—and I am sure I described them better than otherwise had I not been your secretary in the outer office as they swarmed in."

He had not expected the "lavish reception" of the book. It was tempting to take refuge at home with his family, the goats and the solitude. With Helga away at college and Paula off on a visit to Steichen and to speak to Massachusetts goat breeders, he found the dunes "quite lonesome." He especially missed Paula, "the most important cog" in the wheel of his life, but the tranquillity helped restore his energy.

Sandburg and Paula kept their separate lecture and work schedules and reaped their separate honors in 1940. "You have made an honest woman of the Pulitzer Prize," Archie MacLeish wired him in May when the award was announced. Sandburg received his first Pulitzer in history, since books about Washington and Lincoln were still excluded from the award in biography. Sandburg's poetry had yet to be recognized by the Pulitzer board. He and Paula had named their Michigan place Chikaming Farm, and their goats the Chikaming Herd, for Paula's dairy enterprise was flourishing. Paula won trophies at the Illinois State Fair that summer for Best Eight Head for both Nubians and Toggenburgs, and brought home to Harbert not only numerous blue and purple ribbons, but the Grand Champion Toggenburg Silver Cup and the Grand Champion Nubian Golden Cup. Helga had trained the does and kids, and was responsible for the grooming and showing.

Sandburg got a special summons from Archie MacLeish that summer. As Librarian of Congress, MacLeish offered Sandburg the post of Poetry Consultant for the nation's library, the appointment to begin in July 1941. "I have two reasons," wrote MacLeish, "one the personal but not selfish reason of wishing to bring you to the Library of Congress as frequently as possible; the other, the professional reason of wishing to make the Consultantship in Poetry in the Library of Congress a position of the greatest possible distinction and prestige. In other words, I want you to set the job up on a pinnacle for me and at the same time I want to have you around."

MacLeish urged Sandburg to accept, not only because he could make an important contribution in poetry, but because he could work with "Alan Lomax and the boys working with folk song and music." Furthermore, he believed Sandburg would have an "educational influence upon the people's representatives in Congress." He told Sandburg that his presence, his talk, his writing and his thinking "would be invaluable. And the job, once you had held it, would be a job any man thereafter would be proud to hold."

Repeated letters got no response from Sandburg, but MacLeish persisted, in good humor:

> I remember your telling me how your incoming mail went into a goat's nest and only those letters which the goats refused ever got answered. Since I can't imagine a goat refusing a letter from the Librarian of Congress, I have no choice but to shame you with a carbon copy of my letter, which you will find herewith. The question is will you or won't you? You can spend as much time here or as little time as you wish. I am hoping you would want to spend quite a little, but I know what the demands on you are and I should not expect more than some weeks scattered over the year. We could make you comfortable and happy and you could make us happy and proud. What do you say?

Sandburg turned down that and subsequent offers of the consultantship, protesting, "I ain't got the executive ability." Later, MacLeish persuaded William Carlos Williams to do the job.

Personal accolades seemed inconsequential to Sandburg in the face of another gathering "world storm." He attended a reunion of his Spanish-American War comrades that summer, "the only real reunion as to numbers and spirit that we have had in thirty years and probably the last we shall ever hold," he told Harcourt later. But his own past, and Lincoln's, were overshadowed by contemporary events that fall. Sandburg threw himself into FDR's campaign for an unprecedented third term.

With the Second World War wracking Europe, the nation faced excruciating choices in 1940. It was a fiercely contentious time, with congressmen, journalists and ordinary citizens embroiled in vociferous debates about imperialism, isolationism, the nation's duty to the Allies, to itself, to the future. Citizens' groups such as William Allen White's Committee to Defend America by Aiding the Allies launched campaigns around the country. Sandburg, Stephen Vincent Benét and other writers became involved with the Council for Democracy, a group that produced propaganda pamphlets and radio programs about what American citizens could do to make democracy work. The Council issued such publications as *Defense on Main Street, a Guidebook for Local Activities for Defense and Democracy*. Charles Lindbergh was a visible leader of the pacifistic, isolationist American First Committee.

By the summer of 1940 the Nazi onslaught had subdued Denmark, Norway, Belgium, Holland, Luxembourg and most of France. Mussolini chose the moment of France's great vulnerability to attack her from the south. Roosevelt geared up the still-sluggish Depression-era economy for the production of planes and ships so that the nation could be "equal to the task of every emergency." Churchill and the British turned to FDR for material assistance in their lonely battle against Hitler and the Luftwaffe, and began to receive it in the form of fifty American destroyers, vintage World War I. The barter gave the United States leases on British military bases in the Western Hemisphere. FDR also implemented the nation's first peacetime draft.

On election eve 1940 Sandburg was the only political independent to speak on a two-hour national radio broadcast to advocate FDR's reelection. An estimated eighty million listeners tuned in for the program, which ended just before midnight with a five-minute speech by Carl Sandburg. He took his text from Abraham Lincoln's 1864 election campaign, quoting radical congressman and minister Owen Lovejoy, who said of Lincoln, "I am satisfied . . . that if he is not the best conceivable President he is the best possible. I have known something of the facts inside his Administration. . . . And although he does not do everything that you and I would like, the question recurs, whether we can elect a man who would." Sandburg drew vivid parallels between Lincoln and Roosevelt, between the nation in the Civil War and the nation "in this hour of national fate." He spoke to independent voters who "make their final decisions in the deep silence of their own minds and the low whispered prayers of their own hearts."

Sandburg was inundated with requests for scripts of his speech. He had talked it over beforehand with FDR in an hour-long visit to the White House the Sunday before the election. He sent the President a copy of the speech on November 9, at his request. "You might read these quotes sometime in a dark hour when you are under compulsion to make a decision, not between right and wrong," Sandburg told FDR, "but when your course must be for the lesser of two wrongs."

"I have not had a chance since the election to tell you really and truly how much that broadcast of yours closing the 1940 campaign meant to me," the President told Sandburg, who continued to receive "a flock of letters" about the speech. He told FDR that "a few letters and two telegrams curse me as a betrayer—but most of them carry a deep love for you—a love joined with faith and trust. In these hours of ordeal you command loyalties that no one else could."

For the first time in two decades, Sandburg threw himself into politics. He joined Dorothy Parker, Helen Keller and others in sponsoring work on behalf of Spanish refugees. He lent his name to writer Thomas Mann's "association of writers exiled from the Germany of the present and the immediate past," the German American Writers Group. "Should any regime similar to the one prevailing in Germany now by any fate attain the power in this country," Sandburg told Mann, "I do not doubt my choice would have to be that of death or exile." He served temporarily on the board of the Council of Democracy.

And as he inevitably did in times of national or personal crisis, Sandburg examined his own thoughts in the initial privacy of poetry, expressing in a new poem lessons from Abraham Lincoln:

> A Kentucky-born Illinoisan found himself
> By journey through shadows and prayer
> The Chief Magistrate of the American people
> Pleading in words close to low whispers:
> *"Fellow citizens . . . we cannot escape history.*
> *The fiery trial through which we pass*
> *Will light us down in honor or dishonor*
> *To the latest generation . . .*
> *We shall nobly save or meanly lose*
> *   the last best hope of earth."*

Before the end of that momentous year, however, Sandburg's attention was abruptly diverted from international strife to discord at home. Helga, high-spirited, headstrong and almost twenty-two, astounded her family with the news of her marriage to her mother's seventeen-year-old farmhand Joseph Thoman.

Since summer Joe had worked with Paula Sandburg's Chikaming goat herd. He was auburn-haired and good looking. An orphan since the age of six, he had been raised by an aunt in Illinois. Helga had met him at the Illinois State Fair that summer, introduced him to her mother, and "walked off hand in hand" with Joe to get ice cream. Impressed with the young man, Paula hired him to work for her in Harbert. Helga was transferring from Michigan State to the University of Chicago, in part to elude another boyfriend. Once Joe and a state milk inspector drove Helga back to Chicago after a weekend at home. "Joe and Dick (a tall handsome Irishman, at home testing the goats) drove me in," she wrote to her traveling father, "and we did up the Blackhawk. Just had a wonderful Spaghetti Italienne, with garlic and onions, and no drinks. We danced to Raymond Scott, one of my very favorite bandleaders. Dick's a smooth dancer, and of course Joe and I always hit it off like *that* when we shake a leg! I never had a more perfect night."

To Helga, Joe was a good friend and a great dancing partner. They had fun together, but there was no romance. Early in November Joe made an unscheduled trip to Chicago to see her. He told her that her mother was about to send him away from Chikaming Farm. Helga wondered if her father feared that "Mother's herdsman and the milk testers" were having too good a time with their daughter. Helga had her father's restlessness and his need for excitement and varied experience. She had her parents' passion for life. She also had an independent rebellious mind of her own.

There was a way out of that dilemma, she told Joe. She would come home for the weekend of the ninth of November, say she had a dental appointment in nearby South Bend, Indiana, and she and Joe would slip away and get married. That they did. "It is said it takes three days to tie the knot in Indiana," she wrote later. "It can't be done in one Saturday. But an appealing Romeo with curly auburn hair and a dark-haired firm Juliet did." Back home on the Dunes, they told her father first. He took the news quietly, although he must have been disappointed. But Helga recalled that his first words were, "Well, maybe there'll be grandchildren." When they told Paula, she broke into tears and retreated to the third floor for some time alone with Sandburg. "He told her to lay her head on his shoulder," Helga said, "to lie in his arms a while. They might not have chosen Joe, but their daughter did. It was her life."

Composed, Paula was soon her practical self. She gave Joe and Helga the guest room, since it had a double bed, and handed her daughter with "old-fashioned directness" a jar of Vaseline which she said they might need. Helga and her young husband spent their wedding night in the bedroom which the family called the Lincoln Room for its rows of bookshelves housing much of Sandburg's Lincoln library. The jar of Vaseline went untouched, "not," said Helga, "because it wasn't needed but we were unsure of its exact use and had had no explicit directions."

Helga dropped out of college and lived at home, helping Joe in the barns and her father in his workroom. Before long her mother had a small cottage built for them on the property so they could set up housekeeping with more independence. They called it Orchard Cottage, for its location "below the hillside where the tiny orchard of apples and cherries and peaches and plums and nectarines and pears and apricots blossomed in pink and white," Helga said.

Thus the family circle grew. Margaret, Janet and Martha Moorman liked Joe's company. Hardworking as ever, Helga and Joe made a valiant effort to fit their lives to the family. Helga had grown up sharing with her father many of the physical activities fathers and sons traditionally enjoyed—swimming, hiking, horseback riding. At times during her childhood, Helga resented the attention elicited by Margaret's illness. Paula was often preoccupied with Margaret and Janet; their father was such a public man that his attention was pulled in many outer directions. Helga was glad to have her own husband and home to concentrate on, and the cherished freedom of the dunes and all outdoors. Her marriage might baffle and trouble her parents, but the whole family, Joe included, set out to make the best of things, and since Joe was Catholic, Helga became an enthusiastic convert. There were no grandchildren on the horizon, but Sandburg reported that first winter of their marriage that "Helga and her Joe" were planning to get a "sweet laughing St. Bernard dog."

✳

Sandburg vigorously supported Roosevelt, and much of the poetry and prose he wrote then was avowedly patriotic. His work touched the lives of other writers and musicians and took on new life through their work. Norman Corwin, a gifted writer at CBS Radio, worked with composer Earl Robinson on an operatic setting of portions of *The People, Yes,* broadcast in 1941 with Burl Ives performing. Sandburg immediately liked Corwin, and admired his integrity and humility. At forty-one, Corwin was more than two decades Sandburg's junior, but they shared a timeless vision of humanity. While most readers considered *The People, Yes* an American poem, Corwin saw its universality. "The way I see it," he told Robinson, "TPY should be the kind of music-drama which, if translated into the French or the Persian or the Portuguese could play without a single change. . . . Examine the original TPY and see if CS is writing about an American, or even a country. The thing that makes it great is that he is writing about all people everywhere."

Corwin was from Boston, handsome, brilliant, and, like Sandburg, largely self-educated. He was making an indelible mark in the relatively new field of serious radio drama, and his enthusiasm for *The People, Yes* shone in his letters to Sandburg in January 1941. With Corwin's praise on his mind, Sandburg chose a section of the poem to read in a broadcast from the Metropolitan Opera House in New York City on January 25.

Like most Americans, Sandburg had listened to President Roosevelt's 1941 "Four Freedoms" speech, delivered, as it happened, on Sandburg's sixty-third birthday, before both Houses of Congress. In his third State of the Union address, FDR told Congress and the nation that he found it "unhappily necessary to report that the future and the safety of our country and of our democracy are overwhelmingly involved in events far beyond our borders."

Roosevelt outlined his plans for an immediate "swift and driving increase in our armament production," and shared his hope for a world "founded upon four essential human freedoms . . . freedom of speech and expression . . . freedom of every person to worship God in his own way . . . freedom from want," and "freedom from fear, which, translated into world terms, means a worldwide reduction of armaments to such a point and in such a thorough manner that no nation will be in a position to commit an act of physical aggression against any neighbor—anywhere in the world."

On the eve of the nation's entry into World War II, Roosevelt led the country toward a global view, a sense of its own destiny and responsibility as part of the larger world. Simultaneously, Sandburg widened the lens of his poetic vision, contemplating not only national heroes, lingo and heritage, but the great, universal human family.

In that time of international chaos, Sandburg called himself a "Man in a Fog." He could hardly keep up with his own hectic schedule, much less the emerging world agenda. He went to Springfield, Illinois, to make a February 12 CBS Radio broadcast, declining a fee and refusing other broadcasts for pay that Lincoln's birthday. *Life* photograper Bernard Hoffman photographed Sandburg for another article, and Karl Detzer of the *Reader's Digest* interviewed him at length for a story. He got so much publicity then as Lincoln biographer and Poet of the People that he worried that the attention was "overfeeding the country and me." He told *St. Louis Post-Dispatch* editor Irving Dilliard "I am still and yet enough of a hobo so that if I am outside of jails and eating three decent meals a day, and the family provided for, I dont require news treatment or ask for publicity."

As Sandburg avidly followed world events, he was invited to write a weekly news column for the *Chicago Times* Syndicate. For more than two years, he plunged back into journalism, producing the column not as "a watchtower" which shed "light over the national scene, bringing order out of confusion," but as "the best lucid memorandum occurring to the writer for that particular weekend moment of time."

*

There was speculation among his colleagues and readers as to what project Sandburg would tackle next, but he was clear about one thing: "Ain't writing no biog of anybody." For now his attention was split between the darkening world crisis and endless follow-up details associated with the Lincoln books. In March 1941 he urged MacLeish and the Library of Congress to purchase the Herndon-Weik Lincoln collection. His work on *Abraham Lincoln: The Prairie Years* had been handicapped because he did not have access to the papers, then closely held in private hands. They covered "the youth and formative period of Abraham Lincoln— with primary source documents—as nothing else on that period," Sandburg pointed out. The collection represented "the life work of a man who was Lincoln's law partner and office associate for sixteen years, and author of what many writers, including men of vast labors in the Lincoln field . . . consider the greatest biography written by men of Lincoln's own generation."

Sandburg foresaw that Lincoln would be "continuously, endlessly, across the future, a subject for the use of materials of more and more biographies, special studies of certain phases of his personality—and perhaps more important yet the work of the writers having creative imagination, who, with the modern devices of screen and radio, reach audiences running into tens of millions of people." Therefore, he argued, "too much stress cannot be laid to the importance of the creative writer of integrity having access to all possible primary source materials on Lincoln."

In those twentieth-century war days, Sandburg believed more than ever that Lincoln was "the one American figure cherished by the human family the earth over as the foremost incarnation or patriot saint of democracy." MacLeish was persuaded. The Library of Congress bought the collection from G. A. Baker and Company of New York, who had purchased the papers from Jesse Weik's son.

When Alfred Harcourt returned to work after a Florida vacation that spring, Kitty McCarthy, Sandburg's editor, reported that the poet and biographer had "gone into the Silences." But Harcourt saw evidences of activity, he teased Sandburg: "a sheaf of promotion material from The Chicago Times about a weekly syndicated article, copies of Motor City Magazine with some splendid shots of you, and a first-rate study of you by Karl Detzer which comes in by way of Reader's Digest and which I think is good enough for us to publish as a little book." Detzer spent weeks working on the Sandburg story. He talked to Sandburg's *Chicago Daily News* cronies, offering them "free elbow exercises" at a Chicago tavern. Then, he told Sandburg, he "poured them out in front of their hotels at two a.m." He traveled to Galesburg to interview Sandburg's family and friends, sitting on the floor at Mart's house to talk, and interviewing the assistant fire chief who said, "I hear Charley Sandburg's made good *after all*. Guess he done right changin' professions. He never was much of a fireman."

Sandburg lectured, prepared for a May program at the Library of Congress, but concentrated that spring on his *Chicago Times* column, a new, national podium for his opinions. His first column pointed out the folly of trying to see too far, to formulate alternatives in wartime. He reminded his readers of some of the lessons of World War I—of how events suddenly, decisively shook the world into certain courses of action. In war, Sandburg reflected, events rise "out of a fog of imponderables where one man's guess was as good as another's."

Sandburg had "theories and ideas about propaganda that may work out and may not," he told Eugene Meyer of the *Washington Post*. He and MacLeish arranged an American poetry program at the Library of Congress featuring their own poetry, some of it set to music and sung by the exotic French refugee Marianne Lorraine. There were selections from Sandburg's *The People, Yes* and MacLeish's *America Was Promises*, testaments to the vision the two poets shared of the poet's public responsibility to address the "living issues" of his time.

Sandburg agreed that spring to another propaganda project—writing the soundtrack narration for government films. He wanted his words to make a difference, in a variety of media. He was set to write the soundtrack for *Bombers for Britain*, a literary form, he said, "I have not yet tried."

The nation lived in a state of limited national emergency during those uncertain months of 1941, torn between intervention and isolation. On June 7 an All-American Committee of two hundred citizens sponsored a national unity rally at the Chicago Stadium, where 24,000 people packed the main floor and four galleries to hear an all-star cast of fellow citizens talk about the national crisis. Businessmen, labor leaders, artists and politicians spoke. Chicago mayor Ed Kelly was there, and then–University of Chicago professor Paul H. Douglas, a member of the city council and future U.S. senator. Wendell Willkie flew in from New York to speak, and when Judy Garland "stepped up to a mike and let her warm tremulous contralto go on the first line of 'God Bless America,' " Sandburg said, "at least half of the audience on the main floor rose from their seats and joined in the singing."

Just a few weeks earlier the audiences at America First meetings in

Philadelphia and Chicago had "hooted and booed and howled" singers into silence when they tried to sing Irving Berlin's patriotic song. There were rumors that Nazi propagandists were at the root of such protests because the composer was Jewish. Sandburg wrote a news column about the Chicago Stadium rally, warning that "when the long arm of Nazi propaganda reaches from Berlin to Chicago and Philadelphia telling us what songs we can or can't sing, we are merely getting a little preview and foretaste of what that propaganda will hand us when its prestige and power have been fortified and buttressed to the extent we will surely see if and when the British Isles become a Nazi outpost through lack of what we might have determined to send."

He did not mention his own speech in his column, or the fireworks ignited by his attack on one of the most prominent figures in the America First movement, aviation hero Charles Lindbergh, who had spoken vigorously against American participation in the war, to the cheers of America Firsters in New York. When President Roosevelt called Lindbergh a "Copperhead," comparing him to traitors during the Civil War, Lindbergh resigned his army commission. ("The army meant so much to him," his wife mourned in her diary. "It was the open world, his first chance; he blossomed there. How he worked, what it meant to him, he has told me.")

Sandburg lambasted Lindbergh in his Chicago Stadium speech. He did not call Lindbergh by name, but he did not have to:

> The famous flyer who has quit flying and taken to talking, who is proud that he has ice instead of blood in his veins, he has no more notion of what has kept me awake when I wanted to sleep than a Greenland walrus has of the Negro spiritual "Swing Low, Sweet Chariot." He calls me hysterical. He sees others like me shaken and anxious at what has happened to human freedom under the "New Order" in Europe, under the wave of the future. And he calls them hysterical. He wishes us to understand that he is as cool as a surgeon making a diagnosis. . . .
>
> The famous flyer who has quit flying and taken to talking doesn't know that the hysteria he mentions is in part the same anxiety, the identical deep fear that men politically free have always had when there were forces on the horizon threatening to take away their political freedom.

He had met Charles and Anne Morrow Lindbergh a year earlier. They greeted each other with affection and warmth. Mrs. Lindbergh liked Sandburg at once, finding him "so sound, so rooted, so American. As American as Charles." When she read the news account of the attacks Willkie and Sandburg had brought on her husband, she was "shocked beyond words." Willkie's attack was "angry and indignant," she wrote in her diary, "but perfectly fair and decent—on *issues*. But Carl Sandburg says C. is proud that he has ice instead of blood in his veins." She was disillusioned, she wrote, that such an unfair attack could come from a man such as Sandburg, "A poet, a philosopher, a historian, a man who had studied Lincoln's life, who praised Lincoln for remaining true to his conscience, even if every friend left him. Who saw the bitter and unfair criticism of another era. A man of breadth and learning and life, of compassion, of understanding of people."

Lindbergh was the most visible, audible spokesman for the America Firsters, and Sandburg's criticism of him did not abate, despite a flood of protest. "So I am getting letters about how I should not have said that," he wrote in his column June 29.

Sandburg spoke at another national unity meeting in August at Madison Square Garden in New York, under the sponsorship of the Council for Democracy, delivering one of his most often quoted interpretations of democracy. The American democratic system "gives more people more chances to think, to speak, to decide on their way of life . . . than any other system," Sandburg said. It "has more give and take, more resilience . . . more crazy foolishness and more grand wisdom, than any other system. . . . Under no other system can a man be so many different kinds of a fool—and get away with it—and get paid for it. . . . Personal freedom, a wide range of individual expression, a complete respect for the human mind and the human personality—this is the ideal of the democratic system."

While only "fools and idiots want war," Sandburg concluded, "sometimes the issue comes before a nation of people: Will you fight a war now, or would you deliberately choose another later inevitable war, another inevitable bloody struggle for the sake of not losing what we have now?"

Sandburg and Lindbergh were just two voices among millions in the tumult in those days before the Japanese bombing of Pearl Harbor forged a national unity and purpose in one blinding, bloody instant. But Sandburg believed with all his heart, as he had for more than thirty years, that a writer had an obligation to speak to his times. He knew there were dangers in propaganda, but that increased the urgency of getting "your own propaganda across to masses of people." Otherwise, he argued, "by your silence or lack of clarity you are doing the same thing that helped get the intellectuals of Europe where they are."

"There are freedom shouters," he wrote in a poem that year.

There are freedom whisperers.
Both may serve.
Have I, have you, been too silent?
Is there an easy crime of silence?
Is there any easy road to freedom?

✳

"HELLBENT GRANDSON ARRIVED TODAY," Sandburg wired Alfred Harcourt on Thursday, December 4, 1941. Since she had "observed and helped so many does at their birthing" and because she was "so strong," Helga Sandburg Thoman planned to deliver her child at the Sisters of St. Francis Hospital in Michigan City, Indiana, some twenty miles from home. When things did not go well, she asked Joe to get her parents' help. She was taken by ambulance to Passavant Memorial Hospital in Chicago, where Dr. James H. Bloomfield delivered her baby by Caesarean section.

"This is just to say I never met a finer poem than you were yesterday," Sandburg wrote his daughter after his first glimpse of the baby they named Joe Carl. "The next best poem I met yesterday was the little feller who didn't look at me through the glass. But he did yawn twice. . . . When his legs were uncovered for me I noticed they were fine legs and he was trying to tell me something by signals with his toes."

From the first, Sandburg often called his grandson John Carl. He had intended to name his own son John. The Sandburgs usually tinkered with names until they came up with just the right one. Carl had been Charles, and then Charlie, Sandy, Saundy, Cully and, finally, Carl again. Lilian had been Lily and Paus'l before becoming Paula. Margaret was sometimes Marney, sometimes Marne. Helga had been Mary Ellen and Mary Illinois and Mary Alix before they settled on Helga for her, and then there were nicknames. Joseph Carl Thoman, or Joe Carl, eventually became a John, and, later, a Steichen. It was a family in which you eventually grew into your own name.

The whole family exulted that weekend in the baby's arrival. "HAL-LELUJAH FOR THE BOY THAT TOOK STEICHEN AND SANDBURG AND THOMAN TO PRODUCE. WE ARE GETTING DRUNK TO CELEBRATE LOVE AND CON-GRATULATIONS TO ALL AND MAW AND GRANDPA AND GRANDMA AND TO THE AUNTS FROM US ALL. BRUDDER," Steichen wired from Connecticut.

Their joy in Helga's robust baby was grimly overshadowed that weekend by stunning news. It came first over the radio, that lifeline to the world beyond the bright, peaceful dunes of Lake Michigan. "Yesterday, December 7, 1941—a date which will live in infamy—the United States of America was suddenly and deliberately attacked by naval and air forces of the empire of Japan." President Roosevelt's voice, taut with emotion, recited to Congress a litany of Japanese assaults. The President vowed that the nation would "not only defend ourselves to the uttermost but will make it very certain that this form of treachery shall never again endanger us." With that the United States was at war. In an act of swift and deadly surprise, the Japanese quelled the national debate between the interventionists and the isolationists. At Pearl Harbor they killed 2,403 Americans, injured 1,178, demolished 149 planes, destroyed two battleships and crippled four others, and damaged or decimated a handful of other vessels. As far as could be determined, the Japanese lost twenty-nine planes and pilots.

Congress declared a state of war with Japan on December 8, and on December 11 Germany and Italy declared war on the United States. "With confidence in our armed forces," the President pledged, "with the unbounding determination of our people, we will gain the inevitable triumph. So help us God."

It was a Christmas of darkness, Sandburg wrote at year's end, with "the usual millions of lighted Christmas candles" blacked out by war in Europe. Much of the free world, he said, was "wrecked, humanly torn, bleeding, starving." There was the "blazing and unforgettable" Nazi invasion of Russia in June and the Japanese attack on the United States at Pearl Harbor in December, "dealing death from the sky . . . in a savage and undeclared war killing American sailors and soldiers by thousands . . . the least foreseen event of the year."

Pearl Harbor had "with almost a touch of miracle" brought national unity, Sandburg wrote in his last column of 1941. "That it could come so fast, so clean and so complete, was beyond anybody's telling beforehand. . . . In their journey of destiny the American people on December 7 came to a Great Divide. And they crossed over. Millions of plans and projects canceled themselves like writing on sand after a storm wave." The finality of the "Japanese deed at Pearl Harbor," he told his readers, "smote home to every American-hearted listener of the news and the tolling bells of doom."

Now the Nazis throw in with the Japs. Now the pure Aryans of Berlin yoke themselves with the pure Mongols of Tokyo. Now it is four-fifths of the Family of Man signed up for a finish fight against the "New Order" in Europe and the Pacific. The "New Order" will lose. It will be outfought and outthought. The war ending when? That depends on unforeseen events. Within possibility too are several cataclysms, colossal in explosive force and reverberations.

Sandburg had kept his silence on some national issues during the height of the Red Scare after World War I, shaken as he had been by the spy episode. But this was a different war, a different time. He was vigorously outspoken. As a biographer, he had probed the nation's wartime history, finding lessons in the Civil War and the First World War which shed light on this war. Now, as a reporter once again, he interviewed military people, factory workers, families, and observed every possible component of the war effort at home, using his weekly news column to chronicle the progress of the war and to comment on it. There were echoes of his views on earlier wars: "The common man is the main figure in the fighting and the production. The forces working for him are immense. . . . The saying 'It is a people's war' is not empty." Sandburg the reporter roved from the specific wartime story to abstract reflections on the dangers and uses of propaganda, the meaning of freedom, the reasons men fight, among them "our wish, prayer, and dream that sometime, maybe soon, but anyhow sometime, over the whole earth the Family of Man will understand and put into reality the Four Freedoms."

Throughout the war, Sandburg the old idealist spoke out vigorously, in every genre at his disposal: his syndicated column, new poems, radio speeches, propaganda films. For the U.S. Office of War Information, he wrote the script for *Bomber*, a film about the B-26. With editor Elisabeth Bevier Hamilton of Harcourt, Brace, he prepared a one-volume profile of the Civil War, drawn from his Lincoln biography. They called it *Storm Over the Land*.

One of his most visible statements on the war came in "Road to Victory," a photographic exhibition prepared by Steichen, with Sandburg writing the text. "My own feelings of revulsion toward war had not diminished since 1917," Steichen said. "But, in the intervening years, I had gradually come to believe that, if a real image of war could be photographed and presented to the world, it might make a contribution toward ending the specter of war. This idea made me eager to participate in creating a photographic record of World War II." Steichen had tried to persuade the air force to reactivate his status as a reserve officer, but he was turned down, too old at age sixty-three, they told him, for active service. Thus, when David McAlpin of the Museum of Modern Art offered him carte blanche to do a photographic exhibit at the museum, Steichen decided to do a contemporary portrait of America. He called it "The Arsenal of Democracy" until Pearl Harbor threw the nation into war and it became "Road to Victory." By then the navy had solicited Steichen's services. When the call came, he "almost crawled through the telephone wire with eagerness." He was commissioned a lieutenant commander. His camera would take him, and the talented staff he assembled, to cover the Pacific war. But first he and Sandburg completed "Road to Victory," "a procession of photographs" which reported to the nation and the world on "the American people, their home front and fighting fronts, our wartime America."

When the show opened in May 1942 it filled the second floor of the Museum of Modern Art in New York, where it ran for six months before touring the country. A replica of the exhibit shipped to England was sunk en route by an enemy submarine. Undaunted, the sponsors shipped another exhibit, which reached London safely. Other replicas went to Honolulu, Australia and other Pacific ports. Two replica exhibits toured South America, and a paperback book was published for the armed services.

Sandburg had worked for nearly two weeks on the narrative, writing "sometimes desperately, first one and then another text," until he had "a framework of words" which moved "in tempo and theme" with the flow of the pictures. Steichen was "no slouch of an editor," Sandburg discovered. Sometimes he made Sandburg rewrite a sequence five or six times until "he wangled, joked and threatened better texts out of me than I would have believed possible."

The result was a great panoramic mural of pictures and words. "Here is man and what man hath wrought," Sandburg said of his brother-in-law's vision; "here too the sea and the face of the earth, and the American people in their productive and fighting phases. Steichen's faith in his America runs deep. The photographs he chose present a people and a country who have strengths, lights, and faiths to wrestle with any dark destinies ahead." It was, said Sandburg, "a massive portrait and an epic poem of the United States of America at war and on its road to victory."

✳

Helga and Joe Thoman left Chikaming Farm that year to live in southern Illinois in a two-room house with no plumbing, and look for some land of their own to farm. They needed independence from the family, a place of their own. Paula and Sandburg watched their departure tearfully. "Every one of your letters I read first for the facts and the fun," Sandburg wrote to Helga that fall, "and then a second time to see how the red inside heart of you is ticking."

Letters and snapshots moved back and forth between Chikaming Farm in Michigan and Helga and Joe in southern Illinois. Sandburg told Helga he felt "mighty good about how you are now and where you are and the way things are going." He and Paula loved the photographs of their grandson which Helga sent and they understood Helga's need for her own family life: "To love the good old earth and to make a little piece of it behave under your hands, that is to have riches if along with it you have health and strength," her father told her.

Martha Moorman left the Sandburgs to be married, and eighteen-year-old Adaline Polega took her place. She came to call Paula "Mom," and Paula began to think of her as another daughter. By autumn 1942 Joe and Helga were farming fifty acres of land, sharecropping with the widow who owned it. Paula sent the couple two goats to insure that her grandson would have "proper milk." Helga was twenty-four and enthralled with her new life. Her husband, five years younger, was not old enough for the draft, but soon he would join the merchant marine.

The Sandburgs missed Helga, Joe and the baby so much that Paula and Margaret traveled to St. Louis by train in September, where Joe met them to drive them to the farmhouse for a visit. Sandburg joined them for a day and a quiet picnic on the lawn enjoying the baby's antics. The family sang together, as always, and took pictures. Briefly, the war seemed far away.

Sandburg was soon back to a rigorous schedule of lectures, news columns, radio broadcasts. He wrote a sympathetic column on Japanese Americans, citizen and soldiers alike, whose loyalty was doubted. To demonstrate his own faith in them, he hired a secretary and a farmhand who were both Nisei—American-born children of Japanese immigrants.

The American people were living through "heartbreak time." They endured conscription, taxes, rationing, sacrifice. They demonstrated cooperation, survival, heroism, "epics of valor and endurance." They were rediscovering as a people how profoundly they valued freedom and peace. They had learned, Sandburg said, "to be a little sad and a little lonesome, without being sickly about it." As the first anniversary of Pearl Harbor passed, people were singing Irving Berlin's new song, "White Christmas."

Away down under, this latest hit of Irving Berlin catches us where we love peace. . . . While we proceed with our job of making war terrible to the enemy, while we move forward toward killing enough Nazis and Japs to end the war, the hopes and prayers are that we will see the beginning of a hundred years of white Christmases—with no blood spots of needless agony and death on the snow, with no lurking ski troopers in white uniforms on the white snow spitting the merciless music of machine-gun rain and hail.

Where there is will and vision men and women may hope. They may even dream of a century of white peace where tree-tops glisten and children listen to hear those sleigh bells in the snow.

*

By June 1943 Helga and her little boy had returned to Chikaming Farm, for Helga was pregnant again and her doctor advised her to have another Caesarean section. She wanted her Chicago surgeon to deliver this baby, too. Joe was preparing to enter the merchant marine. Sandburg was working with Frederick Hill Meserve on a new Lincoln project, the publication of *The Photographs of Abraham Lincoln*, culled from Meserve's vast collection, with commentary by Sandburg. He had decided to give up his weekly column, and Harcourt planned to publish the pieces, along with poems, speeches and other Sandburg statements on the war, in *Home Front Memo*. Sandburg thought about leaving out "a couple of mean Lindbergh pieces," he said. "Then I put 'em in again because he is the best 1941 exhibit of the respectable American Nazi mind and spirit."

He worked in New York that spring and early summer, and he was eager to get home to Michigan. "I miss the house, the air, the trees, the goats," he wrote to Paula, "and my loved ones and you most of all— love and blessings—" There was a special celebration once he was home. On June 28 Helga gave birth to a baby girl. They named her Karlen Paula. "My second grandchild arrived this week," Sandburg exulted, "so I am feeling affirmative about the firmaments of life."

He dedicated *Home Front Memo* to Stephen Vincent Benét, who died in 1943. "He saw that a writer's silence on living issues can in itself constitute a propaganda of conduct leading toward the deterioration or death of freedom," Sandburg wrote. He was expressing his own creed as well. In an April 1943 column Sandburg had praised Archibald Mac-Leish, Muriel Rukeyser, Alfred Kreymborg, Edna St. Vincent Millay, Ben Hecht and other American poets who, like Benét, wrote prose or poetry on behalf of the war effort. MacLeish had headed the short-lived, controversial Office of Facts and Figures while he was Librarian of Congress, until that clearinghouse for wartime information was superseded by the Office of War Information, directed by Elmer Davis. MacLeish, still Librarian of Congress, was Davis's associate director, and became an Assistant Secretary of State in 1944. He and Sandburg shared a vision of the poet-citizen's duty to be involved in his times and to let his writing "for the moment go forth for the moment, hoping a little good might come of it, and keenly aware it will not do to wait, revise, wait longer, revise yet more." Without calling names Sandburg attacked "two or three major America poets" who seemed to hold themselves "in foxholes of safety and silence."

He went on to write about Ezra Pound, soon to be indicted for treason by the Department of Justice for broadcasting for the Fascists in Italy, where he had lived for years. Sandburg, MacLeish, Ernest Hemingway and other writers thought Pound's broadcasts were "the product of a completely distracted mind" and not "overt acts to incite to violence." As MacLeish put it, Pound "seems to have gone completely to pieces under the pressure of a swollen and dropsical ego. Briefly, he feels he has not been appreciated at home and he has taken it out in babbling correspondence which has now turned into babbling broadcasting which, in form at least, comes awfully close to treason."

One of the major poets most conspicuously absent from Sandburg's list of those who "threw in with what they had" was Robert Frost. For the most part Frost, unlike Sandburg, MacLeish, Louis Untermeyer and others, kept his opinions to himself, or expressed them in private letters rather than in poetry or public forums such as the propaganda work of the Office of War Information. He did not believe that an artist could or should use his talent as an instrument for government propaganda, no matter how worthy the cause. He wrote to his daughter, Lesley, in 1942 about his feelings: "Once you start reasoning you never know where you will end up. That's why I refrain from reasoning too much about the Germans. Louis [Untermeyer] is down living alone in the Webster Hotel on the regular government job that Archie and Carl and Elmer Davis are on. I couldn't bring myself to it if I tried."

As Frost told Untermeyer, laboring away as senior editor of publications at the OWI, he had chosen to abstain, and refused to write propaganda. In August 1944 he wrote a long letter which was actually a poem, explaining his position to Untermeyer:

> I could no more have taken pen to Hitler
> Than taken gun (but for different reason).
> There may have been subconscious guile at work
> To save my soul from the embarrassment
> Of a position where with praise of us (US)
> I had to mingle propaganda praise
> Of a grotesque assortment of allies . . .
>   I'm bad at politics . . .
>
> In District of Columbia dialect
> Im not a big shot. None of you down there
> Would think of me for any liquidation
> (Dread word!) or purge the Sandburg-Browder bloc
> May have in mind. You told me so yourself.
> Nothing I do can matter. I make verse . . .

For Sandburg and Frost this disagreement was another skirmish not unlike their famous 1942 debate over the relative merits of conventional and free verse. In a March *Atlantic* article, Sandburg defended free verse, alluding to Frost's statement that he would as soon play tennis without a net as write free verse. Frost retorted that he was "challenged to single combat by Carl Sandburg. . . ."

During the war, Frost kept quiet, for the most part, and Sandburg stuck his neck out. As he wound up his stint as a columnist for the Chicago Times Syndicate in 1943, Sandburg felt as he had at the beginning that he "had no right to keep silence during a time of chaos and storm."

From time to time, Sandburg was urged to run for Congress. FDR himself told Sandburg he would welcome such a liberal in the House of Representatives. Sandburg had no interest in public office, however, and discouraged such overtures. He was a writer, not an office seeker. He would do what he had long wanted to do—"settle down on the farm here and hold myself to the written and printed word."

As he put the proofs of *Home Front Memo* to bed in New York, Sandburg had an offer for an exciting new project, to be written for a vast, highly visible stage. Voldemar Vetluguin of Metro-Goldwyn-Mayer invited him to dinner one June night at Longchamps Restaurant on Lexington Avenue. Vetluguin and producer Sidney Franklin (*Mrs. Miniver, Random Harvest, White Cliffs of Dover*) had an idea for an epic film about the United States of America. It would not be a "mere motion picture project." It would carry a great, ringing message to the people. "All kinds of people," Vetluguin promised. "Even those who read with their lips moving. Even those who never heard of the Bill of Rights." They wanted Sandburg to write a novel based on Franklin's scenario for the film. After the novel was published, MGM would turn it into a screenplay. They would pay Sandburg a hundred thousand dollars for the job.

He was sixty-five years old in 1943, the celebrated author of poetry, biography, children's stories, news commentary, a folk music anthology. He was a man of letters, still a pioneer wanting to try every possible genre. He had never written a novel. MGM wanted a great American epic to reach the wartime audience. It was a challenge Sandburg could not resist.

MGM expected the novel to be written in nine months. Convinced that he could do it, Sandburg signed a contract with MGM to write "the full and complete story and novel tentatively entitled 'American Cavalcade.' "

He and Frederick Hill Meserve were well along in their collaboration on *The Photographs of Abraham Lincoln*, which would appear in 1944, but by autumn 1943 he was free to travel to Hollywood to discuss the MGM project. In 1944, "still traveling, still a seeker," Sandburg was hard at work on his first novel.

✳

Like every family in the "heartbreak time" of war, the Sandburgs could recite a litany of losses: friends; children of friends; Sandburg's nephew Charles Goldstone, a conscientious objector, killed while driving an ambulance in Europe. While Joe Thoman was overseas, Helga decided she had outgrown that love and marriage, and they were divorced shortly after he came home. Sandburg's brother Mart died in April 1944, just a few months after his wife, Kate, died of cancer.

Opa Steichen, who had stayed on stubbornly in the empty house in Elmhurst after Oma died in 1933, finally consented to come to Harbert to live so that Paula could care for him. She, Helga and the children had gone to visit him and found him "propped up in bed, waiting to die (by the window so the neighbors would see!)." Paula immediately called an ambulance to move Opa to her house. Reluctantly, he gave up his independence, his house, his familiar garden—the tulips, flowering almonds, Persian lilacs—and went to Michigan, as the Sandburgs had long urged him to.

There he rested, gained strength, sat in the sun, enjoyed Helga's children, played cards with Janet and Margaret. He liked to ride into town with Paula on errands. She had found him thin and malnourished in Elmhurst, but he seemed to thrive in Michigan. "Opa seems reconciled to staying with us for the rest of his days," Paula told Carl in a letter, "but he has not forgotten Elmhurst and sometimes he says he wonders if he couldn't manage it there alone again." He was not to return to Elmhurst, however. Sometime in 1944 he suffered a fall, which left him weak and stiff. In early December, 1944, shortly after Edward Steichen reached his bedside, Opa died. He was almost ninety.

Oma had wanted her ashes buried with him, and Paula had kept them in an urn. Now she bought a cemetery lot in Riverside Cemetery, Chikaming Township. There, she and Steichen buried their parents. Steichen brought roses, tore them apart, and flung them over the coffin. "In a box in the casket with him are the ashes of his wife Mary who died in 1933," Sandburg wrote in a simple tribute. "They were life partners of nearly the same age. It was his wish they could share together the same oblong corner of earth. They will be joined in their long sleep and they will face together what they meet of silence or trumpets or changes and resurrections. To this we, the living, can join in saying Amen."

✳

One Sunday afternoon during the summer of 1944 the Sandburgs entertained four truckloads of army trainees who had bivouacked on the lake shore. The Ladies' Aid Society of a local church prepared dinner for the young soldiers, from Fort Custer near Battle Creek. Later Sandburg joined the soldiers on the beach. They sat in a circle around him while he played his guitar and sang. Then he talked to them about his work and his family, and answered their questions. He hoped they would make it through the war. They were the living, breathing counterparts of the young men he commemorated in his poems those days, poems such as "The Long Shadow of Lincoln: A Litany" which he would read as the Phi Beta Kappa poem at William and Mary College in Williamsburg, Virginia, that winter:

> . . . There are dead youths
> with wrists of silence
> who keep a vast music
> under their shut lips,
> what they did being past words . . .
>
> There is a dust alive
> with dreams of The Republic,
> with dreams of the Family of Man
> flung wide on a shrinking globe
> with old timetables,
> old maps, old guide-posts
> torn into shreds,
> shot into tatters,
> burnt in a firewind,
> lost in the shambles,
> faded in rubble and ashes . . .

Like most Americans, Sandburg and his brother-in-law Steichen "threw in" with all they had during the war. Steichen's persistence got him to Pearl Harbor, the Gilbert and Marshall islands and Iwo Jima. He told the story of the U.S. Marines' capture of Kwajalein Island in a book of photographs entitled *The Blue Ghost*. He broke the long-standing navy taboo which forbade officers to carry cameras for making official photographs, and deployed a carefully chosen staff of crack photographers on ships and planes to cover the war across the Pacific. One of the most haunting pictures to come out of that war, or any war, was Steichen's stark portrait of the hand of a dead Japanese soldier buried in the rubble of battle on Iwo Jima, only four fingers visible, clutching for light and air.

✳

Franklin Delano Roosevelt died on April 12, 1945. Sandburg and Steichen, each in his own way, commemorated the President's death. Steichen sent his men out to photograph the funeral and the sorrowing faces of the American people. Sandburg recorded the nation's loss in a poem, "When Death Came April Twelve 1945," remembering another wartime April, another President's demise:

> . . . And there will be roses and spring blooms
> flung on the moving oblong box, emblems endless
> flung from nearby, from faraway earth corners,
> from frontline tanks nearing Berlin
> > unseen flowers of regard to The Commander,
> from battle stations over the South Pacific
> > silent tokens saluting The Commander
> > . . .
>
> Can a bell ring in the heart
> in time with the tall headlines,
> the high fidelity transmitters,
> the somber consoles rolling sorrow,
> the choirs in ancient laments—chanting:
> > "Dreamer, sleep deep,
> > Toiler, sleep long,
> > Fighter, be rested now,
> > Commander, sweet good night."

PART FOUR

THE CONNEMARA YEARS

———— ✻ ————

1945–1946

25. The Eternal Hobo

Give me a quiet garret alone
Where I may sit for a few casual callers
And tell them carelessly, offhandedly,
"This is where I dirty paper."

Thus each poet prays and dreams.
The eternal hobo asks for a quiet room
   with a little paper he can dirty,
   with birds who sit where he tells 'em.

—Carl Sandburg, "Galuppi,"
Breathing Tokens

Carl Sandburg made two significant departures from the past in 1945, one temporary, one permanent. The temporary and ultimately disappointing excursion took him from poetry, biography and journalism to the novel he was writing for MGM. The permanent and much happier leave-taking turned him from his home in the Midwest to a new, spacious house in a far milder climate. Sandburg was the "Eternal Hobo," perennially traveling, seeking, experimenting. He was working as hard in his sixties as he had in his twenties, eager for new challenges. He undertook his first novel in that spirit, wandering into the uncertain terrain of a new and difficult genre. At the same time, he and Paula began to search for a new home for the family, the dairy goat herd, and his work. They were tired of severe winters, not only the fierce snow storms sweeping in from the lake, but the long, bleak season separating autumn from the soft blooming Michigan spring. Paula and Helga "hungered for green pastures" for the goats, Helga remembered. Their dune property, once relatively remote from other dwellings, was now part of a highly developed shoreline community. Strangers were often found on the beach, or climbing the dunes through the Blow to the house, or knocking at a door in search of the famous poet who lived there.

His face and voice were now recognized internationally. On April 3, 1945, Sandburg spoke to millions around the world in a radio broadcast "dedicated to what may well be the last remaining hope for a better world coming out of this war." CBS Radio producer Norman Corwin persuaded him to broadcast from his Michigan living room and asked him to evoke the spirit of Abraham Lincoln. "You are the only man in this country through whose lips the words of Lincoln could convincingly be re-activated," Corwin told Sandburg, "and I rather believe that if Abe's spirit is abroad these days, he might be a little miffed with you for passing this up for anything else."

Sandburg reiterated a favorite theme in the minute and a half allotted to him that April night, quoting Lincoln's December 1, 1862, message to Congress. "We can succeed only by concert. The dogmas of the quiet past are inadequate to the stormy present. . . . Fellow citizens, we cannot escape history. We . . . will be remembered in spite of ourselves. . . . The fiery trial through which we pass will light us down in honor or dishonor to the latest generation. We shall nobly save or meanly lose the last, best hope of earth."

A scant two weeks later, the war was won in Europe. Like millions of other Americans, the Sandburgs celebrated by listening to Corwin's radio drama "On a Note of Triumph," which Sandburg called the "greatest achievement I ever met in a combination of poetry, drama, music." He told Corwin that his program had "the eloquence, the relation of present to future, that Lincoln's House Divided speech had and that Patrick Henry's liberty or Death cry had."

Sandburg mourned that FDR had not lived to see the victory in Europe. Summoning more images of Lincoln, he eulogized Roosevelt in prose, to follow the farewell poem. At least Lincoln had lived to see his war end. Roosevelt's cerebral hemorrhage had taken his life less than three weeks before Hitler committed suicide, and not quite a month before Germany surrendered and the war in Europe was over. "The heart of the man is still now," Sandburg wrote of FDR. "Yet his shadow lingers alive and speaking to the whole family of man round about the earth." He called Roosevelt "a builder with a genius for the solidarity of mankind in his own country and everywhere in other countries."

Sandburg was still in the early stages of work on his novel in 1945. His MGM contract had called for its completion in 1944, but he quickly saw that the job would take far longer than nine months. Immediately, Sandburg chronicled the war's end and later made it part of his narrative. "The end of the war in Europe meant for millions of people less of fear, more of hope," he wrote, "and this was more so in America, the only country at war whose cities stood clean and whole with never a gash from air raids, its shores and countrysides witness of no invasion scar." He spoke in the novel of "the great clock of the war" which "ticked off deaths and dooms by the millions."

That cataclysmic August, Sandburg turned momentarily from his novel back to poetry. He wrote a chilling meditation on wars to come, "The Unknown War." Noting that French field marshal Foch had said "The controlling factor of war is the Unknown," Sandburg concluded the poem with that theme:

> The bombs of the next war, if they control, hold the Unknown blasts—
> the bacterial spreads of the next war, if they control, reek with the
> Unknown—the round-the-curve-of-the-earth guided missiles of the
> next war, should they control, will have the slide and hiss of the Un-
> known—the cosmic rays or light beams carrying a moonshine kiss of
> death, if and when they control, will have the mercy of the sudden
> Unknown.
> We shall do the necessary.
> We shall meet the inevitable.
> We shall be prepared.
> We shall stand before the Unknown,
> aware of the controlling factor
> > the controlling factor
> > the controlling factor
> > > —the Unknown

Punctually at nine-fifteen on the morning of August 6, the B-29 bomber *Enola Gay*, from an altitude of 31,600 feet, dispatched the bomb which decimated four square miles of Hiroshima and killed 60,175 Japanese citizens, including the entire Second Japanese Army. The second atomic bomb exploded at noon August 9, killing 36,000 people in Nagasaki. Just that morning Russia had declared war on Japan. By August 14 Emperor Hirohito had subdued his own unwilling advisers and accepted the terms of the Potsdam Declaration. On September 2 General Douglas MacArthur and Allied representatives met with Japanese officials to sign the papers which outlined the conditions of Japan's surrender and launched what MacArthur rightly pronounced a New Era.

On that momentous day, among other, more routine business at the White House, President Harry Truman, or someone on his staff, dictated a letter to Carl Sandburg, thanking him for the recent gift of an inscribed six-volume set of *Abraham Lincoln: The Prairie Years* and *The War Years*. As he read *The War Years* in "haunts made holy by memories of Lincoln," Truman told Sandburg, "I shall often be reminded of the 'White House loneliness and laughter' which you mention with such feeling."

"Your deeply moving letter about those Lincoln volumes has been framed and put on a wall in our house," Sandburg wrote the President a month later, "because near twenty years in the house was given to those books and your words are a sort of attestation that the work has a living use."

Sandburg had written his first war poetry about forty years earlier, and he took up the theme again in 1945: "Storms begin far back . . ./The anger of the waters lay/breeding, spawning, pent up/and ready to go . . ." In another poem, called "Turn of the Wheel," he wrote, "Geography costs—why does the map of Europe never stay put?"

This war was over. Peace and the New Era had begun. But Sandburg's historical and personal encounters with war had not left him much faith in the durability of peace, as he wrote in the poem "Peace Between Wars":

> . . . Therefore we know
> absolutely
> incontestably,
> the peace we now see
> will run
> till the next war begins
> whereupon peace
> will be ushered in
> at the end of the next war.
> Beyond this
> we know little
> absolutely, incontestably.

✳

One by one, those who had gone away to war came home to their peacetime fates. Since Helga's divorce in the summer of 1945, she and the children had lived at Chikaming Farm in "Orchard Cottage." Her parents put Helga on a salary, and she worked hard helping her mother with the goats and her father with secretarial chores. Steichen, now sixty-six and a navy captain, would serve as director of the U.S. Navy Photographic Institute in command of all navy combat photography until his release from active duty in January 1946. He had created another wartime photography exhibition for the Museum of Modern Art, "Power in the Pacific," had supervised the U.S. Navy film *The Fighting Lady*. He published three books of war photography, *Power in the Pacific, U.S. Navy War Photographs: Pearl Harbor to Tokyo Harbor* (1946) and *The Blue Ghost* (1947), based on his often dangerous experiences aboard the U.S.S. *Lexington*. He had come home from World War I a highly decorated army officer and a pioneer in aviation photography. He came home from World War II a decorated navy officer who had left an indelible imprint on the U.S. Navy Photographic Institute. In 1947 he was appointed director of the Department of Photography at the Museum of Modern Art in New York City.

When Steichen came home to Connecticut after the war, his daughter Kate had planned to greet him with a laurel wreath. When she saw him, however, she recognized that the close-up view of the war had saddened him. She did not give him the wreath. World War I had left Steichen depressed and disillusioned and marked a turning point in his artistic life. World War II had given him his greatest opportunity to record "the true face of war" in hopes of helping to banish war forever. He knew that, because of the work he and his staff photographers had achieved, there never had been anything like the photographic story of World War II. Once again, his war experiences shaped his future work. "During my lifetime our country has had three wars," he said. "I have been a photographer in two of them. I don't want to do it again. I want to photograph the light on the countenances of men and women who are at peace."

His brother-in-law Sandburg had lived the war at home, and "fought" it in the public arena of his newspaper column, his speeches and his occasional poems. From 1943 until long after the war's official conclusion, Sandburg explored in his sprawling novel the nature of war, historic and present, and the meaning of the abstractions Freedom, Liberty, Patriotism and Nationalism.

From the beginning the project was unorthodox, despite the precedents of American writers hiring out to Hollywood to produce scripts, for movies were usually derived from already-published novels. When Sandburg agreed to write the dramatic narrative which Sidney Franklin had named *American Cavalcade*, he accepted Franklin's own outline and vision of the story, as transmitted by Vetluguin. Franklin had been haunted all his adult life by the question "What is America all about?" He wanted to use the movie screen "to explain her meaning not only to one hundred and thirty million Americans," but to people around the world.

Franklin's story started with the premise that "there is such a thing as being influenced by the people who lived in one's house long before one was born." He visualized a hut on a tract of land in the Northeast, which eventually becomes the site of a country estate inhabited by a venerable character modeled on Justice Oliver Wendell Holmes. The Justice is intrigued with the history of the people who lived on the land in the seventeenth century, "those who rebuilt [the house] shortly before the Revolution; and those who slept there on the morning of the Battle of Gettysburg. Each time there was a man and a woman. Each time there was a clash of ideas and emotions." Franklin thought it would be artificial to make the characters of the four separate eras "any blood relation" from generation to generation. Their only link was the land on which they built their respective houses. "In Chapter One our man and woman clash because of various beliefs and lose each other," Vetluguin told Sandburg. "In Chapter Two (Revolution) they meet again, become engaged, but clash once more. He is a Tory. In Chapter Three, they get engaged and married. But then comes the Civil War. She's a Northerner, he's a Southerner." In the final chapter, the romantic interests would be the Justice's daughter and son-in-law. Vetluguin passed on to Sandburg one other scene—the Justice contemplating "the statues of the great and near-great" in the Rotunda of the Senate until "he begins to see the Meaning."

With that outline, the project was launched. Vetluguin discussed it with Frank Morley of Harcourt, Brace, who was enthusiastic. "If Sandburg writes those four dramatic episodes, in no matter what form," Morley said, "you people will have the foundation for a great picture and we will have one of the most beloved books of our time."

MGM gave Sandburg an outline, a handsome contract—and latitude, out of respect for his stature. Inevitably, from the outset of the work, he began to shape Frankin's outline to his own vision. Like all his books, this one would just have to grow in its own time and way. Like the sprawling Lincoln biography, it quickly transgressed its original boundaries. Nine months into the work, when it was supposed to be finished, the novel was still in its seminal stages.

When Sandburg went to Hollywood in 1943 to work at MGM, he could not concentrate at the hotel where MGM housed him. He asked longtime friend Lilla Perry if he could stay at her comfortable house in Los Angeles. "I've been here three days now in all this elegance," Sandburg complained, "and I can't do a lick of work here. . . . I've always been able to work at your house. Can't you find a spot for me?" She had a houseful of people, but gave him her mother's room on the third floor. Soon an MGM limousine deposited the poet, his single suitcase and his briefcase at Mrs. Perry's house. There he worked contentedly. Mrs. Perry knew his ways, even providing two empty wooden apple crates "As a joke and to make his workroom look really homelike. He laughed about it. But he used them!" She saw that he was working "with tremendous zest and interest." He was not tempted by other work, even when Will Rogers, Jr., came to try to persuade Sandburg to write a biography of his famous father.

Back home again in Michigan after his MGM conferences, Sandburg worked steadily, submitting the novel to a gradual, inevitable metamorphosis as he took Franklin's framework into his own imagination and subjugated it to his long immersion in American history. Some of his friends were concerned to hear that Sandburg was writing a novel commissioned and custom-tailored by Hollywood. He told Brenda Ueland not to "give a flickering moment of worry or anxiety about what I will hand them in Hollywood," assuring her it would be "as stubborn and norsk a book as I have ever done." He acknowledged that it was not easy "breaking some of the ground to begin" but he was developing a "framework and content now as far as I have gone that travels in key and tone with my other works [and has] possibly a wider and farther reach." His novel would be like his other books, "each done with the wish that someone else had done such a book for me to read when a youth."

By summer 1944 the first section of the novel was complete enough to share with his Lincoln mentor Oliver Barrett. Sandburg respected Barrett's forthrightness, and thought Barrett, as an attorney, could tell him if his main character was plausible. Following Franklin's wishes, Sandburg created a central character who was a retired Supreme Court Justice. He named him Orville Brand Windom, and, in one of many autobiographical touches, gave him a grandson who called him Bowbong, just as Helga's son called Sandburg "Buppong." The prologue of the novel was set in 1944, in the midst of World War II, and was followed by a self-contained story of the Pilgrims, featuring a philosopher and wood-carver called Oliver Ball Windrow, repeating the initials of the modern protagonist.

Sandburg showed the manuscript to Barrett and asked for honest criticism. He got it. Barrett praised the Pilgrim sequence as a "gripping and thrilling romance" which was "sympathetically and beautifully told" as well as authentic in its details. He found serious problems, however, with the character of the modern-day Justice Windom. Barrett, himself a skilled attorney as well as a Lincoln scholar, sent Sandburg materials as well as advice about how to depict a Supreme Court Justice, who might be "convincingly portrayed as an able, humane and courageous Judge" and who would not "seem a mere mouthpiece or sounding board." Barrett objected to the affectations Sandburg had given his Justice: "His vanity in dying his hair a dusky gold, or wearing a dark reddish brown wig at the age of 78. His claim of having stood on his hands and turned handsprings, a claim belied not only by his age but his weight. His economy in wearing three or four sweaters and an Indian blanket on cold nights to save fuel."

Sandburg completely reconstructed his Justice, but from the outset he had great difficulty creating living, breathing characters in the novel rather than one-dimensional, allegorical figures. He seemed overpowered by the narrative, unable to shape it or to populate it with convincing figures. Skilled as he had been at rendering the vernacular of the people in poetry and biography, he could not seem to capture their realism and vitality in fiction. The narrative began to run away from him, growing beyond control. At the end of the first year's work, Sandburg told Vetluguin, "The book will be a strange one." He had shown parts of it to people at Harcourt, Brace, who were "lighted about it," he said. As for himself: "My feeling is the same as I have had about other books before publishing, that if the country doesn't care about it then it is too bad for the country, and I can stand neglect of it if the public can."

Back in Hollywood in the fall of 1944 to work with Franklin and Vetluguin, Sandburg read part of the manuscript aloud. They told him it was "a great book" and paid him an additional forty thousand dollars on October 31, in accord with their contract. Engrossed in the work, Sandburg did not have time even to consider an offer to write a life of Samuel Gompers for the movies. His MGM contract precluded new projects anyway until this one was complete.

At Lilla Perry's that fall, Sandburg discovered the letters of a young navy officer who quickly became a friend as well as a character in his novel. Kenneth MacKenzie Dodson wrote graphic letters from the Pacific

Theater to his wife, Letha, who shared them with Mrs. Perry's niece, who in turn showed them to her. Enthralled, Mrs. Perry read them to Sandburg, who found them "extraordinarily vivid, the larger part of them unforgettable." He wrote to Dodson about them: "I found myself using parts of them in a novel I am doing which, after publication in book form, Metro-Goldwyn-Mayer will make into a screenplay." He asked permission to quote him, telling Dodson it was good "to meet you through these letters of yours and to know that there are Americans in the South Pacific with your range, sensitivity, vision and hope." Sandburg sent Letha Dodson inscribed copies of many of his books, and, with Ken Dodson's blessing, incorporated him and his letters into the Epilogue of the novel, where he became Kenneth MacDougall. True to promise, Sandburg named him in the acknowledgments, "a true mariner and a man of rare faith in the American dream."

Sandburg and Dodson began a lifelong correspondence in 1945, and Sandburg encouraged Dodson in his aspirations to become a writer. "I hope and trust that all your journals and letters can go into a fireproof vault, to be edited and published at some future time under conditions suitable to you," Sandburg urged Dodson, promising to help. "Your faith in America is like a good poem."

"War leaves a stamp on you," Dodson had written to his wife in one of the passages which so haunted Sandburg that he used it in the Prologue to his novel:

> You take a bath and you don't feel clean. You want a spiritual purge of the whole stinking business. You feel like you'd like to be baptized and have communion. You want to lie on the grass on a windy hill in the summer time and smell the clean drying grasses. . . . You want to have your arms around one very near and dear to you and snuggle your head deep beside your loved one and feel the tenderness of her lips on yours and the clean warm living scent that is her. Then sleep. And there shall be no more war, no parting, no killing, no smell of death. Just peace.

By the summer of 1945 Dodson had been severely injured in the war. He was hospitalized for more than a year, and would never fully recover. In 1953, after five years of work and much encouragement from Sandburg, Dodson would publish his first novel, *Away All Boats*. He dedicated it to Sandburg and to his wife, Letha, and named one of his own central characters MacDougall. Dodson's story about the navy's Attack Transport Service, of which he had been a part, was one of the most successful novels to come out of World War II. It became a big best-seller and a motion picture. Dodson said he would not have been able to write and publish his novel without "the repeated and sustained encouragement received from Carl Sandburg."

✳

By summer 1945, Sandburg's novel was already 400,000 words, the size of three novels, and nowhere near finished. He told Vetluguin he wanted to call it *American Scroll: Storm and Dream*. He packed it with scenes from the gamut of American history, peopled it with a huge cast of characters, historical and fictitious. He augmented his vast Lincoln research with deep studies in the source documents of Colonial history and the Revolutionary War. He wanted to put all of the nation's past into the book. Overwhelming in scale, the novel went "winding, zig-zagging, careening," Sandburg told Brenda Ueland. He predicted it would "be a strange affair."

He was going to have to interrupt the work on the final chapter of the American Revolution sequence, however. After a lifetime in the Midwest and nearly two decades on the Michigan dunes, the Sandburgs, grandchildren, goats and all, were about to move South to Flat Rock, North Carolina. Abraham Lincoln's biographer was going to set up house-keeping in the antebellum summer mansion built by Christopher Gustavus Memminger, first secretary of the treasury in the cabinet assembled by Jefferson Davis to lead the Confederate States of America. As the Second World War drew to a close, the Eternal Hobo set out on one more journey into past and present, this time with his family in tow.

✳

"Moving is a terrific business heavy accumulations of notes and manu-scripts so much of it unfinished and irreplaceable and of course it aint the work—it's all the time the goddam decisions that wear a fellow down," Sandburg complained to his sister Mary late in 1945. It was very difficult and unsettling to be uprooted in the middle of his novel, and he was beset with other work. "Three pieces of writing that I promised to do some 2 years ago I am trying to finish now," he told Vetluguin, announcing his plans to move and explaining where he was in the novel. He was preparing "a sketch of Oliver R. Barrett and his collection of Lincoln manuscripts," which would be published in 1949 as *Lincoln Collector: The Story of the Oliver R. Barrett Lincoln Collection*. He was writing the introduction to Roy Basler's edition of Lincoln's writings and speeches, and he was finishing a "3,500 word commentary on Lincoln's style as speaker and writer and its progressions, this for a cyclopedia of American literature edited by Robert Spiller of Swarthmore." He hoped to have all this work completed by November 20, along with much of his novel.

Paula and the girls did their best to shield Sandburg from the practical headaches of a major move across country—first the decision about where to go, and then the infinite logistical details of getting there. Despite their efforts, Sandburg's concentration was inevitably disrupted. An inveterate saver and keeper, he faced the staggering task of going through a half century's worth of files and papers, deciding what to keep and what to relinquish. Ultimately, he kept almost everything, papers, books, research files, newspapers, clippings—literally tons of material from his long career.

When the Sandburgs finally decided that it was time to leave their house on the dunes for a more spacious house and farm, and milder winters, Paula cast about for a place which would support her thriving goat herd, and, more important, give Sandburg solitude and privacy. In her usual careful, methodical way, she studied mean temperatures, rainfall and other conditions. Climate was of utmost importance. Sandburg, prone to bronchitis, had long escaped to Florida or other warm places during the worst of winter, but Paula and the girls had to stay home, and the farm work increased in winters. The goats had to be barn-fed. Paula and Helga envisioned a more temperate climate, richer pasturelands, a larger country home where the children and the animals would have more space and freedom, and the adults more privacy and warmth. Dana and Steichen had loved western North Carolina since their sojourn in Asheville during Steichen's illness in the late twenties. Paula, too, had good memories of western North Carolina, where she, Margaret and Janet had traveled in 1940.

Near the village of Flat Rock, North Carolina, just outside Hendersonville, they found a paradise. It was called Connemara. At the heart of 245 acres of mountain, meadow and forest land stood a simple, spacious three-story house, built between 1836 and 1838 by Christopher Memminger, lawyer and statesman and the one South Carolinian Jefferson Davis appointed to his Confederate cabinet. Memminger named his estate Rock Hill for the vast granite plateau which had led the Cherokee Indians to call the area Flat Rock. From the winding trail that was called Little River Road, there was a steep, wooded ascent to the house, and the woods behind the house converged upward to Little Glassy and then Big Glassy mountains, named in the literal way of the Indians and the straightforward pioneers who first explored them. When they looked up at the bare rocky face of these mountains, certain angles of sunlight made a looking-glass of the water or ice or minerals shimmering there.

Cherokee Indian warriors and traders had discovered, named and settled the Great Flat Rock in the Blue Ridge Mountains of North Carolina, only to lose it to the white man, the soldiers and pioneers who claimed the territory and whose descendents banished the Cherokees to the Trail of Tears. Pioneer families sold the rugged land to wealthy plantation owners and lawyers such as Memminger, from Charleston, South Carolina, who searched for summer respite from the tropical heat and fevers of the Low Country. Gracious antebellum estates such as Memminger's Rock Hill juxtaposed to primitive mountain cabins meant that a microcosm of the Civil War would be fought there in words and animosity. Stubborn, independent mountaineers supported the Union cause in the shadow of the gracious houses built by Memminger and other leaders of the Confederacy, who gave their all in what they called the War of the Northern Invasion.

For the two decades before the war, the Memminger family and their aristocratic neighbors made the strenuous uphill trek by wagon and buggy from Charleston, two hundred miles to the southeast, in late spring, transporting servants and household goods. The Civil War interrupted the leisure and luxury of Flat Rock summers. Later during those bitter days, when Memminger's fiscal policies failed to stabilize the Confederate economy, he resigned and retreated to Rock Hill in Flat Rock, where he and his neighbors were often vulnerable to attack by the soldiers assigned to protect them, or by deserters from both armies. After the surrender at Appomattox, Union troops pillaged the community. At Memminger's house the wide front steps which led from the front lawn to the main floor were pulled down to make the house a fortress. According to legend, Jefferson Davis entrusted the Great Provisional Seal of the Confederacy to Memminger for safekeeping at Flat Rock. Supposedly, Memminger buried the seal in a secret hiding place on Glassy Mountain. It has never been recovered. In the mists and shadows of these mountain legends, Carl Sandburg could feel completely at home.

He could walk the curving trails Memminger had carefully laid out for treks by foot or small carriage up and down the mountains. Sandburg could ramble in the woods and find pathways such as the one Memminger cut from Rock Hill to the nearby Episcopal Church of Saint John in the Wilderness. After the Civil War, President Andrew Johnson pardoned Memminger for his role in the Confederacy, and Memminger distinguished himself as president of the first Southern company to manufacture sulfuric acid and superphosphates, a turning point in Southern agriculture and commerce. He served in the South Carolina legislature and, as local railroad company president, helped to oversee the construction of a rail line from Spartanburg, South Carolina, fifty miles down the mountain, to Asheville, North Carolina, twenty miles west of Flat Rock. Memminger died in 1888 at the age of eighty-five, having sired seventeen children. Some of his survivors sold Rock Hill to Colonel William Gregg of South Carolina, who never occupied the estate, and sold it in turn to South Carolina textile industrialist Ellison Adger Smyth, who renamed it Connemara because the verdant mountains and meadows resembled those of Connemara, Ireland, home of his ancestors. Smyth had died in the tranquillity of Connemara in 1942.

So it was, in those last days of the war, that the house and barns stood empty, the meadows overgrown and quiet, when Paula and Helga reached western North Carolina in their search for a new home. They looked at other estates and large farms that summer of 1945, but when they saw Connemara they knew they had found the ideal place for a writer, his family and their farm operations. The house stood serenely on the crest of the hill. The vista of far mountains came in and out of focus, depending on the weather. Glassy Mountain protected the rear of the house from winds. There were 245 acres of solitude, privacy, serenity. The barns were far removed from the house, overlooking ample grassy meadows. Sandburg could work far into the night on the third floor of the secluded house, and sleep into the morning undisturbed by the clatter of the goat dairy and the bleating of the herd.

There were flowers and fruit trees, trails to climb, mountains to explore. Connemara was enfolded in the bracing clarity of pure mountain air and great stillness, the "creative hush," as Sandburg called it. While the higher mountains to the north and west bore the brunt of winter snows and wind, Flat Rock nestled in a thermal belt. Winter was a milder season there. The Sandburg women knew they need look no further, particularly when they discovered the price. They could buy Connemara for $45,000. "The health of the missus, the ancient desire of Helga for a farm and horses, the plight of barnfed goats who want pasture, these sent us to N.C.," Sandburg told Lloyd Lewis. "I told 'em I'd go any place they picked and it was just an accident that the Memminger place was there at a price near silly."

Paula skillfully orchestrated the work of moving her husband, three daughters, two grandchildren, several tons of books, papers and manuscripts, and more than thirty championship dairy goats from Michigan to North Carolina. The first priority was to minimize disruption of Sandburg's work on the novel, "a heavy piece of work, a curious involved job that has grown to far larger proportions than expected at the beginning."

In late November, a railroad boxcar loaded with 42,000 pounds of Sandburg "cargo," including thousands of books and papers, set out for Hendersonville. Sandburg told friends that "the missus and daughter Janet and nephew Eric* drove away this morning in a rain with a station wagon and a trailer holding 16 blue ribbon Nubian does and daughters Margaret and Helga with the two grandchildren we are keeping house amid the ruins till a VAN comes sometime before Dec."

Paula, Janet, Adaline Polega and Eric drove to North Carolina first, their station wagon pulling an old trailer carrying some of their best does. Helga, Margaret and the children stayed in Michigan to finish the packing there. Helga shipped twenty-two more goats in November, while her mother supervised the necessary renovations of the house at Connemara. She knew Carl was better off in Michigan, out of the hubbub, where he could go on with his work. When the painting, carpentry and plastering were done and the new house arranged, Sandburg and the rest of the family could move to North Carolina. Paula, Janet and Adaline were enchanted with the place. "We had a long walk up the mountains Sunday," Paula wrote in December 1945 to the family in Michigan.

> We found that our land goes over the top of *Little* Glass Mt and up to the very top of *Big* Glass Mt—at least *a mile* of real climbing from the house. The timber seems *endless*—mostly oak, black gum, yellow pine, white pine, hickory—with dogwood everywhere. The hills will be white with dogwood blossoms in Spring. There are many trails and paths through the mountain—perfect for horseback riding. We walked up & down the mountain for 3 hours—a perfect day—air crisp & winey! How Dad will enjoy these walks! From the top of Big Glassy you see all over Hendersonville and the country about, Smokies & Blue Ridge. A far wider view than that from our porch. And in every direction you are "on top of the World!"

By January 1946 the whole family was settled under the historic roof of the old house on the crest of the hill. "How can the author of *The People, Yes* be a colonel or a poobah?" Sandburg joked, and friends reported hearing him survey the splendid vistas from his lofty front porch and say, "What a hell of a baronial estate for an old Socialist like me!"

With her usual care, Paula had arranged Sandburg's third-floor workroom almost exactly as it had been in the Michigan house, so much so that photographs of the two rooms, from certain angles, are hard to tell apart. Consequently, when Sandburg came home to Connemara for the

* Eric Johnson was the son of Sandburg's sister Mary.

first time, he could walk upstairs into a familiar setting, find his writer's tools and materials accessibly at hand, and get right back to work on the novel. "I could have done a smooth fast piece of work, 75,000 to 100,000 words for MGM, that they would have taken," he told Lloyd Lewis after he had gotten settled that January. But he was doing the book his way, in his own time. "And it will be a book as I want it and they dont interfere."

✳

"I have laid an egg the shape of another long chaotic book," Sandburg joked in a letter to Archie MacLeish before his novel was published. Unfortunately, his appraisal was all too accurate. He was an inveterate researcher, compulsive in his slow, thorough investigation of the social and historical milieu of his story, which spanned three hundred years. For the novel, he dug into the past as rigorously as he had excavated history for the biography. On the third-floor landing outside his work-room at Connemara were shelved hundreds of books on American history. He rummaged through them all, poring over many of them, ingesting thousands of details. Voldemar Vetluguin read the novel in progress, and warned Sandburg not to be seduced by "the formidable mass of research and facts." Sandburg's enthusiasm for his American saga overpowered his capacity to shape, select and mold. Before he knew it, the narrative was swollen with excessive detail.

The problems were apparent to Vetluguin and Sidney Franklin in Hollywood. They were patient, tactful, respectful—yet forthright in their criticism. Unfortunately, Sandburg did not heed their advice along the way. He was having particular trouble with his characters, succumbing, as Vetluguin put it, to the "hypnotic spell of the great historical figures." He urged Sandburg to focus on his fictitious characters "against the background of earthshaking historical events, bloodshed and chaos." The characters needed to be rescued from the maze of Sandburg's historical research so that they, not the facts, would stand in the limelight. Vetluguin offered many practical suggestions about how to heighten dramatic value, and to make characters and events "pay off." Franklin encouraged Sandburg to put his characters through experiences which the modern audience could identify with because they shared them. "Man and woman have always had the same problems," Franklin observed. "The backgrounds and the tools were different—that's all. In that way we humanize our story, and make it understandable to the people that see the picture."

For MGM, the goal of the project was a landmark patriotic movie. The novel was commissioned for that sole purpose. Sandburg understood that, agreed to it contractually, set out to work in good faith on a certain timetable with a prescribed outline. From the outset, however, he was so enthralled with the scope of the story and the challenge of writing his first novel that his version preempted Franklin's and the novel became for him a literary end in itself. He confessed to a friend that he "had no illusions that Hollywood will gather the main drift of it into a picture. But the book will go rolling on."

In Hollywood, Franklin read the early draft and found the central characters stiff, humorless, "too straight and severe." "History and the background get in the way," Franklin told Sandburg.

Sandburg sought advice as he struggled with the sprawling manuscript. Oliver Barrett helped him further define and develop the character and career of the Justice. He admired writer Mary Hastings Bradley's fiction, and asked her to read the book in progress. "The job here goes weaving on," he told her. "I have the kind of admiration for your themes and your craftsmanship—so that all points you make, positive or negative, sink in and have consideration and use." He asked her to examine the book to see if it had "an organic current," for from the first the unity of the four stories was difficult to achieve. Mrs. Bradley was "a friend in time of need . . . and a mainstay when I had moments of groping on this long tough and involved job," Sandburg told her appreciatively. "It made a difference that I had read those two short magazine novels of yours and could put a certain trust in your eye as to workmanship, both style and content." He corresponded with Ken Dodson, who was recuperating from his war injuries in a Seattle, Washington, naval hospital. "Just this week finished the long haul over the hump of Book Three," he wrote to Dodson in autumn 1946, "which leaves only the Epilog."

Sandburg wrestled mightily with characters, plot, narrative structure, unity and dramatic devices, but he had a steady vision of his theme. The novelist in him grew from the same seeds which had yielded the poet and biographer and folklorist. He was a Seeker, he told a friend, of "that hectic mystic imponderable The American Dream and how it will ride thru the Atomic Age!"

✳

A newspaper reporter writing about Carl Sandburg's move to North Carolina noted that he had "acquired an historic estate in which he can commune with ghosts of the Civil War." The house was indeed suffused with the past. Because lumber was scarce during and after the Second World War, Paula had the bookshelves in the Michigan house torn down and the lumber shipped to Connemara, where mountain carpenters filled the walls of the old house from floor to ceiling with sturdy shelves to hold Sandburg's working library of nearly twelve thousand volumes. The history books and other source books for the novel Sandburg clustered on the third floor of the house, within easy reach. He slept in a simple bedroom adjoining his workroom, and could work there late into the night without disturbing anyone or being disturbed by the ebb and flow of family activity. Across the wide landing, Janet and Margaret each had a bedroom, and shared a bathroom. The grandchildren loved the small room on the front of the third floor, with its eaves and deep, dark closets, and its view of the far mountain range. They called the room the Crow's Nest.

Downstairs, on the spacious main floor, there was a living room, simply furnished, the shelves lined with copies of books by Sandburg, including the many foreign translations. His comfortable chair was there, and his guitars, used during family song fests in the evenings after dinner. Margaret played the grand piano in the corner, and later, when they were old enough, gave John Carl and Paula music lessons. The adjoining front room served as Sandburg's downstairs study, a more public office where he could work with a typist, often Helga, on his immense correspondence. Three walls of the room held bookshelves, lined from floor to ceiling with books he had read, all or in part, many of them filled with markers and marginal notes in his bold handwriting. Near his desk stood a table crafted from timber which had been in the White House during Lincoln's residency there. Next to the office Paula had a serene, spacious bedroom. There were twin beds, and Carl often slept there. She kept the tall windows of the house free of curtains to admit the light and air and the majestic views of mountains to the north and soaring hemlocks and pines enfolding other exposures of the house. Sandburg's third-floor rooms overlooked a giant ginkgo tree planted in the nineteenth century.

Helga and the children shared two rooms adjacent to the dining room, where the family gathered later to watch television as well as to take their meals. The literal and symbolic heart of the house was Paula's farm office, tidy and compact. The dark, cool ground floor of the house contained a utility room, and a kitchen with a Swedish Aga stove and specially designed boxes for feeding newborn goat kids. There were two more bedrooms there, and a room filled with shelves, like library stacks, where books and files were stored side by side with equipment for the kitchen and the farm.

Paula had put Helga in charge of running the farm operation at Connemara, selling her the Chikaming herd for a token two hundred dollars and giving her a ten-year lease on the Connemara pastures and barns "in return for supplying the family with milk and butter." They had business stationery printed reading "Chikaming Herd, Connemara Farm, Flat Rock, N.C., Mr. and Mrs. Carl Sandburg, Helga Sandburg Thoman." In addition to the goats, there were horses and dogs, a pony, and a team of gray work horses, with room for all in the spacious meadows.

"I'll tell you about my three daughters when I see you, all three having distinctive personalities and each making a pretty good life of it," Sandburg told Paul Angle during that first year at Connemara. Dilantin and other medications minimized Margaret's seizures. Most of the time she was well and active, although not as hardy as her sisters. She stayed busy with her music, her serious studies—Russian literature, Shakespeare, mythology, the music of Gilbert and Sullivan—and her painting. In addition, she was her father's librarian, able to retrieve very quickly, even from remote shelves in the house, books or materials he needed. Like her father, she worked late into the night and slept into the late morning. Helga, her mother's "Barn Boss," rose before dawn to do farm chores and work with the goat herd. Awkward with people, Janet had an easy and natural grace with the animals, and worked with great physical stamina. Helga was everywhere at once, typing her father's manuscripts, working on the goat breeding records, tending to the incessant work of breeding, birthing and caring for the herd. She encouraged her children to explore the world around them, and, young Paula wrote later, "so wisely set her children free to learn what they could from Connemara."

The children called their grandmother Gramma, pronounced "Grahmah," and their grandfather Buppong, since John Carl tried to say grandpa and came up with Buppong instead. Busy Helga made notes in a journal about daily life at Connemara: "Buppong comes down this morning, I am working, Mom is writing, Janet is doing dishes, Margaret is dusting, Little Paus'l orders him to stand up and then sit down and then stand up again. 'What a house!' he said. 'Women managing everything. Ed should see this. Little John and I, we've got to put up some front!' "

Often Sandburg wrote poems about the grandchildren he prized. "I have seen thee in solitude and self-communion," he wrote to John Carl in 1946.

> Thou hast wandered in thought
> and reverie seeking great meanings.
> I trust now this early the integrity
> of thy mind and its searchings.

> Freckles thou hast and a moonrise
> smile and I value these phenomena
> as precious possessions.

Their Buppong seemed like a father to John Carl and Paula, although he "had a grandfather's tendency toward leniency." Helga noted in her journal how her small daughter followed Sandburg's footsteps at Connemara, and emulated his words: "The road—to hell—is paved—with good intentions—war is war—peace is peace—if all nations—would settle their differences—each must—sacrifice—some principle." John, overhearing, told his mother, "I know where Paula gets that. From her grandfather, not her other father."

The whole family joined in walks over the Connemara trails, singing as they went, and Sandburg and Margaret often walked in the evening. "We didn't just buy two hundred and forty-five acres when we bought Connemara," Paula said more than once. "We bought a million acres of sky, too!" In that spacious world, the Sandburgs felt deeply at home from the first. When Ed and Dana Steichen visited them that first Connemara spring, Sandburg and Steichen sat on the great front porch, twenty steps up from the ground, its pillars framing the mountain view, there "to go over all the world's problems and solve them one by one."

His grandchildren were "almost too good to be true," Sandburg said, "and a fellow wonders what time will bring. They have loveliness and rare lights and shake the house with their promises."

✳

In his workroom under the eaves, Sandburg was struggling with his novel. He had given it three years so far, working at it three times as long as anticipated. He was far from the end of it. It was his major literary enterprise for most of the 1940s, and only time would tell if he had been right to divert his energy from the familiar, successful vehicles of poetry and biography so late in his career.

In the end, he named the novel *Remembrance Rock*, after the giant boulder he planted in the fictitious garden of his main character, Supreme Court Justice Orville Brand Windom. Around the "Remembrance Rock," Windom had scattered earth he gathered from Plymouth, Valley Forge, Gettysburg and the Argonne. After Oliver Barrett's criticism, Sandburg completely transformed Windom, describing him in the novel through the eyes of his daughter-in-law Mimah:

A slash of a wide gargoylish mouth, half-solemn, the upper lip thin as against the heavy and mournful lower lip, the jaws having a flow of lines that joined to shape the chin and it reminded her of battleships, anvils and tall crags. . . . His brown eyes, she knew, could drowse, then bore deep into your own, then drowse again, then dance and flutter at sudden keen interest. . . . He stood five feet eight inches weighing one hundred eighty pounds, thickset and powerful of build, his silvered head of hair, once brick-red in the sun and sunset maroon in shadow, one side of his face at peace in calm and the other side half-snarling and dark with endless combat. . . . His face had the ranging contrasts of his personality, for though he was most of the time grave, calm, slow-spoken, his moods could run to banter and persiflage, the airy fooling of broomstraws in a high wind.

In the Prologue, set in 1944, Windom makes a national radio broadcast, as his daughter-in-law understands, to address "what the American people, the American flag, the American citizen might stand for in relation to the world scene and the widespread Family of Man over the earth."

Windom's speech was the nexus of the novel, as well as a mirror of Sandburg's own worldview during and after World War II, and he often quoted it on public occasions during the next two decades:

> . . . For we know when a nation goes down and never comes back, when a society or a civilization perishes, one condition may always be found. They forgot where they came from. They lost sight of what brought them along. The hard beginnings were forgotten and the struggles farther along. They became satisfied with themselves. . . . It has cost to build this nation. . . .
>
> In a very real sense there is no such thing as a death of thought and energy. . . . Long before this time of ours America saw the faces of her men and women torn and shaken in turmoil, chaos and storm. . . . Yet there always arose enough of reserves of strength, balances of sanity, portions of wisdom, to carry the nation through to a fresh start with an ever renewing vitality. . . . In a rather real sense the pioneers, old settlers, First Comers as some called themselves—they go on, their faces here now, their lessons worth our seeing. They ought not to be forgotten—the dead who held in their clenched hands that which became the heritage of us, the living.

The novel was broken into five parts—the Prologue, set in the 1940s during World War II; Book One, "The First Comers," about the Mayflower, Pilgrim and Puritan years; Book Two, "The Arch Begins," set during the American Revolution; Book Three, "The Arch Holds," about the Civil War era; and the Epilogue, "Storm and Stars," set at the end of World War II. Sandburg's symbolic, recurring faces fit Franklin's plan to cast the same actors in all three segments of the film. Sandburg further augmented Franklin's unifying devices—the casting, and the setting on the same physical site—by giving characters in each story the initials OW—Justice Orville Brand Windom in the 1940s; wood-carver Oliver Ball Windrow and Pilgrim Orton Wingate in Book One; master printer Ordway Winshore in Book Two; pioneer Omri Winwold in Book Three. Justice Windom might have been a reincarnation of wood-carver Windrow, for Sandburg described them in the same terms. Windrow in 1607 looked like Windom in 1944: "He [Windrow] stood five feet eight inches, well over a hundred and eighty pounds, thickset of build, a massive head of hair brick-red in the sun and a sunset maroon in shadow, one side of his face smooth in peace, the other side half-snarling and set for combat. . . . Usually grave, slow-spoken, his moods often ran to banter and persiflage, airy as milkweed floss in a high wind."

Like Windom and Windrow, Ordway Winshore in 1775 wore a split mask, a face with two sides, "one profile giving peace and calm, the other hinting at wrath and turmoil." Omri Winwold in Book Three had hair of a "brick-dust color," "liquid brown" eyes, the stocky physique of his predecessors, and the paradoxical face, two-sided, "one with a storm toss on it and the other utterly at peace."

To this contrived, allegorical unifying device, Sandburg added a more organic symbol, a small bronze plaque crafted by wood-carver Windrow for the woman he loved, who would marry someone else and go with him on the *Mayflower* to the new world, wearing the small bronze plaque on a silver cord around her neck. This symbolic talisman is passed from story to story. On it is inscribed Roger Bacon's Four Stumbling Blocks to Truth, which Sandburg saw as the true impediments to the achievement of the American Dream:

1. The influence of fragile or unworthy authority.
2. Custom.
3. The imperfection of undisciplined senses.
4. Concealment of ignorance by ostentation or seeming wisdom.

During the week of Justice Windom's June 1944 radio broadcast, he is preoccupied with a heavy metal box, more than a foot long and deep, filled with papers. His daughter-in-law worries about him: "She noticed the two sides of his face as never before so vivid in contrast. She had heard of a friend once saying of those two profiles, 'One side, he's been to heaven, the other side he's been to hell,' and it struck her she had never seen the combat profile so doggedly, even viciously, determined in its will and purpose nor the grave calm of the other profile so brightly composed and luminously serene."

There is an ominous, violent storm during which "one fierce crashing prong of fire sent itself straight into an arching majestic oak that had lived too long and clove it in two and shattered the halves and left it a mass of splinters and charred grandeur." Later that night, Windom dies. His grandson Raymond comes home on leave from the army for the funeral, and Raymond and his wife open the Justice's box, which holds three books of a novel Windom had been writing for years in secret. Windom has left his family a note recording his hope that "as you live with these repeating faces that weave a blood-scarlet thread over and through the story of our country—may it be that you find tokens and values worth your time in living with them and my time in the many years I have given them."

Thus the Prologue sets the stage for the novel, supposedly Windom's novel, written to an avowed thesis, the passionate culmination of Sandburg's own idealism. Therein lay the novel's greatest strengths, and its weaknesses, its ultimate popular success and its critical, artistic failure.

Sandburg told Brenda Ueland that the book was "strangely inevitable in its growth and progressions. . . . It has had revisions and changes and next week I put it on ice and about [September] will take it up saying What the hell have we here?"

1946–1949

26. American Dreamer

The war came to its end more than two years ago but a
portrait of America, getting the lights and shadows of the
American Dream past and present, is perhaps more
wanted now than at any previous hour.

—Carl Sandburg to Voldemar Vetluguin, 1947

S andburg was lean and vigorous as he approached his sixty-ninth
birthday. The exhilarating mountain air seemed to breed new energy, most of which he poured into his novel. He loved working
at Connemara, with its "pines tall as Oregon." Paula and Helga had
expanded the herd to ninety-two goats, and Helga was "in a fair milk
selling trade," Sandburg boasted. His grandchildren were "marvels."
He had finished the first main draft of *Remembrance Rock*, including
the Prologue and Epilogue which dealt with "now, terrific Now." It was
time for the manuscript to "age in the wood." Then he could revise it.
He told friends on the West Coast that the screenplay would run three
hours or more. "I build no expectations on what they will do with it,"
he said.

He let his heavy lecture schedule lapse during the years he spent on
the novel, but his grandchildren kept alive in him the fun and play which
had animated his *Rootabaga Stories*. He worked from time to time on
"piles of nonsense things, stories and oddities, fragments, Sayings of the
Hongdorshes." "When zebras change their black stripes to white and
their white stripes to black, is it any use or do they do it just for a
change," he teased. "I suppose I will publish a couple of books of these
sometime about when I am rated as washed up."

Throughout the Connemara years mail for Sandburg poured into the
little Flat Rock post office, sometimes in such volume that it was carried

up to the house in baskets. Sandburg relished letters from his fans. He and Paula tried to answer them, but there were thousands. Over the years he created a series of personable form letters, numbered so he could prepare a tailored response to the readers who took time to write to him. At least he could express his appreciation that way.

"You send a beautifully human letter," read Form Letter #4. "Such fellowship and speech as yours gives rest to my bones and fresh roots for living on." A request for advice got #12 in reply: "My only advice to you is to beware of advice and to be never afraid of toil, solitude and prayer." A request for an interview elicited #20: "If I should give interviews to all the people I'd like to, I would not have time for thinking or writing. What could I tell you that you could not find in the books that I have written?" The writer of a fan letter received #13, personally signed "Faithfully yours, Carl Sandburg": "Your letter is one to treasure. You cover much ground in it and the least I can say is that your words make me feel less useless in this age of chaos. May luck stars be over you."

Occasionally Sandburg lost his temper—in private—with the inevitable autograph seekers. "Please autograph the *FRONT* of the enclosed envelope," one man wrote. Sandburg's exasperation was evident in the bold strokes handwritten on the unreturned envelope: "The serene & blissful gall of a brass monkey."

The nearby *Asheville Times* carried a story in November 1946 about Sandburg's "Epoch-Film," noting that Sandburg had "virtually completed the script for a film, 'American Cavalcade,' which Metro-Goldwyn Mayer plans to produce as a picture covering the main crises in America's growth." According to the newspaper account, Sandburg himself had told the *Times* that "90 percent of the script for the picture has been finished." When the *Times* reporter told Sandburg that the Associated Press had announced that Spencer Tracy would star in the film, Sandburg replied that that was news to him, "which I am glad to get." He told a friend, "And as the picture goes 3-hours or more, it will not be finished till sometime in 1949, if then, as Sidney Franklin takes his time to get what he wants."

Harcourt, Brace found some problems in the contract Sandburg had signed with MGM in 1943, especially in regard to serial and foreign publishing rights, and Sandburg hoped to get MGM to substantially modify the agreement. But with all the headaches, Sandburg believed that the "long journey" of the novel was coming to an end, nearly four years after it had begun.

✻

"Maybe I will see you about July 26 when we creep into the R. T. Lincoln crypt," Sandburg told journalist Junius B. Wood in June 1947. Sandburg was one of four Lincoln scholars chosen to have the first look at the Robert Todd Lincoln collection of his father's papers, sealed at the Library of Congress by direction of the younger Lincoln until twenty-one years after his death. CBS Radio planned to cover the long-awaited opening of the papers. Edward R. Murrow, then vice president and director of public affairs at CBS, arranged the documentary coverage of the event, to be narrated by veteran CBS reporter John Daly. In addition to Sandburg, the Librarian of Congress had invited University of Illinois historian James G. Randall; Paul Angle, then secretary and director of the Chicago Historical Society; and Jay Monaghan, state historian of the Illinois State Historical Library. These four scholars would "lend their counsel in the process of evaluating the material in the collection." Later Murrow and CBS planned to work with Sandburg and the other scholars on a radio documentary which would "bring to the American people a dramatic recreation of the new insights into Lincoln's life which this collection may reveal." In reality, the Robert Todd Lincoln papers shed little new light on Abraham Lincoln's life, but Sandburg took a keen interest in examining the documents page by page, and spent a leisurely time in Washington looking them over and writing a series of newspaper columns about them for the Chicago Times Syndicate. Newspapers across the country carried his Lincoln Letter Series in late July, 1947, enough to produce nearly five thousand dollars in royalties.

Sandburg joined other writers in voicing concern for his old friend Ezra Pound, incarcerated since 1945 at St. Elizabeth's Hospital in Washington, the first American to be charged with treason after World War II. The accusation grew from his tirade of Fascist articles, pamphlets and radio broadcasts, the latter going out over Italian radio in English. Pound attacked Churchill, Roosevelt, American war policy and the Jews. There were increasing doubts about his sanity; even his old literary friends, including MacLeish, Hemingway and Sandburg himself, thought that, at the least, Pound had made "an incredible ass" of himself. After his confinement at St. Elizabeth's, Pound's literary friends remained concerned about his well-being.

Pound had lived in Italy since 1923, and during the war earned much needed income from his radio broadcasts. He became a vigorous exponent of Fascist propaganda, and used his podium to ventilate his passionate political and social beliefs, particularly about monetary reform. In 1941 an errant book review reached Pound in Rapallo, Italy, giving Carl Sandburg credit for writing an economic pamphlet by the communist Dr. Karl Sandberg, so often mistaken for the poet and biographer. Thinking Sandburg had written the Sandberg pamphlet *Money and Democracy*, and endorsing its economic views, Pound congratulated his fellow poet: "Bravo! Carl. And my compliments. It will also improve your poetry no end. I dunno what effect it will have on guitar plain' but I reckon it will help even that."

Sandburg lectured at Hamilton College in Clinton, New York, in 1947, and visited with Pound's son, Omar, who was on the faculty there. "It is greatly to your credit that you spoke up, as you did, about my Father when we met," Omar Pound told Sandburg later, "and I assure you that I appreciated it very highly. . . . I do so hope that you have found it possible to visit him in Washington, D.C., for contact with the outside world is one of his main needs in these days."

For all of the striking differences in their poetry and their politics, Sandburg and Pound had helped each other in the early days. "Good reading good reading," Sandburg wrote in an unpublished fragment of a poem entitled, simply, "Ezra":

> O most excellent reading
> If can easy pass over
> Easy skip idiotics
>   pedantics pomposities
> Good reading sure sure
> I have learnt
>   how to read Ez
> He is my crazy brudder

Brenda Ueland had shared with Sandburg her "complex unscientific thoughts about geniuses." Some were "egoists," who went "around and around themselves, self-revealing." She told Sandburg he belonged in the second group who were "not circular but fly out into the abyss, at a tangent, in love and generosity. They care for others and what is outside." At the age of sixty-two, Pound, who had spent his life in Europe going "around and around" himself, "self-revealing," was a literal as well as figurative prisoner of his own volatile genius. Sandburg's outer journey through the American experience had led him to great public recognition of his work as a poet, biographer, troubadour, journalist. Now, nearly seventy, he had once more flown "out into the abyss, at a tangent, in love and generosity." He was nearing the finish of his first novel. Voldemar Vetluguin, in his rich Russian accent, had told Sandburg it might be a novel, a dramatic epic poem or a new form altogether.

Sandburg was tired. He had given the book all he had. As his seventieth birthday approached, he remembered the Chinese proverb: "At seventy man is a candle in the wind."

✳

Sandburg was having serious difficulties with his huge, often chaotic manuscript, and Paula was worried. He was irritable and increasingly impatient. The book was overwritten, extravagantly embedded with minute detail. Most of the characters seemed trapped in allegory, too wooden in demeanor and speech to be real. There were so many layers of plot and subplot that the effect was one of formlessness. Sandburg knew there were problems, could not resolve them alone, and turned first to friends and then to Harcourt, Brace for help. "It may be that I shall have presented, across a timesweep running back to England in 1609, parts of an American testament," Sandburg wrote to Ken Dodson, whose letters were sprinkled throughout the Prologue and Epilogue.

He was sending sections of the manuscript to his friend Marjorie Arnette Braye for final typing. She had a good editorial eye, and he gave her latitude to help him revise and cut the manuscript. "It is a butchery business we are on," he wrote to her as they neared the end of work on revisions. "You will need at times to be as remorseless as a headsman lopping off the skypiece of an important king. . . . I will be praying here in Flat Rock while you pray in Baltimore."

In January 1948 editor Robert Giroux of Harcourt, Brace went to Connemara to work with Sandburg. Soon after his arrival, Paula took him aside to express her hope that he could help Sandburg finish the manuscript. She told Giroux she had never known Carl to struggle so hard with a book. He was making life difficult for those about him, but Paula worried most that he was suffering a great deal himself. Giroux promised to do his best. His skill as an editor was matched by his tact. He had worked with Edmund Wilson, reputed to be a difficult author, and had prompted William Saroyan to turn a screenplay into his first novel, *The Human Comedy*. Giroux knew that temper "is always a sign of trouble with an author" facing difficult technical problems and that irritability could be "one of the first signs of editorial trouble ahead." "All you can do is try to pour oil on the troubled waters," he observed.

Giroux's visit with the Sandburgs went well. Immediately they made him one of the family. He had breakfast with Paula or the daughters; Janet would take a breakfast tray upstairs for Sandburg. Giroux would sometimes see him in the morning working in his simple double bed under the eaves in the bedroom adjoining his upstairs workroom. Sandburg wore the green celluloid eyeshade which he depended on more than ever as he grew older, for his eyes weakened with time and use and his sensitivity to light grew more painful. Giroux would go up to say good morning, and then leave him there, propped up in his bed with his papers arranged on a work board. Sometimes Sandburg joined Giroux and the family at lunch, but he usually spent the day alone writing and came down at last to join the others for the evening meal. Then he and Giroux would work on the novel.

"It was an enormous book," Giroux remembered. "It really was in a way not a novel in the sense that it was a panorama of American history. He had sets of characters in each era of American history." The novel was "an artificial kind of fiction," Giroux thought but he kept his opinion to himself. The book was nearly finished and Giroux did not have the authority to make major structural decisions about it at such a late stage. Had he come into the work earlier, he would

> have tried to get Carl onto a different blueprint for his book. I thought it was too mechanical. The other fact I had to face as an editor was that it was already a fait accompli. I came in late, after more than half of it had been written, so it was impossible even if I had wanted to suggest a new approach. It would have been very difficult for Carl to follow it. I just knew that would have been disruptive and not pleasing to anybody, so I did the best I could under the circumstances.

Sandburg trusted Giroux, and enjoyed his company. Although he sometimes resisted when Giroux urged him to cut portions of the manuscript, Sandburg yielded. Giroux saw that he tended to overwrite. "His poetic gifts were interfering," Giroux believed. "The prose got too flowery, too lyrical and instead of naturalistic speech, which he was very good at, [the dialogue] got to be poetic." Giroux encouraged Sandburg toward more naturalism and greater economy, and about a third of the manuscript was eventually cut. Even so, the published novel was 1,067 pages long.

"He was a hard worker," Giroux said of Sandburg years later, "very well acquainted with work. . . . It had something to do with his newspaper training. He was a working writer. . . . He was one of the hardest working writers I have ever known in terms of keeping at the job very constantly. This was just second nature to him."

Sandburg called Giroux a keen editor, and Paula thanked him as he left Connemara. Sandburg was in a much better humor, and she and

Giroux believed that the problems with the novel had been resolved as well as they could be.

Giroux carried away memories of the Sandburgs' unique life-style. "I was greatly impressed by the character and the originality of Carl's study and writing room," he wrote in PBS's *The Dial* in March 1982:

> It was a big bare room on an upper floor, with many windows, and it was empty except in the center. There Carl had constructed his personal nest, an oasis bordered by bookcases of various heights, shelves, wooden crates, and a long table. There was a typewriter on a stand. . . . Everything was within easy reach—books, periodicals, typing paper, yellow writing pads, well-sharpened pencils, and so on. The whole construct was a marvelous creation unlike any other writer's den I've ever seen. . . .
>
> Mrs. Sandburg and their daughters—Margaret, Janet, and Helga— made me feel very much at home. They showed me the newborn kids, the goatlings kept in the cellar next to the furnace in the winter months. Once I went to the railroad station in a jeep with Mrs. Sandburg to pick up a crated goat that had been shipped in from the West Coast. The Sandburg family even converted me to goat's milk, which I learned is just as tasty as and much more easily digested than cow's milk. The whole family helped Carl with his researches.

Sandburg was grateful to Giroux for his astute help in "handling and mauling over the manuscript" and, later, the galleys and page proofs. His inscription in Giroux's own copy of *Remembrance Rock* praised his editor as "a man of valor and jests, with patience and frowning & multitudinous materials."

Despite the fact that the project took years instead of months, Sidney Franklin and Voldemar Vetluguin worked cordially with Sandburg. Vetluguin graciously arranged a contract amendment when Donald Brace asked to revise the agreement Sandburg had signed with MGM four years earlier. Sandburg told Vetluguin in retrospect that Franklin's "framework" for the novel appealed to him because it was so similar to an outline he had thought about for a long time. "Much the same idea has fascinated several generations of American novelists and poets," Sandburg wrote, "an epic weaving the mystery of the American Dream with the costly toil and bloody struggles that have gone to keep alive and carry farther that Dream." Originally, the goal was to create a work to "nourish fighting morale" and paint "a portrait of America in its beginnings and now." "I could have written in the course of a year a 100,000 word novel that . . . would have made possibly a fair picture," Sandburg reflected. "Yet the book slowly grew into proportions beyond what any of us had expected." He had spent four and a half years on it. The war was over, but he hoped that the book would be even "more wanted now" than before. He hoped it would "go farther than my Lincoln biography."

Once again Isabel Ely Lord took on the mammoth job of copyediting. This was Sandburg's first major work not shepherded through the publication process by Alfred Harcourt. Sandburg sent galleys to him anyway, and from Harcourt's California retirement came praise like "a high song." Sandburg was relieved and grateful: "You dust off some of the weariness," he told Harcourt.

On the eve of publication of *Remembrance Rock*, Sandburg told one interviewer that there must have been something inevitable about his writing such an ambitious book because "a man exercising his will wouldn't have let himself in for a job that size." Why so late in his remarkable career had he attempted his first novel? "I wrote the longest biography ever written in America," he explained. "I've written six volumes of poetry and a songbag that was something completely new. After all that adventuring why shouldn't I say to myself, 'Here goes for a novel.' This is in the groove of all my other work."

When the novel was published in October 1948, Eugene Reynal, head of the Harcourt, Brace trade department, gave a glittering publication party for Sandburg at his Manhattan townhouse. Reynal's wife, Kay, a fashion photographer, photographed Sandburg at the party where striking models mingled with book reviewers. Sandburg was affable and at home as the center of attention.

With Robert Giroux, Sandburg headed west soon afterward to promote the book in Chicago. Giroux boarded the *Twentieth Century Limited* with an advance copy of *The New York Times Book Review* and its lead review of *Remembrance Rock*. Already Sandburg's friends and fans had flooded his mail with letters of praise for the novel. On the whole, however, critics were not enthusiastic. They called Sandburg's earnest, flawed epic of a novel a failure, "noble in intention," but defective in form, tedious in plot, with static allegorical characters. According to *The New Yorker*, the book was "sonorous, right-minded and passing dull." Historian Perry Miller had written a severe review for *The New York Times*; Giroux realized that Sandburg had not yet seen it. They met as planned in their drawing room on the train, and busied themselves with their luggage. Soon after the train departed for Chicago, Giroux put the review on the seat beside Sandburg. Without a word, Sandburg picked it up and began to read. "The reiteration of his triangular drama is tedious," Miller wrote.

The effect is to show, unmistakably, some of the things a Bard falls short of—when he tries to construct a novel out of no more intelligible or dramatic a comprehension of the past than his blind assurance that "Life goes on. . . ." Whether wittingly or unwittingly, Carl Sandburg has written within the conventions of the panoramic film in technicolor. There is no more disheartening comment upon our era than to discover that at this point in his career the author of "Smoke and Steel" has lent himself to these maudlin devices.

Giroux sat waiting for Sandburg's reaction, expecting him "to blow up, to curse or to say something human." Instead there was absolute silence. "He never said a word about it," Giroux remembered.

> Of course I couldn't say anything. I couldn't console him. I could have said, "Carl, don't pay any attention to your reviews. One shouldn't read reviews. One should measure them. You have a big picture from a publicity point of view." That's the sort of thing I might have said, but I couldn't say anything because he didn't want to acknowledge the fact that it existed so we went all the way to Chicago. . . . No reference whatsoever. When we did begin conversation, he didn't talk about it at all.

The negative reviews came primarily from eastern critics, and did not deter sales in the heartland of the country. Midwestern critics were kinder to the novel, and it sold well, on the strength of Sandburg's name alone. Sandburg's author tour to the Midwest was a great success. "At one extreme the book was hailed as a timeless masterpiece, the Great American Novel," Sandburg told a friend later; "at the other end as a muddled affair for the ashcan." For himself, Sandburg said again, he would not be able to judge the value of his novel until he had "been deep sunk in other work and come back to it with complete detachment."

Back home at Connemara, baskets of mail came up the hill from the small Flat Rock post office, most of it thanking Sandburg for *Remembrance Rock*. One of the letters came from his longtime friend Fanny Butcher of the *Chicago Tribune*, who had given his poetry one of its first favorable reviews back in 1916. "Thank you for affirmations and eloquence," he told her that autumn of 1948.

> As I look back, what happened, I'm sure, is something like this: after being long possessed by it, I wrote a novel of theme and structure such as I wished someone else had written for me to read 40 or 50 years ago so I could have gone on from there. The theme is costly, tangled in dream and death. Tom Wolfe and Ross Lockridge died in their thirties, Stevie Benét at 45. Sometimes I wonder how and why I am ambulant & in my right mind, enjoying certain fool songs more than ever.

Candidates for the Pulitzer Prize in fiction published in 1948 were James Gould Cozzens for *Guard of Honor*; Norman Mailer for *The Naked and* the Dead; Thornton Wilder for The Ides of March; Ross Lockridge for Raintree County; William Faulkner for Intruder in the Dust; and Sandburg for Remembrance Rock. The award went to Cozzens.

Sandburg's novel was never made into a film. The war was over, Franklin had moved on to other projects, and there were changes, including internal dissension, at MGM. The fundamental reason, however, was the book itself—far too complex, too vast for adaptation. In a later era, it might have been a mini-series, but its multiplicity of stories and times far exceeded the original vision, making Remembrance Rock too ponderous and overwhelming to be reduced to a movie script.

Sandburg, the Eternal Hobo, brooded "from fury to sorrow to disbelief" about the book's reception, Helga wrote. Stubbornly, he had followed the book where it led him. It was an odyssey deep into the American Dream, an "American testament." The novel was Sandburg's affirmation of "the works and self-denials of great men with an utter and complete faith in the American Republic they were founding; the windings of doom, strife and prayer out of which came the amalgamated American Union of States fated to become a world power." His novel, like his poetry, was written to a thesis—"Always the path of American destiny has been into the Unknown":

> . . . At Plymouth and Jamestown there was the Unknown of a vast continent of wilderness to be faced. At Philadelphia in the writing of the Declaration and later amid the cold and filth of Valley Forge, there was the Unknown again, no precedents or forerunners to guide. Later in the trials of crossing the Great Plains and pioneering the West coast and in the bloody sectional struggle that hammered national unity into a finality, there was ever the Unknown. And never was it more true than now— the path of American destiny leads into the Unknown.

Slowly, tenaciously, Sandburg had written the kind of book he had to write, heedless of time, precedent, external pressures. His novel, like his work in every other genre, had grown in its own way out of his spirit and experience, the careful elucidation of his national and personal vision. He could be ruefully defensive about its "peculiar press." "About a fourth rated it The Great American novel, an epic and a testament," he told Allan Nevins, who had called it "an impressive and enduring book." Others called it "huge, muddled, overdone, and some the worst novel that had ever come to their hands."

Most critics damned it with faint praise or stinging criticism. "The 1,067 pages of 'Remembrance Rock' made up as dull and tedious a literary performance as has been foisted on the public in many months," wrote the *Newsweek* critic. While no one could quarrel with Sandburg's premise, the *Newsweek* article continued, the book was "an amazing exhibition of how not to write a novel, even the great American novel." Yet his public liked it. "It has ranged from second to sixth in the best-seller score-board," he told Nevins, "and will be kicking up controversy for some time to come."

Despite its major and minor flaws, the novel is a testament to Sandburg's love for his country and for the universal "Family of Man," his last ringing pledge of allegiance. *Remembrance Rock* is also an exercise in courage, for Sandburg had everything to lose and little to gain by undertaking an experiment in fiction so late in his literary career. It was a critical failure, but a bold failure—an ambitious, wholehearted, visionary risk. "I will say everything," he had pledged as a young man, unknown even to himself. He had so endeavored, over the half century of his career, plunging repeatedly into the unknown, diving exuberantly, albeit sometimes heedlessly, into the beckoning streams of new challenge. He was not only a pioneer, but an adventurer and explorer, in his own words a Seeker. Stubborn, garrulous, he migrated from genre to genre, but he was steadfast in vision and belief and in his unifying commitment to The People, who read his work no matter what the critics said about it. "Each time has its plain people and humble folk, lacking both the guile and the desire to lay false exactions upon others," he wrote. As always, the people were Sandburg's best subject and his best audience.

*

He turned seventy-one on January 6, 1949, but did not pause to rest. He moved, as he always had, directly from one project to another. By February he was working "like an old time government mule." His first goal was to complete the book, in collaboration with Oliver Barrett, based on Barrett's outstanding collection of Lincoln materials. Sandburg was writing the text, beginning with an informal and entertaining account of the genesis and development of Barrett's collection. Barrett himself augmented the text and prepared the source documents to be reproduced in the 1949 limited edition, which was so successful that a regular edition appeared in 1950. Sandburg and Barrett worked over the final manuscript together before submitting it to Harcourt, Brace "for the demoniac and hawk-eyed Isabel Ely Lord to plough through it and employ her skilled and unmistakable directions" to the printers, Sandburg said. "I can see her coming from Episcopal services and joyously hurling herself into this mess as an assignment from God."

Once again, Sandburg refused to be hurried. "In closing up this piece of work we must be grave and reverend seigneurs acting with due deliberation and a high score of hustle and bustle." He was determined to make "a sane landing from the long flight" of *Remembrance Rock*. He was still experimenting, pioneering, hoboing, still studying his craft, still learning to write. When Ken Dodson sought his advice about writing, Sandburg offered him as near a credo as he articulated in the late 1940s:

> . . . You are a man of a thousand stories. Find a framework. Then write it. Then overwrite it and cut it down. Let no day pass without writing it. When the going is good with you, your sentences march and hammer and sing low and what is called style is there in simple perfection. . . . You have only to go to your memories and to the wellsprings of your own heart for what is termed material. You have an eye for the vivid and can render it sparely. You can . . . compress great teachings in a few sentences. Most of whatever you now need to be taught will have to come out of your own loving and toilsome practice. . . . Paganini had a formula: toil, solitude and prayer.

Sandburg had written Paganini's formula on a slip of paper which he kept within view in the workroom where he spent his own lonely "loving and toilsome" hours. He was beginning to think seriously about going to his own memories, to the wellsprings of his own heart, to write his autobiography.

Eugene Reynal and Robert Giroux proposed another new project, but Sandburg was skeptical. They wanted him to prepare a volume of his complete poems, with a preface. He had more than eight hundred poems, "or psalms—or contemplations." Why collect them? If he did, which ones should go in, which should be omitted? He had written so many poems over so many years. As he looked at them now, in the cold, clear light of passing time, he could see a body of work "for which I must give the world an alibi or thumb my nose at the world and refuse, in so many words, to testify."

Editors, critics and fans aside, Sandburg would write in his maturity as he had in his youth out of his own burning need to speak. He would have to see if he could balance the old work with the new. Meanwhile, he shared with another would-be writer the insight he had come to nearly a half century earlier: "Those who are bent on writing will go on with it no matter what anybody says."

1949–1951

27. Songs and Scars

Work, love, laughter, pain, death, put impressions on us
as time passes, and we brood over what has happened,
praying it may be an "exalted brooding." Out of songs
and scars and the mystery of personal development, we
may get eyes that pick out intentions we had not seen
before in people, in art, in books and poetry.

—Carl Sandburg, "Notes for a Preface," *The
Complete Poems of Carl Sandburg*, 1950

The seventh decade of his life brought Carl Sandburg public honors
and private sorrows. He became an international celebrity, harvesting the fruits of a lifetime of hard work, yet the public accolades were overshadowed by private losses. "Study the wilderness under
your own hat," he wrote in a poem unpublished until after his death,
"And say little or nothing of how/You are not unaccustomed to thorns."

Always his great capacity for friendship yielded rich fellowships, and
the concomitant risks of pain and loss. Wherever he traveled, he made
himself at home in the houses of friends, usually settling in as the center
of attention while his hosts provided his favorite food and drink, and
accommodated his schedule. Long, frugal years on the road gave him a
preference for such arrangements over the loneliness of hotel rooms and
restaurants. "The only trouble with Sandburg is, that while a guest at
my home, he persisted in staying up until one a.m. both nights he stayed
with me," one old friend confided to another. "He continued to nurse
Old Forrester on the rocks while I wanted to get to bed. He would sleep
until noon the next day while I was up and doing by 7:15 a.m."

Since the *Chicago Daily News* days the ebullient Quaker Lloyd Lewis
had been one of Sandburg's closest friends. Lewis's work on his biography
Sherman: The Fighting Prophet had coincided with Sandburg's Lincoln

researches. They shared materials, techniques and the hard-won understanding of the biographer's prolonged and difficult work. Lewis had written the introduction to Sandburg's *Poems of the Midwest* in 1946, and in 1948 gave *Remembrance Rock* a staunchly favorable review. They shared a friendship with Adlai Stevenson, elected governor of Illinois in 1948. Lewis persuaded Sandburg to speak at Stevenson's inauguration because Stevenson wanted "more than anything else at his inauguration" to have Sandburg, "the greatest interpreter of the prairies to talk to and about the prairie people."

The Stevenson family invited Sandburg to be their special guest during the 1949 inaugural, putting him up in a hotel beforehand and then making him one of their first guests as they moved into the Governor's Mansion. His speech was a highlight of the festivities, and notable for his new vision of Abraham Lincoln as "a world figure, in a certain sense adopted by the whole Family of Man because of what he represented in the name of human freedom."

Lloyd Lewis was working hard that spring of 1949 on his biography of Ulysses S. Grant. Sandburg urged him not to set any "absolute deadline" for the book. For more than three decades, the two men had traded ideas, books, jokes and encouragement. "Do you remember when we agreed that if we had a little less intelligence, of a sort, we would have made a vaudeville team good as McIntyre & Heath or Moss & Hart in *How High Is Up?*" Sandburg asked Lewis in one of the last letters he wrote to him. Lewis died of a heart attack April 21, 1949, his biography unfinished.

"I cry over his going but it isnt a bitter crying," Sandburg told Lewis's widow. "He liked that line in Rem Rock: 'To every man, be he who he may, comes a last happiness and a last day.' " Sandburg brooded over Lewis's death even so. "Just to have had him for that kind of a friend and coworker held something rich," he told Adlai Stevenson. "And that is about all that mitigates your real loss in this hour. He knew the best heart of both you and me away deep."

With Oliver Barrett, Sandburg finished the work on *Lincoln Collector: The Story of the Oliver R. Barrett Lincoln Collection*, "a heavy set of chores," Sandburg said late in 1949. "Never again am I going in for one of these documentary jobs where you check and double check till the walls come falling." Yet it was a job he had to do. "I wouldn't have undertaken it if it were not that Barrett has been friend and counselor across twenty-five years," he told Allan Nevins, "and I am beholden to him in a thousand ways as a beneficient influence." Barrett was in failing health as the book neared completion, but told Sandburg he had lived longer because of their work on the project. Barrett died within months of the book's publication.

Sandburg was still haunted by earlier deaths. On at least two public occasions he paid tribute to Vachel Lindsay by reading Lindsay's poems instead of his own. "Vachel still lives with me," he told the Lindsay family, "and I hope to write impressions of him sometime." Nearing seventy-two, Sandburg was keenly aware of ebbing time. As he said good-bye to intimate friends, he began to contemplate his own history.

He had begun to work on his autobiography, partly at the encouragement of Robert Giroux. Sandburg's older sister Mary now lived in Los Angeles with her son and his family. He visited her there in the fall of 1949, and they talked over their life in Galesburg, remembering their parents and hard times. They spoke of the committee of Galesburg women who had purchased and restored the little house on Berrien Street where August and Clara Sandburg made their first home and where Mary and Carl Sandburg, their eldest children, were born. "I am still not at ease about a non-posthumous [birthplace]," Sandburg had told Adda George, leader of the move to restore the house. "It would require an ego and assurance I don't have. Yet a man must meet more than halfway the clean and fine regard of certain old and tried friends."

Except for occasional trouble with his eyes, Sandburg was as vigorous and fit now as he had been two decades earlier. He was full of plans for books to come. In December 1949 he went to New York for "furious conferences over a book that originates at their suggestion and not mine," he said, "a volume of Complete Poems to be issued in September of 1950." He had to choose which poems to include, and to write a "Preface, Lord help us." He began making notes for the preface on the train to Washington for a visit at the Library of Congress. His pockets were full of notes on other projects—some new nonsense tales about imaginary creatures he christened the Onkadonks; two more novels; one-act plays for high school audiences. He and his editors at Harcourt, Brace were talking about a one-volume condensation of the entire Lincoln biography. In the familiar bold handwriting, he made a tidy list of work to be done after the Barrett book.

In Washington that December, Sandburg consulted with historians and musicologists at the Library of Congress, and went to a party for Robert Frost, in town to record his poems for the Library. "Not having seen Frost in 12 years, and we being old friends, I go over and take a hand in a many sided discussion of the Bollingen award to Ezra Pound," he told a friend. T. S. Eliot, e. e. cummings, W. H. Auden and Allen Tate had been among the poets who helped steer the first national

Bollingen Award to Pound, still incarcerated in Chestnut Ward at St. Elizabeth's Hospital. The Library of Congress was to administer the thousand-dollar prize award; there was speculation that giving it to Pound would force the Department of Justice to free Pound, if not pardon him. The announcement of the award fired a national controversy, resulting in an investigation and the decision to have Yale University oversee the award in the future.

Privately, Frost expressed the view that if "we should admire Ezra for being a great poet in spite of his being a traitor, so we must condemn him for a great traitor in spite of his being a great poet. That works both ways for anybody with a brain." There is no record of Sandburg's position on the Bollingen-Pound question, but in 1958 Sandburg, Frost, MacLeish, Eliot, Hemingway, Dos Passos, Marianne Moore, Auden and other writers would speak in concert on behalf of Pound's release. "It won't hurt Ezra to do a little time," Sandburg said of Pound's confinement during the summer of 1950. "I hope to visit him at St. Elizabeth's and I will tell him that I will read Ezra Pound as long as I live."

Shortly afterward Pound sent Sandburg a postcard:

> S Liz
> 14 Ag.
>
> Ef
>   Ther'z
> z'any visitin'
> done, yu
> gotter dew
> it.
>
>   yrs
>   Ez.

*

Hearty and vigorous, Sandburg enjoyed an active social life on his journeys away from Connemara. During that same December 1949 Washington trip, he socialized with Frost, visited an old friend from the Wisconsin days, William Leiserson (they talked till one in the morning); and attended the Gridiron Dinner with Washington journalist Thomas L. Stokes. ("In the whirl of these circumstances I forgot about the goddam WHITE tie," Sandburg apologized later; "I had no intention of being a white crow in a flock of blacks. I just clean forgot.") He met Millicent Todd Bingham, author of a book about Emily Dickinson. "As that picturesque Amherst wraith of a girl and woman has always fascinated and instructed me," he said, "and as once on a moonlit night I walked with Robert Frost past the Amherst home, I was a little spellbound at Mrs. Bingham's answers to my questions and her questions put to me." He recorded "three fool songs" for the Library of Congress folk music division and consulted on a folk song anthology prepared by Duncan Emrich and Ruth Crawford Seeger, "a Chicago gal who for years was a sort of added informal adopted daughter" to the Sandburgs.

With *Lincoln Collector* launched, he was playing with new nonsense tales and poems for children of all ages, still spinning new stories about his whimsical "Hongdorshes." He was shaping the first draft of the Preface for *Complete Poems.* In February 1950 audiences in Illinois, Michigan, Ohio and New York heard him try to answer the question "What Would Lincoln Do Today?" He shared a Rochester, New York, lecture platform with Eleanor Roosevelt and Ralph Bunche. Although he still preferred to travel by train, Sandburg had quickly taken advantage of the convenience of air travel. "There was a time when I could go along with grasshopper jumps over the landscape," he reflected as he declined many lecture invitations that year, "but not now." Still he kept up a schedule which would daunt much younger men.

Sandburg came home from his strenuous February travels to rest, write and catch up on his correspondence before undertaking his spring lecture tour. He was ill with intestinal flu when Oliver Barrett's widow asked him to write a funeral tribute to "his old friend and co-laborer." Barrett and Edgar Lee Masters died during that same wintry March week. The icy mountain winter was a somber backdrop for mourning the loss of "ancient fellowships."

Later, in Chicago, Sandburg and Ralph Newman, proprietor of the Abraham Lincoln Bookshop, called on Oliver Barrett's widow. "Sandburg himself remains a wonder," Newman told a friend. ". . . he's as vigorous as ever—likes to take long walks, does setting-up exercises regularly, etc." Sandburg was finishing his Preface, nearly 6,000 words long. He worked on the manuscript in several cities, showing it to various friends at various stages. As usual, he felt overworked. "I am the man who was on that train out of St. Louis," he told Archie MacLeish; "—the fifth time he was kicked off he dusted himself and said, 'I'm going to Cincinnati if my pants hold out.' "

When the University of Illinois proposed to award Sandburg an honorary degree in June 1950, he was deeply moved. "About a degree in June I could carry one more if it came from the cornbelt of my native state of Illinois, to which commonwealth I can truly say, 'Of thee I have sung.' " He asked the university to go a step further, however, and award a similar degree to his brother-in-law. Steichen had received an honorary master's degree from Wesleyan University in 1940, Sandburg told Bruce Weirick of the University of Illinois, "but so far America's greatest photographer, a plant breeder extraordinary, hero of distinguished record in two wars, so far he hasn't a Doctorate from a great university." Sandburg thought the occasion would have "dignity, humor and gayety" if Steichen could receive a degree "along with his biographer." Steichen was "a Teacher in the truest sense of that word," Sandburg said. "His influence on me has been immense and incalculable." Nevertheless, he could not persuade officials to let Steichen share the limelight, and did not receive his own honorary degree from the university until 1953. The University of Uppsala in Sweden awarded Sandburg an honorary Ph.D. in June 1950, however, his second honor from a Swedish university and one of a harvest of public awards.

Sandburg's schedule pulled him back and forth across the continent in 1950, and fall found him settled at the Royalton Hotel in New York for final work on *Complete Poems*. He had done some perfunctory work on a *New American Songbag*, published in 1950 by Broadcast Music Incorporated with a foreword by Bing Crosby. He was getting to know other musicians in New York, and enjoying their company immensely. His host and hostess for "long boxcar evenings" of music, talk, good food and drink were artists Gregory and Terry d'Alessio, whose brownstone on Henderson Place on the Upper East Side of Manhattan was the setting for some of the best private parties Sandburg ever got to be the life of. Sandburg and d'Alessio, a superb classical guitarist and editor of *The Guitar Review*, shared a friendship with the master guitarist Andrés Segovia, whom Sandburg had met years earlier in Chicago. Segovia tried in vain to teach Sandburg additional guitar chords and fingerings and occasionally sent him gold guitar strings.

He was at home in a vast web of friendships, kept in touch with old friends—poet Alfred Kreymborg; Ken and Letha Dodson, to whom he dedicated the "New Section" of *Complete Poems*; Ernest Hemingway and his fourth wife, Mary, with whom Sandburg had worked during the *Chicago Daily News* years; French singer Marianne Lorraine Oswald; Adlai Stevenson; Zora Neale Hurston. "Carl was all-out for friendship," journalist Harry Golden recalled. "If Carl was your friend and your son was sick, Carl worried as much as you. If you were depressed, Carl wanted to share your depression as he wanted to share your exhilaration when you were happy. Carl, as a friend, accepted your entire universe, every star, jungle, and person in it."

*

"It was the publishers' idea we shd [should] do this book," Sandburg wrote Archie MacLeish about *The Complete Poems of Carl Sandburg*. "I never for a moment asked about it a lot of these poems have grown up and gone around and have an existence of their own some of them rowdies and I cant change their rowdy ways." The manuscript he was working on included forty new poems, "mostly little fellows," he said.

Harcourt, Brace produced the collected works of T. S. Eliot, e. e. cummings and Sandburg in books which "had a family look . . . a similarity," said Robert Giroux. Each book jacket contained a vivid photograph of the poet. These editions of the collected poems of "three terribly important American poets" turned poetry sales around at Harcourt, Giroux recalled. But it had taken much persuasion to convince Sandburg to collect his work. He worried that some of his poems could be "passed by as annals, chronicles or punctuation points of a vanished period." His Asgard Press books he considered "not worth later reprint," and he offered an apology for some of his other work: "In a six-year period came four books of poetry having a variety of faults, no other person more keenly aware of their accomplishments and shortcomings than myself."

He had finished his work on the book by summer 1950. Like many of his other books, this one was completed to the counterpoint of "world storm," this time the escalation of Cold War tensions as North Korea invaded South Korea on June 25, 1950. "Regrets over the Cold War. Regrets over the goddam internecine warfare in Washington and the USA," Sandburg told a friend.

The "Notes for a Preface" to *Complete Poems* was published in the September 1950 issue of *Atlantic Monthly*. When a radio host of the fifties asked Sandburg during an interview how many poems he had written, Sandburg estimated about seven hundred, and reckoned that that came to about a penny a poem, since *Complete Poems* sold for $6.95. His most quoted poem was "Fog," and he delighted in parodying it for his grandchildren at Connemara: "De fog come on itti bitti kitti footsies," he would tease. "He sit down on Chicago and—whamo—he gone."

Outspoken as always, Sandburg jabbed at literary critics in the Preface as well as in some of the poems in the "New Section" of *Complete Poems*, such as "The Abracadabra Boys." Most critics lauded the body of Sandburg's work in *Complete Poems*, but there were demurrers, some of them delayed and painfully exasperating. "I expected disfavor or short shrift in most reviews and was surprised at what came," Sandburg told poet Thomas Hornsby Ferril, offering some astute self-criticism: "There is a percentage of drivel or overwriting, sometimes 'spewing' or again 'running off the mouth. . . .' But I had to let that percentage ride, with the alibi, 'I wrote it like that then and read proof on it and saw it into print and now I stands mute.' "

He won the Pulitzer Prize in 1951 for *The Complete Poems of Carl Sandburg*, published in the fall of 1950. In 1919 he had shared with Margaret Widdemer the Poetry Society of America Prize, forerunner to the Pulitzer in poetry. His first official Pulitzer had been awarded in 1940 for history, not poetry. "At fifty I had published a two-volume biography and *The American Songbag*," he wrote in "Notes for a Preface" in *Complete Poems*, "and there was puzzlement as to whether I was a poet, a biographer, a wandering troubadour with a guitar, a midwest Hans Christian Andersen, or a historian of current events."

✳

Sandburg was weary from work and travel, but he could not find the rest he needed at home. At times the busy life at Connemara made him impatient. Paula and Helga were running a flourishing dairy and farm, rising early and working late. Paula often sat at her farm office desk until midnight. Helga was in love then with an aspiring writer and actor, who began to spend weekends at Connemara. During the week Art taught drama in a high school more than a hundred miles from Flat Rock. At Connemara, he worked for Sandburg, copying materials and helping with other literary tasks, as well as "projects calling for brawn."

Helga had inherited her parents' remarkable stamina and creative energy, as well as their high expectations. During their courtship, Sandburg and Paula had written of the wonder children their union would produce. With one child lost at birth and two daughters living sheltered and limited lives, Helga was left to fulfill whatever worldly ambitions the Sandburgs might have had for their offspring. A free spirit, Helga gave her own children the wide latitude she herself had enjoyed on the Michigan dunes when her father was absorbed in his career and her mother concentrated on Margaret's illness and Janet's development. She gave her children free rein to explore the wonders of the Connemara hills and woods while she worked with the goats and the farm, rode horseback through the mountains, painted, and began to write poetry of her own, as well as a detailed private journal. Her father encouraged her writing when she summoned the courage to tell him about it.

"Write until you are ashamed of yourself," he urged. Helga was the one who usually drove her father to the train station or the airport when he set out on his frequent journeys, carrying a supply of goat's milk and sandwiches for sustenance en route. Between Sandburg and his youngest daughter there was a fierce bond of love and ego. It would not be easy for him to give her up again to another man, or for her to give up her father in favor of another husband. By autumn 1950, however, Helga and Art had decided they wanted to marry and to work and live at Connemara. But they were not ready to announce their plans. Helga wondered what the presence of another adult male would do to that unorthodox household, especially if he, too, wanted to work at writing.

There were tempestuous times as it was. "It seems Dad was in a storm this afternoon about typewriters clacking in the nights and we are all having it out," Helga wrote in her journal.

This is the note he typed on the Farm Office typewriter while the rest of us went up to his room: "Now is the time for all men to come to the aid of the party we are making a test here as to how this sounds up on the floor above and whether it disturbs sleepers who wish to sleep and get their proper rest. See what I mean? How many times has it been that good people requiring their sleep have been kept awake by a god-dam lowlived sonofagun who didn't know any better than to go on pegging away at his high-power typewriter."

Someone was awake at Connemara around the clock, it seemed. Sandburg and Margaret were nocturnal creatures, working far past midnight into the early morning, often walking the Connemara drives in the evening, singing together as they traced the pathway around the dark lake and up the hill again. Then, like her father, Margaret would sleep far into the morning. Helga rose before dawn to begin the busy work of the farm. In the fresh morning light, the children often took their bowls of cereal to the warm barn to watch the goats being milked. With five busy adults and two active children in residence, and farm workers coming and going, Connemara was a lively community rather than a tranquil mountain estate. The barn was even headquarters for a championship square-dancing team.

While Sandburg was away, Helga and Art began to talk to Paula about marrying, and making a business venture out of Connemara, a dairy and a goat breeding operation. Helga told her mother Art would "forego an interesting and lucrative job somewhere else" if they were given "sole responsibility and the final word on all moves." Paula agreed to lease the land, animals and equipment to Helga and Art. In return they would furnish milk and vegetables for the family, and maintain the long, hilly Connemara drives.

Sandburg spent much of November traveling, lecturing and promoting *Complete Poems*. As always, it was hard for Paula to keep track of him. When word came from Los Angeles that his sister Mary had suffered a stroke, Paula asked Catherine McCarthy at Harcourt, Brace to find Sandburg and give him the news, "As we don't know where Carl is." Family problems were overshadowed by grim events in Korea. General Douglas MacArthur's hopes of bringing his troops home for Christmas vanished in late November when more than 200,000 Chinese troops made it "an entirely new war" by crossing the Yalu, entrapping American and UN forces and inflicting heavy casualties. There were fears of full-scale war with China, and the resurrection of the intimidating specter of the Bomb. The national anxiety about atomic warfare led Sandburg's publishers in New York to dispatch the original Lincoln photographs in their files to Connemara for safekeeping. At the request of the commander-in-chief of the Pacific Fleet, Edward Steichen went back into uniform as an adviser on navy photography in yet another war, and later mounted an exhibition of Korean War photographs at the Museum of Modern Art.

Sandburg returned home December 4, full of talk about the war, and news from Dana and Steichen. Helga met his train, and on the way home broached the matter of her marriage. "I expected questions, at least," she wrote in her journal for that day. "However, his concern seemed to be on the basis of personalities and adjustments. I guess he has seen enough couples trying to adjust and not succeeding. Anyway he said, 'So you're going to get hitched legally.' And I said, 'Yep.'" Sandburg told his daughter he thought she and Art were "well-mated." "He is glad we are staying at the farm," Helga wrote,

> and thinks Art is a genius with the land and tools and also that he will branch out as we get moving. . . . And I'm pleased because I was worried. He kissed me before we left the car. Then when we were upstairs, he started talking to Mother about 'Art-and-Helga's move' and how good we were for each other. I was listening from my desk in the Farm Office and flinching and wincing because I'm used to keeping it all so quiet.

The day after Sandburg's return, Fred Friendly of CBS telephoned from New York to ask Sandburg to appear on *Hear It Now*, a new radio program which would begin December 15. He wanted to come down to Connemara with a CBS crew to record five minutes with Sandburg for the show he and Edward R. Murrow were coproducing. Heading the

CBS production crew which would tape Sandburg on December 9 was producer/director/writer Joseph Wershba, whose sense of humor and joy in life matched Sandburg's. Wanting to take a gift to Sandburg, Wershba arrived at Connemara with a bottle of Old Forrester, according to a CBS colleague, Sandburg's favorite drink. Wershba's engineer met him at the airport, and en route to Connemara told him, "That old son of a bitch. You know what's going to happen. He's going to make you drink some of his goat's milk when you get out there."

"My stomach started to churn," said Wershba. "I said, 'I'll be a son of a bitch if I'm going to drink goat's milk.' I didn't even know what it was. I felt it was lousy, it was warm, makes you nauseous and all that. I said, 'I ain't drinking that!' "

When Wershba and his crew arrived at Connemara, Wershba addressed Sandburg respectfully as Doctor Sandburg. "He got a little embarrassed," Wershba recalled. "He said, 'Oh, don't call me doctor. Call me Carl.' " Wershba gave Sandburg the bottle of whiskey, and immediately Sandburg asked Art to bring three glasses.

"Jesus, no," Wershba said to himself. "We're not going to start drinking before we record. We're going to get drunk. I don't want to do that."

"No, please," Wershba protested aloud.

"Art, there are three little glasses up there," Sandburg went on. "Bring them on down. I think these gentlemen will enjoy some good goat's milk."

Wershba's stomach sank, he said, and his engineer looked at him as if to say "I told you so!"

When the goat's milk came, Wershba gulped it down fast. "I was so amazed that it didn't taste bad I said, 'This stuff is great. It tastes terrific. It's wonderful stuff.' You know, on and on and on."

Sandburg looked at Wershba "under those eyebrows," a mischievous gleam in his blue eyes. "You know," he said to Wershba, "you remind me of that editor of the *Louisville Courier* walking down the streets of Louisville on a Sunday morning with the fat Sunday *New York Times* under his arms and saying to himself, 'I'll read this son of a bitch paper if it kills me!' "

"At that point," Wershba said, "I knew, don't try to pull the wool over this old buddy's eyes. He was as sharp as anybody. He knew immediately that I was probably just glad I didn't throw up on the goat's milk."

The recording session went on for two hours, and Sandburg and Wershba were fast friends from that afternoon on. "I was absolutely on fire, on fire with this man," Wershba said later. "I have been listening to the recordings we made this afternoon," he wrote Sandburg that day from his hotel in Asheville,

> and we have all been stunned by the magnificence, the beauty, the clarity—I speak not only of your reading, but of the reproduction. . . . In short, thank your for your cooperation, thank your family for their friendliness, thank your dog for his silence, thank your cat for foregoing the luxury of meowing for her mistress. . . . Thank your geese for turning off their honking horns—and thank you for introducing me to goat's milk—and I did *so* enjoy it.

Sandburg's mellifluous voice helped launch *Hear It Now*, and he, Wershba and Friendly enjoyed years of fellowship. Wershba urged Murrow and Sandburg to produce a record album of Sandburg reading his poems. "You must do these things soon, Carl Sandburg," Wershba wrote, "because it is a crime that your voice is not abroad in the land these days, as much as it should be."

※

The Korean War unleashed a palpable fear of the New Atomic Age which Sandburg had foreseen years earlier in poems such as "The Unknown War": "In the faint light and smoke of the flash and the mushroom of the first/bomb blast of the Third World War, keep your wits collected." And at the same time, Senator Joseph McCarthy, zealot from Wisconsin, charged that communists had infiltrated the State Department, and set off a chain reaction which reverberated into the future. Wearily Sandburg beheld the current world storm. "Days go by after the news and I go saying, 'What the hell is there to write?' " He spoke about the times in an occasional interview or letter, but did not have the heart for a sustained commentary in journalism or any other format. He burrowed instead in his own boyhood, compiling notes and memories for the autobiography.

Sandburg was aware of his mortality, and of the vulnerability of people who mattered to him. "Alf Harcourt has twice been to Johns Hopkins the past six weeks and nearly crossed over, had the next room to Mencken who too just managed to 'stay this side,' as AH puts it. My sister in Los Angeles had a stroke last week. An 87 year old daughter of a cousin of my father, the only link left in that direction (in this country), she is blind and bedfast most of the time but getting up one day broke one of her pipestem legs." In the background, there was international turbulence which carried an unprecedented immediacy, given the shared world history of the preceding war. "And what are these tabulations as we now slowly move into the longest hardest war this nation has ever seen?" Sandburg reflected somberly. "Well, as I says, what the hell!"

✳

Margaret Ligon of Asheville's Pack Memorial Library wanted to arrange a tribute to Sandburg in 1951, along with an exhibition of his works and related materials. She wrote to people across the country asking for letters speaking of Sandburg. George Jean Nathan answered that he was "a great and noble soul." Eric Sevareid called him "the strongest and most enduring force in American letters today." "Carl Sandburg—Yes," said Brooks Atkinson. "It is part of a reporter's duty to be no man's disciple and to inoculate himself frequently against the disease known as hero-worship," answered Edward R. Murrow. "So far as Sandburg is concerned I am a disciple with the disease and regard my lot as most fortunate."

James Thurber sent along a letter and a drawing entitled "After Dinner Music: Thurber and Sandburg," with a pint-sized Thurber playing a banjo facing a giant-sized Sandburg strumming a guitar. "He may seem as easy to describe as a face carved on a mountain," said Thurber, "but there are vast and complex reaches between the cat feet of the 'Fog' and 'Remembrance Rock.' . . . He was up here not too long ago, playing his guitar and singing, sometimes with me, late into the night, although it seemed early. . . . He is an American institution." Texas senator Tom Connally, no doubt distracted by his duties as chairman of the committee on Foreign Relations, responded with a eulogy:

> The entire nation mourns the recent passing of our beloved poet, Carl Sandburg, who illuminated for us the rich heritage of our American past and the living spirit of freedom which sets our people apart in the world.
>
> While no words of mine can add lustre to his immortal fame, I am glad to join with you people of Asheville, North Carolina, in paying personal tribute to your late neighbor and friend, Carl Sandburg, both for his genius as a writer and for his warm humanity as a man.

Sandburg, alive and well, was vigorously at work in that new year adding "lustre to his immortal fame" and having a good horselaugh at the exaggerated report of his death. That February he launched an authors' series at the New School for Social Research in New York. The programs, arranged by his friend the poet Jean Starr Untermeyer, included William Carlos Williams, Edith Sitwell, e. e. cummings, John Berryman and Robert Fitzgerald, among others. He had a full lecture schedule that spring, working his way by train or plane from the East Coast to the Midwest. The capstone of the year was the long-awaited honor, the Pulitzer Prize for poetry.

But it was a bittersweet year. Another old friend was gone. "A tumult of memories came over me—you winding in and out of them—on the news of Red Lewis passing," he told Harcourt when he heard that Sinclair Lewis was dead. Harcourt had fostered the careers of both men. "First time I met Red was in Chicago shortly after Main Street," Sandburg recalled that spring. "We were with the same [lecture] bureau and he said, 'We are both feaking for Feakins.'"

Another old friend, William T. Evjue of the Madison, Wisconsin, *Capital Times*, the first Wisconsin newspaper to speak out against McCarthy, sent Sandburg a sober greeting in 1951:

> In these days when hysteria seems to have preempted the place of reason, we need men like you to help maintain some semblance of sanity. I am not too hopeful,—I have now seen McCarthyism supplant La Folletteism here in Wisconsin, the state once heralded over the world as the ideal commonwealth.
>
> I hope that you will "git holt of that thar guitar," start out over the country and ask the plain people whom you know so well,—"whereinell are we going?"

Sandburg saw it all as "colossal world drama."

✳

When Helga, thirty-two, and Art, five years younger, were married in February 1951 at Connemara, Unitarian minister Frank Bishop performed the ceremony. Sandburg and Bishop had been classmates and basketball teammates at Lombard College. A bitter mountain cold snap froze the water pipes in the basement at Connemara, and before she dressed for her wedding, Helga worked on the pipes with a blow-torch, her two children watching the proceedings "intently, faces uplifted." Sandburg wanted the event to be a celebration, so friends and family filled the old house. Carnations, roses and champagne denoted the importance of the day, and Helga's children dressed up in new clothes—a pink dress with hoop skirt and black patent shoes for little Paula; gray tweeds, gray shirt, a tie and shiny cordovan shoes for John Carl. Helga wore green velvet and white orchids. Her father gave her away. When young Paula learned that they would have a new last name she protested. "You all can change if you want to—but I'm going to keep my old name!"

Helga was happy: again she had "a handsome herdsman husband," she wrote later. And she would stay at Connemara. "Wasn't I always persuasive with parents and lovers about remaining with my beloved family? I was content."

At first, the old house seemed spacious enough to accommodate the newlyweds and Helga's children; Margaret and Janet; and Carl and Paula, who would celebrate their forty-third wedding anniversary in June. The two gentle maiden sisters lived on the third floor in rooms across the wide landing from their father's. He was away from Connemara much of that spring, lecturing and working on his newest project, his memoirs. "I get it from many points I should do an autobiog," he told Tom Ferril. "That's an assignment to go ahead and forget the present colossal world drama and every day write 'I, I, I' and 'Me, Me, Me,' while singing that ditty of the 1880's 'Listen to My Tale of Woe.' Going to ponder on it, ponder on a lot of imponderables."

His pleasure in the Pulitzer Prize, announced in May 1951, was intense but short-lived. "YOU HAVE MADE AN HONEST WOMAN OF THE PULITZER PRIZE," Archie MacLeish telegraphed. "THE HONOR IS ALL HERS." He and other poets and critics had praised *Complete Poems*. "It's a wonderful record to put down on paper in one man's life time" MacLeish told him, seeing in Sandburg's work "the truth and strength and skill and beauty of a man." The praise was offset by a scathing review which appeared nearly a year after the book was published. In the September 1951 issue of *Poetry*, the magazine which in 1914 gave Sandburg his first serious publication as a poet, his old friend William Carlos Williams took aim at Sandburg's *Complete Poems* with a wounding attack. Sandburg had had his battles with the critics for decades; the general panning of *Remembrance Rock* still rankled. But this unexpectedly negative review from *Poetry* was a particular blow.

Williams gave him fair warning: "I have just finished an 11 page review of your Collected Poems for *Poetry* . . . it's rough but you can take it. . . . You may not like what I have said but one thing I didn't say, I didn't say you were dead."

Sandburg had long admired Williams's work, praising him in the late forties as timeless, "helplessly and intensely grounded in American scenes and people," a poet who "can be read for this hour, this present mankind which he never forgets is both ancient and modern." He left an unpublished poem to Williams among his Connemara papers. It would not have surprised Sandburg for *Poetry* editor Karl Shapiro to dismiss his work. He told Harcourt that spring that if Shapiro accepted some of his new poems for *Poetry* "then on the day of the first prediction of frost next fall I will eat five straw hats."

Williams had admired Sandburg's early poetry, although in an essay in *Others* (July 1919) he disliked the "ataxic drivel" of "Liars." After the publication of *Good Morning, America* he had called Sandburg a writer of "excellent hocus," skillful with language and metrics. Williams had suffered his first stroke in March 1951, and was recovering when he wrote the review charging that Sandburg's poems revealed no technical initiative "other than their formlessness" and no "motivating spirit held in the front of the mind to control them." He believed that Sandburg lacked a basic artistic drive toward "a deeper, more universal discipline, whose function would be to refresh the mind of the poet." Williams mused that while it "may never have entered" Sandburg's mind "that there was anything significant to do with the structure of" free verse itself, "the best of him was touched with fire." "Carl Sandburg petered out as a poet ten years ago," Williams wrote. Except for occasional war poems in the forties, Sandburg had of course published little new poetry since *The People, Yes* in 1936. Indeed, biography and fiction usurped poetry: he had lavished his energy on *Abraham Lincoln: The War Years* and *Remembrance Rock*. "His poems themselves said what they had to say," Williams continued, "piling up, then just went out like a light. He had no answers; he didn't seek any . . . the formlessness of his literary figures was the very formlessness of the materials with which he worked. That was his truth. That was what he wanted truthfully to make plain, that was his compulsion."

According to Williams, Sandburg should have followed his "natural love of violence," demonstrated in *Chicago Poems*; his neglect of that theme kept him from becoming a poet of "great distinction." Williams saw Sandburg's work with Lincoln as the deliberate choice of a single image, exploited in prose, "to carry the whole burden of what he had been saying directly" in the "Human catalogues" in his poetry. Sandburg set poetry "deliberately aside." "He couldn't limit himself to being a poet," Williams suggested; "the facts were too overpowering, he himself was swept off his feet by their flood."

In a conclusion which evoked the charges of propaganda brought against Sandburg's poetry by Amy Lowell and others decades earlier, Williams decided that Sandburg had "abandoned his art" to expose the flaws in "the official democracy" of the nation.

Williams saw the body of Sandburg's poetry as "a monstrous kind of show," "a massive pilgrimage." If Sandburg's poetry had any form, said Williams, it was its very formlessness and shapelessness, "the drift of aimless life through the six hundred and seventy-six pages."

✳

Despite the presence of work composed during World War II, the sixty-five pages of "New Section" which concluded *Complete Poems* were anticlimactic, often disappointing. Here Sandburg gathered random poems dating as early as 1908, many of them excluded from his earlier books. Some of them should have been left unattended in the journals where they first appeared, or in his large files of unpublished work. In 1963 he would publish his last book of poetry, *Honey and Salt*, a volume carefully crafted over time, and invigorated by the passion and wisdom of his later years. But the evidence in *Complete Poems* justified Williams's perception in 1951 that after *The People, Yes*, Sandburg's poetry had shown little development. Indeed, his growth as a poet had been superseded by his interest in biography and fiction.

Sandburg had always been unorthodox. After all, a critic in 1914 had turned to a dictionary definition to be sure Sandburg was even a poet. In his unorthodoxy, Sandburg never fit any prevailing poetic canon—Eliot's, Pound's, Williams's, the modernists', the New Critics'. As critic Helen Vendler has observed, "the evolving [poetic] canon is not the creation of critics, but of poets." Lustrous poet-critics such as Eliot, Pound and Williams found Sandburg facile, intransigent, deficient in form, classical sense, depth. His was the poetry of clarity, not density, obscurity. He did not work with images and allusions, as Eliot and Pound did, or symbols, as Williams did. He was something of a heretic, working outside the prevailing poetic "religion," the cloister, as an "evangelist" of the streets. He never marched in stride with trends in poetry.

Sandburg was not a critic, but his work grew from his own implicit canon, and by the terms of the purposes he set for himself, he succeeded brilliantly. It was brave, tenacious, lonely, honorable work he set out to do—telling the American nation about itself, its weakness and strength, its past and its promise. Perhaps only the son of immigrants could have held so stalwartly to the national vision which Sandburg embraced and expanded to global themes, and probed on an epic scale, in poetry, biography and fiction.

He was always caught between cycles in American poetry, which moved, as Louis Untermeyer saw in the twenties, from an aristocratic to a democratic art, and then back again. Sandburg was no intellectual aristocrat, never pretended or wanted to be. He was, in Untermeyer's words, the "emotional democrat" of American poetry. His poetry was never cerebral, but always felt, deeply felt.

Through the years, critical assessments of Sandburg the poet oscillated from praise to condemnation to, worse, dismissal and neglect. He wrote free verse when it was revolutionary, and kept at it when it went out of fashion. Eastern critics found him too provincial, midwestern. In an age of international modernism, he was unabashedly American. In a time of nervous nationalism, he was courageous and farsighted in his outspoken global view. His passion for social justice blurred the boundary between poetry and propaganda. He wrote the "poetry of the fireside," not the "poetry of the academy." The powerful solidarity of poets and critics in the universities diluted acceptance of the poets of "streets and struggles."

Sandburg was a man of multiple literary identities. For decades, that had its impact on prevailing critical perceptions of his work. Could a writer of biography, fiction, journalism, *children's stories* be taken seriously as a poet? His success in the literary marketplace compromised him in the opinion of those who believed commercial success incompatible with poetic achievement.

From the first, Sandburg had written in a new idiom. As Malcolm Cowley observed, he "turned the Mid-western voice into a sort of music." If he made music, it was, to many critical ears, vulgar, brutal, superficial, hollow. He was a folksy troubadour, a celebrity, an entertainer, not to be taken seriously by some of the literary establishment, despite their respect for him in the seminal years of their mutual struggle. Unlike Pound, Eliot, Stevens, Williams and others, Sandburg advocated no formal theory of poetry. Unlike Frost, Warren, some of the New Critics, and others, he held no university chair. He engaged in no dialectics, just kept writing his way through the maze of his time, subordinating form to subject.

Among poets, he said only half in jest, he was considered a good biographer; among biographers, a fair poet. He paid little attention to rules in any form. "I have known newspaper staffs where a saying ran, 'The way to be a Star Reporter is to break all the rules,' " he wrote defiantly, in his "Notes for a Preface." He could be irreverent toward his art, simplistic (naïve, Williams thought), arrogant, heedless. The New Critics ignored him because they believed he worked by intuition and whim, rather than technique and theory. Yet Sandburg the writer thought profoundly about what he said, and how he said it.

He wrote always for the ordinary man and woman, and for himself, and he did not, like Pound, Stevens and Eliot, have to be explicated. Critics long saw that as a deficiency, as Sandburg ruefully noted. "According to Edmund Wilson," he said, "my trouble is that when I want to write about smoke and steel, I write about smoke and steel and not something else." He objected to the poetry advocated by the New Crit-icism: "It comes in cellophane and has not known the touch of human hands," he wrote. "Certain sacrosanct things that belong in this country and in the lives of its people don't belong in poems, says the New Criticism. A poem should not deal with *action* and not with acting and should have nothing to do with leading men toward acting. It must concern itself with *being*." Sandburg offered Whitman as an antidote: "Now Walt Whitman was perhaps the head spirit of an opposite view-point. He took the word democracy and threw it around like a juggler does a fireball and wrestled it until it came to have something of the elements found in men's hearts." That was Sandburg's pivotal theme, democracy, in a philosophical even more than a political sense.

Perhaps, again, as the son of immigrants, he could see deeper into the precious, vital force of it than his colleagues who were bred to it, who took it more for granted. Eliot and Pound went abroad and stayed there. Frost and MacLeish went and came home. Stevens longed to go abroad, and did so in his imagination. Sandburg and Williams, both children of bilingual households, stayed at home, rooted in the provinces of their native land, finding the cosmos at the center.

Sandburg's was one of the most familiar, loquacious, beloved poetic voices of the century. His old friend and champion Joseph Warren Beach accused him in a Harvard lecture in the 1950s of "*too much soap box.*" Sandburg "too often forgets the distinction between poetry and public-ity," Beach charged, "and indulges too often in the rhetorical arts of the public speaker." Sandburg was in critical "eclipse," said Beach, because he did not interest the dominant minds in criticism of the day.

His poems began to slip out of the anthologies in the fifties, and little critical attention would be given his work in the decades after his death. But, as Gay Wilson Allen pointed out, "No other American writer was at the same time so widely read and heard." Sandburg was a "great celebrity and a superb professional entertainer," Allen went on, but was he a great poet? "At the peak of his productivity—say from 1930 to the entry of the United States in World War II—there seemed little doubt that he was." Sandburg, along with Frost, was "the symbolical 'voice of America,' " Allen concluded, believing that "Sandburg's success as the voice and conscience of his time and generation to a degree Whitman would have envied, is sufficient justification for a critical study of his life and career."

Was he a success or a failure as a poet? Both. If success is measured by the prevailing critical canon, Sandburg was more successful at some times than others. He could be insubstantial, Edmund Wilson thought, of meager emotion, but with "a genuine talent for language" and a "hard-boiled vocabulary and reputation." He could be repetitive, garrulous, sentimental. As he himself said, he could be dated. He wanted to ratify the national identity, to create "simple poems" which spoke to "simple people," to celebrate and console the "plain folk living close to a hard earth." He wanted to reveal the beauty in ordinary language, the rich vernacular of past and present. He was interested in recording language, not in manipulating or transfiguring it.

If success is measured by the respect of peers, Sandburg succeeded and failed. He had the early regard of Pound, Williams and Stevens, the later disapproval of Pound and Williams. He was most revered and emulated by regional poets; black poets such as Arna Bontemps, Frank Marshall Davis, and, most of all, Langston Hughes, who called Sandburg his "guiding star"; and some of the Beat poets (although, Allen Ginsberg said, he was not as influenced by Sandburg as some thought).

If success is measured by the poet's own canon, then Sandburg also succeeded and failed. In his Whitmanesque immersion in the common life of his times grew the seeds of much of Sandburg's success and of his failure. He celebrated and affirmed "swarming and brawling Democracy," wanted to "give back to the people their own lingo," sought from the first "to say everything." The sheer weight of his body of work, its mass, its sincere, ringing, sometimes strident message, appealed to millions of readers and listeners around the world, just as it antagonized many critics. In numbers of books sold, appearances demanded, fan letters received, honors bestowed, Sandburg was one of the most "successful" American poets of the century. He quoted John Synge in his Preface on the importance of poetic feeling for ordinary life and writing poetry of ordinary things, and repeated Synge's telling words about audience, which affirmed his own intent: "Many of the older poets, such as Villon and Herrick and Burns, used the whole of their personal life as their material, and the verse written in this way was read by strong men, and thieves, and deacons, not by little cliques only." He had the same distaste for the literary elite that he had for the economic elite, was the common man's champion in poetry as well as politics.

He reprinted in the Preface his tribute to Stephen Vincent Benét, a mirror of his own creed as a writer: "He wrote often, hoping that men would act because of his words." Sandburg was emphatically a public poet, one who "could sing to give men music, consolation, pleasure" and who could just as vigorously "intone [a] chant or prayer pointing to the need for men to act."

"Each authentic poet makes a style of his own," he reflected. "A poet explains for us what for him is poetry by what he presents to us in his poems." He gave fair notice in the conclusion to his preface: He was still traveling, still a seeker, still becoming a writer. He was not finished yet.

"In a world with so high a proportion of fools, it is neither disgrace nor honor when people say of a finished work, 'I can't understand it,' " he had written back in 1916 about the work of Ezra Pound. "The last word on the merits of it will be spoken by the future." He was willing to entrust all his work to the future—the poetry, the biography, the novel. Toward the end of *Complete Poems*, there are a handful of poems about critics, Sandburg's acknowledgment of their views and his own scorn, and pain. He wrote of the elitist "Enemy Number One," "a handsome mournful galoot" writing for antiquity. He wrote about "The Abracadabra Boys," their "stacks and cloisters," their "sea of jargons" and "passwords." And, in "Many Handles," he wrote of himself and of his own battles:

Beware writing of freedom: the idea is political . . .
Would you accept a thesis in governance of the writing of poems?
Why not listen to these poets on how those ones fall into categories the
    same as eggs or potatoes? . . .
Has not the square stood up and publicly called the circle a sonofabitch
    because of animosities induced by the inevitable mutual contradic-
    tions of form? . . .

He had spoken in his preface of the "great though neglected poem *Piers Plowman*," and he returned to it at the conclusion of "Many Handles":

"Of Piers Plowman, is it permissible he made sad
lovable songs out of stubborn land, straw and
hoe-handles, barefoot folk treading dirt floors?
Should it be the Dark Ages recur, will there be
again the Immeasurable Men, the Incalculable
Women?"

Sandburg was that kind of poet, without apology making his "sad lovable songs out of stubborn land" and "barefoot folk treading dirt floors," singing his enduring faith in "immeasurable men," in "incalculable women," in his nation, in himself.

Wallace Stevens saw poetry as the "supreme fiction" which enables human beings to apprehend reality. For Sandburg, poetry was the supreme myth which enables human beings to endure reality, to survive it, even to transcend it.

---※---

1951–1954

28. A Majestic Old Age

If I live to a majestic old age becoming the owner of a
    farm I shall sit
under apple trees in the summer and on a pad of paper
    with a large yellow
lead pencil, I shall write of these things, lover of mine.

—Carl Sandburg, "Personalia," *Honey and Salt*, 1963

A t home at Connemara, Sandburg loved to work in the bright
sunlight, often taking a chair out to the wide shelf of rock up
the hill just behind his house. All about him were the family.
"My grandchildren, the boy 10 and the girl 8.5, are marvels of genius
and light," he wrote. "Their mother married again and she and her
husband are making a go of the goat herd, running a Siamese cattery on
the side." Outside, down the mountain, tensions heightened in the world
drama. Even to Sandburg's experienced eye, there had never been "such
a vast stage and contrasted players, never such a dizzy diversity of the
hinges of fate."

Sandburg traveled thousands of miles in the autumn of 1951, from
New York to Chicago and Galesburg to Texas, and then West. He stayed
with Lilla Perry in Los Angeles while he talked to his sister Mary about
his autobiography, and then spent time with Ken and Letha Dodson in
Everett, Washington, where Dodson sought his help with the final manuscript of *Away All Boats*. Sandburg told Lilla Perry that there was still
a lot of the bum and vaudevillian in him. His schedule in 1951 had
confirmed that. At home for Christmas and the New Year, he found his
family life in an "uproar" which seldom settled down, leaving him with
"incomplete work" that stayed "incomplete." As tension mounted between Sandburg and Art it was a relief to go back to New York to work
and appear on Dave Garroway's "Today" show.

Sandburg was dispirited that winter of 1952, and not just because of

614

the disrupted serenity at Connemara. Oliver Barrett's collection of papers and books went on the auction block, and Sandburg could do nothing about it. He told a friend, "it is nobody's fault, no one to blame, but I am not easy about it being scattered & never will be. Across 30 years I became part of its corporeal entity." It was one more loss. He was run down, and weary from "having a tough schedule."

Sandburg had counted on Helga to help him with his work, as she had before her marriage. A skilled typist, Helga knew her father's habits, as well as the signals of impatience, anxiety and frustration which came when his work was not going well. She knew how to soothe him and "never contradicted," she remembered. She was an efficient secretary and researcher, and, at times, a helpful critic. During their courtship Art had typed, filed, and "classified," and congenially performed other chores for Sandburg, out of admiration, and with the confidence that the work would advance Art's own literary ambitions.

"The house, large enough before her marriage, is becoming smaller, holding two families now," Helga wrote in ". . . *Where Love Begins*," her 1989 memoir. "The quarters are somewhat close for arguments, for discussions that need space for shouts, door-slammings." She saw an intensifying rivalry between her husband and her father: "The air is electric with two Bears where there was one." Once when Steichen visited Connemara he was surprised to find Art stretched out in Sandburg's favorite chair.

Paula was, as always, the buffer in the family, soothing, mediating, leavening the atmosphere with her cheerfulness. The deep, affectionate bond between Sandburg and Helga held her as close to home as their handicaps held Margaret and Janet. Helga and her father were alike in strong ego and temperament, a fierce passion for life and, now, for writing. Helga had feared that ultimately it would be impossible for her husband to live and work in her father's house, as hard as all of them tried. Loving Helga as he did, Sandburg wanted the plan to work, needed to keep his daughter and the beloved grandchildren under his roof. In the privacy of his journal, however, he put down his growing displeasure with Art:

> He worked in the fields, he worked at repairing this and that, he was a willing worker and it seemed to be a pleasure for him to be joining us in the work—until after the wedding. . . . He would keep asking me if he could help with my correspondence or copying from books or manuscripts. After the wedding he turned all of this over to Helga. And instead of writing his own letters he would dictate them to Helga. Before the marriage, when he came nearly every weekend and we often ate in the kitchen,

there was fellowship, laughter, songs . . . Meantime from month to month a fellowship that there had been between him and me began shading away into something else. He said to Paula, "This place cramps my style." He had been in and out of "this place" for 5 years when he married Helga. He had come into it by way of marriage and on his own terms. He said he believed he could make a go of the goat milk business. For 2 or 3 months he probably did give it the best that he had in him. . . .

Helga and Art finally began to talk of leaving Connemara. Art looked for a job, and Helga began to reduce the size of her Siamese cattery and reorganize other phases of the farm business so she could leave it all in her mother's hands. When Art found a teaching job in Virginia, he went on ahead to find a house for Helga and the children. He sent for them in early summer. The leave-taking was hard for John Carl and young Paula, for Connemara was all the home they remembered. "Fed up with the silences, the tensions," Helga "couldn't go soon enough," she wrote years later. Paula supported the move, saying it was good for Helga and Art and the children to have their "own set-up." Sandburg was visibly unhappy at first, cross, Helga said later. But he saw the wisdom if not the necessity of the move. He gave Helga the names of Washington friends who might help her find a job. His going-away gifts to her were a set of encyclopedias and a bottle of Jack Daniel's. Helga took her father to the train bound for some lecture destination, so he was not at home at Connemara to see them leave, the daughter whose stubborn chin and intense, bright eyes were so like his own, and the two grandchildren who had been his joy and his shadows for nearly a decade.

The grandchildren, transplanted from the fragrant wilderness of Connemara where they had grown up in idyllic freedom, had to adjust to life in a small house with a quarter-acre backyard in a Washington, D.C., suburb. Even there, Helga continued to work for her father, typing the growing manuscript of his autobiography *Always The Young Strangers* as her mother sent it up in segments from Connemara. She did occasional research for her father at the Library of Congress. In that decade of losses the hardest for Sandburg was the departure of his daughter and his grandchildren. He and Paula grieved for them, longed for their voices and faces. The gentle aunts wrote letters full of Connemara news. Margaret moved into the rooms Helga's family had used, and Paula hired farmhands to carry on the work with the goats. Later on, she hired two men with families to live on the place. One of them had two daughters, ages seven and two. "It's good to have children on the place again," she told Sandburg.

John Carl and young Paula would go back to Connemara for summer and wintertime visits at first, riding a Pullman car, exploring the train "from end to end," loving it as their Buppong had all his life. "When the engine pulled into Asheville," Paula remembered, "Gramma, Buppong and Marne [Margaret] would be assembled on the platform. . . . My excitement seemed almost unbearable as Gramma turned the car down the Little River Road and I caught sight of our white-pillared house barely visible through the trees—standing on the steeply sloping hill above the lake." Their grandfather would join them as they retraced the familiar pathways, greeting the farm animals, surveying the gardens, revisiting the moss gardens they had sculpted on the rock where Sandburg sat working on one manuscript or another. He would write them letters when they were away, with whimsical formality and deep affection, signing them "Your everloving Buppong."

He missed them keenly from the beginning, and the pain of their absence would intensify in the future. Because Helga and her children had almost always lived under their roof, Sandburg and Paula were used to being completely involved in their lives. Their interdependency made it difficult, if not impossible, for them to let go of each other. Parents, daughter, grandchildren were inextricably caught, it seemed, in a complicated web of love and need. For Sandburg it was particularly hard to see another man take his daughter and the beloved grandchildren away. "My little exiles the banished ones," he wrote in an unpublished poem:

> the heart keeps turning to them
> memory will not be still
> remembering how and what they were
> the faces and words of them—
> hope works on how and where they are—
> how they laughed and ran and slept—
> their utterly reckless singing gayety—
> their perfections of grace and manner—
> their ease and quiet at going lonely—
> to each of you I say across empty miles
> "whither goest thou little pilgrim?
> do you sometimes remember Gramma and Buppong?"

✳

Sandburg received the American Academy of Arts and Letters gold medal for history and biography in 1952, and went to New York to accept the award, which he called "bullion good at any USA mint or pawnshop." Harcourt, Brace and Company announced at about the same time the upcoming publication of Sandburg's life story, to be called *Always The*

Young Strangers, after a line from one of his poems. This "new, long-awaited work" would appear January 6, 1953, Sandburg's seventy-fifth birthday, when he would be "lifting my light feet over the 75th milestone." By late summer of 1952 the manuscript was finished, and his editor, Kitty McCarthy, traveled to Connemara to help get the final copy in order. Sandburg campaigned for Adlai Stevenson against Dwight Eisenhower in the Presidential election after conventions which, as he predicted, were "a wild night on the moors with plenty of combustibles." He himself tried to "survey the complex scene with calm and persiflage." He believed Stevenson to be the only Presidential contender who truly understood that "the next president, if he is in some degree sensitive, will live in a Golgotha."

According to newspaper accounts, 150,000 people competed for the 22,500 seats available in Madison Square Garden at an October rally for Stevenson. Eleanor Roosevelt was on the platform, with Tallulah Bankhead, Montgomery Clift, Humphrey Bogart, Lauren Bacall, Al Capp and Sandburg. He had known Stevenson for twenty-five years, and spoke eloquently on his behalf. It had been a difficult, even vicious campaign, the kind that Lincoln had known, and other politicians for whom Sandburg had sympathy. Sandburg called Stevenson "a great and a consecrated man, one more embodiment of the finest human flame out of the American past."

He spoke out for Stevenson with the same fervor he had given in 1910 to Eugene Debs, and later to FDR, in a similar Madison Square Garden rally. "From the Great Lakes to the Gulf, Adlai Stevenson sees America not in the setting sun of a black night of despair ahead of us," Sandburg concluded that October night. "He sees America in the crimson light of a rising sun."

Eisenhower's popularity swept him into office. Yet "It was all worth the time and toil," Sandburg told Stevenson afterward. "Yours is a high name now and for a long time." Stevenson would run again, and Sandburg would campaign for him as vigorously. "As for speeches and ideas you're throwing 'em straight or curved, better than ever, the best since Lincoln," he would encourage his old friend four years later.

Sandburg, Stevenson and Lloyd Lewis had shared Chicago parties during the twenties and thirties where, said Stevenson, "anecdotes, Lincoln and music took us far into the night." Sandburg took pride in the democratic spirit of the state of Illinois, whose "three great Governors were of the Catholic, Jewish, and Protestant faiths, Altgeld, Horner, and Stevenson, in order of their service." Horner and Stevenson had been his close friends, and Sandburg's loyalty to his friends was boundless.

With Horner gone, and Lewis, and Barrett, and so many others, the surviving "ancient fellowships" were precious.

The Sandburgs spent a quiet Christmas in Flat Rock, full of anticipation. John Carl and little Paula were coming to Connemara by train December 29 to spend a week. The customary wreaths were made, the house filled with holly. There was an array of traditional Christmas cookies, springerle, butter cookies, pfeffernüsse, anise, as well as chocolate and white fudge and sea foam. With the help of Ella the cook, Paula baked dense, moist fruit cakes studded with currants, white raisins, nuts, dates, cherries and pineapple. Margaret and Janet decorated the Christmas tree in the dining room with ornaments the family had collected over the years.

On Christmas Day Sandburg made a handwritten copy of his new poem, "Names," to be printed on the program for his upcoming seventy-fifth-birthday celebration in Chicago. He sent a copy to Edward and Dana Steichen, for he and Steichen were working together on the text for Steichen's most ambitious photographic exhibition yet. Steichen had asked Sandburg for a poem to accompany the landmark project, a display of pictures made by photographers around the world to show "what a wonderful thing life was, how marvelous people were, and, above all, how alike people were in all parts of the world." Steichen's exhibition of Korean War photographs had been intended to show war "in all its grimness" so that he might incite people "into taking open and united action against war itself." Now he envisioned an exhibit which would express "the oneness of the world we lived in." He found the title for the exhibit in Sandburg's Lincoln biography, in one of Lincoln's speeches—the "Family of Man."

"Nearest I have come so far to a poem on The Family of Man is this enclosure," Sandburg told Steichen and Dana in a letter that Christmas, as he waited for his grandchildren to come home to Connemara. He knew, he said, that the poem was "so damned simple and childish that I expect some people to say it runs over into the silly." "There is only one horse on the earth," it began, "and his name is All Horses."

> There is only one bird in the air
> and his name is All Wings.
> There is only one fish in the sea
> and his name is All Fins.
> There is only one man in the world
> and his name is All Men.
> There is only one woman in the world
> and her name is All Women.

There is only one child in the world
and the child's name is All Children.
There is only one Maker in the world
and His children cover the earth
and they are named All God's Children.

Back in *The People, Yes*, Sandburg had inscribed the words of Hiamovi, chief of the Cheyenne Indians:

"There are birds of many colors . . .
Yet it is all one bird.
There are horses of many colors . . .
Yet it is all one horse . . .
So men in this land, where once were only
Indians, are now men of many colors—
white, black, yellow, red.
Yet all one people . . ."

One of the first tasks Sandburg had given Helga when she moved to Virginia was to go to the Library of Congress to research the Welsh poet Taliesen. Forty years earlier Sandburg had read one of Taliesen's poems. It was on his mind as he worked on his new poem, and he sent Helga a copy of Taliesen's work. Immediately she saw the similarity to "Head One," the long poem-in-progress she had been typing for her father: "Tiller of the mountain, who is that man?—A man," Taliesen had written in the sixth century.

What tongue does he speak? —All.
What things does he know? —All.
What is his country? —None and all.
Who is his God? —God . . .

Two other poets, one Indian and one Welsh, spurred Sandburg's choice of form in "Names," but the idea of universality was one he had explored since his college days. Now he collaborated wholeheartedly with Steichen on the text for "The Family of Man." The metaphor itself would illuminate much of the work they both had yet to create.

For now, the immediate family circle was about to be restored. The prized grandchildren were on their way, and he, Paula and Margaret would be at the train station well ahead of time, to collect them and take them home again to Connemara.

✳

When Carl Sandburg turned seventy-five on January 6, 1953, his friends around the country celebrated at parties in Los Angeles, New York and

Chicago. He and Paula went to the Chicago party, given by his publishers and a host of friends at the Blackstone Hotel. Paula, who normally stayed at home, decided not to miss this special occasion. "If you can take it, I can," she told Sandburg, "and you will never have another 75th birthday and I might have regrets if I didn't go." She had not "gone to any doings," she told Helga, since the Harvard and Yale commencements in 1940 when he received honorary degrees. She would fly home just after the dinner, however, while Sandburg traveled on to Galesburg and then to New York to accept the gold medal of the Poetry Society of America.

Always the Young Strangers, released on his birthday, recounted in vivid detail the first twenty years of his life. Although it became universally popular, it is not an introspective, deeply revealing personal portrait. Instead, it is a lively document of nineteenth-century American life in the heartland. This time reviewers gave Sandburg warm affirmation. Robert Sherwood in *The New York Times* pronounced it the "best autobiography written by an American." Horace Reynolds predicted in the *Christian Science Monitor* that the book might "well prove to be the best beloved of all American biographies." It was hailed as a "many-faceted triumph," and readers and critics alike praised its simplicity and immediacy, its depiction of the warmth and dignity of "ordinary, everyday life," without apology for poverty and struggle. Sandburg was saluted for his "encompassing humanity." His forthright narrative of his boyhood was a disarmingly universal story of coming-of-age. Even readers in China and Japan later found it consonant with their own experience, despite cultural differences.

The gala birthday dinner in Chicago was the setting for a harvest of tributes. Five hundred friends gathered at the Blackstone for the party, orchestrated for Harcourt, Brace by Ralph Newman, still proprietor of the Abraham Lincoln Bookshop and Sandburg's occasional companion on lecture trips and Lincoln quests. The Sponsoring Committee for the celebration included Fanny Butcher, J. Frank Dobie, Harry Hansen, Lloyd Lewis's widow Kathryn, Alfred MacArthur, Robert Sherwood and Eugene Reynal. Lincoln scholars attended, along with journalists, Galesburg citizens, and Quincy Wright, son of Sandburg's college professor and mentor Philip Green Wright, who had died in 1934. Close friends, including his brother-in-law Steichen and historian Allan Nevins, joined Sandburg and Paula at the speakers' table. President Truman sent a tribute, as did writers, politicians, journalists, musicians, people from the wide circumference of Sandburg's life. Governor Stevenson proclaimed Carl Sandburg Day in Illinois, and delivered an eloquent salute to Sandburg at the dinner. "Carl Sandburg is to me the one living man who in his life and in his work epitomizes the American dream," Stevenson said. "Congratulations old man—congratulations *old* man," Robert Frost wrote. "Seventy five years is quite an achievement though nothing of course compared with what you have done for us in prose and verse. . . . Keep grandly on." Swedish king Gustav VI Adolf, through his U.S. ambassador, made Sandburg a Commander in the Order of the North Star. Paula watched proudly as her husband accepted these honors. Steichen took liberties with some lines by poet James Whitcomb Riley in his tribute to Sandburg, saying, "When God made Carl, he didn't do nothing else that day but just sit around and feel good."

When Sandburg took the microphone, he was his exuberant, irascible, outspoken self, expressing his opinions on American movies, literature, television and politics. He stood before his friends in a new black double-breasted suit with "an incongruous blue tie with shiny golden triangles on it" and reflected on the significance of this birthday. "I don't know why I came along here tonight," he mused. "And I thought there would be difficulty about it. I was saying to the Missus yesterday that perhaps the first thing I would say to you good people here tonight would be that at age 65 it would be very hard to take an evening like this. At 55 it would be impossible. At 45 unthinkable. But at 75 when you can see the flickering crimson rays of the sunset—ah, it's not so hard." Thinking back to his long struggle for poetic identity, Sandburg concluded that a "certain amount of recognition or approval or even applause—a certain amount is all right." Yet he thought it was not such a bad thing to have to wait for it. "But I have seen young fellows wrecked in their twenties and thirties on account of it—the recognition, approval and applause. A certain amount of swimming against the stream in youth is good and healthy and natural."

Later, at a press conference, the Sandburgs talked to reporters from newspapers, radio and television. "Mrs. Sandburg, does he talk about his books before he writes them?" one reporter wanted to know.

"Well, he certainly has talked this last book long before he wrote it, not only to our families but I'm sure to all of his friends."

"About half the book I would bring down to the dinner table and read to my grandchildren," Sandburg added, "and they would say, 'more, more.'" He expounded on his literary views, calling Robert Frost "a fine poet most of the time," and admiring the fact that Frost's poems were read by "strong men, farmers, thieves and deacons—and not by little cliques."

"I say to hell with the new poetry," Sandburg said when asked. "They don't want poetry to say what it means. They have symbols and abstractions and a code amongst themselves—sometimes I think it's a series of ear wigglings." He did not mean to suggest that poetry should not have "the quality of mystery," he said. "Readers of poetry are entitled to mystery. And as for abstractions, the Declaration of Independence has a few worth looking at. But this new bunch—if you write a line that means what it says you are in bad, you don't belong."

There was an undercurrent of poetry in *Always The Young Strangers*, and a deceptive simplicity. Sandburg had feared as he began the book that it would "make melancholy reading," but its straightforward treatment of his prairie boyhood was essentially an affirmation of the American Dream. Robert Sherwood wrote that Sandburg had, "By striving to tell no more than an intensely personal story," achieved "the universality of a 'Pilgrim's Progress.' " Sherwood noted that Sandburg had lived the kind of life that "could have turned another sensitive boy into an embittered cynic or a wrecker, but Carl Sandburg registers no grievances; he expresses incessant gratitude for the goodness and kindness that he met with everywhere."

"I have an album of faces in my memory," Sandburg reflected, "faces that were a comfort." As he captured these faces, he drew a graphic portrait of the American experience as it had shaped his life. Many readers pressed him for another volume to carry his story forward from his twenty-first year. "If I live I'll do some kind of sequel to *Always The Young Strangers*," he responded. "Lord knows what it will be like. I'm still groping."

He most definitely did not want a biography written about him while he was living. Yet he was ready to return to biography himself. He recognized that he could not work the long hours he used to, but he wanted to produce a one-volume biography of Abraham Lincoln. Sandburg had been forty-eight when he finished the first two Lincoln volumes, and sixty-one when he wrote the final pages of the sixth. At seventy-five, having contemplated his own personal history, he wanted to turn once again to Lincoln, to "shape out the book that might become widely known as an indispensable classic 1-volume biography of Lincoln." He set to work on what he called a "distillation" of the massive six-volume Lincoln biography, taking into account the new scholarship which had emerged since *The Prairie Years* appeared in 1926 and *The War Years* in 1939.

He was determined not to turn out "a cramped and cryptic summation" of Lincoln's life. He and Catherine McCarthy, his "good right arm," set to work on the project. He kept at it despite illness—influenza and "minor ailments that demanded time and attention," and some medical treatment by his friend and physician Arthur "Jim" Freese in Chicago. Disciplined as ever, he stuck to the work. "I am trying to *UN*write the 6-vol Lincoln into 1-vol," he told novelist Kenneth Dodson. Sandburg hoped by the fall of 1954 to have a "real finished and polished One-Vol Life of Mister Linkern Hisself." The work was strenuous, intense, but it gave Sandburg "solace" and "companionship." "Unwriting" the Lincoln biography immersed Sandburg in a "refresher course" in Lincoln, and, he exulted, Lincoln "kept growing on me."

By summer, deep into the work, Sandburg suffered recurrent dizzy spells. His doctors told him six to eight hours of work a day was too much. He slowed down to three or four hours daily, yet made steady progress. He worked on through the bright mountain summer, looking forward to the arrival of his grandchildren for a few weeks' reunion. "Connemara is lovely as ever," Paula had written to Helga, "but we miss you and especially the children's voices and presences! We hope summer vacation will bring you and the young visitors! No harm in hoping for a long visit—remembering all the shared years." When Helga let her parents know that the children would come to Connemara for three weeks, the Sandburgs rejoiced. "Going to be rich and gorgeous to see you here in July," Sandburg wrote his grandson. "People, animals, trees, plants, fishes and birds, count the days till you come. Buppong."

He wrote a new poem for his granddaughter as a gift for her tenth birthday. "Second Sonata for Karlen Paula" said in part:

> Try standing in the sun, telling your shadow
> "I like you much—you never fail me . . ."
>
> Be jungle dark in your heart
> and then find the black moonlight
> of a silence holding your soft voice;
> "Sleep and peace always wash my heart."

With the grandchildren back in residence, Connemara seemed complete, almost a paradise, with Paula the heart. "Paula is a wonder in all ways as a helpmeet," Sandburg told Alfred Harcourt. "She is steadily reducing the herd but so long as she stays ambulant she will be breeding goats as her brother does delphiniums: it is a genius with her and the goat industry idolizes her for her knowledge and lighted enthusiasms." In Paula's gardens there were zinnias, delphiniums, roses, marigolds, flowers everywhere. Lush vegetables went in abundance from the garden to the dinner table in the cool dining room, or, preserved, into neat jars in the cellar. Janet worked hard in the house and gardens, and at the barn grooming the goat kids for frequent goat shows. Paula gave her a new outfit to wear when, proudly, she led the kids into the show ring. Janet was thirty-seven years old that summer, happily absorbed in Connemara life. Knowing as they did that Janet would always be dependent, the Sandburgs had set up a Social Security account for her, regularly paid her a salary and paid all the required fees and taxes. Janet kept a factual diary of daily affairs at Connemara: "Dad left on the train at three for New York. The sun is shining today. It is nice out." In her childlike handwriting there is a litany of departures and arrivals, dinner guests, weather reports, baseball scores, news about the birthing of kids, the deaths of does or bucks, the consequences of the mountain goat shows she attended with her mother.

"I love this place," she told her father, "and hope we never move from it." She worked endlessly, enthusiastically tending to goats, chickens, gardens, buttermaking, going to sleep early in the fragrant mountain night, and rising before dawn to begin again.

Margaret, the brilliant semi-invalid, could not match her parents or siblings in physical stamina, but she tried hard, working all day in one of the summer flower gardens, tiring, but keeping at it and, according to her mother, showing more endurance than she had in years, and enjoying "all keenly."

"Margaret has become widely read," Sandburg told Harcourt, "a scholar who often surprises me with her erudition, knows the Bible and Shakespeare better than I do." She was her father's reliable librarian, keeping order amidst the seeming chaos of his books and files.

That idyllic summer of 1953, Sandburg lived with Lincoln, and with the family he cherished. He and Paula had been married for forty-five years. Margaret, now forty-two, was their scholar and companion. Her epilepsy could be controlled most of the time by medication. Home, family, books, music, the serene outdoors filled her life. Like her parents, she was avidly outspoken on political matters which stirred her. Gentle Janet was their farmer, and a constant source of cheer. Helga was their rebel, struggling to find herself, to bring up her children, to make her marriage work, to fulfill her own artistic drive. She would join them for a coveted week in August. Meantime, the grandchildren were theirs again.

They roamed the Connemara acres until dusk, ate heartily from the good, simple food that came from their grandmother's kitchen, caught up on all the changes in the goat herd, and slept deeply at night in the small front room on the third floor, still called the Crow's Nest for its wide mountain overlook. They begged their Buppong to sleep with them there, and he cheerfully obliged, settling down on one of the narrow cots at their nine-thirty bedtime, and slipping away when they fell asleep. Young Paula plucked bouquets of flowers that summer, especially the vivid zinnias with their ragged, neon faces. Sandburg celebrated the summer and the flowers in a new poem for his grandchildren, "Zinnia Sonata":

> . . . I have heard zinnias couseling together:
> "Ever the summer is kind to us,
> summer belonging to us as we belong to summer.
> When God said, 'Let there be summer'
> He also said, 'And let there be zinnias
> bathed in colors called from sunsets and early stars' . . ."

✳

Too soon for all of them, Helga and the children had to board the train for the trip back to Washington and Virginia. John Carl had befriended a "large noisy" frog who resided in the Connemara pool. They named him Archimedes. Soon after his departure, Sandburg wrote his grandson a note: "I miss you very much and so do the salamanders and we hope to see you next summer." He signed it "Archimedes."

"If it can be done it is not a bad practice for a man of many years to die with a boy heart," Sandburg had written at the end of *Always The Young Strangers*. His own boy heart was very much alive, and he shared it exuberantly with his grandchildren, delighting in their bright minds, their physical beauty, their sweetness and play. It was hard for the Sandburgs to give them up again. The old house, pristine in the sun, seemed empty without them. The gardens and meadows were too quiet without their shouts and laughter. For weeks, the Sandburgs found mementos of the children, their grandmother said. The four inhabitants of Connemara returned to a more sedate rhythm as summer waned. Sandburg lost himself in the Lincoln work, but looked up now and again to write to Helga and her children. "Dear Snick," he wrote to young Paula that autumn.

> You have on occasion a vehement, picturesque and eloquent flow of speech. I suspect that Shakespeare must have known some young lady somewhat like yourself who as a rebuff to one who had spoken a vile slander, let fly the three words:
> "Filth, thou liest!"
> I send this to you as merely the impression of a moment and a small oddity

that might interest you and to say again pax vobiscum and may the good
Lord guide your footsteps in righteous paths and may you often, if not
ever, do what your deepest clean heart tells you to do.

Buppong

Sandburg sent Helga sheets of Lincoln manuscript to type, paying her
a dollar a page. She worked quickly and mailed the typescript back to
him with praise, finding the new work "positively magnificent, enthralling." He was crafting "The Head One," his ambitious new poem,
reflecting on the universality of life. The text raised poignant questions,
as if he were considering how best to use the remaining years of his
creative life. "I am more than a traveler out of Nowhere," the poet
wrote.

> Sea and land, sky and air, begot me Somewhere.
> Where I go from here and now, or if I go at all
>   again, the Maker of sea and land, of sky and
>   air, can tell.

He concentrated on biography and new poetry till year's end, and then
paused to enjoy the holidays. John Carl and young Paula were coming
back December 27. "Whatever Xmas dreaming we do, is of those precious
days," Paula wrote to Helga of the upcoming visit, and paid for their
train tickets gladly. "Of course, all here are most happy to have the
children with us, lighting up the house. It is really Christmas now!"

✻

The New Year found Sandburg "slugging away" at the one-volume Lincoln. Not only did he want to weave new material and insights into his
Lincoln portrait, he wanted to produce a book which was within the
reach of the general audience, the people for whom he had always written.
"Lincoln was a man of the people," many readers had said to him. "Why
should his life story be told in a book so long that most people don't
have time to read it, and, furthermore, in a book that is financially out
of reach of the common people?"

Kitty McCarthy spent time with him at Connemara working on the
new volume. Sandburg had deep respect and affection for his hard-
working editor, and loved to tease her, deliberately inserting paragraphs
he knew she would cut. At the end of their work, Sandburg gave Harcourt, Brace a manuscript that ran to 430,000 words.

His *Lincoln Preface*, written thirty years earlier but not used until
now, appeared that February in a limited edition to announce the

one-volume Lincoln. The *Preface* was widely reprinted in newspapers on Lincoln's birthday, and Sandburg read it on an ABC Television simulcast. One television reviewer wrote that "the half-hour turned prose into poetry, a TV show into an occasion and a simple scribe into a saint." The editors of the *Saturday Review of Literature* invited Sandburg to read the preface for their series of recordings by noteworthy individuals. His Lincoln Preface filled one side, and excerpts from *The War Years* and *The People, Yes* filled the other. His voice, like his face, was an American landmark.

Sandburg delivered the manuscript for the one-volume Lincoln to Harcourt, Brace himself, carrying it in a bulging leather portfolio. He did not know, he said, whether it was more difficult to be "a writer or an unwriter." He acknowledged that he could not have produced the new book without the help of many people, chief among them Kitty McCarthy. He leaned on her heavily as his "ambassador, negotiator and EDITOR."

Sandburg and Alfred Harcourt celebrated the advent of the one-volume Lincoln, for their Lincoln gamble nearly three decades earlier had paid off handsomely for both of them, financially and otherwise. They had been intimate friends as well as collaborators. Harcourt was much more to Sandburg than "a good and grand book publisher." Harcourt was not to see the new book in print, however, for he died June 21, 1954, at the age of seventy-three. Sandburg would dedicate his one-volume Lincoln "To the departed friends" whose knowledge and fellowship had animated so much of his Lincoln journey—Lloyd Lewis, Oliver Barrett, Steven Vincent Benét, James Randall, Douglas Southall Freeman and Alfred Harcourt, "whose shadows linger and whose fellowship endures."

Sandburg went to the West Coast in January 1954 for another grand tour. On January 30 he addressed a sold-out house at the Philharmonic Auditorium in Los Angeles, giving them songs, stories, opinions, the familiar, jocular one-man show. Ventriloquist Edgar Bergen introduced him to a standing ovation.

On the night of his Philharmonic performance in Los Angeles, Sandburg hoped to see for the first time in more than a half century one of the Galesburg faces which had lived in his memory, "faces that were a comfort." He had written about his old friend Theresa Anawalt in *Always The Young Strangers*: "My eyes would be on her walk and the ways of her head and shoulders long before we met and passed by each other," he remembered in his autobiography.

As she came closer, my eyes fed on the loveliness of her face. I'm sure her face is there in certain Irish ballads of wild fighting over such a face. . . . It wasn't with me a case of love at first sight or the hundredth sight. It just happened that I found her wonderful to look at, a mysteriously beautiful young woman with a sad and strange mouth. We didn't speak to each other there and then on that sidewalk in that block in the Fifth Ward—nor ever afterward. . . . And if this stray item about her should meet her eye, she can't say I've forgotten her.

When Theresa Anawalt read these words she wrote to Sandburg at Harcourt, Brace from Glendale, California. She was there at the Philharmonic that night, and sent a note to Sandburg backstage. "You'd better be good!" she told him. "I'm here in the eleventh row, aisle seat, with ears and eyes alert. I'll come back and see you after the program and when we look at each other after all these years we'll say, 'Well, here we are again!' " Sandburg waited, but she did not come. He found her by telephone later, and thus exchanged his first words with the long-remembered Theresa Anawalt. She had tried to reach him, she said, but he was surrounded by people, and she had given up and gone home.

As Sandburg left the theater that night with friends, bound for a party given in his honor by the Swedish-American Society, a beautiful elderly woman watched him pass, surrounded by people. She was close enough to touch him lightly. Friends who knew the Theresa Anawalt story noticed her, saw her tearful smile, and wondered if she might be the Galesburg girl who had lived in Sandburg's album of memories.

Losses and memories fed a growing loneliness in him, and he brooded about it. The crowds and the celebrity could not assuage it. Usually cordial and jovial with the press, he could be short-tempered then. "Why should I be interviewed?" he snorted when he was besieged by Los Angeles reporters on that winter's trip. "I had enough of that sort of thing in Chicago at my birthday celebration. What do they think I am, a prophet, an elder statesman? Should I know whether we are likely to be attacked by atomic bombs? Who do I think is the most promising young writer in America today? Have I got to decide that? Jesus wept!"

He talked to journalist Ralph McGill about loneliness during a summertime walk at Connemara. "A man must get away now and then to experience loneliness," Sandburg said. "Only those who learn how to live with loneliness can come to know themselves and life. I go out there and walk and look at the trees and sky. I listen to the sounds of loneliness. I sit on a rock or a stump and say to myself, 'Who are you, Sandburg? Where have you been, and where are you going?' "

He had work left to do, poems to finish, an important new project to share with Steichen. He mourned for Harcourt, the absent grandchildren, the inexorable passage of time. He repeated the familiar adage: "The Chinese have a saying that after 70 a man is like a candle in the wind," he told Ralph McGill, "but sometimes the winds are soft . . . and if, when a man comes to die, he has a boy's heart, is that a bad thing?"

✳

1954–1956

29. The Family of Man

Here are . . . the loved and the unloved, the lonely and
abandoned, the brutal and the compassionate—one big
family hugging close to the ball of Earth for its life and
being. . . . A camera testament, a drama of the grand
canyon of humanity, an epic woven of fun, mystery and
holiness—here is the Family of Man!

—Carl Sandburg, Prologue, *The Family of Man*, 1955

"The man not having his moods of lamentations in these days is
not alive and registering to the scenes around him," Sandburg
wrote in 1954. In the "national and international whirl of
events," he wondered "if there is a smell to the political weather that I
have known before: I get to wondering if I will see the Third World
War." The national paranoia spawned by the McCarthy hearings painfully resurrected the past—the Red Scare after World War I, the "tangled
mass of blunders and corruption" in the Civil War era. Sandburg remembered the Union general who wrote to his wife in 1864, "May God
save my country—if there is a God—and if I have a country."

The Sandburgs, like the nation, watched, riveted, as Edward R. Murrow took unprecedented, courageous and careful aim at Joseph McCarthy
on the March 9 broadcast of "See It Now." "It was a week of overwhelming excitement and anxiety for the Murrow people and CBS
management—not knowing what McCarthy would do next," Joe
Wershba of Murrow's staff remembered. "The tension was relieved somewhat Friday night. . . . Murrow was all smiles, even proud-faced. He
unfolded a telegram from his old friend and admirer, Carl Sandburg. The
message was pure Sandburg: 'There's a lot wrong with America, Ed, but
it ain't you.' "

Murrow and Fred Friendly of CBS came to Connemara in the late
summer of 1954 to film an episode of their innovative television news

631

show. "See It Now" had been created in 1951 after the success of "Hear It Now" on radio. Murrow, born in North Carolina, was at home in the Blue Ridge Mountains. He and Sandburg sat on the front porch at Connemara imbibing the view, drinking goat's milk, filling tape recorders with their talk. They tramped the Connemara trails talking in the way of two old friends, seemingly impervious to the television crew with their cameras and microphones. The show, which aired October 5 on the eve of the appearance of the one-volume Lincoln biography, was a recapitulation of Sandburg's career. The opening shot focused on the twenty-eight books Sandburg had published since 1916.

To Murrow's question about why he had spent so much time on Lincoln, Sandburg said, "Oh, the straight-off simplest answer to that is because he was such good company." Murrow asked him to name "the worst word in the English language." "The one word more detestable than any other in the English language is the word 'exclusive,' " Sandburg retorted, elongating the word for emphasis. "Exclusive—when you're exclusive, you shut out a more or less large range of humanity from your mind and heart—from your understanding of them." Sandburg took on contemporary poets, the cerebral poetry which was written "right out of the brain, with nothing of the blood in it, and it's rather pathetic. You need footnotes, and you need diagrams."

When Murrow asked Sandburg whether he wanted to be known as a poet, biographer or historian, Sandburg said without hesitation, "I'd rather be known as a man who says, 'What I need mainly is three things in life, possibly four: To be out of jail, to eat regular, to get what I write printed, and then a little love at home and a little outside.' Those four things, and I don't need to be called either poet, historian, biographer, guitar player, folksinger, minnesinger . . . novelist."

Murrow and his crew interviewed Paula and her granddaughter at the barn with the goats. No, she was not tired of living with Abraham Lincoln for so many years, Paula said with a smile. She found Lincoln "a very lovable character," and her husband had grown more like Lincoln through the years, "and more understanding. He wasn't so understanding when a young man as he is now." She observed that her husband had always "worked for himself, for his own ideal," and he never considered anything else but "what he personally would consider a good book . . . and he would write if there were no one to read."

Hearing Sandburg speak of the enduring, "abiding" Lincoln, Murrow and Friendly began to call him the "Great Abider." When he visited them at CBS in New York, he often overstayed his welcome, lingering until almost air time for Murrow's evening news broadcast. Murrow would get Friendly on the phone and ask him to come get the "Great Abider." "He was a folksinger in motion," Friendly remembered, "a poet, an historian, a lover of America. Like his resonant voice, his life and work resonated with the American experience."

Sandburg and Murrow spoke soberly on and off camera about the problems confronting the world of the fifties. "Most inscrutable world scene that there ever was," Sandburg said. "There never has been a time that there were not clouds upon the horizon in this country and there was one crisis after another that could be named: in the Colonial times, in the American Revolution, and that Civil War—the like of which almost no other country has ever had. And then the two world wars. Over and over again it has looked as though we were sunk as a nation." Citing examples, Sandburg turned to Lincoln's words about a deceptive, incompetent Union Army general, who was, Lincoln told John Hay, "like Jim Jett's brother. Jim used to say that his brother was the damnedest scoundrel that ever lived, but in the infinite mercy of Providence, he was also the damnedest fool. And that," concluded Sandburg, "will go for the demagogues of nearly every generation in American history. And that's that."

Beneath the placid façade of the 1950s there was global turbulence, a chaos of "isms"—Communism, Stalinism, McCarthyism, nationalism. The postwar economic boom in America set loose, as *Fortune* magazine had noted, "a powerful consuming demand for everything that one can eat, wear, enjoy, read, repair, paint, drink, see, ride, taste and rest in." The Cold War and the frightening new Atomic Peril parented a historic worldview and, in the United States, a vital sense of global interaction and responsibility.

An inevitable part of that global perspective was the search-and-destroy mission aimed at enemies, particularly communists, as epitomized by the Russians, recent allies in World War II. Stalin's Iron Curtain might be impenetrable by Western democracy, but his agents could blend into the great, fluid freedom of American society, and did so, despite the McCormack Act of 1938, the Hatch Act of 1939, the Smith Act of 1940 and Harry Truman's Executive Order 9835 in 1946, which allowed inquiry into the political history and philosophy of federal employees. Alger Hiss, Julius and Ethel Rosenberg, Whittaker Chambers, Morton Sobell and other names struck fear in the hearts of loyal Americans. When Senator Joseph McCarthy of Wisconsin had announced in Wheeling, West Virginia, back in 1950 that there were 205 known communists working in the U.S. State Department, the nation was galvanized in the hunt for communists at the doorstep. Seventy-eight percent of Americans polled in 1954 were convinced that it was important to report to the FBI anyone, relative, friend or acquaintance, who was suspected of being a communist or consorting with communists and/or their organizations.

For the most part, Sandburg was uncharacteristically silent in public about "this colossal human drama that shifts in multiple mirrors every day." The old poet and politician, chronicler of the long, weary march of the People, observed with resignation, not even a muted protest, that man was a slow learner, heedless of his past. In his poem "Man the Moon Shooter," he traced the "progress" from the "fights of man from club and sling/to the pink mushroom of Hiroshima," concluding that, "for the looking and listening Family of Man,/ever the prophets are a dime a dozen/and man goes on a moon shooter."

Sandburg's most significant public statement during the mid-fifties appeared in the Prologue to *The Family of Man*, the book based on Steichen's photographic exhibition which would open at the Museum of Modern Art in 1955. Sandburg and Steichen shared a humanitarian vision which transcended politics. They wanted to make a universal statement that would reach the world community. It was for Steichen "the most important undertaking" of his career. "My first concept was in the direction of human rights," he said, "but I soon realized that this also had negative implications. And, at that time, the subject of human rights was becoming an international political football. The real need was for an expression of the oneness of the world we lived in." He had found the "all-embracing theme" for the exhibition in Sandburg's Lincoln biography.

Steichen had always been a "severe" editor when he and Sandburg collaborated, and he was no different this time. Sandburg wrote more than one draft before Steichen was satisfied. "The Family of Man has been created in a passionate spirit of devoted love and faith in man," Steichen said. He conceived the exhibition "as a mirror of the universal elements and emotions in the everydayness of life—as a mirror of the essential oneness of mankind throughout the world."

Back in the spring of 1954, Steichen had gone to Connemara to rest and work for a few days, and to help Paula celebrate her seventy-first birthday. He arrived "looking tired—left rejuvenated," Paula told Helga in a letter. He "conspired with Ella [the cook] to get a Birthday Cake for me May 1st, baked by Ella and decorated with Dogwood blossoms and candles galore by E.J.! He kept the cake in his room!"

The "Family of Man" exhibition was for the Sandburgs and the Steichens a testament to long-held views. Sandburg's poem "Names" ended the Prologue, almost archaically simplistic in those Cold War days of suspicions, subterfuge, curtains and walls:

> There is only one man in the world
> and his name is All Men.
> There is only one woman in the world
> and her name is All Women.
> There is only one child in the world
> and the child's name is All Children.

✳

When Ernest Hemingway won the Nobel Prize for literature in 1954, he was asked to name other writers to whom he, if he were a judge, might give the award. He listed Mark Twain, Henry James, Isak Dinesen, Bernard Berenson, and Sandburg. "I would have been most happy to know that the prize had been awarded to Carl Sandburg," he said. "YOUR UNPRECEDENTED COMMENT ON THE AWARD DEEPLY APPRECIATED & UNDERSTOOD IF ONLY AS FELLOWSHIP BETWEEN TWO ILLINOIS BOYS," Sandburg telegraphed him. "One result of your warm-hearted and record-breaking comment is that you have sent Hemingway readers to Sandburg and Sandburg readers to Hemingway," he wrote to Hemingway that December. "The [New Orleans] *Times-Picayune* printed a letter from a bird saying we're both lousy."

"I got quite a kick out of Hemingway's giving you the Nobel prize," Sandburg's friend Carl Haverlin told him. "If he hadn't been so broke I guess he would have refused it in your behalf."

Sandburg passed along that remark, and sent the Hemingways some of his books, affectionately inscribed. They were still recuperating from injuries from two plane crashes in Africa. "When some books arrive to your four hands I want Mary to hold Always The Young Strangers a half-a minute against the healed ribs," Sandburg wrote. "And that will do for now—with prayers that the healing goes well and fast and the old working strengths come back in full flow and stride."

Sandburg was very much in the national eye that year, with the October exposure on "See It Now," the Hemingway publicity and the attention to *Abraham Lincoln: The Prairie Years and The War Years*, his new one-volume edition. "The cruellest thing that has happened to Lincoln since he was shot by Booth has been to fall into the hands of Carl Sandburg," Edmund Wilson later wrote in *Patriotic Gore* (1962). It was an unfair commentary. Sandburg conscientiously integrated new Lincoln scholarship into the text of the one-volume Lincoln which was skillfully pared from 3,309 pages to 742, supported by an essay including sources and acknowledgments. Historians and critics alike reviewed the book favorably when it appeared in 1954. It was Sandburg's last major book project. His remaining publications were compilations of earlier work, or, in the case of *Honey and Salt* (1963), a collection of poems, many of them begun years earlier, assembled with the help of Paula and his editor. He worked off and on for several years on a second autobiographical volume, which he tentatively called *Ever the Winds of Chance*, but the unfinished manuscript languished among his papers long after his death, until its publication in 1983.

Sandburg opened the Library of Congress Poetry Series that fall, and Archibald MacLeish wrote from Harvard about another award in Sandburg's harvest of honors. "How would you like to get $500 and your travelling expenses and be able to see me, all at once?" MacLeish asked.

> Boston has a thing called an Arts Festival—you know nothing about festivals but you know all about art—at which they give a poetry prize for the biggest and the mostest, and you are it for June 1955. All you would have to do would be to show up here, let me feed you and oil you, and then go in to Boston Common where you would read some of your poems to an audience that would probably run between 5,000 and 10,000. Oh, and one more thing—under the terms of the grant the honored poet is requested either to write a poem for the occasion, as one does for those Phi Beta Kappa poems, or to read a poem not previously read or published. I assume you would rather do the latter, but there is certainly no law against the former.

"Don't put this letter in the wood bin with the goats," MacLeish cautioned, knowing Sandburg's propensity to take his time about answering his mail, "since I need to have an answer sometime within the next millennium." Sandburg accepted immediately. "To say a poem for a crowd gathered on Boston Common would be something to tell the grandchildren about." At year's end the National Arts Foundation named four outstanding international artists for 1954—cellist Pablo Casals, British sculptor Sir Joseph Epstein, French artist Georges Roualt, and American writer Carl Sandburg. He enjoyed the crest of national and international recognition of his work.

Unknown to Sandburg, there were dark undercurrents in that sea of visibility and approbation, not surprising in the prolonged wake of the McCarthy witch hunt. For some indecipherable reason, there was a request to the FBI "To furnish pertinent information concerning Carl Sandburg." Sandburg's FBI file dated back to 1918 and the Borodin episode, one of the oldest Bureau files. In the 1950s it still contained the mistaken allegations that Sandburg was a communist, stemming from the confusion of his identity with that of Dr. Karl F. M. Sandberg. The file had been updated over the years to include newspaper and other sources linking Sandburg to various activities which, given the retrospective alarm of the McCarthy era, were circumspect. The November 1954 report, "unclassified" in 1984, recapitulated the Sandburg information in Bureau files:

> The following information was furnished the State Department in March, 1952:
>
> "Files of this Bureau (line censored) that the name of Carl Sandburg was listed in 1939 as a sponsor of the Veterans of the Abraham Lincoln Brigade. This organization has been cited by the Attorney General as an organization coming within the purview of Executive Order 9835." [Sometimes called the Loyalty Order, and the basis of authority for the Attorney General's List. This order was revoked in part by Executive Order 10450 in 1953.]

The report included a synopsis of other allegedly dangerous activities:

> Washington Times-Herald article dated November 26, 1942, reflects that "2,600 in Chicago Applaud Chaplin Praise of Russia." Charles Chaplin and Carl Sandburg spoke at a meeting at which "our Russian ally" was saluted. The article reflects that Carl Sandburg, poet, stated, that to the outside world Russia had been "immense, chaotic, foglike," but that "now we are acquainted with Russian courage through the most tremendous epic of war that has ever taken place in the shadows and shambles of Stalingrad."

While there was no official "investigation" of Sandburg at that time, the cryptic information in his FBI file, stripped from context, left a lingering shadow. When Sandburg "praised 'Russian courage' in World War II," the Soviets were, after all, allies. The Chicago meeting in November 1942 was sponsored at Orchestra Hall by three hundred "leading Chicagoans." Data on the communist Karl Sandberg remained in Carl Sandburg's file. Marginal notes on certain pages indicate that an FBI staff member questioned the discrepancy between Sandburg and Sandberg, but their merged identities were never clarified.

Oblivious to all this, Sandburg nonetheless began to have some apprehension about going forward with his autobiography. The atmosphere of the 1950s did not encourage resurrection of the socialist idealism he had espoused at the turn of the century. He sent Kitty McCarthy various notes and drafts "from my subterranean cavern of skulls, memoranda, miscellany, monkey business." "Very tentatively I wonder about *Ever the Winds of Chance* to follow *Always The Young Strangers*," he said. ". . . Hell, we dont have to think up a title till we get the doggone book written."

✳

No public honor pleased Sandburg more than having a school named for him. Over the years, more than two dozen Carl Sandburg Schools were christened in his honor. He was there in person for the dedication of Carl Sandburg High School at La Grange and 131st Street in Chicago in the fall of 1954. He was beginning to curtail such appearances, however. He asked Louise Eaton, his lecture agent, to notify people "that I am now 77 and am taking a very limited number of platform engagements" to be determined by "the factors of health, time and certain inexorable work commitments."

He had made a startling discovery about the relatively new medium of television in 1954 when he had been paid five thousand dollars to read his *Lincoln Preface* on Lincoln's birthday. "Fifteen minutes of TV are just as remunerative as and far less wearing than lecture programs all over the country," he exclaimed—and began to favor television appearances over the platform events which had provided much of his bread-and-butter income as well as his audience exposure for nearly fifty years. With television he could widen his audience as well as conserve energy and time. In New York to work on "The Family of Man" that winter, he paid what was supposed to be a short visit to Steve Allen's "Tonight" show, broadcast live on NBC. Sandburg liked Allen and his audience so much that he declined to leave when his guest stint was over, almost displacing actor Charles Coburn, Allen's other guest that night. Allen, Coburn and Sandburg closed the show with a rendition of "Home on the Range" in three-part harmony. "You've made me feel at home here," Sandburg told Allen appreciatively. "I feel I have friends out there in the dark." Sandburg's ad-lib remarks, said Allen, "had the control room in a panic."

An old hand at radio, Sandburg sat for a long interview with John Henry Faulk for his CBS Radio program. Unfortunately, CBS sound engineers failed to preserve the mellow voice and the crisp opinions which would have gone out to CBS listeners on Sandburg's seventy-seventh birthday on January 6, 1955. When Faulk found out that his crew had lost the prized tape, he talked with Sandburg about doing another interview. Sandburg declined, but he asked Faulk to promote "The Family of Man," about to open at the Museum of Modern Art. "Johnny, you're there on the radio in New York," he drawled over the telephone from Flat Rock. "You can influence people. My brother-in-law's having a show at the Museum of Modern Art—'The Family of Man.' He's a genius. It'll enlarge people's lives to see this show. You urge 'em to go. Tell 'em Carl Sandburg told you to do it."

In March, Sandburg appeared again on Dave Garroway's "Today" program. Afterward, reading bundles of letters and telegrams from viewers, he told Garroway, "Everybody was pleased though some had certain mild demurrers." He was a consummate showman, as much at home on television as on the lecture platform. He knew how to work a crowd, to reach out to those "friends in the dark." Sandburg was an actor whose best role was his own persona. Sometime during that period he looked on as his friend Thomas Hart Benton painted a portrait of folk singer Burl Ives, who was playing in Tennessee Williams's *Cat on a Hot Tin Roof.*

"Ives has a good chin," Sandburg said. "I wonder why he covers it with that beard?"

"For the same reason that you let your hair flop down over your forehead," Ives replied. "Because you're a ham—and so am I."

✳

Sandburg was highly visible in 1955, thanks to television, newspapers and his collaboration with Steichen on the text for "The Family of Man" exhibition. Paula joined her husband and brother in New York for the opening of the show on January 24. She was glad to get away from Connemara briefly. She decided at the last minute that she could leave the farm for three days in New York, but did not go to see Helga and her family in Washington. For the first time ever, Helga's children had not spent Christmas at Connemara. "I thought of trying for a short visit with you," she wrote Helga later, "but I decided against risking another day as Margaret's vitality was low and I feared she might neglect taking her medicine regularly which could lead to real trouble. Margaret has not had a seizure for over a year—I felt I had taken enough chances with being away 3 days. Of course I would have loved to see you and the children. But I know you are all well—and it's *here* that I'm really needed."

The Sandburgs and Ed and Dana Steichen had adjoining rooms at the Gotham Hotel. "A great show it is!" Paula exulted after she saw "The Family of Man." That was one of the last visits the Steichens and Sandburgs would enjoy together. Later, when a journalist asked Paula how it was to be married to a genius, she replied that she had a husband and a brother who were geniuses. "I don't see anything crochety in either one of them," she said. "The time a man is difficult is before he's found himself."

As they celebrated the public success of "The Family of Man," the Sandburgs confronted new tensions in their private family life. Leaving Helga and the children in Washington, Art stayed temporarily with his parents in Brooklyn while he tried to establish himself as a television actor. He found small roles, but decided to ask his famous father-in-law to "open some doors for him." When Art telephoned Sandburg at his New York hotel that January, Sandburg told him he was too busy to visit. Art was "enraged and insulted," Helga wrote later. Sandburg resented the "loss" of his beloved grandchildren and his youngest daughter. Helga, beginning to feel restless in her second marriage, had to juggle husband, children, parents, work. Art wanted her to relinquish her government job and do typing at home. He gave up his New York quest and returned to Washington to begin a novel. According to Helga, they had "loud and lordly fights," and he did not want her or her children to communicate with the family at Connemara.

Helga would write candidly about her estrangement from her father in her 1989 memoir, ". . . *Where Love Begins*," and indirectly in some of her fiction. The bitter, often painful silence which lay between them grew not only out of their differences but out of their fundamental kinship. Helga was strong yet vulnerable. Bred deep in the bone were the pride, the stubbornness, the fierce, independent sense of self, and the hunger for expression which burned in her father. Their powerful mutual anger sprang from their immense love for each other. Helga wrote of it passionately in her journal and her books. Sandburg's own journal fragments reveal that he looked at Helga's husband as an intruder.

For nearly four years Helga kept herself and her children from her father, denied him loving access to three of the most important people in his life. Her husband, she said, forbade her to communicate with her family at Connemara, or to send her children there for the coveted visits. Helga loved her husband, occasionally feared his temper, but was "glad of" her "new life and its freedoms." "I like the conventional family scene," she wrote: "Father, mother, son, daughter, dog, cats. I wish for the addition of visiting parents and sisters. It doesn't work. How can it? It is an age-old scene for women, caught between the Young and the Old Bears. The Unfamiliar with whom we journey away from the Familiar. Ruth."

Helga was caught between the powers of husband and father, and her children were hostages in that struggle. There were on all sides regrettable words and silences. Sandburg had once teased Helga and young Paula that if they did not stay at Connemara he would find a new daughter and granddaughter. In a sense he did that over the empty years of the late fifties when he did not see their beloved faces. He lavished on the children and grandchildren of friends and on a series of vibrant, opinionated young women the love, affection and watchful care he had meant to give young Paula, John Carl and the errant Helga. Paula sought to be the pacifist and mediator, but staunchly defended Sandburg. In her own household, Helga saw the mirror image of the conflict between her father and her husband; her husband and her son began to have their own struggles with each other.

Helga was fighting hard to become herself during those years of "The Rift," as she termed it. As the youngest daughter of two extraordinary parents, she had grown up deeply aware of their great accomplishments. If they required less of her two sheltered sisters, they exacted more of her. Until she left Connemara with Art, Helga had in some ways been as homebound as Margaret and Janet. Indeed, their parents' home was a wonderful place, brimming with books, conversation, music, creativity. Interesting people came in a veritable pilgrimage. Their father's literary career brought many worlds into their home, and their mother's industrious, capable work with the long line of champion dairy goats gave her a reputation as solid in her realm as their father enjoyed in his. Connemara in all its facets was a seductive place, and Helga could have gone on and on there, aiding her parents in their work. But she had her own work to do, her own needs, her own self to discover.

Another major grievance, fraught with misunderstanding, had to do with Sandburg's library, and certain books, manuscripts and papers which he had entrusted to Helga's possession in 1954. They had first spoken of the idea during Helga's visit to Connemara that summer. "This was a wonderful idea of Dad's to give [the manuscripts] to you who were at his side preparing the Mss. in the first place," Paula told her then, promising to pack up the materials for shipment to her. Helga had surveyed the books, papers and mementos stored in the ground-floor rooms of the rambling old house. Plain pine shelves filled one large cellar room, giving it the look of library stacks. There stood rows and rows of books, cardboard cartons of books, newspaper clippings, papers. A "fireproof safe . . . its combination never used" protected some manuscripts and papers. Wooden file cabinets burgeoning with more papers stood in the cellar shadows.

Long before their "Rift," Sandburg turned over to Helga "the manuscripts and related material" of *Abraham Lincoln: The Prairie Years*, *Abraham Lincoln: The War Years*, *The American Songbag*, *Lincoln Collector*,

Remembrance Rock, Always The Young Strangers, Early Moon, The People, Yes and other books of poetry, making the act official in a document he signed on August 20, 1954.

Helga and Art had put two government surplus file cabinets and a dehumidifier in the basement of their small Virginia house so that Helga could arrange and store her father's collection. She discussed its value and its future with a friend from the Library of Congress and with Ralph Newman of Chicago's Abraham Lincoln Bookshop, who had been her father's Lincoln material "lookout" for years. Sandburg, too, had told Newman that Helga had some of his papers, and Newman wrote to Helga about his interest in seeing them and "ultimately selling them to someone who would in turn place them in a public institution."

Someone else was courting Sandburg's collection. University of Illinois English professor Bruce Weirick had encouraged Sandburg to let his library go home to Illinois. He had broached the idea to Sandburg and to university officials in the spring of 1950 after Sandburg's sister Esther surprised him with the gift of four portfolio-scrapbooks of clippings, letters and poems, her own record of her brother's life. She and Sandburg wanted to give the collection to the University of Illinois. "For an hour we had high-balls and pored over [the scrapbooks] with great excitement," Weirick told Esther later, "Carl exclaiming all the while: I didn't know I did that; I swear I had forgotten all about that . . . and THINK of Esther being so considerate and thoughtful!" Thinking about how best to display the albums, Weirick conceived the idea of a Sandburg-Lincoln Room at the University of Illinois Library, "with Carl's library, his manuscripts, the Steichen pictures, and a lot of recordings of Carl reading his poems and singing his ballads."

Weirick proposed the idea of having the university purchase Sandburg's library "and making a Sandburg-Lincoln room as a state center for Lincoln and literary pilgrims to come to, and for scholars to use!" In the way of state university machinations, the idea would be a long time coming to fruition.

In March 1955 the new president of the University of Illinois authorized Weirick to discuss the matter with Sandburg, who still liked the idea. He told Weirick he had been offered as much as a hundred thousand dollars for his whole library. Some of the more valuable books and papers would be sold separately, Sandburg feared. The dispersal of Oliver Barrett's collection, and his own difficulties in working with fragmented Lincoln collections, had convinced Sandburg that a library such as his had its greatest value as an entity. He did not want his books and papers to be sent hither and yon. He had built this collection over a lifetime of work. He wanted it to reside in one place for all time, and Illinois was its true home, he felt. He asked Weirick to keep the negotiations secret in the meantime, to keep the book dealers away from his doorstep.

The spring of 1955 was hectic, and it was early June before Sandburg could prepare a description of his library, including the valuable materials he and Paula had shipped off to Helga months earlier. He was finishing the poem he would read in Boston Commons in June and preparing the commencement address he would deliver at the University of North Carolina June 6.

His attention on other things, Sandburg managed to irritate his old friend Archie MacLeish, trying graciously to arrange a dinner in Sandburg's honor during his upcoming Boston visit. "I guess the goats must have gotten my telegram because there hasn't been a word out of you," MacLeish wrote at the end of May. "Either that or silence is to be read as dissent. Or else you just plain can't come." He told Sandburg he had "called off the dinner," yet hoped to see him during the Boston event. Sandburg immediately proposed having a dinner the evening before his Boston Common reading, with only the MacLeishes and the Howard Mumford Joneses. "I remember when together we threw in with all we had and yet we didn't save the country," Sandburg wrote MacLeish in early June. "There will be no illusions about June 12th," the date of his reading. He wanted MacLeish to hear the poem before he read it. He had written and rewritten it, under the tough, frank criticism of his editor Kitty McCarthy.

He called the new poem "Psalm of the Bloodbank," choosing as its theme a line from Acts XVII:26, "And hath made of one blood all nations of men for to dwell on all the face of the earth." In keeping with his absorption in "The Family of Man," the poem spoke briefly and vividly of

> crimson blood streams poured
> together and together
> blended into one likeness,
> mingled in mute communions,
> Catholic in flow with Protestant,
> Nordic in flux with Negro.

As an elder statesman, he deplored the fractured worldview of the Cold War. His poem was a simple testimony to his recognition of the great Human Family which transcended national boundaries and political and economic ideologies. People were made of one blood, belonged to one global family, had to understand that and each other if any were to survive. He read the poem to eight thousand people on Boston Common that June. Archie MacLeish was there to give him the Poetry Prize of the Boston Art Festival, five hundred dollars and words of tribute:

> To Carl Sandburg, poet of the American affirmation . . . a participant in the history of his own troubled generation as well as the recorder of the great American trial. He has been the singer of the city where no one before him thought song could be found, and the voice of the prairie country which had been silent until he came, and all this continent is in his debt—a debt which Boston and New England by this award, acknowledge.

Houghton Mifflin Company of Boston funded the prize, and the audience listened to Sandburg in the rain. "Carl Sandburg's rank as a poet was clearly recognized last night as 8000 persons jammed the Public Garden to hear him read a new poem prepared for the Boston Art Festival," the *Boston Herald* reported the day after.

Back at Connemara, Sandburg turned his attention immediately to his library. By 1955 the antebellum house at Connemara Farm was nearly groaning beneath the weight of tons of books and papers, spilling from the third-floor workroom into files and boxes on the landing and under the eaves. More than fourteen thousand books lined the shelves built into almost every wall of the twenty-two rooms of the house. Sandburg had kept about him the accumulated books, papers and periodicals of a fertile lifetime.

Sandburg and Paula thought it was time to part with much of this sprawling library. They worried about fire, and about safety, and wanted the library to be preserved as it should be. They liked the idea of the University of Illinois in Sandburg's home state. Besides, Paula herself had been a student there for a year before going on to the University of Chicago. The University of Illinois offered thirty thousand dollars for the collection, a figure surely far below its actual value, but the Sandburgs found that agreeable. Sandburg made his own appraisal of the collection, and a rough inventory of its contents. Then he wrote to Bruce Weirick about it, and to Helga. He had shipped some vital materials to her. He needed them to make the collection complete for the University Library. He decided to offer to buy them back.

He went to Washington in late June while Steichen was preparing a "Family of Man" exhibition at the Corcoran Gallery. He decided to talk to Helga face-to-face, and took her out to dinner alone. "That evening

Carl rattles a paper or two beside my glass of wine and proposes to give me $10,000 for my Treasure," Helga wrote in her journal. "Will I budge? The collection is mine! A tie to my past. I refuse. Never." He told her that he had a secret buyer for all the papers, and wanted to include his manuscripts. He wanted all his papers to be in one place. Helga still resisted: "Is there really a buyer, the daughter considers, or is he regretting the gift, due to the shortcomings of the son-in-law? No. The manuscripts were given to me. I have labored on them. Bought new files for them. A dehumidifier for their comfort. They are mine!" Chin to stubborn Swedish chin, Sandburg and his daughter stood at an impasse over the papers. He declined her invitation to visit her family and home, and she took him to the train bound for Baltimore where he planned to stay with his friends Marjorie and Bill Braye. "Life is a series of relinquishments," he told Helga.

She went home alone to tell her husband about her father's offer for his papers. Art composed "a furious letter" pointing out "the Old Bear's specific problems with relationships and life and how he might solve and mend them," Helga wrote. She saw "the frenzied letter" before it was mailed, and, as she recalled it in one of her books, felt "that the catharsis, the purification, for her husband, may give him relief (The Last Word!) and our life will be simplified. I feel the pain and in my fashion, no inclination to stop the tide (King Canute!). My husband returns to his desk and his wrestling with his new manuscript, cleansed of his ire."

The letter caused distress, and anger, at Connemara. Margaret wrote a letter in retort, but did not mail it, and Carl and Paula kept their own reactions from Helga, understanding how hard it was for her to be torn between husband and father. "Let it rest," Carl told Paula and Margaret. He concentrated on preparing his "workshop" for inspection by Weirick and acting director of the University of Illinois Library Leslie Dunlap, who planned to come to Connemara in July. The scope of the material surprised even Sandburg himself.

It included more than three thousand Lincoln books, he told Weirick,

along with hundreds of notes and memoranda, holograph letters of Lincoln and his cabinet members, holograph letters of Grant, Sherman, Lee, Jeff Davis, Alex Stephens, and others, and later FDR, Hopkins, MacLeish, Justices Murphy, Roberts, Douglas, Hughes, Burton, including Truman (3), Stevenson (6), Wallace (2), modern authors from Teasdale, Amy Lowell, Robert Frost, Harriet Monroe, Jim Farrell, Masters, Lindsay, Dreiser, Ole Rölvag [sic], Bob Sherwood, Allan Nevins (8), Douglas Freeman, Steinbeck, Hemingway . . . Eric Sevareid, Ed Murrow . . . a driver's manual for the Model A car autographed by Henry Ford—a drawing of hat, shoes and cane signed by Charlie Chaplin—perhaps 1,000 and possibly 2,000 letters including copies of hundreds of my own letters—eleven pocket notebooks with handwritten entries 1902–1908—. . . several hundred hand written and typed items, large and small, some worth eventual publication—poetry and folksong books with scripts and notes—a large box of notes and overplus from the writing of Remembrance Rock and another box with Lincoln Collection materials—tape recordings . . . a disc of my broadcast election eve 1940—Steichen photographic prints and holograph letters and notes—first editions of all my books including In Reckless Ecstasy, The Cannibal . . . text books I used at Lombard and in grade schools (not all of course but a few quaint ones)—foreign translations such as Always the Young Strangers now to be read in Swedish, Portugese, and Chinese—a slave auctioneer's cane and a blacksnake whip used in slavery days—a library of more than 1,000 stereoscopic photographs, most of them made 1890–1904.

In late June, Bruce Weirick and Leslie Dunlap went to Connemara to take stock of Sandburg's library and to talk to him about its acquisition. They were enchanted with Connemara and the Sandburgs. Weirick and Dunlap spent four days with Sandburg going through the library. "I do not know which was the more overwhelming, the library, or the man it represents, with his running-fire comment on this or that memo, letter, manuscript, and the fifty years of America there revealed," Weirick wrote. "That a poet, ballad collector, singer, and biographer should have had the patience and foresight to collect and sort so much material,— a task to daunt ten librarians—reveals another side of Carl's genius. . . . No one knows how many letters he has, not even Carl, but they are a collector's paradise."

Weirick's original report discussed what he called "The Helga Collection," the manuscripts of books which had been "put in possession of Carl's daughter, Helga." Sandburg was deeply annoyed to read in print about a sensitive episode which he considered a private family matter, and wrote to chastise Weirick, who immediately revised the report, and apologized. "The Helga business is omitted, and I am sorry as all hell that I ever put it in at all. . . . Fortunately, not many are out; those are all with people we trust; and you will be glad to know it has caused no comment at all."

Back in Urbana, Illinois, Weirick lobbied for the Sandburg Room, soliciting letters of support from luminaries such as former governor Adlai Stevenson, Senator Paul H. Douglas, alumnus James Reston, historian Allan Nevins and others. At least ten faculty members opposed the purchase; some of the historians in residence looked askance at Sandburg's "poetization of biography." Internal politics delayed a decision until, at last, Weirick and his allies succeeded in getting the endorsement of the American literature faculty, and the University of Illinois Foundation agreed to allocate thirty thousand dollars for the Sandburg Collection, to be paid in five equal annual installments. The purchase was officially approved January 11, 1956.

It would be April 1956 before the books and papers were actually taken away from Connemara. It was a difficult parting, and the Sandburgs had not expected that the university librarian would want to take so much in the first shipment. Sandburg found it nearly impossible to let go of his books. One by one, he took them from the shelves to give them up, only to reclaim them. "His books were part of him," he had written in *Remembrance Rock* of the autobiographical character Orville Brand Windom.

> Each year of his life, it seemed, his books became more and more a part of him. . . . In the books of Herodotus, Tacitus, Rabelais, Thomas Browne, John Milton, and scores of others, he had found men of face and voice more real to him than many a man he had met for a smoke and a talk. . . . His living thought and heaviest anxieties of many years, along with some of his deepest pleasures of life, had centered in this room, these books, and what he had met in them to make his own.

On May 7, 1956, a moving van arrived at the University Library bearing 150 boxes of Sandburg's books and papers, 8,560 pounds, more than four tons of documentation of a singular American life. Dunlap thought that about two-thirds of Sandburg's library still rested at Connemara, where the old poet believed it should be, understanding that the terms of the sale had given him a life interest in the books and papers, as he himself had implied in his correspondence on the matter.

Sandburg had denied himself food and luxuries in the early days so he could afford the essential sustenance of books. The imposed discipline of thrift made him in all ways a saver. His early exploratory work was still preserved in the small pocket notebooks kept among his papers. The whole, immense journey of Sandburg's life could be traced there in his papers and books. Sometimes he had put little notes inside articles or envelopes to identify them. "I went from the east to the west coast and back again with this," he had written on a scrap of paper tucked into a wallet worn to the curve of his hip. He would never be able to relinquish his "life interest" in these books, papers and artifacts, suffused as they were with his most personal history.

*

The rest of the summer of 1955 was tranquil at Connemara, although too quiet without the grandchildren, the "little exiles" who had not been there for a year. They vacationed that August with their mother and stepfather in the Shenandoah Valley in a rustic cabin loaned by Eric and Lois Sevareid. There they could hunt, swim, pick wild blueberries and blackberries, explore the woods and fields, almost as if they were at Connemara. Their grandfather spent most of August "writing as steadily as ever, only fewer hours at a stretch," Paula said. Margaret was busy with books and gardening and daily walks with her father over the Connemara trails. Janet managed the kids on her own now, and they were doing better than ever, according to Paula. Janet could call each kid by name, and seemed to thrive on the disciplined work of the farm. She and her mother stayed up at night when there was a sick animal to be tended or a birth to oversee. Janet loved going with her mother to goat shows around the mountains. Their prizes were displayed in Paula's farm office; later the trophies and ribbons were interspersed with awards given to Sandburg, an affectionate parity of poetry and goats. Paula was much admired for her success, and local farmers knew they could turn to her for expert advice. She worked steadily to improve the production of her dairy herd, kept meticulous records, and shared her knowledge in animated talks with other breeders and in occasional brisk, practical articles in goat journals. As Bruce Weirick had discovered that summer, "It is a real farm they have at Connemara; it takes work and intelligence, and is no rich poet's toy."

"All the big people are simple, as simple as the unexplored wilderness," Sandburg had written to Paula in 1908. "They love the universal things that are free to everybody. Light and air and food and love and some work are enough. In the varying phases of these cheap and common things, the great lives have found their joy." Life at Connemara was all they could have dreamed of, except for the distance, computed in more than miles, between them and Helga and the children. "My little exiles," Sandburg had written, "the banished ones/the heart keeps turning to them/memory will not be still/remembering how and what they were/the faces and words of them."

In far-off Virginia, Helga was beginning to regret that she had not let her father have "his own manuscripts to complete his collection of papers." "It was unkind," she said of her own decision. "I would get shed of them and their memories and put the money into the market or bonds." She telephoned her mother to talk it over, and then wrote to her father about it. "Yes, the offer is still open, regardless whether the pending deal goes through," he wrote to her on September 21. "I will give you ten thousand ($10,000) in exchange for your entire Manuscript Collection, and I will add $500 extra to cover what work you have done on it." He offered to pay her three thousand dollars as soon as the collection reached Connemara, and to pay a portion of the balance on January 1 of each year from 1956 through 1961, with six percent interest. "Mother thinks there will be no income tax involved for you, as gifts are exempt from income tax. Your collection was a gift from me, and when you return that gift, I give you an equivalent gift in money." He promised, however, to pay any tax there might be. "If you wish to accept this offer on the terms stated above," he wrote very formally, "sign below and keep one copy of the agreement, and return one copy to me together with the paper that I signed on the original gift of my manuscripts."

Helga sent her father the earlier document along with "the agreement and carbon that you sent for signing," adding, "I don't think you and I need signed agreements when no outside party is involved. The terms are satisfactory—I am presuming that this money will in the end be coming from the buyer of the collection."

In the autumn of 1955, Helga sent her father twenty-eight carefully packed boxes of manuscripts, and her mother sent her her first check and an affectionate letter full of Connemara news. They had exported twelve Nubian yearlings to Colombia, South America, and five to Cuba. She had sent saddles and tack to young Paula, who had a horse to ride, and butterfly mounting boards for both John and Paula. "Deep love always from your mother," she said in closing.

Between Sandburg and Helga there was only a deepening silence. He told many friends over those years of estrangement how he loved and missed his daughter, but no words passed between them. Helga turned more and more during that painful time to putting words on paper, in her journal and in fiction. "My tales would be of farms and the ways of country people and animals. There would be goats," she said poignantly, "and a strong-willed girl and a powerful father."

Sandburg lectured in the Midwest that fall, read part of *The People, Yes* on an NBC Television program, and filmed a segment of "See It Now" on the Vice Presidency from Greenville, Tennessee, where Lincoln's successor, Andrew Johnson, once had a tailor shop. He spent a quiet Christmas at home with Paula, Margaret and Janet. The weather was "almost balmy," and the family enjoyed strolling the Memminger Path. "No baby kids this Christmas—but will have some very soon," Paula wrote to Helga. She had sent the children clothes for Christmas, along with other gifts. "Dear Mother," Helga wrote in acknowledgment. "Your Xmas boxes were lavish. . . . *But*: Paula, nearly 13 now, wears a 14 Pre*teen* and wouldn't fit into the beautiful outfits you sent. . . . As to John, the 15½ shirt was perfect but the sweater too small again! O dear! He is a hefty fellow, broad in the shoulders."

"I just made a guess!" Paula explained to young Paula. "It's a year and a half since we saw you, so you've perhaps grown a lot! I hope, with all my heart, that you and John will visit us next summer, like you used to do."

In the Connemara days, young Paula had planted a moss garden near her grandfather's workplace on the big splash of rock behind the house. During the years she had lived at Connemara, she "often appeared by his side, asking him to come and see a sight in the garden," she wrote years later in *My Connemara*. "It's quite a sight, Snick!" her grandfather would say.

> . . . often before returning to his papers he stood on the rock, feet placed apart, and raised the huge oaken armchair over his head and into the air. He seemed of gigantic proportions at such times, although he was only about six feet tall.
>
> Sometimes as I knelt by my garden . . . I would hear a mocking bird singing close by the rock. . . . When the song was at an end, Buppong would solemnly reply to it, whistling his interpretation. I was envious of the way he could warble a note and vary his tune as the grey bird with its white-tipped tail had done.

✳

Sandburg celebrated his seventy-eighth birthday in 1956, "famous so long that he has become respectable," Senator Paul Douglas noted. In a *New York Times* interview, Sandburg mused that sometimes he felt he had lived past his years. He worked only four or five hours a day now, instead of the twelve-to-sixteen-hour days of his youth. At times he had trouble with his memory. He was still physically vigorous and full of projects. In his quiet third-floor workroom he wrote and revised poems, tried to develop the second autobiographical volume, and read widely, marking with narrow slips of paper passages in dozens of books he meant to turn to again. Downstairs in his bright office on the main floor at Connemara, he dealt with his heavy correspondence. He turned one letter over to Paula: "My husband has referred to me your letter regarding the color of his eyes," Paula wrote, "along with a statement that I have seen his eyes in reality more often than he has seen them in a mirror, and therefore I am a more competent witness and testator. Sea-green blended with blue—those are the best words I find for the color of my husband's eyes."

In April of 1956 Sandburg went to New York to receive the first Albert Einstein Commemorative Award in the humanities at Yeshiva University's Albert Einstein College of Medicine. He spoke out on the dangers of "fat, dripping prosperity." Quoting Einstein's statement that "To make a goal of comfort or happiness has never appealed to me," Sandburg suggested that the "element of struggle in life" was a positive force. He saw danger in "the deep desire and main goal of Americans to obtain the articles of comfort and happiness when this goal overrides other motives." "Beware when you fail to remember that man's fate on the earth/is concentrated in the word: Struggle," he wrote in an unpublished poem called "Bewares." When a reporter asked him to identify the principal end in life, Sandburg said, "Before you go to sleep at night you say, 'I haven't got it yet. I haven't got it yet.'"

Columnist Westbrook Pegler, who had caricatured Sandburg in print years earlier, attacked him in his syndicated column that spring for his remarks about America's "fat-dripping prosperity." Pegler identified Sandburg as "a prosperous commercial biographer of Abraham Lincoln whom he resembles in the length of his legs and the close proximity of his buckle to his collar button." Unknown, of course, to Sandburg, someone at the FBI in Washington filed Pegler's article, of all the newspaper footage devoted to Sandburg in 1956, in Sandburg's still-growing FBI file, sending copies to FBI chief J. Edgar Hoover's close aides Louis Nichols and Clyde A. Tolson. That syndicated column was officially "unclassified" in May 1984.

Other journalists were kinder to Sandburg than Pegler had been, among them feisty, controversial Harry Golden of *The Carolina Israelite*. A renegade New Yorker transplanted to Charlotte, North Carolina, Golden had the audacity and courage to champion black civil rights issues in the strife-ridden South. He had met Sandburg in 1948 as one of a crowd of reporters, but did not sit down to visit with him man-to-man until the spring of 1956. They spent nearly eight hours that day walking at Connemara and sitting on the spacious front porch beholding the "sapphire mountains," drinking whiskey and "fresh North Carolina branch water," and talking. Sandburg roared with laughter when Golden teased, "Well, I wonder what old Victor Berger would have said if he had seen this place," and then explained to Golden how an old proletarian had acquired a Southern plantation.

Sandburg was at home that summer trying to work on *Ever the Winds of Chance*, but he viewed it as "a book that may never get written." He was having trouble gathering material for it, and was dissatisfied with his work on the first draft. He continued to read every new book and article pertaining to Lincoln's life and times. He kept crafting poems, burying deep within some of them his own personal anguish.

Downstairs in the farm office, Paula wrote to Helga, pleading for a summer's visit with the children: "Are the children coming to spend a couple of weeks of their vacation with us? It is Buppong's dearest wish and mine, to have our grandchildren here for a visit with us. I'd think, Helga, that you could spare them for two weeks out of fifty-two! . . . I believe that a visit with us is as important for John and Paula as for their grandparents. It was thoughtful of you to remember my birthday—but the only present that I really want is a visit from the children."

Helga wrote back defensively, asking why the family had not visited her in Washington. "Since last July, Dad had been through time and again," she said. "It is hard to believe that his dearest wish could be to see the children. I believe the children are not bean bags to be tossed back and forth between a disunited family . . . I don't know, Mother, where we go from here. I don't look for elemental change or remade personalities. I wonder if you or Dad have any suggestions." In her heart, she would have been "happy to oblige" her parents and her children with a reunion at Connemara, but "at the head of her household," she wrote years later, was "the strong-willed blond-headed Bear" who would not agree for the children to go. Editor Pascal "Pat" Covici, hearing of the rift between the Sandburgs and their youngest daughter, encouraged Helga to write a book about her father.

Sandburg worked in the summer heat, nursing a left shoulder inflamed with bursitis. He, Paula, Margaret and Janet still gathered in the summer twilight to sing. He played the guitar for them, but often he played "at night, in the dark, alone." The days passed slowly for him. "You know," he told an interviewer, "when you're over seventy, a day is an awful lot of time."

The Sandburgs had enjoyed a warm friendship with Asheville *Citizen* editor Don Shoemaker and his family. After they moved to Nashville, Tennessee, Sandburg especially missed their small daughter. "Hearts here beat in unison with yours," he wrote from Connemara. The old house was enlivened in July by the Wershba family, Joe and Shirley and their young son and daughter, Don and Randi. Like Harry Golden and the Shoemakers, they were enfolded in Connemara life as if they were family. The children filled, temporarily, the vast emptiness. Wershba listened as his daughter and the old poet swapped nonsense words and stories.

"Cut out that silliness, Carl Sandburg," Randi giggled during one of those summer afternoons.

"Ah," Sandburg responded pensively. "Without my silliness, I would die."

✳

Carl Sandburg, said Westbrook Pegler, had a "happy knack of backing bashfully into the limelight." Actually, Sandburg enjoyed public accolades up to a point, but effusion quickly made him uncomfortable. He agreed to be the honored guest of *Poetry* in November 1956, but when a longer Carl Sandburg celebration was proposed, he declined, saying "you suggest an event which I would rather be postponing until I am gathered to the shadows where I would hear none of the tumult."

Sandburg traveled to New York in December to record an album of his poems for the Harcourt, Brace textbook department and sign the contract for his first paperback, *Fiery Trial*, the excerpt of Book III of *Remembrance Rock*, "beyond per adventure the greatest Civil War novel ever written and I'm glad that is off my chest." He was back at Connemara for Christmas, and it was Paula's turn to travel. The invitation came from Helga. Gratefully, Paula accepted. "We are going to New York for five days or so after Xmas," Helga wrote. "Would you like to come and stay with the children then? Or better yet, you and dad both?"

He could not go, or would not. Paula did, spending a happy three days with John Carl and Paula, whom she had not seen in nearly two years. "They have 'grown up' since their last visit here," their grandmother said afterward, "so mature—so well-balanced—so sweet-natured as ever!" She took many pictures of her handsome grandchildren to take home. "Buppong says it's almost like a visit, seeing these prints of you & John," she wrote to young Paula afterward. "I had a wonderful visit with you—and you were the gracious hostess. . . . You and John made me very happy and proud."

Friends of the Sandburgs knew then how deeply they missed Helga and her children. The estrangement hurt the close-knit family at Connemara as well as the trio of "exiles" in Washington. Paula's December visit with the children was a first tentative step across a bitter bridge of distance and misunderstanding. The holiday visit to her daughter's home did not reunite the whole family, but Paula rejoiced in it. During that decade of his public celebration of the Family of Man, Sandburg was consoled by his wife's account of the two beloved children and her pride in their growth. But between him and Helga lay such a vast silence that he did not know his daughter was very near to publishing her first novel.

How to assuage his sadness? He filled his days with work, travel, other people. There was one new friend in particular, about Helga's age. They met at a cocktail party in Chicago after *Poetry*'s November Carl Sandburg Celebration. She admired his work, seemed to know it all. Effusively, she praised the concept of "The Family of Man." She told him she had been "digging in" to his books for some time. She said that as an artist he could add only a night to the whole of time, but "yours," she exulted, "is a full-moon night."

Not only was she statuesque and extraordinarily beautiful, but this Chicago businesswoman seemed to understand all his work, even *Remembrance Rock*. He began to write to her and to stay in her elegant Chicago apartment on his trips to the city. She was an idealist, he saw, a kindred spirit. He was enchanted.

1957–1958

30. Yes No Yes No

> . . . To live big is good:
> to deny much is good too
> You would have a bag of gold:
> you might ask a sack of peanuts.
> Be full, not so full, go hungry
> Life is all time yes no yes no . . .
>
> —Carl Sandburg, "Consolation Sonata,"
> *Harvest Poems*, 1960

"I'll die propped up in bed trying to do a poem about America," Carl Sandburg told reporters in 1957 as he celebrated his seventy-ninth birthday. His old friend and physician Jim Freese of Chicago had given him a physical examination, probing "muscular back, broad chest, hard abdomen," after which "Sandburg mischievously whomped his belly with clenched fists."

"How's that, doc?" he asked Freese, who "dutifully noted on his records that at 79, Carl Sandburg—poet, historian, novelist, troubadour—was all to the good."

Joe Wershba, writing for newspapers as well as the CBS Radio Workshop, interviewed him at length for a seventy-ninth birthday profile. Sandburg ranged over a wide landscape of talk. "I don't like the phrase, 'old age,' " Sandburg told Wershba. "Frank Lloyd Wright and I are agreed that we have done some of our best work in our seventies, and Wright has done some of his best work in his eighties." Sandburg did not like to be called "Old Man," because "I have a much younger heart for the things that the young love and enjoy over the world, than most of the poets now setting forth obscurantist lines." He lashed out at modern poets who were antidemocratic, writing not for the common people, but for each other. "They are latitudinous and sepulchral. Most of them ain't never had no fun—just plain fun."

He spoke lovingly of his wife. "Darned good to look at, darned sweet, extraordinary," he said of Paula. "And when I was writing pretty poor poetry, she told me to go on." He told Wershba he was up to 1907 in *Ever the Winds of Chance*, and that he was going through his unpublished poems, destroying those which did not meet certain standards he had set for himself. His publishers and his family objected when he discarded poems, believing "posterity should not be denied."

"What's posterity done for me?" Sandburg retorted. Wershba saw in his "fierce editorial reexamination" of the poems "the artist's passion to leave only the best for posterity's judgment."

Sandburg sang some of his favorite songs during his taping session with Wershba, his voice still sweet, deep and mellow. He still had plenty of fire, Wershba observed, as the poet held forth on the perils of radio and television and criticized motion picture executives who "aim their product at blood, sex, violence, profits, and who ignore the classics." He ruminated on the dangers of nuclear war, and reiterated his faith in the democratic system, the American Dream.

"Of course, I've been asked lots of times, what do you want out of life, Carl, what do you want most of all?" he told Wershba. "All my life, I've been thinking what I want out of 'life.' " He gave the familiar list: singing, staying out of jail, eating "regular," getting what he wrote printed, and "let's say a little love at home, and a nice affection hither and yon over the American landscape."

He got the last that year from audiences across the country, wherever he lectured or appeared on television. He also found it in Chicago, where he began to make his home away from home with businesswoman Donna Workman in her elegant Cedar Street apartment. She had succeeded in meeting Sandburg as she succeeded in other enterprises, by her own avowed formula—aggressive persistence. His poetry and biography and the novel *Remembrance Rock* drew her to him. Through mutual friends Ralph Newman and Patrick Lanham in Chicago, she wangled an introduction to Sandburg at the November cocktail party in Lanham's Chicago apartment. Their friendship was instantaneous.

The electricity between the two had its source in something quite apart from his celebrity and her beauty. They shared the same idealism. In 1951 Donna Workman founded a company to provide jobs for laborers and erstwhile drifters in the slums of Chicago. Idlers, ruffians, tramps or men just temporarily down on their luck could come to her headquarters early in the morning any day of the week, shower, don a clean shirt, eat a decent breakfast, and survey the big board on which jobs were posted daily. They could sign up for work at meat-packing plants, factories and other businesses in need of temporary heavy labor. Donna and her staff handled wages and benefits. She called her business Workman for Workmen. "One man or an army of men," was her slogan. A sign over the portal read "Through These Doors Pass the Finest Workmen in the World." By 1953, she had expanded her flourishing business to the West Coast. *Fortune* magazine applauded her, noting that when she was a student actress at the American Academy of Dramatic Art, classmates such as Kirk Douglas and Jennifer Jones had voted her Most Likely to Succeed.

As soon as he heard about Workman for Workmen, and paused to read the sign above her doorway, Sandburg knew that in Donna Workman he had found a compatriot. Here was an enterprise after his own heart. She was almost single-handedly doing for the downtrodden men of Chicago exactly what he had sought to do for other men in much earlier times.

*

Despite the trappings of power, there is vulnerability in great fame, particularly in old age. Inevitably there are those who are attracted to celebrity, seeking to exploit it, capitalize on it. Yet those who have achieved greatness may still long to be loved for themselves, not their accolades. Especially as they near the end of long lives of relentless work, they can be drawn to attractive, diverting people, sometimes only to be victimized by them. It happened to Sandburg, who for all his hard-earned experience in the world kept a core of innocence and trust. Consequently, besieged by people who wanted to be close to him, he was terribly vulnerable.

There were people who insinuated themselves into his life, seeking to use him. There were others who sincerely cared about his well-being. Much of the time it was difficult for Sandburg to tell one motive from the other. It was not in his nature to be suspicious. Consequently, there were in those later years of his complicated life some enigmatic relationships—such as the dancer who got him to sign over to her the rights to some of his voice recordings. He would be photographed in Hollywood and New York in the early sixties with Marilyn Monroe, with the inevitable fallout of gossip about what was essentially a friendship between a lonely old man and a lonely young woman, more grandfather and granddaughter than anything else. Monroe sent him her poems to read, and he wrote a tribute to her for *Look* magazine after her death.

Donna Workman was another enigma who entered his life in the last years, most likely filling the Helga void, but the appearance of things caused his family, and ultimately Donna herself, great consternation and pain. In the late 1950s she gave Sandburg the same care she gave her workmen, except in intimate, personal ways. She provided refuge from some of the ongoing cares of his life, made him laugh, expedited some of his work, buffered him in Chicago when his schedule was too strenuous. Paula was as always homebound in North Carolina, absorbed in the family and the farm operation. Sandburg and Helga were still bitterly estranged. As he grew older, travel was more intensely wearying and lonely. He disliked hotels. In Chicago, he began to make Donna's apartment home base. The first time he stayed there, he arrived with only a small black imitation-leather suitcase in hand, not even a clean shirt. He looked at her sumptuous apartment, and chose the smallest room for himself, a servant's room with its own bath right off the kitchen. He named it the Caboose. Donna and her housekeeper kept the icebox stocked with things he liked—pitchers of orange juice and tomato juice, goat's milk. "All night long," Donna remembered, "you could hear that icebox swing shut. He liked honey and coffee and pecans and Jack Daniel's."

She bought clothes for him when he needed them, "clean underwear, clean shirts . . . nice sweaters, and scarves, cashmeres . . . always blues and light greys." Donna treated him like a baby, coddling and pampering him. She kept him supplied with vitamins as well as good food, and made him get his teeth fixed by her own dentist, whom Sandburg afterward labeled "the Michael Angelo of dentists."

Sandburg liked to "horizontalize" after a meal, taking a nap for a half hour or so, with a handkerchief covering his eyes. Often he would stretch out to rest with his head in Donna's lap and talk to her "all about the lean days." He never forgot about being poor, she discovered. "In fact," she said, "Carl with all his richness of genius and money, was a perennial *Poor Man*. He *felt* poor. Honest to God poor. . . . The first time he ever took me to dinner, he took me to a beanery, and we had a bowl of bean soup and one of his sandwiches he pulled from a pocket."

Sandburg gave Donna pet names—Evie Mae, and Rose Potato because, he said, she was useful and ornamental. He called her a female Huck Finn, a lady lion tamer. He showed her his most private moods —a bawdy sense of fun; deep melancholy; even tears. She wrote that he could weep as if his heart would break, could "roar like a tiger and a lion put together too," could laugh like a child. He was no saint, she knew, but he was a hard worker, "a lover of life," "a goddam fine decent man."

There was much conjecture about the nature of the relationship between the Poet of the People, almost an octogenarian, and the beautiful, brassy business woman nearly half his age. "You put a wild, childhearted woman, and a sage of a man, who hasn't lost his childheart" together, said Donna, and you have a volatile combination. She gave him "every affection," she said, but "at no point, *at no point*, did *Carl ever ever ever step* out of line."

His creative energy had begun to flag then. "Shall I say I'm through and it's no use?" he wrote in a poem named "Evening Questions," "Or have I got another good fight in me?" Donna rekindled the poetry in him, released in him new energy and vitality. "Dearest, Starlight of my heart," she wrote to him in one note. "Please have only a light bite— until we eat together—for I wish to make something very special for you when I get up." "Donna I love you so—such a deep love," he wrote on a scrap of paper. "I love every day and hour with you," he wrote to her,

. . . Your hands and your eyes are precious to me
I have never seen your voice
But I love every tone and shadow of your voice coming to my ears
Your voice has shadows and colors, I save and keep those, they come to me
    before I sleep and then in dreams they float and I sometimes awake
    saying your name

He left love poems among the ashes in the stove in his third floor workroom—along with rowdy scatalogical poems he wrote or collected, as Lincoln had collected them.

Donna believed at first that Paula welcomed her friendship with Sandburg, but worried later about how the family perceived the relationship. "I am perfectly capable (have always been)," Donna protested, "of platonic friendship with male members of the human family; a friendship full of tender concern and affection."

Donna thought of Sandburg as a father in their multifaceted relationship. "Ours was not a sophisticated 'romance,'" she reflected; "it was children at play, serious children sometimes, mostly, but children . . . and it was camaraderie, and fascination." She saw that Sandburg needed "affection, warmth, and inspiration, and a good deal of prodding, which he wasn't about to take, but did from me, oddly enough." Despite what other people believed about their relationship, Donna was staunch in her interpretation of it:

The fact that Carl could love more than one woman should not be a deterrent . . . and the fact that Carl loved me is well spelled out in his letters to me. There was nothing illicit about it, nothing taken away from his beloved wife, and no taint whatsoever. I brought joy and inspiration to his life, and for this I am glad and as proud as he was about it. And those who are not noble of mind enough to understand this kind of love can go to hell! . . .

What's more, I resent being put down as a seductress. . . . I talk straight and act straight, I always have, I always will. And only a full-blown man can understand and appreciate this kind of woman. Carl did, the others will feel threatened, but that's their problem, not mine. I have a mind, and courage, and drive, and as long as I live, I intend to use *these*, and not the artful ways of a lesser woman. (God will take care of my heart, because it belongs to HIM.)

Donna knew how Sandburg loved his wife and daughters, and how he grieved over Helga. "I had the feeling that in some way I was a sort of stand-in for Helga while they were estranged," she reflected. Sandburg "lamented" that Helga would not let the grandchildren go to Connemara. He and Paula were deeply hurt about that, he told Donna. She knew that he had always liked and trusted women, and believed that his best poems about women reflected his love for Paula, and his commitment to her. "He was tremendously proud of her," Donna said, "always letting you know she was 'valeeeedictorororian' of her class at the University of Chicago." "She was Phi Beta Kappa, you know," he would say.

Donna heard rumors about Sandburg's flirtations with other women over the years, but was loyal in her defense of him. "He was human, wasn't he?" she said. "And why shouldn't he have had all the fun he could cram in his sunset years?" They talked at length about the hardships of his youth in Illinois and hers in an Ohio coal town. They both had struggled "to realize the American Dream," and Donna wanted to be sure that the nation, the "whole world" would remember that "through Sandburg that dream was still there, waiting to become a reality!"

Donna began to take Sandburg's business affairs in hand just as she had done for her workmen. Her motivation was not financial, for she was far wealthier than he. A successful businesswoman, she was totally inexperienced in the world of literary matters. But she instinctively knew that Sandburg had to be engaged in meaningful projects, especially as he brooded over the process of aging, the waning of his creative powers, the transience of life. She also saw that he needed to earn more money to shore up future income for Margaret and Janet so they would be secure after he and Paula were gone. That was always on his mind. Donna quickly busied herself with Sandburg's literary and media projects.

She bought a thousand copies of *The Family of Man*, the book of the exhibit, had Sandburg inscribe special sheets which were then tipped into the books, and mailed them, beautifully wrapped, to heads of states around the world. She tried to shepherd a collaboration between Sandburg and Norman Corwin on a play about Lincoln. She persuaded Sandburg to serve as honorary chairman for the Oliver Wendell Holmes Celebration she was producing for the Chicago Council of Adult Education, in the style of tributes she had mounted to Clarence Darrow and George Bernard Shaw. She set to work on such a tribute to Sandburg himself.

In March 1957 Sandburg signed an agreement to grant Donna "the sole right to produce" the play he and Corwin had talked of writing. It was a contract Corwin never signed. In May Sandburg signed a letter of agreement making Donna his agent for three years "commencing as of May 24, 1957" for three projects: the proposed Chicago Tribute to Carl Sandburg to be held in 1958; the "play on the subject of Abraham Lincoln which I expect to write in collaboration with Norman Corwin within approximately eighteen months from the date of this agreement"; and, in the event Sandburg could reclaim the movie rights, a production of *Remembrance Rock*. Sandburg told Donna he "grieved" about his novel. MGM-Loews had found it "too ponderous and too impossible" to turn into a motion picture in the 1940s, and had shelved it. He loved the book, she said, as a father might love "a baby that hadn't come out right, and he somehow blamed himself, and grieved for the malfunction, and loved it all the more for it." Donna wanted to have a film made from *Remembrance Rock*, and believed producer George Stevens was the one to do it. She sent him a copy of the novel, urging him to consider it. Paula was dismayed that Donna kept Sandburg "too involved in *Remembrance Rock* and hopes for it," Helga recalled years later.

Sandburg trusted Donna, and turned over these rights to her, but she was careful to protect his other literary rights and lecture arrangements. Donna focused on these three projects only. His signature on their contract guaranteed her ten percent of all profits on the projects she envisioned. She invested a lot of her own money in her promotional ideas for Sandburg, picked up the tab when they dined out, subsidized his prolific long-distance telephone calls to Connemara as well as to friends around the country.

As Donna enlarged her dreams for the tribute, she enlisted the ideas of his friends—Norman Corwin; Joe Wershba; Senator William Benton; Catherine McCarthy, his loyal editor at Harcourt, Brace. It would be a colossal, national Sandburg tribute. Catherine McCarthy especially endorsed the project. "I think it's a natural that the Tribute should be centered in Chicago," she told Donna in June 1957, for even though CS is revered and recognized as one of the greats through-out the land (and beyond) his name is synonymous with Chicago. No matter that he now lives in North Carolina, no matter that he now spends more time in New York than in Chicago, he is so definitely a product of the midwest that when one thinks of him one thinks automatically of Chicago. . . . There's a special kind of love Chicago has for him; I've seen it and felt it in a way I have never seen or felt it in New York.

She sent Donna many ideas for Sandburg exhibits, and entrusted to her little-known Sandburg pieces such as his first published essay on Lincoln (1909).

Kitty McCarthy had been working with Sandburg and Paula on a compendium of his work, to be entitled *The Sandburg Range* and published in the fall of 1957. There were excerpts from all the major works, as well as new poems. For the foreword, Kitty chose to reprint an editorial published in the *Boston Globe* when Sandburg received the Gold Medal for History and Biography from the American Academy of Arts and Letters. "Like other towering figures in the great tradition of letters," the piece concluded, Sandburg "has been not one man but many: poet and biographer, essayist and critic, historian and novelist, teller of prose tales for children, and indefatigable bearer of song to the nation as a traveling minstrel."

Sandburg kept his habitual peripatetic schedule that year, crisscrossing the country, leaving to the women who loved him and sustained his work many of the details of it. Paula and Kitty guided the choices for *The Sandburg Range*, and Donna moved steadily forward with her Sandburg projects. "Sandburg believed in the goodness of women, he trusted them," Donna Workman observed. "Was there ever one, in his life, that let him down?"

＊

Helga Sandburg sold her first novel in the late spring of 1957. *The Wheel of Earth* would be published in 1958 by McDowell, Obolensky. In their house in Virginia, she was already deep into work on her second book. Art was teaching English at American University in Washington. Her son, John, "spent his life in his room, now a licensed ham operator," she wrote in her journal. "Paula was showing a neighbor's horse called Ginger in a ring at nearby Bailey's Crossroads, wearing old jodhpurs of mine and a visor cap."

"I've been hoping that you and John would visit us here this summer," Paula wrote to her granddaughter Paula on her fourteenth birthday in

June. "You'd like the smooth front drive now—widened so cars can pass—so smooth for walking which means much for Margaret. Otherwise Connemara is the same as ever."

Yet another summer passed without the presence of the grandchildren to brighten the tranquil days. Sandburg broke the mountain calm with remarks to three thousand members of the General Federation of Women's Clubs who convened in Asheville for their annual convention. According to *Time* magazine reporters, "frosty-haired old (79) Poet Carl Sandburg sat bemusedly while a TV show was praised. Then he took aim at the 21-in.-screen hog caller for the world." He attacked television with relish, as he had done before. "When we reach the stage when all of the people are entertained all of the time, we will be very close to having the opiate of the people," he said. He attacked commercials which were filled "with inanity, asininity, silliness and cheap trickery."

Reporters mobbed Sandburg in the press room after his iconoclastic speech. Asked if he even owned a television set, Sandburg replied that he did, but he also had his "Blab-Off," a remote control device John Carl made and sent him, to get rid of commercials. Furthermore, he owned three radios and two hi-fi sets, and he liked the hi-fi best of all.

Sandburg kept moving about the country in 1957, speaking out on any number of matters which drew his interest—from television to the parole of Nathan Leopold, serving the thirty-first year of his life sentence for the murder of Bobby Franks. Sandburg urged his friend Governor William Stratton of Illinois to consider "immediate and unconditional pardon" for Leopold. "I would add that if he were a neighbor of mine I would want to see him often if only for benefits from association with a great intellect and a rare human spirit," Sandburg concluded. He made the presentation speech at the American Academy for Arts and Letters ceremony when Allan Nevins received the National Institute Gold Medal in History and Biography. He flew over Chicago by helicopter to gather images for a new poem about Chicago, commissioned as "Chicago's unofficial poet laureate" by the Chicago Dynamic Committee to celebrate the city's architectural heritage.

He seemed to be thriving on the strenuous schedule, although it left him little time to write. "But Jesus Christ!" he exclaimed, exasperated when he had to turn down something he really wanted to do. "When and where am I going to get time to finish my unfinished works?" But, he told Allan Nevins, "when you reach five months from four score you will say once in a while, 'By golly, they'd get along without me if I had slipped on a banana peel and fallen across to the Other Shore.' "

＊

Sandburg and Donna Workman had their first serious quarrel in the fall of 1957, nearly a year into their relationship. It had to do with Chicago and United States Steel. In October the city of Chicago celebrated Chicago Dynamic Week, dedicated to "the sound building and farsighted planning of the World's Most Dynamic City." The civic committee coordinating the fete was chaired by Edward C. Logelin, vice president of United States Steel Corporation. They invited Sandburg to write a new poem about the city and to address the Climax Banquet at the Drake Hotel on October 30. They offered him a fee of ten thousand dollars, which he accepted. His new poem, "Chicago Testament," would be inscribed on a plaque which he would give to Mayor Richard Daley at the banquet.

When Donna heard about Sandburg's agreement with the Chicago Dynamic Committee, she was furious. He was working for "former enemies," she charged, recalling his days as a labor organizer and sympathizer. She felt he was "working the wrong side of the street." Their friendship was finished, she told him in a storm. She asked him not to call her anymore.

Sandburg's friend and doctor Jim Freese quickly interceded. Sandburg did not understand her anger, Freese told Donna. He was terribly upset. His health might even be in peril. Donna agreed to see Sandburg and explain her distress. He came to her apartment disheveled, "so tired and worn." She led him into her library, where she kept all his books on special shelves. She asked him to sit down, and moved to the shelves. One by one she removed his books and dropped them at his feet.

"Carl, did you write all of these marvelous books?" she asked.

Puzzled, he nodded his head. He was hawking the wares of the industry he used to attack, she told him, and all for "ten measly grand." She was "wild with anger" that he could appear to forget his own "lament for the steel workers" in *Smoke and Steel*.

"You have whipped me across the face with a black snake whip," Sandburg told her wearily. He talked to Donna about the speech he had agreed to write. He assured her he would speak out in the old way *against* injustice and war, and *for* life. As she saw "what a sensitive instrument he was" and how "the years were heavy on him," Donna resolved never to be so hard on him again.

The speech he gave October 30 transmitted all the zest and fire of the quintessential Sandburg. Dressed in a blue suit with a blue bow tie, his white hair neatly parted in the middle, he spoke to a select audience of 350 people. Donna and other friends were there with the dignitaries to hear Sandburg in a "voice nearly as rich as his poetry and prose" pay homage to the city he loved, he said, "as Victor Hugo loved his Paris, as Charles Lamb loved his London." He read from earlier poems—*Smoke and Steel*; *Good Morning, America*; *The People, Yes*; "Man the Moon Shooter." Then the poet gave way to the orator, burning with the old time idealism:

> If I had not seen the passing of the twelve hour workday and Benjamin Fairless and my friend Phil Murray at a table working out an agreement they signed, I would not be here tonight. I like it and I give it praise that the 21,000 men in the Gary Steel Works have an eight hour day, a five day week, time and a half for Saturday and for Sunday. A few weeks ago I watched close up perhaps a thousand of the workers leaving the plant after the eight hour shift. And I like it and I give it praise that these workers have shower baths and lockers and they can leave their eight hour shift clean of body and in a change of clothes, if they so wish.
>
> My father happened to be a railroad blacksmith. He hammered hot steel and iron on an anvil ten hours a day, six days every week for thirty years, and every night in the year he came home with the smoke of the shop still in his clothes and soaped and scrubbed his hands, face and neck at the kitchen sink. It is now two or three generations back to the time when there was a saying in Pittsburgh and the steel industry, "Old age at forty." In the fact of that time and period being past and gone who can not have a glad and thankful heart about it today?

Before his attentive Chicago audience that night, Sandburg quoted himself in *Remembrance Rock*: "You may become witnesses of the finest and brightest era known to mankind. The nations over the globe shall have music, music instead of murder. It is possible. That is my hope and prayer—for you and for the nations." With that recapitulation, he picked up his guitar, strummed it softly, and sang in the inimitable voice "a couple of hymns as a benediction to the evening service."

✳

Sandburg was nearly eighty, thriving on his role as elder statesman and celebrity poet, willing to pause and take stock of his accomplishments. As a young man he had simultaneously created his poetry and his persona. He had mused in his Lincoln biography that Lincoln had the ability to stand outside himself and observe his own demeanor, as if he were an actor on the stage who could simultaneously act and watch himself acting. In a new poem he was still working on, Sandburg wrote a poignant summary of life:

Your personal doorways know your shadows
and number the times you enter, exit, enter
so often having no lines to say
though you are actor and audience to yourself . . .

Sandburg had made his singular, stubborn way from obscurity to international fame. Many critics relegated him then and later to literary
oblivion in part because he was so uniquely visible and commercially
successful, a popular poet. For the first half century of his career Sandburg
was driven to speak, to sing, to fight the battles inherent in the "great
human struggle." He acted, for the sake of the action, the dream. As
his celebrity grew, he gradually became "actor and audience" to himself,
refining the public image, until the casual shock of hair and the glib
repartee with audiences or newsmen crystallized into one familiar, predictable performance. He created a mask, wore it easily until it became
habitual, until he himself seemed to become the mask. The celebrity
showman often superseded the poet during those harvest years of the
1950s, and Sandburg gave himself up to having a good time, having his
opinionated, uninhibited say, onstage and off.

He spent Christmas of 1957 at home at Connemara with Paula, Margaret and Janet. Helga and her family did not come. Helga's first novel
would soon be in galleys. She was keeping her journal, working on a
new book, watching her second marriage deteriorate. Her children were
caught in a web of conflict and tension. Her husband and her son
stubbornly engaged in what Helga termed "The War of the Bears." She
remembered the night when Art told her son that if he were not home
from his after-school job by ten, he would have to stay out until 2:00
A.M. "Sure enough he does, in the doorway, in the rain. Stubborn.
Silent. A little pale. His dark red curls matted. Asking no quarter, on
his way in life. My hero—my Little Bear."

Hard as those times were, Helga was finding herself, as a woman, as
a writer. When Sandburg's friend David Mearns of the Library of Congress
asked her what was going on between her and her father, she told him
that in middle age, "one must assert one's individuality, one goes his
own path." Had Sandburg read her book, Mearns wondered?

"Oh, my, no," she told him emphatically. "I am not writing as his
daughter, but as a writer. I do not care for his opinion."

Her second novel, published as *Measure My Love*, had for its main
characters "a strong-willed girl (another one)," she said, and this time,
"a weak-willed husband."

"You and the children were especially in our thoughts during this holiday season," Paula wrote Helga after Christmas. She had not seen her grandchildren in a year. Since 1954 Sandburg had hungered for their faces and voices. He had turned to other households bright with the voices of children. Other vibrant young women had stepped into the great space left by his rift with Helga.

"Many things we do not understand," Paula told Helga, "but we love you now and always the same as ever."

✳

Edward Steichen, mourning for his beloved Dana, who had died of lung cancer in June, suffered a debilitating stroke in December 1957. Worn with grief, thin and newly-bearded, he spent some time with his colleague Wayne Miller in California, hoping to regain some of his zest for life. He found the will and energy to write a birthday tribute to Sandburg. *The New York Times* had asked him for it, and it was printed throughout the country. "Dear Carl," he wrote to the man who had been his brother-in-law and friend for half a century: "So you are 80 today. That in itself is something to make one feel good. Many do not last that long. Among those that have reached eighty none has so consistently and continuously devoted himself to the getting to know—and to understand—to love the people, yes, of our land." He was grateful, he said, that when Sandburg married "sweet, lovely" Paula, he had acquired a brother. "I salute you, my brother."

Sandburg enjoyed Steichen's tribute, and all the national fuss over his eightieth birthday. Once the celebrations ended, he plunged again into a rigorous schedule. The University of Illinois Library mounted an exhibit from the Sandburg Collection. He lectured and spoke on radio and television. In recording sessions with Joe Wershba in 1958, he described his life at eighty: "I feel as young as I ever felt in my life. I figure if I can get to 88, then I ought to get to 99. And the reason for that is my recent discovery that three of my great-grandfathers died at advanced ages, all divisible by the number 11. Unfortunately, the precise details are lost in the mists of Swedish antiquity." He joked about it in a press interview: "It's inevitable, it's inexorable, it's written in the Book of Fate that I die at an age divisible by eleven!"

✳

Sandburg lent his strong voice to a controversial cause in February of 1958. He was staying with Donna Workman in Chicago on the eve of Nathan Leopold's latest parole hearing. Donna and Ralph Newman, long a friend of the convicted murderer's family, persuaded Sandburg to go to Stateville Prison near Joliet, Illinois, to speak on Leopold's behalf. Sandburg and Donna traveled by car over treacherous, icy roads to reach the hearing on time. Sandburg wrote out his speech en route, covering small strips of blue paper with words he would use to urge mercy for Leopold.

Sandburg had written letters to and for Leopold, but they did not meet face-to-face until the morning of the parole hearing. Leopold's attorney Elmer Gertz arranged for Sandburg, Donna and Newman to sit down with Leopold for a "long conversation which, of course, made Leopold very happy." The hearing, one of the longest parole deliberations in Illinois history, took nearly the whole day. After Sandburg was called to speak, Gertz remembered, "Everybody wanted to be photographed with Sandburg. He was photographed with every member of the Board, with me, with my son and with everybody else under the sun. The newspaper photographers could not have enough." At the end of that long day, Leopold was paroled by a split vote.

Back in Chicago, Donna and Sandburg celebrated with friends at a dinner party in Donna's apartment. Elmer Gertz and Ralph Newman picked up Leopold when he was released from prison. "The press was waiting and they followed us," Newman said.

> It was like Indians following the wagon train west. I hadn't realized that Nathan Leopold had not ridden in an automobile and certainly not at high speed for many, many years. He became car sick. I stopped so he could become sick near a telephone pole and *Life* magazine had the bad taste to photograph him. I took him to my home in Oak Park where I had some clothes I had bought for him, a new suit. He called many of his friends.

Before he left for Puerto Rico where he would spend the rest of his life working in a hospital, Nathan Leopold called Sandburg to thank him. Sandburg was in New York in March staying with Gregory and Terry d'Alessio on Henderson Place. They were awakened by phone at about two one morning. D'Alessio heard a "high-pitched voice, thin and reedy, almost a whine" ask for Sandburg. The caller identified himself as Nathan Leopold.

D'Alessio could "hear the Sandburg voice over the telephone, just the voice, not any of the words it made, but the music of its rise and fall and gesture into the still air." "Never before had I caught it in such a coloration," d'Alessio said. "Reassuringly, calmingly, comfortingly, Carl was talking to Leopold as to one just awakened from a nightmare."

The next evening "as we played and sang and sipped Jack Daniel's," d'Alessio voiced his misgivings about Sandburg's public defense of Leopold.

"You oughtn'ta get so worked up about it, boy," Sandburg told his worried friend. "It'll come out all right—you wait and see." Sandburg's faith in Leopold was justified by Leopold's thirteen-year-long odyssey of public service in Puerto Rico. He died there in 1971 of a heart attack, at age sixty-six. There had been that irrevocable moment of insane violence, and then forty-seven years of retribution, thirty-three of them in prison, nearly fourteen in exile. Sandburg, the staunch champion of the innate worth of mankind, saw in Leopold's life after 1924 "a struggle toward light."

"I just picture him," he explained later, "as a magnificent struggler."

✳

In 1958 Helga Sandburg won the prestigious *Virginia Quarterly Review/ Emily Clark Balch* prize in short fiction for her story "Witch Chicken." Her novel was close to publication, her marriage in disarray. She had not seen her father in three years, but he haunted her in dreams. In one of them, he had published a book

> in collaboration with my name. Produced it triumphantly with Kitty. It was a dreadful thing with old type and photos. . . . Yet I had to be polite about it, knowing I'd been taken, trying to discern if he truly believed he was helping me . . . or thought he was putting one over, making out on my publicity! These dreams as a rule are very vivid. I hope one day to put them to rest.

Helga refused to let a camera crew travel to Connemara with Fanny Butcher of the *Chicago Tribune* and other book reviewers so that Sandburg could introduce his literary daughter's first book. She feared it would be a fiasco, and she wanted, from the outset of her career as a writer, to stand on her own.

In New York for a series of appearances, including one with the New York Philharmonic at Carnegie Hall, Sandburg talked to Kitty McCarthy about his alienation from Helga. Kitty tried to negotiate a truce and a reunion, hoping that Sandburg and Helga could find a "new relationship." Helga was willing, she said, to meet with her father on neutral ground, but not in Flat Rock, " 'his' arena." She felt that would be fatal to her future career. She was risking a significant promotion of her book at Marshall Field's in Chicago by declining a Connemara meeting with her famous father, for the booksellers there wanted to exploit his Chicago popularity to augment sales of her book.

"These people are looking at tomorrow's sales," Helga wrote in her journal. "I am taking the long view of my literary future & have to be more careful. . . . Am quite frustrated, but clearheaded nonetheless, about this ridiculous CS thing. I get the feeling that his ghost will forever bedevil me."

Through an intermediary came a message that Sandburg would gladly meet with his daughter and introduce her book to Chicago on neutral ground, "provided he gets the two grandchildren." Whether Sandburg actually said this or not, Helga rejected the offer.

That spring marked Helga's first success as a writer, and the demise of her second marriage. She wondered if her "wrath" toward her husband doubled her wrath for her father, "The Grizzly," as she called him. She admired her mother's wisdom in "tending, fostering, pacifying genius!" As the newspapers reported her short-story prize and reviewed her first novel, they inevitably referred to her as Carl Sandburg's daughter. She had not shown her father her work, she told the press, and she did not "wish to trade on his fame." If anybody deserved credit, she told them, it was her husband.

In the privacy of her journal, she despaired. "Would my father's name always be chained inexorably to me?" She was determined to have her own destiny, and to keep it separate from her father's. She set out joyfully on her first author tour. Art wrote notes criticizing her public speaking. In New York for interviews, she was bumped from the Dave Garroway "Today" show because her father was scheduled to appear soon; they did not want to feature two Sandburgs in such close proximity. "I hope to Christ he does not louse me up again," she wrote in her journal. *The Wheel of Earth*, dedicated to her husband, was warmly reviewed. *The New Yorker* called it "a triumph of storytelling." She sent three autographed copies of the book to Connemara, and waited to hear how her family would regard her work. Letters of thanks came from her two sisters and her mother. She did not hear directly from her father. He spoke of her to others, though. "Dearest," he wrote in a note to his wife. "Here's first time you done seen yr daughter in a best seller list. Carlo."

And he spoke of her to the press. What was it like to be famous? he was asked. "It's like a communicable disease—nothing can be done about it," Sandburg replied with a grin. Later he proposed his own question: "Why don't you ask me how I feel about my daughter having a novel out? I believe it is a great novel—extraordinary for a first novel. She's going to write novels as long as she lives."

Helga invited her parents and sisters to visit in May of 1958. Margaret had not been well, and could not travel, nor would Paula leave her until she had improved. But by late May Margaret was better and Paula thought she could get away to Helga's for a two-day visit. Sandburg was in Chicago where he was honorary chairman for Donna Workman's Oliver Wendell Holmes celebration. He had spent the spring traveling; recording several records of his work for Caedmon; narrating the Copland "Lincoln Portrait"; being honored at various places, including the Carl Sandburg Day events in North Carolina, his adopted home state; giving lectures and interviews in several other states. Donna was on his mind. "So often, so incessantly, so continuously with no letup, you are in my thoughts," he wrote to her in one of the more than two hundred notes that punctuated their long friendship; "the reality of you & the shadow, the apparition, haunt me."

He would not travel to Washington with Paula that May to see his daughter and the children. More than three years lay between them now. Paula praised Helga's work in her letters. "We all thought your novel very fine—and the short story *a really great story, an enduring work of art.* . . . I'm very happy to see that you are getting into work that you love—and receiving high praise from the most discerning critics in the field. What could be better than the prospect unfolding for you of a life-work of creative writing?"

Paula proposed that Helga and the children come to Connemara for a summer visit and thus "fulfill the dearest wish of us all—Dad, Margaret, Janet and *your* Mother." Meantime, Paula could travel and would, arriving in Washington by train May 20.

It was a measure of the gulf in family communication that Helga did not know until her mother's visit that Dana Steichen had died a year earlier. Paula told Helga about Steichen's intense, prolonged grief. For a while he had lost his will to live, and his stroke had set him back. But he was stronger now, resuming his work. Further, he had resolved to finish the book Dana was writing at her death, an effort to prove the identity of the mysterious lady Beethoven called "Immortal Beloved." The book appeared in 1959, entitled *Beethoven's Beloved.* Steichen kept "a little shrine" to Dana at their Umpawaug farm—"with Dana's book and fresh flowers and her photograph."

Mother and daughter talked of these matters and many others during their short visit. Paula told Helga she thought her book was a great one—"not the greatest, but great." Her father thought so, too, Helga heard her mother say.

Helga had not known that her former husband, Joe Thoman, now had two children by his second wife, Adaline Polega, formerly the Sandburgs' helper in the house and barn in Michigan. Adaline and Joe and their family had visited the Sandburgs at Connemara now and then, and Paula brought pictures to show Helga. Adaline, who still called Paula Sandburg "Mom," had faithfully brought her children to Connemara, a boy and a girl. But Helga was not ready to take her family back to the old white house standing high off Little River Road. She did wish, however, that John Carl and Paula could meet their stepbrother and stepsister, their own father's younger children, but she thought Art would object.

After her mother's visit, Helga's dreams stirred her to restless, troubled nights. She wanted the dreams "laid to rest. Done with." "A dream last night," she wrote in her journal:

Dad and Mother standing there with me and declaring my independence (again!). I will make my own way, husband or no. And their indulgent smiling faces (frustrating!) and my husband (Joe-Art) laughing. Later saying good-bye politely to them and kissing Dad's smooth cheek and him being busy and hurrying past me. Dreams. I am aware of the implications. I suppose I will always fight the uphill battle. (Sisyphus?) Constantly, the dreams. Dad, Mother, Uncle Ed, sometimes my sisters, in strange angry alien roles, pitted against me. Unfamiliar. Humiliating me in public as well as private groups. Dreamed last night of being seated in a large audience where I am to speak. Suddenly Dad appears in the doorway, a sweater (to disguise himself?) over his head. Mother is with him. With glad hands, he is drawn in by the public, who remove the sweater. He is given a good seat and when Mother looks over at me, I smile in greeting. She turns away. Then he gets up to examine some paintings on the wall and to comment on them in his engaging rambling way. He is taking over my ground. I say, even though mortified, "Hush! Shhh!" And he sits down.

Her father's old friend Norman Cousins published one of Helga's speeches on writing as the November lead article in the *Saturday Review* and inadvertently made one of her bad dreams come true. The magazine cover carried a picture of her father, not Helga herself. Angrily, she telegraphed Cousins to say so:

WAS UTTERLY APPALLED BY NOVEMBER TWENTY-NINE ISSUE PARTICULARLY IN VIEW OF FACT THAT MY OFFER OF EXCELLENT STUDIO PHOTO OF MYSELF WAS SWEPT ASIDE AND THEN [A . . .] KARSH STUDIO PHOTO OF CS WAS EMPLOYED STOP WHERE IS MENTION OF FACT THAT THIS WAS ADDRESS IN CONNECTION WITH PUBLICITY FOR MY NOVEL STOP THIS PIECE WAS NOT A

MEMOIR STOP I AM STUPIFIED THAT PHRASE SUCH AS LIFE WITH FATHER HAS
BEEN USED IN CONNECTION WITH ME STOP WHEN I AM PREPARED FOR MEM-
OIRS BY GOD I SHALL SO STATE AM FURIOUS WITH SRL AND HOW ABOUT IT
HELGA.

Helga seemed blessed with a double portion of the genetic gift for
words, as if both her brilliant, articulate parents had endowed her with
the power of language. She had inherited, too, her father's pride and
sometimes willful stubbornness. They were two of a kind in ego and
temperament, these two writers, father and daughter. He would praise
her work to other ears, but could not yet bring himself to speak to her
directly of his pride. She would work in "rigorous loneliness," as her
father had done, to make her own way. Meantime she had her hands
full with warring husband, children, the new novel and now a full-time
job at the Library of Congress as secretary to the Woodrow Wilson Papers
project.

He father, meanwhile, went on his independent way, filling his time
with work and travel and his heart with surrogate daughters and grandchildren.

✳

The nation would celebrate the hundred and fiftieth anniversary of Abraham Lincoln's birth in February of 1959, and by autumn 1958 Sandburg,
Lincoln's chief spokesman of the time, was inundated with invitations
to write or speak on behalf of the occasion. Archie MacLeish asked him
to write and record a *"son et lumière"* production to be mounted at the
Lincoln Memorial. Sandburg declined the project. "It would sap me of
my last small drops of creative juice," he told MacLeish.

He had enough to do with other work and travel. Paula and Margaret
ventured to the West Coast that autumn. Over the years, Paula wrote
dozens of articles on goat breeding and production for *Better Goatkeeping,
Goat World, Dairy Goat Journal* and other periodicals. Her byline was
respected because her success as a breeder was widely known. She wanted
to attend the American Milk Goat Record Association meetings in Riverside, California, and Margaret was well and strong enough to accompany her. En route, they visited the Grand Canyon and Santa Fe.
Afterward, they saw the Sequoia National Park, and stopped in Galesburg, Illinois, between trains so Margaret could see her father's birthplace.

Meanwhile, Sandburg was comfortably settled in Sherman Oaks, California, in Norman Corwin's guest cottage, which Sandburg christened

"Hacienda the World." He would be there for a month of special events, capped by the Sandburg Tribute at Royce Hall on the UCLA campus, a "star-filled evening" that grew in part from Donna Workman's un-realized dream of an epic tribute in Chicago. Corwin wrote and directed the tribute, and the gala evening on November 23, 1958, was a night after Sandburg's own heart. A Hollywood church choir sang a setting of his poem "Buffalo Bill," the music composed by Irving Gertz just for the tribute. Murrow's "See It Now" film of Sandburg was shown, and an all-star cast read from his work—Burt Lancaster, Jack Lemmon, Anthony Quinn, Eva Marie Saint, Raymond Burr, Glenn Ford, Francis X. Bush-man and others. Sandburg was delighted.

He was also scheduled to appear on "The Milton Berle Show." Corwin had the broadcaster's instinctive foresight to tape the proceedings when comedy writer Hal Kanter came to work with Sandburg on the script for the show. Sandburg sang and expostulated for nearly eight hours, as if he were on the lecture platform. He wanted to talk about Lincoln and atomic war, but he did not want to talk about Ezra Pound ("I'll read the sonofabitch as long as I live") or Elvis Presley ("I wouldn't mention Elvis Presley, even under duress. . . . An insignificant passing phenomenon") or Burl Ives or Bernard Baruch or Albert Schweitzer (". . . Schweitzer doesn't have a much higher place in my book than Elvis Presley. He left Germany when the goddamndest enemy of the German people there ever was, was taking over power. He fled to Africa for safety. He had a career figured out.").

Later, when Corwin discovered that Sandburg was being paid only $3,500 for the Berle show appearance, and that he did the show before he signed a contract, he told Sandburg he needed an agent. Corwin knew that Sandburg should command much larger fees. He recommended an agent who had his "unqualified respect, to say nothing of affection." Her name was Lucy Kroll. Over the years she would represent a host of distinguished artists in various fields—Helen Hayes and Lillian Gish, Charles MacArthur and Ben Hecht, Martha Graham, Horton Foote, James Earl Jones, Robert Fitzgerald and others. She was an expert in literary as well as theatrical film and television projects, and was known for the consistently high quality of her clients and their work. At Corwin's suggestion, Lucy Kroll wrote to Sandburg late in 1958. "There is very little that I can say that could add to my deep feeling for the artist and the fulfillment I have received in my chosen career of representing the artist," she told him. "There is no parity between the agony and the sweat of the creator, and the glory and the profit. I can only add a small measure by protecting the artist and making possible the continuation of his work."

Sandburg decided to follow Corwin's advice and turn to Lucy Kroll. Inevitably, the decision alienated Donna Workman. As soon as Sandburg began to work with Lucy, Donna began to pull away. Saddened, he saw that he was losing her. Life was indeed "all time yes no yes no."

1959–1967

31. Honey and Salt

There are sanctuaries
holding honey and salt.
There are those who
spill and spend.
There are those who
search and save.
And love may be a quest
with silence and content.

—Carl Sandburg, "Honey and Salt,"
Honey and Salt, 1963

H e was eighty-one, looking back on his life, looking ahead. His favorite photograph of himself was Steichen's "Montage," six profiles, reflecting as many selves. Sandburg had had such a montage made cheaply in his youth, suggesting the whole range of his personality: boisterous to brooding, elusive to exultant; some poses studied, artificial, confident; others vulnerable and disarming; at once a full disclosure and withholding of self. "The many-sided self," Paula had called him at the very first. Always, and only for her, he was transparent. To others, himself, he was often an enigma. He was as complicated and as simple in his eighties as he had been in his twenties, pulled in as many directions, almost as frenetically active.

Looking back, there had been the constant, hungry search, suffused with possibility. He had wanted to say everything. Now, still calling himself a seeker, he was an international figure, the national poet, honored, loved by many. Forty thousand school children gave pennies to help support his Galesburg birthplace. He was writing in his great age as he had in youth about the passionate hungers for life, love, knowledge: "There are hungers/for a nameless bread/out of the dust/of the hard earth,/ out of the blaze/of the calm sun." Time was growing short. He had so

676

much left to do. "Has ever been a man praying?" he asked in "Shadows Fall Blue on the Mountains":

> "Make me into a thin
> goblet of glass, oh Lord.
> I fear what my shadow tells me?" . . .
>
> Now the shadow of Shakespeare—
> what did he say to it?
> what did he leave unsaid?
> and how well did he know he left
> millions of shadow soliloquies unspoken?

He wrestled with the shadows of doubt, incompletion, words unspoken. He felt the forthcoming silence, and wrote about it in "Speech," published in his eighties:

> There was
> what we call "words"
> a lot of language,
> syllables,
> each syllable made of air.
>
> Then there was
> silence,
> no talk at all,
> no more syllables
> shaped by living tongues
> out of wandering air.
>
> Thus all tongues
> slowly talk themselves
> into silence.

✳

During the last decade of his life, he was a full-time celebrity, and only a part-time writer. Many people clamored for his attention, sought to superimpose his venerable image on television shows, advertisements, causes, prefaces to books, public occasions, motion pictures. His life was a public circus of entertainment and pilgrimages, and a private sanctuary, as he was writing in a long new poem, "holding honey and salt." There was the sweet honey of fame, adulation, a long life of prolific accomplishment. Harcourt Brace Jovanovich would publish his tenth book of poetry in 1963, his thirty-eighth book to be published there since Alfred Harcourt had founded the firm back in 1919. Sandburg and Harcourt had shared most of those books, as well as the intimate ordeals and public honors of their lives. His last publisher, William Jovanovich, however, did not feel he knew Sandburg, despite their professional association, because they had never shared their troubles. "You never truly know a man until you know his sorrows," Jovanovich said years later, looking back at Sandburg.

The sorrows were deep and plentiful, the salty wound of his long separation from Helga, John Carl and Karlen Paula festering with misunderstanding, exacerbated by his stubbornness, and hers. Helga was his true daughter in temperament, endowed with his passion and his tenacity of will. Those traits empowered much of his success, and Helga's, but they also inflicted pain. In her first marriage in 1940 to Joe, Paula's hired man, Helga had essentially defied her mother. Joe, five years Helga's junior, helped her to leave home and become a farmer, like her mother an artist with all growing life. That time Helga left her mother's house, and proved she could excel at her mother's work. Later, she would try writing, her father's work, and would leave his house to do so. Far beyond the time when most parents and children take their leave of each other, that triangle of Paula, Carl and Helga held together, enclosing Helga's children. Margaret and Janet were worried onlookers, not actors in the drama which riveted the emotions of their parents and sister. Helga's sturdy shoulders bore the whole weight of parental expectation. She craved the life in her parents' home, and fed on it until it nearly suffocated her. Even then, her leave-taking was prolonged and wounding.

Her second marriage was in part of gesture of rebellion against her father. This time, she brought a rival into her father's house. Like Joe, Art was five years younger than Helga. Also like Joe, Art helped to liberate Helga from a life of seductive, loving dependency. She wrote in published poems and memoirs about how they had been lovers, how their marriage disintegrated, how her children were buffeted by the years of contention between Helga and her father, by later years of strife between Helga and Art, and then by John Carl's rebellion. Because of those rocky, bittersweet years, Helga freed herself from her second husband, but, most of all, from her parents and their home.

She spoke candidly in her journal and her books about her fierce, loving rivalry with her father, about becoming a writer on her own, with no help from him, refusing to lean on his name or on his friends. She was so adamant about not exploiting the Sandburg name that young Paula, when asked in high school if Sandburg was her grandfather, denied that he was. Assigned an English report on Carl Sandburg by a teacher who knew the family connection, Paula did just what her classmates did—went to the encyclopedia and took down the information there about her assigned subject, her Buppong, the grandfather who had been father and playmate and idol for the first ten years of her life.

The web of their family love was, like that of all families, immensely complicated. The three daughters saw in essence three different sets of parents, three different homes, as most children bring parents and home into the focus of their particular need and experience. Margaret's parents were all patience and love, intellectually as well as emotionally nurturing. Janet's parents were kind, loving, protective. They gave her an entire, safe universe—the house, the goat dairy, the Michigan dunes and later, the mountains and woods at Connemara—all the world she ever knew or wanted to know. Helga's parents were brilliant, passionate, loving, demanding, exacting. Her father roared, swore, ranted, intimidated, manipulated, usurped, understood. Her mother judged and scolded and looked serenely the other way, beautiful and cheerful and sometimes emotionally remote, absorbed totally in her own work, her husband's genius, Margaret's invalidism, Janet's limitations of mind.

Paula's obsession with genetics was a haunting counterpoint to her own sorrows as a mother—one child stillborn, one child epileptic, one child mentally flawed, her mind arrested in the early teenage years. Paula manipulated the genes of the animals until they approached world-class perfection, forcing them by her steadfast, probing brilliance to transcend themselves. Her brother Ed exacted the same rigorous surpassing of self from the flowers he bred, improving on their creation, manifesting his own voluptuous vision of the universe in the gorgeous delphiniums he patiently and relentlessly grew in his gardens.

The bitter "rift" between Helga and her parents was a well of endless sorrow in the last years of Sandburg's life. She and her father were still at war in 1959, the year of his eighty-first birthday, and one of the supreme occasions of his life.

✳

Sandburg flew to the West Coast in January 1959 as an honored guest on the first cross-continental jet flight, and found it every bit as marvelous as the train which first took him out of Galesburg when he was a boy. In February he was honored as the first private citizen since historian George Bancroft in 1874 to be invited to address a Joint Session of Congress. It was February 12, 1959, the hundred and fiftieth anniversary of Lincoln's birth. Both Houses of Congress, the Justices of the Supreme Court, President Eisenhower's cabinet, members of the diplomatic corps, and other guests were invited to the Capitol at eleven that morning, first to hear actor Fredric March read the Gettysburg Address, and then to hear Lincoln's most visible ambassador in the twentieth century, Carl Sandburg. Helga, who lived in Washington then, was invited, but quickly declined, even though privately she "longed for him." Speaker of the House Sam Rayburn introduced Sandburg as the man who probably knew more about "the life, the times, the hopes and the aspirations of Abraham Lincoln than any other human being," and presented "this great writer, this great great historian" to a standing ovation.

Tall, straight, the old oratorical fire burning strong as ever, forging the poet's words, Sandburg began: "Not often in the story of mankind does a man arrive on earth who is both steel and velvet, who is hard as a rock and soft as a drifting fog, who holds in his heart and mind the paradox of terrible storm and peace unspeakable and perfect." Sandburg filled his speech with Lincoln's own words, letting them weave a portrait of Lincoln's times and the present, the future. "The people of many other countries take Lincoln now for their own," Sandburg told his distinguished audience. "He belongs to them." For millions, Lincoln was a "personal treasure," Sandburg went on. He carried Democracy in "his blood and bones," in "the breath of his speeches and writings," in the "lights and shadows of his personality." His "most enduring memorial" lay in the "hearts of those who love liberty unselfishly for all men."

Sandburg would bring his audience to their feet once more at the finish of his speech. With quiet eloquence, prolonging every syllable, he concluded: "So perhaps we may say that the well-assured and most enduring memorial to Lincoln is invisibly there, today, tomorrow and for a long time yet to come. It is there in the hearts of lovers of liberty, men and women who understand that wherever there is freedom there have been those who fought, toiled and sacrificed for it."

That monumental Sandburg-Lincoln celebration launched an avalanche of "occasions" and from then until 1963, Sandburg seldom retreated into the sanctuary of Connemara with his family, or into the solitude of sustained, reflective work. Two obligations guided him: his and Paula's fundamental concern about securing the future for Margaret and Janet, the family at home; and his self-ordained role as spokesman for the great global "family." He could be seen singing, playing the guitar, or reading from his work on the major television shows of the sixties. Milton Berle, Dave Garroway, Ed Sullivan and Howard K. Smith were his hosts, along with Gene Kelly, who called himself the "dancer of the proletariat," dancing to a poem written for him by Sandburg, the poet of the proletariat.

Lucy Kroll shepherded these appearances, negotiating premium fees and working with Sandburg and Paula to choose the best outlets for his energy. "Believe me we all value your warm-hearted friendship for all the family and your deep understanding," Paula wrote to her in 1960. Sandburg told Lucy, " 'Smart' is not the word for you—you are *keen* and *deep*—*elegant* in the earliest sense of the word." He and Paula quickly grew to love and respect the feisty agent who was becoming one of the family. "Comes by you a letter which is cold swept straightaway business, unimpeachable business with figures and dollar signs complete and scrupulous and only a hydraulic jackass would dare utter any kind of murmur," Sandburg wrote as they worked on some contracts. "And then come lines of fellowship and affection having the colors of a gypsy flame dancer."

Although television gave Sandburg the largest possible audience in the sixties, he still lectured, frequently narrated the Copland "Lincoln Portrait," delivered commencement addresses. He and Norman Corwin worked on the script for *The World of Carl Sandburg*, for Bette Davis and her husband, Gary Merrill, had signed a contract "script unseen" to star in the stage review of Sandburg's work, even though it was going to mean "a strenuous, back-breaking seventeen-week tour of one and two nighters in sixty-seven cities throughout the country."

Engrossed as he was, Sandburg still told dozens of friends how he missed Helga; he could share his anguish with them, but not with her. He missed Donna, too, away in her long silence. "How goes it by you dearest rose, priceless potato?" he wrote, and, in another note later, "What ere betides, I love you." Paula watched that friendship diminish with relief, for it had wounded and embarrassed her. Donna later sold many of her Sandburg papers to Knox College in Galesburg, but kept some for a book she meant to write. Those papers would disappear after she died of lung cancer many years later, alone, and broke, in a small town in New Mexico. Some of the private notes and poems Sandburg sent Donna in that handful of years vanished, lines that in his mind and hers did not ever diminish his love for Paula. Donna would insist until she died that their friendship was innocent, saying of Sandburg then essentially what Brenda Ueland had said about him in the thirties. Despite innuendos about his sexual liaisons, no woman ever came forward to confirm that he was physically unfaithful to Paula, the heart of his life and work since 1908, that spring of their "baptismal rain."

In a letter to Helga many years later, journalist Evelyn Wells wrote about Sandburg's outrage once when he heard about a "publishing friend" divorcing his wife. "He was as great a friend with women as with men,"

Wells noted, "and he got homesick when he was away from his family too long." According to Wells, Sandburg once said, "I could have made an awful fool of myself over women if it hadn't been for my work."

Paula was a great success in her own chosen work, begun late, after her daughters were grown and her husband well-established. Her hundreds of letters over sixty years paint the intimate details of their family life. Her meticulous journals chronicle the bleak despair of Margaret's early illness, the lonely nights at Connemara when Carl was far away and Margaret's voice broke the stillness when there was a seizure, or when, if her medicine was not exactly calibrated, her sleep was torn by frightening dreams. Paula's letters speak of how she missed him during his prolonged absences from home, for months each year, all down the years of his independent, solitary, wearying but often joyful life on the road. "We never tried to 'remake' each other," she told a reporter in 1964. "Where there's love there's concern, a desire to help. But free souls do not try to 'remake' each other." In another, later interview she spoke about the secret to the success of their marriage: ". . . he always wanted me to do what I wanted to do and I always wanted him to do what he wanted."

Paula was by all testimony of her daughters and her friends a serene, deeply contented woman, fulfilled, sparkling with vitality, rejoicing in her life.

And he—until the end, he always traveled, the Eternal Hobo. That part of his life's journey she could not and would not share. Her incessant, loving responsibility for two daughters kept her at home, but then so did her quiet spirit, her intense love for the farm and all of nature, her need for tranquillity, stability, permanence.

The incontrovertible fact, documented everywhere in poems, letters and deeds, was the enduring love Sandburg and Paula shared, and their devotion to their family. Sandburg had only a few years left to ensure that there would be enough money to support Margaret and Janet long after he and Paula were gone. He worked feverishly throughout the 1960s, as long as his health lasted, keeping an inordinately strenuous schedule for a man of his age. "I have no strong will," he confided in Lucy, "but I long ago decided that a deep enough desire, a big enough wanting, is better than the much boasted strong will."

Enthralled with the "beginning" and "promise" of jet flight, Sandburg agreed in the summer of 1959 to do a rare commercial endorsement. He would speak on the American Airlines "Music Till Dawn" radio show and allow the airlines to reprint an essay he wrote about the first cross-country passenger jet flight. Remembering that it took relays of ponies seven days and seventeen hours to rush Lincoln's first inaugural address from St. Joseph, Missouri, to Sacramento, California, Sandburg hoped that "this narrowing of the distance between states and rivers, between countries and the people in them, will cement still further the common country that Lincoln saw as the destiny of America."

As he worked on the American Airlines project, he met Joanna Taub, a beautiful young copywriter. Captivated, he quickly introduced her to Steichen, who was still grieving for Dana. When Steichen suffered another stroke later that year, Joanna nursed him, and they would marry in March 1960, when Steichen was eighty-one, Joanna twenty-six.

Sandburg made his third and final trip abroad in 1959 when he and Steichen set off on a landmark journey to open the "Family of Man" photographic exhibition in the Soviet Union, part of the American National Exhibition sponsored by the State Department and the United States Information Agency. This cultural exchange would bring millions of Soviet citizens to look at the latest American technology, art and lifestyles. Just before Steichen and Sandburg departed, and unbeknownst to him, Sandburg had his last skirmish with the incriminating data in his FBI file, much of it incorrect. Some individual, name censored, tried to block his passport, despite the fact that the State Department had invited Sandburg to make the Moscow trip as a cultural envoy of the American people, awarding him an American Specialist grant under the State Department's International Educational Exchange Service and calling him the "dean emeritus" of the American group which would represent the United States. After his passport was issued, Sandburg managed to lose it en route to Moscow, but was admitted all the same "On Distinction of Man of Letters."

Millions came to see the "Family of Man" exhibit, officially opened by Steichen and Sandburg, Vice President Richard Nixon and Soviet Premier Nikita Khruschev. Clouds of dust filled the thirty-thousand-square-foot American exhibit space as the footsteps of visitors actually wore out the poorly formed concrete floor. More than seventy thousand people visited the American exhibit on one Sunday alone. From Moscow, Steichen and Sandburg went to Sweden. There Sandburg saw his mother's birthplace and searched in vain for his father's. In the farm fields surrounding his mother's birthplace, he gathered a handful of earth and let it fall through his fingers. He told a Swedish cousin, "This is for me holy earth, and I am grateful to Providence that I got the opportunity to come here."

One of his Swedish cousins, a son of Sandburg's mother Clara's half-sister, told him about the letters and pictures Clara sent faithfully to Sweden throughout her lifetime, full of news of life in Galesburg. "Aunt Clara had an unusual gift for storytelling," he told Sandburg. Over the years, her letters had been read again and again, until they were worn to pieces. Sandburg picked wildflowers from the fields in Östergötland, his mother's home county, and found the Swedish names for the flowers surfacing in his memory. Emotionally, and in Swedish, he read from *Always the Young Strangers* on Swedish television. He had an audience with Swedish king Gustav VI Adolf, who awarded him a gold medal.

Sandburg's last journey abroad was a triumph. He was recognized and celebrated everywhere he went—in the Soviet Union, in Sweden, in Paris and London. By mid-August 1959, he and Steichen were homeward bound, "a pair of eminent octogenarians" who served their nation as official "representatives of American culture." Later, Sandburg wrote about his brother-in-law and closest friend. Steichen embodied the American Dream, he said. "Property is nothing. Toils, hardships, and dangers are little or nothing to him alongside of the American Dream. He is no particular hand at patriotic speeches but he has some mystic concept of this country and its flag."

✳

Erect and vigorous, Sandburg strode into his eighties at the pinnacle of his popularity. He was beginning to have trouble with his memory from time to time, forgetting names and places, but he attributed that to weariness. "I am not proud of my forgettery nor do I hang my head in shame," he wrote journalist Virginia Pasley, asking for Terry and Gregory d'Alessio's address, a house he had thought of as home in New York for years. He and Kitty McCarthy put the finishing touches on a new book, a slim collection of previously published poems, arranged now for young people, called *Wind Song*. He dedicated it to John Carl and Karlen Paula, whom he had not seen in five years. He was still writing poetry, although most of the time he was crafting poems already begun rather than creating new ones. He did not mind at all sharing six of them with the "gustatory" readership of *Playboy*, whom he described as an audience of men who loved women and women who loved men. "And that," he declared, "is as it should be."

Sandburg took on two ambitious projects in 1960, boldly attacking new forms in his eighties as he had at sixty-five with his first novel. With Norman Corwin's *The World of Carl Sandburg*, he was headed for the first time to Broadway. With one of his favorite filmmakers, George

Stevens, he was headed for the last time to Hollywood, to work on the screenplay of *The Greatest Story Ever Told*.

Sandburg's last venture writing for the motion pictures was as financially profitable and artistically disappointing as his first, *Remembrance Rock*, but he enjoyed the experience. It was his last major endeavor, for afterward, failing health and mind governed his days. But in mid-July 1960, Sandburg was en route to Hollywood, with Lucy Kroll at his side, to begin work with Stevens on *The Greatest Story Ever Told*. At the outset, Stevens and Twentieth Century–Fox offered Sandburg $125,000, a tremendous boost to the trust fund.

All told Sandburg would spend a year and a half in Hollywood, with occasional visits home and elsewhere. His daily schedule revolved around afternoon story conferences led by Stevens. At first they were focused, almost scholastic, but more often, Sandburg and Stevens engaged in robust dialogue about wide-roving subjects, or Sandburg launched into long monologues before his captive audience of younger men. They began to chafe at his digressions. Stevens insisted that Sandburg enhanced his own conception of the film. To him, Sandburg was a national treasure, a poet and biographer of singular vision who could illuminate his epic film. Some of Stevens's younger staff members, however, saw an old man, admittedly venerable, but rambling, garrulous, more centered on himself than the movie.

After good reviews during its seventeen-week cross-country tour, *The World of Carl Sandburg* opened at the Henry Miller Theatre in New York September 14, 1960, without Gary Merrill. The carefully woven stage review of Sandburg's work, intertwined with music from *The American Songbag*, had been animated by the electricity between Davis and Merrill, but that ended when the couple separated and announced plans to divorce. Onlookers thought the production was never the same after Merrill left. The show opened on Broadway without him, and closed after a three-week run. In small theaters all over the country, however, it was still popular at least thirty years later.

Although the show closed quickly on Broadway, its opening brought a happy family reunion. Suddenly, in August 1960, Helga wrote years later, "The wide canyon of the Rift, in an instant, slams together and it is as if it had not been. Phones and letters are employed. Helga's third novel is going well and will be ready in October. The separation papers are signed. I am on a Georgetown University Writers Conference panel with Katherine Anne Porter, in heaven." Helga had decided once and for all to separate from Art, and get her own small apartment in Washington. "I must have my integrity in trade for loneliness and loss of affection," she told Art in a letter. The separation released her to be herself, to concentrate on her writing, and to rejoin her family, on her own terms. She wrote a "pages and pages" long letter to her mother, and proposed a visit to Connemara. "This exuberance, which I'm sure shows in this letter, is of course due to my fine sensation of release," Helga told her mother. Elated, the Sandburgs began to make plans to see Helga and the children. Even before Helga's letter came, Paula had written to the grandchildren, urging young Paula, seventeen, working as a camp counselor in Pennsylvania, to come to Connemara for a visit. She told John Carl, a rising sophomore at Virginia Polytechnic Institute, that "If Buppong can help in any way at any time" with his college expenses "you know this would be a grandfather's *privilege* and a deeply *rewarding privilege*."

Helga joined her parents and Margaret for the Broadway opening of *The World of Carl Sandburg*, happily reunited with them and her uncle Ed Steichen. As she and her father said good night after the premiere, Sandburg asked Helga if she had brought one of her manuscripts with her. "He asked me! HE ASKED ME!" she exulted in her journal. ". . . HURRAY! I THROW MY CAP IN THE AIR! HURRAY HURRAY He cares!"

She thought her father was "Complex. Unfathomable." She wrote him a long letter that fall: "I'm sorry the years have gone as they have, without you [and the children] knowing each other, but that is the way of it. . . . This is a Delayed Love Letter." Sandburg could not make it home for Thanksgiving, but when he got there for just a day's visit, he and Paula arranged for Helga and the children to fly to North Carolina "at once." All of them were together again at last in the "Golden Place," walking the old trails, talking, singing, hearing Sandburg read aloud, as if they had never been apart. When Sandburg was back in Hollywood, Paula wrote of that happy, healing time in a letter: "The New Order brings back the days at Chikaming and the first years at Connemara." And Sandburg answered Helga's "Delayed Love Letter": ". . . John and Snick [his nickname for young Paula] keep haunting me with their outer and inner loveliness. . . . Jesus! Swipes! It's good to know you under the NEW ORDER!"

Life was honey and salt, gains and losses. The losses, real and imminent, saddened Sandburg. Steichen was slow in recovering from the second stroke. Sandburg's editor and "good right arm" Kitty McCarthy was leaving Harcourt, Brace to lead her own life after many years of dedication to the firm, especially to his work. Worst of all, Sandburg was stricken that Paula was ill in the snow-clad Carolina mountains, and he was far away from her again, in Hollywood. She so seldom complained about anything, but had reluctantly written to him about an "ailment" which confined her to bed, back pain, most likely a sciatic nerve. "I'm glad you call it an ailment and not a disease," Sandburg answered immediately. "All along the Steichens always have had ailments and not diseases. . . . You were warned. I have warned you several times in your office as I found you there, concentrating on this and that. You have a rare, high-power mind. Something of your nervous system operates along with that mind. . . . Anyhow, it's nice that I'm going to be back in February and we'll have a morning walk and an evening walk—holding hands."

*

"Let us talk it over long/and wear cream gold buttons/and be proud we have anger and pride together," Sandburg wrote in one of the later poems, "High Moments." "I have kept high moments./They go round and round in me." The circles of his life were closing, one by one. He and Harry Golden campaigned actively for John Kennedy's election in 1960. It was Sandburg's last political campaign, and he brought to it "anger and pride," the fervor of the early days. He had written a poem about the "later America," finding his nation "yet ever more seeker/than finder, ever seeking its way/amid storm and dream."

The Poet of the People had become inextricably associated with Abraham Lincoln and the themes of American democracy. He liked young John Kennedy, thought he would make a great President, and encouraged him as he had Roosevelt and Truman. Robert Frost, the New Englander, was chosen to speak at the Kennedy inaugural, not Sandburg who had campaigned for Kennedy. Sandburg declined an invitation to the ceremonies, but later gladly wrote the preface to a book of Kennedy's speeches, *To Turn the Tide*.

In May of 1961, with their stepfather no longer part of their family, Helga's teenage children legally changed their names. They had taken Art's last name sometime after he and Helga married. John Carl and young Paula and Helga talked about the name they would use now, and chose their grandmother's maiden name. It would give them more privacy, and liberty to be themselves. "Sandburg would never do," Helga wrote. "Only a daughter can handle living with that." So they became John Carl and Karlen Paula Steichen. Their grandfather approved, and their grandmother "was delighted." In mid-summer, the family at Connemara was "jumping with joy" because young Paula was on her way to spend three weeks at the farm. Sandburg was now taking open pride in Helga's blooming writing career. He wrote to Paula to be sure to send their grandchildren money if they were short of funds. "I remember when you were in tears over that first marriage," he reminded her, "and I said, 'I think it means we are going to have grandchildren, and it may be that they will be exactly what we want.' Now it has happened. You have done well all the way through, and I kiss you a salute to our progeny."

Paula Sandburg was making headlines herself then, worldwide. Jennifer II, one of her Toggenburg goats, had set a "new all-breed record for dairy goats in the United States and a world record for the Toggenburg breed," producing "a record-breaking" 5,750 pounds of milk and 191 pounds of butterfat in 305 days. Helga joined the family in celebrating her mother's achievements. In her private journal Helga wrote about her new contentment in her own free life. "I feel most lovely. I am loved; I don't despair; the stars have meaning; my father loves me and I refuse to be wounded by Freud."

They were a celebrated family, garnering public honors for their work. Helga was invited to lecture abroad on American letters, sponsored by the State Department, and departed for London and Finland. Steichen was honored with a retrospective exhibit of his work at the Museum of Modern Art, three hundred photographs chosen from more than thirty thousand taken during his long career. Carl and Paula Sandburg went to New York to help him and Joanna celebrate.

Sandburg felt more than ever Paula's "personal force" in his life. She and Steichen had been for him "a faculty of many professors in several fields whether the fine arts, genetics or healthy and wholesome mysticism." As always, he delighted in her success. "I tell people you are a champion breeder of a champion, that you are a geneticist, a naturalist, an ornithologist, Phi Beta Kappa and a sweet gal," he wrote her from Hollywood where he was still working as Stevens's consultant. Her letters reached him steadily, with details of Connemara life and often, pictures of the goats. His letters home recounted highlights of his Hollywood life. "MEMO for my Paula," he wrote July 17. "Last Saturday night went for the first time in my life to the Hollywood Bowl, the guest of Mr. and Mrs. Andre Kostelanitz [sic] . . . it was a kind of a Grand Canyon audience, every seat taken, twenty thousand people, to hear an all-Gershwin program. A master of ceremonies . . . suddenly was saying, 'We have present with us this evening a man who has become a legend in his own time, Carl Sandburg' . . . So there we are, 'A legend in our own time.' And what you and I have to say is, 'Jesus, it could be worse.' "

He mourned the death of another legend that year. Ernest Hemingway had taken his own life in July 1961. Sandburg wrote his widow, Mary, praising her "deep quiet strengths" and her "wisdom gathered out of years wonderfully mingled with storm and peace." In October, Sandburg was off to Washington to open the Civil War Centennial Exhibition at the Library of Congress, and to entertain a black-tie audience at "An Evening with Carl Sandburg," sponsored by Jacqueline Kennedy. Robert Frost had given a similar evening's performance in May. Sandburg visited President Kennedy in the White House that week, and held a raucous press conference afterward. The "living legend" quickly discovered that whatever he said made news—and controversy.

He gave Kennedy his wholehearted approval, but Eisenhower was another matter. Reacting to the former President's recent speech attacking President Kennedy's Peace Corps, Sandburg gave reporters his uninhibited opinion: "Ike is talking like a regular Army-trained man in state-craft. He's going to put his foot in his mouth more than he expects." Before press at the Library of Congress, he attacked Eisenhower's position on welfare: "He has yet to know the people of the United States. With him the words 'socialist' and 'socialism' are dirty words . . . but ever since he left the creamery at Abilene, Kansas, he never bought a suit of clothes or a meal. . . . He's lived in a welfare state ever since he left Abilene and went to West Point."

Afterward, the Sandburgs were inundated with mail at Connemara, but Sandburg was not disturbed by the brouhaha after his "crazy press conference."

On the brink of his eighty-fourth birthday, Sandburg was both ebullient and weary, still driving himself relentlessly. He and Harry Golden were promoting Golden's anecdotal biography *Carl Sandburg* in appearances around the country. He had agreed to write the text for a book of photographs by photographer Arnold Newman. Twentieth Century–Fox was about to end financial support for *The Greatest Story Ever Told*, which already far exceeded schedule and budget, but he kept on working with Stevens.

He was tired, and his memory was capricious. He never knew now when it would let him down, erasing names, events, sometimes even his own work. But he had responsibilities. If being eighty-four meant you had to work harder and longer to get the same amount of work done, then that was just the way it would have to be, even if you were "a living legend."

✳

"Can you measure/moments in the sun/when your shadow lays down your shape?" he had written in the poem "Shadows Fall Blue on the Mountains." There were many moments in the sun then, and the shadows of fame, family need and his own vulnerability laid down the "shape" of his life. Margaret was ill again in 1962, this time with severe bursitis. Paula, nearly seventy-nine, helped her fifty-year-old daughter with daily physical therapy to heal a "frozen" shoulder. Hemmed in by winter and illness, it was a bleak season, and they all looked forward to Sandburg's next homecoming from California. He always lit up the house.

He flew into Charlotte, North Carolina, on January 27, but a barrier of snow and fog kept him from Flat Rock until Monday, January 29. He set his own weariness aside in his concern for Margaret and Paula. He was glad to be at home, overjoyed to have Helga there, too, down from Washington, where she had left her job at the Library of Congress. She was now lecturing and writing, visiting Connemara as her lecture schedule permitted. She worked with her father for several days of that winter visit, dealing with "a bushel and a half" of letters and other literary chores.

By the first week in February, Sandburg was saying good-bye to Paula and the daughters again, setting out one more time, as he had for more than a half century, to write and perform. There was no indication on that cold February day of his departure that this leave-taking was any different from a thousand others. He left Connemara for New York, a remarkably youthful and vigorous eighty-four-year-old. He came back to Connemara weeks later, an ill and failing elderly man.

He arrived in New York a few days before his scheduled appearance on "The Ed Sullivan Show." He had been invited to stay with Arnold and Augusta Newman in their apartment near Newman's photography studios. Lucy had negotiated a contract with Simon and Schuster, and Sandburg wanted to begin work with Newman on the text for his new book of photographs. Newman was a younger Steichen, Sandburg thought, and here was a chance to close the circle on his lifelong interest in photography.

When he arrived in Manhattan, he was bone-tired from months away from home in Hollywood, and the constant cross-continental trips for public appearances, especially in connection with Harry Golden's book. He spent hours in a cold, drafty studio rehearsing for yet another television show. He gave a fine performance, reading excerpts from his earlier writings on Lincoln in celebration of Lincoln's birthday. One night early in his visit, he and Newman sat down to talk about the book, and

Sandburg drank whiskey and then cognac in much larger quantities than he customarily did, departing from his old habit of nursing a drink as carefully as he nursed the cigars he cut in halves or thirds before smoking. He awoke the next morning with a raging fever. The worried Newmans quickly brought in a doctor to examine him. The diagnosis: Sandburg appeared to have a virus, aggravated by the alcohol.

Augusta Newman and her housekeeper cared for Sandburg for more than two weeks, getting him through the crisis and finding him a gentle, cooperative patient. He refused to go to the hospital, however, and he did not want to call and alarm Paula in North Carolina, tending to Margaret's recovery and other matters at home. News of his illness inevitably spread among his friends in New York and then to Paula in Flat Rock, terribly distressed to learn so late that he had been so ill. Harry Golden took charge of getting Sandburg home to Connemara.

Sandburg had perennially suffered bronchitis and pneumonia in the winter months, and those symptoms were part of a serious strain of influenza in 1962. But Paula wondered if he might have suffered a slight stroke. He could not seem to rally strength or recapture his customary zest. He tried to write, and to finish the Newman text in those spring days of his recuperation in the Blue Ridge Mountains he loved, but the words would not come.

The Connemara spring helped him heal and grow a little stronger, but when Newman visited Flat Rock in May, he could see that Sandburg was unable to do any more work on the book. He asked Sandburg to consider letting him send Olga Steckler to Flat Rock to tape and transcribe Sandburg's thoughts for the book, for she had typed manuscripts for Sandburg before. His enthusiasm for the project surpassed his physical energy. Ideas came to him, yet his mind would not stay fastened to the work. He was profoundly weary. He tried to summon the old discipline and will. But Sandburg was simply unable to go on.

Work had been therapy and sanctuary for him in the past. Paula, Lucy and Hilda Lindley, his new editor, began to work with him on *Honey and Salt,* a collection of poems to come out in time for his eighty-fifth birthday, but he left most of the decisions to them. By summer he was stronger, and tentatively accepted an invitation to speak at Hebrew University in Jerusalem in the fall with Harry Golden as his traveling companion. He was not well enough to make the trip. He and Golden did make a joint appearance that summer at the Flat Rock Playhouse, the professional summer stock theater just across the way from Connemara. They were greeted by a packed house. After Sandburg read his poems for more than an hour, he managed some songs with the guitar. He did not finish the last song he tried to sing that night. He could not remember the words.

By the autumn of 1962, he had limited his public appearances. For the first time ever, Paula traveled with him as a matter of course, fearing he would wake up in a city and not know where he was. They flew to Seattle for the World's Fair and a warm visit with Kenneth and Letha Dodson, who were sad to see Sandburg so fragile, with so much memory loss. In November, Sandburg and Paula flew to New York so that he could tape "The Bell Telephone Hour." Just as he had done for Fred Friendly earlier in a CBS show about the Supreme Court, Sandburg summoned the old strength and poise for the television camera. Offstage, he was sometimes a shadow of himself, wavering, tentative, often frustrated.

Lucy and Paula joined forces to protect him because sometimes he answered telephone calls and letters and accepted invitations which he then forgot. They shielded him from the public and the press, and turned his attention toward the appearance of *Honey and Salt* and the gala eighty-fifth-birthday celebration his publishers planned at the Waldorf-Astoria.

Helga and young Paula joined the family for Christmas in the gray winter hills. The New Year began with Sandburg's festive eighty-fifth-birthday dinner, attended by Rebecca West, Justice William O. Douglas, Adlai Stevenson, John Steinbeck, Malcolm Cowley, Mark Van Doren, Elia Kazan, Herbert Mitgang and nearly 150 other friends. Just before the dinner, Malcolm Cowley heard a rumor that Robert Frost was dead. Frost lay critically ill in a Boston hospital, having suffered a pulmonary embolism in late December, two weeks after surgery revealed prostate cancer. "This dinner for Sandburg would normally have had a good front page coverage in *The New York Times*," Cowley said. "If Robert Frost had died that day, goodness, the dinner would be pushed off the front page and perhaps out of the paper." Cowley told the journalist who gave him the story, "If you say that to one other person at this dinner, I'll never speak to you or write for you again!' " But it was only a rumor, and, said Cowley, "Sandburg's birthday dinner did get noted on the front page of *The New York Times*."

Mahalia Jackson sang for Sandburg and the crowd that night, and then Sandburg spoke a few words to his friends: "Being a poet is a damn dangerous business. Here and there you are good, and here and there you are not." He was visibly moved by the evening's tribute. "I will live a little longer, a year or two longer, because of it."

Honey and Salt was generally well reviewed. Poet Kenneth Rexroth, however, wondered "Where is the Sandburg who talked of picket lines? Where is the Sandburg who sang of whores?" When he read Rexroth's review in Harry Golden's office, Sandburg told Golden, "I am eighty-five years old. I am not going to talk about whores at my age."

Before the end of January, his old friend and rival Robert Frost would be dead, and on March 1, William Carlos Williams died. Wallace Stevens had gone in 1955. Eliot and Pound were left, but Eliot had long been a British citizen, identified as an "American-born English poet." Pound, liberated from St. Elizabeth's in 1958 with help from his fellow poets, had gone back to Italy, telling Italian reporters upon his arrival, "All America is an insane asylum!"

"I like Eliot, and I like Pound," Frost had told poet Donald Hall in 1962, "but they left us behind. They should have stayed over here." He and Sandburg had stayed, and survived, staunchly rooted to American life, past, present and future. Sandburg and Frost had had their differences, but as he wrote in his inscription to Frost's copy of *Complete Poems*, Sandburg kept a "thankful heart" for Frost's poetry and his fellowship.

Louis Untermeyer, who had known and loved both Sandburg and Frost for decades, observed that Frost was "proud, troubled, and frankly jealous" in nature. He noted that it "took years" for Frost to "recover from the feeling that every living poet was his potential if not his actual rival." Frost was as stalwart in his belief that the "best things and the best people rise out of their separateness" as Sandburg was in his vision of a unified Family of Man. The American public frequently mistook one venerable white-haired poet for the other, especially after the Kennedy inaugural when, sun-blinded, Frost stumbled in reading a new poem and recovered to give an old poem from memory. Sandburg usually managed to respond graciously when people congratulated him for Frost's performance. He insisted that he was not "cool" to Robert Frost.

"We're entirely different in our work," Frost told reporters aboard a plane en route to Israel in 1961. Harry Golden was seated across the aisle from Frost, and wanted to talk to him about Sandburg. "He has a good heart," Frost said, after disparaging Sandburg's haircut. "He says in his poetry that the people say yes. I say the people say yes and no. . . . Our great difference is our approach to poetry. I once said when he introduced me at a dinner that I'd just as soon write free verse as play tennis with the net down. But I have no quarrel with him. He's out there in Hollywood now with his name on the door writing that $5,000,000 picture about Christ, and I suppose that's all right if you want to do that sort of thing."

"Best wishes for the best man to win!" Frost had written on a Christmas greeting to Sandburg in 1953. Sandburg spoke testily of Frost in 1961 in an interview with Mark Harris, who was preparing a magazine article on the two poets, yet reflected with deep compassion on Frost's personal sorrows. "But there is this point," he said. "Frost has had personal tragedy of a kind I have not had in my life." Frost's son had died of cholera at age three; one of his daughters and his sister had been institutionalized with mental illness; another of his daughters died in childbirth; his other son had committed suicide; and his wife's death haunted him with guilt.

Sandburg had known Frost's daughter Lesley and written about her in a poem, and Helga had gotten to know Frost, whom she admired as a man and a poet. When she heard of his death, she wrote "an emotional elegy," and was invited to fly with Stewart Udall, Kennedy's Secretary of the Interior, as part of the official party to attend the memorial service at Amherst College.

"Of the trio of elder poets who were with us when this year began— Robert Frost, William Carlos Williams, Carl Sandburg—the one who remains stood chronologically in the center . . . an American bard in the tradition of Walt Whitman," John K. Hutchens wrote in the *New York Herald Tribune*. "With the deaths of Frost and Williams, American letters suffered grievously, and so the remaining one is to be cherished even more." Sandburg more than any of his contemporaries has been "around and *in* his country, border to border, coast to coast," Hutchens continued. "He is the old America. . . . He is today's America."

Sandburg was venturing into public view only occasionally in 1963, however. He and Paula went to New York in May so that Sandburg could narrate Copland's "Lincoln Portrait" one more time. At rehearsal he received a standing ovation from the orchestra. Paula and Lucy hovered anxiously around Sandburg on the night of the premiere performance with the New York Philharmonic at Lincoln Center. He sat on stage awaiting his cue, his knees covered with a shawl, appearing at times to doze. In reality, the bright lights hurt his weak eyes. But when his turn came, his voice filled the hall. There were many times in private when his memory faded, his attention waned, but on stage, before an audience of the people, he could still be the consummate performer.

When the Sandburgs celebrated their fifty-fifth wedding anniversary at Connemara in June, Sandburg insisted that without Paula, he would have been a bum. That was nonsense, she protested: "Carl Sandburg was so independent he wouldn't have allowed any woman to make a mess out of him. I don't believe there is a woman behind every great man." But she was one of the three greatest influences in his life, he still maintained, along with Steichen and Philip Green Wright. And she was never so important to him as she was in his last years, when his physical and mental powers were diminishing, his voice slowly talking itself into silence.

Helga came to Connemara in the fall, bringing with her a handsome Ohio physician, Dr. George Crile, a widower. Helga's writing career was flourishing. She had just finished her fourth book, *Sweet Music: A Book of Family Reminiscence and Song*, with a preface by her father. Her counterpart of *The American Songbag* wove songs with memories into a vivid portrait of her family history. Absorbed in her work and the life she had made for herself, she had not thought of marrying again, but friends introduced her to George "Barney" Crile, a "world-wide-known and somewhat controversial surgeon, as well as traveler, philosopher and writer," she wrote. He was, as well, "stunningly handsome with graying hair and wild blue eyes and aggressive determination in all ways."

He wrote Sandburg a letter, asking for Helga's hand: "I am Helga's Barney—Dr. George Crile Jr., head of the department of General Surgery at the Cleveland Clinic. I am one of the ones who want to marry your daughter. To be more precise I am the one whom she is thinking of marrying. Helga has asked me to visit you and Mrs. Sandburg at your farm. I hope that this can be arranged, for I want to discuss Helga's and my plans with you and have your approval of our marriage."

"But you're not married," Janet Sandburg protested when Helga and Barney arrived at Connemara and were about to share a bedroom. Amused, Sandburg decided to marry Helga and Barney himself. In a mock-solemn ceremony at Connemara, Sandburg pronounced Helga Sandburg and Barney Crile man and wife. Janet was mollified, and the couple could officially share a room in the lofty old house.

In Barney, Helga found her true mate at last. Her parents and children immediately liked the brilliant, genial doctor. When he and Helga were later married in a civil ceremony, her parents gave their blessings, and a wedding gift of three goats and a Sardinian donkey named Piccolino. It was from the outset a joyous marriage, and Helga would produce more than sixteen books, two more of them about her family. The last one, ". . . *Where Love Begins*," was her catharsis, leaving her luminous, transfigured, free to resurrect all the wonder and pleasure of life in her parents' household.

*

Sandburg passed his days walking the trails and meadows at Connemara, reading, sleeping and resting, sometimes working on poems he had never considered finished. He seldom left Connemara. For Paula, Margaret and Janet, he was, as always, life's center. Paula, now eighty-one, could not keep up with the place as she had before, and the old white house and its gardens and meadows sometimes lay neglected. She was concentrating on Sandburg. Her poet had at last come home to stay.

Beside his bed, Sandburg kept some of the books he loved most, works by Emerson, Whitman, Charles Lamb, Bacon and others. He read them over and over again during the quiet days of his great age, marking significant passages. As he had since youth, he read Bacon. In the essay "Of Great Place," he marked Bacon's lines on fame: "Death presses heavily upon him who, although well-known to others, dies unknown to himself." "There are ten men in me and I do not know or understand one of them," Sandburg had written as a young man. He was, even in his eighties, "still traveling, still a seeker." As he had written in *Always The Young Strangers*, he had kept his "boy-heart" intact. But his memory ebbed, his creative powers almost ceased, and his physical vigor, bred on the enduring prairie, waned with each bout of illness. Slowly he was letting go.

President Johnson invited him to the White House in September 1964 to receive the Presidential Medal of Freedom, as Steichen had the year before. Sandburg was the eldest of a distinguished company honored that day, among them some of his longtime friends—Helen Keller, Edward R. Murrow, John Steinbeck, Ralph McGill, J. Frank Dobie and Aaron Copland. Walt Disney received a medal, as did Lewis Mumford, Reinhold Niebuhr, John L. Lewis, Walter Lippmann, Leontyne Price and others. Frail and proud, Sandburg stepped up smartly to salute the President as he received his medal. "Sixth Illinois Volunteers," he said. It was a fitting honor, and the last time Sandburg would venture far from the sanctuary of home.

*

Honey and Salt, the final volume of poetry published in his lifetime, was notable for its variety and uneven quality. Some of the poems are sentimental caricatures of earlier work. Some are among the finest poems he ever wrote. In his reflections on life, love, death, time, there was indeed honey and salt, whimsy and pain, sentimentalism and strength, glibness and idealism, memory and hope, and a pervading affirmation of universal life. Many poems collected in *Honey and Salt* had been rewritten over time, portions of one poem lifted out and juxtaposed to another, a kind of endless experimenting, tinkering with his poetic universe.

Some of his most beautiful love poetry is gathered here, resplendent with images of love's many faces. "I could love you as dry roots love rain," he writes in "Offering and Rebuff." "Forgive me for speaking/so soon. . . . Love is a fool star." At the root of love—romantic, patriotic, platonic, family love, love for life—was passion:

> . . .
> Passion may hammer on hard door panels,
> empty a hot vocabulary of wanting, wanting . . .
>
> Passion may spend its money,
> its youth, its laughter, all else,
> till again passion is alone
> spending its cries to the moon . . .

He speaks here and in other poems of the encompassing passion for life in all its seasons and mystery. In "Fog Numbers" he reiterated the theme:

> Birth is the starting point of passion.
> Passion is the beginning of death.
> How can you turn back from birth?
> How can you say no to passion?
> How can you bid death hold off?
> And if thoughts come and hold you
> And dreams step in and shake your bones
> What can you do but take them and make them
> more your own?

The poems converging in this final book became a kind of last will and testament. He had long ago forsaken organized religion, "churchianity," but he was a spiritual, sometimes mystical man, given to writing prayers. He constantly discovered in nature not only physical beauty but the transcendental metaphors which helped to decipher life. He explained in the poem "Cahokia," about the Indian:

> . . . And he saw the sun.
> But he didn't worship the sun.
> For him the sun was a sign, a symbol.
> He bowed in prayer to what was behind the sun.
> He made songs and dances to the makers and movers
> of the sun.

It was all there in *Honey and Salt*, his valedictory, his life. He wrote of being a fool, a dreamer, a seeker. "There must be substance here/ related to old communions of/hungering men and women." The finale was "Timesweep," the long poem he had worked over for years, first calling it "Head One." Here he was still trying to puzzle it out, existence, writing at the end as he had at the beginning of his place in the evolutionary scheme of things, giving himself up peacefully to his moment in the immense, timeswept processional of life on this earth. He was kin to every creature since the beginning of life. Like Whitman, he contained the cosmos. All of us do, he deeply believed. "I got a zoo, I got a menagerie, inside my ribs, under/my bony head, under my red-valve heart," he had written back in 1918. He reprised the theme and resolved it in "Timesweep" in 1963:

> Listen and you'll hear it told,
> I am a beast out of the jungle.
> Man, proud man, with a peacock strut
> seeing himself in all his own man-made mirrors.
> Yet I am myself all the animals. . . .

It was a rhapsody, and he took it to absurdity at times, but he was offering his last epic. This time the subject was the creation, immortality. He was prepared for his own death, writing out his eulogy, his hope.

> Since death is there in the marvel of the sun coming up to travel
> its arc and go down saying, "I am time and you are time,"
> . . .
> Since death is there in almost inaudible chimes of every slow
> clock tick beginning at the birth hour there must be a tremor
> of music in the last little gong, the pling of the final an-
> nouncement from the Black Void.

He was "more than a traveler out of Nowhere," he wrote at the end:

> I have been woven among meshes of long ropes
> and fine filaments; older than the rocks and
> fresh as the dawn of this morning today are
> the everliving roots who begot me,
> who poured me out as one more seeker
> one more swimmer in the gold and gray procession
> of phantoms laughing, fighting, singing, moan-
> ing toward the great cool calm of the fixed
> return to the filaments of dust . . .

Finally, death, part of the deep rhythmic cycle of life, was not to be unwelcome, he said in "Atlas, Where Have You Been?":

And the forgetfulness of our own sleep
is strange and beautiful by itself
and sometimes in its shifting shapes
the world is a cradle dedicated to sleep
and what would you rather have than sleep?

And, in "The Gong of Time," there is acquiescence, peace:

Time says hush.
    By the gong of time you live.
  Listen and you hear time saying you were silent
    long before you came to life and you will
    be silent long after you leave it,
    why not be a little silent now?
        Hush yourself, noisy little man . . .

The day he turned eighty-seven, Carl Sandburg was strong enough to perform his customary exercise of lifting a chair over his head, but he did not venture to Washington to accept President Johnson's special invitation to the inaugural. He did not go to Hollywood for the premiere of *The Greatest Story Ever Told*, released in February 1965, starring Max von Sydow as Christ and Charlton Heston as John the Baptist.

In September, Roy Wilkins of the National Association for the Advancement of Colored People made Sandburg a life member of the NAACP, calling him "a major prophet of Civil Rights in our time." The NAACP saluted Sandburg, "who found beauty in brotherhood." He was very proud of the award. It was the only one among hundreds he had received that he kept in daily view.

A painful and debilitating attack of diverticulitis sent him to the hospital in the fall, and his slow recovery was marked by one setback after another. Paula, Margaret and Janet cared for him at home all that winter. In New York, Lucy kept an eye on his business affairs, sending down an occasional contract to Paula for her consideration and for Sandburg's quavering signature, no longer the bold holograph. With journalist and author Herbert Mitgang, Margaret set to work collecting Sandburg's letters to be published by Harcourt Brace Jovanovich. He willingly left the work to others.

Paula moved Sandburg from his bedroom on the third floor to her own spare, bright room on the main floor of the house. There he could sit in a comfortable chair by the bay window overlooking the giant, pungent ginkgo tree and the graceful boxwood grove near the Swedish House. He could listen to classical music on the record player at his elbow, and read and rest, with the comfortable hubbub of the house in the background. His recovery was slow, almost imperceptible, but he was cheerful. He did not seem to realize he was not in perfect health and vigor. Many mornings he would awaken when Paula called him. "Who is it?" he would cry.

"Paula," she would answer in her lilting voice.

Sandburg would laugh and shout, "Too good to be true!" He often asked her where they were—"In New York—or Chicago?"

"We are at home," she would tell him, and he was happy. He still read, and often, as in the old days, read aloud to the family and, now, the ever-present nurse. As the mountain spring warmed the woods and meadows, he began to take slow walks around the house, pausing to examine flowers, stones and leaves, gathering a few in the old way to bring into his room. For the first time in his long life, he was content to be at home.

"Dad is always in good spirits," Paula wrote to Helga in 1966, "always has compliments for everyone and hasn't a worry in the world. Occasionally he gets the idea he has an engagement for an evening performance, but has no worry about it, just takes for granted that he will be there with no concern as to how that will be managed. All this is wonderful for him and for all of us who love him."

There were still invitations, calls for interviews, hundreds of letters. His health became more fragile, his walks shorter, his interludes of sleep longer. By year's end, Paula told friends that his activities were limited. "He spends most of his time reading and listening to music. He is not involved in the present political scene and is serene and content in our family life here."

The serenity was broken from time to time by unpredictable outbursts of temper and frustration. At times the powerful mind, the mischievous humor and the old mystical sense of life were clear as ever. At other times, confused and disoriented, Sandburg did not know his family or nurses or friends who came to visit. Only Paula could steady him. "Come on, Buddy," she would say, "it's time to rest," and she would lead him to the bedroom and sit with him until he slept.

The darkening of his lustrous mind and spirit deepened after a heart attack in June 1967, and then another. Young Paula Steichen came to be with him. Sandburg could barely manage a few faltering steps. He was not revived by the clean bright heat of the mountain summer. The Rose of Sharon bloomed into the wide windows, the birds fed within view, Paula's African violets covered the window sills. In the nearby gardens Steichen's blue delphiniums, named for Carl Sandburg, grew tall in the sun, mingled with Paula's gold lilies. By mid-July, Sandburg was bedfast and silent, seldom recognizing any face but hers.

Paula and his nurses filled his room with music—Chopin, near the end. Someone brought one large, beautiful magnolia blossom. Its fragrance hovered in the air.

Late in the day, Friday, July 21, Sandburg smiled at his wife and spoke to her. Just after nine o'clock in the morning, Saturday, July 22, 1967, the poet's great mind and heart gave way at last to silence and to sleep.

In life, he spoke and sang millions of words. In death, the last word he spoke was her name.

"Paula—"

Epilogue: Shadows

I have love
And a child,
A banjo
And shadows.
(Losses of God,
All will go
And one day
We will hold
Only the shadows.)

—Carl Sandburg,
"Losses," *Chicago
Poems*, 1916

anet did not know her father was dead until she looked down from
her third-floor window and saw the hearse moving soundlessly under
the arch of hemlock trees, taking his body away. For a while, she
wept. Then she went downstairs to help her mother, and to wait for
people to come. Margaret was visiting Helga in Cleveland, and Barney
would bring them back to Connemara.

It was Steichen who persuaded Paula that she had to let the press
know of Sandburg's death. She called Joe Wershba at CBS, who in turn
shared the news with the President and the wire services. Sandburg had
"slowly breathed away," Paula told reporters. "He had a beautiful passing. . . . Now he belongs to the world."

He was hailed as "a national poet, America's greatest since Walt
Whitman." Thomas Lask wrote in *The New York Times* that Sandburg
was "more than a poet, biographer, spinner of tales and wandering
minstrel—he was the American bard."

Family and friends gathered for a simple ceremony July 24, 1967, at
St. John in the Wilderness Episcopal Church in Flat Rock. Esther Wachs,

Sandburg's last surviving sister, came from California, frail and beautiful. Steichen tore a bough from a Connemara pine tree and placed it on Sandburg's coffin. George Tolleson, the young Unitarian minister in charge of the service, read poems by Whitman and by Sandburg to celebrate his life, "life itself, all life on this earth."

Sandburg had outlined a funeral in 1920 in his poem "Finish" in *Smoke and Steel*, and the service in Flat Rock in 1967 followed that design:

> Death comes once, let it be easy.
> Ring one bell for me once, let it go at that.
> Or ring no bell at all, better yet.
>
> Sing one song if I die.
> Sing John Brown's Body or Shout All Over God's Heaven.
>
> Death comes once, let it be easy.

At the finish, there were the songs and the poetry, and one bell for the eighty-nine-year-old singer and seeker. "All my life I have been trying to learn to read, to see and hear, and to write," he had said when he was seventy-two. Echoing the artist Hokusai, he wrote, "It could be, in the grace of God, I shall live to be eighty-nine . . . and speaking my farewell to earthly scenes, I might paraphrase: 'If God had let me live five years longer I should have been a writer.' "

"Life is a river on which we drift down thru an unexplored country," he had written to Paula in the days of their courtship. Together they had explored a century; the heights and depths of his work; the universal yet infinitely diverse patterns of family life; the mysteries of self, soul, being. "You are yourself the *Achievement*," Paula wrote to him in 1908. "We shall do our best *to do something*—to leave some *thing* that we have produced here on earth as a bequest. But we'll remember that *the life we live* is more important than the *works we leave*." Whatever the fate of the mass of work he produced, Sandburg had made his life a work of art—richer and deeper for its flaws; transcendent in its tenacious struggle against the "barriers of the unknown" in poetry, politics, self.

Nearly six thousand people gathered at the Lincoln Memorial in Washington in September 1967 for a national Carl Sandburg tribute sponsored by Chief Justice Earl Warren; Secretary of the Interior Stewart Udall; Secretary of Labor Willard Wirtz; United Nations ambassador Arthur Goldberg; and, from Sandburg's home state of Illinois, Governor Otto Kerner, Senators Everett Dirksen and Charles Percy, and former senator

Paul Douglas. With Margaret, Helga and Barney, Paula Sandburg was there to hear poets Mark Van Doren and Archibald MacLeish give eulogies. President Lyndon Johnson arrived unannounced to praise "this vital, exuberant, wise and gentle man."

Back in the early days of his American odyssey, Sandburg had discovered Whitman's credo, expressed in "Starting from Paumanok": "I am the credulous man of qualities, ages, races;" Whitman wrote. "I advance from the people in their own spirit;/ Here is what sings unrestricted faith."

To the end, Sandburg went on singing his boundless "unrestricted faith." He had said it his own way in *The People, Yes*:

> I am credulous about the destiny of man
> and I believe more than I can ever prove
> of the future of the human race
> and the importance of illusions . . .

On October 1, 1967, Sandburg's ashes were buried at his birthplace in Galesburg beneath a granite boulder called Remembrance Rock. His brother-in-law Edward Steichen died on March 25, 1973, at the age of ninety-four. Lilian Anna Maria Elizabeth Magdalene Steichen, whom Carl Sandburg named Paula, was ninety-four when she died February 18, 1977. Then her ashes joined his in the bright, lonely hush of the prairie.

Key to Abbreviations and Sources

*

Carl Sandburg's Published Works as Cited in Text:

(This list does not include reprints, special editions or translations of Sandburg's published work except when there is a citation in this text.)

ALGU   *Abe Lincoln Grows Up* (New York: Harcourt, Brace, 1928)

AL:OVE *Abraham Lincoln: The Prairie Years and the War Years*, one vol. (New York: Harcourt, Brace and World, 1954)

ALPY   *Abraham Lincoln: The Prairie Years*, two vols. (New York: Harcourt, Brace, 1926)

ALWY   *Abraham Lincoln: The War Years*, four vols. (New York: Harcourt, Brace, 1939)

AS   *The American Songbag* (New York: Harcourt, Brace, 1927)

ATYS   *Always The Young Strangers* (New York: Harcourt, Brace, 1953)

BT   *Breathing Tokens*, Margaret Sandburg, ed. (New York: Harcourt Brace Jovanovich, 1978)

CH   *Cornhuskers* (New York: Henry Holt, 1918)

ChiP   *Chicago Poems* (New York: Henry Holt, 1916)

CP   *The Complete Poems of Carl Sandburg* (New York: Harcourt Brace Jovanovich, 1970)

CRR   *Chicago Race Riots, July 1919* (New York: Harcourt, Brace & Howe, 1919, reprinted 1969)

EM   *Early Moon* (New York: Harcourt Brace, 1930)

EWC   *Ever the Winds of Chance*, Margaret Sandburg and George Hendrick, eds. (Urbana: University of Illinois Press, 1983)

FFF   *Fables, Foibles and Foobles*, George Hendrick, ed. (Urbana: University of Illinois Press, 1988)

FM   *The Family of Man* [Prologue] with Edward Steichen (New York: Maco Magazine Corporation for the Museum of Modern Art, 1955)

GMA   *Good Morning, America* (New York: Harcourt, Brace, 1928)

HFM   *Home Front Memo* (New York: Harcourt, Brace, 1943)

705

HP   *Harvest Poems* (New York: Harcourt, Brace, 1960)

H&S   *Honey and Salt* (New York: Harcourt Brace Jovanovich, 1963)

IN   *Incidentals*, as Charles A. Sandburg (Galesburg, Illinois: Asgard Press, 1907)

IRE   *In Reckless Ecstasy*, as Charles A. Sandburg (Galesburg: Asgard Press, 1904)

J   *Joseffy*, as Charles A. Sandburg (Galesburg: Asgard Press, 1910)

LCB   *Lincoln Collector: The Story of Oliver R. Barrett's Great Private Collection*, with Oliver Barrett (New York: Harcourt, Brace, 1949)

ML   *Mary Lincoln: Wife and Widow*, with Paul Angle (New York: Harcourt, Brace, 1932)

PAL   *The Photographs of Abraham Lincoln*, with Frederick Hill Meserve (New York: Harcourt, Brace, 1944)

PF   *Potato Face* (New York: Harcourt, Brace, 1930)

PR   *The Plaint of a Rose*, as Charles A. Sandburg (Galesburg: Asgard Press, 1904)

PTB   *Prairie Town Boy* (part of ATYS, for children) (New York: Harcourt, Brace, 1955)

PVCS   *Photographers View Carl Sandburg*, Edward Steichen, ed. (New York: Harcourt, Brace, 1966)

RC   *Rootabaga Country* (New York: Harcourt, Brace, 1929)

RP   *Rootabaga Pigeons* (New York: Harcourt, Brace, 1923)

RR   *Remembrance Rock* (New York: Harcourt, Brace, 1948)

RS   *Rootabaga Stories* (New York: Harcourt, Brace, 1922)

SOL   *Storm Over the Land: A Profile of the Civil War Taken Mainly from Abraham Lincoln: The War Years* (New York: Harcourt, Brace, 1942; London: Cape, 1943)

SP   *Selected Poems*, Rebecca West, ed. (London: Cape, 1926; New York: Harcourt, Brace, 1926)

SR   *The Sandburg Range* (New York: Harcourt, Brace, 1957)

SS   *Smoke and Steel* (New York: Harcourt, Brace, 1920)

SSW   *Slabs of the Sunburnt West* (New York: Harcourt, Brace, 1922)

STP   *Steichen the Photographer* (New York: Harcourt, Brace, 1929)

TPY   *The People, Yes* (New York: Harcourt, Brace, 1936)

WP   *The Wedding Procession of the Rag Doll and the Broom Handle and Who Was in It* (New York: Harcourt, Brace & World, 1967)

Key to Abbreviations of Names

For the most part, names are given in full in the notes for ease of reference. The exceptions are those individuals who appear frequently throughout the narrative:

ACH   Alice Corbin Henderson

AH   Alfred Harcourt

CS   Carl Sandburg

HS   Helga Sandburg

JS   Janet Sandburg

LS   Lilian Steichen; who then becomes PS, Paula Sandburg

MS   Margaret Sandburg

PGW   Philip Green Wright

PS   Paula Sandburg (formerly LS, Lilian Steichen)

Helga Sandburg's books are cited by their initials, as follows:

HS, GGR   Helga Sandburg, *A Great and Glorious Romance* (New York: Harcourt Brace Jovanovich, 1978)

HS, SW   Helga Sandburg, *Sweet Music: A Book of Family Reminiscence and Song,* with a Preface by Carl Sandburg (New York: Dial, 1963)

HS, WLB   Helga Sandburg, *". . . Where Love Begins"* (New York: Donald Fine, 1989)

Other works by Helga Sandburg, and works by Paula Steichen and Edward Steichen, are cited as they appear in the notes.

Manuscript Collections

The Carl Sandburg Collection at the University of Illinois Library, Urbana-Champaign, is the most important Sandburg research center in the nation. In addition to several thousand of Sandburg's books, UI houses more than fifty thousand Sandburg papers— letters, manuscripts, journals and other documents of significance. There are smaller but crucial collections of papers at Connemara, the Carl Sandburg Home National Historic Site; at the University of Virginia; at the University of Texas in Austin; and at Knox College in Galesburg, Illinois. Manuscript collections cited in the biography are abbreviated as follows:

CHS   The Chicago Historical Society

CSH   Carl Sandburg Home NHS, Flat Rock, N.C.

CM   The Charlotte-Mecklenburg Public Library, Charlotte, N.C.

DU   Duke University

ES/UI   The Encyclopedia of Sandburgiana, a year-by-year series of notebooks arranged by Margaret Sandburg

HB   Harcourt, Brace Files

HS   The Helga Sandburg Private Collection

HS/UI   The Helga Sandburg Collection at the University of Illinois

HU   Harvard University

ISU   Indiana State University, Terre Haute (Eugene Debs)

IU   Indiana University

JW   The Joseph Wershba Collection

KC   Knox College, Galesburg, Illinois

LC   The Library of Congress

LK   The Lucy Kroll Collection

MCHS   The Milwaukee County Historical Society

MS   The Margaret Sandburg Private Collection

MS/UI   The Margaret Sandburg Collection at the University of Illinois

NEA   The Newspaper Enterprise Association Archive, Cleveland, Oh.

NL   The Newberry Library

SMU   Southern Methodist University

UC   University of Chicago

UD   University of Delaware

UI   University of Illinois

UM   University of Minnesota

UNCC   University of North Carolina–Charlotte (Harry Golden)

UT   University of Texas, Austin, Humanities Research Center

UV   University of Virginia

WSHS   Wisconsin State Historical Society

Sandburg's Poetry

The previously unpublished or uncollected poems are identified in the notes by title and all available information about date and place, as well as variants in existing drafts of the work. Relevant manuscript collections are indicated. Because printers rather than the poet himself sometimes established line lengths and breaks in the first editions of Sandburg's published poetry, *The Complete Poems of Carl Sandburg* (New York: Harcourt Brace Jovanovich, 1970, Revised and Expanded Edition) reflects Sandburg's own final rendition of his published, collected poems. In addition, because that volume is more readily available to most readers, I have used that source for quotation of all Sandburg's published poems contained therein, using the abbreviation CP. I have indicated the name of the volume in which each poem appears. The abbreviation BT indicates that a poem was published in Margaret Sandburg's 1978 edition, *Breathing Tokens*.

Sandburg's Letters

All unpublished letters quoted are identified with the initials of the appropriate repository. Sandburg's published letters appear in three collections, as noted below. While in every possible case I have quoted from the original letter or a photocopy of it, I have cited, for the reader's ease of reference, the volume and page number where the published letter may be found.

PDG   *The Poet and the Dream Girl: The Love Letters of Lilian Steichen and Carl Sandburg*, Margaret Sandburg, ed. (Urbana: University of Illinois Press, 1987).

MIT   *The Letters of Carl Sandburg*, Herbert Mitgang, ed. (New York: Harcourt, Brace & World, 1968).

VA   *Carl Sandburg, Philip Green Wright and the Asgard Press* (Charlottesville: University of Virginia Press, 1975).

Margaret Sandburg and George Hendrick are preparing for the University of Illinois Press a multivolume collection of Sandburg's letters, an invaluable tool for future biographers and students of Sandburg. On occasion, my dating of letters differs from that in the published editions, based on internal evidence or consultations with Margaret Sandburg, Helga Sandburg or George Hendrick. On those rare occasions when the original document varies from the published letter, I have explained in a note.

Because the Sandburgs and the Steichens and some of their correspondents often used idiosyncratic spellings, abbreviations, punctuation and syntax, I have quoted them faithfully, without the constant interruption of [*sic*].

Oral History Interviews

I have used four types of interviews as part of the documentary base of the biography:

First, interviews given *by* Carl Sandburg and other members of the family to other interviewers. They are identified in the notes in each case.

Second, interviews *about* Sandburg conducted by others, so identified in the notes in each case.

Third, interviews I conducted for the Carl Sandburg Oral History Project, identified CSOH Interview by PEN; except for a few restricted interviews, these interviews are available to researchers at UI. Copies of the interviews are deposited for the use of the National Park Service staff at Connemara, CSH NHS.

Fourth, interviews I conducted apart from the Carl Sandburg Oral History Project, identified PEN Interview. The tapes, transcriptions and notes from these interviews will eventually be deposited at UI.

Notes

∗

Preface

xi. "Ain't it hell": CS to Amy Lowell, March 17, 1925, MIT 230.

xi. Connemara background is based on interviews with MS, Paula Steichen, HS, Warren Weber, Louise Bailey, Mead Parce and Judge Frank Parker.

xiii. See "The Abracadabra Boys," CS, CP 643.

xiii. William Carlos Williams, "Carl Sandburg's Complete Poems," *Poetry: A Magazine of Verse* [hereafter *Poetry*], LXXVIII (September 1951), 345–51.

xiv. Helga Sandburg shipped: HS interview.

xiv. Helga Sandburg kept: HS interview.

xv. Sandburg's critics have: Critical reviews are cited in detail throughout the biography.

xvi. "Biography is hell": CS to Paul L. Benjamin, February 13 [1920], MIT 178.

xvi. Sandburg was the: Undated, unpublished fragment, UI.

xvi. Background on Sandburg's youth and family is drawn from ATYS and EWC.

xvii. "hunger for a": CS, "Timesweep," *Honey and Salt*, CP 758.

xvii. "Study the wilderness": CS, "Accept Your Face with Serious Thanks," BT, 154.

xvii. Like Sophia Hawthorne: MS, HS interviews; MS, PDG xii; 54.

xviii. "older than the": CS, "Timesweep," CP 758.

xviii. "Scroll": CP 629.

xviii. The autobiography begins: CS, ATYS 15–30.

xix. He wrote about: Undated, unpublished manuscript, UI.

xix. "If it can": CS, ATYS 436.

Chapter 1: The Young Stranger (1869–1895)

1. "the new people": "Broken-face Gargoyles": Smoke and Steel, CP 185. CS wrote Louis Untermeyer February 5 [1920] that this poem "is one of the best I've ever done and is young America to the World."

1. "When a man looks": Unpublished, undated fragment, UI.

1. "to tell what": Ibid.

1. "first found how": CP xxx.

2. "black marks on": ATYS 59.

2. "Dread in his": ATYS 77.

2. He was about twenty-three: Knox County, Illinois, Department of Welfare Enumeration District record, June 1, 1880, gives August's age as thirty-four and Clara's as thirty "at last birthday."

2. "where there was": ATYS 21.

3. "black" Swede: ATYS 18.

3. was her "*chance*": ATYS 82.

3. "*Det är en*": ATYS 15.

4. "welcome man-child": ATYS 15.

4. Galesburg, Illinois, background is drawn from ATYS; EWC; Earnest Elmo Calkins, *They Broke the Prairie* (New York: Charles Scribner's Sons, 1937); Hermann R. Muelder, *Missionaries and Muckrakers: The First Hundred Years of Knox College* (Urbana: University of Illinois Press, 1984).

5. "The small town": ATYS 280.

5. "Did I know": ATYS 287.

5. "I was born": "Prairie," *Cornhuskers*, CP 79.

6. "insidious menace": ATYS 120.

6. Sandburg's account of the Demorest Medal Contest appears in ATYS 72–74, and in an undated, unpublished fragment, UI.

6. "parents, playfellows, friends": Ibid.

7. "Of course I": Ibid.

7. "They laughed because": Ibid.

8. "day on day": ATYS 80.

8. "layers of muscle": ATYS 80.

8. "City of the": "Chicago," *Chicago Poems*, CP 3–4.

8. "important and independent": ATYS 378.

8. "wild downpour," "fast twister of": ATYS 81.

8. "I picked it": ATYS 81.

9. "Ah! dat iss": ATYS 94.

9. "pushing a plane": ATYS 95.

9. "he could kill": ATYS 95.

9. "At first I": ATYS 95.

9. "I enjoyed their": ATYS 355.

9. "classic as Mona": ATYS 354.

10. "I was more": ATYS 354.

10. "another three-room": ATYS 16.

10. "set himself up": ATYS 21.

10. "Two Swede families": "House," *Cornhuskers*, CP 138. See ATYS 44–48.

10. "a carpenter, a": ATYS 38.

11. "fear of want": ATYS 77.

11. "fagged and worn": ATYS 80.

11. "deep, passionate baritone": ATYS 81.

11. "powerful side fist": ATYS 80.

11. "breakage or spoilage": ATYS 81.

11. "gravel baritone": ATYS 85.

11. "with real respect": ATYS 85.

11. "de Yesse Yames": ATYS 85.

11. "only mildly interested": ATYS 85.

11. "visions and hopes": ATYS 90.

11. "eagerness about books": ATYS 90.

12. "stormed and hurled": ATYS 90.

12. "printed words, written": ATYS 79.

12. "We won't bodder": ATYS 92.

12. "Carl would mean": ATYS 39.
13. "young Republican, a": ATYS 33.
13. "have had in": ATYS 97.
13. "Hard work never": ATYS 98.
13. "How or why": ATYS 99.
14. "Be careful you": ATYS 99.
14. "didn't like quarrels": ATYS 99.
14. "patient and toiling,": "Masses," *Chicago Poems*, CP 5.
14. "He worked thirty": "Jack," *Chicago Poems*, CP 22.
14. "the great brave men": "Clean Hands," *Smoke and Steel*, CP 197–98.
14. "stallions and mares": ATYS 188.
16. "to a faith": ATYS 70.
17. "granted judgment": ATYS 105.
   Sandburg devoted a chapter in *ATYS* to the details of "The Sleeping Mortgage." His friend Wilson Henderson, Superintendent of Public Welfare in Knox County, Illinois, helped him document the event with county records (*ATYS* 108).
17. "wrung from the": ATYS 105.
17. "hardest worry": ATYS 103.
17. "going through": ATYS 103.
17. "He had nothing": ATYS 106–108.
18. He had devoured: Sandburg wrote in *ATYS* and *EWC* about the books he read in his youth and their influence on his life, and later kept notes on his reading in his journals and pocket notebooks.
19. "Illinois and the": ATYS 59.
19. "poor boys who": ATYS 260.
19. "get his first": Lilian Paula Sandburg, "Conversation at Connemara," *Rochester Democrat and Chronicle*, 11/26/64, 8E.
19. "nothing but his": Ibid. and unpublished fragment, UI.
19. "more hopes than": ATYS 232.
20. "first taste of": ATYS 230.
20. "so grand and": ATYS 230.
20. "hard enough to": ATYS 228.
20. "buckwheat cakes": ATYS 220.
21. "a grayish white": ATYS 221.
21. "He is cold": ATYS 222.
21. "It was all": ATYS 223.
22. "I shall cry": "The Right to Grief," *Chicago Poems*, CP 12–13.
22. "My feet were": ATYS 225.
22. "looked as good": ATYS 225.
23. "There was my": ATYS 198.
23. "sweating and puking": ATYS 199.
23. "slightly used": ATYS 233.
23. "having color and": ATYS 206.
23. "hard-and-fast": ATYS 206.
24. "an anarchist": ATYS 206.
24. "tide of feeling": ATYS 207.
24. "widespread American scene": ATYS 208.
24. "doom and fate": ATYS 51.

25. "The past is": CS, "Prairie," *Cornhuskers, CP* 79; CS, "Four Preludes on Playthings of the Wind," *Smoke and Steel, CP* 183.
25. "I was no": ATYS 52.
25. "You know where": ATYS 225.
25. "education in scraps": ATYS 230.
26. "what Lincoln said": ATYS 242.
26. "in winter sunrise": ATYS 242.

Chapter 2: The Dust of the Traveled Road (1896–1898)

27. "I SHALL foot": "The Road and the End," *Chicago Poems, CP* 42.
27. "traveler seeing the": ATYS 378.
27. "dust of the": Ibid.
28. "So this is": ATYS 147.
28. "traveling light": ATYS 378.
29. "shimmering water": ATYS 379.
29. "in wax Jesse": ATYS 379.
29. "heard so much about": ATYS 380.
29. "as a tall": ATYS 381.
29. "She smiled a": ATYS 380.
30. "You're up the": ATYS 380.
30. "I had my bitter": ATYS 375.
30. "too ugly a sight": ATYS 375.
30. *"Sandburg Boy Killed"*: ATYS 375.
30. "actually feeling a": ATYS 375.
30. "all the best": ATYS 376.
30. "if the luck didn't": ATYS 376.
31. "hell to pay": ATYS 245.
31. "a voice, an": ATYS 246.
31. "had it hot": ATYS 247.
31. "the other side": ATYS 247.
32. "My bones tell": ATYS 248.
32. "the scrabbling little": ATYS 377.
32. "the isolation": Unpublished, undated manuscript, UI.
32. Sandburg's journals are part of the CS Collection, UI.
32. "three species of": Dr. Edmund Kelly, *The Elimination of the Tramp* (New York: G. P. Putnam's Sons, 1908), 103–104

    A fascinating body of "tramp" literature documents the international scope of the problem of homelessness, unemployment and vagrancy, especially the study of "trampology" by Josiah Flynt (Willard), *Tramping with Tramps* (New York: Century, 1899); Richard Etulain, ed., *Jack London on the Road: The Tramp Diary and Other Hobo Writings* (Logan: Utah State University Press, 1977); Dr. Ben Reitman, *The Second Oldest Profession* (New York: Vanguard Press, 1931); and Nels Anderson, *The Hobo: The Sociology of the Homeless Man* (Chicago: University of Chicago Press, 1923, reprinted 1965).
33. "become so enamoured": Willard, *Tramping with Tramps*, 302.
33. "an unavoidable nuisance": Willard, 303.
34. "robbery, obstruction of": Kelly, *The Elimination of the Tramp*, 1–3.

34. "surplus labor army," "Into the surplus": London, *The Tramp Days,* 486.
34. "For know that": London, *The Tramp Days,* 318.
34. "I was meeting": ATYS, 391–92.
35. "a young stranger": ATYS 400.
35. "taken to the," "The real tramp": ATYS 382.
35. "at the water": AS, 184.
36. 1895 statistics: *World Almanac, 1897,* 210.
36. "It was night": ATYS 396.
36. "An hour of": ATYS 396–97.
36. "We don't want": ATYS 397.
37. "sharp hunger": ATYS 381.
37. "a little homesick": ATYS 397.
37. "thanked him and": ATYS 398.
37. "marched to the": ATYS 399.
37. "only house in": ATYS 400.
37. "Away deep in": ATYS 400.
37. "I leave you": "The Red Son," *Chicago Poems,* CP 74.
38. "a blank-faced Swede": ATYS 401.
38. "one more apprentice": ATYS 402.
39. "going along with": ATYS 404.
39. "men were called": ATYS 404.
39. "twenty-one years of": ATYS 405.
40. "waved to her": ATYS 405.
40. "patiently cut away": ATYS 407.
   Sandburg drew the details of his war experience from his "Spanish-American War Journal," now part of CS Collection, UI. On May 1, 1898, he wrote to his family from Springfield, Illinois, that George Martin of Knox College "is also writing for the Mail, so I am going to write only once and a while. That letter Thursday was almost all from me, but there is no earthly use of 2 reporters in one co." MIT 3.
40. "swarming flies": ATYS 407.
40. "a second-rank Galesburg": ATYS 409.
41. "a lumber-hauling freighter": ATYS 411.
41. Sandburg recounts the July 25 arrival in detail in his Spanish-American War Journal (UI).
41. "at an unseen": ATYS 414.
42. "in brigades, accompanied": Spanish-American War Journal, July 27, 1898, UI.
   "They came with bugles sounding mess call," Sandburg wrote in ATYS 414.
42. "heavy blue-wool pants": ATYS 415.
42. "elegant" native cigarettes: Spanish-American War Journal, July 26, 1898, UI.
   Sandburg writes in the Journal, but not in ATYS, of being put on commissary detail because he "did not meet" the captain "with the pass the night before" (August 3, 1898).
42. He packed the: Spanish-American War Journal, August 6–8, 1898, UI.
42. "Underwear and pants": ATYS 417.
43. "lean, somewhat faded": ATYS 419.
43. "It wasn't much": ATYS 418.
43. "a nightmare of": Ibid. Recalling that war correspondent Richard Davis had called

the Puerto Rican expedition a "fete des fleurs" in comparison to "the Santiago nightmare," Sandburg wrote that "Santiago was a nightmare, but only by comparison with that nightmare of blood, fever, and blunders" was the Puerto Rican expedition "a feast of flowers." *ATYS* 418.

43. "emaciated and worn": Annals of Knox County, September 1898, quoted in *ATYS* 420.
43. "more bony so": *ATYS* 421.
43. "a good soldier": *ATYS* 421.
43. In the loneliness of, "audiences of shadows": CS ms, UI.
44. "The boast of": Thomas Gray, "Elegy Written in a Country Churchyard," 1751.
44. "Joy always," "Joy," *Chicago Poems*, CP 51.

Chapter 3: An Independent Drifter (1898–1902)

45. "I had wonderings": EWC 11.
45. "you could go": *ATYS* 288.
45. "a tall human skeleton": *ATYS* 290.
46. "in nearly every": *ATYS* 423.
46. "a seasoned soldier": CS to Philip Green Wright, May 24, 1904, UV 62; MIT 18.
46. "I do not remember": PGW, Foreword, *IRE*.
46. "the Terrible Swede": Athol Brown, Unpublished memoir, February 2, 1951, MS/UI.
46. "for it is": Ibid.
46. "two rows of": *ATYS* 423.
46. for seventeen years: *ATYS* 31.
46. "a second floor bathroom": EWC 8.
47. "We were very": EWC 8.
47. "The Old Man": EWC 9.
47. "always smiling": EWC 7.
47. "Often did I": EWC 10.
47. "seen a good": PGW, Foreword, *IRE*.
47. "had a mind": EWC 10.
48. "I was a": EWC 11.
48. "fooling around with": EWC 11.
48. "a tall, noble": EWC 9.
48. "endless piles of": EWC 9.
48. "Jekyll and Hyde": EWC 43–44.
48. "an endless unrest": EWC 121.
48. "it came over him": EWC 129.
48. "from plain folks": EWC 60.
   For excellent detailed views of Galesburg, Knox and Lombard, again see Earnest Elmo Calkins, *They Broke the Prairie* (New York: Charles Scribner's Sons, 1937) and Hermann R. Muelder, *Missionaries and Muckrakers: The First Hundred Years of Knox College* (Urbana: University of Illinois Press, 1984).
49. "to a series": Athol Brown, 2–8.
49. "most coveted": PGW, Foreword, *IRE*.
49. "suspicions that his": EWC 20.
   Sandburg kept journal notes about his reading in college and afterward. See *EWC*

33–44 for his discussion of readings from J. Scott Clark's A *Study of English Prose Writers* and his discovery of Browning, Carlyle, Bacon and others.

49. "in the Illinois": EWC 39.
50. "books and writers": EWC 39.
50. "a ragged, second": EWC 42.
50. "Bone of our": EWC 49.
50. "I am the": IRE.
50. "inside my ribs": "Wilderness," Cornhuskers, CP 100.
50. "everliving roots," "Who are these": "Timesweep," Honey and Salt, CP 758.
51. "overwhelming numbers of": EWC 49.
51. "human heroism lying": EWC 158.
51. "The average man": "The Average Man," unpublished manuscript, UV. (See VA 37–41.) This remarkable early essay was preserved by Philip Green Wright. It is handwritten on seventeen sheets of paper, about 1906–1907, and contains some of Sandburg's earliest considerations of socialism and of Abraham Lincoln.
51. "the first requisite": EWC 42.
51. "it would pay": EWC 42.
51. the Lombard College bell tower: With classmate Athol Brown Sandburg shared the duty of ringing the college bell each hour to announce the beginning of classes. He dramatized the job by carrying a large nickel-plated watch to class and checking it with much ceremony, Brown recalled in his unpublished memoir. Sandburg wrote in EWC that he often studied in the privacy of the college bell tower. After Lombard merged with Knox College the Lombard bell was housed in a bell tower built in 1936 on the Knox campus.
52. "try to": EWC 11.
52. "Maybe what I": EWC 11.
52. "I never had": EWC 72.
52. "what I had": EWC 72.

The account of Douglas MacArthur's preparation for West Point is based on information in William Manchester, *American Caesar: Douglas MacArthur 1880–1964* (New York: Dell, 1978).

53. "measured, pounded, squeezed": EWC 72.
53. "It is with": United States Military Academy to August Sandburg, June 13, 1899, UI.
53. "FAILED EXPLAIN SHORT": Telegram, Charlie Sandburg to Martin Sandburg, June 13 (1899), UI.
53. "You had the": EWC 70 and 75
53. "found that after": EWC 66.
53. "the Terrible Swede," "He wore the": Athol Brown, op. cit.
54. "any person who": Advertisement, Lombard Cannibal (pages unnumbered), Jubilee Year Book 1851–1901, 92 leaves. UV 13.
54. "I did well": EWC 53.
54. "had wide experience": Cannibal (pages unnumbered).
55. "lit up and": EWC 53.
55. "that the laborer": EWC 53.
55. "roll out any": EWC 53.
55. "one of the": Cannibal (pages unnumbered).
55. "insatiable desire": EWC 70.

55. "in the main": Charles August Sandburg, "A Man with Ideals," *Lombard Review*, Vol. 17, March 1901, 109–11, UI.
56. He was growing: Sandburg discussed his study of lecturers and orators in *EWC* 45–58.
57. "the long hair": *EWC* 50.
57. "had fought politicians": *EWC* 51.
57. "all misty" *EWC* 11.
57. "a newspaper reporter": *EWC* 11.
57. "Illinois Prairie": *EWC* 26.
57. "He was lean": *EWC* 29–30.
58. "And the beauty": *EWC* 30.
58. "knew more than": *EWC* 26.
58. "ran toward the": *EWC* 27.
58. "lively free-for-all": *EWC* 31.
58. "We are poor": *EWC* 31.
58. "Viking force": PGW, *IRE*.
58. "richly stored mind": *EWC* 32.
58. "great friend": Unpublished ms, UI.
59. "And there never": *EWC* 32.

When Charlie Sandburg was growing up on Berrien Street, he often saw Wright walking to teach his classes at Lombard. "As a boy I didn't have the faintest dim gleam of a dream that this professor would in less than ten years become for me a fine and dear friend, a deeply beloved teacher," Sandburg wrote in *ATYS* (140–41). He described Wright then as "a mathematician, an astronomer, a historian, an economist, a poet, a printer and a bookbinder, a genius and a marvel" (*ATYS* 141).

59. "selling views": *EWC* 79–85.
59. "the best hotel": *EWC* 81.
59. "Maybe sometime you": *EWC* 85.
60. "what goes into": *EWC* 91.
60. "tall and lean": *EWC* 91.
60. "any two courses": *EWC* 98.
60. "edited and written": *EWC* 98.
60. "homely, freckled, sweet": *EWC* 63.
60. "future was so": *EWC* 64.
60. "I must congratulate": Elbert Hubbard to CS, July 1901, UI.
61. "more keen interest": *EWC* 99.
61. "loud, slangy, even": *EWC* 99.
61. "write in any": *EWC* 109.
61. In a column: See, for instance, Karl August, "Sidelights," *Lombard Review*, Vol. 17, March 1901, 119–20, UI.
61. "the best known": *EWC* 112.
61. stereoscopic photographs or "views": CS wrote in *EWC* (81) that some of his customers as children had heard the term "views" and "wouldn't go along with me and call the new modern product either 'stereographs' or 'stereoscopic photographs.' "
61. "I Am Blind": RS 51.
62. "without convincing each": *EWC* 113.

62. "You say G.": CS to Mary Sandburg, n.d. [appears to be July 1901], UI (MIT 5).
62. "one of the greatest": CS to Mary Sandburg [December 26, 1902, dating based on internal evidence], UI; (MIT 6–7).
62. "newborn": EWC 21.
63. "not only respect": EWC 121.
63. "books, diligence, decency": EWC 12.
63. "puzzled and wondered": EWC 121.
63. "tall elegant human": EWC 116.
63. "What was I": EWC 121.

Chapter 4: Reckless Ecstasy (1902–1904)

64. "I try to": IRE, Epigraph.
64. "with anything": EWC 139.
64. "I was on a horse": EWC 139–40.
65. "migratory roadster": CS to PGW, April 6, 1904, VA 57.
65. "There are ten": EWC 162, from IN.
65. "Some way I": CS to Mary Sandburg, June 2, 1904, UI, MIT 28. Sandburg's letters to his sister Mary are housed at California State University, Northridge. Photocopies are on deposit at UI. Unpublished letters from CS to Mary Sandburg are quoted courtesy MS/UI, and are designated UI.
65. "I am like": CS to PGW, Epigraph for IN; CS to PGW, October 12, 1904, VA 71.
65. "gay and chipper," "only a back-action": CS to PGW, January 20, 1904, VA 53.
65. "the joy of": CS to PGW, October 4, 1903, VA 50.
65. "in this game": CS to PGW, June 14, 1904, VA 63; MIT 29.
65. "disdained harness": CS to PGW, October 16, 1904, VA 71.
65. "evolving a small-sized": CS to Mary Sandburg, January 18, 1903, UI. (Sandburg apparently gave the wrong year date, early in the New Year; see January 18, 1904, MIT 20.)
65. "that vagrant, restless": CS to PGW, February 16, 1907, VA 93.
65. "noble self-denial": CS to PGW, December 19, 1904, VA 80.
65. "frozen, wind-swept": "Charles XII, of Sweden," poem by CS, IRE 17.
66. "a sort of": CS to Mary Sandburg, May 19, 1903, MIT 10.
66. "it takes time": Ibid.
66. "no great, lasting": IN 20.
66. "Take up your": CS, 1902 Notebook, UI; Epigraph, IN 2.
66. "that vast organism": CS to Mary Sandburg (December 26, 1902), MIT 6.
66. "mightiest material works": Ibid.
66. "I have canvassed": Ibid.
67. "The trees now": CS, "The Falling Leaves," The Thistle, November 1902.
67. For background on Elbert Hubbard, see The Note Book of Elbert Hubbard (New York: William H. Wise & Co., 1927); Albert Lane, Elbert Hubbard and His Work (Worcester, Mass.: Blanchard Press, 1901); Felix Shay, Elbert Hubbard of East Aurora (New York: William H. Wise & Co., 1926), as well as EWC, passim.
68. "over the plank": CS to Mary Sandburg, MIT 7.
68. "when the future": Ibid.
68. "Links and Kinks": CS, 1902 Notebook, UI.

68. "could have had": CS to Mary Sandburg, January 19, 1903, MIT 8.
69. "wide Main Street": *EWC* 129
69. "walking, loafing on": *EWC* 128
69. "rioting in social": CS to Mary Sandburg, February 26, 1903, MS; also CS to PGW, December 5, 1904, VA 77; MIT 35.
69. "Vineland was nigh": Ibid.
69. "the avatar of": CS to PGW, n.d. [1903], VA 45.
69. "I wonder": Ibid.
69. "Down in southern": CS, "Millville," *IRE.*
70. "You never come": CS, "Mill-Doors," *Chicago Poems,* CP 6.
70. "You perhaps know": CS to Mary Sandburg, May 19, 1903, MIT 10.
71. "beauty of a": CS, 1904 Notebook, UI.
71. "I have been": CS to PGW, [1903], VA 45.
71. "haunted": CS to PGW, June 22, 1903, VA 46; MIT 12.
71. "designation of which": Ibid.
71. "because you have": CS to Mary Sandburg, November 27 [1903], MIT 18.
72. "I know you understand": CS to PGW, July 14 [1903], VA 47; MIT 14.
72. "two Delilahs and": CS to PGW, June 22, 1903, VA 46; MIT 12.
72. "had seen pictures": *EWC* 147.
72. "I met a": *EWC* 128.
72. "If I could": CS to PGW, December 5, 1904, VA 77; MIT 36. (VA, repository of letters, records date as December 5, 1904.)
72. "Being young and": CS to PGW, July 14 [1903], VA 47; MIT 13.
73. "I do not": "Quatrains Suggested by Zola's 'L'Assommoir,' " CS to PGW [ca. August 1903], VA 49; MIT 17.
73. "what must the": Ibid.
73. "I stood me": Ibid.
74. "something of a brute": CS to Mary Sandburg, December 21 [1903], UI.
74. "I am not": CS to PGW, December 23 [1903], VA 51.
74. "I don't lack": CS to Mary Sandburg, ibid.
74. "There was always": *ATYS* 430 and 432.
75. "It is enough": CS to Mary Sandburg, November 27 [1903], MIT 18.
75. "It's a pity tho": CS to Mary Sandburg, [ca. December, 1903], MIT 19–20.
75. "I have become": CS to Mary Sandburg, January 19, 1903, MIT 8. CS quoted Tennyson's "Ulysses" here.
75. "infinite variety of": CS to Mary Sandburg, November 27 [1903], MIT 18.
75. "I am delighted": CS to PGW, February 11, 1904, VA 56; MIT 23.
75. "What men would": "Complacency"; for full text, see *IRE* 13 or CS to PGW, January 20, 1904, VA 53.
76. "Austerity": *IRE* 13, and CS to PGW, ibid.
76. "you know I've": CS to PGW, February 11, 1904, VA 55; MIT 22.
76. "Now if I": CS to PGW, February 17, 1904, VA 56; MIT 23.
76. "clear in its": CS to PGW, February 17, 1904, VA 56; MIT 24.
77. "set on a": CS to PGW, April 6, 1904, VA 58.
77. "Only the select": CS to PGW, May 15, 1904, VA 61; MIT 26.
77. "enhance the readers'": CS to PGW, April 6, 1904, VA 58.
77. "dulled the nib": CS to PGW, April 28, 1904, VA 59.
77. "Of the making": CS, "Foreword," *Dial of the Heart,* MS, UV. Note the allusion

to Whitman in "Cut these words and they will bleed. There is a man back of them."

77. "all the varied": CS to PGW, May 15, 1904, VA 60; MIT 25.

77. "blankety-blank verse": CS to PGW, April 28, 1904, VA 59.

78. "playing with oratory": CS to PGW, April 6, 1904, VA 58.

78. "breaking away more": CS to PGW, May 24, 1904, VA 62; MIT 27.

78. "eat well and": EWC 129–30.

78. "some of the": CS to PGW, May 24, 1904, ibid.

78. "eschew all literary": CS to PGW, May 15, 1904, VA 60; MIT 25.

78. "acknowledged revolutionists": CS to PGW, June 16, 1904, VA 64.

79. "I rank Hubbard": CS to PGW, December 5, 1904, VA 77; MIT 35.

79. "railroad octopus and": CS to PGW, October 16, 1904, VA 71.

79. "more sane than": CS to PGW, June 16, 1904, VA 64.

79. "long and strong": David Shannon, *The Socialist Party of America* (New York: Macmillan Co., 1955), 1–3.

80. "If you think": CS, "How Long Will It Last?," *Lombard Review*, April 1904, 140–41. CS occasionally contributed to the *Lombard Review* after he left the college.

80. "Then the workmen": Ibid.

80. "It can't last": Ibid.

81. "What is he": This episode, including dialogue, was recorded in Sandburg's letter to PGW, June 1, 1904, VA 62.

81. "that Whitman for": EWC 128.

81. "I will make": Walt Whitman, "Starting from Paumanok," *Leaves of Grass* (Philadelphia: David McKay, 1900), 24. McKay was Whitman's last publisher in his lifetime. This edition is one which was available to Sandburg.

82. "His work throughout": CS, 1904 Notebook, UI.

82. "All seems beautiful": Walt Whitman, "Song of the Open Road," *Leaves of Grass*, 172.

82. "mazy path": CS to Mary Sandburg, June 2, 1904, MIT 28.

82. "one of the blessings": Ibid.

83. "I am the one": IRE 36–37. An earlier draft entitled "An Egotist's Diadem" was sent to PGW. See UV; VA 35.

83. "good expression of": CS to PGW, October 30, 1904, VA 73.

83. "hundreds of experiments": EWC 138.

83. "the more I read": CS to PGW, May 15, 1904, VA 60; MIT 25.

84. "pass thru the": IRE 37.

84. "a man of thought": CS to PGW, July 4, 1904, VA 64; MIT 29.

84. "swung up on": EWC 130.

84. "Unshackling myself from": CS to PGW, August 2, 1904, VA 65; MIT 31.

85. "the ten days": " 'Boes," *Chicago Poems*, CP 70.

85. By the time " 'Boes": In 1903 Sandburg composed a poem which was a half-serious appraisal of Whitman's emerging influence on his poetry. He sent it PGW from Vineland, New Jersey, sometime in 1903. It went in part:

> The likelihood is great that I will never dally with rhyme and meter again,
> And I say this is so because I have been reading Walt Whitman. . . .
>
> (VA 45)

85. "by which police": *EWC* 135.
85. "feeling weak": *EWC* 135.
85. "I took a": *EWC* 136.
85. "Such menus as": CS to PGW, August 10, 1904, VA 66–67.
86. "We had a": *EWC* 136.
86. "measures me true": CS to PGW, August 2, 1904, VA 66; MIT 31–32.
86. "something of the": PGW, Foreword, *IRE*.
86. "Anent the foreword": CS to PGW, August 10, 1904, VA 67.
86. "And when he": PGW, Foreword, *IRE*.
87. "I sent a": CS to PGW, October 6, 1904, VA 69.
87. "I am not": CS to PGW, ibid.
87. "ideas which can": CS, *IRE*, 9.
87. "sonnets and triolets": *EWC* 138.
87. "Lost in flight": From Sandburg's poem "Sometimes," enclosed in a letter to PGW, October 12, 1904:

> How oft, like Cyrano, I've faced a hundred men to fight
> Alone and single-handed thru a nameless, starlit night;
> But unlike Cyrano, when morning stars broke out in song
> Baffled, baggageless and sore, I myself, was lost in flight.
>
> (VA 71)

87. "Spoke to a vast": CS to PGW, November 22, 1904, VA 76; MIT 33.
87. "particularly enjoy dealing": Ibid.
88. "speak for three": *EWC* 137.
88. "easy-going complacent people": CS to PGW, November 22, 1904, VA 76; MIT 34.
88. "heavy pink wove": VA 5.
88. "Great, long, lean": "A Homely Winter Idyll," *IRE* 33.
88. "This morning I": "Experience," *IRE* 15.
89. "I heard the": "Pastels," *IRE* 23.
89. "one who has": Dedication, *IRE* 8.
89. "A man's merits": CS to PGW, December 5, 1904, VA 77; MIT 35.
89. "Of course, I": CS to PGW, December 13, 1904, VA 79.

Chapter 5: A Vagabond Philosopher-Poet (1904–1906)

90. "If I could": CS to PGW, December 5, 1904, VA 77; MIT 36.
90. "zigzagging toward the": CS to Mary Sandburg, January 18, 1904, MIT 20.
90. "infinite variety of": CS to Mary Sandburg, November 27 [1903], MIT 18.
90. "daring, piquant, half-elfish": CS to Mary Sandburg, January 18, 1904, MIT 20–21.
90. "I hope I": CS to Esther Sandburg, October 12, 1904, MIT 32–33.
90. "living a life": CS to Mary Sandburg [ca. December 1903], MIT 20.
91. "I couldn't think": CS to Mary Sandburg, January 18, 1904, MIT 21.
91. "the canny, restless, turbulent": CS to PGW, November 22, 1904, VA 75; MIT 33.
91. "what is significant": CS to PGW, October 6, 1904, VA 69.
91. "studies": Ibid.
91. "living touch": CS to PGW, December 19, 1904, VA 79–81; MIT 37–39.

91. "ache to utter": Untitled prefatory poem, *IRE*.
92. "I see myself": CS to PGW, December 19, 1904, VA 79–81; MIT 37–39.
92. "I have said": Ibid.
92. "So I am": Ibid.
93. "fuzzy-minded and": EWC 138–39.
93. "From the west": EWC 139.
93. "I am living": "The One Man in All the World," *IRE* 36.
93. "By littles and": CS to PGW, January 23, 1905 [CS misdated this 1904], VA 81.
93. "Teaching is more": CS to Mary Sandburg, October 13, 1904, UI.
94. "Any week I": EWC 138.
94. "was no banner": Ibid.
94. "one of my": EWC 140.
94. "I have been": CS to Mary Sandburg [ca. March 1905], MIT 39.
94. "I am sending": CS to PGW [ca. March 1905], VA 82.
94. Invaluable background information for this early Chicago period can be found in Margaret Sandburg's unpublished biographical manuscript, MS/UI.
94. "revolutionary enough to": CS to PGW, December 13, 1904, VA 78.
94. "a faded and": EWC 153.
94. "kept open house": Bruce Calvert, undated typescript 3, ES/UI.
94. "No bum ever": Ibid.
94. "the intelligentsia": Ibid.
95. "same somber gladness": CS to PGW, January 13, 1905, VA 81.
95. "In Petersburg, flows": CS to PGW, January 23, 1905, VA 82. In this letter, Sandburg gives the poem and its date of composition. Note the calendar differences between Russia (O.S.) and the United States (N.S.) in 1905. News of the Russian upheaval reached the United States quickly—on the day itself —thanks to the cable. *The New York Times*, for instance, carried stories about the turbulence January 17, 18, 19, 20, 21, 22, and 23, 1905, and on other days following "Bloody Sunday."
96. "fire them at": CS to Mary Sandburg, April 14 (1905), MIT 40.
96. "What you want": EWC 141.
96. "quiet corner in": EWC 144.
96. "leading journal of": CS, unpublished fragment, UI; courtesy of Margaret Sandburg.
97. "A bum has no": CS, "Open Letter," *Galesburg Evening Mail*, UI clipping, n.d.
97. "farm boys, shoe": CS, "Inklings and Idlings," MS clipping, n.d.
98. "virile spirit": Reese Moyer, Mobile Alabama *Daily Register*, June 18, 1905.
98. "signs of hope": EWC 146.
98. "I showed a": EWC 146–47.
98. "like a ferocious": EWC 151.
98. "earnest, mawkish, rhymed": EWC 151.
98. of William Ernest: CS expressed this view to William Marion Reedy in a letter which has not survived. Reedy alluded to Sandburg's remark in his letter to CS, November 19, 1906, UI.
98. "sent on poems": EWC 151.
98. "remain long in": Oscar Lovell Triggs, quoted in *EWC* 151.
99. "I think to": CS, "A Fling at the Riddle," *To-Morrow*, Vol. I, April 1905, 22.
99. "The desire to": EWC 144.
99. "the Athens of": EWC 148.

99. "as a fireman": *EWC* 152.

99. "I drove my": *EWC* 152.

100. "little hills and," "I love your": CS, "The Red Son," *Chicago Poems, CP* 74.

100. "I shall go": "The Red Son," ibid.

101. "I kissed my": CS, "An Old Woman," *BT* 56.

101. "unduly": CS to PGW, no date [ca. 1905], VA 83.

101. "And men and": CS, "A Fling at the Riddle," PDG 249.

101. "broad blue vista": CS, "Perspectives," PDG 244. Published in *Triggs* magazine, Vol. I, October 1905, 24–25, along with "Backyard Vagaries" and "In Illinois." See Library of Congress bibliography, 32. Also published in *To-Morrow,* Vol. II, no. 10, October 1906, 23.

101. "thin red dollars": CS, "Backyard Vagaries," PDG 245.

101. "In Illinois": CS, "In Illinois," PDG 245.

102. "O my brave soul": Walt Whitman, "Passage to India," *Leaves of Grass,* 346–54.

102. "I am Columbus": CS, "Fragments," unpublished except for PDG, 252–53.

103. "I rode with": *EWC* 153.

103. "both a joy and": Reuben Borough to Margaret Sandburg, n.d., 2, MS/UI.

103. "yet ready to": Ibid.

104. "his first chance": Bruce Calvert, 3.

104. "He could mention": *EWC* 153–54.

105. "the man who": Theodore Roosevelt, quoted in Harvey Swados, *Years of Conscience: The Muckrakers* (New York: World Publishing, 1971), 10. See also Ray Stannard Baker, *American Chronicle: The Autobiography of Ray Stannard Baker* (New York: Charles Scribner's Sons, 1945), 201.

105. "were filling": *EWC* 159.

105. "sources of history": *EWC* 159.

105. "Today 'tis ink": CS, "The Muck-Rake Man," *To-Morrow,* June 1906, Vol. II, 21. This issue of *To-Morrow* also carried work by Maxim Gorky, Carlos Montezuma and Reuben W. Borough.

105. "an admirable stylist": Walter Hurt to CS, April 2, 1906, MS.

105. "strong, wholesome, incisive": Parker Sercombe, *To-Morrow,* April 1906.

105. "almost every manjack": This phrase and the following quotations appear in CS, "Jack London: A Common Man," *To-Morrow,* April 1906, Vol. II, no. 4, 35–39.

106. "another case of": CS, "The Book of the Day," "Views and Reviews," *To-Morrow,* Vol. II, April 1906, 50–55; May 1906, 54–56; June 1906, 22–26; July 1906, 32–36.

107. "The foulest blot": CS, ibid.

107. "the leveling down": Dr. Frank Gunsaulus, quoted by CS, "Views and Reviews," *To-Morrow,* June 1906, 34.

108. "why the preacher": CS, "Views and Reviews," *To-Morrow,* June 1906, 34.

108. "There is a": Ibid.

108. "As the waters": CS, "Little Sermon," *To-Morrow,* Vol. II, July 1906, 7.

108. "monthly magazine for": Masthead motto for *To-Morrow.*

108. "play hell with": CS to PGW, January 20, 1904, VA 54.

108. "twist the tail": CS to PGW, July 4, 1904, VA 64; MIT 30.

109. "a good deal": A. S. Hoffmann to CS, May 15, 1906, UI. With this letter, Hoffmann returned the following Sandburg poems: "The Road and the End,"

"The Great Presence," "Departure," "On Shipboard," "Luck," "Identities," "Vagabond," "Nocturne," "Many Men," "An Overtone" and "Parallel." On May 26, 1906, Hoffmann wrote to Sandburg again; this time he returned the poems "Storms," "Comrades," "Loafer," "Backyard Vagaries," "Balmat" and "The Shadow Child." He told Sandburg his rhythm was smoother, and asked to see more poems. UI.

109. "Strolling along": CS, "Docks," *Chicago Poems, CP* 65–66.
110. "vindictive and scatterbrained": CS to PGW, November 12, 1906, VA 89.
110. "These faces!": CS, "On State Street, Chicago," MS/UI. Margaret Sandburg has identified this as an unpublished poem, noting "This poem is definitely Charles Sandburg and not Carl Sandburg. Charles Sandburg was always just a little artificial." PEN Interview with MS, November 18, 1986.
110. "I lie on": CS, "Loafer", unpublished poem, MS.
110. "I shall foot": CS, "The Road and the End," *Chicago Poems, CP* 42.
111. "You said I": CS, "To a Poet," *BT* 55. The line "Whatever horse you want to ride is yours" suggests that CS had discussed his recurring dream with PGW.
112. For background on William Marion Reedy, see Max Putzel, *Man in the Mirror* (Cambridge: Harvard University Press, 1963).
113. "nervous, well-knit, savory": W. M. Reedy quoted in *EWC*, 149.
113. "certain rough vigor": W. M. Reedy to CS, November 19, 1906, UI.
113. "hunger for a": CS, "Timesweep," *Honey and Salt, CP* 758.
114. "The road I": CS, "Horse Fiddle," *Smoke and Steel, CP* 224.
114. "I suppose . . . that": W. M. Reedy to CS, November 19, 1906, UI.
114. "jumping-off place": Reuben Borough to Margaret Sandburg, n.d., 2, MS.
114. "filling the days": CS to Esther Sandburg [July 31, 1906], MS.
    Sandburg discussed his lectures in a letter to PGW October 27, 1906, VA 87, as they worked on the copy for his lecture circular. He also sought the help of Reuben Borough, who by then lived in Fort Wayne, Indiana. See CS to Reuben Borough, December 19, 1906, MIT 41–42. Sandburg discussed lecture bookings with PGW in a letter October 6, 1906, VA 84; and in the July 31 letter to his sister Esther.
115. "hammering away at": CS to PGW, October 6, 1906, VA 84.
115. "a future looms": CS to PGW, ibid.
115. he would earn: CS to PGW, October 20, 1906, VA 84–85.
115. "pounding, smashing, happy": CS to PGW, ibid.
115. "a masterpiece of advertising": CS to PGW, ibid.
    The Galesburg photographer was Walter Loomis. See illustrations. Seeds, germinations and fragments of Sandburg's lectures appear throughout his Notebooks, UI.
115. "Amid the noise": CS to PGW, October 20, 1906, VA 85.
115. "apothegm or epigram": CS to PGW, ibid.

Chapter 6: Uncharted Seas (1906–1907)

116. "Look at it": CS, *IN*.
    See *EWC* 154 for Sandburg's account of his *Lyceumite* job.
116. "cut out vagabonding": CS to PGW, December 29, 1906, VA 92; MIT 42.
116. "Lincoln and Douglas": CS to *Talent*, December 1906, ES, MS/UI.

117. "was in constant": CS, *Lyceumite* Notebook, MS/UI.
117. "dead level and": William James, quoted in *EWC* 159.
117. "commonplace and so-so": CS, "Unimportant Portraits of Important People," *Lyceumite*, February 1907, 126.
117. "one of those": CS to PGW, February 16, 1907, VA 93.
117. "Three Great Blunders": CS to PGW, ibid.
117. "logic, fact, invective": Ibid.
117. "Civilization and the Mob": See CS, unpublished manuscript, "The Average Man," VA 37–41.
117. "The common people": VA 38.
118. "The average man": Ibid.
118. "He is the": Ibid.
118. "He came nearer": VA 39.
118. "art, and conduct": CS to PGW, March 14, 1907, VA 94.
118. "It is not": CS to PGW, March 14, 1907, VA 95.
118. "militant equalitarians": Reuben Borough, "The Sandburg I Remember," *Journal of the Illinois State Historical Society*, Vol. 59, no. 3, Autumn 1966, 229–51.
119. "go along with the": *EWC* 28.
119. "All not out": CS to PGW, April 13, 1907, VA 95.
     Sandburg's notebooks (UI), his early prose and *EWC* reveal the breadth of his reading. Margaret Sandburg's unpublished manuscript illuminates the matter, and is augmented by her interviews with her father about books which influenced his thought and his work.
119. "Lady photographed at": CS, 1907 Notebook, UI.
119. "geysers of words": *EWC* 160.
120. "His name was": CS, "Dynamiter," *Chicago Poems*, CP 21.
120. "what seems to": CS to Esther Sandburg, ca. March, 1907, MIT 43.
121. "I was tossed": CS to PGW, May 2, 1907, VA 96; MIT 45.
121. "Strange things blow": CS, "Don't Worry," *The Lyceumite*, quoted in *EWC* 156.
121. whom he pronounced: CS to PGW, June 9, 1907, VA 98.
121. "Green-crested hills": CS to Reuben Borough, May 30, 1907, MIT 46.
121. "I have fairly": CS to Reuben Borough, June 4, 1907, MIT 47.
121. "for the fellow": CS to PGW, May 26, 1907, VA 97.
122. "keep up this": CS to PGW, June 9, 1907, VA 98.
122. "There is a": Ibid.
122. "Oratory?": CS Notebook, UI.; Felix Shay, *Elbert Hubbard of East Aurora* (New York: William H. Wise & Co., 1926), 464.
122. "oratory flung by": *EWC* 156.
     See Sandburg's account of preparation of his main lecture, "An American Vagabond", *EWC* 156–57.
122. "to rows of": *EWC* 156.
122. "cool, irreparable type": CS to PGW, June 9, 1907, VA 99.
123. "The American Vagabond": Sandburg describes the lecture in *EWC* 156–57. His copy of *Leaves of Grass* is marked at key passages. Notes and a partial draft of his Whitman lecture have been transcribed by Margaret Sandburg, MS, UI.
123. "Afoot and light-hearted": Walt Whitman, "Song of the Open Road," *Leaves of Grass*, 169.

123. "Take the Train" and subsequent details about Roycroft and East Aurora are based on Shay's eyewitness account, passim, especially 75–80, 90–97.
123. "architectural hodge-podge": Shay, 80.
123. "sanctuary of art and beauty": Ibid.
124. "There will be": Shay, 95.
124. "To be frank": CS to PGW, July 6, 1907, VA 99; MIT 49.
124. "Sandburg knows his": Elbert Hubbard, 1907 Lecture Circular for Charles A. Sandburg, Asgard Press.
124. Sandburg wrote PGW July 6, 1907, "Since I left the Lyceumite, I have changed it [the Whitman lecture] from a strong literary lecture into an oration" (VA 99).
124. "I have dreamed": Ibid.
125. "Understand me, I": Manuscript, MS; UI.
125. "I heard that": Walt Whitman, "To Foreign Lands," *Leaves of Grass*, 13. CS Notebook, UI.
     See CS to PGW, July 6, 1907, VA 99; MIT 49 for Sandburg's account of his Roycroft lecture experience.
125. "They are sort": Ibid.
126. "Conquer the kingdom": *IN* 15.
126. "listened to a": CS to Reuben Borough, June 9, 1907, MIT 48.
126. "I believe in": *IN* 14.
126. "paradox of success through failure": Elbert Hubbard, *The Notebook of Elbert Hubbard*, 15.
126. "Freedom is found": *IN* 9.
127. "I have never": *IN* 8.
127. "this boy heart": *IN* 7.
127. "Failure, as the": *IN* epigraph.
127. "idyllic, rural and": CS to PGW, July 22, 1907, VA 101.
127. "the cream of": CS to PGW, August 12, 1907, VA 103.
127. "Walt Whitman": [CS] unsigned news clipping, *Marshall [Michigan] News*, August 9, 1907, UV. Sandburg quoted himself as saying "Was his (Whitman's) work poetry? Was it art? I don't care what you call it; you don't care what it is called. . . . You know what it does for you—the name doesn't matter." He argued that art "is a matter of individual taste," and concluded the article with an account of two cats who appeared on the lecture platform, one of them rubbing itself "affectionately against the leg of the orator as he was getting well into his subject."
128. "momentarials rather than": CS to PGW, September 7, 1907, VA 105.
128. "Apologia": *IN*.
128. "almost tiresome": CS, ibid.
128. "flimsy agreement": CS to PGW, November 9, 1907, VA 114.
128. "some of the": CS to PGW, September 12, 1907, VA 107.
128. "poetization in prose": Ibid.
128. "Where I talked": Ibid.
129. "Since I saw": CS to Reuben Borough, October 5, 1907, MIT 54.
129. "There are things": CS to Vella Martin, June 25, 1907.
129. "the kind of woman": CS to PGW, January 23, 1905, VA 81.

130. "You will come": CS, "A Dream Girl," *The Lyceumite*, January 15, 1906. Later published in *Chicago Poems*, CP 68, entitled "Dream Girl."
130. "Once more Fate": CS to PGW, September 25, 1907, VA 108.
130. "several good prospects": Ibid.
130. "the long look": CS to PGW, October 4, 1907, VA 111.
130. "I hold firm": Ibid.
130. "It seems to me": CS, *IN* 25.
130. "I believe": CS to PGW, October 4, 1907, VA 110.
131. "premier piece of": CS to PGW, November 9, 1907, VA 113.
131. "false tints": CS to PGW, December 24, 1907, VA 119.
131. "I consider now that": CS to PGW, November 9, 1907, VA 113.

Chapter 7: A Gospel of Freedom to Come (1907–1908)

132. "So there I": Charles A. Sandburg, unpublished fragment, UI.
132. "not a commonplace": Chester Wright, "Sandburg Is to Speak at Opera House," *Manitowoc Daily Tribune*, October 26, 1907.
133. "Speaking to one": [CS,] Lecture Circular, UV, text credited to *Manitowoc Daily Tribune*.
133. "bold, dashing ideas": Ibid.
133. "If America does": Ibid.
133. "The man who": Ibid.
133. "living, palpitating personality": Ibid.
133. "had a great": CS to Reuben Borough, November 6, 1907, MIT 54.
134. "recent immigrants": David Shannon, 61.
134. "a socialist movement": *EWC* 163.
134. "Organize?": Ibid.
134. "Your pay will": Ibid.
134. "I have been": CS to PGW, November 9, 1907, VA 113.
135. "frail, ill-grown plant": PR 5.
135. "my soul is": PR 6.
135. "The spaces I": PR 8–9. Sandburg knew by heart lines from Gray's "Elegy Written in a Country Churchyard," which may have evoked the metaphor of the fading rose: "Full many a flower is born to blush unseen,/And waste its fragrance on the desert air."
135. "poetization in prose": CS to PGW, September 12, 1907, VA 106.
135. "you should receive": Elizabeth Thomas to CS, November 29, 1907, UI.
135. "batten on the": CS to PGW, December 12, 1907, VA 118.
135. "I shall send": CS to PGW, ibid.
136. "Have never gotten": CS to PGW, n.d.; internal evidence suggests November or December 1907 (see CS to PGW, December 24, 1907); VA 103.
137. "to fire into": CS to PGW, ibid.
137. "Remember who you": CS, "A Little Christmas Sermon," *Manitowoc Daily Tribune*, December 24, 1907.
138. "no man can": CS Notebook, UI.
     Background on socialism has been gleaned from Shannon; Theodore Draper, *The Roots of American Communism* (New York: Viking, 1957); Daniel Bell, "The

Background and Development of Marxian Socialism in the United States," in Egbert and Persons, eds., *Socialism and American Life* (Princeton: Princeton University Press, 1952), Vol. I; Nick Salvatore's biography *Eugene Debs: Citizen and Socialist* (Urbana: University of Illinois Press, 1982); and other contemporary sources. Primarily, however, I tried to read the books Sandburg read then, works by Marx, Ferri, Bellamy, William Morris and Kirkup; and to consult newspapers and documents of the period, including Emil Seidel's unpublished autobiography, Wisconsin State Historical Society, Madison. For background on Victor Berger, I am indebted to Sally M. Miller, *Victor Berger and the Promise of Constructive Socialism, 1910–1920* (London: Greenwood Press, 1973) and, especially, Meta Berger's unpublished autobiography in manuscript, WSHS, Madison.

138. "You will come": CS, "Dream Girl," *Chicago Poems*, CP 68.
138. "the woman with": CS to PGW, January 23, 1905, VA 82.
139. Now she stood: PEN interview with MS; MS, PDG, 5–7; HS, GGR, passim.
139. "company of geniuses": LS to CS, n.d. [ca. 1909], UI.
139. "moral philosopher": LS to CS, January 7, 1908, PDG 9. Lilian Steichen's early life is reconstructed from letters; interviews with MS and HS; references to published and unpublished manuscripts by MS and HS: and news clippings, interviews and records in Princeton, Illinois, including an interview with MS on a windy day in Bryants Woods.
140. "saw that city": CS, STP.
141. For several anxious: Account reconstructed by PEN from MS interviews, HS interviews, HS, GGR, 24–25; Paula Steichen, *My Connemara* (New York: Harcourt, Brace & World, 1969), 124–25.
142. "kind of visual memory": LS to CS, PDG [April 12, 1908], PDG 86.
142. Details of Eduard/Edward Steichen's early life are drawn from family interviews; from Edward Steichen's *A Life in Photography* [ALP] (Garden City: Doubleday & Co., 1963); from CS, STP; and from letters, including Steichen's letters at UI and the Museum of Modern Art. I am indebted to HS for the family history and genealogy she compiled.
142. "old old German": LS to CS [April 12, 1908], PDG 83.
142. "splendid peasant constitution": Ibid.
143. "took charge of": Ibid.
143. "delicate and strange": *STP*, reprinted in *SR* 306.
143. "thought one picture": ES, *ALP* (pages are unnumbered; Section 1)
144. "mysterious and ever-changing": Ibid.
146. "as long as": Paula Steichen, *My Connemara*, 127.
146. See MS, PDG, note, 76–77, on Lilian Steichen's education at this time. In a handwritten chronology, LS/PS gave her name as Lilian Mary Ann Elizabeth Steichen.
146. "the highest point": James Huneker, *The Sun*, March 12, 1902. According to a review in the March 30, 1902, edition of the *New York Herald* Steichen's photographs, the first ever accepted in the prestigious Paris Art Exhibition, were "a great triumph."
147. the "old-country" way: HS, GGR 24.
147. "hard for such": LS to CS [April 12, 1908], PDG 83–87.
148. "a proposed new": LS, unpublished ms, UI.

The account of the Socialist Club appears in a letter written by LS to Miss Lane, March 22, 1904, MS, UI.

148. "I am glad": ES to LS, February 9, 1904, UI.
148. "I see in": Ibid.
149. "a young woman": quoted in HS, GGR 86–87.
150. pressed for details: HS, GGR 87–88.
150. "another vague tale": Evidence suggests, although there is no absolute documentation, that the "Important Personality" was Victor Berger, plausible given the contemporary socialist interest in eugenics and an episode surrounding some of the Sandburg-Steichen love letters. As MS records in PDG, 54, she intervened when her mother was destroying pages from a fifty-page letter written by LS to CS [April 6] 1908, "afraid that something in it would be misinterpreted." HS had earlier made a photocopy of the letter, including the two pages missing from the text of PDG. HS had also made a typescript copy of her father's reply to the letter, also missing from PDG. Internal evidence in that letter, and the vehemence of Sandburg's words about Berger, tend to support the conclusion that Berger was the "Important Personality" LS mentioned to HS, later retracting the story. Sandburg wrote angrily of "the voluptuary who must have one woman corresponding to the apple, another to the banana, and yet others to apricots, paw-paws and tangerines, the fellow who cooly reduces this to a scheme and a science, I say to him, 'Take to the red lights and find your comrades of utility and variety,' " (CS to LS [April 8, 1908], HS/UI.)
150. "My dear Mr": LS to CS, January 7, 1908, PDG 9–12.
150. "such aesthetic enjoyment": LS to CS, February 15, 1908.
150. "Your *Dream-Girl*": LS to CS, ibid.
150. "formed in the": CS to LS, February 21, 1908, PDG 13.
151. "to swim, row": Walt Whitman, "A Woman Waits for Me," *Leaves of Grass*, 107.
151. "the intensity of": CS to LS, February 21, 1908, PDG 13.
151. "The poems": LS to CS, February 24, 1908, PDG 15.
151. "Will you tell": Ibid.
151. "Have you really": Ibid.
152. "Would it be": Ibid.
152. "that it wasn't": LS to CS, February 25, 1908, PDG 17.
152. "Of course I": Ibid.
152. "completely upset": LS to CS, February 29, 1908, PDG 20.
152. "strenuous life": Ibid.
152. "arduous labors in": LS to CS, March 3, 1908, PDG 23.
152. "I like to get": LS to CS, February 29, 1908, PDG 20. (S.D.P. = Social Democratic Party.)
153. "I like to hear": LS to CS, March 4, 1908, PDG 25.
153. "I see the": LS to CS, March 7, 1908, PDG 28.
153. "Strong, simple, direct": LS to CS, March 12, 1908, PDG 31.
153. "I'll try always": LS to CS, ibid.
153. "I think for": LS to CS, March 7, 1908, PDG 28.
154. "fine walk in": LS to CS, March 4, 1908, PDG 25.
154. "We will *walk*": Quoted by LS to CS, March 15, 1908, PDG 33.

154. "An artist's temperament": Ibid.
154. "So glad": Quoted by LS to CS, March 16, 1908, PDG 35.
155. "I have been": Ibid.
155. "Wunderkind!": LS to CS, March 17, 1908, PDG 36.
       At this point, they talk about "You," a poem he wrote for her. He promised to read it to her himself "from the rostrum." PDG 37; see epigraph to Chapter 8.
155. "Dear Comrade": LS to CS, March 18, 1908, PDG 38.
155. "Will you bring": CS to LS, March 21, 1908, PDG 42.
155. "battering from town": CS to LS, March 25, [1908], PDG 47.
156. "Dear, beautiful girl-heart": Ibid.
156. "Now she had": Edward Steichen, *Photographers View Carl Sandburg* (New York: Harcourt, Brace, 1966), Preface.
156. "could hear him": Ibid.
156. "poets when they": Ibid.
156. "spending a few": CS to PGW, April 2, 1908, VA 122.
157. "the light in": CS to LS [April 5, 1908], PDG 52.
157. "That boy-heart of": LS to CS, April 9 [1908], PDG 65.
157. "over the bogs": CS to LS, n.d., PDG 67
157. "Oh we know": LS to CS, April 10 [1908], PDG, 71.
157. "the beginning of": LS to CS, quoted by MS, PDG x.
157. "candle in hand": LS to CS, April 10 (1908), PDG 71.
157. "You gave—with": CS, "You Gave," PDG 266.
158. "What a Glory": LS to CS, April 6, 1908, PDG 52.
158. "to the finest": LS to CS, April 10, 1908, PDG 71.
158. "For your face": CS to LS in the poem "On a Wagon," PDG 49.
158. "Dream-Girl-come": CS to LS [April 11, 1908], PDG 81.
158. "I love you": CS to LS [April 5, 1908], PDG 51.
158. "dear hands—good": Ibid.
158. "those lips, those": LS to CS [April 6, 1908], PDG 54.
158. "You are with": CS to LS, n.d., PDG 67.
158. "We are *One*": LS to CS, April 10 (1908), PDG 71.
158. "single separate person": LS to CS, April 6, 1908, PDG 52.
159. "neglected the more": CS to LS, n.d., PDG 67.
159. "After a while": LS to CS, April 10 (1908), PDG 71.
159. "What things are": LS to CS, ibid.

Chapter 8: Hope and Glory (1908)

160. "The touch of": CS, "You," PDG 37.
160. "known each other": April 10 (1908), PDG 71.
160. She understood that: PDG 53; PEN interview with MS.
160. "for two Souls": CS to LS, n.d., PDG 67.
161. "the most beautiful, graceful": Ibid.
161. "sex-question" and: LS to CS, [April 6, 1908], PDG 54. As a previous note indicates, MS kept her mother from destroying this letter. See note, PDG 54. "The real fray was between B & myself," LS wrote (PDG 58–59). "—I understand why he and I could not agree. It is natural for him to be a varietist—because he cannot understand a modern woman—cannot really

love as you & I love. . . . He hasn't that poise of mind & heart and body—
It's too much a matter of body with him."

161. "The strong, beautiful. . . ." CS to LS, [April 8, 1908], HS. The letter continues,
"Had he asked you to transiently gratify him, had it been rash, impulsive,
hot-blooded manhood calling for ministration to something starved, or
uncontrollably roused that would have been different." CS called it "very
cheap duplicity" or "unnatural . . . an eccentricity of genius" to try to perpetuate "male B. blood and that being of no certainty considering *his* age and
yours. . . ."

161. "You glorious man": LS to CS, April 9 [1908], PDG 65.

162. Sandburg worked harder: CS to LS, n.d. [ca. April 1908], PDG 67.

162. "To keep from": Ibid.

162. "Sometime we must": LS to CS, April 11 [1908], PDG 78.

162. "I think we-two": Ibid.

162. "look fresh and": LS to CS [April 15, 1908], PDG 93

163. "We stand with": CS to LS [April 11, 1908], PDG 81

163. "One large room": CS to LS, n.d. [ca. April 1908], PDG 67.

163. "four walls of": LS to CS, April 13 [1908], PDG 89.

163. "You are a *Man*": LS to CS, April 10 [1908], PDG 71.

164. "Sacrifice of self": LS to CS, April 11 [1908], PDG 93.

164. "be identified with" LS to CS, April 13 [1908], PDG 89.

164. "It's unsatisfactory business": LS to CS, n.d., PDG 155.

165. "No, I will": CS to LS [April 21, 1908], PDG 117.

165. "You're a Teacher": CS to LS [April 20, 1908], PDG 111.

165. "which spells—to": CS to LS [April 29, 1908], PDG 151.

165. "windbeaten": CS to LS, April 19, 1908, PDG 107.

166. 29,270: Socialist Party Membership Reports, Socialist Party Collection, Duke University, quoted by Miller, 33.

166. "the here and now": Miller, 32.

166. 21,543: LS to CS [April 15, 1908], PDG 94.

166. "crossed the Rubicon": LS to CS [April 27, 1908], PDG 145.

166. "If you're going": CS to LS, n.d., PDG 149.

166. "I've done with": LS to CS [April 29, 1908], PDG 151.

166. "festival": LS to CS [April 18, 1908], PDG 103.

167. "be a lark": CS to LS, April 21, 1908, PDG 113.

167. "As for household goods": LS to CS, April 20, 1908, PDG 108.

167. "Yes," he had: CS to LS [April 20, 1908], PDG 110.

168. "these bourgeois!": LS to CS, May 4 [1908], PDG 173.

168. "plugging away since": CS to LS [June 5, 1908], PDG 230.

168. "there will be": "Dear Bill" Letter, PDG 262.

168. "I have been": Ibid.

169. "living among shades": LS to CS [May 5, 1908], PDG 176.

169. "love them—talk": LS to CS, May 7 [1908], PDG 181.

169. "the tragic ones": LS to CS, May 11, 1908, PDG 196.

169. "dissipate doubts and": CS to LS, quoted by LS [May 22, 1908], PDG 209.

169. "be foolish and": LS to CS [May 8, 1908], PDG 187.

169. "Honorable High Turnkey": CS to LS, n.d., PDG 236.

170. "You are evidently": Edward Steichen to LS ("Dear Paus'l"), n.d. [ca. spring 1908], UI.

170. "Edward Steichen is": CS to LS [May 9, 1908], PDG 193.
170. "My sister acquired": Edward Steichen, *Photographers View Carl Sandburg*, Preface.
170. "I'm sending a": CS to LS [May 2, 1908], PDG 163.
171. "relics of barbarism": LS to CS, May 28, 1908, PDG 221.
171. "an outward and": LS to CS [June 7, 1908], PDG 231.
171. "You see I": Ibid. On June 8, LS wrote to CS sending nineteen dollars "(what Cash etc. I happen to have hand)," PDG 235.
171. "a splurge": LS to CS, June 8 [1908], PDG 235.
171. "the ring question": Ibid.
171. "As long as": LS to CS [June 9, 1908], PDG 237.
171. "I believe our": LS to CS, June 7 [1909], PDG 231.
172. "I am not": LS to CS [May 13, 1908], PDG 199.
173. "the stolid social": Irving Howe, *Socialism and America* (New York: Harcourt Brace Jovanovich, 1985), 6.
173. one socialist newsman: Frederick Heath, Milwaukee *Social-Democratic Herald*, May 1908.
173. "Hasn't it been": Quoted in CS to LS [May 20, 1908], PDG 206.
174. "Ghosts!—Paula": CS to LS [May 19, 1908], PDG 203.
174. "honey-sweet days": LS to CS [May 20, 1908], PDG 205.
174. "The memory is": LS to CS [May 19, 1908], PDG 204.
174. "The vivid memory": LS to CS [May 20, 1908] PDG 205.
174. "two mad feverish": LS to CS, May 20, 1908, PDG 207 (her second letter to him that day).
174. "Woman-Genius": LS to CS, February 25, 1908, PDG 17.
174. "a solemn declaration": LS to CS, May 30 [1908], PDG 223.
175. "Do you understand": LS to CS, ibid.
175. "great biological function" and following passages: Enrico Ferri, *Socialism and Modern Science* (New York: International Library Publishing Co., 1904), 21–22 ("Lilian Steichen" on flyleaf, MS/UI).
176. "hardy enough, intelligent": LS to CS, May 2, 1908, PDG 166.
177. "*Woman Is the*": CS, "Socialism and Woman Suffrage," PDG 261.
177. "We're equal, Pal!": LS to CS, May 3, 1908, PDG 166.
177. "What the hell": CS to LS [June 1, 1908], PDG 228.
178. "plugging away day": CS to Esther Sandburg, May 25, 1908, MS, UI, PDG 238.
178. "why almost all": Ibid.
178. "I am young": CS, "Middle of May," PDG 268.
178. "a mass of": LS to CS [June 5, 1908], PDG 230.
179. See MS, Afterword, PDG 241–42, for an account of the wedding. Additional material, PEN interviews with MS.

Chapter 9: Dreamers? Yes, Dreamers (1908–1909)

181. "Yes, we are": CS, Journal Note, 1911, UI.
181. "battle for freedom": CS, "Battle for Free Press Is Now on in Circuit Court," *Manitowoc Daily Tribune*, June 20, 1908.
181. "big business men": CS, *Manitowoc Daily Tribune*, June 27, 1908.
181. "monster lecture": Chester Wright, "What's Doing in Manitowoc," *Manitowoc Daily Tribune*, June 30, 1908.

181. "for ultimate freedom": Ibid.
182. "cowbells, horns, tin": CS, "Give Socialist a 'Charivari.' When the Wedding Din Subsides, Organizer Takes Collection," *Daily Socialist*, July 6, 1908.
182. "Indeed you have": Clara Sandburg to Paula Sandburg (henceforth abbreviated PS), July 30, 1908, UI.
183. "any more lonely": PS to CS, PDG 205.
183. "Without being together": PS to CS, PDG 210.
183. "We cannot live": CS to PS [April 21, 1908], PDG 118.
183. "I can hear": Paula to CS, ca. August 1908, UI.
183. "You speak to": Ibid.
183. "The Socialists say": CS, "Lake Shore and Fox River Valley Notes," *Social-Democratic Herald*, February 1, 1908.
184. "industry of the": Thomas Kirkup, *History of Socialism* (London: Adam & Charles Black, 1900), 288.
184. "the child of": Ibid.
184. At the turn: Figures based on U.S. Bureau of Census, Eleventh Census, courtesy Milwaukee County Historical Society.
185. "the frugal, hard-working": quoted in CS Journal, 1907–1908, Collection Records for Lake Shore and Fox River Valley District, UI. See James J. Lorence, " 'Dynamite for the Brain': The Growth and Decline of Socialism in Central and Lakeshore Wisconsin, 1910–1920," *Wisconsin Magazine of History*, Vol. 66, no. 4, Summer 1983, 251–73.
185. "a number of": CS, "Lake Shore and Fox River Valley Notes," *Social-Democratic Herald*, February 1, 1908.
185. The Wisconsin Social-Democrats: A study of the columns by Sandburg, Carl D. Thompson and others writing for the *Social-Democratic Herald* provided the daily details of the Milwaukee movement.
185. "Oshkosh is such": CS, "Lake Shore and Fox River Valley Department," *Social-Democratic Herald*, May 26, 1908.
186. "never attended a": Carl D. Thompson, "State Organizer's Department," *Social-Democratic Herald*, April 25, 1908.
187. "a bit of": Ibid.
187. "If labor will": CS, "Lake Shore and Fox River Valley Department," *Social-Democratic Herald*, July 26, 1908.
187. "The comrades say": Carl D. Thompson, "State Organizer's Department," *Social-Democratic Herald*, Septemeber 19, 1908.
188. She had thought: PS to CS, August 26 and September 2, 1908, UI.
188. "I want you!": PS to CS, September 2, 1908.
188. "I want to": Ibid.
189. "Have walked abroad": PS to CS, n.d. [1908], UI.
189. "The melancholy of": CS to PS, August 25 [1908], UI.
189. "One tree on": Ibid.
189. "We have the": Victor Berger, "Wisconsin Holds State Convention," *Social-Democratic Herald*, June 20, 1908.
190. "piece of socialist": Carl D. Thompson, "How the Milwaukee Socialists Distribute Literature," MS, Socialist Party Collection, Duke University.
190. "good reliable comrade": Ibid.
190. "Comrades throughout": PS to CS [September 11], 1908, UI.

190. "go over that": CS to PS, September 9 [1908], MIT 77.

191. "Do you see": CS, *You and Your Job* (Chicago: Charles H. Kerr & Co., [1908]), 7–8.

191. "When the last": CS, *You and Your Job*, 10. Sandburg wove into *You and Your Job* passages from his notebooks and lectures. See page 6, for instance, for a passage almost surely drawn from his lecture "Black Marks." This pamphlet is a striking example of the fusion of Sandburg's oratory, politics and prose.

191. "Fighting toward one": CS, *You and Your Job*, 25.

191. "ringing speech": Unsigned newspaper clipping, *Social-Democratic Herald*, September 14, 1908.

On September 17, Sandburg spoke in Fond du Lac, opening the meeting by playing graphophone recordings of speeches by Eugene Debs for an audience of "proletarians, but not slummers" who "had some taste of the good things of life and want more!" That speech was covered for the *Social-Democratic Herald* by Lilian Steichen Sandburg. The graphophone was a phonograph using wax records.

192. "It is impossible": Eugene Debs, *Wilshire's*, October 1908, 7.

192. "tired of the": Eugene Debs, quoted in *Social-Democratic Herald*, undated news clipping, CS 1908 Labor File, CSH/UI.

Red Special reports are drawn from a packet of news clippings, CS Collection, UI, most hard to attribute, without datelines and newspaper sources.

192. "All tumbled": CS, "Aboard the Red Special," September 24 [1908], MIT 78.

192. "all about the": PS to CS [September 26, 1908], UI.

193. "His face": CS to PS, "Aboard the Red Special" [September 27, 1908], MIT 79.

193. "*Don't wear yourself*": PS to CS [September 18, 1908], UI.

194. "Am homesick—and": PS to CS, n.d. [ca. October 1908], UI.

194. "I have been": CS to PS, October 19, 1908, UI.

194. "I don't know": CS to PS, October 21, 1908, UI.

195. "unbounded": Carl D. Thompson, "Wisconsin State Organizer's Department," *Social-Democratic Herald*, October 31, 1908.

196. "monkeying with platform": CS to PS [September or November 10, 1908], MIT 79.

196. "company of geniuses": PS[LS] to CS, n.d. [ca. November 1908], MS/UI.

196. "The poems you": PS to CS, n.d. [1908], UI.

196. "a couple of": Ibid.

196. "We both grow": PS to CS [November 1908], UI.

196. "all but broke": PS to CS, n.d. [1908], UI.

197. "I have myself": PS to CS, n.d. [1908], UI.

197. "has either just": CS to LS, n.d. [1908], UI.

197. "I hope the FIVE": PS to CS, n.d. [1908], UI.

197. "direct, sincere": CS, 1908 Lecture Circular.

197. "thorough and eager": Ibid.

197. "one of the": Eugene Debs to CS, November 27, 1908, UI.

198. "We have bills!": PS to CS, n.d. [1908], UI.

198. "wonder poems": Ibid.

198. "The Poems are": PS to CS, n.d. [1908], UI.

198. "If Lillian was": Mary Steichen to Clara Sandburg and family, February 22, 1909, MS.

199. "three acres and": PS to CS [February 17, 1909], UI.

199. "rip up shirts": PS to CS [February 19, 1908], UI.
199. "so calm and": Ibid.
200. "hoeing and ploughing": PS to CS [February 17, 1909], UI.
200. "poetry and romance": CS to PS [February 16, 1909], MIT 84.
200. "love and faith": CS to PS [February 16, 1909], UI.
200. "give the Poet": PS to CS, n.d. [1909], UI.
200. "wait—and work": PS to CS, ibid.
200. "vile, stale": PS to CS, ibid.
201. "Every day, we're": PS to CS [February 19, 1909], UI.
201. "way and will": CS, "February Morning," unpublished poem, UI.
201. "reduced the *crowd*": CS to PS, March 3, 1909, UI.
202. "Dear Sister Esther": PS to Esther Sandburg, May 20, 1909, MS/IU.
202. "The average daily": CS, "The Saloon Smashers," *Wilshire's*, May 1909.
203. "nothing doing at": CS to PS [June 5 or 12] 1909, UI.
203. "confessed everything in": CS to PS, ibid.
203. "had no references": CS to PS, n.d. [1909], MS/UI.
203. "Took me on": CS to PS [June 7, 1909], MIT 86.
203. "I am down": CS to PS [June 7, 1909], MIT 87.
203. "I miss you": Ibid.
203. "Whatever comes, we": PS to CS, n.d. [1909], MS/UI.
203. "quite a cog": CS to PS [June 9, 1909], MIT 89.
204. "I want you": CS to PS, n.d. [1909], MS.
204. "lean ribs and": CS, autobiographical manuscript prepared for Henry Holt & Co., 1915, UI.
204. "feature pieces": CS to Karl Detzer, *Carl Sandburg: A Study in Personality and Background* (New York: Harcourt, Brace & Co., 1941), 81–82.
205. "America has many": CS, "Zig-Zags," *Milwaukee Journal*, quoted in HS, GGR 174–75.
205. "All poets from": Ibid.
     In "The Wisconsin Years," her unpublished biographical manuscript, MS gives a full account of her father's work as a reporter in Milwaukee.

Chapter 10: Fugitives of Pain (1909–1911)

206. "I shall foot": CS, "The Road and the End," *Chicago Poems*, CP 42. This poem, originally entitled "Lands and Souls," was published in Elbert Hubbard's *The Fra* in August 1908 and later in Harriet Monroe's *Poetry: A Magazine of Verse* in March 1914.
206. "liberal radical": CS to PS, n.d. [1909], MS/UI.
206. "TO PITY the": CS, "What Do You Think?," *The Fra*, June 1909; reprinted as broadside.
207. "after what seemed": PGW to CS, August 17, 1909, UI.
207. "one disease whose": CS, "Fighting the White Plague: How the People Are Being Educated to Stamp out Tuberculosis," *La Follette's*, October 1909, 7–8.
208. "one of the": News clipping, n.d., "Illustrated Lecture at Courthouse Tonight," Packet of news clippings, UI.
     CS wrote to Paula throughout December 1909 about the difficulties of the anti-tuberculosis tour. See unpublished letters, UI.

208. "chafing at the": "Drummers Buy Stamps" (West Bend) *Evening Wisconsin*, n.d.

208. "the big heart": CS to PS, December 15, 1909, UI.

209. "the common people": CS, "Lincoln's Birthday," *Social-Democratic Herald*, February 12, 1910.

209. "Already the concentration": Undated news clipping, "Socialism Is Country's Salvation," Packet of news clippings, MS.

209. "almost shabby": Reuben Borough, "The Sandburg I Remember," *Journal of Illinois History*, Vol. 59, no. 3, Autumn 1966, 251.

    August Sandburg's obituary appeared in the *Galesburg Daily Republican-Register*, March 22, 1910.

210. "worker on the": CS, Dedication, *Abraham Lincoln: The Prairie Years*, 1926.

210. See MS, "The Wisconsin Years," unpublished biography, for background on August Sandburg's death. Esther and Martha Sandburg were still living at home at this time. Mary Sandburg lived in Galesburg and worked as a nurse. According to his obituary, August Sandburg was born September 27, 1844, in Osbosocan, Sweden, although records there cannot substantiate that fact, given the uncertainty about the original surname. The obituary indicates that August Sandburg came to the United States in 1869. As earlier noted, Galesburg census records in 1880 gave August's age as thirty-four, as of June 1880. That suggests that he was born in September 1845.

210. "always a bond": CS, *ATYS* 430–32.

211. "It would be": CS, ibid.

212. "event of the": Oscar Ameringer, *If You Don't Weaken* (New York: Henry Holt & Co., 1940), 286.

212. "the principles of": Eugene V. Debs, quoted in Nick Salvatore, *Eugene V. Debs: Citizen and Socialist* (Urbana: University of Illinoise Press, 1982), 246.

212. "Its slums were": Ameringer, 286–87.

213. "our workers to": Emil Seidel, unpublished autobiography, Manuscript Collection, Wisconsin State Historical Society, Madison, 79–80.

213. Seidel's biography, passim, contains an informative account of his mayoral campaign and administration.

    For Sandburg's appointment as Seidel's secretary, see *Milwaukee Journal*, April 12, 1910, 11.

213. "I will show": CS to Reuben Borough, May 5, 1910, MIT 91.

213. "I don't know": ES to PS and CS, n.d. [1910], UI.

213. "I'm sorry I wasn't": ES to PS and CS, n.d. [1910], UI.

214. "come into national": *Lombard Review*, March 1910, 159–60.

214. It was an: Emil Seidel, "Mayor's Message to the Common Council, April 19, 1910," Appendix, Seidel unpublished autobiography, WSHS.

214. "safe place for": Ibid.

214. "For the love": Daniel Hoan, *City Government: The Record of the Milwaukee Experiment* (New York: Harcourt, Brace & Co., 1936), 69.

214. "Why, the Social": Seidel unpublished autobiography, 165.

    For a much fuller treatment of Seidel's administration and Sandburg's role in it, see Penelope Niven (hereafter PEN) unpublished manuscript, UI; MS unpublished biography; HS, GGR. Meta Berger's unpublished autobiography, Manuscript Collection, Wisconsin State Historical Society, Madison, is also revealing of the time.

215. "It is just": CS to PS, n.d., UI.

215. "songs warbled and": CS to PS, n.d., UI.
215. "Cheer up": Elsie Caskey to PS, n.d., MS.
215. "MRS. CARL SANDBURG": *Milwaukee Journal*, September 29, 1910.
215. "many sorry days": Ibid.
216. "If Honest Abe": PS, quoted in typescript, 1910, MS/UI.
216. "I have seen": CS, "The Hammer," was published in *Poetry: A Magazine of Verse* in 1914, but was not included in *Chicago Poems* in 1916. It appeared in "New Section" of *Complete Poems* in 1950, page 650, dated 1910.
217. "His viewpoint is": "Sidelights on Milwaukeans," *Milwaukee Journal*, November 11, 1910, 15.
217. "a literary genius": Ibid. CS, "In the Milwaukee Mayor's Office," *Social-Democratic Herald*, news clipping, n.d., UI.
217. "Governor Wilson has": "What Leading Citizens Think of Wilson," *Milwaukee Journal*, November 19, 1910, 2.
217. "an air of": *Milwaukee Journal*, June 1, 1910, 3.
218. "Prosperity for the": CS, "A Labor Day Talk," *Social-Democratic Herald*, September 3, 1910, 3.
219. "plainest pamphlet printed": George N. Cohen to CS, August 2, 1910, UI.
219. "to put the": Head note to CS, "The 'Municipal Dance,' " *La Follette's*, December 24, 1910, 9, 15.
219. "many strangers within": Emil Seidel, unpublished autobiography, 164.
219. "the sincerity of": William Leiserson to Emily Leiserson, March 24, 1911, Wisconsin State Historical Society, Madison. Leiserson's letters to his wife in March 1911 give a graphic picture of Sandburg at that time—"how thoroly devoted he is to the cause and how completely he forgets himself . . . neglecting to take care of himself & his health" (March 18, 1911).
219. "The right to": PS, "Women Are Glad: Suffragettes Happy Over the Chance to Vote on Bonds," typescript from the *Milwaukee Journal*, [March 10?], 1911, ES, MS/UI. "Milwaukee women, suffragettes in particular, are elated over the opportunity which has been given them to vote for school boards as well as for school directors," the article said, noting their objection to the ruling that there must be separate boxes for their ballots on bond issues. Another Milwaukee suffragette, Edith Webster, reportedly saw no advantage in separate ballot boxes except to correctly ascertain the number of women voters. "We might also discover how intelligently they vote," she said, "or if theirs will be merely a duplication of the men's vote."
220. "writing about a": CS to Reuben Borough, April 15, 1911, MIT 92.
220. "We expect to": Ibid.
220. "She loves blood-red": CS, "Poppies," *Chicago Poems*, CP 60. Paula grew poppies in her garden in Milwaukee, and was working in the garden the evening before her first child was born. PEN interview with MS, October 7, 1986.
220. "Paula is digging": CS, "June," *Chicago Poems*, CP 55. According to MS, "June" was written just before she was born. PEN interview with MS, October 7, 1986.
220. "a girl and": CS to Reuben Borough, June 3, 1911, MIT 93.
220. "The white moon": CS, unpublished poem, MS.
    Part of this poem, revised, appeared as "Baby Face" in *Cornhuskers*, CP 131. "The white moon comes in on my baby's face" was revised to "WHITE MOON

comes in on a baby face," and the last ten lines were omitted. The unpublished draft reads as follows:

To the White Moon

The white moon comes in on my baby's face,
The shafts across her bed are flimmering.
Out on the land the wide white moon shines,
Shines and glimmers against the gnarled shadows,
    All silver with a beauty that flimmers
    Among the slow twisted shadows
Falling across the long road that runs from the house.

I ask you, White Moon,
To keep a little beauty
And some of your flimmering silver
For her who sleeps here
By the window tonight
Where you come in
With your trembling shine
Of light on her little face.

Her little feet will go out
On the long road from the house
One of these days.
Keep a little of your beauty
For her, White Moon,
Falling on the snow
Amid the twisted shadows
Tonight.

220. "Only seven days": CS, "My Baby Girl," *La Follette's*, June 10, 1911, 10.
221. "Gray World of": PS to CS, July 20 [1911], UI.
221. "fruit season": CS to William Leiserson, August 30, 1911, MS.
222. "the conventional themes" and following terms: Walt Whitman, "A Backward Glance O'er Travel'd Roads," *Leaves of Grass*, 545–59.
222. "I SHALL foot": CS, "The Road and the End," *Chicago Poems*, CP 42.
223. "I shall never" CS, "Broadway," *Chicago Poems*, CP 69.
223. "Dreams, only dreams": CS, "Dreams in the Dusk," *Chicago Poems*, CP 65.
223. "The headlight finds": CS, "Old Woman," *Chicago Poems*, CP 69.
224. "I am the": CS, "I Am the People, the Mob," *Chicago Poems*, CP 71.
224. "Woman of a": CS, "Paula," PDG 70.
225. "first-class": Whitman, "A Backward Glance O'er Travel'd Roads," *Leaves of Grass*, 545–59.
225. "these incalculable, modern": Ibid.
225. "There are no": CS, "Languages," *Chicago Poems*, CP 72–73.

Chapter 11: This My City (1911–1914)

227. "And they tell": CS, "Chicago," *Chicago Poems*, CP 3.
228. "one of the": CS, "The Power of Publicity," undated clipping, *Social-Democratic Herald*, 1912, ES/UI.

228. He continued to write free-lance: For a fuller study of Sandburg's journalism during this period, see PEN's unpublished manuscript, UI. In particular, Sandburg wrote a series of thoughtful, forward-looking articles on city planning.

228. "made good beyond": A. M. Simons, quoted by C. L. Edson to CS, January 4, 1912 letter, UI.

228. "some kind of": CS, "They Feel Queer About the New Rebellion," *Milwaukee Leader*, clipping in CS Notebook, UI, n.d.

229. "an insensitive old": CS, quoted by MS in "The Wisconsin Years," unpublished biographical ms.

229. angry that Berger's: For a detailed account of Sandburg's position on *The Leader's* conflict with the Newspaper Writer's Union, see PEN's unpublished manuscript, UI. See also CS to Walter P. Stroesser, August 1, 1912, MIT 93. These events are pivotal in the Sandburgs' departure from organized socialism, as reflected in their lapsed party membership after this time. Sandburg wrote later (Henry Holt biographical statement, 1918) that he had offended "Victor Berger and strictly parliamentary Socialists who don't like 'direct action.' " Sandburg and others, including Oscar Ameringer, later gave the story that Sandburg had actively promoted a Milwaukee streetcar strike, to Berger's displeasure. See John Woods, "Trippers," *Motorman and Conductor*, June 1940, and Ameringer, op. cit., 291. Amy Lowell alludes to the story in *Tendencies in Modern American Poetry* (New York: Macmillan, 1920), 214.

229. "a go": CS to PS, [1912], UI. MS believes they moved first to another Chicago apartment but had to move again because downstairs neighbors objected to the presence of a child.

229. "exploring the paths": PS to CS, n.d. [1912], UI.

229. "Now it is": CS to PS, n.d. [September 1912], MIT 97.

230. "It's been mystically": Ibid.

230. "for even a": CS quoted by Detzer, 87–88.

230. "Dark Period": PEN interviews with MS and HS; HS, GGR, 189.

230. "tribulations various": CS to William Leiserson, February 8, 1913, MIT 98.

230. "no advertising": Ibid.

230. "a really free": Negley D. Cochran to CS, February 24, 1921, UI.

231. "a humility like": CS to Negley D. Cochran, August 8, no year indicated, letter apparently not sent to Cochran, UI.

231. "pounded it into": CS to Negley D. Cochran, May 18 [1926], UI; MIT 238.

231. "probably the best": CS to Negley D. Cochran, January 25, 1921, MIT 196.

231. "the splits and cross-sections": CS to William Leiserson, op. cit.

231. "You might say": CS to Reuben Borough, July 13, 1913, MIT 99.

232. "Margaret wailed, 'Come' ": PS to CS, n.d. [Summer 1913], MS/UI.

232. "Dearest: The moon": CS to PS, n.d. [1913], UI.

232. "generally written first": CS, Henry Holt biographical statement, 1918.

232. "Chicago": CS to Norman Corwin, *The World of Carl Sandburg* (henceforward *WOCS*) (New York: Harcourt, Brace & World, 1961), 32.

232. "must sometime succeed" ms to PEN, 517, PEN unpublished MS, UI. The baby Madeline was born November 13, 1913, according to ms. HS writes of the baby's death in GGR, 190. ms writes of the event in notes to PEN, PEN unpublished ms, UI. Further details, from PEN interview with MS.

233. "I could see": PS to MS, quoted in interview with PEN.

233. "I am singing": CS, "Killers," *Chicago Poems, CP* 36.

233. "The time has": CS, "Never Born," *Smoke and Steel, CP* 265.

233. "the habit of": F. M. Feiker to CS, November 1913, UI.

234. "To be original": CS as Sidney Arnold, "Random Notes and Sketches," *American Artisan and Hardware Record*, December 6, 1913.

234. "Oh things one": CS, "Dust" (1913), *CP* 652.

234. "Give me hunger" CS, "At a Window," *Chicago Poems, CP* 49.

235. "a little clairvoyance": CS, "In Appreciation of Harriet Monroe," *The Courier*, University of Chicago, May 1938, n. pag.

   There are varying accounts of how Sandburg's poems were actually delivered to *Poetry*. See HS, GGR, and Eunice Tietjens, *The World at My Shoulder* (New York: Macmillan Co., 1938).

235. Background on *Poetry: A Magazine of Verse* is based on Harriet Monroe, *A Poet's Life* (New York: Macmillan, 1938); Tietjens, *The World at My Shoulder*; the Alice Corbin Henderson Papers, UT; the Harriet Monroe Papers, UC.

236. "some living in": CS, "In Appreciation of Harriet Monroe," n. pag.

236. "search out and": Harriet Monroe, *A Poet's Life*, 250.

237. "marked an embarkation": CS, "In Appreciation of Harriet Monroe," n. pag.

237. "pitiless reader of": Harriet Monroe, *A Poet's Life*, 317.

237. "sweep and vitality": Eunice Tietjens, 39.

238. "I suggest [Pound]": William Butler Yeats to Harriet Monroe, quoted by Monroe in her account of Yeats's visit, *A Poet's Life*, 329–33.

239. "to get back": W. B. Yeats to Lady Gregory quoted in Kenneth Tytell, *Ezra Pound: The Solitary Volcano* (New York: Anchor Press/Doubleday, 1987), 86.

239. "a tall, somewhat": Eunice Tietjens, 38–42.

240. "a style like": Quotations from Yeats's speech and other details are drawn from *Poetry: A Magazine of Verse*, Vol. IV, no. 1, April 1914, 25–29; and the Harriet Monroe Papers, UC.

240. "highspot": CS to Harriet Monroe, postcard, n.d., UC.

240. "Here are the": CS to Harriet Monroe, March 5, 1914, UC.

   While the enclosure is missing, it is possible that Sandburg's transcription of Yeats's speech is given verbatim in *Poetry*, above.

241. "gay and peremptory": Harriet Monroe, *Poets and Their Art* (New York: Macmillan Co., 1926), 12.

241. "his word goes": Harriet Monroe to William Carlos Williams, quoted in Ellen Williams, *Harriet Monroe and the Poetry Renaissance: The First Ten Years of Poetry, 1912–22* (Urbana: University of Illinois Press, 1977), 56.

241. "I don't doubt": Ezra Pound to Harriet Monroe, April 22 [1913], D. D. Paige, ed., *The Selected Letters of Ezra Pound 1907–1941* (New York: New Directions, 1971), 19.

242. "took a long": Harriet Monroe, *A Poet's Life*, 322

242. "Hog Butcher for": CS, "Chicago," *Chicago Poems, CP* 3.

242. "I was influenced": CS to Norman Corwin, WOCS 32.

242. "They tell me . . .": CS, "Chicago," *Chicago Poems, CP* 3.

242. Amy Lowell and others: Amy Lowell, *Tendencies in Modern American Poetry* (New York: Macmillan Co., 1920), 216.

242. "Desolate and lone": CS, "Lost," *Chicago Poems, CP* 5.

243. "blue burst of": CS, "The Harbor," *Chicago Poems, CP* 5.

243. "in sequence of": Monroe, *A Poet's Life*, 297.

243. "beginning of": Ezra Pound to Monroe, ibid., 300.

243. "roused a veritable": Eunice Tietjens, 38–42.

243. "The typographical arrangement": Ibid., 312.

243. "Next to making": Harriet Monroe, "The Enemies We Have Made," *Poetry*, Vol. IV, no. 2, May 1914.

244. "hard clear style": Harriet Monroe, *Poets and Their Art*, 299.

244. "a kind of": Harriet Monroe, *A Poet's Life*, 318–22.

244. "who came swinging": Ibid.

245. "a stalwart slow-stepping": Ibid.

245. "always kept him": Eunice Tietjens, 38–42.

245. "the rising poet": *The Western Comrade*, May 1914, ES/UI.

245. "For God's sake": William Marion Reedy to Edgar Lee Masters; quoted by Max Putzel, *The Man in the Mirror: William Marion Reedy and His Magazine* (Cambridge: Harvard University Press, 1963), 331.

246. "on scrambling eggs": PEN interview with MS.

246. "tramp to the": Edgar Lee Masters to Theodore Dreiser, April 13, 1914.

246. "many early portrait": PEN interview with MS.

246. "good book for:" Edgar Lee Masters to Theodore Dreiser, April 20, 1914.

247. "At last!": Ezra Pound, *The Egoist*, January 1915.

247. "Get some of": Ezra Pound to Harriet Monroe, October 12 [1914], Paige, 43.

247. "I shall run": William Marion Reedy to CS, November 16, 1914, UI.

247. "one long chronicle": Amy Lowell, *Tendencies in Modern American Poetry*, 175. Amy Lowell praised Masters for his "revolutionary" poetry, but wrote that Masters was "more preoccupied with sex than any other English or American author has ever been" and thought his inclusion in *Spoon River* of "Everything that is coarse and revolting in the sexual life" was "the great blot upon Mr. Masters' work" (174–75).

248. "already shaken out": Edgar Lee Masters to Harriet Monroe, quoted by Monroe in "The Fight for the Crowd," *Poetry*, March 1915.

248. "the sheer brute": CS, "Tribute to Webster Ford," *Reedy's Mirror*, November 1914.

248. "The thirty-second page": E. W. Scripps to Negley D. Cochran, quoted in Negley D. Cochran, *E. W. Scripps* (New York: Harcourt Brace, 1932), 136–37.
   See Cochran's biography of Scripps for full background on *The Day Book*, and PEN's unpublished manuscript, UI, for more detail on Sandburg's career there. Also see Frederick Nash and Gwenna Weshinsky, "Carl Sandburg and *The Day Book*," *American Book Collector*, November/December 1928, 23–34, for an invaluable checklist of 135 CS articles in *The Day Book*.

248. "get the most": Negley D. Cochran, Memo to *The Day Book* staff, June 2, 1914, UI.

249. One day he: CS to Norman Corwin, WOCS 31–32.

249. "Japanese Hokus": Ibid.

249. "The fog": CS, "Fog," *Chicago Poems, CP* 33.

250. "I was rather": PEN interview with MS. See HS memory of this event in *GGR*, 192–93. In January 1968, PS spoke of the incident to Anthony Mancini in an interview for the *New York Post Weekend Magazine* (January 13, 1968, Section 2, 25): "We had a disagreement one time a few years after we

were married, and I said, 'Maybe it's time to consider our pact.' But he
answered, 'And I should go through all that courting again?' So that ended
that."

251. "It's a B": PEN interview with MS; MS to PEN, annotation, PEN's unpublished
manuscript, UI. MS to PEN, April 5, 1985.

251. "After waking at": CS, CP 37.

251. "Dreams go on": CS, "Among the Red Guns," Chicago Poems, CP 37. First published in Poetry, November 1914.

252. "But please send": Floyd Dell to CS, n.d., UI.

252. "the one about Chick Lorimer": see "Gone," Chicago Poems, CP 64.

252. "the American citizen": Ezra Pound to Harriet Monroe, quoted by Williams, 124.

252. Ironically it was: Eunice Tietjens, 38–42.

253. "I was surprised": Eunice Tietjens, ibid.

253. "a multimillionaire club": CS, unpublished biographical statement for Henry Holt,
1915, UI.

253. "that strange vegetable": Karl Detzer, 94

254. "with lifted head": CS, "Chicago," CP 3.

Further context for this singularly rich period of twentieth-century American
literary history can be drawn from the following sources:

Margaret Anderson, My Thirty Years' War: the Autobiography (New York: Covici-
Friede, 1930); Floyd Dell, Homecoming: An Autobiography (New York: Farrar &
Rinehart, 1933); Bernard Duffey, The Chicago Renaissance in American Letters: A
Critical History (East Lansing: Michigan State University Press, 1954.); John Gould
Fletcher, Life Is My Song: The Autobiography of John Gould Fletcher (New York:
Farrar & Rinehart, 1937); Dale Kramer, Chicago Renaissance: the Literary Life of
the Midwest, 1900–1930 (New York: Appleton-Century, 1966); Alfred Kreymborg,
Troubadour: An Autobiography (New York: Boni & Liveright, 1925); Edgar Lee
Masters, Across Spoon River: An Autobiography (New York: Farrar & Rinehart,
1936); Max Putzel, The Man in the Mirror: William Marion Reedy and His Magazine
(Cambridge: Harvard University Press, 1963); Louis Untermeyer, American Poetry
Since 1900 (New York: Henry Holt, 1923); Untermeyer, From Another World: The
Autobiography of Louis Untermeyer (New York: Harcourt, Brace, 1939).

Chapter 12: Blood, Work and War (1914–1916)

255. "Poetry is written": CS to Paul Benjamin, n.d. [1918], UI.

255. "overwhelmed us like": Amy Lowell, Tendencies in Modern American Poetry, v.

255. "Poets have made": Harriet Monroe, Poetry, Vol. IV, no. 6, September 1914,
238–39.

255. "good, bad and indifferent": Harriet Monroe, A Poet's Life, 342.

255. "genuine revolt against": Ibid.

256. "immediately the poet's": Harriet Monroe, Poetry, Vol. IV, no. 6, September 1914,
238–39.

256. "Ten minutes now": CS, "Ready to Kill," Chicago Poems, CP 28. The poem first
appeared in Poetry, as noted in text, and was published in June 1916 in the
International Socialist Review.

257. "The war-atmosphere has": D. H. Lawrence to Amy Lowell, quoted in S. Foster
Damon, Amy Lowell: A Chronicle (Boston: Houghton Mifflin, 1935), 278.

257. "It put me": D. H. Lawrence to Harriet Monroe, quoted in Harriet Monroe, *A Poet's Life*, 345.

257. "in the grass": CS, "Murmurings in a Field Hospital," *Chicago Poems*, CP 38.

257. "The welding together": Amy Lowell, v.

258. "somber trench poems": Harriet Monroe, *A Poet's Life*, 347.

258. "Twenty-one million men": CS, "Statistics," *Chicago Poems*, CP 39.

258. "the great arches": CS, "Salvage," *Chicago Poems*, CP 41.

258. "SMASH down the": CS, "And They Obey," *Chicago Poems*, CP 40.

258. "I am singing": CS, "Killers," *Chicago Poems*, CP 36.

259. "millions of men": CS, "Wars," *Chicago Poems*, CP 42.

259. "Silence,/Dry sobs": CS, "Ashes and Dreams," *International Socialist Review*, May 1915, MS.

260. "I wish you": William Marion Reedy to CS, January 14, 1915, UI.

260. "He is mankind": Ezra Pound, "1915: February," reprinted in *New York Times Book Review*, January 10, 1988.

260. "come out all": Ezra Pound to Harriet Monroe, January [1915], D. D. Paige, ed., *The Selected Letters of Ezra Pound 1907–1941* (New York: New Directions, 1971), 48.

260. "really pulling the": Ibid.

261. "free verse has": Ezra Pound to CS, n.d., UI.

The remarkable unpublished letters of Ezra Pound to CS, housed in the CS Collection at UI, document for the first time Pound's interest in Sandburg, and his influence on CS at this seminal stage of his career.

261. "I don't know": Ibid.

261. "Also you might": Ibid.

261. "peck and annoy": Ibid.

262. "Both were jailbirds": CS, "Jack London and O. Henry," *Smoke and Steel*, CP 230.

262. "This will be": PS to CS, n.d. [1915], UI.

262. "I saw Masters": CS, "Notes for a Review of 'The Spoon River Anthology,' " *The Little Review*, Vol. 2, May 1915, 42–43.

263. "I liked Hubbard": William Marion Reedy to CS, June 21, 1915, UI.

263. "stop a cranky": CS, "Lookin' 'Em Over," *The International Socialist Review*, August 1915.

264. "It was a hell": CS, "The Eastland," unpublished poem, MS/UI.

265. "salesman and crowd": CS to Alfred Harcourt, February 4, 1916, MIT 107.

265. "bought stock in": Ibid.

265. "You come along": CS, "To a Contemporary Bunkshooter," *Chicago Poems*, CP 29.

265. "Who is this": MS, unpublished biography, UI.

265. "blood, work": CS, op. cit.

265. "Runs on the": CS, "Nocturne in a Deserted Brickyard," *Chicago Poems*, CP 55.

266. "I do not": Ezra Pound to CS, n.d. [1915], UI.

266. "Blossoms of babies": CS, "Handfuls," *Cornhuskers*, CP 133.

266. "Of my city": CS, "They Will Say," *Chicago Poems*, CP 5.

266. "I never knew": CS, "The Great Hunt," *Chicago Poems*, CP 50.

266. "Let a joy": CS, "Joy," *Chicago Poems*, CP 51.

267. "I think the": Ezra Pound to CS, ca. November 1915, UI.

267. "In the blue": CS, "Sketch." *Chicago Poems*, CP 4.

267. "I simply want": Ezra Pound to CS, ca. November 1915, UI.

267. "And I saw": CS, "The Mayor of Gary," *Smoke and Steel, CP* 161.

268. "the expression of": J. B. Kerfoot, quoted in *Others,* November 1915.

268. "Sometime ago I": Theodore Dreiser to CS, August 6, 1915, UI.

268. "Such a dandy": CS to Theodore Dreiser, September 1, 1915, MIT 103.

268. When Masters got: CS wrote to Theodore Dreiser with these details September 1, 1915, MIT 193.

268. "Edgar Lee is": Theodore Dreiser to CS, October 19, 1915, UI.

269. CS told MS that this was "the only instance of any work of his coming under a police or censor ban." MS, unpublished biography, UI.

269. "books, plays, poems": Theodore Dreiser to CS, November 29, 1915, UI.

269. "I perform all": CS to Theodore Dreiser, February 13, 1916, MIT 110.

269. "Steer Carl my": Alfred Harcourt to Alice Corbin Henderson, quoted by Harcourt, "Forty Years of Friendship," *Journal of the Illinois State Historical Society,* 45 (Winter 1952), 395–99.

270. "tempt him to": CS to Louis Untermeyer, November 11, 1915, UD.

270. "Building the *Day*": Ibid.

270. "I am slaving": CS to Alice Corbin Henderson, December 15, 1915, MIT 104.

270. "organization efficiency and": CS to Ray Stannard Baker, January 24, 1920, MIT 177.

270. By early January: Sandburg wrote these details to Alice Corbin Henderson, hereafter ACH, January 8 [1916], MIT 106.

270. "I saw at": Alfred Harcourt, "Forty Years of Friendship," 395–96. Alfred Harcourt elaborated on this story in an interview with Lloyd Lewis, ca. July 1948. He urged Henry Holt to publish Sandburg's poems, Harcourt told Lewis, but "he was too conservative an old gentleman to embrace the rugged, revolutionary fire in Carl's work. Holt had a little earlier refused my pleas that we publish John Masefield, and Sandburg seemed more brutal than the Britisher." Thus Harcourt withheld about five "raw" poems, got the manuscript approved, and then "slipped the hot numbers back into the manuscript," gambling that his bosses would "never read the book." "It worked out that way," Harcourt concluded. "If I had been caught, I would have been fired, of course, but the risk was worth it." The interview appeared in Lloyd Lewis's column in the *Chicago Daily News,* ca. January 24, 1948.

271. "a work to": CS contract with Henry Holt, February 5, 1916, UI.

271. "away behind in": CS to ACH, January 8 [1916], MIT 106.

271. "It is rare": Alfred Harcourt (henceforth AH) to CS, January 20, 1916, UI.

271. "For obvious reasons": Ibid.

271. "Are they going": Edgar Lee Masters, quoted by CS to AH, February 4, 1916, MIT 107.

271. "I saw clearly": CS to AH, February 4, 1916, MIT 107.

272. "Holt & Co. are": CS to Louis Untermeyer, February 13, 1916, UD.

272. "I'll vilify you": Louis Untermeyer to CS, February 16, 1916, UI.

272. "The silly cover": Edward Steichen to PS, n.d. [1916], UI.

272. "a civilizing force": Edward Steichen to PS, n.d. [1916], UI, and Steichen, *ALP,* following Plate 62.

273. "to sing, blab, chortle": CS to Amy Lowell [ca. June 10, 1917], MIT 117.

273. "the very heart of": Edward Steichen, *ALP,* following Plate 62.

273. "The dago shovelman": CS, "Child of the Romans," *Chicago Poems*, CP 12.

273. "creative art": CS, "The Work of Ezra Pound, *Poetry*, Vol. VII, no. V, February 1916.

274. " 'Feb.' Poetry just": Ezra Pound to CS, February 17 [1916], UI.

275. "torn to pieces": CS to Amy Lowell, April 2, 1916, MIT 111.

275. She promised to: Amy Lowell to CS, April 20, 1916, UI.

275. "remember that color-bearers": CS to Amy Lowell, April 2, 1916, MIT 111.

275. "Thank you for": Amy Lowell to CS, April 20, 1916, UI.

275. "amid . . . furor": CS to ACH, March 25, 1916, MIT 110.

275. "Rough but *real*": Sinclair Lewis to Alfred Harcourt, quoted in Mark Schorer, *Sinclair Lewis: An American Life* (New York: McGraw-Hill, 1961), 232.

275. "had a holy": CS to ACH, March 25, 1916, MIT 110.

275. "whose services have": CS, prefatory note, *Chicago Poems*.

275. "tradition shattering": *American Library Association Booklist*, Vol. XIII, no. 23, October 1916.

For a full discussion of critical treatment of *Chicago Poems*, see PEN unpublished ms, UI.

276. "one the rather": W. A. Bradley, *Dial*, 61, 528, December 14, 1916.

276. "book of ill-regulated": William Stanley Braithwaite, *Boston Transcript*, May 13, 1916.

276. "all alive, stirring": *New York Times*, June 11, 1916.

276. "vivid with the": Louis Untermeyer, *The Masses*, Vol. VIII, no. 30, July 1916.

276. "one of the": Amy Lowell, *The Poetry Review*, Vol. I, July 1916, 46.

276. "type hap-hazard a": CS, "The Work of Ezra Pound," *Poetry*, Vol. VII, no. V, February 1916.

276. "I am delighted": H. L. Mencken to CS, n.d., UI.

276. "human drive": CS to Louis Untermeyer, June 8, 1916, UD.

277. "The pictures which": PGW to CS, May 28, 1916, UI.

277. "The 'Chicago Poems' ": Ezra Pound to CS, October 11, 1916, UI. Pound liked *Chicago Poems* better than *Spoon River Anthology*, he told CS. Pound thought, however, that Sandburg's "dialect" and "argot" seemed "not the best way, not the most controlled way but simply the easiest way." Yet he urged Sandburg to adhere to his own style: "And I certainly dont want you to use anyone else's face. Elliot's wouldn't become you, for example. . . . Style so far as it is clothing, balls with it, but when it becomes incomparable concentration it is another story" (Pound to CS, ibid.).

277. "I have, of course": CS to Amy Lowell, July 23, 1916, MIT 113.

277. "lyric counterbalance": Amy Lowell to CS, June 2, 1916, UI.

277. "the lyricist in": Amy Lowell, *Tendencies in Modern American Poetry*, 202 and 200–32.

278. "Carl Sandburg has": Harriet Monroe, *Poets and Their Art*, 30–31.

278. "in the cool": CS to Amy Lowell, July 23, 1916, MIT 113.

278. "Masters I haven't": CS to ACH [September 16, 1916], MIT 114.

279. "Ivory domes": CS, "OTHERS (Fantasia for Muskmelon Days)," *Others: A Magazine of the New Verse*, Vol. III, no. 1, July 1916. William Carlos Williams was the editor of this issue. The poem was published in 1978 in BT, 14.

279. "Poor, millions of": CS, "Masses," ChiP, CP 4.

279. "their hunger-deep eyes": CS, "The Harbor," ChiP, CP 5.

279. "muckers": CS, "Muckers," ChiP, CP 10.
279. "long lines": CS, "Working Girls," ChiP, CP 16.
279. "Brooding and muttering": CS, "Nigger," ChiP, CP 23.
279. "romance/and big": CS, "Mamie," ChiP, CP 17.
280. "Lines based on": CS, "Used Up," ChiP, CP 61.
280. "Women of night": CS, "It Is Much," Chip, CP 63.
280. "a broken smile": CS, "Trafficker," ChiP, CP 62.
280. "If it ain't": CS, "Harrison Street Court," ChiP, CP 62.
280. "Let us be": CS, "Soiled Dove," ChiP, CP 63.
281. "Gone with her": CS, "Gone," ChiP, CP 64.
281. "the people—the crowd": CS, "I Am the People, the Mob," ChiP, CP 71.
281. "Tell no man": CS, "Gypsy," ChiP, CP 76.
281. the emotional democrat: Louis Untermeyer, American Poetry Since 1900 (New York: Henry Holt, 1923), 67.

Chapter 13: The Four Brothers (1916–1918)

282. "They are hunting": CS, "The Four Brothers," Cornhuskers, CP 143.
282. "iron-gray": HS, GGR, 218.
282. Her intelligence: Edward Steichen and PS exchanged letters about Margaret's development (UI). Also see George Fox to CS and PS, January 28, 1916, UI, and Frank Wolfe to CS, April 8, 1916, UI.
282. "exploding": Quoted by MS, PEN interview with MS.
282. Details of the Maywood house are based on PEN interviews with MS, and MS's sketches of the house.
283. "It's a girl": CS to ACH, July 9, 1916, MIT 113.
283. "So, the household": CS to ACH [September 16, 1916], MIT 114.
283. "as immortal a": Ibid.
283. "dozing in a": CS, "Dan," Smoke and Steel, CP 264.
283. "Here is a thing": CS, "Home," Chicago Poems, CP 62.
283. "In your blue": CS, "Margaret," Chicago Poems, CP 60.
283. "far silent yellow": CS, "Child Moon," Chicago Poems, CP 60.
283. "The child Margaret": CS, "Child Margaret," Cornhuskers, CP 107.
284. "The two sisters": CS, "Two Sisters," unpublished, UI.
284. "at the evening lamp": Ibid.
284. "sweeping, chaotic, vivid": CS to Amy Lowell, November 17, 1916, HU.
284. "I am for": CS to ACH [September 16, 1916], MIT 114.
284. "In power, range": CS to ACH [October 9, 1916], MIT 115.
284. Chicago Poems had: Two critics in particular, Conrad Aiken and William Stanley Braithwaite, attacked Sandburg and Chicago Poems more than once. Sandburg was deeply angered by Braithwaite's treatment. See PEN's unpublished manuscript, UI, for an extended exploration of the Sandburg-Braithwaite dispute. On December 30, 1916, Sandburg wrote ACH "The lesson of the Braithwaite affair is that I shouldn't dabble in the politics of literature" (UT). While Sandburg bridled at some criticism, he said he could accept the criticism of William Morton Payne at the Dial, John Hervey and others because he respected them and liked them as men (ibid.). "I think it's on the man-to-man

basis and not on art that [Braithwaite] and I have a fundamental antagonism,"
    CS told ACH (ibid.).
284. "the critics are": CS quoted by AL to CS, October 19, 1916, HU.
284. "be roundly swatted": CS to ACH, November 7, 1916, UT.
284. "Can each see": Walt Whitman, "Carol of Occupations," *Leaves of Grass*, 203.
285. "I SALUTED a": CS, "Chicago Poet," *Cornhuskers*, CP 101.
285. "I'll bet more": CS to ACH, November 7, 1916, UT.
285. "any clubs or": CS, Henry Holt biographical statement, 1915, UI.
286. "frank politics of": CS to ACH, May 23, 1917, UT.
286. "Written to be": CS, "Fire Dreams," *Cornhuskers*, CP 130.
286. "I keep on": Ezra Pound to Felix Schelling, November 17 [1916], Paige, 98.
286. In the after-hours: See PEN, unpublished ms, for discussion of Sandburg's work
    for the *International Socialist Review* during this period, and his assumption of
    multiple identities and names as a journalist. There are ample materials to
    support a full-fledged political biography of CS; his ISR association would be
    pivotal in such a study.
287. "between-whiles": CS to Amy Lowell, November 17, 1916, HU.
287. "toward simplicity": Ezra Pound, Paige, 98.
287. "I discount Sandburg's": Ezra Pound to Harriet Monroe, August 21 [1917], Paige,
    115.
287. Most recently, he: See John Tytell, *Ezra Pound: The Solitary Volcano*, 135.
287. "the point is": Ezra Pound to CS, February 22 [1917], UI.
287. "I am very": Martyn Johnson to CS, January 31, 1917, UI.
    See "Brave Art, a Little Bravado, and Much Joy!," CS ms, UI, and "Brave
    Art and a Little Bravado," galleys, UI. CS made two key points in the unpub-
    lished review of Pound's book: He argued that what an artist has to say "about
    life and art, of value and worth anybody's keeping, will be said not in logo-
    machic art theories but in tangible art accomplishments," the closest he
    came to an attack on Vorticism and Pound's "patter about 'isms.'" Second, he
    revealed his own struggle with the critics then: "There is here the manner of
    one isolated and exasperated, feeling himself overforlorn with the struggle to
    penetrate impenetrable 'ivory domes.'" See previous discussion of the poem
    "Others" (BT 14).
287. "I do not": Vachel Lindsay to CS, January 13, 1917, UI.
288. "individual": Conrad Aiken, "Poetic Realism," *Poetry Journal*, January 1917.
288. "forty ways": CS to L. W. Payne, December 3, 1926, MIT 243.
288. "A world that": CS to George Fox, n.d. [1917], MIT 116.
289. "work and war": CS to ACH [November 27, 1917], MIT 123.
289. "silent mass of": Woodrow Wilson, "Peace Without Victory," address to U.S.
    Senate, January 22, 1917.
289. "My people are": CS, "My People," *Smoke and Steel*, CP 266.
290. "the strongest, loneliest": CS to Louis Untermeyer, n.d. [1917], UD. Also see JW
    Papers, August 28, 1984.
290. "one of the": Louis Untermeyer to CS, May 18, 1917, UI.
290. "once a year": CS to AH, n.d., ES/UI.
290. By 1913 Anderson: The others were *Many Marriages*, published in 1922, and *Mary
    Cochran* and *Talbot Whittingham*, unpublished.

290. "finer, more indigenous": ACH to CS, May 12, 1917, UI.

290. "Glancing over some": CS to Amy Lowell, n.d. [ca. June 1917], MIT 119.

291. "The goddam academicians": CS to ACH, May 23, 1917, UT.

291. "The Drift of": CS as Jack Philips, "The Drift of the War," *International Socialist Review*, May 1917, 658–59.

291. "Pile the bodies": CS, "Grass," *Cornhuskers*, CP 136. "Grass" appeared in the *International Socialist Review* in September 1917.

291. "I write your": CS, "Omaha, 1917," UI.

292. "I look at": CS Journal, quoted by Harry Golden, *Carl Sandburg* (Cleveland & New York: World Publishing Co., 1961), 198.

292. "the Daily News": CS, ATYS 379.

292. "curious academy of": CS, Unpublished ms, UI.

293. "The world could": Clarence Darrow, *The Story of My Life* (New York: Grosset & Dunlap, 1932), 218.

293. "The planet is": CS to Harriet Monroe [May 1917]. Quoted in Monroe, *A Poet's Life*, 350.

294. Against his better: For fuller background on the position of the Wisconsin Social-Democrats on the war, see Emil Seidel's unpublished autobiography, op. cit.; Sally M. Miller, *Victor Berger and the Promise of Constructive Socialism, 1910–1920*, op. cit; PEN unpublished ms, UI.

294. "federal marshals corraled": Salvatore, 288.

295. "Men were arrested": Darrow, 218.

295. "I have been": CS to ACH, [November 27, 1917], MIT 123.

295. "whistling 'Yankee Doodle' ": CS, "What Will Tomorrow Bring?" *The Chicago American*, August 7, 1917.

295. "O sunburned clear-eyed": CS, "The Four Brothers," *Cornhuskers*, CP 143.

296. "Advise strategic retreat": Eugene Meyer to Edward Steichen, quoted by Steichen in *A Life in Photography* (Garden City, NY: Doubleday & Co., 1963), no page numbers; opposite Plate 62.

296. The sinking of: Steichen to CS and PS, n.d., UI.

296. "be a photographic": Steichen, *A Life in Photography*, pages following Plate 62.

296. "a symbol of": Ibid.

297. "reading lines, shadows": CS, SP, *The Sandburg Range*, 318.

297. "Through a steel": CS, *Chicago Daily News*, October 2, 1917.
     See CS, *Chicago Daily News* Scrapbook for his clippings of key articles and editorials during this period, UI.

297. felt profoundly the: Sherwood Anderson to CS, April 17, 1917, UI.

297. "the ambulance corps": Malcolm Cowley, *Exile's Return* (New York: Viking, 1951), 38.

297. "I find I": Edgar Lee Masters to Harriet Monroe, quoted in Monroe, *A Poet's Life*, 358.

297. "lifted the inevitable": Walter Lippmann, Ronald Steel, *Walter Lippmann and the American Century* (New York: Vintage/Random House, 1981), 113.

297. "a healthy public": Ibid., 125.

298. "articulate opinion into": Ibid., 126.

298. "a liberal interpretation": Louis Untermeyer, *The Letters of Robert Frost to Louis Untermeyer* (New York: Holt, Rinehart & Winston, 1963), 55.

298. "I have been": John Reed, *The Masses*, quoted in Charles A. Madison, *Critics and Crusaders* (New York: Henry Holt & Co., 1947–48), 519.

298. "conspiring to effect": Untermeyer, 55.

298. "If the Postmaster": Robert Frost to Louis Untermeyer, July 15, 1917, Untermeyer 56.

298. "do or say": Robert Frost to Louis Untermeyer, August 18, 1917, Untermeyer, 58–59.

298. "mess with the": Robert Frost to Louis Untermeyer, June 27, 1918, Untermeyer, 69.

299. "No poet of": Amy Lowell, *Tendencies in Modern American Poetry*, 223–24.

299. "would surpass and": CS to ACH, n.d. [November 27, 1917], MIT 123.

299. "formally opened the": CS, *Chicago Daily News*, October 11, 1917.

299. "Make war songs": CS, "The Four Brothers," *Cornhuskers*, CP 143.

300. "done a fine": George Creel to CS, October 12, 1917, UI.

300. "a magnificent thing": Sherwood Anderson to CS, quoted by HS, GGR 229.

300. "majestically and beautifully": Lloyd Lewis to CS, October 29, 1917, UI.

300. "splendid poem": Edith Wyatt to CS, October 29, 1917, UI.

300. "the greatest poem": Charles Dennis to CS, October 24, 1917, UI.

300. "Your poem": Ben Reitman to CS, October 29 [1917], UI.

301. "The millions easy" and following: CS, "The Four Brothers," *Cornhuskers*, CP 143.

302. "blood-crossed, blood-dusty": CS, ibid.

302. "I sit in": CS, "Smoke," *Cornhuskers*, CP 142.

302. "world storm": CS to PS, n.d. [ca. September 1917], MIT 132.

Chapter 14: World Storm (1918–1919)

303. "Terribly big days": CS to PS, January 30 [1910], MIT 150.

303. "blur and the": CS to PS, November 1 [1918], MIT 144.

303. "Amid the jabber": CS, "May 1915," UI.

303. "I open my": CS, Journal, April 28, 1918, unpublished ts, "Diary Page for April 28, 1918," MS, UI.

304. The charming widow: For background on Harriet Vaughn Moody, see Olivia Howard Dunbar, *A House in Chicago* (Chicago: University of Chicago Press, 1947).

305. "Woke in the": CS, Journal, May 5, 1918, unpublished ts, "Diary Notes, Sunday May 5, 1918," MS, UI.

305. "bigger conceived and": CS to AH, May 3 [1918], MIT 129.

305. "very American": CS to ACH, n.d. [1918], UT.

305. "Of course we": AH to CS, June 13, 1918, UI.

306. "I was born": CS, "Prairie," *Cornhuskers*, CP 79.

306. "In the city": Ibid.

306. "I am here": Ibid.

306. "No pals to": ACH to CS, May 31, 1918, UI.

306. "Tumult. A world": CS to ACH, June 28 [1918], UT.

306. "sparse sales, a": CS to ACH, March 8 [1918], UT.

307. "ten thousand crimes": See CS, "IWW Drive to Discredit U.S. Department of

Justice," *Chicago Daily News*, February 19, 1918; Jack Phillips, "Haywood of the IWW," *International Socialist Review*, January 1918, 343; Jack Phillips, "Speaking of the Department of Justice," *International Socialist Review*, February 1918, 406–407.

307. "many brothers in": CS to ACH, February 20 [1918], UT.

307. "personally directing the": PS to CS, November 3, 1918, UI.

307. "As you know": Sam T. Hughes to CS, July 11, 1918, UI.

308. "It is a go," he: CS to Sam Hughes, July 15, 1918, MIT 130.

308. "It is a go," Hughes: Sam Hughes to CS, July 18, 1918, UI.

308. "I was brought": CS to Sam Hughes, July 22, 1918, NEA. (While this passage appears in MIT 136, it is part of July 22, 1918 letter.)

308. "get down to": Sam Hughes to CS, July 18, 1918, UI.

308. "Go, with your": Ben Hecht, " "Good-by, Carl," *Chicago Daily News* clipping, ES/UI.

309. "was duly and": CS to Sam Hughes, July 22, 1918, NEA.

309. "luminous": CS to PS, n.d. [1918], UI.

309. "There were tears": CS to PS, n.d. [1918], MIT 132.

309. "And again": CS to PS, n.d. [1918], UI.

309. "he may see": CS to PS, September [1918], MIT 138.

309. "the guitars, the": CS to PS, n.d. [1918], UI.

309. "an awful pull": CS to PS, n.d. [1918], UI.

310. "Make me important": CS to Sam Hughes, July 23, 1918, MIT 130.

310. "How about the": CS NEA Notebook, UI, and CS to Sam Hughes, July 22, 1918, UI, NEA.

310. especially after Eugene Debs: Debs was convicted September 12 and on September 14, 1918, was sentenced to ten years in prison. He was incarcerated first in Ohio and then in Georgia in Atlanta Federal Prison.

310. "From the start": Julian S. Mason, July 23, 1918, NEA File, UI.

311. "Well, I suppose": CS to PS, n.d. [1918], UI.

311. "only neutral subjects": CS to Sam Hughes, August 9, 1918, NEA File, UI.

311. "No passport today": CS to PS, August 13 [1918], UI.

311. "Out of my": CS to PS, n.d. [1918], MIT 138.

311. "they are watching": CS to Sam Hughes, August 21, 1918, NEA.

311. He spent time: CS Journal, "Notes for Diary Pages, New York, Saturday, August 31, 1918," UI.

311. "Paula": CS to PS, undated [1918], UI.

312. "New York tries": CS to ACH, September 17 [1918], MIT 141.

312. "I walk on": CS, Journal, "Notes for Diary Pages, New York, Saturday, August 31, 1918," UI.

312. "I can see": CS to PS [September 7, 1918], MIT 133.

312. "I'm saying over": Ibid.

312. "I can't see": CS to PS, Labor Day [September 9, 1918], UI.

313. "I think our": CS to Sam Hughes, September 12, 1918, MIT 134.

Sandburg estimated that "probably thirty daily newspapers, outside of the labor papers using the American Alliance for Labor and Democracy service, and several magazines" printed "The Four Brothers," and hoped that would document his patriotism and support for the war.

313. "shutting down on": Sam Hughes quoted by CS to PS, n.d. [September 1918], UI. Internal evidence suggests September 13.
313. He wrote two: The other poem is "Smoke Rose Gold," *Smoke and Steel, CP* 232.
313. "in the night": CS, "Tangibles," ibid.
313. "backed to the": CS to PS, Labor Day [September 9, 1918], UI.
313. "My own hunch": CS to PS, ibid.
314. "loading on the": CS to PS, n.d. [September 1918], UI.
314. Paula attended to: On September 13, CS wrote to the town clerk of Maywood, Illinois, to clarify his legal name. He had enlisted in the Spanish-American War as Charles August Sandburg, but wanted to officially resume use of his christened name Carl August Sandburg. "The middle name has been dropped for my convenience," Sandburg wrote (UI), "and I suppose it will be a convenience all round if the designation 'Carl Sandburg' is employed." Paula secured a statement September 23, 1918, from Local Draft Board No. 4, Cook County, Illinois, authorizing Carl August Sandburg to leave the United States and certifying that he was not likely to be called for military service (UI).
314. "Have eaten at": CS to PS, September 24 [1918], MIT 140.
314. "Just love and": PS to CS, n.d., UI.
314. "I am taking": CS to PS, Saturday, n.d., UI.
314. "The day John": CS to PS, Sunday [September 1918], MIT 133.
315. "These are great": CS to ACH, June 28 [1917 or 1918?], UT.
315. "probably take longer": CS to PS, Wednesday [October 1918], UI.
315. "Had an hour": CS to PS, October 17 [1918], MIT 143.
315. "Fog on fog": CS, "North Atlantic," *Smoke and Steel, CP* 233.
315. "There was a thrill": CS to PS, November 1 [1918], MIT 144.
315. He knew enough Swedish: CS to PS, October 28 [1918], UI.
315. "five or six": Ibid.
315. "I look forward": CS to PS, November 1 [1918], MIT 144.
316. "Just a hasty": Edward Steichen to John Peter and Mary Steichen and Paula Sandburg, November 5 [1918], UI.
316. "SANDBURG'S THERE": NEA File, October 15, 1918, NEA, UI.
316. "I saw roses": CS, unpublished poem, UI.
317. "the Bolshevik conqueror": Background on Borodin is drawn from Dan N. Jacobs, *Borodin: Stalin's Man in China* (Cambridge: Harvard University Press, 1981).
317. According to some: There are three significant reconstructions of this episode: Karl Detzer (1941), 110–17; Theodore Draper, *The Roots of American Communism* (New York: Viking Press, 1957) 236–38; and HS, GGR (1978), 240–65. Detzer interviewed Sandburg in 1940–41, and Sandburg reviewed Detzer's manuscript before publication. Draper interviewed Sandburg in 1956 and based his account on that April 23, 1956, interview, Sandburg's February 25, 1956, letter, and his informal memorandum (see copy, UI). An investigation of letters to and from Sandburg in 1918–1919 and of extensive NEA files, coupled with the details provided in Jacobs's study of Borodin's activities in 1918, reveals that Sandburg's 1956 recollections deviate in some ways from the 1918 documents and his earlier account.
318. "circulated among all": CS, Detzer 112.
318. "stories regarding the": Ibid., 115.

318. "a report of Dr. Robert Tigerstedt": CS, NEA Notebooks, UC.
318. "We understood each": CS, Detzer, 113
318. "all kinds of": CS, Stockholm Memorandum, UI.
319. "Most of Europe": CS, NEA dateline December 19, 1918, NEA.
320. "husky little new": PS to Harriet Monroe, November 29 [1918], UC.
320. "But it *is*": PS to CS, n.d., MS/UI.
320. "a real, informative": Sam Hughes to Frederick M. Kerby, December 3, 1918, NEA.
321. "even if the": CS to Major Birger Osland, Military Attaché, American Legation, Christiania, Norway, December 11, 1918, UI.
321. "We are at": Quoted by CS, ibid.
321. "a literal fact": CS, ibid.
321. "mass of Russ": CS to PS, n.d. [December 1918], MIT 145.
321. "It would have": CS to Sam Hughes, December 27, 1918, UI.
322. "jottings on interviews": Ibid. This letter describes in detail "every piece of written or printed material" Sandburg transported home in December 1918.
322. "two drafts for": CS, ibid.
322. "U.S. Minister Schmedeman": CS, ibid.
322. "You should be": PS to CS, December 1918, UI.
323. "every piece of written" CS to Sam Hughes, December 27, 1918, UI/NEA.
323. "I was grilled": CS, Stockholm Memorandum, UI. This document also gives the detail of the shaving cream.
323. "I told them": CS to Sam Hughes, December 27, 1918, UI/NEA.
323. "unconsciously being made": Ibid.
323. "carrying funds from": CS to Sam Hughes, January 17, 1919, MIT 147.
323. "communication in a": Ibid.
323. "Isn't it fine": Sam Hughes to Secretary of War Newton Baker, January 1919, CS FBI File, quoted in Natalie Robins, "The Defiling of American Writers," *The Nation*, October 10, 1987, 367. This letter was not released to me by the FBI.
323. "The news too": CS to PS, December 28 [1918], UI.
324. "If it had": Sam Hughes to Frederick M. Kerby, December 30, 1918, NEA. Hughes telegraphed Secretary of the Navy Josephus Daniels January 8, 1919, to protest Sandburg's treatment by the censors and to request return of the confiscated material (UI).
324. "I know that": Sam Hughes to CS, December 31, 1918, UI.
324. "American and British": CS to PS, n.d. [December 1918], MIT 145.
324. "I want to": CS to PS, cablegram, January 1, 1919, UI.
324. "beat on all": CS to PS, n.d. [December 1918], UI.
324. "I have a": Ibid.
324. "I have wished": PS to CS, n.d. [January 1919], UI.
324. "Buddy if you": PS to CS, January 5 [1919], UI.
325. "Never can I": CS to PS, January 17 [1919], UI.
325. "She reaches everywhere": PS to CS, n.d. [1918], UI.
325. "not much the": PS to CS, n.d. [1919], UI.
326. "ten days in": CS to Sam Hughes, January 17, 1919, MIT 147.
326. "glorious homey time": CS to PS, n.d. [January 1919], UI.
326. "two straight nights": CS to PS, January 17 [1919], UI.
326. "one who holds": CS to Sam Hughes, January 17, 1919, MIT 147.

326. "the Military Intelligence": CS, January 28, 1919, MIT 149.
327. but Sandburg did recall: CS, Draper, 236–38.

   I have obtained Sandburg's FBI file, under the Freedom of Information Act, but it does not shed light on this episode. My search of government archives, including the War Department files and the files of the United States Attorney for the Southern District of New York, has not revealed the final disposition of the bank drafts or the confiscated material.

327. "weird, incalculable letters": Detzer, 115.
327. "The czarina letter": CS to PS, n.d. [February 1919], MIT 150.
327. "Of course if": PS to CS, n.d. [1919], UI.
327. "something about Chicago": CS to PS, n.d. [1919], UI.
328. "I haven't had": CS to PS, February 25 [1919], MIT 151.
328. "Your banjo is": PS to CS, n.d. [1919], UI.
328. "Hotels lately tur-a-bul": CS to PS, n.d. [1919], UI.
328. "Every day action": CS to PS, January 30 [1919], MIT 150.
329. "The Liars is": CS to PS, n.d. [1919], UI.
329. " 'Liars'—terrible, yes": PS to CS, n.d. [1919], UI.
329. "A liar lies": CS, "The Liars (March 1919)," *Smoke and Steel*, CP 192.
330. "Wandering oversea singer": CS, "Prayer After World War," *Smoke and Steel*, CP 194.

Chapter 15: Smoke and Steel (1919–1920)

331. "In the blood": CS, "Smoke and Steel," *Smoke and Steel*, CP 151.
331. "I could write": CS to ACH, June 26, 1919, UT.
331. "Carl, only one": Leon Starmont note on CS letter to Sam Hughes, April 14, 1919, UI.
331. "80 per cent of": CS to Sam Hughes, April 17 [1919], MIT 158.
331. "hitching well together": Sam Hughes to CS, May 19, 1919, UI.
331. "We like you": Leon Starmont to CS [May, 1919], quoted in HS, GGR 268–69.
332. "the organized labor": CS to Henry Justin Smith, May 31, 1919, MIT 163.
332. "But what is": CS to Joseph Warren Beach, November 22 [1919], MIT 172.
332. "T.R. of poetry": CS to Amy Lowell, February 15, 1919, HU.
332. "You are one": Amy Lowell to CS, May 9, 1919, UI.
333. "The California thing": CS to Vachel Lindsay, May 21, 1919, MIT 163.
333. "the heartening word": Vachel Lindsay to CS, May 21, 1919, CHS/UI.
333. "The music of": CS to Louis Untermeyer, April 19 [1919], MIT 153.
333. Somehow Sandburg obtained: See George Hendrick and A. Lynn Altenbernd, "Writing about Sandburg and His Literary Friends," *Carl Sandburg, 1878–1978: A Century of America, Non Solus*, no. 5, 1978, 8–13.
333. "How much piffle": Wallace Stevens to CS, October 17 [1919], UI.
333. "as good as": CS to Louis Untermeyer, April 19 [1919], MIT 153.
334. "chant a Chippewa": Harriet Monroe, *A Poet's Life*, 393.
334. "What I am": CS to Lew Sarett, June 6 [1919], MIT 165.
334. "If I am": AH to CS, May 20, 1919, UI.
334. Since the Pulitzer Prizes: For background, see John Hohenberg, *The Pulitzer Prizes* (New York: Colgate University Press, 1974).

334. "fought, bled and very": Sara Teasdale to Harriet Monroe, quoted in HS, GGR 268.
335. "*Poetry* may be": Harriet Monroe, *Poetry*, July 1919.
335. "Sandburg is better": Robert Frost to AH, quoted by AH to CS, October 29, 1918, UI.
335. "Mr. Sandburg is": William Stanley Braithwaite, *Boston Transcript*, January 11, 1919, 9.
335. "that general sense": O. W. Firkins, *The Nation*, January 4, 1919.
335. "racial soberness of": *New York Times*, January 12, 1919.
335. "Art is long!": *Outlook*, December 18, 1918.
335. "He's our Chicago": Ben Hecht, Review of *Cornhuskers*, *Chicago Daily News* [1918], quoted from typescript, ES/UI.
336. "Am back with": CS to ACH, June 26, 1919, UT.
336. "Very physical hysteria": CS to John Lomax, January 9, 1920, MIT 175.
    Chicago background is based on CS, CRR; William Loren Katz, editor, *The Negro in Chicago: A Study of Race Relations and a Race Riot in 1919* (New York: Arno Press & *The New York Times*, 1970); William M. Tuttle, Jr., *Race Riot: Chicago in the Red Summer of 1919* (New York: Atheneum, 1970).
336. "pretty tough hole": Katz, 12.
337. "When Private Little": CS, CRR xiv.
337. "Under pressure of": CS, CRR 5.
337. "returning south of": CS, ibid.
337. "We made the": CS, CRR 9.
337. "a great deal of": CS, CRR 25.
337. "It is the": CS, CRR 26.
338. "At the time": CS, CRR 40–41.
338. "reprehensible, a menace": CS, CRR 47.
338. "You notice there": CS, CRR 56.
338. "8,000,000 copies a": CS, CRR 77–78.
338. "radical" platform: CS, CRR 67.
339. "the proximity of": CS, CRR 69.
339. "death, desertion, divorce": CS, CRR 71.
339. "New things is": CS, CRR 71–72.
339. "He wants to meet" AH to CS, July 21, 1918, UI.
339. "No city or": Joel Spingarn to CS, CRR 80.
340. "constructive recommendations": CS, CRR 6.
340. "as usual": CS, ibid.
340. "attacks and retreats": Katz, 4.
341. "because fear of": "Epitome of Facts in Riot Deaths," *Report of the Chicago Commission on Race Relations*, 1921, 655–67.
341. "On the one": CS, CRR 4.
342. "It's working people": CS, July 29, 1919, UI.
342. "I am a": CS, "Hoodlums," July 29, 1919. I have quoted the original typescript of the poem, which includes the epigraph. "Hoodlums" as published in *Smoke and Steel*, CP 201, dropped the pronoun "we" after "cadavers" and eliminated the expletive "the Son of a Bitch." I have used the line breaks of the early typescript here rather than the arrangement in CP.

342. "They ought to": AH to CS, August 11, 1919, UI.

342. "a booby prize": CS to Amy Lowell, April 2, 1916, MIT 111.

343. Sandburg was not: In his introduction, in a passage Sandburg probably found condescending and, as he said, uninformed, Lippmann called for "race parallelism," saying that since "permanent degradation is unthinkable, and amalgamation undesirable for both blacks and whites, the ideal would seem to lie in what might be called race parallelism." Sandburg had praised some of Lippmann's reporting, telling him that "When you write of actual contacts —when you do real reporting—I get you." CS to Walter Lippmann regarding his *New Republic* coverage of the 1916 Republican Convention is quoted by HS, GGR 273.

343. "get this stuff": CS to Louis Untermeyer, September 26, 1919, UD.

343. "serious and intelligent": Katz, 549; *Booklist*, February 1920, 154.

343. "How much do": Ralph McGill, Preface, CRR, 1969 edition, ix-xvii.

343. "it's come over": CS to Louis Untermeyer, n.d. [ca. March 1920], MIT 183.

344. "Did I see": CS, "Crimson Changes People," *Smoke and Steel*, CP 168.

344. "I saw Man": CS, "Man, the Man-Hunter," *Smoke and Steel*, CP 171. See "Early Lynching" (CS, GMA, CP 395), another poem composed during this period. Even Louis Untermeyer found the language in this poem too harsh, telling CS it would antagonize the Society for Suppression of Vice and other groups. See CS to Louis Untermeyer [ca. March 30, 1920], MIT 183.

344. "We suddenly picked": CS to ACH, September 26, 1919, UT.

345. "many orphans and": CS to Amy Lowell, September 26 [1919], MIT 168.

345. "We mustn't let": AH to CS, August 11, 1919, UI.

345. "I know he": Sara Teasdale to Harriet Monroe, September 22, 1919, UC.

345. "a smoke and": CS to Joseph Warren Beach, November 22 [1919], MIT 172.

345. "men and women": Waldo Frank to CS [ca. October 1919], UI.

345. The country was: See PEN unpublished ms, UI, for discussion of how the Red Scare affected Sandburg's former socialist colleagues, especially Victor Berger, elected to Congress by the Fifth District of Wisconsin, denied his seat by a vote of 331 to 1 by Congress, reelected by the people of Wisconsin's Fifth District, again denied his seat, and eventually returned to Congress after the Supreme Court reversed his conviction of violating the Espionage Act. See *Congressional Record, House of Representatives*, Monday, November 10, 1919, 8218–8262. After Eugene Debs's 1918 conviction of violations of the Espionage Act, Sandburg wrote to William Marion Reedy, "Some day it will get into the histories that the White Terror of this period was a hundred times more cruel than the Red Terror." (CS to William Marion Reedy, March 14 [1919], UI.)

346. He apparently never: PEN interview with MS.

346. "If I have": CS to Romain Rolland [ca. October 1919], MIT 169.

347. "Many things I": CS, "Aprons of Silence," *Smoke and Steel*, CP 176.

347. "grand show!": Emanuel Carnevali, *Poetry*, February 1920.

348. "Indian chants and": Ibid. See PEN unpublished ms, UI, for extended treatment of CS–Carnevali correspondence, including the story of Carnevali's illness. As William Carlos Williams suspected, Carvenali had syphilis. He revealed that in letters to Sandburg (UI).

348. "Frankie and Albert": CS pointed out in AS (75) that "Frankie and Albert" preceded "Frankie and Johnny." "Frankie and Albert" was sung as early as 1888.
348. "that dingy little": Siegfried Sassoon, Siegfried's Journey (London: Faber & Faber, 1945), 294–96.
348. "Carl Sandburg's features": Burton Rascoe, Before I Forget (New York: Doubleday, Doran, 1937), 434–38.
349. "Is this poetry": Unidentifiable clipping source, CS Packet of lecture clippings and reviews, UI.
349. "a new deep": CS to Negley D. Cochran, March 30 [1920], MIT 181.
349. "Amalgamated Clothing Workers": CS to Ray Stannard Baker, January 24, 1920, MIT 177.
350. "I've been trying": CS to Louis Untermeyer, January 3, 1920, UD.
350. "going along slow": CS, ibid.
350. "a cornfed young": CS to Louis Untermeyer, February 5, 1920, UD.
350. "sleeping nearly all": CS to Clyde Tull [February 24, 1920], MIT 179; CS to Louis Untermeyer, February 24 [1920], UD.
350. "cull over and": CS to Louis Untermeyer, March 5 [1920], UD.
350. "I'm sure you'll": CS to Louis Untermeyer, ibid. Sandburg told Untermeyer that his poem "Broken-face Gargoyles" would appear in the Dial and was "one of the best I've ever done and is Young America to the World. . . . I'll leave it to you whether The Liars in the May Liberator last year should go in; too like propaganda, I guess; a Danish poet has done it into Norwegian, Swedish and German." (CS to Louis Untermeyer, February 5 [1920], UD.)
350. "broad vision, profound": Jean Catel, Mercure de France, March 1920.
351. "where to go": CS to Louis Untermeyer, January 3, 1920, UD.
351. "Say, I hear": AH to CS, January 6, 1920, UI.
351. "I wrote to": CS to AH, February 6, 1920, UI.
351. "You're as good": AH to CS, March 4, 1920, UI.
351. "If Harcourt hadn't": CS to Louis Untermeyer, May 29 [1920], UD.
352. "I am lugging": CS to Lew Sarett, April 12 [1920], MIT 184.
352. Modern Library edition: H. B. Liveright to CS, February 2 and 11, 1920.
352. In his preface: In his introduction, Sandburg called Leaves of Grass "the most decisively individual, the most sublimely personal creation in American literary art . . . the most highly praised and the most deeply damned book that ever came from an American printing press as the work of an American writer . . . the most intensely personal book in American literature . . . America's most classic advertisement of itself as having purpose, destiny, banners and bea-confires. . . ." He called Whitman "the commanding instance in shirtsleeve literature . . . the only established epic poet of America. . . ." CS, Introduction, Walt Whitman, Poems (New York: Boni & Liveright, the Modern Library of the World's Best Books, 1921), III–XI.
352. "Sandburg has the": Burton Rascoe, Before I Forget, 434–38.
352. "Today I feel": CS to ACH, May 10 [1920], MIT 186.
352. "It's a book": Ibid.
352. "Don't be such": Sinclair Lewis to AH, quoted in Harcourt's obituary, June 26, 1954.
353. "This office has": Ellen Eayrs, May 12 [1920], UI.

353. "spent most of": AH to CS, May 12, 1920, UI.
353. "Carl, you came": Louis Untermeyer to CS, n.d. [1920], UD.
353. "narrower width of": CS to Donald Brace, July 10, 1920, HB.
354. Steichen was beset: For accounts of Steichen's marital problems, see HS, GGR 276–78; *New York Times*, November 9, 1920, 17, and December 8, 1920, 22.
354. "What can we": CS to Edward Steichen, July 8, no year indicated [ca. 1919 or 1920], MIT 166.
354. "finders in the dark": CS, "Smoke and Steel," *Smoke and Steel, CP* 151.
355. "Sleep is a": CS, "Work Gangs," *Smoke and Steel, CP* 156.
355. "the red death": CS, "Crimson Changes People," *SS, CP* 168.
355. "Drum on your": CS, "Jazz Fantasia," *SS, CP* 179.
356. "The north has": CS, "Helga," *SS, CP* 209.
356. "Your hands are": CS, "Paula," *SS, CP* 216.
356. "I made a": CS, "North Atlantic," *SS, CP* 233.
356. "In the deep": CS, "North Atlantic," *SS, CP* 233.
356. "Since you have": CS, "Put Off the Wedding Five Times and Nobody Comes to It", *SS, CP* 249.
357. "Is the night": CS, "Night's Nothings Again," *SS, CP* 260.
357. "PLAY it across": CS, "Cahoots," *SS, CP* 169.
357. "I go hungry": CS, "Places," *SS, CP* 190.
357. "The road I": CS, "Horse Fiddle," *SS, CP* 223.
358. "And this will": CS, "And This Will Be All?," *SS, CP* 200.
358. "Loosen your hands": CS, "Stars, Songs, Faces," *SS, CP* 207.
358. "DEATH comes once": CS, "Finish, *SS, CP* 267.
358. "I will read": CS, "Fire Pages," *SS, CP* 266.
358. "The woman named": CS, "Four Preludes on Playthings of the Wind," *SS, CP* 183.
358. "I speak of": CS, "Prairie," *Cornhuskers, CP* 79.
358. "My grandmother, Yesterday": CS, "Four Preludes on Playthings of the Wind," *SS, CP* 183.
360. "There will be": CS to ACH, September 12 [1920], MIT 191.
360. "the best enemy": William Carlos Williams, *Kora in Hell: Improvisations* (Boston: The Four Seas Co., 1920).
360. "you punk out": Ezra Pound to William Carlos Williams, September 11 [1920], Paige, 157.
360. "often flirted with": Maxwell Bodenheim to CS, December 12, 1920, UI.
360. "You know how": Sara Teasdale to CS, October 22, 1920, UI.
360. "deep quiet thrill": CS to William Allen White, October 20, 1920, MIT 193.
360. "Of all today's": William Allen White to CS, October 9, 1920, UI.
361. "The book of": Clara Sandburg to CS and PS, n.d., 1920, UI.
361. "an epic of": Louis Untermeyer, *The Bookman*, January 1921.
361. "variance of viewpoint": CS to Amy Lowell, November 1, 1920, MIT 194. CS also said that future critics might write that "I put in too many realities I was familiar with and you not enough."
361. "Reading these poems": Amy Lowell, *New York Times*, October 24, 1920.
361. "Mr. Sandburg has": William Stanley Braithwaite, *Boston Transcript*, October 16, 1920.
361. "Psychiatric Curiosity": Arthur Wilson, *Dial*, January 21, 1921.

361. "sententious garrulity which": Arthur Wilson, ibid.
361. "Who the hell": Louis Untermeyer to CS, January 5, 1921, UI.
361. "rather obviously repeated": Mark Van Doren, *Nation*, December 1, 1921.
362. "many sided self-hood": Alfred Kreymborg, *Our Singing Strength: An Outline of American Poetry, 1620–1930* (New York: Coward-McCann, 1929), 391–92.
362. "fixed, frozen, immutable": CS, "Notes for a Preface," CP xxviii.
362. "Beat, old heart": CS, "Beat, Old Heart," *Slabs of the Sunburnt West*, CP 291.

Chapter 16: To a Far Country of Make-Believe (1920–1921)

363. "I travelled in": CS to A. J. Armstrong, October 13, 1921, MIT 200.
363. "One satisfaction—the": CS to ACH, September 12 [1920], MIT 191.
364. "almost unbelievably ill-informed": William Allen White, *Autobiography of William Allen White* (New York: Macmillan Co., 1946), 105.
364. "required a determined": PS, Unpublished Diary, MS, 2.
365. "The kids are a": CS to ACH, January 20, 1920, MIT 177.
365. "cinema expert, the": CS to ACH, September 12 [1920], MIT 191.
365. "picture words": CS as quoted in Detzer, 141.
366. his amiable boss Henry Justin Smith: Background on CS at the *Chicago Daily News* grows from CS, Unpublished ms, UI; CSOH-PEN interviews with Fanny Butcher, Al Dreier, Donald Russell, Betty Peterman Gole, MS and HS; Charles H. Dennis, *Victor Lawson: His Time and His Work* (New York: Greenwood Press, 1935); Harry Hansen, *Carl Sandburg; the Man and His Poetry*, Little Blue Book #814 (Girard, Kansas: Haldeman-Julius Co., 1925); Ben Hecht, *Erik Dorn* (Chicago: University of Chicago Press, 1963), a novel in which CS appears as a Swedish poet; Lloyd Lewis, *It Takes All Kinds* (New York: Harcourt Brace, 1947); Lloyd Lewis and Henry Justin Smith, *Chicago, The History of Its Reputation* (New York: Harcourt, Brace, 1929); Frank Luther Mott and Ralph D. Casey, editors, *Interpretations of Journalism* (New York: F. S. Crofts & Co., 1937); Henry Justin Smith, *Deadlines: Being the Quaint, the Amusing, the Tragic Memoirs of a Newsroom* (New York: Harcourt, Brace, 1922). See also PEN's unpublished ms and PEN, "Carl Sandburg's *Chicago Daily News* as a Literary Place," UI.
367. "the wayward and joyous": CS to Charles Finger, August 26, 1920, MIT 189.
367. "To tell the": Charles Finger to CS, October 22, 1920, UI.
367. similar letter of disclaimer: See CS, "To the Editors of Chicago Newspapers," n.d., MIT 137. See also PEN, unpublished manuscript and PEN, "The Two Chicago Sandb . . rgs," UI. As we will later see, Sandburg's FBI file contains material erroneously linking Carl Sandburg and Dr. Karl Sandberg.
367. "Hand it to": CS to Louis Untermeyer, October 31, 1920, UD.
368. "You and Mrs. Sandburg": Amy Lowell to CS, September 2, 1920, UI.
368. "a country I knew": Amy Lowell, "To Carl Sandburg," manuscript of poem enclosed with September 2, 1920, letter, UI.
368. "Our letters crossed": CS to Amy Lowell, September 8, 1920, HU.
368. "a lost town": CS, "Three Notations on the Visit of a Massachusetts Woman to the House of Neighbors in Illinois (for Amy Lowell)," unpublished, HU, UI.
369. "a good neighbor": CS to Amy Lowell, September 2, 1920, MIT 190. "We are glad you came and that among our few traditions we have the added one for

the south porch that you supped with us there," he wrote, regretting that "the rainfall began and broke in so you couldn't get the last verse of This Mornin, This Evening."

369. "in the next": CS to Amy Lowell, September 8, 1920, HU.

369. "too many realities": CS, ibid.

369. "dissimilar from anything": Harry Hansen, *Midwest Portraits* (New York: Harcourt Brace, 1923), 46.

370. "spotted with round": CS Review, *Chicago Daily News* (henceforward CDN), October 1, 1920. For reprints of many CS movie reviews, see Dale and Doug Fetherling, editors, *Carl Sandburg at the Movies: A Poet in the Silent Era 1920–1927* (Metuchen, N.J.: Scarecrow Press, 1985).

370. "The riding and": CS Review, CDN, November 4, 1920.

370. "thrilling entertainment": CS Review, CDN, December 14, 1920.

370. His 1920 income-tax: CS and PS 1920 Tax Return, CSH Document, UI.

370. "That afternoon hour": CS to Alfred Stieglitz, December 27, 1920, MIT 195.

371. "You and I": Alfred Stieglitz to CS, January 3, 1921, UI.

371. "into good hands": Alfred Stieglitz to CS, January 12, 1921, UI.

371. The private battles: *New York Times*, November 9, 1920, 17; December 8, 1920, 22; PEN interview with MS.

372. "The wholesale murdering": Edward Steichen, *A Life in Photography*, following Plate 62. See here Steichen's account of how he found in his Voulangis studio one morning "a very free copy of a flower painting" he had been working on. The painting was done by his gardener, a "Brittany peasant," and Steichen thought it "was better than I had been trying to do." This discovery "crystallized" his decision to become a photographer. Fortunately, some of Steichen's paintings survived.

372. "reach into the": Steichen, ibid.

373. For several weeks: This account is based on Paula Sandburg's Unpublished Diary, MS. Paula Sandburg's extraordinary diaries and journals document Margaret's illness through the years. She recorded every pertinent detail—heredity, history of illnesses and accidents, symptoms, observations, her own "Diary of Case." Margaret Sandburg's generous loan of these records provided insights unavailable anywhere else. Her unselfish sharing of such private matters facilitated a fundamental illumination of her father's public life during these years.

373. "The cramped position": PS, ibid.

373. "9: a.m.": PS, ibid.

374. "Margaret is fine": PS to CS, March 4, 1921, UI.

374. "wearily about the": PS, ibid.

374. "drammer, solid melodrammer": CS Review, CDN, October 11, 1920.

374. "the value of": CS, Review, CDN, October 16, 1920.

375. "In these days": D. W. Griffith, quoted in CS Review, CDN, December 14, 1920.

375. "an art rostrum": CS Review, CDN January 18 and 19, 1921.

375. "Before starting for": CS Review, CDN April 23, 1921.

375. It is drawn: See CS Review, CDN, April 16, 1921.

376. "He sets the": CS, "Without the Cane and the Derby (For C.C.)," *Slabs of the Sunburnt West*, CP 302. ". . . A candle/in his left hand throws a slant of light on the dark face," CS wrote in the poem. In the CDN, he wrote, "Here was Charlie in a gray shirt, candle in his right hand, lighting his face and throwing

shadows about the room." "A woman's head of hair shows, a woman's/white face," he wrote in the poem. In the CDN, he wrote, "A woman's head of hair, then a woman's face, appeared." In the CDN counterpart of lines quoted from the poem in the text, CS wrote, "The man in the gray shirt set down the candle, leaped toward the white sheet, threw back the white sheet, put his fingers at the throat and executed three slow, fierce motions of strangling" and "He paused at the door, listening./He stepped out. The door closed. All was dark."

376. "vastly different audiences": CS to Mrs. Stevenson, January 15, 1921, UI.

376. "resonant," "vibrant": Sampling of reviews from Fayetteville, Arkansas, *Daily Democrat*, April 5, 1921; Bloomington, Indiana, *Daily Student (Indiana University)*, March 3, 1921, and other clippings, CSH, UI.

377. "This whole thing": CS to Isadora Bennett Reed, January 26, 1921, MIT 196.

377. "smash that guitar": Malcolm Cowley, "Smash that Guitar," *Brentano's Book Chat*, December 1926. See Cowley to CS, October 6, 1926, UI.

377. "glorious": CS to A. J. Armstrong, April 16, 1921, UI.

377. "entirely lost on": CS to Louis Untermeyer, April 25, 1921, UD.

377. "by the influence": Unsigned student review, "A Poet of the People," Bloomington, Indiana, *Daily Student*, March 3, 1921, 2.

378. She had been well: PS, Unpublished Diary.

378. "mild general convulsion": Ibid.

379. "After a nightly": PEN interview with MS.

379. "When I get 100": CS to ACH, June 29 [1921], UT.

379. "still grinding teeth": PS, Unpublished Diary.

379. Steichen photographed his: This haunting photograph hangs on the landing of the Sandburg home.

380. "The missus has": CS to Louis Untermeyer, August 18, 1921, UD.

380. "the summer we": CS, ibid.

380. "Convulsion with cry": PS, Unpublished Diary.

380. "put the case": PS, ibid.

381. "the most severe": PS, ibid.

381. "He and I": CS to Ellen Eayrs, October 7 [1922], HB/UI. Dr. Emmett Dunn Angell was the author of books on play such as *Basket Ball for Men* [sic] and *Real Games for Real Kids* (Chicago: A. C. McClury & Co., 1923).

382. "It goes slow": CS to Witter Bynner, September 9, 1921, MIT 199.

382. "each a child": CS to Clyde Tull, November 15, 1921, MIT 201.

382. "With me, it": CS to Witter Bynner, December 7, 1921, MIT 204.

382. "an absolute fast": PS, Unpublished Diary.

383. "I was not": PEN interview with MS.

383. "This is only": CS to MS, n.d. [1921], UI.

383. "the railroad tracks": CS, "How They Broke Away to Go to the Rootabaga Country," RS 16.

383. "You asked me": CS to MS, n.d. [December 1921], MIT 205.

383. "Pooch learns": CS to PS, n.d. [December 1921], MIT 215. Internal evidence suggests this dating.

383. "innumerable times": May Massee to Burton Rascoe, December 15, 1921, UI.

384. "I don't care": MS to CS, n.d. [December 1921], UI.

384. Margaret and Helga: PEN interview with MS. MS thought this episode took place in 1921 or 1922, more likely 1922.

384. "and laughed and": PEN interview with MS; MS notes to PEN.
384. "terrible and forbidden": CS to Witter Bynner, December 30, 1921, UI.
384. "Finishing two books": CS to ACH, December 30, 1921, UT.
385. "The going is": CS to Witter Bynner, December 30, 1921, UI.

Chapter 17: Refuge in Rootabaga Country (1922)

386. "Sometime I shall do": CS to Lilla Perry, February 22, 1922, MIT 207.
386. "trading poems and": Vachel Lindsay, *A Handy Guide for Beggars, Especially Those of the Poetic Fraternity* (New York: Macmillan Co., 1916); and Lindsay, *Rhymes to Be Traded for Bread* (Springfield, Ill.: Privately printed, 1912).
386. "poets and friends": Dorothy Dudley, "Notes from the Poetry Society of America Annual Dinner," *Poetry*, April 1922, 53–56.
387. "a mystic sensuous": CS, quoted by Dudley, ibid.
387. "I'd rather climb": CS to Witter Bynner, December 30, 1921, UT.
387. "what seemed beyond": Dudley, op. cit. See Damon, 591, for Amy Lowell's account of the evening.
387. "Buddy": CS to PS, February [7], 1922, MIT 206.
387. "Raw weather and": CS to PS, n.d. [February 14, 1922], MIT 206.
388. "milk—milk": PS to CS, February 7 [1922], UI.
388. "You don't know": MS quoted by PS to CS, March 13, 1922, UI.
388. "In the making of books": CS Journal Note, ca. January 9, 1922, UI.
388. " 'Slabs of the Sunburnt' ": AH to CS, January 11, 1922, UI.
389. "I wanted something": CS to Karl Detzer, Detzer, 155.
389. "seemed to grow": Harry Hansen, *Midwest Portraits, A Book of Memories and Friendships* (New York: Harcourt, Brace, 1923), 71.
389. "baggy or misshapen": Helga Sandburg provided this definition.
389. "When I look": PS, Introduction, *The Sandburg Treasury* (Harcourt Brace Jovanovich, 1970), 7.
389. "Carl thought that": PS, ibid.
390. "forty ways farther": CS, "How They Broke Away to Go to the Rootabaga Country," *RS*.
391. "across prairies": CS, "The Two Skyscrapers Who Decided to Have a Child," *RS*.
391. "I am Blind": CS, "The Potato Face Blind Man Who Lost the Diamond Rabbit on His Gold Accordion," *RS*.
391. "I have the": CS to Helen Keller, October 10, 1929, MIT 269.
391. "flew whonging away": CS, "The Dollar Watch and the Five Jack Rabbits," *RS*.
392. "Feet are as good": CS, "How Six Pigeons Came Back to Hatrack the Horse After Many Accidents and Six Telegrams," *RP*. CS recorded this story and others.
393. "Some of the Rootabaga": CS to Anne Carroll Moore, November 20, 1922, MIT 220.
393. "They fill a": Frank Lloyd Wright to CS, quoted in *SR* 91.
393. "carried away by": Alfred Stieglitz to CS, October 31, 1922, UI.
393. "At breakfast this": Frank J. Coyle (?), April 12, 1924, UI.
394. "One indignant child": *The Nation*, December 6, 1922. See also CS to Mrs. Van Doren, December 11, 1922, UI carbon.
394. "developed a new": *New York Times*, November 19, 1922.

394. "I tell them": CS, "People with Proud Chins," *Smoke and Steel,* CP 210.

394. "The book stacks": CS to AH, May 10, 1922, HB, UI.

394. "most human and": CS to AH, January 17, 1922, HB, UI.

395. "the place of": CS, "The Windy City," *Slabs of the Sunburnt West,* CP 271.

396. "go mile on": CS, ibid.

396. "where everything is": CS, "How They Broke Away to Go to the Rootabaga Country," RS.

396. "where the white horses": CS, "The White Horse Girl and the Blue Wind Boy," RS.

396. "And if a boy": CS, "The Windy City," SSW, CP 271.

397. "That is all": CS, "Black Horizons," SSW, CP 288.

397. "There is no": CS to Ellery Sedgwick, June 30, 1922, MIT 208.

397. There is little: At first I found *Slabs of the Sunburnt West* fragmented and oblique. Then, as I began to study Sandburg's work as a movie critic, I watched as many as possible of the films he reviewed, in the order he saw and reviewed them. Afterward, when I read SSW, it seemed to me that the book was alive with images and words Sandburg encountered in the movies, including short takes, fadeouts and special effects.

398. "Into the blanket": CS, "Slabs of the Sunburnt West," SSW, CP 307.

399. "Skeleton men and": CS, "And So Today," SSW, CP 283.

400. "Mannikins, we command": CS, "Caligari," SSW, CP 298.

400. "mellower Sandburg": *Bookman,* July 1922.

400. "already in danger": *New York Times,* June 4, 1922.

400. "Penetrating, courageous, heartening": Clement Wood, *Nation,* July 26, 1922.

400. "strikingly alive": William Rose Benét, *Literary Review,* July 22, 1922.

400. Arthur Guiterman deplored: Arthur Guiterman, *Independent,* August 5, 1922.

400. "All the best and": William Stanley Braithwaite, *Boston Transcript,* July 29, 1922.

401. "ragged ease": Malcolm Cowley, *Dial,* November 1922.

401. "Dearest Sweetest and": Clara Sandburg to CS and PS, n.d., UI.

401. "Amy Lowell says": Charlotte Markley to CS, May 1, 1921, CSH.

401. "Everything is propaganda": CS to Charlotte Markley, May 4, 1921, CSH, UI.

402. "It is the law": CS, "At the Gates of Tombs," SSW, CP 293.

402. "In the matter": CS to Charlotte Markley.

403. "He's a big": CS to Eugene V. Debs, November 19, 1922, MIT 219. "And some day I hope to get the strong truth about those hands of yours into a poem," CS told Debs in this letter. See PEN Unpublished ms, UI, for more background on the Sandburg-Debs friendship. See also David Karsner, *Debs, His Authorized Life and Letters* (New York: Boni & Liveright, 1919); Salvatore; Schorer; Ray Ginger, *The Bending Cross: A Biography of Eugene Debs* (New Brunswick, N.J.: Rutgers University Press, 1949); HS, GGR; Ralph Chaplin, *Wobbly: The Rough and Tumble Story of an American Radical* (Chicago: University of Chicago, 1948).

403. "Not weeks, nor": CS, "Place Race Problem with Biggest in U.S.," *Chicago Daily News,* September 26, 1922. See also CS, September 5, 1922, MIT 214.

403. "brilliantly conceived travelogue": CS Review, CDN, September 9, 1922.

403. "Dear Daddy": MS to CS, September 19, 1922, UI.

404. "I am going to shape": CS to PS, n.d. [September 28, 1922], MIT 216.

404. "I am going to get": CS to PS, n.d. [September 1922], MIT 217.
404. "Dear Paus'l": Edward Steichen to PS, no date [fall 1922], UI.
404. "Out of the": CS to PS, n.d. [ca. fall 1922], MIT 202. Internal evidence (the reference to the "free show at the Medill School of Journalism") suggests that this letter was written in October 1922 rather than in November 1921.
404. "one of the champion": CS to MS, n.d. [September 22, 1922], MIT 214.
404. "without a million interruptions": PS to CS, n.d. [1922], UI.
404. "renewing a mortgage": CS to Ellen Eayrs, October 7 [1922], HB/UI.
405. "achieved nothing more": PS to CS, October 1, 1922, UI.
405. When Paula had: PEN interview with MS.
405. "Don't you think": PS to CS, quoted by MS, PEN interviews with MS.
405. "And now a matter": CS to AH, October 23, 1922, MIT 218.
406. "real stuff": Edward Steichen to PS, n.d. [1922], UI. Sandburg did not work with Steichen on his "kid's picture book." In 1930, with his daughter Mary Steichen Martin (later Calderone), he published *The First Picture Book: Everyday Things for Babies* (New York: Harcourt, Brace). The picture book he was working on in 1922 involved imaginary creatures he named "Oochens," "that never were on land or sea, and yet they are as alive as alive can be." (ES to PS, ibid.)
406. "Carl Sandburg, the": "Throng Hears Carl Sandburg in Medill Talk," *Chicago Tribune*, October 12, 1922.
406. "a concert, grand opera": William Allen White, quoted on CS Lecture Advertisement, 1922, UI.
406. "old guard": Amy Lowell, Damon, 635.

Chapter 18: A Certain Portrait 1923–1925

408. "For thirty years": CS, Preface, *ALPY*.
408. "How is the": AH to CS, February 28, 1923.
408. "We are plowing": CS to AH, March 18, 1923, HB, UI.
409. Once Paula and: PEN interview with MS.
There are various accounts of Sandburg's work on the Lincoln biography, in addition to the letters of the period; see HS, GGR; Harry Golden, *Carl Sandburg*; Harry Hansen, *Midwest Portraits* and *Carl Sandburg, the Man and His Poetry*; Alfred Harcourt, "Forty Years of Friendship," *Journal of the Illinois State Historical Society*, 45, Winter, 1952; Allan Nevins, "Sandburg as Historian," ibid. Also see Detzer, 141–42, 166–68. Also see "Sandburg and Lincoln: The Prairie Years," in Robert Johannsen, ed., *The Frontier, The Union and Stephen A. Douglas* (Urbana: University of Illinois Press, 1989), 267–84.
409. "fine understanding": Harry Hansen, *Midwest Portraits*, 89.
409. "interest payments on": CS to AH, February 5, 1923, HB/UI.
410. "the Big Book": CS to AH, May 15, [1923], HB.
410. "I'm hoping you": PS to CS, February 25, 1923, UI. PS told CS also that his sister Mary's husband had died.
410. "Paula girl": CS to PS, n.d., UI.
410. "We miss you": PS to CS, n.d., UI.
410. Margaret went away: PEN interviews with MS.

410. "Dear Spink": CS to MS, n.d., MS. May Massee wrote to CS June 25, 1923, "today comes the good news Margaret is going to camp" (UI).
411. "cast frustrated glances": Adlai Stevenson, "A Friend and Admirer," *Journal of the Illinois State Historical Society*, 45, Winter 1952, 297–99.
411. "You haven't written": CS to AH, September 20, 1923, MIT 221.
411. "I know you": AH to CS, September 22, 1923, UI.
411. "We've had not": AH to CS, October 16, 1923, UI.
411. "Old Abe is": CS to AH, October 20, 1923, HB.
411. "kaleidoscopic and telescopic": CS to AH, ibid.
412. Anne Carroll Moore: See Anne Carroll Moore to CS, July 15, 1923, UI, a long handwritten letter to CS after Moore read the galleys for *RP*. Moore reviewed *RP* for *The Nation*, December 5, 1923.
412. "invented a new": *Literary Review*, November 1923.
412. "No one but": Eugene Debs to CS, November 6, 1923, UI.
412. Sandburg's professor: PGW wrote to CS November 13, 1923, UI.
412. "O'Keeffe is sitting": Alfred Stieglitz to CS, October 10, 1923, UI.
412. "The wife and friends": CS to AH, December 8, 1923, MIT 223.
412. "Certainly all of": Clara Sandburg to PS, February 1, 1924, UI.
413. He earned: Sandburg's income is given as reported on tax returns, DU, UI.
413. "the healthiest, boldest": CS Review, CDN, September 1, 1924; see Fetherling, 103. (When I have quoted from the original text of CS Reviews, either in manuscript or from the CDN, I have so indicated. When I have quoted, as in this instance, from the Fetherling edition of CS Reviews, I have cited the page number in that text, for ease of reference.)
413. "epic of the": CS Review, CDN November 3, 1924; see Fetherling, 93–94.
414. "I make my": CS, "Acknowledgments," Unpublished Poem, UI. One draft of this poem suggests it was written as early as 1915.
414. "for I always": Amy Lowell to CS, February 14, 1924, UI.
414. "Sandburg blew in": Amy Lowell to Louis Untermeyer, March 12, 1924, quoted in Damon, 657.
414. "Ada told me": Amy Lowell to CS, April 3, 1924, UI.
414. "I've been thinking about": AH to CS, July 19, 1924, UI.
414. "working like a dog": CS to Cyrene Corwin, May 20, 1924, ES.
415. "illuminated, mysterious personality," and following quotations: CS, *ALPY*, passim.
416. "If there had been any stubborn grandeur": CS, *ALPY*, II, 197–99.
416. "thinker and spokesman": CS, ibid.
416. "Sprinkled all through": CS, *ALPY*, II, 155.
417. "O Memory! thou": Abraham Lincoln, quoted by CS, *ALPY*, I, 311–12.
417. "Of course, when": Abraham Lincoln, quoted by CS, *ALPY*, II, 201–202.
417. "was hungry to understand," and following quotations: CS, *ALPY*, passim.
418. "In the short and simple": Note Sandburg's use of a line from Thomas Gray's "Elegy Written in a Country Churchyard":

> Let not Ambition mock their useful toil,
> Their homely joys, and destiny obscure;
> Nor Grandeur hear with a disdainful smile
> The short and simple annals of the poor.

418. "pioneers are half gypsy": CS, *ALPY*. In *ATYS*, CS had written of "Pioneer and Old-Timers," "There was no standard pioneer cut to a regular pattern. . . . They were living segments of history, specimens and vestiges, breathing evidences in the building of America." *ATYS* 356–57.

419. "It is toil and toil": CS to Clyde Tull, March 25, 1925, MIT 231.

419. "whose times and": CS to AH, August 3 [1924], MIT 225.

419. "It is a book": CS, ibid.

419. "Personally, I find": Donald Brace to CS, August 8, 1924, UI.

419. "strongly inclined to agree": AH to CS, August 21, 1924.

419. "Oh, hell, the": CS to AH, August 3 [1924], MIT 225.

420. "I have been": CS to AH, September 8, 1924, MIT 226.

420. He met Chicago: CS wrote to AH of his meeting with Barrett in a letter September 8, 1924, MIT 226.

420. "droll" request: Oliver Barrett, quoted by CS, *LCB* 9.

421. sometimes stacking them: CSOH-PEN interview with Roger Barrett, son of Oliver Barrett, November 12, 1981.

421. "Forgive a hardworking": CS to Clyde Tull, September 8, 1924, ES.

421. "It's rather thrilling": AH to CS, September 26, 1924, UI.

421. "I wonder how": CS to Sherwood Anderson, November 1, 1924, ES/UI carbon.

421. "There can't be": Sherwood Anderson to CS, quoted in ES/UI.

421. "That's wisdom": CS to Sherwood Anderson, November 1, 1924, ES/UI carbon.

422. "Great stuff": AH to CS, October 15, 1924, UI.

422. "to stay till": CS to PS, November 16 [1924], MIT 228.

422. "clearer and definitely": CS to AH, November 3, 1924, HB.

422. "splendid—great stuff": AH to CS, November 13, 1924, UI.

422. "I am inclined": AH to CS, December 16, 1924, UI.

Chapter 19: Strange Friend (1925–1926)

423. "Almost there were": CS, *ALPY*, II, 285.

423. "tentative experiments": CS, Introduction, Lloyd Lewis, *Myths After Lincoln* (New York: Grosset & Dunlap, 1929), vii.

423. "The embryo of": CS, *ALPY*, I, Preface, vii.

424. "was wonderful": HS to PEN, December 10, 1990.

424. found solace and release: PEN interviews with MS.

425. The Sandburgs considered: CS to AH, November 3, 1924, HB.

425. "I am on the": CS to Amy Lowell, March 17, 1925, MIT 230.

425. "When are we": AH to CS, March 17, 1925, UI.

425. "break precedent and": Virginia Kirkus to Harry Golden, September 21 [1961], UNCC. This letter gives the story of what transpired at *McCall's* and the *Pictorial Review*.

426. "I RECEIVED ADDRESSED": A. J. Armstrong to CS, April 3, 1925, UI.

426. "HARCOURT WIRES BOOK": CS to PS, April 4, 1925, MIT 231.

426. "YOUR WIRE WITH": PS to CS, April 5, 1925, UI.

426. "This is the": CS to AH, April 13, 1925, MIT 231.

426. "Vance begged that": AH to CS, April 4, 1925, UI.

427. "exclaiming at their": Frederick Hill Meserve, "Thoughts on a Friend," *Journal of the Illinois State Historical Society*, 45, Winter 1952, 337–38.

427. " 'sea-change' in their": PS to CS, n.d., MS/UI. See also 1925 ES/UI.
427. "I hope you will": PS to CS, n.d., MS/UI. See also 1925 ES/UI.
428. "misery and monkeyshines": CS Review, CDN, July 21, 1925; Fetherling, 133.
428. "masterpiece": CS Review, CDN, August 4, 1925.
428. "an independent artist": CS Review, CDN, August 21 and August 25, 1925.
428. "a hell of": CS at April 20, 1934 ceremony dedicating the William E. Barton Library of Lincolniana at the University of Chicago.
428. "various persons in": CS to Albert J. Beveridge, September 2, 1925, MIT 233.
428. "He had written": CS, *ALPY*, II, 301.
428. "Yourself and Oliver": CS to Ida Tarbell, September 26, 1925, MIT 234.
429. "Sometime within the": CS to AH, September 1, 1925, Letter 1, HB.
429. "not so much": CS to AH, September 1, 1925, Letter 2, HB.
429. "heart fatigue": AH to CS, September 8, 1925, UI.
429. "a pretty strict": CS to AH, September 15, 1925, HB.
429. "I'm waiting for": CS to AH, ibid.
429. "LINCOLN BOOK COMMITTED": CS to PS, October 31, 1925, UI.
429. "I breathe easier": CS to AH, November 7, 1925, HB, UI.
430. "The gilt top": CS to AH, November 14, 1925, HB.
430. "ask the Almighty": CS to AH, November 24, 1925, HB.
430. "never heard of": CS to AH, November 14, 1925, HB.
430. Dana took some: See Dana Steichen photograph, book jacket.
430. "heights of intelligence": CS Review, CDN, December 15, 1925; Fetherling, 140.
430. "Americans are at": CS Review, CDN, Fetherling, 141.
430. "lights and shadows": CS, *ALPY*, I, Preface, vii.
430. "The wind is": CS Review, CDN, Fetherling, 143.
431. "A biography, sirs": CS, "Biography," *Honey and Salt*, CP 712.
431. "I made an": CS, *Sandburg Range*, 347.
431. "The facts and": CS, SR 356. For a discussion of Sandburg's "A Lincoln Preface," see the article by his editor Catherine McCarthy, *Lincoln Herald*, Spring 1968.
432. "faults and merits": CS, Introduction, Lewis, op. cit.
432. Sandburg believed that: CS to Albert J. Beveridge, September 2, 1925, MIT 233.
432. stood considerable wear: CS to Gamaliel Bradford, February 20, 1928, MIT 255.
432. "For the first": Alfred Frankenstein to CS, October 9, 1926, UI. For fuller discussion of the publication of *ALPY*, see PEN Unpublished ms, UI.
433. Critical reaction to: For fuller analysis of critical response, see PEN Unpublished ms, UI. See also Robert Johannsen's astute analysis, *The Frontier, the Union and Stephen A. Douglas.*
433. "Can we accept": Benjamin Thomas, *Portrait for Posterity: Lincoln and His Biographers* (New Brunswick, N.J.: Rutgers University Press, 1947), 286–89.
433. "one of the great": Fanny Butcher, *Chicago Tribune*, February 3, 1926. See CS to Fanny Butcher, February 4, 1926, MIT 235.
433. "the greatest book": Robertus Love, *St. Louis Post-Dispatch*, February 3, 1926. See Robertus Love to CS, February 3, 1926, UI.
433. "It is Sandburg": Mark Van Doren, *Nation*, February 10, 1926, 149.
434. "an intensely individual": *New York Times*, February 14, 1926.
434. "superpatriots": George Currie, *Brooklyn Daily Eagle* [February 1926], undated news clipping, CSH/UI.
434. "rarely, if ever": Leonard Woolf, *Nation*, May 1, 1926.

434. "It has done": S. L. Cool, *Boston Transcript*, February 6, 1926.
434. "It says much": *Times Literary Supplement* (London), July 29, 1926.
434. "When so many": *International Labor News Service*, February 13, 1926.
435. "tight and rather": George Currie, op. cit.
435. "Sandburg's Lincoln is not": unidentifiable, incomplete news clipping, CSH/UI. Reviews poured in from around the nation and Sandburg kept a vast clipping file. Some articles cannot be attributed.
435. "Out of the": Harry Hansen, *Chicago Daily News*, February 3, 1926.
435. "helped destroy the": C. M. Morrison, *The Literary Review of the New York Evening Post*, February 13, 1926, 1.
435. "The dome of": Knox Reevers to CS, February 18, 1926.
436. "Another critic of": RMH of HB to CS, February 9, 1926, UI.
436. "I saw a": AH to CS, March 29, 1926, UI.
436. "with abridgement, taken": CS to AH, May 17, 1926, MIT 237.
436. "Your Lincoln grows": Eugene Debs to CS, May 22, 1926, UI.
436. "breath and feeling": CS to Eugene Debs, May 18, 1926, ISU.
436. "[That] is most": Debs, May 22, 1926.
436. "You spent a": Negley D. Cochran to CS, March 31, 1926, UI.
436. "You note that": CS to Negley D. Cochran, May 18 [1926], MIT 238.
436. "For two weeks": ACH to CS, February 23, 1926, UI.
437. "Truly a rare": Alfred Stieglitz to CS, April 23 [1926], UI.
437. "I am hugging": Ida Tarbell to CS, February 3, 1926, UI.
437. "You have made": Harriet Monroe to CS, January 31, 1926, UI.
437. "prose poem": PGW to CS from Brookings Institute of Economics, Washington, D.C., January 24, 1926, UI.
437. "I am proud": William Allen White to CS, January 20, 1926, UI.
437. "By God you": Malcolm Cowley to CS, n.d. [1926], UI.
437. his natural, instinctive: For fuller discussion, see PEN Unpublished ms, UI.
438. "to build on": CS, *ALPY*, I, Preface, vii.
438. "high document": Ibid., viii.
438. "imagination, intuition": Ibid.
438. "Going farther": Ibid., xii.
438. "Man is his": Negley Cochran to CS, March 31, 1926, UI.
439. "probably be of": CS to Donald Brace, March 26, 1926, HB.
439. "I have to give up": CS to Arthur Vance, June 15, 1926, UI carbon.
439. "Paper today looks": Henry Justin Smith to CS, August 14, 1926, UI.
440. "People keep asking": CS to Lilla Perry, quoted in Lilla Perry, *My Friend Carl Sandburg: The Biography of a Friendship* (Metuchen, N.J.: Scarecrow Press, 1981), 25–26.
440. "I said that": CS to H.L. Mencken, August 22, 1926, UI carbon.
441. "With *Spoon River*": Louis Untermeyer, *American Poetry Since 1900* (New York: Holt, 1923), 113–32.
442. "To August and": CS, dedication, *ALPY*.

Chapter 20: American Singer (1926–1929)

443. "There is presented": CS, Introduction, AS vii–viii. Morris Fishbein.
443. "great rough song": Lloyd Lewis, "Last of the Troubadours," SR 123–24. Dr. Morris Fishbein was editor of the *Journal* of the American Medical Association.
444. "blunt, direct, odorous": CS, AS 270.
444. "Oh, it's now": CS, AS 271.
444. "It was like": Lloyd Lewis, op. cit.
444. "famous oblong songbook": CS, AS 152.
444. "Picnic and Hayrack": CS, ibid., xxi.
444. "Do you want": H. L. Mencken to CS, December 29 [1925], UI.
444. "I have gone": CS, AS ix.
445. "SEND VERSES FOGGY DEW": D. W. Griffith to Lloyd Lewis, quoted by CS, AS 14.
445. In the Southwest: CS gave the history of his song collection in AS, passim.
445. "midnight prowlers in": CS, AS 26.
445. "comic bucolic monologue": CS, AS 48.
445. "listening to sailors": CS, AS 404.
445. "classical gutter song": CS, AS 75, 78.
445. famous Saturday Night: see Guy J. Forgue, ed., *Letters of H. L Mencken* (New York: Alfred A. Knopf, 1961) and Charles A. Fecher, ed., *The Diary of H. L. Mencken* (New York: Alfred A. Knopf, 1989).
446. "Sandburg may not": Lloyd Lewis, op. cit.
447. "tug of war": David Karsner, *New York Herald Tribune*, April 18, 1926, 7–8, had written "if Sandburg ever gets away from the people he is a dead one. . . . Few poets have come of age in America with more positive knowledge and a keener comprehension of the tug of war for bread than Sandburg."
447. "Just now I": CS to AH, n.d., HB.
447. His job as: CS quoted in interview, *Editor and Publisher*, September 25, 1926.
447. "pegging away at": CS to Donald Brace, March 26, 1926, HB.
448. "Carl is working": PS to AH, March 22, 1926, HB.
448. "Young Frankenstein": Harrison Smith to CS, April 19, 1926, UI.
448. "I'm glad you": CS to Harrison Smith, April 29, 1926, UI.
448. "I hear great": Louis Untermeyer to CS, May 11, 1926, UI.
448. "to discuss how": CS to Clifford Cairns, May 27, 1926, ES/UI.
448. "else it would": AH to CS, June 1, 1926, UI.
449. "It's a tussle": CS to AH, June 29 [1926], HB.
449. "the sad fate": Alfred Frankenstein to CS, August 3, 1926, UI.
449. "He has learned": Rebecca West, ed., SP, Preface, 15–28.
450. "Your Sunday morning": CS to PS, n.d. [1926], UI.
450. MOTHER PASSED AWAY: Martin Sandburg to CS, December 30, 1926, UI.
450. "Dearest Paula": CS to PS, n.d. [ca. January 1927], MIT 244.
450. "There may or may not": CS, Untitled, unpublished Poem, UI.
451. "At one moment": CS, "Souvenir" manuscript, UI.
451. "My heart is": Clara Sandburg, "Souvenir," UI.
452. "Many things I": CS, "Aprons of Silence," *Smoke and Steel*, CP 176.
452. "And since at": CS, "At the Gates of Tombs," *Slabs of the Sunburnt West*, CP 293.
452. "Carl with his": Clara Sandburg, "Souvenir," UI.
452. "As some measure": Frederick Dickinson to CS, January 2, 1927, UI.

452. "Rode back from": CS to AH, quoted in Detzer, 164.

452. "I meant to": Ibid.

453. "kicked around": CS to James Stevens, March 3, 1927, MIT 245.

453. "glad if we": Royal Cortissoz, quoted in John Hohenberg, *The Pulitzer Prizes* (New York: Columbia University Press, 1974), 115.

453. "It has mounted": CS to Vachel Lindsay, April 6, 1927, MIT 246.

453. "Sometimes I think": CS to Freda Kirchway, June 28, 1927, ES/UI.

453. "food, sleep": CS to Arthur Vance, May 17, 1927, UI carbon.

454. "Music engraving is hell": CS to Franklyn Wolfe, May 25, 1927, UI.

454. "there are times": CS to Ralph Steiner, April 6, 1927, UI.

454. "nearly put me": CS to Lillian Rickaby, December 20, 1927, UI.

454. "large study": PEN interview with MS.

454. "I remember vividly": CS to AH, February 28, 1927, HB.

454. "I never was": CS to H. D. Ross, March 3, 1927, UI.

455. "It is a paradoxical": Henry Justin Smith, "It's the Way It's Written," *Chicago Daily News* Reprints, no. 7, 1923; Mott and Casey, eds. *Interpretations of Journalism*, 263.

455. "saw the paper": Ben Hecht, *A Child of the Century* (New York: Simon & Schuster, 1954), 250.

455. "A curious academy": CS, Unpublished manuscript, UI.

455. "human pivot of": CS, ibid.

455. "individual and indigenous": CS to Sam T. Hughes, September 12, 1918, MIT 134.

455. "Dear Harry": CS to Henry Justin Smith, April 25, 1927, MIT 247.

456. "It was always": CSOH-PEN interview with Donald Russell, May 4, 1981.

456. "still toiling": CS to Hazel Buchbinder, March 1, 1927, ES/UI.

456. "If this is": H. L. Mencken to CS, December 9 [1926], UI.

456. "If the harmonization": H. L. Mencken to CS, December 13 [1926], UI.

456. "My recital dates": CS to Frederick Fadner, February 28, 1927, UI.

456. "with becoming poetic": News clipping, CS Lecture File, UI, Quincy, Illinois, February 23, 1927: "Carl Sandburg, Poet, Eludes All Pursuers After Arrival Here."

457. "three or four weeks": CS to Franklyn Wolfe, May 25, 1927, UI.

457. Sandburg's new studio: For fuller background on the Michigan property, see Margaret Sandburg's Unpublished Biographical Manuscript; HS, GGR; PEN's Unpublished ms, UI.

457. "I nearly went": CS to Franklyn Wolfe, May 25, 1927, UI.

457. "The plates for": Howard Clark to PS, June 15, 1927, UI.

457. "invaders from Lakeside": PEN Interviews with MS.

458. "This is the first": PS to AH, July 20, 1927, HB.

458. "You can hardly": AH to PS, July 22, 1927, UI.

458. "I have been": CS to Charles Dunning, August 20, 1927, MIT 250.

458. "twenty-two mile": CS to Oliver Barrett, August 11 [1927], UI. (Beginning in 1927, CS's CDN secretary Betty Peterman typed much of his correspondence, with carbons, which are at UI.)

458. "I have had more": CS to Charles Dunning, op. cit.

458. "Two of the best": CS to Donald Brace, August 26, 1927, HB.

458. "Beat at the": CS, "Bars," *Good Morning, America*, CP 392.

459. "Who put up": CS, "Money, Politics, Love and Glory," *Good Morning, America,* CP 394.

459. "I have thought": CS, "Bundles," *Good Morning, America,* CP 427.

459. "You shall have": CS, "Peace, Night, Sleep," *Good Morning, America,* CP 426.

460. "there are swimming": CS to Oliver Barrett, op. cit.

460. "take great pleasure": Oliver Barrett to CS, August 13, 1927, UI.

460. "I happen to": Theodore Dreiser to CS, August 20, 1927, UI.

460. "worst punished galley": CS to Howard Clark, October 1, 1927, HB.

460. "Dear Mamma & Daddy": MS to CS and PS, September 7, 1927, UI. Background on MS's boarding school experience, PEN interview with MS August 7, 1988.

461. "I gained in": CS to AH, September 23, 1927, MIT 251.

461. "I have run": CS to Albert Wetjen, September 8, 1927, ES/UI.

461. "because I am": CS to Paul D. Paddock, September 8, 1927, UI.

461. "You mention the": CS to Howard Clark, September 22, 1927, HB.

461. Paula kept track: The HB files contain PS's meticulous notes and summary, very like the patient, detailed attention she gave to MS's illness in her Journals.

461. "It would be": AH to CS, September 26, 1927, UI.

461. "the runaway Christmas": AH to CS and PS, October 6, 1927, UI.

462. "There is a": AH, ibid.

462. "I thought you": MS to CS and PS, September 27 [1927], UI.

462. "finally put to": AH to PS, October 20, 1927, UI.

462. "Paula dearest—Songbag": CS to PS, n.d. [October 1927], UI.

462. "I hope something": AH to PS, October 20, 1927, UI.

462. "I am looking": H. L. Mencken to CS, November 8 [1927], UI.

462. "Thanks over": Jake Zeitlin to CS, November 30, 1927, UI.

For background on the Michigan house, see MS Unpublished Biographical Manuscript and HS, GGR. Details here are also drawn from PEN interviews with MS, as well as a visit to the house.

463. "done a great": Jesse Ricks to CS, December 5, 1927, UI.

463. "a noble piece": Frank Dobie to CS, November 24, 1927, UI.

463. "I wish you": ACH to CS, December 19, 1927, UI.

463. "why in thunder": Arthur Vance to CS, December 29, 1927, UI.

463. "heavy and awful": CS to Neeta Marquis, November 30, 1927, ES/UI.

463. "The book nearly": CS to Abby Sutherland, November 22, 1927, UI.

463. "The detail work": CS to H. L. Mencken, November 3, 1927, MIT 253.

463. "tackling books of": CS to Dorothy Scarborough, March 1, 1928, UI.

464. "I have had": CS to AH, December 23, 1927, MIT 254.

464. "It's a noble": AH to CS, February 7, 1928, UI.

464. "advised by competent": CS to Glenn Hughes, December 20, 1927, UI.

464. secretly more homesick: PEN interviews with MS.

464. "I hope I": MS to CS and PS, February 2, 1928, UI.

464. "so that at": PEN interviews with MS.

464. "Janet's defender": PEN interview with HS.

464. "open way encouraged": HS, Unpublished ms, UI, 56.

See HS WLB for her memories of life in Michigan. HS generously loaned the complete, unpublished manuscript of this book. Portions of that manuscript quoted or cited are designated hereafter HS Unpublished Manuscript, UI. See also HS's short story, "The Innocent," in *Children and Lovers* (New York: Harcourt Brace Jovanovich, 1976), 3–17.

465. Janet was Paula's: CS to PS, Wednesday, n.d. [1928], UI.

465. "They will take": PS to CS, n.d., UI.

465. "got very worried": PEN interview with MS.

465. On April 6, 1928: St. Peter's Church Records, Elmhurst, Illinois, provided courtesy of HS.

465. "If you want": MS to PS and CS [May 1928], quoted in HS, Unpublished Manuscript, UI, 62.

465. On the first night: PEN interview with MS; MS notes to PEN.

465. "I have been": CS to Henry [Parks], October 9, 1928, CSH Carbon/UI.

465. "Harvard has more": CS quoting himself to Stewart McClelland, n.d. [ca. 1940], MIT 381.

466. "resting platform having": PEN interview with MS; MS notes to PEN.

466. "a white-haired man": Detzer, 171–72.

466. "four door sedan": CS to Fred Black, September 11, 1928, ES.

CS wrote to PS (n.d., UI), "Will get the car . . . there will be Arabian Sand at our Paw Paw Sand soon." Sandburg named the car "Remorse," according to Fred Black; see Fred Black to CS, October 16, 1928, ES/UI.

466. He was not: See HS on CS's driving, GGR 310–11.

Poems from GMA were published in 1928 in *Ladies' Home Journal, Plain Talk, The New Republic, Poetry, The Saturday Evening Post, The Tanager* and the *Virginia Quarterly Review*. See PEN Unpublished ms, UI, for discussion of many of the poems in GMA, including the influence of poet–railroad agent W. H. Simpson on "Many Hats."

466. "And who made": CS, "Good Morning, America," GMA, CP 320.

466. "the short miserable": Ibid., 434.

467. "Carl, you're imitating": CS to Joseph Warren Beach, March 1933, MIT 288.

467. "The spiders are": CS, "Crisscross, GMA, CP 341.

467. "drunken, death-defying": CS, "Many Hats," GMA, CP 430.

467. "I shall take": CS, "Hungry and Laughing Men, GMA, CP 386.

467. "battlegrounds and workshops": CS, "Explanations of Love," GMA, CP 399.

468. "Speech requires blood": CS, "Precious Moments," GMA, CP 428.

468. "If I then": CS, "To the Ghost of John Milton," GMA, CP 384.

468. "Comes along a": CS, "Many Hats, GMA, CP 432.

469. "Came a lean": Ibid., 434.

469. "I feel that": Conrad Aiken, Preface, *Modern American Poets* (New York: Modern Library, 1927).

469. "no real progression": Edwin Seaver, *New Republic*, December 5, 1928.

469. "fresh combinations": Percy Hutchison, *New York Times*, October 21, 1928.

469. "master his own": Paul Rosenfeld, "Carl Sandburg," *Bookman*, Vol. LIII, July 1921, 389–96.

469. "Not everybody can": Joseph Warren Beach to CS [1928], UI.

469. "Mostly I am": CS to Henry [Parks], October 9, 1928, UI.

470. He told Sherwood: CS to Sherwood Anderson, October 11, 1928, MIT 261.

470. "tunneling": CS to PS, n.d. [November 1928 postmark], UI.

470. "conference with Atlantic": CS to PS, November 27 [1928], UI.

470. "Mr. Angle is": CS to Ellery Sedgwick, November 20, 1928, ES.
470. "entirely authentic": CS, "Lincoln Letters Called Authentic," *New York World*, December 4, 1928.
471. "When I scrutinize": CS, *New York World*, December 4, 1928.
471. "Anyone can go wrong": Paul Angle to CS, December 5, 1928, UI.

    For a complete account of the *Atlantic*-Minor controversy, see Don E. Fehrenbacher, "The Minor Affair: An Adventure in Forgery and Detection," *Lincoln in Text and Context* (Stanford, Calif.: Stanford University Press, 1987) 247–69.

471. "appraise the goddam": CS to Benjamin Thomas, January 12, 1954, MIT 496–97.
471. "Somebody is spoofing": CS to Editor, *Harper's Monthly*, November 20, 1928, UI.
471. "I have been": CS to AH, February 11, 1929, HB.
471. "any lads who": CS to R. P. Walker, January 31, 1927, UI.
471. "our palhood days": John Sjodin to CS, May 1, 1929, UI.
472. "I am 48": Vachel Lindsay to CS, September 16, 1927, UI.
472. "I was so": HS to CS [November 21, 1927], HS/UI.
472. "Dear Swipes": CS to HS, April 15 [1929], UI.
472. "Sunday there were": PS to CS, n.d. [winter 1929], UI.
473. "six months or": CS to Leo Sowerby, March 21, 1929, MIT 264.
473. "It may be": CS to Clark P. Bissett, May 18, 1929, MIT 266.
473. "booked for steady": CS to Arthur [Vance], June 14, [1929], ES/UI.

Chapter 21: A Great Bundle of Grief (1929–1933)

474. "In the darkness": CS, *The People, Yes, CP* 617.
474. "Heavy profit-taking halted": *Omaha World Herald*, October 31, 1929, 1.
474. "bread-line silhouettes": CS, *TPY, CP* 439.
474. "relentless meal ticket": Ibid., 460.
475. "the plain people": Ibid.
475. "mortgages, house rent": Ibid.
475. "seething of saints": Ibid., 471.
475. "The people is": Ibid., 456.
475. "When at thirty-eight": CS to Joseph Warren Beach, April 1, 1930, MIT 273.
476. "too busy with": CS to Arthur Vance, June 14 [1929], ES/UI.
476. "all day": CS, *STP*.

    See PEN Unpublished MS, UI, for much fuller discussion of Steichen's life and career.

476. "idealistic Sandburg": Paul Rosenfeld, *New Republic*, January 22, 1930, 251.

    Also see Mike Gold, *The New Masses*, May 1930. He wrote that "Carl Sandburg advances the thesis that an artist has only two alternatives in America; he must be either a commercial or a revolutionary artist. We agree. We do not agree, however, with Sandburg when he chooses commercial art for himself; glorifies it, in this amazing and shameless essay, and advises the youth to sell their talents to Big Business. Sandburg is in his decadence. Once he believed in the Revolution, and it made him an inspired American poet; now he believes in Big Business, and is a kind of literary Tex Guinan who entertains the fat, idle ladies who hang around women's clubs."

476. "pioneer of motion": See CS on D. W. Griffith, Fetherling, *passim*.

477. "DAVID WARK GRIFFITH": CS telegram to D. W. Griffith [October 1929], UI.
477. Besides, Sandburg had earned: Financial figures are taken from CS-PS 1929 IRS files, CSH.
478. "Griffith called me": CS to Charles Dunning, January 4 [1930], MIT 263. As he often did at the beginning of a new year, Sandburg misdated the letter, absentmindedly writing 1929 instead of 1930. Other documents confirm 1930 here.
478. "Can't you bring": William Allen White to CS, January 11, 1930, UI.
478. "the human family": CS Note, February 2, 1930, UI.
478. "a wild game": HS to PEN, December 10, 1990.
478. "I sent off": PS to CS, n.d. [1930], UI.
478. "The children all": Ibid.
478. "about the livest mag": Ezra Pound to CS, February 7, 1930, UI.
479. "I went in": HS to CS, March 16, 1930, UI.
479. "and then we": Ibid.
479. "I don't know how": PS to CS, n.d. [March 1930], UI.
479. "You have been": CS to AH, n.d., HB.
479. "MR SANDBURG WAS": PS telegram to Elizabeth Manwaring, April 13, 1930, UI.
480. "Fate works oddly": CS to Elizabeth Manwaring, April [no day given], 1930, UI.
480. "Where are the": AH to CS, May 29, 1930, UI.
480. "the work now": CS to Ferris Greeslet, April 1, 1930, ES/UI.
480. "belonged among": CSOH-PEN interview with Martha Moorman Groth, July 30, 1980, UI.
480. "different but very": Ibid.
480. "could stand the": Ibid.
480. "do the real": Ibid.
481. "He didn't do": Ibid.
481. bronze as an: PEN interview with MS.
481. "to sink or": CSOH-PEN interview with Martha Moorman Groth.
481. "Don't mind the": CS quoted by Martha Moorman Groth, ibid.
481. "The Lincoln of": CS to Rupert Hughes, March 21, 1930, ES/UI.
481. "Sometimes it": CS to Fanny Butcher, June 23, 1930, MIT 274.
481. "The work has": CS to Emanuel Hertz, August 29, 1930, UI.
482. "We have not": CS to Martin Sandburg, October 5, 1935, MIT 338.
482. "struggling away at": CS to Ole Rölvaag, January 6, 1931, MIT 275.
482. "long time job": Ibid.
482. "A ballplayer's legs give": CS to Albert Barrows, January 25, 1931, MIT 276.
482. "about three volumes": CS to Ole Rölvaag, February 28, 1931, UI.
482. "Masters and I": CS to William Townsend, March 12, 1931, MIT 277.
482. "Masters has been": CS to Clark Bissett, August 5, 1931, ES/UI.
482. "worthy historian and": CS, Dedication, ALWY I.
483. "Enclosed is the": CS to Paul Angle, n.d., UI carbon.
483. "Held down by": CS to C. B. Hill, August 18, 1931, UI carbon.
483. "doing pretty well": AH to CS, July 8, 1931, UI.
483. "I only hope Red": AH to CS, March 3, 1931, UI.
483. "Dear Janet, How": Mary "Oma" Steichen to JS, June 2, 1931, UI.
484. "I will go": CS to Elizabeth Lindsay, November 13, 1931, MIT 279. For background on Lindsay, see Edgar Lee Masters, *Vachel Lindsay: A Poet in America* (New

York: Scribners, 1935), and Eleanor Ruggles, *The West-Going Heart: A Life of Vachel Lindsay* (New York: Norton, 1959.) See also Stephen Graham, *Tramping with a Poet in the Rockies* (New York: Appleton, 1922); Monroe, op. cit.; Amy Lowell, *A Critical Fable* (Boston: Houghton Mifflin, 1922).

484. "Those were beautiful": CS to William Rose Benét, December 2, 1931, MIT 280.

485. "I took Lysol": Vachel Lindsay, quoted by Masters, based on his interviews with Elizabeth Lindsay; Masters, *Vachel Lindsay: A Poet in America*, 361.

485. the Sandburgs suggested: PEN interviews with MS.

485. "an ambiguous term": Paul Angle to CS, December 9, 1931, UI.

485. Margaret Sandburg was: PEN interviews with MS.

485. "I had no romantic": MS notes to PEN.

485. "Margaret had five": PS to CS, quoted by HS, Unpublished ms, 92–94, UI.

486. "We were very": Ibid.

486. Helga remembered standing: Ibid., 95. PEN interviews with HS.

486. "method of hot": PS to CS, op. cit.; PS Journal, MS/UI.

487. In May of: Henry Justin Smith to CS, May 17, 1932, UI.

487. "I have so": CS to Frederick Babcock, July 29 [1932], MIT 282.
    See PEN Unpublished ms, UI, for fuller treatment of *Early Moon, Steichen the Photographer,* and *Mary Lincoln: Wife and Widow.*

488. "Our Janet was": CS to AH, September 13, 1932, HB.

488. "Your letter with": AH to CS, September 23, 1932, UI.
    See HS, Unpublished ms, UI, and HS, *WLB,* for background on her schooling and Janet's.

489. "long gloom and": CS to AH, October 11, 1932, MIT 283.

489. "I almost feel": CS to Oliver Barrett, n.d. [November 14, 1932], MIT 285.

489. "decisive judgment": CS to AH, n.d. [January 24, 1933], MIT 286.

489. the Nobel Prize: See CS to Ernest and Mary Hemingway, December 8, 1954, MIT 502; Harry Golden, *Carl Sandburg,* 171–72; HS; *WLB,* 195–96.

489. "too much of my": CS to AH [January 24, 1933], MIT 286.

489. "guiding and inspiring": Edward Steichen, Dedication, *A Life in Photography.*

489. "I hope the new": Edward Steichen to Mary Steichen, n.d. [1933], UI.

490. Tragically, Oma received: PEN interviews with MS.

490. "She had been": PS to Edward Steichen, n.d., UI.

490. "Opa, Opa, Opa": Ibid.

490. "a terrifying time": PEN interview with HS.

490. The Illinois church: PEN interview with MS; MS notes to PEN.

490. English was a: PEN interview with MS.

490. "Love and Kisses": John Peter Steichen to CS and PS, on several letters over the years, UI.

Chapter 22: Heroes, Did You Say? (1933–1936)

491. "These are heroes": CS, *The People, Yes, CP* 460.

491. "tangled passion about": CS to Paul de Kruif, February 1, 1938, MIT 359.

491. "best light of": CS to Franklin Delano Roosevelt, March 29, 1935, MIT 317.

491. "All the time": Ibid.

492. "the man grows": CS to ACH, March 17, 1933, MIT 287.

492. "oppressive": CS to AH, February 7 [1933], MIT 286.

492. "paradox or mystery": CS to Lloyd Lewis, March 9, 1938, MIT 314.
492. "ten minute broadcast": CS to AH, July 6 [1935], MIT 331.
492. "At first I": Ibid.
492. "all the elations": CS to Worthington C. Ford, April 22, 1933, MIT 291.
493. "I know all": CS to William Leiserson, April 10, 1933, MIT 289. CS told Leiserson he would "hear no holler from me in case the intake at the door should merely equal that of one of my soap box meetings in Oshkosh which brought forty-two cents."
493. "no goddam contracts": CS to ACH, March 17, 1933, MIT 287.
493. "writing new verses": CS to Joseph Warren Beach, March 31, 1933, MIT 288.
493. "I'm going to": CS to ACH, ibid.
493. "I see many": CS to Raymond Moley, October 20, 1933, MIT 297.
493. "Am sunk fathoms": CS to AH, August 7, 1933, MIT 294.
494. "I kept to one": CS to Archibald MacLeish, October 6, 1933, MIT 297; LC. See PEN Unpublished ms, UI, for extended treatment of Sandburg's association with MacLeish.
494. "And now I": Archibald MacLeish to CS, n.d. [1933], UI. See CS to *The New Republic*, August 26, 1933, MIT 295.
495. "Miss Frances Perkins": Eleanor Roosevelt to CS, December 16, 1933, UI.
495. "courteous offer to" Malvina Scheider to CS, January 12, 1934, UI.
495. "extended me unusual": CS, Foreword, *ALWY* I, xx.
495. "Lincoln corners of": Ibid.
496. "Nobody will read": CS, quoted by Detzer, 200.
496. "more leis than": PS to MS, JS, HS and Martha Moorman, n.d. [1934], UI.
496. The Bacons drove: PEN interview with Ernst Bacon.
496. "Jesus, that's a": Ibid.
    For fuller accounts of the Hawaii trip, see HS, Unpublished ms, UI, and PEN, Unpublished ms, UI.
497. "rebel poets": Malcolm Cowley, —*And I Worked at the Writer's Trade* (New York: Penguin, 1979), 162–75; CSOH-PEN interview with Malcolm Cowley, June 24, 1982.
497. "a little more scabrous": Malcolm Cowley to PEN, ibid.
497. "No use my": Malcolm Cowley to CS, December 11, 1935, UI.
497. "No, I didn't": CS to Malcolm Cowley, January 20 [1936], MIT 309. Once again, CS seemed to write the old year instead of the new; he clearly alludes to Cowley's December 11, 1935, letter here.
497. "When you have": CS to Malcolm Cowley, ibid.
497. As a poet: Malcolm Cowley to PEN.
498. "a lot of": Malcolm Cowley to CS, December 11, 1935, UI.
498. "a heavy maternal": HS, Unpublished ms, UI 105.
498. "six giant grey": Ibid.
498. "became proficient at": Ibid., 106.
498. "No," he said: Ibid.
498. Leona, a half-bred: Ibid.
498. "garden, geese": CS to AH, September 1935, quoted by HS, Unpublished ms, 108.
499. "abolished": Ibid.
499. "Over 200 quarts": Ibid.

499. "The farm here": CS to Oliver Barrett [November 1935], quoted by HS, ibid., 108.
499. "working on an": CS to AH, November 27, 1935, MIT 339.
499. "effloresce": Ibid.
499. "large intelligent horselaugh": Ibid.
500. "I was the first" Brenda Ueland, "While You Are Alive Be Alive," A Brenda Ueland Sampler, Eric Utne, ed., Utne Reader, June/July 1985, 48.
500. "No Cruelty": Brenda Ueland, from an unpublished essay, ca. 1980, ibid., 56.
500. Sandburg told Brenda: CSOH-PEN interview with Brenda Ueland, June 5, 1984, UI.
500. "I have had": Ibid.
500. "best book ever": CS, quoted by Brenda Ueland, If You Want to Write: A Book About Art, Independence and Spirit (St. Paul, Minn.: Graywolf Press, 1987 [reprint of New York: G.P. Putnam's, 1938], xii.) For further background on this extraordinary woman, see Brenda Ueland, Me (G. P. Putnam's, 1939). "I must help you with your book," Brenda told me that June day in 1984. "You need encouragement. You need wild rapturous encouragement." She was right, and she did help me, and still does, through her luminous book If You Want to Write. She died in March 1985, ninety-three years old.
500. "That piece": CS to Brenda Ueland, n.d. [ca. March 1935], MIT 315.
501. "some of the chaos": CS to Benjamin Cardozo, June 30, 1936, MIT 342.
501. "Parts of it": Ibid.
501. "It was the": CS to Paul de Kruif, November 26, 1936, MIT 345.
501. "a ballad pamphlet": CS to Malcolm Cowley, January 20 [1936], MIT 309.
501. Not surprisingly: See CS to Oliver R. Barrett, May 9 [1936], MIT 322.
502. "the masters of": CS to Oliver Barrett, ibid.
502. "greed, fear, brutality": Ibid.
502. "Science, inevitable changes": Ibid.
502. "with the people": Ibid.
502. "to convey the": Oliver Barrett quoted by CS, ibid.
503. "I have been wrong": CS, ibid.
503. "that Felicia, Carlotta": CS to AH, June 3, 1935 (HS believes this letter was written in 1936, and internal evidence—proofs of TPY—confirms that), MIT 330.
503. "Those who will": CS to AH, June 10, 1936, MIT 340.
503. "what the Quakers": CS to George P. West, August 13 [1936], MIT 344.
503. "It has a": CS to George P. West, September 26 [1936], MIT 336. CS seems to have misdated several 1936 letters 1935, perhaps because, as he explained, "This is one of the times when overwork has me down to feeling like a fumbling shadow" (CS, ibid.).
504. "Sometimes it goes": Stephen Vincent Benét, Books, August 23, 1936.
504. "the monstrous efforts": CS to Henry R. Luce, July 3, 1936, MIT 343.
504. "Accordingly, they commenced": CS, TPY, CP 609.
504. "Affirmative of swarming": CS, "Notes for a Preface," CP xxv.
504. "It is dedicated": CS, Unpublished ms, UI.
505. "would have gone": CS to Robin Lampson, December 5, 1936, MIT 346.
505. "The existing prejudices": CS, ibid.

505. "the one word": CS, *TPY*, CP 586.
505. "damned near owe": CAP (otherwise unidentified) to CS, May 19, 1936, UI.
505. "fruition": AH to CS, May 18, 1936, UI.
505. "partly as a" AH to CS, May 29, 1936, UI.
505. "The sad part": Archibald MacLeish to CS [ca. July 1936], UI. This letter is published in R. H. Winnick, ed., *Letters of Archibald MacLeish 1907 to 1982* (Boston: Houghton Mifflin, 1983), 281–82.
506. "The people is": CS, *TPY*, CP 616
506. "hold to the humdrum": CS, *TPY*, CP 616.
506. "Streetwalking jobhunters, walkers": CS, *TPY*, CP 458.
506. "loans and mortgages": CS, *TPY*, CP 459.
506. "And in the air": Ibid.
506. *"The People, Yes"*: CS, *TPY*, Preface, CP 437.
507. "The people of the earth": CS, *TPY*, CP 439.
507. "Five hundred ways": CS, *TPY*, CP 440.
507. "a mumbling poem": CS, *TPY*, CP 579–80. This autobiographical section recalls Sandburg's hobo days.
508. "The people is Everyman": CS, *TPY*, CP 453.
508. "poverty and the poor": CS, *TPY*, CP 608.
508. "hopes of a promised land": CS, *TPY*, CP 593.
508. "Those who have nothing": CS, *TPY*, CP 593–94.
509. "Who shall speak": CS, *TPY*, CP 465.
509. "shrewd and elusive proberbs": CS, *TPY*, CP 471.
509. "Grown in the soil": CS, *TPY*, CP 441.
509. "join in a shout": CS, *TPY*, CP 440.
509. "whimsical fixer": CS, *TPY*, CP 439–40.
509. "the soap boxer pleading": CS, *TPY*, CP 574.
510. "the buyers, the consumers": CS, *TPY*, CP 604.
510. "What is this?": CS, *TPY*, CP 607.
510. "From the four corners": CS, *TPY*, CP 439.
510. "the wandering gypsy, the pioneer": CS, *TPY*, CP 518.
510. "desperate hoper": CS, *TPY*, CP 520. See Section 20, 461, on hope.
510. "riders to work, to": CS, *TPY*, CP 530.
510. "a vast field of faces": CS, *TPY*, CP 588.
510. "To the deeper": CS, *TPY*, CP 616.
510. "the little Family of Man": CS, *TPY*, CP 471.
511. "mortal kinship with": CS, *TPY*, CP 557.
511. "United States of the Earth": CS, *TPY*, CP 578.
511. "search the earth": CS, *TPY*, CP 579.
511. "The people will live": CS, *TPY*, CP 615.
511. "From the four corners": CS, *TPY*, CP 439.
512. "This old anvil": CS, *TPY*, CP 617.
512. "One of the early": CS, *TPY*, CP 464. In an address delivered September 17, 1967, and reprinted as the Introduction to CP in 1970, Archibald MacLeish said, "No one who knew Sandburg would identify this as a self-portrait. Sandburg, though he sometimes slouched, was never underslung" (CP xix). See PEN Unpublished ms, UI, for fuller discussion of *TPY*, including the belief that CS is clearly writing about himself in this passage.

512. "I am credulous": CS, *TPY*, CP 464–65.
513. "The unemployed/without": CS, *TPY*, CP 606–607.
513. "Finished revisions and": CS to Edward Steichen, April 28 [1936], MIT 319. Again, in his weariness, CS must have misdated this letter 1935. I agree with HS that it was written in 1936. HS relied for dating on her journals, and internal evidence supports her view.

Chapter 23: Lincoln? (1936–1940)

514. "Lincoln?/He was": CS, *The People, Yes*, CP 521–23.
514. "all the trouble": PS to Edward and Dana Steichen, March [1937], ES/UI,
514. "down to feeling": CS to George P. West, September 26 [1936], MIT 336.
514. "So much honest": CS to Ida Tarbell, September 30, 1936, UI Carbon.
514. "a big white horned": CS to AH, November 27, 1935, MIT 339.
514. "Mother was wild": HS to PEN, December 10, 1990
514. "We do practically all": CS to George P. West, September 26 [1936], MIT 336.
515. "The eldest daughter": Ibid.
515. "The lake performs": Ibid.
515. "to mush in true": PS to Harriet Monroe, April 6, 1933, UC.
515. "fine evening; of talk": James Thurber to CS, December 1, 1936, UI.
515. "a momentous historic": CS to Bruce Bliven, September 12 [1936], MIT 333. Again, CS seems to have been living so close to Lincoln and *The People, Yes* that he lost track of a year and dated this 1936 letter 1935. HS and internal evidence confirm the error.
515. "print or use": Ibid.
516. "done no shadow": Ibid.
516. "the lowest gloom": CS to George P. West, September 26 [1936], MIT 336.
516. "so that in": CS to Mart Sandburg, December 30, 1936, MIT 347.
516. "He was very sick": PS to Edward and Dana Steichen, March [1937], ES/UI.
516. "more than half": CS to Oliver Barrett, February 22, 1937, MIT 348.
516. "keep clear of": CS to Virgil Markham, n.d. [March 1937], MIT 349.
516. "more than being": PS to Edward and Dana Steichen, March [1937], ES/UI.
516. "had drained his": PS, Ibid.
516. "when General Motors": PS, Ibid.
517. "slow going": CS to Paul Angle, March 5 [1937], CHS.
517. "I told the": CS to Virgil Markham, n.d. [March 1937], MIT 349.
517. "in two eras": CS to Frank Murphy, March 29 [1937], MIT 350.
517. "about sit-down strikes": "Carl Sandburg Visits Toledo to Meet Friends and Talk About Herd of Goats," news article by Walter Leckrone, *Toledo News-Bee*, Toledo, Ohio, March 18, 1937.
517. "the first two": CS to AH, September 1, 1937, MIT 353.
517. "among them some": Ibid.
517. "on the ragged edge": Ibid.
517. "The summer has": CS to Brenda Ueland, September 2 [1937], UI carbon.
517. "Don't let the": Brenda Ueland to CS, September 7, 1937, UI.
518. "dazzling white": HS, Unpublished ms, UI 125. See HS, ibid., passim, and HS, *WLB*, for a vivid account of life in Michigan. Background on this period is drawn from HS, ibid., and PEN interviews with HS, MS and JS.

518. "not following a": HS, Unpublished ms, UI, 126.
518. "It was a": HS, ibid., 127.
519. "For the last": CS to Paul Angle, December 6, 1937, CHS.
519. "cowboy Paul Robeson": "Sandburg Sings American," *Life*, February 21, 1938.
519. "monkeywork": CS to Mrs. Charles J. Bednar, May 28, 1937, MIT 351.
519. "The American people": Charles Beard, defining *isolationism*, quoted in Lois Gordon and Alan Gordon, *American Chronicle: Six Decades in American Life 1920–1980* (New York: Atheneum, 1987), 173.
520. "The heroes": CS, *TPY, CP* 454.
520. "The first world": Ibid.
520. "And after the": Ibid., 455.
520. "the chart of": CS, "Nearer Than Any Mother's Heart Wishes," *BT* 114. According to MS, editor of *BT*, this poem was unpublished in CS's lifetime, probably because of its length. I agree with her that this is one of the best posthumously published poems. Note that its dramatic antiwar stance evokes his earliest war poems.
522. "events of wild": CS, "Foreword," *ALWY* I, vii.
522. "record so stupendous": Ibid.
522. "a thousand vivid parallels": CS to AH, September 22, 1938, MIT 372.
522. "involved or cheap": CS to Lloyd Lewis, September 24, 1938, MIT 372.
523. "It was a hell": CS to Lloyd Lewis, April 22, 1938, MIT 362.
523. "too muddy": CS to Lloyd Lewis, August 20, 1938, UI, MIT 367.
523. "Considering what I've": CS to Paul de Kruif, February 1, 1938, MIT 358.
523. "I cannot think": CS to Julia Peterkin, January 13, 1938, MIT 357. See PEN's Unpublished ms, UI, for full discussion of the role Sandburg and H. L. Mencken played in launching Julia Peterkin's career. Sandburg often visited Mrs. Peterkin at "Lang Syne," her plantation in Fort Motte, South Carolina. See also their letters, UI and IU. Julia Peterkin won a Pulitzer Prize for her novel *Scarlet Sister Mary* (1928).
523. "Sorrow here, too": CS to Robert Frost, March 28, 1938, MIT 361.
524. "pain and suffering": Lawrence Thompson and R. H. Winnick, *Robert Frost: A Biography*, one-vol. edition (New York: Holt Rinehart & Winston, 1981), 373.
524. "A slight woman": CS, "In Appreciation of Harriet Monroe," *The Courier* (The University of Chicago), no. 10, May 1938.
525. " 'classified,' thousands of": CS, Dedication, *ALWY* I.
525. Actually, Margaret remembered: PEN interview with MS.
525. "often threw in": CS, Dedication, *ALWY* I.
525. "For Whitman Lincoln": CS, *ALWY* IV, 385.
525. "Look where [Lincoln]": CS, quotes himself, in CS, "Lincoln, Man of Steel and Velvet," Address before a Joint Session of Congress, on February 12, 1959, and in his unpublished preface; HFM 8.
526. "For the writing of": CS to Catherine McCarthy, June 28, 1941, MIT 406.
526. "Of the involved": CS, "Foreword," *ALWY* I, viii.
526. "sons and daughters": Ibid.
526. "humorously and democratically": CS to June Provine, n.d. [ca. March 1941], MIT 400.
526. "grand human struggler": CS, "Foreword," *ALWY* I, ix.

526. "You were a": CS to Paul Angle, October 18, 1939, CHS.
526. "luminous on lights": CS, Foreword, *ALWY* I, xxi.
526. "favors, errands, loans": CS, ibid.
527. "wildernesses": Ibid., xi.
527. "the most essential": Ibid., x.
527. "tangled, involved": Ibid., vii.
527. "Weaves, inserts": CS to AH, June 2, 1938, MIT 363.
527. "Have finished now": CS to AH, June 30 [1938], MIT 365.
527. "revisions and inserts": CS to George and Marie West, August 20, 1938, MIT 366.
527. "faithfully plodded": CS to Lloyd Lewis, August 20, 1938, MIT 367.
527. "groping": CS to Roy Basler, August 24, 1938, MIT 368.
528. "Wilkes Booth could": CS to AH, August 28, 1938, MIT 369.
528. "the poor reader": CS to AH, September 22, 1938, MIT 372.
528. "rewriting hundreds": CS to Lloyd Lewis, September 24, 1938, MIT 372.
528. "a matter of timing": Ibid.
528. "I belong to": CS to Frank Murphy, September 10, 1938, MIT 370.
528. "They are sharks": CS to AH, September 22, 1938, MIT 372.
528. "Your own character": CS, September 2, 1925, MIT 233.
529. "in terrific highlights": This and the following phrases appear in CS, *ALWY* passim.
529. "Black men could": CS, *ALWY* IV, 386.
530. "among nations counted": Ibid.
530. "the living and actual": CS, *ALWY* IV, 371.
530. "Beyond any doubt": Ibid.
530. "Beyond all the hate": CS, *ALWY* IV, 386.
530. "a storm of steel": Ibid.
530. "Out of the smoke": CS, *ALWY* IV, 387.
531. "garish, vulgar, massive": Ibid.
531. "The ground lay": CS, *ALWY* IV, 388.
531. "more than one": CS, *ALWY* IV, 412.
531. "The estimated figures": CS, ibid.
531. Martha Moorman: CSOH-PEN interview with Martha Moorman.
531. "On May 4": CS, *ALWY* IV, 413.
532. "And the finish": CS to Lloyd Lewis, September 24, 1938, MIT 372.
532. "Carl sat at": Edward Steichen, *A Life in Photography*, following Plate 164.
533. "in token and appreciation": CS, quoted in ES/UI.
533. "The time when": CS to HS, October 15, 1939, MIT 374.
533. "I am slowing": CS to Martha [Dodd], December 20, 1939, CSH/UI.
533. "That son-of-a-gun": CS, *Time*, December 4, 1939.
533. "Never yet has": Charles Beard, "The Sandburg Lincoln," *Virginia Quarterly Review*, XVI (Winter 1940), 112–16.
534. "a monumental undertaking": Robert Sherwood, "Review of Abraham Lincoln: the War Years," *New York Times Book Review*, December 3, 1939, 1.
534. "The poets have": Henry Steele Commager, "Lincoln Belongs to the People," *Yale Review*, no. 29, Winter 1940.
534. "reporter, poet, lover": Max Lerner, "Lincoln as War Leader," *New Republic*, December 6, 1939, reprinted in "The Lincoln of Carl Sandburg," a Harcourt, Brace and Company promotional pamphlet, which also included the Com-

mager review, above, the reviews by Charles A. Beard and Robert Sherwood, and reviews by Lloyd Lewis and Henry Bertram Hill.

534. "You could have": CS to Allan Nevins, December 16, 1939, MIT 379.

535. "a beautiful bright": MS to HS, quoted in HS. Unpublished ms, UI 146.

535. "After the Doctor": CS to Stewart McClelland, n.d. [ca. 1940], MIT 381.

535. "meet them more": Ibid.

535. "When your invitation": Ibid.

535. "And one little": CS to Edward Steichen, December 28, 1939, MIT 380.

Chapter 24: Heartbreak Time (1940–1945)

536. "Any mother might": CS, "Nearer Than Any Mother's Heart Wishes," BT 117.

536. "damned vast manuscript": CS to AH, September 22, 1938, MIT 372.

536. "first real vacation": CS to AH, August 20, 1940, MIT 388.

537. "Your letter arrived": CS to Emil Seidel, January 20, 1940, MIT 384.

537. "lavish reception": CS to Henry Horner, May 5, 1940, MIT 388.

537. "quite lonesome": CS to "Swipes," HS, n.d. [ca. February 1940], MIT 386.

537. "You have made": Archibald MacLeish to CS, May 7, 1940, UI.

537. Paula won trophies: See HS, Unpublished ms, UI, and WLB for accounts of the growing goat herd.

537. "I have two": Archibald MacLeish to CS, June 13, 1940, UI.

538. "I remember your": Archibald MacLeish to CS, July 1, 1940, UI.

538. "I ain't got the": CS to Archibald MacLeish in unidentified news clipping, CSH. CS later served as a Fellow of the Library of Congress in American Letters.

538. "the only real": CS to AH, August 20, 1940, MIT 388.

538. Council for Democracy: see CS, HFM 81–83.

539. "I am satisfied": Quoted by CS, "Election-eve Broadcast," November 6, 1940; reprinted in HFM, 29–30.

539. "You might read": CS to FDR, November 9, 1940, MIT 390.

539. "I have not": FDR to CS, December 3, 1940, UI copy.

539. "a flock of letters": CS to FDR, December 7, 1940, MIT 392.

540. "association of writers": CS to Thomas Mann, December 26, 1939, MIT 380.

540. "A Kentucky-born Illinoisan": CS, "Is There Any Easy Road to Freedom?," HFM 284; CP 624. This poem first appeared in *The Free World*, December 1941.

540. "walked off hand": HS, WLB 94.

540. "Joe and Dick": The account of Helga's marriage is based on HS, Unpublished ms, UI and HS, WLB, 96–100; PEN interviews with HS and MS. HS letter to CS, quoted in HS, Unpublished ms, 155–56.

541. "Mother's herdsman": HS, Unpublished ms, 156.

541. "It is said": Ibid., 157.

541. "Well maybe there'll": HS to PEN, December 10, 1990.

541. "He told her to": HS, Unpublished ms, 157.

541. "old-fashioned directness": Ibid. Also see HS, WLB 97.

541. "not," said Helga: Ibid., 158. I quote here from HS, Unpublished manuscript, rather than WLB, which uses the present tense.

541. "below the hillside": Ibid., 162. Also see HS, WLB 98.

542. At times during: CSOH-PEN interview with HS, November 24, 1980, UI.

542. "Helga and her Joe": CS to Catherine McCarthy, February 19, 1941, MIT 395.
542. "The way I": Norman Corwin to Earl Robinson, January 18, 1941, UI.
542. Sandburg chose a section: HFM 30–33.
543. "Four Freedoms" speech: FDR, "The Four Freedoms," Message to the 77th Congress, January 6, 1941.
543. "Man in a Fog": CS, HFM 275.
543. "overfeeding the country": CS to Catherine McCarthy, February 19, 1941, MIT 395.
543. "I am still": CS to Irving Dilliard, March 12, 1941, MIT 401.
543. "a watchtower": CS, HFM 275.
544. "Ain't writing no": CS to June Provine, n.d. [ca. March 1941], MIT 400.
544. "the youth": CS to Archibald MacLeish, March 6, 1941, MIT 397.
544. "gone into the Silences": AH to CS, April 4, 1941, UI.
544. "a sheaf of": Ibid.
544. "free elbow exercises": Karl Detzer to CS, n.d. [ca. 1941], UI.
545. "out of a fog": CS, HFM 50.
545. "theories and ideas": CS to Eugene Meyer, April 30, 1941, MIT 404.
545. "I have not": CS to Louis Untermeyer, n.d. [June 28, 1941], MIT 407.
545. "stepped up to": CS, HFM 69.
546. "hooted and booed": Ibid.
546. "when the long": Ibid. This column appeared June 15, 1941.
546. "The army meant": Anne Morrow Lindbergh, War Within and Without, 1939–1944 (New York: Harcourt Brace Jovanovich, 1980), 159.
546. "The famous flyer": CS, "Chicago Stadium Speech," June 7, 1941, HFM 33–37. See PEN Unpublished ms for fuller discussion of the Sandburg-Lindbergh controversy.
546. "so sound, so": Anne Morrow Lindbergh, 173.
547. "A poet, a": Ibid.
547. "So I am": CS, HFM 72–74.
547. "gives more people": CS, "The Dream that Holds Us," Speech at Madison Square Garden National Unity Meeting, sponsored by the Council for Democracy, August 19, 1941; broadcast over CBS September 9, 1941 (HFM 37–40).
547. "your own propaganda": CS, HFM 76–78.
547. "There are freedom": CS, "Is There Any Easy Road to Freedom?," HFM 284; CP 624.
548. "HELLBENT GRANDSON ARRIVED": CS to AH, December 4, 1941, quoted by HS, Unpublished ms, UI, 169.
548. "observed and helped": Ibid.
548. "This is just": CS to HS, n.d. [December 5, 1941], MIT 408. According to Janet Sandburg's reliable journal, this letter was written Monday rather than Friday. HS confirmed JS's dating.
548. "HALLELUJAH FOR": Edward Steichen to CS and PS, quoted by HS, Unpublished ms, UI, 170.
549. "the usual millions of": CS, HFM 123.
549. "blazing and unforgettable": CS, HFM 125.
549. "Now the Nazis": Ibid.
550. "The common man": CS, HFM 137.

550. "our wish, prayer": CS, *HFM* 161.

550. "My own feelings": Edward Steichen, *A Life in Photography*, following Plate 22.

551. "a procession of": CS, "Road to Victory," *HFM* 306.

551. "sometimes desperately": CS, *HFM* 307–10.

551. "Here is man": CS, *HFM* 309.

551. "Every one of": CS to HS, n.d. [fall 1942], MIT 411.

552. "proper milk": HS, Unpublished ms, UI 179–80.

552. He wrote a sympathetic column: *HFM*, "Americanized Japanese," November 29, 1942, 222–24. Sunao Imoto was CS's secretary; the farm worker was Kaye Miyamoto.

552. "epics of valor": CS, *HFM* 224–26.

552. "Away down under": Ibid.

553. "a couple of mean": CS to Archibald MacLeish, July 2, 1943, MIT 413.

553. "I miss the": CS to PS, June 18, 1943, MIT 412.

553. "My second grandchild": CS to Archibald MacLeish, July 2, 1943, MIT 413.

553. "He saw that": CS, Dedication, *HFM*.

553. "for the moment": CS, *HFM* 258–60.

553. "two or three major": Ibid.

554. "the product of": Archibald MacLeish to Harvey Hollister Bundy, September 10, 1943, LC.

554. "Once you start": Robert Frost to Lesley Frost, quoted in Lawrance Thompson and R. H. Winnick, *Robert Frost: The Later Years, 1938–1963* (New York: Holt, Rinehart & Winston, 1976), 100.

554. "I could no": Robert Frost to Louis Untermeyer, Untermeyer, ed., *The Letters of Robert Frost to Louis Untermeyer* (New York: Holt Rinehart & Winston, 1963) 335–40.

555. their famous 1942 debate: This March 1942 *Atlantic* article was the preface of *Smoke and Steel. Slabs of the Sunburnt West. Good Morning, America* (New York: Harcourt, Brace, 1942).

555. "had no right": CS, *HFM* 275.

555. "settle down on": CS to Eugene Meyer, April 30, 1941, MIT 404.

555. "mere motion picture": Voldemar Vetluguin to CS, July 7, 1943, UI.

555. "the full and complete": CS, *Remembrance Rock* Document Files, September 2, 11, 13, 1943, UI.

556. "still traveling, still": CS, "Notes for a Preface," CP, xxxi. ("At sixty-five I began my first novel, and the five years lacking a month I took to finish it, I was still traveling, still a seeker.")

556. brother Mart died: Mart wrote to CS and PS January 6, 1944, about Kate's cancer: "Kate you know is of Christian Science faith and not known to us she concealed her troubles to us all" (ES/UI).

556. "Opa seems reconciled": PS to Edward Steichen, September 21 [1944], UI.

556. Oma had wanted: HS to PEN, December 10, 1990.

556. "In a box": CS, Tribute to John Peter Steichen, UI.

557. One Sunday afternoon: This account was drawn from a letter from Howard Berry, one of the young soldiers, to CS, April 5, 1951, UI.

557. "There are dead": CS, "The Long Shadow of Lincoln: A Litany," CP 635. CS read the poem at William and Mary in December 1944; it was published in *The Saturday Evening Post* in February 1945.

557. "threw in" with: CS to Julia Peterkin, July 14, 1943, MIT 415.
558. "And there will": CS, "When Death Came April Twelve 1945," CP 637. The poem appeared in *Woman's Home Companion* in June 1945. According to HS and MS, the magazine had requested the poem.

Chapter 25: The Eternal Hobo (1945–1946)

559. "Give me a": CS, "Galuppi," BT 158.
560. "dedicated to what": Norman Corwin to CS, April 3, 1945, UI.
560. "You are the": Ibid.
560. "We can succeed": CS, quoting Lincoln, CBS Radio Script, April 24, 1945, UI.
560. "greatest achievement I": CS to Norman Corwin, May 15, 1945.
561. "The heart of": CS, quoted by HS, Unpublished ms, UI 226.
561. "The end of": CS, RR 1017.
561. "the great clock": CS, RR 1011.
561. "The bombs of": CS, "The Unknown War," CP 646.
562. "haunts made holy": Harry S. Truman to CS, August 14, 1945, UI.
562. "Your deeply moving": CS to Harry S. Truman, September 15, 1945, MIT 424.
562. "Storms begin far": CS, "Storms Begin Far Back," CP 621.
562. "Geography costs": CS, "Turn of the Wheel," CP 644.
562. "Therefore we know": CS, "Peace Between Wars," CP 640.
563. When Steichen came: Kate's greeting was described in Christopher Phillips, *Steichen at War* (New York: Portland House, 1987), 53.
563. "the true face": Ibid., 54.
563. "During my lifetime": Edward Steichen, quoted in George Bailey, "Photographer's America," *New York Times Sunday Magazine*, August 31, 1947, 39; and Phillips, 54–55.
564. "What is America": Sidney Franklin, quoted by Voldemar Vetluguin (hereafter VV) to CS, July 7, 1943, UI. See PEN Unpublished ms, UI, for extended discussion of the inception and creation of *Remembrance Rock*.
564. "to explain her": VV to CS, ibid.
564. "there is such": Ibid.
564. "If Sandburg writes": Frank Morley to VV, quoted in VV to CS, July 7, 1943, UI.
565. "I've been here": CS to Lilla Perry, quoted in Lilla Perry, 65–68.
565. "give a flickering": CS to Brenda Ueland, June 20 [1944], MIT 412. Internal evidence suggests 1944 rather than 1943.
566. "gripping and thrilling": Oliver Barrett to CS, July 17, 1944, UI. Note the similarity of names in the novel to Oliver R. Barrett.
566. "The book will": CS to VV, July 20, 1944, UI carbon.
566. "a great book": Frank Orsatti to CS, October 31, 1944, UI.
567. "extraordinarily vivid": CS to Ken Dodson, October 30, 1944, MIT 418.
567. "a true mariner": CS, RR, "Notes and Acknowledgments."
567. "I hope and trust": CS to Kenneth Dodson, January 27, 1945, MIT 419.
567. "War leaves a": Kenneth Dodson to Letha Dodson, quoted in Lilla Perry, 73–74; quoted by CS, RR 17.

    The extensive Sandburg-Dodson correspondence and various taped interviews by Kenneth Dodson may be studied at UI.
568. "winding, zigzagging, careening": CS to Brenda Ueland, n.d. [internal evidence

and Brenda Ueland's March 28, 1945, letter, UI, suggest spring 1945], MIT 426.

568. "Moving is a": CS to Mary Sandburg Johnson, n.d. [ca. December 1945], MIT 430.

568. "Three pieces of": CS to VV, n.d. [June 20, 1945], MIT 423.

569. Background on the move from Michigan to North Carolina is drawn from PEN interviews with MS, HS and JS; HS, Unpublished ms, UI, passim.

569. where she, Margaret and: According to MS (PEN interview with MS), when Helga and Joe were married and set off on a short honeymoon, Paula suggested that she, Margaret and Janet should have a "honeymoon" also, and took them on a trip through the South.

569. For background on Connemara, see Louise Howe Bailey's *From "ROCK HILL" to "CONNEMARA": The Story Before Carl Sandburg* (Eastern National Park and Monument Association, 1980). Another invaluable reference is David H. Wallace's *Historic Furnishings Report: Main House and Swedish House at Carl Sandburg Home National Historic Site* (U.S. Government Printing Office, 1984).

571. "The health of": CS to Lloyd Lewis, n.d. [ca. December 1945], MIT 430.

571. "a heavy piece": CS to Russ [n.n.], September 15, 1945, CSH/UI carbon.

572. "the missus and": CS to Helen Page (Stephen A. Douglas's great-granddaughter) and Gale Wilhelm (the novelist), November 19, 1945, MIT 429.

572. "We had a long": PS to CS, HS and MS, December [1945], UI.

572. "How can the": CS to Lloyd Lewis, op. cit.

572. "What a hell": CSOH-PEN interview with Judge Frank Parker, October 30, 1980, UI. Paula Steichen, *My Connemara* (New York: Harcourt Brace & World, 1969), 111.

573. "I could have": CS to Lloyd Lewis, n.d. [January 1946], MIT 431.

573. "I have laid": CS to Archibald MacLeish, Feburary 7, 1947, MIT 438.

573. "the formidable mass": VV to CS, n.d. [ca. October 1944], UI.

573. "hypnotic spell of": Ibid.

573. "Man and woman": Sidney Franklin to CS, October 12, 1944, UI.

574. "had no illusions that": CS to Carl Allen, February 11, 1947, ES/UI.

574. "too straight and": Sidney Franklin to CS, October 12, 1944, UI.

574. "History and the": Ibid.

574. "The job here": CS to Mary Hastings Bradley, June 18, 1946, MIT 432.

574. "an organic current": CS to Mary Hastings Bradley, n.d. [ca. fall 1946], MIT 433.

574. "Just this week": CS to Kenneth Dodson, n.d. [November 1, 1946], MIT 435.

574. "that hectic mystic": CS to Benjamin Thomas, December 28, 1946, MIT 437.

574. "acquired an historic": Unidentified news clipping, quoted in Paula Steichen, *My Connemara*, 6.

576. "in return for supplying": PS Note, December 20, 1945, UI; HS/UI. See HS, Unpublished ms, UI; HS, *WLB*; and Paula Steichen, *My Connemara*, for detailed descriptions of life at Connemara.

576. "I'll tell you": CS to Paul Angle, October 1 [1946], MIT 434.

576. "so wisely set": Paula Steichen, *My Connemara*, Dedication.

576. "Buppong comes down": HS Journal, 1946; quoted by Paula Steichen, *My Connemara*, 15.

576. "I have seen": CS, "John Carl," *My Connemara*, 75.

577. "had a grandfather's": Paula Steichen, My Connemara, 85.
577. "The road—to hell": HS Journal, quoted by Paula Steichen, ibid.
577. "We didn't just": PS, quoted by Paula Steichen, ibid., 101; 178.
577. "to go over": HS, Unpublished ms, UI, 246. Helga Sandburg and Paula Steichen wrote vivid personal memoirs of Connemara life, intimate portraits of a unique American literary family.
577. "almost too good": CS to Lloyd Lewis, September 25, 1946, UI carbon.
577. "A slash of": CS, RR 12–13.
578. "what the American": CS, RR 14.
578. "For we know": CS, RR 19–22.
579. "He [Windrow] stood": CS, RR 33
579. "one profile giving," and following: CS, RR, passim.
579. "1. The influence of": Roger Bacon's Four Stumbling Blocks to Truth, quoted by CS, RR 43 and passim.
579. "She noticed the two": CS, RR 23.
580. "one fierce crashing": Ibid.
580. "as you live": CS, RR 30.
580. "strangely inevitable in": CS to Brenda Ueland, n.d. [ca. May 1947], MIT 442.

Chapter 26: American Dreamer (1946–1949)

581. "The war came": CS to Voldemar Vetluguin, no date [1947], UI carbon.
581. "pines tall as": CS to Helen "Chico" Page, n.d. [ca. 1947], UI carbon.
581. "in a fair milk selling": Ibid.
581. "now, terrific Now": CS to Alvin Thaler, December 20, 1946, UI carbon.
581. "I build no expectations": CS to Helen Page, n.d. [ca. 1947], UI carbon.
581. "piles of nonsense": CS to Myrtle Pope, December 19, 1946, ES/UI carbon.
582. "You send": CS Form Letters, UI.
582. "Please autograph": Paul ——— to CS [October 10, 1946], UI.
582. "The serene & blissful": CS holograph on envelope, UI.
582. "virtually completed the script": "MGM Plans Sandburg Epoch-Film," Asheville Times, November 12, 1946.
583. "Maybe I will": CS to Junius B. Wood, n.d. [ca. June 1947], MIT 442.
583. "lend their counsel": Edward R. Murrow to CS, July 16, 1947, UI.
583. "bring to the": Ibid.
583. "an incredible ass": Archibald MacLeish to Ernest Hemingway, July 27, 1943, R. H. Winnick, editor, Letters of Archibald MacLeish, 316.
584. "Bravo! Carl": Ezra Pound to CS, n.d. [1941], UI. See Tim Redmond, Ezra Pound and Italian Fascism (London: Cambridge University Press, 1991).
584. "It is greatly to": Omar Pound to CS, August 17, 1947, UI.
584. "Good reading good": CS, "Ezra," UI.
584. "complex unscientific": Brenda Ueland to CS, n.d., UI.
585. "a novel, a dramatic": VV to CS, quoted by CS to Edward and Natalie Davison, March 20, 1948, MIT 450.
585. "At seventy man": CS to Fanny Butcher, December 17, 1947, MIT 450.
585. "It may be": CS to Kenneth Dodson, June 6, 1947, MIT 444.
585. "It is a butchery": CS to Majorie Arnette Braye, n.d. [ca. December 1947], MIT 449.

585. She told Giroux: CSOH-PEN interview with Robert Giroux, June 16, 1982.
585. "is always a sign": Robert Giroux to PEN, ibid.
586. "It was an enormous": Ibid.
586. Sandburg trusted Giroux: CS wrote in several letters about his high regard for Giroux. See, for instance, CS to Marjorie Arnette Braye, n.d. [ca. March 20, 1948], MIT 440. (Internal evidence suggests 1948.)
586. "His poetic gifts were": Robert Giroux to PEN, June 16, 1982.
586. "He was a hard": Ibid.
587. "I was greatly impressed": Robert Giroux, "Sandburg Surprises," *Dial [PBS]*, March 1982, 52–55.
587. "handling and mauling": CS inscription to Robert Giroux in his copy of *Remembrance Rock*. See Giroux, "Sandburg Surprises," 54.
587. "Much the same": CS to VV, quoted on *RR* book jacket.
588. "a high song": CS to AH, May 17, 1948, MIT 451.
588. "I wrote the": CS quoted by Anne L. Goodman, "Sandburg's Inevitable Novel," *Books and Bookmen*, October 7, 1948, CS *RR* clipping file, UI.
588. "sonorous, right-minded": *New Yorker*, October 9, 1948, 128.
588. Giroux realized that: CSOH-PEN interview with Robert Giroux, June 16, 1982.
588. "The reiteration of his": Perry Miller, *New York Times*, October 10, 1948.
589. "to blow up, to": CSOH-PEN interview with Robert Giroux, June 16, 1982.
589. "At one extreme": CS to T. V. Smith, February 7, 1949, UI carbon.
589. "Thank you for": CS to Fanny Butcher, November 30, 1948, MIT 452.
590. "from fury to": HS, *WLB* 156.
590. "the works and self-denials": CS, *RR* 1000.
590. "Always the path of American": CS, *RR* 1064.
590. "peculiar press": CS to Allan Nevins, February 3, 1949, MIT 455.
590. "About a fourth": Ibid.
590. "huge, muddled, overdone": Ibid.
590. "The 1,067 pages of": *Newsweek*, October 10, 1948, CS *RR* clipping file, UI.
591. "It has ranged": CS to Allan Nevins, February 3, 1949, MIT 455.
591. "Each time has its": CS, *RR* 887.
591. "like an old time": CS to Oliver Barrett, February 25, 1949, MIT 457.
591. "for the demoniac": Ibid.
591. "In closing up": Ibid.
592. "a sane landing": CS Notes [ca. 1947–48], ES/UI.
592. "You are a man": CS to Kenneth Dodson, April 14, 1949, MIT 459.
592. "or psalms—or contemplations": CS to Thomas L. Stokes, December 26, 1949, MIT 465.
592. "for which I": Ibid.
592. "Those who are bent": CS to V. Y. Dallman, n.d. [ca. March 1949], UI carbon.

Chapter 27: Songs and Scars (1949–1951)

593. "Work, love, laughter": CS, "Notes for a Preface, *CP* xxx.
593. "Study the wilderness": CS, "Accept Your Face with Serious Thanks," *BT* 154.
593. "The only trouble": William Evjue to Harry Sheer, October 20, 1948, WSHS. Evjue was editor of the Madison, Wisconsin, *Capitol Times*.
594. "more than anything else": Lloyd Lewis to CS, November 30, 1948, UI.

594. "a world figure": CS Address at Stevenson Inaugural, January 10, 1949.
594. "absolute deadline": CS to Lloyd Lewis, n.d. [ca. January 1946], MIT 431.
594. "Do you remember": Ibid.
594. "I cry over": CS to Kathryn Lewis, April 22, 1949, MIT 460.
594. "Just to have": CS to Adlai Stevenson, May 4, 1949, MIT 461.
594. "a heavy set": CS to Marjorie Arnette Braye, August 22, 1949, MIT 463.
594. "I wouldn't have undertaken": CS to Allan Nevins, February 3, 1949, MIT 455.
595. "Vachel still lives": CS to Mrs. Wakefield, December 20, 1949, UI carbon.
595. "I am still": CS to Adda George, n.d. [ca. December 1947], MIT 448.
595. "furious conferences over": CS to Thomas L. Stokes, December 26, 1949, MIT 465.
595. some new nonsense: CS Notes, UI.
595. "Not having seen": CS to Thomas L. Stokes, December 26, 1949, MIT 465.
596. "we should admire": Robert Frost, quoted in Thompson and Winnick, *Robert Frost: The Later Years*, 176.
596. "It won't hurt": CS quoted in Harry Golden, *Carl Sandburg* (Cleveland: World Publishing Company, 1961), 168–69.
596. "Ef Ther'z": Ezra Pound to CS, August 14 [1950], UI.
596. "In the whirl": CS to Thomas L. Stokes, December 26, 1949, MIT 465.
597. "three fool songs": Ibid.
597. "There was a": CS to Mr. Wendt, December 18, 1950, UI.
597. "his old friend": CS to Archibald MacLeish, May 12, 1950, MIT 472.
597. "Sandburg himself remains": Ralph Newman to Harlan Horner, March 31, 1950, UI.
597. "I am the": CS to Archibald MacLeish, May 12, 1950, MIT 472.
597. "About a degree": CS to Bruce Weirick, May 2, 1950, MIT 471.
598. "long boxcar evenings": See Gregory d'Alessio, *Old Troubadour: Carl Sandburg with His Guitar Friends* (New York: Walker & Co., 1987). When I asked Gregory and Hilda Terry d'Alessio for interviews for the CSOH, they arranged a reunion of many friends who gathered in their New York house for those "boxcar evenings" when CS was in town. In 1980 I met the d'Alessios, Joseph and Shirley Wershba, Dolores Wilson, Ethel Smith, Olga Steckler and other friends of Sandburg and recorded their memories. During Gregory d'Alessio's interview, he told me about the manuscript, illustrated with his drawings of Sandburg, which was published in 1987 as *Old Troubadour*.
598. "Carl was all-out": Harry Golden, *The Right Time* (New York: G. P. Putnam's, 1969), 319.
599. "It was the": CS to Archibald MacLeish, n.d. [1950], LC.
599. "had a family": CSOH-PEN interview with Robert Giroux, June 16, 1982.
599. "passed by as annals": CS, "Note for a Preface," CP xxv.
599. "not worth later": Ibid., xxx.
599. "In a six-year": Ibid.
599. "Regrets over the": CS to Gregory d'Alessio, July 31, 1950, UI carbon.
599. When a radio: Robert Ron, *Hendersonville Times News*, January 6, 1989.
599. "De fog come": Quoted by Paula Steichen, *My Connemara*, 157.
600. "I expected disfavor": CS to Thomas Hornsby Ferril, January 8 [1951], MIT 467. (Sandburg apparently gave the wrong year date here; internal evidence suggests 1951.)

600. "At fifty I": CS, "Notes for a Preface," *CP* xxxi.
600. "projects calling for": HS Unpublished ms, 301.
601. "Write until you": CS quoted in HS, Journal, April 24, 1950, HS Unpublished ms, UI, 301.
601. "It seems Dad": HS, Journal, October 16, 1950, HS Unpublished ms, UI, 303–304. See also HS, *WLB*, for background on this time.
601. "forego an interesting": HS Journal, October 23, 1950, HS Unpublished ms, UI, 304–305.
602. "As we don't": PS telegram to Catherine McCarthy, November 30, 1950, HB.
602. The national anxiety: HS, Unpublished ms, UI, 307. Later, after General MacArthur had been fired by Harry Truman, CS wrote a poem about MacArthur, not intending it to be published, but simply getting it off his chest, according to MS. The unpublished poem (UI) goes in part:

> MacArthur tells us he is going to fade away . . .
> From the San Francisco show he faded to the Washington
> spectacle, then fading to the New York exhibit
> stupendous beyond all stipends, and in his stride arranging
> to fade away to Chicago and Milwaukee hullabullos, wherefore
> it is not idle to surmise he will go on fading and fading
> away till his name is spoken amid tornadoes of confetti
> at the Republican National Convention in 1952.
>
> MacArthur is one of the fadingest faders that
> ever practiced in public at never dying but just fading
> away.

602. "I expected questions": HS Journal, December 4, 1950, HS Unpublished ms, 306–307.
603. "That old son": CSOH-PEN interview with Joseph Wershba, June 16, 1980, UI.
603. "My stomach started": Ibid.
603. "I have been": Joseph Wershba to CS, December 9, 1950, UI.
604. "You must do": Ibid.
604. "In the faint": CS, "The Unknown War," *CP* 646.
604. "Days go by": CS to Mary Sandburg Johnson, December 10, 1950, MIT 473.
604. "Alf Harcourt has": CS to Marjorie Arnette Bray, December 10, 1950, UI carbon.
605. "And what are": Ibid.
605. "a great and noble": George Jean Nathan, quoted in Harry Golden, *Carl Sandburg*, 108–109.
605. "the strongest and most": Eric Sevareid, ibid.
605. "Carl Sandburg—Yes": Brooks Atkinson, ibid.
605. "It is part": Edward R. Murrow, ibid.
605. "He may seem": James Thurber to Margaret H. Ligon, January 30, 1951, *Selected Letters of James Thurber* (New York: Little Brown, 1981), 197.
605. "The entire nation": Senator Tom Connally, January 19, 1951, Golden, 108.
606. "A tumult of memories": CS to AH, March 28, 1951, MIT 475.
606. "First time I": CS to Hal ———, May 21, 1951, UI carbon.
606. "In these days": William T. Evjue to CS, January 8, 1951, UI.
606. "colossal world drama": CS to Dorothy ———, August 31, 1951, UI carbon.

606. "intently, faces uplifted": Paula Steichen, *My Connemara*, 165. Paula Steichen and HS accounts of the wedding can be found in Paula Steichen, ibid., and HS Unpublished ms, UI and *WLB*.
606. "You all can": Paula Steichen, ibid.
606. "a handsome herdsman": HS Unpublished ms, UI 314.
607. "I get it": CS to Thomas H. Ferril, May 22, 1951, MIT 475.
607. "YOU HAVE MADE": Archibald MacLeish to CS, 1951, UI.
607. "It's a wonderful": Archibald MacLeish to CS, February 14 1951, UI.
607. In the September: See William Carlos Williams, "Carl Sandburg's *Complete Poems*," *Poetry: A Magazine of Verse*, September 1951, LXXVIII, 345–51. (Reprinted in *Selected Essays* [New York, Random House, 1954].)
607. "I have just": William Carlos Williams to CS, June 7, 1951, UI.
607. "helplessly and intensely": CS, Unpublished Fragment [ca. late 1940s], UI. Sandburg's poem to Williams was published in *BT*, 1978, and goes in part:

> Doctor Williams having delivered
> eleven hundred babies
> in Rutherford New Jersey
> also delivered from himself
> eleven hundred poems
> each poem a baby . . .
> thus having two prides
> ever pleasing his heart—
> one the embryo poem
> in his fertile brain-womb—
> the other his obstetric skill
> with no use of forceps
> delivering the brain-child
> to wriggle in black ink on white paper
> Doctor Williams saying often to himself,
> "Good babies make good poems."
>
> (BT 142)

607. "then on the day": CS to AH, May 22, 1951, UI carbon.
608. "excellent hocus": Williams, "Good . . . for What?," *Dial*, March 1929, 250–51. For background on William Carlos Williams, see Paul Mariani, *William Carlos Williams: A New World Naked* (New York: W. W. Norton, 1981).
608. "other than their": William Carlos Williams, *Poetry*, September 1951, 345–51.
609. "the evolving [poetic] canon": Helen Vendler, *The Music of What Happens: Poems, Poets, Critics* (Cambridge: Harvard University Press, 1988), 38.
609. "emotional democrat": Louis Untermeyer, *American Poetry Since 1900*, 67.
610. "streets and struggles": CS, "Notes for a Preface," CP xxvi.
610. "turned the Mid-western": Malcolm Cowley, CSOH-PEN interview, June 24, 1982, UI.
610. "I have known": CS, "Notes for a Preface, CP xxiv. [CS also wrote this to Kenneth Dodson, April 14, 1949, MIT 459.]
610. "According to Edmund Wilson": CS, quoted in Harry Golden, *Carl Sandburg*, 177. [Note, as we shall see later, that CS worked with Harry Golden on this book, furnished key materials, and read and commented on galleys.]

611. "It comes in": CS, reprinted in Harry Golden, ibid., 175–76.

611. *"too much soap box"*: Joseph Warren Beach, Typescript, Harvard University Lecture, LC.

611. "No other American": Gay Wilson Allen, *Carl Sandburg*, Pamphlets on American Writers, no. 101 (Minneapolis: University of Minnesota Press, 1972), 5–6.

612. "a genuine talent": Edmund Wilson, *The Shores of Light: A Literary Chronicle of the 1920s and 1930s* (Boston: Northeastern University Press, 1985 [reprint of Farrar, Straus & Giroux 1952 edition]), 239–40. This essay, "The All-Star Literary Vaudeville," first appeared anonymously in June 1926.

612. "simple poems": CS, "Notes for a Preface, CP xxxi.

612. "plain folk living": CS, ibid., xxvi.

612. "guiding star": Langston Hughes, quoted by Arnold Rampersad, *The Life of Langston Hughes: I, Too, Sing America*, Vol. I, 1902–1941 (New York: Oxford University Press, 1985), 44. See Rampersad, 29 and passim, for discussion of Sandburg's influence on Hughes, and for Hughes's poem to CS:

> Carl Sandburg's poems
> Fall on the white pages of his books
> Like blood-clots of song
> From the wounds of humanity . . .

612. although, Allen Ginsberg: George Plimpton, ed., *Poets at Work: The Paris Review Interviews* (New York: Penguin, 1989), 193.

612. "swarming and brawling": CS, "Notes for a Preface," CP xxv.

612. "Many of the": Ibid., xxvi.

612. "He wrote often": Ibid.

612. "Each authentic poet": Ibid., xxx.

612. "A poet explains": Ibid., xxvi.

613. "In a world": CS, "The work of Ezra Pound," *Poetry*, Vol. VII, no. V, February 1916.

613. "a handsome mournful": CS, "Enemy Number One," CP 641.

613. "stacks and cloisters": CS, "The Abracadabra Boys," CP 643.

613. "Beware writing of": CS, "Many Handles," CP 645.

613. "supreme fiction": See Wallace Stevens, *Notes Toward a Supreme Fiction* (Cummington, Mass.: Cummington Press, 1942), and Stevens, *Transport to Summer* (New York: Knopf, 1947).

Chapter 28: A Majestic Old Age (1951–1954)

614. "If I live": CS, "Personalia," *Honey and Salt*, CP 745.

614. "My grandchildren": CS to Dorothy————, August 31, 1951, UI carbon.

614. the bum and vaudevillian: CS, quoted in Lilla Perry, *My Friend Carl Sandburg: The Biography of a Friendship*, 120.

614. "uproar": CS to Lilla Perry, February 19, 1952, paraphrased in Lilly Perry, ibid., 131.

615. "it is nobody's fault": CS to Mary Hastings Bradley, February 19, 1952, MIT 479.

615. "having a tough": Ibid.

615. "The house, large": HS, Unpublished ms, UI, 318, and HS, *WLB*, 168. See HS, *WLB*, passim, for narration of this period.

615. Once when Steichen: HS, *WLB*, 166.

615. "He worked in": CS Journal, n.d., UI. Also see HS, *WLB*.

616. "Fed up with": HS to PEN, December 10, 1990.

616. "own set-up": HS to Art, quoted in HS, Unpublished ms, UI, 321.

616. "It's good to": PS to CS, n.d. [ca. February 1952], UI.

617. "from end to": Paula Steichen, *My Connemara*, 168.

617. "When the engine": Ibid., 168–70.

617. "Your everloving Buppong": See *My Connemara*, passim.

617. "My little exiles": Untitled poem, 1952, published in Paula Steichen, *My Connemara*, 163.

617. "bullion good at": CS to Archibald MacLeish, May 23, 1952, MIT 482.

617. *Always the Young Strangers*: The title comes from "Broken-face Gargoyles," *Smoke and Steel*, CP 175, which CS called one of his best poems (". . . the new people, the young strangers, coming, coming, always coming . . .").

618. "new, long-awaited": HB Press Release, May 1952, UI.

618. "lifting my light": CS to Archibald MacLeish, May 23, 1952, MIT 482.

618. "a wild night": CS, ibid.

618. "the next president": CS to Adlai E. Stevenson, April 25, 1952, MIT 480.

618. "a great and": CS, Madison Square Garden Rally for Adlai Stevenson, October 28, 1952, printed in King Features Syndicate Release November 6, 1952, byline Alice Hughes, "Carl Sandburg's 75th Birthday Brings His Autobiography," 2.

618. "It was all": CS to Adlai Stevenson, n.d. [November 5, 1952], MIT 486.

618. "As for speeches" CS to Adlai Stevenson, September 25, 1956, MIT 511.

618. "anecdotes, Lincoln and": Adlai Stevenson, "A Friend and Admirer," *Journal of the Illinois State Historical Society*, 45, Winter 1952, 297–99.

618. "three great Governors": CS, quoted in Harry Golden, *Carl Sandburg*, 107.

619. The customary wreaths: Christmas details come from PEN interviews with MS, JS, HS and Paula Steichen, and from Paula Steichen, *My Connemara*, passim.

619. "what a wonderful": Steichen, *A Life in Photography*, preceding Plates 226–30.

619. "Nearest I have": CS to Edward and Dana Steichen, n.d. [ca. December 1952], MIT 487.

619. "There is only": CS, "Names," incorporated later into "Timesweep," *Honey and Salt*, CP 771.

620. "There are birds": CS, *TPY*, CP 563.

620. Immediately she saw: For a full discussion, see HS, Unpublished ms, UI, 326–28; HS, *WLB*, 173–76; 225.

621. "If you can": PS, quoted by CS to Edward and Dana Steichen, n.d. [ca. December 1952], MIT 487.

621. "best autobiography written": Robert Sherwood, *New York Times*, January 4, 1953, 1.

621. "well prove to": Horace Reynolds, *Christian Science Monitor*, January 8, 1953, 7. Not all reviewers liked ATYS. Karl Brown wrote in *Library Journal*, January 1, 1953, "Autobiography, and just about as dull as they come."

621. Even readers in China: In particular, two Asian Sandburg scholars have spoken and written of their discovery of their own lives in Sandburg's: Professor Xian-Zhong Meng, author of "Sandburg's Popularity in China," Unpublished ms, UI, delivered "Poetry and Politics," national Sandburg symposium, October

21, 1988; and Professor Akio Ichise of Osaka, Japan, who has written about and translated Sandburg's work in Japanese.

622. "Carl Sandburg is": Adlai Stevenson Tribute to CS, typescript, Ralph Newman papers.

622. "Congratulations old man": Robert Frost to CS, quoted by HS, Unpublished ms, UI, 337. See PEN Unpublished ms, UI, for an account of the 1950 evening when CS and HS traveled down the mountain from Connemara to Wofford College in Spartanburg, S.C., to hear Robert Frost lecture. Sandburg mused, in a long unpublished memo afterward, that Frost was old. Frost seemed to CS to single him out in the audience and try to engage him in a debate. After Frost's lecture, he did not include CS and HS in a party. Among CS's papers of this period may also be found a rough, shorthand draft of the inscription he wrote in Frost's edition of *Complete Poems*: "For Robert Frost who had many miles to go and went them and who will go into one further range after another—with a thankful heart for his Complete Poems and renewal of fellowship, and pointing to page 379 herein whose implication is unmistakable that Robert Frost's face is worth more than a second look and his poems worth second readings."

622. "When God made": Edward Steichen, quoted in Steichen, *Photographers View Carl Sandburg*, Introduction.

622. "an incongruous blue": "Five Hundred at Dinner for Sandburg," *Chicago Daily News*, January 7, 1953.

623. "By striving to": Robert Sherwood, *New York Times*, January 4, 1953, 1.

623. "I have an": CS, *ATYS* 353.

623. "If I live": CS, quoted by HS, Unpublished ms, UI, 344. See HS, ibid., and PEN Unpublished ms, UI, for fuller treatment of ATYS.

623. He most definitely: See CS to Alan Jenkins, April 23, 1953, MIT 493.

623. "shape out the": CS to Catherine McCarthy, n.d. [ca. 1953], MIT 490.

623. "a cramped and cryptic summation": Ibid.

624. "minor ailments that": CS to Kenneth Dodson, April 2 [1953], MIT 490.

624. "I am trying to": Ibid.

624. "real finished and": CS to Dr. Arthur "Jim" Freese, April 2 [1953], MIT 492.

624. "solace": CS to Gerald W. Johnson, July 30, 1954, MIT 497.

624. "refresher course": Ibid.

624. His doctors told: CS to AH, September 24, 1953, MIT 494.

624. "Connemara is lovely": PS to HS, Unpublished ms, UI, 346.

624. "Going to be rich": CS to John Carl Steichen, n.d. [summer 1953], HS Unpublished ms, 347.

624. "Try standing in": CS, "Second Sonata for Karlen Paula," BT 149.

624. "Paula is a wonder": CS to AH, September 24, 1953, MIT 494.

625. "Dad left on": JS Diary.

625. "I love this": JS to CS, quoted in CS to AH, September 24, 1953, MIT 494.

625. "all keenly": PS to HS, quoted in HS, Unpublished ms, UI 346.

625. "Margaret has become": CS to AH, September 24, 1953, MIT 494.

626. "I have heard": CS, "Zinnia Sonata," BT 144.

626. "large noisy": HS, Unpublished ms, UI 356.

626. "I miss you": CS to John Carl Steichen, n.d. [1953], reproduced in HS, Unpublished ms, UI 356.

626. "If it can be": CS, *ATYS* 436.
626. "Dear Snick": CS to Paula Steichen, n.d. [ca. September 1953], MIT 494.
627. "positively magnificent, enthralling": HS to CS, quoted in HS, Unpublished ms, UI 360.
627. "I am more": CS, "Timesweep," *Honey and Salt*, CP 771. "Head One" evolved into "Timesweep"; although it was not published until 1963, the poem was begun in the early 1950s.
627. "Whatever Xmas dreaming": PS to HS, quoted in HS, Unpublished ms, UI 362.
627. "slugging away": CS to Benjamin P. Thomas, January 12, 1954, MIT 496.
627. "Lincoln was a man": CS, quoted in "Sandburg's Job of Unwriting," *Chicago Sunday Tribune*, December 5, 1954, Part 4, 8 and 26.
628. "a writer or": CS, quoted by Sidney Fields, "Carl Sandburg: The Boy Who Flunked Grammar," "Only Human," *Sunday Mirror*, October 24, 1954, 39.
628. "ambassador, negotiator and EDITOR": CS to Eugene Reynal, quoted in HS, Unpublished ms, UI, 367.
628. "a good and grand": CS to AH, September 24, 1953, MIT 494.
628. "To the departed": CS, Dedication, AL:OVE.
628. "faces that were": CS, *ATYS* 353.
628. "My eyes would": CS, *ATYS* 354–55.
629. "You'd better be": Theresa Anawalt to CS, quoted in Lilla Perry, 144–45.
629. "Why should I": CS, quoted in Lilla Perry, 148.
629. "A man must": CS to Ralph McGill, in McGill, "The Most Unforgettable Character I've Met," *Reader's Digest*, May 1954, 109–13.
630. "The Chinese have": Ibid.

Chapter 29: The Family of Man (1954–1956)

631. "Here are . . . the": CS, Prologue, *The Family of Man*.
631. "The man not": CS to Gerald W. Johnson, July 30, 1954, MIT 497.
631. "It was a": Joe Wershba Notes to PEN.
632. "Oh, the straight-off": CS to Edward R. Murrow, "A Visit to Flat Rock," CBS "See It Now" Transcript, broadcast of October 5, 1954, JW.
632. the "Great Abider": PEN interview with Fred Friendly, July 13, 1989.
633. "He was a folksinger": Ibid.
633. "Most inscrutable world": CS to Edward R. Murrow, n.d., UI carbon.
634. "this colossal human": CS to Gerald W. Johnson, July 30, 1954, MIT 497.
634. "fights of man": CS, "Man the Moon Shooter," CP 680.
634. "the most important": Edward Steichen, *A Life in Photography*, Section 13.
634. "The Family of Man": Edward Steichen, Introduction, *The Family of Man*, henceforth FM.
634. "looking tired": PS to HS, May [1954], quoted in HS Unpublished ms, UI 379–80.
635. "There is only": CS, "Names," Prologue, FM.
635. "I would have": Ernest Hemingway to Harvey Breit, quoted in Carlos Baker, *Ernest Hemingway: A Life Story* (New York: Collier Books, 1969), 527.
635. "YOUR UNPRECEDENTED COMMENT": CS to Ernest Hemingway, quoted in HS, WLB, 196.
635. "One result of": CS to Ernest and Mary Hemingway, December 8, 1954, MIT 502.

635. "I got quite": Carl Haverlin, quoted by CS, ibid.
635. "When some books": Ibid.
635. "The cruellest thing": Edmund Wilson, *Patriotic Gore: Studies in the Literature of the American Civil War* (New York: Oxford University Press, 1962), 115–16.
636. "How would you": Archibald MacLeish to CS, November 23, 1954, UI.
636. "To say": CS to Archibald MacLeish, November 30, 1954, LC.
636. "To furnish pertinent": CS, FBI File. The Federal Bureau of Investigation and associated government agencies provided efficient service in responding to my requests, under the Freedom of Information Act, for FBI files on CS, and to my subsequent appeal. Ultimately, I received nearly fifty pages of an eighty-three-page file. In his research for *Dangerous Dossiers: Policing America's Writers* (New York: Donald I. Fine, 1988), Herbert Mitgang received twenty-three pages of an FBI file and six pages of an army intelligence file on Sandburg. Natalie Robins, at work on a book on the surveillance of American writers, obtained a thirty-one-page file on Sandburg, including the six pages from army intelligence. See PEN, "The Two Chicago Sandb:rgs," UI, for more details of the Sandburg-Sandberg story.
637. "The following information": CS FBI File.
637. "from my subterranean cavern": CS to Catherine McCarthy, n.d. (April 1, 1955), MIT 506. HS, Al Dreier and Joe Wershba have discussed the probability that CS was reluctant, during the feverish days of McCarthyism, to go forward with the story of his days as an organizer during the Social-Democratic era in Wisconsin in 1907–1912, given the American propensity to misunderstand and misinterpret history. Sandburg's socialism had its own identity and meaning in its own unique time. By the 1950s, not even half a century later, younger Americans did not comprehend that, and were too intimidated by current events to judge their own times clearly, much less those complicated earlier years. If Sandburg did not continue his autobiography for political reasons, it was not that he repudiated his past. He certainly did not. He simply wanted his past to be clearly understood. See Sandburg's June 28, 1941, letter to Catherine McCarthy (MIT 406) for his earlier concerns about Karl Detzer's biography of him: "The labor movement and industry in general is, since the days I was a labor reporter, on so vastly different a basis, that I wouldn't like to see a Harcourt Brace book in the hands of college and high school students, putting me on the side of any and all racketeers who call strikes for the payoff. . . . A general trend in the Detzer piece indicates that my interest in the socialist and labor movements was entirely rooted in sympathy for labor and the masses. That was only part of it. I sensed these movements, even when a boy, as having terrific potential power, that they would be worth knowing close-up." For more background on CS's reasons for not going forward with *EWC*, consult HS, Unpublished ms, UI; PEN, Unpublished ms, UI; CSOH-PEN interview with Alvin Dreier, November 23, 1981; and MS and George Hendrick introduction, *EWC*.
638. "that I am now 77": CS to Louise Eaton, January 4, 1955, UI carbon.
638. "Fifteen minutes of TV": Ibid.
638. Sandburg liked Allen: This anecdote comes from CSOH-PEN Interview with Steve Allen, May 2, 1981, UI.

638. Unfortunately, CBS sound: PEN interview with John Henry Faulk, September 2, 1989.
639. "Everybody was pleased": CS to Dave Garroway, March 5, 1955, UI carbon.
639. "Ives has a": "Early Bird . . . Coast to Coast by Hy Gardner," quoted in HS, Unpublished ms, UI 400.
639. "I thought of": PS to HS, quoted in HS, ibid., 404.
639. "A great show": PS to HS, ibid.
639. "I don't see": William A. Emerson, Jr., "Lincoln's Man Sandburg—The Time for Remembering Greatness," *Newsweek*, February 14, 1955.
640. "open some doors": HS, *WLB* 200.
640. "enraged and insulted": HS, ibid.
640. "loud and lordly": HS, *WLB* 199.
640. he did not want: See HS, *WLB* 201.
640. indirectly in some: HS interview with PEN. See, for instance, HS, *Children and Lovers* (New York: Harcourt Brace Jovanovich, 1976), "The Innocent," 3–17; "The Other One," 105–20. See also HS's poetry, *The Unicorns* and *To a New Husband*; and HS, *GGR* and *SW*.
640. Her husband, she said: HS, *WLB* 201, 210, 214.
640. "glad of": HS, *WLB* 198.
640. "Father, mother, son": Ibid.
641. He lavished on: CSOH-PEN interviews with Joe and Shirley Wershba, Gregory and Terry d'Alessio, Majie Failey, Anne Grimes, Al Dreier and others; PEN correspondence with Donna Workman.
641. "This was a": PS to HS, quoted in HS, *WLB* 192.
641. "fire-proof safe." HS, *WLB* 193.
641. "the manuscripts and related": CS Document quoted by HS, *WLB* 193.
642. "ultimately selling them": Ralph Newman to HS, quoted in HS, Unpublished ms, UI 401.
642. "For an hour": Bruce Weirick to Esther Sandburg Wachs, April 9, 1950, UI.
642. "with Carl's library": Ibid.
642. In the way: For background see John Hoffmann, "How the Sandburg Collection Came to Illinois . . . Part I: 1950–1957," *Non Solus*, no. 8, 1981, 25–36.
643. "I guess the goats": Archibald MacLeish to CS, May 27, 1955, UI.
643. "I remember when together": CS to Archibald MacLeish, June 3, 1955, LC.
643. "crimson blood streams": CS, "Psalm of the Bloodbank," *CP* 683.
644. "To Carl Sandburg": Archibald MacLeish, Boston Art Festival tribute, reprinted in the *Boston Herald*, June 13, 1955.
644. "Carl Sandburg's rank": Ibid.
644. "That evening Carl": HS, *WLB* 202.
645. "Is there really": HS, *WLB* 202.
645. "Life is a": CS, quoted in HS, ibid.
645. "a furious letter": HS, ibid.
645. Margaret wrote a: PEN interview with MS.
645. "along with hundreds": CS, Unpublished Manuscript, June 4, 1955, UI. CS also wrote at least two drafts of letters to Helga about the collection. One of them, dated June 5 [1955], proposed paying Helga $15,000 for the manuscript collection in her possession, five thousand dollars at first and a thousand dollars yearly for ten years.

646. "I do not": Bruce Weirick (and Leslie Dunlap), Report on the Carl Sandburg Library, July 4, 1955, UI.

See also Leslie Dunlap, "On Moving Carl Sandburg's Library," January 10, 1978, UI, delivered as a Centennial Address in Galesburg, Illinois, January 1978.

646. "The Helga business": Bruce Weirick to CS, July 26, 1955, UI.

647. "poetization of biography": Quoted in Hoffmann, 28.

647. "His books were": CS, RR 11.

648. "writing as steadily": PS to HS [August 1955], quoted in HS, Unpublished ms, UI 419.

648. Janet could call: CSOH-PEN interviews with JS.

649. "My tales would": HS, Unpublished ms, UI 423.

649. "almost balmy": PS to HS, ibid., 427.

650. "Dear Mother": HS to PS, ibid., 425.

650. "I just made": PS to Paula Steichen, ibid. 426.

650. "often appeared by": Paula Steichen, My Connemara, 88.

650. "famous so long": Senator Paul Douglas quoted in CS Journal Note, UI.

650. In a New York: New York Times, February 14, 1956.

650. "My husband has": PS to Mrs. Guthrie, January 19, 1956, UI carbon.

651. "fat, dripping prosperity": CS quoted by Charles N. Quinn, New York Herald Tribune, April 17, 1956.

651. "Beware when you": CS, "Bewares," an "unpublished cautionary poem" written, CS said, "when members of a graduating class in Crane High School, Chicago, wrote me collectively, asking me what to look out for in life." The poem is published in Norman Corwin, The World of Carl Sandburg (New York: Harcourt, Brace & World, 1961), 25.

651. "Before you go": CS, quoted by Charles Quinn, New York Herald Tribune, April 17, 1956.

651. "a prosperous commercial biographer": Westbrook Pegler, "Poor Talk About Material Riches," syndicated column, Journal-American, May 14, 1956.

651. "sapphire mountains": Harry Golden, "A Day with Carl Sandburg," Carolina Israelite, April 1956. See also Harry Golden, Carl Sandburg and The Right Time.

651. "a book that": Joseph Wershba interview with CS, June 11, 1956.

652. "Are the children": PS to HS, quoted in HS Unpublished ms, UI 432–33.

652. "Since last July": HS to PS, quoted in HS, ibid., 433.

652. "happy to oblige": HS, WLB 214.

652. Editor Pascal: Ibid., 216.

652. "at night, in": CS, Look, July 1956, quoted in HS, WLB 215.

652. "Hearts here beat": CS to Don and Lyal Shoemaker, December 19, 1955, MIT 508; see CS to Shoemaker, March 27, 1956, MIT 508.

See PEN Unpublished ms, UI, for fuller story of Sandburg-Wershba friendship.

653. "Cut out that": Randi Wershba, quoted by her father in CSOH-PEN interview with Joseph Wershba, op. cit. Sandburg here echoes Lincoln's words in a similar situation. CS tells the story in HFM, 11: "My God, man, don't you see that if I didn't laugh I would have to cry?" Lincoln said. Randi Wershba and her small brother Don were two surrogate grandchildren for the Sandburgs. After one visit, Randi wrote a poem for Sandburg.

653. "you suggest an": CS to Donna Workman, September 27, 1956, holograph copy, on her September 18 letter, UI.

653. "beyond per adventure": CS to Virginia Pasley, December 17, 1956, UI copy.
653. "We are going": HS to PS, quoted in HS, *WLB* 217.
653. "They have 'grown' ": PS to HS, ibid.
653. "Buppong says it's": PS to Paula Steichen, quoted in HS, Unpublished ms, UI 440–41.
654. "digging in": Donna Workman to CS, September 18, 1956, UI.

Chapter 30: Yes No Yes No (1957–1958)

655. "To live big": CS, "Consolation Sonata," *CP* 686.
655. "I'll die propped": CS, quoted by UP, *New York Times*, January 6, 1957.
655. "muscular back, broad chest": Joe Wershba, *Washington Post* and *Times Herald*, January 6, 1957. Sandburg once told Wright, "I admire the poetry of your architecture." Wright replied, "And I admire the architecture of your poetry."
656. In 1951 Donna: Background is based on the Donna Workman Collection, Knox College; the Donna Workman papers at UI; PEN correspondence with Donna Workman; interviews with Al Dreier, Elmer Gertz, Ralph Newman and Gene Lovitz, CSOH-PEN, UI.
658. The first time: Donna Workman to Max Goodsill, n.d., Knox College.
658. "All night long": Ibid.
658. "clean underwear": Ibid.
658. "the Michael Angelo": CS, quoted in Donna Workman to Max Goodsill, July 13, 1969, KC.
658. "In fact": Donna Workman to Max Goodsill, October 18, 1967, KC.
658. "roar like a": Donna Workman to Max Goodsill, n.d., KC.
659. "You put a": Donna Workman to Max Goodsill, July 23, 1969, KC.
659. "Shall I say": CS, "Evening Questions," *CP* 723.
659. "Dearest, Starlight of": Donna Workman to CS, n.d., UI.
659. "Donna I love you": CS to Donna Workman, n.d., CSH/UI.
659. He left love poems: A particularly vivid packet of poems labeled in CS's hand "Thoreau King" remains among his papers, CSH/UI.
659. "I am perfectly capable": Donna Workman to Max Goodsill, n.d., KC.
659. "Ours was not": Donna Workman to Max Goodsill, n.d., KC.
659. "The fact that": Donna Workman to Max Goodsill, n.d., KC.
660. "I had the": Donna Workman to Max Goodsill, April 16, 1980, KC.
660. He and Paula: CS quoted by Donna Workman, ibid.
660. "He was tremendously": Ibid. Actually, Paula Sandburg was not valedictorian, although she was an honor graduate.
660. "He was human": Ibid.
660. "through Sandburg that": Donna Workman to Max Goodsill, July 23, 1969, KC.
661. "the sole right": Letter of Agreement, March 19, 1957, UI.
661. "commencing as of May": CS to Donna Workman, May 24, 1957, UI and KC.
661. "grieved": CS quoted in Donna Workman to Max Goodsill, July 23, 1969, KC.
661. "a baby that": Donna Workman, ibid.
661. "I think it's": Catherine McCarthy to Donna Workman, June 13, 1957, KC.
662. "Like other towering": Publisher's Note, *SR* vii.
662. "Sandburg believed in": Donna Workman to PEN, August 19, 1980.
662. "spent his life": HS, Unpublished ms, UI 445.

662. "I've been hoping": PS to Paula Steichen, quoted in HS Unpublished ms, UI 450.
663. "frosty-haired old": *Time*, quoted in HS, Unpublished ms, UI 447. Actress and television personality Arlene Francis also appeared at the convention. See PEN, Unpublished ms, HS, Unpublished ms and Arlene Francis, with Florence Rome, *Arlene Francis: A Memoir* (New York: Simon & Schuster, 1978).
663. "immediate and unconditional": CS to Governor William Stratton, n.d. [ca. July 1, 1957], MIT 514.
663. "But Jesus Christ!": CS to Allan Nevins, August 5, 1957, MIT 515.
664. "the sound building": Chicago Dynamic Committee Letterhead, UI.
664. "former enemies": Donna Workman to Max Goodsill, two letters, n.d., KC.
664. "You have whipped": CS quoted by Donna Workman, ibid.
665. "voice nearly as": *Chicago Daily News*, October 31, 1957.
665. "as Victor Hugo": CS, Chicago Dynamic Speech, Climax Banquet, October 30, 1957, UI.
665. "If I had": Ibid.
665. "a couple of": *Chicago Daily News*, October 31, 1957.
666. "Your personal doorways": CS, "Breathing Tokens," BT 3.
666. "The War of the Bears": HS, *WLB* 222.
666. "Sure enough he": Ibid.
666. "one must assert": HS Journal, December 16, 1957, HS, Unpublished ms, UI 461.
666. "Oh, my, no": Ibid.
666. "a strong-willed girl": HS, Unpublished ms, UI 459.
666. "You and the": PS to HS, January 13, 1958, quoted in HS, *WLB* 223.
667. "Many things": Ibid.
667. "Dear Carl": Edward Steichen, Open Letter to Carl Sandburg, January 6, 1958, *New York Times* and elsewhere.
667. "I feel as": CS to Joseph Wershba, 1958 interview; see Joseph Wershba, album notes, "Flat Rock Ballads" (Columbia, 1959).
667. Donna and Ralph Newman: Details of this event are based on Donna Workman Papers, KC; CSOH-PEN interviews with Ralph Newman, November 14, 1981, and February 25, 1983; and with Elmer Gertz, November 12, 1981.
668. "long conversation which": CSOH-PEN interview with Elmer Gertz, ibid.
668. "The press was": CSOH-PEN interview with Ralph Newman, November 14, 1981.
668. "high-pitched voice": Gregory d'Alessio, *Old Troubadour*, 90–93.
669. "You oughtn'ta get": CS, quoted in d'Alessio, ibid. Nathan Leopold's letters to CS (UI) are of great interest. See Leopold to CS, April 3, 1958 (UI), for an account of his new life in Puerto Rico.
669. "a struggle toward": CS quoted in news article, "The Poet Pleads for a Convict," *New York Post*, February 6, 1958.
669. "I just picture": CS quoted in Associated Press interview, "Sandburg Muses on Fame, Still Writes," May 1958.
669. "in collaboration with": HS Journal, February 19 [1958], HS, *WLB* 225.
669. Helga refused to: See HS, *WLB* 225
669. "new relationship": Ibid., 226.
670. "These people are": HS Journal, March 13 [1958], HS, Unpublished ms, UI 473–74.
670. "provided he gets": HS, *WLB* 226.
670. "wrath": HS, *WLB* 226.

670. "tending, fostering, pacifying": HS, *WLB* 227. "I have witnessed Carl in towering rages . . . but I was never somehow touched," HS wrote further in this passage. "As a child, I saw Paula retreat to the shelter of a closet while the storm raged. That household is directed easily to the pacifying of its hero, the Big Grizzly. Not this one! And sometimes at night I weep in the bushes by our little house's side, thwarted in the image I want of the husband going his way, me mine, and happiness therefore" (HS, *WLB* 227).

670. "wish to trade": HS, Unpublished ms, UI 479.

670. "Would my father's": Ibid.

670. "I hope to Christ": Ibid., 481.

670. "a triumph of": Ibid., 482.

670. "Dearest": CS to PS, reproduced in HS, *WLB* 231.

670. "It's like a communicable": CS, AP Interview, "Sandburg Muses on Fame, Still Writes," May 1958.

671. "So often, so": CS to Donna Workman, May 8, 1958, KC.

671. "We all thought your": PS to HS, April 28, 1958, HS.

671. "fulfill the dearest": PS to HS, May 8, 1958, HS.

671. "a little shrine": HS, Unpublished ms, UI 498.

671. "not the greatest, but": PS to HS, quoted in HS, Unpublished ms, UI 401, and HS, *WLB* 234–35.

672. "laid to rest": HS, *WLB* 235.

672. "A dream last": Ibid.

672. "WAS UTTERLY APPALLED": HS to Norman Cousins, quoted in HS, Unpublished ms, UI 502.

673. "rigorous loneliness": HS, *WLB* 236.

673. "It would sap": CS to Archibald MacLeish, September 18, 1958, LC.

See Corwin, *The World of Carl Sandburg*, 101–102, for details on the UCLA Tribute. Additional accounts may be found in Lilla Perry, HS, Unpublished ms, PEN, Unpublished ms, CSOH-PEN interviews with Norman Corwin, and CS letters to participants, UI. Also see Leonard Karzmar to CS, November 11, 1958, UI.

674. "I'll read the sonofabitch": CS quoted from tape transcription in Norman Corwin, "The Poet & the Gagster," *Los Angeles Times West* magazine, September 24, 1967, 10–14.

674. Later, when Corwin: CSOH-PEN interviews with Norman Corwin, March 25, 1983, and Lucy Kroll, April 29–30, 1983.

674. "unqualified respect, to": Norman Corwin to CS, December 16, 1958, UI.

674. "There is very": Lucy Kroll to CS, December 19, 1958, UI.

675. "all time yes": CS, "Consolation Sonata," *CP* 686.

Chapter 31: Honey and Salt (1959–1967)

676. "There are sanctuaries": CS, "Honey and Salt," *H&S, CP* 706.

676. "The many-sided self": PS to CS, n.d. [1908], UI.

676. "There are hungers": CS, "Timesweep," *H&S, CP* 758.

677. "Has ever been": CS, "Shadows Fall Blue on the Mountains," *H&S, CP* 747.

677. "There was": CS, "Speech," *H&S, CP* 752.

677. "holding honey and": CS, "Honey and Salt," *H&S, CP* 706.

678. "You never truly": William Jovanovich, CSOH-PEN interview with William Jovanovich, June 17, 1982, UI.

678. Because of those: HS writes in *WLB* (259): "The debt to Joe and to Art. To the first for taking me from my family into the golden life of the farm and its reality. To the second so that I was stirred into writing (and also for removing me from the family scene!)."

678. denied that he: PEN interview with Paula Steichen.

680. "longed for him": HS to PEN, December 10, 1990.

680. "Not often in": CS, "Lincoln, Man of Steel and Velvet," Address to Joint Session of Congress, February 12, 1959, reprinted in the *National Geographic*, Vol. CXVII, no. 2, February 1960, 239–41.

680. "dancer of the proletariat": CSOH-PEN interview with Gene Kelly, March 26, 1983, UI. The poem: "Lines Written for Gene Kelly to Dance To," CS, CP 704.

681. "Believe me we": PS to Lucy Kroll, September 5, 1960, LK.

681. " 'Smart' is not": CS to Lucy Kroll, March 28 [1959], LK.

681. "Comes by you": CS to LK, May 9, 1959, LK.

681. "a strenuous, backbreaking": Bette Davis with Whitney Stine, *Mother Goddam* (New York: Berkley Books, 1975), 289.

681. "How goes it": CS to Donna Workman, n.d., KC.

681. "What ere betides": CS to Donna Workman, n.d., KC.

681. Paula watched that: PEN interviews with MS; Alvin Dreier.

681. Donna later sold: The sale took place after Sandburg's death. In February 1959, Donna Workman gave Knox College a "Collection of Books Read by Lincoln." Ralph Newman had assisted her in assembling the collection. See Donna Workman Papers, KC; Galesburg, Illinois, *Post*, February 20, 1959; CSOH-PEN interviews with Ralph Newman.

681. Those papers would: See PEN Unpublished ms and Donna Workman letters to PEN for the nature of these papers, and efforts to locate them.

681. "He was as": Evelyn Wells to HS, quoted in *WLB* 187. See HS, *WLB* 185–89 and 275–76 for her discussion of CS and women. Of interest may be CSOH-PEN interviews with Virginia Pasley, Ethel Smith, Olga Steckler, William Sutton, Brenda Ueland and Dolores Wilson.

682. "We never tried": PS to Robert Spencer, "Conversation at Connemara," Rochester *Democrat and Chronicle*, November 26, 1964.

682. Sandburg had only: CSOH-PEN interviews with Sandburg Trustees Maurice Greenbaum and Judge Frank Parker have been invaluable for background here.

682. "I have no": CS to Lucy Kroll, August 5, 1960, LK.

683. "this narrowing of": CS on the first passenger jet flight across the country, American Airlines Reprint from *Better Homes and Gardens*, 1959, courtesy of David C. Frailey, who wrote, "The Sandburg flight grew from a suggestion I passed along to Better Homes & Gardens." (David Frailey to Jennifer McJunkin, 1989.) For details of Steichen's meeting with Joanna Taub and their eventual marriage, I am grateful to Joanna Taub Steichen, CSOH-PEN interview, June 15, 1982, Restricted Interview, UI.

683. Some individual: CS, FBI Files. Background on the Moscow trip is drawn from an extensive document file, CSH/UI, including Department of State United States Government Grant Authorization 1947–0, June 2, 1959; Department

of State Foreign Service Travel Voucher July 16, 1959–August 4, 1959, and others; see also Tamara Mamedov, Embassy of the Union of Soviet Socialist Republics, to CS, June 1, 1959, UI.

683. "This is for": CS to Swedish cousin, n.n., "Carl Sandburg," unsigned, undated ms, 1–8, UI.

684. "Aunt Clara had": Ibid.

684. "a pair of eminent": Lawrence Spivak, "Meet the Press," NBC, transcription of broadcast taped August 27, 1959, and aired August 30, 1959.

684. "Property is nothing": CS Typescript, quoted in Harry Golden, *Carl Sandburg*, 110–11. According to Golden, CS said, "You have to put this essay I've written in your book" (Golden, 110).

684. "I am not proud": CS to Virginia Pasley, July 2, 1959, UI carbon.

684. "gustatory": CS, quoted in Harry Golden, *Carl Sandburg*, 30.

685. Some of Stevens's: CSOH-PEN interview with William Hale, March 28, 1983, UI; CSOH-PEN interview with George Stevens, Jr., June 11, 1982, UI.

685. "The wide canyon": HS, *WLB* 264.

686. "pages and pages": HS to PS, quoted in HS, Unpublished ms, UI, 601.

686. "If Buppong can": PS to John Carl Steichen, quoted in HS, ibid. 598.

686. "He asked me!": HS, *WLB* 274–75.

686. "Complex. Unfathomable": Ibid., 275.

686. "I'm sorry the": HS, *WLB* 280–81.

686. "Golden Place": HS, ibid., 283.

686. "The New Order": PS to CS, quoted in HS, *WLB* 287.

686. "John and Snick": CS to HS, quoted in HS, *WLB* 301. "Swipes" was CS's nickname for Helga.

687. "I'm glad you": CS to PS, December 30, 1960, MIT 532.

687. "Let us talk": CS, "High Moments," *H&S, CP* 741.

687. "later America": CS, "Ever a Seeker," *H&S, CP* 744

687. "Sandburg would never": HS, *WLB* 290.

688. "I remember when": CS to PS, July 6, 1961, MIT 539.

688. "new all-breed record": HS, Unpublished ms, UI 661.

688. "I feel most lovely": HS Journal, quoted in HS, ibid., 683.

688. "personal force": CS to Harry Golden, June 14, 1961, MIT 536.

688. "a faculty of": Ibid.

688. "I tell people": CS to PS, July 14, 1961, MIT 543.

688. "MEMO for my": CS to PS, July 17, 1961, MIT 544.

689. "deep quiet strengths": CS to Mary Hemingway, October 5, 1961, MIT 548.

689. "Ike is talking": CS, quoted in Associated Press dispatch, "Poet Looks at Presidents," *Christian Science Monitor*, October 26, 1961. See also columns by Russell Baker, *New York Times*, October 26, 1961, and David Lawrence, *New York Tribune*, October 27, 1961.

690. "Can you measure": CS, "Shadows Fall Blue on the Mountains," *H&S, CP* 747.

690. He flew into: CS wrote these details to his sister Esther and her husband, Joseph Wachs, January 30, 1962, UI carbon.

690. Sandburg wanted to begin: Lucy Kroll had negotiated the contract with Simon & Schuster for the proposed book of Newman photographs with text by Sandburg, and Sandburg had begun a rough draft of the text, including biographical

matter on Newman. See Lucy Kroll to Carl Sandburg and Arnold Newman, February 13, 1962, UI and CS manuscript, UI.

690. One night early: CSOH-PEN interviews with Arnold Newman and Augusta Newman, June 18, 1983.

Background on CS's illness is also drawn from interviews with MS, HS, Lucy Kroll, Gregory and Terry d'Alessio, Olga Steckler and Harry Golden. See also HS, *WLB* 304–305.

691. Details on these last years come from a mosaic of sources: the Lucy Kroll papers; PS's letters; interviews with Lucy Kroll, HS, MS, Joe and Shirley Wershba, and Terry and Gregory d'Alessio. See HS, Unpublished ms, UI, and PEN Unpublished ms, UI, for fuller background; also see HS, *WLB* passim.

692. "This dinner for": CSOH-PEN interview with Malcolm Cowley, June 24, 1982.

692. "Being a poet": CS, quoted in unidentified news clipping, CS Clipping File, 85th Birthday, CSH.

693. "Where is the Sandburg": Kenneth Rexroth, quoted in Harry Golden, *The Right Time*, 336.

693. "I am eighty-five": CS to Harry Golden, ibid.

693. "I like Eliot, and I": Robert Frost to Donald Hall, quoted in Donald Hall, "Vanity, Fame, Love, and Robert Frost," *Commentary*, December 1977, 51–61.

693. "proud, troubled": Louis Untermeyer, *The Letters of Robert Frost to Louis Untermeyer*, 372.

693. "We're entirely different": Robert Frost, quoted by Art Buchwald, *New York Herald Tribune*, March 10, 1961.

694. "Best wishes for": Robert Frost to CS, Christmas 1953, UI.

694. "But there is this": CS to Mark Harris, Transcript, August 11, 1961, interview for *Life* (typed transcript, UI).

694. "an emotional elegy": HS, *WLB* 319.

694. "Of the trio of": John K. Hutchens, *New York Herald Tribune*, April 7, 1963.

694. "Carl Sandburg was": PS quoted by Richard C. Bayer, Associated Press, "Sandburgs—Wed 55 Years—Weren't Sure It Would Last," *Buffalo [N.Y.] Domestic News*, June 12, 1963.

695. "stunningly handsome": HS, *WLB* 329. This account of Helga's courtship with Barney Crile is based on CSOH-PEN interviews with HS and Barney Crile, April 24, 1983, UI.

695. "I am Helga's": George "Barney" Crile to CS, quoted in HS, *WLB* 329–30.

695. "But you're not": JS, quoted in HS, *WLB* 330 and CSOH-PEN interviews with HS November 24, 1980, and April 25, 1983, and George "Barney" Crile, April 24, 1983.

Details of Sandburg's last years are based on interviews with MS, HS, Paula Steichen, Joe Wersbha, Gregory d'Alessio and Lucy Kroll. See PEN, Unpublished ms, for fuller treatment. Also see Paula Steichen, *My Connemara*. Paula Sandburg's letters to Lucy Kroll, LK, are poignant and revealing.

696. "Sixth Illinois Volunteers": CS, quoted in Associated Press release, "Medal of Freedom for 30," *New York Herald Tribune*, September 15, 1964.

697. "I could love you": CS, "Offering and Rebuff," *H&S*, CP 740.

697. "Passion may hammer": CS, "The Evening Sunsets Witness and Pass On," *H&S*, CP 716.

697. "Birth is the": CS, "Fog Numbers," *H&S*, CP 723.
697. "And he saw": CS, "Cahokia," *H&S*, CP 715.
698. "There must be substance": CS, "Alone and Not Alone," *H&S*, CP 709.
698. "I got a zoo": CS, "Wilderness," *CH*, CP 100.
698. "Listen and you'll": CS, "Timesweep," *H&S*, CP 758.
698. "Since death is": Ibid.
698. "more than a traveler": Ibid.
699. "And the forgetfulness": CS, "Atlas, How Have You Been?," *H&S*, CP 720.
699. "Time says hush": CS, "The Gong of Time, *H&S*, CP 746.
699. "a major prophet": Roy Wilkins, Executive Director, NAACP, September 1965. In his citation, Wilkins quoted CS, July 26, 1919, on the Chicago race riots.
700. "Who is it?": CS, quoted by PS to Lucy Kroll, February 19, 1966, LK.
700. "Dad is always": PS to HS, March 2, 1966, UI carbon.
700. "He spends most": PS to Ralph [Newman], September 28, 1966, UI carbon.
700. "Come on, Buddy": PS, quoted by MS, PEN interview with MS.
700. heart attack in June: "Carl Sandburg, 89, Poet and Biographer, Is Dead," *New York Times*, July 23, 1967, 1.
701. Someone brought one: See Paula Steichen's account of her grandfather's death in *My Connemara*, 175–78; and HS's narrative in *WLB* 342–59.
701. "Paula": Paula Steichen, *My Connemara*, 176.

Epilogue: Shadows

702. "I have love": CS, "Losses," CP 35.
702. Janet did not: CSOH-PEN interview with Janet Sandburg, August 19, 1981, UI.
702. It was Steichen: CSOH-PEN interview with Joseph Wershba, April 28, 1983.
702. "slowly breathed away": PS, quoted by Joseph Wershba, ibid.
702. "a national poet": Thomas Lask, *New York Times*, July 23, 1967.
703. Steichen tore a: Steichen made this same gesture at the funeral of his old friend and colleague Alfred Stieglitz in 1946. "Tearful Steichen, with a tinge of theatricality that almost misrepresented his genuine grief, laid a pine bough atop the black cloth and moved on," Sue Davidson Lowe wrote in *Stieglitz: a Memoir/Biography* (New York: Farrar Straus Giroux, 1983), 377.
703. "life itself, all life": George Tolleson, quoted by George Tolleson to PEN in CSOH-PEN interview, June 7, 1980, UI.
703. "Death comes once": CS, "Finish," SS, CP 267.
703. "All my life": CS, "Notes for a Preface, CP xxxi.
703. "Life is a river": CS to PS [April 20, 1908], PDG 110.
703. "You are yourself": PS to CS, April 10 [1908], PDG 71.
703. "barriers of the unknown": CS in many places, especially GMA, CP, 318: "Tentative (First Model) Definitions of Poetry"; 15: "Poetry is a search for syllables to shoot at the barriers of the unknown and the unknowable."
704. "I am the credulous": Walt Whitman, "Starting from Paumanok," *Leaves of Grass*, Section 7, 20.
704. "I am credulous": CS, TPY, CP 464.

Selected Bibliography

*

The *Key to Abbreviations and Sources* provides a selected bibliography of the works of Carl Sandburg. For a guide to translations of Sandburg works, see Mark Van Doren, *Carl Sandburg, with a Bibliography of Sandburg Materials in the Collections of the Library of Congress*, Washington, D.C., 1969, and Dale Salwak, *Carl Sandburg: A Reference Guide*, New York, 1988.

Complete citations of numerous articles by and about Sandburg may be found in the notes. These entries are not repeated in the following bibliography, which lists books already cited in the text as well as others pertinent to the context of Sandburg's life and work. It was a necessary pleasure to read deeply the work of Robert Frost, Vachel Lindsay, Ezra Pound, Amy Lowell, Edgar Lee Masters, Archibald MacLeish and a host of Sandburg's literary contemporaries, but space precluded listing all those primary works here.

Aaron, Daniel. *Writers on the Left: Episodes in American Literary Communism*. New York, 1961.

Addams, Jane. *The Second Twenty Years at Hull House*. New York, 1930.

Aiken, Conrad. *Modern American Poets*. New York, 1927.

———. *Scepticisms: Notes on Contemporary Poetry*. New York, 1919.

Allen, Gay Wilson. *Carl Sandburg*. Pamphlets on American Writers, Number 101. Minneapolis, 1972.

Allsop, Kenneth. *Hard Travellin': The Hobo and His History*. London, 1967.

Ameringer, Oscar. *Communism, Socialism and the Church: An Historical Survey*. Milwaukee, 1913.

———. *If You Don't Weaken*. New York, 1940.

Anderson, Margaret. *My Thirty Years' War: The Autobiography*. New York, 1930.

Anderson, Nels. *The Hobo: The Sociology of the Homeless Man*. Chicago, 1923.

Anderson, Sherwood. *Sherwood Anderson's Memoirs*. New York, 1952.

Angle, Paul. *A Shelf of Lincoln Books*. New Brunswick, N.J., 1946.

Bailey, Louise Howe. *From "ROCK HILL" to "CONNEMARA": The Story Before Carl Sandburg*. Washington, D.C., 1980.

Baker, Carlos. *Ernest Hemingway: A Life Story*. New York, 1969.

Baker, Ray Stannard. *American Chronicle: The Autobiography of Ray Stannard Baker*. New York, 1945.

Barnard, Harry. *Eagle Forgotten*. Indianapolis, 1938.

Basler, Roy, ed. *The Collected Works of Abraham Lincoln*. New Brunswick, N.J., 1953–55.

Beach, Joseph Warren. *The Outlook for American Prose*. Chicago, 1926.

Bell, Daniel. "The Background and Development of Marxian Socialism in the United

States." Egbert and Persons, ed. *Socialism and American Life*, Vol. 1. Princeton, 1952.

Blankenship, Russell. *American Literature as an Expression of the National Mind*. New York, 1931.

Boyle, Kay, ed. *The Autobiography of Emanuel Carnevali*. New York, 1968.

Boyle, O.D. *History of Railroad Strikes*. Washington, D.C., 1935.

Boynton, Percy H. *Some Contemporary Americans*. Chicago, 1924.

Brenner, Rica. *Ten Modern Poets*. New York, 1930.

Brooks, Cleanth. *Modern Poetry and the Tradition*. Chapel Hill, N.C., 1939.

Brooks, Van Wyck. *Scenes and Portraits: Memories of Childhood and Youth*. New York, 1954.

Bruns, Roger. *Knights of the Road: A Hobo History*. New York, 1980.

Bruns, Roger A. *The Damndest Radical: The Life and World of Ben Reitman, Chicago's Celebrated Social Reformer, Hobo King, and Whorehouse Physician*. Urbana, Ill., 1987.

Bryan, William Jennings. *The First Battle*. Chicago, 1896.

Cahill, Daniel J. *Harriet Monroe*. New York, 1973.

Calkins, Earnest Elmo. *They Broke the Prairie*. New York, 1937.

Callahan, North. *Carl Sandburg, Lincoln of Our Literature*. New York, 1970.

Cantor, Milton. *The Divided Left: American Radicalism, 1900–1975*. New York, 1978.

Cargill, Oscar. *Intellectual America*. New York, 1968.

Carpenter, Margaret Haley. *Sara Teasdale: A Biography*. New York, 1960.

Chaplin, Ralph. *Wobbly: The Rough and Tumble Story of an American Radical*. Chicago, 1948.

Chase, Richard. *Walt Whitman Reconsidered*. New York, 1955.

Cochran, Negley D. *E. W. Scripps*. New York, 1932.

Corwin, Norman. *A Date With Sandburg*. Northridge, Calif., 1981.

———. *The World of Carl Sandburg*. New York, 1961.

Cowley, Malcolm. *—And I Worked at the Writer's Trade: Chapters on Literary History, 1918–1978*. New York, 1979.

———. *Exile's Return: A Literary Odyssey of the 1920s*. New York, 1951.

———. *The Dream of the Golden Mountains: Remembering the 1930s*. New York, 1980.

Crowder, Richard. *Carl Sandburg*. New York, 1964.

Current, Richard Nelson. *Wisconsin: A Bicentennial History*. New York, 1977.

d'Alessio, Gregory. *Old Troubadour: Carl Sandburg with His Guitar Friends*. New York, 1987.

Damon, S. Foster. *Amy Lowell: A Chronicle*. Boston, 1935.

Darrow, Clarence. *The Story of My Life*. New York, 1932.

Davis, Bette. *Mother Goddam*. New York, 1975.

Debs, Eugene V. *Debs: His Life, Writings, and Speeches*. Chicago, 1908.

Dedmon, Emmett. *Fabulous Chicago: A Great City's History and People*. New York, 1983.

De Kruif, Paul. *The Sweeping Wind*. New York, 1962.

Dell, Floyd. *Homecoming: An Autobiography*. New York, 1933.

Dennis, Charles H. *Victor Lawson: His Time and His Work*. New York, 1935.

Detzer, Karl. *Carl Sandburg: A Study in Personality and Background*. New York, 1941.

Deutsch, Babette. *Poetry in Our Time: A Critical Survey of Poetry in the English-Speaking World 1900 to 1960*. Garden City, N.Y., 1963.

Dodson, Kenneth. *Away All Boats*. New York, 1953.

Donald, David. *Lincoln's Herndon* (Introduction by Carl Sandburg). New York, 1948.

————. *Lincoln Reconsidered: Essays on the Civil War Era*. New York, 1961.

Draper, Theodore. *The Roots of American Communism*. New York, 1957.

Duffey, Bernard. *The Chicago Renaissance in American Letters: A Critical History*. East Lansing, Mich., 1954.

Dunbar, Olivia Howard. *A House in Chicago*. Chicago, 1947.

Durnell, Hazel. *The America of Carl Sandburg*. Seattle, 1966.

Eastman, Max. *Heroes I Have Known*. New York, 1942.

————. *The Trial of Eugene Debs*. New York, n.d.

Edel, Leon. *Literary Biography*. London, 1957.

Eliot, T. S. *The Use of Poetry & The Use of Criticism*. Cambridge, Mass., 1933.

Etulain, Richard, ed. *Jack London on the Road: The Tramp Diary and Other Hobo Writings*. Logan, Utah, 1977.

Fecher, Charles A., ed. *The Diary of H. L. Mencken*. New York, 1989.

Fehrenbacher, Don E. *Lincoln in Text and Context*. Stanford, Calif., 1987.

————. *The Changing Image of Lincoln in American Historiography*. Oxford, 1968.

Ferri, Enrico. *Socialism and Modern Science*. New York, 1904.

Fetherling, Dale, and Doug Fetherling, eds. *Carl Sandburg at the Movies: A Poet in the Silent Era 1920–1927*. Metuchen, N.J., 1985.

Fletcher, John Gould. *Life Is My Song: The Autobriography of John Gould Fletcher*. New York, 1937.

————. *Some Contemporary American Poets*. London, 1920.

Flynt, Josiah. *Tramping with Tramps*. New York, 1899. [See Willard.]

Forgue, Guy J., ed. *Letters of H.L. Mencken*. New York, 1961.

Francis, Arlene, with Florence Rome. *Arlene Francis: A Memoir*. New York, 1978.

Frye, Northrop. *The Modern Century*. Toronto, 1967.

Gavett, Thomas W. *Development of the Labor Movement in Milwaukee*. Madison, Wis., 1965.

Gertz, Elmer. *A Handful of Clients*. Chicago, 1965.

Ginger, Ray. *The Bending Cross: A Biography of Eugene Debs*. New Brunswick, N.J., 1949.

Giroux, Robert. *The Education of an Editor*. New York, 1982.

Golden, Harry. *Carl Sandburg*. Cleveland and New York, 1961. Reprint, Urbana, Ill., 1988.

————. *The Right Time*. New York, 1969.

Gompers, Samuel. *Seventy Years of Life and Labor*. New York, 1957.

————. *The American Labor Movement: Its Makeup, Achievements and Inspirations*. Washington, D.C., 1914.

Gordon, Lois, and Alan Gordon. *American Chronicle: Six Decades in American Life 1920–1980*. New York, 1987.

Gould, Jean. *Amy: The World of Amy Lowell and the Imagist Movement*. New York, 1975.

Grade, Arnold, ed. *Family Letters of Robert and Elinor Frost*. Albany, N.Y., 1972.

Graham, Stephen. *Tramping with a Poet in the Rockies*. New York, 1922.

Gregory, Horace, and Marya Zaturenska. *A History of American Poetry 1900–1940*. New York, 1946.

Gullen, Karen, ed. *Billy Sunday Speaks*. New York, 1970.

Haas, Joseph, and Gene Lovitz. *Carl Sandburg: A Pictorial Biography*. New York, 1967.

Hansen, Harry. *Carl Sandburg: the Man and His Poetry*, Little Blue Book # 814. Girard, Kans., 1925.

———. *Midwest Portraits: A Book of Memories and Friendships.* New York, 1923.

Harris, Frank. *Contemporary Portraits.* 4th ser. New York, 1923.

Hecht, Ben. *A Child of the Century.* New York, 1954.

———. *Erik Dorn.* Chicago, 1963.

Hemingway, Mary Welsh. *How It Was.* New York, 1976.

Henderson, Alic Corbin, comp. *The Turquoise Trail: An Anthology of New Mexico Poetry.* Boston, 1928.

Herndon, William Henry, and Jesse William Weik. *Herndon's Lincoln: The True Story of a Great Life. Etiam in Minimis Major. The History and Personal Recollections of Abraham Lincoln.* Chicago, n.d. [1889].

Herron, George D. *Why I Am a Socialist.* Chicago, 1900.

Hillquit, Morris. *History of Socialism in the United States.* New York, 1910.

Hoan, Daniel. *City Government: The Record of the Milwaukee Experiment.* New York, 1936.

Hohenberg, John. *The Pulitzer Prizes.* New York, 1974.

Howe, Irving. *Sherwood Anderson.* New York, 1951.

———. *Socialism and America.* New York, 1985.

Hubbard, Elbert. *The Note Book of Elbert Hubbard.* New York, 1927.

Jacobs, Dan N. *Borodin: Stalin's Man in China.* Cambridge, Mass., 1981.

Johannsen, Robert. *The Frontier, the Union and Stephen A. Douglas.* Urbana, Ill., 1989.

Johnson, Walter, ed. *Selected Letters of William Allen White.* New York, 1947.

Jones, Howard Mumford, and Walter B. Rideout, eds. *Letters of Sherwood Anderson.* Boston, 1953.

Jones, Llewellyn. *First Impressions: Essays on Poetry, Criticism, and Prosody.* New York, 1925.

Kaplan, Justin. *Lincoln Steffens: A Biography.* New York, 1974.

———. *Walt Whitman: A Life.* New York, 1980.

Karsner, David. *Debs, His Authorized Life and Letters.* New York, 1919.

———. *Sixteen Authors to One: Intimate Sketches of Leading American Story Tellers.* New York, 1928.

Katz, William Loren, ed. *The Negro in Chicago: A Study of Race Relations and A Race Riot in 1919.* New York, 1970.

Kazin, Alfred. *On Native Grounds.* Garden City, N.Y., 1956.

Kelly, Edmond. *The Elimination of the Tramp.* New York, 1908.

Kenner, Hugh. *A Homemade World: The American Modernist Writers.* New York, 1975.

Kirkup, Thomas. *History of Socialism.* London, 1900.

Kraft, James, ed. *The Works of Witter Bynner.* New York, 1979.

Kramer, Dale. *Chicago Renaissance: The Literary Life of the Midwest 1900–1930.* New York, 1966.

Kreymborg, Alfred. *Our Singing Strength: An Outline of American Poetry 1620–1930.* New York, 1929.

———. *Troubador: An Autobiography.* New York, 1925.

Lane, Albert. *Elbert Hubbard and His Work.* Worcester, Mass., 1901.

Lewis, Lloyd. *It Takes All Kinds.* New York, 1947.

Lewis, Lloyd, and Henry Justin Smith. *Chicago: The History of Its Reputation.* New York, 1929.

Lindbergh, Anne Morrow. *War Within and Without 1939–1944*. New York, 1980.

Lindsay, Vachel. *A Handy Guide for Beggars, Especially Those of the Poetic Fraternity*. New York, 1916.

———. *Rhymes to Be Traded for Bread*. Springfield, Ill., 1912.

———. *The Art of the Moving Picture*. New York, 1915.

London, Jack. *The Dream of Debs*. Chicago, n.d. [1910].

Lowe, Sue Davidson. *Stieglitz: A Memoir/Biography*. New York, 1983.

Lowell, Amy. *A Critical Fable*. Boston, 1922.

———. *Tendencies in Modern American Poetry*. New York, 1920.

Lowes, John Livingstone. *Convention and Revolt in Poetry*. New York, Boston, 1926.

MacLeish, Archibald. *Poetry and Experience*. Boston, 1960.

Madison, Charles A., *Critics and Crusaders*. New York, 1947–1948.

Manchester, William. *American Caesar: Douglas MacArthur 1880–1964*. New York, 1978.

Mariani, Paul. *William Carlos Williams: A New World Naked*. New York, 1981.

Massa, Ann. *Vachel Lindsay: Fieldworker for the American Dream*. Bloomington, Ind., 1970.

Masters, Edgar Lee. *Across Spoon River: An Autobiography*. New York, 1936.

———. *Lincoln: The Man*. New York, 1931.

———. *The Tale of Chicago*. New York, 1933.

———. *Vachel Lindsay: A Poet in America*. New York, 1935.

———. *Whitman*. New York, 1937.

Matthiessen, F. O. *Theodore Dreiser*. New York, 1951.

McMurry, Donald L. *The Great Burlington Strike of 1888: A Case History in Labor Relations*. Cambridge, Mass., 1956.

Mencken, H. L. *Vachel Lindsay: The True Voice of Middle America*. Washington, D.C., 1947.

Miller, Sally M. *Victor Berger and the Promise of Constructive Socialism*. London, 1973.

Mitgang, Herbert. *Dangerous Dossiers: Policing America's Writers*. New York, 1988.

Monroe, Harriet. *A Poet's Life: Seventy Years in a Changing World*. New York, 1938.

———. *Poets and Their Art*. New York, 1926.

Monroe, Harriet, and Alice Corbin Henderson, eds. *The New Poetry: An Anthology*. New York, 1917.

Morison, Samuel Eliot. *The Two-Ocean War: A Short History of the United States Navy in the Second World War*. Boston, 1945.

Morris, Edmund. *The Rise of Theodore Roosevelt*. New York, 1979.

Morrison, Theodore. *Chautauqua*. Chicago, 1974.

Mott, Frank Luther, and Ralph D. Casey, eds. *Interpretations of Journalism*. New York, 1937.

Muelder, Hermann R. *Missionaries and Muckrakers: The First Hundred Years of Knox College*. Urbana, Ill., 1984.

Mumford, Lewis. *My Works and Days: A Personal Chronicle*. New York, 1979.

———. *Sketches from Life: The Early Years*. New York, 1982.

Nelson, Raymond. *Van Wyck Brooks: A Writer's Life*. New York, n.d.

Norris, Frank. *The Octopus*. London, n.d.

Overton, Richard C. *Burlington Route: A History of the Burlington Lines*. New York, 1965.

Paige, D. D., ed. *The Selected Letters of Ezra Pound.* New York, 1971.

Perry, Lilla. *My Friend Carl Sandburg: The Biography of a Friendship.* Metuchen, N.J., 1981.

Peterkin, Julia. *Scarlet Sister Mary.* New York, 1928.

Phillips, Christopher. *Steichen at War.* New York, 1987.

Plimpton, George, ed. *Poets at Work: The Paris Review Interviews.* New York, 1989.

Pound, Ezra. *Literary Essays of Ezra Pound.* (T. S. Eliot, ed.) London, 1954.

Preston, William. *Aliens and Dissenters: Federal Suppression of Radicals 1903–1933.* New York, 1966.

Pritchard, William H. *Frost: A Literary Life Reconsidered.* New York, 1984.

Putzel, Max. *Man in the Mirror.* Cambridge, Mass., 1963.

Rampersad, Arnold. *The Life of Langston Hughes: I, Too, Sing America,* Vol. I, 1902–1941. New York, 1985.

Randall, Ruth Painter. *Mary Lincoln: Biography of a Marriage.* Boston, 1953.

Rankin, Henry B. *Intimate Character Sketches of Abraham Lincoln.* Philadelphia, 1924.

Ransom, John Crowe. *The New Criticism.* Norfolk, Conn., 1941.

Rascoe, Burton. *Before I Forget.* New York, 1937.

Redmond, Tim. *Ezra Pound and Italian Fascism.* Cambridge, 1991.

Reitman, Dr. Ben. *The Second Oldest Profession.* New York, 1931.

The Report of the Chicago Commission on Race Relations. Chicago, 1921.

Revolutionary Radicalism, Its History, Purpose and Tactics. Report of the Joint Legislative Committee Investigating Seditious Activities. Albany, N.Y., 1920.

Rexroth, Kenneth. *American Poetry in the Twentieth Century.* New York, 1971.

Rosenfeld, Paul. *Port of New York: Essays on Fourteen American Moderns.* New York, 1924.

Ruggles, Eleanor. *The West-Going Heart: A Life of Vachel Lindsay.* New York, 1959.

Ruskin, John. *Sesame and Lilies and the Political Economy of Art.* Philadelphia, n.d.

Sakel, Manfred. *Epilepsy.* New York, 1958.

Salvatore, Nick. *Eugene Debs: Citizen and Socialist.* Urbana, Ill., 1982.

Sandburg, Helga. *Anna and the Baby Buzzard.* New York, 1970.

———. *Blueberry.* New York, 1963.

———. *Bo and the Old Donkey.* New York, 1965.

———. *Children and Lovers.* New York, 1976.

———. *Gingerbread.* New York, 1964.

———. *A Great and Glorious Romance: The Story of Carl Sandburg and Lilian Steichen.* New York, 1978.

———. *Joel and the Wild Goose.* New York, 1963.

———. *Measure My Love.* New York, 1959.

———. *The Owl's Roost.* New York, 1962.

———. *Sweet Music: A Book of Family Reminiscence and Song.* (Preface by Carl Sandburg.) New York, 1963.

———. *To a New Husband.* New York, 1970.

———. *The Unicorns.* New York, 1965.

———. *The Wheel of Earth.* New York, 1958.

———. *". . . Where Love Begins."* New York, 1989.

———. *The Wizard's Child.* New York, 1967.

Sassoon, Siegfried. *Siegfried's Journey.* London, 1945.

Schelling, Felix E. *Appraisements and Asperities as to Some Contemporary Writers.* Philadelphia, 1922.

Schlesinger, Arthur M., Jr. *History of American Presidential Elections, 1789–1968,* 4 vols. New York, 1971.

Schorer, Mark. *Sinclair Lewis: An American Life.* New York, 1961.

Shannon, David. *The Socialist Party of America.* New York, 1955.

Shay, Felix. *Elbert Hubbard of East Aurora.* New York, 1926.

Simons, Algie M. *Class Struggles in America.* Chicago, 1906.

Sinclair, Upton. *The Brass Check: A Study of American Journalism.* Pasadena, Calif., 1919.

Smith, Henry Justin. *Deadlines: Being the Quaint, The Amusing, The Tragic Memoirs of a News-room.* New York, 1922.

Smith, William Jay. *The Spectra Hoax.* Middletown, Conn., 1961.

The Social Democratic Party of America. N.p., n.d.

Solenberger, Alice. *One Thousand Homeless Men.* New York, 1911.

Sperber, A. M. *Edward R. Murrow: His Life and Times.* New York, 1986.

Spiller, Robert E. *Cycle of American Literature.* New York, 1955.

Stallman, R. W., and Lillian Gilkes, *Stephen Crane: Letters.* New York, 1960.

Stave, Bruce M., ed. *Socialism and the Cities.* Port Washington, N.Y., 1975.

Stead, William T. *If Christ Came to Chicago!* Chicago, 1894.

Steel, Ronald. *Walter Lippmann and the American Century.* Boston, 1980.

Steffens, Lincoln. *The Autobiography of Lincoln Steffens.* New York, 1931.

Steichen, Edward. *The Blue Ghost: A Photographic Log and Personal Narrative of the Aircraft Carrier USS Lexington in Combat Operations.* New York, 1947.

———. *A Life in Photography.* New York, 1963.

———. *Photographers View Carl Sandburg.* New York, 1966.

Steichen, Edward, ed. *Power in the Pacific.* New York, 1945.

Steichen, Edward, ed. *U.S. Navy War Photographs.* New York, 1946.

Steichen, Edward, and Mary Steichen [Martin]. *The First Picture Book: Everyday Things for Babies.* New York, 1930.

Steichen, Paula. "Hyacinths and Biscuits," in *Carl Sandburg Home Handbook 117.* Washington, D.C., 1982.

———. *My Connemara.* New York, 1969.

Steinbeck, Elaine, and Robert Wallsten, eds. *Steinbeck: A Life in Letters.* New York, 1975.

Stevens, Holly. *Souvenirs and Prophecies: The Young Wallace Stevens.* New York, 1977.

Stevens, Holly, ed. *Letters of Wallace Stevens.* New York, 1966.

Stroud, Parry. *Carl Sandburg: A Biographical and Critical Study of His Major Works.* Doctoral dissertation. Chicago, 1956.

Sutton, William. *Carl Sandburg Remembered.* Metuchen, N.J., 1979.

Swados, Harvey. *Years of Conscience: The Muckrakers.* New York, 1971.

Swank, George. *Carl Sandburg: Galesburg and Beyond.* Galesburg, Ill., 1983.

Tarbell, Ida M. *All in the Day's Work.* New York, 1939.

Tate, Allen. *Reactionary Essays on Poetry and Ideas.* New York, 1936.

Thomas, Benjamin. *Portrait for Posterity: Lincoln and His Biographers.* New Brunswick, N.J., 1947.

Thompson, Lawrance. *Robert Frost: The Early Years, 1874–1915.* New York, 1966.

———. *Robert Frost: The Years of Triumph, 1915–1938.* New York, 1970.

Thompson, Lawrance, ed. *Selected Letters of Robert Frost.* New York, 1964.

Thompson, Lawrance, and R. H. Winnick. *Robert Frost: A Biography.* (One-volume edition.) New York, 1981.

Thompson, Lawrance, and R. H. Winnick. *Robert Frost: The Later Years, 1938–1963.* New York, 1976.

Thurber, James. *Selected Letters of James Thurber.* New York, 1981.

Tietjens, Eunice. *The World at My Shoulder.* New York, 1938.

Trueblood, Elton. *Abraham Lincoln: Theologian of American Anguish.* New York, 1973.

Tuttle, William M., Jr. *Race Riot: Chicago in the Red Summer of 1919.* New York, 1970.

Tytell, Kenneth. *Ezra Pound: The Solitary Volcano.* New York, 1987.

Ueland, Brenda. *If You Want to Write.* New York, 1938. Reprint, Saint Paul, Minn., 1987.

————. *Me.* New York, 1939.

Untermeyer, Louis. *American Poetry Since 1900.* New York, 1923.

————. *From Another World: The Autobiography of Louis Untermeyer.* New York, 1939.

————. *The Letters of Robert Frost to Louis Untermeyer.* New York, 1963.

Van Doren, Carl. *Many Minds.* New York, 1924.

Van Doren, Mark. *Carl Sandburg. With a Bibliography of Sandburg Materials in the Collections of the Library of Congress.* Washington, D.C., 1969.

Vendler, Helen. *The Music of What Happens: Poems, Poets, Critics.* Cambridge, Mass., 1988.

————. *Part of Nature, Part of Us: Modern American Poets.* Cambridge, Mass., 1979.

Waldrop, Frank C. *McCormick of Chicago.* Englewood Cliffs, N.J., 1966.

Wallace, David H. *Historic Furnishings Report: Main House and Swedish House at Carl Sandburg Home National Historic Site.* Washington, D.C., 1984.

Weirick, Bruce. *From Whitman to Sandburg in American Poetry.* New York, 1924.

White, William Allen. *The Autobiography of William Allen White.* New York, 1946.

————. *Selected Letters of William Allen White.* New York, 1947.

Whitman, Walt. *Leaves of Grass.* Philadelphia, 1900.

————. *Poems.* (Introduction by Carl Sandburg.) New York, 1921.

Willard, Josiah Flynt. *My Life.* New York, 1908.

————. *Tramping with Tramps.* New York, 1899. [See Flynt.]

Williams, Ellen. *Harriet Monroe and the Poetry Renaissance: The First Ten Years of Poetry, 1912–1922.* Urbana, Ill., 1977.

Williams, William Carlos. *The Autobiography of William Carlos Williams.* New York, 1951.

————. *Kora in Hell: Improvisations.* Boston, 1920.

————. *Selected Essays.* New York, 1954.

Wilson, Edmund. *Patriotic Gore: Studies in the Literature of the American Civil War.* New York, 1962.

————. *The Shores of Light: A Literary Chronicle of the 1920s and 1930s.* New York, 1952. Reprint, Boston, 1985.

Winnick, R. H., ed. *Letters of Archibald MacLeish 1907 to 1982.* Boston, 1983.

Wood, Clement. *Poets of America.* New York, 1925.

Yatron, Michael. *America's Literary Revolt.* New York, 1959.

Acknowledgments

Writing biography is a paradoxical enterprise, at once solitary and communal. I have relied on many eyes and hands beyond my own. First there is my daughter Jennifer, who has lived with me while I lived with Carl Sandburg. Her countless acts of love and generosity have sustained me. I thank my parents for unflagging faith and encouragement, and my father for rainbows. My agent and friend Lucy Kroll has been at my side throughout the writing of this book, and through all the unexpected journeys of my own life these past few years.

Margaret, Janet and Helga Sandburg have given me extraordinary friendship, as well as vast resources of fact and insight. They have offered every measure of help, always saying, "But do what you want with this. It is *your* book." At my request, Margaret and Helga have read various drafts of the manuscript, including the complete final draft. Maurice Greenbaum and Judge Frank Parker, Sandburg Trustees, have given unlimited assistance, encouragement and freedom. I am grateful, too, for the wit and advice of Philip Carson, attorney for the Sandburg family. Dr. George "Barney" Crile has my esteem as writer, friend and physician.

From the outset, this biography has been enriched by the contributions of Joseph Wershba, who shared rare materials, his expertise as a researcher and writer, and his wide knowledge of American history and culture. He set me straight on many matters and read the manuscript in more than one draft. For a decade he has provided encouragement, and he and his family, Shirley, Randi and Don, have brought me closer to Sandburg's humor and humanity.

Many of these pages could not have been written without the support given by my sister Doris Niven Barron; my brother William Olin Niven; and my sister and brother-in-law Lynn Niven Duval Clark and Philip L. Clark. At one time or another my nieces and nephew have worked with me on Sandburg projects. For their help and their affirmation, I thank Lisa Duval Von Sprecken, Shannon Duval, Derek Duval and Ashley Buchanan. I deeply appreciate the cheerful, gracious help Lee Davidson has given me over many years, and her fine understanding of the Sandburgs.

I owe a special debt to Barbara Hogenson of the Lucy Kroll Agency. Norman Corwin has enhanced my understanding of Sandburg and blessed me with his wisdom and friendship. I thank him, too, for reading parts of the manuscript. For his astute and meticulous reading of two complete drafts of the book, I am especially grateful to Dr. George Hendrick, professor of English at the University of Illinois, editor of Sandburg texts and other books, and a distinguished scholar. Dr. John Hoffmann of the University of Illinois Library has provided expert advice on photographs and many other matters. I appreciate his help, and his crucial work over the years with the Carl Sandburg Collection. I thank Dr. Scott Bennett of Johns Hopkins University, formerly of the University of Illinois, who facilitated my work in the early, critical stages.

813

Since my childhood days, when my Aunt Sally and my Aunt Geneva were librarians, I have loved spending time in libraries. Without exception, I have found expert assistance in libraries across the nation. At the University of Illinois Library, Frederick Nash, Mary Ceibert, Louise Fitton and others gave indispensable support. Much of my work was done in Lilly Library at Earlham College in Richmond, Indiana, with the daily help of my friend and colleague Jody Doll. She expedited matters in a thousand cheerful ways, and I thank her. Librarian Evan Farber, Hope Farber and the extraordinary staff of Lilly Library at Earlham eased my way to many resources and gave the Carl Sandburg Collection Development Project a home base in Indiana.

I am grateful for the courtesy and aid extended generously by librarians and archivists across the country. The *Key to Abbreviations and Sources* provides a list, but I should reiterate my appreciation of four important Sandburg research sites: the Clifford Waller Barrett Library of American Literature at the University of Virginia; the Humanities Research Center at the University of Texas, Austin; the Knox College Library in Galesburg, Illinois; and the University of North Carolina at Charlotte. I appreciate Robin Brabham's help there in sharing the invaluable collection of news and journal articles in the Harry Golden Collection. My cousin Dr. Harry Y. Gamble, Jr., of the University of Virginia expedited my work there, and shared my enthusiasm over the revealing handwritten letters from Sandburg to Philip Green Wright.

Two of Sandburg's houses are open to the public—Connemara in Flat Rock, North Carolina, where he died; and the cottage in Galesburg, Illinois, where he was born. Carole Nelson of the Sandburg Birthplace has guided me to important resources. Warren Weber and the staff of the Carl Sandburg Home NHS have given unstinting assistance for many years, and I could not have made this journey without them—Muriel Potts, Bill Berry, Bess Gibbs, Mimi Rabb, Diana Miller, Charlie Hamm and all the remarkable people who have given hospitality and service to thousands of visitors to Carl and Paula Sandburg's house. I am particularly grateful to Judy Hellmich, Curator, who worked with me on photographs for this book. I thank Superintendent Kenneth Hulick. I will always appreciate the help given by the late Benjamin Davis, Superintendent when I began my work. I regret that I cannot put the book into his hands.

Many people have helped me by word and deed over the years: fellow writer Jeffrey Couchman; Lois Sims; Richard Wentworth; Betty Cooper Hirt; David Hirt; Natalie Smith; Joseph Kraemer; James Earl Jones; Stephen and Ann Kroll; Dr. Bob Waller; Peter Sterling; Chan Chandler; Benjamin Wilson; Elinor McLaughlin; Dr. Robert Beavers; Arthur Peterson; Bobbie Cullum; Paula Matthews; Beth Reynolds; Franklin Wallin; Holly Lebed, Jane Harris, Pamela Allen and the wonderful staff of the Lucy Kroll Agency, my "home" in New York; Betty and Ross Parks; Muriel and Les Mark; my unforgettable students at the College for Seniors, North Carolina Center for Creative Retirement, University of North Carolina at Asheville; Johanna Erlenbach and the Friends of Connemara; David and Lin Brown; Ed and Emily Herring Wilson; Doug Wilson; Valerie Kindle; Mead Parce; Molly Pace; Sarah Upchurch Browning; Stewart Browning; Rob Browning III; Bev Rich and Rob Groves; Darma Smoker; Betsy Dillard Stroud; Pete Caudle; Alice, Andrea and Aaron Wiethoff; Wally Bowen; David Solomon; Flora and Corbin Tayloe; Rob and Sarah Martha Tyson; Mark Hardy; Bob Cornman; Robin Farquhar and the staff of the Flatrock Playhouse; Dr. John Broderick; Francis and Jean Ann Reed; June Glenn; Pascal Covici, Jr.; Professor Akio Ichise; Warren Staebler; D. Elton Trueblood; Dr. Ralph Levering; Robert Nelsen; Ronald Peyton Lowery; Mark and Sally Trew; Dr. Robert von Hallberg; Alice Barkley; Maynard Brichford.

I will never forget my friend Susan Leon, whose enthusiasm as an editor helped to launch this book, and saw it through its first submitted draft. Four fellow writers have deepened my understanding of Sandburg and of biography: Louise Bailey, Robert Morgan, Mead Parce and Ann Sperber. Providentially, Dr. Tim Redman and I found ourselves in the same apartment building in the same city. We soon found ourselves working with the same agent, publisher and editor, and sharing papers and insights, for his Ezra Pound and my Carl Sandburg corresponded during the seminal years of their work. Tim has been a catalyst at a crucial time, and I am grateful for his presence in what has become known as the Biography Building.

On many Sunday afternoons for nearly a decade in Indiana, I was blessed with the wisdom and laughter of eight extraordinary women, all writers. I send my gratitude to Sirkka Barbour, Margaret Beidler, Margaret Lacey, Tunie Munson-Benson, Caroline Richards, Jane Silver, Patricia Staebler and Florence Wallin. They made me believe I could and should write this book, and listened while I did.

For indispensable grants and fellowships, I am indebted to the National Endowment for the Humanities, the Eastern National Park and Monument Association and the American Council of Learned Societies. I appreciate the efficient cooperation of the Federal Bureau of Investigation, Department of Justice, in my acquisition of Sandburg's FBI file and my subsequent appeal. Of unique value have been Lucy Kroll's papers in New York and at the Library of Congress, as well as many hours of dialogue.

For illuminating interviews, I deeply appreciate the contributions of Steve Allen, Louise Bailey, Roger Barrett, Clarice Bowen, Mutt Burton, Fanny Butcher, Norman Corwin, Malcolm Cowley, Barney Crile, Gregory d'Alessio, Hilda Terry d'Alessio, Kenneth and Letha Dodson, David Donald, Alvin Dreier, Majie Failey, John Henry Faulk, Fred Friendly, Elmer Gertz, Robert Giroux, Harry Golden, Betty Peterman Gole, Maurice Greenbaum, Anne Grimes, Martha Moorman Groth, William Hale, Charlie Hamm and Benjamin Davis, William Jovanovich, Gene Kelly, Lucy Kroll, Gene Lovitz, Frances and Mason Merrill, Frederick Morgan, Arnold and Augusta Newman, Ralph Newman, Kappie Opper (granddaughter of Negley Cochran), Sophocles Pappas, Frank Parker, Virginia Pasley, Sarah Ronald, Donald Russell, Helga Sandburg, Janet Sandburg, Margaret Sandburg, Martin Sandburg, Jr., Pete Seeger, J. Ray Shute, Ethel Smith, William Smith, Olga Steckler, Joanna Steichen, Paula Steichen, George Stevens, Jr., William Sutton, the Reverend George Tolleson, Mary Leta Tolleson, Brenda Ueland, Joseph Wershba, Randi Wershba, Shirley Wershba, Dolores Wilson, Jake Zeitlin. I felt bereft at the death of Archibald MacLeish, not only for his family and the nation, but because he and I had been corresponding about our forthcoming interview. I am grateful for the letters I received from several of Sandburg's friends, now deceased: Aaron Copland, Gary Merrill, Georgia O'Keeffe, Donna Workman, Brenda Ueland, and his niece, Kate Rodina Steichen. I appreciate, too, the assistance yielded by letters written to me by Robert Penn Warren, A. B. Magill, Leslie Dunlap and E. Caswell Perry, whose mother Lilla Perry wrote about her friendship with Sandburg. I thank Alan Lomax and Norman Rosten for their willingness to help, and Perry Miller Adato for her film vision of Sandburg, and for all she taught me about the joy of research. I also thank Steichen's daughter Mary Steichen Calderone, founder of SIECUS. I treasure an interview with the late Hilda Lindley, Sandburg's graceful editor during the last years of his life.

I have enduring appreciation for Father Keith Rhodes, who has many times come to the rescue, despite hundreds of miles. Grace Mayer of the Museum of Modern Art has greatly enhanced my understanding of Edward Steichen, and stimulating talks with her have been a particular delight. Special thanks go to Jack McJunkin, Jr., and to Cleo McJunkin, who got me to Connemara in the first place. Without Majie Failey I would not have made it to the finish line.

I am fortunate to have had the company and counsel of the late Duane Bogie. I pay tribute in the reality of this book to the memory of my grandparents William Graham and Penelope Marsh Hearon, and Olin and Ellen Walkup Niven; to Mable Ruth Hearon Kelly; to Jack Fain McJunkin, Sr.; and to Andre R. Duval.

Finally, I send my deep thanks to the people at Scribners who made this book out of a long manuscript. Because I typed those fifteen hundred pages myself three times, I keenly appreciate the expert labors of that impeccable scribe Carol Wilson, who prepared the final typescript. I am grateful for the meticulous attention given the manuscript by Ann Keene. Roberta Corcoran deserves daily bouquets of roses and praise. With his artistic vision, his astute questions, and his erudition and skill, my editor Robert Stewart has enriched this book beyond measure.

Index

✳

817

Permissions

*

Joan St. C. Crane, copyright © 1975 by the Rector and Visitors of the University of Virginia published by permission of the University Press of Virginia.

Excerpts from his published and unpublished writings, from his Carl Sandburg Oral History Project interviews, and from his letters and notes to Penelope Niven are published by permission of Joseph Wershba.

Excerpts from the letters of Donna Workman are published by permission of Special Collections and Archives, Seymour Library, Knox College, Galesburg, Illinois, holder of unrestricted rights.

Excerpts from Jacob Zeitlin's letters and his Carl Sandburg Oral History Project interview are published by permission of Josephine Zeitlin, executor.

Excerpts from his published and unpublished writings and from his Carl Sandburg Oral History Project interview published by permission of Malcolm Cowley.

Excerpts from the writings of Floyd Dell and Lloyd Lewis published by permission of the Newberry Library, trustees.

Excerpts from the writings of Vachel Lindsay published by permission of Nicholas Cave Lindsay.

Excerpt from his letter to Carl Sandburg printed by permission of Omar Pound.

Excerpts from the work of James Thurber printed by permission of the Lucy Kroll Agency.

Excerpts from the letters of Alfred Stieglitz published by permission of the Georgia O'Keeffe Estate.

Excerpt from a letter of Alfred Stieglitz that appears on page 437 of this book is published by permission of the Yale Collection of American Literature, Beinecke Rare Book and Manuscript Library, Yale University.

Excerpts from the writings of Amy Lowell published by permission of F. Davis Dassori, Jr., and Thomas H. P. Whitney, Jr., Trustees under the will of Amy Lowell.

For the courtesy of the use of letters by Carl Sandburg held in their collections, the author gratefully acknowledges the Carl Sandburg Collection, the University of Illinois Library, Urbana-Champaign; the Carl Sandburg Collection, Connemara, Carl Sandburg Home NHS; Seymour Library, Knox College, Galesburg; the Houghton Library, Harvard University for Sandburg's letters to Amy Lowell [call no. bMS Lowell 19 (10610)] and to Robert Sherwood [call no. bMS AM 1947 (721)]; Carl Sandburg's letters to Amy Lowell and to Robert Sherwood are quoted by permission of Maurice Greenbaum and Frank M. Parker, Trustees, Sandburg Family Trust, courtesy of Houghton Library, Harvard University; University of Chicago; Special Collections, University of Delaware Library, for Carl Sandburg's letters to Louis Untermeyer; University of Texas Humanities Research Center, Austin, for Carl Sandburg's letters to Alice Corbin Henderson; Harcourt, Brace files for Carl Sandburg's letters to Alfred Harcourt and employees of the firm. All unpublished letters written by Carl Sandburg are published by the permission of Maurice Greenbaum and Frank M. Parker, Trustees.

For their invaluable assistance in clearing permissions the author thanks Peter Jovanovich and Elaine Hopkins of Harcourt Brace Jovanovich; Richard Wentworth and Harriet Stockanes of the University of Illinois Press, Urbana-Champaign; Carley R. Robison, Curator of Manuscripts and Archives, Seymour Library, Knox College, Galesburg, Illinois; and Jeffrey Goldstein of Macmillan Publishing Company.

For permission to reprint photographs, the author is grateful to Helga Sandburg Crile and Paula Steichen Polega; June Glenn, Jr.; the *Palladium Item*, Richmond, Indiana. Thanks go to Helen Williamson of that newspaper, to Jody Barber, and to Helen Lothrop Klaviter, Managing Editor of *Poetry*, for assistance.